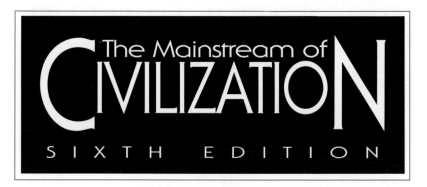

The Mainstream of **CIVILIZATION**

SIXTH EDITION

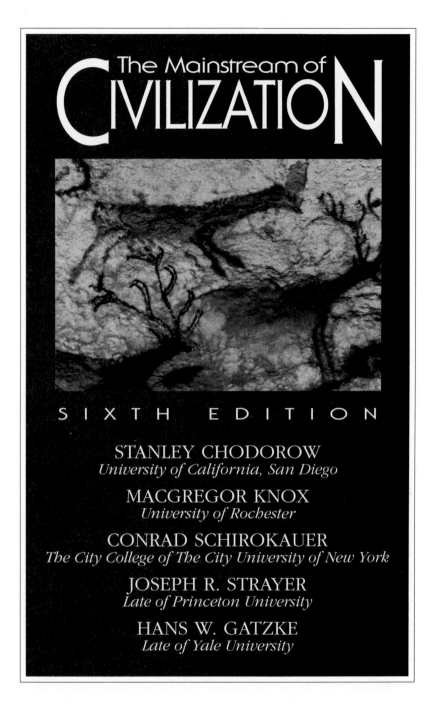

The Mainstream of CIVILIZATION

SIXTH EDITION

STANLEY CHODOROW
University of California, San Diego

MACGREGOR KNOX
University of Rochester

CONRAD SCHIROKAUER
The City College of The City University of New York

JOSEPH R. STRAYER
Late of Princeton University

HANS W. GATZKE
Late of Yale University

THE HARCOURT PRESS

Harcourt Brace College Publishers

Fort Worth Philadelphia San Diego New York Orlando Austin San Antonio
Toronto Montreal London Sydney Tokyo

Publisher	Ted Buchholz
Acquisitions Editor	Drake Bush
Senior Project Editor	Kay Kaylor
Associate Project Editor	Sandy Walton
Senior Production Manager	Kathleen Ferguson
Art Director	Burl Sloan
Picture Editor	Lili Weiner

Cover: Lascaux Caves, Dordogne, France / Art Resource, New York. Background: © Shinichi Eguchi / Photonica

Requests for permission to make copies of any part of the work should be mailed to: Harcourt Brace & Company, Permissions Department, 6277 Sea Harbor Drive, Orlando, FL 32887-6777

Address for Editorial Correspondence: Harcourt Brace College Publishers, 301 Commerce Street, Suite 3700, Fort Worth, TX 76102

Address for Orders: Harcourt Brace & Company, 6277 Sea Harbor Drive, Orlando, FL 32887; 1-800-782-4479 or 1-800-433-0001 (in Florida)

ISBN: 0-15-501197-9
Library of Congress Catalog Card Number: 93-78399
Printed in the United States of America
789012 048 98765

PREFACE

Writing a history of civilization is an almost foolhardy enterprise. But it is easier to do if you have done it before, as the authors of the first four editions of this history, Joseph R. Strayer and Hans W. Gatzke, noted dryly in their preface to the Fourth Edition. We, their successors, had not done it before the mid-1980s. But we did have the robust framework the original authors left to us. In this Sixth Edition of *The Mainstream of Civilization,* we have built on that framework and on the major recasting of the work carried out in the Fifth Edition.

That edition integrated into the text new themes—such as social history and the history of women—that had figured less in earlier editions. Especially in the modern period, it emphasized the great driving forces—technology, demography, economics, and nationalism—that have made the twentieth century immensely different from any earlier age. It sought to explain the origins of key events, such as the Industrial Revolution, the Great Depression, and the World Wars. And unlike its predecessors, it used charts and graphs to present chronological and other quantitative data vividly, new picture captions to integrate the illustrations into the text, new boxed quotations from primary sources (some of them translated for the purpose), and frequent primary-source quotations in the text to convey the flavor of the past.

Yet the Fifth Edition also drew on the greatest strength of earlier editions—their global perspective. Like its predecessors, it sought to follow the "mainstream of civilization" by gradually shifting its geographic focus from the Mediterranean to Europe, and ultimately to the wider world. It offered detailed treatment of the major civilizations east and south of Europe, from Byzantium and Islam to India, China, and Japan. And as that "mainstream" flowed toward the present, the text provided increasingly detailed analysis and narrative in order to make that present understandable. That narrative attempted to convey to readers the texture and flavor of past civilizations and the astonishing variety of human possibilities and accomplishments. It sought to emphasize the interrelationships of all spheres of life, from politics and warfare to economics, art, scholarship, and religion. It sought to suggest at least some of the differing ways in which contemporaries and historians have understood the past. But above all, the text attempted to explain that past, to explain historical change and the recurring patterns visible in the past. Why and how have states, institutions, and ideas risen, flourished, and crumbled into dust? Why did events happen as they did and not otherwise?

This new Sixth Edition, we are confident, has kept the strengths of its predecessors. But it also contains much that is new both in presentation and substance. We have reviewed and rewritten the entire text sentence by sentence for clarity and readability; the result is slightly shorter than the Fifth Edition. We have reorganized Chapters 9, 10, and 11 to group related topics more effectively and to strengthen the narrative line. We have sometimes written new chapter introductions to make clearer how the material presented in topical chapters, such as 24, 25, and 27, fits into our overall chronological and thematic framework. We have rewritten or added subheadings where necessary to group the text into more easily understood segments. And we have revised and updated the bibliographical suggestions at the end of each chapter.

The Sixth Edition also incorporates recent research and new material on topics that range from humanity's origins to the end of the Cold War. We have added material on Hebrew culture to provide a better understanding of the background of European religion. We have reorganized and strengthened the sections on Hellenistic civilization to better explain the transition from Greece to Rome. We have radically rewritten and shortened our chapter on the post-1945 non-Western world to simplify the presentation and bring it up to 1992. Finally, we have rewritten the final chapter almost completely to offer both narrative and interpretation of recent momentous events. We are confident that Chapters 34–36 of the new *The Mainstream of Civilization* offer the best short analysis of the world since the Second World War available in any similar textbook.

The Sixth Edition also comes with a totally recast package of ancillary materials: a testbook (also available in software form) and film guide with learning objectives, 50 map transparencies, and 25 color transparencies of major works of art and architecture. Above all, the Sixth Edition study guide is completely new; it contains new chapter summaries, chapter objectives, time-lines, maps and map questions, identifications, and numerous probing essay questions also designed to serve as topics for class discussion.

This edition, like its predecessors, inevitably draws heavily upon the publications, contributions, and advice of other scholars. We have sought wherever possible to hint at our major debts in the Suggestions for Further Reading that follow each chapter. We owe special thanks to Conrad Schirokauer, City College of the City University of New York, for his contribution of Chapters 6 and 15. We thank Carl Abrams, Bob Jones University; Ron Brown, Charles County Community College; Ann Sumner Holmes, Louisiana State University; Gilberto Ramirez, Auburn University; Randall Rogers, Louisiana State University; Alan Schaffer, Clemson University; and Marian E. Strobel, Furman University, for their perceptive comments and criticisms. And we are profoundly grateful to Everett M. Sims, who edited the final manuscript with tact, decisiveness, and a brilliant choice of synonyms. All have helped to make this book better, but they bear no responsibility for sins of omission or commission and errors of fact or judgment, which belong to the authors alone.

Finally, we remain deeply indebted to the late Hans W. Gatzke. Despite the debilitating effects of a tragic illness, he oversaw with tact and consideration the transition from one "team" of authors to the next. He set ambitious goals for the new team: a major revision and recasting of the book. He shaped the plan for that revision and suggested a number of the new themes that we have attempted to emphasize. To his memory, and to that of the late Joseph R. Strayer, we thankfully dedicate this Sixth Edition.

Stanley Chodorow   MacGregor Knox

CONTENTS

9

THE EMERGENCE OF WESTERN EUROPEAN CIVILIZATION / 221

10

REVIVAL AND REFORM IN WESTERN EUROPE / 251

11

MEDIEVAL CIVILIZATION AT ITS HEIGHT / 279

12

THE RISE OF THE SECULAR STATE / 305

13

EASTERN EUROPE IN THE MIDDLE AGES / 329

14

THE LATE MIDDLE AGES / 351

LIST OF MAPS

INTRODUCTION

History as Foresight and Memory

History is the story of the human past. It is also the only available introduction to the human future. That was how the first critically thinking historian, Thucydides the Athenian, justified his history of the great war between the rival Greek city-states of Athens and Sparta in the fifth century B.C. Thucydides addressed his work to those "who want to understand clearly the events which happened in the past and which (human nature being what it is) will, at some time or other and in much the same ways, be repeated in the future." He added that his book was "not a piece of writing designed to meet the taste of an immediate public, but was done to last for ever."

No modern historian would dare make that claim. Forever is a length of time beyond human grasp, and the tastes of the immediate public now have a weight that Thucydides the aristocrat would have roundly condemned. But Thucydides' book, the most penetrating historical work of the ancient world, has nevertheless survived for 2400 years, and has probably enjoyed more readers in the last three centuries than in its entire previous existence. Thucydides' claim that human affairs follow patterns meaningful to the trained eye has remained the fundamental argument for studying history.

The future is by definition unknowable and unpredictable; events are unique, and never repeat themselves precisely. But they often follow patterns. Individuals are unique, and are free to make their own history. That freedom gives the unfolding of history its element of suspense. But individuals also band together to create societies. Those societies have structures—languages, religions, intellectual traditions, artistic styles, and political, social, economic, and military institutions—that limit how individuals can make history, and that restrict the range of thoughts and actions open to them. Those historical structures operate in consistent and often predictable ways. Historical situations separated by centuries and continents have similarities, and sometimes develop according to a similar logic. Historical analogies—comparisons between one set of historical structures or events and another—are powerful if treacherous tools for probing future possibilities.

Historical analysis inevitably has limits. Evidence about the past is always incomplete. Politics, warfare, religion, philosophy, and art have left more traces than everyday life. The few with power and leisure loom far larger in the surviving sources than the peasants and workers on whose drudgery that power and leisure rested. Men appear in the sources more frequently than women. Societies with writing have left far more behind them than those without. Twentieth-century technology—aerial photography, radio-carbon dating, precise chemical analysis, meticulous archaeological technique—has told us much about voiceless societies and groups, and has broadened our knowledge even of societies that left extensive literatures. Source criticism—close scrutiny of the style, content, context, purposes, and reliability of surviving texts—has deepened our understanding of the written sources and of the societies that created them. The fragmentary nature of the evidence transmitted from the past nevertheless limits the historian's ability to see clearly and to draw valid conclusions. And in the nineteenth and twentieth centuries, the written record has swollen geometrically with the coming of mass literacy and the creation of immense bureaucracies. Too much evidence rather than too little is the burden of the historian of the recent past.

The historian's own values also color and sometimes drastically distort both the selection of evidence and the analysis of ideas and events. The past is the key to the present, but the present can also crush the past. Crusading religions and combative secular ideologies such as nationalism or Marxism-Leninism alter history to fit dogma. Traumatic experiences such as wars, revolutions, or economic catastrophes sometimes lead the historian to seek escape in a largely imaginary and far more pleasant distant past, or to rewrite recent events as a one-way street leading inevitably to the unhappy present. And historians, although their craft should lead them to take the long view, sometimes fall victim to passing fads. The historian's only defenses against ideological distortion and trendiness are the search for detachment and the passionate commitment to the verifiable evidence that has distinguished the best historical writing from Thucydides onward. For history, if painstakingly and honestly written, gives to those who pursue it a sense of the probabilities, of the range of outcomes inherent in a given historical situation. Historical knowledge can teach us how the world works.

That knowledge is also indispensable in a second way. History is memory. Historical knowledge is self-knowledge. It tells us how our world, our own society, and we as individuals got to where we are. Memory can give pleasure, but is also decisive in our lives. For the individual, memory is identity. For society, the "collective memory" or knowledge of the society's past and shared values is equally central. It is part of the glue that binds society together. When a society suffers collective amnesia, when it loses its historical consciousness, the values formed through that society's history erode. That decay undermines the society's political, social, and intellectual cohesion, and may threaten its survival.

In the empires, city-states, monarchies, and tribal polities of the past and in the single-party dictatorships of the present, religion, custom, political indoctrination, and force have usually maintained cohesion. But our own civilization has over the last three centuries evolved a historically unique concept: laws that guarantee the rights of the ruled against the rulers, the rights of individuals against the state. Those laws have given individuals a measure of freedom unprecedented in history: freedom to worship as they please, to follow their economic interests, to pursue private happiness. The victories of rights against the state in the seventeenth and eighteenth centuries and of representative democratic government in the nineteenth and twentieth centuries marked an immense leap forward in human freedom and economic dynamism. But that freedom also carried with it the possibility that its heirs might one day lose it, through forgetfulness of the sacrifices and struggles that has secured it and through ignorance of its historical uniqueness and potential fragility. Historical knowledge can guard against that danger as no other knowledge can.

History as the History of Civilization

Our present comes from our past, but what is the shape of that past? All readers of this book, by the fact that they read the English language, are heirs to a tradition that stretches back to the first millennium B.C., to the Greeks on the one hand and to the Hebrew authors of the Old Testament on the other. That *civilization*—a term coined in the eighteenth century and derived from the Roman word for city, *civitas*—is the civilization of the West, the civilization of Europe.

Civilization above all means cities, a human institution less than 10,000 years old. Cities demand a highly developed peasant agriculture to feed them, architects and laborers to erect them, artisans to people them, bureaucrats to organize and tax them, soldiers to defend them, rulers to rule them, and religious or communal myths and customs to foster loyalty to the existing order. Cities mean a degree of social stratification, of differences between the high and the low, unknown in the hunter-gatherer or cattle-herding nomad societies that preceded them. Cities mean *literacy, organization,* and *specialization* of work. And the degree of literacy, organization, and specialization affects the density of population that a given civilization can support and the character and attainments of that civilization. The Greek city-states were capable of efforts and achievements far surpassing those of the Scythian nomads to their north and of the ramshackle Persian empire to their east.

Cities have meant the intensified development of religion, philosophy, technology, art, and literature. The great religions, from those of ancient Egypt and Mesopotamia through Hinduism and Buddhism to Christianity and Islam, were or became urban civilizations. Philosophy, the quest for the principles and realities underlying human knowledge and existence, was an offshoot of religion that first arose in the Greek cities and in the urban civilizations of China and India. Technological advance—from improvements in tools and weapons to the building of fortifications, roads, and aqueducts—made cities possible, and cities in turn accelerated technological advance. Highly developed art, from architecture and sculpture to ceramics and painting, has been the mark of urban civilizations. And writing, invented for the tax accounting of the bureaucrats and the records of the city priesthoods, eventually made possible the flowering of poetry, drama, history, and science.

Cities have meant common values that bind the inhabitants together, that inspire them to accept the sacrifices—often without immediate or apparent compensating benefits—that specialization and organization impose. Those values can derive from a variety of sources. The great religions, the cult of the nation-state, the modern ideologies that claim to grasp the meaning and destination of history, and the sense of duty toward the community that is the "civic religion" of democracies have all provided the myths and values needed to sustain urban civilization. Those myths and values have been closely related to the type of civilization they spring from and support.

Finally, cities have meant conflict as well as achievement. Hunter-gatherers and nomads raid their neighbors for booty, women, slaves, and cattle. All adult males are by definition warriors. But in urban civilizations, specialization of work extends to warfare: hereditary warrior castes or standing armies and navies that may command the entire resources of the state. Urban civilizations, by virtue of literacy, organization, and specialization, can wield violence far longer and more systematically than their predecessors. That violence led to the formation of *state systems,* of highly competitive groups of rival states. In such systems, as the greatest of Greek philosophers, Plato, bitingly remarked, "What most people call peace . . . is just a name; in fact there is by nature an everlasting undeclared war of all against all." And even within the city walls, fierce conflicts between rival groups among the ruling few or between the few and the downtrodden many have frequently broken the peace.

A history of civilization must therefore try to explain the gradual increase of literacy, organization, and specialization over the last three millennia. Such a history must be a political history, for politics is the key to understanding the nature, growth, and collapse of *states*—the large-scale political units whose character, success, or failure has been a matter of life or death for the inhabitants of all known civilizations. A history of civilization must be an economic and social history, for economic and social relationships shape politics and are in turn shaped by politics. A history of civilization must be a history of art, literature, and ideas—for art, literature, and ideas define and reflect the systems of shared beliefs without which no civilization is possible. Above all, a history of civilization has to explore the interconnections of politics, economics, and ideas that determine the character, development, and fate of civilizations.

And as seen from the late twentieth century, the history of human civilization as a whole centers around the history of the West, the history of Europe. For Europe's civilization, although at first merely one of the world's major traditions, spread outward after 1492 to dominate the entire globe. That outcome was not foreordained, for Europe started late. The earliest civilizations arose as early as 3000 B.C. in the great river valleys of Egypt, Mesopotamia, India, and China. The first recognizably Western civilization only appeared after 1000 B.C. in the Greek city-states of Greece, Asia Minor, southern Italy, and Sicily. The Greeks borrowed much from their predecessors to the east and south, including the alphabet they took from their Phoenician rivals. But the Greeks were unique. In the space of little more than three centuries—the sixth through fourth centuries B.C.—they invented the Western traditions of philosophical, historical, and scientific inquiry. They created the concept of individual freedom. They laid the foundations of Western literature. They made Western civilization self-conscious, inquiring, and *historical*. And in the fourth century B.C., the immense conquests of Alexander of Macedon, heir to a half-barbarian kingdom on Greece's northern border, spread Greek civilization—and Greek-ruled cities named Alexandria—from Egypt to the borders of India.

The successors of Alexander, the Romans, dominated the entire Mediterranean basin for five centuries. In art and literature they borrowed much from the Greeks. In law, statecraft, and military organization they were bold and ruthless innovators who solved brilliantly the problem that had perplexed the Greeks: how to create large-scale and long-lasting political units ruling over citizens and noncitizens alike. The only contemporary civilization that rivaled the brilliance of Rome and the extent of Rome's power was China, which experienced a merciless unification in the same centuries as the Roman conquest of the Mediterranean.

Roman legions, Roman roads, Roman cities, and Roman laws civilized Europe as far east as the great river barriers of the Rhine and the Danube and as far north as the wild borders of Scotland. Rome provided the political order within which a new religion, which blended the Hebrew traditions of the Old Testament with the philosophical conceptions of the Greeks, could spread and prosper. In the fourth century A.D., that new religion, Christianity, became the official religion of the empire. By that point Rome was near collapse. Interrelated and mutually reinforcing pressures from within and without brought the empire down: bloody civil wars, brigandage and piracy, economic decay, plague epidemics, loss of intellectual self-confidence and social cohesion, and vastly increased barbarian pressure on the Rhine-Danube frontier.

In the fifth century A.D., Rome fell to waves of invaders, as the pitiless Huns on their shaggy steppe ponies drove the warlike Germanic tribes across Rome's crumbling frontiers. The western half of the empire collapsed. The unity of the Mediterranean basin was gone. A Greek-speaking remnant of the Empire centered on Byzantium survived in the East for another thousand years, but had small influence on developments in the West. In the seventh and eighth centuries A.D., the Arabian tribes, under the green banner of their new religion, Islam, conquered the eastern Mediterranean and swept across northern Africa to Spain. Those conquests further divided Rome's inland sea—between the heirs of Greece, Rome, and Jerusalem and the heirs of the prophet Mohammed. The *ancient world,* the Greco-Roman civilization of the Mediterranean basin, had ceased to exist.

The new *medieval* civilization that eventually arose in western Europe after the eighth century was thus thrown back on its own resources. It saved only a fragment of its Roman inheritance, as Rome itself had been only a part of the ancient world. And the new rulers of western Europe, the Germanic peoples, had never been part of that world. They only gradually absorbed the fragments of Latin literature and Roman law that Rome had left behind. They were slow to blend with the Latin peoples they had conquered. They and their subjects were equally slow to absorb Christianity. But the fusion over some six centuries of those diverse ethnic and cultural elements ultimately produced a distinctive European civilization.

Once its character was set, medieval Europe developed rapidly. It eagerly received lost Greek texts, decimal numbers, and algebra from its neighbors, the more highly developed Byzantines and Arabs. Many of its basic institutions and ideas, such as universities and representative assemblies, originated in the twelfth and thirteenth centuries. Its centers were in the north, in the triangle bounded by the formerly Roman cities of Paris (*Lutetia Parisiorum*), Cologne (*Colonia*), and London (*Londinium*) and in north Italian cities such as Florence, Bologna, and Padua. Its periphery, from Sicily, Spain, and Ireland to Scandinavia, Poland, and Bohemia, developed more slowly. And beyond that periphery Western influence almost ceased. Byzantium remained apart: Greek in language, despotic in politics, and Orthodox rather than Catholic in religion. Byzantium's influence dominated the southern and eastern Slavic peoples who had moved into eastern Europe as the Germanic tribes had moved west. Byzantium likewise inspired the early Russian state, until Mongol conquerors subjugated Moscow and Kiev in the thirteenth century and forced them to face eastward for more than 200 years.

South and east of Byzantium lay the civilizations of Islam, which began to close themselves off from new ideas just as Europe was beginning its ascent. Still further east lay the great civilizations of India, China, and Japan. Each had characteristic values—religious in India, scholarly and bureaucratic in China, military and bureaucratic in Japan. All three had on occasion borrowed from their neighbors, but they nevertheless tended toward self-absorption and the perfection of existing modes of thought rather than the acquisition of new knowledge. India suffered Moslem conquest, constant wars, and crushing taxation. China after the fifteenth century showed little interest in exploration or seaborne trade. Japan, which had borrowed much from China, fiercely walled itself off after 1600. And after pioneering efforts—gunpowder, rockets, firearms, crucible steel, iron smelting with coke—none of the Eastern civilizations developed a tradition of scientific inquiry and technological innovation rivaling that of the West.

By the fifteenth century, medieval Europe had begun to break out of its original social and religious mold and out of its narrow and rain-sodden peninsula off the Eurasian landmass. Since the twelfth century, Europeans had shown an insatiable scholarly curiosity about distant lands and a thirst for trade and booty. They had shown a fascination with machinery—from clocks and windmills to ships and cannon—rarely seen to the south and east. European scholars had begun to lay the groundwork for the seventeenth-century scientific revolution that immeasurably increased humanity's mastery over nature and transformed its view of its place in the universe.

In the last decade of the fifteenth century, Europeans leapt across the globe—the Spaniards to the Americas in 1492 and the Portuguese around Africa to India in 1498. Europe's new seaborne empires—the empires of the *early modern* age of Western expansion—soon dominated the fringes of Africa and Asia and conquered three newly discovered continents: North America, South America, and Australia.

Then came two further revolutions within Europe itself. The collapse of the French monarchy in 1788–89 opened 25 years of revolution and war that spread the democratic ideas of the French revolutionaries and the notion of nationalism—the political religion of the nation-state—eastward across Europe. Simultaneously, an industrial revolution that transformed humanity's power over nature and over its own existence began in Britain. Those twin revolutions—of mass politics and nationalism, and of engine-powered machines and economic freedoms—have been the driving forces of the *modern* era in which we still live. They transformed Europe and the world. For the first time in history, one civilization brought all others into increasingly direct contact with it, and forced its rivals to adopt its techniques and ideas or go under.

Those rivals ultimately maintained or reasserted their independence—within the framework of the worldwide international system that Europe established—by adopting Western ideas and techniques. The world has not become one; mortal rivalries between states, religions, ideologies, and cultures continue to rend it. But for good or ill a recognizably Western global civilization has taken shape, bound together by an accelerating revolution of science and technology, an ever-expanding world market, and a thickening web of mass communications. That is the present that any history of civilization must seek to explain.

The Origins of Civilization: the Ancient Middle East To ca. 500 B.C.

We live in a complex environment. We are now conscious of being part of a world economy and of being affected by geological, climatic, and human events that occur around the globe. At the same time, we have developed a strong sense of ethnic and racial identity that makes us feel different from one another and even glorifies that difference. Human history has produced this uncertainty about whether we are part of a small group—such as an ethnic community within American society—or of a large one—such as Christianity or Islam—or of the global human community. When we read history, we learn of mass migrations, of the mixture of populations and cultures, of constant change in societies, economies, polities, ideologies. Change has produced our uncertainties. Change is the dominant fact of human life.

Recent findings in archaeology show that the human animal itself is the product of change. The primary force of human evolution has been climatic change, the same force that led to the extinction of the dinosaurs. Hominids, the family of animals that includes human beings, evolved in Africa, probably on the eastern side of the continent: The earliest hominid fossils were found in southern Africa, and the most important were found in the region east of Lake Victoria where the Serengeti Plain runs into the great Rift Valley. The oldest hominid fossil dates to about 3.25 million years ago, but archaeologists have found fossilized footprints made by a two-legged hominid ancestor about 3.75 million years ago.

Bipedalism (walking on two feet) was the first stage in human evolution, and recent studies show that it emerged about the same time the footprints were made,

Average Temperature: 55° F	**Average Temperature: 59° F**	**Average Temperature: 50° F**	**Average Temperature: 59° F**
2.5 Million Years Ago	125,000 Years Ago	18,000 Years Ago	11,000 Years Ago

a period when a major shift in climate took place. At that time, the earth's temperature fell dramatically, and the vast forests in which the ancestors of the hominids lived began to thin out. These animals had developed grasping hands and long arms to facilitate movement through the forest canopy, but they now had to travel from patch to patch of forest. Walking or running on two legs was much more efficient than gamboling along on feet and knuckles. Bipedalism was an adaptation to climatic change.

The next great leap in evolution took place about 2.5 million years ago, when the hominid began to develop a large brain and to make primitive tools. This period too was a time of climatic change, probably caused by the rise of the Himalaya Mountains, which altered wind patterns around the world. That change caused a cooling that produced the first polar ice caps and a drying of the African continent, which further reduced the extent of the forests. About this time, new species of antelopes adapted to the large grass plains emerged, and the vegetarian

hominid of the forests became omnivorous, eating grains, fruits, and meat, whatever was available.

The climatic change that took place 2.5 million years ago triggered a cycle of temperature fluctuations that, in turn, produced a series of ice ages. The ice would cover large parts of the earth for 50,000 to 80,000 years, and then about 10,000 years of relative warmth would cause the ice to retreat to the Arctic. The last ice age ended about 13,000 years ago. Scientists believe that plentiful food resources during the warm periods caused a rise in the hominid population and that when the ice returned only those with the best mental capacities survived. Repeated over 2 million years, this climatic pattern fostered the evolution of a large-brained animal that survived by its mental capacity, rather than its climbing ability, speed, teeth, claws, or physical size.

From about 700,000 years ago, we have evidence that *Homo habilis* (able or competent hominid) was making good tools of flint by striking flakes off a large "core" with a second rock. The flakes could then be shaped into hand-held blades. The tools, found in camps, were used to butcher animals, as the patterns of tooth and blade cuts on the bones show. The animal bones found in these camps show that *H. habilis* was sometimes a scavenger, fighting other carrion-eaters such as hyenas for carcasses, and sometimes a hunter who made the kills, took the meat, and left the remains for scavengers. The tools also reveal a great deal about the evolutionary progress the creature had made since it began to run across fields between clumps of trees. Scholars have learned to make the flint blades and have shown that *H. habilis* was right-handed. This means that the animal had developed a brain divided into two lobes, with the left side usually dominant. (Because of a twist in the brain stem, the left lobe of the brain controls the right side of the body.) Moreover, the skull structure

The Rise of the Himalayas and World Climate

The earth's crust is composed of huge plates—such as the North American plate, the Pacific plate, and the Asian plate. These are in constant movement caused by the continuous creation of new crust in deep ravines on the sea floor, principally in the Pacific and Atlantic oceans. Earthquake and volcanic zones are areas where two plates grind against one another. Millions of years ago, the plate on which India sits collided with the Asian plate causing the edge of the Asian plate to crumple as the Indian plate drove in under it. The crumpled region is the Himalayas, which are still being pushed upward. Geologists estimate that about 2.5 million years ago the range reached a height sufficient to alter worldwide wind patterns. The effect of this change was a cooling trend as cold air circulated to the south around the globe.

THE ORIGINS OF CIVILIZATION: THE ANCIENT MIDDLE EAST TO *ca.* 500 B.C.

3

suggests that the voice box had moved down into the throat, a change required to produce the wide range of sounds needed for speech.

Homo habilis had many of the characteristics associated with modern human beings. It was bipedal, had a bicameral brain, made tools, and ate meat. Most important, it had a sense of time. It could plan its activities—for example, it could go to outcrops in the hills, gather flint, and take it back to camp for use in butchering. It was willing to spend energy on activities that only indirectly produced food. Yet the most recent finds show that *H. habilis* was more ape-like than human in appearance and lived in family groupings similar to those of modern apes, with several females and their young under the domination of a single male. Also, its young matured at about the same rate as those of apes. *Homo habilis* was definitely a transitional animal.

The great evolutionary changes experienced by *H. habilis* led to the next stage of human development, *Homo erectus*. This creature improved his mobility and posture and not only used tools, but also created a toolkit. *H. erectus* also began to migrate out of Africa. Remains of this hominid have been found from western Europe to China (Peking Man) and Indonesia (Java Man). The major finds date from 350,000 years ago and are associated with tools that are crude but of standard form. The common tools suggest that *H. erectus* took his kit with him from Africa; they also demonstrate the stability of human culture at this stage.

The last warm period before our own, about 125,000 years ago, seems to have produced two species of hominids. One of these, perhaps the older one, is called Neanderthal Man *(Homo sapiens neanderthalensis)*, because the remains were first found in the valley (*thal* in German) of the Neander River in northwestern Germany. *Sapiens* means "wise," for Neanderthal had a very large brain and survived by its wits. Neanderthal hunted big game and appears to have practiced a primitive animism—a belief that spiritual beings inhabit inanimate objects and affect human life. The appearance of religion was a ma-

jor development in human evolution. It may have been related to the willingness, which first appeared among the Neanderthal, to care for members of the family or clan who through illness or injury were unable to gather food and protect themselves from predators. Among the Neanderthal skeletons studied by anthropologists are those of cripples who clearly lived long after they had become incapacitated.

The direct ancestor of the today's human beings, the fully modern hominid *(Homo sapiens sapiens)*, emerged about 100,000 years ago, during the last ice age. The first find of this creature was discovered in Cro-Magnon, France, and it is commonly called Cro-Magnon Man. Neanderthal died out about 35,000 years ago, leaving Cro-Magnon in possession of the earth. There may have been interbreeding between the two species while they coexisted, though the evidence is inconclusive. In any case, the two were associated with different climatic conditions. In the Middle East, Neanderthal remains are associated with animals and plants adapted to a cooler climate than those associated with

Homo habilis made tools by striking flakes off of a core.

This bone shows the cut marks of the butchering process.

The Spread of Human Populations, about 10,000 B.C.

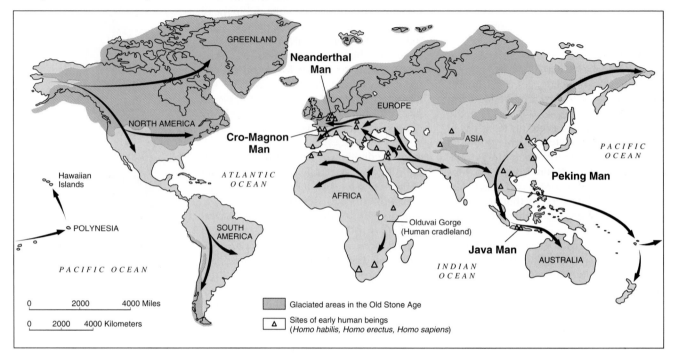

Cro-Magnon remains. This suggests that Cro-Magnon originated in Africa and migrated north during warming trends and retreated to the south when the climate cooled in the mini–ice ages that have occurred repeatedly during the interglacial periods.

The Culture of Early Hominids

Just before the end of Neanderthal Man, about 40,000 years ago, both species of

Climate and Neanderthal Man

Archaeologists discovered the connection between Neanderthal and particular climatic conditions by studying the remains of plants and animals found in their campsites. Many plants are sensitive to temperature and moisture and can be associated with a type of climate. Rodents are even more sensitive to climate than plants, and those that lived with the Neanderthals were cold-weather animals, while those whose remains are found in connection with Cro-Magnon bones and tools were adapted to warm climates.

hominid went through a cultural revolution stimulated, probably, by a rapid warming trend that forced the hominid communities to adapt to new plants and animals. Once started, the process of change gained momentum, so that in a few thousand years it resulted in greater technological advances than had been achieved during the previous 2.5 million years of toolmaking. Both Neanderthal and Cro-Magnon created sophisticated implements of stone, bone, and wood. Among these new tools were blades and spear points of better quality than those of their ancestors, fish hooks, and sewing needles for making clothing—and, perhaps, shelters—from animal skins and sinews. Ultimately, Neanderthal seems to have been unable to adapt to the warming climate, and Cro-Magnon carried on the cultural development, introducing the use of handles for tools and creating ornaments for personal adornment. Cro-Magnon communities also showed an interest in religion. About 30,000 years ago, they began painting elaborate scenes on the walls of caves and making sculptures, probably meant to increase fertility and ensure success in the hunt.

Archaeologists have not found any of the earliest Cro-Magnon dwellings, which must have been lightweight shelters that could be easily carried as the hunting society followed game, such as mammoth (ancestor of the modern elephant) and bison. The earliest known houses, dating from the end of the last ice age about 13,000–15,000 years ago, were found in southern Russia. These were substantial structures built on frames of mammoth bones and associated with storage pits for food, suggesting the existence of large, permanent communities. Why did such communities come into being?

Again, the evidence points to climatic change. According to one hypothesis, the end of the ice age produced a population explosion that forced people to curtail their migrations and to settle down in "home" territories. At the same time, the vast herds of ice-age animals died out as the warming trend reforested a world that for thousands of years had been covered with prairies. In the south—for example, in the Middle East—the warming trend led to the spread of the desert. In the region north of the Dead Sea, people reacted to the encroachment of the desert by settling near the few remaining lakes. As we shall see, that decision led to the most momentous revolution in human history, the invention of agriculture.

Before turning to that story, we must ask one other question: What does the evidence reveal about the social life of the early hominids? So long as the animal relied on the gathering of fruits and other vegetable food for sustenance, there was no differentiation of sex roles, but biology did produce a size difference between males and females. Evolution favored large males, who had an advantage in creating and maintaining a clan—the grouping of a dominant male with several females and their young. Because size had little to do with female ability to reproduce, care for young, or gather food, their genes did not evolve toward largeness.

The shift from a gathering economy to a hunting economy, which *H. habilis* brought about, may have contributed to the role differentiation between males and females in hominid society. Once the species began to hunt large animals, the basic economy was divided into male and female realms. Hunting was a male activity because it required strength and speed,

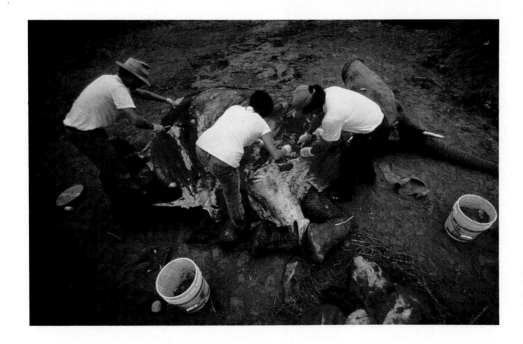

In an effort to understand the ways of ancient people, archaeologists butcher a "mammoth" using primitive tools.

Homo habilis skull: The inside of the skull preserves an impression of the brain that scientists can analyze.

and it was a cooperative activity because a lone hunter could not kill big game. To succeed, the clans had to join together in larger bands, and the men had to learn to cooperate. This development must have produced a social system that permitted families to live together more or less in harmony. Studies of the cranial fossils of *H. habilis* seem to show that their brain, which left its imprint on the bones, had developed the regions that permit human beings to use speech, and this too would be consistent with an economic revolution that demanded cooperation and communal living.

The culture of early hominids from *Homo erectus* to *Homo sapiens sapiens* is called the Paleolithic Culture, or Old Stone Age Culture (400,000–10,000 years ago). Although the economy of Paleolithic peoples was limited to what nature provided, nature was relatively generous. Evidence from hunting camps of the late Paleolithic period suggests that the inhabitants may have "managed" herds of wild animals. The refuse found at some of the camps consists mainly of the bones of young animals, from which archaeologists conclude

that the inhabitants practiced some form of herding and culling. This impression is strengthened by the presence of dog skeletons in the camps. About 20,000 years ago, the hunters either domesticated dogs and used them in controlling the wild herds or, less likely, had already formed a symbiotic relationship—a relationship mutually advantageous to two independent species.

Still, it is clear that the Paleolithic hunter-gatherers did little to manipulate nature. Human beings did not truly domesticate nature until they invented agriculture about 10,000 years ago.

Agriculture and the New Stone Age

Recent finds suggest that agriculture was first practiced in Palestine just north of the Dead Sea. There, about 10,000–11,000 years ago, the Natufians (named for Wadi-al-Natuf, a site in the hills of the region), the people who had reacted to the drying trend by settling down near the remaining lakes, began to sow the grains they had been gathering in the wild for thousands of years.

About 11,000 years ago, the earth went through a mini–ice age that lasted 1,000 years, creating an environment that obliged the Natufians to take nature into their own hands. The cooling trend forced them to choose between moving away or finding a way to produce food where they were. They chose to cultivate wild grains and stayed where they were.

The first farmers cultivated wheat, barley, and other grains, and about 1,000 years later they began to domesticate sheep, goats, and cattle. They used dogs to guard their flocks and kept cats to protect their stored grain from rodents. The communities were larger than those of the hunter-gatherer societies and might contain as many as several hundred people.

In contrast to hunter-gatherer communities, agricultural communities did not require that everybody spend all their time producing food. At the peak periods of sowing and harvesting, everyone in the village would join in the farm work. In between, however, many of the people could engage in other activities. Some be-

Disease and the Agricultural Revolution

The principal result of the agricultural revolution was an enormous growth of the human population. Within a few hundred years, the number of people in agricultural regions had grown to be ten or twenty times larger than the hunter-gatherer economy supported. One result of this population growth and of the new contact with domesticated animals, was the spread of new diseases. The dense populations of the agricultural towns provided pools of hosts that permitted viruses and bacteria to sustain themselves as they could not in the small communities of hunter-gatherers. Even though people developed antibodies against the invaders, large populations always provided unprotected hosts. In addition, constant contact with domesticated animals introduced new diseases. Measles appears to be related to rinderpest, a cattle disease, and to distemper, common among canines; influenza probably came from hogs; smallpox from cowpox. The list of diseases shared by human beings and their domesticated animals is very large.

See William H. McNeil, Plagues and Peoples *(New York, 1976) esp. pp. 31–68.*

came specialists in weaving, making pots or tools, and house building, in what was essentially a revolution of technology and the arts. The villagers produced a wide variety of buildings, implements, and goods, and they engaged in trade. They exchanged stone to be used in the making of tools, and materials such as amber for art or personal ornamentation. The toolkit of these communities was extremely large and beautifully crafted of polished stone. Archaeologists have recognized the epochal change represented by such implements by giving this period a new name, the Neolithic Age, or New Stone Age, to distinguish it from the cruder culture of the Paleolithic hunter-gatherers.

From its beginnings in Palestine, agriculture spread north, east, and, perhaps, south. Some of the earliest agricultural sites are in the hills of northern Mesopotamia (the region between the Tigris and

Euphrates rivers in modern Turkey and Iraq). Agriculture also spread east toward the Indus Valley, where the new technology provided a basis for the first Indian civilization. Whether the agricultural revolution to the south along the Nile stemmed from Palestine or arose independently is not clear, although archaeologists have found ancient evidence that grains figured in the diet of the people of that region. They used metates—a grinding stone—to prepare grains that grew in pools produced by annual floods, so they might have learned to sow their plants independently of the Natufians.

Certainly the Chinese and the Native Americans invented agriculture on their own. About 4000 B.C., the Chinese of the Yellow River Valley developed an agriculture based on millet. The farmers of that region practiced slash-and-burn agriculture, cutting and burning off the forest,

Origins of Agriculture   6000 B.C.

using the fields until the soil became infertile, and then moving on. Around 5000 B.C., the American peoples of central Mexico were growing peppers, squash, pumpkins, and avocados. It is not known when they succeeded in creating hybrid maize (corn), which became their staple crop.

Language and Language Groups

In 1786, Sir William Jones, an orientalist serving with the British government in India, published a work in which he claimed that Sanskrit, the language of the ancient Hindu classics, was related to Greek and Latin. The three languages must, Jones argued, have originated from a common linguistic source, which became known as Indo-European. Jones's study laid the foundation for historical linguistics, which has produced a historical map of language families and their relationships. In the last forty years, Soviet linguists have shown that modern languages preserve the remnants of the prehistoric languages from which they arose and that the great language families—Indo-European, Semitic, Altic (East Asian languages), and Amerind—arose from even earlier languages, leading back to the very first human language. That aboriginal language may have been spoken by *Homo erectus,* the hominid that first moved out of Africa to populate the world.

The reconstruction of the history of language has produced some interesting results. Proto-Indo-European ("proto" means the one before, in this case the language from which Indo-European evolved) and the ancestor languages of the Semitic and Altic families contain words associated with agriculture—for example, the names of domesticated plants. The even more ancient language from which these groups derived, called Nostratic (Our Language), lacks any such words, an indication that it was in use before the agricultural revolution. But Nostratic contains an ambiguous word, *kuyna,* that could mean either wolf or dog. (It evolved into the English word *hound.*) The ambiguity may reveal a stage in the relationship between human beings and canines during which canines first be-

came domesticated and the distinction between the wild and friendly breeds had not yet been established. Clearly, linguistic reconstructions provide a good deal of information about ancient cultures.

The Indo-European family, to which nearly all of the European languages belong, seems to have arisen in Anatolia, a region of modern Turkey. Because surviving traces of Proto-Indo-European contain words that were apparently borrowed from Mesopotamia, the language must have been spoken by people who were in contact with that region. Moreover, the language contains words for mountains and swift rivers as well as for domesticated plants and animals. Anatolia fits this linguistic environment perfectly, and scholars now think that the Indo-European language was carried into Europe by farmers from that region.

When and at what rate the language spread are difficult to determine. The migration may have begun in the third millennium B.C. and progressed at an average pace of one mile per year. At that rate, the speakers of Indo-European would have reached the western limits of Europe in 1,500 years. As they moved west, they broke into subgroups, each speaking a language, or a closely related group of languages—Greek, Italic, Gaelic, German, or Slavic—derived from Indo-European. Shortly after 2000 B.C., the Italic tribes moved into Italy, and the Greeks colonized the Balkans and the region around the Aegean Sea. By 1000 B.C., the Celts (Gaelic speakers) controlled most of Europe. Not long afterward, the Germanic and Slavic peoples migrated into central and eastern Europe and into Scandinavia.

During this same period, Indo-European speakers were migrating into southwest Asia and India. Among these peoples were the Kassites, who invaded Mesopotamia in the early 1500s B.C., and the Sanskrit-speaking peoples, the Aryans, who conquered parts of India about a century later. The Persians also were part of this eastward migration of Indo-European speakers.

During the second millennium B.C., (1800–1200 B.C.), as Indo-European culture and language spread across Europe

Family Tree of Indo-European Languages

PROTO-INDO-EUROPEAN

INDO-IRANIAN
- INDIC
  - *Sanskrit and Prakrits*
    - Romany
    - Bengali
    - Hindi
- IRANIC
  - *Avestan*
  - *Old Persian*
  - Modern Persian

BALTO-SLAVIC
- SLAVIC
  - EAST
    - Byelorussian
    - Russian
    - Ukrainian
  - WEST
    - Slovak
    - Czech
    - Polish
  - SOUTH
    - Serbo-Croatian
    - Slovenian
    - Bulgarian
- BALTIC
  - Lithuanian
  - Latvian
  - *Old Prussian*

Armenian

Albanian

TOCHARIAN
- *Tocharian B*
- *Tocharian A*

ANATOLIAN
- *Hittite*

HELLENIC
- *Mycenaean*
  - *Attic-Ionic*
  - Greek (Koine)
  - *Aeolic*
  - *Doric*

ITALIC
- Oscan
- *Latin—Old German*
  - Romanian
  - Italian
  - French
  - Portuguese
  - Spanish
- Sabine

CELTIC
- *Gaulish*
- GOIDELIC
  - *Manx*
  - Irish Gaelic
  - Scots Gaelic
- BRYTHONIC
  - Breton
  - *Cornish*
  - Welsh

GERMANIC
- NORTH
  - EAST
    - Danish Swedish
  - WEST
    - Norwegian
    - Icelandic
    - Faeroese
- EAST
  - *Gothic*
- WEST
  - NETHERLANDIC-GERMAN
    - HIGH
      - Yiddish
      - Modern Standard German
    - LOW
      - *Old Saxon*
        - Modern Low German (Plattdeutsch)
      - *Old Low Franconian*
        - Dutch
        - Afrikaans
        - Flemish
  - ANGLO-FRISIAN
    - Frisian
    - English

9

and southern Asia, in the ancient heartland in Anatolia, the Hittites were creating a great empire that came to dominate the Middle East.

THE ORIGIN OF CIVILIZATION

In the culture of the Neolithic farmers, as in that of the hunter-gatherers, the skills and knowledge that governed a community's way of life were passed down by word of mouth from one generation to another. Because what was transmitted depended on the capacity of human memory, the sum of cultural knowledge remained relatively constant. Moreover, because the small communities survived by keeping rigorously to their ancient ways, cultural practices changed only slightly through the generations.

Civilization is culture that extends beyond the limits of human memory and the limits of the local community. A civilization—from the Latin adjective for city life (*civilis*)—requires great resources of food and large-scale social and political organization that permits many people to practice arts unconnected with food production. The growth of a civilization results from elaboration of every aspect of village culture. Agricultural production reaches new heights through political organization of the workforce. Trade becomes big business and connects the town to distant places. Religion acquires an elaborate ritual and body of beliefs. The large body of skills and knowledge required for such activities cannot exist without writing. Written records are necessary to maintain control over complex commercial, political, and social activities. They are both the repository and the source of intellectual invention.

The Early Civilization of Old Europe

A transitional phase from the farming culture of the Neolithic Age to an early stage of civilization has been identified in the Balkans and Central Europe. This advanced culture, called Old Europe, was based on large, stable, agricultural villages, and it can be traced back to about 5000 b.c. The people of the region did not, as far as we know, use writing, but they did use pictographic symbols, such as the bird, the bull, and the snake.

The soil of the region was fertile, though the climate was uncertain, and the villages were relatively wealthy. Even the oldest villages had granaries and produced well-crafted pottery for food storage. This economy permitted the Old Europeans to develop a large commercial trade. Their basic toolkit was made of stone, some transported from distant quarries, though they began to use copper very early. Some stone and metal came from the eastern Mediterranean.

These people depended on the regular cycle of the seasons and the fecundity of their animals. Their villages contained shrines and clay models of shrines, and

Old Europe   6000–3500 b.c.

their pottery bore pictures and symbols that served as charms against the fury of nature. The bird goddess, who laid the universal egg, was painted on pottery and represented in figurines, sometimes realistically, but usually abstractly. The snake, which periodically sheds its skin and moves mysteriously, represented the world's turning and the cycle of the seasons. Often depicted abstractly as a spiral, the snake was a common motif in Old European art, as were the bull, the toad, the cross (which in Old Europe and in the hieroglyphs of Egypt represented life), and representations of water as rain, river, and ocean. All these symbols reflected the beliefs of people dependent on nature. Some motifs of Minoan and Greek mythology—such as the bull born of a woman and the bird-goddess aspects of Hera, queen of the gods in the Greek pantheon—have been linked with motifs found in the culture of Old Europe. Old Europe was apparently one of the sources of the civilizations that arose in the eastern Mediterranean.

THE CIVILIZATION OF MESOPOTAMIA, *ca.* 3500–1500 B.C.

The first true civilization arose in lower Mesopotamia, where farming depended on the flooding of rivers rather than on rain. Once agricultural communities learned to use dikes and canals to control and channel the floods, they greatly expanded their food production and, consequently, their populations. The first cities were not, however, merely enlarged agricultural villages; they were a new type of community. They were centers of political order and power and religious worship, and their population was both larger and more specialized than that of agricultural villages. The large urban market created a demand for the best products of the human imagination and fostered new levels of invention and specialization.

The development of cities required a more abundant agriculture than that of the ancient agricultural regions, where the climate and soil were marginal, and a more

certain agriculture than that of Old Europe, where the climate produced cycles of good and bad harvests. When the idea of farming spread into the rich countryside of the lower Tigris and Euphrates valleys during the fourth millennium B.C., the people there had to devise new methods of using the annual floodwaters of the rivers. To construct and maintain irrigation systems required larger and better organized communities than those of the rain-watered uplands. An intricate system of reservoirs was needed to catch the floodwater and a system of canals to distribute it. Failure to perform these operations meant widespread famine, but success in managing the floods produced a stable and prosperous economy that could support a large population. Within such a population, many were free to practice arts not directly connected with the production of food.

Around 4000 B.C., at places like Ur, Tell Shahrain, and Tepe Gawra, the people of Mesopotamia built large, mud-brick towns, each centered on a temple, which was furnished with equipment that took skill and time to make. The centrality of the temple reflected the importance of the priests who served in it. Next to farming, propitiation of the divine powers that controlled the environment was the most important activity of the community.

The sites of settlement in Mesopotamia were in continuous use for hundreds of years—some reveal twelve or more layers of settlement—so we can follow the course of their development closely. The temples were built on large rectangular platforms that rose above the town. About 3100 B.C., the towns began to erect ziggurats—stepped platforms—in place of the older temples. These immense stone works became the dominant features of the first cities. At about the same time, the Sumerians began using copper and silver vessels and producing larger-than-life sculptures, both signs of wealth.

It used to be thought that the Sumerians, who were among the earliest city-builders of Mesopotamia, invented writing in about 3500 B.C. Recent archaeological finds indicate, however, that writing arose more or less simultaneously throughout

Ziggurat at Ur (*ca.* 2250 B.C.).

the region. If any area had a claim on priority, it would be Elam, the hilly area to the north and east of Sumeria, though the evidence is inconclusive.

The First Writing Systems

The earliest form of writing was pictograms, in which concepts and things were represented by drawings. Over time, these pictograms became increasingly abstract, more signs than pictures.

The next stage was syllabic writing, in which signs represented syllables of words. This form of writing has the advantage of representing the spoken language, rather than the physical world, but it has the disadvantage of being tied to language. Thus, one cannot read syllabic script unless one knows the language it represents. Cuneiform was a syllabic script.

Finally, alphabetic writing is based on signs that represent individual sounds, or phonemes, of a language. This script is highly adaptable because, although syllables differ markedly from one language to another, elemental sounds are relatively common among languages, and an alphabet can be easily adapted to fit a large variety of languages (see p. 24).

For an excellent source of illustrations, see Reading the Past: Ancient Writing from Cuneiform to the Alphabet, *intro. J. T. Hooker (Berkeley: UC Press, 1990).*

Everywhere it is found, the earliest writing related to keeping accounts of storing and trading agricultural goods. The temple buildings included the city's storage facilities, and the priests played a central role in the economic life of the communities and in the economic relations among the cities of the region. Writing was the special skill of temple priests. In fact, for hundreds of years writing was used only for purposes of commerce.

About 3000 B.C., Mesopotamian society began to change rapidly. Apparently the cities had succeeded in exploiting their environment and had begun to achieve substantial wealth, indicated by discovery of an increasing number of metal tools and personal ornaments in the excavation layers of this period. Engraved cylindrical seals—used to mark trade goods—bear pictures of chariots and boats, indicating the importance of war and transport, and evidence exists that the Sumerian cities were now being ruled by kings.

Kingship was new at that time. It was the product of wealth, which attracted attacks by the poor tribes of the hills and deserts, and required military protection. But at the same time, the growth of wealth created a market for a wide variety of goods, which in turn created the need for raw materials. To avoid becoming dependent on the regions that could supply the raw materials, the cities often tried to bring them under their control, by war if necessary.

During the third millennium, the cities of Mesopotamia were fortified and kings became prominent. War became a constant in the river valleys. In the royal tombs at Ur, mosaic representations of troops led by a king provide striking evidence of the importance of war in the lives of the people and of the power of the kings.

Scholars are not sure how kingship arose. Some believe that the institution originated in the position of chief priest. Others think it came into being as a result of the rise of warfare. It is clear that the earliest kings served as war leaders, but they also performed religious functions. They were viewed as guarantors of the welfare of the city and its population, which led to the view that they had a special relationship with the gods.

The rise of kings created new uses of writing. To maintain their authority, the kings had inscriptions prepared that memorialized royal deeds. Lists of earlier kings provided proof that the current king derived his authority from an ancient line and that he was the successor of a continuous series that had guaranteed good luck in the harvests and victory in war for longer than any living person could remember. During the later third millennium B.C., scribes recorded the ancient traditions of the people, including the story of a great flood. The Israelites, who traced their history back to the Mesopotamian city of Ur, incorporated that story and others into their own historical tradition.

During the Early Dynastic Period in Sumeria, between about 3000 B.C. and 2370 B.C., each of the small city-states that dotted Mesopotamia was ruled by a king. These communities managed to organize the floodplain agriculture, develop bronze and other metallurgy, and build impressive temples. Eleven of them have been discovered—each the seat of a royal dynasty, and each with a history of alliances and wars.

About 2370 B.C., Sargon of Akkad, the king of the Akkadians—speakers of a Se-mitic language—united the whole region of south Mesopotamia in the world's first imperial state. It appears that over time Sargon and his successors extended their control to Elam in the north and all the way to eastern Asia Minor in the northwest. The Akkadians were the first to use writing, which they inherited from the Sumerians, for purposes other than commerce and temple accounts. In the remains of their cities, archaeologists have found a treasure of literary works that represent the first written record of an ancient people's religious beliefs and historical consciousness.

The power of the Akkadians was broken about 2200 B.C. by raiders from the Zagros Mountains to the east. These newcomers founded a new dynasty, the Third Dynasty, at Ur, which had been one of

Minister or ambassador makes presentation to the king.

The Akkadian Empire   *ca.* 2370 B.C.

the principal cities of the Akkadian empire. For the next century and a half, the kings of Ur dominated lower Mesopotamia, while the other sections of Sargon's former domain went their own ways. During this period, the Mesopotamians developed the pictographic writing they had inherited from the Sumerians and the Akkadians into an abstract form called cuneiform ("wedge-shaped": from the Latin word for wedge, *cuneus*), which was more compact and versatile than the earlier script. The technology, art, and architecture of the Third Dynasty make it the classical period of Mesopotamian civilization.

Just before 2000 B.C., the influence of Ur was broken by new raids of Elamites and Amorites, mountain peoples from the north and east of Mesopotamia. The Amorites were Northwest Semitic people, related to the Canaanites and Israelites. About 1990 B.C. they founded the first dynasty of Babylon, just up the river from Akkad, the old center of Sargon's power. Under their king Hammurabi (r. *ca.* 1792–1750 B.C.), the Amorites, also called the Babylonians, re-created the empire of the Akkadians.

Hammurabi is famous for having issued a great code of law that incorporated earlier codifications by Sumerian and Akkadian kings. Hammurabi's code was more comprehensive than the earlier ones, however, and served as a model for later codes. It provided the basis for economic and social relations. Knowledge of the law made it possible for merchants and subordinate officials of the state to act independently of the king and to plan ahead, and it gave people confidence to try out new ways of doing things within the well-known rules of social tradition.

The Babylonians also produced the first-known mathematics. They solved rather complicated problems in arithmetic and geometry and had some understanding of algebra. Their system of numbers used both base 10 (decimal) and base 60 (sexagesimal). The modern 60-minute hour and 360-degree circle are vestiges of their system of measurement.

Like older agricultural peoples, the Babylonians studied the heavens, because agriculture depended on a knowledge of the seasons. The movements of the sun and moon had long been followed—there is evidence of this in the art of Old Europe—but the Babylonians succeeded in tracking the regular movements of the visible planets as well. They also engaged in astrology, which predicts events on the basis of planetary movements.

Babylonian civilization was not limited to a tiny elite. The very publication of Hammurabi's law code indicates that literacy was widespread. During Hammurabi's reign, Akkadian language, with cuneiform writing, became the medium of commerce and culture throughout the empire. A common Mesopotamian culture and numerous economic ties enabled Babylonian civilization to survive the political collapse caused by the invasion of the Indo-European Kassites from the east about 1595 B.C. This invasion destroyed the First Babylonian Dynasty and gave the Kassites control of southern Mesopotamia for 400 years. Babylon did not again become an important political center until the seventh century B.C.

EGYPTIAN CIVILIZATION, THE PRE-DYNASTIC PERIOD, *ca.* 3800–3100 B.C.

Nine hundred miles to the southwest of Mesopotamia, another river, the Nile, provided a setting for irrigated agriculture. The Nile flows south to north for more than 600 miles, and each year it deposits fertile soil over its floodplains. In the south (Upper Egypt), the band of fertility is rarely more than ten miles wide, but in the north (Lower Egypt), the river forms a large, swampy, fertile delta.

The first agricultural villages in Egypt date from the early fifth millennium B.C., and the implements used by the first farmers show the influence of northern cultures such as Jericho in Palestine, where agriculture had begun at least a thousand years earlier. Though the northerners' influence was significant, the Egyptians preserved much of their own pre-agricultural culture. In fact, one of the characteristics of Egyptian culture was its ability to absorb

Tablet containing the code of Hammurabi, *ca.* 1750 B.C.

external influences without losing its essential nature. At various points in their history, the Egyptians received new technologies from abroad, but absorbed them into a culture that diverged little from its ancient course.

The history of Pre-Dynastic Egypt—which might also be called pre-civilized Egypt—has been divided into several broad periods, representing the development of pottery and other implements. During the last of these periods, from about 3800 B.C. to 3100 B.C., the pace of change quickened, especially in Hierakonpolis (Greek for "City of the Falcon"; the Egyptians called it Nehken), a large community along the Nile in Upper Egypt supported by floodplain agriculture but dominated by the manufacture of pottery and other fine goods.

During the first centuries of the fourth millennium B.C., the population of Hierakonpolis grew to between 2,500 and 10,000. Throughout the settlement, archaeologists have found kilns and pottery "factories," some of them covering more than a quarter of an acre. The factories produced two types of pottery—a coarse ware made of clay mixed with straw and a fine ware called Plum Red Ware that was fired at high temperatures. Natural wind tunnels in cliffs near the town were used as kilns for the fine ware. The town also produced mace heads made of stone, which were used by the rulers of the Nile Valley as symbols of authority.

Most of the dwellings in Hierakonpolis were rectangular and built of mud brick. They were crowded close together, though some seem to have had gardens around them. This suggests that the town was large and wealthy enough to support an elite class. Moreover, in the town cemetery excavators have found large tombs, along with normal-sized ones similar to those found elsewhere in the valley. The elite, probably a merchant elite, dominated this society in death as in life.

The power of Hierakonpolis rested on its pottery works, but its survival depended on agriculture. After about 3500 B.C., the original agricultural economy began to decline as the climate became drier and the savannah (grassland

A Babylonian boundary stone (*ca.* thirteenth to tenth century B.C.), showing an example of cuneiform writing.

Pre-Dynastic Egyptian pottery jar decorated with gazelles and ostriches.

Ancient Egypt

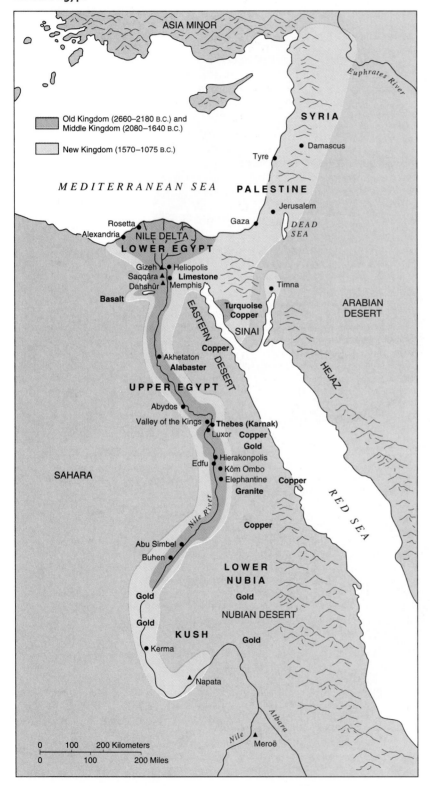

and sparse woods) turned into desert. The population was forced to move closer to the Nile, and the kilns and cemetery were abandoned.

In the ensuing decades, the old elite appears to have used its wealth to establish control over the new villages founded along the river. The villages were likely governed by individual merchant families, but any tendency toward independence was countered by the need for cooperation to control the floodwaters. During this period the ruling elites began large irrigation projects and built palaces, temples, and walled towns. They began to use the symbols of royal authority—particularly the crown and the mace—and conflict among the fortified villages became common. The history of Egypt between 3500 and 3100 B.C. was marked by both war and cooperation among the petty kings. There is also evidence of active trade with the Mesopotamian centers of civilization.

About 3200 B.C., the local kingdoms had grown powerful enough to check each others' ambitions, and constant war became a feature of life in the Nile Valley. During this period, the rulers of Hierakonpolis, which had become one of the royal centers, began again to use the old cemetery, continuing the ancient tradition of worship of the dead. The cemetery was built in the form of a necropolis, a city of the dead, to symbolize the society of the living. It was laid out along a dry stream (a *wadi*), which represented the Nile.

About a hundred years later, Narmer of Hierakonpolis (his name means Catfish) succeeded in unifying the valley. Narmer may have built on the success of his predecessor Scorpion, but the Egyptians regarded him as the first pharaoh, the founder of the First Dynasty.

The cemetery of Hierakonpolis is divided into sections representing the two halves of Narmer's united Egypt. The tombs of the southern section are built of mud brick in the manner of Upper Egypt, and those of the northern section are built of stone in the style of Lower Egypt. A particularly large tomb, on the border between the two sections, may be that of Scorpion. Its position symbolizes the unification achieved by the dynasty of Hierakonpolis.

Dynastic Egypt, ca. 3100–333 B.C.

What we know about the history of unified Egypt comes from the work of a third century B.C. priest named Manetho, who wrote a history of his country in Greek. He grouped the kings into 30 dynasties, from the legendary Narmer (Menes in Greek) to the last native Egyptian pharaoh, Nectanebo II, who died in 343 B.C. With the discovery of the Rosetta Stone in 1799 by Napoleon's conquering army, much older Egyptian historical sources became available. The stone, which is a tablet with parallel texts in Greek and in Egyptian hieroglyphics, provides the key to deciphering the ancient script. Modern historians count 31 dynasties and usually use Egyptian instead of Greek names for the pharaohs, but they follow Manetho's practice of dividing Egyptian history into dynasties. They also divide Egyptian history into long historical periods—the Early Dynastic Period (*ca.* 3100–2700), the Old Kingdom (*ca.* 2700–2150), the Middle Kingdom (*ca.* 2050–1650), and the New Kingdom (*ca.* 1550–1100). Between these kingdoms were periods of political disorder, and after the New Kingdom a series of Middle Eastern empires dominated Egypt for a time.

The full unification of the northern and southern kingdoms took about 400 years (3100–2700 B.C.), during which the foundations of Egyptian civilization were laid. This is the period of the first two dynasties, the Early Dynastic Period. The

The Rosetta Stone, found by Napoleon's troops in 1799, provided the key to deciphering the hierogliphs. It has the text in Greek and Egyptian.

success of these dynasties provided both the resources and the peace necessary for rapid cultural development.

The cemetery at Hierakonpolis, which dates back to about 3800 B.C., already contained artifacts that archaeologists consider characteristic of Egyptian civilization. For example, the arrangement of the cemetery as a necropolis, with wooden or reed houses built over many of the tombs, represented an early stage of the cult of the dead that later came to dominate Egyptian religion. In addition, some Hierakonpolis tombs from this early period contained pots bearing writing-like symbols that may actually be primitive writing, though archaeologists have not yet deciphered them. Painted scraps of a

Wall painting from grave at Hierakonpolis shows men and cattle.

| ca. 3100 B.C. | ca. 2700 | | ca. 2150 | ca. 2050 | | ca. 1650 | ca. 1550 | | ca. 1100 | ca. 650 |

Early Dynastic · Old Kingdom · Middle Kingdom · New Kingdom · 3rd Intermediate Period

1st Intermediate Period

2nd Intermediate Period

papyrus-like plant have also been found in the tombs. The use of papyrus for written records, instead of the stone or clay tablets used in Mesopotamia, provided the Egyptians with a cheap, easy-to-use writing material and greatly expanded their ability to create and circulate lengthy works.

Under the first dynasties, the pace of cultural advance quickened. Early attempts to manage the Nile floods had shown that the river could be a source of great agricultural wealth but that its potential could not be realized until all the projects along its course were managed by a single authority. The unification of Egypt provided that authority, and the wealth of Egypt grew as large-scale irrigation and flood-control projects were organized. To ensure that those activities were set in motion at the proper time, the priests, in close association with the pharaoh, created a precise calendar around the time of unification.

The Egyptians believed that the Nile Valley belonged to the gods. The pharaoh, under whose authority the river was harnessed, was the divine representative of the gods on earth, and it was he who drew wealth from the land. This belief contributed to the power of the priesthood in the society.

The idea that the gods controlled the environment, common to all agricultural societies, had long ago led the Egyptians to contemplate the boundary between the visible world of humans and the invisible world of the gods. The interaction between these two worlds was represented in the belief that, like the cycle of the seasons, the life of a person cycled through life and death—from birth to death to rebirth.

The formal activities at the junctures between these states of existence were analogous to the activities in agriculture. Just as the most important act of the agricultural cycle was collecting and preserving seed for the next year's planting, so the most important moment of a person's life was the preparation for life after death, through which one would pass to rebirth. The Egyptians believed that for this cycle to be completed, the body of the dead person had to be preserved, and evidence of primitive mummifying has been found in the ancient cemetery at Hierakonpolis. One of the most striking aspects of Egyptian culture was the cult of the dead, with its holy book, the Book of the Dead. The Egyptians were especially concerned to ensure that the pharaoh, the embodiment of authority and divinity, would have safe passage from life to death.

The contrast between Egyptian and Mesopotamian civilization is illuminating. While the Mesopotamians first used writing to keep temple accounts and records of commerce, the Egyptians appear to have first used writing in connection with the cult of the dead. If the mysterious symbols on the pots found at Hierakonpolis

Egyptian Hieroglyphs

Hieroglyphs were used longer than any other script. The earliest date from about 3100 B.C., and they were used until the eleventh century after Christ. It was a pictorial script, with most signs representing whole words. Later versions of the script also contained signs signifying single sounds—phonemes—of the language and determinatives, symbols that indicated the precise meaning of a word.

See Reading the Past: Ancient Writing from Cuneiform to the Alphabet, *intro. J. T. Hooker (Berkeley: UC Press, 1990).*

turn out to be examples of the first Egyptian script, this will seem even more likely. Likewise, the Mesopotamians concentrated their engineering skills, celebrated in the biblical story of the tower of Babel (a ziggurat), on building temples, while the Egyptians concentrated on building tombs. Their tombs were far more impressive and technically advanced than the "palaces" built by the great men. For the Egyptians, the transient world of the living was of slight significance compared with the eternal world of the dead.

The principal architectural achievements of the Egyptians were in fact the great pyramid tombs. The first one was built at Saqqara by Djoser (Zoser in Greek), the first or second pharaoh of the Third Dynasty (r. *ca.* 2600 B.C.). This tomb was a stepped pyramid surrounded by an enclosure and outbuildings—a suitable dwelling for the pharaoh after death. Later, the style shifted to smooth-sided pyramids. About a century after Djoser, Khufu (Cheops in Greek) had the Great Pyramid of Giza built as a tomb for himself and his queen. This tomb covered 13 acres and was 482 feet high. It was constructed of more than 2,300,000 $2\frac{1}{2}$-ton blocks of

stone, which had been transported to the site from a great distance.

According to the Greek historian Herodotus (fifth century B.C.), it took 20 years to build the Great Pyramid. Archaeologists estimate that 4,000 stone masons worked steadily through those years and that crews of up to 100,000 men hauled the stone and lifted the blocks into place. The Great Pyramid stands as the most impressive memorial of the Egyptians' view of the passage from life to death.

Controlling the whole lower course of the Nile (about 500 miles long) was a difficult task even for a highly centralized government. After unification, the pharaohs of the Third Dynasty created a large bureaucracy to help with the job and divided the kingdom into districts, called *nomes,* each governed by a royal vizier (nomarch).

This system worked well as long as the central government was strong. But weakness at the center presented an opportunity, and sometimes a necessity, for the local nomarchs to act independently. Although the reasons for one dynasty replacing another are not usually clear, evidence suggests that weakness in the

The great pyramid of Khufu with the Sphinx in the foreground.

central government often gave rise to political turmoil, out of which a strong nomarch or a royal bureaucrat emerged to found a new dynasty.

After the Old Kingdom the pharaohs stopped building pyramidal tombs, not because the Egyptians no longer believed in the cult of the dead, but because power had become too widely distributed throughout the kingdom. The nomarchic system had contributed to the governance of the country, but it had also provided local governors with their own power bases. This duality helps explain why the history of Egypt was both tumultuous and remarkably stable. There was always a class of able men ready to make a bid for control of the central authority, and those who won out were well schooled in the techniques of governing.

Between the great periods of Egyptian history—the Old, Middle, and New Kingdoms—were periods of weakness and, on occasion, subjugation. The Old Kingdom collapsed with the end of the Sixth Dynasty. The following century, from *ca.* 2150 to 2050 B.C., was a period of internal strife. The country was finally reunited by the pharaohs of the Eleventh Dynasty, who founded the Middle Kingdom. The Middle Kingdom may have ended shortly after the explosion of Thera, a volcanic island in the Aegean Sea. The explosion, the largest in recorded history, spewed more than 50 cubic miles of rock and lava into the atmosphere, created a tsunami, or tidal wave, that rose to 800 feet in some places, and produced an artificial winter whose traces are still discernible in the rings of the bristlecone pine of California's Sierra Nevada. Tons of hot ash fell on Egypt, and the tidal wave flooded the Nile delta. These events may have been the basis of the biblical stories of the plagues associated with the rise of Moses among the Hebrews living in Egypt. For nearly a century after this disaster, from about 1630 to 1550 B.C., Egypt was under the domination of the Hyksos, a people of unknown origin who gained control of the Nile delta and eventually formed a new dynasty themselves. But the Hyksos kings—called the Shepherd Kings, an indication that they were a nomadic peo-

ple—were never absorbed into Egyptian society, and Ahmose (r. 1570–1546 B.C.), the ruler of Thebes in Upper Egypt, finally expelled them. Ahmose became the first pharaoh of the Eighteenth Dynasty and founded the New Kingdom.

During the Eighteenth Dynasty Egypt expanded its contacts with the world around it. With the south it carried on a rich trade in gold and ivory; several times the pharaohs campaigned in the Sudan, perhaps to protect that trade. The Egyptians also conquered parts of southwest Asia, and cuneiform documents have been found at Egyptian sites dating from this period. Egyptian influence in Asia lasted until the middle of the twelfth century B.C. and coincided with the great Anatolian empire of the Hittites, against which Egypt fought several wars.

This extended contact with foreigners may have led to the religious experiment conducted by Pharaoh Akhenaton (r. 1379–1362 B.C.), who abandoned the old gods in favor of Aton. This god was represented by a sun-disk and was considered by Akhenaton to be his father. Akhenaton built a new capital city at Amarna and devised a new theology to support his religion. The experiment ended shortly after Akhenaton's death, and his successor Tutankhaton (r. 1361–1352 B.C.) abandoned the cult four years into his reign. Tutankh*aton* then changed his name to Tutankh*amen* and returned to the old capital at Thebes, the center of the cult of Amon. Under this young pharaoh, royal officials undertook major building projects in the capital. The furnishings of Tutankhamen's tomb, which was discovered intact in 1922, seem to reflect his return to the old religion.

In the eleventh century B.C., powerful families from the delta region overthrew the Theban dynasty, and the New Kingdom collapsed. This shift of power to the north shows the effects of Egypt's involvement in the affairs of Asia. The delta region had become the area of contact between old Egypt and its subject territories, and the new dynasties themselves were headed by foreigners. From the tenth to the eighth century B.C., Libyans who had been settled in military camps in the

Chair and mummy case from
Tutankhamen's tomb.

western delta formed new dynasties and dominated the country. Then power shifted to the south. From the late eighth to the middle of the seventh century, Kushites from Nubia in the Sudan held sway. Finally, from the seventh to the fourth century, Persians ruled the country.

After enduring centuries of conquest, probably few Egyptians recognized the finality of the Macedonian conquest led by Alexander the Great in 333 B.C. But from that time on, no Egyptian was able to revive the kingdom of Egypt even for a short time. After Alexander's death in 326 B.C., the Ptolemies, a Greek dynasty, ruled Egypt until the Roman conquest in 30 B.C.

Egyptian Civilization

By the time of the Middle Kingdom (*ca.* 2050–1750 B.C.), the scribes who ran the governmental bureaucracy had established an educational system that permitted talented men of humble origins to rise in the state service. The scribes also created a literary culture, which provided a basis for education in language and rhetoric, and which expressed the values and ideology of the educated elite.

Though the pharaoh was the head of all the cults, the priests of the various gods actually conducted the activities of the cults. Apparently, scribes enjoyed higher status than priests, because the scribes were exempt from the levy of troops and of labor, while the priests, at least those of the lower ranks, were not.

During the New Kingdom, the growth of the Egyptian empire in Asia and the conquest of the Sudan increased the importance of the military elite. The pharaohs received a military education and were supported by a professional officer class, which represented a new, third element in the upper classes of society. It seems that many pharaohs of the New Kingdom chose their wives from leading military families.

Although the early pharaohs appear to have been members of the merchant elite, merchants had little status in the mature civilization of Egypt. Their activities were limited to local markets and low-cost wares. Long-distance and large-scale trade was a state activity controlled by the priests, perhaps because the temples were so richly endowed with land that they were the largest suppliers of the market. The three segments of the upper class—the scribes, the priests, and the military—controlled the wealth of the society.

The upper classes provided a market for a substantial artisan class—woodworkers, metalworkers, artists, and others—in their households. Though the artisans constituted a "middle" class, they were not independent entrepreneurs, and they could not sell their goods in the open market.

Below these classes was the great mass of peasants, whose labor supported the rest of society. The peasants lived in villages and had their own farm plots, but the agricultural wealth of the society rested on the great state projects that controlled and distributed the floodwaters of the Nile. At each of the crucial times in the agricultural cycle, the pharaohs and nomarchs organized a labor draft, or corvée. The peasants formed the core of these great labor forces, but members of the artisan and priestly classes also were enlisted. When the agricultural chores were light, many peasants probably supplemented their income by working on the pyramids or other great building projects. The peasants also provided the manpower for the armies.

Slaves constituted only a small segment of the population. Most were foreign prisoners of war. Upper-class families generally had one or two household slaves, and the pharaohs maintained slave labor forces in the state mines and on some construction projects. Slaves were not commonly used in agriculture, however.

Egyptian society was tightly regulated and highly traditional, anchored in the ideas and artistic styles of the past. Although men dominated society, women were not altogether subordinate. Marriage, as in other ancient societies, was arranged by contract between the husband—or the husband's family—and the father of the bride, but women seem to have had the right to divorce and to make commercial contracts. There was a female

priesthood as well as a male priesthood, and men and women were accorded equal treatment in the cult of the dead.

Egyptian civilization, though often subjected to foreign influence, preserved its distinctive, indigenous character to a great degree. Moreover, it had an enormous influence on the civilizations of other Mediterranean peoples.

Small Kingdoms in the Near East

**THE ERA OF SMALL KINGDOMS,
ca. 1250–750 B.C.**

Between about 1150 and 750 B.C., the absence of any great imperial power in the Middle East enabled several small kingdoms to flourish. Among them were the Phoenician city-states along the eastern coast of the Mediterranean, in present-day Lebanon, and the Canaanite and Hebrew kingdoms of Palestine.

The Phoenicians

The Phoenicians were a people of mixed background who lived in cities along the eastern Mediterranean coast. By about 1100 B.C., Phoenician ships were plying the Mediterranean trade routes, and for the next three centuries Phoenicians controlled commerce in the Mediterranean.

The Phoenicians built a great commercial empire by trading with the established cities of the Mediterranean world and by founding colonies in the western regions. Those colonies, most notably Carthage, near modern Tunis in North Africa, exploited the surrounding regions and helped supply Phoenician industry with raw materials. Phoenician ships regularly voyaged to Cornwall, Brittany, and Ireland for tin to be used in bronze manufacture. Egyptian writings suggest that the Phoenicians may have sailed all of the way around Africa, and some scholars believe that they may even have reached the Americas.

The oldest Phoenician city was Byblos, located on the coast north of Tyre (the largest of the cities), famous for the manufacture of writing materials. The Greek word for book, *biblion,* stems from its name. The Phoenicians helped to refine and spread the Northwest Semitic alphabetical system of writing. This was a great advance over Egyptian hieroglyphics and Sumerian-Akkadian cuneiform because it used simple-to-draw and easily recognizable symbols (letters) to represent sounds. The Phoenician alphabet consisted of 22 letters and was the basis of the three major alphabets now used in the Western world: Hebrew, Greek, and Latin. The Greek alphabet, in turn, was the basis of the Cyrillic alphabet used in Russia and parts of eastern Europe, and an Aramaic version of the West Semitic script formed the basis for the writing systems of India.

About 750 B.C., the Phoenician cities came under the domination of the Assyrian Empire and fell into rapid decline. Many of the leading merchant families migrated to the western colonies, especially to Carthage, which became the center of the Phoenician world until it was destroyed by the Romans in 146 B.C.

The Israelites

Between about 1250 and 400 B.C., the Israelites, or the Hebrews, as they were sometimes called, founded a state in Palestine. If not for their innovations in religion and for their use of the Northwest Semitic alphabet to record them, these people would be only a vague presence in the history of the region, almost indistinguishable from the Canaanites, to whom they were closely related. (Hebrew is a dialect of Canaanite.) In their written record, a collection of books composed between about 1000 and 150 B.C., they chronicled their historical relationship with their God, Yahweh, and that account subsequently influenced Christianity and Islam, the other two great religions of the Mediterranean-European world.

The Israelites traced their origin to Mesopotamia, from which, they believed, their patriarch Abraham had migrated. In fact, they preserved many of the historical and legal traditions of Mesopotamia. The story of the great flood, for example, was known in Mesopotamia, and a fragment of the Babylonian version of the story, dating to the fourteenth century B.C., has been found at Megiddo, a city in Palestine. The legal code of the Israelites was derived in part from the Mesopotamian tradition represented by the laws of Hammurabi.

Yet while the Israelites preserved the memory of a migration out of Mesopotamia, they were really formed as a people in the delta region of Egypt around the town of Avaris, the old capital of the Hyksos, who may have settled them there. During the Hyksos period (1630–1550 B.C.), many Semitic words had entered the Egyptian language. Long after the Egyptians expelled the Hyksos, the Egyptian pharaoh Ramses II (r. 1290–*ca.* 1224 B.C.) rebuilt Avaris as Raamses, the "house of Ramses," and the Hebrew Bible (Exodus 1.11) tells us that the ancestors of the Israelites were pressed into service building that city.

Not long after Ramses' death (date uncertain), Moses emerged as leader of the enslaved peoples living in the area of Raamses (Goshen, Genesis 47.27), and led

Phoenician	Greek	Roman
𐤀	A	A
𐤁	B	B
𐤂	Γ	G
𐤃	Δ	D
𐤄	E	E
𐤅	[Y]	F
𐤆	Z	Z
𐤇		H
𐤈	I	I
𐤉	K	[K]
𐤋	Λ	L
𐤌	M	M
𐤍	N	N
𐤏	O	O
𐤐	Π	P
𐤒		Q
𐤓	P	R
𐤔	Σ	S
𐤕	T	T
	Y	U,V
	X	X
	Ω	

Typical letters of the alphabet in Phoenician, Greek, and Roman forms. The final Greek letter, omega, is pronounced like the Roman long *o*.

Israelite or Hebrew?

We use the names Israelite and Hebrew interchangeably, but the ancient sources indicate that the two are not synonymous. "Hebrew" is used in the Mesopotamian, Hittite, and Egyptian sources to refer to people who came from outside the established community, and the term is associated with personal names belonging to many linguistic groups. In the Bible, the term is used infrequently and then only in the early texts. When the term is used in the Bible, it is nearly always in the mouths of foreigners speaking of the Israelites (Gen. 39.14, 17; Exod. 2.6), or the Israelites themselves are identifying themselves to foreigners (Gen. 40.15; Exod. 3.18).

It appears, then, that "Hebrew" was a name used to describe those elements of the middle eastern population who lived on the fringes of civilized society. The Israelites arose from this nomadic element, but they did not incorporate all who would have been identified as Hebrews in the second millennium B.C.

them out of Egypt. They crossed over the Sea of Reeds, probably an arm of Lake Menzaleh, near what is now El-Qantara along the Suez Canal, into the Sinai Peninsula. There they lived a nomadic life for a generation—40 years, according to tradition—during which Moses created their religion, perhaps borrowing elements from Midianite quarrymen and metalworkers at Egyptian copper mines in the region. According to the Bible, Moses was related to the Midianites on his mother's side (Exodus 18.10–27).

A little before Moses led his people out of Egypt, the Midianites living near Timna in the region of Horeb (one of the names of Mount Sinai) destroyed the Egyptian temple there and replaced it with a tent shrine. This place has recently been excavated and may have been the site of the wilderness tabernacle of Moses mentioned in Exodus 26. Found at the site was a gilded snake image, like the one Moses raised up in Numbers 21.4–9. Moses adopted the local god of Mount Sinai, Yahweh, as the god of his people, Israel (the people of God).

After trying and failing to invade Palestine from the south, the Israelites wandered east through the southern Transjordan and, according to the Bible, made a successful attempt north of the Dead Sea. Archaeological evidence suggests that their settlement of Palestine was much slower and, perhaps, more peaceful than the Bible reports. In any case, during the late twelfth century, Palestine was settled by a group of related tribes—twelve, according to the biblical account—who later identified themselves as Israelites.

The tribes were united under Saul, the first Israelite king (r. *ca.* 1000 B.C.). The biblical text hints at a conflict between religious and secular authority in its account of the warning issued by Samuel, the religious leader who anointed Saul, that the Israelites would regret the act. Not long after this, Samuel named David (r. *ca.* 1000–960 B.C.) as Saul's successor. King David completed the conquest of the Philistines, who lived along the southern coast near Gaza, and the Canaanites, and built his capital at Jerusalem, already an ancient

town site. David's son and successor, Solomon (r. *ca.* 960–930 B.C.), established lucrative trading and diplomatic relations with his neighbors and built a great royal palace and a temple to Yahweh in Jerusalem. But Solomon's strong style of governing created opposition among the tribes, and after his death the ten northern tribes seceded to form the Kingdom of Israel under another dynasty. The two southern tribes remained loyal to the house of David in the Kingdom of Judah. These two kingdoms experienced repeated conquests by three successive empires that dominated Mesopotamia and the eastern seaboard of the Mediterranean between about 750 and 333 B.C.

THE NEW AGE OF EMPIRES, *ca.* 750–333 B.C.

The Assyrian Empire, ca. 750–612 B.C.

The Assyrians, a Semitic people, lived in the highlands of the upper Tigris Valley. By the end of the eleventh century B.C., they had built a powerful army, with which, after 900 B.C., they terrorized and conquered their neighbors. By about 750 B.C., they had won control of all of Mesopotamia. They then moved swiftly to overwhelm Syria, the Phoenician cities, the kingdoms of Israel and Judah, and, finally, Egypt.

From their capital city of Nineveh, the Assyrians ruled by terror, killing and enslaving large portions of their subject populations. They destroyed the ten northern Israelite tribes and made the Kingdom of Judah into an Assyrian dependency.

Although the Assyrians managed to preserve their empire for more than a hundred years, they were not numerous enough to garrison their vast territories, and their systematic cruelty made it impossible for them to control their subject peoples except by force of arms. About 613 B.C., the Babylonians, joined by other conquered peoples, rebelled, and Nineveh fell in 612 B.C. The Assyrian empire collapsed almost overnight.

| *ca.* 750 B.C. | 626 612 | 549 539 | 333 B.C. |

Assyrian Empire

Chaldean Empire

Persian Empire

The Chaldean Empire, ca. 626–539 B.C.

The leaders of the rebellious Babylonians were the Chaldeans, a people from the southern part of Mesopotamia, the region bordering the Persian Gulf. After the fall of Nineveh, the Chaldeans built an empire of their own, centered on the ancient city of Babylon. In 587 B.C., the Chaldean king Nebuchadnezzar overran Judah, which had joined an anti-Chaldean coalition led by Egypt, and destroyed Solomon's temple in Jerusalem. To control the population of the conquered kingdom, Nebuchadnezzar carried off the leading citizens to Babylon. The so-called Babylonian Captivity lasted until the fall of Babylon in 539 B.C. Although the Hebrew prophets saw that event as divine punishment for the Chaldeans' treatment of the people of God, the proximate cause of the fall of Babylon was the rise of the Persians.

The Assyrian Empire   *ca.* 700 B.C.

An alabaster relief showing an Assyrian king on a hunt.

The Persian Empire, ca. 549–333 B.C.

The Persians, an Indo-European people, lived on a high plain east of Mesopotamia, where they herded sheep and raised horses. They lived in a loose tribal federation with the Medes and other neighbors. In 549 B.C., Cyrus, an able military leader, set himself up as king (r. 549–529 B.C.) and brought the various tribes together under his leadership. From his headquarters at Ecbatana north of Mesopotamia, he led his forces first against Anatolia (modern Turkey), which he conquered in 543 B.C., thereby gaining access through the Greek cities of the western coast (Ionia) to the rich trade and advanced civilization of the Aegean. In 539 B.C., Cyrus overcame the Chaldean Empire and brought Mesopotamia, Syria, Palestine, and the Phoenician cities under Persian control. His son Darius (r. 529–486 B.C.) conquered Egypt in 525 B.C.

Cyrus created a new type of empire. Under the close supervision of his government, he permitted the conquered peoples to retain their own customs and religions and their own forms of government. For example, he permitted the Isra-elites to return to Judah, reestablish their kingdom, and rebuild their temple. In each territory, a Persian governor and garrison kept the peace and supervised tax collection.

The Persians left a strong mark on the religions of the Mediterranean. The upper classes followed the teachings of the sixth-century prophet Zoroaster, who taught that the world was under the control of two divine powers, one good and one evil. The two were engaged in a battle that would last 6,000 years, and human beings were free to join one side or the other. Those who allied themselves with the god of good would go to paradise (a Persian word), and the others would be consumed by eternal fire. Although Zoro-astrianism did not spread beyond Persia, it influenced the religions of the Middle East through the Persian imperial system and had immense historical importance. For example, it was from Zoroastrianism that the Israelites took the concepts of the devil, hell, paradise, and the last judgment.

Persian power was first checked by the Greeks in 490 B.C., at the Battle of Marathon. After a serious defeat by the Greeks in 479 B.C., at the Battle of Salamis, Persia ceased to be the dominant power in the Mediterranean. Nonetheless, the Persian Empire survived in the Middle East until Alexander the Great conquered it in 333 B.C., after which Persia became part of the Hellenistic world (see pp. 49–50). In A.D. 224, a native Persian dynasty deeply devoted to Zoroastrianism overthrew the Hellenistic successors of Alexander and recreated the empire in the Middle East. This empire became a formidable opponent of Rome, which by then had extended its power throughout the Mediterranean (see pp. 76–79). At the beginning of the seventh century, after the Roman Empire had collapsed in the West and become weak in the East, the shah of Persia made a new attempt to establish himself as the greatest power in the eastern Mediterranean. He conquered Anatolia, forced its population to convert to Zoroastrianism, and threatened Constantinople, the capital of the Eastern Roman

The Persian Empire   *ca.* 500 B.C.

Lydians paying tribute to the Persian emperor Darius I.

Empire. The emperor Heraclius was able to push the Persians out of his territories and to weaken his enemy (see pp. 173–74). The Arabs, galvanized by their new religion of Islam, destroyed the remnant of the Persian empire in A.D. 637 (see p. 199).

Western civilization, the civilization of the Mediterranean Basin and Europe, is the heir of the civilizations studied in this chapter. The inheritance was transmitted to the Mediterraneans and Europeans in many ways, but principally through trade and the Israelites. The Phoenician traders of the Middle East were well known to the people of Crete and Greece, who got their alphabets as well as many other artifacts of middle-eastern civilization from them. Phoenician colonies in the western Mediterranean also spread culture along with trade goods. The Israelite religious and cultural tradition, preserved in the collection of books called the Hebrew Bible, transmitted an amalgam of middle-eastern thought, a selected part of what might be called the cultural point of view of the Middle East. For two thousand years before Europeans discovered early civilization through archaeology, they knew and had absorbed the basic characteristics of middle-eastern civilization through the Hebrew tradition, which was one of the cornerstones of western civilization.

Suggestions for Further Reading

General

On the geography of human habitation, see L. Febvre, *A Geographical Introduction to History* (1924). Excellent maps, with explanatory notes, for this and other chapters, are in *The Times Atlas of World History,* ed. G. Barraclough (1978).

For an overview of prehistory, see G. Clark, *World Prehistory in New Perspective,* 3rd ed. (1977). W. Howells reviews our understanding of human evolution in *The Evolution of the Genus Homo* (1973). No synthetic work has yet incorporated all of the newest discoveries about human evolution, but on the role of climatic change, see Elizabeth Vrba, ed., *Species and Speciation* (1985), and William Calvin, *The Ascent of Mind: Ice Age Climates and the Evolution of Intelligence* (1991). On the Old Stone Age, see K. P. Oakley, *Man the Tool-maker,* 4th ed. (1958), and F. Bordes, *The Old Stone Age* (1968). On climate and the origins of agriculture, see Ofer Bar-Yosef and F. R. Valla, eds., *The Natufian Culture in the Levant* (1991), and Ofer Bar-Yosef and A. Khazanov, eds., *Pastoralism in the Levant*

(1992). On Neolithic culture, see P. Singh, *The Neolithic Cultures of Western Asia* (1974); J. Mellaart, *Catal Huyuk. A Neolithic Town in Anatolia* (1967); and *The Domestication and Exploitation of Plants and Animals,* eds. by P. J. Ucko and G. W. Dimbleby (1969). On the spread of the agricultural revolution, see J. G. D. Clark, *Prehistoric Europe: the Economic Basis* (1971).

On the origins and differentiation of languages, see the provocative work of Joseph Greenberg, *The Languages of Africa* (1966) and *Language in the Americas* (1987).

On the dating of ancient civilizations, see C. Renfrew, *Before Civilization* (1979). For surveys of Old Europe, see S. Piggott, *Ancient Europe, from the Beginnings of Agriculture to Classical Antiquity* (1965), and C. Renfrew, *The Emergence of Civilization: The Cyclades and the Aegean in the Third Millennium* B.C. (1972). On the culture of Old Europe, see M. Gimbutas, *The Goddesses and Gods of Old Europe,* 2nd ed. (1982).

Mesopotamia

A. L. Oppenheim, *Ancient Mesopotamia* (1964), and H. W. F. Saggs, *The Greatness That Was Babylon* (1962), are detailed surveys of Mesopotamian history. For an appreciation of life in the valleys, see J. Hawkes, *Life in Mesopotamia, the Indus Valley and Egypt* (1973), and G. Contenau, *Everyday Life in*

Babylon and Assyria (1954). S. N. Kramer has translated original Sumerian documents in *History Begins at Sumer* (1959) and *The Sumerians* (1963). For the history of Dilmun, see Geoffrey Bibby, *Looking for Dilmun* (1969).

Egypt

On early Egyptian civilization, see W. B. Emery, *Archaic Egypt* (1961). There are two good surveys of dynastic Egypt. Of them, A. H. Gardner, *Egypt of the Pharaohs* (1961), is the more factual,

and J. A. Wilson, *The Culture of Ancient Egypt* (1956), the more interpretative. For a study of Egyptian monuments, see I. E. S. Edwards, *The Pyramids of Egypt* (1975). H. Frankfort, *Ancient*

Egyptian Religion (1958), largely replaces older standard works on this subject, and P. Montet, *Everyday Life in Egypt in the Days of Ramses II* (1958), is the counterpart of Contenau's book on Babylon.

Syria and Palestine

Informative studies on the non-Hebrew peoples of Syria-Palestine can be found in E. Anati, *Palestine before the Hebrews* (1963); J. Gray, *The Canaanites* (1964); D. B. Harden, *The Phoenicians* (1962); and R. A. H. Macalister, *The Philistines* (1913). Among the best of the many books on the Hebrews, see J. Bright, *A. History of Israel* (1959); W. F. Albright, *The Biblical Period from Abraham to Ezra* (1963); and A. Lods, *Israel* (1932).

Assyrians, Chaldeans, and Persians

The general histories of Mesopotamia mentioned above discuss the Assyrians and Chaldeans. For studies of the Persians and their subjects, see R. N. Frye, *The Heritage of Persia* (1963), and A. T. Olmstead, *A History of the Persian Empire* (1959).

2

GREEK CIVILIZATION

During the second millennium B.C., the civilizations of the Middle East became aware of new peoples in the "far west." This region was the Aegean, where an advanced civilization based on trade had grown up on the island of Crete and surrounding islands. As we saw in the last chapter, this civilization borrowed some of its motifs from Old Europe, the Neolithic culture of the Balkans and central Europe. It contributed a great deal, in turn, to Greek civilization, which succeeded it in the Aegean, and the Greeks established the basic characteristics of European civilization.

CRETE AND MYCENAEAN GREECE

Minoan Civilization

The first great civilization of the Aegean—the Minoan civilization—arose on the island of Crete. Minos was the dynastic name of the Minoan kings, and stories of a fabulously rich King Minos and of Perseus's defeat of the bull-man Minotaur found their way into Greek mythology.

By 2000 B.C., the Minoans had achieved a high level of civilization. Their central city, Knossos, on the northern coast of Crete, had a large population and was the site of a magnificent palace. Their commercial economy was so extensive and so complex they were obliged to keep written records of their transactions. Borrowing from the middle easterners, they devised a distinctive syllabic script to serve the purpose. Using clay tablets, they recorded contracts, sales, and bills of lading in a script that archaeologists call Linear A to indicate that it was the first of two scripts used by the Minoans and that it was written in lines. Linear A has not been fully deciphered, but the symbols clearly represent syllables rather than whole

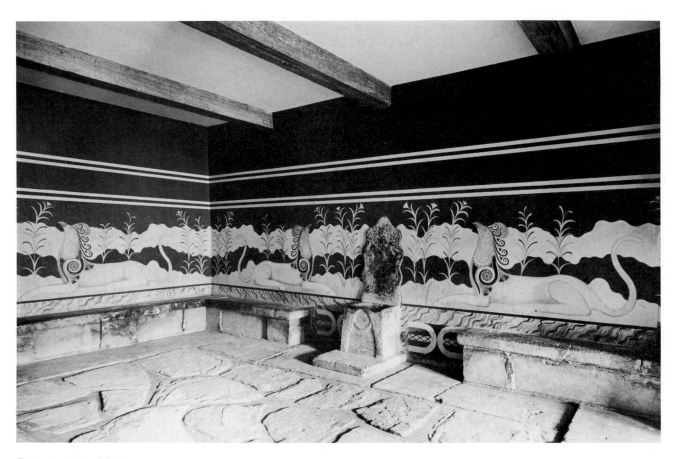

The reconstructed throne room of the palace at Knossos.

words as in pictographic writing. We can often guess at the contents of the tablets by looking at pictographs in the margins that the Minoans used for handy reference.

The Minoans lived in comfortable apartment buildings with indoor showers and flush toilets. The pipes, made of clay rather than metal, were enclosed in the walls and emptied into elaborate sewer systems. The streets were lined with bakeries, smithies, and pottery shops. The partially excavated remains of a few Minoan cities reveal a middle-class society in which, despite the extraordinary wealth of the kings, prosperity was widely shared by the population. People decorated their well-furnished houses with frescoes of human figures and landscapes. Some of the wall paintings depict animals and plants native to the Middle East and the Nile Valley, an indication that this commercial so-

ciety had frequent contacts with those regions. The frescoes also show that women played important roles in Minoan society.

About 1630 B.C., Minoan civilization came to a catastrophic end. The agent of destruction was the explosion of a volcano on the island of Thera, about 150 miles north of Crete. The largest volcanic explosion known in recorded history, it was a hundred times more powerful than the explosion that blew off half of Mount St. Helens in Washington State in 1980. Before the explosion, the island of Thera had risen more than a mile out of the sea; after it, all that was left was a hole more than one-half mile deep surrounded by a remnant of land. The explosion instantly vaporized 50 cubic miles of rock and created a tidal wave that reached 800 feet high along the coasts of Ionia, Greece, and Crete and flooded large areas of the Nile

Delta. Oceanographers have found a layer of ash in the strata of the sea floor. The hot cloud traveled out at hundreds of miles an hour, burned the cities of Crete, and moved eastward. It was still hot when it fell on Egypt, perhaps giving rise to the story of the plague later associated with the escape of the Hebrews (Exodus 9.8).

Survivors of the disaster fled across the sea. The Phoenicians welcomed many of them to their coastal cities, where they entered into commerce. Meanwhile, Greeks from the mainland moved in and resettled some of the old Minoan sites. About this time, Linear B, also a syllabic script, replaced Linear A. An early form of the Greek language has been identified in Linear B inscriptions.

Mycenaean Greece

The Greek homeland embraced the Peloponnesian peninsula, the islands of the Aegean, and the western coast of Asia Minor (modern Turkey), called Ionia. The rocky mountains of the peninsula made communication difficult and favored the settlement of small, independent communities. Across the Aegean Sea, dotted with scores of volcanic islands, the craggy promontories and jagged coast of Asia Minor again favored small, isolated settlements. This was an environment dominated by the sea, and from the earliest days the Greeks were people of the sea.

For more than a thousand years, the small city-states of Greece pursued their independent ways. The communities along the coasts emerged as cosmopolitan societies that absorbed and then surpassed the accomplishments of the Middle East in art and science. Western science, ethics, political thought, aesthetics, and literary criticism all arose from Greek foundations.

Recent excavations on the Greek mainland show that by the sixteenth century B.C., shortly after the destruction of the Minoan cities, the Greeks had developed a sophisticated Bronze Age civilization. Historians call the civilization Mycenaean, from Mycenae, the home city of the Homeric hero Agamemnon (see p. 38).

The Minoans devised a distinctive syllabic script: Linear A *(left)* that was later replaced by Linear B *(right)*.

Deciphering Linear B

Linear B, the script of the Mycenaeans, is found on clay tablets small enough to be held in one hand. The tablets were held in one hand while being written on with the other, and many have finger marks impressed on the back side. The script mixes pictograms, each of which stands for a word, and phonetic signs, each representing a sound.

The scholars who undertook to decipher the script began with a serious handicap—they thought they were dealing with Minoan texts. They could "read" some of the pictograms, such as man, woman, and horse, but they could not tell what language was represented. Then in 1951, amateur scholar Michael Ventris made a breakthrough. He found pairs of words in the texts that he believed represented masculine and feminine forms, and he arranged these in a grid that aligned the words with similar consonants and vowels with one another. If he could find the sound values for some of the signs in some of these words, the grid would help him apply the values to other words. He began to find the sound values when he noticed a group of paired words that seemed to be the names of cities on Crete. He discovered that the names were close to those used by Greeks and he made an analysis of his grid using the sound values that would be true if the language of the tablets was Greek. With this approach, he was able to show that Linear B recorded a form of Greek. Next came the work of understanding the deciphered texts, which required establishing the characteristics of the Mycenaean Greek in which they were written.

The Bronze and Iron Ages

The first metal used was copper, which could be beaten into blades, bowls, and other implements. But copper could not be used for tools used in daily life because it is soft and difficult to melt and cast. The invention of bronze, an alloy of copper and tin, overcame these problems. The hardness of bronze makes it excellent for the manufacture of all sorts of implements, and it can be cast in a multitude of shapes.

The bronze revolution occurred about 3000 B.C. in the Caucasus (the mountainous region between the Black and the Caspian Seas) and in Asia Minor. The emerging civilizations of Mesopotamia and Egypt soon began to adopt bronze, and they completed the transition from stone to bronze by 2000 B.C.

Soon after that, however, bronze became obsolete, as the peoples of Asia Minor learned to use iron. The Hittites were the first Iron Age people, and the rapid expansion of their empire after 1800 B.C. was based on the superiority of iron to bronze. The Indo-European-speaking Celts brought Iron Age culture to Europe (see pp. 8–10).

Mycenaean society was dominated by the petty kings of the towns that had grown up in the fertile valleys of the peninsula. The survival of these communities depended on the strength of their kings, who engaged in constant warfare with one another, and for whom "commerce" included everything from peaceful trade to piracy and looting. Their goals were to accumulate wealth with which to dazzle their followers, to fortify their city against attack, and to demonstrate their greatness by erecting impressive buildings and supporting the arts. The myths dating from these times reflect the feats of these legendary figures, who led their people out of barbarism and helped fashion a civilization strongly influenced by the Minoan.

Mycenaean Greek civilization, like the Minoan, was based on cities, each controlled by a princely family. The cities were typically built around an imposing palace positioned on high ground, and the city held sway over a territory with a radius of six to nine miles. The topography of Greece, with its small fertile valleys cut off from one another by rugged mountains, encouraged this pattern of small, independent, princely states.

The palaces were built around the megaron, a spacious room with a large central hearth. The center of the room was two stories high, and an interior balcony around the walls provided space for living quarters. A covered porch led into the megaron, which was surrounded by corridors that opened off the porch. Beyond the corridors were workshops and storerooms. In addition to serving as a residence for the ruling family, the palace housed government offices and industrial and commercial facilities. The palace compound was surrounded by a wall, and the entry porch itself was fortified. The presence of workshops and storage areas in the palaces suggests that the commercial activities of the Mycenaean city-states came under direct control by the kings. Although information about the commercial economy is scanty, we know that Greek traders brought raw materials, particularly metals, from distant places to be processed in the workshops of the palace compounds.

This was a male-dominated society that drew its wealth from trading and raiding. Yet the tablets, on which commercial transactions were recorded, list forty female occupations, mostly connected with the manufacture and sale of textiles. Names of the craftswomen mentioned on the tablets indicate that some were refugees from other societies. Certain crafts were associated with specific towns, and the women who specialized in a particular craft were referred to by such names as "Tinwasian weavers," "Aswian flaxworkers," and "Milesian spinners." Women of the aristocratic class, however, generally

Six royal graves in Mycenae, the city of Agamemnon, leader of the Greeks at Troy.
Photo courtesy of The Granger Collection

The Aegean World *ca.* 1500–146 B.C.

stayed at home in closely protected quarters.

The Mycenaeans did not build religious shrines, and we have little knowledge of their religion. Nonetheless, the tablets reveal that there were female priesthoods, whose aristocratic members occupied prominent places in the community and who, with their female helpers and servants, exercised control over considerable wealth.

THE SEA PEOPLES, THE TROJAN WAR, AND THE DORIANS

The heroic Mycenaean civilization survived for about 400 years, during which the Greeks became known as traders and mercenaries throughout the eastern Mediterranean. The petty kings of Greece fought one another and made short-lived alliances, like those that figure in the mythological story of the Seven Against Thebes and the epics of the Trojan War. At one time historians thought that the Trojan War was purely legendary, the invention of the eighth-century B.C. poet Homer, whose epics *The Iliad* and *The Odyssey* recount the story of the war and its aftermath. Scholars now think the war actually occurred some time between 1200 and 1180 B.C.

Nineteenth-century scholars saw little historical value in the Homeric stories, beyond the information they provided about Greek society and religion during Homer's lifetime. Then, in 1870, Heinrich Schliemann, a successful German businessman who was convinced that the Greeks had actually laid siege to Troy, began excavations near the Dardanelles in Asia Minor on a mound traditionally thought to be the site of Troy. To the astonishment of the scholarly world, he discovered layer after layer of ancient cities, one of them a large fortified city that had been destroyed around 1200 B.C. and another older and very rich city that had been destroyed around 1800 B.C. Schliemann thought the older city was the Homer's Troy, but it is likely that the more recent city was the city of Priam and Hector.

Next, Schliemann conducted excavation at Mycenae in southern Greece, the legendary home of the Greek leader Agamemnon. There he found a royal palace

Oral Tradition in the Homeric Epics

In an oral tradition of poetry, the poets recite the works from memory. This does not mean that they have memorized poems hundreds of lines long, but that they know the stories and have a collection of memorized poetic elements to use to tell them. The storytelling process is one of relating the action by stringing together the phrases and descriptions from the stock of poetic elements in the poet's repertoire, and repetition of these elements is therefore a basic characteristic of oral poetry.

In the Homeric poems, the remnants of the oral tradition are found in such phrases as "the wine-dark sea" or "the sons of Atreus," which describes the leaders of the Greeks. The poet has whole lines to use for the introduction of characters, such as:

Son of Laertes and seed of Zeus, resourceful Odysseus

which occurs many times in the *Iliad* when Odysseus enters the action. Other traditional elements include the catalog of attributes of the hero, who can run, jump, swim, and fight with magnificent strength, speed, and agility.

Homer constructed from the inherited stock of poetic elements a powerful and wholly new work that expressed the basic moral and social values of the Greeks. The use of writing to record the epics gave the poet the opportunity to fashion the elements of his story more carefully than an oral poet could and gave the poems themselves a permanent existence, which no oral poem could have. These advantages made it possible for the Homeric epics to become classics—that is, works universally recognized as representing in a particularly powerful and complete form the moral, social, and artistic ideas and standards of society.

and evidence of a surprisingly advanced Bronze Age civilization dating back to at least 1800 B.C. Most of what we know of Mycenaean civilization is derived from the work of Schliemann and his successors.

At the time of the Trojan War, the eastern Mediterranean was dominated by the so-called Sea Peoples, who subjected the established societies of the region to constant raids and who, according to contemporary records, even engaged in several great sea battles. Presumably the Sea Peoples were residents of the area who took to piracy when the power of the great states—the Egyptians, the Hittites, and the Minoans—began to decline. Many of them were Mycenaean Greeks, and during the thirteenth century B.C. they helped to spread Mycenaean influence throughout the eastern Mediterranean.

Normally, these Mycenaean adventurers operated in small bands led by the petty kings of their city-states, but occasionally they took part in great expeditions led by the major powers. For example, around 1286 B.C., Mycenaean Greeks fought on both sides of a critical battle between the Hittites and the Egyptians.

The Greek bands also formed federations of their own. In 1233 B.C., they entered into a grand alliance with Sicilians, Sardinians, Lycians, and others against the Egyptian pharaoh Merneptah. Such ventures ended with two great naval battles—one between the Greeks and the Egyptians around 1187 B.C. and the other between the Greeks and the Hittites five to ten years later. The Greeks lost both engagements, and their opponents congratulated themselves on their victory over such formidable adversaries.

Greek mythology memorializes many of the events of the last years of the Sea Peoples, particularly the Trojan War, a conflict with a relatively insignificant enemy. Stories of the war were passed down from generation to generation, and in the eighth century B.C., Homer incorporated many of them into his two great epic poems, *The Iliad* and *The Odyssey*. *The Iliad* tells the story of the war itself, of the heroic deeds and clever stratagems that brought down the city of King Priam after a ten-year siege. *The Odyssey* tells of the adventures of Odysseus, one of the Greek leaders, on his long journey home to Ithaca.

An international team of archaeologists is excavating Troy once again, hoping to discover what prompted the Greeks to attack the city in the first place and why many of the twelve cities built one on top another at the site were destroyed. The city lies inland from a natural harbor along the route to the Black Sea through the Dardanelles, the strait between Asia Minor and Europe. The passage is exceedingly difficult; the current runs south at three miles per hour, and a strong north wind blows almost every day of the year. Sailors often took refuge in the harbor, where they might wait for weeks or even months before getting a chance to run the strait. It seems likely that the Trojans exacted a price for allowing them to wait there unmolested. If so, it would not be surprising if from time to time the cities that depended on the Black Sea trade made common cause to destroy what they must have viewed as the pirate kingdom of Troy.

In the historical memory of the Greeks, the Trojan War marked the end of an epoch. The fifth-century B.C. historian Thucydides (p. 56) wrote, "After the Trojan War Greece was in a state of constant movement and was being settled in a way that left her no peace to grow strong again." The returning soldiers had learned new ways during the long years of siege, and while they were away, many of the kings had been displaced at home by usurpers. Thucydides notes that, following civil wars in many of the cities, the losers had left to found new cities elsewhere. He suggests that these troubles were connected with the arrival of a new people who had taken control of the Peloponnesus about eighty years after the war.

The newcomers were Dorians, Greeks from somewhere north of the Greek peninsula. The Dorian migration coincided with the end of the era of the Sea Peoples. The destruction of some cities, like Pylos in Messenia, may have taken place during this incursion, but on the whole the Dorians seem to have settled down peacefully. In fact, the only evidence of their arrival is the presence of writings in the Dorian dialect from a later period.

THE DARK AGE AND ARCHAIC GREECE, *ca.* 1150–500 B.C.

After the decline of the Mycenaean world, the cities of Greece declined both in number and size, and the Mycenaean ruling class gave way to local aristocracies little given to adventure or innovation. During the period from the late twelfth to the eighth century B.C., the Greeks produced no written records and little art or architecture of any significance. Historians call the period the Dark Age and usually blame the decline on the Dorian invasions, though archeological evidence does not support this conclusion.

Actually, Greek society during the Dark Age (roughly 1150–800 B.C.) was quite stable. For hundreds of years, the ruling families patronized minstrels and poets who preserved traditions reaching back to the heroic era of the Sea Peoples, gradually infusing them with universal themes. The minstrels and poets sang of the relationship between the human and divine worlds and between men and women, of admirable humans and despicable humans, of the limits of human wisdom and knowledge, and of the nature of moral and social life. Whatever troubles disturbed society during the Dark Age were not severe enough to cause a break in the cultural tradition.

Around 800 B.C., a revival of trade signaled that the Dark Age was coming to an end. Several cities on the mainland and in Ionia, the western coast of Asia Minor, emerged as commercial centers. Miletus and eleven other Greek cities set up a trading port in the Nile delta, and Miletus itself operated a string of trading posts along the shores of the Black Sea.

The rise of commerce created a sharp increase in population that upset the social balance of many cities. The cities became crowded, and few of them possessed enough farmland to support a large population. Together, the population pressure and the search for new markets encouraged people to move out and settle

A four-drachma coin from Athens showing Athena and her owl (*ca.* sixth century B.C.).

Scene from a Greek vase (*ca.* 550 B.C.) showing merchants weighing produce. As trade routes multiplied, Greek merchants and producers of wine and oil prospered.

Greek Colonies in Mediterranean and Black Seas

new areas. Greek pioneers ventured into the Black Sea region and into the countries bordering the western Mediterranean. Wherever they went, they founded cities modeled on those they had left behind and also retained their cultural and religious ties with the mother cities. At such places as Byzantium on the Bosporus, Phasis on the eastern shore of the Black Sea, Syracuse and Palermo in Sicily, Taranto and Naples in southern Italy, and along the eastern coast of Spain, the colonists extended the reach of Greek civilization.

The new era, known as the archaic period (800–500 B.C.), began at a time of rising prosperity. In the late seventh century B.C., the invention of coined money, probably in the kingdom of Lydia in Asia Minor, stimulated growth of commerce. Before this, the value of goods had been measured in terms of specific weights of gold and silver, but most of the actual trading had been conducted through barter. Coins were small, standardized pieces of gold or silver stamped to show who had struck them and who guaranteed their weight and content.

Because coins could be used over and over again, they allowed a new kind of trade. Formerly, traders had to trade one product for another and had to transport their trading stocks from market to market. For example, it was common for a merchant who set out to buy luxury goods in a distant port to engage in a series of barters all along the route. First, he would barter in a nearby city whatever goods he had started out with, then he would transport the goods he got in that trade to another city along the route, barter again, and so on all along the way. The successive trades were necessary to pay for his travel expenses and to enable him to make a rapid turnover of his goods, which were often bulky or perishable and could be transported only short distances. But a merchant with a pocketful of coins could travel directly from home to where he could buy the goods he wanted.

But coinage had a cultural significance as well. From early times, the Greeks had sought to possess objects of value that would reflect their personal worth. The prize awarded to the winner of an athletic, poetic, or dramatic contest signified his achievement and therefore his own value. In the story of the Argonauts, associated with Greek expansion into the Black Sea region, Jason had to win possession of the golden fleece, a symbol of royalty, before he could sit on the throne he claimed as his own. Coined money, too, was a sign of value, and "Money makes the man" was an old Greek expression. Even the inscription that identified the person who had issued a coin symbolized his value in society, and eventually emperors and kings claimed the exclusive right to coin money. Even today, the federal government of the United States retains that right as a symbol of its authority.

The Rebirth of Civilization

The economic revival of the eighth century B.C. brought the Greeks, particularly those of Ionia, into renewed contact with the old civilizations of the eastern Mediterranean, and the influence of those civilizations produced profound changes in Greek society. During this period, the Greeks of Ionia adapted the Phoenician alphabet so that it could be used for writing Greek, thereby creating a kind of renaissance of civilized life in the Greek world.

The growth of international trade brought enclaves of foreign merchants to many cities, causing the urban population to become increasingly cosmopolitan. The commercial classes sensed their growing power and began to challenge the authority of the ruling families, and the merchants who came to the cities to buy and sell brought new ideas and new attitudes with them. In a sense, even Homer's great epics of the Trojan War were the results of the new commercial ferment, for in them Homer brought together oral traditions formerly known only in isolated communities.

After Homer, the next Greek poet whose work we have retained was Hesiod, a small landowner who lived in Boeotia in the second half of the seventh century B.C. and who wrote long didactic poems explaining the origins of the gods and describing the life of the farmer-merchant. Life was hard, and Hesiod was cranky. He described his village as "awful in winter, miserable in summer, and no good at any time." And yet he preserved much of what we know of Greek religion and economic life during the archaic period.

Early in the next century, on the Aegean island of Lesbos, Sappho wrote lyric poems that became well known throughout the Greek world and influenced later Roman poets. Her poems, which survive only in fragments, seem to have been written for school girls, and some think Sappho was the mistress of a school for daughters of Ionian aristocrats. A few years later, in the Peloponnesus, where the old, aristocratic-military society remained strong, a Spartan commander named Tyrtaeus (fl. *ca.* 650 B.C.) composed martial songs to inspire his men. Communities throughout the Greek world, from Sicily to the Black Sea, but particularly in Ionia, held poetry contests at regular intervals.

Architecture, too, underwent a revival as many Greek cities rebuilt and enlarged their public buildings. It was during this period that the Greek temple acquired its characteristic design as an oblong building framed by pillars with sculptured figures on the doorposts and along the upper walls. Although early Greek sculpture owed much to Egyptian styles, by the sixth

century B.C. the Greeks had created new ways to represent the human figure. They came to depict figures in frontal view, which the Egyptians did not do, and they highlighted the natural form of the human body. At the same time, realistic scenes showing men and women replaced the traditional geometric designs painted on pottery.

THE GROWTH OF THE *POLIS*

Origins

Both the Mycenaeans and the Dorians lived in communities that were utterly under the control of the kings, around whom all political, social, and economic life revolved. As the king fared, so did the community. After the fall of the Mycenaean world, Greek society underwent a gradual change.

During the course of the so-called Dark Age, small, independent communities began to coalesce into city-states, which were more complex and more powerful entities than the old Mycenaean towns. Each city-state (in Greek, *polis;* plural *poleis*) controlled the country around it, including, in many cases, subordinate towns. But what distinguished the *polis* was the idea that it was the common possession of its members, who at the same time were subject to its authority. Even those who controlled the *polis* were subject to its authority, because their power derived from the city-state's constitution.

For a time the *poleis* were governed by aristocratic clans formed during the Dark Age. As a result, the local kings lost much of their authority and became first among equals within the aristocratic class. Although each clan included the extended noble family and its household servants, it enjoyed the support of citizens from all classes. The clan protected lesser families in disputes, lent them money, and helped them arrange marriages, and in return the client families gave the clan their political allegiance.

Each clan (*genos* in Greek) claimed to have descended from heroes or gods, a claim that entitled it to perform religious

Model of the acropolis in Athens with the Parthenon, the temple to Athena, at the center.

ca. 2000 B.C.	*ca.* 1700	*ca.* 1400	*ca.* 1100	*ca.* 800	*ca.* 600	404	323	Conquest by Rome 146 B.C.
Minoan Civilization on Crete			"Dark Ages"	Archaic Period	Classical Period		Hellenistic Era	
Arrival of Greeks	Mycenaean Civilization in Aegean Area							

Decline of
City-State System and
Conquest by Macedon

functions within the *polis*. The religious life of the clan centered on an ancestor cult, devotion to the gods of the *polis,* and participation in religious ceremonies. Social relations were viewed as part of the religious life of the *polis,* and justice—the regulation of what each person could expect from others and what each owed to others—was negotiated between the clans, with the priesthoods of the *polis's* cults playing the role of mediators.

The clans were keenly interested in matters of family and of succession and of who had the right to participate in religious ceremonies. Each clan, led by the head of its noble family, demonstrated through public expenditures that it deserved its place in society. Thus wealth came to be seen as a requisite for playing the aristocratic role. Public buildings, the equipping of the military, and the sponsorship of festivals and games all depended on the generosity of the aristocrats.

As we have seen, the Mycenaeans had accorded women some measure of independence in society. During the Dark Age, however, the clans relegated women to a subordinate position. The reason, presumably, was to ensure legitimate succession to the positions of leadership. The claim to royal authority in Mycenaean times rested on the certainty that the claimant was the son of the king, and the aristocratic clans adopted that practice to their own society. Women of the lower classes were probably freer than women of the aristocracy, because they had to contribute to family earnings.

This is not to say that all aristocratic women were ignorant and uncultured. Sappho's poetry suggests that girls of the upper classes attended schools to learn literature and music. Moreover, young women were probably expected to contribute to the cultivated society of the aristocratic household and to help with the management of the household as well.

Greek vase of the late sixth century B.C. depicting a foot race. The vase was awarded to the winner of the race at the Panathenaic festival in Athens.

During the seventh century B.C., changes in the social life of the *poleis* affected political organization. Throughout Greece, vast tracts of land were given over to the production of olive oil and wine. Only the landlords with large holdings had the economic wherewithal to produce these commercial crops, because it takes years to bring vineyards and olive orchards to maturity, and the crops must be processed before they can be marketed. The peasants continued to grow grain, but their prosperity was undermined by the import of cheap grain from the Black Sea, Egypt, and Sicily. As time passed, the gulf between rich and poor widened, and traditional values began to erode. The yeoman farmer had been viewed as the ideal citizen of the *polis,* but the decline of that class inevitably led to social conflict.

At the same time, the military was also undergoing change. The armies of the Mycenaeans and their successors in the Dark Age had been little more than disorganized crowds in which each soldier acted pretty much on his own. A battle was a melée in which individual soldiers on one side fought individual soldiers on the other side, and victory was the sum of individual victories. Because speed and agility were all-important, the warriors wore light armor and carried spears and short swords.

Beginning near the middle of the eighth century B.C., soldiers began to wear heavy armor to protect themselves. They added greaves to protect their shins, plate corselets to protect their upper bodies, a closed helmet, and a large round shield *(hoplon)*. The complete array had come into use by about 675 B.C., but not until about 650 B.C. were the heavily armed men (called hoplites, from the name of the shield) organized into a new battle formation, the phalanx. In the phalanx, the soldiers were positioned in tightly structured units several rows deep and fought as a coordinated, disciplined troop. The strategy was for each phalanx to attack the opposing phalanx and to force it from the field. In the line, each man held his shield on his left arm to protect his own left side and the right side of his neighbor. Because the man on the right end of the line was vulnerable, the line tended to swing around toward the right as the end man sidestepped to protect his right flank.

The new arrangements had important social effects. The armies of the past had consisted of small bands of lightly armed peasant-warriors led by aristocratic commanders. Once the armies were organized into hoplite phalanxes, the role of the individual soldier was sharply diminished. All citizens who owned a certain amount of land (five acres in the fifth century B.C.) were obliged to serve, and everyone in the phalanx had the same basic role. Order and discipline had replaced heroism and self-assertion.

The Tyrants

All these changes coincided, roughly, with the rise of tyranny, a new type of political leadership that spread from city-state to

Frieze depicting the hoplite phalanx, each man protecting the man on his left.

city-state during the seventh century B.C. Tyranny—the word was probably borrowed from the kingdom of Lydia in Asia Minor, where the king was called "tyrant"—meant the rule of a single man, as opposed to the rule of hereditary kings or an aristocratic oligarchy (the collective rule of the best men). The Greeks seem to have used the term to describe any leader who ruled without regard for the traditional political system of the *polis*. By the archaic period, the king had become the first among equals in the aristocratic oligarchy. He had some limited functions in the cults of the *polis*. By contrast, the tyrant stood outside the traditional power structure.

Some historians believe that tyranny emerged from the hoplite system, but the earliest tyrants rose to power before the phalanx became the basis of the army. Others argue that the tyrants came to power as representatives of the lower class. The fifth-century B.C. historian Thucydides, who was keenly interested in the causes of historical events, thought that tyranny had grown out of the widening disparity between the economic power of the upper and lower classes. Many modern historians agree.

The notion that the tyrants may have represented the lower class is supported by the actions of some tyrants. In many *poleis,* they altered the political structure to give more power to lower-class citizens. Some of the tyrants themselves seem to have come from the lower class.

In any case, the economic changes of the period clearly favored the ascendancy of the tyrants. In many *poleis,* friction had arisen between those aristocrats who had joined the commercial revolution and those who had continued as landed gentry. The economic interests of the two groups were in conflict, and soon a contest broke out for control of the *polis*. In the ensuing turmoil, a tyrant often seized power, sometimes with the support of the citizens, whose livelihood depended on social order.

Many of the tyrants were experienced politicians, some of them capable rulers, and they wooed the lower classes for support. Typically, they sought to weaken the landowning aristocracy and to bring about reforms that favored the urban commercial classes. Still they failed to cope with the social problems caused by economic change, and few of them remained in power for long. The Greeks were suspicious of tyranny, and in the long run the ancient idea that the community is the source of authority reasserted itself.

The Lawgivers

The social and political troubles of the seventh and sixth centuries B.C. also gave rise to the codification of laws in many *poleis*. In the early *poleis,* which were small and stable, everyone was familiar with the customs and laws transmitted through oral tradition. The heroes of the epic poems were exemplars of social values and lived in accordance with the laws.

The archaic period, however, created situations and relationships that were unknown in traditional law, which, having emerged from agricultural society, did not suit the commercial economy. On occasion, even the conservative aristocratic clans supported men who undertook to reform the laws.

The early law codes were rigid and severe; the word *draconian* testifies to the harsh laws imposed by the Athenian Draco, elected chief magistrate in 621 B.C. Later lawgivers were less severe and were more concerned with the welfare of the poor. For example, about 590 B.C. Solon of Athens established laws that eased the burden of debt on small farmers and prohibited enslavement for debt. Solon's code survived a period of tyranny and formed the basis of a new Athenian constitution at the end of the sixth century, and Solon became a heroic figure in Athenian history. Other cities had similar experiences.

The codes of the lawgivers strengthened social order in the *poleis* and altered the course of society and politics. Formerly, changes in the law had occurred through a subtle and hidden process as the law was passed down in oral tradition from generation to generation. Now, changes in the law resulted from conscious decisions of the citizenry, because written law could be altered only by a formal, public act.

The codification of the laws gave law-abiding citizens a sense that they were part of a community, and loyalty to the *polis* became a paramount commitment. The community was now embodied in its law code, its marketplace, and its public buildings. In short, the *polis* became a republic, and *res publicae* (public affairs) became the dominant concern of the citizens. The words "politics" and "political" both derive from the communal life of the *polis*.

The center of the *polis* was its marketplace, the *agora*. There, the citizens carried on their daily business and kept abreast of everything that affected the life of the city. Young men followed their teachers. Politicians argued about public issues. Artisans and artists sought their clients. The *agora* was the heart of the Greek *polis*.

The Social Life of the Polis

Athens is a convenient example of the society and social life of the *polis* at the end of the sixth century B.C.

From the age of seven to fourteen, the Athenian male was educated with his peers in the *palaestra,* where he learned wrestling and other physical arts, and in the *gymnasium,* where he practiced those arts with older boys and men. He would also learn to read and write, study the Homeric poems, and acquire the rudiments of arithmetic. When he reached age seventeen, so long as his father was a citizen and his mother the daughter of a citizen, he would be enrolled in a *deme,* one of the districts of the city. If his family was rich enough to support him, he might continue his education by following one of the teachers who set themselves up in the *agora*. These studies gave him a detailed knowledge of the laws and honed his skills as an orator, which was good preparation for political leadership.

As a citizen, he had the right and the obligation to serve on the jury, in the assembly, and in a hoplite phalanx or on a ship. He could hold public office, own land, and receive free distributions of grain. If he was wealthy, he was privileged to perform "liturgies," public functions of the greatest importance. They required him to organize and pay for festivals; sponsor poetic, musical, and dramatic performances; and command and pay for a *trireme,* the principal warship of the Athenian navy. As in ancient times, a man's social position depended on his generosity in supporting the *polis,* and wealthy citizens took pride in performing such time-consuming and costly services.

By the fifth century B.C., about half of the Athenian population consisted of citizens, their wives, and daughters. The other half was made up of metics and slaves, mostly metics. Metics were foreigners who lived more or less permanently in Athens and controlled manufacturing, banking, and commerce. They were subject to a head tax, could not own a house or land, and had only restricted access to the courts. All metics had citizen patrons who provided them with legal protection and often participated in their economic activities. Metics could serve as oarsmen in the fleet, where they shared the benches with poor citizens, and in times of trouble they could join the forces defending the city. One measure of the status of metics is that the premeditated murder of a metic was equivalent to the unpremeditated murder of a citizen. Both crimes led to exile.

Slaves were common in Greek society, and even families of modest means owned one or two slaves to help with farming or craft work, such as potterymaking or metalworking, necessary for daily life. Wealthy families might have many slaves, some serving in the household, some serving as pedagogues (guardians of the young boys of the family), and some acting as craftsmen. Some slaves took care of the family's business affairs. Slaves at that level might live independently and even put aside enough money to buy their freedom. Freedmen achieved the status of metics.

A few wealthy men kept crews of slaves that they rented out to individuals or to the state. For example, some of the slaves who worked the state's silver mines at Laurium were leased from private citizens. All in all, slaves made possible the life-style of the upper and middle classes of Athens. Although the slaves of Athens ran away fairly frequently, they never revolted, as did the slaves in Sparta and, later, in Rome.

Social life remained the province of the family, specifically the male head of the household. The Greeks of the fifth century B.C. had inherited the idea that the integrity of the family required that the female members be protected and controlled. Moreover, because men viewed females as wanton and more given to sexual desire than males, they saw to it that women stayed at home most of the time. When the women went out, they were accompanied by escorts, usually trusted male slaves.

Virtually all women in Athens were married, and in the marriage ceremony the father of the bride said, "I give you this, my daughter, for the procreation of legitimate children." This meant, apparently, the correct number and gender of children as well as children proven to be of the husband's begetting. Most men wanted two sons, in case one died, and a daughter. They could order any unwanted infants exposed to the elements and left to die.

Most girls were married between the ages of fourteen and eighteen—typically to men twice their age. The bride brought to the marriage as dowry a portion of her father's estate, which the husband managed but was obligated to return in case of divorce. Under Athenian law, women could get a divorce, but men could get one far more easily.

Greek Religion

Religion, like other aspects of Greek civilization, underwent profound changes through the centuries. The religion of Mycenaean Greece appears to have been based on family cults, perhaps related to ancient fertility rites. Through contact with the Minoans and with other civilized peoples of the eastern Mediterranean, the Mycenaeans became familiar with the idea of universal gods and over time created

their own pantheon (group of gods). Later they introduced legendary heroes to the unseen world of the gods. Mythological figures like Heracles, Theseus, and Medea were never regarded as fully divine, but they constituted a link between the human and divine worlds. The shrine of Apollo at Delphi continued to elevate men to the status of heroes, in a kind of sanctification, down to the fifth century B.C.

By the time of Homer, the pantheon consisted of a family of twelve major divinities living on Mount Olympus. As time passed, these gods absorbed many of the place-gods, the local gods revered by agricultural societies since prehistoric times. As a result, each local version of a god in the pantheon was somewhat different from other local versions. For example, the Apollo of Delphi was different from the Apollo of Delos.

Zeus was the ruler of the gods and the wielder of thunderbolts; his sister and wife, Hera, was goddess of women and marriage. Each god held sway over one or two human activities: Ares was god of war; Athena, goddess of wisdom; Demeter, goddess of the harvest; Apollo, god of music and poetry; Artemis, Apollo's twin sister, goddess of the hunt; and Hephaestos, god of fire and metallurgy. Each city had its own divine patron: Athena was revered in Athens. Artemis was the protectress of Sparta. At shrines dedicated to Apollo at Delphi and on the island of Delos, the god communicated with pilgrims through priestesses who went into a trance while the god spoke in their voice. Greeks consulted these oracles (divine prophecies) to learn about the future.

With the emergence of the *polis,* the community took over the practice of religion and transformed it into a civic function. Communal life centered on religious festivals, and people reaffirmed their sense of community by participating in the cult of the *polis*'s divine patron. This centralization of religion, however, revealed that many of the mythological stories of the gods were inconsistent and even contradictory. Those inconsistencies led many educated Greeks to become skeptical in their attitude toward religion

Marble grave relief of a girl with pigeons (*ca.* 450 B.C.).

Athena, goddess of wisdom, protector of the home and the citadel, is shown in this bronze statue in military dress (*ca.* seventh century B.C.).

and toward the community itself. Moreover, once the sacrifices and other religious rites became a function of the community, they lost much of their emotional power. The early family cults had played a direct role in people's lives; they had guaranteed the success of the family and had preserved the cohesiveness of the clan. The civic religion and formal rituals of the *polis* no longer gave people a sense of belonging at a time when the society of the burgeoning cities was itself growing more and more impersonal. The failure of the civic religion to provide a sense of identity was one of the reasons for the rising popularity of foreign mystery cults in Greece during the fifth century B.C. Those initiated into the cults became members of a select group, with secret knowledge and beliefs unknown to the rest of society.

A procession recorded in marble on the Parthenon (fifth century B.C.). The paraders on their way to the Acropolis carry jars containing sacrificial gifts.

THE RISE OF ATHENS AND SPARTA

During the sixth century B.C., Athens was ruled by a succession of tyrants who destroyed the power of the aristocracy. After the last tyrant was overthrown in 510 B.C., the popular leader Cleisthenes put through a program of far-reaching constitutional reforms. He divided the citizens into ten tribes, with each tribe constituting a cross section of the population, rich and poor, rural and urban. From each tribe, 50 citizens were chosen annually by lot to serve on the Council of Five Hundred. The Council prepared proposals that were submitted to the assembly of all the citizens, which had held legislative power in the *polis* from ancient times. The chief civilian and military officers were elected by the assembly; those offices carried no salary and were open only to the wealthy. Thus, Cleisthenes' new constitution created a mixed government with a balance of power between ordinary and aristocratic citizens. As a result, political life in Athens became more vigorous, and virtually every citizen began to take a deep interest in political issues. In the *agora,* argumentation became an art, and education a means of preparing young men for leadership. Every citizen was expected to participate in government and to contribute the best products of his intellect and judgment to the state.

The new constitution was well suited to the commercial society of Athens. The city had a large fleet of ships that plied the Mediterranean trade routes, and its military power rested on its navy, which relied for manpower on poor and rich citizens alike. Although the hoplite phalanx was an aristocratic force, manned by those citizens who could afford the required armor, the navy gave all citizens, and even metics, a role in the military. Participation in the defense of the state strengthened the claim of poor citizens to political participation, which Cleisthenes' reforms recognized.

Founded on the vigorous commerce of the Aegean and beyond and supported by a good agricultural base in its home territory of Attica, Athens became the dominant commercial power of Greece. By the beginning of the fifth century B.C.,

Athens had emerged as the capital city of a maritime empire and the commercial center of a mainland economy.

The history of Sparta was quite different. Originally, Sparta was an agricultural society located on the fertile plain of Laconia, in the southern Peloponnesus. By the early seventh century B.C., under the leadership of an aristocratic oligarchy, it had achieved dominance over its neighbors. About 650 B.C., one of its subject communities rebelled and launched a ferocious war that raged for 50 years. During this struggle, Sparta evolved into a tightly controlled military state. The entire male population of the *polis* became a standing army, and both the society and the economy of the state were organized to support this military force.

Sparta and the communities under its control constituted the state of Lacedaemon. Society consisted of three classes. The men of Sparta, who numbered fewer than 10,000, possessed full political rights and enjoyed full equality among themselves. The citizens of the subject communities managed their own affairs, but they had no say in the affairs of Sparta itself. The serfs, or *helots,* who may have descended from the pre-Dorian population, worked the farmland that supported the citizen-army.

Life in Sparta was rigidly regulated. Boys left home at the age of seven to begin their military training. They entered the army at age twenty and were then allowed to marry. They could not live with their wife until they were thirty, however, and during those ten years, they lived in barracks. They remained liable for military service until they were sixty years old.

By 500 B.C., Sparta controlled most of the Peloponnesus, either directly or through a system of alliances called the Peloponnesian League. The commercial competitors of the Athenians, such as the Corinthians, found natural allies in the Spartan sphere.

THE PERSIAN WARS, 499–479 B.C.

By the middle of the sixth century B.C., the powers of the eastern Mediterranean had decided that the thriving cities of Greece were ripe for conquest. Soon after Cyrus the Great consolidated his Persian Empire, he moved against the wealthy Greek cities of Ionia, and by about 540 B.C. had brought them under control. Now Persia stood as a formidable threat to the Greeks of the Aegean and the mainland. To withstand that threat Sparta and Athens must band together.

The first encounter of the war involved only Athens. In 499 B.C., the Ionian cities rebelled against the Persians, and Athens sent a fleet to assist them. When the rebellion failed, Shah Darius of Persia, son and successor of Cyrus, dispatched an army to punish the Athenians. In 490, a large Persian army sailed across the Aegean and landed north of Marathon, a narrow passage between the sea and the hills. An Athenian army of 11,000 took its stand at Marathon and in one of the great victories of military history defeated the much larger Persian force.

Humiliated by this defeat, Darius decided to stage a full-scale invasion of Greece. He died before he could do so, but in 480 B.C. his successor Xerxes crossed the Dardanelles with over 100,000 men and marched down the Greek peninsula. The small cities in his path quickly declared their neutrality and left the task of defending Greece to Athens and the Peloponnesian League under Spartan leadership.

This time, the Spartans and their allies formed the backbone of the resistance. A small, Spartan-led force of about 6,000 men took its stand at Thermopylae, a narrow pass. Meanwhile, the Athenians led a fleet against the Persian fleet that was supplying the land force. The sea battle was indecisive, however, and the entire force of heroic men at Thermopylae was killed. The Greeks withdrew to the Isthmus of Corinth and the Bay of Salamis, and the Athenians abandoned their city to the Persians, who looted and burned it.

Soon, under the leadership of a far-sighted politician named Themistocles, the Athenians had rebuilt their fleet, using income from their silver mines at Laurium. Themistocles saw that the Persians would need their navy to control the hundreds of islands and inlets along the Greek coast and to supply their occupying forces. His

Head of a Spartan warrior believed to be King Leonidas, who commanded the Greek force at Thermoplyae (early fifth century B.C.).

The Persian Wars   499–479 B.C.

strategy was to destroy the Persian navy. The Greek fleet, which was two-thirds Athenian, defeated the Persians in the Bay of Salamis, and a short time later the Greek army, led by Sparta, defeated the Persians at Plataea (479 B.C.). Later in the year, the Greek fleet utterly destroyed the Persian navy off Ionia.

The Athenians recovered rapidly from the Persian occupation. During the two or three generations before the Persian War, Athens had already succeeded Miletus and the Ionian cities—then under Persian domination—as the principal commercial power of Greece. Its naval successes against the Persians gave Athens control of the Aegean and enabled it to bring the newly independent cities of Ionia into its orbit. The stage was now set for Athens

Phidippides and the Marathon

The Greek armies used runners to carry messages, and Phidippides was the runner at Marathon. After the victory, he was sent to Athens, a distance of 26 miles, with the news. He delivered the message and dropped dead. Phidippides' feat is commemorated in the marathon race, the longest of the Olympic games. To be fair to Phidippides, he had run from Athens to Sparta a few days earlier to inform the Spartans of the Persian landing. Herodotus says that he covered the 150 miles between the cities in two days.

to launch the brief but brilliant classical age of Greek civilization.

THE AGE OF ATHENIAN DOMINATION AND THE PELOPONNESIAN WAR, 478–404 B.C.

The Athenian Empire

During the struggle against the Persians, the Greek cities of the Aegean formed the Delian League, of which Athens assumed leadership. In 478 B.C., the members of the League met on Delos, its headquarters, to plan for defense against any attack by the Persians. They adopted a plan that called for each member to contribute an annual quota of ships or money. Athens dominated the meeting and won the right to name the admiral of the League and to control the League's treasury, which was kept on Delos.

In time, the navy of the Delian League became almost exclusively Athenian—the great majority of the other members chose to contribute money—and the League itself became an instrument of Athenian power. Gradually, most of the member cities became mere dependencies of Athens, and the League's treasury was moved to Athens in 454 B.C. In short, the Delian League had been transformed into a maritime empire under the control of Athens.

Because Athens had been dependent on foreign grain since the time of Solon (early sixth century) and grew only about a third of its own food supply, its survival depended on control of the seas and its sources of supply. Furthermore, its imperial role lent stability to its commercial economy. Finally, empire brought honor to the city.

After the Persian War, Sparta sought to consolidate its leadership of the Peloponnesian League. Although the Peloponnesian League never competed directly with the Delian League for control of the Aegean, it emerged as a countervailing force to the Athenians. Between 454 and 431 B.C., most of the cities that had not yet joined one of the leagues had to decide which one to join, and the Greek world was divided into two great empires.

A tablet, discovered in 1960 (it was being used as part of a doorway in a house), containing Themistocles' decree outlining the evacuation and defense of Athens in 480 B.C.

Athenian Politics

By the middle of the fifth century B.C., the population of Athens had grown to about 100,000, of whom only 20,000 men were citizens with full political rights. The city's new role as an imperial capital put a strain on the old constitution of Cleisthenes, which had been designed for a small city-state.

One example of the constitution's inadequacy was the growing abuse of ostracism, whose original purpose was to guard against the revival of tyranny. If any Athenian seemed to be gathering too much power, he could be exiled for ten years by a majority vote of the citizens. When someone proposed that a citizen be ostracized, those in favor voted by writing the name of the man on a pottery shard *(ostraka)* and depositing it on a pile in the *agora*. If the shards added up to a majority of the citizens, the man was sent into exile.

After a time, demagogues began to bribe the poorer citizens to vote for the ostracism of their political rivals, thus tilting the balance of power between the

Ostraka, or broken pieces of pottery, on which citizens wrote the names of those they wished to ostracize from Athens (*ca.* 470 B.C.). The names on these pieces are Themistocles, who was later recalled, and Cimon.

classes in favor of the lower economic class. In short, demagogic politicians sought to ostracize one another. Archaeologists have discovered "factories" that produced shards, already inscribed with names of competing politicians. In such a political climate, the calm deliberations envisioned by Cleisthenes degenerated into self-serving plots to drive one's opponents out of the city. By the middle of the fifth century, a long political career had become a rarity.

Given this state of affairs, the career of one political leader, Pericles, is remarkable. Pericles (b. *ca.* 495) came from the family of Cleisthenes and rose to prominence as one of the leaders of a campaign to ostracize Cimon, a popular leader in the 460s. From 463 to 429 B.C., he dominated Athenian politics, and for the last fifteen years of his career won annual election to the position of commander in chief as well. It was Pericles who led Athens during its period of high imperialism.

The Peloponnesian War, 431–404 B.C.

The uneasy coexistence of the two great confederations, the Delian League and the Peloponnesian League, was endangered by their economic relationship and by differences of constitution. The cities of the Peloponnesus provided agricultural surplus and a market for the commercial economy of the Delian League, and thus the two leagues had different interests while being dependent on one another. In addition, Sparta and its allies were conservative aristocratic states with oligarchic constitutions while Athens and its dependent city-states were democracies. Conservative *poleis* tended to ally themselves with Sparta, while democracies sided with Athens. Both leagues worked to intervene in the politics of uncommitted cities to bring aristocratic or democratic elements to power.

War between the two leagues broke out in 431 B.C. over a quarrel between Athens and Corinth, a Spartan ally. The issues were control of the colonies of Corcyra (an island off the coast of Epirus in western Greece) and Potidaea (a coastal city on Macedonia's Chalcidice peninsula) and Athens's decision to exclude merchants of Megara, also a Spartan ally, from the markets of the Delian League. In themselves, these issues were of little concern to both Corinth and Megara, but they loomed large because they followed a series of similar imperialistic actions by Athens.

Pericles' strategy was to abandon the rural areas around Athens, bring the farmers and their families inside the city walls, and rely on the navy to keep the sea lanes open for supplies. The Peloponnesian League had only small naval forces—mostly Corinthian. But in the second year of the war (429 B.C.), a plague broke out in Athens, perhaps as a result of the crowded conditions, and many Athenians died, including Pericles. No subsequent leader achieved Pericles' political power, and the city had no consistent policy or plan of action. Nonetheless, Athens forced Sparta to make peace in 421 B.C.

The peace was soon undermined by the unstable state of politics in Athens. Promises by politicians seeking popular support to open a new war with Sparta led to renewed hostilities. This time, the Athenians took greater and greater risks as competing politicians tried to curry favor by taking bold military action. Finally, they staged a disastrous attack on Syracuse, a great city on Sicily and an ally of Sparta, between 415 and 413 B.C. This failed adventure nearly destroyed Ath-

ens's naval power and brought the temporary collapse of the Athenian democracy. In 411, an aristocratic oligarchy seized power in Athens and opened peace negotiations with Sparta. The oligarchs also hoped to get military support from Persia, which was still the principal force in the eastern Mediterranean and which had maintained its keen interest in Greek affairs. Within the year, however, a popular revolution restored democratic government in Athens, and the war was renewed. A string of losses, culminating in a naval defeat in 405, forced Athens to surrender to Sparta in 404. But by 370 B.C. Athens and other cities had thrown off Sparta's control, and Sparta was too weak to resist.

The Peloponnesian War   431–404 B.C.

THE CLASSICAL CIVILIZATION OF GREECE

The classical age of Greek civilization lasted little more than a century. It began in the early 470s and ended by the middle of the fourth century. Centered in Athens, its first manifestations were in architecture, sculpture, and drama; its last were in philosophy.

Architecture and Art

When the Athenians returned to their ruined city after the Persian War, they undertook a massive rebuilding program. The multitude of construction projects attracted architects, artists, and craftsmen from all over the Greek world. The Athenian festivals became showcases of dramatic poetry and music, and teachers of all sorts appeared regularly in the *agora*.

After coming to power, Pericles took control of urban renewal. He put his friend, the sculptor Phidias, in charge of the building program to ensure that the new public edifices and temples would be adorned with art of the highest order. The centerpiece of the plan was the Acropolis, the citadel of Athens, on which the major religious shrines and public buildings were erected. Dominating the Acropolis was the Parthenon, an enormous temple dedicated to Athena, and one of the most impressive structures of Western civilization.

Back in the sixth century B.C., as we have seen, Greek sculptors had discarded the ancient Egyptian style of sculpture and had begun to represent living forms in great detail. Led by Phidias, the sculptors of fifth-century Athens sought to represent the human body in ideal form. They saw no conflict between the real and the ideal. For them, art represented the perfection of the world as it is and provided an edifying picture of the ideals of form and action.

The Parthenon, covering an area nearly as large as a modern football field, was the crowning achievement of classical Greek architecture. The structure was a model of proportion and grace, and Phidias himself executed the sculptures. The reliefs that formed a frieze along the sides of the temple represented processions, athletic contests, and military exercises, incorporating both secular and religious themes.

Drama and Music

Greek drama grew out of religious festivals in which choruses sang poetic chants and danced as they sang. From at least the archaic period, festivals had served as occasions for poetry contests; the winners became famous men whose names are still known, though their poetry has been lost. By the late sixth century B.C., the festivals, particularly the festival of Dionysus, god of wine and revelry, had taken on a dramatic aspect with the introduction of a lead singer, who sang a story, accompanied by the chorus of singers and dancers. Poets composed dramatic works for the festivals, with a prize going to the best one. Each poet wrote three plays—a trilogy—all performed, sometimes with the poet playing the lead, in a single day.

At first, all the plays were tragedies in which poetry, music, and dance combined to tell the mythical stories from the heroic age of Greece. They explored the limits of human knowledge and power and the tragic conflict of fate with human aspirations. They dealt with the flaws inherent in human beings, the impossibility of living the perfect life, and the unpredictable consequences of one's actions. Beginning in the early 480s, a comedy, an old folk form of theater, was sometimes performed after the tragedies. Eventually, comedy developed into a genre of its own, with its own festival and competition.

The earliest festival dramas were performed in the *agora* with a wagon serving as the stage and with the audience sitting on wooden bleachers. Then, some time in the 460s, after the bleachers collapsed during a performance, the festival was moved to the shrine of Dionysus on the lower reaches of the Acropolis. An area at the foot of the hill was cleared and leveled to serve as a stage, and wooden seats were built in a hollow on the hillside. Finally, about 440, Pericles had the original structure replaced with a stone structure that contained a stage house for the

The Parthenon at Athens.

The theater at the foot of the
Athenian acropolis (restored).

actors that could also provide a support for the painted scenery.

Three of the tragedians famous in the Athenian theater—Aeschylus (525–456 B.C.), Sophocles (*ca.* 496–406 B.C.), and Euripides (*ca.* 480–406 B.C.)—created the foundations of Western drama. Aeschylus introduced a second lead actor in his tragedies to augment their dramatic possibilities. His *Oresteia,* the only trilogy to survive intact, tells the story of what happened to the family of Agamemnon, leader of the Greeks at Troy, after he returned home. His wife, who had taken a lover, murdered Agamemnon in his bath, and his son, Orestes, avenged his father by killing his mother. In the last play of the trilogy, the gods argue over whether Orestes' action was justified and at last agree to rehabilitate him at Athens. As a whole, the trilogy demonstrates that human beings are sometimes trapped in paradoxes, in which actions are neither altogether right nor altogether wrong. It also reveals the tendency of tragedians to link the ancient traditions to Athens, the center of Greek culture.

We have only a tiny fragment of the work of these dramatists. Sophocles wrote 123 plays during his long career, of which only seven survive. We have six by Aeschylus and only 17 by Euripides. We know the names of a few other dramatic poets, but we have nothing at all of their work. Aristophanes (*ca.* 448–*ca.* 380 B.C.), the leading writer of comedies, often lampooned contemporary politicians and their politics.

Greek Historians

Herodotus of Halicarnassus in Ionia (*ca.* 484–420 B.C.), who spent a good deal of time in Athens and was a friend of Sophocles, wrote a history of the Persian War, including the events at Marathon and Thermopylae. Herodotus saw the Persian War as the culmination of a struggle between the Greeks and the peoples of the Middle East for domination of the Mediterranean. He had traveled widely in the Middle East as a merchant and everywhere had picked up local lore. He wrote a history of the Persian War, and in an effort to explain the background of the enemy he wrote a series of historical works in which he set down what he had learned about the peoples of the eastern Mediterranean. Later librarians organized these writings into a single work of nine books.

Thucydides (*ca.* 460–400 B.C.), an Athenian, wrote the history of the Peloponnesian War. Thucydides had served as a general in 424, but because he failed to protect an important city on the border of Macedonia and Thrace, he was exiled from Athens for twenty years. Before this setback, Thucydides had been preparing to write a history of the war, "believing," as he said, "that it would be a great war, and more worthy of relation than any that had preceded it." The enforced leisure of the exile gave him time to write that history and an opportunity to stand back and view the war objectively.

Thucydides thought that the Athenians's relentless pursuit of power had threatened the Spartans and their allies and that, so long as Athens pressed its imperialist aims, the Spartans would have to react. The specific causes of the conflict, the disputes over Corcyra and Potidaea, were not significant; they were only the sparks that ignited the tinder.

Thucydides wrote a history of very recent times, which made it unlike previous histories, including that of Herodotus. Moreover, he told the story through historical personages, creating a drama—what we might call a docudrama—in which the characters themselves explain their policies and the decisions they made. This was his way of conveying what he believed was the objective truth about the war and its causes. In his commitment to the truth he followed the method historians still respect:

With reference to the narrative of events, far from permitting myself to derive it from the first source that came to hand, I did not even trust my own impressions, but it rests partly on what I saw myself, partly on what others saw for me, the accuracy of the report being always tried by the most severe and detailed tests possible. My conclusions have cost me some labour from the

Sophocles, popular fifth-century playwright.

want of coincidence between accounts of the same occurrences by different eyewitnesses, arising sometimes from imperfect memory, sometimes from undue partiality for one side or the other. The absence of romance in my history will, I fear, detract somewhat from its interest; but if it be judged useful by those inquirers who desire an exact knowledge of the past as an aid to the interpretation of the future, which in the course of human things must resemble if it does not reflect it, I shall be content. In fine, I have written my work, not as an essay which is to win the applause of the moment, but as a possession for all time.*

For obvious reasons, Thucydides is considered the father of history. His reference to the lack of romance in his history may be a swipe at Herodotus, who provided romance aplenty and who was quick to believe whatever his informants told him.

Thucydides observed the rule of chronography, the precise determination of the dates of past events, a discipline first practiced in the sixth century B.C. Chronography was based on the regular four-year cycle of the Olympiad, the athletic contest in honor of Zeus, held for the first time in 776 B.C. Fragments of the works of the chronographers preserved in later writings have enabled modern historians to establish the chronology of many ancient events.

Philosophy

From the Egyptians and Babylonians, the Greeks learned the rudiments of astronomy and mathematics. Originally, these subjects had been valued for their usefulness in practical matters, but the Greeks turned them to intellectual ends. For the Greeks, astronomy and the science of numbers raised questions about the nature of the world, and by the early sixth century B.C. they had begun to propound theories to explain such phenomena as matter, time, and the changes observed in

* *The Complete Writings of Thucydides,* ed. by J. H. Finley, Jr., New York: Modern Library, 1951, pp. 14–15.

physical existence. In 585 B.C., Thales of Miletus had accurately predicted a solar eclipse, demonstrating that mathematics was more reliable than myth in explaining the mysteries of the cosmos. Speculation about the history and structure of the earth was a favorite pastime among the educated classes, and by the fifth century there were many competing theories.

As the cultural center of greater Greece, fifth-century Athens attracted a great many intellectuals, and it became fashionable among the upper classes to patronize teachers and thinkers as well as artists and architects. The teachers in particular were interested in politics and instructed their pupils in rhetoric, the art of argumentation, along with other subjects.

Among the teachers of rhetoric were the so-called sophists, who concentrated exclusively on technique and concerned themselves not at all with content. Some citizens regarded the teachings of the sophists as irrelevant and downright dangerous. The real questions, they insisted, were: What policies should guide the state? What were the duties of a citizen? Out of such criticism arose a new concept of intellectual life: philosophy—the love of wisdom, the pursuit of truth.

The first philosopher of note was Socrates (469–399 B.C.), a harsh critic of the sophists who sought to define the duties of the citizen and who devised a method for searching out the truth. He spent his days in conversation with anyone who would talk to him, asking simple questions about what they knew of such matters as love, justice, and the good. Aristophanes, a good friend of Socrates, ridiculed him in *Clouds* (423 B.C.), in which Socrates describes himself as walking "on air considering the sun." "I never understand things in mid-air, except by mingling my intellect and subtle thought with air, which is the same," he says. To some, Socrates must have appeared a charming crank; others saw him as a threat, for he exposed shoddy thought and argument even when it was cleverly presented.

Socrates left no written works. Yet he made a powerful impression on the youth of Athens, who delighted in his challenge to conventional wisdom and pomposity

Socrates, statuette from the Hellenistic period.

Plato (426–347 B.C.), Socrates'
pupil.

as they followed him about the *agora*. The more serious of the young aristocrats recognized him as the personification of philosophy, the search for truth.

Unfortunately, some of those young aristocrats took part in the oligarchic revolution of 411 B.C., and Socrates was suspected of having encouraged them. He seems to have escaped prosecution at the time, but in 401 another faction tried once more to replace the democracy with an oligarchy. This time Socrates was accused of corrupting the young of the city, and in 399 a citizen-jury condemned him to death.

The trial and death of Socrates were described in reports by two of his young followers, Xenophon (*ca.* 430–*ca.* 355 B.C.) and Plato (426–347 B.C.). Plato's account is presented in a series of dramatic dialogues in which Socrates defends himself before the jury and then, while awaiting death in prison, discusses with his friends the question of whether he has an obligation to obey the sentence or would be justified in escaping with their help. He argues that he must obey because he owes his identity as a civilized man to the *polis*. The dialogue form, which Plato used throughout his long career, and which he probably invented, wedded drama with philosophy. In all his works, Plato used the voice of Socrates to develop his arguments, and only in the early dialogues does he portray Socrates as a real-life person.

Plato was related to the man who had led the aristocratic rebellion of 411, and after Socrates death he went into exile. We know he was in Syracuse in 387, after which he returned to Athens to set up a teaching institution near the ancient shrine of Akademos, just outside the city's walls. The school came to be called the Academy, and it was there that Plato spent forty years writing a series of philosophical works that he published as dialogues. In the course of this work, he explored the notion that the moral, political, or physical aspects of the world are only manifestations of ideas that exist eternally in the unseen world of the gods. In this view, called idealism, such objects as tables and chairs are the particular, temporal mani-

festations of the idea or form of table and chair. What we see in the world, Plato said, is but a dim reflection of true, unchanging reality, which is the reality of ideas. The philosopher studies mutable, visible things to learn the nature of immutable, invisible reality. Plato's greatest work was the *Republic,* a long dialogue in which he explores the ideal *polis,* which is ruled by a philosopher-king.

Among Plato's students during the last twenty years of his life was Aristotle, a brilliant young man who eventually succeeded him as head of the Academy. In the age-old pattern of students, Aristotle (384–322 B.C.) came to view his master's work as essentially wrong. Aristotle viewed the objects of this world as real, not as manifestations of unseen forms, and therefore as worthy of careful study for their own sake. For Aristotle, the aim of philosophy was to discover general principles or modes of behavior or patterns of organization. He took an interest in zoology and botany, trying to categorize and order the natural world. He wrote a work on physics in which he sought to describe the universe and how it originated. He sent students all over the Greek world to do descriptive studies of political constitutions—158 in all—and used the data to write a general work on politics that has influenced political theorists from his day to ours. He set the foundations of literary criticism in his *Poetics,* in which he analyzed the great tragedies of the preceding century. Finally, he worked out a method of rational inquiry in a series of treatises on logic that has dominated Western intellectual practice ever since.

In his own time, Aristotle's influence was not limited to the students of the Academy or the readers of his works. He also played a role in the upbringing of the most important ruler of his age. Born in Macedonia, Aristotle had a connection to the royal family of the kingdom, and in about 340 B.C. King Philip appointed him to tutor his son Alexander. Following on his father's success in dominating the mainland Greek city-states, Alexander would soon bring the whole Greek world into his power and spread the influence of Greek culture through the most spectacular series of conquests the ancient world ever saw. To understand Alexander's achievement, we need to follow the history of fourth-century Greece.

THE GREEK WORLD IN THE FOURTH CENTURY B.C.

In 404–403 B.C., Sparta, after its victory over Athens, had placed its representatives in cities throughout Greece, but almost immediately many of the cities had asserted their independence and thrown the representatives out. The Persians, still the dominant power in the eastern Mediterranean and still keenly interested in Greek affairs, encouraged the Greek cities in their struggle against Spartan control. With a provincial capital at Sardis, less than 100 kilometers from the Ionian coast, the Persians remained a factor in Greek politics throughout the fourth century B.C.

While Sparta tried to maintain its hegemony in Greece, new leagues of cities arose in Boeotia, Ionia, and elsewhere to challenge Sparta's power. In 395, Thebes (the leading city of the Boeotian League), along with Athens, Argos, and Corinth, joined in a war against Sparta. Both sides appealed for help to the Persians, who finally threw their support to the Spartans. In 388 B.C., King Artaxerxes II of Persia (404–359/58 B.C.) brought about peace through a treaty that preserved the Peloponnesian League and Sparta's area of control while guaranteeing autonomy to all the other Greek cities. The treaty therefore limited both Sparta's power and that of its major enemies, because it guaranteed the autonomy of the cities on which they had relied for support. Most important, the treaty imposed a common peace on all regions and cities of Greece. Until that time, treaties had settled conflicts only between certain states or leagues.

Between 385 and 378 B.C., however, Sparta violated the treaty by intervening forcefully in the affairs of several cities. In 378, Athens reacted by organizing the Second Sea League (the Athenian-led league, disbanded in 388, had been the First Sea League) in which the member

Aristotle (384–322 B.C.), pupil of Plato and organizer of Greek thought.

cities stood on an equal footing consistent with the treaty of 388 B.C. By the middle of the century, however, Athens had subordinated some of its allies. Finally, Greece was split up into several leagues, of which the most important were the Peloponnesian League, the Second Sea League, and the Boeotian League. Greek politics became a welter of alliances, wars, and peace conferences, usually influenced by the meddling Persians.

Philip II of Macedon (359–336 B.C.), the king who had appointed Aristotle tutor to his son, took advantage of this situation to expand his power to Greece. Like the Persians, he interfered in Greek politics—countering the ambitions of some cities while protecting other cities. By 354 B.C.,

Greek coin bearing the likeness of King Philip, conqueror of Athens.

he had gained access to the Aegean, and in the next decade he pushed east into Thrace and west into Epirus. By the late 340s, he had won control of Thessaly.

Philip's aggressive behavior posed a severe threat to the major Greek cities. Once established in central Greece, he insinuated himself into the affairs of the great shrine of Delphi, which was administered by an ancient league of Greek cities. In Thessaly, he challenged the power of the Boeotians. In Thrace, he threatened to cut off Athens's vital supply of grain from the Black Sea. Thrace controlled the Bosporus and the Propontis, the sea passage to the ports from which, once a year, a great Athenian fleet of some 200 ships fetched supplies of grain. In Thrace, Philip also challenged the Persians, who were now in alliance with Athens. In 340 B.C., when Philip at last gained control of the Propontis, he seized the Athenian grain fleet, precipitating war with Athens. For the next two years, he campaigned against the Athenians and their allies and in 338 defeated them decisively.

Philip dictated the treaty that ended the war. But the Athenians retained their fleet—the largest in the Aegean—and, though the Second Sea League was disbanded under the treaty, Athens held on to some of its overseas possessions. The treaty gave Philip great advantages elsewhere, enabling him, for example, to install garrisons in many cities to preserve the peace. From this time on, although the Greek cities remained independent and continued their habit of shifting from one alliance to another, the Macedonians dominated Greece. They kept a close watch on events in Greece and intervened when it suited their interests, but otherwise they left the Greeks to their political games.

Alexander the Great, 336–323 B.C.

Philip was assassinated in 336 B.C. and was succeeded by his 20-year-old son, Alexander. The young king was conceited, overbearing, undisciplined, temperamental, charming, and brilliant. His soldiers idolized him. He typified the heroic commander, always out in front,

Idealized statue of Alexander, probably the work of an artist of Pergamum in Asia Minor.

exposing himself to danger, and stirring his men to victory. Philip had been a patient schemer, but Alexander was brash and mercurial and carried all before him.

Alexander embraced his father's plan to unify Greece and to lead a Greek-Macedonian army against the Persians. In 334 B.C., he led an army across the Hellespont to Asia Minor, launching a career in which he proved himself to be one of the great military geniuses of history. After defeating one Persian force, he proceeded to Syria and defeated a second one, led by the king himself (333 B.C.). Next year, he conquered Egypt. There, he founded the city of Alexandria, which was destined to become one of the great cities of the Mediterranean world. Following ancient tradition, the Egyptian priests declared Alexander the son of the god Amon, and Alexander incorporated a claim to divinity into his political propaganda.

After winning control of the eastern Mediterranean, Alexander defeated the remnants of the Persian army and declared himself king of Persia. The East was now open to him, and he marched north through the Transoxiana into Turkestan, on the eastern boundary of the Persian Empire. From this crossroads of the Eurasian continent, he led his army into the Indus Valley in the northwest corner of India, campaigning there in 327–326 B.C. and forcing the local rulers into an alliance with him. We know of two Greek cities he built there, but before he could continue his conquest of the East his army mutinied and he had to turn back.

Alexander's military conquests were motivated by a grand plan for creating a great Greek empire. Throughout the territories he conquered, he planted Greek colonies and encouraged the colonists to marry into the local population. Alexandria in Egypt was the most successful of these new centers. Throughout the growing empire, the Greek language and Greek culture were the rule. Alexander hellenized the upper classes of Egypt, Mesopotamia, Persia, and northwest India by encouraging them to accept Greek language and culture, and for 800 years Greek civilization prevailed among the

Alexander's Empire   336–323 B.C.

→ Alexander's route

0   MILES   300

ARAL SEA

BLACK SEA

CASPIAN SEA

MACEDON

Byzantium
Sinope
Nicodemia
Pergamum
Ipsus
Ancyra
Sardes
Athens
Sparta
Corinth
Ephesus
Miletus
Halicarnassus
CARIA
PISIDIA

Maracanda
Alexandria Eschate
SOGDIANA
Zariaspa
BACTRIA
Nicaea
Taxila
GANDHARA

PELOPONNESUS

CRETE

CYPRUS

Antioch

MEDITERRANEAN SEA

Alexandria

Gaza

Sidon
Tyre
Damascus
Jerusalem

SYRIA

MESOPOTAMIA

Gaugamela
Arbela
ASSYRIA

Babylon
BABYLONIA

Susa

MEDIA

Ragae
Ecbatana

Hecatompylus
PARTHIA
Alexandria
Ariorum

Alexander's route

Alexandria
Arachoton

Alexandria
Opiana

LIBYA

Siwah

EGYPT

RED SEA

ARABIA

PERSIAN GULF

Persepolis

PERSIA

CARMANIA

INDIA

ARABIAN SEA

The Partitioning of Alexander's Empire   ca. 300 B.C.

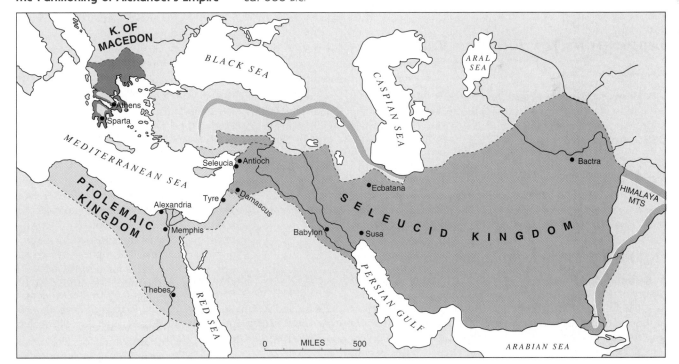

K. OF MACEDON

BLACK SEA

ARAL SEA

CASPIAN SEA

Athens
Sparta

MEDITERRANEAN SEA

Seleucia
Antioch

Tyre
Damascus

Bactra

PTOLEMAIC KINGDOM

Alexandria

Memphis

Ecbatana

SELEUCID KINGDOM

HIMALAYA MTS

Babylon
Susa

Thebes

RED SEA

PERSIAN GULF

0   MILES   500

ARABIAN SEA

political and cultural elites of the Middle East. It did not, however, supplant the native cultures, which continued to flourish among the peasants and urban lower classes.

Alexander died of fever in 323 B.C., at the age of 33, and his great dream of empire vanished with him. After his death, his generals fought for control of the various regions and soon were calling themselves kings. The kingdoms they established maintained control over the native populations and continued Alexander's program of hellenization. Macedon, under Antigonus, retained its domination over the Greek peninsula, but its power over Asia Minor and the Balkans steadily declined. In Egypt, Ptolemeus established himself as king in Alexandria. Situated in the Nile delta, Alexandria profited from the international trade that Alexander's conquests had opened up, and its population reached a million people. Alexandria became a leading center of Greek culture, and its library became famous throughout the Mediterranean world.

The old Persian territories, which stretched from the Mediterranean to the Indus Valley, fell to Seleucus. Beyond the Hindu Kush, the Seleucids lost the territory Alexander had won in India to the new Maurya dynasty of the Ganges Valley, who created the first Indian empire.

The Greeks of the classical age created a new version of human society, of political entities, and of the natural world. Drawing on the centers of civilization in the Middle East, they transformed the ancient world view. From the sixth century B.C. on, they viewed science as an approach to knowledge rather than as a practical aid in tracking the seasons or building shrines. Socrates pioneered the study of human affairs and the nature of the state, and Plato and Aristotle searched for an understanding of the entire universe. Western philosophy, science, and architecture trace their origins to the Greece of the fifth century B.C., and modern political systems are based on Greek models.

Suggestions for Further Reading

General

J. B. Bury, *A History of Greece,* rev. ed. by R. Meiggs (1975), is the most comprehensive history of the ancient Greeks. A. A. Andrewes, *The Greeks* (1967), and F. J. Frost, *Greek Society* (1972), are interpretive works. Complete texts of all the Greek writers are available in the *Loeb Classical Library.* For Herodotus and Thucydides, see Herodotus, *The Persian Wars,* trans. G. Rawlinson (1942), and *The Histories,* trans. A. de Sélincourt (1954); Thucydides, *The Peloponnesian War* (1951).

The Mycenaean Era and Dark Age

On Bronze Age and Minoan civilization, see E. Vermeule, *Greece in the Bronze Age* (1964), and L. R. Palmer, *Mycenaeans and Minoans* (1965). See also A. E. Samuel, *The Mycenaeans in History* (1966). For the period of the Trojan War, see D. L. Page, *History and the Homeric Iliad* (1959).

The Greek World from 800 to 500 B.C.

A. R. Burn, *The Lyric Age of Greece* (1960), presents a detailed history of the politics and literature of Archaic Greece. See also M. I. Finley, *The World of Odysseus* (1954). On the Greek cities of Ionia and of Sicily and Italy, see J. M. Cook, *Greeks in Ionia and the East* (1962), and A. G. Woodhead, *Greeks in the West* (1962). On the political development of Greece in this period, see H. Michell, *Sparta* (1952); A. A. Andrewes, *The Greek Tyrants* (1965); W. G. Forrest, *The Emergence of Greek Democracy* (1966); and A. Lintott, *Violence, Civil Strife and Revolution in the Classical City: 750–330* B.C. (1982). In general, see R. Sealey, *A History of the Greek City States, 700–338* B.C. (1976).

The Fifth Century B.C.

Recent studies of the Persian Wars include A. R. Burn, *Persia and the Greeks* (1962), and C. Hignett, *Xerxes' Invasion of Greece* (1963). On Athens in the Golden Age, see C. A. Robinson, *Athens in the Age of Pericles* (1959); V. Ehrenberg, *From Solon to Socrates* (1968); and W. R. Connor, *The New Politicians of Athens* (1971). On the economic life of the period, see M. I. Finley, *The Ancient Economy* (1973), and K. D. White, *Greek and Roman Technology* (1984). For a comprehensive history of the Peloponnesian War, see B. W. Henderson, *The Great War Between Athens and Sparta* (1927), and D. Kagan, *The Origins of the Peloponnesian War* (1969), *The Archidamian War* (1974), and *The Peace of Nicias and the Sicilian Expedition* (1981).

Social History

For the social history of Greece, see the studies in M. I. Finley, *Studies in Ancient Society* (1974); S. B. Pomeroy, *Goddesses, Whores, Wives and Slaves: Women in Classical Antiquity* (1975); M. Balme, "Attitudes to Work and Leisure in Ancient Greece," *Greece and Rome* 31 (1984) 140–52; J. C. Billigmeier and J. A. Turner, "The Socio-economic Roles of Women in Mycenaean Greece," *Women's Studies* 8 (1981) 3–20; E. S. Stigers, "Sappho's Private World," *Women's Studies* 8 (1981) 47–63; and S. G. Cole, "Could Greek Women Read and Write?," *Women's Studies* 8 (1981) 129–55. For a general study of Athenian society in the classical age, see J. W. Roberts, *City of Sokrates* (1984).

Art, Literature, and Drama

For a thorough history of Greek literature, see G. Murray, *The Literature of Ancient Greece* (1956); A. Lesky, *A History of Greek Literature* (1966); and P. E. Easterling and B. M. W. Knox, eds., *The Cambridge History of Classical Literature,* Vol. 1, *Greek Literature* (1985). For a brief account, see P. Levi, *The Pelican History of Greek Literature* (1985). For an introduction to Greek art, see J. Boardman, *Greek Art* (1964), and G. M. A. Richter, *A Handbook of Greek Art* (1974). For an exhaustive history of Greek philosophy, see W. K. C. Guthrie, *A History of Greek Philosophy* (6 vols., 1962–81); more briefly, see H. D. Rankin, *Sophists, Socrates and Cynics* (1983). On science, see B. Farrington, *Greek Science* (rev. ed. 1961); G. E. R. Lloyd, *Early Greek Science: Thales to Aristotle* (1970); E. D. Phillips, *Greek Medicine* (1973). For an interpretation of Greek religion, see E. R. Dodds, *The Greeks and the Irrational* (1951).

Alexander the Great

The principal ancient sources on Alexander the Great are the *Anabasis* by Flavius Arrian and a much later biography by Plutarch, of which there are many editions. The standard biography of Alexander is U. Wilcken, *Alexander the Great* (1932), but see P. Green, *Alexander of Macedon: A Historical Biography* (1974), and E. Badian, "Alexander the Great and the Greeks of Asia," in *Ancient Society and Institutions* (1966), and R. M. Errington, "Alexander in the Hellenistic World," in *Alexandre le Grand: Image et Réalité,* ed. E. Badian (1976).

3

HELLENISTIC CIVILIZATION, ROME, AND THE MEDITERRANEAN WORLD

With the death of Alexander the Great in 323 B.C., the vast empire he had created began to fall apart, and for a time the eastern Mediterranean was a scene of political fragmentation. By 200 B.C., however, the Persian Empire, Egypt, Asia Minor, and the combination of Macedonia and Greece had come to dominate the region. The Macedonian rulers of these successor states, aware that their survival depended on continuing the program of hellenization that Alexander had begun, had, within a relatively short time, hellenized the upper and middle classes.

And yet, despite the ambitions of those rulers and the pervasiveness of Hellenistic civilization, the next great imperial power arose, not in the eastern Mediterranean, but in the West. A little more than half a century after Alexander's death, Rome, a small city-state in south-central

Italy, had won control over most of the Italian peninsula, including the Greek colonies in the south. Within two hundred years, through a haphazard process of conquest, Rome emerged as master of the entire Mediterranean Basin. Ironically, as Rome imposed its imperial power on the states of the eastern Mediterranean, its culture was eclipsed by that of the hellenized East.

THE MEDITERRANEAN WORLD AFTER ALEXANDER THE GREAT

The Political and Commercial Powers

Throughout the third century B.C., the Hellenistic states that succeeded Alexander's empire continued to dominate the Mediterranean world. The three most powerful

The Mediterranean World during the Hellenistic Era

states in the eastern Mediterranean were Asia Minor, unified under the Macedonian regime centered in Pergamum; Seleucid Persia, which controlled both Mesopotamia and the eastern seaboard of the Mediterranean; and Ptolemaic Egypt, which stretched west from the Nile Delta into Libya. The Greek states remained nominally independent under the control of Macedonia, much as they had been under Alexander's father, Philip II.

In the western Mediterranean, Greek colonies dotted the coastline, their influence extending only a little way into the interior. The colonies of Sicily and southern Italy had pretty much gone their own way after the Peloponnesian War, when the mother cities in Greece were no longer able to keep up the old relationships. These colonies continued to trade with the East, but only Syracuse in Sicily emerged as a significant center of power and culture.

The greatest power in the western Mediterranean was the city of Carthage,

founded by the ancient Phoenicians of Tyre on the north African coast, near present-day Tunis. Carthage traced its origins to the arrival of Queen Dido, sister of Pygmalion, king of Tyre, at the end of the ninth century B.C. Strategically located as a trading center, the city dominated the commercial life of the western reaches of the Mediterranean.

While Tyre and other Phoenician cities were being absorbed by successive middle eastern empires, Carthage expanded its own sphere of commercial influence. It established colonies in southern Spain and drew wealth from the silver mines of the region. It controlled the trade of the north African coast, out to the Strait of Gibraltar, known then as the Pillars of Hercules. It produced rich grain harvests in the surrounding territory, where rainfall was more abundant than it is today. Carthaginian ships sailed to Cornwall and Ireland to trade for metals and may have made their way down the western coast of Africa. Despite its wealth and influence, however, Carthage never became a noteworthy center of civilization.

Massalia (Marseilles), one of the few Greek colonies west of the Italian peninsula, grew to be a serious rival of Carthage. Located on the Mediterranean coast of Gaul (present-day France), east of the Rhone River delta, Massalia was a major center of commerce. It exploited both the coastal and inland regions of southern Gaul and reached out along the coast to found subordinate trading towns at Antibes, Nice, and Monaco to the east, and Agde to the west. It established an inland center at Arles, where the Rhone begins to form its delta, from which it could trade with the tribes of the interior. Traders from Massalia sailed along the Atlantic and North Sea seaboards and probably reached Britain. Like the Carthaginians, they may have sailed down the west coast of Africa, perhaps as far as Senegal.

Hellenistic Civilization

After 200 B.C., an educated merchant could travel from the eastern margin of the old Persian Empire to Massalia and feel more or less at home throughout the entire trip. Artists and teachers found patrons in congenial surroundings throughout this vast region. Everywhere in Alexander's former empire—except in India, where an indigenous empire arose and wiped out Greek influence, aristocrats and merchants shared a uniform, cosmopolitan culture derived from that of classical Greece but influenced by local traditions. Hellenistic culture, like a thin veneer, extended over the myriad cultures of the eastern Mediterranean and the Middle East.

Beneath this veneer, the lower orders of society preserved their ancient ways—their languages, religions, and social habits. The hellenized upper classes modified those traditions to some extent, but the Persian and Egyptian societies, and the native populations of Asia Minor and the Balkans were little deflected from their traditional modes of living.

Hellenistic culture flourished especially in Egypt. In the third and second centuries B.C., Alexandria, the emporium of the eastern Mediterranean and the center for trade with India, was the wealthiest city in the world. Its ruling family, the Macedonian Ptolemies, encouraged artists and scholars and, next to the palace, built a magnificent temple to the Muses (called the Museum) for the study of the arts and sciences. Next to the Museum stood the famous library of Alexandria. Scholars from all parts of the Hellenistic world came to Alexandria, which rivaled Athens as a center of Greek culture. Egyptians made up most of the population, of course, but in the streets one could hear all the languages of the Mediterranean world. More Jews lived in Alexandria than in Jerusalem, and the city became the center of Hellenistic Judaism. Here, the Hebrew Bible was translated into Greek; this version later became the Old Testament of the Christians.

Antioch in Syria, the capital of the Seleucus, who succeeded Alexander in the Persian Empire, was also a great city and trading center. The island of Rhodes prospered as transshipment point for goods headed for the Aegean and goods destined for Black Sea ports passed through Pergamum (near the site of ancient Troy), the home of a group of talented artists. Dozens of other Hellenistic cities were centers of lively commercial, intellectual, and artistic activity.

A sixteenth-century vision of Alexandria at its height.

LA MER MEDITERRANEE.

Art and Literature

Although Hellenistic art lacked the serenity and self-confidence of the sculpture and architecture of fifth-century Greece, it displayed intense emotive power. Occasionally, it sought to impress by mere size, as did the gigantic colossus that stood astride the harbor of Rhodes and the Mausoleum at Halicarnassus in Ionia. Hellenistic sculptors created works that continue today to impress the viewer with their

The Winged Victory of Samothrace.

beauty and power—works such as the Winged Victory of Samothrace, the Venus of Milo, and the Dying Gaul of Pergamum. Hellenistic artists, in their paintings, mosaics, and statues, strove to depict everyday life realistically, showing men and women as they actually lived.

Among the Hellenistic poets, Theocritus (fl. *ca.* 270 B.C.) wrote lyric poetry on pastoral subjects in the *Idylls*, and Apollonius (*ca.* 295–215 B.C.), who may have served as head librarian at Alexandria, wrote an epic in the tradition of Homer, the *Argonautica.* The comedies of the dramatist Menander (*ca.* 342–292 B.C.) have amused audiences for 2000 years and, through their influence on Roman comedy, have influenced Shakespeare and other playwrights up to the present.

Alexandria was the birthplace of literary scholarship. Aristarchus of Samothrace (head of the Alexandria library *ca.* 180–*ca.* 145 B.C.) produced editions of Homer, Hesiod, Pindar, and other poets of the archaic and classical ages and wrote commentaries on many ancient texts. The study of literature was the principal activity of educated Alexandrians, who typically knew the works of Homer by heart. In a popular parlor game, the guests took turns telling a story using only lines and half-lines from the Homeric epics.

Science

Perhaps the most striking achievements of the Hellenistic age were in science. Scientists performed some remarkable experiments—such as Archimedes's studies of propulsion—and developed theories on such questions as the motion of bodies of different size that foreshadowed discoveries during the 1600s. In medicine, geometry, astronomy, botany, and zoology, they brought together the knowledge of the past and supplemented it with observations and findings of their own. Their work preserved for later generations Babylonian, Egyptian, and classical Greek knowledge that would otherwise have been lost.

The Alexandrian anatomist Herophilus (fourth–third century B.C.) identified the nervous system in human beings and came close to proposing a theory of circulation of blood. The astronomer Aristarchus of Samos (b. *ca.* 320 B.C.) was the first to propose that the planets revolve around the sun. Because he believed that the planets follow circular orbits, however, his theory failed to explain the observable pathway of their movements and his successors rejected his theory. And yet his ideas would influence Copernicus in the 1500s. The Alexandrian Eratosthenes (second half of the third century B.C.) wrote poetry, history, and literary commentaries, but he is best known as the mathematician who accurately calculated the circumference of the earth.

Most of the work of these gifted scientists sank into oblivion and the views of Aristotle continued to be regarded as the correct explanations of natural phenomena well into the Middle Ages. Finally, Moslem scholars in the 700s took up Hellenistic science, and through them it reached the West five centuries later.

Interest in mathematics remained strong, however, probably because mathematics could be put to practical use. Euclid (fl. *ca.* 300 B.C. in Alexandria) brought scattered theorems and proofs together into a coherent system of geometry that remains valid to this day. Archimedes of Syracuse (*ca.* 278–212 B.C.) worked out the basic problems of mass and motion and perfected a theory of machines, including the compound pulley and the type of pump called Archimedes' screw. His ideas had many everyday applications, particularly in the construction of war machines. His theoretical treatises, however, were forgotten until they were rediscovered by Europeans in the thirteenth century. They contributed to the scientific revolution centuries later.

Philosophy and Religion

Hellenistic philosophy and religion reflected what was to the educated classes a worldwide society. No longer was life circumscribed within the tiny city-states of the classical period. Now, life could be affected by unforeseen, mysterious events in distant places. In such a world, the efforts of individuals seemed futile, and educated people turned to philosophy and religion in their search for meaning in their lives.

The three most popular schools of philosophy emphasized private virtue and self-discipline rather than participation in public life.

Stoicism, which drew on the ideas of Zeno of Citium on Cyprus (fl. *ca.* 300 B.C.), spoke of a universal law that binds all men together as brothers. Everyone, from slave to king, must do his duty in the station in which he finds himself. Power and wealth, human desires and affections, are dangerous distractions. Public office is not to be sought, though it might be one's duty to accept it. The ideal existence is to live as a private citizen unaffected by political or other external influences.

Epicureanism, based on the philosophy of Epicurus (341–270 B.C.), holds that the wise man should seek the pleasure that arises from right conduct, serenity of mind, and moderation in all things. Ambition and the pursuit of wealth cause more pain than they are worth, and the wise man should avoid forming strong attachments to family, friends, or state.

Cynicism stemmed from the thought of Antisthenes (b. *ca.* 440 B.C.), who taught in the gymnasium called the Cynosarges in Athens. The Cynics doubted the possibility of achieving true knowledge and saw no sense in trying to save a world trapped in ignorance. They believed the wise man should pursue peace of mind and withdraw from worldly concerns.

Ordinary people sought solace in the so-called mystery cults rather than in the formal schools of philosophy that attracted the educated upper classes. The origins of these cults lay deep in the cultures of the societies Alexander had incorporated into his empire. The cults achieved wider visibility through his efforts to integrate Greek and indigenous cultures and by the late fourth century B.C. they were attracting followers throughout the Hellenistic world.

The cults borrowed freely from one another and from older religions of the Mediterranean world and the Middle East. Each cult engaged in elaborate secret ceremonies and claimed that initiates, after

In the sixteenth century, Archimedes was considered the greatest of the ancient scientists. Here is a sixteenth-century imagination of him.

549 B.C.				338	323		*ca.* 30 B.C.

Persian Empire

Independent Greek City-States

Hellenistic Era

Rise and Dominance
of Macedon

performing a ritual purification of their sins, would be admitted to the mystery that opened the way to communion with the god of the cult. Especially popular were the Dionysian rituals from the Greek cities, Isis worship from Egypt, and the cult of the Great Mother from Asia Minor. The communities of believers were small, mystic cells that provided a sense of security and personal worth and a promise of eternal life as antidotes to the helplessness and harshness they experienced in their daily life. Like the formal schools of philosophy, they turned inward and offered an escape from reality.

The Fate of Hellenistic Civilization

The Hellenistic states never achieved military strength, and most of them were weakened by internal dissension and cultural conflict. The Seleucid Empire, for example, soon lost Bactria and Persia, and in 167 B.C. the Jews regained their independence under the leadership of the Maccabees. When Rome became the dominant power in the Mediterranean about 200 B.C.,

Ancient Rome

it annexed the Hellenistic states one by one, and with the seizure of Egypt in 30 B.C. it acquired all of Alexander's empire except Persia.

Despite its political collapse, the influence of the Hellenistic world persisted for centuries. The Romans admired Hellenistic culture and borrowed heavily from it. Greek continued as the language of the upper classes in the Middle East, and Athens and Alexandria were the cultural centers of the Roman Empire. When the Arabs built a great empire around the Mediterranean and in the Middle East during the seventh century, the Hellenistic populations exerted a profound influence on Moslem culture. Hellenism's sphere of influence began to shrink by about A.D. 500, however. In Greece, Asia Minor, and the Levant, it gradually gave way to Byzantine culture (see Chapter 7), which survived until the fall of Constantinople in A.D. 1453.

THE FOUNDATIONS OF ROME AND ITS POWER

Origins

By 1000 B.C., the Italic tribes, including the Latins, had settled most of the Italian peninsula and had begun to clear the forests for agriculture. Soon after 800 B.C., new civilizations arose in the north and the south. In the north, the Etruscans built fortified hill towns on the Lombard plain, in the Apennines, and along the western coast down to Campania. In the south and in Sicily, as we have seen, the Greek colonists founded cities and soon brought the Italic tribes of the area under control.

The Etruscans appear to have been a non-Indo-European people native to the Italian peninsula. Their ultimate origins are obscure, and scholars have been unable to decipher their writing. We do know that the Etruscans achieved a highly

Etruscan sarcophagus (third century B.C.) showing the deceased couple reclining on a couch and pouring libations as if at their own funeral banquet.

Etruscan kitchen utensils: a water bottle and a spoon.

developed civilization and employed sophisticated techniques in painting, terracotta, bronze, and precious metals. Their political organization was, like that of Mycenaean and classical Greece, based on independent city-states. Through trade they came into contact with the Greeks and the Phoenicians, whose culture influenced their own.

Etruscan funerary art—which is mostly what survives—shows men and women as equals; the Greeks regarded the Etruscans as decadent because of the prominence and freedom their women enjoyed. Etruscan society was an aristocratic society based on the family, and the union of men and women brought honor to both partners.

Rome originated as an Etruscan-type city during the late seventh or early sixth century B.C. It is not clear whether the coalescing of the villages into a city was accomplished by the Etruscans or by the villagers themselves as they tried to resist Etruscan encroachment. In any case, the Etruscans eventually gained control of the region, and throughout the sixth century B.C., an Etruscan dynasty, the Tarquins, ruled the small city-state of Rome. About 510 B.C. (Romans later fixed the date at 509), local aristocrats (the *patricians*)

ousted the Tarquins and established a republic.

The Republican Constitution

The patricians devised for the new republic a constitution carefully wrought to prevent another king or tyrant from seizing power. Two elected magistrates, the *consuls*, held executive power, and other officials, also elected in twos or threes, managed the treasury and presided over the legal system. All chief magistrates held office for only one year at a time. In times of emergency, the constitution allowed for the appointment of a dictator who could hold authority only until the crisis had passed and in no case for more than six months.

During the fifth century B.C., the various governmental offices became fixed. From the beginning, the consuls had had assistants called *quaestors*, who were generally up-and-coming young patricians. By the middle of the fifth century, the quaestors had become independent magistrates elected by the assembly. Eventually, there were four quaestors; two managed the public treasury, and two assisted the consuls in handling military finances. By about 435 B.C., two *praetors* had been added to the roster of magistrates. They were responsible for the administration of justice. One of them handled the cases of citizens and governed the city when the consuls were away. The other handled the cases of foreigners.

The electorate of citizens—as in Greece, only males were citizens—constituted an assembly that elected the magistrates, passed laws, declared war, and sat as the final court of appeal in capital cases. Voting in the assembly followed a form of military organization called the centuriate, which probably dated back to Etruscan days. Originally, the centuriate consisted of units of 100 men each, called centuries. Under the Republic, the centuries were of various sizes, and each century had one vote.

The assembly was divided into five classes according to wealth, each class having a prescribed number of centuries. The patricians had 80 centuries; the four lower classes—the *plebeians*—had, collectively, 90 centuries. So it would seem that the plebeians could outvote the patricians. Actually, though, the assembly included groups that did not belong to the five classes. The equestrians (wealthy plebeians who served in the cavalry) had 18 centuries; the artisans (part of the middle class) had 2; and the proletarians (landless men who belonged to no class) had 1. In practice, the equestrians voted with the patricians, and together they held the majority—98 centuries out of 193.

In normal times, the patricians governed the Republic. Only patricians could be elected as magistrates. In addition, the patricians formed a powerful council of former magistrates, called the Senate (from *senex* meaning elder). All those who had served as quaestor, praetor, or consul, became senators as soon as their terms expired. Until the late fourth century B.C., it seems no act passed in the assembly was executed by the magistrates until the Senate had approved it.

The Senate's influence over elected officials rested on class and family ties, as well as on the senators' political experience. The quaestors, holding their first major offices, were the sons, nephews, and cousins of senators. The praetors and con-suls were already senators themselves. Consequently, the Senate usually determined policy, and Senate debates attracted more attention than the activities of the magistrates or the assembly. In fact, the senators also controlled the assembly through a client system. They gave economic and other support—such as legal assistance—to small farmers and city dwellers in return for political support in the assembly, so they rarely had to rely on their control of a majority of the centuries.

The Romans assigned military and civilian powers to the same officials but at the same time differentiated military and civilian functions. Although the consuls were both civilian magistrates and commanders in chief of the army, they could exercise their military authority only outside the city limits. Within the city, civilian government held sway. In the field, the citizen-soldier was subject to strict military discipline, but in the city he was a citizen free to voice his opinion on political matters and to vote as he wished. Moreover, because the consuls held office for only one year, no one could create a political following based on the army.

An able young aristocrat could be elected quaestor at the age of 25 and praetor at the age of 30. At the age of 35, he could stand for the consulship. A man could serve in these offices more than once, but in 342 B.C., the assembly passed a law prohibiting anyone from repeating a term of office, particularly the consulship, within ten years. This law soon proved impractical, however, because Rome became engaged in lengthy military campaigns that required continuous leadership. In 325 B.C., to get around the law, the Senate permitted a consul to continue as a military leader after his term expired by making him *pro consule*—that is, an officer who acted *for* or *as* the consul. In time, the proconsulate became embedded in the power structure of the state.

The patricians led the rebellion against the Tarquins, and they were firmly in control of the Republic. As time passed, however, the plebeians came to resent the patrician monopoly of power. Under the Etruscan king, ordinary citizens could seek royal protection from aristrocratic abuse, and the competition between the king and the aristocracy often made the king sympathetic to their complaints. But under the Republic, the power of the aristocrats went unchecked, and social relations, always rough, grew rougher still. The aristocrats often subjected small farmers to economic pressure or physical violence to force them to become clients or surrender their land. In neither the city nor the countryside were life and property safe any longer.

Patrician control over the workings of government made life nearly intolerable for the lower orders of society. The plebeian was obliged to stand before a patrician judge who was probably related to his opponent by blood, marriage, clientage, or politics. Moreover, at least during the first decades of the Republic, laws were neither written nor published. Consequently, the laws were whatever the aristocratic magistrates said they were. As grievances mounted, with no remedy in prospect, a prolonged struggle set in between the patricians and the plebeians.

The Struggle between the Patricians and Plebeians

Around 470 B.C. the plebeians forced the patricians to consent to election, by an assembly of plebeians, of two independent plebeian magistrates, called *tribunes*. One of these tribunes, in the late 450s B.C., proposed the Twelve Tables, the first written code of Roman law. This transition from unwritten law administered by the patrician magistrates to written law binding on all citizens brought increased security to the populace. Then, in 446 B.C., the old ban on intermarriage between patricians and plebeians was abolished. Even though patrician families were slow to enter into marriages with plebeians, the new openness had a significant effect on the social order in the long run.

For some time, the plebeians had sought access to offices, especially those that carried some measure of military authority, but the patricians had resisted their efforts. About 444 B.C., a compromise was achieved under which the plebeian assembly elected three military tribunes in addition to the two civilian tribunes. Yet this new arrangement continued to favor the patricians: Each year, the Senate decided whether military authority should be granted to the military tribunes or to the consuls; with the senators making the decision, the choice was rarely in doubt. Moreover, because patricians controlled the assembly, and the assembly elected the military tribunes, no plebeian reached that office until 400 B.C., when a difficult campaign made it necessary to choose the

Plebeian Reforms

Enslavement for debt was a constant threat to the poorer peasants of the ancient world. In this passage, the Roman historian Livy (59 B.C.–A.D. 17) shows how the plebeians gained constitutional safeguards against enslavement for debt by refusing to fight in a time of emergency.

An old man suddenly presented himself in the Forum. . . . Though cruelly changed from what he had once been, he was recognized, and people began to tell each other, compassionately, that he was an old soldier who had once commanded a company and served with distinction. . . . "While I was on service," he said, "during the Sabine War, my crops were ruined by enemy raids, and my cottage was burnt. Everything I had was taken, including my cattle. Then, when I was least able to do so, I was expected to pay taxes, and fell, consequently, into debt. Interest on the borrowed money increased my burden; I lost the land which my father and my grandfather had owned before me, and . . . I was finally seized by my creditor and reduced to slavery. . . ."

The man's story . . . caused a tremendous uproar, which spread swiftly from the Forum through every part of the city. . . .

On top of this highly critical situation, came the alarming news . . . that a Volscian army was marching on Rome. . . . For [the plebeians] it seemed like an intervention of providence to crush the pride of the Senate; they went about urging their friends to refuse military service. . . . [One of the consuls then issued] an edict, to the effect that it should be illegal . . . [to] imprison a Roman citizen. . . . As a result of the edict, all "bound" debtors who were present gave their names on the spot, . . . and in the ensuing fight with the Volscians no troops did more distinguished service.

From Livy, The Early History of Rome, *trans. by Aubrey de Sélincourt (Baltimore: Penguin Books, 1960), pp. 113–16.*

This head of a statue of Hermes (*ca.* 500 B.C.) was part of a group of terra-cotta figures that adorned the roof of a temple of Apollo in Veii. It became a spoil of war when Veii fell to besieging Romans in 396 B.C.

best-qualified men, regardless of social class.

By then, plebeians had finally begun to break down the barrier to election to the regular magistracies—the quaestorship, praetorship, and consulship. In 421 B.C., they became eligible for election to the quaestorship, although the patricians still controlled the assembly, which elected quaestors. Finally, in 367 B.C., plebeians became eligible for the consulate, the highest office in the Republic, and the military tribunate was abolished. Under the law of 367 B.C., one consul was to be patrician and one plebeian, though no plebeian was elected to the office until 340 B.C.

The struggle persisted for generations, with the patricians resisting every effort by the plebeians to win a share of power. When the patricians did make a concession, it was invariably occasioned by the exigencies of war—first, wars fought to defend the new republic and, later, wars of expansion. The tradition of aristocratic authority was embedded in the history of early Rome. This was a community created and governed by a small class of men who considered themselves the best among the citizenry. They felt they had an obligation to govern and a right to preserve their power. As they saw it, the prosperity of the Roman state and the welfare of all citizens depended on their leadership.

THE GROWTH OF ROMAN ITALY, *ca.* 500–265 B.C.

The Expansion of Roman Power

In the early days, Rome's prosperity rested on agriculture, and for centuries Romans continued to revere the rural way of life. Like Sparta, Rome trusted its defense to an army of citizen-farmers.

When the Republic was founded, Rome controlled a territory of about 300 square miles, with a diameter of less than 20 miles. The Republic inherited the powerful position of the Etruscan kings among the towns of Latium. With the expulsion of those kings, the towns asserted their independence and, about 496 B.C., formed the so-called Latin League and rebelled against the Republic. Still threatened by the Etruscans to the north, the Romans entered into treaties with the League instead of trying to suppress it. Latins and Romans received rights in each other's courts and pledged to assist each other in times of emergency. Together they created a powerful army and achieved domination over central Italy. Wherever the combined forces won a battle over local tribes, they established a colony of veterans to consolidate their power.

Rome's settlement with the Latin League influenced Roman policy toward other peoples as well. By entering into

Cities of the Latin League   *ca.* 400 B.C.

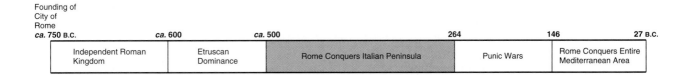

Founding of
City of
Rome
ca. 750 B.C.   *ca.* 600   *ca.* 500   264   146   27 B.C.

| Independent Roman Kingdom | Etruscan Dominance | Rome Conquers Italian Peninsula | Punic Wars | Rome Conquers Entire Mediterranean Area |

that settlement, Rome took a step toward opening its citizenship to outsiders. Having created a category of citizenship for conquered peoples, Rome ultimately became a city-state with the citizenry and power of an empire.

Not long after Rome's accommodation with the Latin League, the Etruscans in the north were weakened by the invasion of a new people, the Celts. The Celts were iron-using Indo-Europeans who, starting in the sixth century B.C., had spread out from the area just north of the Alps. In successive waves of migration and conquest, they had gained control of most of the continent from Spain to western Russia. The Galatians in central Asia Minor were Celts, as were the Gauls who moved into Italy beginning about 450 B.C.. After conquering the Etruscan cities in the Lombard plain, the Gauls pressed south into the peninsula. The Romans seized the opportunity to challenge Etruscan power in central Italy, and, between about 405 and 396 B.C., Rome and its Latin allies besieged the Etruscan city of Veii. With the fall of the city the balance of power shifted permanently from the Etruscans to the Romans.

The Gauls pushed on to the south, however. Around 390 B.C., they defeated a Roman army and seized the city of Rome; only the citadel held out. But the Gauls had reached the limit of their southern drive. After sacking the city, they returned north. Rome took a generation to recover from this disaster, and not until the 360s B.C. did Roman armies again go on the offensive. By about 350 B.C., Rome had completed its conquest of the Etruscans by annexing southern Etruria, their last stronghold.

After this success, the Romans consolidated their control over central Italy. Between about 340 and 338 B.C., they fought the Great Latin War, and defeated the Latin League. The citizens of the Latin cities were then incorporated into the citizenry of Rome. From this time on, the Romans often granted citizenship to conquered peoples in Italy, a practice that added to their manpower and gave their former enemies a stake in Roman affairs.

Now the Romans turned their attention south to the Italic tribes. These tribes had occupied the Apennines and the plains of south-central Italy around 1000 B.C., and they had emerged as strong powers when the Greek cities of southern Italy declined during the fourth century B.C. They spoke Oscan, a language related to Latin much as French is related to Spanish or Italian. The most powerful of the Italic tribes were the Samnites, who controlled much of south-central Italy, including the plain of Campania.

About 325 B.C., the Romans turned on the Samnites and launched a long series of wars against them. The Samnites allied themselves with the remnants of Etruscan power and forced Rome into a two-front war. Although Rome lost most of the early battles, its superior military organization and firm control over its allies brought victory at last. During these difficult campaigns the Romans prolonged the military service of its consuls by creating the proconsulate. By 290 B.C., Samnite power was broken. After a little mopping up, Rome assumed control of all of Italy except for the Gallic cities in the Po Valley and the Greek city-states in the south.

After the Samnite Wars, some of the Greek city-states allied themselves with Rome, while others allied themselves with Epirus, a partially hellenized kingdom on the eastern shore of the Adriatic. Around 280 B.C., King Pyrrhus of Epirus sailed across to Italy to support his allies. Although he won numerous battles against the Romans, he lost the war. In winning one of his battles, he lost so many men that his victory was worse than defeat. Since then, a disastrous victory has come to be known as a pyrrhic victory. By 265, the Greek city-states had accepted Roman hegemony.

The Roman Military System

In the course of these long years of war the Romans created a first-rate military system and cultivated an ethos of perseverance. Their military system was based on the legion, an infantry unit of about 4,300 men, which was subdivided into smaller units for maneuverability. At first, the officer corps was made up of young patricians, but after the expansion of plebeian power wealthy plebeians came to serve as officers too. The officer corps was led by the consuls.

The legion was a highly flexible body manned by well-disciplined soldiers. When divided into its constituent units, it could be deployed in a wide variety of formations. The smaller units were under the close control of their officers, and the chain of command made it possible for the legionary commander to coordinate the performance of the whole. It was the best-organized and best-disciplined army of the ancient world.

Because Rome controlled rich farmlands capable of supporting a large population, it enjoyed a clear superiority in manpower over its enemies. Not even the strongest states of the Mediterranean world could withstand the steady pressure that Rome could exert.

ROMAN EXPANSION OVERSEAS

The Punic Wars, 264–146 B.C.

When it subjugated the Greek city-states of southern Italy, Rome inherited their ancient struggle with Carthage for control of Sicily and the western Mediterranean. The war between Rome and Carthage was similar to the contest between Sparta and Athens: land power versus sea power. Carthage was the greatest naval power in the Mediterranean, whereas at the beginning of action Rome had no navy at all. The so-called Punic Wars (from *Poenicus*, Latin for Phoenician) between Rome and Carthage dragged on for more than eighty years.

The First Punic War broke out in 264 B.C., only a year after Rome had completed its conquest of southern Italy. This time, Rome was bent on winning control of Sicily, one of the great breadbaskets of the Mediterranean. To win this prize, Rome first had to build a fleet and learn the arts of naval warfare. It developed a ship that enabled its troops to board enemy ships and use the skills they had learned as infantrymen. After some early victories, Rome lost three fleets in storms. With a fourth fleet, the Romans defeated

A wall painting from Pompeii depicting the warships of the ancient Mediterranean.

Early Italy *ca.* 275 B.C.

the Carthaginians off western Sicily in 241 B.C. and took control of the island.

After this defeat, Carthage turned its attention to Spain, and to the rich silver mines and farmlands it possessed there. Once again, Carthage and Rome fell into conflict. For more than a thousand years, southern Gaul (France) and Spain had

Founding of City of Rome					
ca. 750 B.C.	*ca.* 600	*ca.* 500	264	146	27 B.C.
Independent Roman Kingdom	Etruscan Dominance	Rome Conquers Italian Peninsula	Punic Wars	Rome Conquers Entire Mediterranean Area	

played a prominent role in Mediterranean trade, and Rome had become well-established there, principally through an alliance with Massilia, Carthage's rival. A strengthening of Carthaginian power in Spain was a serious threat to Roman interests. The Second Punic War began in 218 B.C. with a Carthaginian attack on a northern Spanish city allied with Rome.

Had it not been for the brilliance and daring of Hannibal, the Carthaginian general, the war might well have been fought in Spain, or even in north Africa. As the war began, Hannibal marched through southern Gaul and crossed the Alps with a large army and fifty war elephants. For the first two years of the war, the Romans tried to pin down Hannibal's army without engaging in open battle. Then, in 216 B.C., two inexperienced Roman consuls decided to confront Hannibal. At Cannae, in eastern Italy, north of Bari, he inflicted one of the worst defeats Rome ever suffered. Nearly 70,000 Roman soldiers died in the battle, and 10,000 Roman prisoners of war were sold into slavery. After Cannae, Hannibal spent thirteen years ravaging the Italian countryside, defeating one Roman army after another. At one point he threatened Rome itself. But Rome's allies in central Italy forced him to spend most of his time in the south, where he found support among the Italic peoples. The Romans controlled the sea and denied Hannibal reinforcements from Africa. For thirteen years, the two sides were stalemated.

In 203 B.C., the Romans sent a gifted general, Scipio Africanus, into the field. Scipio first took the war to Spain and won the province for Rome. He then invaded North Africa itself, forcing Hannibal to rush to the defense of Carthage. After a difficult campaign, Scipio finally defeated Hannibal in 202 B.C. at Zama, a few miles from Carthage, and imposed surrender terms on the Carthaginians. Carthage ceded Spain to Rome, paid a heavy war

This third-century B.C. coin bears one of the few known contemporary portraits of Hannibal. The elephant appears on the reverse.

indemnity, and agreed to limit its fleet henceforth to ten ships.

Fifty years after the end of the Second Punic War, Carthage had recovered some of its wealth but was no longer a military threat to Rome. Nonetheless, the Romans had bitter memories of Hannibal's depredations, and for years the Roman Senate had debated whether Carthage should be destroyed. Finally, in 146 B.C., Rome moved against its old enemy. Carthage fell after a six-month siege, and every inhabitant was either killed or enslaved. The city was razed, its fields sown with salt, and the surrounding territory made into a Roman province. Rulers elsewhere in North Africa were forced to become clients of Rome.

Rome and the Hellenistic East

Although Roman expansion in the western Mediterranean was a matter of long-term strategy, it is difficult to find a compelling reason for the extension of Roman power to the eastern Mediterranean. Actually, Rome was drawn into eastern affairs by degrees, as one state after another asked for assistance against its rivals. The wealth of the East was attractive, of course, but Rome moved hesitantly and repeatedly refused to annex defeated states, making them independent client kingdoms instead.

Rome's first experience in the East had been its war with King Pyrrhus of Epirus during the 270s B.C. Later, during the Second Punic War, when the Macedonians lent support to Hannibal, Rome attacked and defeated them. Then, as time passed, the successor states to Alexander's empire—Ptolemaic Egypt, Seleucid Persia, Macedon, the leagues of Greek cities, and the small kingdoms in Asia Minor—repeatedly involved Rome in their affairs.

Exasperated, the Romans in 167 B.C. plundered Macedon and Epirus and sold thousands of their inhabitants into slavery.

They destroyed Corinth for its disobedience and sold much of its population into slavery. And they plundered Athens and brought thousands of its young men to Italy as slaves. By the late 140s B.C., Macedon had become a Roman province; the Greek cities were under Roman control; Asia Minor had become a Roman protectorate; and Egypt and Syria remained independent but were obliged to get Roman approval before acting in foreign affairs.

THE CONSEQUENCES OF EXPANSION

Governing the Provinces

The expansion of Roman power led to an expansion of Roman government. The constitution, which had been designed for a small city-state, now had to be altered to suit the governance of vast territories populated by foreign peoples. Previously, the consuls had served both as generals and as heads of the civilian government. But now the armies were often active in several theaters of war at once, and the state needed additional military leaders. As we have seen, Rome filled that need by creating the office of proconsul. Most of the provinces had military garrisons, and it became common to unite provincial administration with military command under the proconsuls. Separation of military and civilian power, one of the distinctive features of Roman government, was not exported to the provinces.

Military control enabled unscrupulous proconsuls to enrich themselves at the expense of the provincials, and in 149 B.C. Rome established a special court to try those who were suspected of corruption. The court soon fell under the influence of Roman politicians, however, not unlike what had happened to ostracism in Athens (see pp. 51–52). Once a proconsul returned to Rome, he could be sure that his political enemies would sue him for corruption.

Some of the older provinces had only token peace-keeping garrisons, and their governors concerned themselves mainly with civilian affairs. More recently acquired provinces and those threatened by enemies of Rome were under military government. Generally, however, the Roman governors kept small staffs and left local affairs to local leaders. Many of those leaders learned Latin, arranged for their sons to have a Roman education, and built Roman-style houses and public buildings. Thus they served as a link between the Romans and the native populations, which preserved many of their linguistic and cultural traditions.

Some provincial city-states enjoyed complete autonomy, though in close alliance with Rome. Elsewhere, Roman governors intervened only when necessary or profitable to do so. In North Africa and in some parts of the Middle East, the Romans permitted the old kingdoms to continue as client kingdoms. The rulers had control over internal affairs, but they had to act in accord with Rome's foreign policy and to seek Roman approval on succession to the throne. On the whole, Roman provincial government was less burdensome than that of earlier conquerors, and it succeeded in keeping the peace. Under Roman rule, the Mediterranean world enjoyed a period of extraordinary prosperity and peace, the *Pax Romana* (Roman Peace).

Economic, Social, and Political Change

By 146 B.C., Rome had become the capital of a great Mediterranean empire. Wealth poured into Rome, mainly to the benefit of the upper classes, and as time passed the difference between rich and poor grew wider and wider. In the old days of the city-state, the difference had been less noticeable, because the estates of the aristocrats were little larger than the farms of the yeomen, and all were prosperous. But the effects of empire transformed the Roman economy. The small farmers, unable to compete with the cheap grain brought in from Sicily and Spain, grew increasingly dependent on the noble families. Those families in turn bought out the ruined farmers and concentrated on producing

A stooped farmer takes his produce to the market.

wine and olive oil for export. Consequently, Roman Italy came to rely on the provinces for most of its food supply.

Economic change triggered social and political change. By the middle of the second century B.C., many of the farmers who had once formed the backbone of the Roman population had moved to the city. There they constituted a new element in Roman life—the urban mob. For a time, the noble families of their old districts continued to support them in the traditional manner and preserved the old client system in the assembly, but ambitious politicians soon wooed them away with offers of largess, including promises of land reform, which would provide the former farmers with acreage. But promises of reform were not kept, and the mob became a fickle electorate.

Imperialism advanced the fortunes of the traders and manufacturers who emerged from the equestrian class. With the movement toward empire, the equestrians derived new political and economic power from the growth of trade and from the imperial tax system. Instead of setting up a centralized tax bureau, the Roman government sold the right to collect taxes in the provinces. Companies of equestrians bid for the contracts that carried the right, and the winning bidders managed

to earn a handsome profit after covering the contract price. Tax collectors (called publicans) have never been popular, but those who collected taxes in the Roman provinces earned special hatred.

And yet, the Romans' readiness to grant citizenship and its attendant privileges won the loyalty of many provincials. Typically, the provinces were organized around cities that had emerged from small towns. The Roman governors usually permitted the local aristocracy to manage the political and economic affairs of the cities, and members of the city councils were awarded Roman citizenship. In this way, many provincial leaders became loyal Romans, legally equal to Romans by birth.

Finally, many of the prisoners taken in the Roman conquests were, according to the common practice, sold into slavery. As in classical Greece, most of the Roman slaves seem to have worked as household servants or as assistants to craftsmen. Others, especially those seized in the Hellenistic states of the eastern Mediterranean, were skilled artisans, and some were well educated. Many Roman families acquired Greek slaves as teachers for their children. Some slaves were put to work in distant mines, and a few were used in manufacturing, though there was little large-scale manufacturing at the time. It is not clear

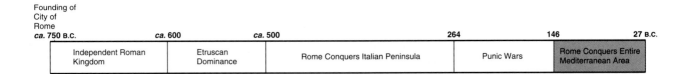

Founding of City of Rome ca. 750 B.C.		ca. 600		ca. 500		264		146		27 B.C.
Independent Roman Kingdom		Etruscan Dominance		Rome Conquers Italian Peninsula			Punic Wars		Rome Conquers Entire Mediterranean Area	

whether the laborers on the great landed estates were slave or free, but the senatorial families are known to have had a great many slaves. Apparently all but the poorest families were slave owners.

Many slaves managed to win their freedom, either because their owners freed them voluntarily through the practice of manumission, or because they managed to buy their freedom. Freedmen continued to be obligated to the family of their former owner, and cadres of freedmen performed various services and contributed to the treasury of wealthy families.

Unlike the cities of Greece, Rome admitted freed slaves to citizenship. Although freedmen could not serve in the army, they could serve as oarsmen in the imperial fleet. Their children enjoyed full citizenship. The long process of creating the empire brought hundreds of the thousands of slaves to Italy, and by the end of the first century B.C., many Roman citizens were descendants of foreign slaves. Although Rome did not grant full citizenship to all the peoples it conquered, its liberal practices bound most of those defeated to its constitution and laws and reduced the incidence of rebellion.

Expansion of the Roman Republic beyond Italy   First Century B.C.

Literary, Artistic, and Religious Change

Even before the eastern wars, educated Romans had been influenced by Greek culture. The subsequent influx of thousands of Greeks and others from the hellenized East literally transformed Roman civilization. Many artists, philosophers, and craftsmen arrived as slaves and worked their influence within and through the great families. Greek became the second language of educated people, and Greek poetry, literature, and art dominated Roman culture.

The more conservative Romans warned that these alien influences would undermine traditional Roman values. In their view, Rome had achieved its greatness as a result of its unique virtues, and to imitate foreign styles was tantamount to admitting that Romans were culturally inferior. Other Romans, however, were enthusiastic hellenizers, and some even went so far as to denigrate the old Roman culture. The disagreement between the two camps ran deep and showed itself in politics as well as cultural matters. Conservatives insisted that it was hellenization that had brought about the rise of the urban mob and had fostered other undesirable changes in Roman politics.

The conservatives were waging a losing battle. Roman artists became slavish imitators of Greek models. In fact, much of our knowledge of Greek sculpture comes from Roman copies made during this period. In architecture, too, Greek styles had come to replace Roman styles by about 200 B.C.

Greek influence is apparent in Roman literature as well. In fact, one of the first long poems written in Latin was a translation of Homer's *Odyssey*. The Romans also admired Greek drama, and the first Roman plays were written in Greek. Later, when the leading playwrights chose to write in Latin, they still based their work on classical or Hellenistic models. The works of Menander, the Greek playwright who wrote comedies in late fourth century B.C., were particularly influential, and many early Roman comedies are essentially reworkings of his plays.

The first Roman historians were already writing in Greek around 200 B.C. About 168 B.C., Cato, a senator who strongly opposed the Greek influence, used Latin when he wrote the first major history of Rome. Ironically, Cato's aim was to elevate Latin prose to the level of Greek. Perhaps the best account of Rome's rise to power, however, was that of Polybius (*ca.* 202–120 B.C.), a Greek who spent considerable time as a hostage in Rome and saw himself as a latter-day Thucydides. The Romans themselves emphasized the parallels between Rome and Athens. They dated the expulsion of the Tarquins to coincide almost exactly with the Athenians' expulsion of the last tyrant and Cleisthenes' creation of the democratic constitution (see p. 48).

In religion, the Romans created a pantheon that accommodated many local gods of the peoples they conquered. After their conquest of Greece, they combined their own pantheon with the Greek pantheon, identifying as best they could the twelve gods of Olympus with their own

The Roman Gods

Although Roman religion derived from the religion of the Italic peoples and the Etruscans, it was common among the ancients to equate the gods of different peoples. At the beginning of the second century B.C., the poet Ennius listed the twelve main Roman gods as representations of the Greek gods of Olympus. They were:

Roman	**Greek**
Jove (Jupiter)	= Zeus (king of the gods)
Juno	= Hera (marriage, queen)
Minerva	= Athena (handicrafts, war)
Mars	= Ares (war)
Apollo	= Apollo (prophecy)
Venus	= Aphrodite (love)
Mercury	= Hermes (trade)
Diana	= Artemis (hunting, woods)
Vesta	= Hestia (hearth)
Ceres	= Demeter (grain)
Vulcan	= Hephaestus (fire, smithing)
Neptune	= Poseidon (sea)

gods. During the second century B.C., the eastern mystery cults began to attract a following in Rome and the western Mediterranean, though they did not influence Roman religious life significantly until after the end of the republican period (after 30 B.C.).

So long as the patricians dominated Roman society and politics, Rome's traditional civic religion, led by a patrician priesthood, remained the dominant religion. By the second century B.C., however,

the old religion was losing its grip on the Romans, who were turning more and more to the eastern cults.

Roman jurisprudence showed only slight Greek influence. From the earliest times, the Romans took special pride in their law and government. After the codification of the law in the Twelve Tables, Roman law developed into an impressive body of legislation. Much of it had to do with such constitutional questions as whether plebeians would be eligible for

This fresco found in a villa on the outskirts of Pompeii depicts initiation rites of a Dionysian mystery cult, but they are rendered in such a way as to make precise interpretation difficult for the outsider.

election to the magistracies. The edicts issued by the praetors, however, defined the cases the judges would hear and dealt mainly with private law. Each new praetor reissued the edict pertaining to his court, altering and extending the legal remedies available to citizens and foreigners to reflect changes in the society and economy of the city and empire. The praetors were under constant pressure from litigants to accept new claims, new remedies, and new procedures. In a sense, the Roman legal system developed in response to the clamor of litigants and was consequently flexible in dealing with the myriad legal disputes of an imperial society. By the end of the republican period, the texts of the edicts had become pretty well fixed and were re-issued annually with only minor changes.

Unlike modern systems, the Roman legal system was neither centralized nor run by professional lawyers. When a complainant brought a case before the praetor, the praetor merely decided whether or not the complaint was actionable. If he decided it was, he appointed a private citizen, usually a patrician or at least a wealthy and educated man, to judge the case. The judge could proceed in almost any way he chose—there were no established rules of procedure or evidence—but he had to meet the high standards of the praetor in handling the case. A judge who mishandled a case, either through incompetence or prejudice, was subject to severe penalties.

Litigation was part of everyday life, and most patricians were well versed in legal matters. Some of them became known as legal experts and were called on to advise judges, litigants, and even the praetors themselves. Starting in the first century B.C., these experts produced commentaries on the praetorian edicts and wrote treatises on various aspects of the law. They did not work for pay, however, and in no sense constituted a legal profession. The practice of law was simply something a gentleman did.

THE COLLAPSE OF THE REPUBLIC, 146–59 B.C.

The Society of the Late Republic

The vast changes in Roman society that came in the wake of empire finally weakened the political framework of the Republic. Many Romans, like Cato, clung to the ancient values of the farmer-citizen, but by the middle of the second century B.C., Roman society was far different from what it had been in the early days. The influx of foreigners had transformed the society of the capital city, and the countryside had undergone a social and economic revolution. Agriculture had become specialized in the production of olive oil and wine, and only the great landowners had the capital and the commercial contacts needed to make these crops profitable.

The upper classes, who were the main beneficiaries of the imperial conquests, acquired immense wealth and sought to acquire whatever land they fancied by whatever means. They lent money to the small farmers to plant, not, as of old, in keeping with the patron-client relationship, but so they could seize the farmers' land in the event of a bad harvest, sickness, or other disaster. Often, they helped disaster along. Accounts from later times tell of large landowners who permitted their flocks to destroy the crops of lesser neighbors and sent their crews to destroy irrigation ditches at crucial times

A funerary relief showing a man and his wife, a portrait of an ancestor, and an attribute of the man's profession (first century B.C.).

of the year. During the late third and early second centuries B.C., small farmers found it almost impossible to survive.

As land and wealth became concentrated in the hands of the upper classes, thousands of small farmers deserted the countryside and made their way to Rome. Sometimes they sought redress, though often that meant appealing to the very people who had deprived them of their land. Sometimes they sought a new livelihood. The population of Rome swelled with displaced farmers and their families living in unwholesome tenements. Poor and wretched as they were, they were Roman citizens, and many conservative politicians equated their fate with the decline of Rome itself.

The Gracchi

The leaders of the conservative faction were Tiberius and Gaius Gracchus, grandsons of the great Scipio who had defeated Carthage. They believed that the yeoman farmer was the foundation of Rome's greatness, and that the only way to save the state was to institute land reform that would return the farmer to his farm. Realizing they could never win the Senate to their cause, Tiberius Gracchus decided to work through the plebeian magistracy. In 133 B.C., he won election as tribune of the people and immediately proposed legislation to redistribute public land. Although the law would not have deprived the senatorial families of their estates, it so happened that the public land itself was at the disposal of these same families under favorable long-term leases. Not surprisingly, the senators vigorously opposed the law. The conflict precipitated a constitutional crisis, because it raised questions about the respective powers of the Senate and the tribunes. Moreover, according to an ancient constitutional principle, no proposal opposed by the Senate could be enacted into law. When the Senate persuaded another tribune to veto the enacted law, Tiberius, in an unprecedented move, had him voted out of office. Tiberius then ran for a second term as tribune, another violation of custom and a direct

threat to the Senate's power. If a man could hold office indefinitely, the state's ability to check popular power would be destroyed. At last, a group of senators prompted their clients to stage a riot, which ended in the lynching of Tiberius Gracchus.

Ten years later, Gaius Gracchus overcame senatorial opposition and won election as tribune. He revived his brother's proposal for land reform and actually managed to set up colonies of small farmers on public land. To win a wide political base, Gaius sought the support of the urban mob by enabling people to purchase grain from the state at half price. He sought the equestrians' support by giving them control over the juries that heard cases of corruption in tax collecting. Finally, he responded to the old complaint of Rome's Italian allies, particularly of the Samnites, that they, like the Latins, had contributed much to Rome's success, but had never received full rights as citizens. It was Gaius's proposal to grant them citizenship that brought him down. His own supporters were split on the issue, and during the conflict that erupted, Gaius, like his brother before him, was murdered.

Marius and Sulla

The animosities generated by the Gracchi disrupted relations among the Senate, the tribunes and assembly, and the equestrians, and henceforth every proposal met with strong opposition from one quarter or another. The Republic's stability was further imperiled by the rise of independent military power, a consequence of Rome's indulgence in imperialism.

In 107 B.C., Rome was embroiled in a difficult war with a former ally in North Africa, and in desperation the citizens elected as consul Marius, an ambitious equestrian from a rural area. Already famous as a general, Marius quickly brought the African war to a successful conclusion. In 104 B.C., he was called on to meet a new threat. Indo-European tribes, the Germans, had come out of the northern European forests to invade Gaul and now threatened northern Italy. After they defeated several Roman armies that defended the peninsula, Marius was re-elected consul five years in a row (104–100 B.C.) to meet their threat.

In order to build an army strong enough to deal with the Germans, Marius violated the ancient rule that only land-owners could serve in the military and recruited landless men. Formerly, soldiers supported themselves, at no expense to the state. Marius rewarded his men by dis-tributing to them the booty won in battle and by settling them on conquered land. In so doing, he created an army loyal to its general, the source of its reward. More-over, he transformed army service into an attractive career for the poor and dispos-sessed by giving them the prospect of a new start in life. In sum, Marius profes-sionalized the army and set it on the path to independence from the civilian govern-ment it was supposed to serve. The army also acquired an aggressive stance on Rome's dealings with foreign powers, be-cause the soldiers' rewards were won through conquest.

In 90 B.C., Rome's Italian allies, disap-pointed by the death of Gaius Gracchus in their quest for full citizenship, rose in rebellion against the Romans. Marius again assumed military command in this so-called Social War (war with allies—

socii in Latin). After two years of conflict, Sulla, one of Marius's former officers, emerged as the most prominent figure in Roman politics.

Sulla was serving as consul in 88 B.C. when the Romans ended the Social War by granting full citizenship to the Italians. While the war was going on, Mithradates, king of a small Hellenistic state, was trying to create a Hellenistic empire in Asia Mi-nor. In 88 B.C. he instigated the massacre of 80,000 Romans in Greek cities along the coast of ancient Ionia.

Although still consul, Sulla marched on Rome to prevent Marius from receiving the command against Mithradates. Suc-cessful, he moved against Mithradates the next year and, after three years of hard campaigning, succeeded in putting down the rebellion. His long absence from Rome gave his enemies opportunity to under-mine his authority, and in 83 B.C. he again marched on the city. By now, the army had become a force to reckon with in Roman politics. In 82 B.C., Sulla was named dicta-tor to resolve a crisis he himself had pre-cipitated. He proscribed thousands of his enemies—put a price on their heads and confiscated their property. He then distrib-uted the property among his veterans. He installed supporters in the Senate and tried to weaken the powers of the tribunes and the popular assembly. In 79 B.C., he retired from public life and died the follow-ing year.

New Leaders: Pompey, Crassus, and Cicero

After Sulla, the chief object of a political career in Rome was a provincial military command, which brought great wealth and control of a loyal army. Following Sulla's retirement, one of his officers, Pom-pey, emerged as the leading general and politician. His chief rival was Crassus, who had made a huge fortune in questionable real estate dealings in Rome. In 71 B.C., while Pompey was putting down a rebel-lion in Spain, Crassus, though not much of a general himself, snuffed out a dangerous slave rebellion led by a former gladiator named Spartacus. Conflict between the

Sulla, dictator of Rome from 82 to 79 B.C.

two generals was avoided when they were both elected consuls for the year 70 B.C.

In the next few years, a third political figure, Cicero, entered the scene. Cicero was a member of the equestrian class and came from the same town as Marius. None of his ancestors had ever served as a magistrate, so he was a "new man" in town, an unusual figure in Roman politics. But he parlayed his extraordinary skill as a lawyer and orator into a distinguished senatorial career. In fact, Cicero has served as the model for aspiring orators to the present day. He wrote treatises on rhetoric and philosophy that set out the basic rules of public speaking and also set a new standard of Latin prose. His works ultimately became part of the standard fare of every student of the Latin language.

Cicero rose to prominence after he successfully prosecuted a spectacularly corrupt provincial governor named Verres. Throughout his political career, he tried to maintain his political independence. Nonetheless, when obliged to choose between Pompey and Crassus, Cicero threw his support to Pompey. The alliance with Pompey led to Cicero's election as consul in 63 B.C., and during his year in office he put down a conspiracy led by Catiline to seize control of the state. As he had after his prosecution of Verres, he published his speeches made against Catiline and his supporters, thus keeping his name before the public.

In 74 B.C., Mithradates rebelled again. This time, the Romans provided for stable military command in the East by permitting Pompey to remain there for more than a decade and by commissioning him to reorganize imperial government throughout the eastern Mediterranean. By the time he returned to Rome in 62 B.C., he had created a new Roman province in western Asia Minor, had converted Syria into a province, and had put the rest of the Near East under new client kings, including the Jewish Herodians.

When he returned to the capital, Pompey discovered that the Senate was unwilling to ratify all the arrangements he had made or to honor the promises he had given. In the struggle that ensued, he al-

lied himself to a powerful urban politician named Gaius Julius Caesar.

Bust of Pompey showing him late in life.

THE END OF THE REPUBLIC, 59–30 B.C.

The Rise of Caesar, 59–52 B.C.

Caesar, the scion of an ancient patrician family, had won huge popularity with the Roman mob and while doing so had piled up huge debts. This gave Crassus, whose political power had dwindled after his consulship, a chance to reassert himself. He paid the young man's debts and helped him win rapid political advancement. In 60 B.C., Caesar convinced Pompey and Crassus to join him in a triumvirate, the so-called First Triumvirate. This alliance helped Caesar to win election as consul for the year 59 B.C. Once in office, he saw to it that Pompey's arrangements in the East were ratified and that Pompey's veterans were properly rewarded with public land. He also distributed land to his own urban supporters.

For his own reward, Caesar received a military command, though a less promising one than the command that had made Pompey's reputation. Caesar took command of Gaul, the weak link in Rome's western provinces. The Romans controlled only a narrow strip of territory along the Mediterranean coast, Transalpine Gaul, which linked Cisalpine Gaul (Gaul on the Italian side of the Alps) with the province of Spain. North of Transalpine Gaul, Gallic and German tribes posed a constant threat. Stabilizing this region was essential, but it was an unrewarding assignment for Caesar. The Gallic tribes had none of the wealth of the kingdoms Pompey had conquered in the East.

In 58 B.C., Caesar received a five-year proconsular command, later doubled in length, that included both Cisalpine Gaul and Transalpine Gaul. He immediately launched a campaign to pacify the tribes north of Transalpine Gaul. As he marched north, he saw new enemies further north, and in the end he subdued the whole of Gaul, which he organized as a province.

Bust of Julius Caesar showing him at the time of his assassination.

Caesar in Gaul   58–49 B.C.

Moreover, he made two expeditions to Britain, where his Gallic foes often took refuge with their Celtic allies, and he crossed the Rhine several times to push the Germans back. He commemorated these campaigns in *Commentaries on the Gallic War*, a model of terse Latin prose that helped establish his fame.

Crassus also received a military command through the triumvirate and led an army against the Parthians, the Roman name for the Hellenistic successors of the Persian empire. In 53 B.C., the Parthians destroyed Crassus's army and killed Crassus himself, leaving Pompey and Caesar as Rome's political leaders. Pompey had returned to Rome by now, and Caesar was still trying to pacify the new province of Gaul.

Caesar and Pompey, 52–48 B.C.

In 52 B.C., Pompey was elected sole consul to put down mob violence in Rome. This extraordinary power gave him an advantage over Caesar, who depended on the Senate and assembly to legitimate his command. Pompey and Caesar had begun to drift apart even before Crassus's death. So long as Caesar remained in command of a fiercely loyal army, Pompey could not feel secure. So he tried to deprive Caesar of his command. Friends of Caesar in Rome blocked this attempt, but it was now clear that the two were enemies. The Senate tried to arrange a settlement by calling on both of them to give up their commands. When Caesar refused, the Senate ordered Pompey to march against him.

One of Caesar's assets as a general was his ability to act swiftly, and he did so now. On March 1, 49 B.C., he crossed the tiny Rubicon River, the border between Cisalpine Gaul and the territory of Rome itself, and began a civil war against Pompey. The Senate had assumed that Pompey would be able to raise an army quickly, but few of his veterans were settled in Italy, and he fled to Greece, accompanied by most of the senators. Rome was open to Caesar. After a year of indecisive fighting, which mostly went in Pompey's favor, Caesar defeated Pompey at Pharsalus in 48 B.C. Pompey escaped to Egypt, where the Ptolemaic king ordered him executed in a bid for Caesar's favor. For the next three years, Caesar and his lieutenants campaigned against Pompey's supporters in Spain, North Africa, and the East.

Caesar in Power, 48–44 B.C.

Caesar was named dictator in 48 B.C. Though this was a republican title, many Romans were aware that political reality had changed dramatically. Caesar held the *imperium*, the supreme military power, and was styled *imperator* (from which the word *emperor* derives), the supreme military commander. Thus he united military and civil authority not as the consuls had under the Republic, but as Sulla had 35 years before. His power derived from his military command rather than from election to civilian office.

Once in power, Caesar undertook reforms similar to those attempted by Sulla and Pompey. He settled his veterans on public land and tried to end corruption in

Richly embossed helmet of an aristocratic warrior of Gaul, at the time of Julius Caesar's conquest.

the provincial administrations. He enlarged the Senate and even seated some provincial nobles there. The full incorporation of provincials into Roman government and society was still far in the future, however. He reformed the calendar, adopting the Egyptian year of 365 days with the addition of an extra day every four years to keep it synchronized with the solar year.

His reforms gained him support in Italy and in the provinces, where romanization proceeded rapidly. But the old senatorial class continued to oppose him. Caesar had tried to conciliate them by permitting many scions of the old families to retain their positions in the Senate, but that strategy had failed. The senators viewed the new government as a direct challenge to their ancient rights and an unconstitutional usurpation of power. At last they formed a conspiracy under the leadership of Brutus and Cassius, and Caesar was assassinated in the senate house on the Ides of March (March 15), 44 B.C.

Caesar was not in power long enough to reveal his intentions. It remains unclear whether he planned to set aside the ancient republican constitution or to try, like Sulla, to reform it. Whatever his intent, his death created a political crisis in which any hope that the Republic would be restored was lost.

Civil War and the Second Triumvirate, 44–30 B.C.

In the chaotic political situation that followed Caesar's death, Mark Antony, Caesar's chief lieutenant, won the support of Caesar's veterans and much of the Roman mob. Brutus had hoped to revive senatorial government, but the old system had broken down completely, and he and his co-conspirators found themselves with little support. Octavian, Caesar's grandnephew and adopted heir, a frail 18-year-old, received the support of Cicero and other senators who thought they could control him. But when Octavian had won sufficient support among the Roman mob, he suddenly joined Mark Antony and another of Caesar's former lieutenants, Lepidus, in the Second Triumvirate. Late in

44 B.C., the three led an army on Rome, where the assembly granted them full power for five years.

The new triumvirs began by ordering a bloody proscription against those who had opposed them. Like Sulla, they confiscated the property of those they proscribed and distributed it among their soldiers. Cicero, a personal enemy of Antony, was forced to commit suicide. Brutus and Cassius, who had escaped to Macedonia, were hunted down and were defeated and killed at the Battle of Philippi (in Thrace) in 42 B.C.. The triumvirs then offered favorable terms to the conspirators' army and quickly put an end to the civil war, at least temporarily.

Now the triumvirs had to deal with one another. Antony came out on top. He had the largest army and held command of the wealthy East. Octavian got Italy,

The Murder of Caesar   44 B.C.

The Lives, *written by the Greek historian Plutarch around* A.D. *100, supplies valuable information on Greek and Roman history, particularly on the confusing years of the late Republic. As may be seen from this passage, Plutarch's* Lives *served as a source of Shakespeare's play* Julius Caesar.

When Caesar entered, the senate stood up to show their respect to him, and of Brutus's confederates, some came about his chair and stood behind it. . . . Tillius, laying hold of his robe with both his hands, pulled it down from his neck, which was the signal for the assault. Casca gave him the first cut in the neck. . . . Those who were not privy to the design were astonished, and their horror and amazement at what they saw were so great that they durst not fly nor assist Caesar, nor so much as speak a word. But those who came prepared for the business enclosed him on every side. For it had been agreed that they should each of them make a thrust at him, and flesh themselves with his blood; for which reason Brutus also gave him one stab in the groin. Some say that he fought and resisted all the rest, shifting his body to avoid the blows, and calling out for help, but that when he saw Brutus's sword drawn, he covered his face with his robe and submitted, letting himself fall . . . at the foot of the pedestal on which Pompey's statue stood. . . .

From Plutarch, The Lives of Noble Grecians and Romans, *trans. by John Dryden, rev. by Arthur Hugh Clough (New York: Modern Library, n.d.), pp. 892–93.*

A coin commemorating the death of Caesar. One side bears the portrait of Brutus; the other side shows the assassins' daggers flanking the cap of liberty.

and Lepidus got Gaul and Spain. In time, Octavian forced Lepidus into retirement and won control of all the western provinces. Meanwhile, Antony entered into a love affair with Cleopatra, the Egyptian queen, and granted her large portions of the eastern provinces. Cleopatra was unpopular in Rome, and Antony's relationship with her cost him a great deal of support. Antony also opened a war with the Parthians and weakened his forces while gaining nothing.

By 32 B.C., Octavian had consolidated his hold over Italy and the West and was ready to move against Antony. He secured a decree from the assembly relieving Antony of his command. In 31, after a year of skirmishing, the two met in a great naval battle at Actium, on the Adriatic coast of Greece. There Octavian's fleet, commanded by the capable Agrippa, decisively defeated Antony and Cleopatra. The two fled to Egypt, where first Antony and then Cleopatra committed suicide.

Actium put an end to the civil wars that followed Caesar's death and left Octavian without rivals. On January 13, 27 B.C., he proclaimed the restoration of the Republic. The proclamation was a sham, but it enabled Octavian to establish a new state, republican in name, but a military dictatorship in fact.

The real genius of the Romans was not in conquest but in law and government. They anchored their society on a system of law, and from an early date dealt with the peoples they conquered according to law. They asked how the law should apply to the conquered. Over time, that emphasis led both their allies and their subjects to think of their position in the empire in legal terms. True, Rome planted garrisons in conquered territories and put down rebellions, but the real conflicts were over the legal rights of groups and individuals and the legal responsibilities of Roman officials. In short, the Romans created a new type of empire, a vast city-state in which ancient ideas of citizenship and government were played out on an international scale.

Suggestions For Further Reading

Hellenistic Period

There is an excellent new survey of Hellenistic history and civilization in P. Green, *Alexander to Actium: The Historical Evolution of the Hellenistic Age* (1990). On the hellenization of the East, see M. Avi-Yonah, *Hellenism and the East: Contacts and Interrelations from Alexander to the Roman Conquest* (1978). On Ptolemaic Egypt, see A. K. Bowman, *Egypt after the Pharaohs, 332 B.C.–A.D. 642* (1986), and P. M. Fraser, *Ptolemaic Alexandria* 3 vols. (1972). M. Hadas, *Hellenistic Culture: Fusion and Diffusion* (1959) is a general introduction. On the Hellenistic philosophical schools, see A. A. Long, *Hellenistic Philosophy:*

Stoics, Epicureans, and Sceptics (1974). For a general introduction to Hellenistic art, see C. Havelock, *Hellenistic Art: The Art of the Classical World from the Death of Alexander the Great to the Battle of Actium,* rev. ed. (1981); on sculpture, see M. Bieber, *The Sculpture of the Hellenistic Age* rev. ed. (1961). On Hellenistic science, see G. E. R. Lloyd, *Greek Science after Aristotle* (1973), and E. J. Dijksterhuis, *Archimedes,* trans. C. Dikshoorn (1987). On the classical scholarship of the Hellenistic period, see R. Pfeiffer, *History of Classical Scholarship from the Beginnings to the End of the Hellenistic Age* (1968).

Roman Political History

There are many reliable texts devoted to Roman history. Among the best are H. H. Scullard, *History of the Roman World from 753 to 146 B.C.,* 3rd ed. (1961); F. B. Marsh, *History of the Roman World from 146 to 30 B.C.,* 3rd ed. (1961); and H. H. Scullard, *From the Gracchi to Nero: A History of Rome from 133 B.C. to A.D. 68* (1975). For a shorter work, see A. E. R. Boak,

A History of Rome to A.D. 565, revised by W. G. Sinnigen (1977). On Pompey, see P. Greenhalgh, *Pompey: The Republican Prince* (1981). On Julius Caesar, see M. Gelzer, *Caesar: Politician and Statesman,* trans. J. Lloyd (1975). On Mark Antony, see E. G. Huzar, *Mark Antony: A Biography* (1978). The reign of Octavian will be treated in the next chapter.

Etruscans and the Roman Republic

On the Etruscans, see H. H. Scullard, *The Etruscan Cities and Rome* (1967), R. Bloch, *The Etruscans* (1958), and H. Hencken, *Tarquinia, Villanovans and Early Etruscans* (1968). O. J. Brendel, *Etruscan Art* (1978), is excellent. L. Bonfante uses Etruscan funerary art to reveal Etruscan society in "Etruscan Couples and their Aristocratic Society," *Women's Studies* 8 (1981) 157–87. R. Bloch, *The Origins of Rome* (1966), and H. H. Scullard, *The Etruscan Cities and Rome* (1967), treat the early history of Rome. On the early conquests, see E. T. Salmon, *Samnium and the Samnites* (1967), and *Roman Colonization under the Republic* (1969). Two works treat the development of Rome's overseas empire: R. M. Errington, *The Dawn of Empire* (1972), and E. Badian, *Roman Imperialism in the Late Republic* (1968). On the social history of the period, see the studies by M. I. Finley, *Studies in Ancient Society* (1974), P. A. Brunt, *Social Conflicts in the Roman Republic* (1971), and K. R. Bradley, *Discovering the Roman Family: Studies in Roman Social History* (1991).

On aspects of Roman culture, see P. Grimal, *Hellenism and the Rise of Rome* (1968); W. G. Arnott, *Menander, Plautus and Terence* (1975). A rich sampling of selections from ancient Roman sources is collected in the first volume of N. Lewis and M. Reinhold, eds., *Roman Civilization* (1951).

THE ROMAN EMPIRE
27 B.C.–A.D. 476

*O*ctavian's proclamation of the restoration of the Roman Republic in 27 B.C., actually marked the beginning of a new era. True, the Senate was restored, consuls and other magistrates were elected once again, and the assembly met from time to time. But these familiar forms of republican government cloaked a military dictatorship. Octavian still held the *imperium,* the supreme military command, and still had the backing of the army. After 14 years of civil war, he had swept the empire clean of challengers and could afford to give honor, if not substance, to the old institutions. He introduced his supporters into the Senate and accepted from them the position of *princeps* (first citizen)—that is, the man who spoke first on any issue before the Senate. When Octavian spoke, the senators listened. The period during which Octavian and his immediate successors controlled the government of Rome is called the Principate.

Shortly after the restoration, the Senate voted to bestow the title *Augustus* on Octavian. This was a title ordinarily used for gods, and a person called *augustus* was looked upon with awe and reverence. In this political usage, it emphasized Octavian's role as the beneficent protector of the state. In a masterstroke of propaganda, Octavian adopted the title as his name, thereby enhancing his authority while avoiding the charge that he was violating constitutional principles as Caesar had.

THE PRINCIPATE OF AUGUSTUS, 27 B.C.–A.D. 14

The Organization of Imperial Government

The backbone of Augustus's power was the army, which was made up of 25 legions of about 6,000 men each and an equal number of auxiliary units of provincial troops. Augustus kept the legions at

(OPPOSITE) MEDALLION DEPICTING EMPEROR THEODOSIUS I (R. 379–395).

27 B.C.	A.D. 14		68	96		A.D. 180
Principate of Augustus	Julio-Claudian Emperors		Flavian Emperors	The "Five Good Emperors"		

near full strength; he had about 250,000 men under arms at all times. Because the soldiers received large cash bonuses and an allotment of land when they retired after twenty years of service, they were completely loyal to their commander in chief.

Once he had consolidated his power in the government, Augustus turned his attention to the provinces. During the civil wars, the contenders for power had vied for control of the provinces and had pitted them against one another. Once the wars were over, Augustus assigned his military lieutenants to govern all the provinces in which military garrisons were stationed. The tax revenues collected in each province supported its garrison.

Yet, recognizing that the Senate had a right to participate in governing the provinces, Augustus appointed senators to govern those that were thoroughly pacified, which meant that the Senate controlled the richest, most romanized provinces. He also permitted the local elites to carry out most of the functions of government and continued the old practice of permitting semi-independent client kingdoms on the Empire's fringes to control their internal affairs.

In fact, Augustus encouraged local autonomy throughout the Empire. In Gaul, his governors helped transform the old tribal centers into romanized cities, from which they governed the surrounding region. The Romans devoted substantial sums of money to constructing public buildings in the provincial cities and made a great effort to romanize the tribal aristocracy. In Spain and North Africa, they planted cities in areas where they wanted to encourage agriculture; the North African province eventually had about 300 *municipia,* towns with the legal status of cities, though most of them were little more than agricultural villages. In the

The ruins of public structures at Djemila, Algeria.

East, the ancient city-states were permitted to govern themselves under Roman supervision. In short, the Empire was a collection of city-states under a centralized government in Rome.

Augustus's Social Program

The great theme of the Augustan program was "restoration." He restored peace in Rome and in the Empire, he restored the Republic and the provincial governments, and he sought to restore the fabric of traditional Roman society. He passed legislation to restore the family unit by encouraging marriage and childbearing. Moreover, he made a point of governing through the traditional magistracies and the Senate. All in all, he projected a thoroughly conservative image designed to link himself with the hallowed past of Cato, Cicero, and other heroes of the Republic.

In his efforts to restore traditional Roman religion, Augustus revitalized the old civic cults and reestablished the priesthoods, which had been decimated by the civil wars. After waiting for the old incumbent to die, he himself assumed the role of Pontifex Maximus (highest priest). Meanwhile, he prohibited practice of the mystery cults, which had gained strong followings in Rome during the preceding century (see p. 83).

Augustus's legislation relating to family life reveals a great deal about what had happened to Roman society during the last years of the Republic. Traditionally, Rome was a society of families, each dominated by a patriarch. The male head of the family, the *paterfamilias,* had supreme authority over all members of the household. He owned all the family's property and determined whom his sons and daughters could marry, where they would live, and what professional or economic goals they would pursue. A man who bought something from or lent money to another man whose father was alive was taking a big risk, for the son had no legal right to sell what belonged to his father, and the father was not responsible for his son's debts.

Daughters had even fewer rights than sons. Every woman had a male guard-

Wall painting from Pompeii depicting wealthy Roman women.

ian—usually her father, husband, or a male relative—and she could make decisions about such matters as marriage or buying and selling property only with the guardian's approval and assistance. Women were expected to spin and weave and perform all the household chores. In legend and funerary inscriptions, those who had produced many children were held in high honor.

By the time of Augustus, upper-class women may have been familiar with the domestic arts, but only slaves actually engaged in them. Upper-class Roman women often became patronesses of the arts and sometimes played a role in politics. Some were excellent businesswomen. In practice, most women seem to have had considerable freedom to manage their own affairs. A study of Cicero's wife, Terentia, reveals that she managed substantial property holdings by herself and even kept knowledge of her business dealings from her husband. When Augustus ruled that women who had borne three children would no longer need a guardian, he apparently repealed an old law that no longer had much force.

Augustus's view of the aristocracy emphasized duty to the state, hard work, avoidance of luxury, and traditional family values. He tried to bring the debauched, extravagant members of the upper classes to heel by passing sumptuary laws to control ostentatious expenditures and to encourage marriage and large families. During the last decades of the Republic, some upper-class Roman women practiced contraception and abortion, and many of them refused to marry. To ensure the succession of their property, some elderly women adopted adult men, often young lovers. Augustus's effort to change such behavior met little success.

The lower-class families of Rome needed no law to restrain them from ostentation or lascivious living. All members of the family shared the burdens of earning a living. Women tended shops, worked the fields, and ran the household. Augustus's program concerned itself only with the elite elements of society.

The Golden Age of Latin Literature

During the Augustan restoration, Latin literature achieved its highest level of excellence. Although Greek culture remained a powerful influence, Augustus and his associates patronized a group of writers and poets whose loyalties were rooted in the late republican period. As we have seen (p. 87), Cicero had achieved fame as an orator and essayist, and his prose had set a standard that was to stand for centuries. Caesar's history of the Gallic campaigns became a model for the sparse style of the man of action. Writers who grew up in the times of Cicero and Caesar did their mature work under Augustus.

The leading historian of the Augustan period was Livy (59 B.C.–A.D. 17), who wrote a monumental history of Rome from its origins to the age of Augustus. Though most of that history has been lost, enough remains to show that Livy celebrated the traditional virtues of Roman society that Augustus was trying to restore.

The poets of the late Republic set the basis for the achievements of their Augustan successors. Catullus (87–54 B.C.) wrote lyric poetry that was often of an intimate, sometimes sensuous, nature. Lucretius (99–55 B.C.), perhaps the greatest poet of the republican period, wrote *De rerum natura* (Concerning the nature of things),

Roman bust of Vergil.

a great work extolling the virtues of Epicurean philosophy. Lucretius was too speculative and abstract to appeal to the Romans, however, and had little influence on other poets.

The poets of the Augustan period sometimes chose to write on political themes, and when they did, they revealed some ambivalence toward the Augustan achievement. Horace (65–8 B.C.), Propertius (*ca.* 50–*ca.* 16 B.C.), and Vergil (70–19 B.C.) all wrote poems in which they dealt with the horrors of civil war and with the ethical problem of basing a new society on violence. But they and other poets, including Ovid (43 B.C.–A.D. 18), also wrote love poetry, pastoral idylls, and poems with mythological themes. Ovid was a friend of Horace and Propertius, but unlike them he never chose to extol the ancient Roman virtues so cherished by Augustus. In A.D. 8, after the publication of his *Ars Amatoria* (The Art of Love), Augustus banished him to a small town on the western shore of the Black Sea, where he died ten years later. Augustus considered this poem, and perhaps Ovid's behavior, lacking in the high moral character that he sought to restore to Roman life.

Of the poets of the early Empire, Vergil was surely the greatest. He was born near Mantua in the Lombard plain, and, after receiving his education in Cremona, Milan, and Rome, he returned to his ancestral farm. In 41 B.C., the government confiscated his property and gave it to the soldiers who had defeated Brutus and Cassius at Philippi. Vergil moved to the Campania, where his patron was Maecenas, one of Augustus's lieutenants, and also patron of Horace and Propertius. In the 30s B.C., after Vergil had published two poem cycles dealing with rural life, Augustus asked him to compose a work glorifying Rome and the achievements of the *imperator*.

For the last eleven years of his life, Vergil worked on the *Aeneid,* a great epic tale of the origins of Rome and made an analogy between Aeneas, legendary founder of the city, and Augustus. But Vergil rejected the Augustan propaganda that Rome's greatness rested on its moral superiority. In war, particularly in civil war, basic moral principles were necessarily violated, and no state founded on war could claim the moral high ground. Aeneas's success in founding Rome rested on violation of the principle, "War down the proud, spare the weak." Augustus had violated this principle many times during the wars that brought him to supreme power.

THE SUCCESSORS OF AUGUSTUS, A.D. 14–68

Because Augustus had retained the republican constitution, there were no rules to determine who would succeed him. Nonetheless, Augustus made it clear that his successor must be from his own family, the Julians. Consequently, during the last two decades of his reign, members of the imperial family constantly jockeyed for position. An atmosphere of intrigue affected the reigns of virtually all of Augustus's successors, often paralyzing them with suspicion and fear. Yet, the imperial government would flourish for centuries.

When Augustus died in A.D. 14, he was succeeded by Tiberius, an able administrator and general who had grown embittered by Augustus's refusal, during his lifetime, to name him as successor. Although Tiberius, a Julian by marriage, came from a distinguished senatorial family, the Claudians, many senators resented his elevation and intrigued against him. It did not help that he set high standards for his administrative assistants and removed many incompetent or dishonest scions of senatorial families from the civil service. After a struggle broke out in his family over who would succeed him when the time came, several suspicious deaths occurred. Fearful for his own life, Tiberius eventually left Rome for the safety of Capri, an island in the Bay of Naples. With Tiberius off the scene, Rome seethed with intrigue. When he heard about it from his spies, he ordered his lieutenants to execute several officials and senators on charges of treason. Tiberius died in 37.

His successor, Caligula, won the hearts of Romans as a young boy, when he often appeared in the company of his elders at official events. People expected great things of him as emperor. But Caligula was insane, and his whimsical cruelty and incompetence in military affairs finally led the palace guard (the elite corps of the army) to put him to death. His reign lasted only four years (r. 37–41).

For a short time after the death of Caligula, the Senate tried to reassert its authority and to restore the Republic in fact as well as in name. But by now real power had resided in the army for a century, and soon the palace guard that had done away with Caligula found someone to take his place. This was Caligula's uncle Claudius (r. 41–54), a scholarly, sickly man of 51 who had survived intrigue by pretending to be a harmless fool. Claudius turned out to be a more capable ruler than anyone expected. He initiated the conquest of Britain and continued the ancient Roman practice of extending citizenship, by making all those who served on provincial city councils citizens of Rome. As an administrator, he established four permanent bureaus, each headed by a freedman of the imperial family (usually a Greek). Senators still commanded the armies and governed the provinces, and equestrians still handled most of the Empire's financial affairs, but Claudius had established the foundations of the imperial bureaucracy that would eventually control the government.

Claudius's good sense did not extend to family matters. He married his niece Agrippina, an evil woman who poisoned him in 54 so that Nero, her son from a previous marriage, could succeed him. For a time, Nero (r. 54–68) acted under the guidance of his tutor Seneca, a philosopher and writer of high standing, and Burrus, master of the palace guard. But in 62, after the death of Burrus, Seneca retired, and the young emperor fell under evil influences.

Nero was a megalomaniac who fancied himself a poet and artist. Rumor said he set a great fire that destroyed much of Rome in 64 to create a brilliant backdrop for a recitation of his poetry. This story is certainly false. Nero cast the blame on a tiny community of Christians in the city

A coin with the bust of Claudius (*ca.* A.D. 50).

and ordered them killed. According to tradition, St. Peter lost his life in this early persecution.

During his last years, Nero became increasingly fearful of intrigue. In 65, he forced Seneca to commit suicide on suspicion that he had participated in a plot.

Agrippina, Claudius's wife, with her child Nero.

Later, he condemned to death his mother, the poet Lucan, and the general Corbulo, who had defended the eastern frontier against the Parthians. He also executed many senators and confiscated their wealth. Obsessed by threat of intrigue, he paid no attention to the administration or to the army, and in 68 the legions rebelled. Nero was quickly overthrown and committed suicide, ending the Julian succession. A brief civil war followed among the main segments of the army, each comprising several legions. Each unit vied to raise its general to the imperial throne.

THE EMPIRE AT ITS HEIGHT, 69–180

The troubles of 68–69 revealed the weakness of the Augustan political system. The armed forces controlled all power, and each army was loyal to its own commander. So long as the emperor was popular and competent, he could command the loyalty of all the units and preserve order. But when the emperor was weak, as under the later Julians, each army looked to its local commander to provide the rewards of service. The various corps put forward their own candidates after the death of Nero, and there were four "emperors" in one year.

Vespasian, commander of the eastern legions, emerged victorious. He was a self-made man, with foresight and good judgment. Recognizing the need for competence at the top, he trained his sons to be worthy of the role of *imperator*. He wanted his successor to rise through the army ranks, to be experienced in the affairs of empire, and to know the provinces well. After Vespasian, for more than a hundred years, the emperors rose through service in the army.

Vespasian ruled for ten years and was succeeded by his able son Titus (r. 79–81), who had served as co-ruler since 71. Titus was succeeded by his brother Domitian (r. 81–96), who began well but grew increasingly suspicious and arbitrary as time went by. In 96, his wife had him poisoned and the line of Vespasian came to an end.

27 B.C.	A.D. 14	68	96	A.D. 180
Principate of Augustus	Julio-Claudian Emperors	Flavian Emperors	The "Five Good Emperors"	

In this difficult situation, the Senate managed to elevate one of its own members, the elderly Nerva, to the imperial throne. Nerva, recognizing the danger that the state would face when he died, adopted an able legionary commander, Trajan, as his successor (r. 98–117). The practice of adopting an able man as heir and successor continued for four generations and produced the "five good emperors." These were wise and capable administrators, and under them the Empire prospered in peace.

Yet, these emperors instituted certain changes that served to weaken the Empire. The most important was in the military. Under Augustus and his immediate successors, the frontier armies had been mobile, able to make swift forays across the borders. The second-century emperors stationed the legions in permanent camps behind fixed, fortified frontiers. In northern Britain, for example, the emperor Hadrian (r. 117–138) built a wall across the island to keep out the northern tribes. Along the Rhine and Danube frontier, the Romans build a line of fortress camps and watchtowers. The armies that manned these fortifications had to be much larger than the mobile ones, and from the second century on they absorbed an increasing share of the Empire's wealth.

The years of unbroken peace during the second century encouraged farmers in various regions of the Empire to specialize in crops that could be sent to market. Earlier, the ready availability of grain from Sicily had motivated Italian farmers to turn to the production of olives and wine. Now, grain from Egypt and North Africa competed with grain from Sicily, and Gallic wine competed with Italian wine. In short, the regions of the Empire were becoming increasingly interdependent, making them more and more susceptible to any disturbance of the peace. No such disturbance occurred during the second cen-

Nero as emperor.

tury, but in the next century a multitude of troubles erupted.

THE CRISIS OF THE THIRD CENTURY

Political and Military Weakness

The last of the "good emperors," Marcus Aurelius (r. 161–180), had to spend a great deal of time away from Rome dealing with renewed unrest among the Germanic tribes across the Rhine-Danube border. Trier, a city near the border, became his second capital. The trouble was partly the fault of the Romans themselves. By establishing a static defensive line along the border and ceasing to stage forays across the border to keep the Germanic tribes

Vespasian, founder of the Flavian dynasty.

Trajan (*ca.* a.d. 100).

off balance, they had permitted the tribes to gather strength. Moreover, they had contributed to that strength by trading with the tribes and by encouraging them to join together in confederations. The Romans found it easier to deal with large confederations than with a multitude of small tribes, and the Germans, even those far from the frontier, were gradually drawn into the Roman sphere of influence.

The Roman strategy worked for about a century, but starting at the end of the second century, the northern border defenses came under continual pressure. This put a strain on the military system and its supply system and strengthened the position of the local commanders. When under attack, the border armies looked to their commanders for leadership rather than to the emperor. So long as the emperors chose competent and experienced successors who could control their lieutenants in the field, the legionary commanders remained loyal and obedi-

ent. But when Marcus Aurelius passed the imperial power on to his incompetent son Commodus (r. 180–192), a rift opened between the central government and the border armies. When Commodus was assassinated, the events of 68–69 were repeated and legions put up their respective generals as candidates for the imperial seat. Out of the strife, Septimius Severus (r. 193–211) emerged to establish a new dynasty, which ruled from 193 to 235.

The brief civil war altered the balance of power in Roman government. Although the emperors had always risen to power through the army, the civilian government set policy and determined how the legions were to be used. From 193 on, the army determined policy. On his deathbed, Septimius is reported to have advised his son to ensure for himself the affection of the army and to ignore the civil government and the classes that supported it. Whether or not the story is true, under the Severan dynasty the army governed the Empire.

The Roman Empire at Its Height   a.d. 117

During the brief civil war that followed the death of Commodus, however, the legions had withdrawn from the frontiers, weakening the defenses, and the Severan emperors were unable to reestablish the defense line created by the second-century emperors. When Septimius Severus died in 211, he was in northern Britain pacifying the Caledonian tribes that had been raiding the British province from Scotland. His sons quickly ended the campaign because they had to return to Rome to take over the government. On the Danube, the Germanic tribes, repelled by Marcus Aurelius in the 170s, but now organized in large confederations, reasserted themselves soon after Septimius's death. To the north, in the lower Rhine Valley, a group of related tribes, called the Franks, formed a confederation of their own. To the south, along the upper Rhine, a confederation of Alemans emerged, and, to the east, along the lower Danube, the Goths formed from tribes that appear to have migrated from southern Scandinavia. The Goths even managed to put together a pirate fleet in the eastern Mediterranean. In the Middle East, the Parthians renewed their pressure on the Empire after 224, when the Sassanid dynasty overthrew the old hellenistic Seleucid state.

Under all these attacks, the imperial system, already weak, broke down. The number of demands made on the emperor, even if he was competent and energetic, could not be met. Again, the troops turned to their commanders for the rewards of service.

When the last of the Severi was assassinated in 235, the powerful border armies took over the Empire. Between 235 and 285, they created and killed 26 emperors and at least as many unsuccessful contenders. The troops concerned themselves only with their own interests and regarded the emperor simply as the guarantor of their well-being.

Economic and Political Problems

In fact, by the third century, maintaining the vast army had become a heavy burden on the government. In 212, the emperor Caracalla (r. 211–217) issued a law that

The emperor Marcus Aurelius (r. 160–180) entering Rome in triumph (detail from the column of Marcus Aurelius in Rome).

granted citizenship to all free men in the Empire and thus made them liable for military service and the payment of certain taxes. By this time, virtually all tax receipts were going to supply the vast border armies, and most taxes were being paid in

Third-century tomb relief showing an affluent banker and two struggling Roman laborers. The Roman economy was weakened by the gap between the wealthy few and the poor masses.

kind—that is, in grain or other produce rather than in coin—at stations along the military roads that ran throughout the Empire. The goods were then transported to the military installations at the border. But even this enormous supply could not support the hundreds of thousands of troops, and the state began to purchase great quantities of agricultural products in the market. The great landowners were the main beneficiaries of those purchases.

The government took over other sectors of the economy as well. Many goods were manufactured in state factories, including all weapons and most army clothing. Goods were sent to the troops through the government transport system, which virtually monopolized large-scale transportation. The government also organized and subsidized the provisioning of major cities, which meant that independent merchants were left to deal in a few widely available low-value raw materials such as timber, wool, and flax, and in ordi-

nary tools and implements. They could also deal in luxury items such as spices, jewelry, and fine wines, but that trade was only a small part of the economy. Most of the traders in luxury goods were Orientals, including Syrians and Jews, who had connections in the eastern Mediterranean cities through which spices and the oils used in perfumes passed, some of them from as far away as India and China.

The civil wars of the third century put enormous stress on this government-dominated economy. Armies on the march repeatedly disrupted the operation of farms and the collection and transport of produce, and severe inflation set in. Now the armies began to compete for tax revenues as well as for the imperial throne and subjected the people in the provinces to repeated demands for taxes—demands backed by military force.

The main victims of this crisis were the provincial aristocrats who governed the towns; they were responsible for the

Roman Trade Routes at Height of Empire

whole system of tax collection and government. Under the Roman system, the local government, run by a council (*curia*, pl. *curiae*) made up of the leading men of the town, collected taxes, maintained roads and bridges, and conducted all other government business in the district. Every man with property of a certain value was obliged to serve as a *curialis* (pl. *curiales*) of his *municipium* and, with his colleagues, was personally responsible for performing government functions. In practice, during normal times, the members of the *curia* had townspeople carry out most of their duties. During the civil wars, however, so many people were financially ruined that city councils had trouble finding anyone to perform public services or to pay taxes, and their personal liability became a very heavy burden.

Many of the *curiales,* who had once regarded their position as a sign of economic and social distinction, escaped their obligations by retiring to their country estates. As a result, the government of a great many provincial towns simply collapsed. From time to time, during periods of relative tranquillity, the imperial government tried to reestablish the municipal governments, but with little success.

Actually, the imperial government opened up another avenue of escape for the *curiales.* Civil servants were exempt from service in the *curiae,* and a great many local aristocrats won appointment to the imperial bureaucracy from emperors eager to please. As a result, the two governments dwindled as the bureaucratic class grew. Moreover, the civil wars and the swift comings and goings of emperors kept the bureaucracy in constant turmoil, torn by shifting loyalties and competing claims. With each new emperor, the civil servants appointed by the last one were purged, though some of them managed to survive.

IMPERIAL SOCIETY, FIRST TO THIRD CENTURIES

Rural Life

What was life like during these centuries? Even during times of tranquillity, the lives

Roman Military Weakness   Late Second Century

of ordinary men and women were not always peaceful. In the countryside, most people lived in small villages, many of them wholly owned by upper-class landlords. Outside the villages, thieves roamed

Municipal Services in the Greco-Roman Cities

What are today regarded as the municipal services *par excellence* are not very frequently mentioned in antiquity. . . . The first duty of the *astynomi* [controllers or *curiales* of the towns] was the care of roads and bridges, both in the city itself and in its territory. They had to prevent encroachments on the public highway; the . . . law laid down minimum widths for country roads, thirty feet for a main road, twelve feet for a byroad. They had to remove obstructions; shopkeepers were allowed to display their wares outside their shops, but not in such a manner as to block the traffic. They had to prevent rubbish being tipped into the streets. . . . Landowners and householders were responsible . . . for the paving of the roads on which their property fronted, and the *astynomi* had to enforce this obligation. . . . Another care of the *astynomi* was drainage. Progressive cities had a regular system of drains, running under the streets, which carried off both surface water and sewage. . . . For their water-supply all ancient cities relied to some extent on wells and rain-water cisterns, and it was the duty of the *astynomi* to see that the owners of these kept them in good order.

From A. H. M. Jones, The Greek City *(New York: Oxford University Press, 1940), pp. 212–13.*

A roman vegetable stall and its owner.

the land. Many villages had watchtowers, and almost all of them posted guards night and day. Farmsteads outside the village were situated well off the road and were fortified with walls and watchtowers. There was no police force, either in the cities or in the countryside, and the armed forces took action only during major insurrections.

At the bottom of the social hierarchy were the shepherds, who worked for either peasants or landowners and lacked even the protection afforded by the peasant villages. When the shepherd was out in the fields watching his sheep and goats and accompanied by his powerful mastiff, he had to be on constant guard against roving bands of rustlers. When he came to the village, he lived in a rundown section, referred to as the Shepherds' Quarter.

The peasants, by far the largest class in the Empire, were not much better off. Many of them, if not most, were tenant farmers working under the harsh supervision of the landowners' bailiffs and accountants. These men, unfettered by conscience and unrestrained by the landowner, could keep for themselves anything beyond what the landowner demanded from the tenants. The few records that survive, mostly from the province of Egypt, reveal the bitter conflict that raged between peasants and landlords. At times, desperate villagers, who were being ruined by the high rents and exactions, physically attacked the hated bailiffs.

There is some evidence of a small rural middle class of prosperous farmers and villagers, but farmers who owned their own plots were scarcely better off than the tenant farmers. Their holdings were likely to be small and poor (records remain of men who owned one-sixth of an olive tree and one-tenth of a small house), and their powerful, upper-class neighbors were a constant threat. Many of the landowners held an assortment of small parcels of land rather than a large, coherent estate, and they did whatever they could to force the farmers off the land to enlarge and consolidate their enormous holdings. The records show farmers complaining that powerful neighbors had turned animals loose in the fields to ruin their crops, or had sent work crews in to harvest their crops before they themselves could harvest them. Many of the farmers simply gave up and sold or abandoned their land to the great landowners.

If a powerful neighbor did not ruin a farmer, the state itself might do so. The government taxed districts on the basis of their total production, without taking into account the exemptions granted to many upper-class holders. Most of the tax burden fell on the small farmers. With the enormous growth of the armies, taxes grew heavier and heavier, and from time to time the government had to lighten the load to keep whole districts from being deserted as the farmers gave up and migrated to the cities.

To add to their hardships, rural families were constantly threatened by famine. The military roads ran straight to the borders, rarely providing connections between regions along the way. Consequently, a poor harvest in one region might mean starvation, even though a nearby region was enjoying a good harvest.

Although the evidence is spotty, it shows that overcrowding was the norm even in the countryside. In Egypt, records show that 25 people, more or less closely related, lived in one house. Unwanted infants were often abandoned, commonly left on the village dungheap where well-to-do families might pick them up to be raised as slaves. Such people were known as people "of the dungheap" throughout their life.

Urban Life

In such conditions, it is not surprising that wealth and talent were concentrated in the cities. The rents, taxes, and food produced in the countryside flowed to the cities, and often the countryfolk starved while the townspeople lived comfortably. Because the best craftsmen left the villages for the city, only simple implements were produced in the country. Rural folk relied on peddlers for things that required skill and good materials to make. With few exceptions, the great landowners lived in magnificent houses in the city and left their country holdings in the hands of bailiffs.

During the imperial period, great urban estates covered one-third of the city of Rome, and public buildings occupied another quarter of it. Ordinary folk lived in densely populated neighborhoods, usually arranged in blocks. The density of the larger Roman cities has been calculated at about 200 people per acre. Today in Europe, 150 people per acre is considered dense, and 250 per acre a slum. People spent as much time as possible in the streets, and only the existence of public areas made city life bearable. Every incident on the crowded streets instantly drew a crowd, and a person was never far from violence.

Property ownership in the cities was much like that in the countryside. The multistory tenements in which most city-dwellers lived were owned by large landowners who often let the buildings run down. Indeed the buildings were so badly built that they often collapsed. Cicero wrote to a friend about the collapse of two buildings he owned; he decided to rebuild them in the hope of getting a good return on his investment. Crassus (p. 86) made a fortune in Roman real estate. He created a private fire brigade, and when a building caught fire, his men would arrive,

This marble relief pictures a small Italian city as it looked in the days of the early Caesars. Blocks of two- and three-story tenements are enclosed by the ancient town wall. At the right, the country villas of the wealthy, with their gardens and colonnades, sprawl across the nearby hillsides.

strike a deal for the property, and then put out the flames.

Block associations organized by the city residents served as the basis of the census and of the government's tax system. These associations, which met at the corner cafe, took care of all sorts of business: They helped families in trouble, functioned as burial societies, and organized youth athletic clubs. Tradespeople and artisans formed associations of their own. People who worked in the same craft or trade—butchers, booksellers, cobblers, and so forth—usually lived in the same part of town, and buyers knew where to go to find what they wanted. The trade associations lobbied government officials on measures that affected their business. In fact, clubs and associations of one kind or another were ubiquitous in city life. Organizations supported shrines, promoted athletics, and served dozens of other purposes. A foreigner entering the city always headed for the shrine his countrymen had set up, confident that he would find someone there to help him.

The greatest cities of the Empire were Rome and Alexandria, each with nearly a million inhabitants. Antioch and Carthage (Carthage was recovering from its destruction by Rome) were next, with populations of several hundred thousand. About six other cities had populations of 75,000, and a great many had populations of about 20,000. Many cities, such as most of those in North Africa, were cities in name only. They had the status of *municipium* but were in reality simply agricultural villages.

In both country and city, the gulf between rich and poor was extreme, with only a small middle class at the economic center. Virtually all wealth was in land and loans. Senatorial families rarely participated in commercial activities, because they could make 6 percent annually on their loans, doubling their money every twelve years. Along with their vast holdings in land, rich men could afford to sit back and let their fortunes grow.

The turmoil of the third century made life more difficult for everyone, but Roman society remained remarkably stable. Although the great estates continued to grow larger, peasant agriculture remained the backbone of the economy. And although the cities had their troubles, the urban elite remained strong.

Culture and Society

The local aristocracies constituted the largest class of educated people in the Empire, and their education was remarkably similar from one end of the Roman world to the other. That similarity served to narrow the linguistic and cultural differences between the Latin West and the Greek East. Although Greeks did not study Latin unless they aimed to pursue a military or legal career—all official documents sent to the East were accompanied by a Greek translation—all educated westerners during the first and second centuries were fluent in Greek. The disruptions of the third century, which concentrated everyone's attention on local affairs, seem to have weakened the status of Greek as a universal language, however. By the fourth century, the corpus of Greek philosophy, science, and theology was being translated into Latin for the benefit of educated westerners who had not learned Greek.

Much like the upper classes of Hellenistic society, the aristocracy of the Roman Empire was a thin veneer over a great

A model of the Roman Forum, the heart of the imperial capital. The Forum, originally a market area, contained the main temples of the city, the Senate House, and other government buildings.

range of peoples with vastly different cultures. In fact, the Empire was a patchwork of ethnic societies. Because Latin and Greek were virtually the only written languages (Syriac and Hebrew were rare exceptions) and the only ones taught in schools, it is difficult to identify the linguistic patterns prevailing across the Empire. It seems likely, however, that the indigenous populations continued to speak their own languages. Several dialects of Celtic (from which modern Gaelic and Breton derive) were spoken in Gaul and Britain, and several native languages continued to be used in Asia Minor. Syriac and Coptic (the Egyptian language) also continued in common use. Thracian, the language spoken by tribes living in the southern Balkans, was still spoken in the fourth century, and modern Albanian is probably a survival of the language spoken by the ancient Illyrians.

Thus, the Empire accommodated two more or less distinct levels of culture. At one level were the leaders of the imperial government and the classes that served it, controlling a vast realm united by the Mediterranean and by a network of roads that carried communications, goods, and armies. The education, institutions, and tastes of this class were remarkably homogeneous; theirs was the culture known as Greco-Roman. At the second level were the myriad populations that maintained their pre-Roman customs and languages, even while living under the imperial government.

Although the upper classes were culturally unified, they were highly stratified. Under the Empire, with its vast imperial bureaucracy and many subject peoples, Romans and provincials alike developed a fondness for honorific titles to demonstrate their position in society and in government. In the late third century, the highest class, the senators, bore the title *clarissimi* (most distinguished), while the high judges of imperial courts were called *eminentissimi* (most eminent) and their immediate subordinates, *perfectissimi* (most excellent). The prestige that went with these titles declined as the emperors bestowed them on more and more public servants in return for faithful ser-

vice. In the late third century, approximately 500 senators were *clarissimi*; but by the middle of the sixth century, several thousand could claim that title. The same happened with other titles. Moreover, there was a proliferation of new titles— for example, *spectabiles* (nobles) and *viri illustri* (illustrious men). Such titles also defined the privileges accorded to their holders.

There were middle-class titles also, but these defined obligations rather than privileges. At the top were the *curiales,* the members of the municipal councils (see p. 103). The superintendents of state factories, which dominated the industrial economy of the Empire, were substantial men with appropriate titles of their own. They ranked above the merchants, who, even when they were successful, rarely rose into the class of *curiales*. On the whole, merchants were on the same social level as the craftsmen who worked in the state factories.

THE RISE OF CHRISTIANITY

During the last century of the Republic, Rome was flooded with mystery cults from the eastern provinces. Augustus tried to stamp them out, but they continued to grow in number and influence under the Empire. Yet, their influence was slight compared to that of Christianity. Originating in Palestine and other regions of the eastern Mediterranean as a religion antagonistic to Rome, Christianity had become by the late fourth century the predominant religion of the Empire.

Christianity emerged from Judaism at a time of ferment in that ancient religion. A split in the Jewish community had opened up between those who had assimilated into Hellenistic society and those who had preserved their Semitic identity. Symbolic of that split was the translation of the Hebrew Bible into Greek in Alexandria in the second century B.C., evidence that many Jews no longer knew Hebrew and were practicing their religion in Greek. Moreover, several conflicting sects emerged within Judaism itself.

A Roman girl with a writing tablet is depicted in this fresco from Pompeii (*ca.* A.D. 70).

After Pompey organized the eastern provinces (74–62 B.C.), the Jews lived in a semiautonomous client kingdom until the death of the last king, Herod the Great (r. 37–4 B.C.). The Romans then took over direct administration of the kingdom and made it part of the province of Syria. As long as the Jews had their own king, they had debated how their kingdom would achieve its historical destiny as defined by the Hebrew Bible. Now, the argument shifted to how to deal with the Romans, who the Jews believed stood in the way of that destiny. While the majority of the Jewish population accommodated itself to Roman rule, some of the religious sects were fanatically anti-Roman and agitated ceaselessly for rebellion. The Romans' insensitivity to Jewish sentiments sometimes provoked violent demonstrations and occasional acts of rebellion.

The first significant rebellion occurred at the beginning of Roman rule. In 4 B.C., the Romans announced that a census would be taken, following a practice initiated by Augustus as a basis for taxation. The Hebrew Bible prohibits the numbering of the people of God, and the Jews rebelled. The Romans put the rebellion down, and the Jews had to limit their activity to guerrilla warfare until A.D. 66. At that point, a great rebellion erupted that took the Romans four years of hard fighting to subdue. They then tried, unsuccessfully, to destroy the Jews' sense of identity by destroying the city of Jerusalem and its temple. The last great Jewish rebellion took place in 135. Thereafter, the Romans tried to cope with the Jewish problem by forcing many Jews to emigrate to other parts of the Empire. During this time of troubles, the Romans crucified thousands of Jews as subversives and conceived a strong dislike for the Jews and their troublesome religion.

Between about A.D. 26 and 29, Jesus of Nazareth attracted a small following among the Semitic Jews of Galilee, a part of the ancient kingdom of Samaria (see p. 26). But, like all Jews, Jesus regarded Jerusalem as the center of Judaism, and in 29 he led his followers to the city. According to the Christian scriptures, his followers eventually came to regard him as the Messiah, the anointed of God (in Greek, the Christ), who would lead the Jews to glory and establish the kingdom of God on earth. They associated Jesus with the Savior prophesied in the Bible by Isaiah (7:14).

Religious figures such as Jesus were common in Judea at that time—John the Baptist had built a following shortly before Jesus did. Such figures made both the Romans and the Jewish leaders nervous, because they often stirred up anti-Roman agitation or actual insurgency. When Jesus arrived in the environs of Jerusalem, he fell under suspicion, and the Romans soon arrested and crucified him. Crucifixion was the Roman punishment for insurgents.

The death of Jesus caused most of his followers to lose their faith in him as the Messiah. The committed few, however, believed that he had been resurrected after three days, and it is that belief that lies at the heart of Christianity. The believers, under the guidance of Peter (one of the first members of the sect), worked out an interpretation of the ancient prophesies to account for the death and resurrection of Jesus.

A small community of Christians soon came together in Jerusalem, where they were persecuted by the Jews but pretty much ignored by the Romans. At first, the sect grew modestly and slowly, if at all, and attracted only other Semitic Jews. Then the conversion of a hellenized Jew named Saul radically changed its fate.

Saul, who changed his name to Paul after his conversion, preached the message of Jesus to great numbers of hellenized Jews who had migrated to the great cities of the eastern Mediterranean. There, they had attracted many Gentiles who came to their prayer services and became familiar with the Jewish religion without actually becoming Jews. In these mixed communities Paul and his assistants found many of their converts.

By the time Jerusalem was destroyed by the Romans in 70, Christianity had spread to Antioch, Alexandria, Rome, and many lesser cities. The Christians formed small communities—much like the familiar urban associations. They met for com-

Symbol of Christianity, incorporating the Greek letters *chi* and *rho* (the monogram for Christ that forms the shape of the cross) and *alpha* and *omega* (meaning *beginning* and *end*).

mon worship—focused on a ritual meal modeled on the last supper of Jesus—in the houses of their richest members, and they performed works of charity toward their poorest members. At first, these communities seem to have had little formal structure, except that elders (presbyters) organized their worship and social work.

The Semitic Christians believed that Jesus was the Messiah who had come to save the Jews. Paul, aware that converts in the Hellenistic population would not respond to such a nationalistic mission, preached that Jesus came not to lead Israel to victory over its enemies, but to save mankind. The Semitic Christians emphasized the human Jesus and the continuity of their religion from Judaism. Paul emphasized the divine Jesus, the Savior of all who had faith in him, and the break with the Jewish past. The Semitic Christians continued to follow the dietary and other religious laws of Judaism. The Greek Christians could see no reason to obey those laws, and Paul argued that belief in Jesus as the Messiah freed one from the law of the Hebrew Bible, which became for Christians the Old Testament. These differences between Paul and the Semitic Christians led to a conflict, recorded in the New Testament (Acts 15), that was settled in Paul's favor. Henceforth, the church preached to both Jews and non-Jews, and Christianity emerged as a universal religion based on faith in Jesus rather than obedience to Mosaic law.

For the first century and a half, the Romans regarded Christianity as just one of the multitude of eastern mystery cults. Like those cults, Christianity emphasized individual religious experience and a personal, emotional, and intimate contact with the deity. Like them, it offered communion with the deity in this life, and promised union with the deity after death. Like them, it used sacraments, ritual acts that prepared the initiated for communion with the deity, and it had a body of doctrine that explained the mystery by which the deity survived death. In fact, Christianity absorbed several ideas and practices from the mystery cults, probably at the suggestion of Christians who had previously belonged to one of them.

Christianity had several advantages over the cults, however. First, it drew on the ancient Judaic heritage, which gave it a strong sense of identity. Second, it had originated in part from an interpretation of the Hebrew Bible, and that experience enabled it to integrate new ideas into its body of beliefs.

Third, Christianity was not a secret society. The Christians had inherited from the Jews a sense of community as evidenced in their open refusal to honor the Roman gods and their consistent attitude toward the Roman government. Christians were adamant in their refusal to render unto Caesar what was God's. Finally, Christianity, despite its Judaic origins, was deeply influenced by Hellenistic beliefs and ideas. It was thus both ancient and modern, a Judeo-Greco-Roman religion.

These unique characteristics complicated the relationship between Christianity and the Roman state. Every good Roman believed in the existence of gods who lived in an invisible world and had power over human affairs. The welfare of the state depended on the favor of those gods, and to ensure that favor, sacrifices (the ritual slaughter of animals) must be performed in which every member of the community participated. The Jews had refused to take part in such sacrifices for centuries, but the Romans recognized the Jews as a separate people with a separate religion, and they had always been tolerant of such "native" traditions. Some Roman officials, including Pontius Pilate, the governor of Judea (26–36) who had ordered the execution of Jesus, liked to bait the Jews, but on the whole the Romans left the Jews in peace.

The Christians were a different matter. Although they had originated as a Jewish sect, they had disassociated themselves from the Jews, particularly after the great Jewish rebellion of 66–70, and by the second century most Christians were gentiles. Consequently, because the Christians were not a distinct ethnic minority following an ancient religious tradition, the Romans would not tolerate their refusal to participate in the sacrifices. Before the end of the first century, a law was passed making it a capital offense to be

The Formation of the New Testament

The New Testament consists of 27 parts written between the 50s and the early second century. These works were not the only ones written and circulated among the Christian communities during the century after Jesus's death. But they were the ones eventually recognized by the church as divine revelation. The formation of the canon, or list, of books with scriptural authority took place in the mid-third century. It occurred in response to several challenges within the Christian community. Some bishops, such as Papias of Hieropolis in Asia Minor (d. *ca*. 130) claimed that his memory of the sayings of the apostles was sufficient for knowledge of the new religion. Writers of the second and third centuries pointed out inconsistencies in Papias's recollections and their contradictions to written testimony such as Paul's letters and the gospels. Marcion (d. *ca*. 160) claimed that the god of the Old Testament was different from the god revealed by Jesus, and his followers renounced the Old Testament as irrelevant to Christians. The Gnostics, a heretical group that believed that Christianity consisted not in faith in Jesus alone but in knowledge of his message, claimed that writings containing the wisdom constituted the holy book.

In response to such challenges, and particularly to counter the Marcionites, orthodox Christians began to define their holy scriptures, choosing works that affirmed the continuity between the Old and the New Testaments and that were connected with the apostolic age. The slow process of distinguishing the true from the false testament finally ended with the definition of Athanasius, bishop of Alexandria (r. 328–373), who listed the 27 books still included in the New Testament. Jerome (see p. 120) accepted this list when he translated the Bible into Latin. Officially, however, the New Testament was not defined until the Council of Trent in 1546.

a Christian, and for generations people circulated rumors that Christians engaged in immoral rituals during their services.

Suspicion of the Christians intensified during the third century, when assaults on the Empire made Romans eager for some show of divine favor. In 250, the emperor Decius ordered all Romans to participate in sacrifices and to obtain certificates showing that they had done so. This order was tantamount to official persecution of the Christians. In most places, the authorities permitted Christians either to ignore the order or to get a certificate through official connivance. But a few Christians made a public show of their refusal to conform and were executed. The persecu-

tion came to an end when Decius was killed by the Germans in 251 but was revived in 257 when the emperor Valerian ordered new prayers for success against the Persians. When Valerian was captured by the Persians in 260, persecution virtually disappeared for forty years.

By this time, the Christian communities were growing rapidly and were becoming influential in many towns. As local government weakened during the civil wars, many social functions, particularly caring for the poor and settling disputes that did not lead to a law suit, were left to private groups. The Christian congregations were well suited to perform those functions, and in doing so they gained many new adherents. The heads of the congregations, the bishops, became increasingly visible and respected in the urban communities.

The optimism and complacency generated by two generations of steady growth made the next persecution particularly traumatic. Known as the Great Persecution, it lasted from 303 to 311. To understand its place in Roman history, we must turn to the reign of the emperor Diocletian.

THE RESTORATION OF ORDER: THE REIGN OF DIOCLETIAN, 284–305

The prolonged crisis of the third century disrupted, but did not destroy the Roman army or the Roman bureaucracy. The potential for recovery remained, and restoration of peace and order became the goal of those seeking the imperial throne. The first step was taken by the emperor Aurelian (r. 270–275), who put an end to civil war and started to shore up the border defenses. His successors carried on his work, though the armies continued to make and unmake emperors at a rapid pace. In 284, Diocletian, general of the Illyrian legions, came to power and brought the work of restoration to a successful conclusion.

Diocletian abandoned Rome as his official residence and moved his court to cities closer to the frontiers of the Empire,

A.D. 96	180	284	305
The "Five Good Emperors"	Century of Disorder	Diocletian	

eventually settling at Nicomedia in north-western Asia Minor. From these provincial capitals, he rebuilt the frontier fortifications and enlarged the army. At the same time, he broke the army down into smaller units and relieved the commanders of responsibility for supplying and paying their troops, which made it more difficult for them to use army backing in a bid for power.

In addition, he decided to share his power with Maximian, whom he named coemperor. Both took the title Augustus. Later he created two assistant emperors and designated them as heirs to the imperial title; they were both called Caesar. Diocletian's powerful personality dispelled the potential for conflict in this new arrangement.

Further, Diocletian increased the number of provinces from 50 to 100 and organized them into 13 dioceses. Under this reorganization, the new administrations were more effective in governing the provinces than the old one had been, and they absorbed some of the functions formerly handled by the municipal councils. Still, the curial class retained its claim to office, and Diocletian and his successors tried to close off the avenues by which its members were escaping their obligations. When those efforts failed, the municipal councils began to be replaced by imperial officials—in the West in the early fifth century and in the East toward the end of the century.

In an effort to stabilize the society of the Empire, Diocletian issued a series of laws designed to create a rigid caste system. Sons were now required to follow the occupations of their father. And farmers, both tenant and free, were required to remain on the land they had been occupying when the 290 census was taken and were obliged to register sons with the census-takers. The caste system was imposed on other occupations as well, including bakers and sailors. These actions ensured that the census would be kept current, making it more reliable as a basis for taxation. The civil wars had inflicted heavy damage on the state-run industries, and taxes were more important than ever as a source of funds. Diocletian had his financial staff adjust the tax levies every year on the basis of the census. The tax rate doubled between 324 and 364.

In economic affairs, Diocletian tried to check the inflationary spiral that had set in during the civil wars. He reformed the currency, and, when that effort failed, he issued a decree fixing the prices of many goods. That policy failed as well, even though the penalty for violating it was death.

The Great Persecution of the Christians was part of Diocletian's comprehensive program of restoration. His aim was to restore the pagan cults, particularly the imperial cult that had long served to unify the Empire. When the Christians refused to participate in the rituals of the cult, he turned against them in 303. Subsequent Christian accounts of the persecution exaggerated the number of believers who were martyred, but the experience must

Diocletian and his coemperor stand in front, embracing each other; the two Caesars stand behind them (St. Mark's Cathedral, Venice).

The Administrative Divisions of Diocletian   Third and Fourth Centuries

THE EMPIRE IN THE FOURTH AND FIFTH CENTURIES

The Fourth Century

have been a profound shock to the Christian communities. For more than forty years, they had been left in peace, growing steadily under the able leadership of the bishops. They were gradually being assimilated into Roman society, and in many places they played an important role in their communities. Then, just as peace and order were returning to society at large, they were again subjected to persecution, which lasted until 312.

Diocletian retired in 305, apparently convinced that he had completed his ambitious program of restoration. He forced his coemperor Maximian to retire as well, and the two Caesars succeeded to the imperial throne. The dynastic ambitions of these men led to a new civil war eventually won by Constantine, son of one of the successors to Diocletian and Maximian. Constantine won control of the western provinces of the Empire in 312 and emerged as sole emperor in 324.

Aside from rejecting Diocletian's commitment to divided authority, Constantine followed most of his policies. He ruled first from Milan and then from a new city built on the site of the ancient Athenian colony at Byzantium on the Bosporus, later renamed Constantinople. From Milan, he had ready access to the troubled western borders along the Danube and Rhine Rivers. And from Constantinople, he had ready access to the wealth of Asia Minor and could deal with the renewed threat of the Persians, who were once again pressing on the eastern borders.

He could also look back to Europe, where the Germans were on the attack again. Along the Rhine-Danube frontier, the Roman armies were seriously short of manpower, and the government had to rely more and more on the use of foreign troops. From ancient times, the Romans had supplemented the legions with auxiliary troops of provincials, but the distinction between Roman and provincial disappeared after the emperor Caracalla granted universal citizenship in 212 (see p. 101). Now the Romans began to make pacts with the German kings whereby German tribes could settle on Roman territory in return for serving as a military buffer against other Germans. The tribes enlisted in this way were called *foederati* (allied or confederated peoples), and by the later fourth century they constituted the bulk of the Roman army in the West. Consequently, German kings and military commanders became generals in the Roman armies, and large numbers of Germans became at least partially romanized.

In the long run, this process of federating and romanizing the Germans smoothed the transition to a new society following the collapse of imperial power in the West. But in the short run it made border conditions uncertain and unstable. The federated tribes did not break off relations completely with their fellow Germans on the other side of the border and, especially in times of peace, there was considerable commerce back and forth. Consequently the loyalties of the *foederati* could not always be relied on when tribes from across the board staged attacks against Roman positions.

The Romans coped as best they could by playing the tribes off against another. But that was a chancy business, and in the second half of the fourth century frontier defenses broke down repeatedly. Franks, Alemans, Burgundians,

The Germanic Migrations   Fourth to Sixth Centuries

Lombards—all peoples whose names survive in modern Europe—fought their way into the Empire, were driven back, and came again. The greatest incursion of all was the massive influx of Visigoths toward the end of the fourth century.

Goths, a group of tribes that had migrated from Scandinavia to the plains of southwestern Russia (the Ukraine), had been troubling the Empire for a century and a half, but the imperial armies had fought them off. In the course of their migrations, they had divided into two large groups, the Ostrogoths and the Visigoths. In 375, both groups were suddenly overrun by the Asiatic Huns.

The Huns were a nomadic people from Central Asia who normally lived in small bands that ranged over a large territory in search of pasturage for their flocks. Over the centuries, they had become expert horsemen and had acquired most of the equipment needed for cavalry warfare, including horseshoes and stirrups. Occasionally, a strong leader would bring the bands together into a great horde that would force everyone in its path to join or be killed. Around the middle of the fourth century, the Huns attacked China and were driven back. They then turned west, meeting little resistance. In 375, they rode onto the plains of southern Russia and crushed the Ostrogoths.

The Visigoths immediately packed up and tried to escape. The Roman emperor Valens (r. 364–378) gave them permission to settle inside Roman territory, in present-day Bulgaria, on condition that they become *foederati* and defend the border. He promised to keep them supplied during the defense, but he broke his word. Soon the Visigoths renounced their allegiance, abandoned the border, and began to plunder the Roman provinces to the south, in the direction of Constantinople. Valens declared war and led an army against them. The war ended in 378 in a pitched battle at Adrianople, in which the Visigoths defeated the Romans and killed the emperor. For the next year, the victors wandered about pillaging towns in Greece and Macedonia. Finally the new emperor, Theodosius I (r. 379–395), managed to settle the Visigoths as *foederati*

Stilicho the Vandal general in the service of Rome. Although he is a barbarian, he wears Roman clothing (panel of an ivory diptych, *ca.* 410).

along the lower Danube. Meanwhile, the Huns had been moving west and soon settled in the Hungarian plain, the only extensive grasslands in Europe.

The Fifth Century: The End of Imperial Authority in the West

Soon after the death of Theodosius in 395, an ambitious king, Alaric, united the Visigoths and tried to gain control of the Balkans. Unable to take the fortified cities, he failed. Then, in 407, he led his people out of the Balkans toward Italy, which was defended by troops led by the romanized German, Stilicho, a former lieutenant of Theodosius. To meet the threat, Stilicho withdrew troops from the Rhine frontier and left its defense to Frankish *foederati*, who failed to hold the line. Moreover, he also paid no attention to the Roman commander in Britain, who, apparently seeking his own advancement, led his army across the English Channel and left Britain to defend itself against Caledonian and German marauders.

For a time, Stilicho kept Alaric from breaking into Italy. But in 408, he fell victim to an intrigue in the imperial court, and the defenses collapsed. The Visigoths now moved onto the Lombard plain and marched on Rome, which they took in 410. Though they did little damage, the event made a fearful impression on their contemporaries, not only in Italy but throughout the western provinces.

Alaric had no intention of staying in Rome. He needed land for his people, which Rome, surrounded by marshes and dependent on grain supplies from Egypt, North Africa, and Sicily, could not provide. So the Visigoths moved south, put together a fleet, and prepared to sail across the sea to the rich territory of North Africa. But Alaric died before they could get under way, and the fleet was destroyed by a storm. So the Goths turned about and headed for southern Gaul. There they settled down and established a kingdom that eventually extended into Spain.

Meanwhile, Stilicho's tribe, the Vandals, left the northern frontier and set off for Spain, cutting a marauding swath through Gaul. Then, in 428, under a young king, Gaiseric (r. 428–477), they crossed into North Africa and began a conquest of the Roman provinces there. Once settled, they built a fleet and disrupted the shipping on which Italy relied for grain. They even attacked Italy itself many times, and "vandalism" became a byword for wanton destruction.

At about the same time, the Franks, a large confederation of tribes living along the lower Rhine, moved westward. The Romans resisted for a time, but in time the Franks were able to establish themselves in northern Gaul. The Burgundians, a confederation from southern Germany, moved through the Jura Mountains and the Alps into the east-central part of Gaul.

Then the Huns came on stage again. After overcoming the Ostrogoths in southern Russia, they had formed a loose confederation with tribes of Slavs and Germans. In 433, this confederation was consolidated by a charismatic king, Attila. In the early years of his reign, his troops served the Romans as mercenaries against the Germans—in one battle they nearly obliterated the Burgundians—but in the 440s, he turned to plundering the Empire. He pillaged the Balkans and reached the walls of Constantinople. Then he turned west to Gaul. Along the way, his troops earned a reputation for slaughter and rapine, and he himself became known as "the scourge of God." In 451, Attila was finally turned back from western Gaul, and he retreated into northern Italy. There, in 452, he sacked the great city of Aquileia, whose refugees fled to the swamps and islands at the head of the Adriatic Sea and founded villages that eventually became the city of Venice. At this point, Leo I (440–461), the bishop of Rome, led an embassy to Attila's camp and persuaded him to withdraw from Italy. When Attila retreated, Leo got the credit. But because the Huns were already exhausted and sick with malaria, it seems likely that Attila's decision had little to do with Leo's intervention. Attila died in 453.

By the 470s, Italy was the only western territory of the Empire that remained under direct imperial governance, and the imperial government at Milan was decrepit. Throughout the fourth century, the Empire had usually been ruled by two emperors—one in the West and one in the East—Theodosius I was the last emperor to rule both parts. The emperors in the East had maintained their authority in Constantinople; but the emperors in the West had fallen under the influence of their German generals. In the early 470s, the western emperor was a puppet of Orestes, the German commander in chief. And in 476, Odoacar, another German commander, led a rebellion that overthrew both Orestes and his puppet emperor. Breaking with precedent, however, Odoacar did not enthrone a new emperor of his own. Instead, he had himself elected king by the German troops and turned Italy into a Germanic kingdom. In Gaul and Spain, the Franks, Visigoths, and Burgundians also were establishing independent kingdoms.

The emperor in Constantinople had no choice but to recognize these kingdoms. By doing so, he made them agents of Roman authority and kept alive the idea of an Empire unified under imperial authority, even though much of it was governed by autonomous rulers. Henceforth, the eastern emperors were determined to regain authority over the West, and in the late 480s the emperor Zeno (r. 474–491) commissioned the Ostrogothic king Theodoric, who had been raised in Constantinople, to reconquer Italy on his behalf. After the death of Attila, the remnants of the Ostrogoths had settled along the Danube as *foederati* and had thrived there. Theodoric entered Italy in 489 and within four years had conquered the peninsula and had killed Odoacar. But instead of restoring the imperial government in Milan, he did what other German kings had done; he established an Ostrogothic kingdom in Italy (see Chapter 5).

THE CHRISTIANIZATION OF THE EMPIRE

The Conversion of Constantine

Constantine, during his struggle for control of the West following Diocletian's death (see p. 112), fought a crucial battle for control of Rome at the Mulvian Bridge, just north of the city. After winning the battle, he became convinced that Jesus had helped him to victory. A year later, in 313, he issued an edict of toleration of Christianity and forced his colleague in the East, Diocletian's successor Licinius, to confirm the decree. Issued at Milan, it is known as the Edict of Milan.

Although Constantine was not actually baptized until 337, on his deathbed, his behavior indicates that he considered himself a member of the church from the time of his conversion. From 313 on, he surrounded himself with church leaders and was soon taking an active part in church affairs. Christians still constituted only a small minority of the Empire's pop-

Colossal head of Constantine, from his basilica in Rome (*ca.* 320).

ulation—about 10 percent in the East, and about 5 percent in the West. So it seems that Constantine embraced Christianity because he truly believed in Jesus, not because it was the politically astute thing to do.

Christianity was no longer an obscure cult, however. During the late third century, it had gained considerable strength in the cities, the centers of imperial society and government. When civic government collapsed during the civil wars, the Christian churches had taken on the government's social functions, thereby attracting several leading families who added to their prestige. So Constantine cast his support to a movement that could support him in turn: a church that linked the aristocracy with the lower classes in a cohesive organization.

Constantine permitted the churches to become corporations, entitled under Roman law to own property. Soon many of the private houses in which the Christians met were incorporated as churches. Moreover, Constantine authorized bishops to act as judges in disputes brought to them by their parishioners. As the church gained social and legal status, Christianity moved rapidly toward becoming the predominant religion of the Empire.

Constantine and the Unity of the Christian Movement

Constantine concerned himself with many of the thorny problems that arose during the early years of the Christian movement. Some of those problems stemmed from consequences of the persecutions, others from theological disputes over the nature of Jesus.

The first major controversy was over the priesthood of the western, particularly the North African, church. On one side, the Donatists, followers of the North African priest Donatus, claimed that the only true Christians were those who had resolutely resisted the imperial government during the persecutions. The Donatists held that priests and bishops who had hidden or had connived with imperial officials to avoid persecution were not legitimate officers of the church and that

Christians should avoid their masses and refuse to obey them. On the other side, the majority of bishops and church members argued that accommodation had been the only reasonable course under the circumstances. The dispute disrupted the African churches and affected many of the churches in Europe.

How was such a controversy to be settled? One means of settlement could be found in the church's doctrine of episcopal authority. In the second century, Irenaeus (ca. 120–ca. 200), bishop of Lyon, had propounded the theory that bishops derived their authority from their succession from the apostles. According to Irenaeus, the apostles had transmitted their personal knowledge of Jesus and his message to their successors in the churches they had founded and that each bishop had handed down the tradition to his successor. As the number of churches grew, the apostolic tradition passed from community to community, so that, in theory, the totality of the churches, represented by their bishops, possessed the totality of the Christian tradition.

Acting on this theory, in 314, Constantine summoned the bishops of Africa and the West to a council at Arles to deal with the dispute. The council decided against the Donatists, establishing the doctrine that the efficacy of the sacraments was independent of the personal character of the priest. Thus, even if the offending bishops and priests had been stained by their actions during the persecutions, Christians were justified in treating them as priests until and unless the church itself judged them unworthy. This decree established the principle that a priest's legitimacy was legal rather than spiritual in nature and that obedience to the church was a legal obligation.

Most theological conflicts arose in the East, where Christians from different ethnic and social backgrounds understood the Christian message in different ways, and where the educated classes introduced troublesome philosophical considerations into the new religion. Steeped in Hellenistic philosophy and accustomed to reading texts critically, educated easterners struggled to synthesize their own

Constantine's Religious Beliefs

The official policy of the Empire after 312 was toleration, as shown in a letter sent in the name of both Constantine and his coemperor to the governor of Bithynia in 313.

. . . we resolved to make such decrees as should secure respect and reverence for the Deity; namely, to grant both to the Christians and to all the free choice of following whatever form of worship they pleased, to the intent that all the divine and heavenly powers that be might be favorable to us and all those living under our authority.

But Constantine showed stronger personal convictions in a letter written only a year later to the governor of Africa, dealing with the problem of schism in that province.

Since I am assured that you are also a worshipper of the supreme God, I confess to your Excellency that I consider it absolutely wrong that we should pass over in insincerity quarrels and altercations of this kind, whereby perhaps the supreme divinity may be moved not only against the human race, but even against me myself, to whose care He has entrusted rule over all earthly affairs. . . . For then, and only then, shall I be able truly and most fully to feel secure . . . when I shall see all men, in the proper cult of the Catholic religion, venerate the most holy God with hearts joined together like brothers in their worship.

From Great Problems in European Civilization, *ed. by K. M. Setton and H. R. Winkler (Englewood Cliffs, N.J.: Prentice-Hall, 1954), pp. 75, 79.*

philosophical leanings with writings circulated among the churches and expounded in the preaching of the bishops. Theology—the representation of revealed truth in a systematic manner—originated among Hellenistic Christians and Jews. Notable among them was Philo the Jew (born ca. 10 B.C.), an Alexandrian who tried to reconcile Jewish doctrine and law with Greek philosophy. Later Christians followed his lead.

Origen (ca. 185–ca. 254), for example, also an Alexandrian, produced the *Hexapla,* in which he compared six versions of the Hebrew scriptures in parallel columns. He then used the comparisons as a basis for biblical commentaries. Origen sought to synthesize Neoplatonism, one of the main strands of Hellenistic philosophy, with Christianity. Although his contemporaries challenged some of his views, later Christians recognized him as one of the fathers of the church, a man who was inspired by God and whose writings were therefore authoritative in doctrinal matters.

Another controversy among the early theologians was over the nature of Jesus: Was Jesus man, God, or both? The Alexandrian priest, Arius (*ca.* 256–336), proposed the theory that, although Jesus was both human and divine, he was not wholly human or wholly divine, but rather a unique individual created by God. This theory violated the Christian view that Jesus was both God incarnate and fully human (that is, subject to all the conditions of human life, including death). Arius's view, called Arianism, set off a heated debate in the eastern part of the Empire.

Constantine chose not to intervene in this controversy until after he had consolidated his power in 324. Then he acted quickly. The unity of the church depended on agreement about what to believe; the peace and stability of the Empire depended on the unity of the church, which strongly supported Constantine's political program.

In 325, Constantine summoned a new council of more than 300 bishops to Nicaea in northwestern Asia Minor and presided over the council's sessions himself. Because of its size and the critical questions of faith it addressed, Christians consider the Council of Nicaea to be the first ecumenical—that is, universal—council of the church. The council, by confirming that Jesus was both fully man and fully God, made a start toward formulating the Christian creed. The creed was not fully enunciated until the Council of Chalcedon in 451, but it is called the Nicene Creed.

The council also established two important principles of ecclesiastical organization—first, that a council of bishops held the supreme authority in deciding matters of Christian doctrine and church law, and, second, that the emperor, as the supreme secular ruler, played an important role in church affairs. The first of these principles gave the church a means of settling disputes and contributed to its survival as a universal institution. The sec-

ond undermined the New Testament position that the Christians' obligation to Caesar was distinct from and often in conflict with their obligation to God.

The Progress of Christianity after Constantine

With the exception of Julian (r. 361–363), the fourth-century emperors adhered to the Christian religion and remained involved in its affairs. Nonetheless, strong opposition to the religion existed among members of the conservative senatorial class who linked the ancient rights of the Senate to the old pagan cults. As the church grew stronger, its opposition to the pagan cults became a serious threat, and the conflict came to a head in the 370s and 380s. Educated men on both sides wrote tracts defending their own positions and arguing strongly against that of their opponents. The emperors, meanwhile, refused to ban the pagan practices, because the senatorial class was an important component of the Empire and a bulwark of political stability. At last, however, in 390, the emperor Theodosius I declared Christianity the official religion of the Empire and ordered the destruction of the pagan altars.

Some of the responses to the pagan opposition to Christianity turned out to be significant documents in the subsequent life of the church. For example, the North African bishop Augustine (354–430) formulated what became the accepted view of what it means to be a Christian and the role of Christianity in human history. Augustine had been attracted to many philosophies before he converted to Christianity in his early thirties, while teaching rhetoric in Rome. After his conversion, he returned to North Africa, where he eventually become bishop of the little town of Hippo. About ten years after his conversion, he wrote his *Confessions,* in which he explored the meaning of that experience. How had he, a man who had entertained false philosophies and had engaged in sinful ways, been able to recognize the truth of Christianity? What had happened to his former self after the conversion? In answering these questions, he

A late Roman wall painting of St. Augustine in a church in Rome.

explained how God saves human souls and how Christians atone for the sin that weighs down all human beings since Adam sinned against God and was expelled from the Garden of Eden.

Augustine wrote many works in addition to his *Confessions.* Together, they constitute the basis of much of Christian theology. Perhaps his greatest work is *The City of God,* which he wrote over a period of twenty years in response to pagan attacks on Christianity. In it, he proposed a Christian theory of history and a Christian approach to understanding human society. Augustine died while leading the defense of his city against a Vandal attack.

The Growth of the Church as an Institution

During the fourth and fifth centuries, bishops appointed priests, deacons, and many lesser officials to help in governing their churches. Each bishop had complete authority over his subordinates and over the property owned by his church. Yet, no effective agency existed to bring the individual churches into a coherent organization. The emperor could call a council to deliberate questions of doctrine, but the church itself had no way to resolve disputes. In theory, all bishops, as successors of the apostles, were equal. But whose opinion would prevail when they disagreed?

The apostolic churches—churches actually founded by the apostles—claimed precedence in disputes over doctrine, but those churches often disagreed among themselves. To support their positions, the leading apostolic churches cited the status of their founders. Alexandria, for example, claimed to have been founded by Paul; Antioch and Rome claimed to have been cofounded by Peter and Paul. Rome won the contest when it came up with the so-called Petrine Doctrine, based on passages in the New Testament (principally Matthew 16:18–19) indicating that Jesus had chosen Peter as the leader of the apostles. Moreover, according to tradition, Peter had been head of the Roman church and had died in Rome. So the bishops of Rome claimed to have inherited his primacy and appropriated for themselves the title of pope (*papa,* meaning father), which had been widely used by bishops throughout the church. Pope Leo I, who led the delegation to Attila the Hun in 452 (see p. 115), was the first to enunciate the doctrine in its entirety. In the West, where Rome was the only apostolic see (seat of a bishop, diocese), the Petrine Doctrine was gradually accepted. But in the East, the great episcopal powers—particularly Antioch, Alexandria, and Constantinople—never accepted it.

Throughout the late imperial period, Christianity remained primarily a religion of the cities. As a religion created by educated Greeks, it had little appeal for the peasants of the countryside, and it took a long time for the church to proselytize the vast agricultural population of the Empire.

ROMAN CULTURE DURING THE MIGRATIONS

The eastern provinces of the Empire survived the invasions of the Germans and the Huns virtually unscathed, and the Persian threat that had troubled the eastern border in the third century did not again arise until the early seventh century. Consequently, during the fifth century, the East with its Hellenistic culture remained the most stable region of the Empire (see Chapter 7).

In the West, even as barbarian kings took over the old Roman provinces during the late fourth and early fifth centuries, the sophisticated Latin culture managed to survive. Though aware of the danger, people went on writing books of philosophy, theology, and history and kept up an active correspondence with one another. This was the time when Augustine wrote his *Confessions* and *City of God.* It was the time when Ambrose, a well-educated man high in the imperial service, became bishop of Milan, the principal western capital, and exerted a wide influence in Christian circles. Ambrose also led the final assault on the paganism of the upper classes.

This was also an important time in the history of the papacy. Pope Damasus

St. Augustine on the City of God

Accordingly, two cities have been formed by two loves: the earthly by the love of self, even to the contempt of God; the heavenly by the love of God, even to contempt of self. The former glories in itself, the latter in the Lord. For the one seeks glory from men, but the greatest glory of the other is God, the witness of conscience. . . . In the one, the princes and the nations it subdues are ruled by the love of ruling; in the other, the princes and the subjects serve one another in love, the latter obeying, while the former take thought for all. The one delights in its own strength, represented in the persons of its rulers; the other says to its God: "I will love Thee, O Lord, my strength." And therefore the wise men of the one city, living according to man, have sought for profit to their own bodies or souls, or both, and those who have known God "glorified him not as God, neither were thankful, but became vain in their imaginations, and their foolish heart was darkened. . . ." For they were either leaders or followers of the people in adoring images, "and worshipped and served the creature more than the Creator." But in the other city there is no human wisdom, but only godliness, which offers due worship to the true God, and looks for its reward in the society of the saints, of holy angels as well as holy men, that God may be all in all.

From St. Augustine, City of God, *in* Basic Writings of St. Augustine, *ed. by Whitney J. Oates, Vol. II, p. 274. Copyright 1948 by Random House, Inc. Reprinted by permission.*

At various times and places, the invasions and migrations of the Germans had a disruptive effect on the community of educated men, which was at most a small coterie. The Vandals virtually destroyed Latin culture in North Africa. But in most regions it declined only gradually. In Spain, for example, the Visigoths, who had been converted to Arian Christianity while still in Russia, persecuted orthodox Christians but did nothing to suppress cultural activities. In Gaul, the literary culture dwindled during the later fifth century as the migrations of the Franks and Burgundians forced the old provincial aristocracy to retire to the isolation of their estates. In Italy, neither Odoacar nor Theodoric had much effect on the life of the educated elite; in fact, Theodoric appointed many educated Romans to government posts.

The Romans created an empire that endured for seven centuries during which they imposed political, economic, and cultural unity on the entire Mediterranean world. Reminders of their extraordinary achievement survive in the ruins of their monuments and in the cultural and political entities that emerged in the centuries following the eclipse of the Empire.

The Romans created a literary tradition, governmental forms, and a jurisprudence that continue to influence Western societies. By dividing the Empire into eastern and western halves, Diocletian and his successors created the basis for the two regions to develop separately. The remainder of this book deals primarily with the history of the western half, but it is well to remember that Islamic culture also owes much to Greco-Roman culture. We will look at what happened in the eastern Mediterranean and the Middle East in Chapters 8 and 13.

(r. 366–384), who laid the groundwork for the Petrine Doctrine that Pope Leo I was to enunciate seventy years later, commissioned Jerome, one of Augustine's learned contemporaries and correspondents, to translate the Bible into Latin. A partial translation, made in North Africa, was already available, but it was faulty. Jerome's translation later become the standard, or vulgate (common), version.

Suggestions for Further Reading

General

On the transition from the Republic to the Empire, R. Syme, *The Roman Revolution* (1939), a classic, offers an exciting account of the social as well as the political changes wrought by Augustus. On the early Empire, see F. B. Marsh, *Founding of the Roman Empire* (1927), and M. Hammond, *The Augustan Principate in Theory and Practice* (1933). For the second century, see M. Hammond, *The Antonine Monarchy* (1959). For comprehensive histories of Roman literature, see J. W. Duff, *A Literary*

History of Rome to the Close of the Golden Age, 3rd ed. (1963); and *A Literary History of Rome in the Silver Age,* 3rd ed. (1964). See also E. J. Kenney, ed., *The Cambridge History of Classical Literature, II: Latin Literature* (1982). For a general intellectual history of late antiquity, see H. Marrou, *History of Education in Antiquity* (1948).

For a general history of the later Roman Empire, see H. M. D. Parker, *History of the Roman World from A.D. 138 to 337* (1935); A. H. M. Jones, *The Later Roman Empire* (1964); and M. Grant, *The Climax of Rome* (1968). F. Millar, *The Emperor in the Roman Empire 31 B.C.–A.D. 337* (1977), is a massive study of the role of the emperor in Roman government and life. The classic social and economic history of the Empire is M. Rostovtzef, *The Social and Economic History of the Roman Empire,* rev. ed. (1957). See also, R. MacMullen, *Roman Social Relations* (1974). M. I. Finley, *The Ancient Economy* (1973), and *Studies in Ancient Society* (1974), are also excellent. On social stratification and the legal system in the imperial period,

see P. Garnsey, *Social Status and Legal Privilege in the Roman Empire* (1970). On women in Roman society, see S. B. Pomeroy, *Goddesses, Whores, Wives, and Slaves* (1975), and J. P. Hallet, *Fathers and Daughters in Roman Society: Women and the Elite Family* (1984).

For the frontier provinces, see F. Millar, *The Roman Empire and its Neighbors* (1968), and, on provincial administration, see G. H. Stevenson, *Roman Provincial Administration* (1939). On the army, see J. B. Campbell, *The Emperor and the Roman Army 31 B.C.–A.D. 235* (1984). E. N. Luttwak, *The Grand Strategy of the Roman Empire* (1976), analyzes the military approaches the emperors took to defending the Empire's borders. On the cities, see F. F. Abbott and A. C. Johnson, *Municipal Administration in the Roman Empire* (1926), and A. H. M. Jones, *The Cities of the Eastern Roman Provinces* 2nd ed. (1971). For an interesting attempt to reconstruct late Roman tax policy and its social and economic consequences, see W. Goffart, *Caput and Colonate: Towards a History of Late Roman Taxation* (1974).

Christianity

On the rise of Christianity, see J. Lebreton and J. Zeiller, *The Emergence of the Church in the Roman Empire* (1962), and R. L. Fox, *Pagans and Christians* (1986), which puts Christianity in the context of Roman religion. On this subject, see also T. R. Glover, *The Conflict of Religions in the Early Roman Empire* (1960); R. MacMullen, *Paganism in the Roman Empire* (1981), and *Christianizing the Roman Empire (A.D. 100–400)* (1984); J. Ferguson, *The Religions of the Roman Empire* (1970); and T. D. Barnes, "Legislation against the Christians," *Journal of Roman Studies* 58 (1968) 32–50. On the persecutions, see

W. H. C. Frend, *Martyrdom and Persecution in the Early Church* (1967). The world of late Roman religion is illumined by Peter Brown, *Religion and Society in the Age of Saint Augustine* (1969), and *Society and the Holy in Late Antiquity* (1982). On Constantine, see R. MacMullen, *Constantine* (1969), and J. Eadie, ed., *The Conversion of Constantine* (1971), which surveys opinion about the emperor's motivation. The best biography of St. Augustine is Peter Brown, *Augustine of Hippo* (1967). Augustine's *Confessions* and *City of God* have been published in many editions.

The Fall of the Empire in the West

E. Gibbon's monumental, *The Decline and Fall of the Roman Empire,* ed. by J. B. Bury (1886–1900), has been the classic treatment of the subject since 1776. As a general history, it should now be supplemented with A. H. M. Jones, *The Later Roman Empire, 284–602,* 3 vols. (1964). For a history of the third century crisis and Diocletian's reestablishment of stability, see R. MacMullen, *Roman Government's Response to Crisis A.D. 235–337* (1976), and S. Williams, *Diocletian and the Roman Recovery* (1985). In *End of the Ancient World* (1931)

F. Lot attributed the fall to economic causes. For a recent survey of the invasions, see L. Musset, *The Germanic Invasions* (1975). Most recent studies have focused on specific aspects of the German migrations. See M. Todd, *The Northern Barbarians, 100 B.C.–A.D. 300* (1976); E. A. Thompson, *The Early Germans* (1965), *The Visigoths in the Time of Ulfilas* (1969), and *Romans and Barbarians: The Decline of the Western Empire* (1982). For contrast, see R. Van Dam, *Leadership and Community in Late Antique Gaul* (1985).

5

THE TRANSFORMATION OF THE WESTERN ROMAN EMPIRE

In 476, when the Roman emperor Romulus was supplanted by Odoacar, his German commander in chief, probably no one was aware that an epochal event had taken place; surely no one would have spoken of the "fall of the Roman Empire." To contemporary Romans, probably the only significance of the event was that the Empire now would once again have a unified government.

For a long time, German leaders had exercised governmental authority in the western provinces under imperial authority. So Odoacar, though a usurper, could be considered a romanized German king who would soon be recognized by the imperial court in Constantinople. Instead, the emperor Zeno sent another German, Theodoric the Ostrogoth, to oust Odoacar, but that action seemed to reaffirm the authority of the emperor. In fact, after Theodoric had taken control, Zeno's successor,

Anastasius (r. 491–518), recognized him as the provincial governor of the Italian provinces.

Even the disappearance of the imperial court in the West seems to have made little impression on the Romans. They had become used to German domination of the army and of the court. Moreover, the German kings in the provinces still relied on the old elite to run the government. For their part, the Germans viewed themselves as the perpetuators, not the destroyers, of the Empire in the West.

Yet, the cultural unity of the Empire soon began to erode under the new order. The members of the Roman aristocracy had already begun to lose touch with their counterparts in the East, and the old homogeneity of upper-class culture was fast disappearing by the end of the fifth century. By the late sixth century, it had become clear that no reunification with the East would occur, and cultural transition began. New vernacular languages and new forms of culture—the beginnings of medieval civilization—began to evolve. Ironically, the Christian church, a quintessentially Roman institution, was a principal agent of that change.

THE GERMAN "SUCCESSOR STATES" IN EUROPE

By the sixth century, Germanic kingdoms governed the western territories of the Roman Empire. The oldest was the Visigothic kingdom, which had arisen in southern Gaul and Spain during the 420s and 430s. Not long afterward, the Burgundians had created a kingdom in the western Alps, down toward the Rhone River. In the early 490s, Theodoric (r. 493–526) had founded an Ostrogothic kingdom in Italy. And about the same time, Clovis (r. 481–511) had set up a Frankish kingdom in Gaul after establishing his authority over the

Franks along the lower Rhine. By the time of his death in 511, Clovis had driven the Visigoths out of Gaul, confining them to the Iberian peninsula. In the 440s, small bands of Angles and Saxons, Germanic peoples from southern Scandinavia, had begun settling in Britain and by the sixth century had established several Anglo-Saxon kingdoms on the island. The indigenous population, descendants of the Celtic tribes conquered by the emperor Claudius during the first century (see p. 97), fled to Cornwall, Wales, and Ireland rather than accept life under the Germans.

Among these peoples, the Visigoths and the Burgundians were already Christians when they invaded the imperial territories. The Visigoths had been converted to Arianism during the fourth century, while still living in southern Russia. The conversion of the Burgundians to Arianism cannot be traced to a specific time and place. Neither of these peoples had given up their Arianism when the Council of Nicaea declared it heretical (see p. 118),

The Germanic Kingdoms   *ca.* 500

and once they had settled down in the Empire they and the leaders of the official church treated one another as heretics.

The Franks and the Anglo-Saxons, by contrast, came to the imperial lands as pagans, and their conversion to official Roman Christianity facilitated their integration into the old Roman society. It also set them at odds with the Arian Visigoths and Burgundians.

Nonetheless, the Visigoths and Burgundians readily absorbed Roman culture and preserved much of the Roman way of life. In the process, however, they began to lose their identity. During the sixth century, the Eastern Empire destroyed the Ostrogothic kingdom of Italy and the Vandal kingdom of North Africa, and the Franks conquered the Visigoths and the Burgundians in southern Gaul. But the Franks and the Anglo-Saxons, who had remained relatively unaffected by Roman culture, created kingdoms that developed into the strongest states of medieval Europe. Italy and Spain retained their old Roman names; they did not become "East Gothia" and "West Gothia." But the Franks imposed their name on Gaul, which became France, and the Angles imposed theirs on part of Britain, which became England.

The Settling of the Germans

Just how the Germanic tribes managed to settle down and acquire land in the Roman provinces is not altogether clear. Contemporary sources, mainly law codes issued by German kings, seem to indicate that the German soldiers received a portion—half or two-thirds—of the lands owned by the provincials, and historians have generally assumed that the land must have been expropriated by the Germans. If that is what happened, the Germans would have become farmers. In fact, much of the population of the new Germanic kingdoms seems to have consisted of yeoman farmers.

But such wholesale expropriation would have raised stronger protest than is evident in the Roman sources of the period. Recently, historians have suggested that the apportionment reported in the Germanic law codes refer not to land but to tax revenues. The Germanic tribes, as *foederati,* appear to have been treated in accordance with the ancient rules governing the settlement of Roman armies. Those rules specified that the provincial landlords owed the armies hospitality, including quarters and tax revenues. In the case of the Germans, landlords provided troops with houses and plots, but the army, under its tribal king, took over revenues that had once been due to the Roman state. Moreover, it appears that the apportionment mentioned in the Germanic

---

Relations between Romans and Germans

The Burgundian Lex Gundobada *(ca. 484) deals mostly with crimes committed by Germans, specifying the penalties to be imposed in each type of case. But the code was written for a mixed Roman-Burgundian society and must occasionally treat cases involving members of both populations. These are typical of the passages historians use to study the process of Germanic settlement in the old Roman provinces.*

LEX GUNDOBADA

54.1: It was commanded at the time the order was issued whereby our people should receive one-third of the slaves, and two-thirds of the land, that whoever had received land together with slaves by the gift of our predecessors or ourselves should not require a third of the slaves nor two parts of the land from that place in which hospitality had been assigned him. . . .

[Hospitality was the system by which, in return for their service, foederati *were assigned portions of land and slaves or tenant farmers. It was based on the old Roman law pertaining to the settlement of soldiers.]*

55.1: As often as cases arise between two Romans concerning the boundaries of fields which are possessed by barbarians through the law of hospitality, let the guests of the contestants not be involved in the quarrel. . . .

55.5: But if a contention has been raised concerning the boundaries of a field which a barbarian has received intact with slaves by public gift, it is permitted him to settle the case by Roman law. . . .

From K. F. Drew, The Burgundian Code *(Philadelphia: U. of Pennsylvania Press, 1972) 62–63.*

A German king *(above)* and his bishop. From an early manuscript copy of Alaric's code of law.

codes was not between Germans and Romans, but between the German king and his troops. In most places, the king received one-third of the tax revenues, and his men received two-thirds. For the provincials, it appears, the settlement of the Germans only changed the recipients of the taxes they paid.

Apparently the Germans became landowners only gradually, through intermarriage or through victory in war. Roman landlords found it impossible to remain neutral in the incessant civil wars that plagued the Germanic kingdoms during the sixth century, and the victorious kings seized the land and wealth of their enemies and parceled it out to their supporters. Gradually, the rulers and their armies were integrated into the rural society of the European provinces.

The Burgundians and the Visigothic Kingdom of Spain

By the early sixth century, the Burgundians occupied a small kingdom on the western slopes of the Alps stretching down to the Rhone River, and the Visigoths controlled Spain and Septimania along the southwestern Mediterranean coast of Gaul. But these two kingdoms played an important role in the creation of medieval culture because they provided a bridge between the Roman and the German cultures.

The Burgundians and the Visigoths were the most romanized of the Germanic tribes because they had been christianized before entering the Empire, and they settled in the most thoroughly romanized of the western provinces. Their kings preserved much of the old Roman system of government and seem to have thought of themselves as rulers within the Empire, rather than as kings of independent kingdoms. Consequently, they tried to reconcile the social and legal differences between the two populations—Roman and German. The Burgundian king Gundobada (r. 474–516) published parallel codes of Germanic law (*Lex Gundobada,* The Law of Gundobad, *ca.* 484) and Roman law (the *Lex Romana Burgundionum,* The Roman Law of the Burgundians, after 484). In the Visigothic kingdom, Eu-

ric (r. 466–484) issued a code for his German subjects (*Lex Visigothorum, ca.* 483), and his successor Alaric II (r. 484–507) issued one for the Roman population (*Lex Romana Visigothorum,* 506). The Roman law in these codes was a vulgarized version of the system that Justinian's lawyers would later include in the *Corpus Iuris Civilis* (see p. 170). The Germanic codes consist of ancient customary law with traces of Roman influence. Together, these codes comprise the source of most of what we know about the settlement of the Germans in the Roman provinces.

Although the Burgundian and Visigothic kings tried to provide good government to the Roman population, their Arianism caused constant trouble between the Germans and Romans in their kingdoms. The orthodox Franks found support among the Roman population when they conquered the Gallic territories of the Visigoths and destroyed the Burgundian kingdom.

In Spain, the Visigoths also faced religious opposition from the Roman population, and by the 580s acceptance of the official doctrine became a means for members of the royal family and their aristocratic supporters to justify a claim to the throne. To remove this ground for rebellion, Recared I (r. 586–601) converted to official Christianity immediately after his succession. Thereafter, the king and bishops of the official church joined in a program of legislation and reorganization that aimed to incorporate the Visigoths into the church. Recared held a series of church councils that issued laws of lasting influence in the European church. The program to create a unified church in Spain also stimulated educated Romans to write comprehensive summaries of church doctrine and lore. The most important of the writers was Isidore of Seville (*ca.* 560–636) whose *Etymologies* was an encyclopedia of knowledge inherited from classical civilization. It became a basic medieval reference work.

Throughout that century, disputed successions to the throne and aristocratic rebellions weakened the Visigothic kingdom. The end came abruptly in 711, when Moorish armies crossed over from North Africa. After this disaster, Christians in the northern hills of Asturias and Galicia managed to establish small kingdoms, but the rest of the Christian population fell under the governance of the vast Arab Empire that had begun to emerge during the 620s (see Chapter 8).

The Ostrogothic Kingdom of Italy: The Continuation of Roman Culture

The Ostrogothic kingdom of Theodoric was in many ways the most successful of all the barbarian kingdoms. Theodoric, who had been raised in Constantinople, was a Roman citizen and had held the office of consul before Zeno sent him to conquer Italy. Finding Italy ruined by decades of war and misgovernment, Theodoric launched a public works program and took measures to revive agriculture and trade. He also tried to stabilize relations among the new Germanic kingdoms by arranging a series of marriage alliances. He himself married a Frankish princess; he married his sister to the king of the Vandals, his two daughters to the Visigothic and Burgundian kings, and a niece to a Thuringian king.

In his own kingdom, he tried to preserve whatever he could salvage of Roman civilization and Roman government by engaging members of the leading Roman families as advisers and ministers. At the same time, however, he sought to preserve the distinction between his Ostrogothic army and the Italo-Roman population by prohibiting the Italo-Romans from joining the army and by forbidding Ostrogoths to attend schools where they might be romanized. He also preserved the Arianism of the Ostrogoths, which helped to maintain the distinction between the two groups. His reliance on the senatorial families obliged him to tolerate their religion and their church, but he sensed that they were intolerant of his Arianism.

Two of Theodoric's Roman administrators, Cassiodorus (*ca.* 490–*ca.* 585) and Boethius (*ca.* 480–524), are commanding figures in the intellectual history of Europe. Cassiodorus, renowned for his learning, served Theodoric and his successor as quaestor, consul, and head of the civil service. A little after 540, he retired to his estate near Bari in southern Italy and founded a monastery, called the Vivarium, where he and his monks sought to preserve Roman civilization by creating a library and copying ancient works. He had already won recognition as a historian and a grammarian by publishing a world history and a guide to writing official documents. At the Vivarium, he turned to theological works, including a dissertation on the soul. His most important work was *An Introduction to Divine and Human Readings,* a compendium of classical learning, intended for the education of his monks. He also wrote a history of the Ostrogoths, which has been lost.

Boethius came from a senatorial family of high standing in Rome. His father and his sons—and he himself—all served as consuls. After his father's death, he was reared in the household of Symmachus, a leading Christian senator and a descendant of the leader of the pagans back in the 370s (see p. 118). Boethius married Symmachus's daughter.

Boethius published books on arithmetic and music in his early twenties, at an age when, as a contemporary said, most people were students, not teachers. Theodoric, in a letter drafted by Cassiodorus, asked the young Boethius to design a sundial and a waterclock for the palace. Theodoric also asked him to recommend a harpist to be sent to Clovis the Frank. In 510, the king named Boethius consul, a largely ceremonial post that left plenty of time for other pursuits. During his year in office, he worked on a translation of Aristotle's treatises on logic. (Another consul, who published an edition of Vergil during his year in office, had complained about the distractions caused by his official duties.) In 522, Theodoric appointed Boethius's sons consuls, though they were only boys, and appointed Boethius as head of the civil service, an office that carried real authority.

Boethius's grand project was to translate all the works of Plato and Aristotle into Latin. In the translations he completed he introduced illustrative examples to make the texts more palatable to Roman readers, who were not passionate readers of philosophy. In many of these examples

Gold coin of Theodoric, Ostrogothic king of Italy in the early sixth century.

he showed how logic could be applied to questions of Christian theology, thereby helping to ensure the survival of logic as a branch of medieval learning.

Boethius never completed his great project because he fell victim to suspicions that obsessed Theodoric in his old age. Theodoric had become convinced that the Romans were plotting with Constantinople to invade Italy, using his Arianism as a pretext. In 524, he accused Boethius of treason and condemned him to death. While in prison awaiting death, Boethius wrote his most famous work, *The Consolation of Philosophy,* in which he engages in a dialogue with Lady Philosophy, who leads him from despair to "that true contentment which reason allied with virtue alone can give." In this little book he makes an eloquent argument for the superiority of spiritual over material values.

Theodoric's kingdom did not long survive his own death in 526. The invasion he had feared came in 536, and Theodoric's successor was unable to organize any effective resistance. After suffering a series of defeats, the Ostrogoths established a new dynasty that struggled for twenty years against the army from the East.

The war devastated the peninsula. Cities were taken and retaken, and the countryside was ravaged. The population of Rome declined by perhaps 90 percent. To make matters worse, a plague struck the Mediterranean region in the 540s and persisted into the 570s. When the Eastern Empire finally won control of Italy in the 550s, it took over a ruined land that was easy prey for new invaders.

In 568, the Lombards, a northern Germanic people who were among the least romanized of all the Germans, invaded Italy and by 572 had won control of most of the peninsula. They had been mercenaries in Italy some twenty years before and now had come back to serve their own purposes. As invaders, they were only loosely united, and after winning control they founded several states. The Lombard king established his capital in Pavia, while his leading aristocrats settled in central and southern Italy. The government in Constantinople managed to retain a few enclaves, notably Ravenna and its environs. Rome, though surrounded, also held out, loyal to Constantinople but hardly subject to it.

The Rise of the Franks

The Franks first appear in history during the third century, when they were raiding deep into Gaul, even into Spain. At the beginning of the fifth century, when Stilicho withdrew his legions from the Rhine to defend Italy against the Visigoths (see p. 114), he organized the Franks into *foederati.* But instead of defending the frontier, the Frankish kings occupied northern Gaul and permitted the Vandals, Suevi, and Alans to sweep through the province on their way to Spain. The Vandals eventually crossed over to North Africa, the Suevi settled in present-day Portugal, and the Alans settled in Spain, though some of them joined the Vandals in the crossing to Africa. During the fifth century, the Franks, now divided into two tribal confederations, controlled both sides of the Rhine: the Ripuarian Franks on the east bank of the Rhine and the Salian Franks on the west bank.

Within the confederations, constant warfare erupted among the petty kings who led the tribes. The competition was finally ended by Clovis, a Salian Frank who succeeded to a tribal kingship in 481. Only fifteen years old at the time, he was a scion of a royal family that claimed descent from the legendary king Merovech; the line is called the Merovingian line. The family's capital was at Tournai in present-day Belgium. Clovis (r. 481–511) soon started to consolidate the Salian tribes and then unified all the Franks under his kingship, expanding Frankish territory. In 486, he destroyed a Roman principality, the "kingdom of Soissons." In 496, his army annihilated the Alemanni in southwestern Germany. In 507, he defeated the Visigoths in a great battle and took control of most of southern Gaul. Theodoric, by occupying Provence and helping the Visigoths hold on to Septimania, prevented Clovis from reaching the Mediterranean.

The center of Frankish power was in northern Gaul, where the Roman popula-

Childeric, father of Clovis and an early king of the Franks, from a signet ring found in his tomb. His long hair and his spear are signs of royal authority.

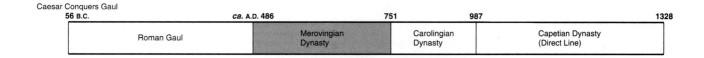

Caesar Conquers Gaul				
56 B.C.	*ca.* A.D. 486	751	987	1328
Roman Gaul	Merovingian Dynasty	Carolingian Dynasty	Capetian Dynasty (Direct Line)	

tion favored the heathen Franks over the Arian Visigoths and Burgundians who had settled in the central and southern part of the province. To keep the bishops of Gaul from stirring up rebellion, Clovis encouraged them to think that he might convert to Roman Christianity. Around 498, he finally did convert, along with about 3,000 of his men, thereby gaining a decisive advantage for himself. He was the only ruler among the Germanic kings who belonged to the official church, and the bishops and their flocks gave him their support. To amalgamate his Frankish and Roman subjects, he issued a great law code, the *Lex Salica* (usually dated 507–511), which reconciled their legal systems.

Clovis died in 511, the most powerful of all the Germanic kings. His four sons divided up the kingdom and proceeded to add to its territories. They conquered the Burgundians in 534. Two years later, they took Provence and reached the Mediterranean, thereby opening their kingdom to trade with the eastern Roman Empire, with which they became allied against the Ostrogoths. They also extended Frankish power in Germany, conquering Thuringia in 531.

The brothers fought incessantly, however, until by 558 only Chlotar I (r. 511–561) was still alive. He spent his last three years ruling a united kingdom, but when he died, his four sons divided it up once again. Most of them died young, leaving their wives as regents for their infant sons. Continual internecine warfare in the kingdom lasted until 613, when Chlotar II (r. 584–629), a grandson of Chlotar I, emerged as sole ruler. But the long struggle had taken its toll on royal power. To win the support of the noble families, the kings had given them large tracts of land and many royal rights. By 613 the kingdom was no longer controlled by the monarchy but by the leading noble families. Under Chlotar's only son Dagobert

(r. 629–639), the royal family made a modest recovery, but the future belonged to the great noble families.

The first century of Merovingian rule was chronicled by Bishop Gregory of Tours (538–594) in his famous *Ten Books of Histories.* Clovis's conversion to Christianity had won him and his heirs the support of the bishops, most of whom, as members of the old provincial aristocracy, enjoyed great prestige among both the Franks and the Gallo-Roman landowners. Gregory was a member of that class. Portraying Clovis as a treacherous man, he told of one occasion on which Clovis bewailed his lack of relatives "not because he grieved at their death but with the cunning thought that he might perhaps find one still alive whom he could kill." Yet in summing up Clovis's career Gregory declared: "God was laying low his enemies every day under his hand, and was increasing his kingdom, because he walked with an upright heart before Him, and did what was pleasing to His eyes." Gregory was equally complimentary of Clovis's grandson Guntram (r. 561–593), of whom the best that could be said was that he murdered somewhat fewer people than his brothers did. "One would have taken him," Gregory says, "not only for a king, but for a priest of the Lord."

The decline of royal power left the way open for the aristocratic families to take control. The greatest prize was the position of mayor of the royal palace; originally, the mayor was the official who managed the king's private affairs. The Franks did not distinguish between private affairs and public affairs, however, so the mayor came to control government as well. After Dagobert, the mayor was the real king.

By 700 the kingdom of Clovis had been split into an eastern, largely Germanic kingdom called Austrasia, a western, more romanized kingdom called

The helmet (reconstructed from fragments) of a seventh-century Anglian king. From the Sutton Hoo treasure, one of the great archaeological discoveries of this century, found under the untouched funeral mound in East Anglia.

Out of these struggles one family emerged to reunite the Frankish kingdom and to transform it into the cradle of a new western European civilization. This family—the Carolingians, named for its most famous member, Charles the Great, or Charlemagne (from Latin, Carolus Magnus)—gained control of the Austrasian mayoralty in the early seventh century. Under Pepin of Heristal, Austrasia defeated an alliance of the Neustrians and Burgundians at the Battle of Tertry in 687. Pippin then became sole mayor of the whole kingdom. By the time he died in 714, the Frankish kingdom was again, as it had been under Clovis, the most powerful of the successor states in the West.

Neustria, and a weak southern kingdom called Burgundy, which was the most romanized of all. Southwest Gaul (Aquitaine) and southeast Germany (Bavaria) were virtually autonomous. In each of the major parts of the kingdom was a mayor of the palace who was constantly threatened with rebellion among his own supporters and with competition from rival mayors. The wars fought among the sons and grandsons of Clovis were now carried on by the mayors.

The Anglo-Saxons in Britain

As we have seen (p. 114), the Romans had pulled their troops out of Britain in 405, when Stilicho was consolidating his armies to protect Italy from the Visigoths. The romanized Celts then slowly reasserted their native culture, while at the same time preserving many elements of Roman culture. In the middle of the fifth century, Angles and Saxons began to arrive in Britain from the North Sea region. These Germanic peoples were hardly distinguishable from one another linguistically or culturally. They were pagans, almost untouched by Roman civilization.

The Celtic population, which had gained a sense of cultural identity during the fifty years following the withdrawal of the Romans, resisted the Anglo-Saxon incursions, but, for the most part, the resistance failed. As the newcomers settled in, much of the Celtic population retreated to the west. Finally, early in the sixth century, a military leader whose name has come down to us as Arthur organized a last heroic counterattack. Arthur was not a king—though legend has made him one—but a captain whose authority rested on what remained of the old Roman military system. He managed to stem the Anglo-Saxon advance for about a generation, but he lost his life in the struggle. After his death, no Celtic leader emerged to take his place.

Bust of a young German warrior of the type the Romans fought. The soldier wears a necklace believed to have magic power.

The Celts settled down in Cornwall, Wales, and Ireland, and a small group crossed to Brittany, where a form of the ancient Celtic language is still spoken. They took with them the remnants of Roman civilization, leaving to the Anglo-Saxons only the remains of the abandoned Roman cities. In their new homes, the Celts lost much of their romanized way of life, but preserved certain remnants of Roman civilization, including the study of Greek. Celtic society was based on extensive kindreds and retainers under the authority of a clan head. In Scotland, where some of the Celts settled, many of the clans survive to this day.

Meanwhile, the tribes of the Angles and Saxons each founded their own kingdom. In the Midlands, groups of Angles founded the kingdoms of Mercia, Norfolk, and Suffolk. North of the Humber River, they founded the kingdom of Deira, centered on York, and the kingdom of Bernicia further north. In the south, Saxon tribes established several small kingdoms—Sussex, Essex, and Wessex. Tradition associates the kingdom of Kent, across from the northern coast of Gaul, with the Jutes, but this people has not been identified, and historians now believe the distinctive society of Kent may have resulted from its close links with the Continent.

As time passed, several of the smaller kingdoms were absorbed by their neighbors, and by the middle of the seventh century there were seven Anglo-Saxon kingdoms. In the south were Kent, Wessex, Sussex, and Essex; in the Midlands were Mercia and East Anglia (the combination of Norfolk and Suffolk); and in the north was Northumbria (the unified kingdoms of Deira and Bernicia). A kind of weak union of the kingdoms existed by virtue of their recognition of a senior king called the *bretwalda,* whose function is hard to determine from the surviving records but who probably mediated disputes and organized common defense. Britain was not fully unified until the tenth century.

Still, the Anglo-Saxons shared a language, a religious tradition, and a culture. And when they were converted to Christi-

The Anglo-Saxon Kingdoms of England
Seventh Century

anity, the influence of the church extended across the boundaries of the kingdoms, though local bishops were appointed by their kings and were loyal to them.

GERMANIC SOCIETY

The Germans, who had originated in Scandinavia and northern continental Europe, were a group of related peoples who spoke similar, though not identical, languages. The Romans first encountered the Germanic tribes in the forests of northern Gaul and Germany, and the earliest references to them are in Julius Caesar's *Gallic Wars* (52–51 B.C.) and Tacitus's *Germania* (A.D. 98). Caesar's account deals with his campaigns against the tribes that had settled in northwestern Gaul, a region Caesar had conquered during his proconsular

The Pagan Gods of the Germans

Most of what we know of the Germanic pagan gods comes from Old Norse sources dating from the twelfth century. Those stories tell of two tribes of gods, the Vanir and the Aesir, and of a war between them. After the war, the tribes made peace and exchanged hostages. In that way, some of the gods of the Vanir joined the Aesir, which became the main tribe. The major gods were:

Odin (Aesir): poetry, wisdom, chief of the gods = Roman Mercury
Thor (Aesir): order = Roman Jupiter
Loki (Aesir): deception, evil
Frigg (Vanir): wife of Odin = Roman Venus
Freyr (Vanir): fertility of the fields
Freyja (Vanir): sister of Freyr, love, fertility, magic

An artifact of the migration period. Ostrogothic gilt bronze buckle with jewels (sixth century). The style is Germanic.

tenure (58–49 B.C.). In *Germania,* Tacitus drew on reports he had received from his father-in-law, Agricola, who had served in Germany. Of the two, Tacitus's is the more reliable work, but both were influenced by the view that the Germans represented an early stage in an evolutionary process that led to Roman society and culture.

Historians have tried to build a picture of the earliest Germanic culture by drawing on Germanic law codes and literature. But that effort is bound to fail, because from early times the peoples who came to be called Germans were influenced by the Celts and, probably, by the Greeks. By the time we hear of them, they had a pantheon strikingly similar to, though more primitive than, the pantheons of some Mediterranean societies. Certainly the origins of the Germanic pantheon are rooted in the same Indo-European sources as those of the Greeks and the Italic tribes. There is no way to tell what stems from the common sources, what is original, and what was borrowed from other cultures.

The same is true of the social and economic systems of the Germanic tribes. To archaeologists, Germanic villages of the first century look virtually identical to villages of the Gauls and the Slavs. They all had similar toolkits and agricultural practices, and they all had absorbed some measure of Roman culture through trade.

After the Romans had conquered some of the tribes, Roman cultural influence spread rapidly into the northern European forests, diminishing to the north and the east. Because Roman records and accounts deal only with the southern Germans, it is nearly impossible to identify the characteristics of the original Germanic society.

It appears that a significant difference existed between the eastern Germans and the western Germans. The easterners, mainly Visigoths and Ostrogoths who had settled on the plains of southern Russia, converted to Christianity in the later fourth century. The biography of an early Gothic saint describes a society of small agricultural villages dominated by elders. Villagers resisted outside influence. Everyone knew everyone else in the community. Foreigners were suspect and were usually driven off, and social relations were regulated by a sense of community and by personal relationships rather than by law.

By the time the Romans came into contact with the western Germans, who lived closer to the Roman Empire along the Rhine and upper Danube, the Germans had evolved a tribal society dominated by kings. Tribal members appeased the gods through the kings, whose authority rested on a claim that they were descended from the gods. For example, the Anglo-Saxon kings claimed descent from Woden (or Odin), the god of war and poetry. That association gave them great authority, but it also gave them fearful responsibility. They were the guarantors of the tribe's good fortune. When tribal luck went bad, the king was blamed, and a run of bad luck could result in his deposition or even sacrifice. His successor had to be a member of the royal family (the *kingling* or kin) who also could claim descent from Woden.

When they created *foederati,* the Romans relied on tribal kings to lead the federated troops. Consequently, the Romans did all they could to strengthen the power of the kings, though by so doing they weakened the idea that the kings' power depended on divine favor. By the time the Germans began to establish kingdoms in the western provinces, their kings had benefited from generations of Roman support and influence.

Germanic communities both beyond and within the imperial borders ascribed great importance to status. Every man's worth was determined by birth, wealth, and personal behavior. A man could improve his status by achieving economic success, by creating a family, and by acting honorably. The status he enjoyed affected a man's immediate family, and their behavior in turn affected his own status. Worthy service in time of war, success in trading, and a good marriage all affected the status of the man and his kin. Sons and daughters married whomever their parents chose for them, so it is not surprising that conflict between parents and children over marriages was a common theme in Germanic myth and literature.

When a man was insulted or injured in some way, he was obliged to recover his honor. One way to do so was by blood feud—inflicting an injury to match the one suffered—but the law provided a more peaceful means. It defined each man's rights and specified the penalties for common injuries. The community had a great stake in making the law work, because in a small society blood feuds would inevitably spread from family to family. In early medieval literature, the community often encourages—even forces—disputants to settle their differences according to the law. The kings stood behind the system of compensation and codified it in their legal codes.

At the center of Germanic society was the family or kin group. The kin group supported its members, shared their status, and guaranteed that they would live up to their obligations. If a man was unable to pay compensation for some wrong he had done, the law specified that his family was obliged to pay. The obligation fell first on his father and brothers. If they could not come up with the full amount, the obligation fell on his paternal and maternal relatives to the third degree—that is, all those descended from his grandparents. As a last resort, the man could seek support from his neighbors. If all failed, the man's life was forfeit, which usually

The crown of King Recceswin of the Visigoths (ca. 660).

meant that the offended party or his family could seize him and either enslave him or kill him. Enslavement seems to have been the more common course, and the enslaved criminal (called a *thrall* in Old German) is a common character in early Germanic literature.

Another important unit in Germanic society was the neighborhood. According to the Frankish *Lex Salica*, published in the early sixth century, no one could take over a vacant farm unless all the neighbors consented; the objection of even one neighbor was enough to keep the newcomer out. However, this rule did not apply to the son, daughter, or other heir of the former owner.

The law governing occupancy of a vacant property stemmed from the late

Two Ostrogothic brooches. The one below is made of gold inlaid with emerald and garnet and marks the zenith of the Ostrogothic style; the one at right, made after the defeats of 552–553, is poor in quality and crudely decorated.

Roman tax system, which treated estates and villages as fiscal units. When a piece of land fell vacant, the members of the community would search about to find someone to take over the previous owner's share of the tax burden. Otherwise, it would fall on them. The provision that a man could turn to his neighbors for help in paying a penalty rested on the same idea. His failure to pay might mean that he would be no longer able to meet his share of the communal tax burden. The idea of neighborhood was an ancient element of Indo-European society. Hesiod, a Greek poet of the seventh century B.C., once wrote, "If any trouble arises in your place, neighbors come as they are, but relatives dress for the journey."

A man's promise to honor a settlement or to come to court and obey its ruling was guaranteed first by his family and then by his neighbors. Those were the people, particularly the kin, who would have to stand in his place should he default. Consequently, no one would trust a man who was without kin or without a following among his neighbors; he could do no business, and no one would accept his suit for marriage.

To a large extent, the social life of the Germans reflected their military organization. The men of the villages were members of the army, and their relationship with the king was that of soldier to general as well as subject to ruler. The military relationship was not a formal relationship, however. Rather, a man's loyalty to his king was a personal matter. At the highest level, the king's associates formed a coterie, called the *comitatus*. They fought at his side, counseled him, and drank with him. His mead hall was the center of their world. (Mead is a strong wine made from honey.) Moreover, each nobleman had his own coterie of soldiers drawn from the neighborhood of his estate, who related to him as he did to the king. The army of the tribe was composed of these units.

Women in Germanic Society

Germanic society was dominated by men, in large part because status was a function of one's forcefulness, which depended on physical strength. Men controlled property, trade, and the arrangement of marriages.

Nonetheless, the Germans recognized that women played an important role in society not only as mothers, sisters, and wives, but also as actors in social relations. Women controlled the household and often stirred the men to action. In Germanic literature they upheld the family's interests. In the *Nibelungenlied* (Song of the Nibelungs), for example, the queens goaded the men into acts of treachery that led to the destruction of the Burgundian royal house. In the Icelandic saga, *Njal's Saga*, women stir the family conflicts that lead to the collapse of society. These works were written down in the twelfth and thirteenth centuries respectively, but they related stories that had been passed down from the early Middle Ages.

Marriage customs in early Germanic society differed little from those of the Greeks and Romans. Literary evidence suggests that the man usually took an active role in searching for a bride, whereas the woman was obliged to follow the will of her father or male relatives. In most marriages, it seems that the man was a good bit older than the woman.

Nonetheless, women had certain rights under Germanic law. In legal actions, the relatives of the mother counted as much as the relatives of the father, and females inherited almost equally with their male siblings. Under the *Lex Salica,* property that a woman brought to a marriage went back to her family if she died without heirs. And if a couple had no heirs, the property they acquired during their marriage was divided equally between the wife's family and the husband's family.

The church, reflecting Greek and Roman attitudes, viewed women as weak and dangerous—weak, because they were considered likely to surrender to sexual desire; dangerous, because they could lead men into licentious behavior. The Germans had a more pragmatic view. Tacitus reports that the Germans expected women to share the burdens of earning a living and wanted them to take an active role in society and in the family. Further, he says that the Germans looked on women as having a special holiness, a quality that led people to seek their advice. Among some Germanic peoples, it seems to have been common for a king to marry the wife of his predecessor. In Sweden, charismatic power was thought to flow from the goddess Freyja through the queen to the king.

THE GROWTH OF CHURCH INSTITUTIONS

The Bishops and Clergy

By the second century, Christian communities had evolved a hierarchical organization that survives in developed form to this day. The church based its organization on the Roman administrative system, which centered on the city. Under Diocletian (r. 284–305), the municipal districts were reorganized as dioceses (see p. 111), and the church's organization changed to reflect the new arrangement. The territorial units of the church are still called dioceses (or sees).

The highest official of each church was the bishop (Latin, *episcopus*). From an early date, the bishop was assisted by various officials. Priests (Greek, *presbyters,* meaning elders) ministered to the spiritual needs of the community. Deacons took care of nonspiritual chores, such as maintaining church buildings and looking after any other property the church acquired. The deacons also distributed alms to the poor. Lesser officials—exorcists, cantors, readers, and others—performed a host of special functions. Together, these officials constituted the bishop's *familia,* his family or household.

Outside this official church organization, monasticism, a wholly different kind of Christian life, developed. At first, monasticism was a more or less independent phenomenon, but eventually it was integrated into the church and became an important influence on its development.

The Beginnings of Monasticism

Christian monasticism originated among simple laymen in Egypt during the latter part of the third century. For several decades, the stresses of village life during a time of civil strife in Roman society had driven many Egyptian villagers into the desert wilderness. (It is important to understand that in the ancient and medieval worlds, a desert was not a hot, barren waste, but rather a place where men did not live, a wilderness.)

Religion played a role in these withdrawals. Several Middle Eastern religions encouraged withdrawal from society, and the New Testament contains passages that encourage it (Mark 10:21–25; Romans 13:14; 1 Corinthians 6:13–20). But the Christians among the hermits of the desert got no encouragement from the church hierarchy.

The earliest Christian monks engaged in such practices as fasting, vigils, wearing rough clothing (such as hairshirts), avoiding baths (which they associated with the immoralities of the Roman public baths), and celibacy. Their asceticism represented rejection of the material, sinful life of contemporary society. Rejecting affluence and comfort, they practiced

A Northumbrian cross (*ca.* 700).

poverty and self-deprivation. Rejecting family life, they practiced celibacy.

The leading figure among these "desert fathers" was Anthony (251–356), a man of great sanctity and austerity and exceptional longevity. He and his fellow monks lived in scattered huts and caves. They might look in on one another from time to time and might even come together for worship on major church holidays, but most of the time they lived alone.

To live as Anthony did required an iron constitution and immense determination, and he must sometimes have felt the urge to leave the straight and narrow path. Many of the men who went to the desert faltered and returned to the comforts of home. Early in the fourth century, a disciple of Anthony named Pachomius created a monastic community in which men could live together and practice an ascetic life of prayer. Within a few generations, cenobitic monasticism (life in a *cenobium,* or community) became the dominant form of monasticism.

Pachomius drew up a rule, a set of regulations, for his monastic community that emphasized moderation. The community was to be led by an abbot (father). Pachomius also provided for common worship by the monks, thus combining asceticism with observance of the sacraments. Because only bishops could ordain the priests who administered the sacraments, the monasteries came under episcopal control at the outset.

The Origins of Western Monasticism

The idea of monasticism reached the West around 340, when Athanasius, patriarch of Alexandria and Anthony's first biographer, was living in exile in Italy. One of the earliest monasteries in the West was founded on the island of Lérins, near Marseilles, toward the end of the fourth century. Under one of its first abbots, John Cassian (d. 429), who had spent time in Pachomius's monastery, Lérins became the model monasticism for the West. John wrote two important books—the *Institutes,* which explained the rule of Pachomius's monastery, and the *Collations,*

which contained sayings of the desert fathers that John thought would inspire and instruct his monks.

Around 360, Bishop Martin founded a Pachomian type monastery at his episcopal church in Tours. He served both as abbot of the monastery and as bishop of the diocese, and the monks functioned as his episcopal *familia.* This union of monasticism with the regular hierarchy of the church became a model of ecclesiastical organization in the West. Augustine of Hippo founded a monastery in his episcopal church, and monk-bishops became common in European and North African churches.

Martin of Tours was also the first to send monks out into the world as missionaries. Christianity had made rapid progress in the cities, but not in rural areas, and the monks Martin deployed proved effective in bringing country people into the church. The most active missionaries, however, turned out to be Celtic monks from Ireland and northern Britain. To understand how this came to be, we must look briefly at the history of the Celtic church.

Celtic Monasticism

The Celtic population of Roman Britain had been partly Christianized during the third and fourth centuries. The Celtic church was already in place when the Anglo-Saxons invaded Britain in the late fifth century, and by that time the Celts had already begun their missionary work. The most famous missionary was the monk Ninian, who prepared in Rome and Tours for his mission (*ca.* 397) among the Picts of Galloway (southwestern Scotland). But the missionary movement was interrupted for a generation by the Anglo-Saxon invasions and was not revived until about 440, when Patrick (d. 461) began to preach among the Celts of Ireland. Patrick was a monk who was said to have spent time on the Continent, perhaps at Lérins, and he dedicated twenty years of missionary work toward the goal of establishing the Celtic church.

This new church united the Celtic clan organization with episcopal monasticism.

The chief administrative unit of the Celtic church was the monastery, and each monastery served the spiritual needs of a single clan under the leadership of the abbot. The bishop, whose duties were wholly sacramental, was subordinate to the abbot.

Although Celtic monasticism was based on the Pachomian model, the Celtic monks displayed a penchant for extreme asceticism and a zeal for missionary work, perhaps a legacy of Ninian and Patrick. Before 565, the Irish monk Columba had founded a monastery on the island of Iona in the Irish Sea, and from that monastery the conversion of the Picts continued and the conversion of the Angles of Northumbria began. In Britain, the monks from Iona founded the famous monastery of Lindisfarne, and Celtic monks were soon spreading Christianity among the rural population on the Continent. Between 585 and 615 Columbanus, a monk from Iona, founded a monastery at Luxeuil, which, with its 600 monks, was the monastic metropolis of the Frankish kingdom. He then traveled on to Italy, where he founded a monastery at Bobbio, between Genoa and Pavia. These houses and their daughter houses became major centers of education and culture.

Between 550 and 650 Celtic monasticism had a powerful effect on the western Christian world. But it clashed with the basic values of many westerners, to whom asceticism was irrational and suspect. Moreover, the monks rejected the conservatism and conformity valued in Rome and in the romanized provincial cities. As time passed, westerners who favored monasticism gradually introduced changes that made monasticism more acceptable to their society.

The Growth of the Monastic Rule

Monastic life was defined and governed by a set of regulations called a rule (from Latin, *regula,* meaning rules). Augustine wrote a rule for the monks of his monastery, and Bishop Caesarius of Arles (*ca.* 470–542) wrote one for nuns. These short, well-organized guides were written for communities living under the direction of a bishop. Yet, even in the West, most monastic communities were not governed by bishops. A need existed for a more comprehensive rule that would meet the requirements of independent communities. That need was filled by Benedict of Nursia (*ca.* 480–543), an Italian monk. After living among the unregulated hermits in the valley of Subiaco, east of Rome, Benedict founded a monastery at Montecassino between Naples and Rome. There he wrote a rule, influenced by John Cassian's works, that was a masterpiece of simplicity and comprehensiveness. Eventually virtually all monastic life in the West came to be regulated by Benedict's rule, and Benedict is considered the "father of western monasticism."

The main features of Pachomian monasticism were communal worship and the observance of poverty, chastity, and obedience. Communal worship, *opus Dei*

The Rule of St. Benedict

Chapter 3: Whenever an important matter is to be undertaken in the monastery, the abbot should call the entire community together and should set forth the agenda. After hearing the various opinions of the brothers, he should consider them all and then do what he thinks best.

Chapter 5: The first degree of humility is prompt obedience . . . These disciples [the monks] must obediently step lively to the commanding voice—giving up their possessions and their own will and even leaving their chores unfinished.

Chapter 33: The vice of private ownership must be uprooted from the monastery. No one, without the abbot's permission, shall dare give, receive, or keep anything. . . .

Chapter 48: Idleness is an enemy of the soul. Therefore, the brothers should be occupied according to schedule in either manual labor or holy reading.

Chapter 64: Always remember, concerning the election of an abbot, that he should be elected by the entire community, in fear of God, or, if that proves unsatisfactory, by part of the community, however small, who would choose more rationally.

From The Rule of St. Benedict, *trans. A. C. Meisel and M. L. del Mastro (New York: Image Books, 1975).*

(the work of God), was also the main feature of Benedictine monasticism, but Benedict introduced four new elements into his rule: First, it consisted of general regulations, rather than specific rules and examples. Consequently, it could be adapted to a wide variety of conditions. Second, it directed that the abbot be elected by the members of the monastic community but consecrated by the local bishop. Consequently, the abbot possessed divinely ordained power that put him above the monks, as an intermediary between them and God. Third, to the vows of poverty, chastity, and obedience, Benedict added the vow of stability. According to this vow, a monk could not leave the monastery without the abbot's permission, a prohibition that strengthened the abbot's power and the community's solidarity. Finally, the Benedictine rule required the monks to perform manual labor, so that the community would be self-sufficient.

Although Benedict did not mention intellectual labor in his rule, the life of the monastery demanded it. The work of God required that the monks know how to read, which meant that the monastery would have a library and a scriptorium for copying books. Although in Benedict's own time the monks would have learned to read and write in secular schools or at home, the later decline in literacy meant that the monasteries had to maintain their own schools for novices. Within a century after Benedict's death, the monasteries had become the principal intellectual centers of Europe.

From the beginning, monasticism attracted women as well as men. Many seventh-century biographies tell of holy women who withdrew from society to live as nuns, sometimes to escape the influence of their families or to avoid an unwanted marriage. For women as well as for men, monasticism offered an alternative to life in society. In most cases during this period, the communities of women were attached to and under the protection of monasteries, and some monastic houses had both men and women in them. According to the biographies, it often happened that a holy man who had helped a woman to escape secular life would enter into a spiritual relationship with her that paralleled the married state both had rejected.

In 580, after Benedict's monastery at Montecassino had been destroyed by the Lombards, the monks fled to Rome, where the new monasticism attracted many young men from the upper classes. One of them was the future Pope Gregory I (r. 590–604), who gave up a promising career in the imperial administration to found a Benedictine monastery on land owned by his family in the city. After he became pope, Gregory wrote a work called the *Dialogues,* in which he told the story of Benedict's life and accomplishments. With Gregory's support, Benedictine monasticism spread steadily and during the ninth century supplanted all other monastic rules in Europe.

Gregory I and the Papacy

After Leo I (r. 440–461) put the Petrine Doctrine in its final form (see p. 119), the bishops of Rome gradually established

St. Benedict giving his Rule to his monks. This eighth-century drawing is the oldest known representation of St. Benedict.

their primacy. Although the great apostolic sees in the East never accepted the claims, except when it suited their interests, the western churches eventually looked to Rome for direction in matters of doctrine and discipline. The western bishops often appealed to the pope for support in their disputes with one another, and in the course of resolving those disputes, the popes built up a body of precedent they used as proof of their primacy. Gregory I was crucial in this process.

Although Gregory had turned away from secular service to become a monk, he did not remain withdrawn from the world of affairs. For some twenty years he advocated a variety of reforms in the Roman church and then, in 590, was elected pope at the age of fifty. This was an unusual election, because Gregory had not risen through the papal bureaucracy and, by Roman standards, was very young. Those elected pope during the sixth century were commonly old men who had progressed slowly through the bureaucracy.

The election of Gregory was a response to the critical situation facing the church of Rome in the late sixth century. The Lombards had conquered most of the Italian peninsula and had surrounded Rome, which remained loyal to the eastern emperor. The Lombards held strongly to their pagan beliefs and were vehemently anti-Roman in their attitude. Moreover, the imperial government in the city was weak. The church was providing much of the government of the city, and it needed vigorous leadership.

As pope, Gregory set about converting the Lombards and restoring the finances of the papacy. With the work of conversion proceeding well, he turned his attention to the church, which had been severely weakened during the Gothic wars of the mid-sixth century. He brought poor bishoprics together to form strong ones, established new bishoprics where none had existed, and reorganized and restaffed the papal bureaucracy.

In his letters to subordinates, Gregory spelled out the principles of ecclesiastical organization, and in his commentary on the Book of Job he set the standard for

A self-sufficient monastery. Its produce included fish bred in the *vivarium* shown in the foreground. A *vivarium* was often taken as a symbol of a monastery. The fish represented the monks—note their faces.

pastoral work. Priests, bishops, and popes still turn to his writings in their efforts to understand the nature of their duties.

Gregory also fostered the spread of Christianity throughout the Germanic world. When the Visigothic king Recared I converted to official Christianity (see p. 126), he turned to Gregory for help in rebuilding the Spanish church, which had been persecuted and weakened by Recared's predecessors. Around 595, the presence of Anglo-Saxon slaves in Rome apparently reminded Gregory that Britain had once been part of the Roman Empire, and he decided to send missionaries to the former province. In 597, the Roman monk Augustine (not the great Christian writer) arrived in Kent with a small entourage. Here again, Gregory provided advice to the missionaries and wrote many letters in which he instructed them on how

Purse lid from the Sutton Hoo treasure. Note the depiction of Daniel and the Lions, revealing the influence of Christianity, *ca. 675.*

to deal with the Germans. In reply to questions on what to do about pagan customs, for example, Gregory advised that they be incorporated into Christian practices whenever possible. Thus, certain pagan rituals, including the blessing of the fields during the planting season, found their way into the English church. Likewise, many of the pagan shrines were transformed into Christian churches, with the new religion supplanting the old in its most important venerated places. Gregory's letters on these matters became a kind of handbook for missionaries and enhanced the authority of the pope among the Germans.

The Conversion of the Germans and Its Effects

Following the lead of Martin of Tours, Gregory enlisted monks in his campaign to convert the Lombards and Anglo-Saxons and to spread Christianity to the isolated villages of the countryside. Yet the speed with which the Germans were converted was largely the result of their own religious tradition. The Germans regarded their kings as intermediaries between the divine world and human world. So when a king accepted a new god, his subjects followed suit. The conversion of Clovis, for example, brought virtually all the Franks into the church.

In Anglo-Saxon England, with no single king, the missionaries had to proceed kingdom by kingdom. This turned out to be a slow process, because it made religion a source of competition among the kings. Pagan kings defended their traditional religion against Christian kings, and Christian kings tried to step up the pace of conversion.

Irish monk-missionaries had been working north of the Humber River for about thirty years when Pope Gregory's emissary Augustine arrived in Kent. After proving his spiritual powers in a series of tests with pagan priests, Augustine converted King Ethelbert of Kent, who was married to a Christian princess from the Frankish royal family. Ethelbert's people followed their king into the new religion. But rival kings stubbornly resisted conversion, and it was more than fifty years before Christianity finally triumphed in Britain.

Even then, however, religious problems persisted. The tribes north of the Humber had converted to Celtic Christianity, which preserved liturgical practices given up on the Continent and followed a religious calendar that Gregory I had replaced. The tribes of the south and the midlands had converted to Roman Christianity. The matters at issue between them were settled in 664 by the Council of Whitby, which established the primacy of the Roman calendar and liturgy. After that, only scattered resistance came from Celtic monasteries in the north.

The centrality of the king in Germanic society and the view that the king served as an intermediary between man and God made the Old Testament of particular interest to German converts. The Christian communities of the Mediterranean region, on the other hand, had emphasized the New Testament, believing that Old Testament law had been superseded by faith in Jesus, as Paul had preached (see p. 109). With the conversion of the Germans, however, Christian intellectuals began to look more closely at the Old Testament, using it to demonstrate points of doctrine and to explain the sources of Christian ethics and political theory to the Germans. Moreover, they brought the Germans to an awareness of Greco-Roman civilization, which had a profound effect on Germanic society.

The idea of a corporation did not exist in Germanic law. But in Roman law, the church was a corporation with rights and privileges unfamiliar to the Germans. In Germanic law, only members of the community could own land, and the law specified who would inherit land when its owner died. Moreover, persons unattached to kin or community had no standing in law, for they had no one to guarantee their conduct or stand surety for them should the need arise. After conversion of the Germans, the church and its clergy had to be somehow integrated into this society of kin and community. On the Continent, the provincial populations had learned to live under Roman law, accepting the church as a landowner and its clerics as members of the community. When the Visigoths, Ostrogoths, Franks, and other Germanic peoples settled down in the provinces, they simply accepted the *status quo,* and their kings confirmed it in their law codes.

In Britain, integration of the church in Anglo-Saxon society was more difficult. Ethelbert of Kent had to find a way to enlarge the concept of community to include the clerics of his new religion. The people of his kingdom had had little contact with Latin culture, and when, at the urging of the missionary Augustine, Ethelbert issued a law code (*ca.* 606), it was written in Anglo-Saxon. Unlike the codes issued by the kings on the Continent, Ethelbert's contained no Roman law. Its purpose, however, was the same as that of the continental codes: to integrate the elements of the community into a cohesive whole under royal authority. In Kent, most in need of integration were the Christian clergy, who had no kin and, therefore, no value in society. Ethelbert's code assigned a value to the clergy for purposes of compensation. Moreover, by incorporating Kentish customary law, it provided a comprehensive legal framework for the new Christian community.

The problem of land ownership took longer to solve. Under normal circumstances, the opinion of neighbors and fam-

A writ from the first Anglo-Saxon King, Edward the Confessor, for Westminster Abbey (1065).

ily members decided a dispute over the ownership of land. But the church had no property rights under the law, because all such rights stemmed from the family through which the rights had passed. During the 630s, the Anglo-Saxon kings created a new form of land ownership based on a written charter rather than on the witness of family and neighbors. It was called *bookland,* because it rested on possession of a charter or book—that is, a written instrument—which conveyed rights in land. Only the king could issue a charter, because law flowed from God through the king. If a man wanted to give land to the church, he "booked" it by getting a charter from the king. He then handed the charter over to the church, which could produce the document if its rights were ever challenged. This was a major innovation in property law.

Thus, the Christian church brought Roman and Germanic ideas and ways of life together into what was to emerge as medieval civilization.

During the sixth century, western society and politics underwent a profound transformation. The Germanic kingdoms established themselves as successors to

Roman political power and began amalgamating their culture with that of the provincial populations. The Christian church, by converting the Germans, served as the principal agent of that amalgamation. At the end of the century, Pope Gregory I ensured the prestige and authority of the Roman church by leading the effort to convert the Germans. He also instituted reforms in the fiscal administration and liturgy that were accepted throughout the West. Henceforth, Rome was the undisputed source of guidance in doctrine, liturgy, and organization. The idea of imperial unity survived in the realm of religion.

By contrast, the civilizations of China, India, and the eastern Roman Empire remained largely intact. Religion, language, and political ideology continued along their ancient paths, and newcomers were absorbed into the dominant culture without deflecting it from its traditional course. Only in the Middle East, where a new religion, Islam, came into being, was there a cultural transformation similar to that of the West. Like the Europeans, the Arabs were deeply influenced by Greco-Roman civilization, which they reshaped to fit their new religion. The next chapters look at the civilizations of the East.

Suggestions for Further Reading

General

For general histories of the Germanic invasions and studies of early Germanic society, see the works cited at the end of the Chapter 4. On the relations between the old Roman population and the Germans, see S. Dill, *Roman Society in Gaul in the Merovingian Age* (1926); W. Goffart, *Barbarians and Romans, A.D. 418–584: The Techniques of Accommodation* (1980); and G. Ladner, "On Roman Attitudes towards Barbarians in Late Antiquity," *Viator* 7 (1976). J. M. Wallace-Hadrill, *The Barbarian West, 400–1000* (1952), is an excellent brief survey. A series of new studies gives a close look at several of the kingdoms: T. S. Burns, *A History of the Ostrogoths* (1984); C. Wickham, *Early Medieval Italy: Central Power and Local Society 400–1000* (1981); E. James, *The Origins of France: From Clovis to the Capetians 500–1000* (1982); and P. J. Geary, *Before France and Germany* (1987). The most important source for the history of the Franks is Gregory of Tours, whose work has been published as *The History of the Franks* (1974, and other editions). For the history of the Anglo-Saxons, see Bede, *The Ecclesiastical History of England* (many editions). F. M. Stenton, *The Anglo-Saxons*, 2nd ed. (1947), is an excellent general history. N. Howe, *Migration and Mythmaking in Anglo-Saxon England* (1989) studies the historical memory of the Anglo-Saxons. On the Goths, see H. Wolfram, *History of the Goths* (1988). On the Visigoths, see Thompson's *The Goths in Spain* (1969); P. D. King, *Law and Society in the Visigothic Kingdom* (1972); and R. Collins, *Early Medieval Spain: Unity in Diversity 400–1000* (1983).

Germanic Society

The picture of Germanic society has been altered by the study of A. C. Murray, *Germanic Kinship Structure* (1983). See also E. A. Thompson, *The Early Germans* (1965). The best modern studies of the early Germanic idea of kingship are J. M. Wallace-Hadrill, *Early Germanic Kingship in England and on the Continent* (1971); P. H. Sawyer and I. N. Wood, eds., *Early Medieval Kingship* (1977); and H. A. Myers (with H. Wolfram), *Medieval Kingship* (1977), which covers the whole subject up to the late Middle Ages. M. McCormick, *Eternal Victory: Triumphal Rulership in Late Antiquity, Byzantium, and the Early Medieval West* (1986) shows how Roman imperial ideas of rulership survived in early Germanic kingship. Much of what is known of early Germanic society derives from study of the law codes: See K. F. Drew, *The Burgundian Code* (1949), and *The Lombard Laws* (1973); and T. J. Rivers, *Laws of the Alamans and Bavarians* (1977). On the condition of women in the early period, see S. Wemple, *Women in Frankish Society: Marriage and Cloister 500–900* (1981) and S. M. Stuard, ed., *Women in Medieval Society* (1976). There is a chapter on the early medieval household in D. Herlihy, *Medieval Households* (1985). See also J. Chapelot and R. Fossier, *The Village and House in the Middle Ages* (1985).

The Early Church

For a comprehensive history of the early Church, see K. Baus and H. Jedin, *History of Church History,* Vol. 1 (1965), and J. Danielou and H. Marrou, *The Christian Centuries,* Vol. 1 (1964). Both of these works amply treat the growth of ecclesiastical institutions. On the development of Christian liturgy, see J. A. Jungmann, *The Early Liturgy to the Time of Gregory the Great* (1959), and G. Dix, *The Shape of the Liturgy* (1960). The standard study of Gregory the Great's pontificate is still F. H. Dudden, *Gregory the Great,* 2 vols. (1905). For his intellectual and spiritual program, see C. Straw, *Gregory the Great: Perfection in Imperfection* (1988). For an appreciation of Gregory's achievement against the background of the early medieval papacy, see J. Richards, *The Popes and the Papacy in the Early Middle Ages 476–752* (1979). On the formation of the Papal State, see T. F. X. Noble, *The Republic of St. Peter: The Birth of the Papal State 680–825* (1984). On early monasticism, see P. Rousseau, *Pachomius* (1985) and *Ascetics, Authority and the Church in the Age of Jerome and Cassian* (1978). For a provocative study of celibacy, see P. Brown, *The Body and Society: Men, Women, and Sexual Renunciation in Early Christianity* (1988). For translations of early saints' lives, see H. Delehaye, *The Legends of the Saints* (1962), and E. S. Duckett, *The Wandering Saints of the Early Middle Ages* (1958). For an interpretation of the monastic ideal, see P. Brown, *Society and the Holy in Late Antiquity* (1982). The Rule of St. Benedict has been published in many editions. C. H. Lawrence, *Medieval Monasticism: Forms of Religious Life in Western Europe in the Middle Ages* (1984) is a good general survey.

6

INDIA AND CHINA IN ANTIQUITY

Civilization in South and East Asia emerged later than in Mesopotamia and Egypt but well before it emerged in Greece and Rome. India and China resemble each other in their antiquity, their duration, and the vast extent of their cultural influence, but in many respects they represent a study in contrast. Furthermore, even though India, unlike China, shared in a broad and diffuse Indo-European heritage, it developed a civilization as distinct from those to the West as it was from that of China. Contact between civilizations is a fascinating theme, but the primary interest of Indian and Chinese civilizations lies in their own history, their cultural achievements, and in the wealth of material they offer for the study of the comparative history of civilization.

INDIA

The Indian subcontinent, stretching from the Himalayan Mountains to the tropical beaches of the south, is a vast area inhabited by peoples with strong regional and local traditions. In the course of time, sufficient unity developed so that we can speak of an Indian civilization, but within that civilization there has always been great diversity. The interplay of the factors making for and against unity is a major theme of Indian history.

Civilization in India dates to the third millenium B.C. when a sophisticated culture flourished, centered in the Indus River Valley. Over a territory of half a million square miles, some 300 sites have been investigated, most of them near rivers that sustained agriculture and provided transportation. The most impressive sites are those of Mohenjo-Daro and Harappa, the former a city of 25,000–30,000 inhabitants. Laid out on grids and capped by citadels, these two cities were complete with granaries and advanced drainage systems, and the presence of separate industrial areas points to class differentiation. Small square seals found as far away as Sumerian Mesopotamia attest to a flourishing commerce. These seals were probably used by merchants to mark their wares. Some are decorated with real or imaginary animals; others bear abstract symbols, including the Greek cross and the swastika. Written inscriptions on the seals have not been deciphered, although the script is generally considerd to be in a language belonging to the family of Dravidian languages still used in South India. The technological repertoire of the cities included wheel-made pottery, cotton spinning, and metallurgy. The impressive bath at Mohenjo-Daro, similar to water tanks in later Hindu temples, may attest to the importance of religion, but no temples have been uncovered from this period.

Environmental factors such as devastating floods, a shift in the course of the Indus River, and exhaustion of soil fertility may have accounted for the demise of this civilization. A decline in social organization followed, as mirrored in later city planning. By the time the crude Aryan tribal peoples entered the subcontinent, the old civilization was gone, leaving in its wake impoverished localized cultures.

Early Aryan–Indian Society

The Aryans began to enter India in substantial numbers through the Hindu Kush mountains around 1500 B.C. They were tribal peoples related to the inhabitants of Iran, and they spoke Sanskrit, an Indo-European language which became the classic language of India. They were a vigorous, indeed tumultuous and warlike people, not unlike the Greeks. Originally pastoral, as time passed they also turned to agriculture. They gradually achieved dominance, first in the Indus Plain, then in North India. After 1000 B.C. the Aryans

also raided in the region beyond the Vindhaya Mountain Range, which separates North from South India. Although ultimately the North Indian culture profoundly influenced that of the South, the various southern regions never lost their cultural or linguistic identity. Today, South India continues to be dominated by peoples speaking Dravidian languages unrelated to the Indo-European tongues of the North.

In the beginning the Aryans were divided into warriors, priests, and commoners, but as they settled down, their social organization became more complex. There developed what became India's classic division of society into four social orders *(varnas)*. The *varna* system was classic in the sense that it became the model of how society was conceived, how it was supposed to be structured, even when actual social stratification was more complicated.

The warriors *(kshatriyas)* originally had pride of place, but the classic order ranks priests *(brahmans)* first with warriors second. Other Aryans were included in the third *varna,* that of the *vaishyas,* a term later used for merchants and cultivators. Members of these three orders were entitled to full membership in society as symbolized by the sacred thread granted to boys in an induction ceremony. This status was denied to the dark-skinned conquered people who formed the fourth order, the *shudras,* who were reduced to serfdom and forced to perform menial tasks. Still further down in social status were those whose work was considered polluting: attendants at cremation grounds, those who worked with animal carcasses, leather workers, and others. Later they became known as "untouchables," beyond the pale of Aryan society.

As political integration proceeded and Aryan influence spread, the interaction between India's various communities grew in complexity and extent. The process by which major components of North Indian culture were spread is frequently termed "Aryanization," but the influence was not all one way. The *varna* system did not operate everywhere in the same way. Another institution developed that

Statuette of a man, perhaps a priest, wearing an ornamental robe, from Mohenjo-Daro *(ca.* 2500 B.C.).

directly molded people's lives and made for a diversity of lifestyles and beliefs. This was *jati*, or caste.* *Jatis* were endogamous (intermarrying) groups that shared a common religious heritage, traditional values, dietary rules, and, characteristically, a common occupation. The *jati* to which people belonged gave them their sense of community and determined the pattern of their lives. Like membership in a family, membership in a *jati* was a matter of birth: *jati* means "birth." One could no more change one's *jati* than one's family. To be expelled from one's *jati*, to become an outcast, was the worst possible fate, for no other *jati* would accept such a person.

The origins of this institution are unclear. It is quite likely that some *jati* may have grown out of occupational groups. Others may have been tribal in origin. Fear of strangers, traditional marriage patterns, and dread of ritual pollution may all have contributed. Although the tendency was for the individual *jati* to be grouped under the five major social orders (the four *varna* and the Untouchables), the division was, as often as not, imperfect. There were regional differences in the dynamics of social relations and status as well as groups imperfectly assimilated into the *varna* system. And, like other institutions, *jati* experienced historical changes; there were splits, changes in mores and practices, and changes in the social status of individual *jati*.

Unfortunately, a good deal of the history of caste remains obscure. On the one hand, the *jati* system allowed aboriginal tribes and other groups to become part of Indian society while maintaining their own traditions and way of life. Not forcing people to assimilate made for tolerance and produced a notably pluralistic society in which people of diverse customs and beliefs could peacefully coexist. By the same token, however, the *jati* system also reinforced strict social differentiation between groups and inexorably bound the individual to the group. Although much has changed in the long course of history,

more than three thousand *jati* attest to the continuing importance of this institution in India today.

Religious Developments

The success of the brahmans (priests) in gaining first place in the social hierarchy suggests the importance of religion in early India. Like other Indo-European peoples, the Aryans worshiped a number of gods—some more important than others. As the civilization grew in complexity and sophistication, the old rituals and formulas no longer met everyone's religious needs, and there appeared a tendency toward abstract thought and a posing of such questions as those concerning the nature of being and nonbeing, questions which were to be central to India's loftiest religious and philosophical discourses.

These religious concerns were expressed in the *Upanishads*, a group of religious treatises of the eighth and seventh centuries B.C. The *Upanishads* contain the religious speculations of teachers working in the traditions of the *Rig Veda*, an ancient collection of hymns handed down orally from generation to generation and written down in its present form around 600 B.C. Because the *Upanishads* do not stem from a single source, they contain diverse ideas, but they do agree on one central theme: the invisible but essential "soul" within each of us *(Atman)* is identical with the world-soul *(Brahman)*, the underlying reality of the world. Failure to realize this truth condemns people to be prisoners of their illusions and chains them to an unending cycle of birth and rebirth. Death provides no relief, for it is merely a stage, an interlude between lives. Release comes only when the individual Atman is rejoined with the Brahman, attainable only after comprehension is achieved through disciplined effort, meditation, and/or various spiritual exercises.

The individual fate of those who do not attain release is governed by the law of *karma*, according to which every action brings forth a reaction, not only in this life but in the next. Thus a person who has led a good life but still falls short of the perfection needed for release will at least

---

*Although *varna* is sometimes also translated as "caste," this is misleading because it confounds a social order and a kinship group.

enjoy a favorable rebirth. But a wicked person might come back as a pig, a goat, or even an insect. In later Indian thought, various theories were advanced to account for the operation of *karma*. Different behavioral conclusions were drawn (for instance, it reinforced a tendency toward vegetarianism), but the concept of

---

Vedic Hymns

Origins of the Four *Varna*

When they [the gods] divided the Man,
into how many parts did they divide him?
What were his mouth, what were his arms,
what were his thighs and feet called?

The brahman [priest] was his mouth,
of his arms were made the warrior.
His thighs became the vaisya [merchants and cultivators],
of his feet the sudra [servants] was born.

The moon arose from his mind,
from his eye was born the sun,
from his mouth Indra and Agni [the war god and the fire god],
from his breath the wind was born. . . .

◆ ◆ ◆

Hymn of Creation

Then even nothingness was not, nor existence,
There was no air then, nor the heavens beyond it.
What covered it? Where was it? In whose keeping?
Was there then cosmic water, in depths unfathomed?

Then there was neither death nor immortality,
nor was there then the torch of night and day.
The One breathed windlessly and self-sustaining.
There was that One then, and there was no other. . . .

But, after all, who knows and who can say
whence it all came, and how creation happened?
The gods themselves are later than creation,
so who knows truly whence it has arisen?

Quoted in A. L. Basham, The Wonder That Was India *(London: Sidgwick and Jackson, 1954; New York: Macmillan, 1968), pp. 241, 247–248.*

---

karma itself was accepted as a basic truth not only by ordinary folk but by all traditional Indian thinkers and holy men.

Most of the era's men of religion stayed within the Vedic tradition, but there were some important exceptions. One was Vardhamana Mahavira (*ca.* 540–468 B.C.), the founder of Jainism, a religion that teaches nonviolence and is centered on the belief that everything is animated. Even more influential was Gautama Siddhartha (*ca.* 563–483 B.C.), also known as Sakyamuni, who achieved religious illumination and became the Buddha, the "Enlightened One." He then spent the remainder of his life sharing his insights with others. His disciples renounced the world, took vows of chastity and poverty, and formed communities of monks and nuns. The idea of monasticism had such deep appeal to people of religious vocation that it spread not only to regions east of India but also west to the Middle East.

At the core of the Buddha's teachings were the Four Noble Truths: that life is suffering; that the cause of suffering is craving or desire; that to stop the suffering the desire must be stopped; that this is accomplished through the Eightfold Path (right views, right intention, right speech, right action, right livelihood, right effort, right mindfulness, and right concentration). Like his contemporaries, the Buddha taught that salvation lay in release from reincarnation, but he denied the existence of a soul and taught that what we think of as the self is merely a temporary aggregate of the material body, the sensations, perception, predisposition, and consciousness. It is a momentary cluster of qualities lacking any underlying unity. Transmigration, in this view, does not involve a substance but rather it is like the passing of a flame from one lamp to another until it is finally extinguished. The state of Nirvana, which literally means "extinguished," was the ultimate goal.

Another major difference between the orthodox Vedic traditions and Buddhism was that Buddhism rejected the hereditary claims of the Brahmans. For Buddhists, birth did not determine worth. This attitude naturally appealed to merchants, warriors, and others offended by the pretensions of the priesthood. As Buddhism developed, it acquired other features which enhanced its appeal and won it patronage. Its greatest Indian patron was the third emperor of the Mauryan Empire.

The Mauryan Empire, 321–181 B.C.

In a gradual process over many centuries, tribes and tribal confederations coalesced into more complex political organizations. By mid-sixth century B.C., there were sixteen kingdoms that we know by name. The largest of these was the Magadhan state, which from its base in the eastern Gangetic Plain (the plain formed by the Ganges River) expanded to become paramount in North India. In the meantime, India's northwest became part of the great Achaemeneid Empire of Persia, which was destroyed by Alexander the Great in the fourth century B.C. When the power of Alexander's empire receded, the Magadhan state, under the Mauryan dynasty, took its place. The Mauryans then expanded until they ruled over the entire Indian subcontinent, except for the extreme south.

The empire had a complex administrative structure. It built public works (es-

The Mauryan Empire   ca. 250 B.C.

pecially roads and irrigation facilities), maintained an army, and collected taxes. Theoretically, all land belonged to the emperor. Cultivators paid about a third of their crop in taxes and were charged for the use of government water. There were also numerous levies on merchants and craftsmen, many of whom lived in Pataliputra (modern Patna), a cosmopolitan city whose bazaars offered goods from places as far away as China, Mesopotamia, and Asia Minor.

Much of the empire's success has traditionally been ascribed to Kautilya, the author of the *Arthashastra* (Treatise on Material Gain), India's prime text on practical politics and administration. It contains a good deal of sound, practical advice (for instance, officials should be selected on the basis of merit, and the king should devote himself to his tasks), but it

The Buddha was at first not pictured in human form; his presence here is indicated by the tree in the upper left corner (detail from a pillar at Sanchi, first century B.C.).

also offers frank counsels of expediency. A notorious example is its advice to the ruler that he employ spies to inform him of what is happening in the state and also to spread propaganda for him.

Emperor Ashoka (r. 269–232 B.C.) is perhaps India's most famous ruler. Converted to Buddhism, Ashoka did much to advance the religion. He sponsored a great Buddhist council, sent out missionaries, and erected numerous stupas, Buddhist reliquary mounds. The largest of these, that at Sanchi, stands 56 feet tall and was later encased in sandstone and supplied with a beautifully carved railing and gateways. The lion column he erected to commemorate the Buddha's first sermon has become a symbol of India, adopted in the twentieth century to decorate the state seal of the Republic of India. In his patronage of Buddhism, Ashoka has been compared to Emperor Constantine and his support of Christianity in Rome, but the Indian monarch also maintained religious tolerance throughout his farflung empire. In the edicts he had inscribed on rocks and special pillars, he displayed the imperial paternalism appropriate to a universal ruler. "I consider my work to be the welfare of the whole world," he proclaimed in one edict.

A half-century after Ashoka's death, the Mauryan Empire was in collapse. Its last ruler was assassinated by a general who had to content himself with ruling over a much-diminished state in central India. It would have taken an exceptionally strong ruler to organize a political machine and inspire the wide loyalty needed to maintain as huge and disparate a domain as that of the Mauryas, a domain with few economic or institutionalized political bonds that might have made for a more permanent union.

Political Division, 180 B.C.–A.D. 320

The next 500 years in India were complicated politically, but they were a time of cultural brilliance, economic growth, and increased contacts with other cultures.

The entrance of a succession of foreign peoples into India was a major source of the period's instability. We have already noted the invasion of Alexander the Great; the ultimate legacy of Greek interest in India was the formation of a number of Indo-Greek states, some of which issued bilingual coins. However, the most successful people to inhabit India during this period were the Kushans, who entered the subcontinent from Central Asia in the first century A.D. and created an empire that lasted until 240. The Kushan empire was the only one ever to straddle the Hindu Kush and Baluchi Hills and become a major power in both Central Asia and India. Most of the lucrative trade along the Silk Route from China to Europe passed through the Kushan empire in the north, while, at the same time, maritime trade flourished in the south. Hoards of Roman coins found in South India, beyond the borders of the Kushan empire, substantiate the complaint of Pliny the Elder that the trade was causing a gold drain in Rome.

The Kushans were converted to Buddhism and eventually spread their new faith to Central Asia and to China. Under the Kushans, the first statues of the Buddha appeared, executed in an Indo-Roman style that spread to the east. The growth of Buddhist art was only one of a number of ways in which Buddhism was gradually transformed and its appeal broadened. Another major development was the growth of worship of a number of Buddhas and *bodhisattvas,* beings who, on the threshold of Nirvana, postpone their own salvation in order to help others. Such figures attracted the pious veneration of the common folk even as Buddhist theorists developed subtle and profound doctrines that supplied spiritual and intellectual nourishment to those who dedicated their lives to the religious quest. These developments coalesced to constitute Mahayana Buddhism, and it was largely in this form that the religion spread from the Kushan empire to East Asia, while the older Theraveda (or Hinayana) form prevailed to the south.

Running parallel to the changes in Buddhism were changes that transformed the traditional Vedic religion into Hinduism. With Hinduism, as in Buddhism, worshipers felt the need for divine beings that were accessible to them, and there developed a rich pantheon of gods and deities even as Hindu saints and philosophers pointed to an ultimate unity underlying all diversity. Of the three main Hindu deities—Brahma (The Creator), Vishnu (The Preserver), and Siva (The Destroyer but also a Creator)—the latter two became the main wings of Hinduism, inspiring sects that gained a vast number of devoted adherents who regarded their gods as representative of the Absolute. Vishnu was believed to have appeared in nine incarnations. His ninth incarnation was as the

Buddha, suggesting that Buddhism was simply part of a great Hindu whole. Vishnu also incarnated himself as Rama, hero of India's great epic, the *Ramayana,* and as Krishna, an important figure in the Hindu pantheon.

Vishnu appears as Krishna in the *Bhagavad Gita (The Song of the Lord),* which was inserted into the great and much older epic, *The Mahabharata.* In the *Gita,* Krishna appears as the charioteer and friend of a warrior named Arjuna, who, greatly distressed to see friends and relatives lined up in the enemy ranks as a

The Buddha (detail of a relief from Gandhara, second century A.D.).

A stone relief of an amorous couple from a sculptured cave temple at Karli, A.D. 100.

The Ends of Man

Some say that dharma [virtue] and material gain are good, others that pleasure and material gain are good, and still others that dharma alone or pleasure alone is good, but the correct position is that the three should coexist without harming each other.

From Sources of Indian Tradition, *ed. by Wm. Theodore de Bary and others (New York: Columbia University Press, 1958), p. 213.*

battle is about to begin, lays down his bow. But Krishna urges him to perform his sacred duty *(dharma)* as a warrior, telling him that everyone has a social role that must be fulfilled. As long as one does so purely for the sake of duty and without attachment, he will not incur bad *karma*.

There are other subtle and profound concepts in the *Gita,* the most widely studied and revered Hindu text. One that fits in well with India's system of castes and social orders is the concept that people's *dharma* differs according to their social

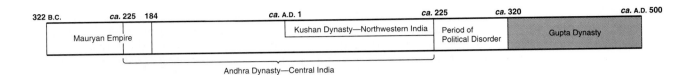

| 322 B.C. | ca. 225 | 184 | ca. A.D. 1 | ca. 225 | ca. 320 | ca. A.D. 500 |

Mauryan Empire

Kushan Dynasty—Northwestern India

Period of Political Disorder

Gupta Dynasty

Andhra Dynasty—Central India

group, and that salvation lies in everyone's following his *dharma* without regard for self-benefit. The basic idea that different duties and life-styles pertain to different groups of people was also involved in the theory of the four stages of life, which were prescribed as the ideal for members of the upper three *varnas*. First came the stage of the earnest student, diligently following the instructions of his teacher. Next came the phase of the householder, with all the joys and responsibilities of an active secular life. Love and pleasure *(kama)*, as well as material gain *(artha)*, were among the accepted goals of life. However, there came a time to retire from the active life of the householder and to partially withdraw into the forest to meditate. This was followed by the final stage, that of the ascetic wandering free from all human bonds, concerned only with the soul's liberation. Many, indeed most, householders did not actually end their lives in this manner, but it had its attractions in a land which honored ascetics and respected the religious quest.

The Guptas, ca. 325–550

Like the Mauryan Empire, that of the Guptas was based in the Gangetic Plain. From there they expanded west to the Punjab, northwest to Kashmir, east to Bengal, and established themselves as a presence in the south. However, the south was not fully incorporated into the empire; defeated rulers were largely reinstated in their lands as tributaries. There were also rulers in distant places such as Sri Lanka who, in theory, accepted Gupta overlordship and sent the emperor gifts, but who were well beyond the range of its authority.

The dynasty reached its greatest height of well-being under Chandra Gupta II *(ca. 375–415)*, even though it had not attained its greatest geographical extent.

The account of Fa Xian (Fa Hsien), a Chinese monk who visited India at this time, testifies to the safety of travel and the general prosperity of the realm. He tells of cities with fine mansions, and that in Pataliputra (Patna) were "houses for dispensing charities and medicine." He also reports, optimistically, that no one in the kingdom killed animals, drank intoxicating liquor, or ate onion or garlic—no one except "wicked men" who had to warn others of their approach by striking a piece of wood so they could avoid contamination.

It was a time of prosperity and, at least at court, luxury, for there were great feasts with drink served in ruby cups or cups in the shape of dancing peacocks. The quantity and quality of Gupta coins attest to the importance of commerce. India's trade with China and Southeast Asia was on the increase, and trade with the West remained significant. Merchant and artisan guilds prospered. The fiscal basis

The Gupta Empire   *ca.* A.D. 400

of the state included a land tax and various supplemental levies. There was also a government monopoly on salt and metal mines. Once again, as under the Mauryans, there was a complex administrative hierarchy and a strong network of government agents and spies.

The last great Gupta emperor was Skandagupta (455–67), who repelled the Hunas (Huns) who invaded India from Central Asia. After his reign, however, the dynasty went into decline. The throne was weakened by succession disputes, a recurrent problem in India where there were no clear rules of primogeniture (succession by the eldest son). In the end, the state was unable to withstand repeated attacks from the Huns.

The Gupta period is celebrated less for its political achievements than for its cultural brilliance. India's greatest playwright, Kalidasa, most probably served at the court of Chandra Gupta II. Notable advances occurred in mathematics and astronomy. The numerals later introduced into Europe by the Arabs and consequently known as Arabic numerals were actually Indian in origin, as was the decimal system. In 499 an Indian astronomer calculated the value of *pi,* determined that there are 365.3586805 days in a year, and argued that the earth is round, that it revolves around its own axis, and that lunar eclipses occur when the earth's shadow falls on the moon. However, these theories were disputed by other astronomers. As elsewhere, astronomy remained firmly wedded to astrology..

Along with a flourishing literary and intellectual culture, the visual arts also reached new excellence. The most lasting achievements were made under religious auspices. Although the Gupta rulers generally favored Hinduism, Gupta artists created their masterpieces in Buddhist sculpture. They achieved a classic style not only in the sense that it served as a touchstone for later artists, but also in that it achieved a perfect balance between the transcendental and the human in idealized figures representing the Buddha. India's finest wall paintings also date from this period, although they were produced in the south, beyond the bounds of the em-

pire. These are the world-famous Buddhist caves at Ajanta, which are decorated with secular as well as religious scenes and constitute a narrative art of the highest quality.

South India

The fact that both of India's great empires were based in the north should not obscure the contributions of the south to the development of Indian civilization. Inscriptions began to appear in South India in the second century B.C. and a century earlier in Sri Lanka. During the first three centuries A.D., anthologies of poetry were compiled in Tamil, a major Dravidian language. The nucleus of the culture that produced this literature was a short distance south of modern Madras. The early Tamil poems describe a complex culture of farmers and townspeople—more than 100 towns are mentioned, as are numerous occupations. Politically the Tamil-speaking area was long divided between three competing states until the Pallavas (roughly 315–800, with their high point around 600) achieved dominance. Over the centuries the Tamil and other southern cultures were deeply influenced by Sanskrit culture without, however, losing their identities. The interaction between the southern cultures and those of the north forms a major theme in the study of South India.

The Spread of Indian Culture

By the middle of the sixth century, Indian influence had spread far beyond the subcontinent. It was a gradual and selective process of cultural diffusion. The peoples of Southeast Asia did not have Indian culture forced upon them. Local rulers, impressed by the achievements of Indian civilization and valuing the power of Indian knowledge and religion, selected and adapted certain Indian institutions to their own distinct cultural patterns.

The influence of India was deep and permanent in all regions of Southeast Asia, with the exception of the Philippines and North Vietnam. The figures of Borobudur, the great eighth-century Buddhist monument in Indonesia, clearly show the influence of Gupta sculpture, and elsewhere South Indian influences were also much in evidence. In later centuries, the temples at Pagan in Burma and the magnificent structures in the jungles of Cambodia were to attest to the appeal of Hinduism, as well as Buddhism. The largest religious building in the world is Angkor Wat in Cambodia. Dedicated to Vishnu, this Hindu temple was built in the first half of the twelfth century. It is a walled complex measuring approximately 4,900 × 4,200 feet and is surrounded by a moat 650 feet wide—just as the world, in Indian eyes, is surrounded by the ocean. The balustrades in the first interior section are in the shape of nine-headed snakes, referring both to an ancient snake cult and to Vishnu's rainbow, the magic bridge that leads to heaven. Relief carvings on the wall portray stories of Rama and Krishna, the two most prominent incarnations of Vishnu.

Although Angkor Wat was built much later than the period we are concerned with here, it symbolizes the enormous influence of Hinduism in the lands to India's east. Yet the influence of Buddhism was to be the more lasting; to this day it is the dominant religion of the Southeast Asian mainland and Sri Lanka. As a proselytizing religion of great force, Buddhism also spread from India through Central Asia to China, where it eventually had great impact.

CHINA

Archaeologists have uncovered a number of Neolithic cultures in China, but it was in the Shang period (*ca.* 1600–1027 B.C.) that the first real civilization emerged. As in India, the first substantial cities and states appeared in the north. A good indication of Shang organizational power was its ability to mobilize the manpower needed to build a wall estimated at 2,385 feet long, 60 feet wide, and 30 feet high surrounding an early capital city. It has been calculated that this wall took 10,000 laborers, working 330 days a year, 18 years to complete.

A ceremonial vessel in the form of an elephant (Shang dynasty).

A view of the temple of Angkor Wat, built in the twelfth century by the king of Cambodia.

The Spread of Buddhism   Sixth Century B.C. to Sixteenth Century A.D.

With the Shang, China entered the Bronze Age. The finest products of the period are bronze vessels unsurpassed in their artistry, as befitted their use in solemn sacred rites. Many such vessels have been found, along with jades and other precious objects, in Shang tombs of the rich and powerful. The remains of people buried alive also have been found in these tombs. In one case, a chariot was discovered, complete with horse and driver; in others, entire entourages accompanied the deceased in death. The victims were non-Shang barbarians, captured in war and reduced to slavery, who were believed to accompany the dead on a journey to the afterworld.

Of more permanent influence was the development of the Chinese system of writing during this period. The earliest Chinese characters were pictograms (stylized pictorial representations) and ideograms (visual representations of a thing or concept), but most characters were more complex, consisting of an element that indicated a category of meaning and another that functioned as a phonetic indicator. Unfortunately, the pronunciation of the language later changed so that today the phonetic element is not necessarily a reliable guide to pronunciation. The early characters were used to inscribe oracle bones and tortoise shells used for divination. Command of the written language was the prized possession of a privileged group, and full literacy, until modern times, remained the possession of an elite minority who prided themselves on working with their brains rather than with their hands.

Although the written language was associated with the perpetuation of social distinctions, it helped overcome geographical barriers. People who spoke mutually unintelligible languages could still communicate with each other in writing, particularly after the form of characters was standardized in 221 B.C. Thus today, even though Cantonese and Mandarin speakers cannot converse with each other, they can communicate in writing and they can read the same books and journals. Similarly, scholars in Korea, Japan, and Vietnam acquired a command over China's literary culture even though they were unable to speak Chinese.

When the Shang were overthrown by the Zhou (Chou)* around 1027 B.C., at first no break occurred in cultural continuity because the Zhou represented a variant of Shang culture. They even produced bronze vessels similar to those of their predecessors. However, the inscriptions on the vessels, as well as the decorations and artistic effects, gradually changed, indicating a process of secularization that transformed them into treasured family heirlooms. At the same time, burial practices changed, and the immolation of humans and animals in the tombs of the powerful became increasingly rare.

The Zhou did not attempt to govern directly the area they conquered. Instead, they invested members of the royal house, favored adherents and allies, with the authority to rule over more than a hundred separate territories without interference from the Zhou king. These subordinate rulers received ranks later systematized into a hierarchical order. They were obliged to render military service and tribute. In practice, these positions were hereditary under a system of primogeniture, but with each generation the succession to a local lordship had to be legitimized by formal royal investiture. Some of these Zhou arrangements resembled those of the feudal system that later developed in Europe and Japan.

We are inadequately informed about the political structure of local village life or the economic relations between those who cultivated the soil and their rulers. However, we can learn something from the folk poetry included in the *Book of Songs,* which was compiled around 600 B.C. and was later accepted as one of the classics of Confucianism. Some songs

*This text uses the *pinyin* system of romanization, followed in parentheses by Wade-Giles. An exception is that some common geographical names appear in their earlier customary forms.

show ordinary people at work: the men clearing weeds from the fields, plowing, planting, and harvesting; the girls and women gathering mulberry leaves to feed the silkworms, making thread, carrying food out to the fields for their men. There is much about the staple crop, millet—both the eating variety and that used for brewing. We hear about wheat, barley, and rice, and men building a house, stamping down the earth between planks to make the walls. There are joyful celebrations of granaries full of grain and references to men gathering thatch for their roofs. Mention is made of lords' fields and private fields, and a "bailiff" is referred to, but the details of the system remain hidden. There are also poems of complaint against the government. One compares tax collectors to big rats. Another tells of the hardships of military service, men constantly on the march, day and night without rest, living like rhinoceroses and tigers. Sometimes a soldier survives the dangers of war and returns home only to find that his wife has given him up for dead and married another. Among the most appealing in their freshness and the innocence of their language are the love poems, for this was a time when girls and

Chinese calligraphy. (*Left*) A rubbing from one of the ten "Stone Drums," an example of the Great Seal style of writing, which evolved in the latter part of the Zhou dynasty. (*Right*) A rubbing from a stone inscription of the Han dynasty, inscribed in the Official Style.

Bronze wrestlers (Zhou dynasty).

young women were not yet restricted by the rules of etiquette from free expression of their longing for their sweetheart or their wish to be married.

The Age of Philosophers

As the bonds that tied the lords to the Zhou king weakened, power eroded, and by the ninth century B.C. the Zhou kings were unable to prevent the local rulers from fighting each other. Nor could they check the incursions of non-Chinese barbarians. To evade the latter, in 771 B.C. the capital was moved from Shaanxi (Shensi) east to the Luoyang (Loyang) region. After this move the Zhou "king" nominally continued to reign for another 500 years, until 256 B.C., but actually he exercised no military, political, or economic power. China was now divided among competing states. During the aptly named "Warring States Period" (403–221 B.C.) the competition between the states became increasingly more desperate and ruthless. With strong states subduing and annexing the weaker, the number of states diminished. The successful states grew ever bigger and more formidable until the process reached its logical conclusion and only one huge state remained.

Confucius (*ca.* 551–*ca.* 479 B.C.), a contemporary of the Buddha, lived relatively early in this period of accelerating change. Distressed by the disintegration of the political and moral order, he sought to put the world back together again and hoped to find a ruler who would implement his ideas. When this failed, he turned to teaching. Confucius saw himself not as a creator but as one who merely transmitted the traditional wisdom and values of civilization. He was a creative transmitter who understood the tradition in terms suitable for his own age and thereby revitalized and transformed old values. A good example is his redefinition of nobility as a quality acquired through virtue and wisdom, not through birth. For Confucius, the ideal man is humane, wise, and courageous. He is motivated by virtue, and the ultimate virtue is *ren (jen),* a term sometimes translated as "benevolence" or "humaneness," but for which there is no exact

English equivalent. *Ren* is the ground for all other virtues, the condition of being fully human in dealing with others. The written Chinese character for *ren* consists of the symbols for "man" and "two."

Morality and the achievement of social harmony were at the core of Confucius's concerns. He urged people to observe the *li,* a term meaning sacred ritual, ceremonial, and propriety, as well as good manners. The *li* were part of the precious heritage of antiquity, imbued with an aura of sacred reverence. When performed with true sincerity, life is truly human and civilized. When everyone follows the *li* and carries out his or her social role with genuine devotion, harmony will ensue. There will then be no need for coercion, no need for laws or punishments. Of crucial importance to achieve this was the initiative of the ruler who, by following the advice of a perfectly virtuous minister, could make government benevolent and win over the people.

Among the virtues and *li* emphasized by Confucius were those related to the family. He placed special importance on filial piety, the wholehearted obedience a

The Chinese States at the Time of Confucius   *ca.* 500 B.C.

Ancient symbol *Yi,* which stands for "changes." One of the five Confucian classics is the *Classic of Changes.*

child owes a parent. The obligations toward a father have priority over those owed a state: a son should not turn in his father for stealing a sheep. The relationship between father and son formed one of the classic Five Relationships of Confucianism. The others were ruler/minister, husband/wife, elder/younger brother, friend/friend. They entail reciprocal obligations between people of superior and inferior status and illustrate the importance of the family. Even the two that are not familial were thought of in family terms: the ruler/minister relationship was compared to that between father and son, that between friends is analogous to that between elder and younger brother. The Confucian view of society was thus paternal and hierarchical.

Confucius and his followers also believed there was only one valid and true, eternal way. The Way was open to all, but only the morally and intellectually cultivated could understand it. The idea that there might be a number of legitimate ways to live one's life and conduct affairs was foreign to the Chinese, who at that time had no contact with other highly developed and literate civilizations radically different from their own.

Confucius's ideas were not widely accepted for many centuries, but ultimately he proved to be one of the world's truly seminal thinkers. His person became a model to be emulated by later Confucians. As he appears in the *Analects,* discourses written by his disciples, he was a man of moderation: gentle but firm, dignified but not harsh, respectful but at ease. One passage gives an account of his intellectual and spiritual progression, culminating at the age of seventy when he was able to follow his heart's desires without transgressing against morality. The Confucian sage personified these characteristics and perfected his moral wisdom to the point that he automatically did what was right.

Confucius was only the beginning of Confucianism. He left many issues unsettled, and his philosophy permitted various interpretations. His later followers, such as Mencius and Xunzi, further developed his teachings, partly in response to challenges from other schools, such as that

Confucius on Government

Zi-gong asked about government. Confucius said "Sufficient food, sufficient armament, and sufficient confidence of the people." Zi-gong said, "Forced to give up one of these, which would you abandon first?" Confucius said, "I would abandon the armament." Zi-gong said, "Forced to give up one of the remaining two, which would you abandon first?" Confucius said, "I would abandon food. There have been deaths from time immemorial, but no state can exist without the confidence of the people."

Analects *12:7. From* A Source Book in Chinese Philosophy *by Wing-tsit Chan (Princeton, N.J.: Princeton University Press, 1963), p. 39, with Wade-Giles transcription changed into* pinyin *here and in all boxes.*

founded by Mozi (Mo Tzu, *ca.* 470–391 B.C.), who taught the practicality of universal love. Mencius (371–289 B.C.) is famed for his view that human nature is fundamentally good but that this goodness has to be cultivated and nourished. Xunzi (Hsün Tzu, 298–238 B.C.) is associated with the opposite view, that people are naturally selfish but nevertheless have the potential to become good. Although for different reasons, education was of essential importance for both men. Consistent with these positions, Mencius stressed the need for benevolence in government, while Xunzi more readily accepted the need for laws and punishment. Mencius is also famous for developing the older idea of the mandate of Heaven, according to which a dynasty ruled only as long as it ruled properly. When a regime lost the mandate, rebellion was justified, and an evil ruler forfeited the right to rule.

Although Confucians put a premium on social harmony, the thinkers known as Daoists (Taoists) sought to understand the eternal order of the universe. Daoism deals with the unconditioned, unnameable source of all reality that transcends being and nonbeing by standing above and beyond all distinctions. The first great Daoist classic, the *Dao De Jing (Tao Te Ching)* or *Laozi (Lao Tzu),* is cryptic, paradoxical, and highly suggestive. Among its themes there is a preference for the nega-

Divine seal of Laozi used in Daoist magic.

I I I I I I I I I I I I

Zhuangzi (also called Zhuang Zhou)

Once Zhuang Zhou dreamt he was a butterfly, a butterfly flitting and fluttering around, happy with himself and doing as he pleased. He didn't know he was Zhuang Zhou. Suddenly he woke up and there he was, solid and unmistakable Zhuang Zhou. But he didn't know if he was Zhuang Zhou who had dreamt he was a butterfly, or a butterfly dreaming he was Zhuang Zhou. Between Zhuang Zhou and a butterfly there must be *some* distinction! This is called the Transformation of Things.

The fish trap exists because of the fish; once you've gotten the fish, you can forget about the trap. The rabbit snare exists because of the rabbit; once you've gotten the rabbit, you can forget the snare. Words exist because of meaning; once you've gotten the meaning, you can forget the words. Where can I find a man who has forgotten words so I can have a word with him?

From Chuang Tzu: Basic Writings, *trans. by Burton Watson (New York: Columbia University Press, 1946), p. 45 and p. 140, respectively.*

tive over the positive, nothing over something, weak over strong, nonaction over action. It teaches silence is more meaningful than words and ignorance is superior to knowledge; in sum, "Those who know do not speak; those who speak do not know." This view of the limitation of language is shared by Zhuangzi (Chuang Tzu), author of the second great Daoist classic that bears his name. Zhuangzi had a keenly developed sense of paradox, as when he argues for the usefulness of the useless: when the able-bodied young men of the village are marched off to war, it is the hopelessly deformed hunchback who stands by the side of the road waving them off. Another theme he pursues is the relativity of everything.

The Unification of China

During the period from 771 B.C. to 221 B.C., momentous and rapid changes took place in all areas of human activity. Warfare is a good example. No longer were battles fought by gentlemen in chariots; now most of the fighting was done by foot sol-

diers, peasant conscripts commanded by professional officers. Armies grew enormously. Some are said to have numbered a million men, although that may be an exaggeration.

Armies had to be fed and supplied. To support the forces, an increase in agricultural production was achieved by reclamation projects, irrigation, and technological changes, including the introduction of iron. There were also changes in management and administration as states adopted systems of taxation and labor services. Land became a commodity to be bought and sold. Commerce increased along with the size of states and the development of roads. Metallic currencies appeared, replacing the cowrie shells used earlier. Among the items of trade were various kinds of textiles, metals, woods, bamboo, jade, and regional specialties. Urban centers grew and expanded until they required new city walls.

As ever, social change was inseparably linked to military, economic, and political change. Merchants and generals were not the only new professionals. It took a skilled diplomat to steer a state through the treacherous waters of international relations, someone with an eloquent voice to win a debate. Faced with internal and external challenges, rulers tended to pay more attention to a man's competence than to his pedigree. Old families declined, and new ones grew in importance.

Faced with a world of disturbing and baffling change, many Chinese turned for guidance to what they perceived as a much better past, but some, such as Han Feizi (Han Fei Tzu, d. 233 B.C.), held that new problems demanded new and drastic solutions. These so-called Legalists stressed the rationalization of administration, the improvement of managerial techniques, and the strict enforcement of punitive laws. Their theories, which were applied by the state of Qin (Ch'in), unified China in 221 B.C.

The Qin was located in the west of North China, the same region from which the Zhou had conquered North China. This area was economically able to support a strong military and political apparatus, and it was well situated strategically, protected by mountains whose passes were easy to defend and yet provided access to the east. It was something of a buffer region between the Chinese and various warlike tribal peoples. Making the best of this situation, the Qin toughened its armies by fighting the tribesmen. At the same time it drew on the administrative and technological expertise developed in the more sophisticated, centrally located states. Under Legalist influence the state was divided into districts governed by a centralized bureaucracy and financed by a direct tax on the peasantry. A system of mutual responsibility was introduced, with harsh penalties for criminals and those who failed to report a criminal. Everything was designed to make the state wealthy, strong, and disciplined.

The First Empire: Qin and Han

The unification of China by the Qin was the beginning of about four hundred years of imperial rule, even though the Qin Dynasty (221–207 B.C.) itself barely survived the first emperor, Qin Shihuangdi (Ch'in Shih Huang-ti). He and his Legalist adviser, Li Si (Li Ssu) applied to the whole domain the policies first enacted in the state of Qin, including the division of the state into administrative districts governed by a bureaucracy. The integration of the realm also was furthered by a program of road building, standardized official coinage, standardized weights and measurements and script, and suppression of scholars and writings critical of the new order. Qin hostility toward Confucianism was reciprocated in kind, so that once Confucianism prevailed, the Qin acquired the most negative reputation of any Chinese dynasty.

The traditional image of cruelty and oppression may well be exaggerated, but it seems clear that the regime tried to do too much too fast. Its ambitions found physical expression in vast building projects, including an enormous underground imperial mausoleum. The Qin also linked segments of earlier walls to protect its territories. Traditionally this has been considered the ancestor of China's famous Great Wall, but that famous and imposing struc-

A life-sized terra-cotta figure of an armored archer of the Qin dynasty. This is one of more than 7,000 such figures unearthed from the tomb of the first emperor of China.

ture, the remains of which are still extant, dates from the much later Ming Dynasty.

After the death of its founder, the Qin soon disintegrated, but it left foundations on which the Former Han (202 B.C.–A.D. 8) and the Later Han (A.D. 25–A.D. 220) erected more lasting edifices.

In many respects Han China was comparable to Imperial Rome. Both were great empires with powerful armies ranging far beyond the heartland: Han forces even crossed the Pamir Mountains. Both are celebrated for practical accomplishments, as in civil engineering: the Han maintained 20,000–25,000 miles of highway radiating out from the capital. They also made advances in shipbuilding (the axial rudder), medicine, astronomy, and agriculture. Intellectually, both empires built on the achievements of their predecessors and were noted more for the synthesis of old philosophies than for producing strikingly new ones. Both also excelled in writing

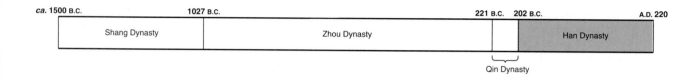

ca. 1500 B.C.	1027 B.C.	221 B.C.	202 B.C.	A.D. 220
Shang Dynasty	Zhou Dynasty		Han Dynasty	

Qin Dynasty

history. China's greatest historian was Sima Qian (Ssu-ma Ch'ien, *ca.* 145 B.C.– *ca.* 90 B.C.) whose *Records of the Grand Historian* is a literary masterpiece as well as a work of careful scholarship.

In China, as in Rome, it took great political ability to create and maintain a huge empire over a long period of time. But there was no counterpart in the Han to the Roman development of law. Instead, the Chinese relied on a bureaucracy staffed by men who shared a common education, a common fund of historical references, and a common set of largely

Confucian values. To help mold these men there was an imperial university where, under the Later Han, 30,000 students were studying mostly Confucian texts. Imperial Confucianism did not preclude employment of pragmatic Legalist military and political policies, but it did provide the dynasty with legitimacy and could prompt ministers to faithful service. The Confucian ideal was one of unselfish public service, not unthinking compliance with the whims or policies of a ruler. Most officials came from families of notables who dominated the local power structure and who

The Han Empire   100 B.C.

could thus afford a measure of political as well as intellectual independence.

The system operated best with a balance between central and local power. Because the wealthy and powerful were also the most apt to evade taxes, the state had a stake in preventing an undue concentration of landownership. But attempts to limit the size of landholdings failed, as did the attempt to stabilize grain prices through government purchases when grain was plentiful and cheap, for resale when it became scarce, causing prices to rise. For its own finances, the government drew heavily on agriculture but also collected commercial taxes and operated salt and iron monopolies.

As in Rome, in weak hands the throne itself became a source of political instability as various groups maneuvered for influence and control. In the Han, the families of imperial consorts became exceedingly powerful, and it was a member of one such family who, after serving as regent for a child emperor, overthrew the Former Han but did not succeed in establishing a lasting dynasty of his own. Instead, after a period of turmoil and fighting, a member of the imperial Han family established the Later Han in A.D. 25.

The Han established a Chinese presence in North Korea and North Vietnam, but the most challenging foreign policy problem was how to deal with the nomads who lived beyond the northern and northwestern frontiers. Nomadic peoples, like the Altaic-speaking Xiongnu (Hsiung-nu), were formidable opponents because of their skill in warfare. For them war was merely a special application of the horsemanship and archery skills they practiced every day in guarding their flocks. Their mobility was an asset in defense as well as attack, for, traveling light with their flocks and tents, they could elude Chinese military expeditions and avoid destruction or control. Chinese measures to deal with these troublesome neighbors ranged from military suppression to conciliation by means of gifts and marriage alliances, so that the nomads would accept tributary status. Tributaries had to acknowledge Han supremacy but profited by an exchange of presents and the opportunity

to trade. Much of this trade was conducted in markets along the borders. Chinese exports included lacquerware, ironware, bronze mirrors, and silk, which first reached Europe over the famous Silk Road. The Chinese also did whatever they could to foster disunity among the tribal people; "using barbarians against barbarians" became a permanent part of their foreign policy.

China in Disunity, 220–589

Disrupted by internal strife, in fiscal trouble because of a shrinking tax base, and beset by foreign challenges, the Han came to an end in 220. Beginning early in the next century, a succession of nomadic peoples carved out states in North China. Some of these, notably the Northern Wei (386–534), attained a good measure of success, but none matched the Han in du-

Han earthenware tile.

Pottery tile rubbing depicting hunters and peasants (Han dynasty).

When the Han fell, a whole civilization seemed to have collapsed. A spiritual and intellectual, as well as political vacuum was created. Some of China's most brilliant and talented men responded by turning to Daoism or to discovering new meaning in poetry, calligraphy, and painting. Others, both humble people and aristocrats, were attracted to Buddhism, which addressed itself more directly to human suffering than did any of the components of the native Chinese tradition. In the north, Buddhism also benefited from the patronage of rulers who, as foreigners themselves, could sympathize with a foreign religion.

Buddhism took many long years to overcome its foreignness in China, years during which Buddhist missionaries patiently labored to translate and explain the Buddhist teachings. It was a formidable task to render the highly inflected Indian languages and discursive Indian writings into uninflected and terse Chinese, to find Chinese equivalents for concepts such as *karma* or Nirvana, and to bridge the gulf that separated Indian and Chinese perceptions of the meaning of life and the nature of the universe.

The greatest of the translators was a Central Asian, Kumārajīva, who, early in the fifth century, directed a staff of about 1,000 monks. In a vivid comment on the translator's predicament, he once compared his work to that of a man who chews rice and then gives it to another to swallow. By the end of the period of disunity, the labors of such men had made Buddhism palatable to the Chinese, but not until after reunification in 591 did they feel sufficiently familiar with the faith to develop it in ways of their own.

For a time Buddhism provided a link between China and India, yet there remained distinct differences between the historical-minded Chinese tradition and the focus in India on the ultimate. The contrast between the two civilizations is also apparent in their different political histories. At the end of the sixth century, India was again politically fragmented, whereas China had entered one of its great ages of imperial unification.

ration or extent. To enjoy their Chinese conquests, the nomads required a more sophisticated political system than the tribal organization they brought from the steppes. They had to rely on Chinese administrators who knew how to operate a tax system, keep records, and run a government. There was also a tendency for the nomads themselves to become more like the Chinese. This not only jeopardized their cultural heritage but tended to alienate those nomads who had remained on the steppe.

Warfare and devastation in the north stimulated vast migrations to south China, especially into the Yangtze region, which underwent great economic development, foreshadowing the time when it would become China's rice bowl. Politically the south remained under Chinese control, but the southern states were unstable and weak. When reunification came, it was, as always, from the north.

Suggestions for Further Reading

India

A gold mine of authoritative information is *A Historical Atlas of South Asia* (1978), ed. J. E. Schwartzberg, which contains historical essays and bibliographies. A. L. Basham, *The Wonder that Was India,* 3rd ed. (1985), is a lucid and balanced account of Indian civilization. S. Wolpert, *A New History of India,* 3rd ed. (1989), is a good survey, although stronger on modern India. A good compedium for intellectual history is *Sources of Indian Tradition,* 2nd ed. (1988), edited and revised by Ainslee T. Embree. Edward Said, *Orientalism* (1978), has stimulated rethinking of how Indian history is analyzed and perceived. A good but demanding recent example of post-Orientalist theory and practice is provided by Ronald Inden, *Imagining India* (1990). Diana L. Eck, *Banaras: City of Light* (1982), is a multifaceted account of India's most holy city. On India's greatest playwright, see Barbara S. Miller, *Theater of Memory: The Plays of Kalidasa* (1984). For readings on Southeast Asia, see Chapter 15.

China

C. Blunder and M. Elvin, *Cultural Atlas of China* (1983), provides an attractive and stimulating introduction to many aspects of Chinese civilization. *Heritage of China: Contemporary Perspectives on Chinese Civilization* (1990), edited by Paul S. Ropp, is a collection of interpretive essays by leading scholars. Kwang-chih Chang, *The Archaeology of Ancient China,* 4th ed. (1986), is authoritative, as is *The Cambridge History of China,* Vol 1, *The Ch'in and Han Empires 221* B.C.–A.D. *220* (1986). Also recommended on topics not represented in Ropp's anthology are Sarah Allen, *The Shape of the Turtle: Myth, Art, and Cosmos in Early China* (1991), and B. Watson, *Ssu-ma Ch'ien: Grand Historian of China* (1958). Also recommended are three anthologies of translations: *Sources of Chinese Tradition* (1960), by W. T. de Bary et al.; Wing-tsit Chan, ed., *A Source Book in Chinese Philosophy* (1963); and P. B. Ebrey, *Chinese Civilization and Society: A Sourcebook* (1981). A general survey is provided by C. Schirokauer, *A Brief History of Chinese Civilization* (1991), and *A Brief History of Chinese and Japanese Civilizations,* 2nd ed. (1989), which include suggestions for further reading.

Buddhism

Heinz Bechert and Richard Gombrich, *The World of Buddhism* (1984), is a well-illustrated introduction. Another good place to begin reading about Buddhism and other religions is the *Encyclopedia of Religion* (1987), M. Eliade, general editor. Two well-regarded books on Buddhist thought are Paul Williams, *Mahayana Buddhism: The Doctrinal Foundations* (1989), and Roger J. Corless, *The Vision of Buddhism: The Space Under the Tree* (1989). For China, see *Buddhism in Chinese History* (1959), by A. F. Wright. Buddhist materials are also included in the source books listed above.

Reference

Ainslie T. Embree et al., *Encyclopedia of Asian History* (1988), is a useful reference. For studies on specific topics see *Bibliography of Asian Studies,* published annually by the Association for Asian Studies, Inc.

7

THE BYZANTINE EMPIRE

ollowing the loss of the western Roman Empire to the Germans, the Eastern Empire gradually evolved into a distinctive civilization, a successor to the Hellenistic civilization created by Alexander the Great. That civilization is called Byzantine and its political manifestation is called the Byzantine Empire. Both were centered in the city of Constantinople (present-day Istanbul), which Constantine the Great had built on the site of the ancient Athenian colony at Byzantium.

Though civilization proceeded along separate paths in the East and in the West, there was constant interaction between the Byzantines and the westerners during the period from the sixth century to the fifteenth. The idea of the Roman Empire never died, and both the Byzantines and the Europeans sought, from time to time, to reunite its two parts. Moreover, the Byz-

antine Empire served as both link and buffer between Europe and the Middle East, where momentous events in the seventh century changed the history of the Mediterranean Basin, indeed of the world. Finally, East and West were linked by Christianity. Over time, the eastern church and the western church deviated in liturgical practice, theology, and political status, but, like the idea of the Roman Empire, the notion of a single church of Christ never disappeared, and the two churches were often in close contact.

Throughout its history, the Byzantine Empire struggled with formidable political and cultural problems. Diocletian's decision to locate the imperial court in the East in the late third century was dictated by the need to protect the rich eastern provinces from the Persian threat, a threat that persisted until the start of the seventh century. It was then replaced by a greater threat—

(OPPOSITE) INTERIOR OF HAGIA SOPHIA, THE PRINCIPAL CHURCH IN CONSTANTINOPLE, BUILT BY EMPEROR JUSTINIAN I IN THE 530S AFTER RIOTS HAD DESTROYED THE CENTER OF THE CITY.

this time, from the new Arab-Islamic empire that destroyed Byzantine power in the Middle East and curtailed Byzantine movement in the eastern Mediterranean. While trying to cope with the Islamic threat, the Empire found itself challenged in its European provinces by the Bulgarians. And, to complicate matters even further, the ancient division between the Semitic culture and the Hellenistic culture in the eastern provinces gave rise to severe religious controversies.

Heresies of the Eastern Church

The emperors in Constantinople had to face a series of heresies that divided the church. Most of them were based on a view of Jesus that emphasized one of his natures, human or divine. The official church believed that Jesus was fully human and fully divine. The major heretical movements were:

Arianism: Followers of this heresy believed that Jesus was a created being and therefore not fully divine. Arians believed that God was unique, so that Jesus, the Son of God, could not be God. Arianism was condemned in 325 at the Council of Nicaea.

Nestorianism: The Nestorians admitted that Jesus had two natures, human and divine, but believed that the natures were separate. For them, the divine nature of Jesus could not be united to or mixed with his human nature, because the two were categorically different. Nestorianism was condemned in 451 at the Council of Chalcedon.

Monophysitism: The Monophysites (from the Greek, *monophysis* meaning "of one nature") believed that Jesus had only one nature in which the human and divine were inexplicably united. They were condemned at the Council of Chalcedon for failing to recognize that Jesus was both fully human and fully divine, one person with two natures.

Monotheletism: This heresy originated in the court of the emperor Heraclius, who wanted to win the support of the Monophysites while remaining true to the doctrine of the Council of Chalcedon. Monotheletism admitted the dual nature of Jesus, but said that he had one will (Greek, *monothelema* meaning "one will"). For the Monothelites, the unity of Jesus's will meant that he was one person, even if he had two natures. The official church held that the will was a function of the nature of a being, so if Jesus had two natures he also had two wills. Monotheletism was condemned in 680 at the Council of Constantinople.

Yet, as we shall see, Byzantine civilization achieved brilliant artistic, intellectual, and governmental successes. And it survived for a thousand years.

THE EASTERN ROMAN EMPIRE AFTER THE LOSS OF THE WEST

The changes that created the Byzantine Empire began in the fifth century. The principal change was from a Roman military government to a Greek civilian government. After centuries of Roman rule, the old Hellenistic culture of the East reemerged.

During the fifth century, many hellenized Egyptians and Syrians—who had been excluded from service in the Roman government—made their way to Constantinople to take posts in the imperial administration. The influx of hellenized easterners accelerated under Emperor Anastasius (r. 491–518), the ruler who recognized Theodoric the Ostrogoth's authority in Italy (p. 127). The officials of Anastasius's government—financial wizards, advisers, and lesser administrators— were well-educated men who regarded civil service as a career. During this time Constantinople changed from being the capital city—the place where the emperor and his government were located—to being the "ruling city," the metropolis that dominated the cultural life of the Empire. Constantinople replaced Rome as the intellectual and cultural center of the world and was often referred to as the New Rome.

Meanwhile, trouble broke out again when Persia, under a revived Sassanid dynasty, began to stage successful attacks on the eastern borders. To meet the threat, Emperor Zeno I (r. 479–491), instead of putting together an army of mercenaries from among the Ostrogothic tribes to the north, marshalled his troops from the Isaurians of southern Asia Minor. Zeno's successor, Anastasius, also relied on armies recruited from the eastern regions.

The populations of the eastern provinces, though mostly Christianized, had kept their ancient religious traditions alive in a number of unorthodox theologies, of which Arianism was an example (p. 118). Because the trade of the East provided a ready medium for exchange of religious ideas, the eastern cities became hotbeds of religious disputes over the nature of Christ, the sacraments, and other issues. Anastasius, beset by the constant threat of invasion, tolerated the variety of religious ideas while seeking to reconcile them to the creeds enunciated by earlier ecumenical councils, such as the Council of Nicaea (325). Although the popes in Rome railed against such compromises, Anastasius refused to condemn and eradicate the heretical sects. He looked on religious differences as a political matter rather than a spiritual matter.

Anastasius left a full treasury and an efficient civil service. But the army reasserted itself after his death and installed as emperor a soldier from the Balkans, Justin I (r. 518–527). This shift back to a military government was short-lived, however. Justinian, Justin's nephew and successor, had been educated in Constantinople by Anastasius's court bureaucrats and had become thoroughly hellenized.

When he succeeded Justin in 527, he inaugurated a decade of exuberant cultural and political revival.

The Early Years of Justinian's Reign

Justinian (r. 527–565) was a reformer whose goal was to restore the Empire to its former glory. One of his first steps was to appoint a commission to revise and codify the Roman law. During the golden age of Roman law, from the reign of Augustus (r. 27 B.C.–A.D. 14) to A.D. 200, a succession of great jurists had shaped the system and had formulated its basic doctrines, in the centuries that followed a vast accumulation of laws, judgments, and learned commentaries had piled up. By Justinian's time, it would take a lifetime to read the law and another lifetime to master it. Judges were often stymied in trying to settle cases as the contending parties cited conflicting laws and opinions to support their cases.

Earlier emperors had tried to end the confusion by commissioning law codes.

Expansion of the Byzantine Empire under Justinian

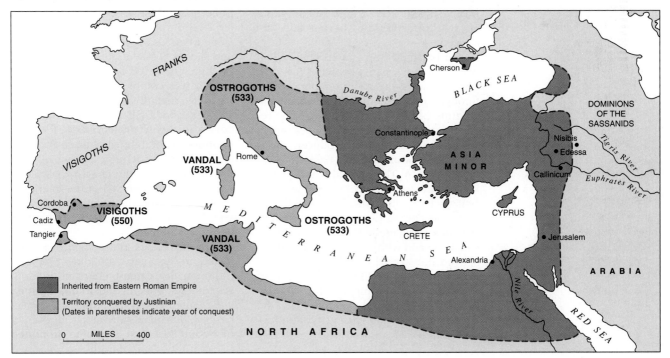

But none of the codes—such as that of Theodosius II, published about 480—dealt with the whole corpus of legislation and commentary. The members of Justinian's commission, led by law professors from Beirut, tried to weave a new fabric from the welter of tradition. In 534, they produced a comprehensive code called the *Corpus Iuris Civilis* (the Body of Civil Law), which contains one of the most sophisticated legal systems ever created. This code was symbolic of Justinian's goal of achieving a reunited, well-governed empire.

In 532, however, mob violence erupted in Constantinople in protest against high taxes and corruption in the government. Coping with the Persian threat, together with the growth of the bureaucracy, had led to a steady rise in the tax burden on ordinary citizens, and their growing frustration and anger finally exploded in riots. Back in the 480s, Emperor Zeno, fearing an Ostrogothic attack on the city, had armed the clubs that supported the teams that played in the games at the Hippodrome (the city stadium) to serve as a militia. Now these clubs, well organized and well armed, joined forces to loot and burn the city. The violence finally subsided, leaving Justinian with a city whose center had been totally destroyed.

Justinian now recognized that he had to find some alternative source of revenue. The simplest way to raise money was through conquest. In 533, Justinian sent an army to North Africa to begin the reconquest of the western provinces. Africa was an important grain producer, and it would provide an excellent base for a military operation. The general whom Justinian named to lead the troops was the brilliant Belisarius, who had helped suppress the riots in Constantinople. Belisarius took Carthage in the first year of the campaign and within a short time had destroyed the Vandal kingdom established in North Africa in 430. The collapse of Vandal power prompted the Moorish tribes to seek their independence, and the Byzantine forces did not pacify the province until 548.

Meanwhile, in 535, Belisarius took Sicily and reached Rome a year later. At this point, however, he fell from favor and was forced into retirement. The Ostrogoths now launched a determined war of resistance. Unable to hold Rome, the Byzantines set up their capital in Ravenna, a city on the Adriatic Sea well protected on the land side by extensive marshes and readily accessible by ships from Constantinople. By 556, after twenty years of war, most of Italy was under the control of the Byzantine governor in Ravenna. But, as we have seen (p. 128), in 568, three years after Justinian's death, new Germanic invaders, the Lombards, entered Italy and quickly overran most of the peninsula.

The Origins of Byzantine Art

Back in Constantinople, Justinian devoted himself to rebuilding the city on a magnificent scale befitting the city that ruled the world. He built public baths, new government buildings, and aqueducts and cisterns to supply the city with water. He dedicated 25 churches in the city and its suburbs. His crowning achievement was the church of Hagia Sophia. The church that originally stood on this site had been built by Constantine and had been reconstructed around 400. Justinian commissioned two Greeks, Anthemius of Tralles and Isidore of Miletus, to build a new kind of church centered on a great dome. The church was completed in just six years. Its dome rises 184 feet above the pavement and, with half-domes on either side, covers an area of 100 feet by 250 feet. The enormous lateral thrust of these domes is supported by great buttresses, which from the outside make the church look like a great pile of masonry. But the interior is light and airy, and the ceilings are covered with brilliant mosaics. Hagia Sophia was dedicated in 537.

Byzantine art and architecture originated in Justinian's building program. Although the earliest churches in Constantinople, built in the fourth century, were patterned on the elongated Roman basilica, Justinian's architects devised a new form based on the dome supported

Engraving showing Constantinople in the mid-fifteenth century, just before the Turks conquered it.

by half-domes. In time, the arrangement of the domes became fixed. The central dome covered the crossing point formed by four half-domes radiating symmetrically as a Greek cross—that is, a cross with arms of equal length. On the inner surfaces of the domes, artists executed frescoes or mosaics that also became standardized over time. The whole program of architecture and interior decoration solidified by the tenth century and remained virtually unchanged until the midfifteenth century when the Empire was conquered by the Turks.

The Byzantine church represented the cosmos. Inside, a representation of God the Father dominated the highest reaches of the central dome with the angels and archangels pictured below him. The walls of the church were covered with pictures of the saints arranged according to the importance of their feasts in the liturgical calendar. In the West, as we shall see, the decoration of churches was intended to provide instruction to the laity. In the Byzantine realms, it was intended to represent the universe under God's rulership.

The Byzantine style of representation suited the purpose of the art. It emphasized the spiritual presence of the figure rather than its physical portrayal. Unlike the naturalistic art of Greece and Rome, Byzantine art represented human figures in a flat, static pose that emphasized line and color. Frequently using a flat gold background, Byzantine artists gave the human figure a formal, somewhat abstract form with large, staring eyes that emphasized the spiritual aspect of the person represented. In the best work, the contrast between the flat monochrome background and the vigorously drawn and highly colored figure creates a three-dimensional illusion; the figure seems to be in front of the background.

Byzantine art exercised a powerful effect on Western art. The Byzantine churches built in Ravenna during the sixth century became models for later Western artists. The art in the churches of southern Italy also influenced westerners. During the twelfth century, when Europeans began to study Byzantine scientific works, Byzantine book illuminations began to influence Western artists. Art historians trace some aspects of early Renaissance painting to Byzantine influence.

The Last 25 Years of Justinian's Reign

The flamboyant spirit of the 530s ended with the revival of war with the Persians

Byzantine gold wedding ring (*ca.* fifth century).

Hagia Sophia, built *ca.* 535. The minarets were added after the Ottoman Turks captured Constantinople in 1453.

Procession of saints and martyrs, Sant'Apollinare Nuovo, Ravenna (*ca.* 574).

and with trouble in the Balkans. In 540, Shah Khusro I of Persia attacked the eastern provinces and, after taking the great city of Antioch in Syria, offered to sell it back to Justinian. The emperor rejected the offer. At about the same time, Slavic tribes moved into the Balkans and destroyed Byzantine authority there. These disasters deprived the Empire of two vital resources: from Syria it had drawn commercial wealth, and from the Balkan provinces it had drawn manpower. Then, in 542, an epidemic (of what sort is unknown) broke out in Constantinople and recurred over the next two years.

Faced with these misfortunes, Justinian was obliged to reduce the campaign in Italy to a holding action and to curtail his ambitious building programs. He experimented with a series of innovative tax measures and reorganized the military, which now had to make do with less money and manpower. The Byzantine commanders devised new mobile tactics for small forces, and in a major test the new model army executed a brilliant campaign in 552 that broke the last Ostrogothic resistance in Italy. In the East, Justinian compensated for the shortage of manpower by building a string of strategically placed fortifications, and used diplomacy instead of force whenever he could.

By the 560s, he had held off Khusro I, had defeated the Ostrogoths, had pacified and fortified North Africa, and had constructed an elaborate series of alliances along the Danube to limit the Slavic invasions. These accomplishments came, however, at significant expense. When Justinian dismantled the government's transport system to reduce expenditures, farmers in the interior of Asia Minor were forced into bankruptcy. The farmers had become economically dependent on the transport system.

The economic strain created by the wars and by Justinian's ambitious building program had depleted the imperial treasury, and it was empty when Justinian died in 565.

The crises also led to a concentration of power resting on the emperor. In reducing the size of the imperial bureaucracy, Justinian had taken onto himself much of the work of government. By the end of his reign, he simply had too much to do. To maintain his successes would have taken even more concentration and energy than he had spent in achieving them. Justinian's successor, Maurice (r. 582–602), was an able administrator, but he could not cope with simultaneous disasters in all quarters. The Lombards had invaded Italy; the Danubian alliances disintegrated as the Slavic Bulgars and the Altaic Avars (related to the Huns) began to put pressure on the border; and the Persians became aggressive once again.

FROM EASTERN ROMAN TO BYZANTINE EMPIRE

Under Maurice's successor Phocas (r. 602–610), the Byzantine world collapsed. The Bulgers and the Avars overran the Balkans and Greece. Asia Minor became a Persian province (a satrapy) in which the Persians carried out an anti-Christian campaign. When Phocas died, the Eastern Roman Empire consisted of the city of Constantinople, the marshlands around Ravenna and Rome, Sicily, Apulia and Calabria in southern Italy, and the North African provinces. Constantinople was virtually impregnable on its promontory, but it appeared incapable of reviving the Empire. Heraclius (r. 610–641), Phocas's successor, even thought of fleeing to North Africa but remained instead in Constantinople and began a campaign of reconquest in eastern Asia Minor.

The prospect was not promising. Heraclius spent more than a decade rebuilding the army and preparing for a long campaign. In 622, he sailed south to Ionia and began a war of attrition against the Persians. After four years of bitter fighting against superior forces, his troops broke the military strength of the Persians and reconquered Asia Minor. Thereupon, Heraclius forced the population to reconvert to Christianity. In 627, he led his army on a raid into the heart of Persia, prompting the Persian nobility to assassinate the shah, Khusro II, in 628. By that time, Heraclius had reestablished Byzantine control over Syria, Palestine, and Egypt.

This run of successes soon came to an end. Heraclius had managed to win back the eastern provinces with a small, well-trained army, but to defend them he would need a large, costly army. The Persian occupation and the long war had ruined the economy of the eastern provinces, and they could not support such a force. The provinces, once the richest in the Empire, were now a drain on the imperial treasury. At the end of his life, Heraclius had to watch a new eastern power, the Arabs, seize much of what he had won.

Nonetheless, Heraclius had reestablished the Hellenistic world and had preserved it as the heartland of Christendom. During the seventh century east–west trade had revived, and eastern churchmen—including the first great archbishop of Canterbury in England, Theodore of Tarsus (r. 669–690)—were playing an important role in the Roman church. Moreover, the eastern emperors continued to influence that church, in which many of the members of the clergy were actually Greek-speaking. And the Byzantine governor of Ravenna was still in control of Rome, even though the land between had fallen to the Lombards.

After Heraclius's death, his successors were unable to hold the borders of the Empire. The Arab expansion, the continuing settlement of the Slavs in the Balkans, and the establishment of a Bulgar kingdom north of the Danube made it impossible for them to continue the work Heraclius had begun. The Arabs built a fleet in the Mediterranean that challenged Byzantine naval supremacy, and they repeatedly attacked Constantinople itself between about 669 and 677. The Byzantines withstood these assaults and managed to hold Asia Minor, but they soon lost the provinces along the eastern seaboard of the Mediterranean. By the end of the seventh century, the Empire was nothing more than a late Hellenistic state with outlying provinces.

The Heraclian dynasty came to an end in 711, when its last emperor was murdered in a palace rebellion. After six years of anarchy, a provincial administrator and general, Leo the Isaurian, ascended the imperial throne as Leo III and founded a new dynasty. Leo (r. 717–741) came to power at a critical moment and was uniquely qualified to meet the threat of a great land and sea siege of Constantinople

The Byzantine Empire   SEVENTH AND ELEVENTH CENTURIES

by the Arabs (717–718). The new emperor was born in northern Syria and knew Arabic. In his youth, his family had been forcibly removed to the Bulgarian border, and so he knew that troubled region as well.

Actually, the Arabs had helped Leo to the imperial throne. Early in 717, when they invaded the eastern province Leo was governing, he seems to have made a deal with them. If they promised to support him, he would seize the throne and as emperor would bow to their demands for territory or tribute. When the Arabs withdrew, Leo stormed the capital and became emperor.

But when the Arabs invaded Asia Minor again, Leo negotiated with them until he had gained the advantage and then he turned on them and defeated them. The crucial moment in the defense of the capital came when the Bulgars arrived and destroyed the Arab army. Shortly after this, Leo defeated the Arab fleet and began his reign as the savior of Constantinople. He followed this triumph with a series of campaigns against the Arabs in eastern Asia Minor that halted their hundred years of conquest. Syria and North Africa had been lost, but the Empire had consolidated its position in Asia Minor, the Balkans, and Greece.

Emperor Leo represented the landed aristocracy of Asia Minor against the court and the bureaucracy that had held sway since Anastasius. Once in power, he carried out the most important reforms since Justinian. He commissioned new law codes, including an abridged and modernized Greek version of the *Corpus Iuris Civilis*. He regularized the system of administrative districts, called *themes*, and by so doing significantly improved the quality of government. He also instigated a movement against the use of religious images (icons) called iconoclasm (hatred of icons).

The effect of these changes in the political, economic, and cultural orientation of the Empire—from a Mediterranean power to a state straddling Europe and Asia Minor, from a commercial economy to an agricultural economy, and from a bilingual society to a Greek society—constituted the final transition from Eastern Roman Empire to Byzantine Empire. The transformation had begun under Anastasius in the late fifth century and was completed under Leo III and his successors in the eighth century. Although the political and economic influence of the Byzantines in the West was diminished, the two halves of the old Roman Empire still carried on relations. The Byzantine government considered itself the only legitimate successor of the Roman imperial government, and religion continued to serve as a link and as a source of conflict between East and West.

THE CONTROVERSY OVER ICONOCLASM

Christianity had been established in Byzantium before Constantine I rebuilt the city, but once it had become the capital of the Empire its church also had become one of the leading sees. Constantine had regarded himself as the thirteenth apostle and the church in Constantinople had claimed the status of an apostolic church (p. 116) from the fourth century on. Its bishops took the title "patriarch," which was used by the bishops of the apostolic sees in the East—Jerusalem and Alexandria—and claimed authority over all the churches in the Empire. But the emperors regarded the church as a department of their government and controlled selection of patriarchs. Iconoclasm arose within the Byzantine church.

The Origins of Iconoclasm

In 726, nine years after he came to power, Leo the Isaurian stood in the porch of his palace and destroyed a famous picture of Christ. That act caused riots in Constantinople and in the western parts of the Empire, but the armies and the people of the eastern provinces accepted it without protest. The difference suggests that Leo was acting in accordance with his Syrian origins and that iconoclasm reflected a profound difference between Semitic religious views and Greco-Roman religious views.

The Hellenistic world had accepted the use of religious images in prayer and worship as part of Christian observance. The pagan Greeks had used idols in their religious rituals, and Hellenistic Christians had followed their lead. Plato had said in the *Symposium* that the contemplation of beautiful objects led one to the contemplation of beauty itself, and the assimilation of Platonic thought into Christianity suggested a similar role for icons in Christian worship. A beautiful image of Christ helped the worshiper rise from contemplation of the world to contemplation of the world's Maker.

The Semitic tradition ran counter to the Greek in this matter. In the Hebrew Bible, the second commandment states that men should make no images of the divine, and that prohibition survived in some Semitic Christian communities, as well as in Judaism and the new religion of Islam. The use of images in the Greek churches of the Middle East, which by the eighth century were under the protection—usually benevolent—of the Islamic ruler in Damascus. But from time to time the Arabs turned on the Christians, criticizing the use of icons, among other things. In 723, the caliph Yazid II—unhappy with the Christians after his failed siege of Constantinople in 717–718—ordered the destruction of representational art of whatever kind everywhere in his realm. In short, iconoclasm was a commonly held attitude throughout the eastern Mediterranean.

Monks, Icons, and the Theory of Imperial Government

In Constantinople, the Christian monks led the protest against Leo's destruction of the image of Christ. Monasticism had spread more swiftly in the East than in the West. In fact, by the eighth century people in the East were complaining that too many of their best young people, men and women, were being lost to monasteries.

Eastern monasticism was dominated by Basil (329–79), a monk who had risen to become bishop of Caesaria in Syria. About fifty years after the founding of Pachomius' community (p. 136), Basil created a carefully worded constitution of monasticism that set a balance between worship and work and identified the three basic values of monastic life: poverty, chastity, and obedience. By the time of Leo III, Basilian communities had been founded in many eastern cities and were playing an active role in the affairs of both church and state.

The influential role of monks was demonstrated during the conflict over the use of icons. Leo apparently viewed the opposition to iconoclasm as an attack on his authority, and in 730 he issued an edict prohibiting the use of icons. In this edict he asserted the idea of Caesaropapism, which held that as Christ's representative on earth, the emperor had authority over

This illumination of the crucifixion and resurrection in early Byzantine style comes from a Syriac translation of the Gospels.

religious affairs as well as secular affairs. This idea was rooted in Constantine's assumption of responsibility for church disciplinary and doctrinal unity in the councils of Arles (314) and Nicaea (325). It contradicted the theory of papal authority (the Petrine doctrine; p. 119), which held that the pope was the sole vicar of Christ on earth and that religious authority and secular authority were distinct and separate.

That Leo saw the controversy in this way is not surprising. In developing an argument against iconoclasm, the monks had emphasized the separation of church and state—a view at variance with the Byzantine position. Leo and his son Constantine V (r. 741–75) were therefore strongly antimonastic—Constantine fanatically so.

Under Constantine V, the controversy over icons entered a new phase. Constantine, an intellectual and a connoisseur of art, devised a theological rationale for the iconoclastic position. He cited early Christian writers, including Eusebius, the biographer of Emperor Constantine I, who had said that the divine is not describable. From this, Constantine V argued that when a painter paints a picture of Christ, either he paints only the human form of God or else he paints both the human form and the divine form. If the former, the painter commits heresy by depicting Christ as only a human being. If the latter, he commits heresy by giving the divine a human, and therefore limiting, form. In this argument, Constantine V assumed that the image and the object depicted were one and the same and argued that the God-man Christ could only be represented in the sacrament of the Eucharist, in which the bread and the wine became His body and blood.

In 754, Constantine V called a council to Constantinople, and under his forceful guidance the members of the council adopted his position on icons. Ironically, his opponents, the iconodules (lovers of images), claimed as their intellectual champion a Syrian Christian named Mansur, better known as John of Damascus (d. after 746), who wrote the classic defense of icons— namely that once God had become man in Christ, it became permissible to represent Him in His incarnate form.

When the monks rejected the council's pronouncements, Constantine V responded by closing monasteries, drafting monks into the army, and forcing monks and nuns to marry and to take ordinary jobs. He recognized, however, that the controversy might precipitate a serious political division between the eastern and western parts of his Empire, and to prevent such a rift he married his son Leo to an Athenian, Irene, who supported the use of icons in worship. When Constantine died in 775, Leo IV moderated, but did not give up, the official position on iconoclasm. Leo died in 780, leaving a ten-year-old son as his heir, and the power of government passed to the empress Irene. Under her influence, the government began to move slowly toward restoration of icons, and in 787 she called a new council in Nicaea that reversed the iconoclastic decrees of 754.

From that time on, both the government and church favored the use of icons, though the old iconoclastic feelings remained strong in southern and eastern Asia Minor, from which the bulk of the

An iconoclast whitewashing an image in a Byzantine church (from a ninth-century psalter). In 730 Leo III issued an edict forbidding the veneration of images. For a hundred years thereafter, icons, mosaics, and frescoes in churches were destroyed or whitewashed.

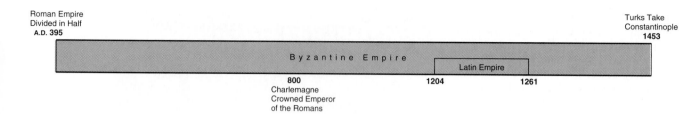

army was recruited. Consequently, the imperial court had to deal constantly with the politics of the controversy, and the court's position depended on the views of those in power. The final restoration of icons in Christian worship came in 843, but even then the government proceeded carefully. More than twenty years passed before the government moved in any overt fashion to restore images to the churches of Constantinople.

The decline of iconoclasm in the Empire was a result of both demographic and cultural changes. Demographically, expansion of the Arab Empire in Syria and in the eastern parts of Asia Minor diminished the role of Semitic Christian communities in Byzantine affairs. Culturally, a revival of secular Greek learning among the upper classes helped spread neo-Platonic ideas.

Although the struggle over iconoclasm had begun as a reflection of the ethnic diversity of the Byzantine Empire, it survived long after that diversity waned. Iconoclasm prompted a deep religious controversy between the monks, who rejected secular influence in religious affairs, and moderate churchmen, who accepted the union of ecclesiastical and secular authority in the emperor. This conflict between radicals and moderates became a perennial political problem in the Byzantine church and contributed to the later schism between the Greek and Latin churches.

THE BYZANTINE EMPIRE BETWEEN EAST AND WEST

When Leo III deflected the massive Arab invasion in 717, he did serious damage to the Arab fleet. The Arab army, however—after suffering heavy losses in engagements with Leo's Bulgarian allies—had made an easy retreat across Asia Minor. As a result, the Arabs continued their raids into Byzantine territory throughout Leo's reign, obliging him to spend much of his time leading armies to meet the threat. Meanwhile, the Slavs were migrating steadily across the Danube frontier and settling in Macedonia and Greece. The Slavs were pagans and were not converted to Christianity until late in the ninth century.

In eastern Asia Minor, where the Islamic and Byzantine worlds met, Leo's reign was an age of dashing military leaders whose feats were memorialized in heroic legends on both sides. The central government of neither the Byzantine Empire nor the Islamic Empire paid much attention to events in the border provinces.

Leo III's son Constantine V managed to consolidate the eastern frontier, but while he was doing so, the Lombards overthrew the Byzantine government in Ravenna (*ca.* 750). Constantine ignored the loss, for he recognized that maintaining Byzantine power in Italy was peripheral to the main interests of his government. This was a new attitude. Earlier, Leo III had punished Pope Gregory II (r. 715–31) for condemning iconoclasm by depriving him of jurisdiction over the churches of Dalmatia (the coastal area of modern Croatia) and southern Italy. This was a blow to the papal treasury. Moreover, it introduced jurisdictional and territorial elements into the conflict over iconoclasm.

Pope Zachary (r. 741–52) did not immediately recognize the significance of Constantine's new attitude toward Italy. When the Lombards, after taking Ravenna, turned on Rome, Zachary followed age-old custom by appealing to the emperor for help. When Constantine ignored his appeal, Zachary turned to the Franks, who had much to gain by undertaking the protection of the papal church (pp. 224–25). In fact, in 753, Zachary's successor entered into an alliance with the Frankish royal house that had momentous results for the history of western Europe.

In the second half of his reign Constantine V devoted virtually all his attention to the Bulgars, who had begun to carve a pagan empire out of the Empire's Balkan provinces. Constantine mounted nine campaigns against the Bulgars and was remembered, even by his enemies, as a successful general.

Constantine's successors were less successful. His son Leo IV survived him by only five years. After his death, the empress Irene, a cruel woman, controlled the government for her son, Constantine VI, who was ten years old when his father died (780). In 797, when Constantine VI finally tried to assert his independence, Irene had him blinded.

Irene retained power and signed her official acts "Irene Emperor." But people everywhere, except at court, felt that the Empire was without an emperor. The advisers of the Frankish king Charles the Great (Charlemagne), noting what they perceived as a vacant throne in Constantinople, urged him to resurrect the imperial title in the West. The Roman Empire had been ruled from Constantinople for centuries, and here was a chance to restore control to Rome. On Christmas day 800, Pope Leo III crowned Charles Emperor of the Romans. In 802, a rumor circulated that Charles might marry Irene, a union that would have reunited the Empire and consolidated Charles's position as emperor.

Although many people in Constantinople must have shared the westerners' view that Irene had usurped imperial authority, they regarded Charles's coronation as the presumptuous act of a barbarian who simply did not understand what it meant to be emperor. They believed that an emperor was elected by Christ, not by a pope. Though they viewed Irene as unacceptable, they thought the true emperor could only be elected in

Early map of Constantinople (fifth or sixth century).

Constantinople, not in Aix-la-Chapelle (Aachen), where Charles had his capital. Charles tried to pressure the Byzantines into recognizing him as emperor by seizing Venice, the Byzantine gateway to Europe. The Byzantines, who were engaged in more immediate dangers, responded by opening a long series of negotiations designed to get Venice back, to protect their western borders from attack by the Franks, and to resolve the legal and political dispute over the imperial title. In 813, the year before Charles died, a treaty was signed that recognized Charles as Emperor *of the Franks*.

In the meantime, the last years of Irene's rule were disastrous. The Arabs, taking advantage of the political disarray in Constantinople, invaded Asia Minor in 798 and reached the Aegean. The Byzantine government was paralyzed by competition among court officials, and Irene had drained the treasury by suspending taxes in an effort to win popularity. She was deposed in 802 by her minister of finance, Nicephorus, who declared himself emperor.

The Empires of Charlemagne and Byzantine   *ca.* A.D. 800

Irene and Nicephorus (r. 802–11) were both unfortunate to have ruled during the reign of the greatest king of the Franks, Charles (r. 768–814), and the greatest ruler of Islam, Harun al-Rashid (r. 786–809). Harun seized every opportunity to encroach on the Empire, and his great campaign of 798 was only the most spectacular of his many ventures. During Nicephorus's reign, Charles and Harun intensified the threat to Constantinople by exchanging embassies. After the death of Charles and Harun, their successors were occupied with internal political troubles, and the danger to the Empire faded. Leo V (r. 813–20) managed to restore a measure of stability to the frontiers, but during his reign the first signs of an important socioeconomic change in the Empire began to emerge.

Byzantine Society and Economy and the Founding of the Macedonian Dynasty

The Byzantine army and navy drew their manpower from the conscription of peasant-soldiers in the administrative districts (*themes*) of Asia Minor. The interior prov-

inces provided infantry troops, while the maritime provinces supplied the fleet. Since the seventh century the Byzantine emperors had been careful to safeguard the prosperity of the yeoman class that provided their military manpower. When the provinces were devastated by war, famine, or disease, the emperors had repopulated them with contingents of small farmers drawn from tribes along the imperial borders. That practice had given the imperial forces remarkable stability.

In the early ninth century, however, the devastations of the Bulgars and Arabs ruined so many of the small farmers that the policy was no longer effective. The rural aristocracy, which had provided the military leadership of the provinces, created great estates by buying out the ruined farmers, who either became tenants or migrated to the cities. Though the process was slow, it did great damage to the Empire's economy and its military establishment. Moreover, it increased the power of the aristocratic generals, because their soldiers were now their tenants.

During this time, the Arabs made new incursions into the Byzantine territories. They took Crete and used it as a base for disrupting Byzantine shipping in the Aegean and the eastern Mediterranean. At the same time, North African Moors began a conquest of Sicily, which had been under Byzantine control since the time of Justinian. The Byzantines tried several times to enlist the Franks in an alliance against the Moors, but inevitably negotiations faltered over the question of the imperial title. By the early tenth century, the Moors controlled both Sicily and southern Italy.

The mid-ninth century was a period of weakness in Byzantine government. The government was conducted by a shaky regency for Michael III (r. 842–67), an alcoholic homosexual. After 852, the regents were Basil, formerly an Armenian stableboy, who may have been Michael's lover, and Bardas, Michael's uncle. Basil, an illiterate, was a man of towering stature and impressive strength in a court often dominated by eunuchs. Bardas was a man of great culture and a patron of the intellectual and artistic community in Constantinople. In 866, Basil murdered Bardas and took control of the government. A year later, when Michael went mad and threatened him, Basil had him killed and declared himself emperor.

An illiterate ruler in a highly literate society, Basil I founded a dynasty that brought the Byzantine Empire to its highest level of prosperity and culture. Though Armenian by ethnic origin, Basil had been born in Macedonia and was called "the Macedonian." The dynasty he founded is called the Macedonian dynasty.

Byzantine Culture and Relations with the West in the Mid-Ninth Century

During the ten years of his co-regency, before Basil had him murdered, Bardas sponsored a brilliant flowering of art, literature, and science. He brought about a renaissance of classical studies to which we owe the preservation of many ancient Greek literary and philosophical works. The center of this renaissance was Photius, a friend of Bardas who became patriarch—that is, head of the church of Constantinople. Bardas reestablished the secular university in Constantinople,

while Photius reformed the education of the clergy. Photius, the most learned man of his age, put together a monumental work called *Myriobiblion* (*The Library*), a compendium of history, philosophy, and theology. Among his associates in the court school were two world-renowned scholars, Leo the Mathematician and Constantine the Philosopher. The Islamic ruler in Baghdad invited Leo, whom Bardas named first rector of the university, to his court, which had an avid interest in mathematics and astronomy (p. 208). Constantine became a missionary to the Slavs and created a script for writing the Slavonic language (pp. 332–33). The university Bardas founded continued as a center of education, scholarship, and culture for two centuries.

In 858, Pope Nicholas I (r. 858–67), an intransigent, forceful man who was allied with the enemies of Photius, launched an investigation into how Photius had become patriarch of Constantinople. During

Interior view of St. Mark's cathedral, Venice. The mosaics were done by Byzantine artists (tenth century).

the inquiry, Nicholas suggested that it was time to restore to Rome the dioceses that the Byzantine emperor Leo III had removed from Roman jurisdiction in 731 (p. 178). Photius, who did not recognize the jurisdiction of the pope, replied that the emperor, Michael III, was not willing to do so.

What Nicholas had in mind was not just the recovery of long-lost territory and income but control of a whole new sector of Christendom. The Slavs and the Bulgars were ready to become Christians, and the Bulgarian Khan Boris was negotiating with both Frankish bishops and Constantinople about which church he should commit his people to. Nicholas wanted to recover Dalmatia to use as a base for missionary activity in eastern Europe. Photius sent his own missionaries to Boris and to Moravia, and in 865 Boris submitted to Constantinople. But the competition for the Slavs and the Bulgars, to which the

dispute over Photius's elevation was related, continued for the next six years, until at last the Bulgarians were committed to the Eastern church.

In the meantime, Nicholas found occasion to spell out for the Byzantine emperor and his patriarch the full theory of papal authority, relying on a document known as the *Donation of Constantine*. This document purported to record the donation of Rome and the western half of the Roman Empire that Constantine I (r. 312–37) made to Pope Sylvester I (r. 314–35) when Constantine moved his capital to Byzantium. Actually, the document had been written in the West some time during the first half of the ninth century, but it was not exposed as a forgery until 1440. Photius replied to Nicholas's argument in a learned, elegant document in which he refuted the *Donation* on every point. He argued that Constantine had retained both his spiritual authority and his secular authority when he moved to Byzantium and that the patriarch, as the emperor's principal ecclesiastical official, enjoyed status at least equal to that of the pope. This argument went back to Constantine I's claims to apostolic status made when he established his capital in Constantinople.

At this time, Basil I deposed Photius, thereby making rapprochement with the papacy possible. But Pope Nicholas had died, and his successor did not pursue the matter. Despite countless attempts to resolve it, the so-called Photian Schism between the Eastern and Western churches persists to this day.

THE MACEDONIAN PERIOD

Basil I

Basil I (r. 867–86) was determined to recover the West for the Empire. First he tried to engage the Frankish king of Italy, Louis II, who called himself emperor, in an alliance against the Moors, whose strongholds in southern Italy threatened Louis as well as the old Byzantine cities. But when Louis's claim to the imperial title proved an obstacle, Basil proceeded by himself. Under the great admiral Niceph-

---

The *Donation of Constantine*

Constantine tells how Pope Sylvester I cured him of leprosy. In gratitude Constantine accepts baptism and decrees

that the sacred see of blessed Peter shall be gloriously exalted above our empire and earthly throne. . . . And the pontiff who presides over the most holy Roman Church shall be the highest and chief of all priests . . . and according to his decision shall all matters be settled . . . for the worship of God or the confirmation of the faith.

We convey to the most blessed pontiff, our father Silvester, universal pope, both our palace [the Lateran] and likewise all provinces, places and districts of the City of Rome and Italy and of the regions of the West, . . . bequeathing them to the power and sway of him and his successors.

Wherefore we have perceived that our empire and the power of our government should be transferred to the regions of the East . . . for it is not right that an earthly emperor should have authority . . . where the head of the Christian religion has been established by the Emperor of heaven.

From the Donation of Constantine, *as quoted in* Select Documents of European History, *ed. by R. G. D. Laffan (London: Methuen, 1930), Vol. 1. pp. 4–5.*

orus Phocas, Byzantine forces made steady, though difficult, progress in southern Italy while the Moors consolidated their hold over Sicily. Following the example of Photius, Basil sent missionaries to the southern Slavs who had settled Dalmatia and Greece and established provincial administrations along the eastern coast of the Adriatic Sea, entering into close ties with Venice.

While pursuing his goal in the West, Basil also carried on a series of campaigns in the East. Here his armies regained strategically important territories and cities and kept the Arab armies at bay. By coordinating land and sea operations in the eastern Mediterranean he was able to maintain the upper hand against the Arab fleets. He defeated the pirates of Crete several times and may even have occupied the island for a while. In sum, Basil made an excellent start on reestablishing the Empire's territorial integrity and its military superiority against its traditional enemies.

Basil also undertook important governmental reforms. He commissioned the writing of a manual of administrative practice, which served as a guide to the bureaucracy until the publication of *On the Administration of the Empire*, written by Emperor Constantine VII, Basil's grandson. He also commissioned a new law code to clear away the clutter and confusion caused by the controversy over iconoclasm and the accumulation of cases and learned treatises.

In 879, Basil began to lose his sanity. Control of the government fell to the patriarch and other leading court figures. This was a time of intensive palace intrigue, which ended in 886 when the mad emperor was assassinated—probably by friends of his twenty-year-old son Leo. Unlike his father, Leo V (r. 886–912) was a highly educated, scholarly man.

Leo V

Like his predecessors, Leo V faced difficult military problems throughout his reign. In the eastern Mediterranean the Arab fleets had recovered and were once again doing great damage to coastal cities and shipping. Following Basil's example, Leo made the navy the Empire's principal military force. However, in 911 most of the Byzantine fleet was lost in a great battle with the Arabs.

Greek fire, a mixture of quicklime, petroleum, and sulfur that ignited when it came in contact with water, was introduced into the Byzantine navy after 675. It was a very effective weapon against the Arabs (detail from a fourteenth-century manuscript).

Meanwhile, the Bulgarian frontier was quiet. Though the Khan Boris (r. 852–89) had converted to Christianity in 865, many of his people remained pagans, and the last years of his reign were disturbed by religious conflict. In 889, Boris abdicated in favor of his eldest son Vladimir, a pagan. At this point, a civil war broke out that lasted until 893, when Vladimir was overthrown by his Christian, Byzantine-educated brother Symeon. These internal struggles kept the Bulgars occupied for a time. After consolidating his power, however, Symeon engaged in new attacks on the European provinces of the Empire.

Throughout these years of turmoil, Leo still managed to carry out important administrative reforms. He established new provinces in southern Italy and upper Mesopotamia, and he strengthened the *themes* to serve as the first line of defense against the Arabs' ceaseless raids. He completed the legal code begun by his father and issued 113 edicts designed to promote good government in church and state. He understood the importance of the church, and to ensure its loyalty to the crown he named his younger brother, Stephen, patriarch. From this point on, the Eastern church was not only a department of state but also an appendage of the imperial family. Finally, he regulated commerce through publication of the *Book of the Eparch*. The eparch was the leading official of Byzantine government, and the book spelled out his jurisdiction over guilds and corporations. Byzantine writers called the emperor "Leo the Wise."

The end of Leo's reign was troubled by a controversy over his fourth marriage. Both religious and civil law prohibited a man from marrying even a third time, unless it was absolutely necessary for continuation of his family; fourth marriages were out of the question. By 905 Leo had been married three times and was still without a male heir. When his mistress gave birth to a male in September of that year, he was determined to legitimize the child. He sought a dispensation from the legal prohibition and eventually forced the patriarch to permit him to marry the boy's mother. The patriarch's acquiescence set off a sharp debate within the church.

Romanus and Constantine VII

Leo V died in 912 and was succeeded by his seven-year-old son Constantine VII. Leo's dissolute brother Alexander now competed with Constantine's mother for control of the regency government. The competition encouraged the Bulgarian Symeon to claim the imperial title for himself, and when he was denied the title he launched a destructive war that raged for eleven years (913–24). In 919, a military commander named Romanus seized control of the government, married his daughter to the young emperor, and had himself crowned co-emperor with his son-in-law. Romanus (r. 920–44) entered into an alliance with the Slavs in the Balkans against Symeon of Bulgaria, and by the time the old khan died in 927 the Bulgarian threat had been contained.

Meanwhile, the eastern armies had been waging a brilliant campaign against the Arabs, putting the Byzantines on the offensive in the East. Moreover, the Empire established itself in Armenia and pushed into the Caucasus, the mountainous region between the Black Sea and the Caspian Sea. In the north, Romanus fought a war against the Russians, which ended in a lasting treaty (945).

When Romanus was overthrown by his own sons, the mob in Constantinople demanded that Constantine VII be named sole emperor. Then nearly forty years old, he had spent his life as a scholar while his father-in-law ruled as co-emperor. Still uneasy about his legitimacy, Constantine VII took the title Porphyrogenitus ("born in the purple"—that is, as the legitimate heir).

During Constantine VII's reign as sole emperor (944–59), literature, science, arts, and crafts flourished under his patronage. The period is considered the golden age of the renaissance that had begun nearly a century earlier under Bardas. Court scholars produced manuals of military strategy and books of law, philosophy, history, and theology. Many of these works were made up of snippets from the great works of the past, and, because many of the originals have been lost, we owe a debt to the mid-tenth-century compilers for preserving at least parts of them. Constantine himself compiled a great work on the ceremony of the Byzantine court, which is the principal source of our knowledge about those rituals. He also wrote a book on the history and practice of imperial administration and diplomacy, mentioned above, to guide his son Romanus II.

Following his grandfather Basil's example, Constantine VII carried on negotiations with the European kings, the successors of Charles the Great, and in 949 the German king Otto I (r. 936–73) sent an embassy to Constantinople. A proposed marriage was arranged between Romanus II and Otto's daughter, and tutors were sent to Otto's court to teach the young girl the Greek language and Byzantine manners. The marriage never took place, however, because Romanus rashly married another woman. The plan to link the German and the imperial houses was realized in the next generation, when Otto II (r. 973–83) married Theophano, daughter of Romanus II.

In the years from 959, when Constantine VII died, to 976, when his grandson Basil II succeeded to the throne, the military aristocracy was growing more and more powerful. Since the ninth century, when the strength of the yeoman class had declined (p. 180), the aristocracy had exercised economic and political control of the provinces. In 963, the naval commander Nicephorus Phocas, a descendant of the admiral who had served Basil I, seized power and in 969 was succeeded by the aristocratic general John (r. 969–76). Together these two men restored the Byzantine military system and recovered territory that had been lost by the Empire. But the idea that the emperor must be legitimate remained strong, and John's successor was Basil II, a peculiar man who is considered the greatest of the Byzantine emperors.

Basil II

Basil II (r. 976–1025) never married and seems to have avoided women. Although he grew up in a society that set a high value on the cultured life, Basil was totally uninterested in education, learning, and the arts. He was an ascetic, a man out of place; he was also a military genius.

Like Constantine V in the eighth century, Basil went out against the Bulgarians year after year. At one time he repatriated 14,000 Bulgarian prisoners of war, all of whom had been blinded. He was known as "the Bulgar Slayer." He also pacified the Russians, with the help of a force of Varangian (Scandinavian) troops. About 989 he entered into a treaty by which the Russian prince of Kiev would become a Christian and marry a member of the imperial family. Basil transformed the Varangians into an elite imperial guard. In the medieval Scandinavian sagas, service in the guard was considered a sign of high birth and great ability as a warrior, for the emperor was said to accept only men from the best families who had proven themselves in war.

At the turn of the eleventh century, Basil II campaigned successfully against the Arabs of Syria and moved forcefully into the provinces south of the Caucasus. In 1001, he entered into a ten-year truce with the Islamic ruler in Baghdad.

At home, Basil turned his attention to the military aristocracy, which, as we have seen, had become a dominant force in Byzantine society. The consolidation of small holdings into huge landed estates had ruined the small farmers, the ancient basis of Byzantine prosperity. Moreover, the landed aristocracy had a strong instinct toward independence and viewed the central government with suspicion and hostility. The reforms of the *themes* under Leo V at the beginning of the tenth century had further strengthened the provinces and their leading aristocratic families, and since that time most of the periodic rebellions against the central government had been fomented by the landed aristocracy. The destitution of the yeoman class, in addition to reducing the manpower available to the Empire, had widened the gap between rich and poor.

On January 1, 996, Basil issued a decree that required the great landholders to produce documentary proof that they had owned their land for at least 75 years.

If someone was occupying formerly government land, as shown by records in the imperial archives, he had to produce proof of ownership going back 1,000 years. That meant he would have to come up with an authentic document that had been preserved in the family since the reign of Augustus (r. 27 B.C.–A.D. 14)! With the support of the army and the populace, Basil managed to enforce this radical legislation and in doing so reduced many great families to poverty. A few years later, he added to the burden of rich landowners by requiring that they make up any deficit in the tax collections from the villages under their control. The law hit the churches hardest, but Basil ignored their protests and pleas for relief.

These measures halted the economic decline of the Empire for a generation and served to weaken the power of the aristocracy. After Basil's death in 1025, however, the great families recovered. Between 1025 and 1081, the civilian bureaucracy and the provincial military artistocracy competed fiercely for control of the Empire, each side setting up emperors who supported it. The bureaucracy found its emperors among members of the Macedonian dynasty, while the aristocrats put up men from their own ranks. Through most of this period, the bureaucracy held the upper hand. It tried to weaken the aristocracy by reducing the size of the army. When the Macedonian dynasty died out in the middle of the century, the Empire's military establishment was in ruins.

BYZANTIUM AND THE WEST

The Foundation of the Commenian Dynasty

During this same period, while competition for power was weakening the Empire, its enemies were making inroads into the imperial territories. In the West, the Normans—from Normandy in northern France—conquered southern Italy (p. 274), driving out the Byzantines and the Arabs alike. In the North, the Patzinaks, an Asiatic people, threatened the Danubian border. Most serious, in the East, the Seljuk

Turks, who had come out of Central Asia, attacked the eastern provinces of the Empire (see pp. 211–12).

When the Turks devastated large areas of Asia Minor, an aristocrat named Romanus Diogenes seized the opportunity to mount the imperial throne. In 1071, he mustered what was left of the Byzantine army and met the Turks at Manzikert. There he suffered a disastrous defeat and was himself captured. After promising to pay a huge ransom, he discovered that the civilian bureaucracy had staged a coup d'état. Consequently, the promise he made to pay tribute to the Turks, which might have given the Empire some respite, went by the boards. That same year, the Normans captured Bari on the west coast of southern Italy and were in a position to invade Greece.

During the next decade, rival claimants to the Byzantine throne entered into alliances with the Turks and the Normans, hastening conquest from both the east and the west. In this time of crisis, the Ducas family, which had been supported by the bureaucracy, allied itself with the greatest of the aristocratic generals, Alexius Comnenus, who married a Ducas princess and became emperor in 1081.

By the time Alexius (r. 1081–1118) came to power, the Normans had crossed the Adriatic and were trying to conquer Epirus. Their leader, Robert Guiscard, wanted to become emperor himself. To deal with the Norman threat, Alexius made peace with the Turks and the Patzinaks, granting them, as vassals of the imperial throne, the territories they had already conquered. He then entered into an alliance with the Venetians, who since the tenth century had been building their commercial and maritime strength. The Venetians agreed to help the Byzantines in return for a monopoly of trade in the imperial territories. With this assistance, Alexius managed to drive the Normans out of Epirus.

Since the 1070s the Byzantine emperors had been appealing to the western powers for help against the infidel Turks. The Turkish conquest of Jerusalem in 1077 added urgency to the appeal, but not until 1095 was Pope Urban II (r. 1088–99)

able to organize a great crusade of Western knights to reconquer the Holy Land.

Although the fall of Jerusalem induced the westerners to join the battle against the Turks, Alexius's real purpose was to use the westerners to reconquer his lost territories in Asia Minor. He had little interest in the Holy Land. When the crusaders arrived at Constantinople, however, he found that their leaders were headstrong men determined to establish independent Latin principalities in the Holy Land. The crusaders passed through Asia Minor to engage the Turks in Palestine. When the westerners had won the major cities there, Alexius found that he had yet another enemy in the Middle East.

Like his diplomatic policies, Alexius's economic policies produced ambiguous results. He restored the value of the currency after decades of decline, but he also doubled taxes, which were already heavy. Moreover, the Venetian monopoly of trade kept prices artificially high. Late in his reign, Alexius tried to counter Venetian power by granting trading privileges to Venice's rival, Pisa, but this move merely intensified competition between the two cities.

Alexius also tried to strengthen the army by increasing the number of land grants made in return for military service. In the long run, this practice further increased the number of large estates and the power of the provincial military aristocracy. Those consequences did not surface until after Alexius's reign, however.

Finally, Alexius was a vigorous supporter of scholarship, at least of that aimed at the recovery of the past rather than at the discovery of new knowledge. Not surprisingly, the greatest works produced during his reign were histories. Michael Psellus wrote an exhaustive history of the Empire, the *Chronographia*, and Alexius's daughter Anna wrote a history of his reign. These works are valuable sources for modern historians.

The First Collapse of the Empire

The struggle to restore the Empire faltered during the last two decades of the twelfth century. After Alexius's death in 1118,

the Byzantines had failed to escape the Italians' commercial control, and rising power among the provincial aristocracy had led to creation of independent armies throughout the provinces. Between 1181 and 1204, the Serbians, one of the Slavic peoples that had settled in the Balkans, created an empire, and the Bulgarians reasserted their power. Meanwhile, the Norman rulers of southern Italy continued to covet the imperial crown, and in the late 1180s the German king Henry VI inherited the Normans' goals when he mounted their throne (p. 319).

In 1204 the pope assembled another great crusade—the fourth—and the Venetians were engaged to ferry the crusading army to the Holy Land. Over the years the

A Crusader's View of Byzantium

Odo of Deuil, the author of this piece, was a historian of the Second Crusade.

And then the Greeks degenerated entirely into women; putting aside all manly vigor, both of words and of spirit, they lightly swore whatever they thought would please us, but they neither kept faith with us nor maintained respect for themselves. In general they really have the opinion that anything which is done for the holy empire cannot be considered perjury. . . . When the Greeks are afraid they become despicable in their excessive abasement, and when they have the upper hand they are arrogant. . . .

Constantinople itself is squalid and fetid. . . . People live lawlessly in this city, which has as many lords as rich men and almost as many thieves as poor men. . . . In every respect she exceeds moderation, for just as she surpasses other cities in wealth, so too does she surpass them in vice. . . .

[The bishop of Langres] added that Constantinople is Christian only in name and not in fact . . . and that her emperor had ventured a few years ago to attack the [Crusader] prince of Antioch. . . . "Though it was his [the emperor's] duty to ward off the nearby infidels by uniting the Christian forces, with the aid of the infidels he strove to destroy the Christians."

From Odo of Deuil, De profectione Ludovici VII in orientem, *trans. by V. G. Berry (New York: Columbia University Press, 1948), pp. 57, 65, 69.*

A Byzantine View of the Crusaders

Anna Comnena, the author of this piece, was the daughter of the Emperor Alexius I.

Now he [the emperor] dreaded the arrival of the Crusaders, for he knew their irresistible manner of attack, their unstable and mobile character, and all the peculiar . . . characteristics which the Frank retains throughout; and he also knew that they were always agape for money, and seemed to disregard their truces readily for any reason that cropped up. . . . The simpler-minded Franks were urged on by the real desire of worshipping at our Lord's Sepulchre, but the more astute, especially men like Bohemund . . . had another secret reason, namely the hope that . . . they might by some means be able to seize the capital itself. . . . For the Frankish race . . . is always very hotheaded and eager, but when it has once espoused a cause, it is uncontrollable.

From Anna Comnena, The Alexiad, *trans. by E. A. S. Dawes (London: Kegan Paul, 1928), pp. 248, 250.*

Women of the Byzantine Imperial Family

Imperial women played an important role in Byzantine affairs. They were well educated and often exercised great political power. Here is a description by Anna Comnena, daughter of Emperor Alexius I (1081–1118), of her paternal grandmother Anna. The younger Anna wrote an excellent history of her father's reign.

[At the beginning of Alexius's reign] He [Alexius] really longed that his mother rather than himself should take the helm of the state. . . . Therefore in all daily business he did nothing, not even a trifling thing, without her advice. . . . When . . . Robert's [the Norman ruler of Italy] crossing in Epirus forced Alexius to leave the capital [he entrusted] his mother single-handed with the imperial government. . . . For my grandmother was so clever in business and so skilful in guiding a State, and setting it in order, that she was capable of not only administering the Roman Empire, but any other of all the countries the sun shines upon. She was a woman of wide experience and knew the nature of things. . . . To put it concisely, the situation was as follows, he indeed had the semblance of reigning but she really reigned— moreover she drew up laws, administered and directed everything; all her orders, written or unwritten, he [Alexius] confirmed by his seal or by word. . . . "

From Anna Comnena, The Alexiad, *trans. by Elizabeth A. S. Dawes (New York: Barnes & Noble, 1967), pp. 82, 83, 85–86.*

westerners had come to resent the Byzantines for a good many reasons: The Venetians resented Byzantine tampering with their trading privileges; church leaders resented Byzantine reluctance to reunite the two churches; and the military leaders of the crusade resented Byzantine attempts to take over the Latin principalities in the Middle East. Hence the Venetian Doge Dandolo found it easy to convince the crusaders that they should besiege Constantinople on behalf of the Venetians. He counted the attack on the city as partial payment for the cost of transportation, which the crusaders could not afford. Constantinople fell to the crusaders in July 1204.

Although the Westerners established an emperor of their own in Constantinople, the Empire had ceased to exist. In western Asia Minor, Byzantine émigrés set up the Empire of Nicaea. To the east was the Sultanate of Iconium, part of the old Seljuk Empire. In the northeast, survivors of the Comnenian dynasty established the Empire of Trebizond. On the Greek peninsula, the Despotate of Epirus became an independent Byzantine state, while Athens became the center of a Frankish duchy. Venice controlled most of the major coastal cities and their surrounding territory. In 1261 a Byzantine general, Michael VIII Paleologus (r. 1259–82), recaptured Constantinople and founded a new dynasty, which presided over the last two centuries of the Byzantine Empire.

THE AGE OF THE PALEOLOGI EMPERORS

That the Empire survived as long as it did under Michael Paleologus and his successors is evidence of the diplomatic skills of the Paleologi. The Empire was constantly threatened from all sides. In the West, the Normans in southern Italy were succeeded first by the Germans and then by the French, and these successors continued to seek the imperial crown, repeatedly plotting with Byzantine dissidents and the heirs of the Western emperors of Constantinople to retake the city.

The Westerners justified their designs on Constantinople by arguing that the

The Latin Empire of Constantinople   1204–61

easterners were heretics and schismatics who did not recognize the primacy of the Roman church. So Michael VIII decided to negotiate with the pope over the unification of the Eastern and Western churches. The negotiations resulted in an agreement, embodied in an act of union, which was announced at a great church council held in the French city of Lyon in 1274. But the agreement raised a storm of protest in the East, and people of every class and condition ended up in imperial prisons. The act of union had failed.

Despite Michael's success in keeping his enemies at bay, his realm was only a minor state among all those that had been established by westerners and Turks on the old territories of the Empire. It was exhausted both militarily and economically. Michael's successors faced new enemies, the Serbs in the West and the Ottoman Turks in the East. During the fourteenth century the Serbs established a powerful state that included Bulgaria and most of the Empire's Balkan provinces, and the Ottoman Turks conquered all of Asia Minor. By 1329, the Empire controlled only a few cities along the western coast of Asia Minor, and the Turks sat across the Bosporus in view of Constantinople.

The following decades were a time of civil war and palace intrigue in Constantinople, with the Ottomans extending their conquests into Thrace and Thessalonica. By the end of the fourteenth century, the Ottoman Turks had defeated the Serbs and their allies in several battles and had surrounded Constantinople. At this point, the Mongols, a people from eastern Asia led by Timur (called Tamerlane in the West), swept down on the Ottoman Turks and crushed them in 1401. But the Empire was too weak to take advantage of the situation. The Ottoman Turks eventually recovered from the disaster, and in 1453 Sultan Muhammed II brought a powerful army, supported by artillery he had acquired in the West, against Constantinople. After nearly two months of attacks and bombardment, he took the city on May 29. The last Byzantine emperor, Constantine XI, a capable man who had tried to cope with an impossible situation, died in the fighting. By 1461, the Turks had conquered all the remnants of Byzantine power, and the Empire was no more.

BYZANTINE GOVERNMENT

At the center of Byzantine government was an extensive, elaborate bureaucracy. Entry into the civil service rested on education, and the bureaucrats created a system of secular education focused on the study of Greek literature, philosophy, and science. Students began by learning Greek grammar and by memorizing Homer's epics and other great works. Normally, students completed this stage by age fourteen and then went on to study rhetoric, philosophy, and science. This system produced an elite of highly educated men. Although the small group of aristocratic families that dominated the bureaucracy had assurance that their sons would be properly educated for government service, any talented young man could gain access to the academic program and enter the power elite.

The bureaucracy was divided into departments. The chancellor ran the department responsible for all state correspondence. The postmaster general headed the department that operated the Empire's extensive communications system. And the *Sacellarius* (treasurer) headed the financial department. Lesser officers, too numerous to list, were supported by bureaucracies of their own. Most officers of the imperial household were eunuchs, who could be trusted because they could never usurp the imperial throne; both social custom and law determined that only men who could produce heirs could be legitimate emperors. Military officers had no place in the bureaucracy and were in constant competition with the civilian officeholders.

The military served as governors of the provinces, or *themes*. At the beginning of the ninth century, there were ten *themes*; by the end of the century, 26; and by the end of the twelfth century, 52. The emperors continually subdivided the *themes* to prevent the military aristocracy from using them as power bases and kept the governors under close surveillance. For example, a financial officer in each *theme* reported directly to the imperial government. In addition, the emperors maintained an effective intelligence network staffed by professional spies.

The center of government was the emperor. The Byzantines considered themselves the direct heirs of the Romans, and like the Romans they entrusted absolute power to the emperor. In both Roman law and Byzantine law, whenever the imperial throne was vacant, power resided in the people. In theory, the people elected the emperor and transferred their power to him. This fiction was symbolized in the rituals that accompanied the raising of a new emperor to the throne. The people in attendance at the ceremony yelled an acclamation that proclaimed the transfer of power from them to the emperor.

The Byzantine emperor was viewed as the vicar of Christ on earth, head of the church as well as of the state (Caesaropapism). He appointed the patriarchs of Constantinople and other bishops, and he promulgated both civil and ecclesiastical statutes. Although a divinely ordained emperor could not legally be removed, rebellion against him was justified. A successful rebellion was a sign from God that it was time to change emperors. An unsuccessful rebellion was viewed as treason against both God and emperor.

To symbolize this divine autocracy, the Byzantines developed an elaborate court ceremony patterned on the liturgy of the church. Every appearance and every act of the emperor was carried out according to a rigid ritual that dramatized the majesty of the imperial office. At the same time, the ceremonies prescribed the manner in which the emperor was to behave and reminded him of his responsibility to uphold justice and good government. Although Byzantine history is full of scoundrels, palace revolutions, and intrigue, Byzantine government was more stable and more consistent in both theory and practice than that of any other Mediterranean state.

BYZANTINE SOCIETY

The Empire embraced both the society of Constantinople and the society of the provinces. During its classical age, from the eighth to the twelfth centuries, the population of Constantinople ranged between 500,000 and 800,000. It was divided into three classes—the bureaucrats, the commercial class, and the poor. The commercial class, which included merchants, tradesmen, and small shopkeepers, was by far the largest. The bureaucratic class was smaller but still numbered in the thousands. The poor class may have numbered around 30,000.

Although the commercial class was huge, its upper crust of merchants never evolved into a powerful force in society or the state. Until the eleventh century, the government rigidly controlled all commerce by regulating the trade guilds. When government control broke down at the end of the eleventh century, the Venetians and other Italians took over Byzantine commerce.

The breakdown of government control extended to the countryside as well. Until the late eleventh century, the government had obliged the rural districts to supply specified quantities of foodstuffs to Constantinople. And it had kept food prices low, making it possible for people with low incomes to survive in the city. Moreover, the emperor, the church, and the leading citizens of the city carried on an extensive program of charities. Giving to the poor became a regular practice among upper-class families, and throughout the city were many hospitals and charitable institutions of various kinds. In a sense, the poor constituted a professional class, and companies of beggars carefully guarded the best places to beg.

Even so, life was hard for the lower classes. With the demise of government control over the countryside, food prices rose sharply. Clothing, which had always been expensive, became even more costly. Housing was grossly inadequate. Thousands of people slept in archways and in any sheltered spot they could find. Garbage and sewage fouled the streets, and disease was endemic. Not surprisingly, the sale of perfumes and aromatic herbs was brisk among the wealthy to mask the odors and to guard against disease.

Although the late Roman and Byzantine law gave women substantial rights, Byzantine women were constrained by elaborate rules of etiquette. Respectable women wore veils whenever they left

A Byzantine lady of rank (late fifth or early sixth century). Note her elegantly draped mantle and the snoodlike bonnet of the imperial type.

home, and they were expected to show diffidence toward guests in their homes. Constraints often led to secret liaisons and falls from respectability. Among lower-class women, prostitution was common. The owners of taverns and baths often maintained brothels, and pimps were easy to find. Historians estimate that at any given time there may have been thousands of prostitutes in the city.

Out in the provinces, life was hard but healthier than life in the cities. Until the middle of the ninth century, as we have seen, the central government repopulated devastated areas and curtailed the growth of the great estates. As a result, the rural population became multicultural, and the military officers who trained and led the peasant-soldiers were obliged to become familiar with at least one vernacular language.

The yeomen farmers lived in villages of from 50 to 500 people, depending on

Early Byzantine jewelry contained Hellenistic and Roman features. The clasp of this late-sixth-century necklace, for example, is of a Hellenistic type, while the cylindrical slides between the pendants are a late Roman feature.

the productivity of the land, and each family owned its own land. Some men escaped country life by entering the army or by seeking an education. Rural monasteries ran schools for talented young men, preparing them to enter the bureaucracy or the church.

Over the centuries from the sixth century to the fifteenth century, the eastern half of the old Roman Empire evolved into an imperial state that exercised a powerful influence on the political, economic, and cultural history of the Mediterranean Basin. From Scandinavia to Baghdad, the Byzantine Empire centered in Constantinople was regarded with awe and envy. For Europeans, it was a nostalgic reminder of the Roman Empire, the ideal state they still hoped to resurrect one day. For the rulers of Islam, the Empire was a formidable enemy that commanded their unwavering attention and absorbed immense resources. The Empire protected the Europeans from the Arabs until 1453, when it ceased to exist.

For a thousand years the Byzantine Empire withstood invasion and attack on all sides. And, during those centuries of turmoil, it produced a memorable civilization. Byzantine art and architecture influenced all the civilizations of the Mediterranean, and Byzantine scholars preserved Hellenistic learning for posterity. Byzantine government was a model of efficiency and its educated bureaucrats set forth the tasks and functions of government in classic works. In short, Byzantine civilization was an essential ingredient in the evolution of Western culture.

Suggestions for Further Reading

General

The leading general histories of the Byzantine Empire are G. Ostrogorsky, *History of the Byzantine State*, 2nd ed. (1968), which focuses on political history, and *Cambridge Medieval History*, Vol. 4 (2 parts), ed. J. M. Hussey (1966–67), which contains excellent articles on all aspects of Byzantine history and culture. On the early period, see A. H. M. Jones, *The Later Roman Empire*, 2 vols. (1964). On Constantine, see the works cited in Chapter 4. P. Charanis treats Anastasius I in *Church and State in the Later Roman Empire* (1974). On Justinian, see J. W. Barker, *Justinian and the Later Roman Empire* (1966), and R. Browning, *Justinian and Theodora* (1971). On the Heraclian dynasty, see R. Jenkins, *Byzantium: The Imperial Centuries, A.D. 610–1071* (1966).

On Iconoclasm, see E. J. Martin, *History of the Iconoclastic Controversy* (1930); S. Gero, *Byzantine Iconoclasm during the*

Reign of Leo III (1973) and *Byzantine Iconoclasm during the Reign of Constantine V* (1977). On Irene, see C. Diehl, *Byzantine Empresses* (1963). For a history of the Byzantine church, see R. M. French, *The Eastern Orthodox Church* (1951); G. Every, *The Byzantine Patriarchate (451–1204)*, 2nd ed. (1962); and H. Margoulias, *Byzantine Christianity: Emperor, Church, and the West* (1970). On Caesaropapism, see E. Barker, *Social and Political Thought in Byzantium* (1957), and D. J. Geanakoplos, "'Caesaropapism' in Byzantium," in *Byzantine East & Latin West* (1966). On the relations between East and West, see F. Dvornik, *Byzantium and the Roman Primacy* (1966), and *The Photian Schism* (1950); H. Pirenne, *Mohammed and Charlemagne* (1939); and C. Brand, *Byzantium Confronts the West: 1180–1204* (1968). On the fourth crusade, see D. Queller, *The Fourth Crusade* (1977), and on the Byzantine recovery after 1261, see D. J. Geanakoplos, *Emperor Michael Paleologus and the West* (1959). For a history of the Bulgarians, see S. Runciman, *A History of the First Bulgarian Empire* (1930), and on eastern Europe, see F. Dvornik, *The Making of Central and Eastern Europe* (1949), and M. Spinka, *A History of Christianity in the Balkans* (1933).

Byzantine Civilization

For a picture of classical Byzantine civilization, see A. Toynbee, *Constantine Porphyrogenitus and his World* (1973); J. M. Hussey, *Church and Learning in the Byzantine Empire 867–1185* (1937) and *The Byzantine World*, 2nd ed. (1961); and S. Runciman, *Byzantine Civilization* (1933). On Byzantine art, see D. Talbot Rice, *The Art of Byzantium* (1959). On the economic life of Byzantium, see the articles in the *Cambridge Economic History of Europe*, Vol. 1 (1942). A. P. Kazhdan and A. W. Epstein, *Change in Byzantine Culture in the Eleventh and Twelfth Centuries* (1985), cover a wide range of topics, including society, daily life, education, art, and government. The classic study of Byzantine government is J. B. Bury, *The Imperial Administrative System in the Ninth Century* (1911). See Michael Psellus, *Fourteen Byzantine Rulers* (*Chronographia*), trans. E. R. A. Sewter (1966), and *The Alexiad of Anna Comnena*, trans. E. R. A. Sewter (1969). D. J. Geanakoplos, *Byzantium: Church, Society, and Civilization Seen Through Contemporary Eyes* (1986) contains a large collection of sources.

End of the Byzantine Empire

On the capture of Constantinople by the Franks, see K. M. Setton, *A History of the Crusades*, Vol. 2 (1962). On the Latin period, see M. Angold, *A Byzantine Government in Exile: Government and Society under the Laskarids of Nicaea, 1204–1261* (1975). On the fall of the Byzantine Empire, see D. M. Nicol, *The Last Centuries of Byzantium, 1261–1453* (1972), and P. Wittek, *The Rise of the Ottoman Empire* (1938).

8

ISLAM AND THE RISE OF THE ARAB EMPIRE

From the middle of the seventh century on, the Arab Empire, founded on the religion of Islam, served as a counterweight to the Byzantine Empire in the eastern Mediterranean. The Islamic religion drew heavily on the Judeo-Christian tradition and Islamic culture absorbed a great deal of Hellenistic philosophy and science.

The rise of Arab power wiped out the Persian Empire and negated the successes of the Byzantine emperor Heraclius. Before they appeared on the stage of history, the Arabs had lived in tribes on the fringes of the Byzantine and Persian worlds. Then, unified by their new religion, the tribes had become a formidable force that swept out of the Arabian Peninsula to conquer the whole Middle East, North Africa, and Spain.

THE EMERGENCE OF THE ISLAMIC WORLD

The Arabian Peninsula in Ancient Times

We know a great deal more about the origins of Christianity than we do about the origins of Islam, mainly because Christianity arose from a literate society whereas Islam emerged from a largely illiterate society. There is no body of Arabic literature that we can turn to in search of the seminal ideas of Islam.

The Arabian Peninsula had been known to the great civilizations of the ancient world for millennia. The Sumerians imported spices from Yemen and Oman in the south of the peninsula, and the Romans controlled the north and northwest

(OPPOSITE) POTTERY BOWL FROM IRAN, TENTH CENTURY.

and traded along the western coast. The Romans called the southern region Arabia Felix (Arabia the Fortunate), because it was the source of rare goods like myrrh (the basis of incense), perfumes, and medicines. The Persians held the northeast, with trade routes down the eastern coast and through the Persian Gulf, and they too traded for the spices of the south. Most important, the Arabian Peninsula lay athwart the trade routes between the Mediterranean world and the Far East.

The ancient kingdom of Yemen exercised direct control of trade at the midpoint of those routes and dominated the interior of the peninsula. During the third century, however, Yemen encountered strong competition from Abyssinia, on the African shore of the Red Sea. With Roman support, the Abyssinians had gained control of Yemen by the beginning of the fourth century.

During the fifth century, missionaries from Egypt converted Abyssinia to Christianity, and the Abyssinians in turn forced the Yemenites to accept Christianity. Seizing the opportunity, the Persians interfered in Yemen and fueled religious and political resistance to the Abyssinians. The Byzantines, who had inherited Roman interests in the region, supported the Abyssinians in this contest. Finally, in the 590s, when the Persian armies were beginning their final assault on the Byzantine Empire, the Yemenites reasserted their independence from the Abyssinians.

The Arabian kingdoms in the southern part of the peninsula, as well as the imperial powers of the Mediterranean had tried repeatedly to win control of the interior deserts so that they could control the trade routes, but none of their political arrangements had lasted for very long. The nomadic Bedouins had clung to their independence and to their ancient pagan culture and had ignored the meddling of outside powers. The Abyssinians had had some success, however, because their bishops had managed to establish bishoprics in some of the larger camps during the early seventh century. Perhaps as a result of that experience, several of the tribes came together in a confederation and defeated Persia in 604 or 611—the date is uncertain. The defeat meant little to the Persians, but it taught the Arabs that unity brought strength.

On the western coast of the peninsula, several towns served as way stations along the trade routes. Members of various tribes lived in each town, and the town itself was a kind of coalition of tribes. Medina and Mecca, two of the most important towns, were active in the international trade and cooperated in trying to keep the Bedouin tribes in the surrounding area under control. The role of these traders grew stronger as the imperial powers to the north weakened one another in constant war. At the beginning of the seventh century, the tribes' demonstration that they were capable of taking independent action, together with their victory over the Persians, gave rise to an Arab ethnic movement among the Arabs throughout the peninsula. The coastal cities led the movement, and Mohammed, who was born around 570 into one of the leading tribes of Mecca, became its principal figure.

Pre-Islamic Arabian Towns

Arabian towns originated in two ways, as settlements of an oasis and as religious precincts. Medina and Mecca illustrate the types perfectly.

Medina is located in an oasis, which gave it its wealth. The town's population was organized into tribal groups, each controlling a district of the town-oasis, with its housing, shops, and agricultural fields. The organization of the town differed greatly, therefore, from that of Hellenistic, Persian, and Roman towns. There was no central government, just a council of tribal elders that dealt only with matters that had to be faced in common, including defense, roads, and external affairs. All other matters were left to the tribes.

Mecca was founded on a holy shrine, the Ka'aba, a black rock cube. The shrine was tended by holy men, and because the men of the desert visited it regularly, the local tribes settled around it to profit off the pilgrims. Within the area immediately around the shrine, no one was permitted to bear weapons, so the holy precinct became a place where feuds could be settled. The holy men served as arbitrators and go-betweens. Thus, from ancient times Mecca was a holy place that played an important role in the politics of western Arabia.

Mohammed and the Creation of Islamic Religion

Around 610, Mohammed began to tell friends and relatives about his religious experiences. He felt that he was in direct communication with God and that God was revealing to him both God's nature and the obligations of men and women to God. Around 613, Mohammed began to speak of the revelations in public, and a small following formed around him. Most of the townspeople, however, were hostile to him, and eventually he was driven from Mecca.

The basic tenets of Mohammed's religion are that Allah, the name for God in Islam, is good and omnipotent; that Allah will judge all men on the last day and assign them either to heaven (the garden) or to hell (the fire); that men should be grateful to and should worship Allah for making the world as it is; that Allah expects men to be generous with their wealth, which comes from him; and that Mohammed, as the prophet of Allah, warns men that the last judgment is coming. These tenets, though clearly influenced by the Jewish and Christian religions, were not copied directly from them.

The leading merchants, offended by a teaching that urged all men to be generous with their wealth, tried to get the members of Mohammed's tribe to silence him. But the tribe protected him until about 619, when there was a change in its leadership. The new chief, himself a prosperous merchant, tried to force Mohammed to cease his preaching. Mohammed refused, and in 622, failing to find another protector, he left Mecca for Medina, where he found powerful supporters.

The journey to Medina, known as the *hegira* (journey), was later considered the founding event of Islam, as the crucifixion of Jesus was the beginning of Christianity. In fact, Moslems—those who follow the teachings of Mohammed—reckon their years from the *hegira*. (In English, the dates are followed by "A.H."—"After Hegira.") In Medina, Mohammed created an Islamic community and established the rules by which such a community should

Mecca and the Background of Islam

As a holy place, Mecca gave its inhabitants an opportunity to deal with the Bedouins on religious grounds. Mohammed's grandfather, Hashim, took advantage of this to create a large alliance based on the Ka'aba, the holy rock of Mecca. He persuaded the tribes along the trade route on the western coast of Arabia to honor special holy days of Mecca as days of truce, and, over time, he extended both the number of holidays and the number of tribes that honored them. In this way, he brought peace and prosperity to the trade route.

Hashim's religious and trade alliance depended on the willingness of the Meccans to keep their own greed in check, to maintain both their cooperation and the good will of the Bedouins. By Mohammed's time, that self-control had broken down, and many of the Bedouin tribes had left the alliance. One aim of Mohammed's preaching was to restore the restraint at the base of his grandfather's system.

live. He instituted dietary rules similar to those of the Jews and prohibited the drinking of wine, gambling, and usury. (In modern speech, "usury" refers to the charging of exorbitant interest, but in Islam and in medieval Christianity it referred to the charging of any interest.) He set up a legal system that substituted arbitration for blood feuds, prohibited infanticide, and regulated inheritance so that the rights of orphans and widows were secure. He put limits on polygamy and divorce: A man could not have more than four wives at one time, and a divorced wife was not to be sent away penniless.

Soon after his arrival in Medina, Mohammed and his followers began attacking caravans going to and coming from Mecca, and by 628 the attacks had evolved into a routine war of attrition. Then, with about 1,500 followers, Mohammed joined the annual pilgrimage to the holy shrine of the Ka'aba, a cube of black rock, in Mecca. When the Meccans refused to let him in, he negotiated with them and got them to agree that he could return the next year and that they would evacuate the town for three days during his stay.

During the following year, Mohammed proceeded to incorporate Bedouin tribes from the surrounding area into the

The holy Kaaba in modern Mecca is the most sacred Islamic shrine.

Islamic state of Medina. When he returned to Mecca in 629, its leaders recognized the futility of resistance and submitted to Islam and to his authority. The leaders of the Meccan tribes now began to serve as leaders of the Islamic state, though its administrative center remained in Medina.

The Founding of the Arabic Empire

War was endemic among the Bedouin tribes until Mohammed redirected their passion for war towards religious objectives. In time, Islamic leaders devised a rationale for wars fought for Allah. Such a war was called a *jihad* (holy war).

In 630, Mohammed himself led an army north against the Byzantine provinces. He also encouraged Bedouin attacks on the Persian Empire, already weakened by Heraclius and by the murder of Shah Khusro II (628). Before his death in June 632 Mohammed had extended Arabic influence into the kingdom of Yemen, which became part of the Islamic state when its population converted.

The death of Mohammed created a crisis, because he had made no provision for a successor. But the crisis was resolved when the leaders of the state, the men who had followed Mohammed to Medina in 622, elected one of his earliest followers, Abu Bakr, as caliph (representative or vicar of the prophet). Abu Bakr (r. 632–34) completed the work of bringing the Arabic tribes into the Islamic state and prepared the way for expansion of Arabic power beyond the peninsula.

His successor, Omar (r. 634–44), launched the conquests that helped create a new empire. Damascus fell in 635, Jerusalem in 638, and soon the Arabs were in control of all of Syria and Palestine. Jerusalem, along with Medina and Mecca, became a holy city of Islam. In 637, the Bedouin alliance that had earlier defeated the Persians seized the imperial Persian capital at Ctesiphon. Soon the Arabs were in control of the entire Persian Empire. Now they began to push east, and in 643 Arab raiders from Persia reached India. Meanwhile, between 640 and 642, Arab forces conquered Egypt—though the Byzantines held on to Alexandria until 646—and moved on along the North African coast as far as Tripoli. In the Mediterranean an Arab fleet defeated the Byzantines, and by the middle of the seventh century the Arabs had occupied Cyprus. The Arab navy kept constant pressure on Constantinople until Leo the Isaurian destroyed it in 718 (p. 175).

This new empire was governed by a theocracy, and as Mohammed had done the caliphs exercised both spiritual and secular authority. The central government ruled the newly acquired provinces through colonies populated by Bedouin tribes. Mohammed had tried to suppress the tribes altogether to create a unified Islamic society, but his successors left the tribes intact, satisfied with their loyalty to the Islamic state. Under Omar and his successors, the tribes became agents of the government. They lived isolated from the conquered populations and carried out their military and administrative functions from a distance. Each colony had a governor appointed by the central government in Medina.

Though a theocracy, the Islamic government did not enforce conversion to Islam. Non-Moslems had to pay a heavy

The Growth of the Islamic Empire   632–750

land tax and could not serve in the government, but they suffered no other disabilities. Aloof from their subjects, the Arabs came to view their empire as "a garden protected by our spears." Waging war by land was their special talent. When they needed a fleet, they ordered the subject populations to build and man the ships.

THE ISLAMIC COMMUNITY

Mohammed's mission lasted from about 610 until his death in 632. His followers memorized his revelations—called *koran*—but the uncertainties of oral transmission were recognized early, and the third caliph, Othman (r. 644–56), had them recorded in the *Koran,* the holy book of Islam.

Part of Mohammed's legacy was his ways (*sunna*) as head of the *umma,* the community of Islam. After his death, the inner circle of officials around the caliphs engaged in frequent discussions about what this or that action meant for the governance of the state. As a result, an extensive body of stories and commentaries relating to the *sunna* grew up. Unlike the revelations, these items could not be set

Mohammed choosing Ali as his heir.

down in simple form, and over time the *sunna* tradition became an elaborate body of lore relating to the nature of Islamic government and society.

As in any theocracy, religious disagreement in the Islamic state nearly always had political consequences, and vice versa. For example, the first civil war in the *umma* originated in a dispute over the succession to the caliphate. Omar, the second caliph, had confirmed that election by the inner circle of government officials should determine the succession. But when Omar was murdered by a Persian slave in 644, the electors faced a difficult choice. They all agreed that the succession must remain within the Hashimite clan, to which Mohammed had belonged (named for Mohammed's grandfather). But that clan included both direct descendants of Hashim and those who joined the clan through marriage. In 644, the leading members of the clan were Ali, Mohammed's cousin and son-in-law, and Othman, a member of the Ommayyad clan, who had married two of Mohammed's daughters.

The decision went to Othman, who, though a wealthy and urbane man, proved unable to deal with the growing financial problems of the Empire. Othman's enemies, encouraged by Ali, accused him of violating the *sunna*. In 656 Othman was murdered by a faction that included men of high standing in Ali's party.

The murder led to a civil war between Ali and Mu'awiya, a relative of Othman and governor of Syria. Mu'awiya demanded the blood revenge permitted by the *Koran*. After inconclusive skirmishing, the choice of a new caliph was handed over to two arbitrators, who disagreed. At this point, a group of fanatical supporters of Ali called Kharijites ("those who withdrew or rebelled") withdrew from his army, claiming that arbitration was contrary to the *Koran*. Ali had most of the Kharijites massacred, but in 658 one of them murdered him. Mu'awiya was then elected caliph and managed to persuade Ali's sons to acquiesce in the new regime. He then moved the capital of the Islamic state to Damascus and did away with the practice of electing the caliph.

The contest between Mu'awiya and Ali led to an enduring division within Islam between the Shiites (the party of Ali) and the Sunnis (the party of the Ommayyads). Ali's claim to the caliphate rested on his hereditary rights, but he also claimed to be a stricter follower of the *Koran* and the *sunna* than Mu'awiya was. The party of Mu'awiya responded that the Ommayyads preserved the truly orthodox *sunna* and that their victory made the Sunnis the orthodox party of Islam. The remnants of the Kharijites also developed distinctive religious views and remained a force in the Islamic world.

Even after the Ommayyads gained control of the caliphate, the Islamic state remained divided and difficult to govern. Arabic society was tribal at base, and even Mohammed had failed to suppress the ancient tribal authority. The first caliphs seem to have recognized the permanence of that authority, and, as we have seen, they used the tribes to help govern the newly conquered territories. Significantly, this practice seems to have arisen in Persia, which had been conquered by tribal armies. Those armies had been settled at Kufa and Basra in lower Mesopotamia in camps that soon became substantial tribal cities, like Mecca and Medina themselves.

Though we can speak of a *Pax Islamica* (Islamic Peace), the Arab Empire never achieved the administrative and political unity achieved by the Roman Empire and the Persian Empire, or by its contemporary, the Byzantine Empire. In the vast stretches of the Arab Empire, it seems that a tribal society simply worked best and that a formal imperial system conducted by a distant central government was an impossibility.

From the very beginning of the Islamic state, the Arabs regarded themselves as the people of Allah, and Islamic law granted them substantial privileges—including freedom from taxation and the right to serve in the army and in government. Those privileges were denied to other ethnic groups even after their conversion to Islam. Consequently, opponents of the caliph could always count on the support of the *mawali,* as the non-Arab converts were called.

THE OMMAYYADS

Further Conquests

The Ommayyad dynasty (661–750) signaled the ascendancy of the urban aristocracy over the Bedouins who had carried out the early conquests under the theocracy of Medina. Mu'awiya and his successors resumed the policy of conquest, though at a slower pace. They were interested in organizing and exploiting the territories they won, and that took time. They had only slight success in Asia Minor, where the Hellenistic population led by the Byzantine emperor put up stiff resistance. In the north, however, Arab armies reached the Caucasian Mountains between the Black Sea and the Caspian Sea and pushed into Samarkand, where they could control the trade route from central Asia to India and the Middle East. In India, around 710, they crossed the Indus River and established a loosely governed territory in the Sindh (modern Pakistan). Over the next generation the Arab governors suppressed the local rulers and organized the territory, including portions of the Punjab and Kashmir, into a province of the Empire. The local populations managed to check further expansion, but contemporary sources indicate that they did not fully recognize the seriousness of the threat.

At the end of the seventh century, Arab armies moved westward from Tripoli. Here they met strong resistance from

Early Islamic calligraphy. Calligraphy was highly developed by Moslem artisans in part because of the religious proscription on representational art.

An Islamic coin (698–99), the first silver coinage struck of purely Islamic type. The inscription in the center of the coin reads: "There is no God but God alone; no one is associated with him." The insistence on God's oneness and the denial of an associate to him is directed against the Christians and their doctrine of the Trinity.

ca. 570	632	661	750		1258
Life of Mohammed	First Four Caliphs	Ommayyad Dynasty		Abbasid Dynasty	

the Byzantine garrisons supported by the Berber tribes of the North African desert. Carthage finally fell to the Arabs in 698 after they had defeated the Byzantine fleet that was bringing reinforcements. Following this success, the Berbers converted to Islam and joined the march westward. Morocco was occupied within the next ten years. In 711, the Berber leader Tarik led a force across the Straits of Gibraltar (gib-al-Tarik, "the rock of Tarik") into Visigothic Spain.

Because the attack came at a time when the Visigothic kingdom was experiencing internecine war, victory was relatively easy. Within a few months, Toledo, the capital of the kingdom, fell to the invaders. With the help of Arab reinforcements from North Africa, the army occupied some of the fortified cities that had held out, including Seville. After pausing briefly to consolidate their conquests, the new Islamic rulers took control of the entire peninsula, except for a narrow strip along the southern foothills of the Pyre-

nees, where the Christian kingdom of Asturias clung to a precarious existence. In 720, the Moors (as the Spanish called the North Africans and their Arab allies) moved into Septimania and converted it into a base for raids to the north. Throughout the eighth century, the Franks struggled to push the Moors back into the Iberian Peninsula.

Ommayyad Society and Culture

Under the Ommayyad dynasty, the Arabs continued their lenient policy toward the conquered peoples. They taxed non-Moslems heavily but otherwise left them alone. Nonetheless, the pace of conversion to Islam accelerated during the seventh and eighth centuries, perhaps because the non-Arabs wanted to escape taxes.

The loss of taxes created a fiscal problem and caused many caliphs to insist that the new converts continue to pay them. Otherwise, the caliphs soon discovered,

The Great Mosque in Damascus, Syria, begun in the late seventh century.

they could not balance the budget. This policy annoyed the converts and made them a ready audience for opponents of the government. In fact, many of the converts turned to Arab noblemen for protection and support, creating a kind of client class dependent on Arab leaders.

Surprisingly, it was the language of the Arab nomads that won out over the languages of the subject peoples, many of whom were highly civilized. That was less surprising in Syria and Palestine, where the populations spoke related Semitic languages, than it was in Persia, Egypt, and North Africa. The Ommayyads contributed to the ascendancy of Arabic by making it the official language of government, but a more powerful influence was the emergence of an Arabic intellectual and literary culture during the Ommayyad period.

Poetry was the most popular literary genre, as it had been in pre-Islamic Arabia. Ommayyad poets wrote romantic and satirical poetry, as well as odes extolling the good life. There were Christian poets as well as Moslem poets, a reflection of the caliphs' policy of toleration.

The new imperial bureaucracy also adapted Arabic to the prosaic needs of government. To make Arabic, a language of the desert, function as an official language, the educated bureaucrats enlarged its vocabulary and gave it a formal grammatical structure. The new grammar made the language more precise and regular and enabled foreigners to learn it more quickly. The improved language also served as a good medium for theology, philosophy, and history. The earliest intellectual works in Arabic date from the end of the Ommayyad period. Though few of those works survive, quotations from them were often incorporated into later writings.

The Arabic tradition in architecture and in the decorative arts also emerged under the Ommayyads. In Damascus, they built a great mosque, a place of prayer, in a form influenced by the Roman basilica, with a long nave and side aisles. The design was copied in mosques elsewhere in the Empire. In Jerusalem, the Ommayyads built a huge mosque on the site sacred to the Jews, the Dome of the Rock, which enclosed a vast central space. This building too was imitated elsewhere.

A distinctive style of domestic architecture was favored for the desert palaces where the Ommayyads spent much of their time. Many of these palaces, of impressive size and richly decorated, contained apartments, private mosques, baths, and formal gardens. During this period, the contrast between town and desert became an established feature of the Islamic culture. Paradoxically, the city

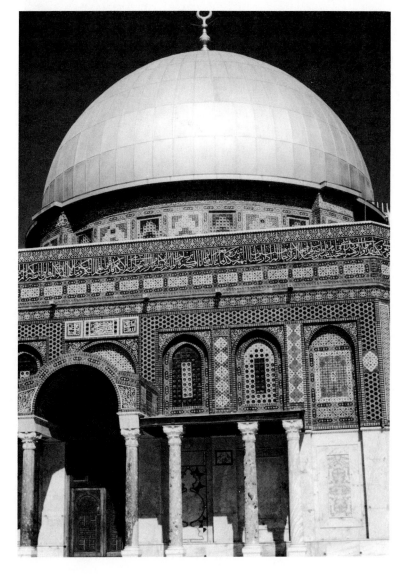

The Dome of the Rock in Jerusalem. This mosque was built on the spot from which Mohammed was believed to have ascended to heaven.

Detail from a portal of an Ommayyad palace in Syria (*ca.* 720).

populations of Syria, Iraq, and Egypt embraced the Arabic language and Arabic culture, while the Arabs themselves kept to the desert and cherished their ancient Bedouin ways. The great palaces and hunting lodges of the Ommayyads symbolized the appeal of the desert but were in fact islands of urban comfort.

The Ommayyad caliphs maintained the distinction between Arabs and non-Arabs long after the actual power of government had passed into the hands of *mawali* officials and generals. By the eighth century, the *mawali* constituted a majority of the community of Islam, suggesting that a major change in the nature of the caliphate was imminent.

THE RISE OF THE ABBASIDS

The Collapse of the Ommayyad Caliphate

Although the Ommayyads made claims to orthodoxy, their court scandalized many Moslems. The palace at Damascus and the desert resorts of the caliphs were centers of luxury that offended hardy Arab tribes-

men and gave the *mawali* an opportunity for complaint. Moreover, the Ommayyads associated with non-Moslems and copied Byzantine governmental institutions that were unfamiliar and suspect to men of the desert. Their concern for the large Christian and Jewish communities of Syria, and the presence of educated Christians and Jews in the government, often in high positions, contributed further to the popular view that the Ommayyad government was verging toward the secular.

The Ommayyads were even accused of favoring the *mawali* community over the Arabs. Faced with almost constant financial crisis, the Ommayyad caliphs introduced new tax and financial schemes to bring the budget under control. These schemes proved particularly offensive to the subject populations, which had become progressively islamicized. Furthermore, the caliphs seemed unable to exercise regular administrative control over the provinces. Often the provincial governors, feeling their position threatened, rebelled against the central government with the support of their tribal contingents and the local *mawali*. Each time, the rebellious governor justified himself by charging the caliph with heterodoxy.

The endless war with the Byzantines also provoked opposition. During a century of conflict, the balance of victories had gone to Constantinople, with the caliphs investing enormous resources without winning either spoils or territory. The great naval and land defeats at Constantinople in 717–18, when Leo the Isaurian outsmarted and outfought the caliph's superior forces (pp. 174–75), were only the most spectacular examples of failure. Even though the caliphs' armies had some successes in the East—with the establishment of Moslem states in the Transoxiana and in the Indus Valley—few of the Ommayyads could claim to be noteworthy conquerors.

The main opposition to Damascus was centered in Iraq, the old heartland of the Persian Empire. It was in the Persian province of Khurasan, however, on the plains south of the Oxus River, that the last rebellion against the Ommayyads took

ca. 570	632	661	750		1258
Life of Mohammed	First Four Caliphs	Ommayyad Dynasty		Abbasid Dynasty	Mongols Take Baghdad

place, in the aftermath of a civil war among rivals within the Ommayyad clan. In 747, when the victor in this war, Marwan II (r. 749–50), tried to consolidate his power over the provincial governors, the governor of Khurasan Abu Muslim, of Persian descent, rebelled.

In this rebellion, tribal and religious rivalries joined with *mawali* anti-Arab sentiments. Khurasan had been converted by Shiite missionaries from Kufa in southern Iraq, the center of Shiism. Abu Muslim therefore declared that he was rebelling in the name of the Shiite *imam* (leader of prayers, religious leader) Ibrahim, a descendant of al-Abbas, an uncle of Mohammed (hence Abbasids). He thus brought the Shiites into his rebellion against the Sunni caliphs. Moreover, Kufa had been established by Yemenite tribesmen who favored the Shiites and the hereditary rights of the house of Mohammed had never been satisfied with the Ommayyads, whom they considered outsiders. Thus, by allying himself with the Shiites, Abu Muslim took advantage also of the ancient tribal rivalry between the Yemenites and Ommayyads.

The Ommayyads succeeded in imprisoning Ibrahim, who died in captivity, but they could not muster an army that could defeat Abu Muslim's forces. In November 749, Abu Muslim had Abu'l-Abbas, Ibrahim's brother, declared caliph in Kufa. Early in 750, Abu Muslim defeated and executed Marwan.

The first official act of the Abbasids was a systematic massacre of the Ommayyad clan, missing only one young boy. That boy, Abd al-Rahman, escaped with his supporters to Spain, where he established an independent Ommayyadc caliphate at Cordova. Thereafter, Spain remained outside the political power of Baghdad.

THE ABBASID CALIPHATE

The Abbasids represented the old Arab leadership and had in fact claimed the caliphate by virtue of their being members of Mohammed's tribe. And yet their accession accelerated the integration of the *mawali,* particularly the Persians, into the society and politics of the *umma.* The second Abbasid caliph, al-Mansur (r. 754–75), built a new capital a few miles from the old Persian capital at a place with the Persian name of Baghdad. Doing so, he completed the transition from an Arab Empire to an Islamic Empire.

Al-Mansur relied principally on Persian officials, and Abbasid government was soon run by a Persian bureaucracy under a new official, called the *wazir* or *vizier,* a kind of prime minister. The Persian *wazir* Khalid b. Barmak established his family as the leaders of the bureaucracy, and until 803 Barmakids were the most powerful members of the government. The court adopted many of the old Persian ways, and the caliphs, like the old Persian shahs, became inaccessible in a palace community of officials and eunuchs.

Soon after they came to power, the Abbasids turned away from their traditional support of Shiites and began to favor the Sunnis. By this time the Sunnis constituted the majority of Islam, and Shiism was deeply divided. As a result of this shift, however, the dynasty faced two Shiite rebellions early in its history.

Al-Mansur succeeded in restoring control over the provinces, except in Spain and the Maghrib (Tunisia, Algeria, and Morocco). In the Maghrib, the ancient Berber tribes asserted their independence once again, as they had under Roman domination. They defeated every force sent out by the central government, partly because the war between the Byzantine and Arab fleets made it impossible for the caliphs to secure supply lines to the distant province.

For a time after the move from Damascus to Baghdad the hostility between the caliphate and the Byzantines declined, but in the late eighth century it flared up once again. The Byzantine emperors were still trying to consolidate their eastern provinces and their eastern frontier, and warfare resumed in that region.

Although Al-Mansur's son, al-Mahdi (r. 775–85), fought the Byzantines with considerable success, he had to concentrate most of his attention on the internal affairs of the Islamic state. He was particularly challenged by a religious movement called Manichaeanism. The Manichaeans were followers of Mani, a third-century Persian priest who had brought Zoroastrianism, the old Persian religion, together with Christianity in a kind of amalgam. The result was a belief in two world powers, one good and one evil, locked in a titanic struggle for supremacy. The sect had troubled both Islam and Christianity for centuries. Augustine, one of the fathers of Latin Christianity (pp. 118–19), went through a Manichaean phase in his youth, and the sect reappeared in Europe in the late eleventh century. Al-Mahdi carried out terrible purges ostensibly of Manichaeans, but most of the people he killed were not Manichaeans at all. He seems to have used the Manichaean threat as an excuse for ridding Islam of both its religious enemies and his own enemies.

Al-Mahdi was particularly taken with Persian customs and ceremonies. He

Hunting scene woven into a seventh-century fabric.

Islam *ca.* 888

spent most of his time in leisure pursuits, leaving the government to be run, and run well, by his Barmakid *wazir* and Persian secretaries. Under al-Mahdi the Baghdad court became a famous center of art and entertainment.

Westerners became aware of the splendor of the Islamic court during the reign of Harun al-Rashid (r. 786–809), who received two embassies from the Frankish king Charles the Great. In turn, al-Rashid sent spectacular gifts (including an elephant) to Charles. The purpose of these exchanges seems to have been to plan a joint attack on Ommayyad Spain, though that attack never occurred. Al-Rashid carried out massive raids in Asia Minor and reached the Aegean Sea in 798 when the Byzantine government was in disarray under Irene (pp. 179–80).

Al-Rashid was obliged, however, to recognize the *de facto* independence of the Maghrib and to grant the governor of the province independent authority in return for a substantial annual tribute. He also agreed to let the governorship become a hereditary position. Thus was born the Aghlabid emirate of North Africa, which acted aggressively toward Christendom a couple of decades later. Aghlabid forces undertook the conquest

of Sicily in 827, attacked Rome in 846, and menaced the coastal cities of Italy throughout the ninth century.

Under al-Rashid, the Barmakids continued to run the government and to dominate the cultural life of the Islamic Empire. The Barkamids tried to effect a settlement between the Abbasids and the Shiites, and they encouraged active discourse on law, philosophy, and theology in the hope of finding a common ground for reconciliation. As a result of these efforts, the Barmakids were suspected of favoring the Shiites during the Shiite rebellion, and the family fell from power in 803.

After al-Rashid's death in 809, the political cohesion of the Empire dissolved. Khurasan became independent under a Persian dynasty (820). A rebel leader set himself up in Azerbaijan (the region around the southern shore of the Caspian Sea) and could not be put down. Refugees from Spain, fleeing from internal conflict there, took Crete from the Byzantines and held it for 135 years. They also stirred up unrest in Egypt. The spiritual authority of the caliphs was still recognized, but their political power had diminished to the point where they were becoming just one of many dynasties in the Empire.

Early mosque and minaret,
Samara, Syria (*ca.* 850).

However, under al-Rashid's successors the court remained a center of intellectual activity. Al-Rashid's son, al-Ma'mun
(r. 813–33), founded a university, the
House of Wisdom, and built several ob-
servatories for the study of astronomy. He
encouraged theologians to turn to Greek
philosophy in their search for ways of reconciling the many strains of Islam.

The Appearance of the Turks

The Turks were a group of Asiatic tribes
that had moved into Turkestan, the region
north of the Transoxiana, and first appeared in Islamic history toward the middle of the ninth century. The caliphs,
remembering all the undependable armies that had plagued their predecessors,
created an army of Turkish slaves. During

the 840s, that army grew to such an enormous size—some sources say 70,000
men—and so disrupted life in Baghdad
that the caliph Mutawakkil (r. 846–61)
built new quarters for the government and
the army at Samara, some distance from
the city.

The Turks were loyal to the caliph's
family, though they sometimes became
embroiled in family conflicts. In 861, Turkish officers killed Mutawakkil, who was
then in conflict with one of his sons. The
following decade was a time of anarchy.
Eastern Persia broke away immediately
upon Mutawakkil's death and retained its
independence until about 910. Tulun, a
Turk who was provincial governor in
Egypt and had at his command a large
slave army, seized control of the province
in 871; his family retained control until
905. But trouble with the Turkish slaves

paled beside that caused by black slaves in southern Mesopotamia. In 868, they started a dangerous revolt.

As in other ancient societies, slavery was common in the Islamic world. The *Koran* condoned slavery but also encouraged emancipation. Most slaves served either as soldiers or as personal secretaries and servants, and a good many of them gained their freedom. In the lower valleys of the Tigris and Euphrates, however, masses of black African slaves worked on sugar plantations under horrible conditions. When they rebelled in 868 the caliphs were powerless to put them down. A reign of terror raged over the region until 883, when the rebellion was crushed.

Following the end of the rebellion the Empire experienced a brief period of recovery under the Abbasid caliph al-Muktafi (r. 902–08). Under his successors, however, the provinces failed to satisfy the central government's demands for taxes and instability set in once again. In 924, the government put a military officer, the Turk Mu'nis, in control who transformed the government into a military dictatorship. He held the title *emir,* and from that point on the caliphs exercised only religious authority.

Throughout these troubled years, the power of the army, now led and manned primarily by Turks, grew steadily. What finally forced the government to surrender its authority to the army was the rise of the Isma'ili movement in North Africa.

THE ISMA'ILIS AND THE RISE OF THE FATIMID CALIPHS

The Isma'ili party was a splinter group of the Shiites. Al-Husain, the first martyr of Islam, was a son of Ali by Fatima, and the imams of his line succeeded one another without incident for six generations. Then, however, the imam Ja'far disinherited his eldest son and presumed heir, Isma'il, for not obeying the tenets of Islam. Ja'far named his younger son Musa as next in line for the imamate. Although Isma'il died before his father, a small party of Husainites insisted on Isma'il's right of succession and became "the Seveners"

(that is, seven generations), or Isma'ilis. Musa succeeded as imam in 765, and his line lasted until the twelfth imam disappeared in Baghdad in the 870s. The followers of that imam, who constituted the main body of Husainites, were known as "the Twelvers."

The Isma'ilis believed that Isma'il was the *mahdi,* the hidden imam who would return to lead Islam to the true religion. In 909, a group of Isma'ilis seized control of North Africa and, believing Ubaid Allah al-Mahdi to be the *mahdi,* proclaimed him caliph in opposition to the Abbasid caliph. Ubaid and his successors were known as Fatimids, because they were descendants of Fatima.

The Fatimid caliphs were determined to replace the Abbasids as the true leaders of Islam. Ubaid's son, al-Ka'im (r. 934–46), built a fleet that terrorized the central Mediterranean and attacked the coast of France and Italy. He also made a third attempt—the first two under Ubaid had failed—to conquer Egypt as a stepping stone to Baghdad. Egypt was finally conquered in 969 by al-Ka'im's grandson, al-Mu'izz (r. 953–75).

By 959, al-Mu'izz had won control of almost all of North Africa out to the Atlantic Ocean and had confined the Ommayyads of Spain to small enclaves near Gibraltar. During the first fifteen years of his reign, al-Mu'izz, with the help of two of his ministers, neither of them Arab, established the Fatimid military and administrative systems, which lasted into the fifteenth century. The architect of his military system was a general named Jawhar, an islamicized Greek slave who had led the conquest of North Africa and then of Egypt. Recognizing the strategic importance of the Nile Delta and the danger posed by the Byzantines, who had recaptured Crete (961), Jawhar and al-Mu'izz built a new capital at Cairo, which soon became known as one of the most beautiful cities in the Mediterranean world.

The architect of the administrative system was al-Mu'izz's *wazir* Ya'qub b. Killis, an islamicized Jew from Baghdad who served both al-Mu'izz and his successor al-'Aziz (r. 975–96). Through enlightened taxation and other well-conceived

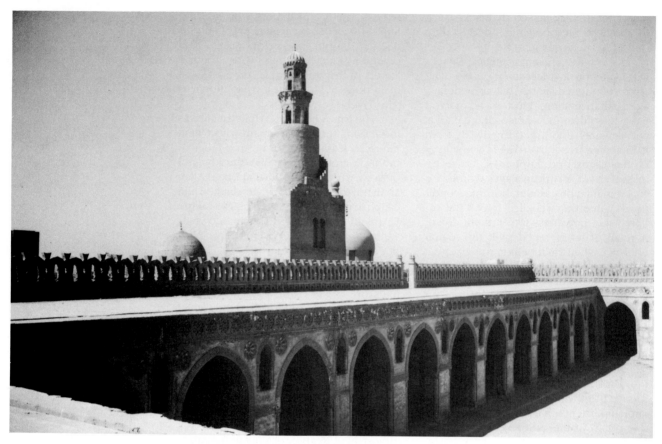

The ibn-Tulun Mosque in Cairo,
Egypt (eighth century).

measures, Ya'qub encouraged traders to travel through Egypt and the Red Sea on their way to the Far East and built a navy to protect Egyptian ports. Alexandria became once again, as it had been in Hellenistic and Roman times, one of the world's great emporia, and the new commercial powers of Italy—Amalfi, Venice, and Genoa—sent their merchants there to buy silk and spices for the expanding European market.

The Fatimids drew on the whole Mediterranean world in building their success and in bringing brilliance to their court. Al-'Aziz married a Christian, named Christians to high office, and permitted Jews and Christians to live in his realm without persecution or constraint. He also created a Turkish slave army to control the Berber troops that Jawhar had brought to Egypt. Al-'Aziz died in 996 at the age of 41, and under his son Al-Hakim (r. 996–1021),

who was then 13, the caliphate soon fell into decline.

Al-Hakim persecuted Jews and Christians and executed, one after another, the ministers and generals he appointed. He would slip out of the palace secretly at night, and during one of his excursions he disappeared. His body was never found.

The Fatimids' push to Baghdad had already lost momentum, for three reasons: First, the resurgence of the Byzantines under Basil II (r. 976–1025) kept the Fatimids pinned down in Egypt and North Africa (pp. 185–86). Second, the Fatimids had become more and more conservative and as a result had lost the support of the fanatical Isma'ilis who controlled the land between Egypt and Baghdad. Finally, the Abbasid caliphate of Baghdad, supported by the Turkish emirs, had grown strong enough to resist the Fatimid threat.

THE RISE OF THE TURKS

The Background

The Turkish slave armies had given evidence of their power on several occasions during the ninth century, particularly in the 860s when they made and unmade caliphs at will. By 924, as we have seen, a Turkish emirate controlled the central government in Baghdad. After 945, however, Turkish power was checked by the Buyids, a family from Azerbaijan that seized power in Baghdad and installed its own candidate as caliph.

The Buyids were Shiites aligned with the Twelvers against the Isma'ilis (the Seveners). When they took control of Baghdad, however, they accommodated themselves to Sunni orthodoxy, which still dominated the *umma*. The Buyid family itself was rarely united, and during its dominance the provinces of Iraq and Persia were often governed by contesting members.

Competition among the Buyid rulers meant peace for outsiders living in the caliphate. The Christians, for example, most of whom were members of sects considered heretical by both the eastern and western churches, played a role in the cultural life of the caliphate and reinforced the influence of Greek learning on Arabic intellectuals. And the Jews during the tenth and eleventh centuries were much better off in the Middle East and Spain than were their coreligionists in Europe. In fact, both Jews and Christians found employment as teachers and government functionaries during these years.

Buyid power was limited to Iraq and the region along the southern flank of the Caucasus. To the west, the Hamdanid dynasty controlled northern Syria and upper Mesopotamia from the old city of Aleppo. The Hamdanids patronized artists and scholars and helped keep the Buyids in check. To the east, the Samanids, the first native Persian dynasty since the Arab conquest, controlled Khurasan.

The Samanids encouraged revival of Persian as the language of science and poetry. And their court poets and writers created a language called "New Persian," or Farsi. Although it was written in the Arabic alphabet and contained many Arab words, Farsi was nonetheless truly Persian, and it remains the language of Iran to this day.

The Samanids sent out missionaries to the Turks living beyond the Transoxiana. Ironically, that good work prevented the Samanids from fighting off the Turks when they began to move into the Transoxiana, because it was impossible for them to conduct a holy war, a *jihad*, against fellow Moslems. Between 999 and 1004, the power of the Samanids collapsed under the Turkish attacks.

The Turkish Dynasty of Ghazna: Afghanistan and India

Still further east, in the region that is now Afghanistan, a Turkish military leader in service to the Samanids established a dynasty at Ghazna. The Ghaznavids, as they were called, rose to power on the ruins of Samanid authority and gained control of the southern and eastern regions of Persia under the great ruler Mahmud (r. 998–1030). Mahmud was the patron of Firdawsi, a Persian poet whose great epic poem, the *Shah-nama*, is considered one of the masterpieces of Islamic literature.

Mahmud took over the small Islamic principalities that had been established in the Indus Valley early in the eighth century and had remained in place for three centuries without expanding their influence. They continued to be important in the trade between India and the Middle East, although the bulk of that trade now went by sea to Fatimid Egypt. Mahmud used these states as a basis for annual campaigns to the east, beyond the Indus. These campaigns opened India to Moslem missionaries and opened the Islamic world to the cultural influence of India.

Another Islamic intellectual who attracted Mahmud's patronage was al-Biruni (973–*ca.* 1050), who ranks with Aristotle in the breadth of his interests and achievements. Al-Biruni fell under the influence of Indian culture, an influence that is apparent in his works on mathematics and astronomy. He also wrote a remarkable book (*ca.* 1030) on India that remains an

The Eastern Islamic World

important source of our knowledge about medieval India.

The Coming of the Seljuk Turks

Mahmud pushed west as well as east. By the end of his reign, he had gained control of Khurasan and was ready to make an attempt on Iraq, where the Shiite Buyids still held sway. His plan was to reunify the caliphate under Sunni power, but that plan was spoiled by the irruption of the Seljuk Turks.

The Seljuks, named for an early chieftain, were nomadic people who had broken away from the main Turkish confederation that controlled the Transoxiana. In the 1020s, they moved into Khurasan and threatened Ghaznavid power. Mahmud's son and successor, Mas'ud I (r. 1030–40), tried to halt their advance,

but in 1040 they defeated him in a decisive battle. Persia was open to the Seljuks, and Ghaznavid power shrank to the territories that are now Afghanistan and the Punjab in India, which Mahmud had organized as a Moslem state.

The Seljuks proceeded to implement Mahmud's plan themselves. In 1055, they invaded Iraq and occupied Baghdad. In the decades that followed, they established an empire within Islam, with a new form of political power. Instead of setting up an emirate, which was technically a governorship under the authority of the caliph, the Seljuks set up a sultanate, which was an independent political power loyal to the caliph.

Under Sultan Alp-Arslan (r. 1063–72), the Seljuks destroyed the Byzantine army at the battle of Manzikert (1071), in Armenia, and in 1077 his successor Malik-Shah (r. 1072–92) took Jerusalem. Their conquest of that holy city finally prompted a crusade that the Byzantines had tried to organize after their defeat at Manzikert (p. 186). Malik-Shah also took Damascus (1076) and established a powerful empire in the Middle East. Although the Seljuks managed to check the advance of the Fatimids, they were unable to conquer Egypt. Consequently the schism between the caliphs in Baghdad and those in Cairo continued until the rise of the Ottoman Turks in the fifteenth century.

Islamic Culture under the Seljuks

The Seljuks had been exposed to Persian culture by the Samanid missionaries, and once in power they encouraged Persian as the court language and were soon using it even in everyday life. Malik-Shah left the running of his empire to a brilliant Persian *wazir* named Nizam al-Mulk (1018–92). Nizam had served Malik-Shah's father, Alp-Arslan, and had acted as regent for Malik-Shah when he succeeded to the sultanate at the age of thirteen.

Nizam and Malik-Shah staged a Sunni renaissance after the long years of Shiite rule under the Buyids. In 1067, Nizam founded a school of law that became the intellectual center of Sunni Islam. One of the students, al-Ghazzali (1058–1111), became dissatisfied with the formalism of the law and went on to become the principal theologian of Islam. He wrote a massive work in which he stressed the importance of prayer and charity, and his ideas became the basis of the modern Sunni religion.

Al-Ghazzali turned away from philosophical and scientific speculation about the world and concentrated instead on the experience of the individual Moslem. In part as a result of his influence, the classical age of Islamic civilization is said to have ended around 1200.

During the reign of Malik-Shah a splinter group of Isma'ilis settled in the mountains of northern Persia around the fortress of Alamut, not far from modern Tehran. The leader of this group, Hasan-i Sabbah, hoped to find support for an anti-Seljuk (and anti-Sunni) rebellion. When he failed to do so, he organized a terrorist movement and sent agents to kill government officials and rulers throughout the sultanate. Orthodox Moslems, who believed that these agents chewed *hashish,* Indian hemp, before embarking on these suicide missions, called the terrorists "Assassins," from the name of the drug. Nizam al-Mulk died at the hands of an Assassin in 1092. Hasan-i died in 1124, but his movement lived on and for generations the Assassins were feared in the Islamic world.

After the death of Malik-Shah, the Seljuk empire broke into fragments under the control of individual leaders. There were Seljuk states in Asia Minor, Khurasan, Kirman (southwest of Khurasan), and Iraq. These states were so beset by internal problems that they were unable to resist the European invaders of Syria and Palestine, who arrived in the First Crusade in the late 1090s. As a result, the crusaders were able to establish the Latin kingdom of Jerusalem, which lasted for several generations.

Saladin and the Recovery of the Mediterranean Lands

Zengi, the Turkish governor of Mosul on the upper Tigris River, launched a counterattack against the Christians, and his recapture of Edessa in 1144 prompted a call for the Second Crusade. His son Nur al-Din (r. 1146–74) succeeded in confining the Europeans to small enclaves on the Mediterranean coast. A gifted ruler, Nur al-Din earned a reputation for good government and justice. Under his rule the Kurds, a people from northern Iraq, rose to prominence in the government and in the army, and one of their leaders, Saladin, emerged as a powerful military figure under Nur al-Din. Saladin led the defense of Egypt against attack by the Franks, who coveted Egypt's wealth and its control of trade with the East. By 1169, Saladin had taken over Egypt himself.

Saladin soon restored Egypt to peace and prosperity and expelled the Franks from Damietta, where they had established themselves during the Second Crusade (1147–49). After Nur al-Din's death in 1174, Saladin won out over rivals to succeed him in Mosul. Saladin (r. 1174–93) defeated the Byzantines in 1176, and after the emperor Manuel's death in 1180 the Byzantines became preoccupied by dynastic conflicts. This freed Saladin to concentrate on Palestine. In 1187 he invaded the Latin kingdom of Jerusalem and crushed its army, leaving the Christians with only the fortress city of Tyre and a strip of coast between Acre and Jaffa. In Europe, the call went out for a Third Crusade.

Saladin was known as a good ruler and a man of courtly manners. He put together a loosely united empire that included North Africa, Egypt, and the coastal regions of the Middle East up to Armenia. His family, the Ayyubids (named after Saladin's father, Ayyub), ruled this empire for sixty years after his death in 1193. Under the Ayyubids, Egypt remained prosperous, though not militarily strong. The commercial cities of Italy were permitted to trade there, ensuring Egypt's position in international trade.

THE MONGOL INVASION

In northern Persia and the Transoxiana, Khwarazm and its Seljuk government collapsed under assault by Oghuz tribesmen who appeared out of the central Asian steppes. At the same time, the Ghaznavids were overthrown by Ghurids, tribesmen from the foothills of the Hindu Kush who had recently converted to Islam. A new Persian dynasty, whose rulers used the old Persian title "shah," arose in Khwarazm and by the end of the twelfth century drove the Ghurids back beyond the Indus River.

In the first decades of the thirteenth century this dynasty, which was Shiite, tried to seize Baghdad, but in the midst of this effort the shah made a fatal error by ordering his men to massacre a caravan of merchants from central Asia. The merchants were Mongols, from an empire ruled by Chengis (Ghengis) Khan. To avenge the massacre, Chengis Khan attacked the Transoxiana in 1220 and overran it, using Chinese engineers to take the fortified towns by siege. In two years of campaigning, he totally destroyed the Kwarazmite state and then returned to Mongolia.

The next generation of Mongols launched a new phase of expansionism. They conquered Russia and pushed on into eastern Europe, reaching the Adriatic in 1241. Fourteen years later, the Mongol army, a composite of Mongol, Turkish, Armenian, and Georgian troops, moved into Persia and the Middle East. After destroying the Isma'ili Assassins, they marched on Baghdad. When the caliph failed to respond quickly enough to a demand that he open the gates, the Mongol army stormed the city and demolished it. According to the most conservative estimate, the Mongols slaughtered 800,000 people. Only Christians were spared, presumably because there were some Christians in the besieging army. The Abbasid caliphate, weakened by centuries of conflict, at last came to an end in 1258 when the last of the line surrendered to the Mongols.

By 1260, the Mongol army was in Syria, perhaps planning to set up a Mongol khanate in the Middle East. But when news arrived of the Great Khan's death in Mongolia, most of the army withdrew to the Caucasus to await the succession. The Mamluk Turks, who had won control of Egypt in 1250, now moved to halt the Mongol advance, and in late 1260 a Mamluk army routed the Mongol forces in Syria at Ain Jalut, near Nazareth, and broke the momentum of the Mongol conquest. Mamluk Egypt emerged as the most powerful state in Islam and remained so until the rise of the Ottoman Turks in the fifteenth century.

ISLAMIC SOCIETY AND ECONOMY

The Arabs came from a tribal society, and in the early years of the empire even their cities were controlled and organized by the tribes. But the towns had enough governmental organization to operate elaborate water systems and to maintain roads and fortifications. In time, the tribes lost some of their power and the towns became like those of other ancient cultures. The tradespeople lived in specific quarters, centered on the main mosque, and there is some evidence that they were organized into something like craft guilds. But we know almost nothing about those organizations.

The towns provided the major markets for wares and produced most of the manufactured goods. Long-distance traders brought in their goods by caravan and stored them in warehouses provided by the central government. After paying a duty on their cargoes, they sold their goods to the local townspeople. Wherever there was a caravansary (an inn for the caravans), the long-distance trade was kept separate from the local market, which was controlled by the town's own merchants.

Transactions were carried out by means of financial instruments that are still used in world trade. For example, Arab merchants used the letter of credit to transfer funds from one end of the Empire to the other. A merchant in one city would pay the bearer of a letter of credit a sum of money in full confidence that it would be paid over to his agent in another city. So long as there was a stable flow of goods in both directions, the principal merchants could assume that the accounts would balance. The Arabs also invented a kind of promissory note that evolved into the modern bank check. In fact, the word "check" probably derives from an Arabic word.

Islamic society was more tolerant of ethnic diversity than either Byzantine or European society. The Arabs intermarried with the local populations, and migrating peoples constantly added to the mix. Because most caliphs were the sons of slave women or of the lowborn wives of their royal sires, there was little room for the emphasis on racial purity that was so common in Constantinople and in the Germanic kingdoms.

The caliph's family served as a model for ordinary families in the society. The *Koran* permitted Moslems to have four wives and accepted the keeping of slave concubines. In practice, only wealthy men could afford to keep several wives and concubines, but most men above the lowest class had at least one wife and one concubine. So the typical Moslem household was large, with the wives and concubines, all their children, and the

The Moslem's Behavior around Women

Mohammed ordered women to cover their beauty, lest they become a cause of sin.

And let them [women] not display their beauty and ornaments except what [must ordinarily] appear thereof. And let them draw their garment over their bosoms and not display their beauty except in the presence of their husbands, or their own fathers, or their husbands' fathers, or their own sons, or their husbands' sons, or their own brothers, or their brothers' sons, or their sisters' sons. . . .

Koran 24:31

In his treatise (thirteenth century) about the duties of the muhtasib, *the law enforcement official of the medieval Islamic town, al-Ukhuwwa tells the muhtasib how to regulate the relations between men and women. The passage is headed "Reprehensible Conduct."*

The muhtasib must prevent people from placing themselves in dubious situations and from incurring suspicion. He must be timely in his warning and not hasten to punish. . . . The muhtasib may not interfere with a man and woman standing conversing in a frequented street and where their conduct shows no sign of offence. In an unfrequented street and in cases of doubt he must forbid them to continue yet must not be in haste to punish, for the woman may be closely related to the man. He must warn the man to keep the women of his family out of dubious situations. . . . The muhtasib must visit the places where women congregate, such as the thread and cotton markets, the riverbanks, and the doorways of the women's bath-houses. Any young men found there without lawful business must be punished by the muhtasib.

From The Ma'alim al-Qurba, *ed. and trans. by R. Levy (London: Luzac, 1938), pp. 9–10.*

household slaves. Most families had at least one or two slaves.

Moslem households were ruled by males, just as the desert tribes had been. Life in the desert depended on the cohesiveness of the group, and that in turn depended on the character of the leader. The quality of his leadership brought either honor or shame to the tribe and to himself and influenced the degree of respect the tribe commanded from other tribes. Islamic society continued to ascribe high value to the honor of men. Status, a measure of respect a man won from others, determined his every prospect—his

The caravansary at Siras-Kayser Road, Turkey. Merchants set up their booths under the arches. Centralization of foreign commerce made government control possible.

Moslem Values and the Behavior of a Prince

In the late eleventh century, Kai Ka'us Ibn Iskandar, ruler of a principality south of the Caspian Sea, wrote a treatise on how to be a prince for his son and heir. His advice gives a good picture of conventional Islamic social values, but it also contains advice to act expediently when necessary.

Much as you would not be parsimonious over kindly words, so also, if you have the means, do not begrudge your material largesse; men are more often beguiled by money than by words. Be on your guard against places of doubtful repute and flee from a companion who sets an evil example in conduct and thought. Do not of your own accord venture into dubious situations, and go only to places where, being sought, you may be discovered without shame. . . . The basis of all virtues consists of knowledge, discipline of the flesh, piety, truth, pure faith, innocuity, sympathy and modesty. As for modesty, although it is said "Modesty is part of faith," yet it may frequently happen that bashfulness is a misfortune to men. Do not therefore be so shamefaced as to cause failure or injury to your own interests. . . . Do not be over-hasty in shedding innocent blood, and regard no killing of Moslems to be lawful, unless they are brigands, thieves and grave-robbers or such whose execution is demanded by the law. . . . Yet do not neglect your duty where blood must rightfully be shed, for the general welfare demands it and out of remissness evil is born.

From A Mirror for Princes: the Oabus Nama, *trans. by R. Levy (New York: Dutton, 1951), pp. 23, 30, 88.*

success in trade and his chances of marrying well. Because every slight or injury was a challenge to a man's honor that had to be avenged, feud was endemic in Islamic society.

In Islamic law, women and men had virtually the same rights, but in everyday life men played the dominant role. Any improper approach to a man's wives or female servants was damaging to his status. It was injurious for someone even to mention the name of a man's wife in public. So women were closely protected and wore a veil whenever they left their home.

Within the household, all women and children lived in separate quarters called the harem. Several competing "families" lived in the harem, with each woman vying with the others to win favor with the head of the household for herself and her children. Mothers instructed their daughters in the household arts and in sex, to help them win favor with future husbands. Whatever influence the women had over the head of the household was exercised within the confines of the harem.

The inaccessibility of women may have contributed to the commonness of homosexual relations among Moslem men. Islamic society was tolerant of homosexuality, though foreigners found it scandalous. Although the percentage of men who were exclusively homosexual was probably no greater than in other societies, many Moslem men who ordinarily had relations with women also had occasional relations with men.

Perhaps the society's liberal attitudes toward racial and ethnic differences allowed men and women opportunities to rise from poverty and lowly status to wealth and, in the case of men, power. The Islamic aristocracy was less exclusive than its counterparts in the Byzantine Empire and Europe. Men often took wives and concubines from families less well placed than themselves, and their children enjoyed all the advantages of the household. Moreover, the educational system gave some talented young men an opportunity to enter the bureaucracy; others could grow rich through commerce. Islamic society was a society of self-made men.

ISLAMIC CIVILIZATION

Islamic civilization began in the attempt to turn the Arabic language into a medium of governmental and intellectual activity. Then it was transformed into a hybrid civilization by the revival of Persian literature and culture under the Saminids and the Seljuk Turks. Nonetheless, the acceptance of Arabic as the language of religion consolidated the Islamic world into a single intellectual community, and the availability of an inexpensive writing material—paper—sped the process along. The Chinese had used paper since about A.D. 100, but it did not become known to the Mediterranean world until 751, when Chinese prisoners of war were brought to Samarkand, north of the Transoxiana. From there, the use of paper spread to Baghdad, where a papermill was founded in 793, and then to Egypt (900) and Spain (950). The Europeans learned of paper from Spain, but as late as the thirteenth century paper was rare in Europe. By reducing the cost of written materials, the use of paper broadened the community of writers and readers.

Islamic civilization absorbed the philosophical and scientific traditions of Hellenistic culture, the astronomical and medical science of Persia and its predecessors in Mesopotamia, and the mathematics of India. ("Arabic" numerals came from India and were first used by Islamic writers in the late ninth century.) It also incorporated contributions from various ethnic groups in the population. The Syrian Christians were the heirs of the Hellenistic civilization and had translated many important Greek works into Syriac, including the works of Aristotle and other Greek authors. When those translations were subsequently translated into Arabic, they exerted a significant influence on Islamic philosophy and theology. Western Europeans rediscovered Aristotle through contact with Islamic and Jewish scholars in Spain, Sicily, and the Latin kingdom of Jerusalem and also received elaborate commentaries written by Moslem scholars. The most important of these commentaries were by the physician and scientist Ibn Sina (or Avicenna, 980–1037) and the philosophers al-Kindi and Ibn Rushd (or Averroes, 1126–98).

Ibn Sina was a Persian from Samarkand, al-Kindi was an Arab, and Ibn Rushd was a Moor from Spain. Although people from all over the Islamic world contributed to Islamic civilization, it was dominated by the Persians. The first great Islamic historian, Tabari (d. 923) was Persian, as were the mathematician and poet Omar Khayyam (d. 1123), the scientists al-Biruni (d. *ca*. 1050) and Ibn Sina, and the first scholar of comparative religion, Shaharastani (d. 1153). After the reemergence of Persian culture under the Samanids and Ghaznavids during the tenth century, Persian poetry and literature experienced a renaissance that continued under the Turks.

Advances in western Europe in the science of optics during the thirteenth century owed a great deal to discoveries made by Islamic scientists in their efforts to treat eye diseases, which were so prevalent in North Africa and the Middle East. Arabic medical works became available in Latin translations late in the twelfth century and served as the basis of medical study in Europe for centuries.

The study of medicine touched not just physiology and pharmacology, but all sciences: astronomy, physics, chemistry, botany, and optics. Arabic physicians dealt both with the bodily humors (fluids), which they believed caused disease when present in improper proportions, and with astronomical powers that they believed affected worldly events. Astrology, an ancient Babylonian science, had been kept alive by the successive civilizations of the Middle East and had spread throughout the Mediterranean Basin in Roman times. Christian writers of the late Roman period, notably Augustine (d. 430), condemned belief in astrology as a superstition, but the Arabs considered it a science. The influence of astrology grew in the West after Arabic medical texts became available to European physicians.

The Mongol invasion did serious damage to the Islamic civilization, as did the conquest of Spain by the Christians, who by the thirteenth century had pinned the Moslems down in the southern region of the peninsula. These events sharply reduced the intellectual activity in the two most vibrant centers of the Islamic world. Meanwhile, al-Ghazzali's theology (p. 213) had a deadening influence on philosophical and scientific pursuits. Ibn Rushd's work on Aristotle and on theology was meant as an answer to al-Ghazzali's school of thought, but it could not turn the tide. Because he argued that philosophy and religion were separable and contained different truths, he was condemned both in Islam and in Christendom, both of which insisted on the oneness of truth. For example, Ibn Khaldun (1337–1406), one of the most profound thinkers of Is-

lam, regarded all true knowledge as consistent with religious knowledge.

After about 1200, few creative minds were at work in Islam. Intellectual activity continued in places such as Egypt, which had escaped Mongol and Christian conquest, but the activity was repetitive and derivative at best, much like that of the later Byzantines. The true heirs of Arabic civilization were the Europeans, for whom the translations of Arabic works created an intellectual revolution during the twelfth and thirteenth centuries (see Chapter 11).

Today, most Westerners know little more about Islamic culture than what they perceive in the anti-Western fundamentalist movements of the contemporary Middle East. But we should be aware that Islam gave rise to a brilliant civilization that stretched from India to Spain and that influenced European civilization in countless ways. During the classical period, from the ninth to the twelfth century, Arabic poets, scientists, and philosophers were among the greatest in the world. They were making major advances in science and technology at a time when Europe was dominated by uneducated warlords and when no city in Europe could compare in size, intellectual activity, or commerce with even modest urban centers in the Islamic world. Arabic leaders who came into contact with Western crusaders found them unspeakably uncouth. By that time, Europe was approaching an intellectual renaissance of its own, but it would be a long time before Europe achieved the level of sophistication already achieved under Islam.

Suggestions for Further Reading

Islamic Religion

The basic source of Islamic religion is the *Koran* itself. A good translation is that of A. J. Arberry, *The Koran Interpreted* (1955). For a general history, see the *Cambridge History of the Islam,* 2 vols. (1970), a collection of excellent articles on all aspects of the civilization. M. G. Hodgson provides both a survey and an interpretation of Islamic history and civilization in *The Ven-* *ture of Islam,* 3 Vols. (1974). J. J. Saunders, *A History of Medieval Islam* (1965); H. R. Gibb, *Mohammedanism: An Historical Survey* (1949); P. K. Hitti, *History of the Arabs,* 6th ed. (1958); B. Lewis, *The Arabs in History,* 4th ed. (1958); and F. Rahman, *Islam,* 2nd ed. (1979), are good brief surveys. B. Lewis published a large collection of sources in *Islam,* 2 vols. (1974).

The Arab Empire

On early Arabian history, see P. Crone, *Meccan Trade and the Rise of Islam* (1987). De Lacy O'Leary, *Arabia before Muhammad* (1927); M. Rostovtzeff, *Caravan Cities* (1932); and B. Thomas, *Arabia Felix* (1932), are still valuable. For a modern appreciation of Mohammed, see H. N. Kennedy, *The Prophet and the Age of Caliphates* (1986); T. Andrae, *Mohammed, the Man and his Faith* (1952); and W. M. Watt, *Muhammad at Mecca* (1953) and *Muhammad at Medina* (1956). On the early conquests, see F. M. Donner, *The Early Islamic Conquests* (1981), and, for an appreciation of the military achievement, see J. Glubb, *The Great Arab Conquests* (1961). On the historical role of the Prophet's sayings and practices, see A. Guillaume, *The Traditions of Islam* (1924), and P. Crone and M. Hinds, *God's Caliph: Religious Authority in the First Centuries of Islam* (1986).

The standard history of the Ommayyad dynasty is J. Wellhausen, *The Arab Kingdom and its Fall* (1927), which also gives a detailed account of the Abbasid revolution. See also the book by H. N. Kennedy cited earlier. On the problem of conversion to Islam and the economic aspects of relations between Moslems and non-Moslems, see D. C. Dennett, *Conversion and the Poll-Tax in Early Islam* (1950). For specific regions of the Arab Empire, see P. K. Hitti, *A History of Syria* (1951); S. Lane-Poole, *A History of Egypt in the Middle Ages*, 3rd ed. (1924); A. B. Chejne, *Muslim Spain, Its History and Culture* (1974); T. E. Glick, *Islamic and Christian Spain in the Early Middle Ages* (1979); L. P. Harvey, *Islamic Spain, 1250–1500* (1990); B. Lewis, *The Origins of Ismailism: A Study in the Historical Background of the Fatimid Caliphate* (1940) and *The Assassins: A Radical Sect in Islam* (1967); H. A. R. Gibb, *The Arab Conquests in Central Asia* (1923); and A. K. S. Lambton, *Islamic Society in Persia* (1954). D. S. Richards, *Islam and the Trade of Asia* (1971), shows the shift in interest toward the East under the Abbasids. On the Turks, see W. Barthold, *Turkestan down to the Mongol Invasion,* trans. of 2nd ed. (1958); D. Talbot Rice, *The Seljuks in Asia Minor* (1961); and C. E. Bosworth, *The Ghaznavids* (1963).

Islamic Society and Civilization

For studies of Islamic society, see the work of Hodgson, cited above and articles in the *Cambridge History of Islam*. The broadest treatments are R. Levy, *The Sociology of Islam* (1957), and I. M. Lapidus, *A History of Islamic Societies* (1988); see also, W. M. Watt, *Islam and the Integration of Society* (1961). N. Abbot, *Two Queens of Baghdad* (1937), focuses on life in the Abbasid court. S. Goitein, *A Mediterranean Society,* 4 Vols. (1967–80) is based on the discovery in Egypt of a treasure of Jewish documents, but, because the Jews were a well-assimilated minority, it reveals a great deal about the whole Islamic society and economy of the Near East. See also, A. Udalvitch, *Partnership and Profit in Medieval Islam* (1967); B. Lewis, *The Jews of Islam* (1984); and B. Ye'or, *The Dhimmi: Jews and Christians under Islam* (1985).

On Islamic civilization, see G. E. von Grunebaum, *Classical Islam, 600–1258* (1970) and *Medieval Islam: A Study in Cultural Orientation,* 2nd ed. (1953); see also, H. A. R. Gibb, *Arabic Literature,* 2nd ed. (1963); and the essays published in R. M. Savory, ed., *Islamic Civilization* (1976). On special topics, see R. Walzer, *Greek into Arabic, Essays on Islamic Philosophy* (1962); C. Elgood, *A Medical History of Persia* (1951); A. J. Arberry, *Revelation and Reason in Islam* (1957); and S. H. Nasr, *Science and Civilization in Islam* (1968). H. A. R. Gibb and H. Bowen, *Islamic Society and the West,* 2 vols. (1950 and 1957), explore the impact of the West on Islam. On the same general subject, see B. Lewis, *The Middle East and the West* (1964) and *The Muslim Discovery of Europe* (1982). For Western views of Islam, see N. Daniel, *Islam and the West: The Making of an Image* (1960), and R. W. Southern, *Western Views of Islam in the Middle Ages* (1962). In general, see T. Arnold and A. Guillaume, eds., *The Legacy of Islam* (1931).

9

THE EMERGENCE OF WESTERN EUROPEAN CIVILIZATION

As we saw in Chapter 5, the amalgamation of Germanic society and Christianity during the sixth and seventh centuries transformed the European provinces of the Roman Empire into a western Christendom unified in a church centered on the Roman pope. That amalgam became the basis of a new European civilization in the eighth and ninth centuries, when the Carolingians, the successors of the Merovingians, created new social and legal institutions and amassed wealth that enabled them to attract men and ideas from all over Europe. The Carolingian dynasty was named for its most famous member—in Latin, Carolus Magnus—in French, Charlemagne. We will call him by his English name, Charles the Great. By the time the dynasty collapsed in the mid-tenth century, the political and cultural foundations of modern Europe had been established.

The age in which these events took place is called the Middle Ages, the period between the collapse of the western Roman Empire in the fifth and sixth centuries and the beginning of the Italian Renaissance in the late fifteenth century. The term "Middle Ages" was coined by Renaissance thinkers who viewed themselves as heirs of Roman civilization and saw the age between the end of Roman civilization in the West and their own time as a benighted "dark age." As we shall see, they exaggerated the intellectual and artistic poverty of medieval Europe, which produced the foundations of their own "modern" civilization.

THE RISE OF THE CAROLINGIANS

The Mayors of the Palace under the Late Merovingians

By the early seventh century, the Merovingian dynasty founded by Clovis (r. 481–511) had declined, and its kings no longer exercised real authority. Dagobert (r. 629–39) was the last Merovingian who actually

The Frankish Kingdom   *ca.* 700

ruled his kingdom. After his death, though a succession of weak Merovingian kings still occupied the throne, the mayors of the palaces governed the various parts of the kingdom—Austrasia, Neustria, and Burgundy. That the Franks permitted weak kings to remain on the throne was an indication of how thoroughly they had absorbed Roman legal and political ideas. The old Germanic idea of kingship precluded a weak man from sitting on the throne; the king must lead his army to victory and protect the interests of his people. By contrast, the Romans had a legalistic view of authority that emphasized the legitimacy of the ruler rather than his competence.

The late Merovingians combined the Roman and Germanic views. They preserved the old Germanic notion that the king was a special person who stood between the community and God, but they accepted the Roman idea that power could be exercised by officials under royal authority, as well as by the king himself.

The idea that men other than the king could perform the functions of the king was the basis of the authority held by the mayors of the palace.

During the second half of the seventh century, the mayors of the various royal palaces contended for control of the Frankish kingdom. Although the Franks viewed the kingdom as if it were property to be distributed among the legitimate sons of the king when he died, they insisted that the kingdom itself remained a single entity, no matter how many kings ruled its various parts. In the civil wars of the sixth and early seventh century, it was the Merovingian kings themselves who sought to unify the kingdom under a single ruler. In the later seventh century, the struggle was carried on by the mayors of the palaces fighting on behalf of their titular kings. In 687, Pepin of Heristal, a forebear of the Carolingians who had been mayor of the palace in Austrasia since 680, ended the civil wars by defeating the mayors of Neustria and Burgundy at the battle of Tertry. By the time Pepin died in 714, he had unified the kingdom and restored the authority of the central government.

Pepin bequeathed the mayoralty to his two young grandsons. But a group of aristocrats, led by men from Neustria and Burgundy, rebelled, and the regents lacked the power to put them down. In the chaos that ensued, one of Pepin's illegitimate adult sons, Charles, defeated the aristocrats, did away with his nephews, and seized power. A hard man and seasoned warrior, Charles (r. 719–41) earned the nickname Martel, "the Hammer."

In addition to trying to keep the unruly aristocrats under control, Charles had to cope with efforts by the Moors in Spain to seize Frankish territory. The Moors had conquered the Iberian peninsula in 711, and in 720 they captured Narbonne, the capital of the ancient Roman province of Septimania. From that city as a base, they carried out raids against Aquitaine, a rich province in the southwest of Gaul. For decades, the dukes of Aquitaine had maintained their independence from the Merovingian government, but, faced with these devastating raids, Duke Eudes now turned to Charles for help. Around 732, Charles

Gold fibula decorated with paste and precious stones (seventh century).

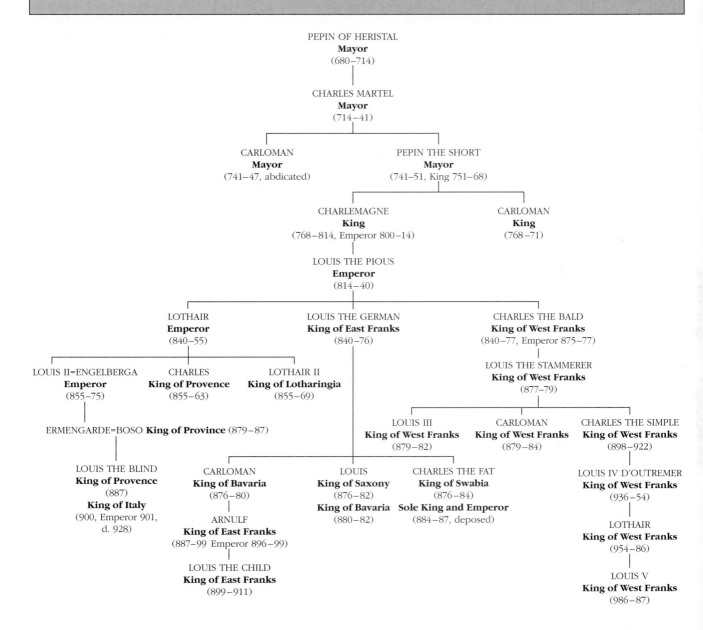

THE CAROLINGIANS

PEPIN OF HERISTAL
Mayor
(680–714)

CHARLES MARTEL
Mayor
(714–41)

CARLOMAN
Mayor
(741–47, abdicated)

PEPIN THE SHORT
Mayor
(741–51, King 751–68)

CHARLEMAGNE
King
(768–814, Emperor 800–14)

CARLOMAN
King
(768–71)

LOUIS THE PIOUS
Emperor
(814–40)

LOTHAIR
Emperor
(840–55)

LOUIS THE GERMAN
King of East Franks
(840–76)

CHARLES THE BALD
King of West Franks
(840–77, Emperor 875–77)

LOUIS II=ENGELBERGA
Emperor
(855–75)

CHARLES
King of Provence
(855–63)

LOTHAIR II
King of Lotharingia
(855–69)

LOUIS THE STAMMERER
King of West Franks
(877–79)

ERMENGARDE=BOSO **King of Province** (879–87)

LOUIS III
King of West Franks
(879–82)

CARLOMAN
King of West Franks
(879–84)

CHARLES THE SIMPLE
King of West Franks
(898–922)

LOUIS THE BLIND
King of Provence
(887)
King of Italy
(900, Emperor 901,
d. 928)

CARLOMAN
King of Bavaria
(876–80)

LOUIS
King of Saxony
(876–82)
King of Bavaria
(880–82)

CHARLES THE FAT
King of Swabia
(876–84)
Sole King and Emperor
(884–87, deposed)

LOUIS IV D'OUTREMER
King of West Franks
(936–54)

ARNULF
King of East Franks
(887–99 Emperor 896–99)

LOTHAIR
King of West Franks
(954–86)

LOUIS THE CHILD
King of East Franks
(899–911)

LOUIS V
King of West Franks
(986–87)

defeated a large Moorish army near Poitiers that had been on its way to plunder the rich church of Tours, which contained the shrine of St. Martin, the monk-bishop (p. 136). From this time on, the Moors remained on the defensive in southern Gaul and Aquitaine accepted the rule of the royal government.

Charles encouraged the Irish and Anglo-Saxon monks who were carrying on the missionary work of Columbanus and his confreres (pp. 136–37) and became closely associated with Wynfrith, the greatest among them. Wynfrith was a monk from Wessex who, after visiting Rome in 718 and winning papal approval of his work, had taken the Roman name Boniface. He founded the monastery of Fulda in central Germany as a missionary base and for two decades was the most prominent churchman in the Frankish kingdom. In 722 Pope Gregory II (r. 715–31) consecrated Boniface as a missionary bishop to Germany, where he worked under the protection of Charles Martel. And in 751 Pope Zacharias (r. 741–52) consecrated him as the first Archbishop of Mainz, which subsequently became the principal diocese in Germany.

It may have been through Boniface that Pope Gregory III (r. 731–41) approached Charles Martel in 739 for help against the Lombards, who were threatening Rome. The pope had asked Constantinople for help, but the emperor had ignored his plea. Relations between the papacy and Constantinople were severely strained at the time by the controversy over iconoclasm (pp. 175–78). Moreover, the Byzantine armies were busy fighting wars against the Ommayyad caliphate and the Bulgarians. Charles, too, turned down the pope's request for help against the Lombards. The Lombard king, Luitprand, had aided the Franks in their war against the Moors, and Charles had sent his son Pepin III to the Lombard court to cement relations between the two royal families. Charles had nothing to gain by helping the pope.

When Charles Martel died in 741, the mayoralty went to his sons, Pepin the Short (r. 741–68) and Carloman (r. 741–47). Like their father, they supported Boniface in his missionary and reform efforts, including his plan to establish Benedictine monasticism (pp. 137–38) as the principal form of monasticism in the Frankish kingdom. Frankish monasticism existed in a bewildering variety of forms at the time, and the disarray disturbed right-thinking churchmen like Boniface. Further, because people associated political unity with religious unity, the confusion threatened the unity of the kingdom. Shortly after they succeeded to the mayoralty,

Pepin and Carloman summoned councils in which Boniface tried to bring to the monasteries some degree of uniformity. Then, in 747, Carloman, who had become caught up in the reform movement himself, retired to a monastery, first in Rome and then at Montecassino, the mother house of Benedictine monasticism, leaving Pepin the Short in control of the kingdom.

The Making of a New Royal Family

Under Charles Martel, the king had been reduced to a nonentity, and during the last years of his life Charles had actually ruled without a king. When Pepin and Carloman succeeded to the mayoralty, however, they felt they needed a king to establish their legitimacy. A search throughout the kingdom produced a distant relative of the royal family, who in 743 was crowned as Childeric III. But after governing for a time, Pepin decided that he had no need for Childeric, who was living a dissolute life under virtual house arrest. So he took the revolutionary step of transferring royal power to himself, with the support of the aristocracy.

To replace the ancient dynasty was a tricky matter. Pepin lacked the divine character that the Germans attributed to their kings, and the right to be God's minister on earth rested not on the exercise of power, but on hereditary right. In his search for a way to overcome this defect in his legitimacy, Pepin turned to the pope, whose goodwill he had gained by his support of Boniface.

In 749 or 750, Pepin wrote to Pope Zachary and asked the question: "Was it right that the king of the Franks, though he had no power, nevertheless occupied the royal office?" Zachary answered that Pepin, who was in fact exercising royal authority, was indeed king, and in 751 the Frankish bishops anointed him in the manner in which the Old Testament kings had been anointed. This was a ceremony practiced in Spain, and the idea may have been brought to the Frankish kingdom by refugees from the fallen Visigothic kingdom. But it was unprecedented in the

Frankish kingdom. The anointment was a symbolic declaration that Pepin possessed the divine character of a king and was the true heir of the Merovingians.

The Franks and the Papacy

The warm relationship between Pepin and Pope Zachary led to a change in the Frankish attitude toward the war between the papacy and the Lombards. In the winter of 752–53, Zachary's successor, Stephen II (r. 752–57), asked Pepin for help against Aistulf, the Lombard king who had recently conquered Ravenna, the last Byzantine stronghold in Italy.

Pepin invited Stephen to his kingdom and in January 754 met with him at Ponthion, a royal residence east of Paris on the Marne River. At the meeting, Pepin promised to help Stephen, and in the spring he persuaded the Frankish aristocracy to support this new policy toward the papacy. At Easter, Pepin promised the pope, who had remained in the Frankish kingdom, that he would restore the territories of the papacy. In July, at Saint Denis, Stephen himself anointed Pepin and anointed his wife and sons as well, naming Pepin *patricius Romanorum* (patrician of the Romans) as special protector of the Roman see. The anointment of Pepin's sons confirmed the legitimacy of the new dynasty.

Over the next year or so, Pepin negotiated with Aistulf, but the talks failed to produce what Pepin had promised. In 755, Pepin invaded Italy and in 756 forced the Lombards to restore to the pope the territory centered on Ravenna. The restoration was recorded in a document, now lost, that was deposited in St. Peter's. Known as the "Donation of Pepin," it later served as the basis of papal claims to secular authority in central Italy.

CHARLES THE GREAT AND THE CAROLINGIAN RENAISSANCE

Charles the War Leader and King

Pepin died in 768, leaving the monarchy to his sons, Charles, who became known

as "the Great," (Charlemagne, from the Latin, *Carolus Magnus*) and Carloman. These brothers did not get along well, and the Franks might have experienced another round of civil wars had Carloman not died suddenly in 771. His widow and children took refuge with the Lombard king, Desiderius, who renewed Lombard claims to the territory that Pepin had donated to the papacy. This gave Charles a double incentive to respond to Desiderius's challenge: By defeating the Lombard king, he would honor his father's alliance with the papacy and at the same time would eliminate competing claimants to the crown. He invaded Italy in 773. Within a year he had conquered the Lombard kingdom and in 774 he took the crown of the Lombards for himself. Carloman's widow and children disappeared.

Charles was a warrior king. For 32 years (772–804), he led a campaign almost every year against the pagan Saxons on

Charles the Great's Conquests and Empire 814

The Golden Psalter, presented to Charles the Great by Pope Hadrian I (*ca.* 780–95).

disputes, and reviewed his army. Because the councils were attended by the leading men of the kingdom, Charles's pronouncements were immediately conveyed to those who were affected by them or who had to carry out his orders. Charles also issued numerous capitularies (so called because they were divided into chapters, *capitula*), which regulated the administration of royal and ecclesiastical estates and dealt with other functions of government. To implement these regulations, he used the countship, a late Roman office that combined military and civilian authority, and appointed counts throughout the kingdom. Although the counts were royal officials, they were not entirely dependent on the central government for their power. Their standing derived as well from their own ancient families and landed estates, so that even under the powerful Charles they could not always be trusted to be loyal. Consequently, Charles appointed *missi dominici* (men sent by the king) as special agents of his government. These men traveled regular circuits to check up on the counts and the bailiffs who managed the royal estates.

The *missi* usually traveled in pairs, a layman and a cleric, a reflection of Charles's concern with ecclesiastical as well as with secular affairs. Here too, he was following in the footsteps of his father and grandfather. Under Charles Martel many bishoprics and abbeys were actually controlled by secular men who drew on the great wealth of the church to provide him with support. Despite their reliance on the church for political support, however, Pepin and Charles both claimed that, as king, they were God's vicar on earth.

The Carolingian Renaissance

As time passed, Charles grew concerned that the churches of the kingdom, which had developed independently, differed from one another in many significant ways. Boniface had failed in his attempt to consolidate the monasteries under the Benedictine rule, and the old variations in practice and tradition remained a source of disunity throughout the Frankish church. The liturgy and even the doctrine

the northeastern border of his kingdom and finally brought them under control. He was helped by missionaries whom he supported and who cemented his alliance with the church. In the southwest, Charles continued his father's and grandfather's wars against the Moors. Between 778 and 801 he established a strong buffer territory along the southern flank of the Pyrenees—the Spanish March. During the campaign of 778, the Moors ambushed his rear guard as he was returning home. The story of that engagement was memorialized in the great medieval epic *The Song of Roland*. On the eastern frontier, Charles brought the Bavarians under his power in 787 and established another buffer, the Ostmark (East March), between his kingdom and the restless Slavic tribes of eastern Europe. The Ostmark formed the core of what later became Austria. About 796, Charles crossed the eastern frontier and crushed the Avars, seizing from them an immense treasure of gold. This campaign put Charles in touch with the western frontier of the Byzantine Empire.

Charles matched these military successes with successes in government. He followed his father and uncle in using councils, which he adapted to all sorts of purposes. While presiding over them, he issued legislation for the church, settled of the bishoprics often differed. So Charles decided to undertake a major church reform.

The reform movement was centered in the royal court at Aix-la-Chapelle (Aachen), the ancient Carolingian estate that Charles had made his capital. Charles had become interested in reform early in his reign, and almost from the beginning he had invited intellectuals to his court. In 774, while he was in Italy after defeating the Lombards, Pope Hadrian I (r. 772–95) had presented him with a copy of the papal collection of canon law. In the 780s a number of scholars took up residence at the court, and Charles himself studied with them. It was said that he had difficulty learning Latin, but he was interested in the scholars' learned discussions.

The influence of the Anglo-Saxon missionaries continued under Charles the Great. Their leader was a monk named Alcuin (*ca.* 735–804), who had come to Aix-la-Chapelle in 781 at Charles's invitation. Alcuin had been educated in York— a great intellectual center—and he stood in a line of scholars that reached back to the Northumbrian monk Bede (*ca.* 672– 735), one of the most important scholars of the Middle Ages (pp. 242–43). Under Alcuin, Charles's court became a seedbed of ecclesiastical reform and an influential intellectual center.

The goal of the reform program was to train a new generation of clerics whom Charles would appoint to the principal bishoprics and abbeys of the realm. The

A small bronze statue of Charles the Great or his grandson Charles the Bald. He wears a crown and carries an orb, symbol of royal power (ninth century).

pope had sent Charles a sacramentary giving the order and content of the Mass along with a carefully prepared copy of the Benedictine Rule. In an effort to standardize liturgical practice, the court scholars used these works to produce model texts from which certified copies were made for churches throughout the realm.

in patria pax inuiolata inregno·
& dignitas gloriosa regalis palatii·maxi
mo splendore regiae potestatis· oculis
omnium luce clarissima coruscare
atꝗ splendescere · qua splendidissi
mi fulgoris maximo pfusa lumine

Lowercase letters and a bold, rounded design were characteristic of the elegant Carolingian handwriting, which is the basis of modern type (detail from a ninth-century manuscript).

That effort met with only moderate success, and in 816–17 Charles's son Louis tried again to impose the Benedictine Rule on all monasteries of the realm, again with moderate success.

Alcuin and his fellow scholars thought that the success of the reform movement depended on their attempt to reestablish the intellectual tradition of ancient Rome. What they accomplished was a true renaissance, the rebirth of a civilization of the past. Bits and pieces of Roman civilization had survived in isolated places in England and Spain during the centuries of barbarian rule, but the Roman tradition had been debased and had lost much of its cultural authority.

Alcuin, who was best known as a teacher, developed a curriculum based on that of Rome for the court school. He divided the seven liberal arts, as defined by the late Romans, into the *trivium* and the *quadrivium*. The *trivium* included grammar, dialectic (logic), and rhetoric. The *quadrivium* included arithmetic, geometry, astronomy, and music (which was thought to derive from the structure of the universe). Alcuin recruited a great Italian grammarian, Peter of Pisa, to come to Aix-la-Chapelle, and produce new editions of Roman works on grammar. Paul the Deacon, another Italian, came to the court to seek the release of his brother, whom Charles had imprisoned, and stayed on for a couple of years compiling a book of model sermons for pastors. Meanwhile, Alcuin undertook a new edition of Jerome's Latin translation of the Bible, which had become riddled with errors in the course of nearly four centuries of copying. The work was finished by his students after his death. Alcuin's edition established Jerome's translation, which had competed with an earlier North African version, as the vulgate (*vulgatus,* meaning common) Bible of Europe.

The reform effort inspired by Charles continued throughout his reign, spurred on by his legislation in the Capitularies of 789, 802, and 811–13. The first of these contained a summary of the most important sections of the papal law book Charles had received in 774 and a general statement of the aims of the reform. Its principal effect was to establish the idea that law was the basis of religious life—in other words, that religious life should be regulated by a coherent body of written rules. Previously, religious life had been based on local custom, which was the product of communal practices and the personal preferences of the bishops who had governed the dioceses over the centuries. The Capitulary of 802 reaffirmed the authority of the papal law book, and the Capitulary of 811–13 dealt with various aspects of the reform in detail.

The palace school produced numerous new editions of Roman works as well as new works patterned on them. During the 780s (the exact date is unknown), Charles issued instructions to monasteries and cathedrals to make copies of the old manuscripts in their possession. The scripts used in Merovingian and early Carolingian times were difficult to read and full of puzzling abbreviations and letter forms. This lack of uniformity in scribal practice had contributed to the corruption of the texts as they were copied again and again. At some of the monasteries, particularly the monastery of Corbie (north of Amiens), a clear, easy-to-read script had begun to emerge by the middle of the eighth century, and Charles's instructions to increase production brought it to perfection. For the first time, the monasteries developed distinctive house styles based on standardized ways of writing taught to the scribes. Modern scholars can often date ninth-century manuscripts on the basis of their script.

The new script, called Caroline Minuscule, used few ligatures (connected letters that could become mysterious in the hands of artful or minimally competent scribes) and few abbreviations. The monastic scribes used this script to produce a large library of beautifully written copies of ancient texts in their scriptoria (writing rooms). When the humanist scholars of fifteenth-century Italy were searching for works of classical literature, they mistook these Carolingian manuscripts for ancient copies, because of their clarity and beauty. In their zeal for ancient civilization, they revived the Caroline Minuscule and established it as the script of scholarship and culture. This script continues to be used today: The type you are reading is based on Caroline Minuscule.

The Coronation of Charles as Emperor

After Charles seized the Lombard crown in 774, Pope Hadrian I gave him the title earlier conferred on Pepin: *patricius Romanorum* (patrician of the Romans). But the time came when Charles made claims to spiritual authority that his father probably never entertained, such as sending out clerics as *missi dominici* and taking the lead in the reform of the Frankish church. Around 794 Charles declared himself "rector of the Christian people," a title that suggests Caesaropapism (pp. 176–77). Like Leo III and Constantine V in Constantinople, Charles, though not a cleric himself, thrust himself into the theological debates of his age.

With the golden treasure he had seized from the Avars in 796, Charles built a "second Rome" at Aix-la-Chapelle, using craftsmen and materials imported from Italy to create a palace and a church modeled on the Byzantine structures at Ravenna. The grand style of the Byzantines was also suggested by his entry into international politics when, in the 790s, he sent and received embassies from the caliph Harun al-Rashid (probably to discuss their common enemies, the Moors in Spain). By the mid-780s, intellectuals at the court had already begun to use the word *imperium* (imperial authority) to describe the authority Charles exercised.

After the empress Irene had her son Constantine VI blinded in 797, both easterners and westerners regarded the imperial throne as vacant. Why not, they asked, resurrect the Roman Empire with Charles as emperor? In 800 Pope Leo III (r. 795–816), threatened by political opponents in Rome, called on Charles, the *patricius Romanorum,* for help. Charles responded by setting off to Rome.

In December 800, Charles summoned a council of churchmen in Rome to deal with the dispute between Leo and his opponents. The assembled churchmen declared that they were unable to make a

---

The Coronation of Charles the Great

800

Now when the king upon the most holy day of the Lord's birth was rising to the mass after praying before the tomb of the blessed Peter the Apostle, Leo the Pope, with the consent of all the bishops and priests and of the senate of the Franks and likewise of the Romans, set a golden crown upon his head, the Roman people also shouting aloud. And when the people had made an end of chanting praises, he was adored by the pope after the manner of the emperors of old. For this was also done by the will of God. For while the said Emperor abode at Rome certain men were brought to him who said that the name of Emperor had ceased among the Greeks, and that there the Empire was held by a woman called Irene, who had by guile laid hold on her son the Emperor and put out his eyes and taken the Empire to herself. . . . Which when Leo the Pope and all the assembly of the bishops and priests and abbots heard, and the senate of the Franks and all the elders of the Romans, they took counsel with the rest of the Christian people, that they should name Charles king of the Franks to be Emperor, seeing that he held Rome the mother of empire where the Caesars and Emperors always used to sit.

From Chronicle of Moissac, *trans. by J. Bryce,* The Holy Roman Empire *(New York: Macmillan and St. Martin's Press, 1911), p. 54.*

---

judgment, because the pope, as successor to St. Peter, could be judged by no one. That opinion confirmed the hierarchical view expressed in the Petrine Doctrine, on which papal authority rested. To clear himself of the charges that his opponents had leveled against him, Leo merely took an oath declaring his innocence. With that, the case was closed.

A couple of days after these events, Charles and his entourage went to St. Peter's church, the basilica built by Constantine I just outside Rome, to celebrate Christmas Mass. When Charles rose from prayer at the altar, Pope Leo placed an imperial crown on his head and the congregation shouted the traditional acclamation to the emperor. So began the conflict between Charles and the Byzantines over the imperial title (pp. 179–80).

According to Charles's biographer Einhard, Charles said that he would not have gone to church that day if he had known what Pope Leo had in mind. It is hard to believe that Leo had tricked

Interior of the Palatine Chapel,
Aix-la-Chapelle (Aachen).

Gold coin bearing the likeness of
Irene, empress in Constantinople
from 797 to 802. She was the
first woman to assume sole rule
over the Byzantine Empire,
taking the title of emperor. Her
rule provided the pope with an
excuse to crown Charles the
Great emperor in 800 to fill the
allegedly vacant throne.

Charles, though he may have persuaded
him to go through with a scheme that
Charles later regretted. Charles did not use
the title until 801, and in 806 he divided
the empire among his three sons. This was
traditional for a Frankish king, but it was
inconceivable to the imperial court in Constantinople, which was now convinced
more than ever that Charles did not understand the nature of imperial authority.
Nonetheless, Nicephorus, who had seized
power from Irene in 802, was in a difficult
position. He engaged Charles in tortuous
negotiations that finally, after Nicephorus
had been overthrown, led to a treaty by

which the Byzantines agreed to address Charles as Emperor of the Franks and by which Charles agreed that the emperor in Constantinople was still the Emperor of the Romans. Neither Charles nor his successors ever used the title Emperor of the Franks, however.

Charles was survived by only one of his sons, Louis, who inherited both the kingdom and the title Emperor of the Franks. Louis's sons and grandsons competed for possession of that title, and it continued to be a source of friction with the Byzantine court.

THE DECLINE OF THE CAROLINGIANS AND NEW INVASIONS

The Disintegration of the Carolingian Kingdom

Louis (r. 814–40) was a merely capable man who succeeded a giant, and his reputation has suffered accordingly. His image was not helped by his nickname "the Pious," which he earned by associating with churchmen and monks. In fact, one of his first acts as king was to reform the morals of the royal court, which under his father Charles had become a rather licentious place.

While his father ruled, Louis had been King of Aquitaine, where he had come to know a monk named Benedict of Aniane, a monastic reformer. When Louis became emperor, he invited Benedict to Aix-la-Chapelle and carried on Charles's program of church reform, particularly as it related to the monasteries. Louis held a series of councils to work out the details of various reform measures, and in 816–17 he and Benedict tried to impose the Benedictine Rule on all the monasteries in the realm. The Rule was ultimately accepted, though many of the old monasteries held on to their ancient rules for many years. Louis was not a vigorous patron of learning, and the pace of the renaissance started by his father slowed during his reign.

Louis came to power at the age of 36, when his three sons were virtually adult. In 817, following Charles's precedent, he

Louis the Pious, son of Charles the Great. The words in the poem written across the portrait can also be read as a crossword puzzle, so that the letters in the cross and halo also form verses.

divided the kingdom among his sons, who became kings of various parts of the realm. This arrangement, though it guaranteed the succession, failed as a strategy for governing the vast domain. During the 820s, the sons began warring with one another and with their father, and in 833 they defeated him in battle. Lothair, Louis's oldest son, imprisoned him in the monastery of St. Medard of Soissons, and the leading churchmen of the realm, at Lothair's urging, declared Louis unfit to rule and deposed him. After several months, powerful nobles and churchmen returned to Louis's camp and helped him to regain the throne. But he had to do penance before the churchmen would recognize his legitimacy.

The Division of Charles the Great's Empire

The Treaty of Verdun 843

Aix-la Chapelle

Paris

TO LOUIS

TO CHARLES

TO LOTHAIR

Pavia

Rome

MEDITERRANEAN SEA

0   MILES 200

The Treaty of Mersen 870

Aix-la Chapelle

Paris

EAST FRANKISH KINGDOM

WEST FRANKISH KINGDOM

KINGDOM OF ITALY

Pavia

Rome

MEDITERRANEAN SEA

The events of these years did great damage to the prestige of the royal house as the various aristocratic families played Louis and his sons off against another and seized for themselves royal lands and royal privileges. Moreover, the church-

Lothair I in Roman dress seated on his throne (*ca.* 817).

men's humiliation of Louis reinforced the church's claim that it had the right to participate in crowning the emperor. Charles himself had crowned Louis as emperor in 813. But in 816 Louis was crowned again, this time by Pope Stephen IV (r. 816–17), who had journeyed to Reims to perform the ceremony. Then, in 824, Louis sent Lothair to Rome to be crowned as emperor by Paschal I (r. 817–24). These precedents served to support the church's claim.

After Louis's death in 840, his son Louis (r. 840–76) inherited Germany; he was called Louis the German. Charles (r. 840–77) inherited West Frankland; he became known as Charles the Bald. And Lothair (r. 840–55) inherited a middle kingdom that stretched from the Netherlands (Frisia) in the north through the region west of the Rhine (later called Lotharingia after Lothair's son Lothair II) and Provence to Italy. Lothair also inherited the title of emperor, which he had actually held since 824. In theory, the three held joint power, but immediately after their father's death they renewed their civil war. In 842, Louis and Charles formed an alliance against Lothair. To ensure that their armies would understand the terms of the alliance, Louis took his oath in the Romance language that was then spoken by the West Franks, while Charles took his oath in Old German. The written record of

Louis's oath is the earliest evidence of the use of the Old French language.

The war that stemmed from this alliance ended in the Treaty of Verdun in 843, by which the Frankish kingdom was divided into three independent parts. Louis and Charles agreed to recognize the superior authority of Lothair, who retained the imperial title, though they usually treated him as an equal. Lothair in turn tried to force his brothers to respect his authority. When Lothair died in 855, his holdings were divided among his three sons. Lothair II (r. 855–69) received the northern portion; Charles (r. 855–63) received Provence; and Louis II (r. 855–75) became king of Italy and emperor. When Lothair II died without a legitimate heir, his uncles, Charles the Bald and Louis the German, fought over his part of the "middle kingdom." In 870 the two brothers made a treaty at Meersen that called for Lotharingia to be divided between them. The division was made according to the number of cities and bishoprics in each section, rather than along a natural boundary. Since then, West Frankland (France) and East Frankland (Germany) have continued to vie for control of the region.

The Viking and Magyar Invasions

These endless conflicts opened the way to new invaders. As far back as 793, a raiding party of Northmen from Norway or Denmark had attacked and destroyed the famous English monastery of Lindisfarne. When Alcuin, who was living at the Frankish court, heard about it, he was shocked by the destruction of this distinguished spiritual and intellectual center. As raids continued over the years, Charles the Great fortified the Frisian coast against the marauders. In 810 a large Danish force broke through these defenses; but for several years afterward, power struggles that followed the murder of the Danish king kept the Danes otherwise occupied.

The new invaders were Vikings—"those who go abroad." They usually were beyond the control of the Scandinavian kings. In Scandinavian society men were expected to spend some time at sea trading and raiding before settling down to

life as a farmer. The raiding parties arrived along the coast in their swift longboats and descended on the populace without warning. After seizing whatever they could find of value, they fled.

Some of the Vikings traveled up the broad, slow-moving rivers of northern Europe and carried out raids deep in the interior. In 834, a large band sailed up the Seine and sacked Paris, and another sailed up the Elbe and destroyed Hamburg. In the succeeding decades, Viking bands established settlements in Brittany and raided up and down the Atlantic coast. They even made their way into the Mediterranean and sacked Seville, in the heart of the powerful caliphate of Cordova.

During the second half of the ninth century, the rise of a strong monarchy in Norway under Harald Finehair drove many aristocratic clans that opposed royal power to Iceland and England. In southern England they banded together in a force known as the Great Army, which by the 870s had taken over several of the

Section from the Strasbourg Oaths, earliest examples of the dialects that became French and German. The oath was taken by Louis the German and Charles the Bald in 842, when they agreed to oppose their brother Lothair. The first paragraph gives the oath in French, taken by Louis, the second the same oath in German, taken by Charles. *The oath of Louis:* "For the love of God and the salvation of the Christian people and our common salvation, from this day forward, in so far as God gives me knowledge and power, I will succour this my brother Charles in aid and in everything, as one ought by right to succour one's brother, provided that he does likewise by me, and I will never undertake any engagement with Lothair which, by my consent, may be of harm to this my brother Charles."

A rune stone (*ca.* ninth century) found in Scandinavia. The carving is distinctly Viking: Within an elaborate border are two panels, one showing a chieftain on a horse and the other a Viking ship on a voyage.

Remains of a Viking ship at Osberg, Norway.

Anglo-Saxon kingdoms and was threatening the others. Alfred (r. 871–99), king of Wessex, spent most of his reign fighting the Great Army and finally forced it to stop its expansion. Large contingents of the Northmen then settled in a band of territory in eastern England, called the Danelaw (the area subject to Danish law), which Alfred's successors brought under their control. Old Danish, a language closely related to Old Norse, had a strong influence on the development of English.

Some of the members of the Great Army crossed over to the continent where, using northwestern Gaul as their base, they raided deep into Frankish territory. After a generation of warfare, the West Frankish king Charles the Simple (r. 898–922), great-great-grandson of Charles the Great, made peace with Rollo, one of the Viking leaders. Under the terms of the peace, Rollo converted to Christianity, became a vassal of Charles with the title of count, and agreed to defend the kingdom against other Vikings. Charles granted Rollo the lands on which his men had already settled. (That territory became known as Normandy, because the Europeans called the Vikings "Normans" or "Northmen.") These events were among the last of the Viking invasions. Before the

end of the ninth century, however, a new wave of invasions had begun.

The new invaders were Magyars, ancestors of the Hungarians. Linguistically, the Hungarian language does not belong to any known language group; the Finnish language is its only linguistic relative. The Magyars seem to have originated in central Asia. They first appear in history in 895, when the Byzantines set them upon the Bulgarians, thus introducing them into eastern Europe. In a short time, the Magyars had conquered the Hungarian plain, once occupied by the Huns and Avars, and were raiding deep into Germany and Italy. During the first half of the tenth century, they were known as the scourge of Europe. In 955, Otto I of Germany defeated them at Augsburg, and they settled down in what is now Hungary.

THE ORIGINS OF FRANCE

When Charles the Great and then Louis the Pious divided the Frankish kingdom among their sons, they were following the precedent set more than a half-century earlier, when Pepin the Short had had his sons anointed as kings by Pope Stephen. The idea was to ensure the succession of

Invasion of the Northmen, the Moslems, and the Magyars   Eighth to Tenth Centuries

the Carolingian family and to keep the kingdom unified though under the rule of three kings. The Treaty of Meersen (870) in effect sanctioned the independence of the three parts of the kingdom—West Frankland (the future France), East Frankland (the future Germany), and Italy (to which the imperial title was attached).

Caesar Conquers Gaul

56 B.C.	*ca.* A.D. 486	751	987	1328
Roman Gaul	Merovingian Dynasty	Carolingian Dynasty	Capetian Dynasty (Direct Line)	

870
Treaty of Mersen

West Frankland
(France)

Charles the Bald and his Descendants

As we have seen, when Louis the Pious died in 840, his son Charles the Bald (r. 840–77) was king of West Frankland. In the late 850s and early 860s, factions of the nobility rebelled against him, and his brother Louis the German invaded the kingdom at their invitation.

In an effort to strengthen his position, Charles granted lands, abbacies, and royal offices to the great men of his realm, including the bishops, who could offer him substantial support from their seats in the major cities of the kingdom. But this practice only strengthened the recipients of the grants. So long as they supported Charles, the monarchy was strong. But when some of them withdrew their support, Charles found himself in trouble. As a result, the power of the monarchy declined under Charles.

Charles did manage to achieve some notable successes, however. He defended his realm against the Vikings, sometimes by paying them enormous sums of silver. He also reformed the coinage and continued the Carolingian practice of issuing capitularies.

Most significant, Charles revived the Carolingian renaissance, which had slowed under his father. He was a great patron of artists and commissioned some of the masterpieces of the early Middle Ages. Archbishop Hincmar of Reims (r. 845–82), the leading churchman of the kingdom, once compared Charles with the kings of the Old Testament, and several of the illuminated Bibles commissioned by Charles contain portraits that associate him with those kings and with God.

Those parts then began to follow separate courses.

Charles was succeeded by his son Louis II the Stammerer (r. 877–79), whose mind was not much quicker than his tongue. Louis tried to secure his grasp on the kingship by giving away still more royal honors and offices to powerful lay and ecclesiastical figures. He died only sixteen months after his coronation.

The aristocratic factions that had emerged under Charles the Bald now declared themselves in support of one or the other of Louis's teenaged sons, Louis III and Carloman. (Another son, Charles, was born after his father's death and did not figure in the contest for power for several years.) Hugh*, a Welf who had risen to power under Charles the Bald, wanted Louis III to succeed as sole ruler because he was sure that he could dominate the kingdom through Louis. The other main faction, led by Gauzlin, the royal chancellor (responsible for issuing documents and for royal correspondence), and Theudebert of Vermandois wanted to divide the kingdom between the two sons. Gauzlin and Theudebert won the contest by inviting Louis the Younger, son of Louis the German, to invade the kingdom. After defeating Hugh, they paid Louis the Younger to leave (see chart on p. 223).

In 882, Louis III won a major victory against the Vikings, but soon afterward he died in a fall from his horse while chasing a girl. Carloman died two years later in a hunting accident. Because Charles the Simple, Louis the Stammerer's last son, was only five years old at the time, the West Frankish nobles invited Charles the Fat, Louis the German's youngest son and

Charles the Bald enthroned from the St. Emmeram Gospels (Regensburg). The hand of God above his head instills him with divine authority.

---

* The Welfs were an ancient noble family that rose to prominence under Charles the Bald. In the eleventh century, they became dukes of Bavaria and remained active in German and Italian politics for centuries.

by then king of East Frankland, to become king of West Frankland as well. Charles accepted and for the next three years ruled the Frankish kingdom as sole king. Actually, both parts of the kingdom were governed by the nobles, and Charles the Fat was so ineffective that he was forced to abdicate in 887. In East Frankland, the nobles, exercising a right they did not have, elected as king Arnulf (r. 887–99), an illegitimate scion of a branch of the Carolingian line. In West Frankland, the nobles, also taking matters into their own hands, broke with precedent and chose a non-Carolingian ruler, Odo.

The Rise of the Capetians, Counts of Paris

The family of Odo (r. 887–98) had risen to prominence as a result of Charles the Bald's largesse. Odo's father, Robert the Strong (d. 866), had received many countships and abbacies from Charles and had been one of Charles's favorites. His power was centered in Paris. When Odo succeeded his father as count of Paris, he proved himself by defending the Paris region against the Vikings, and as king he continued to fight the Vikings. Odo relied heavily on his brother Robert throughout his reign. After Odo's death, and the death of Odo's infant son, Robert became Odo's heir.

By the early 890s, Robert of Paris had become a *marquis,* a royal officer superior to all the counts in the region. This title had once designated a royal officer responsible for a march (a border region). Thus Odo continued the Carolingian policy of relying on the aristocracy to conduct government. Over time, the kingdom became a collection of semiautonomous principalities ruled by aristocrats.

That the great men of the realm regarded Odo's kingship only as a brief interlude in the history of the Carolingian monarchy became apparent in 893. They rebelled against Odo and had Charles the Simple, now fourteen years old, crowned king. Odo quickly put down the rebellion, and Charles withdrew to Lotharingia. But when Odo died on January 1, 898, Charles was accepted as king. Odo's brother Robert was one of the young king's principal

supporters, and Charles rewarded him handsomely for his loyalty.

Although Charles the Simple (r. 898–922) was dependent on the aristocratic factions, he had some noteworthy successes of his own. His action against the Vikings was impressive, and he dealt from strength in making the treaty with the Viking leader Rollo in 911. In that same year, the nobles of Lotharingia chose him as king, rejecting the non-Carolingian East Frankish king, Conrad of Franconia. From that time on, Charles spent most of his time in Lotharingia, leaving the aristocrats in West Frankland, including Robert of Paris, to govern their territories with little interference.

By 920, Charles's neglect of West Frankland and his favoritism toward certain Lotharingian aristocrats led to a rebellion orchestrated by Robert, who was elected king of West Frankland in 922. Charles met Robert in battle in June 923, and, though Robert was killed, his forces won the battle. About a month later, Ralph, son of Richard the Justiciar of Burgundy, was elected king, and shortly afterward Herbert of Vermandois captured and imprisoned Charles the Simple, who died in prison in 929.

Ralph (r. 923–36) concentrated on strengthening his power in Burgundy and continued the practice of awarding lands and offices to noblemen elsewhere in the kingdom to ensure their loyalty. In fact, they accorded him little more than token recognition of his kingship. The most powerful nobleman in the kingdom was Hugh the Great, Robert's son, who ruled the Paris region as count. When Ralph died, Hugh supported Charles the Simple's son, Louis IV, and received the title "Duke of the Franks" as a sign of his power in the kingdom.

Louis IV (r. 936–54) grew up in England, where his mother, sister of the king of Wessex, had retreated after Charles's capture in 923. Louis soon fell out with Hugh and other powerful nobles and was especially determined to break the power of his former supporter Hugh the Great. He might have succeeded had he not died in a fall from his horse in 954.

When Louis's son, Lothair (r. 954–86) ascended the throne, Hugh the Great was the most powerful man in the kingdom, but Hugh's death in 956 left Lothair free to rule on his own. Actually, he spent his reign in constant struggle with the nobles, working tirelessly to set them against one another and to win over their subordinates.

Lothair was succeeded by his son, Louis V, the last Carolingian ruler of West Frankland. He began his reign under the guidance of his mother and of Hugh Capet, the oldest son of Hugh the Great. Once he was free of their guidance, Louis carried on his father's struggle with the nobles. He died without leaving an heir in an accident in 987.

Now the West Franks elected Hugh Capet as king. Like Ralph before him, Hugh (r. 987–96) concentrated on his own region, centered on Paris, and permitted the great men of the kingdom to rule their own principalities with little interference. He was content with their recognition of his kingship. It has been said that his greatest success was in passing the crown on

to his son, Robert. And it is true that the Capetian dynasty endured until 1789.

THE RISE OF THE GERMAN EMPIRE

Henry I

The East Frankish Carolingian line died out in 911, with the death of Louis the Child, who had succeeded his father Arnulf in 899 at the age of six. Instead of reuniting East and West Frankland by accepting the rule of Charles the Simple, the easterners elected Duke Conrad of Franconia as king (r. 911–18). Conrad spent the seven years of his reign vainly trying to assert his authority over the men who had elected him, and on his deathbed he named Duke Henry of Saxony as his successor. Assuming that Henry would be no more forceful than Conrad I, those same men elected him king.

The end of Carolingian rule in East Frankland led to a definitive split between the two main parts of the old Frankish empire, West Frankland and East Frankland. From 911 on, Germany as such became the successor of East Frankland. The last Carolingian rulers of West Frankland might have aspired to reunite the empire, but the loss of the eastern realm was permanent, and the two began to evolve separately.

In 918, the royal house of Germany was in dreadful financial trouble. Powerful nobles had gained control over hundreds of royal estates, which had provided the economic basis of Carolingian power, to such a degree that when Conrad died, only 180 royal estates remained. The dukes of Saxony had been among the most successful usurpers; only five royal estates were left in Saxony. When Henry ascended the throne and added his family holdings to those of the royal house, the number of royal estates held by the German king jumped to about 600.

Henry I (r. 918–36) has been criticized for ignoring the affairs of his kingdom while concentrating on adding to his ducal power. Actually, he devoted considerable attention to his royal obligations. He pushed back the northern Slavs and began

German Expansion to the East
800–1400

German Expansion to the East, 800–1400. Legend: Germanized before A.D. 800 / Germanized between 800 and 1400 / German minorities by 1400

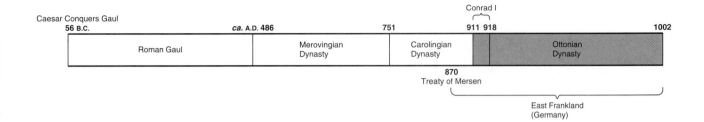

Caesar Conquers Gaul
56 B.C.

ca. A.D. 486

751

Conrad I

911 918

1002

| Roman Gaul | Merovingian Dynasty | Carolingian Dynasty | Ottonian Dynasty |

870
Treaty of Mersen

East Frankland
(Germany)

an eastward expansion based on missionary activity and colonization. Henry and his successors supported missionary activities in eastern Europe and established new colonies populated by Germans. Many of the major cities of Poland and Czechoslovakia began as German colonies in the tenth and eleventh centuries.

Henry also built up a cavalry force to deal with the swift-riding Magyars, who were raiding his kingdom almost every year. In 933, his cavalry inflicted the first defeat on the raiders. Meanwhile, Henry worked assiduously to force the dukes to recognize his authority. He forced the Swabians to accept his nominee as duke; he made a marriage alliance between his family and the family of the duke of Lotharingia; and he struggled to regain control of the old royal estates. He also initiated a policy of appointing supporters to bishoprics and major monasteries whenever he could. In this way, Henry tried to tie the wealthiest and most influential ecclesiastical institutions of the realm to the monarchy. He was the most effective German king since Louis the German.

Otto I

When Henry died, his son Otto I (r. 936–73) became king by hereditary right, though he was formally elected in accordance with the precedent of Conrad's election in 911. Building on his father's success, Otto strengthened the monarchy and continued Henry's effort to bring the Slavs into the church. As part of that program, he carried on the colonization of the eastern frontier and supported establishment of the bishoprics of Magdeburg and Prague. During the first five years of his reign, he put down several serious rebellions led by dukes and substantially reduced ducal power in Bavaria, Swabia, and Lotharingia. In 939, he annexed Franconia to Saxony. His strategy was to put members of his own family in control of the duchies, though he soon discovered that they too had a penchant for rebelling against the central government to advance local interests. So he adopted Henry's idea of using the churches as a basis of royal authority.

To gain control of the churches, Otto had to assert his authority over the appointment of bishops. This authority had once been held by the Carolingians, but it had long ago been usurped by the dukes and other nobles. After reclaiming it, Otto used the royal chapel as a training ground for clerics who later became bishops. Once they had taken up their position as

Ivory plaque showing Otto the Great offering a model of Magdeburg Cathedral to Christ (late tenth century).

heads of episcopal churches, he granted them land and privileges, which provided them with the wealth and power to help him. He also assumed control over the appointment of abbots in the richest monasteries, and they too became agents of royal authority.

Through these policies Otto ensured that the best-educated and most able men in the kingdom would be loyal supporters of his monarchy. Moreover, by seeing to it that the rule of celibacy was enforced among the higher clergy, he reduced the likelihood that bishops would try to launch dynasties of their own. All in all, Otto arranged matters so that the bishops would counterpoise the nobles in their districts and remain loyal supporters of royal authority. The success of these policies was demonstrated in 982, when Otto's successor Otto II campaigned in Italy with an army in which 76 percent of the soldiers had been provided from church-held lands.

Otto I was the most powerful king in Europe, and his court was a center of intellectual and artistic life. In 951, he married the heiress to the throne of Italy— partly to prevent the king of Burgundy from marrying her—and announced that he was assuming the title of emperor, which had been vacant since 924. But

Germany and Italy at the Time of Otto the Great   962

when the pope expressed his hostility to the idea, and when a rebellion broke out in Germany, Otto was obliged to return home. Over the next decade he was occupied with the continuing threat of Magyar raids.

In 961, when the new pope, John XII (r. 955–64), appealed to Otto for help against an Italian usurper, Berengar of Friuli, who claimed to be king of Italy, Otto crossed the Alps for a second time. After dealing with Berengar, he again sought the imperial crown, and at last, in 962, Pope John crowned him Emperor of the Romans. But relations between Otto and the pope soon soured. As emperor, Otto felt that he could assert the same rights in the papal church as he had in the German bishoprics, and John objected. In 963, Otto drove John from Rome and presided over a council that deposed him and elected a pope more to Otto's liking. Otto rigged the election of two other popes during his reign, setting important precedents for later debates over the relationship between secular and ecclesiastical authority.

From 962, Otto spent most of his time in Italy trying to consolidate his position as emperor. He had better success in that effort at home than he did in Italy. The Byzantines did recognize his new title, however, and he achieved the long-sought alliance between the western and eastern imperial houses by arranging the marriage of his son Otto II to the Byzantine princess Theophano.

Otto II, Otto III, and Archbishop Gerbert

Otto II (r. 973–83) spent most of his reign in Germany, trying to cope with widespread rebellions against the monarchy. Otto I had kept the great men in line, and they hoped to regain some of their power under the new king. When Otto II died, they made some progress in that direction. Otto left an infant heir, Otto III (r. 983–1002), in whose name the government was run by the queen mother Theophano and by Adelaide, Otto I's elderly widow.

Although Otto III's authority was recognized immediately in Italy, the regents had to give up a great deal to the German

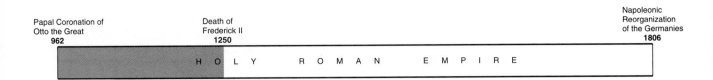

Papal Coronation of
Otto the Great
962

Death of
Frederick II
1250

Napoleonic
Reorganization
of the Germanies
1806

HOLY ROMAN EMPIRE

dukes and magnates to win their recognition. Young Otto III was raised in a court deeply influenced by his Byzantine mother, and when he became king, he dreamed of restoring the Christian empire of Constantine the Great. He was encouraged in this dream by a scholar named Gerbert, who had been Otto II's tutor and who was reputedly the most learned man in Europe.

Gerbert (*ca.* 945–1003) was born in Aurillac in Aquitaine. He studied in Spain, where he learned some mathematics and astronomy from the Moslems. He then traveled to Italy, where he met Otto I, who named him tutor to Otto II. From this time on, he had a close relation with the German royal family. About the time Otto II became king, Gerbert went to Reims in West Frankland to study logic with a famous teacher, and he was soon teaching philosophy at the cathedral school in Reims. About 980, he returned to Otto II's court, and Otto appointed him abbot of the great Italian abbey of Bobbio, near Piacenza. But Gerbert made the mistake of trying to revamp the monastery's financial system, which was controlled by the local nobility, and soon returned to Reims. There he became involved in West Frankish politics, eventually coming down in support of the house of Capet against Charles of Lotharingia, brother of Lothair, the last Carolingian king. With Hugh Capet's support, Gerbert became archbishop of Reims in 991. But some controversy arose over the appointment, and he eventually returned to Italy. There Otto III appointed him first as archbishop of Ravenna and then, in 999, as pope.

Gerbert took the name Sylvester II to signify that he and Otto III were renewing the cooperation between emperor and pope that had prevailed between Constantine I and Sylvester I. In 1000, Syl-vester authorized the establishment of an independent archdiocese in Poland and crowned Stephen king of Hungary. He also brought King Olaf Tryggvason of Norway and his new church into the orbit of papal authority. The dream of rebuilding the empire faded when Otto III died childless in 1002. Sylvester died the next year.

Nonetheless, Gerbert's career was of enduring importance. By bringing teaching and scholarship to the service of the highest authority, he demonstrated that the acquisition of learning was a viable road to success. Moreover, his experience in Spain opened up a world of knowledge formerly unknown to the West. Gerbert was credited with introducing Arabic numerals to Europe; he also reorganized the study of logic. Sophisticated in both political and intellectual matters, Gerbert helped seed a cultural revival that would blossom eventually into the renaissance of the twelfth century.

Ivory plaque showing Otto II, his wife Theophano, and their son Otto III kneeling before Christ (*ca.* 980).

The four provinces of Slavinia, Germania, Gallia, and Roma *(left)* paying homage to Otto III *(right)*, from the Reichenau Gospels (tenth century). Note that Otto wears a Roman imperial costume, not a Germanic one.

Page from the earliest manuscript of *Beowulf* (eleventh century).

ANGLO-SAXON ENGLAND

Anglo-Saxon Culture

By the end of the seventh century the Anglo-Saxon kingdoms had been fully converted to Christianity and had achieved political stability. During the eighth century, they were carrying on an active trade with the Continent and enjoyed a period of prosperity and cultural activity under Offa of Mercia (r. 757–96), the *bretwalda* or chief king among the seven kingdoms.

Although Offa looked on Charles the Great as a leader and model, it was England, not the Frankish kingdom, that had emerged as the intellectual center of northern Europe during the eighth century. At the beginning of the century, the monk Bede from Jarrow in Northumbria rose to prominence and set a tradition that would eventually include Alcuin and other intellectual leaders of early medieval Europe.

Bede (*ca.* 672–735) wrote commentaries on both the Old Testament and the New Testament and helped establish the practice of biblical commentary. He also wrote works on astronomy and intro-

duced the dating system based on the birth of Christ, invented by a Greek writer of the sixth century, that we still use today. His most important work was the *Ecclesiastical History of the English People,* our principal source of information about early Anglo-Saxon history. Bede's greatest contribution was as a teacher, however. His pupil, Egbert (d. 766), became head of the cathedral school in York and then archbishop of the city, which under him became the intellectual capital of England. Egbert's student Aelbert succeeded him as archbishop and appointed his favorite student Alcuin (see p. 227–28) as head of the cathedral school.

As England changed from the pagan warrior society of the migrations to a settled Christian society, poets set down in writing some of the ancient stories that had been recited in the halls of kings for generations. One of those poems was *Beowulf,* an anonymous work that tells of a heroic king who lived in southern Scandinavia before the migrations. The version we have comes from a manuscript that dates from around A.D. 1000, but the earliest version was written about 725. The great battle poems *Maldon* and *Brunanburh* date from the ninth century, though they achieved their final form in the tenth century. Toward the end of the ninth century, King Alfred the Great (r. 871–99) translated Bede's *Ecclesiastical History of the English People* from Latin into Anglo-Saxon and ordered Anglo-Saxon translations of works by Boethius and other Latin writers. Apparently he also commissioned the writing of the *Anglo-Saxon Chronicle,* a history that was continued into the twelfth century.

Anglo-Saxon Government

As we have seen (p. 234), King Alfred defeated the Great Army of the Vikings, and his successors brought the Danelaw, virtually the whole eastern half of England, under control early in the tenth century. Alfred's royal house of Wessex had brought the Anglo-Saxon kingdoms together into the united kingdom of England. To buttress their position, the kings instituted a program of church reform that brought Benedictine monasticism to England and bestowed monastic constitutions on the bishoprics. Henceforth, the clergy of the bishoprics were to be members of the monasteries located in the cathedral churches. The kings also set in place new institutions of local government so effective that they survived for centuries and still appear in modified form in county governments of the United States.

The tenth-century kings divided the country into shires, or counties, headed by shire reeves, or sheriffs, who were royal officials. The shires were subdivided into smaller units called hundreds. These units were judicial as well as administrative units: The sheriff raised soldiers for the army, managed the royal estates in the shire, made sure that the roads, bridges, and any fortifications were kept in good condition, and judged disputes between the king's subjects. The sheriff presided over the shire court, which met twice a year, and oversaw the hundred courts, which met about once a month. Fortified towns were organized as boroughs, with courts of their own.

England from Alfred the Great to Edgar

Powerful as the sheriffs grew over time, they never became independent of the king. Though they came to rank as nobles, below the earls, who were the companions of the king and who were each responsible for several shires, the king could replace a sheriff who failed to do his job loyally and efficiently. By the end of the tenth century the English king had a representative in every part of the country, and during the next century England came to rival Germany as the most powerful kingdom in Europe.

MEDIEVAL SOCIETY: THE GROWTH OF FEUDAL INSTITUTIONS

Until recently, historians referred to medieval society as a "feudal society." The term "feudal" was coined in the eighteenth century to describe a society based on the fief (*feudum* in Latin), a property held by a man in return for services, primarily military service, rendered to its owner, a king or a lord. Although its holder did not own the fief, it was granted to him for life. The services due were personal in nature, including the obligation to attend the lord's court, to support him in arranging marriages for his children, to give him advice about the affairs of the region, and to join him in war. The relationship between lord and subordinate (eventually called a vassal), provided the subordinate with a means of support and thus enabled him to serve his lord.

Peasants held their land from the fiefholder in return for furnishing him with labor and part of their produce. The fief-holder could eject a peasant from his land whenever he felt like doing so. In short, medieval society was seen as a hierarchical structure based on a descending order of rights and obligations.

In recent years historians have revised this view of medieval society, pointing out that simple ownership of land existed side by side with fiefholding, and medieval society now appears to have had a more complex structure than was once believed. Still, feudal institutions did play a distinctive role in medieval society.

Those institutions were based on the notion of "tenure"—that is, one's right to occupy land. Tenure might consist of freehold (outright ownership), leasehold for a finite term, or a right subject to the will of the landlord (villeinage). In the Middle Ages, the right to use a farm or mill often entailed a chain of tenures: the possessor of the property held it by one kind of tenure from another person who held it by another kind from another, and so on. For example, a friend of the king might receive land as a fief and grant some parts of it as fiefs to his supporters, some parts of it under lease to clients, and other parts "in villeinage" to peasant farmers.

In a typical peasant village, some families had freeholds and others were leaseholders or villeins. There were also cottagers, families without land who lived in cottages that belonged to someone else. Cottagers usually kept a small vegetable garden and supplemented their meager living by working for others. A person's legal status depended on the nature of his tenure. Freeholders and leaseholders were freemen with full legal rights. Villeins were subject to the authority of those from whom they held their land. Cottagers were subject to the authority of the lord of the village.

Other aspects of medieval society had little or nothing to do with land tenure, including the personal relationship between lord and vassal, the fragmentation of political authority, and the devolution of royal authority into private hands.

Vassalage derived from an old Roman institution called commendation, by which one person would voluntarily commend himself to another. The act created a legal relationship between them that required the superior party to protect the inferior party and required the inferior to show loyalty and provide assistance to the superior. The man who commended himself became the *fidelis* (faithful man) of the other and took an oath of fealty to him. For example, a small farmer facing ruin might commend himself to a great landowner. That act would lead to a subject tenure, which would enable the farmer to go on using the land.

Twelfth-century seal depicting a vassal giving homage to his lord.

Obviously, commendation was not something that great men ordinarily entered into, and until the eighth century a stigma attached to the idea of a subject relationship, which was then called vassalage. To be sure, an aristocrat owed allegiance to his king, a relationship that derived from the ancient relationship between the Germanic war leader and his warriors, which Romans called the *comitatus*. But obedience and loyalty within the *comitatus* were honorable relationships between free men and their king.

During the eighth and ninth centuries, the idea of the *comitatus* gradually merged with vassalage. In 757, for example, Pepin the Short caught the Duke of Bavaria in a web of intrigue and treason and forced him to commend himself as a vassal. In 787, Charles the Great forced that same Duke of Bavaria to acknowledge his status as a royal vassal. As the device came into use as a means of disciplining presumptuous subjects, the stigma began to wear off.

The idea of feudal tenure derived directly from the Roman law of property. Under Roman law, a person could grant land as a *benefice,* under which the grantee held the land on favorable terms while the grantor retained ownership. In Roman times such grants were made for a definite term, but by the seventh century, under the Merovingian successors to Roman authority in Gaul, benefices were usually made for the life of the grantee. By the tenth century, the fief (as the benefice came to called) had become hereditary. The lord still granted the fief for life, but he always granted it to the eldest son of the previous holder.

The original purpose of the benefice was to cement relations between grantor and grantee. But under Charles Martel and Pepin the Short, it became common to combine the granting of a benefice with a commendation—in effect, creating a lord-vassal relationship. Because the benefice was a way of providing the vassal with a means of support, a man could actually increase his wealth by becoming a vassal. As a result, by the late ninth century a feudal hierarchy was beginning to

---

The Ceremony of Becoming a Vassal   1127

This description comes from the period when feudalism was fully developed. It is detailed because the leading men of Flanders had just accepted a new count after a disputed succession. Homage (the specific obligation of the vassal) is carefully distinguished from the more general obligation of fidelity. By the twelfth century it was assumed that most vassals had fiefs.

On Thursday, homages were done to the count. First, they did homage in this way. The count asked [the vassal] if he wished to become his man without reserve, and the latter answered: "I do." Then, joining his hands together, he placed them in the hands of the count, and they bound themselves to each other by a kiss. Then the man who had just done homage pledged fidelity . . . to the count in these words: "I promise on my faith to be faithful from now on to count William and to observe [the obligations of] my homage completely, in good faith, and without deceit." This he swore on the relics of the saints. . . . Finally, with a little stick that he held in his hand, the count gave investiture of fiefs to all those who had . . . promised security, done homage, and taken the oath.

From Galbert of Bruges, De Multro Karoli comitis Flandiriarum, *ed. by H. Pirenne (Paris, 1891), p. 89.*

---

emerge. Many members of the old aristocratic families who held large tracts of land by freehold chose to become vassals of the king to receive a benefice. About the same time, the word "benefice" was giving way to the term "feudum," or fief.

Under a fief, the service a vassal owed to the king was usually military service. He was bound to serve in the king's army for a certain period—eventually forty days per year. He had to serve at his own expense, which meant that the income from the fief was usually great enough to cover expenses. The smallest military fief was the knight's fief or, as it came to be called in English, the knight's fee. Fiefs were valued according to the number of knightly soldiers they could support, and many were much larger than the knight's fee.

The idea of the knight's fee was not so different from the old Roman idea that anyone who owned a piece of land had an obligation to serve in the army. And

Mailed knight with large shield and spear used by foot soldiers.

A feudal knight accompanying a traveling king (eleventh century).

remember that the Byzantines had tried to ensure the prosperity of yeoman farmers so that they would have an adequate supply of military manpower (see p. 180). Of course, the landholdings in the West were much larger than those in the East, and the fiefs had to support a new kind of soldier. Although the yeomen continued to serve as the backbone of the medieval army, heavily armed mounted knights—professional soldiers—emerged as its elite troops.

The Medieval Military System

The emergence of the new warriors rested on the introduction of a new technology, the use of horseshoes and stirrups. There is disagreement about when these implements came into use. The Huns had been using them in the fifth century, but in Europe their use probably coincided with the appearance of the mounted knights during the eighth century. Horseshoes made the horse a reliable military vehicle, and stirrups gave the rider the support and leverage he needed to fight on horseback.

In an expansion of the vassalage-benefice system, Charles Martel and Pepin the Short built up their new troops by forcing the churches and monasteries to grant benefices to royal vassals, thus bringing the ecclesiastical powers into the

military system. Henry I and Otto I were able to incorporate bishops and abbots into their government because for generations the officials of the church had been supplying knights to the royal armies and were already members of the feudal aristocracy.

Feudal Government

The distinction between military and governmental functions did not exist in early medieval society. It was assumed that the military elite, the king's companions, were also part of his government. In this way, the new feudal hierarchy functioned much like the ancient *comitatus,* which also combined military and governmental functions. The difference was that the *comitatus* was made up mostly of young men who lived with the king but ceased to play a role in royal government when they went home to their farms and estates, whereas the members of the feudal hierarchy held land from the king and were part of his government both at court and at home.

The governmental functions of the early medieval kings were conducted from royal estates spread around the kingdom. Under Charles the Great, the royal bailiffs and counts governed their districts from seats on the royal estates and supported themselves from the income of the estates. Consequently, the rights of government in each district were associated with specific properties, and when the late Carolingians gave away those properties during the civil wars, the powers of government went with them.

In France, where the royal government had been powerless to cope with the bands of Viking raiders that struck without warning, local men had organized the defense of their districts and in the process had arrogated governmental authority to themselves. Some of these men held fiefs, others did not, so the fragmentation of governmental authority into the hands of locals was not related to the emergence of the feudal system. On the eastern frontier, by contrast, the threat posed by the great Magyar armies required a centralized defense that enhanced the power of the German kings and made it possible for Otto I to revive the *imperium* of Charles the Great.

Up to the end of the eleventh century, no region of Europe was totally dominated by feudal institutions. In most regions, some land was held by fiefholders and some by men who held their estates through ancient freehold tenure. Many great men held estates under both systems. The rise of truly feudal states in England and in the Latin kingdom of Jerusalem resulted from conquests that will be discussed later (see pp. 274–75).

LIFE IN EARLY MEDIEVAL SOCIETY

For most people, life was hard in the early Middle Ages. The peasants struggled to produce enough food to feed themselves and their lords, who sometimes had large households that ate a great deal but produced nothing. The lower classes suffered from malnutrition, which stunted their growth and intelligence. No system existed to move foodstuffs readily from one area to another when drought or flood wiped out the crops, so the peasants suffered frequent famines while the upper-class families moved from estate to estate living on the produce of their lands.

The military society of the early medieval kingdoms was dominated by men, and most feudal institutions rested on relationships between men. As hereditary tenure grew more common, however, it became possible for the daughters as well as the sons of a vassal to inherit his fief. Consequently the feudal relationship between lord and vassal was altered to give the lord the right to approve the marriage of the vassal's daughters. An orphaned heiress became the ward of the lord, who could marry her to whomever he wished. It was imperative that the lord choose as vassals only those who were likely to carry out their feudal duties loyally and properly. At the same time, marriage to the daughter of a vassal provided up and coming young men with an entry into the feudal hierarchy, and many men who had

achieved some standing during the Viking period followed this route. In fact, many of the aristocratic families of later times originated from such marriages.

Still, women remained subordinate to men under the law. A woman could not buy or sell property on her own. Whatever she brought to a marriage had to be given over to be managed by her husband. She could not appear in a court of law unless her husband or a male relative accompanied her and acted on her behalf. Although she might influence her family's decision about whom she was to marry, the power to decide resided with her father or with male relatives.

Reality did not usually conform to law, however. The mistress of a feudal household was often left to manage its affairs herself. The husband was often away at the royal court or visiting his other properties, and in his absence the bailiffs reported to her and took orders from her. Moreover, she supervised the education of the children and advised her husband on political matters.

If we turn our attention from the countryside to the cities, we would see that city life was not so different from rural life. Townspeople relied on the market rather than on farming for their livelihood, but they kept gardens and at harvest time many of them went out to the surrounding villages to help bring in the crops. Just as the villages were subject to their lords, so towns were under the control of lords, usually the bishops, who collected fees and taxes from the town market and town court as well as tolls from the local bridges. The lord of the town organized the townspeople for the defense and for the maintenance of the roads and bridges. Townspeople owed service to their lord much as the country villagers owed services to theirs. The early medieval kings came to recognize the commercial potential of the towns only after becoming aware of the prosperous Italian cities that were growing wealthy from the eastern Mediterranean trade. It would be a long time, however, before cities became a significant feature of the economy of northern Europe and before the ways of city life influenced the general society.

Infants were swaddled in the Middle Ages to protect their "loose" limbs and bodies. Here two thirteenth-century nurses hold swaddled infants.

Suggestions for Further Reading

General

On the rise of the Carolingians, see P. Geary, *Before France and Germany* (1988), and J. M. Wallace-Hadrill, *The Barbarian West, 400–1000* (1952). The best work on the Carolingian period is R. McKitterick, *The Frankish Kingdoms under the Carolingians* (1983). On the missionaries, see W. Levison, *England and the Continent in the Eighth Century* (1946), and C. H. Talbot, *Anglo-Saxon Missionaries in Germany* (1954), which treats the relationship between Pepin the Short and Boniface and provides a view of religious life in the eighth century. On Pepin's coronation, the most recent study is M. J. Enright, *Iona, Tara and Soissons: The Origins of the Royal Anointing Ritual* (1985).

Charles the Great

On Charles the Great, see the almost-contemporary life by Einhard, *Life of Charlemagne* (several editions, some with the later life by Notker). For a survey of the Frankish empire, see H. Fichtenau, *The Carolingian Empire* (1957), which emphasizes social conditions. D. Bullough, *The Age of Charlemagne*, 2nd ed. (1973), is a well-illustrated survey. For studies of Frankish institutions, see F. Ganshof, *Frankish Institutions under Charlemagne* (1968) and *The Carolingians and the Frankish Monarchy* (1971). On the economic history of the period, see R. Latouche, *The Birth of the Western Economy* (1961), and G. Duby, *The Early Growth of the Medieval Economy* (1974). For the different views of the coronation of Charles, see R. E. Sullivan, ed., *The Coronation of Charlemagne: What Did It Signify?* (1959). On the relations between the Franks and the papacy, see T. F. X. Noble, *The Republic of St. Peter: The Birth of the Papal State, 680–825* (1984). On the way people of the period lived, see P. Riché, *Daily Life in the Age of Charlemagne* (1978).

Later Carolingians

On Charles the Bald, see the studies in J. L. Nelson and M. T. Gibson, eds., *Charles the Bald: Court and Kingdom* (1981). On the ecclesiastical politics of the ninth century, see P. McKeon, *Hincmar of Laon and Carolingian Politics* (1978), and J. L. Nelson, "Charles the Bald and the Church in Town and Countryside," *Studies in Church History* 16 (1979): 103–18. On the Carolingian view of kingship, see W. Ullmann, *The Carolingian Renaissance and the Idea of Kingship* (1969), and J. M. Wallace-Hadrill, "The *Via Regia* of the Carolingian Age," *Trends in Medieval Political Thought*, ed. B. Smalley (1965). On the origins of the nobility, see the essays in T. Reuter, ed., *The Medieval Nobility* (1978), and D. H. Green, *The Carolingian Lord* (1965). P. Sawyer, *The Age of the Vikings*, 2nd ed. (1971), gives a good picture of the Viking invasions. See also, J. M. Wallace-Hadrill, *The Vikings in Francia* (1975). On Viking civilization, see J. Brønsted, *The Vikings* (1960). C. A. Macartney, *The Magyars in the Ninth Century* (1930), is a scholarly study of the origins and wanderings of the Magyars.

The Carolingian Renaissance

On the origins of the Carolingian Renaissance, see M. L. W. Laistner, *Thought and Letters in Western Europe, 500–900* (1966); P. Riché, *Education and Culture in the Barbarian West* (1976); and L. R. Reynolds and N. G. Wilson, *Scribes and Scholars*, 2nd ed. (1974). For a survey of the Renaissance, see J. Broussard, *The Civilization of Charlemagne* (1969). On Charles the Bald as a patron, see R. McKitterick, "Charles the Bald (823–877) and his Library: the Patronage of Learning," *English Historical Review* 95 (1980): 28–47 and *The Uses of Literacy in Early Mediaeval Europe* (1990). K. J. Conant, *Carolingian and Romanesque Architecture* (1959); A. Grabar and C. Nordenfalk, *Early Medieval Painting: From the Fourth to the Eleventh Century* (1957); and J. Hubert, *Carolingian Art* (1970), give surveys of Carolingian art.

West and East Frankland (France and Germany)

For an overview of the period in which the Carolingian dynasty ended, see R. S. Lopez, *The Tenth Century* (1959). On the history of West Frankland (France) in the period, see E. James, *The Origins of France: From Clovis to the Capetians, 500–1000* (1982). For a general introduction to the history of the Ottonian empire, see G. Barraclough, *The Origins of Modern Germany* (1947); J. Fleckenstein, *Early Medieval Germany* (1978); and B. H. Hill, *The Rise of the First Reich: Germany in the Tenth Century* (1969). K. J. Leyser, *Rule and Conflict in an Early Medieval Society: Ottonian Saxony* (1979), provides a view of politics and social relations in tenth-century Germany.

Feudalism

On the growth of feudal institutions, see F. L. Ganshof, *Feudalism,* 3rd ed. (1964), which gives a good account of "classical feudalism" from the Carolingian period on. J. R. Strayer, *Feudalism* (1965), emphasizes political factors. For the role of feudal- ism in medieval society, see G. Duby, *Rural Economy and Country Life in the Medieval West* (1968), and G. Fourquin, *Lordship and Feudalism in the Middle Ages* (1976).

Women and Society

For studies of women in early medieval society, see P. Stafford, *Queens, Concubines and Dowagers: The King's Wife in the Early Middle Ages* (1983); S. Wemple, *Women in Frankish Society* (1981); and S. M. Stuard, ed., *Women in Medieval Society* (1976), which is a collection of articles on the various roles played by women. See also, A. M. Lucas, *Women in the Middle Ages* (1983); E. S. Duckett, *Women and their Letters in the Early Middle Ages* (1964). On childrearing, see L. deMause, ed., *The History of Childhood* (1974).

10

REVIVAL AND REFORM IN WESTERN EUROPE

By the end of the Carolingian period, what had once been the kingdom of Charles the Great consisted of three separate kingdoms—the realms that would become France, Germany, and Italy—ruled by monarchs with only a vestige of the power that Louis the Pious had left to his sons. Each kingdom was divided into powerful duchies whose rulers acted independently while pretending to support their king. When, in the tenth century, the Saxon dukes in Germany and the Capetian counts in France became kings, they were more assiduous in strengthening their own ancestral principalities than they were in trying to restore royal authority.

During the tenth century only a trickle of long-distance trade found its way to the towns, and urban populations were on the decline. Secular authorities controlled the churches, and the bishops and abbots were little more than feudal lords busily engaged in managing their estates and leading their troops rather than in ministering to the spiritual needs of their parishioners or following the Rule of St. Benedict. Even the papacy had lost much of its stature. After Otto I imposed his control on the church of Rome, the papacy had fallen into the hands of the Roman aristocracy, who used it as a pawn in advancing their dynastic and political strategies. For a moment, under Sylvester II (r. 999–1003), the papacy recovered its international standing, but after his death the Roman families began to buy and sell the throne of St. Peter once again. Finally, the cultural centers of the Carolingian age were without their former luster, and only a few scholars were left to keep Latin learning alive.

Yet, despite this depressing state of affairs, agriculture, the basis of the European economy, began to improve and population growth began to pick up, which fostered a revival of trade. A Burgundian monk launched a program monastic reform that would eventually rekindle intellectual life and reform the church as a whole. And the new kings would slowly turn to the business of ruling their kingdoms.

THE AGRICULTURAL ECONOMY AND SOCIETY

Village Agriculture

The agricultural economy of the Middle Ages was based on the villages, many of which had existed since Roman times. The land of western Europe, which had once been heavily forested, had deep, rocky soil capable of producing rich crops if properly cultivated.

From time immemorial, life in the villages had been controlled by the great landowners. Most of the villages had grown up on the sites of old Roman villas that had been taken over by the new Germanic aristocracy. The lord of the village held part of the fields, controlled the pasturage and woodland, and required the villagers to work his domain. The villagers were under a variety of obligations to the lord, and sorting out who owed what kind of labor service was a matter of great interest.

The confusion arose from the different tenures by which the various families held their land. Many of the families owned their land outright, some held land by villeinage tenure, and some were cottagers with no land at all (see p. 244). The luckier families held strips of land distributed here and there in the common fields that were worked by all the villagers. At harvest time, each family claimed the produce of its own strips. The cottagers worked for others, often for the lord of the village.

Because some strips of land were more productive than others, most of the families held some good land and some poor land. Good luck, good husbandry, or a good marriage gave some families more than others, and every village had poor families and relatively well-to-do families. A run of bad luck, however, such as the death of the husband, or the failure to produce offspring, or a disastrous lawsuit, could alter a family's fortunes. All lived in fear of disaster.

The market square of a thirteenth-century town.

The lord's domain and the village together constituted a unit called a villa or manor. To develop the manor into an economically viable entity, the lords built mills, fish ponds, smithies, and other "industrial" works. Millers and smiths held their respective manufactories from the lord and paid a rent in kind. The rights of villagers to take fish from the ponds were similar to their rights to let their pigs forage and to collect firewood in the woodland or to graze their cattle in the common pasture. Patches of woodland were measured by the number of pigs they could support. Although the typical manor was not altogether self-sufficient, it was a stable, productive economic entity.

The diet of the villagers consisted mainly of bread and cereals, with little meat. The lord kept for himself the right to hunt in the woodland, and what meat the villagers had came from pigs and cattle. But the pasturage always seemed inadequate to provide enough hay to feed the animals through the long winters. Moreover, the fields yielded only about four grains for every seed planted. (Today's U.S. farms yield about 25 to 1.) Consequently, the entire grain crop had to be saved for human consumption and for the next year's planting. The villagers often indulged in great feasts in late winter or early spring—which in pagan times had been associated with fertility cults—in which they consumed animals that would probably have died anyway for lack of fodder.

The Agricultural Revolution

In ancient times, villagers had learned to leave half their fields fallow each year to given them a chance to recover needed nutrients. Cattle grazed on the unplanted fields and helped to replenish them with their manure. The two-field rotation system was used for centuries across northern Europe. At last, however, innovations arose that triggered an agricultural revolution.

One major innovation was the introduction of the heavy wheeled plow. This plow had been used in a few places in late Roman times and may have been invented by the Celts of northern Gaul, though it has been found in early Germanic settlements as well. The simple scratch plows the Romans brought north with them had worked well enough in the dry regions of the south, where deep plowing would have exposed too much soil and would have allowed the moisture to evaporate. But in the moist climate of northern Europe, the heavy wheeled plow fitted with a moldboard could cut deep into the soil and turn it over to bring the nutrients to the surface.

This new tool had a profound effect on village life as its use spread throughout northern Europe during the ninth and tenth centuries. It proved expensive to maintain, however, because the rocks dropped by the glaciers of the ice ages often damaged the plowshare. So the villagers began to band together to buy and maintain their village plow. They needed skilled smiths to keep it in good repair, and the smiths created other farm tools as well.

Pulling such a heavy plow took a great deal of animal power, and teams of six to eight oxen were not uncommon. To put such teams together, several families would pool their resources, another incentive toward cooperation. The more powerful plow increased the yield from old fields and made it possible to bring new fields under cultivation. Consequently, food production climbed steadily from the ninth through the twelfth centuries.

A second great innovation was the introduction of horses to replace oxen as the source of power. Though horses generate a bit less power than oxen, they pull at twice the speed. The use of horses not only increased the amount of plowing

Illustration from an eleventh-century manuscript depicting plowing and sowing.

done each season but permitted the farmers to go out much further from the village before beginning their day's work. The disadvantage of horse power is that horses are more susceptible to disease and injury than oxen.

The change from oxen to horses depended on two technological advances—the use of horseshoes and the development of an improved collar that would enable a horse to pull the heavy plow without injury. The Huns had used horseshoes, as had the Carolingian cavalry. The hooves of horses are quite fragile, and iron horseshoes protected them from the breakage and hoof rot caused by the rocky, moist soil of northern Europe. Horseshoes made it possible to use horses for transport as well as farm work. But until the invention of the new collar, horses could not pull wagons or plows of any great weight because the old harnesses cut across their windpipe. During the ninth century, a new collar, which rested on the horse's withers (the highest points of the shoulder blades), came into use, enabling horses to perform both farm and team work.

Although horses were expensive to maintain, their use gradually spread over Europe during the eleventh century. That development had several important effects. It increased the efficiency of land transport, both for commerce and for military campaigns, and encouraged the growth of an industry served by guilds of teamsters. Moreover, it led to road improvements that in turn opened up new commercial opportunities for crossroads communities. It also advanced the agricultural expansion that was steadily pushing back the medieval forest.

A third technological innovation was the introduction of the three-field rotation system. Although this change took place only slowly in the old villages, which were reluctant to abandon their traditional ways, it was favored by farmers in the new settlements. The shift to three-field farming was complete by the thirteenth century.

The new system expanded the amount of land in production while preserving the old principle that land should be left fallow to recover. This system kept two-thirds—instead of half—of the fields in production at any one time. It also encouraged the villagers to adopt a new scheme of crop rotation, because now they had two large fields to plant instead of just one. They usually planted one field in winter wheat, which they harvested in July, and then let that field rest until the following spring, when they sowed it with a summer crop. After harvesting that crop in the fall, they plowed and sowed the field again in winter wheat. They planted the other two fields according to the same pattern but on a different cycle, so that in any year, one-third of the land was in winter wheat, one-third was in summer grain, and one-third was lying fallow. Over every three-year period, each field lay fallow for a year and a half. In many regions, the summer crop was a legume, such as soybean, which restores nitrogen to the soil.

Horse in harness pulling a harrow (detail from a thirteenth-century manuscript illustration).

The Three-Field System

	Field A	Field B	Field C
First Year	FALLOW until the fall Sow wheat in the fall	Harvest wheat in July FALLOW from July until the spring	Sow oats in the spring Harvest oats in the fall FALLOW until the next fall
Second Year	Harvest wheat in July FALLOW from July until the spring	Sow oats in the spring Harvest oats in the fall FALLOW until the next fall	FALLOW until the fall Sow wheat in the fall
Third Year	Sow oats in the spring Harvest oats in the fall FALLOW until the next fall	FALLOW until the fall Sow wheat in the fall	Harvest wheat in July FALLOW from July until the spring

So the yield increased even more than would be expected from the extra land kept in production.

The three-field system succeeded only where an even distribution of rainfall throughout the year permitted a summer crop to grow and only where farming was done on a village basis. In the Mediterranean region the summers are too dry for growing crops, and in Scandinavia the rocky soil and the short growing season are not conducive to the existence of villages. So the Mediterranean villages stuck to the two-field system, while in Scandinavia most farming occurred on individual homesteads.

THE REVIVAL OF TRADE AND TOWNS

Commerce and the Settlement of Jews in Europe

The political and economic crises of the late Roman period, together with the Germanic invasions, had reduced the size and the economic importance of European towns. Because many of the Germanic kings chose to spend their time on royal estates scattered across the countryside, the towns ceased to enjoy the central role they had enjoyed under the Romans. This was particularly true in northern Europe.

In Italy, the Gothic wars of the sixth century devastated the cities, and it was more than two centuries before they again became major centers in the Mediterranean trade. In Spain, the Moslem conquest cut off the old cities of Valencia, Seville, and Granada from the former European provinces of the Roman Empire and brought them into the Mediterranean commercial system of the Arabic Empire. Not until the slow Christian reconquest of Spain during the eleventh and twelfth centuries did these cities renew contact with the West.

The collapse of Roman power had led to a decline in international trade, which contributed to economic depression in the cities. In ancient times, the long-distance trade had been mainly in grain, but through much of the Middle Ages it was mainly in luxury goods from the eastern Mediterranean. During the sixth through the eighth century, the towns had become local market centers and seats of episcopal administration, hardly conducive settings for population growth or cultural activity.

The later Carolingians tried to revive international trade. They encouraged Jewish merchants to emigrate from Italy to the northern cities by offering them special privileges and protection. The Jews maintained their connections with Jewish communities in commercial centers throughout Italy and the Mediterranean.

The Jews in Northern Europe

The Jews tended to settle into their own sections of town and formed a distinctive cultural community. Jewish religious practice required that they live near the synagogue—the place of worship and study—in buildings centered around a courtyard. On Saturdays, the sabbath, Jews are not permitted to work, cook, or handle money, but they can carry on ordinary activities within their own home. The rabbis defined the courtyard communities as "homes," so their inhabitants could get along on Saturdays. Because the Jewish community was under the protection of the king, it enjoyed a special legal status. All of these features of Jewish life contributed to the isolation of the Jews from the surrounding population.

During the late ninth and tenth centuries, they shipped to southern markets the agricultural surplus produced by the great northern estates. With local markets tied to international trade, the late Carolingian economy experienced a vigorous revival.

Merchants who engaged in long-distance trade had to have safe repositories for goods and funds in the towns they did business in and had to be familiar with the local markets and the men who ran them. Jewish merchants solved those problems by maintaining contact with Jewish communities in various towns and by sending their sons and nephews to be

A manuscript illustration of the barter economy.

their representatives in distant towns. Robbers knew that if they attacked a Jewish merchant, they would have to answer to the royal authorities. They also knew that they would have difficulty peddling the goods they stole. Once a theft was reported, everyone would be on the lookout for the rare goods—the spices, silks, and jewels—that could be easily identified as having come from the merchant's stocks.

The merchants needed substantial amounts of capital to purchase expensive goods in the eastern markets and to cover the cost of shipping them to the West. They borrowed most of their capital from the great landlords, who accumulated money by selling their agricultural surplus in the local markets. In fact, until the late eleventh century Jews were more likely to be borrowers than lenders. But when the crusaders, most of whom were knights with modest holdings, needed to finance their journey to the Holy Land, they turned to Jewish and other merchants for loans secured by the produce of their estates. From the middle of the twelfth century on, the great lords began to borrow money to cover the cost of building their grand fortified castles. And monasteries borrowed money to build their impressive new churches. Thirteenth-century bishops were often concerned about the indebtedness of the churches and monasteries in their dioceses, and many merchants evolved their businesses away from trade into banking.

The Recovery of the Italian Cities

The recovery of the Italian cities began around 800. Venice, on the Adriatic coast, had already been an active center in the trade between Europe and the Byzantine Empire. Founded in the fifth century by refugees fleeing the Huns, the city had come under Byzantine influence during the period in which Ravenna was the capital of Byzantine power in Italy. The city declined during the period of iconoclasm, because the controversy disrupted trade between the eastern and western parts of the Mediterranean (see pp. 175–78). The end of iconoclasm eased relations with the West, and during the ninth century

Medieval Trade Goods   Tenth to Twelfth Centuries

several northern Italian cities, including Venice, had grown slowly as trade with the recovering Byzantine Empire grew stronger.

After the Fatimid caliphs conquered Egypt in 969 and reformed the Egyptian fiscal system to encourage trade (see pp. 209–10), the recovery of the Italian cities gathered momentum. Amalfi (south of Naples), Venice, and Genoa were soon active trading partners of Egypt, and the new wealth spread to secondary markets in Italy and northern Europe. This was the time of the Viking raids, and Italian merchants benefited from the disruption of the trade routes from the eastern Mediterranean through the Baltic Sea and Russia to the Black Sea. The Vikings had moved down the Dnieper River from the Baltic and settled at Kiev. From the late tenth century on, Italian merchants be-

came numerous in Europe, forming the nucleus of a substantial Christian merchant class.

By the middle of the twelfth century, the Italians had come to dominate long-distance trade in Europe. The Italian cities were well positioned to take the lead in international commerce. The breakdown of Carolingian authority began much earlier in Italy than in the north. Even under Lothair, the son and successor of Louis the Pious, Italy found the yoke of royal authority relatively light. One of the reasons for the prosperity of the Italian cities was that they were relatively free of the onerous fiscal impositions of the great aristocratic landholders.

Given all these advantages, the Italian cities responded vigorously when trade began to pick up toward the end of the tenth century. Moreover, through their

An Early Medieval Merchant

When the boy had passed his childish years quietly at home [in Norfolk, England], he began to follow more prudent ways of life, and to learn carefully and persistently the teachings of worldly forethought. He chose not to follow the life of a husbandman but . . . aspiring to the merchant's trade, he began to follow the peddler's way of life, first learning how to gain in small bargains and things of insignificant price and thence . . . to buy and sell and gain from things of greater expense. For in his beginnings he was wont to wander with small wares around the villages and farmsteads of his own neighborhood, but in process of time he gradually associated himself by compact with city merchants. . . . At first he lived for four years as a peddler in Lincolnshire, going on foot and carrying the cheapest wares; then he traveled abroad, first to St. Andrews in Scotland and then to Rome. On his return . . . he began to launch on bolder courses and to coast frequently by sea to the foreign lands that lay about him. . . . At length his great labors and cares bore much fruit of worldly gain. For he labored not only as a merchant but also as a shipman . . . to Denmark and Flanders and Scotland; in all which lands he found certain rare wares, which he carried to other parts wherein he knew them to be less familiar and coveted by the inhabitants. . . . Hence he made great profit in all his bargains, and gathered much wealth in the sweat of his brow, for he sold dear in one place the wares which he had bought elsewhere at a small price.

From Life of St. Godric of Finchale, *trans. by G. G. Coulton,* Social Life in Britain from the Conquest to the Reformation *(Cambridge: Cambridge University Press, 1925), pp. 415–17.*

The Industrial Cities of Flanders

In Flanders, the cities of Bruges, Ghent, St. Omer, and Ypres also were emerging as centers of commerce and industry. Under its counts, Flanders achieved political stability quite early, and the combination of domestic security and rich farmland encouraged both trade and population growth. But the trade was smaller both in volume and in value than the Italian trade. It consisted mostly of raw materials, particularly wool and wood, brought in from England and Scandinavia.

Wool was the basic clothing material of western Europe. But to turn raw wool into cloth took a great deal of work by a variety of specialists. The wool had to be cleaned and carded, spun into thread, woven, smoothed by shearing off the knots and rough spots, and dyed. The production of high-quality cloth required the services of well-trained, experienced craftsmen. The market for good cloth grew stronger as wealth from agricultural production increased, and Flanders emerged as the center of textile production and the most thoroughly urbanized region of medieval Europe. Until the advent of the industrial revolution in the eighteenth century, textile manufacture continued as the most important industry in western Europe.

The Incorporation Movement

Except in Italy and Flanders, medieval towns were small and slow to grow. Nonetheless, starting in the tenth century the older towns showed some signs of growth and new towns were being founded in certain regions. Most of the new towns were located inland from the coastal ports by kings eager to expand the agricultural economy of their realms.

Although the new towns were under the direct control of the kings, the older towns were still subject to local feudal lords. Towns that had grown up around monasteries were subject to the jurisdiction of the abbot, and those around old villas were under the authority of the lord of the villa. The local lords imposed a variety of taxes, tolls, and market fees on

connections with the cities of the eastern Mediterranean they became familiar with several advanced business techniques. From the Arabs they learned how to form partnerships in which a group of men invested various sums for a period of years. The records of such companies specify the kind of business to be undertaken, the shares of the individual investors, and the partners responsible for conducting the business. Partnerships enabled the Italians to accumulate much more capital for their enterprises than the northern Europeans could put together with their borrowed funds. The Italian cities built huge fleets that made regular voyages to Constantinople, Alexandria, and Acre. As trade increased, the fleets grew larger and larger, and Italian merchants became the masters of the Mediterranean.

the merchants who traveled from town to town and thereby hindered the growth of the commercial networks on which trade depended. At the end of the eleventh century, merchants and kings came together to devise a way of removing these obstacles to trade.

The device they came up with was the royal charter of incorporation, under which the king would grant the merchants of a town a charter that gave them the right to govern themselves as an independent corporation under royal law and protection. The town would pay for the privilege to incorporate and would agree to pay taxes into the royal treasury, but the town fathers, who were invariably the leading merchants, could arrange to have the taxes collected in a way that would not discourage commerce.

By the early twelfth century, as a result of trial and error, a model charter of incorporation had been perfected. The model was copied over and over again and the charter movement spread rapidly across Europe. By freeing towns from their feudal obligations, the charter created conditions conducive to the growth of commerce and industry. Any person under some feudal obligation to another was freed from his servile condition after living in an incorporated city for a year and a day. It was said that "city air makes one free."

The newly incorporated cities were run by the merchants, who formed guilds to organize and control commercial activities. Their guildhall commonly served as the city hall as well. But various craftsmen—butchers, weavers, smiths—formed guilds of their own and competed with the merchants for political power. In industrial cities—like those in Flanders—the craftsmen's guilds were especially powerful, and riots often broke out between guilds competing for political advantage.

The Fairs and the Ways of Trade

After unloading the goods they had imported from the East, the Italian merchants packed them up again and transported them north over the Alps by pack train. Commerce in Italy concentrated in the cities. But in the north it took place at great seasonal fairs held in towns that had grown up as transit points along the trade routes. The fairs may have come into being as a result of the foreign merchants' ignorance of local markets and their fear that they would be at a disadvantage trying to do business in them. The great fairs made it possible for sellers and buyers to come together on an equal footing. In any case, northern Europe was too vast for merchants to cover by traveling from town to town, and the fairs served as focal points throughout the vast economic network of the Continent.

The greatest of the fairs were held in Champagne, which lay across the river valleys leading south to the Mediterranean and north to Paris, the English Channel, and western Germany. Here, merchants bringing textiles and wool from Flanders and England met with Italian merchants bringing goods from the eastern Mediterranean. The French merchants brought wines; western Germans brought metal products; northern Germans brought furs. Over time, the merchants adopted the practice of settling their accounts when they met in Champagne, thus making the fairs the money market as well as the commodity market of the West.

To settle their accounts, they used the bill of exchange, a device that may have originated in Fatimid Egypt. The bill was a promise to pay. It was also negotiable, which meant that the recipient could use it to pay his own debts. Suppose merchant A owed merchant B 100 shillings, and merchant C owed merchant D 100 shillings. A gave B a bill of exchange promising to pay his debt, and B sold it to C for 100 shillings; C used it to pay his debt to D, who then went to A and collected 100 shillings, the amount he promised to pay, as evidenced by the bill. The convenience of using such a credit instrument is obvious if A and D were merchants of one town and B and C were merchants of another town. No money was shipped from one place to the other—along routes infested with highway robbers—but both A and C paid their debts. As gathering places for merchants from all over Europe, the

An illustration from a fifteenth-century book shows women engaged in the textile industry: carding, spinning, and weaving.

Money changers are portrayed in the stained-glass window at Le Mans Cathedral (thirteenth century).

Local and Regional Trade

By the twelfth and thirteenth centuries local and regional trade had grown more important than long-distance trade in the commerce of Europe. All over Europe towns supported local markets on which the surrounding villages relied for marketing their surplus produce. Gradually, the towns transformed their economic power into political power over the villages that supplied them with raw materials and bought their manufactured goods. As the towns—now cities—became territorial powers, they displaced the feudal lords in the surrounding region. By the thirteenth century, most of the lords were outside the orbit of the cities.

Urban Life

The growth of the towns during the twelfth century and afterward came mostly from migration from the surrounding region and from more distant regions. The villages had been gaining in population for centuries, and young people were attracted to the exciting life and economic opportunities they were sure they would find in a nearby city. Larger cities drew population from smaller cities, and a few cities, like Paris and Bologna, drew population from all over Europe.

Incorporated towns, which most towns were by the end of the twelfth century, were governed by a council and mayor elected by the merchants. Below the merchants was a substantial middle class of artisans—shoemakers, butchers, leather workers, textile makers, and the like—who tended to live in separate quarters of town. The more noxious trades, such as butchering and leather tanning, were located away from the main part of town. From the late eleventh century, earlier in some places, independent artisans organized into guilds, which were similar to the associations of craftsmen in Roman cities. Through their own elected officers and councils, the guilds set product quality standards and restrictions on competition. They also collected funds to assist the families of members who became disabled or died. Along the way, they set up

fairs provided a perfect opportunity for settling accounts with bills of exchange, which were always written on a specific currency, such as Venetian ducats or Flemish gilders, that was well known and widely trusted.

The growth of commerce created a special class of men. Among men who lived all the time in the same community and whose status depended on their obligations to others, the question was always, "Whose man are you?" With merchants, however, who traveled constantly, the answer to that question was of no consequence. Even if a merchant owed loyalty and service to someone in his hometown, that meant nothing to someone 500 miles away. So merchants became known as a special class—bürger in Germany, burgesses in England, bourgeois in France. All these names stemmed from *burg*, the old German name for a fortified town.

some simple financial institutions, much like banks, to serve their members.

Most guilds were local in nature, extending their power only to the city walls or into the adjacent countryside, but a few were international in scope. The teamsters, for example, who were engaged in both regional and distant activities, maintained a loose organization that extended over a large area. And the stonemasons, whose highly specialized craft could not be supported in any one market, even those of Paris or London, traveled from job to job and formed a loose guild-like organization. Unlike the local guilds, both of these international guilds were made up of men who worked for others.

In the early period of guild activity, entry into a guild was relatively easy. A young boy—twelve or thirteen years old—was taken on by a master craftsman as an apprentice. In effect, he then became a member of the master's family and was trained in the master's shop. After several years spent on the simple, repetitive tasks of the trade, the young man rose to the status of journeyman. He was still subject to the direction of the master, but now he performed as a craftsman in the shop. When he had reached full maturity, he could set up on his own as a member of the guild. This system worked well so long as journeymen could expect to become masters in due time. In the later Middle Ages, however, guild membership tended to become hereditary, and relations between journeymen and masters often turned sour. This development was probably caused by changes in manufacturing practices that threatened guild monopolies and by economic decline in the fourteenth century (more on this in Chapter 14).

Jurisdictional disputes often arose among the guilds, as they do among trade unions today. For example, a horse harness contains both metal and leather: should it be made by leather workers, metalworkers, or both? In addition, the guilds competed with one another for political influence and sometimes formed alliances to challenge the merchants' guild for control of the town's government.

As international trade grew, money changing became increasingly important.

If the merchants were the patricians of the towns—as they were often called—then the laborers were the proletariat. The laborers were at the bottom of the social order. In addition to apprentices and journeymen there were day laborers hired to work on the roads, bridges, and walls of the towns. The position of the day laborers was always precarious. They might be working on a construction project one day and helping out with the harvest the next. They lived poorly, but so long as the economy continued to expand, as it did from the late eleventh through the thirteenth century, they were relatively peaceful members of the town population.

Family Life in the Cities and Towns

The core of the urban family consisted of the father, mother, and children, along with the apprentices and journeymen. The family was a social unit, an economic unit, and an educational unit. Although families were usually headed by men, women too could be heads of household. Some women succeeded their deceased husband as "master" and took his place in his guild. The apprentices and journeymen were then subject to her. Others worked in the textile industry, mostly as spinners and weavers. Women of all classes were expected to run their households efficiently, and in upper-class families that function took on the character of a profession.

During the fourteenth century a wealthy merchant of Paris wrote a book to instruct his young bride on her duties. She was never to go out unaccompanied and was always to walk calmly and look straight ahead. She should focus her eyes on the ground in the middle distance. She should be patient and calm when her husband was silly or difficult and should counsel him when he was about to do something foolish. The husband also instructed his wife on how to manage the steward and the servants and how to see to the food and wine. The book included instructions on what to do when the wine was sour or bitter or muddy or when the white wine looked red. The helpful man also provided his wife with recipes for stews and spicy preserves of nuts, vegetables, and fruit.

The birthrate was probably higher among upper-class women than among lower-class women. Upper-class women did not nurse their own infants. Instead, the infants were usually "put out" to a wet nurse in the village. Middle-class infants were usually wet-nursed at home by a live-in nurse.

At all levels of society, babies were delivered by midwives. These women also took charge of the newborn infant, rubbing its body with salt, cleansing its mouth with honey, and swaddling it. A thirteenth-century writer explained that swaddling was necessary because an infant's limbs were so "fluid" that they might become deformed unless they were closely bound. Women were advised to put their babies in cradles, because the common practice of taking them to the parental bed often led to their being suffocated during the night. The mother rocked the cradle, pre-chewed the infant's food, played games with the children, and taught them to talk. She also instructed them in religion and morals. The father's job was to train his sons for work and to arrange good marriages for both his sons and his daughters. It appears that the father was often much older than the mother and must have appeared a rather distant figure to his children.

Impoverished single women and those widows who were unable to carry on their husbands' business and were unsupported by a guild, were at the bottom of the social scale and led a troubled life. The widow struggling to make ends meet was a common figure in folk tales.

Prostitution was common, and medieval governments frequently issued regulations concerning that behavior. The main subjects were sanitation, living conditions, and working hours. One theologian argued that prostitutes, like other workers, deserved what they earned, but he agreed with the common view that prostitution was evil and that prostitutes should give up such employment. Churchmen found in prostitution a symbol of the evils of worldly society.

Single women and widows of the upper classes could escape their predicament by entering convents, which did not accept women of the lower classes, and many widows did so after their children had grown up. They usually brought an endowment to help the convent meet expenses. There were frequent complaints that convents would not accept applicants unless they paid an entry fee, but the practice was never stopped.

THE RURAL NOBILITY

The nobility of the Middle Ages had been established in the eighth and ninth centuries, with the amalgamation of the old provincial aristocracy of the Roman Empire and the aristocracy of the new Germanic kingdoms. During the late ninth and the tenth centuries, many men who had risen to power as local leaders against the Vikings married into the older aristocratic families and produced the class of warriors who fought in southern Italy, Spain, and the Holy Land during the eleventh century.

Until the late eleventh century, many towns were under the control of local lords who dealt directly with the growing classes of merchants and craftsmen. These nobles never viewed the townspeople as quite honorable, because they did not perform military service or serve as companions to the king. Moreover, they did not fit into the "regular" social hierarchy, which stretched from the king through the great lords to the knights and peasants. Yet, the nobles and the townspeople were obliged to associate with each other so long as the nobles governed the towns. With the incorporation of towns under royal char-

A midwife helps deliver a baby in the Middle Ages.

ter, however, many local lords retreated to the adjacent countryside and the distance between the classes grew wider. They now led different ways of life—rural and urban—and had different economic interests.

From the late eleventh century on, Europe's unruly military aristocracy began to settle down and adapt to the political life of the medieval kingdoms. These were the years that produced the code of chivalry. This code embodied the virtues of knighthood as formulated by churchmen during the Peace of God movement of the previous century in which the church had tried to designate classes of the population—including women, children, and clergy—that the knights must protect from violence. According to that code, the knight was an honorable man loyal to his lord, courteous to women, gentle with the poor and the less fortunate, and generous. Though there were vast differences in wealth and station within the military aristocracy, from simple knight to king, all were seen as following a single calling under a single code.

Rearing a Knight

At the age of about seven, the sons of knights began their schooling in the arts of war and in the proper conduct for members of their class. They first learned to ride a horse and began playing games with toy weapons. When they reached the age of twelve or thirteen, they were trained to take part in exercises on horseback and were instructed in the use of weapons.

In his later teens, such a boy became a squire, the servant of a knight. Under the knight's tutelage, he continued his education and also took care of the knight's horses, armor, and weapons. Although no rule dictated when a squire became a knight, it usually happened when the squire was in his early twenties. The young man knelt before the lord of his knight in a pledge of fidelity, and the lord took the young man's sword and hit him on each shoulder. In the later Middle Ages, this ceremony might become quite elaborate, with the young man spending an all-night vigil in a chapel, wearing special robes and armor, and with the delivery of ceremonial speeches. But in the twelfth and thirteenth centuries it was still a simple ceremony.

Few knights inherited land or title. Most of them were knights-errant who drifted about the kingdom, attaching themselves to landed men when they could. They participated in tournaments, fought wars, and went off on crusades. During the tournament season, from late spring to fall, tournaments occurred somewhere every few weeks, and the knights-errant traveled from one to another. The tournaments were mock battles in which many were seriously injured or killed. The object of the tournament was to capture one's opponents and hold them for ransom. Good fighters could make a decent living on the tournament circuit. Many lords formed teams to participate in the tournaments and provided their men with horses and arms. The participation of teams added verisimilitude to the tournaments. As in real cavalry battles, victory went to the men who fought most bravely and most skillfully. The church disapproved of tournaments and denied burial in consecrated ground to men who died fighting in them.

The goal of all landless knights was to receive a fief from a lord or to marry an heiress. The goal of the fathers of heiresses was to marry their daughters to men with large inheritances. Knights who failed to win an estate carried on as knights-errant for as long as they could and then retired to the countryside as bailiffs or estate managers for the great landholders. They became important figures in the rural hierarchy, and many of them probably married the daughters of prosperous peasants.

Home Life of the Nobility

Most of the landed nobles lived in a manor house or in a motte-and-bailey castle. The manor house was usually a large timber structure surrounded by vegetable gardens and village fields.

The motte-and-bailey castle was a more substantial establishment. The motte was a large mound of from one to six acres in area surrounded by a wooden palisade. The bailey was a courtyard or

A stone "shell keep" on a motte surrounded by a ditch or moat.

open space adjacent to the motte and usually much larger in area. The bailey too was enclosed by a palisade. Depending on the terrain, the motte or the bailey, or both, might be surrounded by a ditch or moat outside the palisade. In the center of the motte was the donjon or keep, a strong wooden tower with slits through which archers could shoot. The ground floor (and sometimes the cellars) were used for storage, and the living quarters were on the upper floors. The tower was entered by way of a stairway to the second floor that could be pushed away in times of danger. Except for the largest castles, the keep was the only building on the motte. All the other buildings—barracks for the garrison, storehouses, stables, workshops, and the chapel—were in the bailey.

Only the greatest lords could afford stone castles, which were built according to a plan much like that of the motte-and-bailey castles. The Tower of London was the keep of a stone castle that William the Conqueror built shortly after coming to England. From it, his garrison could survey the city of London and the surrounding countryside.

Life in the castle revolved around the affairs of its lord. Here he held court to decide disputes among his fiefholders and tenants and entertained the great men who passed by. When he was not away on a campaign with the king or attending the king's court, he spent his time hunting

and managing his estate. During the long winter evenings he listened to professional storytellers and singers or played chess and other games. The members of this class were rough men familiar with violence who lived in a society of professional soldiers. They were quick to defend their own rights and to seize those of weaker men. Many of them ate and drank too much and became quite fat, particularly after giving up wars and tournaments.

Knights-errant retired about the age of 35, and until then they were considered "youths." Because they did not marry until after retirement, they tended to marry women much younger than themselves, and an age difference of twenty years was not uncommon. At the highest levels of society, however, marriage between children as young as seven was legally permissible, and many young boys were married to older girls. Under church law, a marriage was not valid unless the parties to it consented and consummated it. Children could renounce a marriage when they reached fourteen, the age of consent, but if they waited any longer the courts generally ruled that their failure to protest sooner counted as tacit consent.

The wife of the lord usually ran the estate, and many wives were excellent managers. In the great families, the households were very large, with stewards, cooks, stablemen, servants, and family retainers. The women of such families often played a significant role in the politics of the realm and acted as important patrons of the arts. The women of the French royal family were the ones who encouraged the authors of the literary romances that appeared toward the end of the twelfth century (see pp. 297–98).

REFORM OF THE CHURCH

The Condition of the Church in the Eleventh Century

By the middle of the eleventh century many of the institutions of the church had been secularized and were in need of reform. For more than a hundred years, the

Twelfth-century ivory chessmen from the Island of Lewis: Queen, King, and Bishop.

German kings had been appointing bishops and abbots who, though usually men of character and ability, were loyal to the monarchy and often engaged in secular affairs. Moreover, the kings had often granted lands and rights to the bishops, making them part of the feudal structure and obliging them to do homage and take an oath of fealty to the monarch.

Even the parish churches and lesser monasteries had become secularized. Before the Germans converted to Christianity, many of them had maintained private temples and shrines on their properties. After conversion, the lords had renewed that practice by building private churches in the villages adjacent to their estates. Under Germanic law, those churches belonged to the lords, who were therefore entitled to appoint the priests and collect the church income, which consisted of first fruits (an offering from the harvest) and tithes, a tenth of the produce of the land. The lords often appointed parish priests who had not been educated for the priesthood and who might even be serfs of the lord. Consequently, the condition of many rural parishes was scandalous.

Before the Germans were converted to Christianity, the inheritance of an estate had been determined by Germanic folk laws according to rules that no one could alter. In effect, the estate was owned by the family rather than by the man who happen to be head of the family. With the advent of the Christian church a new element entered into this system of inheritance. As we have seen (p. 141), during the seventh century the kings created a new form of landholding called *bookland,* whereby the church could own land under a royal charter. This new form of tenure was available only to the church. By 700, however, large landholders had figured out that by establishing a monastery on their estate they could get a royal charter for the land that they granted as the monastery's endowment. But, because they had complete control over the monastery they had created, they could reclaim the chartered lands any time they wanted to. By this clever ruse, the large landholders evaded the Germanic folk law and assumed power to bequeath their land

Bronze figure of a monk writing on the tail of a monster, on which he is seated (from a cross or candlestick base, north German or English, *ca.* 1150).

to heirs of their own choosing. Soon, churchmen were complaining that the landholders were founding captive monasteries just so they could get a royal charter for their land. As might be expected, monasteries created in this fashion were rarely dedicated to contemplation, prayer, and poverty.

The Establishment of the Reform Movement

In 910, Duke William of Aquitaine asked the monk Berno to found a monastery on his estate at Cluny in Burgundy. Berno agreed to do so on condition that William not interfere with the life or property of the monastery. Racked by guilt for his many sins, William accepted this condition. In fact, he arranged to put the new monastery under the protection of the pope, so that his heirs would not interfere with it either. The new monastery soon became famous, and other nobles asked its leaders to set up similar houses on their lands. And already-established houses asked Cluny to send monks to help them institute reforms of their own. By the eleventh century, under a series of talented, long-lived abbots, Cluny had become the hub of hundreds of reformed monasteries and had inspired reform movements among monasteries in Germany and England.

When the Cluniacs turned to Rome for protection from the heirs of their founders and other aggressive nobles, they discovered that the papacy had become the target of the dynastic and political ambitions of the leading families of Rome. Further, they saw that the popes were men lacking in vision, without pastoral character or genuine religious interests. The Cluniacs soon raised a cry for reform that was echoed by the leading bishops of Europe and finally won the support of King Henry III of Germany (r. 1039–56).

In 1046 Henry marched to Rome to receive the imperial crown from the pope. There he found three self-styled popes contesting for the papal throne, each supported by one of the aristocratic factions. In an action that recalled Otto I, Henry summoned a council of churchmen, who deposed all three of them. He then installed a German as the legitimate successor of St. Peter, and that pope crowned Henry emperor. Soon after Henry returned to Germany, the new pope died mysteriously and Henry appointed Bruno, bishop of Toul, who took the name Leo IX (r. 1049–54). Under Leo, the Germans began the reform of the Roman church and reestablished its spiritual and disciplinary leadership of Christendom.

The church leaders responsible for that reform held councils to render their program into church law. They prohibited the buying and selling of ecclesiastical offices, clerical marriage, and lay interference in ecclesiastical affairs. They also sought to gain control over the city of Rome, from which the papacy drew most of its revenues. The architect of that effort was a Roman monk named Hildebrand, who for two decades, starting under Leo IX, served as the archdeacon, or principal administrative officer, of the Roman diocese. Through his influence with some of Rome's leading families, Hildebrand gained control of most of the ancient shrines in the city, which produced substantial revenue as pilgrimage sites.

The Investiture Controversy

The reformers' views of the church's role and structure were set down by the German monk Humbert, who had come to Rome with Leo IX. According to Humbert, the church was superior over secular authorities because it was responsible for the spiritual welfare of the people, while the emperor and kings were responsible for their material well-being. The church was to secular authorities as the sun is to the moon, he wrote, implying that they received their authority from the church as the moon receives its light from the sun. In support of this claim, the reformers cited the Donation of Constantine (see p. 182) and the bishops' deposition of Louis the Pious (see p. 231). Humbert further pointed out that Christ had established the church as a hierarchical

Cluniac Monasteries   Tenth and Eleventh Centuries

962		1002 1024		1125	1152		1254
Ottonian Emperors		Salian Emperors		Period of Imperial Weakness	Hohenstaufen Emperors		

Henry II

1073   1122
Investiture
Conflict

institution, with the pope, as successor of St. Peter, at the apex of the hierarchy.

Similar views were expressed by the north-Italian monastic reformer, Peter Damian, who justified Henry III's participation in the reform movement and his appointment of the reform popes. Damian argued that, because royal authority like papal authority derives from God (citing the example of the Old Testament kings and St. Paul's *Letter to the Romans* 13), kings have a role to play in spiritual as well as secular government. Though the king cannot perform the sacraments, he is responsible for the well-being of the church. Only when a king, or a lesser secular official, acts against the interests of the church by appointing evil or incompetent men or by seizing church property is the church justified in resisting secular participation in ecclesiastical affairs. By this argument, Henry III's actions were not only justified but deserving of applause.

Henry III died in 1056, and left his son Henry IV, a boy of six, as his heir, under a regency. Taking advantage of this situation, the great feudal lords rebelled, hoping to recover some of their autonomy; the regents had to rely on the bishops and monasteries for support. Consequently, they seized every opportunity to appoint loyal men to church posts, and these men were not always of the sort the reformers in Rome would have preferred. The papal court became increasingly estranged from the regents.

In 1059, Pope Nicholas II (r. 1059–61) issued new reform legislation aimed at the practices of the German kings and emperors. It prohibited the investiture (installation) of priests and bishops by laymen and declared that henceforth popes would be elected by the college of cardinals. This new electoral college represented the clergy of the diocese of Rome, because under ancient law those

clerics who had the right to say Mass in the churches of the Roman diocese were called cardinals. Gradually during the tenth and eleventh centuries the number of cardinals had been fixed to those bishops, priests, and deacons who had been "incardinated" in the oldest churches of Rome. By 1059, all of these men were supporters of the reformers. With only slight modifications, the electoral system conducted by the college of cardinals is still in use today. After 1059, the cardinals became increasingly important as administrators in Rome and as ambassadors, or legates, to all the provinces of the church.*

During most of the 1060s, though the German government was in no position to challenge the new decrees, it effectively ignored them and continued to treat the German church as part of the royal government. When Henry IV (r. 1056–1106) came of age in 1066, he made the royal appointment and investiture of bishops a cornerstone of his political program. The act of investiture, during which the bishop swore an oath of fealty to the king and received from him the ring and shepherd's crook symbolic of episcopal authority, guaranteed the relationship on which the king relied for support against his enemies.

Meanwhile, the aristocratic opponents of the king sided with the reformers, who forced them to obey the papal decrees. In particular, they had to agree that the priests of their own private

---

The church was organized into provinces, each with an archbishop and bishops who were subordinate to him. Thus the province of Canterbury contained most of the bishoprics of southern England and the province of Reims contained many bishoprics of northern France. The bishops always tried to maintain their independence of the archbishop of their province. Papal legates were generally sent to represent papal authority in one or more provinces. They were superior to the archbishops and bishops of the province.

churches would be appointed and invested by the proper ecclesiastical authorities in accord with church law. This requirement prompted the lords to divest themselves of their private churches, sometimes turning them over to reformed monasteries, which they viewed as ecclesiastical institutions. But soon those monasteries were under attack for taking control of the churches. In other cases, the lords gave up the right to collect church income and to install priests but kept the right of patronage that permitted them to nominate priests. The bishop of the diocese almost always accepted their nominations, though disputes over the installation of priests were common. From 1060 to 1160, virtually all rural parish churches that had once belonged to the lords of the villages became church property under control of the local bishop.

Pope Gregory VII

In 1073, when the archdeacon Hildebrand became pope as Gregory VII (r. 1073–85), the reform movement entered a new phase. While his predecessors had been engaged in diplomacy to get first the regency government and then Henry IV to obey the reform decrees, Hildebrand had been engaged in a struggle to establish papal power in the city of Rome. Though a master of city politics and a committed reformer, he was no diplomat.

At the beginning of his pontificate as Gregory VII, he reaffirmed the reform decrees, particularly the prohibition of lay investiture. Then, in June 1075, Henry IV reasserted the ancient rights of the monarchy in ecclesiastical affairs. For Henry, the church was the basis of royal power, and he was determined to control the appointments to its highest offices. At the end of 1075, Gregory threatened Henry with excommunication—which would prevent him from entering a church and would prohibit all Christians from dealing with him—if he did not obey the papal decrees.

Henry reacted by summoning his loyal German bishops to a council at which they prepared a letter attacking Gregory as a false pope and demanding

Manuscript illustration of Gregory VII. Photo courtesy of The Granger Collection.

that he give up his usurpation of the Roman see. Gregory responded by first excommunicating and then deposing Henry. That action triggered a new rebellion of the German magnates against Henry, and for a time it looked as if he might indeed lose his throne. In January, Gregory traveled to Germany to attend a great council that was scheduled to approve his action against Henry. Along the way, he stopped at the castle of Canossa in northern Tuscany, and Henry suddenly appeared to beg forgiveness and absolution from the sentence of excommunication. As a pastor, the pope had no choice but to absolve him. But by doing so, he destroyed the grounds on which he had deposed the king.

Officially, Henry was now an obedient son of the church, and the rebellion in Germany quickly disintegrated. Gregory turned back to Rome, having lost the trust of many of the magnates in Germany who had counted on him for support in their rebellion.

The absolution at Canossa merely demonstrated the limited usefulness of excommunication as an instrument of political policy without resolving the underlying issues between the pope and king. When the continuing dispute over investitures led Gregory to excommunicate Henry again in 1080, his action was largely ignored in Germany.

The Consequences of the Investiture Controversy

The controversy over investitures lasted for 47 years (1075–1122), changed the course of history in Italy and Germany, and revolutionized the relationship between the ecclesiastical and secular authorities in Europe. During the controversy the German kings invaded Italy several times and delayed the reestablishment of papal power. For their part, the popes fomented a series of rebellions in Germany that kept the kings off balance for much of the period and impeded progress toward a strong monarchy.

Both sides spun out theories about the nature of secular and ecclesiastical authority. The papacy, adopting Humbert's position, argued that the church led by the pope was the highest human authority because it was responsible for the highest human goal—salvation. Henry's supporters, following Peter Damian's theory of dual authority, maintained that both secular authority and ecclesiastical authority were divinely ordained. The compromise that ended the investiture controversy in 1122 was based on the theory of dual authority. Henceforth, disputes between the two centers of authority were resolved according to the peculiarly Western idea that both church and state have limited authority. No other civilization has recognized a spiritual authority independent of the secular power.

Religious Life: New Monastic Orders

The resolution of the contest between church and state was not the only outcome of the reform movement. As a result of the reformers' efforts the pope became more and more powerful in church affairs, and by the twelfth century papal legates were active in many parts of Europe. The reformers also improved the education of priests and established the principle that priests could not marry. By the late twelfth century, married clerics had become rare, except in Scandinavia.

The reform movement also stimulated a religious fervor that affected all levels of society and led to a new expansion of monasticism. Cluniac monasticism, though it required that individual monks remain poor, permitted the monasteries themselves to accumulate wealth. Over the two centuries since they had been founded, the Cluniac monasteries had grown into wealthy institutions, with the monks living in sumptuous surroundings. Cluny itself had become the largest landowner in Burgundy.

Within the monasteries, as St. Benedict had ordained, the monks still came together seven times a day for communal prayer services, or offices. They were to spend the rest of the day working to support the community. In the Middle Ages, when people believed that God was more likely to listen to the prayers of holy men

---

Principles of Gregory VII ca. 1075

This document was certainly drawn up in Gregory's circle, and probably by the pope himself. It expresses the views of those who were trying to increase papal power in both church and state.

1. That the Roman church was founded by the Lord alone.
2. That only the Roman pontiff is rightly called universal.
3. That he alone can depose or reestablish bishops.
4. That his legate, even if of inferior rank, is above all bishops in council; and he can give sentence of deposition against them. . . .
12. That it is permitted to him to depose emperors. . . .
18. That his decision ought to be reviewed by no one, and that he alone can review the decisions of everyone.
19. That he ought to be judged by no one.
20. That no one may dare condemn a man who is appealing to the apostolic see.
21. That the greater case of every church ought to be referred to him.
22. That the Roman church has never erred nor will ever err, as the Scripture bears witness.
23. That the Roman pontiff, if he has been canonically ordained, is indubitably made holy by the merits of the blessed Peter. . . .
24. That by his precept and license subjects are permitted to accuse their lords. . . .
27. That he can absolve the subjects of the unjust from their fealty.

From Dictatus Papae Gregorii VII, *trans. by E. Lewis,* Medieval Political Ideas *(New York: Knopf, 1954), Vol. II, pp. 380–81.*

---

than to the prayers of ordinary folk, the men who donated money and land to monasteries demanded that the monks pray for them in perpetuity. As time passed, the monks came to spend virtually all day in church praying for patrons. The Cluniac liturgy became extremely elaborate, and the monasteries built large, ornate churches in which the monks used richly decorated ritual implements and books.

Starting around the middle of the eleventh century, perhaps influenced by the papal reform movement, some monks withdrew from the monasteries to live as hermits. Ecclesiastical authorities, complaining that they had no way of knowing

Henry IV before journeying to Canossa. Miniature from an early twelfth-century manuscript of the life of Countess Matilda of Tuscany. Henry, kneeling, asks Abbot Hugh of Cluny and Countess Matilda to intercede for him with Pope Gregory VII.

An illuminated liturgical book from Spain (thirteenth century).

whether these men were really living a holy life, put pressure on them to come together in communities. In Italy, several communities were formed in which the monks lived solitary, ascetic lives of prayer except when they worked together to support themselves. Peter Damian entered one such community, Fonte Avellana, as a young man and became its prior in 1043. The most famous hermit communities were the Charterhouse (La Grand Chartreuse), from which the Carthusian order stems, and the Camaldoli, which gave rise to the Camaldolese order.

The largest and most influential of the new monastic orders was the Cistercian order, which followed the Benedictine Rule. About 1098, a group of monks withdrew to a desolate place in Burgundy called Cîteaux (Cisterciensis in Latin; the name means marshy place). Determined to live an austere life, they renounced the ownership of property both for themselves and for their community, and they stressed the role of manual labor in monastic life. The harsh region to which they withdrew demanded that they work hard just to survive, and after several years the number of monks at Cîteaux had dwindled. Then, in 1112, when it seemed that the community was about to fail, a young man named Bernard (*ca.* 1090–1153) arrived with relatives and friends to join the house. Bernard, a genius with extraordinary personal magnetism, soon attracted others to Cîteaux. In 1115, he led a group of monks to found a daughter house at Clairvaux, where he served as abbot for the rest of his life. In those four decades, the Cistercian order grew to more than 350 houses, and Bernard became a leading figure in Europe. He wrote hundreds of letters and many commentaries on books of the Bible. In 1145 a former member of his community at Clairvaux became pope as Eugene III.

Unlike the Cluniacs, the Cistercians founded a true order of formally related monasteries. Although many monasteries had copied Cluny's rule and practices, and many had asked Cluny to send monks to give them guidance, those houses were not subject to Cluny in any formal way. By contrast, all of the Cistercian houses were founded by one of the older houses: Clairvaux was a daughter house of Cîteaux; Clairvaux in turn had many daughter houses; and many of those had daughter houses of their own. All followed the same rule, and every year the abbot

Cistercian Monasteries   Twelfth Century

Cistercian monks shown living by their own labor. Illuminated capital letter from a manuscript of St. Gregory's *Moralia in Job,* written at the mother house of Cîteaux in the twelfth century.

of the mother house visited each of its daughter houses to make certain that it was following the rule in every particular. Also once a year, all the abbots of the order gathered at Cîteaux to review the rule and to hear the cases of abbots who had been found wanting.

But as the Cistercian order grew and as the fame of its monks' holiness spread, its monasteries, like the Cluniac monasteries, received valuable gifts from pious donors. Within a generation, the Cistercian houses had grown wealthy. No longer were they committed to life in the wilderness, for society followed them wherever they established themselves. By the middle of the twelfth century, Cistercian abbots were playing an influential role in ecclesiastical and secular politics throughout Europe.

About the time the Cistercians were building their order, other forms of religious life were emerging. Attached to cathedral churches were priests called canons who performed the divine offices—the daily series of prayers—in the church and assisted the bishop with the management and the pastoral work of the diocese; the canons were the descendants of the ancient *familia* of the bishop (see p. 135). By the late eleventh century, many of them had accepted a monastic rule and become regular clergy (from the Latin *regula,* meaning rule). Small groups of canons in many of the rural churches followed suit. The canons lived much as monks did, but they were priests who performed pastoral duties. In the early twelfth century, a German priest founded an order of canons regular at Prémontré (the Premonstratensians) and created a new

form of religious life, the order of priests destined to influence the organization of the church as a whole.

The new interest in monastic life affected women as well as men. For generations, convents had received widows and the unmarried daughters of noble families, but now they also began to receive women who chose to enter them instead of marrying. The Cistercians created an order of nuns who followed their rule, and there also developed various orders of canonesses who lived according to the same rule as the canons but did not perform priestly duties.

Although most of the men and women who lived in monasteries and convents were members of the noble classes, the movement also stimulated a religious enthusiasm among the lower classes. During the twelfth century a host of preachers wandered from town to town urging the townspeople to give up their worldly life and live like the apostles. A few of these preachers formed communities that lasted for years. The followers of a preacher named Waldo, for example, left everything behind to live a common life and to help convert others to holiness. The bishops became concerned about the orthodoxy of the Waldensians, as they were called, because they had had no formal training and had no authority from the church. Moreover, they were often critical of the wealth and worldliness of the church. The Waldensian movement endured for centuries and was never formally condemned by the church.

THE CRUSADERS

When Byzantine military power collapsed after the battle of Manzikert in 1071 (see p. 186), the imperial court in Constantinople appealed to the pope and the western kings for assistance. Although these leaders had little interest in recovering territory for the eastern emperor and hardly understood the role the Empire had played as a buffer between Europe and the Arabic Empire, they agreed that something had to be done about the Moslem conquest of Jerusalem (1077). Still, it took them nearly two decades to put together an army to advance that cause.

In 1095, Pope Urban II (1088–99), seizing the opportunity to assert papal leadership of all Christendom, proclaimed a crusade against the Turks. At a great council in Clermont, France, he preached a famous sermon in which he urged the assembled knights to raise an army to help Constantinople fight the infidel. The effect was startling. Thousands of knights took the cross, which became the symbol of the crusaders—the warriors who had dedicated themselves to fight for Christ.

There were several reasons for this surge of religious fervor among the usually hard-bitten, self-interested knights. First, since the late tenth century, bishops had tried to protect their parishioners from the horrors of war by inducing knights to observe a truce toward certain groups in the population. The movement, called the Peace of God, began in central France and

was led by associations of knights who swore not to attack peasants, merchants, or churchmen. The bishops also tried to get the knights to forswear all fighting on feast days, but this so-called Truce of God was far less effective than the Peace of God. The great lords supported the movement because it helped keep the lesser lords and knights under control. The Peace of God may have served as the inspiration for the chivalric code that was featured in the vernacular literature of the twelfth century.

Moreover, Europeans had already moved against Moslem states closer to home in something like the *jihad*—the Moslem's holy war. For example, the Normans had led a kind of domestic crusade against the Moslems in southern Italy and Sicily and by the middle of the eleventh century had set up independent principalities there. In fact, Robert Guiscard (*ca.* 1015–85), the leader of the Normans

Crusade Routes   1096–1270

Urban's Speech at Clermont   1095

I exhort you . . . to strive to expel that wicked race [the Turks] from our Christian lands. . . . Christ commands it. Remission of sins will be granted for those going thither. . . . Let those who are accustomed to wage private war wastefully even against believers go forth against the infidels. . . . Let those who have lived by plundering be soldiers of Christ; let those who formerly contended against brothers and relations rightly fight barbarians; let those who were recently hired for a few pieces of silver win their eternal reward. . . . The sorrowful here will be glad there, the poor here will be rich there, and the enemies of the Lord here will be His friends there. Let no delay postpone the journey . . . when winter has ended and spring has come . . . enter the highways courageously with the Lord going on before.

Adapted from Fulcher of Chartres, History of Jerusalem, *trans. by M. E. McGinty (Philadelphia: University of Pennsylvania Press, 1941), p. 16. Fulcher was at Clermont and went on the First Crusade.*

peninsula. The Iberian Crusade attracted men from France and other regions who in 1080 took Toledo, the former capital of the Visigothic kingdom. By the thirteenth century the emirate of Granada was all that remained of Moorish Spain.

Finally, during the investiture controversy many members of the aristocracy had sided with the reformers against the kings. Particularly in Germany, they were aware that if the church achieved its independence of the king, the monarchy would be weakened and the aristocracy would grow stronger. Consequently the knights and the members of the lesser nobility gathered at Clermont responded with great enthusiasm to Urban II's appeal for a crusade. After about a year of organizing, thousands of knights gathered in eastern France to march to Jerusalem. Significantly, no kings joined them.

In the meantime, thousands of lesser folk set off for the East on their own. When they arrived at Constantinople, the emperor was horrified. He had expected a disciplined army, not a peasant mob, to help him reconquer Asia Minor and the Holy Land. To get rid of this scourge, he had the peasants ferried across the Bosporus, where they were massacred by the Turks. Few survived to join the march on Jerusalem.

The crusading army proper was led by several great lords from France, who spent much of their time feuding while on the march across the Balkans and Asia Minor. When the army arrived at Constantinople, the emperor discovered that it was almost as disorganized and unruly as the peasant mob, quite unlike the well-disciplined Byzantine army. He was also dismayed to find that the westerners had come, not to serve him, but to stage a raid across Turkish territory to Jerusalem. After he declined their services, they set off on their own.

In their trek eastward, the crusaders suffered disease, hunger, and, in two battles with the Turks, heavy casualties. The leaders continued to feud, and when the crusaders arrived at their destination they split up into separate forces and attacked different targets. One force succeeded in

in Calabria, had grown so strong that he was able to mount expeditions aimed at seizing the Byzantine throne (see p. 186). His successor, Roger I (r. 1085–1111), completed the conquest of Sicily in 1091.

In Spain, meanwhile, the collapse of the caliphate of Cordova in 1031 opened the way for the Christian states on the southern flank of the Pyrenees to move against the independent emirates on the

Medieval knights besiege a city. The troops fight before the city gate, while the besieging army catapults missiles into the city.

taking Jerusalem in 1099, and the rest took other major cities. By 1100, a string of crusader states stretched from Antioch in the north to the Dead Sea in the south.

The condition of these states was precarious, and from time to time the Moslems made serious inroads into them. At such times the westerners called out for reinforcements, and the churchmen back home set about raising new crusades. In the 1140s, Bernard of Clairvaux preached a crusade and even got the kings of France and Germany to promise that they would join it. Louis VII of France (r. 1137–80) actually went all the way to Palestine but accomplished little after arriving.

After Saladin retook Jerusalem in 1187, the church leaders preached a Third Crusade. This time the German and English kings led the crusaders, but it all ended badly. Frederick I of Germany (r. 1152–90) died along the way, and Richard the Lionhearted, the English king (r. 1189–

99), set out for home after an inconclusive campaign. He was captured on the way, and the English had to raise a huge ransom to free him.

Though all these twelfth-century crusades were ostensibly aimed at Palestine, the crusaders occasionally staged attacks on the Nile delta of Egypt, which, under the Fatimid caliphs, had become the richest and most powerful Moslem state. Though the attacks were thrown back, they disrupted the lucrative trade that had grown up between Egypt and the cities of Italy. So, when a Fourth Crusade, aimed specifically at Egypt, was organized in 1202, the Venetians, who had been contracted to provide transport, diverted it to a Byzantine port that was competing with Venice for trade. Soon the crusaders were on their way to Constantinople itself. They took the city in 1204 and established a Latin empire there that lasted until 1261 (see pp. 187–88).

Suggestions for Further Reading

The Medieval Economy

For a good general survey, see R. H. Bautier, *The Economic Development of Medieval Europe* (1971). On the agricultural economy of medieval Europe, see N. Nielson, *Medieval Agrarian Economy* (1976); G. Duby, *Rural Economy and Country Life in the Medieval West* (1968) and *The Three Orders: Feudal Society Imagined* (1980); and M. Bloch, *French Rural Society* (1966). The first three volumes of the *Cambridge Economic History of Europe*, ed. by M. M. Postan (1952–66), contain excellent articles on agriculture, commerce, and industry. The second edition of Volume 1 is much improved over the first edition. See also R. Lennard, *Rural England* (1959). On the agricultural revolution, see L. White, Jr., *Medieval Technology and Social Change* (1962), and J. Gimpel, *The Medieval Machine* (1976).

On the revival of trade, see R. S. Lopez, *Medieval Trade in the Mediterranean World* (1961) and *The Commercial Revolution of the Middle Ages* (1976). C. Cipolla, *Before the Industrial Revolution*, 2nd ed. (1980), is a good one-volume survey based on recent scholarship. A. R. Bridbury, *Economic Growth. England in the Later Middle Ages* (1962), brings W. Cunningham, *The Growth of English Industry and Commerce* (1910), up to date, but the older work remains useful. P. Boissonade, *Life and Work in Medieval Europe* (1929), is also still valuable, but J. Le Goff, *Time, Work, and Culture in the Middle Ages* (1980), has given a modern perspective on many of the same issues. R. de Roover, *Money, Banking and Credit in Medieval Bruges* (1948), is a readable introduction to the operations of the Italian merchant-bankers in Flanders. A. Sapori, *The Italian Merchant in the Middle Ages* (1970), is an excellent general work; see also S. Thrupp, *The Merchant Class of Medieval London* (1948).

Urban Development

On the rise of the cities, see H. Pirenne, *Economic and Social History of Medieval Europe* (1937). F. Rörig, *The Medieval Town* (1967), and M. M. Postan, *The Medieval Economy* (1972), are very good on the towns. C. T. Smith, *An Historical Geography of Western Europe before 1800* (1978), is very good on the growth of the cities. F. Lane, *Venice: A Maritime Republic* (1973), is the best account of the rise of a major trading city. On England, see S. Reynolds, *An Introduction to the History of Medieval English Towns* (1977). There is also interesting material in I. Agus, *Urban Civilization in Pre-Crusade Europe,*

2 vols. (1965), which contains translations of rabbinical *responsa* (legal opinions). See also, J. W. Parkes, *The Jew in the Medieval Community: A Study of his Political and Economic Status* (1938). On life in the cities, see M. Girouard, *Cities and People: A Social and Architectural History* (1985), and J. and F. Gies, *Life in a Medieval City* (1969), which focuses on Troyes and the fairs of Champagne. For studies of individual cities, see C. N. L. Brooke, *London 800–1216: The Shaping of a City* (1975); G. Williams, *Medieval London* (1970); J. W. F. Hill, *Medieval Lincoln* (1948); P. Llewellyn, *Rome in the Dark Ages* (1971); R. Brentano, *Rome Before Avignon* (1974); D. Herlihy, *Medieval and Renaissance Pistoia* (1958); P. Strait, *Cologne in the Twelfth Century* (1974); and D. Nicholas, *The Domestic Life of a Medieval City: Women, Children, and the Family in Fourteenth-Century Ghent* (1985).

Medieval Society

For a general survey, see G. Duby and P. Aries, *A History of Private Life*, vol. 2 (1989). For the earlier period treated in this chapter, see H. Fichtenau, *Living in the Tenth Century* (1991). The manual written in the fourteenth century by a bourgeois man for his young wife has been newly translated in *A Medieval Home Companion: Housekeeping in the Fourteenth Century*, trans. by T. Bayard (1991). For studies on women of all classes and conditions, see M. W. Labarge, *A Small Sound of the Trumpet: Women in Medieval Life* (1986); M. C. Howell, *Women, Production, and Patriarchy in Late Medieval Cities* (1986); and *Sisters and Workers in the Middle Ages*, ed. by J. M. Bennett et al. (1989). See also D. Herlihy, *Women in the Middle Ages* (1971); J. Ferrante, *Women as Image in Medieval Literature* (1975); and V. L. Bullough, *The Subordinate Sex: A History of Attitudes toward Women* (1973). D. Herlihy, *Medieval Households* (1985), places women in the context of medieval domestic life. E. Power's *Medieval Women* (1975) contains imaginative recreations of women's lives. For essays on childrearing, see L. deMause, ed., *The History of Childhood* (1974).

The life of the nobility is recounted in S. Painter, *William Marshal* (1933), and G. Duby, *William Marshal* (1985). See also G. Duby, *The Chivalrous Society*, trans. by C. Postan (1977), and J. Burke, *Life in the Castle in Medieval England* (1978). On the origins of the code of chivalry, see C. S. Jaeger, *The Origins of Courtliness: Civilizing Trends and the Formation of Courtly Ideals, 923–1210* (1985). On women of the aristocratic class, see M. W. Labarge, *A Baronial Household of the Thirteenth Century* (1965).

Ecclesiastic Reform

On the monastic background of the eleventh-century reform movement, see H. E. J. Cowdrey, *The Cluniacs and the Gregorian Reform* (1970). On the ideologies of the reform movement and German kings, see G. Tellenbach, *Church, State, and Christian Society in the Time of the Investiture Controversy* (1940). For a general study of the investiture controversy, see U. R. Blumenthal, *The Investiture Controversy* (1988). On the polemics of the controversy, see I. S. Robinson, *Authority and Resistance in the Investiture Contest* (1978). For a survey of the reform, see R. W. Southern, *Western Society and the Church* (1976), and for the effect of the investiture controversy in Germany, see H. Fuhrmann, *Germany in the High Middle Ages* c. *1050–1200* (1986). On Cluniac monasticism, see B. Rosenwein, *Rhinoceros Bound: Cluny in the Tenth Century* (1982); N. Hunt, ed., *Cluniac Monasticism in the Central Middle Ages* (1971) and *Cluny under Saint Hugh (1049–1109)* (1967); and G. Constable, *Cluniac Studies* (1980). For the English background of the monastic reform, see D. Knowles, *The Monastic Order in England* (1951). For a survey of the whole period, see C. N. L. Brooke and W. Swaan, *The Monastic World 1100–1300* (1974). On the conflict of values between Cluniac and Cistercian monasticism, see D. Knowles, *The Conflict between St. Bernard and Peter the Venerable* (1955). On the spirit of the new monasticism of the twelfth century, see J. Leclercq, *The Love of Learning and the Desire for God* (1961).

The Crusades

On the idea of the Crusade, see C. Erdmann, *The Origins of the Idea of Crusade*, trans. by M. W. Baldwin and W. Goffart (1977), and J. Riley-Smith, *The First Crusade and the Idea of Crusading* (1970). For a study of the preaching of the Crusades in Europe, see P. J. Cole, *The Preaching of the Crusades to the Holy Land 1095–1270* (1991). A. C. Krey, *The First Crusade* (1921), gives a very good picture of the Crusade from the accounts of eyewitnesses and participants. For a readable account, see S. Runciman, *A History of the Crusades*, Vol. 1 (1951). M. L. W. Baldwin, ed., *The First Hundred Years* (1955), Vol. 1

of *A History of the Crusades*, ed. by K. M. Setton, is a collection of essays by leading historians of the crusades. On the Latin kingdom in the Levant, see J. L. La Monte, *Feudal Monarchy in the Latin Kingdom of Jerusalem* (1932), and J. Prawer, *The World of the Crusaders* (1972), which emphasizes the social and intellectual life of westerners in the Levant. On the conquest of Constantinople by the crusaders, see D. E. Queller, *The Fourth Crusade* (1977). The primary sources on the Crusades have been published in many collections. See especially, E. Peters, ed., *The First Crusade* (1971), and J. Muldoon, ed., *The Expansion of Europe: The First Phase* (1977). For an enlightening view of the Crusades, see F. Gabrieli, *Arab Historians of the Crusades* (1969). On the Crusade in Spain, see R. I. Burns, *The Crusader Kingdom of Valencia* (1967), and on the Crusades in the Baltic region, see E. Christiansen, *the Northern Crusades* (1980).

MEDIEVAL CIVILIZATION
AT ITS HEIGHT

*A*fter 1150 the results of the economic and political revival of the eleventh and early twelfth centuries began to become apparent in western Europe. As agricultural production expanded, the rate of population growth picked up. Farm produce and other goods moved along the rivers and over newly improved roads. The roads were busy with travelers: merchants with their goods; students on their way to Paris or Bologna; agents seeing to the business of their lords; peasants carrying their produce to market. The wealth accruing from the marketing of surplus farm goods encouraged the growth of cities and supported a large class of educated men who transformed the practice of government. It also triggered vast new architectural projects. Monasteries erected gigantic churches in the new Gothic style; merchant guilds built spa-

cious guildhalls; and feudal lords built imposing stone castles. Most of the medieval buildings still standing were built or started in the second half of the twelfth century.

THE MEDIEVAL CHURCH AT ITS HEIGHT

The Growth of Papal Government

The eleventh-century reform movement produced an independent church government that came to resemble secular government in many ways. In the second half of the eleventh century, popes began to use cardinals as agents of papal authority, sending them as legates to churches throughout western Europe. At the beginning of the twelfth century, the cardinals began to take over the organs of papal

(OPPOSITE) THIRTEENTH-CENTURY RELIQUARY OF SILVER WITH GILT. THE RELIQUARY HELD RELICS OF A BISHOP-SAINT.

government, creating a bureaucracy to manage its political and economic concerns. By the middle of the century, the church had become a polity with its own legal system and government and was on its way to becoming a highly bureaucratic institution with vast wealth and power.

The first phase of this development was the growth of the ecclesiastical legal

Contemporary mosaic portrait of Pope Innocent III, from the old basilica of St. Peter in Rome.

system. The church had jurisdiction over a great many cases that are now handled by secular courts, including cases having to do with marriage, the legitimacy of children, and the validity of oaths and promises. Church courts also had jurisdiction over clergy and monks and handled any criminal cases involving them. The pope was the highest ranking judge in this legal system, and any litigant could appeal from his bishop to the papal court. By the end of the twelfth century, the papal court was hearing thousands of cases every year. The legal system of the medieval church had a profound effect on the secular legal system of the Middle Ages, which in turn served as the foundation of modern systems.

By calling councils to legislate and promulgate their programs the early reform popes had made the council one of the principal instruments of church government. After Pope Calixtus II (r. 1119–23) and Henry V of Germany (r. 1106–25) settled the investiture controversy in 1122 (see pp. 266–69), the pope had summoned a great council at the Lateran Palace, the papal residence in Rome, to celebrate the event and issue legislation related to the investiture of bishops and other favorite themes of the reformers. And when a schism caused by a divided vote in the college of cardinals was finally resolved in 1138, Pope Innocent II (r. 1130–43) held a second Lateran Council to decide what to do about the actions of his former opponents who had ordained priests and granted church offices. Again, in 1179, following an eighteen-year-long dispute between two claimants to the papal throne, Pope Alexander III (r. 1159–81) held a third Lateran Council. This council revised the law of papal elections (originally set by a church council in 1059; see p. 267) by introducing the idea of majority rule. Henceforth, the election of a pope required a two-thirds majority of the college of cardinals; this rule is still in effect.

Pope Innocent III

Pope Innocent III (r. 1198–1216) made frequent use of the legal and governmental powers of the papacy. A vigorous man who became pope when he was only 37 years old, Innocent often interfered in the politics of the European kingdoms and was never at a loss in justifying his interference. For example, he argued that because he was the one who crowned the emperor, he had the right to decide who was best qualified for the position. As the high priest of Christendom, responsible for the salvation of every man, he insisted that he had to act whenever he detected the presence of sin in any political dispute. Innocent always had a ready-made justification for acting as arbiter, and he acted as arbiter repeatedly.

When Emperor Henry VI of Germany and Italy died in 1196, he left a young child as his heir. Following the boy's succession as Frederick II, rival claimants made a bid for the throne and a civil war broke out. In a demonstration of his papal power, Innocent decided that both were dangerous to papal interests and threw his support to Frederick, whom he thought he could control (see pp. 320–21).

Again, when King John of England (r. 1199–1216) refused to accept Stephen Langton as archbishop of Canterbury, Innocent excommunicated him for interfering with ecclesiastical authority. After John submitted and became a vassal of the pope, Innocent sought to protect him from the barons who were trying to force him to accept the *Magna Carta* (see pp. 310–11). Innocent also found occasion to assert his authority in France, Spain, and eastern Europe.

From the mid-twelfth century on, the church had been beset by recurrent heresies—belief systems contrary to church doctrine—perhaps as a result of the reform movement of the eleventh century and the religious fervor it engendered (see pp. 265–66). By Innocent's time, heretical sects were common in Italy and southern France. Many of the sects were merely anticlerical, charging that priests were ignorant and immoral and that the church had been corrupted by wealth. Others were theologically heretical, claiming that baptism of children was invalid or challenging some other doctrine. The most important of the sects, that of the Cathars, was not Christian at all. The Cathars were

Clama ne ceffef quafi tuba exalta uocem tuam. ani 7 domui Jacob peccata eo?. Unde apt's inquit epl mee a fanguine omium tutm. no eni fubifug quomi confilium det. Mundu fergo a fanguine ipo?. no ei cum noluffet. q2 cum increpate delinquntef noluerit. tot occidit. Cum ttaq; in ttemendi die udtcii de ut debeanf reddere rationem. qnenam 7 de omi uerbo ot

Detail from a page of Innocent's Register showing two wolves, one in friar's clothing, probably assisting in a heretical mass. The page deals with the church's power to punish sinners.

Manichaeans, followers of an ancient religion that combined Zoroastrianism with elements of Christianity and other religions (see pp. 205–06). After being purged by the caliphs of the tenth century, some of the surviving Manichaeans migrated from the Middle East to India (where there are still Manichaeans). Others moved west into the Byzantine Empire and began to migrate to Europe during the eleventh century, settling in northern Italy and southern France.

The Cathars believed that all material things had been created by the god of evil, and all spiritual things had been created by the god of good. They formed their own church, in which they followed a simple ritual and relied on leaders renowned for their learning and asceticism.

Innocent sent missionaries to convert the Cathars, but when peaceful means failed, he proclaimed a crusade in 1207. The crusaders were recruited in northern France and were led by Louis, the son of the French king. When it became clear that the crusaders were bent on conquering the south, which had never obeyed the French king, many of the Catholic lords of the region threw their support to the Cathars. The war was vicious. The northerners salted the fields of the countryside, rendering them unproductive for hundreds of years, and massacred thousands. By 1215, the northerners had incorporated the region into the French kingdom.

Many of the Cathars continued to practice their rites in secret, however. To search them out, Innocent established a new court, called the Inquisition, at the Fourth Lateran Council, held in 1215.

The Inquisition used an old procedure provided for in canon law whereby the judge both investigated the case and ruled on the innocence or guilt of the defendant. The judge could bring suspected criminals or heretics before his court on the mere rumor of guilt. But he had to observe stringent rules of evidence that in effect made it necessary to get a confession in order to convict. This requirement led to the use of torture as a legitimate means of extracting a confession from an alleged heretic. The Inquisition encouraged informers and false accusers, and in the hands of fanatical inquisitors it sometimes brought terror to an entire region. Generally, however, the church supervised the inquisitors carefully to ensure that they followed canonical procedure.

The popes of the thirteenth century built on the successes of Innocent III. For example, in 1234 Pope Gregory IX (r. 1227–41) published a great collection called the *Decretals* that incorporated many of Innocent's judicial decisions and many of the decrees passed by his councils, along with more than five hundred decisions and decrees from the second half of the twelfth century, that became one of the basic texts of canon law. And Gregory's successor, Innocent IV (r. 1243–54), one of Europe's greatest lawyers, held a great council in Lyons in 1245 that produced important legislation to supplement and advance the legislation passed under Innocent III. During the thirteenth century the papacy achieved the height of its political and religious authority.

The Franciscans and
The Dominicans

At about the time Innocent III was preaching the crusade against the Cathars, two saintly men—the Italian Francis and the Spaniard Dominic—took a quite different approach to heresy. By simple preaching and by living exemplary Christian lives they and their followers sought to confirm people in their orthodox beliefs. Pope Innocent recognized the value of the preaching orders founded by Francis and Dominic and gave them his support.

Francis (*ca.* 1182–1226), the son of a wealthy merchant of Assisi, experienced a religious conversion as a young man and gave all he owned to the poor. He became a mendicant—a wandering beggar—preaching the Christian message as he imagined the apostles themselves had done.

Francis soon attracted others to his mission. These first Franciscans were simple men who were at ease with common people. But as time passed, scholars and professional men came to dominate the order, which had been approved by Innocent III in 1209. By the middle of the thirteenth century, Bonaventure, a leading theologian, was minister general of the Franciscans, and the order had become a powerful force throughout Christendom. Among its members were some of the leading intellectuals of the age, including the scientist Roger Bacon.

Dominic (*ca.* 1170–1221) was a trained theologian, who approached heresy as an intellectual problem. He set out to create an order of mendicant preachers trained to refute the arguments of the heretics. Innocent approved the order in 1215. From the first, many intellectuals were attracted to the Dominican Order, which developed a string of schools and became influential in the universities (p. 291). The great Aristotelian scholar, Albert the Great (see p. 296), became a Dominican in 1223, and his student Thomas Aquinas joined the order as a young man. The order also attracted Raymond of Peñafort, who compiled the *Decretals* of Gregory IX and wrote the constitution of the Dominican Order.

The Dominicans developed preaching into an art. They wrote manuals on preaching that outlined ways of approaching various audiences, and much of what we know about the popular beliefs of the late Middle Ages comes from

St. Francis strips off the garments he wore as a well-to-do young man and renounces all worldly goods. Painting by Giotto (1266?–1337) in the church of St. Francis of Assisi.

such books. But the training in Christian doctrine and argument that the Dominicans received made them excellent judges of heresy, and many of them became inquisitors.

Both mendicant orders became closely associated with the papacy, and soon Franciscans and Dominicans were being labeled as agents of papal authority. The popes used them as legates, agents, and judges and gave them freedom to preach wherever they wished. That grant of freedom conflicted with the right of bishops to control the priesthood in their dioceses, and many bishops began protesting to the pope that the mendicants were violating their rights. But the popes steadfastly supported the friars—as the mendicants were called (from Latin *fratres*, meaning brothers), who were indeed loyal supporters of papal authority.

THE RENAISSANCE OF THE TWELFTH CENTURY

The reform movement of the eleventh century (see pp. 265–66) had stimulated a cultural awakening that matured into the golden age of medieval civilization. Both the intellectual energies and the artistic impulses of the twelfth-century renaissance derived from a desire to recover the glories of ancient Roman culture.

The reformers, in an effort to improve the education of clerics, encouraged research and intellectual activity. Monasteries and cathedral libraries were searched for precious books, which were copied and distributed to rising academic centers. The conflict between the reformers and the German kings lent urgency to the research effort as both sides searched for historical precedents and the opinions of church fathers. The search for vestiges of ancient culture reached into Spain, southern Italy, and Syria, which had been intellectual centers under the Arabs. In all of these places, Jewish scholars were busy translating Arabic works of philosophy and science into Latin.

ROMANESQUE AND GOTHIC ART AND ARCHITECTURE

Romanesque

The economic revival of the eleventh and early twelfth centuries provided Europeans with the means to replace their modest churches with grand new churches built of stone and adorned with handsome sculptures. As one observer said, Europe was "clothed in new churches." At first, the builders and their master masons tried to recreate the style they associated with old Roman buildings. This style—called Romanesque—was based on the arch. They designed churches shaped like a

cross, the so-called cruciform plan. The basic design called for a nave with aisles on either side crossed at a right angle by a transept. The cross was completed by a continuation of the nave beyond the transept that ended in a round or square apse. The ceiling was formed by an arched vault that tended to emphasize the vast internal space of the church and the sweep of the nave toward the alter just beyond the transept. The church was oriented so that the alter and apse were at the east end; the main entrance to the nave was at the west end.

Some of the Romanesque churches were immense. The monastic church at Cluny, with a vaulted ceiling about 160 feet high, was the largest church in Christendom until St. Peter's in Rome was rebuilt in the sixteenth century. They were also marvelously ornate, the exterior walls bright with whitewash and the interior walls covered with colorful murals depicting the life of Christ and other scenes from the Bible. The murals served as a Bible for the faithful, most of whom were illiterate. The capitals of the great pillars supporting the vault were richly decorated with naturalistic sculptures of everything from plants and animals to saints.

The building boom occasioned by these ambitious projects gave rise to a class of professional stonemasons who eventually organized themselves into a craft guild. The members of this cadre of craftsmen traveled from one building site to another, participating in the design and construction of the splendid new churches. Over time, they became sophisticated masters of technique and design and developed an artistic consciousness attuned to innovation and creativity. The churchmen who employed the masons also encouraged innovation, because it set their church apart from those being built elsewhere and satisfied their desire to create a unique monument to their piety.

Gothic

In 1150 a completely new style of architecture made its appearance in the monastic church of St. Denis near Paris, which for centuries had been the burial place of the

French kings. Abbot Suger (*ca.* 1091–1152), an educated man experienced in affairs of government, had served as regent while King Louis VII was away on the Second Crusade, and as abbot of St. Denis he was a distinguished figure in the kingdom.

Suger wanted to flood his new church with light, which emanated from God. But the round arch used in Romanesque churches produces great outward pressure that must be absorbed by exceptionally thick walls—twelve feet in some instances. And those walls could not be weakened by having large windows cut through them. Masons had already experimented with pointed arches, with more nearly vertical thrust, which therefore do not require massive walls. Suger's masons based the design of the church at St. Denis entirely on the pointed arch with great windows piercing the walls. The new architectural style was called Gothic, because Italian critics of the sixteenth century associated it with the "Gothic," or Germanic, Middle Ages.

The stained-glass windows of St. Denis were designed as illuminated murals and served the same function as the wall paintings of older churches. The designers of the church also introduced a new style of sculpture—carefully proportioned though somewhat abstract. Altogether, St. Denis revolutionized architectural and artistic taste of churchmen and patrons, although Romanesque churches continued to be built in some regions until the end of the century.

Gothic emerged as the dominant architectural style of the Middle Ages, eventually acquiring an angular, ornate character that emphasized height and complex vaulting. As time passed, the sculpture became increasingly realistic, and, curiously, the plants and animals depicted in stone "matured." In the sculpture of early Gothic churches, the plants and animals tend to be young, but as the tradition aged so did the flora and fauna.

More churches were built in these centuries than in any other period of European history. By the middle of the thirteenth century, the cities were competing to build the largest and most spectacular cathedrals—bishops' churches—ever built. For example, the city fathers of Beauvais decided to build the loftiest

Abbot Suger depicted in a stained-glass window at St. Denis (twelfth-century).

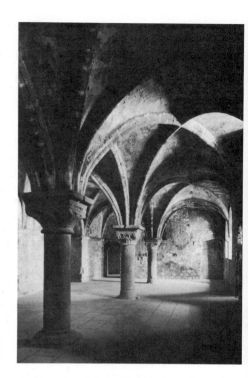

(Left) Barrel vault, church of St. Savin (eleventh century). Although no light could be admitted in the upper part of the nave, the vault could be covered with fine Romanesque painting. (Center) Groin vault formed by the intersection of two barrel vaults, Mont-Saint-Michel (twelfth century). The walls could now be pierced with windows. (Right) Rib vault, Mont-Saint-Michel (late Romanesque). Ribs made it easier to design and build a groin vault, but the effect is still heavy.

(Left) Early Gothic rib vault, Mont-Saint-Michel. Greater height and light are now being exploited. (Right) Rib vaulting on a grand scale, the nave of Chartres Cathedral (1194–1220). Great height and light have been achieved; the upper (clerestory) windows are larger and more useful than those at floor level.

Two representations of the Visitation. *(Left)* Romanesque façade of the abbey church of St. Pierre at Moissac (twelfth century). *(Right)* Gothic façade of Reims cathedral (late thirteenth century). The Romanesque work is linear and heavily stylized, like a manuscript illustration. The Gothic sculpture is more naturalistic.

church in Christendom, and for years their master masons struggled to overcome the technical difficulties of building an unprecendently tall structure in stone. They finished their work in the mid-1250s, but thirty years later the nave collapsed. Recent studies have shown that the collapse was caused by winds that weakened the mortar in the walls.

In effect, the architects of the era were trying to extend the principles of height and light embodied in the first Gothic church at St. Denis. They emphasized vertical lines and steadily increased the size of the windows. In the small royal chapel of Sainte-Chapelle in Paris the walls consist almost entirely of magnificent stained glass supported by a few slender mullions. Even in the larger churches, there was far more glass than stone at the upper (clerestory) level. To make the walls strong enough to bear the lateral thrust, arched buttresses were built along the exterior. These flying buttresses are a characteristic feature of Gothic churches.

The great portals of the cathedrals were covered with hundreds of statues of Christ, the Virgin, apostles, and saints. The windows told stories or interpreted a moral in brilliant colors that shifted as the day proceeded. At Chartres the cathedral windows depict the continuity between the Old and New Testaments by portraying a prophet carrying an evangelist on his shoulders. Typically, the capitals of the pillars inside the cathedrals, along with the walls and roof are adorned with sculptures of animals and plants so realistic that they have been used to study medieval flora and fauna.

Technically, Amiens is perhaps the most perfect Gothic cathedral of all though many prefer the massive solidity of Notre Dame of Paris or the less unified but more interesting style of Chartres, which was built in stages over a century. As the Gothic style spread to England, Germany, and other countries, it underwent modifications dictated by local taste. Only the Italians preferred to stay with the Romanesque style, modeling their churches on the basilica of Santa Maria Maggiore in Rome (fifth century) or Justinian's churches in Ravenna (sixth century).

THE INTELLECTUAL RENAISSANCE

Philosophy and Theology

The rediscovery of philosophy as a formal method of enquiry led to extraordinary advances in theology, law, and science. Dialectic, as logic was called, made it possible to order what was known and then to make new inferences from that knowledge.

Gerbert of Aurillac (Pope Sylvester II; see p. 241) had revived interest in the so-called Old Logic, an elementary system of logic based on Aristotle's treatises, the *Categories* and *On Interpretation*, which were known in the West in Boethius's translations (see pp. 127–28). By the end of the eleventh century, the study of dialectic had gained momentum and was being taught by famous teachers in schools at Laon, Tours, and Chartres. The Italian philosopher/theologian Anselm (1035–1109), who emigrated to Normandy and was appointed Archbishop of Canterbury in 1087, provided a striking example of the power of logic when he created the ontological argument for the existence of God. This proof rested on a definition of God as a being greater than any being that can be conceived, from which it followed by logical deduction that God must exist (because otherwise one could conceive of a greater being).

Among the students of the time was Peter Abelard (*ca.* 1070–1141), a prodigy who earned a reputation as a troublesome genius by challenging his teachers and pointing out how muddled their thinking was. By his early twenties, he was teaching himself, wandering from school to school lecturing on Aristotle's logic. Around 1113, he decided to study theology and went to Laon to study with a famous teacher there. Disappointed, he went on to Paris, set himself up as a teacher, and soon fell in love with one of his students, Heloise, the niece of a powerful Parisian cleric. They had a son and were secretly married, but on learning of the affair, Heloise's uncle had Abelard castrated. Abelard then entered the monastery of St. Denis, and Heloise became a nun at a convent near Paris.

At St. Denis, Abelard continued his studies. Although Anselm and a few others had used logic in their approach to theological problems, the prevailing method was to collect relevant passages from the church fathers and to present them as the answer to a particular theological question. Abelard discovered a great many contradictions in the patristic writings and worked out a new method for dealing with them. In the book *Sic et Non* ("Yes and No"), he set down a series of theological questions, arranged the patristic texts on both sides of each question, and used logical analysis to reconcile the differences. This new method was the foundation of scholasticism, an intellectual practice that eventually became the standard approach in medieval schools. But the immediate effect of Abelard's book was to call into question the opinions of the church fathers, who were considered to have been inspired by God. In 1120 Abelard's work was condemned, and he was expelled from St. Denis. After spending some time in a monastery in the wilds of Brittany, he returned to Paris and resumed his teaching. By the late 1130s, he again faced condemnation for his views.

The Problem of Universals: Reason versus Revelation

Abelard participated in the most important philosophical debate of his age, over the problem of universals. The Old Logic had raised a fundamental issue about the relationship between what is seen and what is unseen. Porphyry, a Greek philosopher who wrote an introduction to Aristotle's *Categories* in the late third century, had noted that it was not clear whether classes of things (universal terms) in the physical world were real in the same way as things themselves. It was possible that classes of things were only mental constructs that were useful in categorizing entities. For example, if we observe various individual dogs and treat them as the category *dog*, is the category a real thing, like the dogs themselves, or is it only an idea that permits us to accommodate the multiplicity of dogs found in the world? In time, philosophers who thought that universals were real came to be called realists, while those who thought that only concrete objects were real came to be called nominalists (because they considered nouns like *dog* to be only names, *nomina*).

The question about the nature of reality underlying the realist-nominalist debate had great significance for Christian thought. The problem was that human reason could not, it seemed, corroborate Christian revelation; indeed, it might even contradict revelation. If only those things that we can observe are real, then how can we understand the reality of God as revealed in the Bible? A form of this question arose in the late eleventh century, when Lanfranc (archbishop of Canterbury 1070–89 and teacher of St. Anselm) and Berengar of Tours (d. 1088) engaged in a controversy over whether Christ was really present in the bread and wine of the Eucharist. Berengar, a nominalist, held that only the bread and wine existed as real objects, while Lanfranc, a realist, argued that the body and blood of Christ were real in the bread and wine after the priest had consecrated them.

The realist-nominalist controversy reached a new stage with Peter Abelard, who tried to resolve it by concentrating on the distinction between a thing and the word that designates it. He suggested that nouns that designate universals, such as *dog*, are neither mere words, as the nominalists held, nor things-in-themselves, as the realists argued. Instead, they were concepts in the mind that had an objective reality derived from a process of mental abstraction. When one sees several dogs, one discovers the concept *dog* by a mental abstraction from the actual animals to the class of animals. This concept is real in a different way from the actual animals it designates.

The ecclesiastical authorities did not view Abelard's resolution as satisfactory because it did not explain the reality of God. According to that resolution, God was real neither as a particular being nor as a mental abstraction. How, then, was God real? The failure of Abelard's argument to answer this question led to its being condemned as heretical. The apparent conflict between reason, exemplified by logical thought, and revelation remained a problem for many philosophers.

Only the realists could get around the problem, essentially by ignoring it. By accepting the idea that concepts are real in the same way as things observed in the physical world are real, the realists ignored the difficulty that logic could not show this to be true. But at least they could remain orthodox in their Christian belief in revelation, and by the late twelfth century the philosopher/theologians had moved on to other metaphysical questions. These questions too centered on the nature of reason and revelation, but they arose, not from the realist-nominalist controversy, but from the study of Aristotle's metaphysical and scientific treatises, which came to the West accompanied by the commentaries of Arabic thinkers.

The Two Approaches to Intellectual Work

Scholasticism attracted many followers and became the basis of the mainstream of medieval philosophy and theology, but it did not go unchallenged. Among the leading opponents of Abelard and his school was the Cistercian monk Bernard of Clairvaux (see p. 271), who held that the purpose of intellectual work is to enhance spiritual experience. Further, he insisted, that purpose imposed both form and limitation on the work. Because the Bible is the basis of divine revelation, it must be the principal object of study. And that study must consist in a contemplation of

Abelard on Scholarship

. . . Investigation is the first key to wisdom: it is the kind of industrious and repeated inquiry which Aristotle, the wisest of all philosophers recommended to his students in saying: "It is difficult to solve problems with confidence unless they have been frequently discussed. It is not useless to express doubts about some matters." For through doubting we come to inquiry and through inquiry we discover the truth, as Truth Himself said: "Seek and you will find, knock and the door will be opened to you."

◆ ◆ ◆

St. Bernard on Abelard

We have in France an old teacher turned into a new theologian, who in his early days amused himself with logic and who now gives utterance to wild imaginations upon the Holy Scriptures. . . .

There is nothing in heaven above nor in the earth below which he deigns to confess ignorance of: he raises his eyes to heaven and searches the deep things of God and . . . brings back unspeakable words which it is not lawful for a man to utter. He is ready to give a reason for everything, even for those things that are above reason. Thus he presumes against reason and against faith. For what is more unreasonable than to attempt to go beyond the limits of reason? And what is more against faith than to be unwilling to believe what cannot be proved by reason? . . .

And so he promises understanding to his hearers, even on those most sublime and sacred truths that are hidden in the very bosom of our holy faith. He places degrees in the Trinity, modes in the Majesty, numbers in the Eternity. . . . Who can endure this? . . . Who does not shudder at such new-fangled profanities?

Translated from Sic et Non, *ed. by V. Cousin,* Ouvrages inédits d'Abélard *(Paris: Imprimerie royale, 1836), p. 104; translated from* Patrologia latina, *Vol. 182, cols. 1055–56.*

could produce a truth that was independent of revelation. He believed there were two sources of knowledge about God and the world—biblical and "scientific"—and the two were compatible and consistent with one another. Drawn by this heady stuff, young men flocked to Abelard's lectures. Bernard, who believed that the way to truth was through the monastic profession, viewed Abelard as a dangerous influence on the young.

These two approaches represented two intellectual milieus, both of them popular and powerful in the twelfth century. The monastic orders were growing rapidly and were attracting men of great ability and personal magnetism. The monks led a special way of life and had a special way of achieving knowledge, and they constituted a strong moral force in the political and social life of western Europe.

By contrast, Abelard and men like him occupied teaching positions in the cathedral schools, which educated future clerics. But their influence went beyond the confines of church schools. When Abelard sought a position in the cathedral school of Paris, the bishop refused to let him teach there. So Abelard taught under the aegis of a monastic house in the city, and hundreds came to hear his lectures. Other masters took advantage of the pool of students to set themselves up in Paris, which soon became the leading intellectual center in Europe. Not having the specific task of training clerics, these independent masters developed philosophical and scientific curricula that provided students with skills and knowledge useful to secular rulers, and many of them subsequently entered the service of kings and great lords.

The Origins of Universities

By the late twelfth century so many masters were teaching in Paris that they decided to form a separate guild, or *universitas* (the Latin word for guild). The exact date is unknown, but by 1200 the guild had existed for some time. Each master was an independent entrepreneur who offered his courses for pay just as a leather craftsman offered his goods for sale. Students who attended a master's lectures or

the meaning of the sacred text, which contains the whole truth about God and the created world. In short, Bernard was insisting on the use of reason to attain the mystical experience of oneness with God. Many Cistercians and other monastic thinkers followed Bernard's mode of theological discourse, which consisted mostly of sermons on biblical passages.

To Abelard, using logic to analyze sense perceptions of the created world took private instruction from him paid him directly. The guild regulated the fees charged, the rental rate of rooms, and, most important, the standards of entry to the guild. A person admitted as a teaching master had to pass an examination, a practice that eventually led to the definition of a curriculum that would prepare students for entry to the teaching profession.

The guild of masters was the beginning of the university, an institution of higher learning based on the cooperative activities of teachers. In its early days the guild was subject to episcopal control, but by the early thirteenth century the masters were seeking independence. The conflict between the guild and the bishop was primarily over the election of the rector, the chief official of the guild, and it was some time before the masters established the principle that they alone had the right to choose their leadership.

As they developed, universities came to offer instruction not only in the liberal arts, based on dialectic, but in theology, law, and medicine. Each of the professional faculties formed their own guild. The theology curriculum was centered on the work of Peter Lombard (*ca.* 1100– *ca.* 1160), the master of the cathedral school in Paris (later bishop of the see) and the author of a scholastic treatment of church doctrine called the *Four Books of Sentences*, which contained the opinions of the church fathers. Lectures consisted of reading the *Sentences* along with commentaries on the text.

Unlike the mystical theologians, who continued to flourish in the monasteries, the scholastic theologians took a speculative, systematic approach to the Bible. In the late twelfth century, the Englishman Stephen Langton, then a professor at Paris but later the archbishop of Canterbury (r. 1207–28), introduced the chapter and verse divisions into the text of the Bible. Once this was done, scholastic commentators could cite passages with precision, making it easier to carry on systematic study and to debate the meaning of particular passages.

The curriculum in law was based on Justinian's *Corpus Iuris Civilis* (Body of Civil Law; see p. 170) and on a parallel

Medieval Schools and Universities   1100–1250

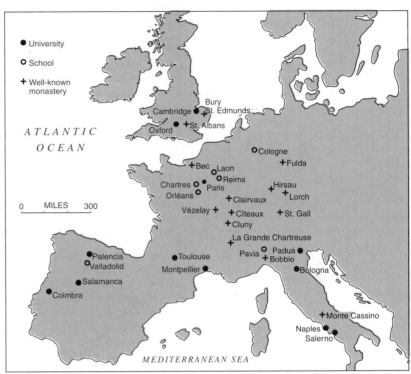

compilation of church law, which came to be called the *Corpus Iuris Canonici* (Body of Canon Law). The discovery of the *Corpus Iuris Civilis* in Italy during the later eleventh century had revolutionized thinking about law. The coherent, sophisticated legal system embodied in Justinian's code soon prompted the setting up of a law school by legal scholars in Bologna who reintroduced the idea that law was not just a collection of old legislation but a logical system based on principles of justice. The discovery of Justinian's code also fostered the study of secular law, now firmly positioned in the grand tradition of Roman jurisprudence.

Church, or canon, law dated back to the fourth century, after the emperor Constantine recognized the church as a legal institution under Roman law (see pp. 116– 17). Canon law was based on Roman law, just as the administrative structure of the church was based on the Roman diocese. After the collapse of Roman authority in the West, canon law absorbed many of the elements of Germanic law. Then, in the eleventh century, the contestants in the investiture controversy turned to the sources of canon law in their search for proof of their arguments. Their efforts produced vast collections containing many contradictory provisions and ideas. By the end of the eleventh century, several experts in canon law, including Ivo, the bishop of Chartres (r. 1090–1116), declared that the conflicting doctrines and ideas found in the canons somehow had to be reconciled.

That goal was finally reached around 1140, when Gratian, who was teaching canon law at Bologna, published a great compilation of canon law, appropriately called *The Concordance of Discordant Canons*. In compiling this work, Gratian had followed Abelard's scholastic method. It soon gave rise to a school of canonical jurisprudence and formed the first part of the *Corpus Iuris Canonici*.

The excitement engendered by the rediscovery of Roman law and by the emergence of a new school of canonical jurisprudence made Bologna an important center of legal studies, and during the late twelfth century a university was founded in the city. The goal of a student of law was the doctorate, though most students studied only long enough to prove their worth to an employer, such as the church, a king, or a duke.

Unlike the guild in Paris, whose members were teaching masters, the members of the Bolognese guild were students. The student guild established the curriculum and regulated the activities of faculty and students alike. It required masters to proceed in an orderly fashion through all the material to be studied in a course and would not permit a master to leave the city during term without posting a bond to ensure that he would return. Although the guild of teaching masters eventually became the model for universities in the West, the student guild was favored for a long time by schools of professional studies such as law and medicine, in which the students were commonly in their thirties and already advanced in their education. The University of Montpellier in southern France, for example, was founded on the model of the student guild in the early thirteenth century.

Formal studies in medicine rested on Arabic science (see p. 217). The first center of medical study in the West arose in Salerno, a city south of Naples, where Europeans came into contact with Arab influences. By the twelfth century, Bologna had become a center of medical studies, and students eventually founded a university there. A medical university was founded in Montpellier in 1221. Through the faculties of these early schools of medicine the West became acquainted with Aristotle's scientific treatises.

The course to a doctorate was long. Few received their degree before they were forty. When a student had completed his course of study and his adviser deemed him ready, he stood for the doctorate. That meant going to a public place, usually the steps of the cathedral or, after the university acquired its own building, in front of the university hall, and standing there all day answering any question put to him by the people who happened by. A panel of faculty members observed and judged his performance and, if they were satisfied with it, awarded him the doctorate. The student was then admitted to the guild of his faculty and received a license to teach in the university.

Aristotle's Scientific Treatises and the Problem of Reason versus Revelation

The Arabs had begun to study Aristotle in the tenth century, and an active school of Aristotelian philosophers and scientists in Baghdad studied and annotated Aristotle's scientific treatises (see pp. 217–18). When the Latin translations of those treatises reached the West, they were accompanied by the commentaries of the Arab scholars.

Aristotle believed that the world had always existed, that it was without beginning or end. That view was in direct contradiction to the Judeo-Christian-Islamic notion of the Creator-God. Arabic and Jewish philosophers had already confronted this conflict between Aristotle and revealed truth and had responded to it in three ways. Some ignored the problem, much as the Christian realists did, and some tried to explain away Aristotle's assumptions about the eternality of the world. Others, led by the Arabic philosopher Ibn Rushd (Averroës in Latin; 1126–98; see p. 217), proposed that there were two truths, one accessible through observation and logical analysis and the other through divine revelation. So Averroës declared that the problem was a false one and that both truths were true. To reconcile them into one truth about the world was beyond the capacity of human beings.

The appearance in the West of Aristotle's *Metaphysics* accompanied by Averroës's commentary set off a storm in the church. In 1215 the ecclesiastical authorities banned their study. And in 1231 Pope Gregory IX appointed a commission of scholars to review all the works of Aristotle and all the commentaries on those works and to purge them of error. Despite the papal ban, university faculties in Paris, Bologna, and Naples (founded in 1224) continued to teach Aristotle—whom scholars called "The Philosopher"—and the controversy over the two truths carried on into the later thirteenth century. To reconcile Aristotle with Christian revelation was the great problem of the thirteenth-century philosophers.

The man who achieved that reconciliation was Thomas Aquinas (1225–74), who created a systematic explanation of the world that matched the structural perfection of a Gothic cathedral. Aquinas brought reason and revelation together in a grand synthesis of the Christian world view.

Saint Thomas Aquinas

Aquinas, the son of a southern Italian nobleman, entered the Dominican order as a young man. His intellectual ability was soon recognized, and he studied at various Dominican houses. At last he was sent to Paris, where the Dominicans had a study center and where Dominicans had begun to become professors in the university. In 1252, Aquinas received his doctorate in theology at the age of 27 and was

elected to a professorship at the university. A university professorship lasted for three years, during which time the professor was to give a course based on Peter Lombard's *Sentences*. The best of the courses were published as theological commentaries or treatises. After completing their course, the professors left the university for other duties. Many of them became deans of cathedral chapters or bishops; some rose to become cardinals or popes—like Cardinal Robert of Courson (*ca.* 1160–1219) and Pope Innocent IV.

Aquinas, after completing his professorship, taught for a time at Dominican houses in Rome, Bologna, and Naples. Then, in 1268, he was recalled to Paris

St. Thomas Aquinas, detail from the Crucifixion, by Fra Angelico (1387–1455). Although this representation was made two centuries after Thomas lived, it seems to accurately depict his large head and bearlike appearance.

for a second professorship, an unheard-of honor. Throughout his lifetime, he was renowned for his extraordinary intellect.

Aquinas argued that through reason alone men can achieve only a partial understanding of the world. To achieve complete understanding, both reason and revelation are necessary. Using the scholastic method of argument, he set out to show that the two approaches, and the truths attainable through each, are consistent with one another. As he saw it, the role of reason is to make deductions from first principles, those being the truths about the world found in the Bible, and from the data of sensory experience. According to the medieval view, religion is not just a system of belief but a body of knowledge about the material and spiritual universes.

Aquinas's method of reasoning represents the ultimate refinement of the scholastic analysis that Abelard introduced in the early twelfth century. Aquinas built

a vast analytical structure concerning the nature of God, man, and the universe in which each topic is taken up in logical order. During his second professorship at Paris he produced the *Summa Theologica*, a large work divided into three parts, each subdivided into Questions dealing with general topics. There are more than six hundred such Questions. Each Question is broken down into Articles, or specific queries, beginning with "Whether. . . ." For example, Question 94 of the second part is titled "Concerning Natural Law," and the fifth Article of this Question is headed, "Whether natural law can be changed?" The specific queries are answered through a series of opposing arguments. In this example, Aquinas set down all the arguments and authorities (mostly patristic texts and Aristotle) to support an affirmative answer (natural law can be changed) and then listed the arguments and authorities in support of a negative answer. He then proceeded to reconcile the arguments and authorities by showing

A university lecture, as portrayed in a fourteenth-century Italian miniature. Attention to the lecturer is not undivided; several students are talking, and one is certainly asleep.

that the contradictions between them were only apparent.

Aquinas's vision of a unified understanding of God and the universe and his systematic presentation of that unity made his work exceptionally persuasive. It led to his early canonization as a saint and to his being regarded as the leading philosopher of Catholicism. Yet not all of his contemporaries shared his views. The most eminent Franciscan philosopher, Bonaventure, who received his doctorate in the same year as Aquinas, thought Aquinas put too much emphasis on reason and relied too heavily on Aristotle and other Greek (that is, non-Christian) philosophers. Bonaventure emphasized will, following Augustine, who believed that his will to salvation had brought about his own conversion. For Bonaventure and his followers, systematic knowledge of the world was less important than an understanding of the way man's will engenders God's act of salvation.

In any case, Aquinas's arguments were too technical to have much influence on laymen, and they led to a distancing between ordinary people and the doctrines of the church. That distancing strengthened the tendency toward the secularization of life that emerged in the late thirteenth and fourteenth centuries.

The Revival of Science

Scientific knowledge had declined to a low ebb in late antiquity and the early Middle Ages. As we have seen, the first stirring of revival occurred in eleventh-century Salerno, when scholars first became aware of Arabic treatises on medicine. Arabic works on medicine and other sciences had been translated in the kingdom of Sicily and in Spain by Jewish scholars who had mastered Arabic and Latin.

Through the influence of these translations, the first three sciences of the *quadrivium*—arithmetic, geometry, and astronomy—were transformed from elementary studies into the mathematical disciplines that are necessary for advanced scientific work. About 1126, for example, Adelard of Bath translated Euclid's *Geometry* into Latin and introduced the West to

---

The Reconciliation of Christian and Classical Philosophy

This extract from the Summa Contra Gentiles *by St. Thomas Aquinas shows how a thirteenth-century scholar was able to use the ideas of Aristotle.*

We have now shown that the effort to demonstrate the existence of God is not a vain one. We shall therefore proceed to set forth the arguments by which both philosophers and Catholic teachers have proved that God exists.

We shall first set forth the arguments by which Aristotle proceeds to prove that God exists. The aim of Aristotle is to do this in two ways, beginning with motion.

Of these ways the first is as follows. Everything that is moved is moved by another. That some things are in motion—for example, the sun—is evident from sense. Therefore, it is moved by something else that moves it. This mover is itself either moved or not moved. If it is not, we have reached our conclusion—namely, that we must posit some unmoved mover. This we call God. If it is moved, it is moved by another mover. We must, consequently, either proceed to infinity, or we must arrive at some unmoved mover. Now, it is not possible to proceed to infinity. Hence we must posit some prime unmoved mover.

From On the Truth of the Catholic Faith. Summa Contra Gentiles, *trans. by A. C. Pegis (New York: Doubleday, 1955), p. 85.*

---

trigonometry by translating the works of the Arabic mathematician al-Khwarizmi (*fl. ca.* 825). About twenty years later, another Englishman, Robert of Chester, translated al-Khwarizmi's *On the Restoration and Opposition of Numbers*, which Arab scholars called "The Book" (*Al Gebra*). The word algebra itself comes from that phrase.

In astronomy, Ptolemy's *Almagest* (second century) was translated around 1160 in Sicily from a Greek manuscript that the Byzantine emperor had given to the king of Sicily. A little later, Gerard of Cremona, working in Toledo, made a translation of the work from Arabic; this translation was preferred, because the Arabic scientists had corrected Ptolemy's original text with their own, more accurate observations. Gerard remained in Toledo for twelve years (*ca.* 1175–87), during which time the city became the chief center of translation. He himself translated more than seventy treatises into Latin and, with other translators, introduced the West to physics, optics, mechanics, biology, meteorology, and psychology. Together, they translated most of the scientific works of Aristotle, along with the Arabic commentaries.

By the early thirteenth century, Aristotle's works had become the textbooks of European science. Albert the Great (1193–1280) was the first to master the whole corpus of Aristotle. He wrote 21 large volumes, most of them devoted to commentaries on Aristotle's scientific treatises. He was particularly concerned with the reconciliation of Aristotle's philosophy with Christian theology, as was his more famous student, Thomas Aquinas.

Oxford was one of the most important centers of science in the thirteenth century. The first rector of the University of Oxford, Robert Grosseteste (1168–1253), did important work in optics. When Grosseteste became bishop of Lincoln in 1235,

he assembled a school of translators, Jews and Christians, to translate scientific works. He designed an optical illusion for the new cathedral he built in Lincoln that can still be seen, which makes it seem there is an aisle where there is only a wall. Grosseteste's successor as the leading scientist at Oxford was Roger Bacon (*ca.* 1220–92), who described eyeglasses, airplanes, self-propelled ships, and a process for making gunpowder. He also conducted experiments, though they were rather crude in design and produced inconclusive results.

It was the work of these and many other thirteenth-century scholars that made possible the scientific revolution of the sixteenth century. While remaining faithful to the work of Aristotle, medieval scientists reintroduced the idea of scientific discovery and experiment.

History and Vernacular Literature

The twelfth and thirteenth centuries were a time of intense literary activity, both in

The side aisle of Lincoln Cathedral (thirteenth century). Bishop Robert Grosseteste designed the side wall, with its line of arches, as an optical illusion. In certain lights, created by the windows opposite, the wall gives the illusion of an additional aisle.

Latin and the vernacular languages. The great monastic writers of the twelfth century, such as Bernard of Clairvaux (see p. 271), were brilliant stylists whose Latin sparkled with rhetorical flourishes. About the middle of the twelfth century, it became common for writers to publish collections of their letters, which were consequently treated as a literary form. Others wrote Latin poetry in imitation of the ancient poets, and university students wrote satirical poetry celebrating youth and youthful pursuits, particularly drinking and womanizing, while attacking the church and the secular powers. The student poets were called Goliards, from Golias, their mythical king (in Old French, *goliarde* meant gluttony).

The principal form of medieval Latin literature was history. Ever since the time of Eusebius (early fourth century), Christians had seen in history the working out of God's plan for the world. In the early Middle Ages, Gregory of Tours and Paul the Deacon had written extensive histories of the Germanic peoples who had inherited Roman authority in the West, and during the Carolingian renaissance Einhard and Notker had written biographies of the Carolingian kings. During the eleventh century, when both sides in the investiture controversy (see pp. 266–69) were carrying on historical research to justify their positions, many monks and priests wrote histories of their churches. And in the twelfth century, kings began to patronize writers who would glorify their deeds and ensure their place in history. Otto of Freising (*ca.* 1114–58) in Germany, Geoffrey of Monmouth (*ca.* 1100–54) in England, and Guillaume le Breton (*ca.* 1159/69– after 1226) in France wrote histories that gave historical legitimacy to the royal dynasties of their kingdoms. Counts and bishops also sought to have their acts recorded in local histories.

Outside the circle of monks and scholars, there was a flowering of vernacular literature. The Germanic peoples had possessed an oral literary tradition made up of epic cycles centered on some heroic figure, like the Celtic hero Arthur or Charles the Great. Only a few of those stories, including the Anglo-Saxon poem *Beowulf* (see p. 242), had been written down before the early twelfth century. But from that time on many of the epics were recorded. The first was *The Song of Roland*, an epic about an incident that took place in Charles's campaign against the Moors in Spain. About the middle of the century, a German poet wrote down the *Nibelungenlied* (Song of the Nibelungs), an epic based on the story of Attila the Hun's destruction of the Burgundians (see p. 115).

Soon, however, poets gave up epics for romances. Romances told of the quest of chivalric knights for a high position in feudal society, a good marriage, and a large estate. The new literary genre was created in France but soon spread throughout Europe. Its earliest patrons were the women of the family of King Louis VII of France (r. 1137–80), particularly his first wife Eleanor of Aquitaine and their daughter Marie of Champagne. Most of the early romances were based on the Arthurian cycle, a series of stories about the knights around the Celtic hero Arthur. Once the romance emerged as the most popular literary style, writers of every language and every country used it. About 1200, a German author (identity unknown) rewrote the *Nibelungenlied* as a romance, and that is the form in which we have the story. The greatest of the early writers of romance was Chrétien de Troyes (*fl.* 1160–90), who wrote romances based on the exploits of Perceval, Lancelot, Erec, and Cligès. By the end of the century, German writers such as Gottfried von Strassburg and Wolfram von Eschenbach were copying the style— Gottfried with *Tristan und Isolde* and Wolfram with *Parzival*. In England, the popularity of the romance endured for centuries, as represented by *Sir Gawain and the Green Knight* (fourteenth century) and Sir Thomas Malory's *Le Mort d'Arthur* (late fifteenth century).

The romance may have grown out of the tradition of the minstrels, or troubadours, professional singers who entertained the households of the great lords. Their songs began to be written down in the late eleventh century. It was around that time that the chivalric code took shape, and knights learned to sing the old songs as part of their education. Some of them, including Eleanor of Aquitaine's grandfather William of Poitou, were themselves accomplished poets. William was the first to write down his lyrics.

The troubadours promoted *courtoisie*—gallantry, gentility, and generosity—as part of knightly virtue and made romantic love—a nonphysical devotion that ennobled both the man and the woman, especially the man—a central virtue of the true knight.

In a typical romance, the heroic knight sets out to perform military feats that will make him worthy of a woman's love. Throughout his encounters he tries to reconcile the violence of his deeds with the gentleness of romantic love. Once romantic love had become intimately associated with the idea of knighthood, every knight felt obliged to fall in love. And, because love meant romantic love, the object of his affection might well be a married woman. Marriage was a dynastic or political affair that had nothing to do with romantic love.

In *The Art of Courtly Love*, a book written some time between 1174 and 1186, Andreas Capellanus systematized the romantic ideals in a set of rules, the first of which was "Marriage is no real excuse for not loving." He described a mythical "court of love" that decided cases involving lovers' rights against each other.

This literature of courtly love placed women on a pedestal and prescribed their behavior, especially toward men. More and more, the image of women conveyed by the romances diverged from their real life, in which their role as surrogates for their husbands in the management of the family estates continued to dominate.

In contrast to the literature of the nobility, the *fabliaux* that became popular with the bourgeoisie were brief tales told in a realistic vein. One purpose of the *fabliaux* was to amuse, and their humor was often crude and broad. Stock characters included hypocritical, unscrupulous monks and priests, the innkeeper with a beautiful daughter but no common sense, and the wealthy merchant who was sharp in trade and stupid in everything else. Whereas the women of the romances rarely took part in the action of the story, the women of the *fabliaux* played important roles and were often portrayed as clever, if not always ethical. The heroes were usually wandering scholars or poor but quick-witted commoners who outwitted aristocrats and merchants. Closely related to the *fabliaux* were the fables, in which a moral was added to the story. The characters of the fables were animals that represented stock human types. The most famous fables were known collectively as the *Romance of Reynard*, in which Reynard the Fox played approximately the same role as the protagonists of the *fabliaux*.

The Rules of Courtly Love

Writing in the third quarter of the twelfth century, the cleric Andreas Capellanus described the nature of courtly love, the new ethos of upper-class society and of the romance literature with which it was enamored. In his work, Andreas imagined a Court of Love that would decide cases brought by forlorn lovers, and for this court he prescribed rules that would help it discern true love, some of which follow.

    I.   Marriage is no real excuse for not loving.
   II.   He who is not jealous cannot love.
   IV.   It is well to know that love is always increasing or decreasing.
  VIII.   No one should be deprived of love without the very best of reasons.
   X.   Love is always a stranger in the home of avarice.
   XI.   It is not proper to love any woman whom one would be ashamed to seek to marry.
  XIII.   When made public love rarely endures.
  XIV.   The easy attainment of love makes it of little value; difficulty of attainment makes it prized.
  XVI.   When a lover suddenly catches sight of his beloved his heart palpitates.
  XIX.   If love diminishes, it quickly fails and rarely revives.
  XXV.   A true lover considers nothing good except what he thinks will please his beloved.
  XXIX.   A man who is vexed by too much passion usually does not love.
  XXXI.   Nothing forbids one woman being loved by two men or one man by two women.

From Andreas Capellanus, The Art of Courtly Love, *trans. by J. J. Parry (New York: Norton, 1969), pp. 184–86.*

Dante

The poet Dante Alighieri (1265–1321) was one of the first serious writers to use the Italian language, which up to then had been used only for *fabliaux* and other popular literature. He wrote in the Tuscan dialect, which he helped to establish as the standard form of Italian. As a student of philosophy, Dante had studied the works of Aristotle and Thomas Aquinas, and he was fully conversant with the Latin poetic tradition. He was born in Florence, and as a young man he earned a reputation as a lyric poet. His greatest work, however, was the *Divine Comedy*, an epic poem divided into three parts and one hundred sections or *canzone*. He also wrote two notable treatises in Latin, one defending his use of the vernacular, the other a strong plea for preserving the empire, which he considered the only viable form of government.

Dante had a troubled life. Having become deeply involved in Florentine politics, he was permanently exiled from the city in 1302 and wrote the *Divine Comedy* in exile. Like Aquinas, Dante was convinced of the unity and significance of all human experience. Thus, at least as a poet, he could view his own experience in the context of man's relationship with God.

In the *Divine Comedy*, Dante imagined a journey through Hell, Purgatory, and Heaven to the beatific vision of divinity. The journey is patterned on the descent of Vergil's hero Aeneas into the underworld, and Dante made Vergil his guide through Hell, the domain of the eternally damned, and through most of Purgatory, where souls purge themselves of sin before ascending to Heaven. In these sections of the poem Dante made frequent allusions to classical and contemporary poetry and history and placed himself alongside the greatest poets of western civilization. The events of the journey parallel the Christian liturgical calendar—specifically between Good Friday and Easter in the year 1300. Dante drew on the courtly romances of medieval literature by setting out on his quest with the help of Beatrice, a young girl he had fallen in love with but who died before any real

relationship could develop between them. It is Beatrice who sends Vergil to guide Dante in his journey. Thus Dante united all the main traditions of medieval literature, just as Aquinas had united Aristotelian and Christian philosophy. Dante's poem sums up the medieval idea of man's salvation, so we should look at its basic outline.

In the *Divine Comedy*, Dante, in the middle of his life—that is, about 35 years old—finds himself in a dark wood, sensing that he has swum across a swirling body of water. He is standing at the base of a mountain, but when he tries to climb it, seeking the sun, he is driven back by animals that symbolize his sins. He then meets Vergil, who leads him down into Hell, which is the way one must approach the light of truth. This is the route Augustine followed in his *Confessions* on his way through error and sin to conversion.

In Hell, Dante finds the sinners who did not ask forgiveness before they died. Near the entrance are the ancients, who, though not sinful, did not know the true God and are relegated to a sort of limbo until the Last Judgment. Lower down are those who sinned against themselves, such as gluttons and suicides. Then come those who sinned against others—thieves, murderers, and such—and finally, those who sinned against authority, Cassius and Brutus, who murdered Julius Caesar, and Judas, who betrayed Christ. Dante imagines these three figures in the mouth of the behemoth Satan, the ultimate symbol of sin as the one who sinned against God.

After this vision, Dante and Vergil climb down the body of Satan, through the ice in which it is embedded, and then turn to climb up the inverted leg of Satan to the base of the mountain of Purgatory. Thus the descent has actually been an ascent.

In Purgatory, souls who had confessed their sins and asked God for forgiveness but who had not completed a penance before dying now purge themselves through suffering. As Dante and Vergil climb up the mountain, they first meet sinners who are more heavily burdened than those higher up, and they find that the climb gets easier as they approach the top, shedding the weight of sin. At the top, Dante has a vision of the corrupt

Dante and his guide, Vergil, visiting the circle of Hell to which usurers have been relegated (illustrated from a fourteenth-century Italian manuscript).

church and of the Antichrist and his armies who will battle Christ and his forces at the end of time. He then sees the victorious Christ presiding over the Last Judgment. The pilgrim now enters the Garden of Eden, having cleansed himself in the river Lethe (which wipes out the memory of sin) and in the river Eunoë (which prepares him for entry into Heaven). He has left sinfulness behind and become perfect as Adam was before the fall. Vergil is left behind, beyond the river Lethe, unable to achieve perfection, because he did not have faith in Christ.

From the top of Purgatory, Dante enters Heaven, which is a spherical universe, with neither beginning nor end, symbolizing eternity. Here Dante is alluding to a medieval definition of God as a three-dimensional circle whose center is everywhere and whose circumference is nowhere. To Dante, it appears that the structure of Heaven is a series of concentric spheres that correspond to the Ptolem-

aic view of the universe, and as he proceeds through them he is guided by Bernard of Clairvaux (renowned as a mystic who had himself achieved the beatific vision). He meets the saints of Christian history (including Augustine and Aquinas) and learns that the division into spheres is only an illusion. Here, Dante draws on the ideas of contemporary physics. Finally, he achieves the beatific vision, the sight of "the love which moves the sun and all the stars." It is a vision of man, made in God's image, within a circle. The way to God is through human life, and the mystery of Augustine's conversion and of Dante's descent in order to ascend are explained. Human beings journey to God through the dark ways of human life, and the miracle of salvation is that such a route can lead to perfection.

The *Divine Comedy* was recognized as a classic almost immediately, and it has remained an important source for an understanding of the medieval world view.

The Significance of Vernacular Literature

Although the Anglo-Saxon poems of the early Middle Ages were in a sense the first examples of literature written in a vernacular language, they had little influence on medieval culture. The main tradition of vernacular literature was launched with the advent of twelfth-century masterpieces like the *Song of Roland*.

Vernacular literature introduced themes that are still common in western literature, such as romantic love and the effort to reconcile nature and civilization. And in dealing with those themes medieval poets created most of the poetic forms that have become traditional in the West. Moreover, vernacular literature helped to weaken Latin as the universal language. Portions of the Bible were translated into French during the twelfth century, and several histories had been written in French by the early thirteenth century. If French could be used for such purposes, it could also be used for official documents, and during the thirteenth century royal letters and government documents were often written in French. The same was true of the use of vernacular languages in other countries, a trend that gave each country a sense of its own identity and contributed to the rise of nationalism.

Finally, vernacular literature instructed people at all levels of society—from aristocrats to town dwellers—in the manners and mores of civilized life. True, many thirteenth-century knights were ig-norant and brutal, but many people took the style of life depicted in the romances and poems as a model for their own behavior.

Dante's Divine Comedy

THE INSCRIPTION ON THE ENTRANCE TO HELL

Through me you pass into the woeful city
Through me you pass into eternal pain
Through me you go amid those lost forever.
Justice it was that moved my Great Creator;
Power divine and highest wisdom made me
Together with God's own primeval love.
Before me there was nothing save those things
Eternal, and eternal I endure.
All hope abandon, ye who enter here.

THE FINAL VISION

O grace abundant, through which I presumed
To fix my gaze on the eternal light
Which near consumes who dares to look thereon.
And in those depths I saw, bound up by love
Into one volume, all the universe. . . .
Here vigor failed the lofty vision, but
The will moved ever onward, like a wheel
In even motion, by the love impelled
Which moves the sun in heaven and all the stars.

From Dante, Inferno, *canto 3;* Paradise, *canto 33, trans. by H. F. Cary (London: Bell, 1877).*

Suggestions for Further Reading

The Church at its Height

On the later medieval Church, see S. R. Packard, *Europe and the Church under Innocent III* (1927), and C. Edwards, *Innocent III: Church Defender* (1951). The best biography is H. Tillman, *Pope Innocent III* (1980). For an excellent study of Innocent's relations with England, see C. R. Cheney, *Pope Innocent III and England* (1967).

On the origins of heresy, see J. B. Russell, *Dissent and Reform in the Early Middle Ages* (1965), and R. I. Moore, *The Origins of European Dissent* (1975). On particular heretical movements, see S. Runciman, *The Medieval Manichee* (1947), which traces the history of the dualist heresy, and E. W. McDonnell, *The Beguines and Beghards in Medieval Culture* (1954). On the crusade against the Cathars in southern France, see J. R. Strayer, *The Albigensian Crusades* (1971); W. L. Wakefield, *Heresy, Crusade and Inquisition in Southern France* (1974); and J. Sumption, *The Albigensian Crusade* (1978). On St. Francis, see P. Sabatier, *Life of Saint Francis of Assisi* (1894), and O. Engelbert, *Saint Francis of Assisi*, 2nd ed. (1966), which has a good bibliography. Two important works on the development of the Franciscan order are R. Brooke, *Early Franciscan Government* (1959), and M. D. Lambert, *Franciscan Poverty* (1961). The latter work traces the controversy over the Franciscans' claim that neither individual monks nor the order owned anything, even though they used property and goods. See in general, J. Moorman, *A History of the Franciscan Order* (1968). B. Jarrett's *Life of Saint Dominic* (1924) is rather adulatory. P. Mandonnet, *Saint Dominic and his Work* (1944), emphasizes the spirit and work of the Order. For a general history of the order in its early period, see W. A. Hinnebusch, *History of the Dominican Order* (1966).

Twelfth-Century Renaissance

On the renaissance of the twelfth century, see the classic work by C. H. Haskins, *The Renaissance of the Twelfth Century* (1927). This work has been brought up to date in R. Benson, G. Constable, and C. D. Lanham, eds., *Renaissance and Renewal in the Twelfth Century* (1982). For an interpretive study, see R. W. Southern, *The Making of the Middle Ages* (1953), and essays by the same author in *Medieval Humanism and Other Studies* (1976). On Abelard and Bernard, see E. Gilson's *The Mystical Theology of Saint Bernard* (1940) and *Heloise and Abelard* (1948). B. S. James, *Saint Bernard of Clairvaux* (1957), focuses on Bernard the man. For a general study of twelfth-century theology, see M. D. Chenu, *Nature, Man, and Society in the Twelfth Century*, trans. by J. Taylor and L. K. Little (1968).

Gothic Architecture

On the development of Gothic architecture, see E. Panofsky, trans., *Suger on the Abbey of Saint Denis* (1946). E. Male, *The Gothic Image* (1913), is a classic study of Gothic art. For interpretive essays, see E. Panofsky, *Gothic Architecture and Scholasticism* (1951), and O. von Simpson, *The Gothic Cathedral* (1956). On the social context, see G. Duby, *The Age of the Cathedrals: Art and Society, 980–1420*, trans. by E. Levieux and B. Thompson (1981). For a study of the stone masons, see J. Gimpel, *The Cathedral Builders* (1961). P. Frankl, *Gothic Architecture* (1963), is the best treatment of Gothic art in the High Middle Ages. He traces the development of the style in all areas of Europe. See also the studies of individual cathedrals: A. Temko, *Nôtre-Dame de Paris* (1955), and A. E. M. Katzenellenbogen, *The Sculptural Program of Chartres Cathedral* (1959).

Philosophy, Science, and Literature

On medieval philosophy, see D. Knowles, *The Evolution of Medieval Thought* (1962), and the articles in *Renaissance and Renewal in the Twelfth Century*, cited earlier. On later medieval philosophy, see N. Kretzmann, A. Kenny, and J. Pinborg, eds., *The Cambridge History of Later Medieval Philosophy: From the Rediscovery of Aristotle to the Disintegration of Scholasticism, 1100–1600* (1982). On medieval logic, see A. Broadie, *Introduction to Medieval Logic* (1987), and D. P. Henry, *Medieval Logic and Metaphysics: A Modern Introduction* (1972). On Abelard and his influence, see D. E. Luscombe, *The School of Peter Abelard* (1969). The introduction of Aristotle and his Arabic commentators is covered in F. Van Steenberghen, *Aristotle in the West* (1955); R. J. Lemay, *Abu Ma'shar and Latin Aristotelianism in the Twelfth Century* (1962); and F. E. Peters, *Aristoteles Latinus: The Oriental Translations and Commentaries in the Aristotelian Corpus* (1968). On Thomas Aquinas, see the biography by J. A. Weisheipl, *Friar Thomas d'Aquino: His Life, Thought, and Work* (1974). On Thomism, see M. De Wulf, *Philosophy and Civilization in the Middle Ages* (1922). The best scholarly treatment of Thomas and his influence is E. Gilson, *History of Christian Philosophy in the Middle Ages* (1954). For the universities and their intellectual life, see G. Leff, *Paris and Oxford Universities in the Thirteenth and Fourteenth Centuries* (1968).

There are two monumental histories of medieval science: L. Thorndyke, *A History of Magic and Experimental Science*, 8 vols. (1923–58), and G. Sarton, *Introduction to the History of Science*, 3 vols. (1927–48). But the best history of medieval science is A. C. Crombie, *Medieval and Early Modern Science*, 2 vols. (1959). On the introduction of Arabic science in the twelfth century, see C. H. Haskins, *Studies in the History of Medieval Science* (1924); B. Stock, *Myth and Science in the Twelfth Century* (1972); and the works on the introduction of Aristotle cited earlier. In *Robert Grosseteste and the Origins of Experimental Science 1100–1700* (1953), Crombie argued that the scientific method developed long before Galileo. This view is not universally accepted. For a history of mechanics in the Middle Ages, see M. Clagett, *Archimedes in the Middle Ages*, 4 vols. (1964–80). J. Gimpel, *The Medieval Machine* (1976), treats the history of medieval technology. R. P. Multhauf, *The Origins of Chemistry* (1967), replaces all earlier studies.

On the historical writing of the Middle Ages, see S. Vryonis, Jr., *Readings in Medieval Historiography* (1968), which treats Latin, Byzantine, and Moslem historians. W. T. H. Jackson, *Medieval Literature* (1966), is a general treatment of medieval literature. P. Dronke, *Medieval Latin and the Rise of the European Love-lyric* (1968), is very useful. See also F. J. E. Raby, *A History of Secular Latin Poetry in the Middle Ages*, 2 vols. (1957). R. S. Southern, "From Epic to Romance," *Medieval Humanism and Other Essays* (1976), provides an interpretation of the literary history of the twelfth century in a brief essay. R. S. Loomis, *The Development of Arthurian Romance* (1963), is a good general introduction to the origins of the romance. For French literature, see U. T. Holmes, *A History of Old French Literature*, rev. ed. (1962). See also Holmes's *Chretien de Troyes* (1970). For Germany, see J. G. Robertson, *A History of German Literature* (1947). The best critical study of the vernacular literature of the twelfth and thirteenth centuries is E. Curtius, *European Literature and the Latin Middle Ages* (1963), which has excellent bibliographic materials. Many of the romances have been translated. F. Goldin provides ample collections of medieval lyrics in *Lyrics of the Troubadours and Trouveres* (1973) and *German and Italian Lyrics of the Middle Ages* (1973). See also Andreas Capellanus, *The Art of Courtly Love*, trans. by J. J. Parry (1941).

Many editions exist of Dante's *Divine Comedy* and other classics of medieval literature. See especially, C. Singleton, *The Divine Comedy*, 3 vols. (1970–75), which contains the original Italian, a facing-page translation, and commentary.

For a history of vernacular culture as a whole, see A. W. Ward and A. R. Waller, *The Cambridge History of English Literature*, Vol. 1 (1907), and E. Vossler, *Medieval Culture: An Introduction to Dante and His Times*, 2 vols. (1929).

12

THE RISE OF THE SECULAR STATE

lthough the church was the dominant political power during the thirteenth century, the kings continued the consolidation of their power that had begun in the twelfth century. By 1300, the church found itself facing secular powers strong enough to resist its claims to interfere in their business. Throughout the thirteenth century, however, the idea of secular power was still inextricably intertwined with Christian doctrine. People still believed that the king's authority derived from Christ, and they could not conceive of legitimate royal power wholly divorced from the church. Yet by the end of the thirteenth century, the monarchies had achieved both ideological and actual independence from the church.

THE EFFECTS OF ECONOMIC CHANGE ON THE CHURCH

Even as the power of the church was at its peak, changes were taking place that

would undermine its position and ultimately lead to its subordination to the secular state. The growth of trade and commerce was accompanied by a rise in prices that affected people living on fixed incomes more severely than it did those who were actually engaged in trade. The church and many aristocratic landowners were particularly hard hit by inflation. In the Middle Ages, because rents were fixed in perpetuity, landowners who rented their land to peasant farmers were badly squeezed by rising prices. During the thirteenth century, they took back their land whenever they could and farmed it themselves, leaving the farmers with plots too small for them to take advantage of the high prices in the market. Many of the farmers grew discouraged and moved to the cities.

As the church tried to cope with the rapidly increasing urban population, it encountered a shortage of parish priests to minister to the spiritual needs of the people. By the middle of the thirteenth century Franciscans and Dominicans were

(OPPOSITE) THIS IS A TABLE OF CONTENTS IN GOTHIC SCRIPT, FOR A SECULAR LAW BOOK OR TREATISE.

helping the priests and providing a good deal of the ministry in the cities. These mendicants won a reputation for holiness, and people flocked to their churches. Wealthy people gave them gifts, and soon the mendicant orders themselves were wealthy. The prominence of the mendicants in the cities angered the bishops, who claimed that only they could authorize priests to preach in their dioceses (see p. 283). In the end, the papacy and the mendicants prevailed because the papacy could claim universal authority in the church, but not before the prestige of the church had been seriously damaged.

Prosperity created another problem for the church. Wealth engendered pride and callousness among the newly rich members of society, and the church strove, with some success, to bring them a heightened sense of social responsibility. It condemned profiteering and neglect of the poor, and created many charitable institutions—such as hospitals for the homeless and destitute as well as for the sick.

The church accepted the idea that a man who invested in a commercial enterprise was entitled to a return on his money, but it denounced the practice of lending money for interest. As the medieval economy tended more and more to become a money economy, many moneylenders amassed huge fortunes. That some of them left substantial endowments to charitable institutions did not alter the fact that they were in violation of church doctrine. With money becoming more important to society than inherited status, men found it difficult to follow the teachings of the church and to put its interests ahead of their own.

Churchmen themselves were affected by these economic changes. To support themselves at the level to which they had grown accustomed, ecclesiastics sought and received multiple offices. When it became apparent that even members of the papal curia were having trouble living on their fixed incomes, the popes gave them offices in churches throughout Europe. A member of the curia might hold an office in one or more Italian bishoprics, one in England, and another in France. He would

collect income from all of them, without performing any of the functions they entailed. He might appoint a substitute, to whom he would pay a low wage, but in most cases the far-flung offices went without a head. Bishops who faithfully carried out their duties complained about this papal practice, but in vain.

The church was criticized for its financial policies. As time passed, the income tax on the clergy, first imposed by Innocent III, was levied with increasing frequency and at rising rates. Fees were imposed or raised on papal letters, legal documents, court costs, and on confirmations of appointment to high church offices. Because a high percentage of church income derived from tithes (one-tenth of produce) and other payments by the laity, they felt much abused by the additional fees imposed by the ecclesiastical bureaucracy. The church was criticized for being too eager to raise money and too ready to grant spiritual benefits in return for cash payments. The more zealous wing of the Franciscans urged the clergy to give away all their property and to lead lives of poverty. Actually, the Franciscan order itself was acquiring large amounts of property while trying to disguise the fact by vesting title in trustees. Even popes and bishops with an appetite for reform found that they could do little to alter the church's financial system, and many people came to suspect that the church was no different from the rapacious secular governments of the period.

ENGLAND

The Creation of the Anglo-Norman State

During the eleventh century, the Normans had led the reconquest of southern Italy and Sicily and had participated in both the reconquest of Spain and the crusades to the Holy Land. But the Norman achievement that had the most far-reaching implications was the conquest of England in 1066.

England had been in the Scandinavian orbit since the late ninth century, when the Great Army of Vikings battled Alfred of Wessex for control of the island. Even after Alfred had defeated the Vikings, Scandinavians continued to view England as part of their world. In the early eleventh century, after driving out Edward, the son of the previous Anglo-Saxon king, Ethelred the Ill-Counseled (r. 978–1016), the Danish king Canute (r. 1016–35) incorporated England into a vast Scandinavian empire. Edward went into exile in Normandy, the country of his mother Emma, daughter of the duke of Normandy. When the Scandinavian empire collapsed in 1042, Edward ascended the English throne.

The Danish kings had mostly left the Anglo-Saxon aristocracy in place during their reign, and Edward (r. 1042–66) found himself surrounded by Anglo-Saxon earls eager to participate in the governance of the country. But Edward was more comfortable with the Norman friends he had brought with him to England, and his reign was troubled by competition between the two groups of aspirants. The leader of the earls was Godwin of Wessex, who persuaded Edward to marry his daughter.

When Edward died without an heir in 1066, Godwin's son Harold claimed the throne on the basis of a weak hereditary right—his sister was the widowed queen. His political claim was a good bit stronger—he had the support of the Anglo-Saxon aristocracy. Edward's cousin, Duke William of Normandy, claimed the throne for himself and prepared an invasion to pursue that claim. William landed on the English coast near Hastings in 1066 and overcame Harold and the Anglo-Saxon army in the battle of Hastings. In a remarkably short time, William had assumed control of the entire country.

William set about creating an almost entirely new political system in England. He dispossessed most of the old Anglo-Saxon nobility and granted their lands in fief to his own men. Henceforth, all land in England was held by feudal tenure from the king, and the fiefholders—the tenants-in-chief—granted some of the land in fief to their own supporters and companions. Within a few years, the Normans had transformed the country into a model feudal hierarchy.

Even though he replaced the Anglo-Saxon aristocracy, William the Conqueror (r. 1066–87) claimed to be the rightful heir of Edward and sought to preserve the old laws and governmental system of Anglo-Saxon England. In doing so, he and his two sons, William II (r. 1087–1100) and Henry I (r. 1100–35), used the institutions of local government (see p. 243) to force the population to accept and obey the royal government. They installed Norman

Silver penny bearing the likeness of William the Conqueror.

A section of the Bayeux Tapestry, which told the story of the Norman Conquest of England (1066) from the Norman point of view. Here, Harold, who claimed the English throne in 1065, takes an oath to William of Normandy promising that he would support William's claim to the throne.

Norman troops on horseback engaging Anglo-Saxon foot soldiers in battle (detail from the Bayeux Tapestry, late eleventh century).

England after the Norman Conquest   LATE ELEVENTH CENTURY

sheriffs in the shires and held the courts of the hundreds responsible for keeping the peace in their districts.

Henry II and the Origins of Common Law

Under the Norman kings, England was the best-governed and most politically unified kingdom in Europe. But England was only one part of the territory under their control. William I had remained duke of Normandy after becoming king of England, and his sons followed his example. Henry I died in 1135, leaving as heir his daughter Mathilda, who was married to Count Geoffrey Martel of Anjou, with whom she had a son, Henry. On her father's death, Mathilda claimed the English throne and the duchy of Normandy for Henry.

Both claims were challenged by Stephen of Blois—the grandson of William I through his daughter Adele. A faction of the Anglo-Norman nobility favored Stephen, in part because of their traditional enmity toward the men of Anjou, the Angevins. With the support of that faction, Stephen was able to take the English throne. But his reign (1135–54) was troubled by almost constant civil war over the succession. Then, toward the end of his reign, an agreement was worked out:

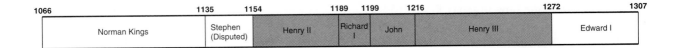

1066		1135	1154	1189	1199	1216	1272	1307
Norman Kings		Stephen (Disputed)	Henry II	Richard I	John	Henry III	Edward I	

Mathilda would permit Stephen to rule in peace, and Stephen, whose own son had just died, would declare Mathilda's son Henry to be his heir.

Meanwhile, young Henry had succeeded his father as count of Anjou and had married Eleanor of Aquitaine, the heiress of the duchy of Aquitaine, the largest and richest duchy in the French kingdom. Thus, when Henry succeeded Stephen as king of England and duke of Normandy in 1154, he was ruler of the largest kingdom in all of Europe. When he had added Brittany to his realm, the empire included England and more than half of the kingdom of France.

Henry II (r. 1154–89) traveled constantly around his vast realm keeping the barons in line and building royal power in England. He spent the first few years of his reign settling the affairs of the kingdom after the disruption caused by the twenty-year civil war over the succession. As he traveled about, he installed his own men as sheriffs and ordered the demolition of castles built by the barons without royal permission. In many places, finding that Stephen and Mathilda had granted the same fief to two different claimants, he issued a writ (a royal order) to the local sheriff instructing him to decide which had the best right to the fief.

These writs gave rise to complicated legal proceedings that sometimes went on for years. Under Anglo-Norman law, the question of right was decided in a trial by battle, but the courts were slow to authorize that procedure. In 1164, to speed things up, Henry decreed new remedies for settling disputes over property.

Those remedies contained three features that eventually transformed English law. First, they pertained only to the right of possession of disputed land, not to the right of ownership. They bypassed the question of who owned the land and the old procedure by which that question was decided. In practice, of course, as soon as the sheriff had decided the issue of possession, the loser gave up the case.

Second, the writs required an old but rarely used procedure—the jury trial. The practice of having a jury decide points of fact had arisen in the early Middle Ages as part of the inquest, the procedure by which a landowner checked on the rents due him. For example, when the king wanted to determine the ownership of various properties in a village and how much the villagers owed to the lord of the village, he would empanel a group of the leading men, make them take an oath to tell the truth, and have them answer questions about the issue. It was assumed that the information produced by the members of the jury (the word comes from the Latin *juratus,* which means sworn) would be accurate, for no one would let another understate his obligations or overstate his rights. Henry's writs put this procedure to a legal purpose by ordering the sheriff to empanel a jury of the disputants' neighbors to answer questions about who had the best right to possess the disputed property.

Third, the writs were "returnable." This meant that someone to whom a writ had been issued could "return" it to the king's sheriff, bringing about the case that

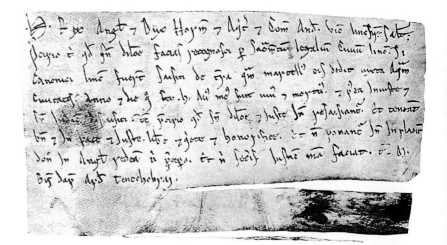

A writ from Henry II to the sheriff of Lincoln, instructing him to summon a jury to determine a land dispute between a layman and the canons of Lincoln. The sheriff is to restore the land to the canons pending the outcome of the trial.

England and France at the Time of Henry II   1154–89

Held by Henry II as vassal
of the king of France

Held by other vassals
of the king of France

0   MILES   100

ferred to the king for decision. Over time, a "case law" developed in the king's court that was binding throughout the kingdom—as opposed to "customary law," which was valid only in a particular hundred or shire court. That case law became known as *common law.*

John and Magna Carta

Henry II's sons, Richard I, "the Lionhearted" (r. 1189–99), and John (r. 1199–1216), lacked their father's political skills. Richard was a warrior who spent his entire reign, except for ten months, either participating in the Third Crusade or fighting King Philip II of France (r. 1180–1223). Despite Richard's neglect of government, however, Henry's astute political arrangements continued to function smoothly.

John, by contrast, was a poor soldier but a shrewd administrator. Early in his reign he lost Normandy, Anjou, and most of Aquitaine to Philip II and spent the last twelve years of his reign trying to get them back. He was constantly in need of money to pay for his campaigns and squeezed revenue from every source he could. On occasion he would impose heavy fines on men he suspected of plotting against him and might even seize their property. His military failures and the repressive measures to which he resorted prompted the English barons to rebel against him in 1215. The rebellion succeeded, and John was obliged to sign the *Magna Carta* (Great Charter) at Runnymede just outside London on June 15, 1215.

The Charter contained 63 chapters covering a wide variety of topics. Among its main provisions was John's promise not to demand taxes without "taking counsel with the kingdom," which meant consulting with the barons. Further, he promised not to convict any freeman of a crime without a trial by his peers and not to charge litigants for bringing cases to his court. He also promised to consult with his vassals and bishops before undertaking campaigns. Although the purpose of the *Magna Carta* was to protect the barons and the ecclesiastical lords, it established the principle that the government of En-

would decide if the complainant had been unjustly dispossessed. Because this practice put the king's law at the disposal of anyone who had a complaint, it generated a huge number of cases, many of them having to do with problems that had never arisen before. When a case came up for which no precedent existed, it was regland was based on law and that the king as well as his subjects were bound by the law.

Henry III

The signing of the *Magna Carta* seemed to be a defeat for the monarchy in England, but John's son, Henry III (r. 1216–72), reissued it, and royal government grew stronger under him. Henry's financial ministers strengthened the administrative and judicial institutions of the country and created new types of taxation. His chancellor, who oversaw the royal courts, devised additional writs to bring more cases into the courts. Moreover, the church's condemnation of trial by ordeal (see the box) at the Fourth Lateran Council of 1215 (see p. 282) increased the number of cases that came to the royal courts because they had a procedure—the jury trial—that was acceptable to the church. The ordeal was the preferred procedure of the courts where customary law was enforced, and once they were deprived of their procedure they lost business because people conceived of a court and its procedure as one and the same.

All these developments were summed up in a remarkable treatise on English law based on the research that Henry de Bracton, a royal judge, did in the records of the royal courts. (The treatise was attributed to Bracton, but scholars are not convinced he wrote it.) Written in the 1250s, this treatise gave a clear, logical, and thorough explanation of the common law through use of precedents and general principles. The author's familiarity with Roman law helped him to bring together hundreds of individual cases into a comprehensive, coherent reference book. Partly as a result of that achievement, the common law has maintained its identity as a legal system up to the present time.

Despite these advances, there was constant conflict between Henry III and his barons. The barons were trying to gain control of the central government to protect their rights—particularly to limit taxes—and often declared that they were defending the realm against a foolish and spendthrift monarch.

Excerpts from Magna Carta   1215

We [John] have conceded to all free men of our kingdom, for us and our heirs forever, all the liberties written below, to be held by them and their heirs from us and our heirs: . . .

12. No scutage [redemption of military service] or aid [grant to the king] shall be taken in our kingdom except by the common counsel of our kingdom. . . .

14. And for obtaining the common counsel of the kingdom, for assessing an aid . . . or a scutage, we will cause to be summoned by our sealed letters the archbishops, bishops, abbots, earls and greater barons, moreover we will cause to be summoned generally by the sheriffs . . . all those who hold of us in chief [the other vassals] for a certain day . . . and place . . . and once the summons has been made the business shall proceed on the assigned day according to the advice of those who are present, even if all those summoned have not come. . . .

39. No free man may be seized, or imprisoned, or dispossessed, or outlawed, or exiled . . . nor will we go against him or send against him except by the legal judgment of his peers and by the law of the land.

40. To no one will we sell, to no one will we deny or delay right and justice.

Translated from W. Stubbs, Select Charters *(Oxford: Clarendon Press, 1921), pp. 294 ff.*

Henry had inherited the throne as a child, and the government had been run by regents until he came of age in 1225. At that time the barons persuaded him to reaffirm the *Magna Carta,* granting him a tax in return. The version of 1225 was little changed from that of 1215, but it was accepted by everyone as the law of the land and marked an auspicious beginning for the young king.

Harmony prevailed until the 1240s when the barons raised a protest against Henry's foreign policy. In addition to pouring money into vain attempts to reconquer the lost French territories, Henry was naming his French relatives and friends to bishoprics and to important secular offices. And he was permitting the pope to draw large sums of money out of

Judicial Ordeals

People in the Middle Ages believed that ordeals revealed God's judgment of the issue of a case. They were used in criminal cases to determine the guilt or innocence of the accused. After hearing testimony the court assigned the proof by ordeal to the accused or accuser, depending on which one seemed to have the best case. Usually, the accused had to undergo the ordeal.

There were three basic forms of ordeal—hot iron, water, and compurgation (the swearing of innocence with a number of "oath helpers").

Hot iron: A piece of iron was heated until it glowed. Then the person undergoing the ordeal picked it up in his bare hand and carried it a certain distance and dropped it. The hand was bandaged, and if the wound was clean after three days, then the person was innocent. If it was infected, he was guilty. (A similar ordeal used boiling water, from which the person had to lift an object.)

Water: The person was tied up with his knees against his chest and lowered into a tub of water. If he sank, the water was deemed to have "accepted" him, and he was declared innocent. If he floated, the water had rejected him, and he was found guilty.

Compurgation: The court ordered the person to swear an oath declaring his innocence. Depending on the status of the person and the nature of the case, the court assigned up to 72 others from the community to swear that the man's oath was true. To prove the principal oath-taker innocent, all of the swearers had to pronounce the oath without mistake. A verbal stumble by any of them proved him guilty.

An early copy of the Magna Carta with the royal seal.

England to fight a war against the German rulers of Italy. The barons had no interest in the French territories; they resented Henry's French friends; and they saw no reason why the donations of pious Englishmen should go to the pope. They were supported in their opposition to foreign intruders and foreign entanglements by many lesser landholders and by a surprising number of clergymen.

In his efforts to overcome his chronic shortage of money, Henry played into the hands of the barons. Ordinary income from the royal domain was barely enough to keep the royal government afloat even during peacetime, and the *Magna Carta* made it difficult to raise additional revenues without the consent of the barons. If Henry wanted to wage war, he had to

levy taxes. But after 1240 the barons refused to let him do so. Nevertheless, Henry went ahead with an ambitious project to help the pope conquer Sicily. The English clergy, under papal pressure, came up with some money to advance the cause, but not enough. By 1258 Henry was hopelessly in debt and his foreign policy was a complete failure. In desperation he appointed a committee of barons to help put matters right.

The barons promptly set about making policy and appointing officials to carry it out. The committee soon split into factions, however. The barons were united in their opposition to Henry, but found it hard to agree on a policy of their own and resented anyone who sought to assume leadership. When the ablest member of the committee, Simon de Montfort (Henry's brother-in-law), gained control of the government, he found that the barons had deserted the cause of reform. In 1265, Henry's eldest son, Edward, raised an army and killed Simon in battle, thereby restoring Henry's authority.

This episode was significant for two reasons. First, it set a pattern that was to be repeated in England many times in the next two centuries. Again and again, the barons would seize control of the government only to split into factions and lose control once again. Second, it speeded up the emergence of a representative assembly. Henry and the barons each summoned knights from the shires and representatives from the towns as well as great lords and high churchmen to give them support in assemblies.

The Origins of Constitutional Government

In the early thirteenth century, several elements began to coalesce into what was to emerge as constitutional government. In the realm of theory, church lawyers began to apply the Roman law of corporations to church organization. They used the principle that "what touches all, ought to be approved by all" to support the right of the clergy and the members of a monastery to participate in the affairs of the church. At about the same time they were discussing how to deal with a vacancy in

Manuscript illumination of the coronation ceremony from a Coronation Order (text of the ceremony) written between 1272 and 1325. The king may be Edward II.

the office of a bishop or an abbot. The old canon law said that the bishop was the ruler of his see and the abbot was the ruler of his monastery. But who was the ruler during a vacancy? The lawyers found the answer in the Roman law of corporations: the members of the church or monastery collectively exercised the power until a new leader was installed. That conclusion gave further impetus to the idea of representation. The officers of a corporation or those appointed by them could act on its behalf and could represent it before others.

The idea that the state itself was a legal community like a corporation spread to many areas of Europe during the early thirteenth century. In many places, rulers called on barons and representatives of the towns to lend their support to the government. Pope Innocent III called together the barons and representatives of the towns in the areas under papal control, the so-called Papal States of central Italy, and the kings of Spain and Hungary summoned meetings of their own. But adherence to the idea was strongest in England.

In England, a meeting called for such purposes came to be called a *parliament* (literally "talk-fest"). The parliament was an enlarged meeting of the king's council, which normally consisted of the king's tenants-in-chief—the great men, both lay and clerical, who held fiefs directly from the king. Under feudal law, these men owed the king advice and counsel, and

An illustration of a parliament under Edward I. Edward is flanked by King Alexander of Scotland and Prince Lewellyn of Wales, who were subordinate to him.

the king was bound to consult with them on business that concerned them—essentially the business of the realm. At a parliament, this inner group was joined by other barons and important men, to ensure that actions would receive support throughout the kingdom. The king also heard important appeals while sitting in parliament and would ask those in attendance to help him decide difficult cases and to support his decisions.

Knights of the shires—sheriffs, royal bailiffs, and tax collectors—were often invited to attend the parliaments. Awed by the occasion, they usually gave the king their support and went home to report what had taken place. Both Henry III and Simon de Montfort followed this practice. In 1265, Simon, to compensate for his loss of baronial support, went even further by inviting the towns to send representatives. These precedents were not forgotten. In 1268, after Simon's death, Henry III summoned both knights and townsmen to a parliament, hoping to win their political and financial support in return for being included in such an august assemblage of great men.

Edward and the Development of Parliament

Although the foundations were laid under John and Henry III, the principles of constitutional government were established under Henry III's son, Edward I (r. 1272–1307). Constantly in need of money to fight his wars with the Scots and the French, Edward summoned several parliaments to ask the barons and the towns for financial support. After calling both knights and townsmen to a parliament in 1275, for the next twenty years he summoned such representatives only rarely. The core of a parliament was still the king's council, made up of high officials, bishops, and barons. In 1295, however, Edward again summoned knights and representatives of the towns to a full meeting (the "Model Parliament"), and from that time on they were frequently present. Edward could probably have managed with the approval of the barons alone, but he found that the full parliament assured wider support for his actions.

Edward also found that working with a parliament was an efficient way of doing business. He and his officials could take care of all sorts of business at one time and in one place. However, it was advantageous to obtain parliamentary sanction whenever possible, for actions taken in parliament carried great prestige. Edward controlled parliament as effectively as he did every other branch of government, and he could not have foreseen that he was nurturing a powerful institution that might one day develop a will of its own.

The knights and townsmen Edward summoned to parliament seem to have viewed their role as largely passive: "to hear and to obey," as some of the early summonses put it. Any opposition came from the barons. In 1297, when Edward pushed through a new tax at a council meeting that did not include knights and townsmen, the barons protested and forced him to promise that in the future he would levy taxes only "with the common assent of the whole kingdom." This was not quite an admission that parliament had to grant permission to levy taxes, but it implied that the assent of a large number of people was needed; and clearly the easiest way to obtain such assent was in parliament.

The idea of constitutional government—that government has limited authority and is subject to law—originated

1060	1108	1137	1180	1223 1226	1270	1285	1314
Philip I	Louis VI	Louis VII	Philip II Agustus	Louis IX	Philip III	Philip IV	

Louis VIII

in the distinction between ecclesiastical power and secular power established in the course of the investiture controversy (see pp. 266–69). Europeans, having accepted that distinction, were prepared to set limits on the authority of both popes and kings. The question of when a king or pope controlled the law and when the law controlled him was basic to a constitutional system of government. In answering it, lawyers, both ecclesiastical and secular, helped to define a system of government that was unique in the world. The parliament of thirteenth-century England was the institutional realization of that system.

THE GROWTH OF ROYAL POWER IN FRANCE

Because of the strong opposition of the great lords, royal power emerged more slowly in France than in England. Until the twelfth century, the French kings could only rule the kingdom through the great lords who were virtually autonomous in their counties and duchies. Louis VI (r. 1108–37) was the first to make progress in making royal power felt outside the county of Paris—the so-called Ile de France.

Louis VI and Louis VII

Philip I (r. 1060–1108) had issued few grants to individuals or ecclesiastical institutions outside the Ile de France. Philip's son Louis VI increased the number of grants issued from an average of three or four each year to about twelve, an indication that he was taking a more active role in the affairs of bishoprics and monasteries throughout the realm. Moreover, he ruled that all bishops who were not already under the protection of some great lord were to accept the king's protection, an assertion that substantially augmented

royal power. Henceforth, bishops dissatisfied with the performance of local magnates could turn to the king for relief.

By taking advantage of his opportunities, Louis added substantially to the number of his *fideles*—that is, the men who took an oath of fealty to him. He recognized that he could not insist, as the Carolingians had, that everyone in the kingdom owed him allegiance, but he worked

The Expansion of the Royal Domain in France   1180–1314

steadily to extend his circle of vassals. His chief adviser, Abbot Suger of St. Denis (abbot 1122–52), eventually fashioned a theory of royal authority that harked back to the Carolingian idea of kingship. In his biography of Louis, written shortly after the king's death, Suger asserted that all men in the kingdom were subject to the king, either directly or indirectly. Lesser men were subject to Louis through the greater men who were his *fideles*. The king himself, Suger said, was subject to no one; his only obligation was to St. Denis, the patron saint of the monarchy and the kingdom. Here Suger was making a subtle distinction between the French king and the English king. The English king at the time was also the duke of Normandy, and, as a duke, he was subject to the French king. Thus Louis had been superior to Henry I of England. Though Suger's theory was never accepted by the majority of the French nobility, it justified Louis's efforts to impose his authority on the dukes and counts of the kingdom.

Louis himself was at his best in managing practical affairs. Toward the end of his reign, he extended the reach of royal authority by arranging the marriage of his heir Louis VII (r. 1137–80) to Eleanor of Aquitaine, heiress to the richest duchy in the kingdom. After ascending the throne, young Louis staged a royal progress to Aquitaine to dramatize his role as monarch. He was the first king to visit Bordeaux in 300 years. But Eleanor was a strong, independent woman, and the marriage was not a success. In 1147, she accompanied Louis on the Second Crusade (see p. 275) and along the way engaged in a dalliance with her cousin the count of Toulouse. Louis decided to have the marriage annulled and succeeded in getting the church's judgment of annulment in 1152. A year later Eleanor married Louis's great rival, Henry of Anjou, soon to become Henry II of England.

Louis VII continued his father's policies and seized every opportunity to extend his authority. During Louis VI's reign, the abbot of Cluny had placed his abbey and its daughter houses under the protection of the French king, because the local counts were seizing the abbey's possessions. In 1166 and again in 1171, Louis VII responded to the abbot's complaints about the local nobility by marching into Burgundy, the first time a French king had visited the duchy since the middle of the tenth century. To give Cluny more permanent protection, Louis left a group of royal officers in the duchy to serve as the nucleus of royal authority. Whenever he was able to interfere in the affairs of bishoprics in other parts of the kingdom, he installed royal officials to ensure that his arrangements lasted. By the end of his reign, half the bishoprics of the kingdom were under royal protection.

Philip II Augustus

Yet the work of building royal authority in France progressed only slowly while Henry II and Richard I of England retained their holdings in France and continued to regard Louis VII and his son Philip II Augustus (r. 1180–1223) as no more than suzerains. After John succeeded Richard I as king of England, the picture changed.

In 1203, John made the mistake of violating feudal law by mistreating one of his vassals in France. The injured baron appealed to Philip, John's overlord, and Philip summoned John to his court. When John refused to appear, Philip declared that he was a contumacious vassal and deprived him of his fiefs—Normandy, Anjou, Brittany, and most of Aquitaine. In 1204, when Philip moved to take control of those areas, the barons gave him their support.

Philip II was an exceptionally able ruler, well deserving of the title "Augustus" bestowed on him by later historians. He had inherited a kingdom with an annual income equivalent to about £60,000 of silver and left it with an income of £438,000. He accomplished this feat through his wise management of the territory he had wrested from John. He permitted the duchies and counties to retain their own laws and institutions of government, but at the same time he divided them up into small districts governed by men from his own court. Thus Normandy kept its law and its court system but was divided into thirteen administrative districts, each governed by a royal bailiff. Philip treated the bailiffs well enough, and they in turn demanded less from the people than the barons had. Philip gleaned an additional measure of popularity from this policy and strengthened his hold on the kingdom. His practice of governing through royal officials served as the model for later governments on the Continent.

Philip was succeeded by his son Louis VIII (r. 1223–26), who had been an active participant in government before his father's death and had led the crusade against the heretics in southern France that resulted in the annexation of that region (see p. 281). But Louis's reign was cut short by his premature death, and it was left to Louis IX to continue his grandfather's work.

Louis IX (St. Louis)

Louis IX (r. 1226–70) managed to put down a few halfhearted rebellions early in his reign, and for the rest of his life no one dared challenge his authority. He was not an arrogant man, however. Rather, he was imbued with the ideals of the Christian ruler, which held that the king should be good, generous, and conscientious. He settled France's longstanding conflict with England by arranging a generous treaty that let the English king retain the coastal district in Aquitaine (around Bordeaux). He kept faith with all men, even with Moslems. In France, he submitted all disputed questions to his courts, and he discouraged his administrative agents from overstating the reach of royal power. He insisted that his subjects observe his prerogatives and rights, but he was scrupulous in observing the rights of others. Throughout his reign he was known for his honesty and fair dealing.

Louis was a pious man, but he held the church to his own high standards. He refused to join Pope Innocent IV (r. 1243–54) in the attack on Frederick II (see p. 321), and he rejected the demand of the French bishops that he punish men who refused to bow to their ecclesiastical

---

St. Louis as Described by Joinville

Jean de Joinville, a noble of Champagne, was a friend of St. Louis and went with him on his crusade of 1248.

This holy man loved God with all his heart, and imitated his works. For example, just as God died because he loved his people, so the king risked his life many times for the love of his people. . . . He said once to his eldest son: . . . "I beg you that you make yourself loved by the people of your realm, for truly, I would rather that a Scot came from Scotland and governed the people of the kingdom justly and well than that you should govern them badly. . . ." The holy king loved the truth so much that he kept his promises even to the Saracens.

A friar told the king . . . that he had never read that a kingdom was destroyed or changed rulers except through lack of justice. . . . The king did not forget this lesson but governed his land justly and well, according to the will of God. . . . Often in summer he went to sit down under an oak-tree in the wood of Vincennes, after hearing mass, and made us sit around him. And all those who had suits to bring him came up, without being hindered by ushers or other people. And he would ask them: "Does anyone here have a suit?" And those who had requests would get up. . . . And then he would call Lord Pierre de Fontaines and Lord Geoffroi de Villette [two of his legal experts] and say to one of them: "Settle this affair for me." And if he saw anything to correct in what they said on his behalf, he would do so.

From Jean de Joinville, Histoire de Saint Louis, *ed. by N. de Wailly (Paris: Firmin Didot, 1874), pp. 11, 34.*

---

punishments. He felt that, as a Christian king, he could himself provide for the spiritual and material welfare of his people.

Louis's concern for law and justice led to a strengthening of the royal judicial system. Since time immemorial, in France as in England, each community had lived under its own customary law, passed down from generation to generation. Louis did not interfere with customary law that dealt with strictly local matters—for example, rules governing the inheritance of property or the penalty for theft. Rather, his royal courts dealt only with matters that concerned the interests of the crown. These matters included litigation over royal lands and rights, disputes over who had the obligation to maintain bridges and roads, and the handling of disturbances of the king's peace.

As time passed, the jurisdiction of the royal courts extended further and further, and the theory of the Christian ruler seemed to give Louis almost universal authority. Nearly every crime came to be seen as a disturbance of the king's peace. Out of this extension of royal power rose one of the great institutions of the French monarchy, the Parlement of Paris—the king's own court, staffed by his closest advisers. It never became an assembly, as the parliament in England. Rather, the Parlement of Paris heard appeals from the decisions of the king's local bailiffs and from the feudal courts of the great lords. In feudal law, these courts were independent of the king's court, but the Parlement managed to establish its position as a court of appeal, which served as a legal basis for royal claims to supremacy over all subjects.

Statue of Louis IX, in the church of Mainville in Normandy.

The bailiffs' courts were even more zealous than the Parlement in upholding royal rights. No exact boundary between the privileges of local lords and the rights of the monarch had ever been drawn, and on issues for which no clear precedents existed, it was only natural that the bailiffs should rule in favor of the king. Although the Parlement often modified the more extreme claims of the bailiffs, the net result was a further increase in royal power. Still, most people felt that Louis had saved them from the demands of local lords and saw him as the one who had suppressed disorder and brought peace.

As a Christian ruler, Louis was a zealous crusader against the enemies of Christendom. The Moslems had taken Jerusalem in 1187, and all efforts to recover it had failed. Emperor Frederick II had arranged a treaty that restored the city to Christian control, but it had lasted only a short time. In 1248 and again in 1270 Louis led crusades to recover Jerusalem. The first expedition seemed to have some chance of success, but after an early victory Louis's army had been cut off from its supplies and forced to surrender. The second expedition was hopeless from the start, for Louis let himself be talked into attacking the outlying Moslem state of Tunis, which had been interfering with western shipping in the Mediterranean for centuries. Soon after landing, Louis and many of his men died of fever.

The church declared Louis IX a saint during the 1290s as part of a general settlement of disputes between the papacy and Philip IV (r. 1285–1314), Louis's grandson. Louis's commitment to justice and order had created a vast reservoir of support for his dynasty, and now his accomplishments had been officially recognized by the church. Some of those who succeeded him on the throne were evil, and some were weak, but for centuries loyalty to the king was the strongest political force in France. The king stood as the symbol of unity and good government; he alone could settle provincial differences and override local ambitions. Though France remained strongly Catholic, loyalty to the state began to overshadow loyalty to the church.

962	1002 1024	1125	1152	1254
Ottonian Emperors	Salian Emperors	Period of Imperial Weakness	Hohenstaufen Emperors	

Henry II

1073   1122

Investiture Conflict

THE RISE AND FALL OF ROYAL POWER IN GERMANY

The Hohenstaufens

The building of royal power in Germany was beset with problems similar to those in France. When Henry I (r. 918–36) was elected to the throne, his power was based primarily on his own duchy of Saxony. To extend that base, the monarchy had to bring the other duchies under control. Henry and his son Otto I (r. 936–73) made substantial progress toward that goal (see pp. 238–40). But building a strong monarchy in Germany was difficult because in principle the king was chosen through an election by the dukes.

Henry I's predecessor Conrad I (r. 911–18) and Henry himself were elected by the dukes. And even though Otto I and his heirs inherited the crown, they still achieved their elevation through a formal election. Whenever the direct line of male heirs failed—as it did in 1002 when Otto III died without heirs—the electors exercised genuine power and a real election took place. Whenever that happened, the leading ducal families competed fiercely for the crown.

The Hohenstaufens* emerged victorious from such a competition in 1152, when Frederick I Barbarossa (r. 1152–90) became king. Frederick, who was Duke of Swabia, set out to restore royal power, which had been weakened by the competition. His first step was to marry the heiress of the kingdom of Burgundy. Then in 1154 he went to Rome to receive the imperial crown, to which he had a claim as the successor of Otto I. As emperor, he claimed authority over northern Italy, a

---

* The Hohenstaufen descended, in the female line, from Henry V (r. 1106–25). They took their name from their ancestral castle in Swabia.

source of tax revenues that would help him to overpower the German dukes. By firming up his control over a collection of territories stretching from Swabia to Rome, Frederick managed to acquire real authority in Germany as well. In 1180, he deprived his principal rival, Henry the Lion, Duke of Saxony and Bavaria, of all his fiefs. But Frederick could not wholly destroy Henry's power base, because Henry remained the richest duke in Germany on the basis of the lands he owned outright. Although the duke had to go into exile after he lost his fiefs, he eventually returned to his position of influence in Germany.

Frederick's strategy of basing his power as king of Germany on his role as emperor inevitably embroiled him in Italian affairs. Northern Italy was divided into city-states that were always ready to assert their independence and resented having to pay taxes to Frederick. And both the papacy and the kingdom of Sicily, which viewed Frederick as a threat, were eager to support any opposition to him. To secure his empire's southern flank, Frederick arranged the marriage of his son Henry VI (r. 1190–97) to the daughter of the king of Sicily. When the male line of the Sicilian kings failed, young Henry inherited that crown, and the Hohenstaufens found themselves split between their interests in the north and the south even more than before.

Frederick died in 1190 while traveling to the Holy Land on the Third Crusade, and Henry VI succeeded him. But Henry died young in 1197, leaving an infant heir, Frederick. Now it fell to the German electors to choose a king. The competition led to a civil war between Henry VI's brother, Philip of Swabia, and Henry the Lion's son, Otto of Brunswick. Pope Innocent III asserted his right to choose the one best

Late twelfth-century gilded reliquary bearing the features of Frederick I Barbarossa.

qualified to occupy the imperial throne (see p. 281). He threw his support to Otto IV (r. 1197–1215), who secured his hold on the throne when Philip was murdered in 1208. But when Otto broke his promises to the pope in 1209 by invading the kingdom of Sicily, which young Frederick was ruling as a vassal of the papacy, Innocent switched his support to Frederick. Determined to prevent the unification of Italy under a single king, Innocent stirred up a rebellion in Germany against Otto and in favor of Frederick.

Germany and Italy at the Time of the Hohenstaufens   1138–1250

Otto returned home in 1212, and in 1214, with the support of King John of England, he invaded France in retaliation for Philip II's support of Frederick. At the battle of Bouvines in Flanders, Philip defeated the combined forces of England and Germany. In England, the defeat precipitated the crisis that led to the signing of the *Magna Carta*. In Germany, it cost Otto his crown: he was deposed by an assembly of the dukes and other nobles in 1215. Frederick II (r. 1215–50; in Sicily, 1197–1250) was now king of Germany. But the long civil war had weakened the monarchy, and the dukes were able to force concessions from him.

Frederick II and the Papacy

By birth and upbringing, Frederick II was an Italian. Though he had spent a few years in Germany after becoming emperor, he never felt at home there and never exercised much power over the German dukes. Apparently deciding that he could do nothing with Germany until he had brought Italy fully under his control, he abandoned almost all authority to the dukes. All he expected from Germany was a steady supply of soldiers for his Italian wars.

In Italy, his first move was to eliminate all opposition in his hereditary kingdom of Sicily by transforming it into a nearly absolute monarchy. Then he began to revive the imperial claim to rule central and northern Italy. Thanks to factional quarrels within and among the Italian towns, he managed to acquire substantial territory in those regions. Some of the northern cities became so alarmed by his success that they revived the Lombard League, which had fought Frederick I in the twelfth century. Frederick crushed the League's forces at Cortenuova in 1237, and for the moment he appeared to be in control of the whole peninsula.

However, the papacy was still determined to preserve the independence of the Papal States, which stretched from Rome to Ravenna, by keeping Italy divided. No pope could believe that an emperor who ruled all Italy would respect the papacy's right to govern the Papal States, especially in view of the long history of imperial meddling in papal affairs. Pope Innocent III, who had crowned Frederick II emperor, kept the empire in turmoil rather than risk that danger, as did his successors.

Frederick was a brilliant, inquisitive man who exchanged friendly letters with Moslem rulers, dabbled in science and magic, and was suspected of having written a book called *The Three Impostors: Moses, Jesus and Mohammed*. To convince the world that he was an orthodox ruler, he took the cross and went on a crusade. Moreover, he was the first to condemn heretics to death by burning them at the stake. Yet his actions raised more doubts than they settled. After taking the cross, he waited for years before leaving on the crusade and the pope excommunicated him for violating his oath. When he finally arrived in the Holy Land, he chose to negotiate with the Moslems rather than fight them. He managed to arrange a treaty that gave the Christians control of Jerusalem for a few years, but the pope renewed his excommunication anyway.

When it became clear that Frederick intended to solidify his control of the Italian peninsula, Pope Gregory IX (r. 1227–41) took drastic measures and called a council in Rome to deal with the problem. But Frederick intercepted the fleet bearing the prelates and captured or drowned most of them, an act that did nothing to improve his reputation for piety. Gregory's successor, Innocent IV (r. 1243–54), a famous lawyer, succeeded in holding a council at Lyons in 1245, which declared that Frederick had forfeited all his possessions and that neither he nor any member of his family should ever again be permitted to rule in Germany or Italy. Innocent proclaimed a crusade against Frederick and imposed a tax on the clergy to pay for the armies to carry it out.

This papal attack on Frederick destroyed the last vestiges of central government in Germany. The dukes refused to obey either Frederick or an opposing ruler elected by a faction that favored the pope. Germany became a loose confederation of states under the control of the dukes, who could either accept or reject the poli-

Portrait of Emperor Frederick II, from a manuscript of his treatise, *The Art of Hunting with Falcons.*

cies made by the king. No German emperor after Frederick exercised any real authority, except over his family holdings.

Frederick held on to most of the territory he had acquired in Italy. After his death in 1250, however, the cities of northern and central Italy asserted their independence, though the kingdom of Sicily remained loyal to his sons. The papacy might have settled for this state of affairs, but it had been too badly frightened to take any chances. So the popes carried on a war against the "viper brood" of Hohenstaufens until the hated family had been ejected from Sicily and Naples. They preached crusades, levied taxes on the clergy to cover their expenses, and sent cardinals out with armies to battle Frederick's heirs. And when they found they could not do the job by themselves, they

In 1241 Frederick's fleet captured (or drowned) two cardinals and a hundred bishops who were on their way to a council summoned by Pope Gregory IX to depose the emperor. This manuscript illustration shows Frederick in the ship on the left, though actually he was not present. On the right, his soldiers attack the prelates in a ship bearing the papal ensign of the keys of St. Peter.

litical ends, and people found it difficult to distinguish the pope's actions from those of a secular prince. One could argue that if it was proper for the pope to tax the clergy to defend his territories, it was equally proper for a king to tax the clergy to defend his kingdom.

Moreover, the popes had won their victory over the Hohenstaufens by creating political instability in both Germany and Italy, and in the long run the church itself was weakened by that instability. With no one in Germany strong enough to protect them, the bishops had to fight and intrigue to protect themselves from the rapacious dukes and local lords. Nor was the German government strong enough to deal with the heresies that sprang up in the fourteenth century, which opened the way for Luther's revolt against the papacy in the sixteenth century.

In Italy, the absence of a strong central government enabled the powerful city-states to dominate the surrounding districts. Genoa and Venice, which controlled the lucrative eastern trade, remained fairly stable and even established colonies in the Aegean and on the northern shores of the Black Sea. But the inland cities, including wealthy trading centers such as Florence and Pisa, were plagued by factionalism and were constantly at war with one another.

turned to England and France for help. Their attempt to involve Henry III of England in the struggle failed and led to the baronial rebellion of 1258 (see p. 312). They were more successful in France. Louis IX reluctantly permitted his brother, Charles of Anjou, to attempt the conquest of the kingdom of Sicily. Charles, aided by crusade privileges for his troops and financed by crusade taxes, defeated the last Hohenstaufen ruler of Sicily in a swift campaign in 1266. A grandson of Frederick II made a desperate attempt to regain the kingdom, but his forces were crushed in 1268, and the young man was executed. The papacy had finally rid Italy of the Hohenstaufens.

The Consequences of the Struggle

In winning this political victory, the papacy had lost much of its moral prestige. Many people had questioned the decision to depose Frederick II—Louis IX himself had maintained a careful neutrality in the struggle—though the church clearly had a case against him. But Frederick's heirs posed no great threat, and it seemed vindictive of the papacy to harry them for two decades. Throughout that time, moreover, it was apparent that the church was using its spiritual authority to achieve po-

The situation was no better in the kingdom of Sicily. In 1282, Peter III of Aragon, who had married the daughter of the last Hohenstaufen king of Sicily, took advantage of a rebellion against the French ruler and seized the kingdom. Although Peter never acquired Naples or the mainland territories of Sicily, which remained in the hands of a younger branch of the French royal family, the kingdom of Naples was itself torn by quarrels over the succession.

In Rome, whether the popes recognized it or not, the destruction of imperial power left political chaos in its wake. The emperors had often helped the popes control the local nobility, for if the emperor wanted to have influence in Rome he was better off supporting the pope than trying to control the local lords. With imperial authority gone, the state of affairs in and around the city deteriorated for the papacy. Members of the Roman nobility were trying to strengthen their hold on the region around the city; small towns around Rome were struggling for independence and for more territory; and Rome itself was divided among the great families. As a result, the pope's position was desperate. He could either flee Italy and lose the prestige associated with the city of Rome or he could stay and participate in the petty politics as a minor prince. In fact, the church was feeling the effects of the rise of the secular states throughout Europe. None of the great thirteenth-century popes ever became a saint, though several kings were canonized. And one of those saintly kings, Louis IX of France, probably exercised greater moral influence over the Europe of his day than did any churchman.

ENGLAND, FRANCE, AND THE PAPACY IN THE LATE THIRTEENTH CENTURY

English Foreign Policy under Edward I

In England, the central government had grown strong by the end of the thirteenth century. After the baronial rebellion of 1258–65, Edward I had reestablished royal authority and was determined to increase it further. Edward was a hardworking, intelligent ruler who chose capable men to serve his government. He was also a man of terrifying rages—the dean of St. Paul's Cathedral in London dropped dead of fright during a dispute with him—and few men dared to contradict him openly. Yet he was careful to keep the support of the propertied classes, both the aristocracy and the townsmen, which he needed in his plan to become supreme ruler of the British Isles—England, Scotland, Wales, and Ireland. He avoided getting involved in affairs on the Continent, except when he went to war with the king of France over France's attempt to seize the duchy of Aquitaine, the last of the English holdings in France. Instead, Edward I concentrated on the conquest of Wales and

Scotland, a policy that pleased the aristocracy. He kept his administration under firm control and was never overpowered by a baronial council.

Edward completed the conquest of Wales that William the Conqueror's barons had begun long before. He replaced the last native prince of Wales with his own infant son, thereby creating a precedent that has endured to the present day—the heir to the English throne is the Prince of Wales. But Scotland proved more troublesome. Edward first installed a puppet king, but when he tried to act independently Edward deposed him and tried to rule the country himself. He was unable to maintain a large enough army in Scotland to suppress dissent, and the Scots rebelled, first under William Wallace and then under Robert Bruce. The rebellion was still raging when Edward died in 1307, and the Scots won their independence at Bannockburn in 1314.

France under Philip IV the Fair

In France, royal power followed a different course. At the end of the thirteenth century, the French barons were still struggling to preserve the right to govern their own holdings. Not particularly interested in what was going on in Paris, they just wanted to keep the central government from interfering with their affairs. The chief problem of the French king was not to keep the counts and dukes from trying to dominate his council but to see that they enforced his orders and his rights.

That problem came to a head during the reign of Philip IV, called Philip the Fair (r. 1285–1314), the grandson of Louis IX. Like his grandfather, Philip was a pious man, upright in his private life and imbued with a sense of divine mission. But he was narrow-minded where Louis had been magnanimous and grasping where Louis had been merely firm. He increased the number of bureaucrats enormously and encouraged them to expand royal authority whenever they could. He would condone any expedient to break the power of a local lord who tried to retain some measure of independence. Lesser vassals

Edward I of England (1272–1307) on this throne (illustration from a fourteenth-century manuscript).

were unable to resist, but the more powerful vassals responded with indignant refusal. Consequently, Philip spent a good part of his time warring with his greatest vassals, including the king of England (as duke of Aquitaine) and the count of Flanders. Though he won some land from both, he never took the rich textile cities of Bruges and Ghent from Flanders nor the flourishing port of Bordeaux from Aquitaine.

Edward I had been reasonably successful raising money for his wars from Parliament; Philip the Fair had a harder time. The French had never been subjected to a general tax, whereas the English had been paying national taxes since the end of the twelfth century. In any case, France had no central assembly like the English parliament to impose a uniform tax on the whole country. Instead, royal agents had to negotiate with each region, and often with each lord or each city within each region. Although France was at least four times larger than England in both area and population, it is doubtful that Philip's tax revenues ever matched those of Edward.

That shortage of funds helps explain France's military weakness during the next hundred years. It also explains why the French representative assembly, the Estates General, never became as powerful as the English parliament. Philip was the first king to call a meeting of the Estates General, but he never asked it for a grant of taxes. He knew that the country would pay little attention to a tax levy ordered by Paris. The lack of power over taxation remained one of the chief weaknesses of the Estates General. Philip had much better luck negotiating tax levies with local leaders. Though the negotiations were tedious, they made it possible to play one region off against another. The royal negotiators would win assent to a tax in an area by indicating that a neighboring area had agreed to pay it and that the royal government would favor the region that agreed to pay with trade monopolies and protection from bandits. The king's bureaucrats became extremely persistent and skillful in conducting these negotiations.

Thus England had emerged as a strongly united country in which the king and the propertied classes cooperated in carrying out policies that they both approved of. Though France was united more by the royal bureaucracy than by common interests, the propertied classes usually trusted the king on policy matters. And in both countries some of the ideas that distinguish the modern state were beginning to appear: The welfare of the state is the greatest good; the defense of the realm is the greatest necessity; opposition to duly constituted authority is the greatest evil. As one of Philip's lawyers remarked: "All men, clergy and laity alike, are bound to contribute to the defense of the realm." People who were beginning to think in these terms were not likely to be impressed by the appeals and exhortations of the papacy.

The Struggle with Pope Boniface VIII

After the death of Pope Nicholas IV (r. 1288–92), the cardinals had had great difficulty choosing a pope. Finally in 1294 they agreed on a most unlikely candidate, Peter Murrone, a hermit who lived on the slopes of Mount Vesuvius near Naples and who took the name Celestine V. Though he was a truly spiritual man, he could not manage the vast machinery of papal government or the complexities of international politics. As the church drifted, calls came for his abdication, and before the end of a year Celestine had indeed abdicated, the only pope ever to do so. The cardinals, chastened by the experience, then elected one of their leading members, who took the name Boniface VIII (r. 1294–1303).

Boniface was an able canon lawyer and a veteran of political conflict. Sensing that the rise of secular authority was posing a serious threat to the papacy, he set about restoring the independence and authority of the church. He made no claim that had not already been made by his predecessors, but the climate of opinion had changed. Many people now believed that their chief duty was to support their king rather than to obey the pope. As a

Pope Boniface VIII receives St. Louis of Toulouse, a grandnephew of St. Louis of France and son of Charles II of Naples. The representation of the pope corresponds to other pictures of him. Fresco by Ambrogio Lorenzetti, Siena (*ca.* 1330).

result Boniface was defeated in a head-on clash with the kings of England and France—a defeat from which the medieval church never recovered.

The issue was clear: Were members of the clergy to be treated as ordinary subjects of the king, or were they to be responsible only to the pope? Specifically, could they be taxed for the defense of the realm without the pope's consent? The kings of England and France were always short of funds, and they were strongly tempted to tap the resources of the church. The popes themselves had provided a precedent for taxing the clergy when they raised money for their political battles against the Hohenstaufens. When Edward I and Philip the Fair drifted into war over Aquitaine in 1294, they both asked their clergy for a grant of taxes. They were outraged when Boniface prohibited those grants in 1296, and they stirred up public opinion against the clergy as disloyal members of the community. Further, they both seized church property and forbade any transfer of money to Rome. Edward virtually outlawed the English clergy. In the end, the harassed churchmen begged the pope to reconsider and remove his ban. Grudgingly, Boniface did so in 1298.

The Issue between State and Church   1302

Boniface VIII says in the Bull Unam Sanctam:

Both the spiritual sword and the material sword are in the power of the Church. But the latter is to be used for the Church, the former by her; the former by the priest, the latter by kings and captains, but by the assent and permission of the priest. The one sword, then, should be under the other, and temporal authority subject to spiritual power. . . . If, therefore, the earthly power err, it shall be judged by the spiritual power. . . . Finally, we declare, state, define and pronounce that it is altogether necessary to salvation for every human creature to be subject to the Roman pontiff.

One of Philip's ministers, speaking for the king, says:

The pope pretends that we are subject to him in the temporal government of our states and that we hold the crown from the Apostolic See. Yes, this kingdom of France which, with the help of God, our ancestors . . . created—this kingdom which they have until now so wisely governed—it appears that it is not from God alone, as everyone had always believed, that we hold it, but from the pope!

From Select Documents of European History, *ed. by R. G. D. Laffan (London: Methuen, 1930), p. 117; from C. V. Langlois,* St. Louis, Philippe le Bel, et les derniers Capetiens directs *(Paris: Hachette, 1911), pp. 149–50.*

Worse was to follow. In 1301 Philip the Fair imprisoned a French bishop on a flimsy charge of treason and refused to obey a papal order to free him. Boniface cited the old principle of canon law that the clergy were not subject to secular courts and threatened to punish the king and his agents. It was at this time that Philip called the first Estates General to assemble at Paris (1302). The assembly gave him its full support and emphatically rejected papal authority over France. When the dispute continued, Philip, through his minister, Guillaume de Nogaret, accused Boniface of immorality and heresy and appealed to a general council to condemn him. Local assemblies throughout France endorsed Philip's plan—the nobility and the bourgeoisie enthusiastically, the clergy reluctantly but almost unanimously. Philip certainly had the support of the people. Though they may not have believed that the pope was guilty of treason, they believed that the church was corrupt and that the pope had no right to interfere in the internal affairs of France.

Assured of support at home, Philip now embarked on a high-risk venture. In 1303 he sent Nogaret to Italy with a small force to join Italian enemies of the pope. Together they staged a surprise attack on Boniface's summer home at Anagni and succeeded in capturing him. They probably hoped to take Boniface back to France to stand trial before a church council, but they were unable to carry out such a plan. The Italians had no great love for the pope, but they cared even less for the French. The people of Anagni and the neighboring areas freed Boniface after a few days, and the French retreated through hostile country. The shock of the experience was too much for Boniface— he was in his eighties—and he died soon after.

Force had been used against earlier popes, but after the assault at Anagni the church became cautious. No one in France—or anywhere else, for that matter—seemed disturbed by what had happened, and Nogaret remained Philip's favorite minister. Now that it was clear that the papal court would have to deal with

Philip, the college of cardinals elected a pope who was at least acceptable to him, though not his own candidate. Clement V (r. 1305–14) yielded to Philip on every matter and even allowed that Philip had acted out of good motives in seizing Boniface. The power that Innocent III had bequeathed to his successors was but a memory.

THE POPES AT AVIGNON

After being elected pope, Clement V set off for Rome from Bordeaux, where he had been archbishop. But after learning that the city-states of Italy were at war and that the Papal States were unsafe, he decided to stop off at Avignon, a small city in the Rhone Valley. Clement apparently planned to continue on to Rome as soon as order had been restored, but as things turned out, Avignon became his permanent residence. Philip and the French cardinals urged him to stay on, and conditions in Italy continued chaotic. So Avignon remained the seat of papal government for more than seventy years.

The long exile in France (1305–78) is known in church history as the Babylonian Captivity—an allusion to the Babylonian captivity of the Jews in the sixth century B.C. Avignon was situated in a small principality that was not subject to the French king, but it was certainly kept under his watchful eye. Surprisingly, however, the popes who succeeded Clement V at Avignon were less subservient to the French kings that he had been, and many of them were excellent administrators. During its time in Avignon, the papacy developed into the largest government in Europe, with an elaborate and powerful bureaucracy and a large income. But the pope was supposed to be the bishop of Rome, and some of Europe's leading intellectual and spiritual figures urged the popes to return to the Holy City. As successful as the papal government was in Avignon, the scandal of the Babylonian Exile damaged the prestige of the pope as the spiritual leader of Christendom.

Suggestions for Further Reading

Economy

On the economic changes that took place in the thirteenth and fourteenth centuries, see the works cited after Chapter 10. M. M. Postan, *Medieval Trade and Finance* (1973), is a general work. R. S. Lopez and I. W. Raymond, eds., *Medieval Trade in the Mediterranean World* (1955), contains much interesting source material. See also A. R. Lewis, *Naval Power and Trade in the Mediterranean* (1951) and *The Northern Seas* (1958). On the merchant class, see the works cited in Chapter 10 and E. M. Carus-Wilson, *The Medieval Merchant Adventurers,* 3rd ed. (1967).

England

W. L. Warren has written two excellent works on the Angevin kings in *Henry II* (1973) and *King John* (1961). See also J. Gillingham, *Richard the Lionheart* (1978). A. L. Poole, *From Domesday Book to Magna Carta,* 2nd ed. (1955), provides an excellent general history. The most thorough treatment of *Magna Carta* is W. S. McKechnie, *Magna Carta* (1914), which studies the document chapter by chapter. For a shorter treatment, see J. C. Holt, *Magna Carta,* 2nd ed. (1990). On English history in the thirteenth century, see F. M. Powicke, *King Henry III and the Lord Edward,* 2 vols. (1947), and *The Thirteenth Century* (1953). For the later period, see M. McKisack, *The Fourteenth Century* (1959). The classic history of medieval common law is F. W. Maitland and F. Pollock, *The History of English Law,* 2 vols., rev. ed. by S. G. F. Milsom (1968). This work is brought up to date in J. H. Baker, *An Introduction to English Legal History,* 2nd ed. (1979). See also D. M. Stenton, *English Justice from the Norman Conquest to the Great Charter* (1964). A large collection of sources for the history of common law was published in J. H. Baker and S. F. C. Milsom, *Sources of English Legal History* (1986).

Constitutional Government

All works on medieval England cited above contain much material on the growth of constitutional government. See also J. E. A. Joliffe, *Angevin Kingship* (1955), which traces the growth of royal power in England and the development of the institutions of government through the twelfth century. On the idea of kingship in relation to law and political thought, see the classic by E. H. Kantorowicz, *The King's Two Bodies* (1957). For a survey of the institutions of constitutional government, see G. L. Haskins, *The Growth of English Representative Government* (1948); A. Marongui, *Medieval Parliaments: A Comparative Study* (1968); T. N. Bisson, *Assemblies and Representation in Languedoc in the Thirteenth Century* (1964); and F. L. Carsten, *Princes and Parliaments in Germany* (1959).

France

On France, see the works cited in Chapter 10, particularly J. Dunbabin, *France in the Making, 843–1180*.(1985), and E. M. Hallam, *Capetian France, 987–1328* (1980). On Philip II Augustus, see A. Luchaire, *Social Life in France at the Time of Philip Augustus,* trans. E. B. Krehbiel (1912). On Louis IX, see J. R. Strayer, *The Administration of Normandy under St. Louis* (1932), and W. C. Jordan, *Louis IX and the Challenge of the Crusade* (1979). For a comprehensive history of Philip IV the Fair, see J. R. Strayer, *The Reign of Philip the Fair* (1980). On the conflict between Philip and Pope Boniface VIII, see C. T. Wood, ed., *Philip the Fair and Boniface VIII* (1967), which contains a selection of historians' work on the subject. On Boniface VIII, see T. S. R. Boase, *Boniface VIII* (1930).

Germany

On the rise and fall of the Hohenstaufens, see G. Barraclough, *The Origins of Modern Germany* (1947); H. Fuhrmann, *Germany in the High Middle Ages, c. 1050–1200* (1985); J. B. Gillingham, *The Kingdom of Germany in the High Middle Ages* (1979); and J. Leuschner, *Germany in the Later Middle Ages* (1980). On Frederick Barbarossa, see M. Pacaut, *Frederick Barbarossa* (1969), and P. Munz, *Frederick Barbarossa: A Study of Medieval Politics* (1969), which takes the questionable view that Frederick was a "rational" politician whose every action was carefully calculated. The classic study of Frederick II is E. H. Kantorowicz, *Frederick II* (1931). T. C. Van Cleve, *The Emperor Frederick II* (1972), is also highly recommended. On the formation of the late medieval empire, see J. Bryce, *The Holy Roman Empire* (many editions), and C. Bayley, *The Formation of the German College of Electors* (1949).

The Avignon Papacy and the Late Medieval Church

The classic work on the late medieval church is A. C. Flick, *The Decline of the Medieval Church,* 2 vols. (1930). See now, F. Oakley, *The Western Church in the Later Middle Ages* (1979). On the Avignon period, see G. Mollat, *The Avignon Papacy* (1963), and Y. Renouard, *The Avignon Papacy* (1970).

13

EASTERN EUROPE IN THE MIDDLE AGES

*U*p to this point, eastern Europe has been mentioned only as a region through which various peoples moved from central Asia into western Europe. In the third century, the Huns created an empire based in Hungary. In the seventh century, the Avars followed suit. In the ninth century, the Magyars succeeded the Avars, establishing a kingdom that survives as a modern state. To the north, the Slavs followed the Germans into the forests of Poland and mountains of Bohemia and Slovakia. To the south, they moved into the Balkans.

Clearly, then, the peoples that migrated into eastern Europe formed kingdoms much as those in western Europe, though the eastern states rarely escaped the interference and influence of the western European rulers. The Franks and their successors in Germany took a keen interest in eastern Europe. The popes sought the conversion of the peoples there. The westerners found themselves in competition with the Byzantines, and both faced resistance from eastern European rulers who sought to create independent states that could take their place within the political system of the Continent.

THE SLAVS

The civilized peoples of the Mediterranean first came into contact with the Slavs at the end of the fifth century and the beginning of the sixth century. Slavs originated in the north between the Vistula and Dnieper rivers and had followed the Germans into southern Russia and eastern Europe during the third century (see pp. 113–15). They did not appear on the borders of the Roman Empire until later, after the Germanic tribes had moved on to the south and west. By the early sixth

(OPPOSITE) THE THRONE OF IVAN THE TERRIBLE. THE STAFF WAS A SYMBOL OF IMPERIAL AUTHORITY.

century, the Slavs were in control of Lithuania, the Ukraine, central Russia, Poland, Bohemia, and Slovakia and had moved south toward modern Yugoslavia. During these early migrations, they often fell into conflict with the Avars and Sarmatians who stormed out of the central Asia in successive waves and set up short-lived empires in southeastern Europe. Following the collapse of those empires, the Slavic tribes gradually absorbed their remnants.

By the sixth century the Romans were fighting the Slavs along the Danube frontier and settling some of them as *foederati* (see p. 113) to help repel further incursions from the northern forests. But like the Germanic *foederati* before them, the Slavic tribes sometimes broke their contract with the Roman government, and in the seventh century Constantinople was threatened by Slavic armies.

THE SOUTHERN SLAVS

When Heraclius (r. 610–41) mounted the throne in Constantinople, he needed allies against the Persians (see pp. 173–74) and enlisted the Slavic Serbs and the non-Slavic Croats, who were eager to escape the domination of the Avars. He persuaded the Croats to settle in the old Roman provinces of Illyricum along the Dalmatian coast and in Pannonia to the northeast. And he persuaded the Serbs to settle in eastern Illyricum. This whole region had been devastated by the Avars early in the seventh century, and Sirmium, the one-time capital of Pannonia, had ceased to exist. Though the Roman population had been Christian, hardly a church or a bishopric remained intact.

Heraclius now set about ensuring the loyalty of these pagan settlers by having them converted to Christianity. Because the ancient churches along the Dalmatian coast had been under the ecclesiastical jurisdiction of Rome, he asked the pope to send missionaries to the Croats. Pope Gregory I (r. 590–604; see pp. 138–40) had already been trying to reestablish the church in Illyricum, but no one made much progress until Honorius I (r. 625–38) sent out missionaries from Rome and Ravenna. Slowly, the missionaries rebuilt the ecclesiastical system, with Spalato (Split) as the center. It was this ecclesiastical province that the Byzantine emperor Leo III (r. 717–41) removed from papal jurisdiction when the popes opposed his iconoclasm (see p. 178).

Meanwhile, Heraclius arranged for missionaries to be sent to the Serbs. Although some of those missionaries came from Bari, the capital of Byzantine Apulia, it appears that survivors of the old Christian population of Pannonia took the lead. Recently discovered archaeological evidence reveals that the Serbs began building churches in significant numbers only in the early ninth century, by which time they must have been fully Christianized.

Behind the Croats and Serbs came the non-Slavic Bulgars from central Asia, who had, like the Croats, settled in southern Russia among the Slavs and had been absorbed into the Slavic culture. They may have arrived as part of the Hunnish horde that invaded the region in the 370s. In any case, they moved into the Danubian region of the Empire in the sixth and sev-

The Settlement of the Croats and Serbs   SEVENTH CENTURY

enth centuries and became particularly troublesome during the reign of Heraclius. Under the first known Bulgarian khan (king), Kurt, or Kuvrat (r. 605–65), the Bulgars created a state that the Byzantines called Great Bulgaria.

It was under the auspices of the Bulgarian khanate that Serbs moved south and established independent communities in the mountainous regions of central and northern Greece, particularly around Thessalonika. The Byzantines, under constant pressure from the Persians and the Arabs, made no effort to recover these regions, and for centuries the Christian population lived in isolated pockets surrounded by Slavic settlements. Not until late in the ninth century did the Byzantine government manage to bring the Slavic intruders under its power and begin to convert them to Christianity. In time, they became fully christianized and so completely assimilated that their language left few traces in Greek.

MORAVIA AND THE CENTRAL EUROPEAN SLAVS

Slavs between East and West

The Slavic settlements in Pannonia lay across the rich trade routes of central Europe, where they seem to have formed a loose confederation of principalities centered on the revived towns of Sirmium (now called by the Slavic name Morava; in Latin, its region was called Moravia) and Belgrade, among others. The picture that emerges, though the evidence is meager, is of a group of petty princes constantly jockeying for position, rather like the Franks before the rise of Clovis (see p. 128).

These central European Slavs were constantly threatened with invasion by their neighbors—the Germans to the west and north, the Avars to the east, and the Byzantines to the south. From early on, the Bavarians, a Germanic tribe settled in southern Germany and Austria, meddled in their affairs and sent missionaries to convert them to Christianity. Then, after Charles the Great (r. 768–814) assumed control of Bavaria (788), the Moravians

Greater Moravia   NINTH CENTURY

and their neighbors began to fall under Frankish influence. By playing the Franks off against the Avars, however, the Slavs managed to preserve some measure of independence and continued to resist conversion. But when Charles the Great crushed the Avars in 796, the Slavs fell entirely under Frankish influence.

To resist the pressures that were acting on them from every side, and to preserve what they could of their cultural identity, the small tribes of Moravians and their Slavic neighbors began to join together in loose political federations. They soon discovered that they could play the Byzantines off against the Franks as they had the Avars. In the early ninth century, the Moravians and their neighbors had achieved enough self-confidence to try to launch an independent Slavic state. But Charles the Great was determined to prevent them from doing so. In 803 he forced the capitulation of both the Moravians and the Bohemians, who lived in the Carpathian Mountains north of the Danube. He then set about consolidating his control by sending missionaries to convert the

Mounted warrior with a captive
(detail from a gold vessel from
the ninth century found in
Sînnicolau Mare, Romania).

for a Slavic state. In fact, in 817 a Bavarian geographer reported that Moravia had eleven fortified "cities," a report that archaeologists have recently confirmed. Nonetheless, by the time of Mojimir's death, around 845, most of Moravia had become Christian, with a church organization subject to the Frankish bishops of Germany.

Following his death there was a brief pagan revival that aimed to recapture the cultural heritage of the Slavs and to renew the quest for independence. Many Slavic leaders thought Mojimir's strategy of accommodating the Frankish influence to achieve his ends had been a failure. Louis the German stepped in, however, and put Mojimir's nephew Rastislav (r. 846–70) in power. He proved the leaders wrong. Soon Louis became engrossed in the conflicts with his brothers (see pp. 232–33), and the Moravian prince was free to go his own way. By about 850, Rastislav was the ruler of a virtually independent state that included most of the old province of Pannonia, with influence as well over Bohemia and Hungary. To keep Louis off balance, Rastislav supported Louis's son Carloman in his rebellion in the early 860s.

Though Louis had installed Rastislav as a puppet king, he now found himself with a rival rather than a trusted ally on his southeastern frontier. To counter Rastislav, he suggested to the Bulgarian khan Boris that they form an alliance against him. In search of an ally of his own, Rastislav turned to Rome, apparently hoping that the pope would help him meet the threat and at the same time free the church of Moravia from Frankish control. Pope Nicholas I (r. 858–67) did not respond, however, because he was already having trouble with Louis and chose not to make matters worse.

In 862 Rastislav sent an embassy to Constantinople with a request for assistance from the emperor Michael III (r. 842–67):

Our people has renounced paganism and is observing the Christian law, but we do not have a teacher to explain to us the true Christian faith in our own language in order that other nations

defeated Slavs, just as he and his predecessors had done in northern and eastern Germany.

But the Moravians, under their leader Mojimir, seem soon to have slipped away from Frankish control, and in 820 Louis the Pious and his son Louis the German embarked on a new campaign that brought the Slavic princes back into the Frankish orbit in 822.

Still, Mojimir managed to stay in power and nurture the Slavic dream of creating an independent state. In 818 he had agreed to convert, though he may not have done so until 822 after convincing his tribal leaders to accept the religion of their conquerors. He may have accepted conversion merely as a way of mollifying the Franks while continuing with his plans *even, seeing this, may imitate us. Send us therefore, Master, such a bishop and teacher, because from you emanates always, to all sides, the good law.*

Behind this request was another message: Though there were many Frankish missionaries in Moravia, their purpose was to impose the authority of the pope on the Slavs instead of helping them to establish a church of their own. Actually, Rastislav's request was also a plea for a political and military alliance, for religion and politics were regarded as one. A Moravian church allied with Constantinople would mean a political alliance as well. Michael did send missionaries to create the alliance, but it produced little political result. It did, however, contribute significantly to the preservation of Slavic culture.

The Mission of Constantine (St. Cyril) and Methodius

Emperor Michael thought he had just the man for Rastislav. Constantine the Philosopher (*ca.* 826–69), as he was called, was then about 35 years old and was teaching in an ecclesiastical college in Constantinople. He had been born in Thessalonika in 826 or 827, the son of a Byzantine military officer on the staff of the provincial governor. After his father was killed fighting the Slavs, young Constantine had become the ward of Theoctistus, the *logothete* or prime minister of the Empire. Theoctistus took him to Constantinople and enrolled him in the court school, where he studied under Photius, the future patriarch and the most learned man in the Empire (see p. 181). Within a short time, Constantine earned a reputation for learning and linguistic ability. He had learned Slavic as a child in Thessalonika, and he may have learned Arabic as well. When he was about 28 years old, he succeeded Photius as the principal teacher of philosophy at the university. Some evidence indicates that the emperor sent him to Baghdad in 851 to debate religious questions with Moslem scholars.

In 856, the Khazars, a central Asian people who had carved out an empire in southern Russia, asked the emperor to send a theologian to participate in a debate among Christians, Moslems, and Jews. The emperor summoned Constantine from the monastery he had entered and sent him north, along with his brother Methodius, to participate in the debate. On the way, Constantine stopped in the Crimea to learn Hebrew and Samaritan from the Jews living there. While he was in Khazaria he translated most of a Hebrew grammar into Greek, and on his return to Constantinople he took a teaching post in one of the city's many ecclesiastical colleges. There he continued his study of Hebrew and Samaritan and was often called on to interpret inscriptions and texts written in unfamiliar languages and scripts.

Constantine's fame as a participant in ecumenical debates and his familiarity with both Greek and Slavic made him well qualified to carry out the mission to Rastislav. Methodius, who also had learned Slavic as a child, accompanied his brother to Moravia. The Byzantines were eager to establish a foothold in Moravia, but they had no interest in setting up a church in competition with the Franks. That might happen in time, but it would involve working through some complicated politics with the western powers,

Constantine's Embassy to the Khazars   856

including the papacy, which claimed jurisdiction over the Slavs. So Constantine and Methodius busied themselves with their missionary work, and Rastislav's request for a bishop went unanswered.

Constantine left for Moravia in 863. But before setting out he invented an alphabet with which to write the translations of the scriptures and the missal, which gave instructions and the prayers for the Mass, into the Slavic language. That alphabet was well suited to Slavic phonology. The earliest works in Slavic were written in this alphabet, and only much later was it replaced in the eastern Slavic countries by an alphabet based on Greek characters, now called Cyrillic even though Constantine, who later took the name Cyril when he reentered a monastery, had nothing to do with it. In most western Slavic countries, the alphabet of Constantine was eventually replaced by the Latin alphabet, which is ill suited to Slavic. Constantine's alphabet is now used only in isolated Eastern Orthodox institutions in Dalmatia and Montenegro.

Using this new alphabet, Constantine and Methodius translated the missal, the psalter, and some other basic liturgical works into Slavic. This meant that Slavic Christians—unlike western Christians—would use their own language in the Mass and in other liturgical ceremonies, such as baptism and marriage. Conservative churchmen argued that only Hebrew, Greek, and Latin were acceptable languages for the liturgy, because those were the languages that Pilate had ordered used for the inscription on Christ's cross. Constantine referred to those churchmen as disciples of Pilate.

The Frankish missionaries in Moravia derided the books translated by Constantine and Methodius as foreign innovations. The brothers responded by translating a missal based on the Roman practice. This missal was essentially the same as the Latin missal used by the Franks, but because it was in Slavic the Moravians favored it over the Latin. Many of the Byzantine liturgical instructions and prayers translated by Constantine became part of the Slavic liturgy.

In making his translations from the Greek, Constantine sought to capture the literary quality and texture of the original. In so doing, he created a literary language for the Slavs and revealed himself as a gifted poet in his own right. His translations marked the beginnings of a literate culture among the Slavs and advanced their language as a vehicle for sophisticated thought.

Constantine and Methodius left Moravia in 867 and headed for Venice, where they expected to take a ship to Constantinople. But the political situation in the Empire had changed during their absence. Basil had murdered Bardas, the patron of their own patron Photius, and had deposed Photius as patriarch (see pp. 182–83). So they accepted an invitation to Rome from the pope. There they lived in a Byzantine monastery and waited for news from home. Constantine went on working, but his health, which had been poor for many years, grew worse. Concluding that he would never return to Constantinople, he joined the monastery and took the name Cyril. He died in Rome in 869 and is known in church history as St. Cyril.

Constantine designed the Glagolitic alphabet for the Slavic language. It is still used in a few isolated monastic communities in the Balkans. The Cyrillic alphabet, named after Constantine's religious name, was designed later. It is based on the Greek alphabet.

modern European	Latin	runes	Greek	Cyrillic	Glagolitic
A	A		A	Д	+
B	B	ᛒ	ß	Б(v) Б(b)	Ʊ ᚼ
C	Ɔ	ᚲᛆᚾᚴ	ᚲᛆ	Г	⅍
D	D	ᛞᛈᛈᛈ(tk) ■ᛉ⊠	DΔ⊙	Д	⅍
E	Ɛ	ᛖᚨᚱᚨ	ᚠ	E	З
F	F	ᚹᚹᛈᛈ	φ F	Ф	⊞
G	G	ᚿ ✦			
H	ᛒ	ᚾᛃᛛᚾᛃ	H	H(i)	𝔛 Ƭ
I	I	I	I	I(i)	ᛞℳ(g̃)
J					
K	ᚴ	Ψ	k	K	ᚼ
L	ᚴ	ᛑ	ᚴ	Λ	ᚨ
M	ᴟ	ᛗ	M	M	ᚴ
N	N	ᛉᛏᛉᛚ	N	H	℘
O	O	ᛉᚫᛉ	o ◇	O	ᛁᵒ
P	ᚨ	ᚾᛉ(ᚲ)	ᚱ	П	ᚱ
Q	Q		Q		
R	ᚨ	R R	ᚱ	Ɵ	ᚿ
S	ᚠ	ᛣ	ᛣ	С	ᛏ
T	T	ᚾ	T	T	ᛗ
U	V	ᚾᚾ	V		
V					
W		ᚱ ᚱ			
X	X	X (ʒ)	X	X (h)	ᚼ
Y	Y	ᛃᛃᚨᛚ	ᚎ	Y (u)	⌀
Z	Z	ᛁᛏ(ik,oo)	ᚎ	Жᚴᛚᛋ(w3H)	ᚼ ⋄ ᛉ
NG		ᛇ Ϥ (ng)	⌐ +		
value	o st tt ts ch sh ŭ	y	i è yu ya ye (ye)	ǫ yǫ yа ya kh ps θ(th,f)	
Cyrillic	Ш Ѱ Ц Ч Ш Ъ	ЪІ ЪН	Ь Ѣ Ю Ѥ ІА Ѧ Ѩ Ж Ѫ Ѯ Ѱ Ѳ		
Glagolitic	ᛟ ᚹ Ѱ ᚠ Ш⊖ ⌐Ƭ ᚼᛉ ⋄ᛋ ⌐ᚨℙ	Ꝋ ᚼᚼᚼ	ᚔ		

The Results of the Mission

Although Constantine and Methodius did not bring the Moravians into the jurisdiction of the church of Constantinople, they had a profound influence on the country's religious practices. In 864 Khan Boris of Bulgaria accepted baptism under the auspices of the Byzantine emperor, and the Bulgarians became part of the Eastern Orthodox church. Soon the liturgical translations of Constantine and Methodius were being used in Bulgaria. At about the same time (864–66), Byzantine missionaries converted the Kievan Russians. Although that conversion did not last, for a while it looked as if all the Slavs would come under the Byzantine church.

But Moravia's political future was with the West. From early times the Franks had looked upon the central European lands as satellites, and the Carolingian kings had done their best to subjugate them. Try as he might, Rastislav was unable to maintain his independence from Louis the German, who constantly interfered in his realm. This failure led Rastislav's own nobility to abandon him. In 870, they captured him and turned him over to the Franks, who blinded him and locked him up in a monastery.

Immediately, another pagan revival was attempted in Moravia, but it was soon put down by Sventopolk, Rastislav's nephew, who had been among his uncle's most formidable enemies. Sventopolk had the support of the Franks, who put him in power in Rastislav's realm. In the first year of his rule in Moravia, Sventopolk asked Rome to send a bishop to establish an independent Slavic church subject to Rome. Pope Hadrian II (r. 867–72) sent Methodius, who had remained in Rome after Constantine's death, and Methodius became Archbishop in Moravia, with his seat in Morava.

Sventopolk then struck out in every direction, creating a state that later historians called Great Moravia. He won control of Croatia down to Istria and the Dalmatian coast and of Bohemia north of the Danube. He also conquered the remnants of the Avar principalities to the east. Meanwhile, Methodius established an indepen-

dent Moravian church and did missionary work in Bohemia and Poland. Sventopolk was at last crowned king of Moravia some time between 880 and 885 and reigned until his death in 894.

Throughout his reign, Sventopolk maintained reasonably good relations with the Franks. He had been on friendly terms with Arnulf of Carinthia even before Arnulf became king of the East Franks in 887 (see p. 237), and events soon solidified their friendship. About 890, the Magyars, who had come out of central Asia to settle Hungary, arrived in Pannonia and initiated the raids that would make them the scourge of central Europe. At a meeting in 890, Arnulf gave Bohemia in fief to Sventopolk, probably in return for his help in defending East Frankland from the marauding Magyars. Sventopolk proceeded to extend his power over Slovakia in the northern Hungarian plain and entered into an alliance with the Magyars. The result of these actions was that Arnulf turned against him, and in 892 and 893 Arnulf led armies into Moravia and devastated everything in sight.

When Sventopolk died in 894, a civil war broke out between his young sons. The East Franks and the Magyars entered the fray, because Moravia formed an important buffer zone between them. Within a few years, the Magyars had overrun Moravia and made it the base for their raids on Bavaria and Italy. Great Moravia had died with Sventopolk.

BOHEMIA

Bohemia was a duchy settled by Slavs in late Roman times. It centered on the castles of Prague, which straddled the Moldau River. From as long ago as the paleolithic period, hunters had frequented the passes through the Carpathian Mountains and the river valleys below them, and each year they had returned to their camps along the migration routes of the great ice-age mammals—the mammoths, rhinoceros, and buffalo. Later, these routes had been incorporated into the Amber Road, the trade route along which precious amber (fossilized pine sap) was carried from the

Baltic to the Mediterranean. The Carpathian Mountains were rich in minerals. Salt had been mined there since the paleolithic period, and the Celts had extracted metal ore from the Carpathians and the northern Alps.

The Bavarians had exercised control over the pagan Slavs of Bohemia even before Charles the Great took over Bavaria in 788. For a long time, the Bohemians refused to be converted to Christianity, and not until the 820s did the Frankish missionaries begin to win converts in the border areas. In the late ninth century, the Bohemians were caught for a time between the Franks and the Moravians, but after the destruction of the Moravian state

Bohemia
ELEVENTH TO TWELFTH CENTURIES

by the Magyars they fell completely under Frankish domination. Both Henry I (r. 918–36) and his son Otto I (r. 936–73) encouraged Germans to set up colonies in Bohemia to strengthen German control and to advance the acceptance of Christianity, but not until 973 was Otto able to establish a bishopric in Prague.

For many years the German kings kept the duchy of Bohemia under subjugation by constantly interfering with the dynastic plans of the dukes. Though the agents of German meddling were usually the dukes of Bavaria, almost every German king during the eleventh and twelfth centuries was at one time or another personally involved in Bohemian affairs. The Bohemians, whenever they could, played Germany, Poland, and Hungary (the Magyar state) off against one another in an effort to win some measure of independence. In 1158, the duchy became the Kingdom of Bohemia when Emperor Frederick I Barbarossa rewarded Duke Vratislav II for his assistance in an Italian campaign. In the fourteenth century, after the collapse of the Hohenstaufen monarchy (see p. 322), the Kingdom of Bohemia fell to the Luxembourg family, which had succeeded to the imperial throne of Germany. From that point on, the fate of Bohemia was determined by the imperial family's dynastic strategy. Emperor Henry

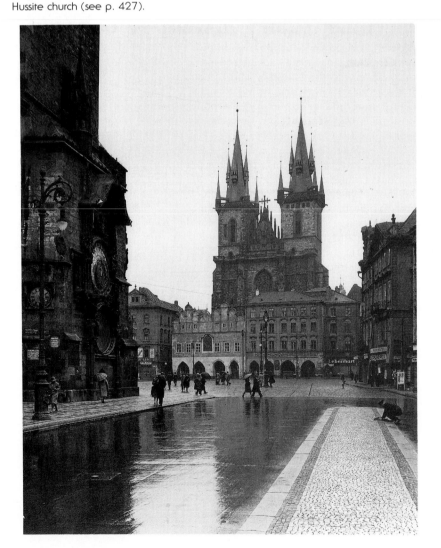

The Tyn Church *(center)* and Astronomical clock *(left)* in Prague. The Tyn Church was founded in the fourteenth century by Germans living in Prague and became the main Hussite church (see p. 427).

Poland in the Middle Ages

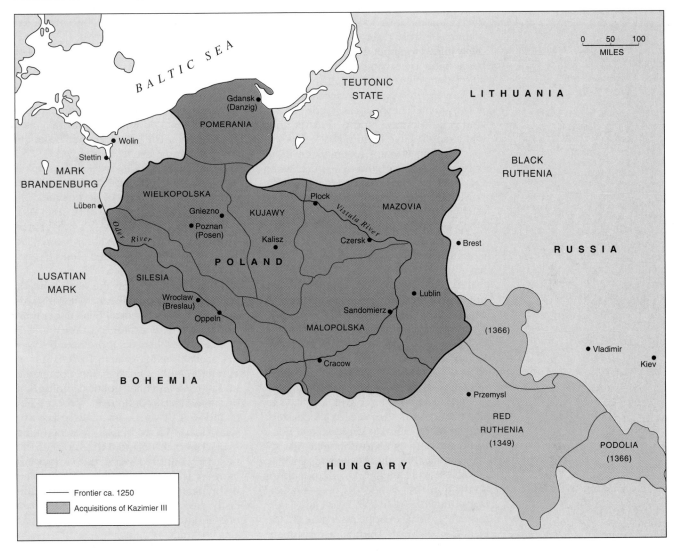

VII of Luxembourg (r. 1309–13) gave Bohemia to his son John (r. 1313–46), who passed it on to his son Charles IV (r. 1346–74), who was elected emperor in 1347. In the fifteenth century, Emperor Sigismund of Luxembourg (r. 1410–37) arranged the marriage of his daughter Elizabeth to the Habsburg Albert II of Austria (emperor 1438–39). When Sigismund died without a male heir, Bohemia passed through his daughter to the Habsburgs (see next section), who eventually created a central European empire that lasted until World War I (1914–19).

POLAND

Poland, the westernmost Slavic region, is situated on a vast plain that stretches from the Atlantic to the Ural Mountains of Russia. It has no natural barriers either to the east or to the west. On the south it is bounded by the Tatra Mountains, a branch of the Carpathians, and on the north by the Baltic Sea. In part as a result of its vulnerability, this vast area, larger than any other European country, has suffered frequent invasion and political instability through the centuries. The Kingdom of

Poland arose from the unification of several tribal domains, which survived as duchies in the kingdom. Throughout the country's history these regions have variously joined together in a federation, have been ruled by a single king, and have allied themselves with foreign and domestic powers in opposition to the central government. The political history of Poland is bewildering, and periods of unity and strength have been rare.

The first attempt to unify the tribes occurred in the early ninth century, when the ruler of the Polanians of Wielkopolska, centered on Poznan and Gniezno, established his hegemony over the regions of Kujawy, Malopolska, and Mazovia. That ruler, who was called Piast, is a semilegendary person, who seems to have succeeded in setting up a dynasty that maintained two seats of power—one in Gniezno and the other in Cracow, the city of the Vistulanians of Malopolska. This dynasty, which historians call the Piast, or Polanian, dynasty, dominated Poland from the time of Louis the Pious (r. 814–40) until 1370, when Kazimierz III the Great died.

Otto I's efforts to convert the Slavs to Christianity and to colonize the eastern frontier of the German kingdom extended to Poland as well as to Bohemia. Shortly after subjugating the Bohemians in 950, Otto turned his attention to Brandenburg on the north-central border between Germany and Poland. In 961, he received permission from the pope to establish the bishopric of Magdeburg as a missionary outpost, and he began to encourage his subjects to migrate into the area. Duke Mieszko I (r. *ca.* 963–92), having observed the forcible conversion of Bohemia and its incorporation into the German kingdom, sought baptism directly from the pope and by doing so was able to maintain some measure of independence. Still, hoping to stay on good terms with the German king, he may have acknowledged the superiority of Otto III in 984. Mieszko succeeded in gaining control of Pomerania, which gave Poland an outlet to the Baltic Sea.

Mieszko's son Boleslaw I the Brave (r. 992–1025) solidified the relationship with Otto III, who visited Gniezno in 1000

and established an independent bishopric there. With that act, Otto revealed that he expected the Poles to be substantial partners in his empire.

Boleslaw extended the boundaries of the Polish state to the east and to the west. In the west, he added Lusatia up to the Saal River (a tributary of the Elbe), and in the east he reached the Dnieper and incorporated Red Ruthenia and Kiev into his kingdom. The pope crowned Boleslaw king of Poland just before he died (1025), but the ability of Boleslaw's successors to claim that title depended on the strength of the German monarchy at the time. The next Polish king, Boleslaw II (r. 1058–79), took advantage of Henry IV's preoccupation with the investiture controversy (see pp. 266–68) and crowned himself king in 1076.

The presence of the independent bishopric at Gniezno meant that Christianity would spread from a Polish rather than from a German center. As time passed, Gniezno established subordinate bishoprics at Płock in Mazovia in 1076, Lubus in Lusatia in 1128, and Wolin in Pomerania in 1140. Meanwhile, political unification under the Piasts continued to proceed until the end of the reign of Boleslaw III, who failed to have himself crowned king (r. as Duke of Poland 1102–38). For the next two hundred years, the various regions of the former kingdom were ruled by branches of the Piast family that steadfastly asserted their independence from one another.

Polish Society and the German Colonization

Under the Piast princes Polish society was dominated by noblemen living on sizable estates associated with peasant villages. The villagers were freemen who paid rent and were obligated to serve in the duke's army. As in the West, the Polish army consisted of a troop of mounted knights and peasant foot soldiers. Apparently, the peasants had not been reduced to servile status.

The eastern half of the North German Plain, from the Elbe River to the Urals, was only sparsely populated, and it seems

The farmers of eastern Europe were still using primitive methods, such as this unwheeled plow, in the thirteenth century.

that the Germans' more advanced farming techniques—such as the heavy wheeled plow, the use of horse power, and three-field rotation—had not penetrated this far. Here the peasants were still using the hook plough, a simple wooden implement that worked only in sandy soils and produced little reward for great effort. When the Polish lords and princes became aware of the superior technology of the West, they encouraged German peasants to colonize their land. Typically, they would hire a so-called locator to round up hundreds of German peasants and transport them to the east. There the locator would find a suitable site and settle the peasants in a new village. Each peasant would receive a homestead, and the locator would receive an estate and would become the mayor of the village. He would also preside over the village court, which heard less-important cases. Important cases or charges of serious crime were heard by a district court presided over by a representative of the prince.

To attract settlers, the princes offered low rents, light labor obligations—typically two to four days a year—and exemption from military service except in defense of the district. Often rent payments were suspended for the first ten or fifteen years to give the villagers a chance to make a good start in their new environment. The locator held a hereditary title to his estate and to his office as mayor and could pass them on to his heirs.

The extent of colonization varied from region to region. In the early thirteenth century, the Piast prince Henry I of Silesia (r. 1231–38) brought more than 10,000 German peasants to his province and settled them in 400 villages. His province became a patchwork of village communities, some under Polish law, some under German law. The settlers and their descendants held tenaciously to their native ways, and the Germans of Silesia are still a distinct ethnic community.

The Poles also encouraged the founding of new cities. Following the practice of the Germans, they gave their cities legal codes based on the law of Magdeburg, which assured them of substantial autonomy and freedom from feudal obligations.

During the thirteenth century even older Polish cities like Poznan and Cracow were brought under German law. To encourage the growth of the new cities, the Piast princes encouraged the settlement of merchants from Germany and the Baltic, and several Polish cities, including Gdansk (Danzig), Cracow, and Wroclaw, became members of the Hanseatic League, a confederation of Baltic cities that controlled northern trade during the thirteenth and fourteenth centuries.

The Polish princes also encouraged Jews to immigrate from Germany and Austria. In 1264, Prince Boleslaw V of Cracow (r. 1243–79) issued a General Charter of Jewish Liberties, which ensured the legal rights of Jews and permitted them to travel without restriction and to practice their religion without interference. Although some cities refused to abide by the charter, its issuance led to the emergence of a wealthy and powerful Jewish community in Poland. In the late Middle Ages, the Jews acted as a separate community with their own rabbis and secular leaders who dealt directly with the princes and lesser authorities.

The Reunification of Poland

Despite the years of political disunity, agriculture and trade flourished and by the late thirteenth century Poland had become relatively strong. Wladislaw I of Mazovia (r. 1306–33), sensing that the time had come to reunify the country, slowly began the process. Led by the archbishop of Gniezno, the Poles set about ridding themselves of the Germans. In 1320, in Cracow, Wladislaw was crowned King of Poland, the first Polish king since Boleslaw II in the eleventh century. He then tried to reclaim Kujawy and Pomerania from the Teutonic Knights (see pp. 341–42). Though he failed in that attempt, he left a strong kingdom to his son Kazimierz III (r. 1333–70).

Kazimierz began his reign by entering into a truce with the Teutonic Knights and arranging a treaty with the kings of Bohemia and Hungary. He paid the Bohemian king John of Luxembourg to give up his claim to Poland and agreed to arbitrate the status of Silesia. The arbitration went

Kazimierz III (from a seventeenth-century engraving).

in favor of Bohemia, and Kazimierz renounced the province in 1339. When he finally made a formal peace with the Teutonic Knights in 1343, he acquired Kujawy but gave up Pomerania. With the security he had gained through these settlements, he turned to other fronts. He successfully challenged the Bohemians for Swidnica, west of Silesia, gained control of Mazovia, Red Ruthenia, and the dukedom of Russia. In Red Ruthenia, he was challenging Lithuania and Hungary. By the end of his reign, Kazimierz had enlarged and unified the Polish state and had earned the sobriquet "the Great."

Yet Kazimierz was much more than a warrior king. In 1347, he issued a great codification of Polish law that served as the basis for legal reforms until the eighteenth century. He also created a royal bureaucracy to ensure the proper administration of the law, encouraged trade, and had fifty fortresses built across the country. As the condition of the country improved, many Polish cities undertook the construction of new buildings. Cracow, for example, tore down its old wooden buildings and replaced them with stone and brick buildings around a market square 200 yards on each side. By 1363, a new cathedral had been completed and a new royal castle was under construction. The renovation of the ancient St. Mary's

The square of a late medieval city.

church on the market square was begun; it took fifty years to complete.

In 1364, Kazimierz founded the University of Cracow, the first non-German university in eastern Europe. There he established chairs in the arts, medicine, and law; he named eight professors of law, reflecting his own deep interest in the subject.

During that same year Kazimierz hosted a meeting of five kings and five dukes in Cracow to discuss a new crusade against the Saracens. The meeting was prompted by the visit of Peter of Lusignan, king of Cyprus. Though the meeting produced no crusade, it furnished evidence of Kazimierz's prestige in the international community.

Kazimierz had many children, including several sons, but only his daughters were legitimate. Early in his reign, he arranged for King Louis of Hungary to succeed him if he died without a male heir, and immediately after his death Louis seized the kingship despite the opposition of the Polish churchmen and nobles. The Piast dynasty was at an end.

Under Louis (r. 1370–82) Poland entered into a long-lasting alliance with Hungary. He had no interest in preserving the strength of the Polish monarchy and consequently granted the nobles royal rights and land to keep them happy. By the end of his reign he had severely weakened the monarchy. He left no heir. With the concurrence of the Polish nobility, he was succeeded by his daughter Jadwiga, who was only eleven years old in 1382. (An older daughter was married to the emperor Sigismund of Luxembourg, who thereby added Hungary to his home kingdom of Bohemia.) Jadwiga was supposed to have married William of Habsburg, prince of Austria, but the Poles refused to accept a German king. Instead, she was married to Jagiello of Lithuania, creating a union of the two states and establishing a new dynasty in the process.

LITHUANIA-POLAND

The Lithuanians were an ancient Baltic people related to the Latvians and the Prussians. The Balts, as the members of this ethnic group have been called since the nineteenth century, were Indo-European peoples distinct from the Germans and Slavs. Latvian and Lithuanian are their only surviving languages. The Baltic tribes settled in northwestern Russia and along the eastern shore of the Baltic Sea, perhaps as early as the third millennium B.C. We know almost nothing about their history until the thirteenth century, however, when the Teutonic Knights began to subjugate them and forcibly convert them to Christianity.

The Teutonic Knights

The Order of St. Mary's Hospital in Jerusalem was one of several knightly orders founded in the Holy Land in the twelfth century to defend the new Latin states and to protect Christian pilgrims. The Order of

St. Mary's was made up of German knights who eventually became known as the Teutonic Knights. When Saladin took Jerusalem in 1187 (see p. 214), the Knights left the Levant and returned to Europe, looking for a crusade nearer home. After a short sojourn in Transylvania in Hungary, they were invited by the north German lords to help subjugate and convert the Pomeranians and Prussians, who lived along the Baltic coast. They arrived in Prussia in 1226 and began conquering the local tribes two years later.

The Knights, a highly organized group, had created an advanced administrative system while in the Levant. They now set about erecting a string of impregnable fortresses and, through the use of calculated cruelty, systematically reduced the pagan Prussians. By the early fourteenth century, the Teutonic Knights had

The Teutonic State and Lithuanian Empire   FOURTEENTH CENTURY created a powerful, well-run state in Prussia centered on the fortress of Marienburg.

Like the Poles, the Knights encouraged German immigration to their realm with offers of low rents and special concessions. They too used locators to settle new villages in their thinly populated region, and large parts of their state became Germanized. But unlike the Poles, the Knights encouraged the Prussian and Slavic peasants already in their realm to adopt the advanced agricultural methods of the Germans and to become Germanized. Gradually, the Prussian language and culture disappeared.

Beyond Prussia, the Knights conquered Samogitia, Courland, Livonia, and Estonia and forced the inhabitants to convert to Christianity. Though they still professed to be crusaders leading a monastic life, the Knights earned a reputation for viciousness and rapaciousness.

The Lithuanians

Toward the middle of the thirteenth century, under their leader Mindaugas (d. 1263), various Lithuanian tribes joined together to resist pressure of the Teutonic Knights. Under Mindaugas's successors, the Lithuanians extended their frontiers south and east into Russia, and in the first half of the fourteenth century Gedymin (r. 1316–41) created a powerful grand duchy centered on Vilna. He conquered all the land between the Baltic and the Black Sea, incorporating the Russian principalities of Smolensk and Kiev into his state. Lithuania now stood as the greatest state of eastern Europe. The Lithuanians saw themselves as the last practitioners of the ancient religion based on a pantheon headed by Perkun, the god of thunder. To them, the Christian god was a German god.

In 1377, Jagiello (r. 1377–1434) inherited the grand duchy at the age of 26. Notwithstanding his youth, Jagiello perceived that he was in great danger. The powerful state of Poland was now allied with Hungary, and the Teutonic Knights were at the height of their power. Searching for a way of safeguarding his duchy, he agreed to accept Christianity from the Poles and to marry their queen Jadwiga. The Poles welcomed this arrangement, because it eliminated a dangerous enemy and countered the power of the Habsburgs to the south and the Teutonic Knights to the north. In 1386, Jagiello was baptized, married to Jadwiga, and crowned King of Poland.

Under Jagiello, the Poles and Lithuanians were united in a single state, by far the largest and most powerful in eastern Europe. In 1413, the Polish and the Lithuanian nobles agreed to settle all matters of dispute in a joint assembly, and the Poles won the right to vote in the election of the Grand Duke of Lithuania.

Throughout the fifteenth century the neighbors of Poland-Lithuania were in a state of disarray. The Luxembourgs of Bohemia were preoccupied by disputes with their cousins in Hungary and with the Habsburgs of Austria. The Ottoman Turks, who had moved into southeastern Europe after taking Constantinople in 1453 (see p. 189), were trying to put down the resistance of the survivors of the Byzantine Empire and of the southern Slavs. To the east, the Mongol horde had split up into several unpredictable tribal states, and the Russian principalities were small and weak (see the next section). The Teutonic Knights were the only formidable enemy, and the Poles and Lithuanians fought them from 1409 to 1422, from 1454 to 1466, and from 1519 to 1521. Then suddenly, with the arrival of Luther's Reformation in Prussia, many of the Teutonic Knights switched to the new religion. In 1525, the Knights ceased to be a secular power, though to this day they continue to exist as a Catholic service organization with headquarters in Vienna.

Under Jagiello and his successors, who held the titles of King of Poland and Grand Duke of Lithuania, the Poles converted Lithuania to Christianity, bringing it into the mainstream of European civilization. Beginning with Zbigniew Olesnicki, bishop of Cracow (r. 1423–55), a remarkable series of Polish bishops pursued the mission in Lithuania while serving the kings at home. With the support of the nobility and the church, Jagiello reestablished the University of Cracow, which had ceased to exist after the death of Kazimierz, and encouraged cultural and economic activity. Salt production, metal production, and trade all increased, and Poland became a major supplier of raw materials. With the collapse of the Teutonic Knights, the Poles finally gained control of Gdansk and acquired a direct outlet to the Baltic through which they could ship goods to western Europe. The Polish kings were major patrons of the arts and sciences; Copernicus (1473–1543) was trained at the University of Cracow and conducted his revolutionary work in astronomy in East Prussia, which had become a fief of the Polish crown.

The fortunes of the Polish-Lithuanian state began to wane in the late sixteenth century. Moscow had succeeded in uniting the Russian principalities and had begun to behave aggressively toward its western neighbors. The last of Jagiello's successors, Sigismund II (r. 1548–72), was defeated by the Russians in the east, the Bohemians and Austrians in the south, and the Germans in the west. After his death the crown went first to the prince of Transylvania, a mountainous region in southeastern Hungary, and then to the king of Sweden. Poland-Lithuania was ruled by Swedish kings until the late seventeenth century.

RUSSIA

Throughout the Middle Ages, Russia was a sparsely populated region traversed by waves of migrating peoples. In the ninth century, Vikings traveled down the Dnieper River under their leader Ruric and settled at Kiev, which may already have been a trading center under the Khazars or even earlier. The Vikings made Kiev an important station on the trade route over which goods from the eastern Mediterranean traveled to northern Europe and Scandinavia. This trade brought the Kievan Rus, as the Vikings of the area were called, into contact with the Byzantine Empire, and in the spring of 860 the Kievans led a coalition of Slavic tribes in a surprise attack on Constantinople. In typical Viking

---

The Rus

In 860 the Rus led a large coalition of Slavic tribes in an attack on Constantinople. Not only were the Byzantines surprised by the attack, but they also had no knowledge of the Rus and their allies. The earliest description of the Rus comes from Ahmed ibn-Fadhlan, an Arab traveler of the first half of the tenth century.

I saw the Rus, when they arrived to trade and camped at the River [Volga]. I have never seen [people] with more perfect bodies than they had. They were like palm trees, blonde, with ruddy cheeks, and white skin. They wore neither jacket nor caftan; but the man wore a *kisa* [a kind of robe], which he wrapped around one shoulder off to one side so that one of his arms protruded from it. And each of them had an axe, sword, and knife, from which he was inseparable. . . . And from his nails to his neck he had green trees, figures, and other things painted on his body.

As regards their women, each wears on her breast a little box, either of iron or silver, copper, gold, or wood, corresponding to the wealth and position of her husband. . . . And around their necks were chains of gold and silver. . . .

The *Rus dirhem* [monetary unit] is a grey squirrel [pelt] without fur, brush, front and back paws and head; and the same goes for sables. If something was missing, the monetary value of the skin was less. They also use them for trade transactions and they cannot be exported because they exchange them for wares. They do not have scales, only standard metal bars. They use a measuring cup for buying and selling.

From I. Spector and M. Spector, eds. Readings in Russian History and Culture *(Palo Alto, CA: Pacific Books, 1965), pp. 14–15.*

---

fashion, the attackers appeared along the sea walls of the city in 200 small ships.

The Byzantines, shocked into awareness of the danger to their north, sent an embassy to the Khazars of the Crimea with whom the emperor hoped to form an alliance against Kiev; this was the embassy in which Constantine and his brother Methodius participated before being sent to Moravia (see p. 333). In the late 860s, the Byzantines also sent missionaries to Kiev. The mission succeeded at first, but it triggered a pagan reaction, which also succeeded. When Christian missionaries reappeared in Kiev in the 980s, they had to start from scratch. The Grand Prince of Kiev, Vladimir I (r. 980–1015), converted

The Church of the Savior at Novgorod (twelfth century). This is an early example of what became a typical style of ecclesiastical architecture in Russia.

During the twelfth century, after the Italians opened up new trade routes between Europe and the eastern Mediterranean (see p. 257), nomadic Pechenegs had arrived in the Ukraine from central Asia and raided the cities and countryside around Kiev. As a result, the center of power shifted to the north, and by the late twelfth century the principality of Suzdal had emerged as the strongest of the many small Russian principalities. During this time the town of Moscow was founded.

Early in the thirteenth century, Chengis (Genghis) Khan (*ca.* 1167–1227) had unified the Mongol tribes on the borders of China and had begun a western push across the steppes of central Asia. When Chengis Khan died, his khanate was divided among his sons, who continued his conquests. By 1234, one Mongol contingent had conquered Korea, and others had moved west into Russia. Another Mongol army crossed the Transoxiana into the Middle East, taking Baghdad in 1258 and Damascus in 1260. Later in 1260, the Mamluk Turks of Egypt defeated the Mongol invaders (see p. 214). The western contingent took Kiev in 1240 and reached the Adriatic Sea in 1242. At that point the Mongol leaders turned back and settled their army in the lower Volga Valley. They permitted the Russian principalities there to govern themselves but demanded heavy annual tribute and insisted on controlling the succession to the princely thrones.

The Mongol conquest cut the Russians off from the West but opened up contact with the advanced societies of the East. Then, in the fourteenth century, the Mongol empire broke up and Russia became isolated from both East and West. From then on, Russia's relations were mostly with the so-called Golden Horde—the Mongols living in the Volga region. Those Mongols dealt with any threat to their authority and failure to pay the tribute by destroying towns and massacring entire populations. To avoid such reprisals, the Russian princes asserted absolute control over their populations. They won the loyalty of the lesser nobles by permitting them to subjugate their peasants. Just when peasants in the West were beginning to achieve freedom from the obliga-

in 988, and the permanent Christianization of Russia proceeded from that date.

Russian society was transformed by conversion to Christianity. The church brought a literate culture to the Russians, but, as an alien institution it created a problem for Kievans, who were governed by customary law that did not cover the church. To fit the church into the community's life, the prince issued a statute that recorded and codified the customary law, with modifications introduced for the benefit of the churchmen.

ca. 800		1241	ca. 1400	1613
	Kievan Russia	Mongol Regime	Rise of Muscovy and Creation of Russian Empire	

tions of villeinage, the Russian peasants were being bound in serfdom.

During the fourteenth century, the principality of Moscow, which had become the center of the old principality of Suzdal, developed into the strongest state in Russia. For several generations, only one surviving heir to the Muscovite throne remained when the reigning prince died. So the successions were orderly, and Moscow avoided the strife that weakened many other states. Moreover, the bishop of Russia—the so-called metropolitan bishop—had moved his seat from Kiev to Moscow, suggesting that the Muscovite princes were the protectors of the church.

The Golden Horde soon came to work through the prince of Moscow in its dealings with Russians everywhere and accorded him the title Grand Prince to symbolize his role. Unwittingly, by so doing, they gave the various principalities a sense of unity and created a potential threat to their own power. They probably little suspected that the subject states might ever challenge the power they had endured so long, but late in the fourteenth century the Grand Prince of Moscow himself led a rebellion to throw off the Mongol yoke. A Russian army defeated the Mongols in 1378, but the Golden Horde struck back and destroyed the city of Moscow a few years later. During the next century, the Muscovite state began to absorb the neighboring principalities one by one, and at last, under Ivan III the Great (r. 1462–1505), it annexed the Republic of Novgorod, which controlled all of northern Russia. Now the Grand Prince was in a position to challenge the Golden Horde once again, and during the sixteenth century the Russians gradually took over the Mongol territories in the lower Volga region. Meanwhile, they were moving against Poland-Lithuania and claiming Kiev and its region as their patrimony. By the end of the century, Russia—once a tiny state of about 500 square miles—had become the largest empire in Europe.

With the rush of conquest and consolidation, the power of the Grand Prince of Moscow had risen steadily. The peasants had already lost their rights, and now most of the nobles lost their independence and

Alexander Nevsky

Throughout the first half of the thirteenth century the Russian city-states were threatened by Lithuanians, Swedes, and Prussians. After the arrival of the Teutonic Knights in Prussia, they became a great threat. One of the early heroes of the struggle against the Germans was Prince Alexander Nevsky of Novgorod. The Chronicle of Novgorod reports his great battle of 1242 on the frozen Lake Peipus (here called Chud) against the Knights and Prussians (men of Chud).

A.D. 1242. *Knyaz* [Prince] Alexander with the men of Novgorod and with his brother Andrei and the men of the lower country went in the winter in great strength against the land of the Chud people, against the *Nemsty* [German foreigners, the Teutonic Knights], that they might not boast, saying: "We will humble the Sloven race under us," for Pskov was already taken. . . . And when they came to their land, he [Alexander] let loose his whole force to provide for themselves. And Domash Tverdislavich and Kerbet were scouring [the country] and the *Nemsty* and Chud men met them by a bridge; and they fought there, and there they killed Domash . . . and others with him, and others again they took with their hands, and others escaped to the troops of the *Knyaz*. And the *Knyaz* turned back to the lake and the *Nemsty* and Chud men went after them. Seeing this, *Knyaz* Alexander and all the men of Novgorod drew up their forces by Lake Chud [Peipus] at Uzmen by the Raven's Rock; and the *Nemsty* and Chud men rode at them driving themselves like a wedge through their army; and there was a great slaughter of *Nemsty* and Chud men. And . . . God helped *Knyaz* Alexander. And the *Nemsty* fell there and the Chud men gave shoulder, and pursuing them fought with them on the ice, seven *versts* [about four and a half miles] short of the Subol shore. And there fell of the Chud men a countless number; and of the *Nemsty* 400, and fifty they took with their hands and brought to Novgorod.

From B. Dmytryshyn, ed., Medieval Russia: A Source Book, 900–1700 (New York: Holt, Rinehart and Winston, 1967), pp. 123–24.

The Growth of the Grand Principality of Moscow   1300–1584

Grand Principality
of Moscow, ca. 1300

Acquisitions to 1462

Acquisitions to the death
of Ivan III, 1505

Acquisitions to the death
of Ivan IV, 1584

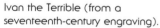

Ivan the Terrible (from a
seventeenth-century engraving).

became servants of the crown. The greatest men in the land could be put to death on the mere suspicion of disloyalty, and bishops who offended the sovereign were sent into exile. When Ivan the Great married Zoe, the niece of the last Byzantine emperor, he began to think of himself as successor to the Caesars and styled himself Autocrat and Sovereign of All Russia. Sometimes he called himself "tsar" (a Russian form of Caesar). That title did not become official, however, until the reign of Ivan IV the Terrible (r. 1533–84), one of the bloodiest tyrants in history, who massacred nobles and ordinary people on the smallest pretext and killed his own son in a fit of rage.

Russia was still a backward country, with none of the technology and commerce that had long fueled the economic development of western Europe. Russian peasants were still farming the poor soils of the north with their primitive tools and had not yet opened up the rich black earth of the Ukraine. Russia was also far behind the West in science and technology, and in scholarship and literature. Only after 1600 did the Russians embark on the economic and cultural advancement of their country.

HUNGARY

Hungary is situated on a true prairie, a flat grassland bordered by mountains on the north, south, and west. The region was ideally suited to the horsemen who rode west from the Asian steppes. The Huns, Avars, and Magyars all made it the center of short-lived empires. As we have seen, the Magyars, the last of these invaders, arrived late in the ninth century and for sixty years engaged in destructive raids deep into the western countries. They contributed to the collapse of the Moravian state, and their armies marched through Germany into France. Then in 955 Otto I of Germany defeated a large Hungarian army near Augsburg, and the raids came to an end. The Magyars settled down on their plain and began the slow process of building a state of their own. (The name Hungary derives from the name the western Europeans gave to the Magyars, Ugri or Ungri.)

Both the Byzantines and the western Europeans sent missionaries to Hungary and in 975, Geza (r. 972–96), the great-grandson of Arpad, the first known Hungarian chieftain, was baptized by western missionaries. Under his son Stephen (r. 996–1038) the country itself was converted to Christianity and, with the help of the papacy, established an organized church. In 1000, Stephen won from the pope the right to crown himself king, an act that made the kingdom a fief of the papacy and ensured Hungary's independence from its German and Slavic neighbors. Stephen was declared a saint in 1083.

The history of the Arpad dynasty (907–1301) is marked by constant strife between the rival claimants to the crown. In the twelfth century, following the practice of other eastern European rulers, the kings brought in peasants from the west to colonize their sparsely populated lands. Germans settled in northern and central Transylvania, and the Szekels, a people related to the Hungarians, settled in eastern Transylvania. These colonies were free communities governed by a provincial governor called a *voivode*.

In 1241, invading Mongols devastated the country and razed its cities. The popu-

---

The Court of Ivan the Terrible

In 1553 the Englishman Richard Chancellor visited Moscow. He had been seeking a northern passage to China and, failing, went to Moscow where he was received by Tsar Ivan. His description of the city and court follows.

The [city of] Moscow itself is great: I take the whole town to be greater than London with the suburbs: but it is very rude, and stands without all order. Their houses are all of timber, very dangerous for fire. There is a fair castle, the walls whereof are of brick, and very high: . . . the Emperor [Tsar] lies in the castle, wherein are nine fair Churches, and therein are religious men. Also there is a Metropolitan with diverse Bishops. . . .

The Emperor's or Duke's house neither in building nor in the outward show, nor yet within the house is so sumptuous as I have seen. It is very low built in eight squares, much like the old buildings of England, with small windows, and so in other points.

. . . I came into the Council chamber, where sat the Duke himself with his nobles, which were a fair company: they sat round about the chamber on high, yet so that he himself sat much higher than any of his nobles in a chair gilt, and in a long garment of beaten gold, with an imperial crown upon his head, and staff of crystal and gold in his right hand, and his other hand half leaning on his chair. . . .

From B. Dmytryshyn ed., Medieval Russia: A Source Book, 900–1700 *(New York: Holt, Rinehart and Winston, 1967), p. 188.*

---

lation was reduced by an estimated 60 percent, and in some areas inhabitants of whole communities either fled or were massacred. After the Mongols retreated to Russia, King Bela IV (r. 1235–70), who had taken refuge in Dalmatia, returned and began to rebuild the kingdom. But the disruption had been so severe that it was beyond his powers to restore the kingdom to what it had been. Many of the local lords acted with utter independence while claiming that they were still loyal to the crown. After the death of Bela's son, Ladislav IV (r. 1272–90), the nobles had to search about for a male member of the Arpad dynasty and finally found Andrew III (r. 1290–1301) in Italy. Andrew proved to be a good king, but he died without an heir and the nobles had to turn elsewhere for a successor.

The aspirants to the Hungarian throne were Charles Robert of Anjou, Wenceslas of Bohemia, and Otto of Bavaria. Wenceslas won out and managed to unite Bohemia, Poland, and Hungary under his rule. He was assassinated in 1306 and was succeeded by Charles Robert in 1308. Charles Robert (r. 1308–42), whose mother was an Arpad, was himself a scion of the royal house of Naples, which Charles of Anjou, the brother of Louis IX of France, had seized from the successors of Frederick II in 1266 (see p. 322). Still a boy when the Hungarian nobles elected him, Charles Robert grew up in Hungary.

Matthias I, the last native king of Hungary (from a seventeenth-century print).

The reigns of Charles Robert and his son Louis (r. 1342–82) were a time of prosperity for Hungary, Bohemia, and Poland. The Hungarians were working the gold mines in the Transylvanian Alps at full capacity, with about 40 percent of the production going to the king. Charles Robert and Louis patronized the arts, built grand buildings in the cities, and extended the kingdom. Louis, who was independently wealthy, was prodigal in granting rights and privileges to the nobility, and of course the nobility professed undying loyalty to him. In 1370, after the death of Kazimierz III, Louis was elected king of Poland and continued his liberal ways in dealing with the Polish nobles.

Louis left two daughters, Maria and Jadwiga, who inherited Hungary and Poland respectively. As we have seen, Jadwiga's marriage to Jagiello of Lithuania led to the founding of a new dynasty and to a lasting union with Lithuania. Maria was married to Sigismund of Luxembourg, who had himself crowned king of Hungary in 1387. From this time on, Hungary was a prize in the competition between the Luxembourgs and the Habsburgs of Austria, with the successors of Jagiello stepping in whenever they could. When Sigismund died, he left only a daughter. When she married Albrecht of Habsburg, Albrecht was accepted as king in Hungary. Then, when Albrecht died, in 1439, the nobles turned to Wladislaw Jagiello of Poland, who died fighting against the Ottomans in 1444.

He was succeeded by Albrecht's son Ladislav (r. 1444–57), but the real ruler of Hungary during Ladislav's reign was Janos Hunyadi, a great general. Hunyadi led the fight against the Ottomans until his death in 1456 and was then succeeded as general by his son Matthias Corvinus, who was elected king after Ladislav's death.

Matthias (r. 1457–90), the last Hungarian king of Hungary and a man of exceptional ability, held off the Ottomans and other enemies, rebuilt the cities, and assembled a huge collection of art, jewelry, and manuscripts. Using the wealth of the gold mines and whatever he could squeeze from the peasants, he brought

Silesia, Bohemia, and lower Austria under Hungarian control. But after his death, in 1490, those provinces fell away and the kingdom declined under a succession of weak kings. The Hungarian alliance with Poland remained in effect, but the Habsburgs proceeded to incorporate the rest of eastern Europe into their growing empire.

Suggestions for Further Reading

General

On the early Slavic migrations and culture, see F. Graus, "Slavs and Germans," in *Eastern and Western Europe in the Middle Ages,* ed. by G. Barraclough (1970). All the essays in this book are useful. In general, see F. Dvornik, *The Making of Central and Eastern Europe* (1949), and A. P. Vlasto, *The Entry of the Slavs into Christendom* (1970). Dvornik's *Byzantine Missions among the Slavs* (1970) is extremely useful for the settlement and conversion of the Croats and Serbs and for the mission of Constantine and Methodius. I. Boba, *Moravia's History Reconsidered* (1971), made the case that the Moravia of the mission was centered on Sirmium/Morava south of the Danube. On the history of the Bulgars, see R. E. Sullivan, "Khan Boris and the Conversion of Bulgaria. A Case Study of the Impact of Christianity on a Barbarian Society," *Studies in Medieval and Renaissance History* 3 (1966), and, from the Byzantine perspective, R. Browning, *Byzantium and Bulgaria* (1975).

Bohemia

Both Dvornik and Boba have much to say about the early medieval history of Bohemia. See also A. H. Hermann, *A History of the Czechs* (1975). Because of its close connection with Germany, comprehensive histories of medieval Germany have a good deal of information about Bohemia.

Poland

Norman Davies, *God's Playground: A History of Poland,* 2 vols. (1982), sets a new standard. *The Cambridge History of Poland,* 2 vols., ed. by W. Reddaway (1941, 1950) remains useful. For the late Piast period, see P. W. Knoll, *The Rise of the Polish Monarchy: Piast Poland in East Central Europe 1320–70* (1972). On Lithuania, see C. R. Jurgela, *History of the Lithuanian Nation* (1948), which historians consider flawed. O. Halecki, *The Borderlands of Western Civilization* (1952), is useful on Lithuania. See also J. R. Koncius, *Vlautas the Great, Grand Duke of Lithuania* (1964). *Baltic History,* eds. A. Ziedonis, W. L. Winter, and M. Valgemäe (1973), contains several articles of interest.

The Teutonic Knights

F. L. Carsten, *The Origin of Prussia* (1954), is the best work on the state created by the Teutonic Knights. For a general history of the order, see C. Krollmann, *The Teutonic Order in Prussia* (1938), and K. Gorski, "The Teutonic Order in Prussia," *Medievalia et Humanistica* 17 (1966). See also W. Urban, *The Baltic Crusade* (1975), which treats the Knights' conquest of Livonia and Estonia. For a broader view of the northern crusades, see E. Christiansen, *The Northern Crusades* (1980).

Russia

For a comprehensive survey of Russian history, see G. Vernadsky and M. Karpovich, *A History of Russia,* 5 vols. (1943–69). N. V. Riasanovsky, *A History of Russia,* 4th ed. (1984), and G. Vernadsky, *Russia at the Dawn of the Modern Age* (1959), are good one-volume surveys. See also F. Nowak, *Medieval Slavdom and the Rise of Russia* (1930). On the first entry of the Russians into Mediterranean history, see A. A. Vasiliev, *The Russian Attack on Constantinople in 860* (1946). On the Mongols in Russia, see G. Vernadsky, *The Mongols and Russia* (1953), and on the rise of Moscow, see J. Fennell, *Ivan the Great of Moscow* (1961). J. Blum, *Lord and Peasant in Russia from the Ninth to the Nineteenth Century* (1961), is an excellent study of social history. There is also a great deal of social history in D. H. Kaiser, *The Growth of Law in Medieval Russia* (1980). On the Khazars, see D. M. Dunlop, *The History of the Jewish Khazars* (1954).

Hungary

For a brief survey of the history of Hungary, see D. Sinor, *A Short History of Hungary* (1959), and C. A. Macartney, *Hungary: A Short History* (1962). On the early period of Magyar settlement, see C. A. Macartney, *The Magyars in the Ninth Century* (1930). On the Ottoman threat, see P. Coles, *The Ottoman Impact on Europe* (1968).

14

THE LATE MIDDLE AGES

The fourteenth and fifteenth centuries were a time of chaos in western Europe. Decade after decade, Europeans were beset by drought, arctic winters, economic depression, war, rebellion, and plague. Neither ecclesiastical nor secular governments seemed capable of easing the distress, and at times the whole structure of European society seemed to be crumbling. Yet the social and political institutions that emerged from this troubled time turned out to be the most powerful in the world. The science and technology, the great navies and armies, the government institutions and the business structures that were to give Europe world supremacy for 400 years all took shape during the stretch of history marked by the Hundred Years' War, the Black Death, and the Great Schism.

THE TROUBLES OF THE FOURTEENTH CENTURY

Climate, Economic Depression, and Population Decline

From the eleventh century to the end of the thirteenth, the economy and population of Europe had been growing steadily. Peasant villages prospered and new lands were put under cultivation or reclaimed after centuries of neglect. The cities and their lords, looking to a bright future, undertook ambitious projects such as draining the Roman marshes and building dikes in the Netherlands. Though much of the land they brought into production was marginal, the projects seemed justified by the needs and opportunities of the time.

Then, around the middle of the thirteenth century, just as medieval civilization was reaching its height, a mini–ice

European Population[a]
A.D. 900–1300

A.D. 900

Iberian Peninsula	4,000,000
France	5,000,000
Italy	4,000,000
Germany/Scandinavia	4,000,000
British Isles	1,500,000
	18,500,000

A.D. 1100

Iberian Peninsula	7,000,000
France	6,200,000
Italy	6,000,000
Germany/Scandinavia	4,500,000
British Isles	2,000,000
	25,700,000

A.D. 1300

Iberian Peninsula	9,500,000
France	14,000,000
Italy	9,300,000
Germany/Scandinavia	11,500,000
British Isles	5,300,000
	49,600,000

[a]*Figures exclude eastern Europe.*

level. As the population declined, it grew weaker and more susceptible to disease.

The poor harvests triggered an economic depression that affected every region and every class. The cities had become dependent on the agricultural surplus, which had been reliable and substantial for many decades and had provided the main commodities for trade. The kings and barons relied for their income on the produce of the farmland or on land rents. And the large landholders, who had taken back their land from leaseholders to farm the lands themselves, suffered along with the peasants.

In the wake of the poor harvests, inflation set in, raising the prices of food and other farm products such as wool and flax. The higher prices in turn drove up the prices of manufactured goods. People on fixed incomes struggled to make ends meet, and a noticeable rise in government corruption occurred as officials came to depend on bribes and gifts as part of their income. People everywhere complained of the venality of the government and the church, and the moral authority of both declined.

The Bubonic Plague

Then, in 1348, bubonic plague swept across Europe. Bubonic plague is a bacterial disease spread by fleas that have bitten infected rats. It originated in southeast Asia and spread along the trade routes to the Middle East. From there it jumped to Constantinople, then to Italy, and then to all of Europe. In just two years, the plague killed about a third of the population; in some places the mortality rate was 80 percent. This first onslaught earned the name The Black Death, but the disease continued to appear here and there until around 1700.

The effect was enormous. Villages and farms were abandoned, and the labor force withered. Many of the peasants who survived migrated to the cities to replace workers who had died. The condition of the peasants who stayed in the countryside seems to have improved for a short time. They could now demand high wages

age set in. It was felt first in the far north, in Greenland, where communities established by Icelanders centuries before had to be abandoned. In 1258 the Icelanders officially declared that they would no longer try to ship goods to Greenland. In Europe, the change was felt later. Toward the end of the century, a series of bad harvests put an intolerable strain on the over-extended farmlands of Europe and brought widespread famine. By 1300, the population had ceased to grow and was even beginning to decline. Even worse famine struck in 1315–17 and had a devastating effect on the peasants, who had already lost their earlier prosperity and were living not far above the subsistence

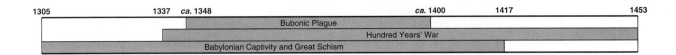

1305		1337	*ca.* 1348		*ca.* 1400	1417	1453

Bubonic Plague

Hundred Years' War

Babylonian Captivity and Great Schism

for their labor on the lords' demesnes enabling them to purchase the land of the peasants who had died, or to buy a release from their feudal obligations. For a few years everyone had more money, with incomes rising a bit faster than prices. But the prosperity was illusory, based on inflation rather than on an expanding market, and soon production fell to the level of demand.

In the cities, employers trying to reduce costs sought to roll wages back to the level of 1348. The kings supported them. England, for example, enacted the Statute of Laborers (1351) and other laws that required workers to accept customary wages (that is, the wages prevailing before the plague) and fixed the prices of food and other basic necessities at the 1348 level. Other kingdoms passed similar legislation.

Wages in the countryside continued to rise, however, and landholders tried to hold their peasants to the customary labor services they were obligated to supply, including plowing and harvesting, mending fences, and constructing buildings. In fact, lords now demanded that their peasants provide those services that in the past the peasants had usually managed to avoid. Some lords, finding labor costs too high to make farming cost-effective, leased their estates and let others worry about the problem.

In either case—whether the lord enforced customary services or converted the entire manor into rent-paying tenancies—the interests of the peasants and the landholder clashed. The peasants agitated for the commutation of the customary services into cash rents, because they would be better off either selling their crops or working as paid laborers. As time passed, the landholders tried to compensate for their declining income by enforcing their rights over the manorial commons, such as the meadows, fisheries, pastures, and woods, and by demanding the customary payments for the use of mills, ovens, and other "appurtenances." At last a demand arose for the abolition of all manorial obligations.

The lot of the workers in the towns and cities was no better than that of the peasants. Employers, craft guilds, and government officials all conspired to keep wages low and to protect local markets from outside competition. After the plague, artisans found it harder than ever to gain admittance into the craft guilds, and the gulf between masters and workers widened.

Miniature painting of a fourteenth-century pewterer turning a jug on a lathe, from the *Guild Book* of the Twelve Brothers' Foundation in Nuremburg.

The Black Death in England

Then that most grievous pestilence penetrated the coastal regions by way of Southampton and came to Bristol, and people died as if the whole strength of the city were seized by sudden death. For there were few who lay in their beds more than three days or two and a half days; then that savage death snatched them about the second day. In Leicester, in the little parish of St. Leonard, more than three hundred and eighty died; in the parish of the Holy Cross, more than four hundred, and in the parish of St. Margaret, more than seven hundred. . . .

And the price of everything was cheap, because of the fear of death, there were very few who took any care for their wealth, or for anything else. For a man could buy a horse for half a mark [about 7 shillings] which before was worth forty shillings, a large fat ox for four shillings, a cow for twelve pence, a heifer for sixpence, a large fat sheep for four pence. . . . And the sheep and cattle wandered about through the fields and among the crops, and there was no one to go after them or collect them. They perished in countless numbers everywhere, for lack of watching . . . since there was such a lack of serfs and servants, that no one knew what he should do. For there is no memory of a mortality so severe and so savage. . . . In the following autumn, one could not hire a reaper for less than eight pence [per day] with food, or a mower at less than twelve pence with food.

From Henry Knighton, Chronicle, *in* The Portable Medieval Reader, *ed by J. B. Ross and M. M. McLaublin (New York: Viking, 1949), pp. 218–19.*

The merchants and aristocrats responded to the disorder by behaving more harshly and more inflexibly than before. The medieval notion that everyone in the community had both rights and duties gradually gave way to the notion that the upper classes had all the rights and none of the duties.

As the turmoil and unrest intensified, people became susceptible to all sorts of fears and rumors. From the mid-fourteenth century on, several spiritual movements arose proclaiming that the end of the world was nigh. Even before the plague, in 1327, a rumor had spread in France that Jews and lepers were plotting to overthrow Christendom, and many people had lost their lives in the riots and trials that followed. In the latter part of the century, groups of flagellants wandered the countryside preaching the end of the world and scourging themselves with whips and ropes. Artists featured the figure of Death in their paintings, and villagers paraded through the streets in the "dance of death." Many preachers declared that God was punishing Christendom because the popes had withdrawn to Avignon.

Neither the workers nor the peasants had any legal means for improving their lot, and discontent grew. The Flemish towns experienced rebellions in 1255, 1267, 1275, 1280, and 1302, and everywhere in Europe the towns suffered riots and unrest throughout the fourteenth century. In Florence, the *popolo minuto*—the "little people"—rebelled against the government in 1378 in the so-called Ciompi rising.

In France, the peasants staged a rebellion in 1358, killing hundreds of nobles and their families and burning their manors. In the Peasants' Revolt of 1381 in England, rebellious mobs caused widespread damage and called for social reforms that would have transformed English society.

THE AVIGNON PAPACY AND THE GREAT SCHISM

Papal Government at Avignon

The city of Avignon, where Clement V (r. 1305–14), the former archbishop of Bordeaux, settled (see p. 326), was French in everything but political allegiance. It was an imperial city—with a charter from the emperor—situated in a county of Provence that belonged to the papacy. Clement V filled vacancies in the college of cardinals with Frenchmen, who in 1314 elected another French pope and stayed where they were. Until the end of the Avignon papacy, all the popes and most of the cardinals were French.

On the whole, the Avignon popes were able men, though not outstanding religious figures. Their talents lay in administration, law, and finance, and under them the centralization and bureau-cratization of the church, begun in the eleventh century, reached its culmination. For example, John XXII (r. 1316–34), who believed that the papacy had to have the financial resources to stand up against the secular powers, developed a financial sys-tem that funnelled a great deal of the money taken in by the church to the papal curia. The curia also strengthened its con-trol over all church business. The result-ing proliferation of offices and officials made the papal government the largest in Europe and helped consolidate its con-trol over ecclesiastical offices throughout Christendom. From this time on, anyone who sought a post in a bishopric had to apply to the papacy; consequently, the bishops, who were themselves pa-pal appointees, lost control over their own sees.

The papal government at Avignon was divided into four main branches: the chancery, the *camera apostolica* (the ap-ostolic chamber), the Datary, and the judi-ciary. By the fourteenth century, the papal chancery, the first to develop, consisted of seven offices that prepared and dis-patched routine administrative correspon-dence and documents. It also received petitions for papal action, reviewed the qualifications of candidates for ecclesiasti-cal offices, and had official custody of the curial records.

The *camera apostolica* had emerged as a separate financial department dur-ing the thirteenth century, and under John XXII and his successors it expanded enormously. Its administrative head was the treasurer, and its policy-making head was the chamberlain. The title indicates that the chamberlain was once a house-hold officer of the popes, and he was still chosen from the pope's personal entou-rage. At Avignon, the chamberlain became in effect the prime minister of the papacy. He handled most of the instructions sent to papal legates and ambassadors and nearly all the private and secret correspon-dence of the popes. He also controlled the papal mint, the tax collectors, and the papacy's extensive courier system. More-over, he was responsible for the receipt and auditing of all papal revenues and

Manuscript illustration of the crucial point in the meeting of Richard II with the main body of the rebels during the Peasants' Revolt of 1381. Its leader, Wat Tyler, is being struck down by one of Richard's men.

supervised a court that heard disputes over papal finances.

The Datary was set up as a separate department in the first half of the four-teenth century to take over some of the chancery functions. It handled petitions that did not require judicial action. In cases that involved no dispute, the Datary disposed of appointments to benefices (income-producing properties), dispensa-tions from provisions of the canon law (especially in routine cases of irregularities in marriages), and the granting of papal approval for the disposition of church property or offices.

The papal judiciary was an elaborate court system. The highest court in that system was the Consistory, which con-sisted of the pope and all the cardinals. The Consistory referred most cases that came before it to judges in the diocese or province from which they came—the judges-delegate—or to one of the lesser tribunals of the curia. Any number of cardinals could consitute a court to hear a particular case, but such courts tended to refer cases to trained auditors. Routine cases were handled by the *Rota*. A panel of auditors chosen from the judges who made up the *Rota* heard each case, and judgment was pronounced by all the judges after they had reviewed the evi-dence and the arguments. At any stage in

Death was a favorite subject for illustration in the late Middle Ages. Shown here is the Dance of Death from a manuscript of *ca.* 1400. Death, playing a trumpet decked with the papal banner of the keys of St. Peter, summons a pope.

the proceedings, a case could be referred to a special tribunal called the *Audientia* for a ruling on technical points and on the authenticity of the documentary evidence. Litigation in the papal courts was complicated and expensive and consequently was ideal for defendants who sought to delay the settlement of a case.

The pope and cardinals spent most of their time running the vast machinery of the papal government, and the cost of running the bureaucracy led them into what some critics denounced as rapacious practices. Disaffected by the wealth and worldliness of the Avignon papacy, many intellectuals withdrew their support. One of them was Petrarch (1304–74), the poet and scholar who coined the term "Babylonian Exile" (see p. 326). Saint Catherine of Siena (1347–80) bombarded the papacy with letters demanding that it return to Rome, and in a dispute with John XXII the emperor Ludwig IV of Bavaria (r. 1314–47) denounced the papacy as an institution subverted by political ambition and ill-gotten wealth.

As time went by, pressure intensified for the popes to return to Rome. Conditions in Rome, long subject to internecine conflict among the noble families and their supporters, improved during the reign of Pope Innocent VI (r. 1352–62), and in 1356 the treaty that ended the first phase of the Hundred Years' War (see below) led to the release of marauding bands of mercenaries who disrupted the peaceful atmosphere of Avignon. Urban V (r. 1362–70) returned the curia to Rome for a time, but after three years of vain attempts to reestablish papal authority in the Holy City, he went back to Avignon. Gregory XI (r. 1370–78) also returned to Rome, but he too failed and planned to retreat to Avignon. He died before he could do so, however, and left the cardinals in Rome threatened by a mob demanding election of an Italian pope. After electing the archbishop of Bari, many of the cardinals retreated to Avignon anyway. But the new pope, Urban VI (r. 1378–89), turned out to be a reformer determined to put an end to the corrupt practices of the curia. The Avignon contingent, seeking to preserve the system that had brought them wealth and

power, declared Urban's election invalid on the grounds that it had been held under the coercion of the mob. They then elected the Frenchman Robert of Geneva as Clement VII (r. 1378–94). Thus arose the Great Schism in the medieval papacy.

The Great Schism

With two popes, each claiming the authority to tax, the cost of running the papal government became doubly burdensome. To make matters worse, the popes hurled anathemas at each other, and the cry of scandal was added to other complaints. The secular rulers of Europe lined up on one side or the other depending on their own political interests. The French and their allies—Scotland, Navarre, Castile, Aragon, and various German dukes—supported Clement in Avignon. The enemies of France—England, Flanders, Portugal, the emperor Wenceslas, most of the German dukes, Bohemia, and Hungary—supported Urban in Rome. The Italian city-states were divided and regularly switched their allegiance from one pope to the other.

To resolve the schism, some churchmen proposed that both popes resign and that the combined colleges of cardinals elect a new pope. But the cardinals did not trust one another, and the popes themselves refused to take the first step toward this solution. Other churchmen, led by the members of the theology faculty at the University of Paris, suggested that a general council be called to decide the issue. This was an attractive idea, but it was not clear whether canon law permitted a council to depose a pope. For hundreds of years, at least since the reform movement of the eleventh century (see pp. 265–66), the church had emphasized the supremacy of the pope in ecclesiastical affairs. The pope was the supreme judge who "judges all and is judged by no one." He was the supreme legislator; no ecclesiastical law was valid without his approval. He was the one who summoned and presided over councils. As far back as the ninth century, when Leo III (r. 795–816) was charged with crimes, the bishops assembled by Charles the Great had declared that they could not judge the pope; only God could do so (see p. 229).

Twelfth-century canonists had already wrestled with the issues raised by this hierarchical view of the church. They had wondered what would happen if the pope, who was a man like other men, committed a crime or fell into theological error. How would the church deal with such a crisis? By the beginning of the thirteenth century, the canonists had worked out a theory that Jesus's promise in the statement "You are Peter . . . and the gates of Hell shall not prevail [against Peter and the church]" (Matt. 16.18)—that is, Peter or the church would never fall into sin— did not apply to the pope, Peter's successor, but to the church. If this interpretation was true, then a general council could be called to deal with an errant pope.

This idea was revived at the time of the Great Schism. The churchmen wanted to call a council to decide who was the true pope but were unsure of how to go about calling one. Some argued that the emperor could summon it, citing the example of Constantine I who had summoned the Council of Nicaea (see p. 118). Others thought that the college of cardinals could summon it. But many of them thought that only the pope had the authority to summon a council.

Given the failure of the churchmen to agree on how to summon a council, the schism dragged on. When Urban and Clement died, in 1389 and 1394 respectively, each college of cardinals elected its own pope, and both of them continued to claim the title.

In 1409, members of the so-called conciliar movement took the first step toward solving the problem by convincing the cardinals on both sides to cooperate in a council to be held at Pisa. Five hundred prelates came to the council and proceeded to depose both popes—Benedict XIII (r. 1394–1423) of Avignon, and Gregory XII (r. 1406–15) of Rome—as "schismatics and notorious heretics." Then they authorized the assembled cardinals to elect a new pope. The cardinals elected Alexander V (r. 1409–10). Benedict and Gregory promptly denounced both the council and the newly elected pope and,

The Great Schism   1378–1417

Land giving allegiance to Rome

Land giving allegiance to Avignon

Shifting and divided

with the support of their secular backers, continued as before. Alexander died while the council was still in session, and the cardinals immediately elected yet another pope, John XXIII (r. 1410–15). To the surprise of all, John asserted that as pope he had a higher authority and declared the council at an end. The churchmen left Pisa having accomplished nothing.

There were immediate calls for a new council, and finally, in 1414, John XXIII summoned a general council to meet at Constance. The council met and soon proceeded to depose all three popes. Gregory XII had anticipated the council's action and had sent out a call to the council himself, on the grounds that he was the true pope. He then abdicated (1415). John XXIII was forced to abdicate the

A manuscript illumination showing an antipope receiving his crown from the devil and in turn crowning an emperor as a pledge of mutual support against the true head of the church.

same year.* Benedict XIII, the Avignon pope, who was then 87 years old, refused to step down and retreated to his castle in Spain, where he died in 1423 still maintaining that he was the true pope. In 1417, the council elected a new pope, Martin V (r. 1417–31).

Seeking to confirm its place in the church's constitution, the council passed a decree that declared that a general council represented the whole church, held its power directly from Christ, and must be obeyed by all men including the pope in matters pertaining to the faith, the abolition of schism, and reform. Having established its legitimacy as a divine institution

* John, though he had called the council and had given it legitimacy, was not considered a true pope. So when in 1958 a new pope took the name John, he was designated the twenty-third of that name, John XXIII (r. 1958–63).

of the church, the council passed another decree requiring that a general council be held every five years.

As a cardinal, Martin V had supported the conciliar movement, but as pope he worked hard to reestablish papal supremacy over the councils. He and his successors succeeded in rendering the councils that met after Constance ineffective, but the Great Schism and the conciliar movement had in effect destroyed the medieval papacy. The popes no longer commanded the extraordinary prestige and power they had commanded since the eleventh century, and the papacy gradually declined to the status of an Italian principality.

ENGLAND IN THE LATER MIDDLE AGES

The expansionist policies of Edward I (see p. 314) had severely strained England's resources, and it was predictable that a reaction would set in after his death in 1307. The reaction was more acute than it might have been, however, because his son Edward II (r. 1307–27) proved a weak-willed, incompetent ruler. Instead of taking up the reins of government, he left them to civil servants and personal favorites. Finally, a group of barons, calling themselves the Lords Ordainers, obliged Edward to accept the Ordinances of 1311, which curtailed the authority of the royal household and required approval by Parliament of appointments to high government offices and of important policy decisions. The defeat of Edward's armies by the Scots at Bannockburn in 1314 further discredited him and left the barons in almost complete control of the government. But they too proved incompetent, and in 1322 a royalist party restored Edward to power. He immediately nullified the Ordinances but publicly acknowledged the validity of the idea that important legislation should be enacted in Parliament. Soon, however, Edward again succumbed to the influence of favorites. His farcical reign climaxed when his queen Isabelle ran off with her lover Mortimer, with whom she then led a successful rebellion against her husband. Edward was imprisoned and executed in 1327.

Edward III (r. 1327–77) was still a minor when he succeeded to the throne, and Isabelle and Mortimer ruled as regents. In 1330 the young king overthrew the regency in a *coup d'état* that cost Mortimer his life and Isabelle her freedom. Edward then took over the government and appeased the barons with minor concessions. In 1333 he defeated the Scots at Halidon Hill. Although the battle was of no great importance, it taught Edward that a war was a good way of distracting the barons from domestic grievances. He was soon to test that lesson in a war with France.

The Hundred Years' War: The First Phase

As we have seen, war between England and France had broken out under Edward I and Philip the Fair and had led to the defeat of the papacy as arbiter of what kings could do in their own kingdoms (pp. 324–25). During the 1290s and the early 1300s neither Edward nor Philip had been in a position to mount a major campaign. Philip had been occupied with Flanders and with building up his power over the great feudal lords of his realm, and Edward had been intent on the conquest of Scotland, which had not gone well. Under Edward II, the war with France had petered out.

Edward III took it up again in 1340. There were many causes of conflict— competition over trade in Flanders (which depended on English wool), French support of Scotland, and the old English claim to Normandy and other French territory. But the immediate cause of the war was Edward's claim to the French crown

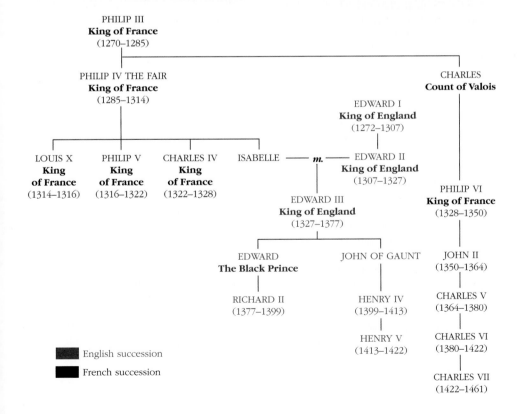

THE FRENCH AND ENGLISH SUCCESSIONS

PHILIP III
King of France
(1270–1285)

PHILIP IV THE FAIR
King of France
(1285–1314)

CHARLES
Count of Valois

EDWARD I
King of England
(1272–1307)

LOUIS X
King of France
(1314–1316)

PHILIP V
King of France
(1316–1322)

CHARLES IV
King of France
(1322–1328)

ISABELLE —— *m.* —— EDWARD II
King of England
(1307–1327)

PHILIP VI
King of France
(1328–1350)

EDWARD III
King of England
(1327–1377)

EDWARD
The Black Prince

JOHN OF GAUNT

JOHN II
(1350–1364)

RICHARD II
(1377–1399)

HENRY IV
(1399–1413)

CHARLES V
(1364–1380)

HENRY V
(1413–1422)

CHARLES VI
(1380–1422)

CHARLES VII
(1422–1461)

English succession

French succession

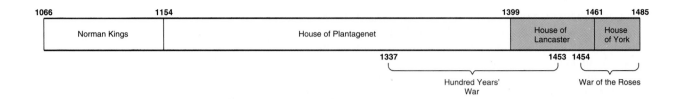

1066		1154		1399	1461	1485
Norman Kings		House of Plantagenet		House of Lancaster	House of York	

Hundred Years' War 1337 — 1453

War of the Roses 1454 — 1485

The Battle of Sluys in 1340 established English control of the Channel. This illustration from a copy of Froissart's *Chronicles,* which recount the first half of the Hundred Years' War, shows an English ship engaging a French vessel.

through his mother. The king of France at the time was Philip VI (r. 1328–50), descended from Philip III (r. 1270–85) through Charles of Anjou, Philip the Fair's brother. And Edward was Philip the Fair's grandson. No matter how the lawyers figured these relationships, Edward III was one degree closer to the French throne than Philip VI. But there were two problems: First, Edward's claim descended through a female, and the French lawyers argued that one who could not inherit the crown could not transmit it. Second, the French royal council would not accept Edward as king.

The war began with an amazing string of English victories. Edward won a naval battle at Sluys (1340), which gave him control of the English Channel. Then his army nearly annihilated the French army at Crécy (1346) and went on to capture Calais, which was to remain an English port for two centuries. Ten years later, his son Edward, called the Black Prince, defeated the French at Poitiers and captured King John of France. That battle ended the first phase of the war (1340–56). In the treaty that followed, the French agreed to pay a huge ransom for the release of their king and to cede about two-fifths of their country to the English. Edward III had reconquered most of the territories his ancestor King John had lost to the French in 1204.

Between the major battles of the war, the English conducted campaigns marked by systematic destruction. (A nineteenth-century historian published a list of substantial buildings destroyed that required two large volumes.) Moreover, in battle the English troops were armed with the highly effective longbow, a weapon developed during Edward I's reign. This weapon propelled an arrow with great power, had a long range, and could be reloaded rapidly. It could even penetrate chain mail. At Crécy, 15,000 English bowmen nearly wiped out 60,000 mounted French knights.

After the treaty of 1356, France fell into economic decline. The burden of the heavy ransom, together with the ravages of the Black Death, brought ruin to peasants and merchants alike and led to the great uprising of 1358, which was put down only after much bloodshed (see p. 354). The end of the war also led to the release of many mercenaries who turned to banditry and plagued cities and towns throughout the country, including Avignon.

England after Edward III

Edward, the Black Prince, predeceased his father, and Edward III was succeeded by his grandson Richard II (r. 1377–99). Richard was a boy when he became king, and the government was run by relatives and barons whose ineffectiveness prompted the peasant rebellion of 1381 (see p. 354). When Richard came of age in 1386, he set about restoring royal authority.

But Richard faced serious obstacles. Since the early days of the Hundred Years' War, most of the armed forces that England put into the field had been private companies paid by the king but recruited and commanded by the barons. That meant that any lord with a taste for war could maintain his own little army at government expense, a dangerous situation. Moreover, in trying to gain control of the government Richard had exiled the leading barons who opposed him and had confiscated their land. That action had united the barons who remained in England and had actually weakened Richard's position. In 1399 the barons rose in rebellion under Richard's cousin Henry of Lancaster, one of the barons Richard had deprived of his land and exiled a few years earlier. At a session of Parliament known as the Great Parliament, Henry had Richard deposed and then mounted the throne as Henry IV (r. 1399–1413). Richard died in prison.

The Hundred Years' War: The Second Phase

The Lancastrian kings, who ruled from 1399 to 1461, never quite lived down the violence by which Henry IV had seized the crown. Henry himself had to put down two dangerous rebellions, and his son Henry V (r. 1413–22) tried to rally the kingdom behind him by renewing the war with France. Henry V was a brilliant commander, and in 1415 at Agincourt in Normandy his small army of bowmen destroyed a French army of mounted knights. He was also the first to use siege artillery against walled cities (see p. 373).

After Agincourt, Henry entered into an alliance with the Duke of Burgundy—the most powerful lord in France after the king—and the French king Charles VI (r. 1380–1422) was obliged to accept a treaty. In 1421, according to that treaty, Charles disinherited his son, married his daughter to Henry V, and recognized that any son born of that union would inherit the French throne. When both Charles and Henry V died the next year, the two thrones were inherited by nine-month-old Henry VI.

The coronation led to a bitter struggle among the infant's uncles and cousins over who would govern in his name. Still, the English managed to deal with Charles VII, the disinherited son of Charles VI, when he renounced the treaty of 1421. They forced him to flee south of the Loire, and for a time it looked as if the English would be able to reinstate the terms of the treaty. Then the tide was turned by the appearance of a young woman, Joan of Arc.

Joan believed that she had been sent by God to rescue Charles VII and the French kingdom from the English. After overcoming the skepticism of the French court, she led a French force to victory at Patay near Orléans in 1429. Soon afterward, the English captured her and burned her as a witch. (The judgment was reversed and Joan was canonized as a saint in 1929.) At this point, the alliance between England and Burgundy broke down, and the French embarked on a war of attrition against the English. By 1453, only the port city of Calais remained in English hands, and the war came to an end.

The Hundred Years' War   1337–1453

During the long war the old French aristocracy had been decimated by the English victories, and with the return of peace Charles VII named many members of the bourgeoisie as counselors and royal servants. His son Louis XI (r. 1461–83) continued that practice, and in his able hands France emerged as a strong bureaucratic state ruled by a king unfettered by the claims of baronial families.

In England, royal authority had been weakened by the competition over the regency during Henry VI's childhood, and the weakness was prolonged by Henry's mental instability. Throughout his adult life, he alternated between sanity and insanity and never succeeded in establishing a stable government. Moreover, the English setbacks during the closing years of the war created dissension among the men who might otherwise have made up for his shortcomings.

The War of the Roses

The main contestants for power in England were the House of Lancaster and the House of York, the oldest line of descent from Edward III. When Lancastrian Henry VI died in 1461, the Yorkists tried to install their leader, the Duke of York, as king. Civil war broke out over the succession. That war has long been known as the War of the Roses, because it was thought, mistakenly, that the symbol of the House of Lancaster was a red rose and that the symbol of the House of York was a white rose. The war, which went on until 1485, was the last attempt by the barons to take over the government. But it destroyed everyone who took part in it—the House of Lancaster, the House of York, and many of the great baronial families. So when Henry Tudor—an indirect, illegitimate, half-Welsh descendant of John of Gaunt (Edward III's son) seized the throne as Henry VII in 1485, he was in a position to build a new monarchy, relatively unchallenged by the baronial factions.

Henry VII (r. 1485–1509) was an excellent politician and administrator. He continued the policies of his predecessors, encouraging commerce and industry and running a frugal, effective government. Every king since Edward III had recognized that as long as England produced only raw materials—such as wool for the Flemish textile mills—it would never develop a strong industrial base. So they encouraged the migration of textile workers to England and protected the English textile industry as it grew. They also encouraged the expansion of English shipping. England was still far behind Flanders in textiles and behind Italy in shipping, but a good start had been made under Henry VII's policies. In the 24 years of his reign, Henry established the Tudor dynasty and prepared the way for a century of peace and prosperity in England.

The Development of Government Institutions

Three important institutional developments took place in England during the fourteenth and fifteenth centuries: the rise of the justices of the peace, the strengthening of Parliament, and the emergence of an independent judiciary.

Edward III had created the office of justice of the peace to help the sheriffs and feudal lords with the work of enforcing the law. The justices were usually well-to-do local landholders of the class that had long borne the responsibilities of local government. They were the knights of the shires who served as members of Parliament. Like sheriffs and tax collectors, the justices served without pay; their reward was status and the respect of the community. By the middle of the fifteenth century their power had grown to the point where they controlled local government. They arrested criminals and tried people accused of minor offenses. (Major cases were tried by circuit judges from the king's court.) They were responsible for enforcing the rules and regulations issued by the central government. They were expected to collect information for the King's Council and to report plots against the government. In practice, the justices of the peace often followed the orders of the most powerful baron in the district. Under the Tudors, however, the justices of the peace, with their wide knowledge of local affairs, became the chief agents of the crown in the counties.

Meanwhile, during the years of weak monarchs and wartime turmoil from Edward II to Henry VI, Parliament had emerged as an indispensable part of the government. Weak kings and usurpers alike sought its support. Moreover, Parliament was regarded as the most representative institution in the country. When Edward III and Henry IV asked Parliament to ratify the depositions of Edward II and Richard II respectively, it appeared that Parliament's assent was necessary even in matters concerning succession to the throne. Further evidence of the growing power of Parliament was that all laws having to do with taxation had to be submitted to it for approval.

The structure of Parliament also changed with the passing years. About 1340 the knights of the shires, who represented the counties, and the burgesses, who represented the towns, joined forces to form the House of Commons. Previously, the knights and the burgesses had acted separately in presenting petitions to the king and in approving taxes. Now Parliament consisted of two houses—the House of Lords and the House of Commons. And the House of Commons, unlike the assemblies of other countries, included nobles as well as commoners. The knights of the shires were landlords who sometimes married into the baronial families; some of them became barons themselves. Their presence in the House of Commons gave it far more influence than a mere assembly of burgesses like the French Third Estate (see p. 324). With the knights leading the House of Commons, the cooperation of the lords was usually forthcoming. So when both houses attacked a minister of the king, they could usually force him out of office.

By the fifteenth century, every important act of government had to be approved by Parliament. So well established had Parliament become that it survived even the period of strong kingship that began under the Tudors in 1485. But Parliament only gave legal validity to acts of government; it did not make policy, which was still the province of the king and his

An English court in the later Middle Ages. This miniature is from a law treatise of the reign of Henry IV (early fifteenth-century). At the top are the five judges of the Court of King's Bench; below them are the king's coroner and attorney. On the left is the jury, and in front, in the dock, is a prisoner in fetters, flanked by lawyers. In the foreground more prisoners in chains wait their turn. On the center table stand the ushers, one of whom seems to be swearing in the jury.

ministers. For example, Edward II and Richard II were not deposed by an act initiated by Parliament; Parliament merely ratified the actions of a few great barons. Not until the seventeenth century did Parliament begin to formulate policy.

Finally, as the result of a blunder committed by Edward III, the English judiciary achieved independence from the crown. In 1340, Edward became enraged when a shortage of funds temporarily halted his campaign in France; he returned home and fired all his ministers, including the royal judges. When Parliament, and the country at large, raised a cry of alarm, Edward was forced to restore the judges to their positions. It was clear that the English

Lawlessness in
Fifteenth-Century England

John Paston was the son of a royal judge and well-to-do landowner in Norfolk. His father had bought the manor of Gresham, but in 1448 Lord Molyns claimed it, though he had no right to it. John Paston tried to settle the claim peacefully, but Molyns's men seized the manor house and Paston moved to another "mansion." While he was seeking help from his friends, Paston's wife was left to defend their home. She wrote her husband this letter late in 1448.

Right worshipful husband, I recommend me to you and pray you to get some cross-bows and windlasses to wind them with and arrows, for your house here is so low that no one could shoot out of it with a long-bow, even if we had great need. I suppose you could get these things from Sir John Falstaff [a friend of the Pastons]. And also I would like you to get two or three short pole-axes to guard the doors and as many jacks [padded leather jackets] as you can.

Partridge [leader of Molyns's men] and his fellows are sore afraid that you will attack them again, and they have made great preparations, as I am told. They have made bars to bar the doors crosswise, and they have made loop-holes on every side of the house to shoot out of both with bows and with hand-guns. The holes made for hand-guns are scarcely knee-high from the floor and no one can shoot out of them with a hand bow.

[Margaret Paston apparently took all this as a matter of course; she then turned to an ordinary shopping list.] I pray you to buy me a pound of almonds and a pound of sugar and some cloth to make clothes for your children and a yard of black broad-cloth for a hood for me.

The Trinity have you in His keeping and send you Godspeed in all your affairs.

Put into modern English from Norman Davis, ed., Paston Letters *(Oxford: Clarendon Press, 1958), pp. 9–10.*

King's Bench and the Court of Common Pleas. The King's Bench heard cases that directly pertained to the king and his interests, such as criminal cases and disputes over royal rights. (Crimes had come to be viewed as violations of the king's peace. They had formerly been regarded merely as injuries to a citizen to be avenged, preferably through law suit, by the injured party.) The Court of Common Pleas heard appeals of cases initiated by royal writs issued to litigants and that had been heard first in a shire or circuit court (see p. 309). In general, these were civil cases rather than criminal cases. All the judges of both the King's Bench and the Court of Common Pleas were appointed by the King.

Under Henry II and his successors, the royal courts were viewed as the means by which the king exercised judicial authority. That authority was limited, however, by the customary law dispensed by the age-old local courts. Englishmen continued to view the royal courts as belonging to the king (they still do) but they came to regard the law itself as a guarantee of specific rights. As far back as 1215, in the *Magna Carta,* the barons had asserted that all Englishmen had the right to a trial by a jury of their peers; the king could no longer ignore that right when it suited him, as King John had done. In 1328 Parliament had passed and Edward III had accepted the Statute of Northampton, which stated that no royal command should interfere with the course of the common law. In 1340, when Edward violated that statute by firing the royal judges, the reaction of the people made it clear that the judiciary was an arm of government and that it was not subject to the whims of the king.

Ironically, this turn of events tended to limit the role of the courts. In the thirteenth century, the royal judges, as officers of the king, had exercised wide discretion in dealing with the cases that came before them. In effect, they made law as they judged cases. Once the judiciary became independent of the king, however, judges refused to hear cases that lacked precedents. Their motive was to protect themselves from the charge that they were usurping political authority. They could claim that they were not making law and

regarded the judges not just as royal appointees, but as officers of the government responsible for dispensing justice. The event marked a fundamental shift in their view of the judicial system.

That system dated back to the royal court established by Henry II (r. 1154–89). During the thirteenth century, the royal court had split into two branches, the

987		1328	1589
	House of Capet	House of Valois	

consequently were not engaging in policy decisions, which were properly the province of political agents such as the king and Parliament.

FRANCE IN THE LATE MIDDLE AGES

In France, as we have seen (p. 359), when the sons of Philip the Fair died, leaving only daughters to succeed them, Edward III had stepped forward to claim the French throne. The rule that the French invented to prevent succession by or through a woman was designed not only to bar Edward's claim but also to prevent any French baron from gaining the throne by marrying a reigning queen. In 1328, the barons put Philip of Valois, cousin of the last king and nephew of Philip the Fair, on the throne. Because Philip (r. 1328–50) owed his position to the barons, he had to spend most of his reign bestowing favors on his benefactors and keeping peace among warring factions. As a result, the loyalty to the crown that had emerged during the thirteenth century began to erode, and rebellions and acts of treason plagued the country. It was this state of affairs that contributed to the French defeats during the first phase of the Hundred Years' War.

Philip's son John (r. 1350–64) had no better fortune. The loss of territory and the heavy ransom levied after his capture by the English at Poitiers caused widespread dissatisfaction and in 1358 set off a bloody peasant rebellion called the *jacquerie*. (The nobles called all peasants *jacques*.) That same year, the Estates General, led by the Paris bourgeoisie, tried to take over the government. The attempt failed, because the Estates had had little experience in government and because their leaders received no support from the nobility. John's son Charles V (r. 1364–80) regained a good measure of royal au-

thority by suppressing his opponents at home and by inflicting a series of defeats on the English.

Charles VI (r. 1380–1422), who succeeded Charles V, was strong in neither mind nor character and after 1390 suffered intermittent spells of insanity. During his reign, government was conducted largely by princes of the royal family who quarreled bitterly over offices, pensions, and land grants. In 1419, when the duke of Burgundy, the king's cousin, was assassinated by followers of the duke of Orléans, the king's brother, the quarrels turned into civil war and the new duke of Burgundy allied himself with the English. In addition

Charles V, king of France.

The only known contemporary portrait of Joan of Arc.

Road building in rural France (*ca.* 1448).

to Burgundy, the duke had acquired Flanders and other provinces of the Low Countries, which made him the most powerful prince in France. His defection to the English proved disastrous. It was during this period of civil war that Henry V of England made his rapid conquests in France and forced Charles VI to disinherit his own son and to recognize any future son of Henry as heir to the French crown.

The Defeat of England

Charles VII (r. 1422–61) faced an almost hopeless situation when his father died. He had been disinherited, and the largest and richest part of France belonged to the English and their Burgundian allies. His army was weak, and he was not using it effectively. Then, in 1429 the peasant girl from the eastern frontier, Joan of Arc, appeared at court and announced that heavenly voices had ordered her to drive the English out of France (see p. 361).

Soon Charles had another stroke of good fortune. England under Henry VI was torn by factional strife, and in the competition for control of the royal government the leader of one of the factions offended the duke of Burgundy. The duke returned to the French cause in 1435. His defection weakened the English and facilitated Charles's recovery of northern France.

Joan of Arc had revitalized the ancient view that the French kingdom was holy and deserved the unswerving support of the people despite generations of misgovernment. Her belief that "to make war on the holy kingdom of France was to make war on the Lord Jesus" was shared by people of all classes. Despite civil war, treason, and treachery, a feeling of national pride began to stir among the French people. Throughout the chaos and confusion of the early fifteenth century the French clung to their faith in the French monarchy and in the Christian religion, foreshadowing the union of monarchy and religion on which the absolutist states of the early modern period were to be built.

The Restoration of Royal Power

All the battles of the Hundred Years' War had been fought on French soil, and whole areas of the country had been intentionally devastated by the English armies. Even during periods of peace, troops of unemployed mercenaries had terrorized and plundered the countryside. Perhaps because of the extent and the intensity of the suffering, royal power was restored more rapidly and more completely in France than it was in England. A king who showed any promise of putting an end to the disorder was accorded almost unlimited power to levy taxes. As soon as Charles VII had the English on the run, he began to levy taxes at will, without asking consent from the Estates General. His task was made easier by the fact that the Estates General was seldom called into session, and when it was called it had little authority. The real power lay with the provincial and regional assemblies, with the Estates of Normandy or of Languedoc rather than with the Estates General. And Charles was able to overcome the fragmented opposition of those local assemblies.

The same bemusement with provincial matters also deferred the French nobles from seeking to entrench themselves in the central government, which remained the preserve of the king and his bureaucrats. Thus the Hundred Years' War

The Reconquest of Spain

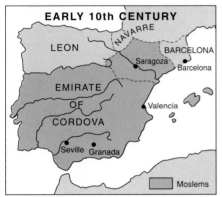

EARLY 10th CENTURY

LEON · NAVARRE · BARCELONA · Saragoza · Barcelona · EMIRATE OF CORDOVA · Valencia · Seville · Granada · Moslems

MID-12th CENTURY

LEON AND CASTILE · NAVARRE · ARAGON · Saragoza · Barcelona · PORTUGAL · Valencia · ALMOHADS · Seville · Granada · Moslems

LATE 15th CENTURY

NAVARRE · CASTILE AND LEON · ARAGON · Saragoza · Barcelona · PORTUGAL · Valencia · Seville · Granada · GRANADA · Moslems

reinforced a tendency that had long been apparent in France—the tendency toward a strong king at the head of a bureaucratic state with all other political forces weak and divided. This French pattern would become the model for the rest of Europe during the early modern period.

SPAIN IN THE LATE MIDDLE AGES

Starting in the eleventh century, the kingdoms of Aragon, León, and Castile reclaimed the peninsula from the Moors, and the Moorish caliphate centered on Cordoba disintegrated into a collection of independent states. By the fifteenth century, Moorish holdings had been reduced to the little kingdom of Granada.

Like the rest of western Europe, Spain was wracked by civil wars in the late Middle Ages. The competition between the principal kingdoms, Castile and Aragon, was exacerbated by the lack of any fixed rule of succession in either kingdom. So whoever sat on either throne was almost sure to be challenged by a rival claimant. Moreover, because many kings of the period came to the throne as minors, frequent quarrels erupted over the regency and attempts by members of the royal family to displace the legitimate king with someone of their own choosing. Because peaceful reigns were rare, the Spanish kings had little opportunity to participate in European politics. At one point, the

kingdom of Castile became a pawn in the Hundred Years' War when the reigning king, Pedro I (r. 1350–69), was challenged by his illegitimate half-brother, Henry of Trastamara. The English supported Pedro, and the French supported Henry. The fate of the two claimants depended on the tide of war. In 1366, the French were in ascendancy and Henry mounted the throne. The next year the tide of war shifted in favor of the English and Pedro was back in power. He was killed in battle in 1369, and Henry ruled until his death in 1379. But throughout his reign Henry was constantly challenged by the kings of Aragon, Navarre, Portugal, and Granada.

The kingdom of Aragon had less trouble with successions, because it controlled a small empire from which it could provide for the younger sons of the royal house. They could be given the kingdom of Majorca (the Balearic Islands) or Sicily (and eventually Naples) in Italy.

Nevertheless, the disorder persisted in most parts of the peninsula until John II of Aragon married his son Ferdinand (r. 1479–1516) to Isabella, the heiress of Castile (r. 1474–1504). The union of the two crowns (1479) did not result in the actual merger of the two kingdoms, but it brought a large measure of security to the people of Spain.

On the whole, the Catholic Kings (as Ferdinand and Isabella were called) followed the French model; they allowed

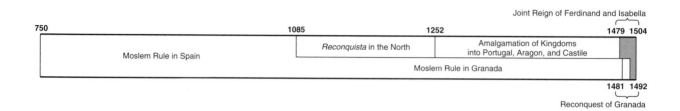

750		1085	1252		Joint Reign of Ferdinand and Isabella 1479 1504
	Moslem Rule in Spain	*Reconquista* in the North	Amalgamation of Kingdoms into Portugal, Aragon, and Castile		
			Moslem Rule in Granada		

1481 1492
Reconquest of Granada

A fifteenth-century Swiss halberd.

each province to keep its time-honored customs but appointed officials of the central government to do the governing. The Catholic Kings did not bear that title in vain; in a society of mixed ethnic population—Moors, Jews, and Christians—they made the Christian religion the test of loyalty. Jews and Moslems, even after they had converted, were suspected of secretly adhering to their old faiths, and some of them were driven into exile. The instrument of religious oppression was the Inquisition (see p. 282), which in Spain alone among the countries of Europe was a tool of the monarchy. The Spanish Inquisition was known for its harsh methods and penalties and for its use of the charge of heresy to achieve political ends. In 1492 Ferdinand and Isabella finally conquered Granada, which completed their conquest of the whole peninsula except Portugal, and forced the Moorish population to convert to Christianity. That same year they expelled the Jews from their kingdom.

The Jews and the Moors had accounted for a large part of Spain's skilled labor and they had dominated commerce, but the loss suffered by the country as a result of their suppression was not immediately apparent. By 1500, Spain was the strongest kingdom in Europe. It financed the exploration and conquest of the New World under the aegis of Isabella and the Castilians, and Ferdinand emerged as the arbiter of European politics. Even far-off England found it advisable to ally itself with Spain.

GERMANY IN THE LATE MIDDLE AGES

The history of the remainder of western Europe during the late Middle Ages paral-

leled that of France and England. Everywhere there were rebellions, civil wars, and attempts to take over neighboring lands. But all this activity brought surprisingly little change. The political map of Europe in 1450 looked very much as it had in 1300, and most of the governments were pretty much the same.

In Germany, however, change was more evident. During the fourteenth century the peasants and townsmen of Switzerland gradually gained their independence from the Habsburg family, which had ruled this part of Germany, along with Austria, for many generations. The Swiss created an army of well-disciplined infantrymen armed with long pikes with which they could repel a charge by the elite cavalry troops of the German army. By the fifteenth century French kings and Italian princes, including the pope, were hiring whole companies of Swiss infantrymen.

The Swiss were also demonstrating the possibility of republican government to a Europe that had little confidence in democracy. Up to then, the only noteworthy republics had been the faction-ridden Italian cities, which at that very moment were losing their independence to tyrants, and the German towns that had tried and failed to form a permanent confederation and had remained weak and isolated.

But the Swiss Confederation, though loosely knit, endured. Each district, or canton, retained its own institutions, and no canton was ruled by a feudal lord. The towns were governed by wealthy burgesses, but the peasant cantons, where the movement for independence had begun, were almost pure democracies.

Change was also apparent in the Low Countries. During the fifteenth century the dukes of Burgundy gradually

Hapsburg and Luxembourg States

gained control over all the provinces of the Low Countries, roughly the area of modern Belgium and the Netherlands. Acquisition of the Low Countries, one of the richest and most urbanized sections of Europe, by the house of Burgundy removed their fate from that of the rest of Germany. As they gradually achieved a sense of national identity, however, their wealth made control of their country the object of a long series of wars that began in the fifteenth century and has continued into the twentieth.

Meanwhile a new power center was rising on the middle Danube as a product of the peculiar electoral habits of the German princes. By the fourteenth century

the number of princes taking part in imperial elections had been reduced to seven. Fearful of bestowing the title on any truly powerful prince, for some time they chose as emperors counts with small holdings. Though the title carried no real power, it bore enough social prestige to enable the emperors to marry heiresses of important thrones. It was by this route that the Habsburgs, petty princes in western Germany who had served briefly as emperors around 1300, managed to acquire the duchy of Austria and nearby counties. A little later, the count of Luxembourg, an equally obscure prince, was elected emperor and arranged a marriage through which his son acquired the kingdom of

Bohemia. Later Luxembourg emperors acquired Silesia and eventually Hungary. When the last male of the Luxembourg line died in 1438, his closest heir was the Habsburg duke of Austria. The union of the vast holdings of the Luxembourgs and the Habsburgs marked the beginning of the Habsburg empire, for five centuries one of the great powers of Europe (see pp. 336–37).

ART, LITERATURE, AND SCIENCE

During the late Middle Ages, art, literature, science, and technology all advanced, but advanced unevenly. We find a great many imitative and second-rate works alongside brilliant and historically important works. The most noteworthy advances were made in the arts and literature.

The Arts

After the thirteenth century, Gothic architecture had become imitative and overly ornate, and few churches of the fourteenth and fifteenth centuries are of commanding quality. One late medieval style is called

King's College Chapel, Cambridge: A fine example of the English perpendicular style of Gothic architecture.

the Flamboyant, for obvious reasons. In England, architects developed a Gothic style, called the Perpendicular, that emphasized height and soaring lines. The chapel of King's College, Cambridge, is an excellent example of the Perpendicular style.

Manuscript illumination reached new heights during the fifteenth century. The rich court of Burgundy supported talented artists who executed ambitious programs of illumination. Many of the manuscripts are so-called "books of hours," popular collections of readings from the service books of the church that were used as personal prayer books by the laity. In the wealthy households of the nobility, artists created superb works of calligraphy and illustration that have survived in whole or in part. The illustrators of these books introduced a realistic style that had a significant influence on future artists. Their detailed, realistic renderings of everyday life are an important source of information about the period.

It was during the fourteenth century that portrait painting first appeared in western Europe, along with the first attempts to treat landscapes with freshness and authenticity. Here again the most talented artists were those patronized by the dukes of Burgundy. The artists of the Flemish school of painting, which emerged in the late fourteenth and early fifteenth centuries, were the first artists to paint in oils and were worthy rivals of the Italian painters of the early Renaissance. The best-known Flemish painters—the van Eyck brothers, van der Weyden, and Memling—combined meticulous attention to detail with genuine religious feeling. Among the masterpieces of the period are Jan van Eyck's painting of Giovanni Arnolfini and his bride (1434) and his *Man in a Red Turban* (1433) which is a self-portrait.

Literature

In literature, the narrative poems derived from the romances of the twelfth century now emerged as fantastic stories (like those parodied by Cervantes in *Don Quixote;* see p. 471), and lyric poetry declined into society verse. Yet some authors demonstrated deeper psychological insights into human behavior, and there was notable improvement in the quality of prose writing. When Nicolas Oresme (*ca.* 1325–82), a scholarly French bishop, set about translating Aristotle's *Politics,* he had to invent or redefine a great many words, and in doing so he enriched the French language.

Geoffrey Chaucer (*ca.* 1340–1400), who began as a translator and adapter of French works, matured into one of England's most talented poets. His most famous work, the prologue to the *Canterbury Tales,* reveals his skill in describing individual characters and his wit in depicting human foibles. His characters include the "perfect, gentle Knight," the poor parson who taught Christ's lore "but first he followed it himself," the earthy Wife of Bath who had buried five husbands, and scoundrels such as the Miller and the Summoner. He may have met such characters while working in the royal customs service in the port of London, but it was through his genius that he translated such experiences into literary masterpieces like the *Canterbury Tales* and *Troilus and Criseyde.* Though Chaucer saw through pretense and sham, he had an affection for the world and its characters. His talents were recognized during his lifetime, and he rose quickly in society under the patronage of John of Gaunt, uncle of King Richard II.

The poet Francois Villon (1431–*ca.* 1463) was less fortunate. In his poetry he showed how close French society was to cracking under the strains of war during the first half of the fifteenth century. Though he cast his poems in the old forms, he depicted life in taverns and thieves' dens rather than courtly society. He confessed that he was a friend of the thieves and prostitutes of Paris and was himself convicted of crime. Villon expressed bitterness over his wasted life, however, and spoke of the hopes and fears of poor people and outcasts—the piety of an old woman, the last thoughts of men condemned to hang. The tendency toward realism, already evident in Chaucer, is even more apparent in Villon.

An example of the early Flemish style. These panels come from a triptych by Gerard David (*ca.* 1460–1523).

As church control over religious life declined, writers produced numerous devotional works for lay readers: meditations, visions, moral tracts, and the books of hours. Among the religious writings of the period was the *Imitation of Christ,* ascribed to Thomas à Kempis (1379/80–1471). It was a guide to the Christian life that emphasized the simple life and devotion to spiritual matters as the ideal. In the late Middle Ages it was the most-read religious work after the Bible.

The Vision of Piers Plowman by William Langland (*ca.* 1332–*ca.* 1400) is one of the first important works written in English after the Norman Conquest. Little is known of Langland, except that he lived during the fourteenth century and came from peasant stock. The language of *Piers Plowman* is archaic, but it is clearly English, not Anglo-Saxon. *Piers Plowman* is evidence of the widespread desire to transform religion into a strong social force. Langland's work criticized people of every class for their worldliness and selfishness; only by a return to the principles of the Gospel could the world be saved. There is nothing anti-church in the poem, but it clearly alludes to the failure of the ecclesiastical authorities to respond to the aspirations of ordinary people.

A fifteenth-century representation of Chaucer from the Ellesmere manuscript of the *Canterbury Tales.*

Science

We know little about what was being done in the sciences during the fourteenth and fifteenth centuries, and historians have usually disparaged what we do know as unoriginal and unimportant. Nonetheless, there were scientists of originality whose work had lasting value. Columbus based his ideas about geography on books written in the fourteenth and early fifteenth centuries. The reaction of some philosophers and theologians to Thomas Aquinas's views of the world freed scholars to some extent from their adherence to the Aristotelian ideas he had incorporated into his theological system. That freedom permitted wider speculation on scientific questions, particularly questions having to do with motion. Fourteenth-century scholars raised many of the issues that Galileo eventually used in revolutionizing the science of physics in the sixteenth century. For example, mathematicians at Oxford came extremely close to solving the problem of acceleration, and the French scholar Nicolas Oresme considered the possibility that the earth rotated.

From the twelfth century on, western scholars relied mainly on the work of the Greeks and the Moslems for knowledge of the world, but there were always some who were interested in science. That interest led eventually to the great discoveries of the early modern period. Copernicus and Galileo were trained in universities that used the methods and books of the late Middle Ages.

European civilization is an amalgam of Roman, Judeo-Christian, Celtic, Germanic, and countless other influences. As such, it has never had a single world view that could hinder the probing of the human mind. In China, a philosopher of Thomas Aquinas's stature might have become an unchallenged authority, but in the West he was subjected to searching critical appraisal. European society is comfortable with opposing points of view, as its literature and its politics show. In *Parzival* (*ca.* 1208), for example, Wolfram von Eschenbach contrasts the courtly with the divine, the Christian with the pagan, and deals fairly with non-Christian values even while showing the superiority of Christian values. In politics, the struggle between ecclesiastical authority and secular authority divided the European consciousness and enabled people to think of political order from the spiritual as well as the secular point of view.

Such attitudes are essential in scientific investigation, which relies on willingness to think about the world in new and unorthodox ways. Though comfortable with contradictions, Europeans worked hard to resolve them by focusing their attention on details. For example, they eventually resolved the problems of constitutional law that they encountered in struggling with the Great Schism by making small changes in the way they viewed the relationship between pope and council. Similarly, scientific thinkers concentrated on details, on observations and explanations of small things, confident that their studies would eventually produce results. And so they did, by revealing the inadequacy of currently accepted theories and by opening the way for Copernicus, Galileo, and Kepler to come up with new theories to explain the observations.

Technology

The Europeans of the Middle Ages were great innovators in technology. They

An early gun, lighter and more portable than the first cannon. The gun was placed on a forked stand and was braced against the ground by its long tail (illustration from a German manuscript, *ca.* 1405).

seized on inventions from the East, such as the stirrup, the horseshoe, and paper, and invented new implements of their own, such as the horse collar and the mechanical clock. The Chinese probably invented gunpowder, and they were using cannons about as early as the Europeans. But the Chinese were content with the primitive weapons they first created, and the Europeans carried on experiments in an effort to improve accuracy and reliability. The first European cannons often blew up in the face of the men who fired them, but by the end of the fifteenth century they had become fairly reliable.

The use of cannons meant that the castles of the nobility were no longer impregnable, and the military might of the nobility declined accordingly. Moreover, cannons were expensive, and only kings and great lords could afford to equip their troops with them. Thus the introduction of cannons tended to concentrate power in the hands of a few powerful men, especially the kings.

The use of cannons and the invention of smaller firearms stimulated advances in other branches of technology. Early gun barrels were extremely unreliable, but steel makers devised new metallurgical techniques and were soon producing higher-quality metal. To produce truly round barrels that could deliver the full effect of the charge, gunsmiths came up with better tools and more precise measuring instruments.

The increased demand for metals led to technological advances in mining and smelting as well. In the early Middle Ages, most ores had been drawn from easily accessible surface deposits. But by the late Middle Ages, miners in Germany, Bohemia, and Austria were sinking their shafts deeper and deeper and were pumping ground water out of their mines. Inventions like the cylinder pump, which drained the mines, prompted inventions in other industries. The principles employed in the invention of the cylinder pump, for example, led eventually to the invention of the steam engine.

The fifteenth-century invention of printing by means of movable type also owed much to advances in metallurgy. To

Early mechanical clockworks (*ca.* 1500). The first clocks had only one moveable hand.

cast usable type requires a metal that will take the exact shape of the mold into which it is poured. German metallurgists answered that need by creating an alloy that expands as it cools and fits the mold precisely. In 1453 Johannes Gutenberg produced the first European printed book, the Bible, using type cast with the new alloy.

Through patient experimentation and research, western Europeans also made great strides in navigation and seamanship. By the end of the thirteenth century they had ships that could tack against the wind and survive the violent storms of the Atlantic. Navigators could find their latitude, though not their longitude, by sightings of the stars and the sun; they knew that the earth was round and that the distance to the rich lands of the East was not impossibly great. French and

Spanish seamen reached the Canary Islands by the early fourteenth century at the latest, and by 1400 Portuguese sailors had made their way down the African coast, claiming Madeira and the Cape Verde Islands for their king.

Meanwhile, the Chinese were sending expeditions into the Indian Ocean, where they found rich countries and profitable trade; the Europeans had discovered only barren islands and disease-ridden coasts. The Chinese abandoned their efforts after a time, however, whereas the Europeans persisted. Still, it was almost two centuries before they reached the rich trading centers of the Orient and the treasures of the New World.

Almost as significant as the advances in navigation was the invention of the mechanical clock. The first clocks, which appeared in the fourteenth century, were not highly accurate. But clock design improved immensely with the discovery of the principle of escapement—the system by which the train of gears moves only a precise distance before it is checked and then released to move the same distance again. In the long run, the invention of reliable clocks had a profound effect on western Europeans. The precise measurement of time became a matter of great concern, a concern that for centuries differentiated European society from other societies. The insistence on precise measurement was a sign of the Europeans' uniquely rational attitude toward the world. The technological and scientific advances of the late Middle Ages stemmed from a desire to master nature rather than merely adjust to it, and the mechanization of the world picture, as one historian has called it, affected their approach to the workings of society and political institutions as well as to natural phenomena.

Suggestions for Further Reading

Economy and Society

On the economic depression of the fourteenth century, see the works cited in Chapters 10 and 12, particularly the *Cambridge Economic History*. See also M. M. Postan, *The Medieval Economy and Society* (1972), on the economic condition of peasants before the plague. On the bubonic plague, see P. Ziegler, *The Black Death* (1969), and R. S. Gottfried, *The Black Death* (1983). *The Black Death: A Chronicle of the Plague,* ed. J. Nohl, trans. C. H. Clarke (1924), contains a collection of contemporary sources. C. Cipolla, *Cristofano and the Plague* (1973), gives a graphic picture of a community's response to the plague, although he is studying a later epidemic. For a study of the effects of the plague, see *The Black Death: The Impact of the Fourteenth-century Plague* (1983), which contains the papers given at a conference at SUNY Binghamton; B. H. Putnam, *The Enforcement of the Statutes of Labourers during the First Decade after the Black Death 1349–1359* (1908); and on the effects in one locale, J. A. Raftis, "Changes in an English Village after the Black Death," *Mediaeval Studies* 29 (1967). For a sampling of the views on the effects of the plague, see W. Bowsky, ed., *The Black Death* (1971). For a general interpretation of the social unrest in the late Middle Ages, see R. H. Hilton, *Bondmen Made Free* (1973). *Social Unrest in the Late Middle Ages,* ed. F. X. Newman (1986), and *The English Rising of 1381,* ed. R. H. Hilton and T. H. Aston (1984), contain essays on the popular movements.

Avignon Papacy

See the work of A. C. Flick cited in Chapter 12. On the Avignon period, see G. Mollat, *The Avignon Papacy* (1963), and Y. Renouard, *The Avignon Papacy* (1970). On the Great Schism and the conciliar movement, see W. Ullmann, *Origins of the Great Schism* (1948); B. Tierney, *Foundations of the Conciliar Theory* (1955); and E. F. Jacob, *Essays in the Conciliar Epoch,* 3rd ed. (1963).

England

For late medieval England, see M. McKisack, *The Fourteenth Century* (1959), and E. F. Jacob, *The Fifteenth Century* (1961). S. Waugh, *England in the Reign of Edward III* (1991), is an excellent study of social and economic conditions. There are excellent histories of individual reigns: W. M. Ormrod, *The Reign of Edward III* (1990); B. Bevan, *Richard II* (1990); J. L.

Kirby, *Henry IV of England* (1970); R. A. Griffiths, *The Reign of Henry VI* (1981); and S. B. Chrimes, *Henry VII* (1972). On the history of Parliament, see P. Spufford, *Origins of the English Parliament* (1967), and R. G. Davies and J. H. Denton, eds., *The English Parliament in the Middle Ages* (1981). On justices of the peace, see B. H. Putnam, *Proceedings before Justices of the Peace* (1938).

France

On late medieval France, see P. S. Lewis, *Later Medieval France: The Polity* (1967). R. Vaughn, *Philip the Bold* (1962), *John the Fearless* (1966), *Philip the Good* (1970), and *Charles the Bold* (1973), give a history of the rise of Burgundian power. On Burgundy at its height, see J. F. Kirk, *Charles the Bold, Duke of Burgundy,* 3 vols. (1864–68), which treats the man in relation to his times. On the culture of the Burgundian court, see O. Cartellieri, *The Court of Burgundy* (1929), and P. Calmette, *The Golden Age of Burgundy* (1962).

The Hundred Years' War

E. Perroy, *The Hundred Years War* (1951), is the best short history. H. Lucas, *The Low Countries and the Hundred Years' War* (1929); K. Fowler, ed., *The Hundred Years War* (1971); H. J. Hewitt, *The Organization of War under Edward III* (1966); and J. B. Henneman, *Royal Taxation in Fourteenth Century France, 1322–1356* (1971). J. Keegan, *The Face of Battle* (1976), provides a brilliant description of the battle of Agincourt (1415). On Joan of Arc, see L. Fabre, *Joan of Arc,* trans. G. Hopkins (1954), a fine biography that presents a fascinating picture of France in the later period of the Hundred Years' War. See also the documents of the trial of Joan translated in *Jeanne d'Arc,* ed. T. D. Murray (1920). G. Pernoud, *Joan of Arc by Herself and Her Witnesses,* trans. E. Hyams (1966), presents a broad picture of Joan's mission and effect.

Spain and Germany

On late medieval Spain, see R. Altimira, *A History of Spain* (1949), and H. J. Chaytor, *A History of Aragon* (1933). R. I. Burns has studied the process of reconquest in *The Crusader Kingdom of Valencia: Reconstruction on a Thirteenth-Century Frontier* (1967), *Islam under the Crusaders: Colonial Survival in the Thirteenth-Century Kingdom of Valencia* (1973), and *Medieval Colonialism: Postcrusade Exploitation of Islamic Valencia* (1975).

On late medieval Germany, see G. Barraclough, *The Origins of Modern Germany* (1947); J. Leuschner, *Germany in the Later Middle Ages* (1980); and C. Bayley, *The Formation of the German College of Electors* (1949).

The Arts, Literature, and Science

On late medieval art, see J. Evans, *English Art 1307–1461* (1949); E. Panofsky, *Early Netherlandish Painting* (1953); L. Baldass, *Jan van Eyck* (1952); and M. Meiss, *French Painting in the time of Jean de Berry,* 2 vols. (1967–68), *Painting in Florence and Siena after the Black Death* (1951), and *The Limbourgs and their Contemporaries* (1974). J. Harthan, *The Book of Hours* (1977), is a history and commentary on the art of the books and contains many color plates. For a history of vernacular culture, see A. W. Ward and A. R. Waller, *The Cambridge History of English Literature,* Vol. 1 (1907). On Chaucer, see D. W. Robertson, *A Preface to Chaucer: Studies in Medieval Perspective* (1962). See also the works cited in Chapter 11. On late medieval science, see the works cited in Chapter 11. On the clock and other mechanical devices, see J. Gimpel, *The Medieval Machine* (1976). For the technology of firearms and sailing, see C. Cipolla, *Guns, Sails and Empires* (1965).

15

SOUTH AND EAST ASIA
CA. A.D. 600–1600

During the millennium considered in this chapter, the civilizations of South and East Asia continued to develop in their own distinctive ways. Even the two momentous events that transformed much of Eurasia during this period—the spread of Islam and the creation of the world's largest empire by the Mongols—affected India and China very differently. Meanwhile, the history of Southeast Asia continued to reflect—but not to mirror—that of India, while in Northeast Asia Japan fashioned its own culture and institutions under the stimulus of Chinese civilization.

INDIA

After the Guptas, India was divided into a number of states of varying duration and geographical extent. In studying this complex period, it is useful to distinguish North India from South India, even though some states for a time bridged this gap and even though major differences existed *within* each area.

In South India power tended to be focused in two major centers. One was the Western Deccan, where the rugged terrain of Maharashtra produced tough fighters. There the Chalyukas of Badani (their capital), beginning with Pulakeshin I (r. 535–66), developed an empire that reached its largest extent under Pulakeshin II (610–42). After this emperor was killed in battle, the Chalyukas were overthrown by the Rashatrakutas who seized Badani in 752. Their empire was even larger than that of the Chalyukas, but their most permanent monument is to be found at their capital of Ellora where they sponsored one of the world's greatest temples.

(OPPOSITE) MINIATURE MODEL HOMESTEAD (CLAY) FROM A MING DYNASTY TOMB (1368–1644).

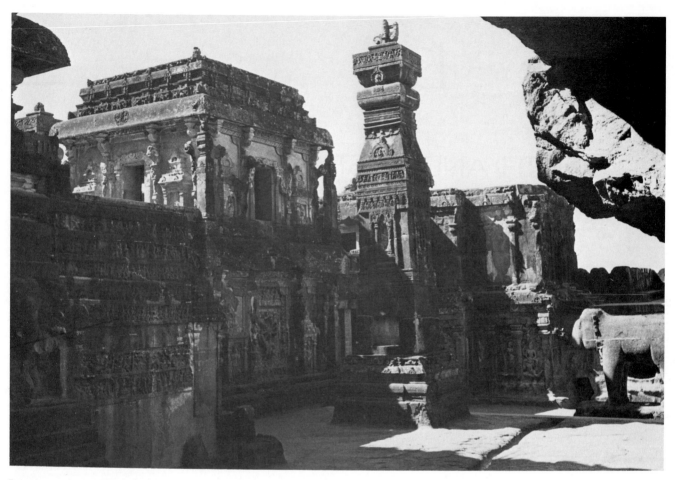

Temple pavilion at Ellora, hewn from natural rock (eighth century).

The second southern power center was in the Tamil-speaking area of the Co-romandel Coast region. Here first the Pallavas (roughly 250–910, with their highpoint around 600) and then their Chola successors (844–1279, highpoint eleventh century) built their states. One reason for taking special note of these two states is that they played an influential role in Southeast Asian history. The Tamil area over which they ruled was a major source for the diffusion of Indian culture to the region. The Cholas, moreover, were able to launch several naval expeditions to Sri Lanka (Ceylon), and in 1020 they even concluded a successful maritime campaign against the Sumatran-Malay state of Shrivijaya.

The southern states, particularly that of the Cholas, were among the most extensive and long lasting of the Indian states during this period. Although they differed in structure, they were all centered on the sacred authority of the king, who was identified with Indra and other deities. Consecrated in solemn enthronement ceremonies, the king commanded the reverent submission due to the protector of the world. One Cholas institution that provided an important ritual and ideological link between the center and outlying regions was that of special villages on the plains governed by *brahman* assemblies but also including residents of other castes. The *brahman* priests were linked to the center of authority by their religion while at the same time they provided religious services to the peasant castes, with whom they formed close ties.

This relationship between the *brahman* and the peasantry was facilitated by the growth of devotionalism that had already appeared earlier in Hinduism. This movement, particularly in the South but by no means limited to that region, incorporated local deities into the Hindu pantheon and formed a religion basically congenial to settled cultivators. This faith inspired fervent hymns dedicated to Shiva and Vishnu performed in song and dance in Tamil temples. Their main themes were love for God and the personal inadequacy of the devotee. These hymns helped to fire the vitality of Hinduism and to undermine the appeal of Buddhism and other rival faiths.

Hinduism was also strengthened on the philosophical level, most notably by Shankara (*ca.* 788–820), India's most famous philosopher, whose basic teaching was an absolute monism. Although a southerner, Shankara wrote in Sanskrit and traveled widely in India, including the North, debating challengers, founding schools, and generally spreading his ideas.

Political fragmentation was characteristic of the North as well as the South. Here too, particularly from the eleventh century, a king exercised only a general overlordship over local warriors outside the area controlled directly by the throne. In a system somewhat similar to Western feudalism, the obligations of these warriors included financial payments, the use of the king's currency, military service, and attendance at the king's court as well as recognition of the king's sacred authority. A local warrior might also be obliged to offer his daughter to the king in marriage. Among the most notable northern rulers were the Rajputs ("Sons of Kings"), who were probably at least partly of central Asian descent but who were fiercely dedicated to the values associated with India's warrior (*kshatriya*) tradition. The Rajputs were able to stem the tide of Arab Islamic expansion in the eighth century. They and other Hindu rulers in North India maintained their independence until the establishment of the Delhi Sultanate.

The Moslem Invasions and the Delhi Sultanate

The first substantial and lasting Moslem presence in India came early in the eighth century when Arabs annexed Sind, the Indus delta region separated from the rest of India by desert. They incorporated their conquests into the Umayyad Empire and soon recognized Hindus as *dhimmis* (protected people, second-class subjects liable for special taxes, see p. 384). The Arabs were prevented from further expansion primarily by the Gujara-Pariharas (*ca.* 750–1027), who created an empire rivaling that of the Rashatrakutas in the South. However, Arab expansionism was only a minor episode in the broad sweep of Indian history. As ever, the main threat came from the northwest.

As we have seen, tough Hunna invaders from central Asia put an end to the Gupta Empire. Such incursions of warlike people from the northwest remained a major theme in Indian history, but with the coming of Islam a new element was added. Now the warrior peoples were imbued with a fierce sense of holy mission; they brought into India a world view that in many essential respects clashed with the native Hindu tradition. The Moslem faith in one God, one prophet, and one book contrasted with the complexity and tolerance of Hinduism, and a wide gulf

Nataraja Shiva as Lord of the Dance (Chola period, twelfth or thirteenth century).

The Rajput Code

A widow speaks to the page who witnessed her husband's death.

"Boy, tell me, ere I go, how bore himself my lord?"

"As a reaper of the harvest of battle. I followed his steps as a humble gleaner of his sword. On the bed of honor he spread a carpet of the slain, whereon, a barbarian his pillow, he sleeps ringed by his foes."

"Yet once again, boy, tell me how my lord bore himself?"

"Oh mother, who can tell his deeds? He left no foe to dread or to admire him."

She smiled farewell to the boy, and adding, "My lord will chide my delay," sprang into the flames.

As quoted in H. G. Rawlinson, India: A Short Cultural History *(New York: Appleton-Century, 1938), p. 202.*

existed between the hierarchical Hindu view of society and the Islamic belief that the ideal social order consisted of an essentially egalitarian community of believers. The interaction between Islam and Hinduism, often marred by misunderstandings, tension, and conflict, was to become a major theme in the history of the subcontinent.

By the eleventh century the region to India's northwest was under the control of warlike Turkic peoples who penetrated deep into India on raids from their base in modern Afghanistan. The most bloody and destructive of the raiding expeditions were those conducted by Mahmud of Ghazni (971–1030), who used the wealth looted from India to turn his own capital in eastern Afghanistan into a major center of Islamic culture.

For several centuries Turko-Afghan invaders were content to return to their home territory beyond the passes carrying their loot with them. But in the last quarter of the twelfth century a new group of Turko-Afghans appeared and in 1206 founded the Delhi Sultanate, which was to last for 320 years. The victory of Islam was accompanied by the wholesale de-

The Moslem Conquest of India
1192–1320

struction of Buddhist temples and centers of learning. Moslems had long resented Buddhism, which, like Islam, was a proselytizing religion. Buddhism had already suffered a serious blow in 751 when Islamic forces inflicted a severe defeat on a Chinese army on the Talas River near Samarkand, thereby hastening the end of the period when Buddhism flourished along the central Asia trade routes. Now the Turko-Afghans effectively destroyed a Buddhism already weakened by Hindu opposition and competition. The result was that the faith virtually disappeared in India until 1956 when a substantial number of Untouchables converted to Buddhism.

The Delhi Sultanate was founded by a Turkish slave-general, a Mamluk of the type prominent also in Egypt during this same period. The Mamluk dynasty (1206–90) was the first of five dynasties to rule in Delhi during the Sultanate. At this time, Turks, many of them slaves, and other foreigners filled key positions in the military and political establishments. In 1221, Chengis (Genghis) Khan, the great conqueror, led a Mongol expedition to the banks of the Indus but then withdrew from India. However, the Sultanate maintained a large army ready in case the Mongols returned. Military leaders were compensated for their service by grants of income from tax-exempt lands.

The Sultanate's decision to maintain a large army was only one of the ways the Mongols influenced the history of the subcontinent. Another was that, being cut off from central Asia, the rulers in Delhi necessarily concentrated their energies on India. Also, by destroying urban centers in central Asia and Iran, the Mongol conquests brought to India numerous refugee scholars, artists, and religious teachers who carried with them much of the high culture of their homelands. Notably, this included Persian as the prime literary language, which became the language of India's Moslem elite. But Persian influence was not confined to literature; it was apparent in architecture, textile design, and generally in court life and ceremony.

After the Mongol threat receded, the Sultanate's armies were occupied first in plundering expeditions and then in subduing much of the rest of India. The regime reached the height of its power under the second and third dynasties, the Khajli (1290–1320) and the Tughluq (1320–1414). It achieved its greatest territorial extent under the second Tughluq sultan, Muhammad (r. 1325–51), when most of India (except for Kashmir, the lower Indus Valley, and parts of the Rajput area) temporarily accepted Delhi's overlordship. However, the Sultanate had overextended itself and lacked the means to consolidate its conquests into a functioning empire. Nor did it have the power to compel the allegiance of distant tribute-paying vassals. Thus in 1336 the Hindu kingdom of Vijayanagar was founded, a state that remained the major southern power for two centuries and lasted for three. Like earlier Indian kings, the Vijayanagar rulers exercised a loose, ritualized overlordship over local chiefs and communities rather than presiding over a bureaucratic apparatus, as in China.

Elsewhere Moslem leaders also declared their independence. One of them proclaimed himself Sultan of the Deccan (South India) in 1347 and founded the Bahmini Dynasty, Vijayanagar's rival. It should be noted, however, that even though Vijayanagar appealed to Hinduism for its ideology, it regularly employed Moslems in its armies, just as Moslem states did not hesitate to employ Hindus.

A low point in the Sultanate's fortunes came in 1398 when Timur (Tamerlane) invaded India and sacked Delhi—the same Timur who checked the advance of the Ottoman Turks in the West. Under the fourth dynasty, the Sayyid (1414–51), Delhi remained weak, unable to prevent various regional rulers from establishing their own sultanates even in North India. The Sayyid dynasty was replaced by the Afghan Lodi (1451–1526), but it remained for a new group of foreign conquerors to match and surpass the earlier achievements of the Sultanate.

During the Sultanate period, Islam was firmly established in the Indian subcontinent, although the majority of Indians remained Hindus. The main agency for the spread of Islam was not

Moslem and Hindu in the Fourteenth Century

Ala-ud-Din [sultan of Delhi, 1296–1316] was a king who had no acquaintance with learning and never associated with the learned. He considered that policy and government were one thing and law another. "I am an unlettered man," he said, "but I have seen a great deal. Be assured that the Hindus will never become submissive and obedient until they are reduced to poverty. I have therefore given orders that just enough shall be left them of grain, milk, and curds from year to year, but that they must not accumulate hoards and property."

From the Moslem historian Barani, as quoted in H. G. Rawlinson, India: A Short Cultural History *(New York: Appleton-Century, 1938), p. 228.*

Tree of Life and Knowledge (southern India, Vijayanagar period, 1336–1546).

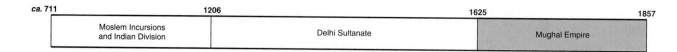

ca. 711	1206	1625	1857
Moslem Incursions and Indian Division	Delhi Sultanate	Mughal Empire	

the Sultanate and its military and civilian organs; nor was it the *ulama,* that is, "the class of state-supported judges, theologians, and preachers who were collectively responsible for upholding Islamic orthodoxy" in India as elsewhere in the Moslem world. Instead, the prime spreaders of Islam were Sufis, mystics not employed by the state. These men of religion belonged to various orders and varied widely in their methods and personalities: "Some of them wielded swords, others the pen, others a royal land grant, and still others a begging bowl. Some were introverted to the point of reclusive withdrawal, others extroverted to the point of militancy. Some were orthodox to the point of zealous puritanism, others unorthodox to the point of heresy."* This quotation, taken from a study of the Sufis in a single Indian state, suggests the adaptability and variety of Islam's holy men but also the dangers of overgeneralization.

*Richard M. Eaton, *Sufis of Bijapur 1300–1700* (Princeton: Princeton Univ. Press, 1978), p. 283.

A Portrait of Akbar by His Son

My father always associated with the learned of every creed and religion: especially the Pundits and the learned of India, and, although he was illiterate, so much became clear to him through constant intercourse with them, that no one knew him to be illiterate. . . . In his august personal appearance he was of middle height, but inclining to be tall; he was of the hue of wheat; his eyes and eyebrows were black and his complexion rather dark than fair; he was lion-bodied with a broad chest, and his hands and arms long. On the left side of his nose he had a fleshy mold, very agreeable in appearance, of the size of half a pea. . . . His august voice was very loud and in speaking and explaining had a peculiar richness.

Memoirs of Jahangir, *trans. Rogers and Beveridge (London, 1909–14), pp. 33–34 as quoted in H. G. Rawlinson*, India: A Short Cultural History *(London: The Cresset Press, revised ed. 1952), pp. 317–18.

Many people came to Islam through peaceful conversion, not holy war; naturally many of the converts came from among those lowest in the Hindu social hierarchy. There was also a trend for Hindu devotionalism and Islamic mysticism to converge, as in the teachings of Kabir (1440–1518), a Moslem weaver, who asked, "If God be within the mosque, then to whom does this world belong?" He won many followers; his verses, written in the vernacular, drew on both Persian and Sanskrit to express themes derived from both traditions. Another syncretist was Nanak (1469–1538), the founder of Sikhism, who was born a Hindu but rejected caste and taught devotion to God. Under a succession of *gurus* (teachers) the Sikhs, spurred on by Mughal intolerance, later developed into a militant community in Nanak's home area, the Punjab (in the northern Indus Valley).

The Mughals

The Mughal empire was founded by Babur (1483–1530), but it was his grandson Akbar (1542–1605) who secured its future and constructed its institutional foundations. Babur and Akbar were Iranicized Turko-Mongols and as such continued certain policies of the Delhi Sultanate, including the furtherance of Persian culture. Akbar was unusual in marrying Rajput princesses—most of the Mughal emperors had Iranian consorts, including the lady buried in the world's most beautiful and perhaps most lavish mausoleum, the Taj Mahal. (Although designed by two Persian architects, this mid-seventeenth century building represents a blend of Persian and Indian elements.) Akbar's marriage policy was just one example of his general inclination toward religious tolerance and toward seeking to reconcile those he could not subdue by military force. The orthodoxy of his religious views has long been argued, but his sense of divine mission is apparent in his characterization of a king

The Mughal Empire 1605

as "a light emanating from God, a ray from the world-illuminating sun." His good will toward Hindus was expressed not only in his own religious attitude but more concretely in his abolition of the tax levied on non-Moslems, and he further placated Hindus by forbidding the slaughter of cows.

Akbar divided the empire into provinces, and his government was conducted by *mansabdars*. These officials were holders of a *mansab*, a military rank defined in terms of the number of troops its holder was obliged to supply. The *mansabdars* were supported by *jagirs*, assignments to collect revenue for the government as well as their salaries and expenses from designated lands. These lands were frequently scattered, subject to reassignment, and not hereditary. One reason for the Mughal success was that the emperors granted *jagirs* to, and thereby made allies of, a diverse elite including Rajputs and Afghans, Turkish and Iranian immigrants, South Indian Moslems, and prominent Hindus as well as Moslems from conquered regional states. The system was designed to prevent *mansabdars*

from turning into local power-holders, but it was hard on the people who actually worked the land because the holder of a *jagir* had no incentive to develop land he would soon lose. His interest was not in the well-being of the peasantry but in garnering the maximum revenue in the shortest possible time.

A substantial minority of townspeople were Moslem, but the great majority of peasants were Hindus as were the revenue collectors. Aside from paying their taxes, the villagers had little contact with

Akbar inspecting building operations of Fathpur Sikri (illumination from the Akbarnama manuscript, ca. 1590).

the state; kinship and village groups remained dominant in their lives. Even in the cities, the state rarely interfered directly in people's lives, and various communities and groups enjoyed a substantial degree of autonomy. For example, when the Portuguese became the dominant seapower along India's western coast, the merchants of Gujarat in northwest India dealt with the Europeans quite independently of their sultan, who remained unconcerned as long as his own prerogatives were not involved. The land-oriented Mughal rulers were similarly indifferent.

The Mughal empire reached its greatest geographical extent under Aurangzeb (1657–1707), a controversial ruler known for his strict adherence to Islam. His reim-position of the tax on nonbelievers was just one of the measures resented by Hindus. However, religious resentments were a less-serious problem than the developing crisis in the state's political economy. Most damaging was a growth in the number of *mansabdars* far in excess of the availability of *jagirs* with which to reward them. Pressures on the peasantry increased and there was rural unrest, but the discontent of the elite proved most dangerous to the regime. The succession after Aurangzeb of weak, uninspiring men to the throne and a general decline in administrative efficiency also placed strains on the loyalty of the empire's servants, undermining Mughal military power at a time when it was increasingly challenged

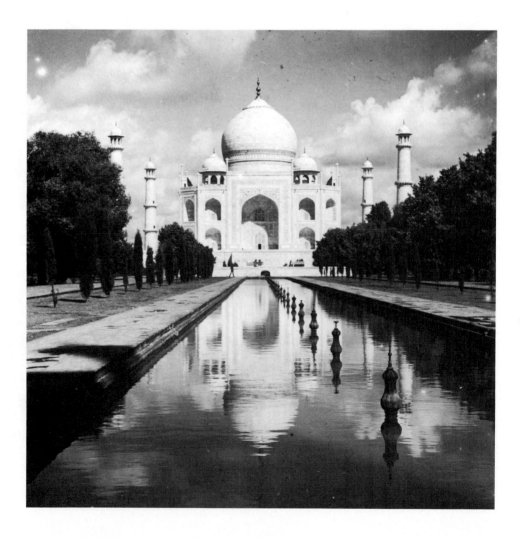

The Taj Mahal (seventeenth century).

by Marathas from India's west and by Afghans and Iranians from beyond the passes. In 1739 Nadir Shah (r. 1736–47), who ruled Iran, became the last foreign conqueror to enter India, devastate the North, and sack Delhi. Although after that a titular emperor remained in Delhi, actual power was in the hands of local potentates.

In 1765 one of these local rulers granted the British East Indian Company the right to collect revenue in his domains, and eventually the British became heirs to the Mughal empire. Up to this time, Europeans accepted and worked within the Mughal system. Although they had earlier gained control of the seas and thereby influenced India's trade and economy, and although individual Europeans helped to introduce new methods of warfare into India, they had remained largely peripheral to the mainstream of the subcontinent's history.

SOUTHEAST ASIA

Much of the diffusion of Indian culture described earlier (see Chapter 6) took place during the period discussed in this chapter. Other major events, such as the decline of Cambodia and changes affecting states of interior Java, were largely determined by internal developments. But Southeast Asia was also affected by Mongol expansionism and by the spread of Islam.

Although Mongol ambitions extended to Southeast Asia and Khublai Khan attempted to force Southeast Asian states into submission, the Mongols did not establish themselves in the area. The giant armada that Khublai sent against Java—where his troops landed in 1293—and the armies that he dispatched into what is modern Vietnam—where Hanoi was occupied three times—affected the local balance of power but did not drastically alter the course of history. Further west, the Mongols, after mastering the techniques of elephant warfare, defeated and conquered Pagan (1287). Yet, their efforts to control Burma failed, and old patterns of mutual dependence as well as conflict between the Burmese monarchs and the Buddhist monastic community continued to dominate Burmese history. The more immediate aftermath of the Mongol irruption was to leave Burma divided. This along with the collapse of Angkor, the other great mainland empire, opened the way for the creation of numerous small states and the emergence to new prominence of Thai rulers, although their states remained fragile because they were held together only by the personal relationship between king and elite.

In contrast to the fleeting impact of the Mongols, Islam became a permanent force in the Malay Peninsula and maritime Southeast Asia. The first Moslems in the area were doubtlessly traders, and Islam generally spread along the trade routes. Its fortunes were greatly increased by the growth of Malacca, whose ruler is said to have converted to Islam in 1414. Malacca, which commands the straits of the same name, became a great center of trade linking Sumatra, Java, and most of the other islands of modern Indonesia to far-off China, India, and ports of the Red Sea. The city participated in a giant international commercial network whose other major center was Gujarat, birthplace of many of the Moslem missionaries who came to Southeast Asia. Islam served as a link between Malacca and small states along the coasts of Sumatra and Java as well as ports in India and points west. Legends from Java, unlike those from Malaya, suggest a

Europeans Arrive in Malacca

After a while there came a ship of the Franks from Goa trading to Malaka; and the Franks perceived how prosperous and well populated the port was. The people of Malaka for their part came crowding to see what the Franks looked like; and they were all astonished and said, "These are white Bengalis!" Around each Frank there would be a crowd of Malays, some of them twisting his beard, some of them fingering his head, some taking off his hat, some grasping his hand. . . .

From Sejarah Melayu or Malay Annals, *trans. by C. C. Brown (New York: Oxford Univ. Press, 1970), p. 151.*

gradual process of conversion to Islam. Generally the diffusion of Islam was a gradual, uneven process that continued for many centuries and still continues.

In this connection, it is well to bear in mind the great vitality and powers of expansion exhibited by Islam during the fifteenth century, the era of the fall of Constantinople, at the other end of Asia, in 1453. Europe's rise to global supremacy came later, but the vanguard of European expansionism, the Portuguese, did arrive in Southeast Asia at the beginning of the sixteenth century. They seized Malacca in 1511 but were unable to maintain its commercial prominence. Instead, the trade was dispersed to the benefit of, among others, the sultanates of Johor at the tip of the Malay Peninsula and of Aceh on Sumatra. The first Dutch expedition reached the East Indies in 1596; a precursor to a much more ambitious effort than that of the Portuguese, it initiated a new age in the history of the islands that became modern Indonesia.

Seated court lady, sculpture of the Tang period (618–906).

THE COSMOPOLITAN CIVILIZATION OF CHINA

The Tang Dynasty, 618–907

China was reunified in 589 by the Sui dynasty, which laid the foundations on which the Tang (T'ang) built one of China's most illustrious dynasties. Under the Tang, Chinese power once again extended to the Pamirs, and the influence of Chinese culture profoundly affected distant Japan. Within China, the south was more fully integrated into the society because the rich ricelands of the lower Yangzte River were now linked to the capital in the north by the Grand Canal built by the Sui.

The central government was organized into six ministries: Personnel, Revenue, Rites, War, Justice, and Public Works. These ministries reflected the range of government concerns and were to be retained by subsequent regimes into the twentieth century. Staffing the government were officials of aristocratic background. Most officials entered the civil

service through family connections even though the Sui initiated a government examination system, which the Tang continued. Indeed, the Tang was the last great age for the hereditary high aristocracy.

The magnificence of the Tang was well expressed in its capital, Changan (Ch'ang-an, modern Xian or Sian). Encompassing about thirty square miles, it was the largest planned city built anywhere in the world. Its roughly one million inhabitants also made it the most populous city in the world in its day; another million people lived in the area outside its walls. In accord with tradition, Changan was oriented so that both the city and the imperial palace faced south. Leading up to the palace and the government complex was an avenue 500 feet wide, well designed to impress envoys from lesser lands with the might and grandeur of the Chinese empire. The people of the city lived in rectangular wards, each a self-contained unit surrounded by walls, with entry provided through a gate that was closed each night.

Tang culture was doubly cosmopolitan: first, in that China was open to cultural influences from India and the distant west; second, in that China itself was the cultural model for the other settled societies of East Asia. Both aspects were reflected in the numerous foreigners in Changan. Some were students, including approximately 8,000 Koreans said to have been in Changan in 640. Other foreigners were engaged in commerce, coming from such distant lands as India, Iran, Syria, and Arabia. At Changan's West Market exotic foods and beverages were on sale, and one could watch performances of foreign acrobats, magicians, and actors. Stylish Tang ladies sported foreign coiffures, while painters and potters enjoyed rendering the outlandish features of the "barbarians" from distant lands. In keeping with the robust and cosmopolitan spirit of the age, a favorite pastime of its aristocratic ladies and gentlemen was polo, a game that originated in Persia. Women's participation in such athletic activities is worth emphasis in light of the very different ethos that prevailed later.

Changan was a religious as well as political center. Manichean, Nestorian, and Zoroastrian temples testified to Tang tolerance, but their congregations were largely foreign. The opposite was true of the many Daoist and even more numerous Buddhist establishments. This was the golden age of Buddhism in China. Just as its pagodas dominated the capital's skyline, the Buddhist faith dominated the intellectual and spiritual horizon.

In the countryside, Buddhist temples performed important economic functions by operating mills and oil presses, maintaining vaults for self-deposits, and performing other banking services, including pawnbroking. The temples also held much land, and they profited from their connections with wealthy patrons who sought to evade taxation by registering land under a temple name. Some temples provided medical care; others entertainment. Architecture flourished, and Chinese Buddhist

sculpture reached a classical highpoint. At their best, Tang sculptures blend Indian delight in the corporality of mass with a Chinese sense of essentially linear rhythm.

The Tang was also the classic age of Chinese poetry, producing a number of excellent poets, including the two who came to be admired as China's best, Li Bo (Li Po, 701–63) and Du Fu (Tu Fu, 712–70). Li Bo was a free spirit who preferred to compose verse in a free style of his own rhythmic and verbal patterns. One of his favorite themes was wine, and there is even a story, most likely spurious, that on a nocturnal drinking expedition on a lake he fell into the water while trying to fish out the moon and drowned. Du Fu, in contrast, was particularly effective in a style of verse governed by elaborate rules of tone and rhythm as well as verbal parallelism. He wrote on many themes but is

Stone relief of a horse and groom from the tomb of a Tang emperor.

Tang guardian lion of marble and polychrome (*ca.* 618–906).

most admired for his social conscience and compassion. Some of his most moving poems describe the suffering and hardships of ordinary people. He could be severe in his political and social commentary:

> Inside the red gates wine and meat go bad;
> On the roads are bones of men who died of cold.*

*Quoted in A. R. Davis, *Tu Fu* (New York: Twain, 1971), p. 46.

An example of Chinese calligraphy. This stone rubbing was made from an inscription in the Regular Style by Ouyang Xun, a scholar and calligrapher of the Tang period.

These lines are from a long poem Du Fu wrote shortly before the dynasty was shaken and almost destroyed by the rebellion of An Lushan, a general stationed in the Northeast. The rebellion began in 755—only four years after defeat of a Tang army on the banks of the Talas River opened Central Asia to Islam—and it lasted until 763. Although the dynasty rallied after the defeat of An Lushan and made some important reforms, the general tendency was for regional military governors to assert their independence. Secular culture continued to flourish, but Emperor Wuzong (Wu-tsung 840–46), beset by financial problems, was unable to resist the temptation of the wealthy Buddhist establishment. In the resulting persecution, monastic lands and wealth were confiscated, monks and nuns returned to lay life, and Buddhist economic power was broken. The government did not concern itself with questions of belief, and the anti-Buddhist policy was promptly reversed by Wuzong's successor, but great damage had been done.

During its last fifty years the dynasty was beset by factionalism and growing eunuch power at court, mistrust between officials in the capital and those in the field, mismanagement, corruption, and incompetence. Bandit gangs, refuges for the desperately poor and dislocated, increased in number, size, and ambition. Forming themselves into confederations, they progressed from raiding to rebellion. Power, whether bandit or "legitimate," went to the strong and the ruthless. Even though the dynasty made occasional gains, each rally was followed by further decline. In the end, Changan was ruined. The city, which the first Han emperor had made his capital over a thousand years earlier, would never again be China's seat of power.

The Song Dynasty, 960–1279

China was reunited by the Song (Sung). This dynasty did not match the Tang in military power or geographic extent. Indeed, after 1127 North China was lost to the alien Jurchen Jin (Chin) state but continued in the south as the Southern Song.

However, what makes the Song of crucial importance is the emergence of some of the basic features of late imperial China. Major developments included the formation of new elites in place of the old hereditary aristocracy, dramatic economic growth, and the creation of a new intellectual synthesis.

The turbulence that accompanied the decline and fall of the Tang destroyed the old aristocratic families and opened the way for new men who based their prestige on literary learning, their power and status on office holding, and their wealth on land ownership. Although these attributes did not necessarily overlap, when all three were present they reinforced each other: wealth enabled a family to educate one or more sons; education was the key to office; and office provided opportunities for the acquisition and retention of wealth.

After the loss of the North in the twelfth century, the tendency was for elite families to concentrate on strengthening their local roots by assuming leadership in local matters and forming marriage ties with similar families. To distinguish the new elite from the old aristocracy, scholars often refer to them as "the gentry." A further and vital distinction is between the office-holding upper gentry and the local gentry families, whose leaders served as intermediaries between their communities and the state.

The civil service examination system now came into its own as the preferred path to office. It linked the local and central elites, did much to validate the state's claim to meritocracy, and bestowed personal prestige on those able and fortunate enough to win a degree. The examinations were open to all men, excluding only a small minority such as the sons of criminals and the like, but, even though printing reduced the price of books, most candidates came from families of some

means or status. Structurally the system provided for an orderly progression through a series of written tests (three in the Song, more later). These began at the local level, included an examination in the capital, and culminated in a palace examination held under the emperor's personal auspices. The government went to great lengths to secure impartiality; papers were identified by number and copied by clerks before being submitted to the readers, who were thereby prevented from identifying the author of a paper through his calligraphy. For centuries, the battle of wits between would-be cheaters and the authorities was pursued with great ingenuity on both sides. Despite occasional scandals, the system enjoyed a reputation for honesty.

In the absence of the old aristocratic counterweight, the throne gained in power, but Song officials were by no means faceless bureaucrats. They had their own moral code and political views. Bureaucratic politics, however, tended toward factionalism. Factions could consist of men who agreed on policy matters, but

The Song and Jin Empires
TWELFTH CENTURY

Detail from *Clearing Autumn Skies over Mountains and Valleys,* Song landscape scroll attributed to Guo Xi (Kuo Hsi, *ca.* 1020–90).

Detail of a handscroll showing scenes of daily life in the Southern Song dynasty (thirteenth century).

they were likely to form around personal relationships and temporary alliances. The ultimate power of decision rested with the emperors, who usually ruled by manipulating rather than intimidating their officials. The most outstanding political figure of the Song was not an emperor, but Wang Anshi (Wang An-shih, 1021–86), an official whose vision of integrating state and society remains controversial. Many of his measures dealt with fiscal and economic matters. He intended to help the small farmer, for instance, by establishing a program of state farm loans. Other reforms

dealt with military and personnel problems. Some of his measures involved an increased use of money and thus represented a response to broader economic trends. However, his program ran into strong opposition, and Wang lost office seven years after he had initiated the reforms.

The increased use of money, including the first appearance of paper money, was but one aspect of impressive economic growth. This included progress in papermaking, book production, ceramics, tea processing, shipbuilding, and a spectacular advance in the production of coal and iron. Coal and iron were mined in North China in an arc from southern Hebei (Hopei) to northern Jiangsu (Kiangsu). Iron was also carbonized to make steel for weapons, drilling bits for digging wells, and chains for supporting suspension bridges.

Because coal and iron were found in the north, production declined drastically when North China was lost to the Jin, but advances in agriculture benefited the South. Yields were increased by the use of improved tools, advances in water control, wider application of fertilizers, and introduction of new strains of rice, most notably an early-ripening variety native to central Vietnam. In the southeast it became common for a rice paddy to produce two crops a year, either two harvests of rice or one of rice followed by a crop of wheat or beans.

With increased production commerce flourished. Large ocean-going ships were built to carry several hundred passengers. They were navigated by compass, steered by an axial rudder, protected by watertight bulkheads, and armed with small rockets. After the loss of the North, the government derived considerable revenue from foreign trade, which it encouraged by maintaining harbors and canals, building breakwaters, erecting beacons, operating warehouses, and even setting up hotels. The government encouraged ceramics export, and the discovery of Song shards not only throughout South and Southeast Asia but also in the Middle East and along the east coast of Africa attests to the wide popularity of the Song product.

Cities flourished; foremost among them was Hangzhou (Hangchow), the capital after the fall of the North. Its merchants, organized in guilds, offered their customers all kinds of products ranging from the staples of life to exotic perfumes and fine jewelry. Like the earlier Song capital in the North and unlike Changan of the Tang, Hangzhou grew haphazardly and featured all the attractions of a lively and thriving center of culture and entertainment, as well as the grimmer aspects of urban life—fire and crime. Hangzhou seems to have merited the praise it received from the cosmopolitan Venetian Marco Polo. Even though he saw the city late in the thirteenth century when it was no longer the capital, he described it as, "without doubt the finest and most splendid city in the world."

Song intellectual and artistic life was varied and lively. This was the classic age of landscape painting. Most influential was a revival of Confucianism that took

Porcelain winepot of the Song dynasty.

understanding the world. This constellation of values and ideas, often called Neo-Confucianism in the West, was an organic system in which each aspect reinforced the others. It is called Neo-Confucianism to distinguish it from earlier forms of Confucianism, but its formulators and practitioners thought of themselves simply as Confucians. More than that, they believed that they had retrieved the true meaning of the tradition, lost since Mencius. The most influential Neo-Confucian was Zhu Xi (Chu Hsi, 1130–1200) and his most influential writings were his commentaries on the *Four Books: The Analects, The Mencius,* plus *The Great Learning* and *The Doctrine of the Mean,* two chapters of the *Record of Rites* singled out by Zhu Xi.

Although influenced by Daoism and Buddhism, the Neo-Confucians rejected the two rival doctrines as fundamentally antisocial and immoral in advocating withdrawal from society and seeking purely personal (and therefore selfish) salvation. To Confucians social values were real and compelling, and the old concept of *ren* (*jen,* humaneness) received new emphasis.

Associated with Song Neo-Confucianism was an emphasis on moral seriousness and a moralism that made heavy demands on men and women. Moralists insisted that widows should not remarry and honored the woman who remained faithful to her betrothed even though he died before the marriage could take place. Yet, we must not exaggerate the influence of theorists on people's actual conduct. In practice, even among the elite (though not among royalty), most widows did remarry.

Also traceable to the Song is the beginning of foot-binding, a procedure that caused agonizing pain. Tiny feet were thought to enhance a young woman's attractiveness even as they deterred her from straying into mischief. To restrict foot growth, feet were wrapped tightly in bandages so that over time, the four toes of each foot were bent into the sole, and sole and heel were brought as close together as possible. Although foot-binding was later practiced widely, it was apparently uncommon during the Song and was never part of the Confucian social pro-

many forms. It inspired reformers like Wang Anshi, led to a revival of classical scholarship, and stimulated new achievements in historical studies and philosophical thought. The new Confucianism was at once a creed that gave meaning to the life of the individual, an ideology supporting state and society, and a philosophy that provided a convincing framework for

The Neo-Confucian Creed

Heaven is my father and Earth is my mother, and even such a small creature as I find an intimate place in their midst.

Therefore that which fills the universe I regard as my body and that which directs the universe I consider as my nature.

All people are my brothers and sisters, and all things are my companions.

Opening lines of "The Western Inscription" by Zhang Zsai (1020–77), from A Source Book in Chinese Philosophy, *trans. and compiled by Wing-tsit Chan (Princeton, N.J.: Princeton Univ. Press, 1963), p. 497.*

710	784		1185	1333	1573	1868
Nara Period	Heian Period		Kamakura Shogunate	Ashikaga Shogunate	Tokugawa Shogunate	

gram. The dynasty's leading female poet, Li Qingzhao (Li Ch'ing-chao, 1094–*ca.* 1152), never mentioned it.

The tone of Song civilization was profoundly civilian, but for many years it sustained itself against external threats by maintaining a large, well-equipped, if not always effective, army. The Song also entered into treaties with neighboring states that sometimes entailed payments and furthered its own interests by playing these states off against each other. After it lost the North, it survived in the South protected in part by its naval supremacy and by the difficulty northern cavalry had operating in the South with its paddies and waterways. Even after the Mongols conquered North China in 1234, the Song held out another 45 years before succumbing to those formidable world conquerors.

The Mongol Yuan Dynasty, 1279–1368

Even before Khubilai Khan (r. 1260–94) completed the conquest of China, he transferred his capital from Mongolia to Peking (Beijing), adopted the Chinese name "Yuan" for his state, and instituted Chinese court ceremonial. Thus he was careful to give at least an appearance of ruling in the Chinese manner. But his ambitions were not limited to China; we already noted his expeditions to Southeast Asia and to these must be added naval expeditions to Japan. To the west, he maintained control of Mongolia but was forced to give up an ambition to control central Asia. As a result, the Yuan was essentially a Mongol regime in China, not the Chinese part of a wider Mongol empire.

To prevent dependence on Chinese officials, the Mongols made a point of employing foreigners, mostly central Asians, though the most famous is Marco Polo. The Mongols accorded highest status to

Two Song ladies. Cave 165, Maijishan, Gansu.

Mongols. Next came Mongol allies, including central Asians and men from Southwest Asia, such as Turks, Persians, and Syrians. The third status group included inhabitants of North China, the native Chinese or descendants of other groups such as the Jurchen. At the bottom were the southerners who had resisted the Mongols longest and continued to be regarded with suspicion. This fourfold division of society affected recruitment and appointment of officials, conduct of legal cases, and taxation.

The Yuan generally accorded military officials preference over civilians, and the provinces had a great deal of autonomy. Because the Mongols were slow to reinstitute the examination system and to patronize scholarly learning, men who in other periods would have become scholars turned to other occupations such as medicine, fortune-telling, and the theater. It is no accident that this was the classic age of Chinese drama. Painting also flourished; the idea that a painting reveals the character of the man who created it existed in the Song, but it was prevalent under the Yuan and inspired work in a great variety of styles. Even though China was once again open to foreign influences and hospitable to travelers from afar, this had no appreciable impact on the world of the scholar-painter, nor did the writings of Marco Polo and his successors show any awareness, let alone appreciation, of the art of the Chinese literati. Although there was a Catholic archbishop in Beijing and relations across the great Eurasian land mass were often cordial, these relations had a low priority on both sides of the world, for the distances were enormous and both Europe and China faced more immediate challenges and opportunities closer to home.

The Ming Dynasty, 1368–1644

The declining years of the Yuan saw the emergence of regional power centers and popular rebellion. One leader of rebellion, Zhu Yuanzhang (Chu Yuan-chang, r. 1368–98), emerged victorious and founded the Ming dynasty. He was a harsh and vigorous autocrat who personally decided all significant matters and even some not so significant. During the later days of the Ming, too, the effectiveness as well as the tone of government was to a large degree determined by the character of the emperors and their devotion to the work of government. Ming government thus ranged from the energetic efficiency of the first two emperors to the laxity of some of the Late Ming rulers, one of whom did not hold an audience for more than 25 years.

Meanwhile, the local gentry presided over local society that continued to move to its own rhythms. Prominent gentry lineages maintained cohesion by compiling lineage genealogies, maintaining ancestral halls and graveyards, conducting ceremonial sacrifices to lineage ancestors, and maintaining general guides for the conduct of lineage members as well as formal lineage rules. A penalty for severe infractions of these rules was expulsion.

The Ming was generally a period of economic growth and considerable prosperity. It was also capable of strong military assertiveness; from 1405 to 1433,

---

The Complaints of the Ming Founding Emperor

In the morning I punish a few; by evening others commit the same crimes. I punish these in the evening and by the next morning again there are violations. Although the corpses of the first have not been removed, already others follow in their path. The harsher the punishment, the more the violations. Day and night I cannot rest. This is a situation which cannot be helped. If I enact lenient punishments, these persons will engage in still more evil practices. Then how could the people outside the government lead peaceful lives?

What a difficult situation this is! If I punish these persons, I am regarded as a tyrant. If I am lenient toward them, the law becomes ineffective, order deteriorates, and people deem me an incapable ruler. All these opinions can be discerned in the various records and memorials. To be a ruler is indeed difficult.

Proclamation of the Hong Wu Emperor from Patricia B. Ebery, Chinese Civilization and Society: A Sourcebook *(New York: The Free Press, 1981), p. 125.*

The Ming Empire
Fourteenth to Seventeenth Centuries

ished. Wang Yangming (1472–1529) stands second only to Zhu Xi in influence and importance. He insisted on the importance of inwardness and is also famed for his doctrine of the unity of knowledge and action. For Wang, knowing and acting were not only inseparable, they were two dimensions of a single process.

The Late Ming was an exciting time intellectually and artistically, but it was also a period of political decay that took a heavy toll in government efficiency and finally led to its collapse. It was ended by popular uprisings, but the real heirs of the dynasty were not Chinese rebels but Manchu leaders in the area northeast of

Porcelain jar of the Ming period showing ladies playing a game of *weiqi* (*go* in Japanese).

seven great maritime expeditions, commanded by a Moslem eunuch, were launched to Southeast Asia but also reached the Indian Ocean, Arabia, and the east coast of Africa. These expeditions illustrate Chinese strength in the fifteenth century, but, because they were an economic drain, they were discontinued, leaving the Europeans to take the lead in world navigation and discovery.

Printing, which had been invented in the Late Tang and spread during the Song, continued to expand in the Ming, along with literacy. Bookshops did a brisk business; among their best sellers were collections of model examination papers used by candidates to cram for their tests. But they also sold encyclopedias, colored prints, novels, and collections of short stories. There were also guides explaining the classics in simple language and books of moral instruction. Most prized by those who love Chinese literature are the Ming novels. Despite their literary excellence, they did not win respectability until the twentieth century. In traditional China, reading a novel was a surreptitious pleasure, something students did when their teacher was not looking—or vice versa.

This period also made notable contributions to drama, painting, and ceramics, and Neo-Confucian thought also flour-

China who were constructing a state in the Chinese manner. They established China's last dynasty, the Qing (Ch'ing, 1644–1911), which sought and won legitimization by ruling in a Chinese manner and continuing many Ming institutions while preserving special privileges for the Manchu elite.

Both the Ming and the Qing were much more concerned with China's Inner Asian frontiers, home of the Mongol and other nomadic invaders, than they were with European maritime expansionism. Indeed, under the Qing China reached its greatest territorial extent. As elsewhere, the first Europeans to arrive in Chinese waters were the Portuguese, whom the Chinese kept at arm's length because they could not drive them off. In 1557 they were allowed to use Macao in return for an annual payment. Of more interest to the Chinese court and officials were Jesuit missionaries who brought with them European science and technology as well as religion. By demonstrating the superiority of their astronomical predictions, they managed to displace Moslem and Chinese experts and established themselves in the Bureau of Astronomy, an important and prestigious office. The Jesuits even made some notable converts and were not seriously affected by the change of dynasties. However, they were there on Chinese terms, and the mission petered out in the middle of the eighteenth century when an impasse developed between the Qing emperor and the pope.

JAPAN

A major theme in Japanese history is the interplay between native and imported elements. In Japan's early history, culminating in the Nara Period (710–84), Chinese influence was enormous. Nara itself, Japan's first capital, was a miniature Changan; the court and political structure were modeled on those of China; writing, Buddhism, and Confucian moral values were among the Chinese imports. Yet, Japan never became just a smaller China. Here geography helped, for, while close

enough to the continent to receive its influences, Japan was far enough away not to be dominated by it. Other factors, too, made for the integrity of Japanese culture, including a language completely different from and unrelated to Chinese, a strong native animistic religion (Shinto), and a special aesthetic tradition. Furthermore, even during the Nara period, the Japanese state and society had their own character.

One difference between Japan and China was the role of the emperor. The Japanese emperor, unlike his Chinese counterpart, had an irrevocable sacred mandate based on divine descent. Thus, the Mencian idea that the mandate could be lost was disregarded. Political change in Japan took the form, not of deposing the emperor, but of controlling him; after the Nara period the emperor retained his religious aura and his powers of legitimization without any real political authority. In somewhat similar fashion, descent remained a major source of status in Japan.

The Nara period was followed by the Heian period (794–1185), when the capital was established in Kyoto and many Chinese imports were modified or discarded. Now, although Chinese remained the official written language, Japanese was written without depending solely on Chinese characters to render Japanese sounds. Instead, linguistic elements without Chinese equivalents were written in a syllabary *(kana)* with Chinese characters retained for nouns and the stems of verbs and adjectives to avoid confusion between homonyms. Art and architecture also departed from the international Tang style of the Nara period and became more Japanese in their concern with the texture of natural materials, especially wood, and a general penchant for asymmetry. The political system also contained a certain asymmetry as, behind the facade of imperial institutions, power came to rest in the hands of those (primarily the Fujiwara family) who held extensive rights in private, tax-exempt estates free from government interference.

This period was famed for its aristocratic culture when noble gentlemen and

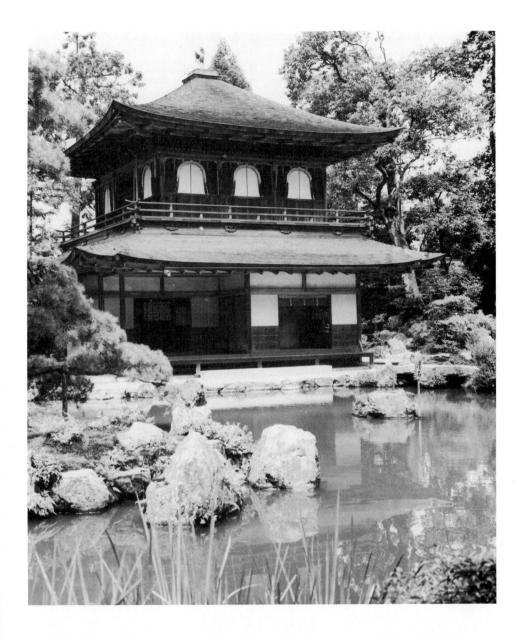

The Silver Pavilion at Kyoto combines both Japanese and Chinese elements.

ladies devoted their lives to beauty and love. One product of this culture was the world's first major psychological novel, *The Tale of Genji,* written by Lady Murasaki. Prince Genji had perfect taste, wrote a beautiful hand, was exquisitely graceful, was ever sensitive to the beauty and sadness of nature's changing moods, and was responsive to the delicate emotions of his many ladies. What he lacked were the martial virtues of the warrior.

The Kamakura (1185–1333) and Ashikaga (1336–1573) Shogunates

During the Kamakura period the warrior class emerged and gradually occupied center stage. Although there had earlier been a provincial warrior aristocracy, these men had been willing to serve civilian masters until the Heian system broke down and warriors were called in to the capital to help settle a political dispute.

After some years of turmoil, a peculiarly Japanese institution emerged: the shogunate. The shogun derived his military power from the loyalty of vassals in an essentially feudal system but received his title and legitimacy from the emperor. For a time, the shogunate honored the economic rights of the old Kyoto establishment, but the balance of power now shifted to the military. In theory, the shogun was subordinate to the emperor but in practice the shogun had the upper hand.

The first shogunate got its name from Kamakura, a village in eastern Japan far away from the imperial court in Kyoto. The choice to keep warriors away from the charms of the imperial capital was a deliberate attempt to preserve the values of the warrior: valor, manly pride, vigor, and undying loyalty. Yet, such loyalty had to be rewarded. This was easily accomplished when the shogunate was fighting recalcitrant Japanese whose lands could be seized and reassigned. But there were no such spoils when the Mongols were

defeated in 1271 and 1284. Worse still was the shogunate's inability to reward the forces it maintained for many years in anticipation of a third Mongol attack that never came.

An attempt at imperial restoration followed the collapse of the Kamakura shogunate, but its real successor was the shogunate established by the Ashikaga family in Kyoto. In many respects, particularly in culture, the ensuing period represented a fusion of the aristocratic culture of the capital and the traditions of the samurai (the Japanese term for *warrior*). A great cultural flowering occurred in this age of Nō drama, of tea masters and Zen aesthetics, of excellent pottery, of the classic Japanese garden, and of fine architecture drawing on Song as well as on native Japanese forms. However, politically the Ashikaga period degenerated into a century of warfare (1467–1573) followed by a shorter period (1573–1600) of unification and ended with the establishment of the last and strongest shogunate.

Interior of a house in Yoshiwara during the Tokugawa period (eighteenth-century woodcut print).

The Tokugawa Shogunate, 1600–1868

Under the Tokugawa the shogunate was once more separated from the imperial court in Kyoto. The shogun's capital was Edo, modern Tokyo. There, the shogunate's officials kept a close watch over regional lords who were burdened with new obligations—including an obligation to spend alternate years in Edo and leave wives and children behind as hostages when they did go back to their domains. Yet, within these domains the local lords were free to pursue their own administrative and economic policies.

A number of Tokugawa policies were meant to ensure a stable future. Thus a freezing of class lines drew a clear line between samurai and commoners. The most visible sign of samurai privilege was the exclusive right to wear a sword, yet in a time of peace his duties were largely civilian. Accordingly, the samurai were sent to school to attain at least a degree of Chinese learning, and the shogunate patronized Neo-Confucianism as a philosophy appropriate for the new age.

Intent on stability, the Tokugawa shogunate was not about to tolerate interference from abroad. At first, Portuguese ships and Jesuit missionaries had been warmly received in Japan, but this changed as Japanese leaders became aware not only of the dangers of European expansionism—as exemplified by the Spanish seizure of the Philippines—but also of the subversive potential of foreign influence. In 1606 Christianity was declared illegal, and in 1614 there was a serious campaign to expel missionaries. Many of the 300,000 Japanese Christians suffered grievously under Tokugawa persecution. In 1637–38 a rebellion in Shimabara, near Nagasaki, was fought under Christian slogans against a lord who combined merciless taxation with cruel religious suppression. Furthermore, trade as well as Christianity was seen as potentially subversive because it would benefit the coastal lords. Consequently, the Tokugawa prohibited not only the foreign religion but expelled all foreigners from the country and only allowed the Dutch to send an annual vessel to a tiny artificial island in Nagasaki harbor. Moreover, Japanese were prohibited from traveling abroad.

In the long run, of course, the Tokugawa shogunate did not achieve the stability envisioned by its architects. They, no more than anyone else, could stop change. Indeed, their very success in ensuring peace and tranquility led to unprecedented economic growth. Cities such as Edo and Osaka grew and developed their own distinct urban culture. An increased use of money and a new economy baffled the samurai and undermined the social and political order. By the middle of the nineteenth century, many felt that Japan was ripe for change.

However, in the seventeenth century it would have taken superhuman clairvoyance for a statesman in Japan, China, or India to realize that European civilization represented anything but a minor problem. In all three countries, leaders could look back on traditions that had withstood the test of time and contemplate the future with confidence. Little could they know that the future was to bring radically new challenges.

Suggestions for Further Reading

General

For a comparative perspective, see E. L. Farmer et al., *Comparative History of Civilizations in Asia,* 2 vols. (1977, 1986). Also see the general works suggested for Chapter 6.

India

The New Cambridge History of India promises to be a major resource. It begins with "The Mughals and Their Contemporaries" and will consist of eight volumes, two of which have been published to date: M. N. Pearson, *The Portuguese in India* (1987), and Burton Stein, *Vijayanagara* (1989). Also by Stein is *Peasant, State, and Society in Medieval South India* (1980), a major advanced analytical study. Two highly regarded books deal with Islam in India: Aziz Ahmad, *Studies in Islamic Culture in the Indian Environment* (1964), and Sheikh Mohamad Ikram, *Muslim Civilization in India* (1964). A more specialized study is R. M. Eaton, *Sufis of Bijapur 1300–1700: Social Roles of Sufis in Medieval India* (1978). P. Spear, "The Mughul Mansabdari System," in E. Leach and S. N. Mukherjee, *Elites in South Asia* (1970), is a concise account of that complicated system.

Southeast Asia

D. G. E. Hall, *A History of South East Asia,* 4th ed. (1981), remains authoritative. Anthony Reid, *Southeast Asia in the Age of Commerce, 1450–1680.* Vol. I: *The Lands Below the Wind* (1988), treats the region as a single cultural zone. It conveys the texture of life and discusses the influence of Islam and Christianity. The first volume of *The Cambridge History of South East Asia* is scheduled for publication in 1993. C. Geertz, *Negara: The State in Nineteenth-Century Bali* (1980), is helpful in thinking about earlier Indianized states of Southeast Asia. R. Winstead, *The Malays: A Cultural History* (1950), is a standard treatment. *Sejarah Melayu 'Malay Annals'* (1970), trans. C. C. Brown, is sometimes tedious but includes passages of great charm. D. K. Wyatt, *Thailand: A Short History* (1984), is definitive. M. Aung-Thwin, *Pagan: The Origins of Modern Burma* (1985), is "must" reading for the history of that country. Robert H. Taylor, *The State in Burma* (1987), devotes 65 pages to the precolonial state. M. C. Ricklefs, *A History of Modern Indonesia* c. *1300 to the Present (1980),* is a solid account.

China

Two volumes of *The Cambridge History of China* deal with the periods discussed in this chapter, Vol. 3, Part 1 (1979) on the Sui and Tang, and Vol. 7, Part 1 (1988) on the Ming. Also recommended are A. F. Wright, *The Sui Dynasty* (1978), and A. F. Wright and Denis Twitchett, *Perspectives on the T'ang* (1973). E. O. Reischauer, *Ennin's Travels in T'ang China* (1955), is an account by a Japanese monk. A Cooper, *Li Po and Tu Fu* (1973), is a fine introduction to these great poets.

Much scholarly attention has been paid to the Song in recent years. Among the good books on major facets of that period are J. W. Chaffee, *The Thorny Gates of Learning in Sung China* (1985); P. B. Ebrey, *Family and Property in Sung China: Yüan Ts'ai's Precepts for Social Life;* R. P. Hymes, *Statesmen and Gentlemen: The Elite of Fu-chou, Chiang-hsi in Southern Sung* (1986); and Paul J. Smith, *Taxing Heaven's Storehouse: Horses, Bureaucrats, & the Destruction of the Sichuan Tea Industry* (1991).

For the Yuan, see M. Rossabi, *Khubilai Khan: His Life and Times* (1987); J. W. Dardess, *Conquerors and Confucians: Aspects of Political Change in Late Yüan China* (1973); and J. D. Langlois, ed., *China under Mongol Rule* (1981). C. O. Hucker, *The Traditional Chinese State in Ming Times* (1961), is succinct and definitive. Arthur Waldron, *The Great Wall of China: From History to Myth* (1990), is an authoritative account of the Ming dynasty's, and China's, most famous structure. It clarifies China's policy toward her nomadic neighbors and links past and present as well as history and myth.

For a fascinating account of a major Qing emperor, see J. Spence, *Self-Portrait of K'ang-Hsi* (1974). Philip A. Kuhn, *Soulstealers: The Chinese Sorcery Scare of 1768* (1990), provides insights into how the Qing government functioned as well as the mind-set of high and low. A number of books relate the social and economic history of the late imperial period to modern Chinese developments. An exceptionally useful and stimulating survey is Lloyd E. Eastman, *Family, Fields, and Ancestors: Constancy and Change in China's Social and Economic History 1550–1949* (1988).

Japan

The Cambridge History of Japan (1989–) is a good place to begin reading in depth. Also recommended is H. P. Varley, *Japanese Culture: A Short History,* 3rd ed. (1984). Tsunoda et al., *Sources of Japanese Tradition* (1958) is a valuable anthology. The Kodansha *Encyclopedia of Japan* (1983) is a useful reference. For a recent compilation, see the "Suggested Readings" in Conrad Schirokauer, *A Brief History of Japanese Civilization* (1993).

Contacts with Europe

Recommended for China are Thomas H. C. Lee, ed., *China and Europe: Images and Influences in Sixteenth to Eighteenth Centuries* (1991) and J. Gernet, *China and the Christian Impact: A Conflict of Cultures* (1985). C. R. Boxer, *The Christian Century in Japan* (1951), is well written and informative. Also see G. Ellison, *Deus Destroyed: The Image of Christianity in Early Modern Japan* (1973), and Vol. 4 of *The Cambridge History of Japan*.

16

THE REVIVAL OF EUROPE

One of the most striking aspects of the late Middle Ages is that political leaders and scholars created so much that was new and exciting while society as a whole was suffering war, famine, and plague. Institutions that had stood for centuries gradually lost prestige and authority, but at the same time the seeds of a new era were being sown. In England, Parliament moved toward its modern status, and the idea that the judiciary should be independent of royal power won acceptance. Capitalism began to emerge as an economic system suitable for commerce and agriculture.

The writers and scholars of the fourteenth century were the first to recognize the vast distance between the culture of the classical world and the culture of their own time. Earlier scholars had thought of themselves as the continuers of ancient civilization; scholars of the new era thought of themselves as recoverers of that civilization. For them, ancient civilization had ended in the fifth century, when the Visigoths, Ostrogoths, and Franks overran western Europe. Scholars of the fifteenth and sixteenth centuries first referred to the thousand years dating from the end of the Roman Empire as the "middle ages."

With this new awareness came a new historical consciousness. Earlier historians, following the lead of Augustine (see p. 118), had divided history into epochs marked by crucial events in the relationship between man and God: History began with the Fall of Adam; the flood and Noah's rescue marked the beginning of a new epoch; Moses and the making of the covenant between God and the Jews marked a third epoch; the incarnation of God in Jesus inaugurated the current epoch; the Second Coming would bring all history to an end. Now, however, people

(*OPPOSITE*) SANDRO BOTTICELLI'S *ALLEGORY OF SPRING* SHOWS THE CLASSICAL INFLUENCE IN RENAISSANCE ART. BOTTICELLI WAS A MEMBER OF THE CIRCLE OF PLATONISTS GATHERED AT THE ACADEMY BY LORENZO DE MEDICI. THE IDEALIZATION OF THE HUMAN FIGURE IN ART IS "PAINTED PLATONISM."

were tracing the course of history according to intellectual and artistic milestones, not according to phases in the spiritual condition of humanity. At the moment, they were conscious of a revival of ancient civilization. Jakob Burckhardt, a Swiss historian of the nineteenth century, called that revival a renaissance.

Recently, however, historians have suggested that Burckhardt's term is somewhat inappropriate. True, there was a sharp break with medieval philosophy and a revival of classical learning, but in many other respects life in the fifteenth and sixteenth centuries was pretty much an extension of what life had been in the late Middle Ages. The economic and political changes that set in had little to do with the new ideas in scholarship and the arts. They were the consequences of a natural evolution from late-medieval society. The same is true of religious institutions, which went through profound changes in the sixteenth century. The next chapter is about those changes.

THE BACKGROUND OF THE RENAISSANCE

The new era opened against a background of economic depression, social unrest, and religious malaise. As we saw in Chapter 14, the droughts and famines that struck Europe toward the end of the thirteenth century had set off a decline in population that continued into the first half of the next century, and at midcentury the already weakened population was ravaged by the bubonic plague. During the next half-century the labor force continued its decline, a decline hastened by the breakdown of the manor and the guild. The structure of government and of society itself weakened, and the upper classes, led by the kings, tried desperately to preserve their privileges and fortunes by instituting drastic measures to keep prices and wages from rising. Europe was in woeful condition.

During the fifteenth century, institutions recovered their stability. The papacy regained much of its power with the defeat of the conciliar movement, even though it no longer exercised the universal authority it had once wielded. The monarchies of England and Spain began to bring their kingdoms under central control, and by the end of the century the French monarchy was following their lead. The population began to grow again, and technological advances gave the economy new impetus. Europeans turned more adventurous and by the end of the century had rounded Africa to reach the East Indies and had found their way to the Americas.

The seeds of this recovery had taken root in Italy toward the end of the fourteenth century. During the two centuries between the death of Dante (1321) and the sack of Rome by mutinous imperial troops (1527), Italy's influence over the rest of Europe had grown enormously. Italians set the style in architecture, sculpture, and painting; they dictated the literary taste and the educational practices that Europeans would follow for centuries. Northern Europeans flocked to Italy to study engineering, art, politics, and business, and Italians frequented the courts of princes and kings throughout Europe—even in remote Moscow. Italian navigators ventured out on bold explorations of uncharted waters.

Several reasons explain why it was Italy that pioneered the way into the new era. In close contact with the advanced civilizations of the Byzantine Empire and Islam, the Italian cities had begun to flourish as early as the tenth century, when northern Europe was just completing its move into feudalism. Because its focus was essentially rural, feudalism provided little impetus for the growth of cities. In Italy, feudalism never became very strong, and by the early fourteenth century it existed there in name only.

Moreover, because of the conflict between the papacy and the German empire a unified monarchy never emerged in Italy. Consequently, many of the medieval institutions that dominated the northern kingdoms never gained a foothold there. In intellectual matters, Italy was never dominated by scholasticism, as were the universities of the north, and Gothic architecture and sculpture had little influence in Italy. Thus, because the Italians' intellectual and artistic proclivities were outside the paradigms of medieval civilization, Italians were more receptive than northerners were to new ideas and to new ways of viewing the world. Also, though they experienced the famines and plagues of the fourteenth century, the cities of Italy were large enough, rich enough, and strong enough to recover more quickly than the cities of northern Europe.

THE CITY-STATES OF NORTHERN ITALY

The main business of the northern Italian cities was international trade. A third of the population of Florence, for example, was engaged in importing wool, making finished cloth, and selling it in foreign markets. Nearly all the people in Venice and Genoa depended for their livelihood either directly or indirectly on trade with the Levant and with northern Europe. Not surprisingly, affairs in the northern Italian cities were largely in the hands of bankers, export merchants, and textile manufacturers.

The political power of the cities reached deep into the adjacent region, which meant that they could act in the manner of urban principalities—that is, as city-states. Feudal lords in the neighborhood soon joined the city elite. And as the small market towns and villages of the countryside (called the *contado*) were annexed, some city-states came to control domains of several hundred square miles.

By the late twelfth century, the population of the city-states was divided into classes defined partly by social and partly by economic criteria. The merchant bankers—called the *popolo grasso,* or "fat people"—constituted the ruling class. The craftsmen, shopkeepers, and other members of the lesser bourgeoisie—the *popolo minuto,* or "little people"—made up the largest class. The lowest class consisted of poor day laborers, who had little say in the political life of the cities. Well-to-do families and craft guilds supported hospitals and other service agencies to take care of this indigent class. To be associated with these institutions brought a certain social cachet.

Unlike the class groups in the northern cities, the classes in the Italian cities rarely organized themselves into cohesive political entities. This was because in virtually every Italian city political parties supported either the emperor or the pope in their endless struggle for power, and the membership of those parties cut across class lines. These parties were descendants of the eleventh-century *patarini,* groups of townspeople who had fought the bishops for political control. Because most of the bishops were appointed by the emperor, the *patarini* had usually allied themselves with the papacy.

In the twelfth century, supporters of the Hohenstaufen emperors came to be known as Ghibellines, while supporters of the papacy were called Guelfs. Ghibelline was the Italian version of Waiblingen, the name of one of the Hohenstaufen castles; the Guelfs took their name from the Welfs, the family of the Bavarian dukes who were traditional rivals of the Hohenstaufens. Every city had its Ghibellines and Guelfs. By the thirteenth century, however, the parties, which continued to be known by their old names, no longer concerned themselves with the conflict between the pope and the emperor. They were only competitors for control of the cities, which had governments elected by all citizens who owned a certain amount of property.

Each party was led by one of the leading families of the city. The party that was out of power at the moment tried to win the support of the *popolo minuto* by blasting the incumbents and by promising to undertake a program of reform if elected. Occasionally, as in Florence in 1378, some reforms really were carried out after a transfer of power. Such reforms lasted only a short time, however, before they were scrapped in a new election or *coup d'état.*

The never-ending turmoil caused by the struggle between the Ghibellines and Guelfs drove many leading citizens from their cities. Whenever an able man won power and succeeded in restoring order by dictatorial means, he was hailed by the populace and accorded widespread

Equestrian statue of the condottieri Captain Bartolommeo Colleoni, who tried to create a state between Milan and Florence in the fifteenth century.

support. Such despots, as they were called, gained control of many Italian cities in the last fourteenth and fifteenth centuries and continued to command support even though they exiled, imprisoned, and executed their opponents. They managed to stay in the public's good graces by improving the city's public services, strengthening its defenses, imposing equitable tax systems, and seeing that the streets were safe. Many of them engaged architects and sculptors to build and adorn magnificent public buildings. They also wooed the public by waging wars with rival cities.

The despots had a hard time raising forces to fight a war, however, because the merchants and shopkeepers of the city, though eager to expand their markets, had no stomach for battle. Moreover, the despots suspected that they might be making trouble for themselves if they armed the townspeople. They hired mercenary troops called *condottieri,* who were well trained and fairly reliable so long as they were paid on time. In a showdown, however, the *condottieri* tended to be more loyal to their captain than to the man who was paying them, and some of the captains managed to seize power for themselves.

War and Diplomacy

In time, the city-states of northern Italy became so independent and so powerful that they were engaging almost constantly in wars and alliances with one another. By the early fifteenth century, they had begun to send ambassadors to the courts of Europe to report on potential allies and potential enemies. This was the beginning of modern diplomacy.

In the second half of the century, the five leading states—Venice, Milan, Florence, the Papal States, and the Kingdom of Naples—entered into a kind of "balance of power" with an unwritten understanding that no one of them would be allowed to become strong enough to threaten the others. Later, when France and Spain intervened in Italian affairs, they too began to engage in the practice of diplomacy and soon were working out a balance of power of their own. By the mid-sixteenth

century, resident ambassadors were common throughout western and central Europe, and France and Spain were maintaining a rough balance of power.

Milan, Venice, and Florence

Milan, the largest city in the Po Valley was the exemplar of the classic Italian city-state. At the end of the fourteenth century, Milan was ruled by Gian Galeazzo Visconti, a despot who made Milan into a leading manufacturing and trading city and who almost succeeded in uniting all of northern Italy under his power.

Venice, Italy's greatest commercial center, had risen to prominence in the ninth century as a Byzantine protectorate. Along with other interests in the eastern Mediterranean, it controlled the trade with Constantinople and Fatimid Egypt (see pp. 186–88). Built on a meager cluster of islands in the Adriatic Sea, Venice had never been touched by feudalism and was the first Italian city to hazard life under a republican constitution. Its government, the most stable in Italy, was conducted by a small council of merchants—the Council of Ten—led by a head of state called the doge. Every ounce of energy of the Venetian state and of the Venetian people was devoted to commerce. Venetian history included no revolutions but more than a few conspiracies. Venetians proclaimed their city, "the most serene republic." Until Venice began to acquire territory on the mainland during the fifteenth century, the city was relatively isolated from Italian politics.

Florence had outstripped its rivals Pisa and Siena as the leading city of Tuscany during the eleventh century. Florence, like Venice, was a republic. Its citizens took pride in their constitutional government and scorned their rivals for tolerating the rule of despots. They were particularly proud of having resisted Gian Galeazzo Visconti's attempt to take over their city.

Florentine society and politics were dominated by wealthy merchant bankers and textile manufacturers. Florentine bankers were regarded as the most astute on the Continent, and Florentine textiles

The Italian City-States   1454

The rise of the Medici: Cosimo de' Medici has the look of the wily businessman.

as the finest to be had. Unlike Venice, however, Florence was the scene of endless political intrigues and conspiracies, with the losers usually being forced into exile. (Dante suffered that fate.) The victors repeatedly tampered with the constitution in an effort to hold onto their position. Finally, in 1434, a party led by the banker Cosimo de' Medici (1389–1464) took control of the city. Cosimo was a political boss who preferred to work through others and used bribes and threats to ensure that his supporters won election to city offices. His son Piero (1416–69) and his grandson Lorenzo the Magnificent (1449–92) followed his ex-ample, and Florence enjoyed sixty years of stability.

Although the Medici were not themselves despots, they behaved in the manner of despots by strengthening the defenses of the city and by patronizing the best artists and architects of the age. The first three Medici made Florence the center of the Italian Renaissance, and their descendants, who remained prominent in the city until the eighteenth century, were faithful patrons of the arts. They allied their family with the leading families of Europe, and two of the Medici became queens of France.

The palace of the Medici in Florence. Cosimo began construction of it in 1444.

ITALIAN URBAN CIVILIZATION

Baldassare Castiglione (1478–1529) in *The Courtier* defined the Renaissance man. The courtier combines the chivalric virtues—physical dexterity and strength, courage, skill in combat, courtesy—with the new virtues—knowledge of the classics, appreciation of art and literature, eloquence, and good taste. Above all, the courtier has grace; he excels effortlessly in everything he undertakes.

During the Middle Ages, courtliness had been associated with high birth. But the Renaissance courtier could be a self-made man, for talented and ambitious men were accorded considerable mobility. The *condottieri* captain Francesco Sforza (1401–66), for example, who overthrew the Visconti family to become Duke of Milan, founded a dynasty that ruled for a century. Leonardo da Vinci and the scholars Lorenzo Valla and Aeneas Silvius Piccolomini (who became Pope Pius II) were not highborn but were said to have *virtù,* a term that meant more than "virtue" in the modern sense; it also meant "virtuosity," that combination of genius and determination that made for greatness in statesmanship, art, and literature. Eventually, *virtù* came to mean the quality that makes for success.

Individualism

Above all else, the Italian Renaissance valued individualism. The Italians had never felt the full weight of feudal obligations, and their wealth came from commerce rather than from landed estates. That meant that their assets were readily available, making it possible for them to move from place to place whenever they found their situation oppressive or boring.

Mobility provided individuals with the opportunity to act independently and favored the man with the talent and courage to strike out on his own. Many merchants, craftsmen, scholars, and artists moved away from their hometowns, where they could find support from family and friends, to places where the market was good or patrons were ready to hire them, but where they would be on their

---

A Man of Virtù

Benvenuto Cellini, a Florentine goldsmith and sculptor, had struck medals and coins for Pope Clement VII (1523–34). He claimed that he had been insulted by a jeweler named Pompeo (who also worked for the pope), and after several quarrels, Cellini stabbed Pompeo to death in a street brawl. Clement VII had just died; Cardinal Farnese was elected pope on October 13, 1534, and took the name of Paul III.

After he had put affairs of greater consequence in order, the new Pope sent for me, saying that he did not wish any one else to strike his coins. To these words of his Holiness one of his gentlemen named Latino Juvinale [a Humanist] answered that I [Cellini] was in hiding for the murder of Pompeo of Milan, and set forth what could be argued for my justification in the most favorable terms. The Pope replied: "I know nothing of Pompeo's death but plenty of Benvenuto's provocation, so let a safe-conduct be at once made out for him." A great friend of Pompeo's was there; he was a Milanese called Ambrogio [Ambrogio Recalcati, a papal secretary]. This man said: "In the first days of your papacy it is not well to grant pardons of this kind." The Pope answered: "You know less about such matters than I do. Know then that men like Benvenuto, unique in their profession, stand above the law."

From Benvenuto Cellini, The Life of Benvenuto Cellini, *trans. by John Addington Symonds (New York: Scribner's, 1926), p. 144.*

own. Benvenuto Cellini (1500–71), a sculptor and goldsmith who described his violent and colorful career in his *Autobiography*, was an excellent case of the individualistic ethos occasioned by the mobility in Renaissance society. Cellini assumed that autobiography, which had been a rare literary genre in the Middle Ages, was a natural form of expression: "All men of whatsoever quality they be, who have done anything of excellence, . . . ought to describe their life with their own hand." He declared that ordinary laws of morality were meant for ordinary people, not for geniuses such as himself, and he claimed that the pope had once absolved him of murdering a man because the pope understood that he was above the law.

Secularism

The second characteristic of Renaissance society in Italy was its secular tone. People were endlessly interested in the things of this world—commerce, the design of houses, styles of dress, food and drink, and the enjoyment of leisure. In his *Decameron* (*ca.* 1350), Giovanni Boccaccio told one hundred stories featuring characters taken from contemporary society. The work provided a model for Italian prose writing but also presented personality types that reveal the interests and ideals of behavior of the period. Boccaccio's characters are not irreligious or anti-Christian, but they scorn the hypocrisy of priests and monks; they rejoice in the triumph of clever people over clerical busybodies; and they seem to say that paying attention to the affairs of this world is quite appropriate for the people who live in it. The secularism of the *Decameron* consisted of two components—a preoccupation with worldly affairs and a contempt for false spirituality and asceticism.

Humanism

Humanism derived from the study of classical literature; the humanist was a classical scholar. It was not the mere act of studying the classics that made the humanist but the implication that one who

---

Petrarch on the Classics and Christianity

You are well aware that from early boyhood of all the writers of all ages and races the one whom I most admire and love is Cicero. You agree with me in this respect as well as in so many others. I am not afraid of being considered a poor Christian by declaring myself so much a Ciceronian. [This is an allusion to a famous vision of St. Jerome in which God told him: "You are a Ciceronian and therefore not a Christian."] To my knowledge, Cicero never wrote one word that would conflict with the principles proclaimed by Christ. If, perchance, his works contained anything contrary to Christ's doctrine, that one fact would be sufficient to destroy my belief in Cicero and in Aristotle and in Plato. . . .

Christ is my God; Cicero is the prince of the language I use. I grant you that these ideas are widely separated, but I deny that they are in conflict with each other. Christ is the Word, and the Virtue and the Wisdom of God the Father. Cicero has written much on the speech of men, on the virtues of men, and on the wisdom of men—statements that are true and therefore surely acceptable to the God of Truth.

From a letter to Neri Morando, 1358, in Petrarch's Letters to Classical Authors, *trans. by M. E. Cosenza (Chicago: University of Chicago Press, 1910), pp. 18–19.*

---

did so was interested in the highest ideals of human behavior. Humanism was the study of man though the examples provided by classical literature and ancient history. As far back as the fourteenth century, the poet/scholar Petrarch (1304–74) had revived classical literary forms and had imitated the styles of the ancient writers. Later humanists followed his example, spurred on by Boccaccio's biography of Petrarch.

Led by Petrarch and Boccaccio, Renaissance Italians conceived a passion for everything relating to classical antiquity. Knowledge of classical literature was an indication of true gentility, and the humanists were held in high honor. Many humanists held positions as secretaries in the royal courts of Europe and as teachers of the children of noble families. Generally, they were self-made men who earned a living through their learning. Enthusiasm

Benvenuto Cellini did this bust of Bindo Altoviti about 1550.

Young student reading Cicero
(detail from a painting by
Vincenzo Foppa).

One humanist educator wrote, "We call those studies liberal which are worthy of a free man . . . that education which calls forth, trains, and develops those highest gifts of body and of mind which ennoble men." That is still the goal of liberal education.

Historical Consciousness

Petrarch and his fellow humanists were well aware that the Roman civilization they admired was quite different from their own and were careful to distinguish between the past and present. They could talk of the "fall of Rome" and of the "dark age" that separated the glorious time of Augustus, Vergil, and Cicero from their own. This was a new consciousness that enabled the humanists to see themselves and their society in historical context, which is a characteristic of the modern view of individuals and society.

FAMILY LIFE

The ideals of Renaissance family life were those of upper-class urban families— the families of bankers and merchants. The *populo minuto* imitated these ideals to the extent that their finances permitted.

Men got married rather late, usually to much younger women, and the husband was unchallenged head of the household. Because of the disparity of age, widows were almost as common as widowers. (Until modern times, men generally outlived their wife because of the frequency with which women died in childbirth.) A man was expected to have established himself as an upstanding member of the community before marrying, and his purpose in marrying was to have children who would carry on his family line and his profession. The role of the wife was to advance her husband's career by exhibiting her beauty, culture, and social grace. Consequently, it was important that women be faithful and virtuous, and a woman's virtue was a common theme in Renaissance literature. The need for a woman to remain faithful to her husband was so urgent that it even survived his

for the classics intensified after 1395, as scholars fled westward from Constantinople to escape the Ottoman Turks, who were advancing across Asia Minor. In Italy the Greeks found students eager to study the Greek language and Greek literature, and Lorenzo the Magnificent founded a Platonic Academy in Florence for the study and teaching of Greek philosophy. By the end of the fifteenth century a few Italians were studying Hebrew and Arabic in addition to Greek.

The humanists turned their attention to education as well. The secular schools of the Middle Ages had concentrated on preparing young men for a career in commerce. They taught reading, writing, and arithmetic, and little else. And the main purpose of the ecclesiastical schools had been to train clerics and monks; their intellectual standards were high, but of course all study focused on theology.

The humanists of the fifteenth century rediscovered the "liberal arts" that liberate the mind and the imagination through the study of great literature and philosophy. To that study they added training in behavior and athletic skill, thereby realizing the ancient goal of *mens sana in corpore sano* ("a sound mind in a sound body").

death. A man was advised to discourage his wife from remarrying after his death by arranging that his property would go to her only "if she remains a widow and lives with her children." Of course many widows did remarry, and families were often quite large.

A young woman married to an older man often had to cope with difficult circumstances. There might be little or no difference between her own age and the age of her husband's older children, and she might become embroiled in controversies between the various sibling groups. She might also be obliged to accept her husband's illegitimate children into the household and sometimes the children of his brothers or sisters as well. During prolonged absences of her husband, she was expected to manage the servants and their children, raise her children, run the household, and keep the family, the relatives, and the staff at peace.

Infants were normally put out for two years to a wet nurse—usually peasant women in the *contado*. When returned to the family household, they had to get to know their siblings and their parents and find a place for themselves in the family group. Many diaries from the period evidence the feelings of alienation and fear that often accompanied this entry into the home.

Between the ages of two and seven, children were almost exclusively under their mother's care. The father remained rather distant except in times of crisis, as when the child or the mother became seriously ill. The father entered the child's world when the child was ready to begin formal education, usually at the age of seven.

Boys were sent to a boarding school, where they spent three or four years learning to read and write both in Latin and the vernacular. They then spent another year or so studying accounting and business procedures and finally were placed as apprentices with a merchant or banker. Girls were educated at home in the household arts and in reading and writing.

Women were expected to come to their marriage with a dowry, and in Florence and many other cities parents could

How Children Should Be Raised

The Dominican Friar Giovanni Dominici (ca. 1356–ca. 1420) wrote a treatise on childrearing.

Children should be accustomed to eat coarse food, to wear cheap and common clothes. . . . They should also learn to wait on themselves, and to use as little as possible the services of maid and servant, setting and clearing the table, dressing and undressing themselves, putting on their own shoes and clothes and so forth.

After a boy reaches three years of age, he should know no distinction between male and female other than dress and hair. From then on let him be a stranger to being petted, embraced and kissed by you [the mother] until after the twenty-fifth year. Granted that there will not take place any thought or natural movement before the age of five . . . do not be less solicitous that he be chaste and modest always and, in every place, covered as modestly as if he were a girl.

Quoted by James Bruce Ross, "The Middle-Class Child in Urban Italy, Fourteenth to Early Sixteenth Century", The History of Childhood, *ed. by L. deMause (New York: Psychoanalytic Press, 1974).*

invest in dowry banks. They deposited a specified sum when their daughter was very young and let the fund grow through the accrual of interest until it was redeemed.

Women of the middle classes participated more directly in their husbands' affairs. From the little evidence we have, it appears that middle-class families emulated their betters by putting their children out to a wet nurse and providing them with a formal education. The men married late, and widowhood was common in this class. Some women found work in manufacturing—perhaps as weavers—and many women seem to have owned their own shops.

THE RENAISSANCE

Literature, Philosophy, and Scholarship

The early humanists tended to imitate the genres and styles of classical literature—letters, orations, moral essays, and poetry,

A seventeenth-century engraving showing a peasant father feeding his infant child.

Renaissance scholars created the discipline of critical scholarship, which calls for a careful linguistic and historical analysis of the literature of the past. Lorenzo Valla (*ca.* 1405–57) used linguistic analysis to prove that the Donation of Constantine (see p. 182), on which papal claims to temporal authority rested, was a crude forgery of the early Middle Ages. He also compared several Greek manuscripts of the New Testament with Jerome's vulgate translation (late fourth century) and uncovered many errors and distortions in the translation. His scholarly approach to literary texts influenced later scholars, including Erasmus (see p. 432), who produced the first critical edition of the Greek New Testament.

Social and Political Thought

Though most of the social and political thinkers of the Renaissance simply paraphrased the Greek and Roman classics, a few of them did original work. Leon Battista Alberti (1404–72), for example, in his *On the Family* analyzed the structure and interests of Florentine families. He reports that they prized prudence, thrift, foresight, and comfort; had strong family feeling and little interest in the affairs of society as a whole; and aspired to a house in the city and an estate in the country to produce the family's food. Alberti's account is one of the earliest treatments of what later came to be called the bourgeois virtues.

Baldassare Castiglione's *The Courtier* (written 1513–18, published 1528), as we have seen, dealt with the ideals of the noble class. Drawing on his experiences at the court of the duke of Urbino, Castiglione reformulated the ideal of "the gentleman." Though his work owed much to the chivalric tradition of the Middle Ages, it spoke of the goals of a liberal education and the idea that "nobility" derives from character rather than from the accident of birth.

Perhaps the greatest political theorist of the Renaissance was Niccolò Machiavelli (1469–1527), who combined wide reading in the classics, particularly history, with wide experience in politics. He served Florence as an ambassador to

for example. They also created new forms, however, such as the sonnet and the essay.

Renaissance philosophers drew heavily on the work of Plato, which had been introduced to the West by refugee Byzantine scholars in the 1390s. The leading members of the Platonic academy founded by the Medici were Marsilio Ficino (1433–99) and Pico della Mirandola (1463–94), who tried to reconcile Plato and Christianity much as Thomas Aquinas had tried to reconcile Aristotle and Christianity (see pp. 293–95).

France and as secretary of the state during a period when the Medici were out of power. When they returned to power in 1512, Machiavelli retired to his country estate. There he studied political history and reflected on what causes political breakdown, how political leaders obtain and hold power, and what can be learned from history.

In his long, rambling *Discourses on Livy* (Livy was a famous Roman historian) and in his brief essay, *The Prince,* Machiavelli sought to describe political life as he saw it, rather than as it should be. His analysis of the strengths and weaknesses of various types of constitutions shows that he favored the republican form of government, like that of Florence. In *The Prince,* however, he concentrated on the behavior of heads of state and their use of power. The book ends with a plea that Italians unify their country, throw out the foreign invaders, and recreate the glory of ancient Rome. *The Prince* became a grammar of political and diplomatic practice and was translated into many languages. Its realistic account of the world of politics and international relations earned Machiavelli a reputation as a proponent of dictatorship. Actually, although he believed that a strong, centralized state was desirable, he insisted that it must operate under a constitution suited to the character of the people. And the most educated populace would be best served by a republican constitution.

The Arts

Soon after the humanists rediscovered Roman literature, Renaissance architects turned their attention to Roman architecture. There were Roman buildings or their ruins everywhere, and architects set about analyzing the principles of design the Romans had followed. The greatest of the early Renaissance architects was Brunelleschi (*ca.* 1377–1446), who designed numerous churches with symmetrical design and stately facades. The most impressive example of Renaissance architecture was the church of St. Peter in Rome, which replaced a fourth-century basilica built by Emperor Constantine I. The largest church

A late sixteenth-century portrait of Niccolò Machiavelli by Santi di Tito. The artist has tried to suggest both the intellectual brilliance and the shrewdness of the man.

in Europe, St. Peter's was the work of several architects—including Bramante, Michelangelo, and Bernini—from 1506 to 1615.

Renaissance painting was strongly influenced by the techniques of Giotto (1276–1337), Dante's favorite painter, who introduced a sense of volume in his representations of figures and their surroundings, especially in a series of frescoes (paintings done on fresh plaster) in the church of St. Francis in Assisi. During the fourteenth century Italian painters had also become familiar with the realistic style favored by the Flemish painters of the Burgundian court. That style was raised to a new height by Masaccio (1401–*ca.* 1428), who suppressed irrelevant details and concentrated on the emotional aspects of the scenes he painted.

In the Middle Ages, painting and sculpture had usually been regarded as adjuncts to architecture. But during the Renaissance they emerged as independent forms of expression. Italian painters still painted frescoes on the walls of

Machiavelli on Cruelty and Clemency

Is it better to be loved than feared or feared than loved? It may be answered that one should wish to be both, but it is much safer to be feared than loved when one of the two must be chosen. Men on the whole are ungrateful, fickle, false, cowards, covetous. As long as you succeed, they are yours entirely. They will offer you their blood, property, life, and children when the need is distant, but when it approaches they turn against you. And a prince who, relying entirely on their promises, has neglected other precautions, is ruined. . . . Men have fewer scruples in offending one who is beloved than one who is feared, for love is preserved by the link of obligation which, owing to the baseness of men, is broken at every opportunity for their advantage, but fear preserves you by a dread of punishment which never fails.

Nevertheless, a prince should inspire fear in such a way that if he does not win love, he avoids hatred; because he can endure very well being feared while he is not hated, and this will be true as long as he abstains from taking the property of his subjects or their women. But when it is necessary for him to take the life of someone, he must do it with proper justification and for manifest cause, and above everything he must keep his hands off the property of others, because men more quickly forget the death of their father than the loss of their heritage.

From Niccolò Machiavelli, The Prince, *trans. by W. K. Marriott (London: Dent, n.d.), pp. 134–35.*

some patrons treated artists as common servants, many artists earned handsome commissions and lived as independent and honored members of society.

In their efforts to achieve realism, Renaissance painters studied the laws of perspective and human anatomy, and their notebooks and sketches contain countless studies of proportion and space and treatments of the human torso and limbs. They observed facial expressions and body posture so that they could reveal the exact emotional state of figures they portrayed. Leonardo da Vinci (1452–1519), for example, in his painting *The Last Supper,* departed from tradition by depicting, not the moment when Christ says to the apostles, "This is my body . . .," but instead the dramatic moment when Christ announces, "One of you will betray me." By conveying the psychological state of each apostle, he achieves tremendous dramatic power.

Da Vinci's wide-ranging curiosity extended to the workings of mechanical devices as well as to the workings of the human body. He created designs for a helicopter and a self-propelled vehicle and made studies of perspective, light, and optics.

Michelangelo followed Da Vinci in searching for the psychologically charged moment. His painting of the Creation on the ceiling of the Sistine Chapel in the Vatican is focused on God's animation of Adam. And in his statue of Moses, Michelangelo portrays him at the moment when he catches sight of the Golden Calf, sitting tense, with a fierce expression, trying to control his rage over his people's idolatry.

Throughout these examples we find the Renaissance emphasis on human beings as they live here and now, in this world—troubled, striving, with unknown potential. Pico della Mirandola remarked in a famous *Oration* on man's dignity (1486) that God had given man something he had given to no other creature—freedom. All other creatures have their set patterns of behavior, but man's nature and destiny, Pico declared, are in his own hands. The people of the Renaissance had not lost their belief in God, but they gave new meaning to the Judeo-Christian idea that man was made in God's image: Like

churches and monasteries, but they turned more and more to easel painting, creating pictures to be hung on the wall and enjoyed for their own sake. Though they still favored religious themes, they often drew on classical sources for their subjects, reflecting the influence of humanism.

Sculptors, too, turned to classical models for inspiration. Donatello (1368–1466), for example, was the first sculptor since Roman times to model a freestanding nude figure. His *David* opened the way to the creation of a succession of great sculptures that culminated in the masterpieces of Michelangelo (1475–1564). These works revived the Greco-Roman fascination with the beauty of the human body.

Many Renaissance artists achieved substantial public recognition and social prestige through their work. Although

God, man is a creator, a creator of his own character and his own destiny.

Along with artists and writers, the urban courts of Italy employed hundreds of musicians, craftsmen, mechanics, and engineers. Working together in a relatively small space, these specialists often cooperated and advanced one another's endeavors. Artists and physicians shared their knowledge of human anatomy. Painters worked out the principles of perspective and contributed to the study of mathematics. Physicians studied astronomy, because in medieval medicine the stars were thought to affect health. In fact, many of the instruments used to observe the stars were designed by physicians.

During the sixteenth century Italy was the center of European cultural life. Northern Europe had begun to recover from the famines and plagues of the late Middle Ages, but northerners with an interest in the arts and humanism traveled to Italy to study. No northern city approached Florence, Venice, or Rome as a center of artistic and intellectual life.

ECONOMIC GROWTH IN NORTHERN EUROPE

The wealth of Italy was based primarily on trade and industry, and from the thirteenth century to the sixteenth century, Italy was the banking center of Europe. The wealth of the nations of northern Europe was based primarily on agriculture and mineral deposits. To be sure, northerners engaged in commerce and industry, and many cities had substantial communities of merchants and manufacturers; Flanders, for example, produced excellent cloth for which there was a lively demand. But agriculture was the main source of wealth, for northern Europe is one of the richest agricultural regions on earth, and the extensive network of rivers made it possible to move the produce to the markets at low cost.

During the fifteenth century, a series of technological advances fueled a new burst of economic activity in the North. And the new industries such as cannon founding and printing required large ini-

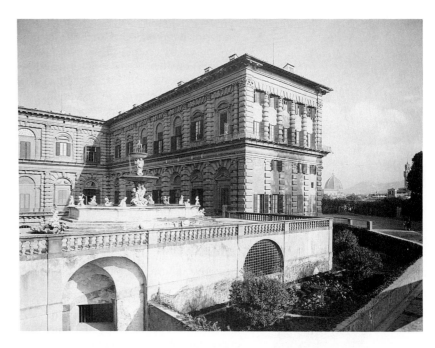

The Pitti Palace in Florence, now an art museum, was built by the early Renaissance architect Filippo Brunelleschi for the merchant Luca Pitti.

tial investments in plant and machinery. From the start, these industries were organized as capitalistic enterprises—that is, enterprises in which wealth was used to create new wealth. This was a departure from medieval practice, when most wealth was used to buy "consumer" goods and was rarely accumulated to invest in improvements and increased production.

The managers of these capitalistic enterprises drew their workers from both town and countryside and created a large, mobile labor force that was subject to the vagaries of an economy that neither they nor their workers could control. Consequently, the workers were wealthier and at the same time less secure than medieval peasants and craftsmen had been.

Progressive landlords tried to introduce capitalism into agriculture by producing only the most profitable crops and animal products. Particularly in England—where wool production was well established—many landlords fenced in, or "enclosed," open fields that had formerly been reserved for the use of villagers, and some of them even enclosed cultivated land to accommodate huge flocks of sheep. At the beginning of the sixteenth

Donatello's *David* (*ca.* 1430–32). Compare this statue with the *David* by Michelangelo on the opposite page.

century, Thomas More, chancellor of England, complained that the enclosure movement was ruining the small farmers and was creating a class of "sturdy beggars" or "vagabonds" who posed a problem for town governments. Actually, the reason for the vagabonds was the growth in population. After two centuries of decline, population growth had resumed, and it outpaced the creation of jobs. Town governments built prisons and workhouses to house the tramps.

The wealth produced by the new industries tended to find its way to a few hands in a few places. For a brief time, the most powerful banking house in northern Europe was that of the Fuggers of Augsburg in southern Germany. Jakob Fugger (1459–1525), banker to the Habsburgs of Austria (see p. 370) and to the popes, could invest in Austrian mines and Spanish colonies and carry on dealings with every part of the continent. From about 1476 to 1576, however, the real center of banking was Antwerp (now in Belgium), with Lyons in second place. In the following century, Amsterdam took over the lead. By the later sixteenth century, financial power was shifting from Italy to the north.

Leonardo da Vinci's design for a helicopter. The man uses a crank to flap the wings.

POLITICAL CONSOLIDATION AND CENTRALIZATION

Toward the end of the fifteenth century, the nations of northern Europe began to recover from the disastrous effects of war and plague. The War of the Roses (1455–85) produced a strong new dynasty in England (see p. 362), and after the end of the Hundred Years' War in 1453 the French kings were able to recover their power. In Germany, though the emperor remained weak, the marriage alliances contrived by the imperial family spread their influence across the Continent. And Spain too established a power base with the wealth extracted from its new colonies. In short, the kings of northern Europe were drawing close to achieving the absolute power that had eluded their medieval predecessors.

France

Although Charles VII (r. 1422–61) managed to drive the English from nearly all of their French territories, he was not a particularly effective ruler. He was, however, good at choosing able men to work for him (he was known as Charles "the Well-served") and getting them to strengthen the monarchy for him. In 1438, he asserted his authority over the French church by means of the Pragmatic Sanction of Bourges (see p. 428). In the 1440s, he solved his need for money by getting the Estates General to agree to a broad-based tax on land, which he continued to collect on his own authority thereafter. He organized a small but strong standing army (not more than 25,000 men). And he won the support of the merchant class, from which he recruited some of his best royal officials.

Charles's son Louis XI (r. 1461–83) was an able ruler who left the monarchy stronger than it had been since the early fourteenth century. He was a master of diplomacy—he was called "the Spider" because of his ability to trap his enemies in a web of intrigue—and won the admiration of Machiavelli. Louis's greatest enemy was Charles the Bold, duke of Burgundy (r. 1467–77), who outmaneuvered him while at the same time helping him to rid France of the last English troops. But Louis finally succeeded in stirring up Charles's eastern neighbors, and Charles died fighting a battle with Swiss pikemen.

The richest part of Charles the Bold's inheritance, the Netherlands, went to the Habsburg emperor Maximilian (r. 1493–1519) by way of his wife Mary, Charles's daughter. But the strategically located duchy of Burgundy went to Louis. Louis also married his son Charles VIII (r. 1483–98) to the heiress of Brittany, thus bringing the last feudal duchy under French control. Louis continued his father's policy of encouraging trade, maintaining the loyalty of the merchant class, and keeping firm control of the aristocracy and the church.

During the first years of his reign, however, Charles VIII spent most of his

Michelangelo's *David* (*ca.* 1501–04). Instead of representing David after his victory over Goliath, as Donatello had done, Michelangelo chose to represent him watching the approaching foe, with muscles tensed in gathering strength.

Michelangelo's statue of the horned Moses. The horns represent the rays of light that symbolize the divine inspiration of Moses as receiver of the Ten Commandments.

An early printing press, as shown in an early sixteenth-century French print.

gon (r. 1479–1516) and Isabella of Castile (r. 1474–1504) enabled them to carry out a common foreign policy and helped them to transform their joint kingdoms into a European power. Another marriage at about that time further enhanced the position of Spain. The emperor Maximilian and his wife Mary of Burgundy had a son, Philip, who was heir to Austria through his Habsburg father and heir to the Netherlands through his mother. Philip married Joanna, the daughter of Ferdinand and Isabella, and their son, Charles, eventually became king of Spain (r. 1516–56) and ruler of the Netherlands, Austria, Milan, Naples, and the Spanish colonies in the New World. In 1519, the German princes elected him emperor as Charles V (see pp. 437, 457).

At the end of the fifteenth century, Spain was not yet wealthy or fully unified. The kingdoms of Aragon and Castile clung to their old institutions and to their own languages. The Spanish armies, however, were among the best in Europe. Then, with Columbus's discoveries in the New World, gold and silver streamed into the kingdom and transformed Spain into the leading power of sixteenth-century Europe (see pp. 453–58).

England

Henry Tudor (Henry VII, r. 1485–1509), who brought the War of the Roses to an end, succeeded in reestablishing peace and proved himself one of the ablest kings in English history. The ranks of the aristocracy had been thinned during the wars, and Henry filled them out with men loyal to his monarchy. He kept England out of foreign wars, encouraged trade, restored royal revenues, and eliminated all pretenders to the throne.

Henry's son, Henry VIII (r. 1509–47), inherited a full treasury, a united nation, and a relatively efficient administration. He introduced humanist learning to England and helped foster the English Renaissance. With the help and advice of his ruthless chief minister, Cardinal Wolsey, he issued numerous statutes to reform the Common Law and to correct abuses. His reign was one of the most innovative periods in the history of the English law.

time consolidating his control of the country. Once that was done, he was ready to renew some of the ancient claims of the French monarchy. In 1494 he invaded Italy and asserted his claim to the kingdom of Naples as the heir of Charles of Anjou (see p. 322). The Spanish monarchy, which also had a claim to Italy, reacted quickly to the French invasion. For the next half-century, foreign armies ranging across Italy destroyed the prosperity and independence of the city-states. Eventually, Spain won out and made the kingdom of Naples a dependency of the Spanish crown. Though the French monarchy had suffered severe financial losses in the wars, it remained one of the most influential powers in Europe.

Spain

As we have seen, the momentous marriage (1469) between Ferdinand of Ara-

War of the Roses

1399	1454	1485	1603
House of Lancaster	House of York	House of Tudor	

1461

Henry married Catherine of Aragon, thereby joining England to the grand alliance of families associated with the royal house of Spain. But he and Catherine had only one daughter. Foreseeing a dynastic crisis, Henry sought to rid himself of his wife. When the pope refused to grant him a divorce, he proclaimed the Act of Supremacy in 1534, declaring himself the head of an English church free from the authority of the pope. Chancellor Thomas More, a humanist scholar and brilliant lawyer who succeeded Cardinal Wolsey in 1529, refused to accede to the king's assertion of authority and retired from his office in 1532. When he continued in his opposition to the king's remarriage and the Act of Supremacy, he was convicted of treason and was beheaded in 1535.

The Consolidation of Royal Power

During the sixteenth century, the European monarchs overcame the nobility, the representative assemblies, and the church in their determination to strengthen their power. They overcame the nobility either because it had been weakened by war, as in England, or because it could not afford the cost of the new military technology. Most of the kings compensated for the loss of the nobility by creating bureaucracies made up of educated, loyal men who strengthened royal finances by means of innovative taxes and sound financial management.

The representative assemblies—the Estates General in France, the Cortes in Spain, and Parliament in England—had achieved great power and influence during the fourteenth century, when the kings needed their help in dealing with the endless wars and the dire effects of the plague. In the fifteenth century, however, the power of the assemblies declined everywhere except in England. In most cases,

they themselves were to blame for their decline. Once the kings were no longer dependent on them for financial aid, the parochial interests of the delegates came

Jakob Fugger with his bookkeeper. The cabinet in the rear lists the names of cities where Fugger had branch offices—Innsbruck, Nuremburg, and Lisbon, among others (detail from a painting by Matthaus Schwartz, 1516).

Los Reyes don fernando y doña y sabel yla R.... almisata su hija doña Juana.

Illumination of Ferdinand and Isabella of Spain—known as the "Catholic Kings"—with their daughter Joanna.

realm and for all sections of the country, it was hard to ignore. Moreover, it was an excellent source of support in time of need. When Henry VIII was trying to get the pope to grant him a divorce, for example, he summoned Parliament and asked for its support. By 1600, as a result of the frequent use Henry VIII and his successors made of it, Parliament had risen to a position of great influence in English government. By that time the representative assemblies on the Continent were hollow bodies under the control of absolute monarchs.

Finally, the monarchs overcame the church by preempting the appointment of prelates, by taxing the clergy without the permission of the pope, and by monitoring the appeal of cases to Rome. The kings of England and France had established the right to tax the clergy by 1300 (see p. 325), and the French king asserted the right to appoint prelates in 1438 in the Pragmatic Sanction of Bourges. In the Concordat of Bologna (1516) the pope granted Francis I (r. 1515–47) the right to nominate members of the higher clergy and to settle most ecclesiastical disputes that arose in France. The power to nominate amounted to the power to appoint. Even Ferdinand and Isabella, the Catholic Kings, asserted their right to appoint, to tax, and to reform the clergy within their kingdoms. In England, Henry VIII's Act of Supremacy (1534) gave him complete power over the church in one stroke.

The consolidation and centralization of power also proceeded in Norway and Sweden during the fifteenth and sixteenth centuries, and in Russia Ivan the Terrible (r. 1533–84) ruthlessly destroyed the power of the Russian nobility (see p. 346). But the process did not take place everywhere. Italy made no movement toward formation of a central government—to the dismay of Machiavelli—and in Germany the emperor was no more than a figurehead. When Charles V became emperor in 1519, his real strength lay in his position as duke of Austria, lord of the Netherlands, and king of Spain. In becoming emperor he gained some prestige, many responsibilities, but little power. Consequently, no one in Germany could resist the exactions

into play and destroyed the effectiveness of the assemblies. As the power of the kings rose during the fifteenth century, they manipulated the assemblies by playing the various factions off against one another, and the delegates began to avoid attending the meetings. The Estates General and Cortes met less and less frequently after the end of the fifteenth century.

In England, Henry VII used the Parliament to help establish his power. Once he was in control, however, he rarely called it into session. Nonetheless, because it spoke for all the privileged classes of the

Sir Thomas More, after Hans Holbein (1527).

of the papacy, which escalated steadily as the popes found themselves challenged elsewhere.

This lack of central authority in Germany was to be crucial in the sixteenth century. It contributed to the success of the Protestant Reformation, which became mixed up in the competition among the German princes. And it obliged the emperor to rely entirely on his hereditary domains in meeting the threat of the Ottoman Turks (see p. 189), who under Suleiman the Magnificent (r. 1520–66) captured Belgrade, took most of Hungary in the battle of Mohacs (1526), and almost seized Vienna in 1529.

Suggestions for Further Reading

General

The classic work on the Renaissance is J. Burckhardt, *The Civilization of the Renaissance in Italy* (1860). For a recent survey, see D. Hay, *The Italian Renaissance* (1977). W. K. Ferguson, *Europe in Transition: 1300–1520* (1963), emphasizes social and economic history. For a revolutionary view of the economic background of the Renaissance, see R. S. Lopez and H. A. Miskimin, "The Economic Depression of the Renaissance," *Eco-*

nomic History Review 14 (1962), and the response by C. Cipolla, "Economic Depression of the Renaissance?" *Economic History Review* 16 (1963–64). For an overview, see A. Molho, *Social and Economic Foundations of the Italian Renaissance* (1969), and G. Huppert, *After the Black Death: A Social History of Early Modern Europe* (1986).

Italian Politics and Society

Recently, historians have written a series of works on individual Italian cities. See G. Brucker, *Renaissance Florence* (1969); D. Herlihy, *Pisa in the Early Renaissance* (1958); W. M. Bowsky, *The Finances of the Commune of Siena* (1970); D. S. Chambers, *The Imperial Age of Venice: 1380–1580* (1970); and C. M. Ady, *Milan under the Sforza* (1907). See also R. de Roover, *The Rise and Fall of the Medici Bank* (1963). For a general view, see D. Waley, *The Italian City Republics* (1969).

The classic work on the origins of modern diplomacy is G. Mattingly, *Renaissance Diplomacy* (1955). For background, see D. E. Queller, *The Office of Ambassador in the Middle Ages* (1967). On Renaissance warfare, see C. Oman, *History of the Art of War in the Sixteenth Century* (1937), and M. Mallett, *Mercenaries and their Masters* (1974).

On the Renaissance family, see L. deMause, ed., *The History of Childhood* (1974); J. Gage, *Life in Italy at the Time of the Medici* (1968); C. L. Lee, Jr., *Daily Life in Renaissance Italy* (1975); G. Brucker, *Giovanni and Lusanna: Love and Marriage in Renaissance Florence* (1986); and P. Aries, *Centuries of Childhood* (1962), a revolutionary work that uses art to show how views of children changed over time. *The Portable Renaissance Reader,* ed. by J. B. Ross and M. McLaughlin (1953), contains a selection from Alberti's *On the Family,* as well as other works. See J. Gadol, *Leon Battista Alberti: Universal Man of the Early Renaissance* (1969).

Humanism

On the origins of Renaissance humanism, see C. Trinkhaus, *The Poet as Philosopher: Petrarch and the Formation of the Renaissance Consciousness* (1979). On the humanist movement, see P. Kristeller, *Renaissance Thought,* 2 vols. (1961, 1965), and C. Trinkhaus, *The Scope of Renaissance Humanism* (1983). H. Baron, *The Crisis of the Early Italian Renaissance,* 2 vols. (1966), is an important treatment of the relationship

between humanist thought and Florentine history in the early fifteenth century. On Renaissance political thought, see J. W. Allen, *Political Thought in the Sixteenth Century* (1928), and F. Chabod, *Machiavelli and the Renaissance* (1958). For an excellent biography of Machiavelli, see S. de Grazia, *Machiavelli in Hell* (1989).

Art and Architecture

There are many histories of Renaissance art and architecture. See P. and L. Murray, *The Art of the Renaissance* (1963); P. Murray, *Architecture of the Italian Renaissance* (1963); and E. H. Gombrich, *The Story of Art* (1953). See also Gombrich's article on the Medici as patrons of art in E. F. Jacob, ed., *Italian Renaissance Studies* (1960). For the early period, see R. Fremantle, *Florentine Gothic Painters from Giotto to Masaccio* (1975),

and M. Meiss, *Painting in Florence and Siena after the Black Death* (1973). See also M. Baxendall, *Painting and Experience in Fifteenth Century Italy* (1972); J. R. Hale, *Italian Renaissance Painting from Masaccio to Titian* (1977); J. Pope-Hennessy, *An Introduction to Italian Sculpture,* 3rd ed., 3 vols. (1986); and R. Wittkower, *Architectural Principles in the Age of Humanism,* 4th ed. (1988).

Economic Growth

For a general history of the European economy, see the *Cambridge Economic History of Europe,* 3 vols. (1952–66). Volume 1 deals with agriculture; volume 2 with commerce and industry;

and volume 3 with economic organization and policy. H. A. Miskimin, *The Economy of Early Renaissance Europe* (1969), is a good short survey. R. Ehrenberg, *Capital and Finance in* the Age of the Renaissance (1928), is the standard study of the Fuggers. See also E. Power and M. M. Postan, eds., *Studies in English Trade in the Fifteenth Century* (1953), and A. R. Bridbury, *Economic Growth: England in the Later Middle Ages* (1962). On the low countries; see H. Van Der Wee, *The Growth of the Antwerp Market and the European Economy* (1963). E. Eisenstein, *The Printing Press as an Agent of Change* (1979), is a good account of the invention and its effect.

France, England, and Spain

On late medieval France, see the works cited in Chapter 14. See also P. M. Kendall, *Louis the Eleventh* (1971); F. Pegues, *Lawyers of the Last Capetians* (1962); and J. H. Shennan, *The Parlement of Paris* (1968). On Spain, see the works cited in Chapter 14. On England, see the works cited in Chapter 14, and S. B. Chrimes, *Lancastrians, Yorkists, and Henry VII* (1964).

17

Religious Reform and Revolution in Western Christendom

As we have seen, religious institutions were changing in the late Middle Ages. By the sixteenth century, the national churches of Europe were essentially under the control of the kings and the status of the pope had dwindled to that of an Italian despot. Many people had grown suspicious of the church and contemptuous of its leaders. So outraged had they become by the church's incessant demands for money that many had stopped attending church services altogether. This did not mean that their interest in religion had waned; it meant simply that they were looking elsewhere for religious guidance. Evangelical preachers abounded and attracted enthusiastic followings who applauded their charge that the church had grown worldly and corrupt. It did not help that the church was a demanding landlord to peasants and townspeople throughout Europe.

The new class of capitalistic merchants and industrialists also was at odds with the church, which had never managed to incorporate business ethics into its system of values. The church still shared the view of the ancient Romans that business was inevitably corrupting and morally suspect, and it still imposed the Judaic injunction against usury (charging interest on loans). Throughout the Middle Ages, merchants had often borrowed money to finance their business and had resorted to ruses to escape the charge of usury. With the rise of capitalism, the tension between the commercial classes and the church intensified, because capitalism was based on the idea that money invested in an enterprise ought to produce a return. Moreover, businessmen were angered by the church's failure to practice what it preached, pointing out that many church officials were themselves greedy and unscrupulous.

One of the questions put to students in debating practice was, "Can an archdeacon be saved?" (The archdeacon was the principal administrative officer of a bishopric.)

EFFORTS TO REFORM THE CHURCH

Late Medieval Reform Movements

The state of the church during the papal stay in Avignon and the Great Schism (see pp. 354–58) seemed so dismal that many laymen began to seek salvation on their own. They did not break openly with the church; they simply ceased to rely on it. They came together in groups, small at first, such as the Brethren of the Common Life in the Low Countries and the Rhineland, to encourage one another to lead a devout Christian life and to seek direct contact with God through mystical experiences. The Brethren produced some impressive works of devotion, like the *Theologica Germanica* (the "German Theology"), that influenced later reformers. They also founded schools that contributed to the educational revival of the fifteenth and sixteenth centuries; Erasmus (see p. 432), for example, was educated in a Brethren school. Conservative churchmen looked on these reformers with suspicion, but most of the groups managed to remain within the bounds of orthodoxy.

A more radical element wanted to mount a thoroughgoing reform of the church, preferably directed by laymen. As early as 1324 Marsilius of Padua, in his *Defensor pacis,* had argued that the state should control the church just as it controlled other organizations, like guilds. If the state could regulate physicians, he reasoned, it could also regulate priests. The church condemned Marsilius's book, but reformers continued to be inspired by his ideas.

Another critic of the church was the Oxford professor John Wycliffe (*ca.* 1320–84). At first concerned with questions having to do with the ownership of private property, Wycliffe became convinced that the church was being corrupted by wealth and that the state should take over its property holdings. The secular rulers applauded this suggestion, of course, and protected Wycliffe from the wrath of the clergy. Wycliffe went on to question the orthodox doctrine that the bread and wine in the communion service are transformed into the body and blood of Christ. He ended up by attacking the whole administrative structure of the church as corrupt and unauthorized by the Bible. He also encouraged his followers to translate the Bible so ordinary people could understand its message without the mediation of the clergy.

Though Wycliffe had no intention of launching a popular movement, his ideas spread rapidly beyond the scholarly circles for which he wrote. Preachers carrying the Wycliffite English Bible traveled about the country telling people about his radical proposals. Many of those preachers became social reformers as well and gained an impressive following among the lower and middle classes in England. Their preaching contributed to the radicalism that triggered the great Peasants' Rebellion of 1381 (see p. 354). When the king and nobles put down the rebellion, they took care to suppress the radicals as well. But the suppression was not wholly successful. The radicals—called Lollards (from the Dutch word *lollaert,* meaning mumbler, which was used to describe religious radicals on the Continent)—went underground and continued to foment unrest until the English Reformation of the sixteenth century.

Such reform movements drew much of their strength from the decline of the church after the Great Schism. In 1395 the French became so exasperated with their pope, Benedict XIII of Avignon, that the French clergy, under pressure from the government, withdrew their obedience from him for five years. This was the first instance of a strategy that was to have a fateful future: the rejection of papal authority by the clergy of a large nation under pressure from the secular government.

John Huss

Even after Wycliffe's death, his ideas continued to exercise great influence on the

Continent as well as in England. The English king Richard II (r. 1377–99) married Anne of Bohemia, and Czech students began to come to England to study. When they returned home, they carried Wycliffe's teachings with them. In time, those teachings found a home at the University of Prague (founded 1348).

In 1402, John Huss (*ca.* 1369–1415), a brilliant young professor at the university, emerged as a leader of the Czech reformers. In his preaching he drew on the teachings of Wycliffe: Faith must be based on the Bible, which is the only source of authority; Christ, not the pope, is the true head of the church; salvation comes from God through Christ, not through ritual ceremonies and a corrupt priesthood. In 1414 Huss was excommunicated by the pope. But he remained at liberty, and his ideas were accepted by a majority of the Czech people.

In that same year, Huss was invited to defend his ideas at the Council of Constance (called to resolve the Great Schism; see p. 357). He eagerly accepted and traveled to Constance under the emperor Sigismund's guarantee of safe conduct. On his arrival he was charged with heresy and was imprisoned, the emperor's guarantee notwithstanding. In fact, Sigismund withdrew his protection as soon as the charge of heresy was leveled. The leaders of the council ordered Huss to recant his views in public, but he stood firm. In the dramatic trial that followed, the issue was whether the Bible and the individual's conscience were the source of religious authority, as Huss argued, or the Catholic church was, as the council insisted. Not surprisingly, the council fathers condemned Huss to death and ordered that he be burned at the stake. He was executed outside the walls of Constance in May 1415.

The following year, the council condemned a follower of Huss, Jerome, to be burnt at the stake, and before the council disbanded in 1418 civil war had broken out in Bohemia. Not until 1436 were some of the more conservative Hussites and the church able to reach an agreement. The agreement recognized a Bohemian church with control over its own ecclesiastical appointments and with its own liturgical practices, notably the right to offer the cup as well as the bread to communicants. For the first time, the Roman church had entered into an agreement with condemned heretics after excommunicating them and preaching a crusade against them.

A pair of woodcuts by Lucas Cranach the Elder contrasting Jesus and the pope. On the left, Jesus is driving the moneychangers from the temple; on the right, the pope is taking money for indulgences.

THE PAPACY'S TRIUMPH OVER THE CONCILIAR MOVEMENT

Though the Council of Constance succeeded in ending the Great Schism, it was unable to institute any meaningful reform, which had been one of its principal goals. The English and German delegates tried in vain to get the council to consider reform before turning to the election of a new pope; the other delegates were more interested in healing the schism first. Once Martin V (r. 1417–31) had been elected, the council leaders waved aside the mild report of a committee they had set up to study church abuses and declared the council ended without ever taking up the question of reform. So the fifteenth-century church continued to countenance corruption under the leadership of a pope who set a standard of worldliness.

The leaders of the council at Constance had decreed that the church must summon a general council every five years. But Martin V saw to it that the decree

1305	1378	1409	1417	1447	1527

Babylonian Captivity

Great Schism

Conciliar Movement

Renaissance Papacy

was ignored. At a time when most European kings were humbling their parliaments and their nobles, the popes chose to abolish regular councils and to humble the princes of the church, the cardinals. By the time Nicholas V (r. 1447–55) became pope, the possibility that the church might evolve into a limited monarchy had vanished. Since that time, every general council has been under the control of the pope.

That victory left the papacy stronger in some respects, weaker in others. No

Julius II (r. 1503–13), the warrior pope, painted by Raphael.

one within the church could any longer challenge the power of the pope, but the pope was now isolated from leaders of opinion—both clerical and lay—particularly in northern Europe. The period of the concordats followed (see p. 420). In France, Charles VII in effect created a national, or "Gallican," church, restricting the pope's power to appoint and tax the clergy. In England and Spain, the kings followed suit, but in Germany, which lacked a central government strong enough to stand up to the pope, the papacy retained its rights of appointment, taxation, and jurisdiction.

The period between the accession of Nicholas V to the papacy (1447) and the sack of Rome by imperial Spanish troops (1527) is often called the age of the Renaissance papacy. During that period, many of the popes were well-educated patrons of humanists and artists, while others were despots; some were both. Nicholas V founded the Vatican library, one of the world's great repositories of books and manuscripts. Pius II (r. 1458–64), before his election as pope, had been a celebrated Sienese humanist, Aeneas Sylvius Piccolomini. Julius II (r. 1503–13) initiated the rebuilding of St. Peter's. Sixtus IV (r. 1471–84) was said to have died in a fit of rage at the conclusion of a peace settlement; and Julius II was known as "the Warrior Pope." Alexander VI (r. 1492–1503) tried to carve a principality out of the Papal States for his illegitimate son, Cesare Borgia.

The papacy had often been embroiled in politics during the Middle Ages, but in those days politics meant international politics, with grand principles of political authority at stake. The Renaissance popes, by contrast, were embroiled mainly in Italian politics, with only dynastic interests at stake. In time, the papacy became thoroughly Italianized. (In fact, since the end of the Great Schism in 1417, only two non-Italians have ever been elected pope, in 1522 and 1979).

THE PROBLEMS OF THE RENAISSANCE CHURCH

The Renaissance church had problems elsewhere besides in the papal curia where venality and nepotism reigned. Most of the bishops and archbishops of the church were of noble birth, and many of them had been appointed to their office by a king or a pope as a reward for their loyal service rather than for their piety or administrative ability. Typically, the newly appointed bishop paid a substantial part of his first year's income to whoever it was who had appointed him. Not only was this contrary to canon law, it gave the bishop a strong incentive to siphon off as much money as he could from his diocese. Moreover, many bishops and archbishops held more than one office—which also was contrary to canon law. In a diocese with an absentee bishop, the bishop's income was drained from the local economy, and the diocese was left to the mercy of the greedy priests and secular lords. One bishop is said to have visited his bishopric only once, to be buried.

Even conscientious bishops found that they had little power to appoint competent clergy or to reform abuses within their dioceses. Much of the power that had formerly belonged to the bishops had either fallen into the hands of local laymen or the pope. Consequently the parish priests tended to be ignorant and immoral. Moreover, because the priests had to raise money to pay taxes to their bishop and to local laymen, they became almost as rapacious as their superiors. Normally the income of a church consisted of tithes (that is, a tenth of the income of parishioners), first fruits (a small share of the early harvest), and oblations (gifts from parishioners). By the sixteenth century priests were augmenting that income by charging a fee for baptisms, marriages, and burials.

Monastic orders had also lost prestige. Many monasteries in the cities performed as parish churches because the population had grown too large for the parish priests to handle. This activity involved the monasteries in the affairs of the world, and they followed the example of the priests in squeezing their congregations for money. By the late fifteenth century, the monastic orders were no longer attracting pious novices but men who wanted to serve parishes and to rise to positions of power and wealth in society. The monks acquired a reputation for living rich and secular lives.

The most common complaint leveled against the church was that it sold spiritual benefits for money. The church was land rich, but cash poor, and it had to find ways to support itself. But the methods it used to raise money and the purposes to which the money was allegedly put—wars, rich living, and the like—outraged many of the faithful. Clergy at all levels were criticized, but the papacy was considered the worst offender.

The sale of indulgences was the practice that aroused the most heated criticism, although it was far from the most important source of papal income. An indulgence was a remission of the temporal penalty for sin imposed by a priest in the sacrament of penance. Christians were required to confess their sins and receive penance (a penalty) at least once a year. Penances ranged from saying prayers to going on a crusade or a pilgrimage; the severity of the penance depended on the seriousness of the sin and the condition of the sinner.

During the Middle Ages, the practice of commuting a penance with a money payment had become common, and in the fourteenth century the popes devised a doctrine that held Christ and the saints had accumulated a "treasury of merits" from which Christ's vicars—the popes—could dispense benefits to the faithful through indulgences. In the fifteenth century, Sixtus IV (r. 1471–84) expanded this doctrine by claiming that the pope had the power to release the souls of the dead from the penances they were undergoing in purgatory—the state in which the soul purged its sins before being admitted to paradise. Sixtus's pronouncement transformed the traffic in indulgences into a booming business and a real moneymaker. It was hard for people to resist an opportunity to ease the suffering of the soul of a dead parent or spouse. Yet when it became clear that the money from the sale of indulgences was going not to pious purposes but to war and ostentatious living, many laymen concluded that the church was selling salvation for profit.

RESPONSES TO CORRUPTION

Criticism and Reform of the Church in the Fifteenth Century

Many church leaders of the late fifteenth century were of course conscientious, pious men who found it difficult to answer the criticism leveled at the church. Not only were the abuses undeniable; the status of churchmen in general had declined. The Europe of 1500 was more secular in its outlook than the Europe of 1400. Imbued with the ideas of the Renaissance, many people now considered a career in business, politics, or the arts to be as attractive as a career in the church and no less likely to lead to salvation.

Moreover, during the fifteenth century the lower and middle classes had come to embrace a popular piety accompanied by religious practices that verged on superstition and idolatry—the cults of the saints, for example, and the veneration of relics. In what one historian has called the "supersaturated" religious atmosphere of the fifteenth century, perceptive church leaders came to realize that the church was vulnerable to troublesome questions: What is the essence of Christianity? Is it the ritual and the elaborate hierarchy? Is it the veneration of relics or participation in a pilgrimage? Or is it loving one's neighbor and living simply, as Christ lived?

Church leaders were well aware of the new power of secular rulers to appoint bishops, tax the clergy, and limit papal control over the churches in their realms. And they knew that the kings could initiate religious reform of their own, often for political purposes. In fact, reform by royal command was sometimes well motivated and effective: In Spain, Cardinal Jiménez de Cisneros (1436–1517), backed by Ferdinand and Isabella, carried out many church reforms early in the sixteenth century. But always the danger remained that reform by a secular ruler, no matter how

well motivated, might result in state control of the church and its property.

Several reform movements were launched within the church, none of them effective. The Brethren of the Common Life, as we have seen, pursued its quiet way of life and founded schools to educate a new Christian elite, but it had little effect on the church. In Florence between 1494 and 1498, one of the most remarkable preachers of the age, the Dominican Savonarola, tried to reform the inhabitants of one of the richest and most secular cities in Europe. He preached repentance and piety and attacked both secular and church leaders. Savonarola held to the medieval view that the church itself was divinely constituted and could never be in need of reform, but that when the individuals who served it grew corrupt they should and must be reformed.

That idea of reform had already begun to disappear. The intention of the leaders of the councils of Constance (1414–18) and Basel (1431–37) had been to reform the church by assigning substantial power to councils and by making the pope a limited monarch. Even more radical, John Huss preached the reform both of individual Christians and of the church as an institution. But the church demonstrated its unreadiness for such reform: it ignored the conciliar movement and had both Huss and Savonarola burned as heretics.

Christian Humanism

Humanism, which, as we have seen, extolled the eloquence and power of the ancient authors, spread from Italy to northern Europe during the fifteenth century and was well established there by the early sixteenth century. Northern Europeans came to Italy to study with humanists, books and translations were shipped north from Italy (some of the most important printing presses were in northern Italy), and Italian humanists kept up a lively correspondence with their northern counterparts.

The humanism that took root in northern Europe is often called Christian humanism to distinguish it from the

Italian variety, but the name is somewhat misleading. Even though the Italian humanists were primarily interested in pre-Christian authors, they were themselves Christians and never denied their Christian faith. The fact that the northern humanists were more interested in the early Christian authors and writings suggests that in some sense they were more "Christian" than the Italians, though at base their interests were the same.

In their studies of the New Testament, the Christian humanists sought to explore the faith of the apostles as revealed in the language of the biblical account. They concentrated especially on the letters of St. Paul, which constitute a substantial body of material. They also studied the works of the church fathers—Greek writers such as Origen and Gregory of Nazianzus and Latin writers such as Augustine and Jerome. There they found straightforward, detailed explanations of the Christian faith free of the abstruse theological accretions of medieval commentators and scholastic theologians. They held St. Jerome in the highest esteem, because his Latin was closest to that of Cicero and because he was the most accomplished literary scholar of the western church fathers.

The main goal of the Christian humanists was to retrieve the original texts of Christianity. During the Middle Ages, intellectuals read the Bible only with the aid of learned commentaries, just as they used a technical gloss when they read legal, medical, or philosophical texts. All the major works were accompanied by a standard commentary, called a *glossa ordinaria,* that became in effect part of the works themselves. The humanists scorned those commentaries, which were often ungrammatical, dense, and rich in jargon. They sought instead the eloquence of the early church writers, who spoke in the original voice of Christianity.

The Christian humanists first set out to produce accurate texts of the Bible and the early Christian writings. In Spain, Cardinal Jiménez set scholars to producing a monumental edition of the Bible in which the original Hebrew and Greek texts appeared in parallel columns with the Latin. In Germany, Johann Reuchlin (1455–1522) promoted the study of Hebrew as a means of understanding the Old Testament, while a group of German Dominicans—who saw such study as a threat to the authority of the church—sought to destroy all books written in Hebrew.

The Christian humanists were in a sense conservative in their attempt to get back to the original texts, but they were radical in their conviction that the individual human being had a unique spiritual capacity. They called for translations of the Bible into the vernacular so that ordinary people could participate in the Christian experience and understand the need for reform. In France, Jacques Lefèvre d'Etaples (1455–1536) translated the New Testament into French (1523). In England, Thomas More (1477–1535)—the royal chancellor who was executed in 1535 for his loyalty to the Roman church

A Catholic, Sir Thomas More, on the Church

The true Church of Christ is the common known church of all Christian people not gone out nor cast out. This whole body both of good and bad is the Catholic Church of Christ, which is in this world very sickly, and hath many sore members, as hath sometime the natural body of a man. . . . The Church was gathered, and the faith believed, before any part of the New Testament was put in writing. And which was or is the true scripture, neither Luther nor Tyndale [translator of the New Testament into English] knoweth but by the credence that they give to the Church. . . . The Church was before the gospel was written; and the faith was taught, and men were baptized and masses said, and the other sacraments ministered among Christian people, before any part of the New Testament was put in writing. . . . As the sea shall never surround and overwhelm the land, and yet it hath eaten many places in, and swallowed whole countries up, and made places now sea that sometime were well-inhabited lands, and hath lost part of his own possession in other parts again; so though the faith of Christ shall never be overflown with heresies, nor the gates of hell prevail against Christ's Church, yet in some places it winneth in a new people, so may there in some places by negligence be lost the old.

From The Workes of Sir Thomas More *(London: Scholar Press, 1978), pp. 527, 852, 853, 921.*

(see p. 419)—detailed in his book *Utopia* the ironies and hypocrisies of society and called for the spread of true Christianity through education.

Erasmus

The acknowledged leader of the Christian humanists was Erasmus of Rotterdam (*ca.* 1469–1536), who in his youth had attended a school run by the Brethren of the Common Life. He was committed to the study of early Christian writers and had absorbed the ideals—though not the secular interests—of the Italian humanists. Erasmus devoted his life to scholarship, in the conviction that knowledge would help save the church.

Erasmus, by Holbein.

After making an exhaustive comparison of ancient manuscripts, Erasmus produced the first critical edition of the Greek text of the New Testament (1516). In his preface, he urged that his work be used as the basis for new translations of the Scriptures into the vernacular languages. He summarized the goal of Christian humanism with this statement: "I utterly dissent from those who are unwilling that the sacred Scriptures should be read by the unlearned translated into their vulgar tongue, as though Christ had taught such subtleties that they can scarcely be understood even by a few theologians, or, as though the strength of the Christian religion consisted in men's ignorance of it." In countless letters and books Erasmus proclaimed a "philosophy of Christ"—the love of God and neighbor that to him was the essence of Christianity.

Erasmus, through his intellect, learning, literary skills, and lively sense of humor, had an enormous influence on his contemporaries. He acknowledged the Renaissance commitment to life in this world by insisting that the love of God and neighbor be expressed through a life of good works. He ridiculed monks and priests who insisted that withdrawal from the world was the ideal form of the Christian life. He also rejected ceremonies and fasts as routes to heaven by imagining what Christ might have said: "I promised [to Christians] the inheritance of my Father, not to cowls, prayers, or fasts, but to works of charity."

Although Christian humanism demonstrated the power of education to bring about reform, it was far too intellectual to arouse the interest of the general population.

LUTHER'S REVOLT

On October 31, 1517, an Augustinian friar named Martin Luther (1483–1546), who was professor of Bible in the little University of Wittenberg in Saxony, submitted 95 theses—or propositions—to his colleagues to serve as the material for a debate on the subject of indulgences. Luther had become outraged by the efforts of a Dominican friar named Tetzel to hawk indulgences to the residents of Magdeburg with the following sales pitch: "So soon as coin in coffer rings, the soul from Purgatory springs." Though the proceeds were supposed to go toward the building of the new church of St. Peter in Rome, half actually ended up with the archbishop of Mainz and the Fugger banking firm of Augsburg (see p. 416).

Luther's theses, which were immediately printed and debated throughout Germany, caused a sensation. They touched on a note of resentment that was ready to be sounded:

> There is no divine authority for preaching that the soul flies out of purgatory immediately the money clinks in the bottom of the chest. . . . It is certainly possible that when the money clinks in the bottom of the chest, avarice and greed increase. . . . All those who believe themselves certain of their own salvation by means of letters of indulgence will be eternally damned, together with their teachers. . . . Any

Erasmus's Preface to His Edition of the New Testament

I utterly dissent from those who are unwilling that the sacred Scriptures should be read by the unlearned translated into their vulgar tongue, as though Christ had taught such subtleties that they can scarcely be understood even by a few theologians, or, as though the strength of the Christian religion consisted in men's ignorance of it. The mysteries of kings it may be safer to conceal, but Christ wished his mysteries to be published as openly as possible. I wish that even the weakest woman should read the Gospel—should read the epistles of Paul. And I wish these were translated into all languages, so that they might be read and understood, not only by Scots and Irishmen, but also by Turks and Saracens. To make them understood is surely the first step. It may be that they might be ridiculed by many, but some would take them to heart. I long that the husbandman should sing portions of them to himself as he follows the plough, that the weaver should hum them to the tune of his shuttle, that the traveller should beguile with their stories the tedium of his journey.

From Erasmus, "Paraclesis," Novum Instrumentum, *trans. by Frederic Seebohm, in* The Oxford Reformers *(New York: Dutton, 1914), p. 203.*

O Ihr deutschen mercket mich recht/
    Des heiligen Vaters Papstes Knecht/
Bin ich/vnd br ing euch ist allein/
    Zehn tausent vnd neun hundert care in/
Gnad vnd Ablaß von einer Sünd/
    Vor euch/ewer Eltern/Weib vnd Kind/
Sol ein jeder gewehret sein
    So viel ihr legt ins Kästelein/
So bald der Gülden im Becken klingt/
    Im hup die Seel im Himel springt/

Contemporary caricature of Johann Tetzel hawking indulgences. The last line of the jingle is: "So soon as coin in coffer rings, the soul into heaven springs."

Christian whatsoever, who is truly repentant, enjoys plenary remission from penalty and guilt, and this is given him without letters of indulgence.

At this time, Luther was 34 years old, the brilliant son of a prosperous peasant turned miner who had been able to afford a university education for his son. As a young man, Luther had experienced several emotional crises and had eventually decided on the life of a friar. Though it was the age of humanism and the new learning, he chose to live a religious life and to pursue scholastic learning, which still dominated the university curriculum.

Luther found no spiritual solace in the prayers, confessions, and penances of the monastic community, however. He sought forgiveness of his sins but found no assurance of God's forgiveness in the ceremonial acts of worship. Instead, he became increasingly guilt-ridden and doubtful about his ability to save himself.

Suddenly he came to an understanding of what St. Paul had meant when he said that a man is saved not by obeying the Jewish law but by his faith in Christ alone. He realized that he had been trying to satisfy God by scrupulously observing church ritual, which was no less demanding and no more effective than the Jewish law against which Paul had preached. He found it unthinkable that human beings, corrupted by sin, could win God's favor by performing some good deed or sacramental act. He came to believe that God alone can save people's souls and that all the sinner can do is to have faith in the possibility of God's forgiveness.

In working out the revolutionary implications of his new understanding, Luther slowly came to the view that ceremonies and sacraments, pilgrimages and indulgences—everything the medieval church called "good works"—were irrelevant at best and dangerous at worst. His first act was to deny the efficacy of indulgences, causing sales of indulgences in Germany to drop off sharply. When the Dominicans, the chief dealers in indulgences, persuaded Pope Leo X (r. 1513–21) to condemn Luther's theses, he was gradually driven into denying the authority of the pope. He also came to believe that John Huss had been right on certain points, despite his being condemned by the Council of Constance, and this belief led him to deny the authority of councils as well.

At last Luther was summoned to appear before the emperor Charles V at an imperial diet (council) held at Worms in April 1521 to defend his theses. Like John Huss a century earlier, he was given a guarantee of safe conduct on his journey to Worms. There he declared to the emperor and assembled dignitaries that he was bound by the authority of the Scriptures and by his own conscience rather than by the authority of the pope or council. He could not recant his theses, he said, because his conscience was "captive of the Word of God" and because it was "neither safe nor right to go against conscience."

The emperor permitted Luther to return to the protection of Frederick, the Elector of Saxony, and until his death in 1546, Luther remained in Wittenberg

Luther on Justification by Faith

For the word of God cannot be received and honored by any works, but by faith alone. Hence it is clear that, as the soul needs the word alone for life and justification, so it is justified by faith alone and not by any works. For if it could be justified by any other means, it would have no need of the word, nor consequently of faith. . . .

It is evident that by no outward work or labor can the inward man be at all justified, made free and saved, and that no works whatever have any relation to him. And so, on the other hand, it is solely by impiety and incredulity of heart that he becomes guilty and a slave of sin, deserving condemnation; not by any outward sin or work.

Therefore the first care of every Christian ought to be to lay aside all reliance on works, and strengthen his faith alone more and more, and by it grow in the knowledge, not of works, but of Christ Jesus, who has suffered and risen again for him.

From Martin Luther, On Christian Liberty, *trans. by H. Wace and C. A. Buchheim, in* First Principles of the Reformation *(London: Murray, 1883), pp. 107–08.*

teaching, preaching, and writing. In his new view of Christianity, the active life of a merchant or a housewife was as spiritually rewarding as the life of a monk or a nun, and he himself married a former nun, with whom he had six children. Meanwhile, the revolt against the papacy that he had initiated gathered momentum and spread across northern Europe. By the late sixteenth century, the unity of western Christendom had been shattered.

Luther's Work

Luther's religious thought contained three main, closely related principles: salvation through faith rather than through good works, the ultimate authority of the Bible, and the priesthood of all believers. Luther wrote hundreds of letters and tracts defending his ideas, but his greatest literary accomplishment was his German translation of the Bible (completed in 1534). He wanted to put the Bible into the hands of every German, for he was convinced that there was no essential difference between a priest and a layman. A dedicated layman reverently reading the Scripture was closer to the divine truth than a worldly pope proclaiming the dogma of the church. Thus a pious layman could serve God as well as a priest or a monk. The literary quality of Luther's translation was so impressive that the work is considered to have been the foundation for the modern language known as High German.

Luther's original protest had been purely religious in nature, but by 1520 he was appealing to German nationalism. "What has brought us Germans to such a pass that we have to suffer this robbery and this destruction of our property by the Pope?" he asked. That question drew a quick response from princes eager to confiscate church property, from businessmen unhappy over papal taxation and over ecclesiastical rules governing business practices, and from devout laymen and priests shocked by the corruption of the church. Though the purpose of his revolt was to enable people to reconcile an honest life with the highest spiritual aspirations, some people seized on it for their own selfish purposes.

IV. D. Pl. I.

T. Buys, inv. et delin.   *Reinr.* Vinkeles *sculp. 1782.*

Luther burns papal bulls, symbolizing his rejection of papal authority.

Luther had no intention of setting up an independent church to compete with the church of Rome. But at last he became convinced that the church founded by Christ had strayed from its true path after the conversion of Constantine, when the church became entangled in worldly affairs, and that the bishop of Rome was not

Title page of the first German translation of the Bible, by Martin Luther, printed in 1534 with the approval of the Elector of Saxony.

the true vicar of Christ but the Antichrist. He wanted the church to return to the pure faith and the simple religion of the apostles. In the purified church there would be only two sacraments—baptism and communion—rather than the seven sacraments of the Catholic church. There would be a simplified ritual in German rather than in Latin, and there would be more emphasis on the congregation's participation in the service. Luther wrote many hymns in which he incorporated these ideas, and those hymns are still sung today.

The split between the "Lutheran" and "Catholic" churches occurred gradually and without Luther's explicit approval. The conflict over the nature of the true church continued unresolved until at last each church embraced its own beliefs and rejected the beliefs of the other.

THE SPREAD OF LUTHERANISM

Unlike the failed reforms of the fifteenth century, Lutheranism—one of the most radical movements in Christian history— spread quickly across northern Europe. One reason for its rapid acceptance was the availability of the printing press, which Gutenberg had invented in the middle of the fifteenth century (see p. 373). Luther and his followers wrote hundreds of tracts and had them printed for widespread distribution. The nineteenth-century historian Leopold von Ranke calculated that in 1523 Luther and his supporters published nearly 400 books and pamphlets.

Another reason for the rapid acceptance of Lutheranism was the early support of the humanists. The humanists were themselves reformers, and they saw in Luther's program many of the principles they were espousing. Like them, Luther rejected the commentaries of the medieval theologians and sought to return to the unadorned text of the Bible. And like them, Luther respected the church fathers and attacked the financial abuses of the church. But while the humanists criticized the medieval commentators for obscuring the text of the Bible with their graceless prose, Luther criticized them for their

faulty theological opinions. And while the humanists valued the church fathers for what they said about the faith of the early Christians, Luther valued them for their simple, direct explications of the meaning of the biblical text. For Luther, the sole source of authority was the Bible, particularly the New Testament.

Further, the humanists wanted to reform only the practices of the church, while Luther and his followers came to view the church itself as illegitimate. Erasmus and Cardinal Jiménez, for example, concentrated on freeing the biblical text from the clutter of the medieval commentaries, whereas the Protestants (as Lutherans were called after 1529, when they presented a "protest" at an imperial diet) claimed that the Scripture was the sole basis for faith and for an understanding of Christ.

The difference is further illustrated by a comparison between a reform document that the cardinals, inspired by the humanists, presented to Pope Paul III (r. 1534–49) in 1538 and Luther's *Address to the Nobility of the German Nation* (1520). After affirming the authority of the church, the cardinals urged the reform of the parish churches, the elimination of nonresident bishops, a restriction on the sale of indulgences to one sale a year, and a reform of the judicial system. Luther complained about the same abuses, and in much harsher language, but he sought to eliminate their root causes. For example, the cardinals urged strict enforcement of the rule of celibacy to ensure the chastity of clerics; Luther argued that clerics should be permitted to marry.

Despite the differences between the humanist cardinals and Luther, many leading humanists, including Erasmus and Thomas More, supported him at first. More broke with him in 1523, in his *Letter against Luther,* and Erasmus broke with him in 1524.

Luther also received early support from many priests and monks, especially in the German cities. The cities had many grievances against the church: it controlled their prime real estate, and it insisted that the clergy be exempted from local taxes. Moreover, the church's tax levies fell most heavily on the urban populations. In city after city, conservative members of the clergy were quietly replaced by followers of Luther. Because so many of the cities held imperial charters, the reformed churches were in effect state churches, and in another decade or so Lutheranism would be established as the state religion by some of the German princes.

The peasants too responded to Luther's message at first, but they lost interest after the Peasants' Rebellion of 1524–25. Although the aims of the rebellion had to do with social reform—the abolition of serfdom and the burdens of the manorial system—the rebels interpreted Luther's pronouncements as support for their program: "Therefore do we find in the Scripture that we are free," they argued, "and we will be free." In a bitter condemnation of the rebels, Luther replied that the freedom he was speaking about was spiritual not social, and the rebels felt he had betrayed them. As time passed, Luther and his supporters found themselves caught between the reactionary Roman Catholic church and the radical lower classes.

Finally, Germany's lack of centralized government prevented its resistance to the spread of Lutheranism. Although the emperor Charles V (r. 1519–56) never wavered in his orthodoxy, he was preoccupied with trying to hold his vast dominions together and with repelling military threats on every side. From 1522 to 1559, Charles and his son Philip were fighting a series of wars with France, while Charles and his brother Ferdinand, Duke of Austria, were trying to stem the advance of the Turks up the Danube Valley.

Not until 1547—the year after Luther's death—did Charles turn his attention to Lutheranism, which by then had been accepted by about half the German principalities. He launched a confused religious war against the princes who supported Luther that dragged on until 1555, when he permitted his brother Ferdinand to conclude the Religious Peace of Augsburg. That peace allowed the free cities and principalities of the empire to choose between Lutheranism and Catholicism and bound them to respect each other's

Contemporary engraving depicting a noble lady and her son kneeling before peasant rebels to plead for their lives during the Peasants' Rebellion (1524–25).

choice. Essentially, the agreement made religion the prerogative of the ruler of each principality; anyone who disagreed with his ruler could migrate to another principality.

The Peace of Augsburg constituted the first official recognition that western Christendom was in a state of disunity and would remain so. In the end, northern Germany became mostly Protestant; southern Germany remained Catholic. Outside Germany, Lutheranism took root only in Scandinavia, where Denmark, Norway, and Sweden became Lutheran by midcentury. The German provenance of Lutheranism limited its appeal abroad, where another form of Protestantism, that of John Calvin, won acceptance.

OTHER PROTESTANT MOVEMENTS

In addition to Wittenberg, other important centers of reform were Zürich, Basel, Strasbourg, and especially Geneva. In each of these cities a form of Protestantism emerged that was significantly different from Lutheranism. The so-called "reformed" churches that resulted had a more highly developed system of theology and church organization and put greater stress on the moral conduct and political action of their members than did the Lutheran churches.

Bucer and Zwingli

Among the early leaders of these Protestant movements were the humanists Martin Bucer of Strasbourg (1491–1551) and the Swiss scholar Ulrich Zwingli (1484–1531). As a Dominican friar, Bucer had been influenced by the humanism of Erasmus. Once he became familiar with Luther's views, however, he left the Dominican order and married a nun. He was excommunicated in 1523, and from 1524 to 1548 he led the reform movement in Strasbourg, where he introduced various liturgical changes. Throughout the years he participated in colloquies held in Worms, Regensburg, and Hagenau aimed at reconciling Catholicism and Protestantism and also was active in trying to reconcile Lutheranism with other Protestant movements, particularly the one led by Zwingli.

Zwingli, who was born in a rural village in the Swiss Alps, studied classics in Basel. He too fell under Erasmus's influence and was especially attracted to the idea of a renascent Christianity based on the Scriptures. Zwingli became a priest, beginning as a village parson in 1506, and rose to become the "people's priest" in Zürich (1518). In this prestigious position, which enabled him to stay abreast of the ideas of the day, he became familiar with the activity of Martin Luther. Historians still debate the extent of the influence of Luther's ideas on Zwingli. Zwingli himself claimed that he had arrived at Luther's basic ideas on his own before reading Luther's works.

As in many other cities, the reform movement in Zürich proceeded by stages. In 1522, some of the citizens violated the church's dietary laws during the Lenten season, and the city council appointed a commission to investigate. The bishop of Constance, who had jurisdiction over Zürich, protested that he had the exclusive right to judge matters of religious discipline, but the commission, of which Zwingli was a member, proceeded anyway. The commission's report was equivocal, but Zwingli soon published a sermon in which he argued that, because Christians were free from the law, as St. Paul said,

they did not have to obey dietary rules imposed by the church. A person's faith, he argued, had to do with his or her beliefs and motivations, not with the observance of actions prescribed by the church. Luther, of course, had reached the same conclusion.

In 1523, the city council of Zürich, in an effort to dispel public confusion and unrest, announced a debate on questions of religion. Zwingli prepared for the debate by drawing up a list of 67 conclusions on matters of doctrine, morals, and church discipline. His main ideas reflected that the Scriptures alone were the basis of true Christianity, and they carried the day. After this, Protestantism was widely accepted in Zürich. The question now became whether the paintings, stained-glass windows, and sculptures should be removed from the city's churches. Zwingli's position was that once the church members had become true Christians they would no longer need such outward signs of faith, and he suggested that the images be removed gradually. The people were less patient, however, and in 1524 they stripped the interiors of the churches—whitewashing the walls, pulling down the crucifixes, and destroying the windows and sculptures. Finally, in 1525, the reformers, with Zwingli in the lead this time, replaced the Mass with a simple service in commemoration of the Last Supper. The city council supported their action by issuing a law that did away with the Mass altogether.

Calvinism

John Calvin (1509–64) was born in Noyon, France, and as a young man was sent to the University of Paris to study law. He was more interested in humanism than in law, however, and soon dropped his legal studies to concentrate on Greek and Latin. In 1532, he published a commentary on Seneca's treatise *Concerning Clemency.* Around this time he had what he later called a conversion to Protestantism, and in 1534 he moved to Basel, where there were many Protestants. In Basel, he wrote a theological treatise, called the *Institutes of the Christian Religion,* which he intended to be a comprehensive treatment of the Protestant religion. The first edition of this work, only six chapters long, was published in 1536. Calvin then revised and enlarged the work until the fourth edition, with eighty chapters, was published in 1559. The *Institutes* was the first systematic presentation of Protestant theology.

Calvin visited Geneva in 1536. He had no intention of staying until Guillaume Farel (1489–1565), a leading Protestant who had introduced Protestantism to the city two months before, persuaded him to become his assistant. Together, Farel and Calvin undertook a vigorous program of reform that aroused opposition because of their impatience and the strictness of their approach. In 1538, a majority of Catholics were elected to the city council, and Farel and Calvin were driven from the city. Farel went to Neuchâtel, where he remained the rest of his life. Calvin went to Strasbourg, where he came under the influence of the moderate reformer Martin Bucer.

Apparently, Protestantism had taken root in Geneva, however, because in 1541 the city council invited Calvin to return. Although he seems to have done so reluctantly, he remained there until his death in 1564. During those years, he worked diligently for reform in the church of Geneva and gradually asserted his power over the city council itself. By the late 1550s, Geneva had become a virtual theocracy—a city-state governed by the clergy.

Building on Luther's doctrine of salvation by faith alone, Calvin constructed a system that emphasized the sovereignty of God and the depravity of man. At the center of that system was the doctrine of predestination: God, through his inscrutable will, destined some men to be saved and others to be damned. Consequently, the idea that one can win salvation by performing "good works" is absurd. Calvin also held that a true and fervent faith in Christ and the Scriptures was a sign that one was among the elect of God and that the performance of good works was evidence of that faith.

In 1559, Calvin established an academy in Geneva comprising schools of arts, law, medicine, and theology. Perhaps because of his own fame, he was able to attract an excellent faculty, and within a few years the academy was flourishing, with more than 1,500 students from all over Europe. Geneva itself became a model for Presbyterian or Reformed churches in France, England, Scotland, the Netherlands, the Rhineland, Bohemia, and Hungary, and later for churches in North America and Dutch South Africa.

Calvin advocated that each local church should have a ruling body composed of ministers and elders (or presbyters) who were to meet regularly in councils (called synods) with the officials of the other churches in the district. Because Calvinism was particularly resistant to secular control, it never became "nationalized," as Lutheranism had. Moreover, because it possessed a systematic theology, it could be adopted by reformers everywhere.

Sketch of John Calvin drawn by a student, perhaps during a lecture.

Calvin on Predestination

Predestination we call the eternal decree of God, by which he has determined in himself, what he would have to become of every individual of mankind. For they are not all created with a similar destiny; but eternal life is foreordained for some, and eternal damnation for others. . . .

In conformity, therefore, to the clear doctrine of the Scripture, we assert, that by an eternal and immutable counsel, God has once for all determined, both whom he would admit to salvation, and whom he would condemn to destruction. We affirm that this counsel, as far as concerns the elect, is founded on his gratuitous mercy, totally irrespective of human merit; but that to those whom he devotes to condemnation, the gate of life is closed by a just and irreprehensible, but incomprehensible, judgment. . . .

How exceedingly presumptuous it is only to inquire into the causes of the Divine will; which is in fact, and is justly entitled to be, the cause of everything that exists. . . . For the will of God is the highest rule of justice; so that what he wills must be considered just, for this very reason, because he wills it.

From John Calvin, Institutes of the Christian Religion, *trans. by John Allen (Philadelphia: Westminster Press, 1930), Book III, Ch. 21, pars. 5, 7; Ch. 23, par. 2.*

By the 1550s Calvinists were in many parts of Europe, but they constituted a majority only in Geneva and Scotland. Elsewhere, they formed a well-organized minority that left its mark on society. Calvinism gave rise to Puritanism in England, to the Huguenots in France, and to the Dutch Reformed church. It served as the militant wing of Protestantism.

THE RADICALS

Other reformers had more radical agendas linked to the social unrest of the period. In Germany particularly—where capitalism was making rapid progress—workers and peasants hard hit by economic change turned to old ideas of social and religious reform. During the 1520s in Switzerland and in the upper Rhine Valley, little groups of people came together and proclaimed that the only true church was a voluntary association of believers, not an official institution like the churches of the Lutherans or the Catholics. Holding that baptism was a sign of belief, many of these groups insisted that only adults could be baptized—an idea that dated back to certain heretical groups of the twelfth century. Their opponents called them Anabaptists, or re-baptizers. The Anabaptists had a simple liturgy and generally interpreted the Bible literally. Most of them refused to take an oath—in court or elsewhere—or to accept public office or serve in the army. Some of the groups practiced the sort of communism described in the second chapter of Acts (2:44–47).

The Anabaptists were persecuted by Catholics and Protestants alike. After being driven from southern Germany, many of them found their way to the Netherlands, Bohemia, Poland, and England. It was during the seventeenth century in England and in the English colonies in America that the ideas of the Anabaptists were fully realized. Modern Baptists (who practice only adult baptism), Congregationalists (who recognize the autonomy of local congregations), and Quakers (who rely on an "inner light") all trace their origins to the sixteenth-century Anabaptists.

The more rigid Protestants objected to all religious paintings and sculpture as leading to idolatry. In this engraving of 1579, Calvinists are pulling down statues of saints and destroying stained-glass windows.

ANGLICANISM

Although several kings took over their national churches during the late Middle Ages, they were not motivated by a desire for reform. In England, though the breach with Rome signaled by the Act of Supremacy in 1534 was followed by change, Henry VIII did not intend to depart from orthodox Catholic belief and practice. He made it clear that he would continue to suppress heresy, whether Lutheran or Anabaptist. Still, he found that he could not seal England off from Protestantism or maintain his break from Rome without the support of Protestant sympathizers. To evidence his willingness to compromise he approved the distribution of an English translation of the Bible.

By the time of Henry's death in 1547, a Protestant clergy had emerged within the English church under the leadership of Thomas Cranmer, archbishop of Canterbury (r. 1533–53). Under Henry's son, Edward IV (r. 1547–53), Cranmer set about transforming the English church into a Protestant church. He assembled the best parts of the Catholic liturgy and translated them into English to form the majestic Book of Common Prayer (1549). In his first version of his collection he tried to accommodate both Catholics and Protestants, but he satisfied neither. So he issued a fully Protestant version in 1552. This prayer book eventually became a literary symbol of Anglicanism, as Luther's Bible and Calvin's *Institutes* had come to symbolize Lutheranism and Calvinism.

The advance of Protestantism in England was further accelerated by Henry VIII's dissolution of the monasteries. Because the monasteries belonged to international orders, they were incompatible with the new national church headed by the king. Furthermore, monasticism had lost much of its appeal, and many of the houses were no longer abiding by the rules of their orders. Beginning in 1536, Henry confiscated the properties of the monastic communities and incorporated them into the crown lands. By 1539, the dissolution of the monasteries was complete. Although the confiscations virtually doubled the royal income, it was still not

enough to support the monarchy's costly wars. Consequently, Henry and his successors gradually sold the old monastic properties to aristocratic families, who thereby acquired an economic interest in preserving the breach with Rome.

The Protestant reformation in England came to a halt in 1553, when Henry's oldest child, Mary, daughter of Catherine of Aragon, came to the throne. To vindicate her mother, Mary tried to reunite

---

I I I I I I I I I I I

Radical Protestantism:
The Teaching of Menno Simons

Menno Simons (1496–1561) was one of the ablest leaders of the radical wing of the Reformation. Simons's followers formed the Mennonite church, which still exists. His ideas also contributed to the development of the Baptist church. He never summed up his doctrine in a single document; it has to be put together from scattered pamphlets.

We do not find in Scripture a single word by which Christ has ordained the baptism of infants, or that his apostles taught and practiced it. We say that infant baptism is but a human invention. . . . To baptize before that which is required for baptism, namely faith, is to place the cart before the horse.

Never should any commandment be observed which is not contained in God's holy Word, either in letter or in spirit.

The regenerated do not go to war nor fight. . . . How can a Christian, according to Scripture, consistently retaliate, rebel, make war, murder, slay, torture, steal, rob, and burn cities and conquer countries?

Where have you read in the Scriptures, that Christ or the Apostles called upon the power of the magistracy against those who would not hear their doctrine or obey their words? . . . Faith is a gift of God, therefore it cannot be forced on anyone by worldly authorities or by the sword.

We must be born from above, must be changed and renewed in our hearts and thus be transplanted from the unrighteous and evil nature of Adam into the righteous and good nature of Christ, or we cannot be helped in eternity by any means, divine or human.

From "Selections from the Writings of Menno Simons," in The Medieval World and Its Transformations, *ed. by G. M. Straka (New York: McGraw-Hill, 1967), Vol. II, pp. 463, 466, 467, 468, 470.*

Title page of Daniel Featley's *Description* of 1645, known also as "The Dippers Dipt," a satirical view of the Anabaptists.

she was an educated, intelligent woman, and she knew that she would have to be patient. She had the Book of Common Prayer revised once again, to make it acceptable to Catholics and Protestants alike. She refused "to make windows into men's souls," as she put it—that is, she would persecute only those who openly and persistently opposed her. Even after the pope excommunicated her in 1570, she tolerated Catholics so long as they refrained from political activity. But she treated as a traitor anyone who challenged her right to the throne.

Elizabeth's moderate policies did not please all her subjects. Radical Protestants continued to demand that the English church be purified of all traces of Catholicism. These "Puritans" were strong in Parliament, and the queen occasionally had to deal harshly with them, but they helped to establish the idea that patriotism required independence from Rome.

The Anglican church viewed Presbyterianism—which was dominant in Scotland and had made some headway in England—with suspicion and was contemptuous of the Baptists. During the seventeenth century, the Anglican church became progressively more conservative, and today many Anglicans insist that their church is not "Protestant" at all. Rather, they argue, it was the Catholic church that strayed from the true path and Henry VIII and Cranmer who preserved the church of Christ.

THE CATHOLIC REFORMATION AND THE COUNTER REFORMATION

The leaders of Protestantism thought of themselves as reformers, and the movement they set in motion is still known as the Protestant Reformation. Catholics, of course, viewed them as rebels and their reformation as a revolt. For them, true reformation could take place only within the church. Churchmen and pious laymen had been calling for reform ever since the fourteenth century, but the Protestant challenge heightened the pressure and helped to precipitate a great new reform movement in the middle of the sixteenth

the English church with Rome. She canceled all antipapal legislation, deposed Cranmer, purged the church of his supporters, and had Cranmer and about 300 other Protestants burned as heretics. Mary's reign of terror (she was known as Bloody Mary) and her marriage to Philip II of Spain offended her English subjects as inhumane and as an affront to their patriotism. As a result, Protestantism came to be identified with patriotism in the public mind.

Mary died in 1558, and Elizabeth, the daughter of Henry VIII and his second wife, Anne Boleyn, succeeded to the throne as Elizabeth I (r. 1558–1603). Elizabeth understood that her legitimacy as queen depended on the validity of Henry's divorce and on his Act of Supremacy. But century. Historians call that movement the Catholic Reformation, or the Counter-Reformation. Actually, these were two different movements. The Catholic Reformation was a reform of the church, while the Counter-Reformation was a Catholic response to the Protestants. That response was vigorous; the church used torture and imprisonment as well as gentler means of persuasion to bring wayward Catholics back to orthodoxy.

The pressure for the reform of the Catholic church had produced some action even before Luther sounded his pro-test. In the late fifteenth century, the Oratory of Divine Love was founded in Genoa as a lay brotherhood similar to the Brethren of the Common Life in the north. The Oratory sought to encourage a simple Christian life among laymen and to reform the clergy, who were gradually admitted to it as members. The movement spread to other Italian cities, and by the second quarter of the sixteenth century it had become the main source of ideas for reform within the church.

The impetus toward internal reform coincided with a decline in the political

Europe after the Reformations

Engraving showing the third session of the Council of Trent (1562–63). An amphitheater was set up in the church of St. Maria Maggiore.

power of the papacy. The last of the politician popes of the Renaissance was Clement VII (r. 1523–34), who rejected calls for reform and acted like a traditional Italian despot. To counter the power of the em-

peror Charles V, Clement entered into an alliance with Francis I of France. But with the sack of Rome in 1527 by undisciplined imperial troops, Italy came under imperial control and the political aspirations of the papacy vanished. Clement's successor, Paul III (r. 1534–49) turned his attention to reform and named cardinals who themselves were eager for reform. Eventually he summoned a great council to the city of Trent—which was under German control—to work out a reform program.

The Council of Trent met in three sessions—1545–48, 1551–52, and 1562–63. Toward the end of the first session, Emperor Charles V urged the council to open direct negotiations with the Protestants. To thwart that proposal, the pope moved the meeting to Bologna, knowing that no Protestant would appear in a city under papal control. For its second and third sessions, the council returned to Trent. In the third session, it issued a series of reform decrees.

Among those decrees was a declaration that salvation was indeed granted by God alone and that salvation resulted from faith, but that good works were a demonstration of faith and a confirmation of the working of God's mercy in the doer. The council also asserted that ultimate religious authority resided *both* in the Bible *and* in tradition, as interpreted by the Roman Catholic church. It urged that seminaries be established to train priests, and those seminaries did in fact foster a gradual reform of the priesthood. Finally, it ruled that clerics could not hold multiple offices and reaffirmed the absolute supremacy of the pope over the clerical hierarchy.

The second and third sessions of the council were dominated by Philip II of Spain (r. 1556–98), who was determined that Spain would resist the Protestant threat. He emerged as the leader of the Counter-Reformation, promoting the revival of a militant church throughout Europe. The spearhead of the Counter-Reformation was a new order founded by Ignatius of Loyola (1491–1556), a Spaniard of Basque descent. While serving as a soldier in the wars between the Habsburgs

Ignatius of Loyola, founder of the Jesuit Order, holds a book with the text "to the greater glory of God."

and the French, Ignatius had suffered a severe wound and had spent months recuperating. During his convalescence, he had read several books on the lives of the saints, the only reading material at hand, and had decided to become a Christian knight in the service of the Virgin Mary. As he found his way into his new life, he worked through a series of "spiritual exercises," which he later recommended to his followers. The exercises called for intense concentration on the most vivid details of hell and of the life and death of Christ as a means of strengthening one's will toward salvation. While Ignatius was studying at the University of Paris (John Calvin was a fellow student), he enlisted nine of his friends to become the nucleus of a new order called the Society of Jesus. Pope Paul III approved the order in 1540, and its members became known as Jesuits.

The Jesuits wore no distinctive habit; they dressed as their work required. They swore an oath of allegiance to the pope and underwent rigorous training for hazardous assignments. They carried out secret missions in Protestant regions, where they would be executed if caught. Through their clandestine operations, they strengthened the pope's control over the church; they ran the best schools in Europe; and they reclaimed most of Bohemia, Poland, Hungary, and southern Germany from Protestantism.

The inquisition was revived as an instrument of church reform when Ferdinand and Isabella instituted a royal inquisition in Spain in 1480. Their lead was followed by the Habsburgs in the Netherlands in 1523 and by Spanish powers in Italy in 1542. In 1559, the papacy instituted a system of censorship known as the Index. This was a list of printed books that Catholics were forbidden to read. The Index was approved, with some modifications, by the Council of Trent in 1563.

The Catholic Reformation brought new vitality to the church and enabled it to close ranks against the Protestants. By the second half of the sixteenth century a strong church, reorganized and backed by Spanish power, faced an array of Protes-

Luther tweaks the beard of Calvin as both of them pull the hair of the pope. This satirical engraving presents a Catholic view of the Reformation controversy.

tant organizations that had already begun to compete with one another for followers.

The Results of the Reformation

Some of the results of the Protestant Reformation are clear: It split Christendom into several competing churches. It halted the trend toward secularism that had been evident in the late Middle Ages. After Luther, all issues were religious issues and for the next century the most serious conflicts in Europe were religious conflicts.

Modern historians have debated the political, economic, and cultural effects of the Protestant Reformation. Did it foster capitalism by recognizing the possibility of serving God in one's secular calling and by extolling the bourgeois virtues of thrift and self-discipline? Did it help kings create absolute monarchies by supporting the idea that royal power came directly from God? Did it deflect the course of art history by cleansing the medieval churches and refusing to decorate the new churches? The historical record does not furnish answers to these questions, but the effort to answer them has produced some influential historical works.

Suggestions for Further Reading

Background of the Reformation

Several works put the Reformation in a historical context. See S. Ozmont, *The Reformation in Medieval Perspective* (1971); G. Strauss, *Pre-Reformation Germany* (1972); and J. Bossy, *Christianity in the West, 1400–1750* (1985). On the background of Protestantism, see H. Oberman, *The Harvest of Medieval Theology* (1963), and A. McGrath, *The Intellectual Origins of the European Reformation* (1987). J. Huizinga's *The Waning of the Middle Ages* (1924) is the classic work on the cultural changes during the fourteenth and fifteenth centuries.

The Religious Upheaval

On the Hussite movement, see M. Spinka, *John Huss and the Czech Revolution* (1941); F. G. Heymann, *John Zizka and the Hussite Revolution* (1955); and H. Kaminsky, *A History of the Hussite Revolution* (1967). On the spread of humanism, see P. O. Kristeller, "The European Diffusion of Italian Humanism," *Renaissance Thought II* (1965), and L. Spitz, *The Religious Renaissance of the German Humanists* (1963). On Erasmus, see J. Huizinga, *Erasmus* (1952), and R. H. Bainton, *Erasmus of Christendom* (1969). For a specialized study of Erasmus's reform views, see J. B. Payne, *Erasmus: His Theology of the Sacraments* (1970). Erasmus's writings are widely available; see, for example, J. P. Dolan, ed., *The Essential Erasmus* (1964).

There are many histories of the Protestant Reformation. H. Holborn, *A History of Modern Germany: The Reformation* (1959), is excellent on Germany. See also B. Moeller, *Imperial Cities and the Reformation* (1972), and G. Strauss, *Luther's House of Learning* (1978). L. W. Spitz, *The Renaissance and Reformation Movements,* Vol. 2 (1971), is an excellent brief history. J. Lortz, *The Reformation in Germany,* 2 vols. (1969), gives a fair statement of the Catholic view. A. G. Dickens, *The German Nation and Martin Luther* (1972), emphasizes the urban nature of the Reformation. H. J. Hillerbrand, *The Protestant Reformation: A Narrative History* (1964), contains a good anthology of contemporary writings.

On the spread of Protestantism, see S. Ozment, *The Reformation of the Cities* (1975). On Zwingli, see W. P. Stephens, *The Theology of Huldrych Zwingli* (1986). On the iconoclasm of the Protestant movement, see C. M. N. Eire, *War Against the Idols* (1986), and C. Christensen, *Art and the Reformation in Germany* (1980). W. Bouwsma, *John Calvin* (1988), is a fine biography and introduction. F. Wendel, *Calvin, The Origin and Development of his Religious Thought* (1963), is an excellent introduction. On the radicals, see G. H. Williams, *The Radical Reformation* (1962); F. H. Littell, *The Free Church* (1958); R. H. Bainton, *The Travail of Religious Liberty* (1951); and C. L. Clausen, *Anabaptism: A Social History* (1972). The best work on England is A. G. Dickens, *The English Reformation* (1964). J. J. Scarisbrick, *Henry VIII* (1968), is a brilliant work. For the Puritans, see P. Collinson, *The Elizabethan Puritan Movement* (1967).

An excellent discussion of the Catholic Reformation is H. Daniel-Rops, *The Catholic Reformation,* 2 vols. (1961). See also A. G. Dickens, *The Counter Reformation* (1969). For the Council of Trent, the definitive work is H. Jedin, *History of the Council of Trent,* of which the first two volumes appeared in English translation in 1957.

Results of the Reformation

On the economic, political, and cultural consequences of the Reformation there are wide differences of opinion. The starting point of modern debate was an "essay" by M. Weber, *The Protestant Ethic and the Spirit of Capitalism* (1905). *Protestantism and Capitalism: The Weber Thesis and Its Critics,* ed. by R. W. Green (1973), is a convenient collection of selections from the literature. See also L. W. Spitz, *The Reformation: Basic Interpretations* (1972), and R. Kingdon and R. Linder, *Calvin and Calvinism: Sources of Democracy* (1972). For a readable and perceptive survey of the period, see A. G. Dickens, *Reformation and Society in Sixteenth-Century Europe* (1966).

18

THE AGE OF DISCOVERY

Tn the early Middle Ages, Europeans knew of the world beyond the horizon only from the works of the ancient geographers. Then they learned something more through their contacts with the Arabs, Moors, Vikings, Magyars, and Mongols. But they had only the vaguest notions of East Asia, except that it was the source of the spices and curiosities that the Arabs brought to market. And they knew nothing at all of the southern hemisphere or the vast American continents.

Consequently, the explorations of the late fifteenth century had a revolutionary effect on their consciousness of the world and their place in it. For the first time in history they had direct experience of all the inhabited continents of the world and of the people who lived on them. By the middle of the sixteenth century, European intellectuals were pondering the question of how to deal with people who had built impressive civilizations without the benefit of divine revelation or Christian sanction.

THE EMERGENCE OF OCEANIC TRADE

The Early Voyages

In 1400, Europeans knew scarcely more about the world than the Romans had, for only a few of them had ever ventured beyond the Mediterranean Basin. The crusades had enlarged the vision of western Europeans somewhat, but not beyond the limits of the ancient world.

Only the Scandinavians had caught a glimpse of far horizons. Their sagas tell of voyages of Leif Ericson and other bold Viking seamen to North America. During

(OPPOSITE) ASTROLABE—USED IN ANCIENT TIMES TO CALCULATE THE POSITION AND ANGLE OF THE STARS. IN THE MIDDLE AGES IT BEGAN TO BE USED FOR NAVIGATION.

the eleventh century, the Icelanders established settlements on Greenland and around Hudson Bay and apparently coasted down the eastern shores of North America. The Hudson Bay settlements seem to have been abandoned after a short time, but the Greenland settlements survived until the middle of the thirteenth century, when a cooling trend in the earth's climate made them uninhabitable. The last official contact between Iceland and the Greenland settlements took place

(Top) Mediterranean war galley with lateen sail *(ca.* twelfth century); *(middle)* lateen-rigged vessel, much like Columbus's *Niña* (early fifteenth-century); *(bottom)* Spanish galleon of sixteenth century, the typical long-distance ship for Spanish commerce.

in 1258, though there is archaeological evidence that English sailors were still visiting them at the end of the century.

Meanwhile the Italians were opening up an overland trade route to China. The Polo family of Venice, and Franciscan friars as well, demonstrated that China could be reached by land across the vast steppes of central Asia. Marco Polo *(ca.* 1254–1324) traveled to China with his father and uncle in 1271 and remained at the court of the Mongol emperor for more than fifteen years. On his return in 1295, he wrote an account of the journey that was widely read in Europe and contributed greatly to the Europeans' knowledge of the East and stimulated their interest in Chinese civilization. But after the collapse of the Mongol empire in the fourteenth century, the overland route to China was no longer safe, and the demand for eastern wares was satisfied by Arab sailors operating in the Indian Ocean who brought spices and textiles to Alexandria and Beirut to be distributed by the Venetians to European markets.

By the end of the sixteenth century, these uncertain contacts with the East had been replaced by a regular trade of worldwide proportions. The ocean had become a busy highway on which Europeans controlled all the traffic, and it was becoming clear that the empires of the future would be built on mastery of the seas. When the first ship to circumnavigate the globe sailed into its home port in 1522, Europeans had already begun to build a network of trade around the earth that would bring all the civilizations of the world under their influence in the centuries ahead.

The Preconditions for Exploration

The age of exploration could not have occurred before revolutionary advances had been made in the design of ships and in the tools of navigation. The Vikings had made short voyages across the North Atlantic—Greenland was only a twelve-day sail from Norway—but in their small, open boats, even those trips were daring. What made the western explorations possible was a rare climatic condition that occasionally gave Scandinavian sailors a hazy glimpse of land beyond the horizon. From the western coast of Iceland they could "see" Greenland: In the winter, when the water is colder than the air, land far beyond the horizon—over the curvature of the earth—is sometimes reflected in the sky, giving would-be explorers confidence that they will reach land just beyond the range of sight.

But the Scandinavians' boats were too small and too unseaworthy to permit regular contact with the settlements in Greenland and North America. Before Europeans could push out across the Atlantic and plant colonies linked to the mother country, they needed more seaworthy ships and more reliable navigational aids.

It was a long time before oceangoing ships became available, however. The oar-propelled galleys of the Mediterranean served well enough in coastal waters, but sailors rarely struck out into the open sea—and then only to cross such narrow stretches as the passage between Sicily and North Africa. By the thirteenth century, Genoese and Venetian galleys were venturing out into the Atlantic to Morocco and Flanders, but they still hugged the coastline going and coming. To sail the open sea, mariners needed ships with sails rather than oars, and with broad, round hulls rather than the long, narrow hulls of the oar-propelled galleys. The fifty or more rowers who manned a galley burned up an enormous number of calories each day and consequently required vast amounts of food—far more than a galley could carry. Only sailing ships with small crews could make voyages across the Atlantic that lasted for months.

By the fifteenth century the Portuguese had designed such a vessel. The squat, three-masted caravel had two masts with the square sails favored by the Europeans and one mast with the triangular lateen sail favored by the Moslems. The square rigs were best for running before the wind, while the lateen rig was better suited to sailing close to the wind. The caravel was slower and less maneuverable than the galley, but it had more space for cargo and provisions for long voyages.

Mariners had had means of determining their direction of sail and their po-

sition for centuries. The astrolabe (already in use in the eleventh century and perhaps as early as the third century B.C.) enabled them to determine latitude by measuring the elevation of the sun and stars. The compass (used in Europe by the thirteenth century) gave them their direction in cloudy weather when the sun and stars were obscured. (No way to determine longitude precisely developed until the eighteenth century, when Edmund Halley—for whom the comet is named—devised a reasonably accurate method.)

The exploration of the oceans required substantial financial resources to construct and man the oceangoing vessels. City-states—from the Phoenicians to the Italians—were the original providers of shipping, but transoceanic voyages required resources far beyond the capacities of city-states. Only after the European monarchs had consolidated their power and unified their countries did there exist powers with enough wealth to man and equip fleets of oceangoing vessels. Thus, after 1400 the kingdoms gradually replaced the cities as the major supporters of shipping.

The Motivations for Exploration

The motivations of individual European ship captains varied, but it is clear that they had both religious and worldly motives. Christians believed that the longed-for end of the world would not take place until all were converted to Christianity. The desire to convert all the peoples of the world was always part of the motivation of explorers and their patrons.

One motivation for exploration was the desire to find new trade routes to East Asia. The spices used to preserve meats and make them palatable—pepper from India, cinnamon from Sri Lanka (Ceylon), ginger from China, nutmeg and cloves from the East Indies—were absolute necessities in an age without refrigeration. The Arabs controlled the trade between Alexandria and East Asia. The Venetians controlled it between Alexandria and Europe. And these monopolies made those necessities extremely expensive. The monarchs of western Europe were

Drawing of an early compass, designed by Agricola (Georg Bauer, 1494–1555), the father of mineralogy.

Toynbee on the Age of Discovery

Since A.D. 1500 the map of the civilized world has indeed been transformed out of all recognition. Down to that date it was composed of a belt of civilizations girdling the Old World from the Japanese Isles on the north-east to the British Isles on the north-west. . . . The main line of communication was provided by the chain of steppes and deserts that cut across the belt of civilizations from the Sahara to Mongolia. For human purposes, the Steppe was an inland sea. . . . This waterless sea had its dry-shod ships and its quayless ports. The steppe-galleons were camels, the steppe-galleys horses, and the steppe-ports "caravan cities." . . . The great revolution was a technological revolution by which the West made its fortune, got the better of all the other living civilizations, and forcibly united them into a single society of literally world-wide range. The revolutionary Western invention was the substitution of the Ocean for the Steppe as the principal medium of world-communication. This use of the Ocean, first by sailing ships and then by steamships, enabled the West to unify the whole inhabited and habitable world.

From Arnold J. Toynbee, Civilization on Trial (New York: Oxford University Press, 1948), pp. 67–70.

eager to find a way to lower the cost of importing them.

Another motivation was the need to find new sources of precious metals. The only way Europeans could pay for imports from Asia was with gold or silver bullion. Asians had no interest in accepting lumber or foodstuff in payment, and in any case such products were too bulky or perishable to be used in long-distance trade. By 1400 the gold and silver mines of Europe, which had never been especially productive, were nearly exhausted. To support the steady flow of gold and silver to Asia, European monarchs were eager to locate new sources of supply.

THE FIRST EXPLORATIONS

By the late fifteenth century many bold mariners along Europe's Atlantic coast were eager to set sail. They had the motivation, the ships, and the instruments they needed to venture out onto the unknown sea. They also had enough information—

most of it wrong—to make success seem likely. They took as fact Ptolemy's estimate that the circumference of the earth was about 8,000 miles. That meant that Japan and China lay only a few thousand miles west of Europe. And because they believed that Africa was much smaller than it is, they thought they could sail around it and soon arrive in Asia. In short, they reckoned that they could sail either east or west and reach their destination in a reasonable amount of time.

Portuguese Exploration

Prince Henry the Navigator (1394–1460), the young son of King John I of Portugal (r. 1385–1433) contributed a great deal to the scientific and seafaring knowledge of the day through his work at a remarkable observatory at Sagres on Cape St. Vincent, at the tip of Portugal. He devoted his life to organizing, equipping, and sending out fleets to explore the coast of Africa, and he had a notion that he could outflank the Moslems and discover lands they knew nothing about. But his main goal was to find gold—a goal he realized when his fleets reached the Gold Coast of Africa in the 1450s.

After Henry's death, the Portuguese lost interest in exploration for a time. They did discover and settle clusters of small islands in the Atlantic—the Madeiras and the Azores. Although the islands did not prove very profitable, the discovery showed that there was land to be found eight hundred miles out in the Atlantic and encouraged further exploration.

Henry's interest in voyages of discovery was taken up again by his grand-nephew, King John II (r. 1481–95), who encouraged Portuguese explorers to find an all-water route to India. By 1488 Bartholomeu Dias had discovered the Cape of Good Hope, and in 1497 Vasco da Gama rounded the Cape with four ships. He reached Calicut on the Malabar Coast of India in 1498 and was back in Lisbon with two of his ships in 1499. In 1500 Pedro Álvares Cabral led a large fleet to Brazil and then sailed on to India, where he established the first Portuguese trading stations. At first the Portuguese met with a hostile reception from the Hindus and the Moslems of India. Da Gama was not impressed by Indian civilization and apparently said as much. Several of Cabral's men were killed by Moslems. But within a few years the Portuguese had built a commercial empire in India under the bold leadership of Afonso de Albuquerque (1453–1515), who served as governor of Portuguese India from 1509 to 1515.

Albuquerque had already been active in the area before he became governor. He had conquered Goa, a coastal region in western India, which he later made his capital, and had established strategic fortresses in East Africa to disrupt the Arabs' trade with India. (The Arabs had established themselves along the East African coast in the Middle Ages and used the ports as staging posts for their trade in the Indian Ocean.) As governor, he seized Malacca to control the trade between the Spice Islands and the Indian Ocean, and took over Ormuz, an island in the Persian Gulf from which he could disrupt Arab shipping. He tried but failed to take Aden, which would have given him control of the Red Sea, through which the Arab-Venetian trade passed. By the time Albuquerque died, Portugal had taken control of much of the spice trade and had established strategic bases all the way from Africa to the East Indies.

That success was short-lived, however. Although Portugal drew large profits from these early ventures, it lacked the resources to maintain permanent colonies in India and to support the navy required to protect its trade. Italian, German, and Flemish bankers soon took over the Portuguese trade, and even the spices that still arrived at Lisbon were sent on to Antwerp for distribution. The burden of empire had grown heavy by the time Portugal fell under Spanish control in 1580.

Columbus and Spanish Exploration

In 1484, before the Portuguese had reached the Cape of Good Hope, a Genoese sailor named Christopher Columbus (1451–1506) had tried in vain to persuade the Portuguese king, John II, to back him

Vasco da Gama.

The Portuguese as others saw them: African bronze sculpture of a Portuguese man.

in a voyage of exploration to the west. Relying on the accounts of Portuguese sailors and on Ptolemy's estimate of the size of the earth, Columbus was convinced that he could reach Japan (then called Cipangu) by sailing due west. But he could find no one to back him with ships and money. The Portuguese were content to follow up the explorations of Henry the Navigator along the coast of Africa, and Ferdinand and Isabella were busy with the conquest of the kingdom of Granada, the last Moorish stronghold on the Iberian peninsula.

In January 1492, Granada fell to Spain, and Ferdinand and Isabella turned to other matters. After much hesitation, and against the advice of her counselors, Isabella agreed to back Columbus. With one brilliant voyage the Spanish reached the New World.

Columbus landed in the Bahamas on October 12, 1492, thinking he had come

The World of the Voyager

Christopher Columbus, the Genoese sailor who sailed west in search of Japan and found the New World. This portrait of Columbus is thought to be the closest existing likeness of him. It is a copy, made in about 1525, of an earlier painting that has been lost.

upon some islands in the Japanese archipelago. Throughout four voyages, until his death in 1506, he remained convinced, even after reaching the mainland, that he had reached Japan and China and gave the name "Indians"—at that time a general term for East Asians—to the people he found.

It was a fellow Italian, Amerigo Vespucci (1454–1512), head of a branch of the Medici bank in Seville, who recognized what Columbus had discovered. After voyages in 1499 and 1501, Vespucci described what he saw in letters that were published and read throughout Europe. In one he referred to the great southern continent in the west as *Mundus novus*, a New World. Later mapmakers labeled both the northern continent and the southern continent "America," after Amerigo.

Incidently, it was Vespucci's letters that inspired Thomas More to write his *Utopia* (see pp. 431–32).

The Treaty of Tordesillas, 1494

Spain and Portugal competed for possession of the western continents from the very beginning. (Portugal's claim rested on the voyage of Cabral in 1500.) To avoid going to war, they turned to the pope, Alexander VI, to settle their claims. Alexander, who was himself a Spaniard, drew a line of demarcation 100 leagues (about 300 miles) west of the Cape Verde Islands (off the coast of West Africa), which clearly favored Spain. Dissatisfied, the Portuguese persuaded the Spanish to negotiate the Treaty of Tordesillas (1494), which drew a line of demarcation from pole to pole 370 leagues west of the Cape Verde Islands.

The Portuguese assumed that the line applied only to the western hemisphere (it gave them Brazil, though they did not know it at the time), while the Spanish assumed that it went clear around the earth. According to their interpretation, the Spanish could claim the Moluccas, the heart of the Spice Islands, and part of what is now Indonesia. Given the progress the Portuguese were making in the East Indies, the conflicting interpretations of the treaty might have led to war after all. But Spain became so occupied with its new possessions in the Americas that in 1527 it sold its claims in the eastern hemisphere to Portugal.

The Spanish remained determined to find a westward route to the Orient, however. When the Spanish explorer Vasco Núñez de Balboa sighted the Pacific Ocean from the Isthmus of Darien in Central America, the Spanish thought that somewhere they might find a passage across the New World. In 1519, the Portuguese navigator Ferdinand Magellan—with Spanish backing—negotiated the treacherous straits off the southern tip of South America and sailed across the Pacific only to be killed by natives in the Philippines. His navigator, Sebastian del Cano, brought one of Magellan's five ships back to Lisbon in 1522 by way of the Cape

of Good Hope. This was the first ship to circumnavigate the world.

THE SPANISH EMPIRE IN THE AMERICAS

While Magellan was on his historic voyage, Spanish conquistadors discovered and overcame wealthy civilizations in Mexico and Peru. The most notable of the conquistadors were Hernando Cortés and Francisco Pizarro. In 1519–21 Cortés conquered the formidable Aztec Empire in Mexico with 600 men, sixteen horses, and a few cannon, and in 1533–34 Pizarro, with an even smaller force, conquered the Incan Empire in the Andes Mountains of Peru.

The Aztecs and the Incans were wealthy, sophisticated peoples, but they were no match for the Spaniards. The Spanish troops were small, but well disciplined and daring, and their leaders took advantage of every opportunity. Moreover, both the Aztec and the Incan empires were highly centralized, and once

Cortés accepting the surrender of Quauhtemoc, last king of the Aztecs. The artist was a Spanish-trained native from Tlaxcala, who chronicled Cortés's conquest for Mexico. Notice the mixture of European and Indian styles.

the rulers had been disposed of there were no local leaders to take over. Even more destructive than the military superiority of the Spaniards were the diseases (especially smallpox) they brought with them. The native populations had no natural defenses against those diseases, and soon they were so reduced in numbers that resistance was impossible.

Though it is difficult to estimate the size of the population of Mexico before the conquest, it appears to have been at least 25 million. It had dropped to about 6 million by 1540, to 4 million by 1563, and to 2.5 million by 1600. By about 1650, it had reached 1.5 million. Thereafter, it climbed gradually and reached a little more than 3.5 million in 1793. By contrast, the population of goats, sheep, and cattle that the Spanish introduced into Mexico rose dramatically in the second half of the sixteenth century. From 1550 to 1620, the number of goats and sheep rose from about half a million to 8 million, while the number of cattle rose from about 10,000 to 100,000. The small plots once tended by the native farmers had been taken over by great herds of range animals that destroyed the vegetation and reduced the land to a desert.

Spain's new empire overseas created conflict between groups with different interests and different goals. The settlers who went out to the New World wanted to build a manorial system based on the old European model, using the forced labor of the native population. They were unwilling to take orders from the Spanish government or to serve its interests. The government in turn wanted to exercise absolute power over the colonies and to exploit the rich sources of precious metals it knew to be there. The friars wanted to convert the native population to Christianity.

The fact that the native population was civilized but non-Christian raised serious theological and moral questions. Spanish scholars turned for answers to the works of medieval thinkers who had speculated about whether the biblical texts that specify that rulers receive their authority from God (such as 1 Samuel 9–31 and Romans 13) applied to rulers who did not

accept or did not know the Bible. Questions also arose regarding marriages of the natives. The church considered marriage to be a sacrament in which God joins husband and wife. Were the marriages of heathens valid? Medieval theologians and lawyers had declared that marriages of non-Christians were valid but not licit. In other words, the union was created by God but the marriages were not recognized by the church. The distinction they were making was between acts performed in accordance with natural law (which stems directly from God) and acts performed in accordance with human law (which stems only indirectly from God, through the medium of human institutions). The sixteenth-century Spaniards made much of this distinction. They concluded that the Indians lived by natural law alone but that they were God's people even without the benefit of the church. The leading proponent of this theory was a Spanish Dominican, Bartolomé de Las Casas (1474–1566).

Las Casas had gone to the New World in 1502 to convert the heathens and had soon become engaged in a struggle to win them better treatment. He and his fellow missionaries wanted the converts to be treated as fellow Christians, and he made several trips to Spain to win support for that goal. In the early 1520s, he took part in a program to found free cities for Christianized Indians. But when the project failed, he returned to Spain and retired to a Dominican house. In retirement, he wrote many learned works promoting his scheme as well as a long *History of the Indians.*

In the end, a compromise was worked out among the conflicting interests of the settlers, the government, and the friars. The settlers were permitted to use the forced labor of the Indians, but under the regulation of the government. The friars were given freedom to evangelize and Europeanize the native population. By contemporary standards, these policies were quite humane, and the Spanish came close to achieving what the Portuguese had failed to accomplish in the East and what the English never attempted in North America: the Christianization and

Europeanization of a whole native population.

Nonetheless, the main goal of the Spanish Empire was economic exploitation. With the discovery of rich silver mines in Mexico in 1545, the Empire gave itself over to the extraction and shipment of silver. After 1564, a silver fleet of twenty to sixty ships would gather every spring in Havana harbor to be convoyed by warships to Seville. And every spring the government officials would wait anxiously until the bullion was safely landed; silver was the key to Spain's power.

Despite their obsession with silver production, the Spanish were also aware of the agricultural potential of their holdings. The wet lowlands of the Caribbean were well suited to sugar cane cultivation, and sugar became an important commodity. When it turned out that the Indian workers were highly vulnerable to disease, however, the Spaniards began to import black slaves from Africa. Eventually, many Spaniards and Indians intermarried, and the mestizos—offspring of mixed marriages—outnumbered the purebred of either race. The Africans, however, remained enslaved outside society.

IMPERIAL SPAIN: THE REIGN OF PHILIP II

With the wealth from its colonies in the New World, Spain became the most powerful nation in Europe. And with the succession of the Habsburg emperor Charles V (r. 1516–56) to the Spanish throne through his mother Joanna, the daughter of Ferdinand and Isabella, Spain acquired a new role in European affairs. Charles, who had inherited Austria through his father, Maximilian, and the Netherlands through his mother, Mary of Burgundy, was elected emperor in 1519. He used Spanish money and Spanish troops to counter the Protestant heretics, to protect Austria from the Turks, and to extend the Spanish conquest of the New World. Although these ambitious enterprises taxed Spain's resources, under Charles and his son King Philip II (r. 1556–98), the nation proved almost equal to the

Las Casas on the American Indians in the Sixteenth Century

It has been written that these peoples of the Indies, lacking human governance and ordered nations, did not have the power of reason to govern themselves—which was inferred only from their having been found to be gentle, patient and humble. It has been implied that God became careless in creating so immense a number of rational souls and let human nature, which He so largely determined and provided for, go astray in the almost infinitesimal part of the human lineage which they comprise. From this it follows that they have all proven themselves unsocial and therefore monstrous, contrary to the natural bent of all peoples of the world.

. . . Not only have [the Indians] shown themselves to be very wise peoples and possessed of lively and marked understanding, prudently governing and providing for their nations (as much as they can be nations, without faith in or knowledge of the true God) and making them prosper in justice; but they have equalled many diverse nations of the world, past and present, that have been praised for their governance, politics and customs, and exceed by no small measure the wisest of all these, such as the Greeks and Romans, in adherence to the rules of natural reason.

From Bartolomé de las Casas, Apologética historia de las Indias, *in* Introduction to Contemporary Civilization in the West, *3rd ed. (New York: Columbia University Press, 1960), Vol. 1, p. 539.*

Contemporary map showing Spain as the head and crown of sixteenth-century Europe.

task. The sixteenth and early seventeenth centuries were the golden age of Spain.

In 1555–56 Charles V divided the Habsburg holdings between his brother Ferdinand and his son Philip. To Ferdinand went the Habsburg possessions in Austria, Bohemia, and Hungary, along with the imperial crown (still elective in theory, but by now always bestowed on a Habsburg). To Philip went the crowns of Castile and Aragon—still technically separate, but united since the death of Isabella (1504) and Ferdinand (1516). With Spain went its possessions in the New World, the kingdom of Naples, and the duchy of Milan (in effect control of all Italy), and the Netherlands. For a century and a half the "Austrian Habsburgs" and the "Spanish Habsburgs," were separate ruling houses that cooperated closely in matters of dynastic policy. Even though Philip's realm included the Netherlands, it was more tightly knit and centralized than that of his uncle.

Although Philip was the scion of a central European family, he was thoroughly Spanish in speech, thought, and character. After 1559, when the Habsburgs concluded peace with France, he spent all his remaining years in Spain. Though conscientious, he was distrustful of his advisers, unable to delegate authority even in minor matters, and rigorously Catholic in religion. His goal was to restore the unity of Christendom with the Spanish king as its temporal head.

Europe about 1560

Economic Policy

After the discovery of the Mexican mines, the value of the annual shipments of silver rose dramatically. In the early years it amounted to something less than $300,000; by about 1550 it had risen to more than $4,000,000; and by 1600 it was about $12,000,000. Then a steady decline set in, and by about 1660 the average value was down to $1,200,000. The crown's share was about one-quarter of the total.

As a result of the influx of bullion into Spain, prices rose steeply after centuries of relative stability. By the middle of the sixteenth century, inflation was rampant and had spread to the rest of Europe. It has been estimated that prices in Spain quadrupled in the course of the century.

The rise in prices outstripped the rise in tax revenues, and Philip II was forced to repudiate his government's debts three times—in 1557, 1575, and 1596. These repudiations, which were tantamount to declarations of bankruptcy because Philip was announcing that he could not and would not repay his debts, sent shock-waves through the financial institutions of Europe. Besides damaging Spain's credit, the inflation ruined its infant industries, which had appeared robust early in the century. Because inflation developed first and rose fastest in Spain, its industrialists were at a disadvantage in the international market, and Spain suffered a regular trade imbalance. Spanish industry languished, and bullion flowed out of the country. When the silver mines in America began to peter out in the mid-seventeenth century, the Spanish economy had already been ruined, and the nation quickly declined into a second-rate power.

Religious Policy

Philip II's religious views were the most intolerant of his time. He once said that he would rather be king of a desert than of a land of heretics. His grandparents, Ferdinand and Isabella, had already forced the Moors to convert to Christianity, had expelled the Jews from their kingdoms (1492), and had delegated to the Spanish Inquisition responsibility for see-

On Philip II of Spain

The pallor of his complexion was remarked on by all observers, and most of them drew the proper conclusion, namely, that it indicated a weak stomach and lack of exercise. Reddened eyes were a penalty of his excessive devotion to the written word both day and night. . . . Reading and writing occupied the major portion of Philip's day. . . . He had taken deeply to heart his father's injunction to direct everything himself, and never to give his full confidence even to the most faithful of his ministers, and the natural result was that his time was completely occupied with receiving and answering reports and letters. . . . Reports, reports, and even more reports; Philip was literally submerged with them in his later years, and moreover he did not stop at reading them; he annotated them, as he went along, with comments on matters as absurdly trifling as the spelling and style of the men who had written them—all in that strange, sprawling hand of his, one of the most illegible hands of an age more than usually replete with chirographical difficulties.

From R. B. Merriman, The Rise of the Spanish Empire in the Old World and in the New *(New York: Macmillan, 1934), Vol. IV, pp. 21–24.*

ing that the converts remained Christian. Nonetheless, it was widely believed that the Moriscos (Moslems who had converted to Christianity) continued to practice Islam in private. In 1566, Philip ordered them to stop using the Arabic language, to give up their traditional dress, and to stop taking hot baths, as was their custom. Three years later, when the Moriscos rebelled in protest against this suppression of their cultural heritage, Philip savagely put down the rebellion and drove them out of Andalusia, where most of them lived. Many of them left Spain for North Africa, depriving Spain of their contributions as leaders of Spanish agriculture and industry.

Philip's actions were part of a comprehensive anti-Moslem policy. Philip led the struggle to control the Turks in the eastern Mediterranean, though with only limited success. In 1570 the Turks took Cyprus from the Venetians, and in 1571 a combined Spanish and Venetian fleet defeated the Turks at Lepanto in the Gulf of Corinth. Though the victory was hailed

The baptism of Moslem women, from a Spanish relief (1520).

throughout Europe, the Christian forces failed to follow it up.

For a short time after Lepanto, Philip was at the height of his power and prestige. But the moment was brief. During the last quarter of the sixteenth century, his dream of a revived Catholic Europe under his authority was shattered by the revolt of the Netherlands, the rise of English seapower, and the accession of a former Protestant to the throne of France.

THE REVOLT OF THE NETHERLANDS

In the sixteenth century, the 3 million people in the seventeen provinces of the Netherlands constituted one of the most prosperous populations in Europe. The comfortable houses of Bruges, Ghent, Antwerp, and Amsterdam had been built with the profits of a flourishing textile industry and a far-flung commercial net-

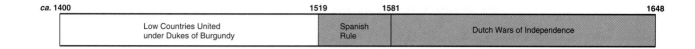

ca. 1400		1519	1581		1648
	Low Countries United under Dukes of Burgundy		Spanish Rule	Dutch Wars of Independence	

work. Though the provinces had been united under the personal authority of the dukes of Burgundy during the preceding century, there was little sense of nationalism until Charles V became duke. Charles was the closest thing to a native ruler the united Netherlands had ever had, but once he became emperor he sacrificed the interests of the Dutch and Flemish cities to his imperial aims and prompted the first stirrings of nationalism in the provinces.

Under Philip II, religious tension added to the Netherlanders' alienation from Habsburg rule. The Netherlands were a crossroads of ideas as well as of commerce, and the teachings of Luther and Calvin had early taken root there. By the 1550s, well-organized Calvinist minorities existed in most of the cities.

Philip's intransigent religious policies were bound to alienate many of his Dutch and Flemish subjects. Their urban-commercial culture had for centuries been out of tune with the church's restrictive attitude toward business practices, and they had adopted an attitude of moderation in religious matters. That attitude had enabled them to countenance the rise and survival of such groups as the Brethren of the Common Life (see p. 426) and it was totally at odds with the king's religious fanaticism. To make matters worse, Philip violated the traditional limits of his authority as duke of the provinces by interfering in the internal affairs of the cities. In 1566 Calvinist mobs went on a rampage, breaking images of the saints and smashing stained-glass windows in Catholic churches throughout the Netherlands.

Philip sent the duke of Alva with about 10,000 Spanish regulars to suppress the iconoclasts, and Alva set up a regime that came to be known as the "Council of Blood." He boasted (with some exaggeration) that during his six years in the Netherlands (1567–73), he executed 18,000 people. His government also confiscated enormous tracts of land and imposed a 10 percent sales tax that seriously injured commerce.

Alva's measures served only to solidify resistance, and by 1572 the Dutch had found a leader in William the Silent, prince of Orange, the wealthiest landowner in the provinces. Although William lost almost every battle he fought against the Spanish, he had political wisdom, integrity, and patience. He also had a deep hatred of religious fanaticism. Dutch nationalism grew stronger under his leadership, helped by the actions of the Spanish themselves. In 1576, the Spanish responded to Calvinist excesses by staging a frightful sack of Antwerp, known as the "Spanish Fury." Frightened, the seventeen provinces rushed into an agreement to form a united front against Philip—the so-called Pacification of Ghent (1576).

The united front was led by moderate Calvinists and Catholics, but soon religious fanatics on both sides seized control. In the savage civil war that ensued, the Calvinists—who were better organized than the Catholics—gained the upper hand. The Catholics fled south to the ten Walloon provinces that were under the protection of the Spanish troops, while the Calvinists moved north to the Dutch provinces. In 1579 those provinces formed the Union of Utrecht, which ultimately evolved into the United Provinces, or the Dutch Netherlands, and declared their independence from Philip II in 1581. The

Example of propaganda badge worn by Dutch "Sea Beggars." The insurgents' hatred of Catholicism is expressed in the inscription: "Better the Turks than the pope."

The Division of the Netherlands   1581

southern provinces remained under Habsburg rule until 1830, when they became the kingdom of Belgium.

The Rise of the Dutch Netherlands

After declaring their independence, the Dutch Provinces struggled for two generations before achieving real independence. William the Silent was assassinated in 1584, and his successors carried on his able, disinterested leadership. Although the "United Provinces" was never more than a loose confederation, the Dutch fought with a fierce stubbornness whenever the need arose.

In 1578, Philip II, angered by the Pacification of Ghent, sent the duke of Parma—one of the age's best military leaders—to remedy the situation. But the Dutch privateers—"Sea Beggars"—joined with the English to control the English Channel and prevent Parma from resupplying the Spanish troops. This meant that Parma and Philip were in conflict with England—where Philip had once been Queen Mary's royal consort. This struggle led to the Spanish decision to send a great flotilla to clear the English Channel (see

p. 464). The defeat of that armada ended any chance Spain might have had to reconquer the Dutch provinces. Not until 1648, however, did Spain formally recognize Dutch independence.

Dutch Prosperity

The Dutch emerged from the conflict with Spain as the most powerful commercial nation in Europe. By the early seventeenth century they were building more ships—and better ships—than all other nations combined. It was said that they built 2,000 per year, and they were taking over more and more of the carrying trade of Europe and of the world. During the war with Spain, the Dutch had closed off Antwerp—which was under Spanish control—by damming its harbor, and Amsterdam had become the commercial and financial capital of Europe.

The Dutch handled much of the grain trade of the Baltic and a large part of the carrying trade of England, France, Italy, and Portugal. When Philip II closed Lisbon to the Dutch—after seizing the Portuguese crown in 1580—the Dutch went directly to the source of spices in the Moluccas. In 1602 the Dutch East India Company was formed and was soon operating out of headquarters at Batavia on the island of Java. By the middle of the seventeenth century the Dutch had taken over Portugal's richest holdings in the East, and in 1652 they set up a colony at the Cape of Good Hope to serve as a way station on the route to Asia. A few decades earlier, they had almost ousted the Portuguese from Brazil and had founded the colony of New Amsterdam on Manhattan Island in the Hudson River (1624), which became the center for a large Dutch carrying trade in the New World. When the French and English began to develop their own overseas empires in the seventeenth century, they found the Dutch ahead of them wherever they went.

ELIZABETHAN ENGLAND

Elizabeth I (r. 1558–1603) was the last of the direct descendants of Henry VII Tudor

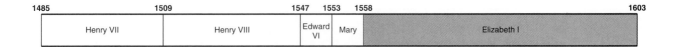

1485	1509	1547	1553	1558	1603
Henry VII	Henry VIII	Edward VI	Mary	Elizabeth I	

(r. 1485–1509; see p. 418). She was a cautious, reflective ruler whose instinct was to temporize and compromise. Although she could never submit to papal authority—the pope had declared the marriage of her mother, Anne Boleyn, to Henry VIII invalid—she followed a moderate religious policy and was conservative in matters of theology and liturgy.

Elizabeth temporized and compromised in foreign policy too. She tried to avoid committing herself, kept a dozen intrigues afoot to give herself an avenue of escape, and seems to have aimed at avoiding war at any cost. The chief foreign danger to the realm was the French influence over Scotland. Elizabeth's cousin, Mary Stuart, Queen of Scots, had married the heir to the French crown in 1558, and the alliance between the French and Scots promised to be troublesome.

But when the Scotsman John Knox returned from Geneva and began preaching Calvinism in 1559, he undermined the influence of Catholicism and the French. This time Elizabeth made a quick decision and allied herself with the Calvinist party in Scotland. By 1560, the Kirk (the Scottish church), the pro-English party, and Knox were in control, and the French had lost their foothold in Scotland.

In 1561, Mary Stuart returned to Scotland after the death of her husband, hoping to reestablish Catholicism along with her own authority. But she faced unbending opposition from Knox and the Kirk, and after a second marriage that turned out badly she was forced to abdicate in 1567. A year later Mary fled to England, where Elizabeth received her coolly but permitted her to stay. Mary soon became the center of French and Spanish plots against Elizabeth who kept a watch on her but refused to imprison or execute her. Then in 1587, when Elizabeth's ministers presented her with incontrovertible evidence of Mary's complicity in an assassination plot, Elizabeth reluctantly consented to Mary's execution.

The Conflict with Spain

Although there were many reasons for conflict between Spain and England—particularly English support of the Dutch—Philip II and Elizabeth I remained on good terms for more than twenty years. That stretch of tranquillity gave English industry and commerce a chance to expand and grow strong. When the inflationary spiral ruined Spanish industry, the English were ready to supply the Spanish colonies with manufactured goods. In 1562, an aggressive merchant named Sir John Hawkins was the first Englishman to carry goods from England and slaves from Africa directly to the Spanish settlements in the New World. The Spanish sought to prevent such direct traffic, which drew profit from their colonies and brought nothing to the mother country, and in 1569 Sir John and his cousin Sir Francis Drake were almost sunk by a Spanish fleet. In revenge, Drake seized that year's silver shipment from Peru to Spain. Then, from 1577 to 1580, he duplicated Magellan's voyage around the world, demonstrating the vulnerability of the Spanish Empire. Meanwhile, other English mariners probed the coasts of North America in search of a Northwest Passage that would outflank the Portuguese route to the East Indies.

It was the revolt of the Netherlands that finally broke the peace between Spain and England. For centuries, the English had had close commercial ties with the Low Countries; Flanders, for example, had long been the best customer for English wool and other goods. Moreover, Englishmen sympathized with their fellow Protestants in the United Provinces, and English privateers—the Sea Dogs—cooperated with the Sea Beggars, their Dutch counterparts, in disrupting Spanish shipping and communications. For their part, Philip II's ambassadors in England were deeply involved in plots against Elizabeth's life, one of which, as we have seen, led to the execution of Mary Stuart.

Elizabeth I of England, and her signature. The silver medal commemorates the defeat of the Spanish Armada.

The Armada

When the Spanish Armada challenged the ancient lords of the English on their own grounds, the impending conflict took on the aspect of a judicial duel in which as was expected in such duels, God would defend the right. . . . So when the two fleets approached their appointed battleground, all Europe watched. For the spectators of both parties, the outcome, reinforced, as everyone believed, by an extraordinary tempest, was indeed decisive. The Protestants of France and the Netherlands, Germany and Scandinavia saw with relief that God was, in truth, as they had always supposed, on their side. The Catholics of France and Italy and Germany saw with almost equal relief that Spain was not, after all, God's chosen champion. From that time forward, though Spain's preponderance was to last for more than another generation, the peak of her prestige had passed. . . . So, in spite of the long, indecisive war which followed, the defeat of the Spanish Armada really was decisive. It decided that religious unity was not to be reimposed by force on the heirs of medieval Christendom, and if, in doing so, it only validated what was already by far the most probable outcome, why, perhaps that is all that any of the battles we call decisive has ever done.

From Garrett Mattingly, The Spanish Armada *(Boston: Houghton Mifflin, 1959), pp. 400–01.*

Then in 1588 Philip decided to make a bold attempt on England itself. He assembled an enormous fleet, the so-called Invincible Armada, and sent it north to clear the English Channel and prepare the way for an invasion of England by the duke of Parma, who was engaged in operations against the Dutch. The English met the Armada with smaller, faster ships that could fire at longer range than the Spanish ships, and when the Armada anchored off Calais to await Parma, English fire ships caused panic among the Spaniards. The Armada fled north, and the English attacked again off Gravelines, scattering the Spanish ships. North Sea storms completed what the English had started, and fewer than half of the Armada's ships struggled home by sailing north and west around the British Isles.

The victory lifted the morale of Englishmen and Protestants everywhere. It ended the threat of a Spanish conquest of England and made it impossible for the Spanish to reconquer the United Provinces. When a peace was finally signed in 1604, the English and the Dutch met the Spaniards as near equals.

THE FRENCH WARS OF RELIGION

The rise of Spain and the relatively peaceful reign of Elizabeth I in England relied in part on the weakness of France, the largest and most populous nation in Europe. From 1562 to 1593 the French were embroiled in civil and religious strife that the monarchy was powerless to control.

Although France was the largest nation in Europe under a single monarch, it

The British fleet attack the Spanish Armada.

was less unified than either England or Spain. The aristocracy was still powerful, and the provinces still held on to their local customs and privileges. The divisiveness grew even more severe with the spread of Calvinism into France.

The French Calvinists—nicknamed the Huguenots (the origin of the name is unknown)—had about 2,500 churches. Huguenot congregations formed a small but well-organized and aggressive minority supported by people at the highest levels of French society. Arrayed against the Huguenots were the Catholic aristocracy, the University of Paris, and the Parlement (high court) of Paris. The monarchy itself was opposed to the spread of Calvinism, because it could not control the Protestant churches as it did the Catholic church under the Concordat of Bologna (1516).

After the death of King Henry II, husband of Mary Stuart of Scotland, in 1559, royal authority fell into the hands of the Queen Mother, Catherine de' Medici, who controlled the French government during the reigns of Henry's two weak brothers—Francis II (r. 1559–60) and Charles IX (r. 1560–74)—and during the reign of Henry's son Henry III (r. 1574–89). Catherine was an astute ruler, but she lacked formal authority and was powerless to prevent the religious fanatics—both Calvinist and Catholic—from making war on one another. Discontented nobles and the provinces sided with the Calvinists. The monarchy and most of the nobility sided with the Catholics. Both sides appealed for foreign support—the Huguenots to the English and Dutch, the Catholics to Spain. England and Spain actually sent troops, mostly at the beginning and the end of the wars.

The fighting was savage, and large areas of France were devastated. Though the Catholics won most of the battles, they could not destroy the Huguenots. In 1572 Catholic fanatics convinced Catherine that

they could put an end to the strife with one decisive blow. At two o'clock in the morning of St. Bartholomew's Day (August 23), armed bands of Catholics attacked and killed several Huguenot leaders who were in Paris for the wedding of the Huguenot Prince Henry of Navarre and the king's sister. The St. Bartholomew's Day Massacre touched off an explosion of violence that soon spread to other cities. Between late August and October, more than 10,000 Huguenots—3,000 in Paris alone—were murdered. The events intensified religious hatred in France and across Europe. Pope Gregory XIII and Philip II of Spain hailed the massacre as a milestone in the fight against

Religion and Patriotism

A Spanish ambassador reporting the words of a French Catholic in 1565:

Nowadays Catholic princes must not proceed as they once did. At one time friends and enemies were distinguished by the frontiers of provinces and kingdoms, and were called Italians, Germans, Frenchmen, Spaniards, Englishmen, and the like. Now we must say Catholics and heretics, and a Catholic prince must consider all Catholics of all countries as his friends, just as the heretics consider all heretics as friends and subjects whether they are their own vassals or not.

An English Protestant writing in 1589:

All dutiful subjects in this land desire with all their hearts the continuance of God's religion; the preservation of Queen Elizabeth; and the good success of the English navy. These particulars, I grant, are not expressed in flat in the Lord's Prayer; but they are contained within the compass of, and may be deduced from the petitions of that excellent prayer. Whosoever doubteth of this is void of learning.

As quoted in Erich Marks, Die Zusammenkunft von Bayonne *(Strassburg: K. J. Trübner, 1889), p. 14; as quoted in Benjamin Hanbury,* Historical Memorials Relating to the Independents *(London: Congregational Union of England and Wales, 1839–44), Vol. I, p. 71.*

Protestantism, but Protestants throughout Europe were horrified.

The wars dragged on for twenty years, growing more and more confused and purposeless, until the Huguenot Henry of Navarre came to the throne as Henry IV (r. 1589–1610). Although Henry was the nearest male heir to the crown, his relationship to Henry III was quite distant, and he had trouble making his claim stick. The Catholics took over Paris, and Spanish troops from the Netherlands moved into France led by the duke of Parma. After four years of fighting and maneuvering, Henry decided to renounce his Protestantism and become a Catholic, which he did in 1593. He did not, however, turn against his former co-religionists. Five years later he issued the Edict of Nantes, which granted the Huguenots freedom of conscience, freedom of worship, equal civil rights, and control of approximately 200 fortified towns. The Edict constituted the first official recognition that two religions could coexist within one nation.

The Effects of the Wars of Religion

In the world of Philip II and Elizabeth I, religion had a strong influence on political and social conflicts. The conflicts them-

selves grew out of economic changes that predated the Protestant Reformation, but religious convictions embittered every issue and made moderation impossible. Some monarchies that had been moving toward the consolidation of power— for example France and Germany— were weakened by the religious strife. Others— such as Spain and England— were strengthened. In Spain, Charles V and Philip II championed the cause of embattled Catholicism. In England, after Mary tried to reverse the reformation that grew out of the Act of Supremacy, Protestantism became associated with patriotism.

Just as the Great Schism in the Roman church (1378–1417) had motivated thinkers to devise a new constitutional theory of the church—conciliarism—so the wars of religion inspired new political theories. French theorists, for example, created a doctrine of political obligation that justified rebellion against constituted authority under certain conditions. And Protestants in Germany, the Netherlands, and France cited that doctrine to justify their rebellion against monarchs whom they accused of seeking to subject them to a false religion. After a generation of religious war, the French writer Jean Bodin (1530–96) developed a new, secular theory of political sovereignty that justified obedience to properly constituted authority without appeal to religious doctrine. That theory had a powerful influence on later political thought.

A less benign result of the religious paroxysm was a terrifying witch-craze in Europe that began in the mid-sixteenth century and lasted nearly a century. During the craze, thousands of people— mostly women—were burned at the stake or hanged as witches. The horror seems to have begun when the religious passions set off by the Protestant and Catholic Reformations got mixed up with ancient, pre-Christian superstitious beliefs and practices. Almost every community had its wizard and cunning woman to whom neighbors turned when the ministrations of priest or physician did not avail. From time to time during the Middle Ages, such women had been convicted of malevolent

Massacre of St. Bartholomew's Day, 1572 (detail from a painting by an eyewitness, François Dubois).

witchcraft—that is, of attempting to use occult means to inflict death or disease on others.

During the sixteenth century, the number of people accused of witchcraft increased dramatically. The accused were tortured into confessing the most fantastic acts—participating in obscene "witches' sabbaths" and creating diabolical schemes to harm their neighbors. Because they were also forced to name their accomplices in their pacts with the Devil, one arrest led to others. Often dozens, even hundreds, in a single community were burned at the stake.

By 1660 the craze was subsiding, and by 1700 it had all but disappeared as religious passions cooled and as toleration became the norm. Moreover, the rise of modern science led educated people to suspend belief in miracles, invisible spirits, and occult forces. The century-long witch-craze was one of the most tragic episodes in the history of Europe.

THE EUROPEAN WORLD IN THE LATE SIXTEENTH CENTURY

The Condition of the Peasants

Although we have been concentrating on urban life in the last two chapters, the vast majority of Europeans lived in the country during these years. By the end of the sixteenth century, significant changes had occurred in the economic and social condition of the peasants. In France and western Germany, the peasants' lot had improved. In Spain, eastern Germany, and other eastern European countries, it had deteriorated.

In most of western Europe, the disastrous plagues of the fourteenth century had undermined the old feudal system whereby peasants were obliged to perform services for their lords. As a result, life in the villages and regular cultivation of the fields broke down. When conditions began to improve in the fifteenth century, landholders granted favorable terms to the peasants to induce them to return to the fields. Some of the landholders had been ruined by the plagues and

Illumination from a Book of Hours (Flemish, *ca.* 1500) shows peasants harvesting grain.

had sold their land to their own peasants. By the late sixteenth century about 5 percent of the peasants in France and western Germany owned their own land, and another 5 percent remained bound in serfdom. The rest of them leased the land they worked. Increasingly, however, the law permitted them to sell or grant their rights in the properties they leased.

In 1480, the king of Castile released all peasants from serfdom and gave them proprietary rights in their land. But within a couple of generations the royal government was encouraging the importation of cheap grain, and the Castilian peasants derived little benefit from their emancipation. The peasants of Aragon, who had not been released from serfdom, also suffered under the government's policy. By the late sixteenth century, peasants throughout Spain were caught up in a serious economic depression.

When the condition of the peasants in Europe finally began to improve, the condition of the eastern peasants continued to sink lower and lower. In northeastern Germany, for example, a region of large estates with access to rivers to carry crops to market, the landholders imposed full-fledged serfdom on their peasants in the late sixteenth century. In Russia, Tsar Ivan the Terrible (r. 1533–84) rewarded his noblemen for service to the state by granting them large estates with the right to force the peasants into serfdom (see p. 345).

Urban Life in the Sixteenth Century

As far back as the twelfth century, the towns and cities of Europe had begun to achieve virtual independence through charters granted by kings and emperors. The charters freed them from the control of the feudal lords and gave them the right to govern themselves. By the sixteenth century, the cities had become independent in both political and economic matters, and their influence was felt throughout Europe.

One historian has compared citizenship in the early modern city to membership in a club. Every aspect of life was regulated by special associations under the control of the city council. Craft guilds and religious fraternities governed the lives of their members and provided social security.

A young man could expect to be elected to a lower office in his guild about six years after becoming a master and to a higher office after another eight years. The principal officers of the major guilds were almost assured of an important position in the city government.

Most cities had religious confraternities or brotherhoods that cut across membership in the various guilds. These organizations were responsible for staging city-wide festivals in cooperation with the guilds, and the fact that men from all walks of life participated in these events helped reduce the potential for conflict among the guilds. Officeholders in a brotherhood often moved to positions in the city government.

Cities were usually divided into wards to facilitate the conduct of government. Each ward was responsible for ensuring security within its boundaries and for providing a certain number of men for the city militia. The wards also furnished men to stand night watch on the city walls and at the gates. Although some wards were dominated by one of the guilds (for example, butchers and tanners usually settled along a river), in most neighborhoods the population was quite mixed, with the rich living alongside the poor. About a fifth of the urban population, more in large cities, consisted of day laborers and other poor people who were not members of any guild. They did, however, have acknowledged status in their ward.

Usually the city gates were opened at 4 A.M. and closed at 8 P.M., about an hour after the workday ended. During the night a curfew was imposed on the city to discourage crime and keep the peace. Saturday was payday, when workers got off early, and Sunday was a day of rest. *Children's Games*, painted by the Flemish artist Pieter Bruegel the Elder (*ca.* 1525–69), suggests what a typical Sunday may have been like in a sixteenth-century city.

Because men did not marry until they had set themselves up as substantial citizens, there were usually many young men about town. Rape, including group rape, was common, and the authorities were always on the watch for such offenses. The larger cities usually had a public

Pieter Bruegel's *Children's Games.*

brothel in which the women were licensed. Even prostitutes who worked the streets were licensed and wore badges to prove it. The public bathhouse was another place where young upper-class men could find prostitutes.

In many cities young men's associations patterned themselves on the religious brotherhoods, though their purpose was anything but religious. The members amused themselves at the expense of the "establishment," and their officers bore such titles as Prince of Youth and Abbot of Fools.

Women played an important role in the sixteenth-century city not only as wives but as craftspeople and merchants. Their principal role was as wife and mother, but a craftsman could not function—indeed, some guilds would not permit him to function—without a wife. She raised the apprentices and often ran the shop where the master's products were sold. Although the guilds guarded their craft secrets jealously, members were permitted to share them with their wives.

Many women also participated in the commercial life of the cities. They engaged in silk weaving, retailing, and brewing and often functioned as agents for foreign merchants. They were accorded no role in city government, however, or in other public business.

ART, LITERATURE, AND SCIENCE

Art

Renaissance art reached its zenith in the first two decades of the century with the memorable accomplishments of Leonardo da Vinci (1452–1519), Raphael (1483–1520), Albrecht Dürer (1471–1528), and Michelangelo (1475–1564). In the last years of his life, Dürer, influenced by Luther's view that the style and subject matter of the Renaissance were too pagan, simplified his work and concentrated on biblical scenes. In the next generation, the German painter Hans Holbein the Younger (1497–1543) was a talented portraitist who traveled to Switzerland and England to execute commissions. He settled in England as a court painter and created portraits of Henry VIII, Thomas More, and other prominent figures.

Michelangelo also abandoned the high Renaissance style after 1520 and developed a new style that departed from the serenity of his early work. For example, his ceiling frescos in the Sistine Chapel, painted around 1510, are organized in carefully planned panels with figures reminiscent of the classical sculpture that inspired the Renaissance, and the Genesis story is represented in a series of static images. By contrast, his wall fresco of the Last Judgment in the same chapel, painted during the 1530s, is a crowded scene of twisted bodies in which the action of condemnation and salvation of souls is captured in dynamic fashion. In sculpture, too, Michelangelo proceeded from observance of the classical ideals of the Renaissance, through a rebellion against proportion and graceful lines, to the creation of tortured shapes of great emotional power.

Some artists, like the Venetian painter Titian (*ca.* 1477–1576), continued to work in the Renaissance style. Others favored a new style known as Mannerism, because they painted in the manner of (the late) Michelangelo. Two of the most notable Mannerists were Tintoretto (1518–94) and El Greco (*ca.* 1548–1614). Tintoretto was a Venetian who tried to combine the style of Titian with the late style of Michelangelo. He painted scenes of saints and miracles and executed some large wall paintings. His works convey a sense of movement and action, similar to that of Michelangelo's Last Judgment. El Greco (Domenicos Theotocopoulos, born on the island of Crete) studied in Venice and Rome and eventually settled in Spain, where he hoped to become a court painter. But Philip II favored the work of second-rate Spanish Mannerists, and El Greco (as the Spaniards nicknamed him) never found favor in Madrid, Philip's new capital. El Greco was a highly original artist who paintings exude a strong mystical aura and whole sparse, elongated figures project great tension and strength.

The Flemish artist Hieronymus Bosch (*ca.* 1450–1516) painted dark, foreboding

Virgin with Sts. Ines and Tecla, by
El Greco.

showing agricultural labors appropriate to
each month of the year. In his few religious paintings, such as the "Slaughter of
the Innocents," he depicts the moment
before the crucial scene occurs, so that
the viewer is caught up in suspense. His
son Pieter also painted scenes of peasant
life, along with works depicting hell, and
Jan favored landscapes and still lifes.
Members of the Bruegel family were still
painting well into the eighteenth century.

Literature

In literature, the sixteenth century was
the great age of drama. Medieval drama
evolved from the religious festivals at
which the guilds staged plays dealing with
the lives and miracles of the saints. University students too had been putting on plays
since the thirteenth century. At first their
plays were based on the stories of biblical
figures, such as Daniel and Herod. But
during the fifteenth and early sixteenth
centuries the students turned to secular
dramas fashioned on Roman models and
intended for educated audiences. The
great age of theater began in the 1570s
when actors and playwrights in England
and Spain formed professional companies
that played to the general public.

In London, several companies were
founded in the 1570s, and two playwrights attracted an enthusiastic following Thomas Kyd (1558–94) and Christopher Marlowe (1564–93). Kyd's *Spanish
Tragedy* and Marlowe's *Tamburlaine*
were the first popular successes of the
English stage. Kyd's play, about a father
who exacts revenge for his son's death,
established revenge as a favorite theme
of English tragedy. Marlowe's plays are
dominated by powerful, romantic figures
who control the action. He was the first
playwright to use blank verse in dramatic writing.

It was Marlowe's contemporary,
William Shakespeare (1564–1616), who
emerged as the greatest English poet and
dramatist. Shakespeare wrote his plays for
a company of twenty or so actors, the Lord
Chamberlain's Company (later called the
King's Company), that continued to perform for more than two decades. Theater

works on religious themes that exaggerate the physicality of human life. Modern scholars have discovered in them a
complex, visual language that reflects
Bosch's mystical view of the world. The
Bruegels—Pieter the Elder (*ca.* 1525–69),
Pieter the Younger (1564–1637), and Jan
(1568–1625)—preferred to paint scenes
from everyday life. Pieter the Elder favored rural scenes, including a series

companies were expected to present a play six afternoons a week throughout the year and consequently had to keep about fifty plays in their repertory. Shakespeare must have written many plays that were never published, because he considered them the property of his company. Eighteen of them, however, were published in illegal editions during his lifetime. After his death, his friends published his surviving manuscripts in a folio volume in 1623. The first edition of Shakespeare's work contained 36 plays; since then scholars have added another, *Pericles*, on the likelihood that some of the scenes in it were written by Shakespeare. The plays consist of tragedies (*Hamlet* and *King Lear*), comedies (*Taming of the Shrew* and *As You Like It*), and histories (*Richard III* and *Henry V*). Shakespeare took his themes from classical and English history and from Italian works, which had become popular in England early in the sixteenth century.

The typical theater of Shakespeare's London was a large, round building without a roof that could hold as many as 3,000 people. In Shakespeare's Globe Theatre, the audience stood in the pit below the stage or in the boxes along the walls. Admission to the pit cost only a penny or two, which meant that watching a play was one of the most inexpensive pastimes in the city. Admission to the boxes cost much more.

There were smaller theaters as well, such as Blackfriars, where Shakespeare's company also performed. These were rectangular buildings that could hold only a few hundred people. Admission to these theaters was more expensive than admission to open theaters, and the plays written for them appealed to a more sophisticated audience. It is estimated that English playwrights wrote more than 6,000 plays between 1580 and 1640, about 2,000 of which have survived.

In Spain, the theater became popular soon after the middle of the century and, as in England, experienced a great increase in popularity during the 1570s. Spanish plays combined dramatic scenes with interludes of dance and musical entertainment. Unlike the English companies, the Spanish companies employed women as entertainers and actresses. The Spanish playwright Lope de Vega (1562–1632) wrote about 1,500 *comedias*, of which 500 have survived. In writing this stupendous number of plays he used only a few plot lines, but he achieved spectacular fame and great success.

By contrast, the greatest literary figure of sixteenth-century Spain, Miguel de Cervantes (1547–1616), led a life of hardship and penury. He began writing plays in the early 1560s, but after getting into trouble with the law he ran off to Rome. There he enlisted in the navy that Philip II was forming to fight the Turks, and he distinguished himself at the Battle of Lepanto (1571; see p. 459). In 1575, while on his way back to Spain to seek an officer's commission, he was captured and enslaved by the Turks of Algiers, and for the next five years he repeatedly tried to escape while his family tried to raise a ransom. Finally freed, he returned to Spain and took a job in the royal bureaucracy in Seville. Accounting was not his strong suit, however, and he was constantly in trouble with his superiors. He left the royal service in 1600.

While still working at his job in Seville, Cervantes began to write again and won first prize for poetry in a contest held in Zaragoza in 1595. After leaving government service, he spent three years writing a great satire on the chivalric romances that had become phenomenally popular in Spain. This work, *Don Quixote*, which recounts adventures of a knight and his squire, became immediately popular. Philip III (r. 1598–1621), observing a young man convulsed with laughter over a book, is said to have remarked that the young man was either crazy or was reading *Don Quixote*. The work was first translated into English in 1612 and has been translated into more languages than any other book except the Bible. Toward the end of his life, Cervantes published the first short stories to be written in Spanish, in a work titled *Twelve Exemplary Novelas* (1613).

Although theater did not become popular in France until the seventeenth century, French writers of the sixteenth century contributed to the foundations

A contemporary drawing (1596) of the Swan Theatre in London.

of modern literature. Michel Montaigne (1533–92), a French nobleman educated as a humanist, created the genre of the essay after retiring from the royal court in disgust over the fanaticism engendered by the wars between the Huguenots and the Catholics. In his *Essays,* Montaigne explored human nature in a manner both witty and wise.

Science

During the sixteenth century Nicholas Copernicus (1473–1543), Tycho Brahe (1546–1601), Johannes Kepler (1571–1630), and Galileo Galilei (1564–1642) combined theory with experimentation and observation to transform the medieval world view. Copernicus, who was educated at the universities of Padua and Cracow, spent most of his adult life in a monastery in Prussia trying to resolve the discrepancy between the observed movement of the planets and the Ptolemaic view that the planets and the sun orbit the earth. Eventually, in a work published the year of his death, he proposed that the earth and the other planets circle the sun.

Copernicus's heliocentric theory did not gain wide acceptance until late in the century. In fact, the Danish astronomer Tycho Brahe made careful observations of the movement of the planets in an effort to demonstrate the validity of the Ptolemaic view. Instead, they led him to the conclusion that Copernicus was right and that the discrepancy between the observed movements and the Ptolemaic theory was even greater than Copernicus had thought.

Copernicus had still subscribed to the ancient view that the planets move in circular orbits. Brahe's observations were not entirely consistent with that view, however, and his assistant, Johannes Kepler, eventually demonstrated that the planets follow elliptical orbits and provided a mathematical explanation for their movement.

Galileo, a professor at the University of Padua, confirmed Copernicus's theory by using a telescope he built after hearing about a spyglass that had been invented in Holland. The telescope, which magnified objects thirty times, enabled him to make many revolutionary discoveries. He was the first to observe the mountains on the moon, the rings of Saturn, and the components of the Milky Way. He also provided mathematical explanations of the movement of physical objects and described the behavior of the pendulum in clocks. In his most famous experiment he dropped objects of different weights from the leaning tower of Pisa to show that all objects fall with the same rate of acceleration and then devised a mathematical formula for the universal rate of acceleration of falling objects. Galileo once remarked, "The book of nature . . . is written in mathematical characters."

In Chapter 21, we will deal with the scientific revolution of the sixteenth century in greater detail.

Suggestions for Further Reading

Geographical Discovery

For a detailed account of the geographical discoveries of the fifteenth and sixteenth centuries, see J. H. Parry, *The Age of Reconnaisance* (1963). For the technological basis of the explorations, see C. Cipolla, *Guns and Sails in the Early Phase of the European Expansion* (1966). For the Mediterranean background of oceanic navigation, see M. E. Mallet, *Florentine Galleys of the Fifteenth Century* (1967), and F. C. Lane, *Venetian Ships and Shipbuilders of the Renaissance* (1934).

Effects on Europe

On the effect of the discoveries on Europe, see J. H. Elliott, *The Old World and the New* (1970). H. H. Hart, *The Road to the Indies* (1950), describes the Portuguese expeditions; J. B. Brebner, *The Explorers of North America, 1492–1806* (1933), and A. P. Newton, *The European Nations in the West Indies, 1493–1688* (1933), treat exploration in particular areas. The best account of Columbus is S. E. Morrison, *Admiral of the Ocean Sea,* 2 vols. (1942). For an overall view, see Morrison's

The European Discovery of America (1971). For good histories of the early Spanish colonies, see C. H. Haring, *The Spanish Empire in America* (1947); L. Hanke, *The Spanish Struggle for Justice in the Conquest of America* (1949); and R. Cameron, *Viceroyalties of the West* (1968).

Spain

On Spain in the sixteenth century, J. H. Elliott, *Imperial Spain, 1469–1716* (1964), is excellent. R. T. Davies, *The Golden Century of Spain, 1501–1621* (1937) and *Spain in Decline, 1621–1700* (1956), are sometimes controversial but good accounts. For the effect of imperialism on Spanish government, see J. H. Parry, *The Spanish Theory of Empire in the Sixteenth Century* (1940). E. J. Hamilton, *American Treasure and the Price Revolution, 1501–1650* (1934), is the starting point for studies of the economic effects of empire. See also C. Cipolla, *Money, Prices and Civilization in the Mediterranean World* (1967). The classic work on the Armada is G. Mattingly, *The Spanish Armada* (1959). F. Braudel, *The Mediterranean and the Mediterranean World in the Age of Philip II*, 2 vols. (1972–73), is a masterpiece.

The Netherlands

The best history of the Dutch rebellion is P. Geyl, *The Revolt of the Netherlands, 1555–1609* (1932) and *The Netherlands Divided, 1609–1648* (1936). For a well-written biography of William the Silent, see C. V. Wedgewood, *William the Silent* (1944), and on the English involvement in the rebellion, see C. Wilson, *Queen Elizabeth and the Revolt of the Netherlands* (1970).

Elizabethan England

There is a wealth of good scholarly books on Elizabethan England. See J. Neale, *Queen Elizabeth I* (1952). C. Read's thorough biographies, *Mr. Secretary Walsingham*, 3 vols. (1925), and *Mr. Secretary Cecil* (Lord Burghley), 2 vols. (1955, 1960), provide detailed information about the politics of the period. For a social history, see A. L. Rowse, *The England of Elizabeth* (1950) and *The Expansion of Elizabethan England* (1955). On the English explorations, see J. A. Williamson, *The Age of Drake*, 3rd ed. (1952).

France

There is not much work in English on sixteenth-century France. J. W. Salmon, *Society in Crisis: France in the Sixteenth Century* (1975), is the best general treatment. J. E. Neale, *The Age of Catherine de' Medici* (1943), and H. Pearson, *Henry of Navarre* (1963), are useful. On the government, see N. M. Sutherland, *The French Secretaries of State in the Age of Catherine de Medici* (1962). J. W. Thompson, *The Wars of Religion in France, 1559–1576* (1909), is still useful. For brief scholarly accounts, see F. C. Palm, *Calvinism and the Religious Wars* (1932), and A. J. Grant, *The Huguenots* (1934). On the development of French political thought during the civil wars, see W. F. Church, *Constitutional Thought in Sixteenth Century France* (1941).

Social History

On rural life in the sixteenth century, see E. Le Roy Ladurie, *The Peasants of Languedoc* (1974), and M. R. Weisser, *The Peasants of the Montes* (1976). N. Z. Davis covers various aspects of French social history in a series of essays in *Society and Culture in Early Modern France* (1975). See also L. Febvre, *Life in Renaissance France* (1979). G. Huppert, *After the Black Death: A Social History of Early Modern Europe* (1986), concentrates on urban society. There are several excellent studies of individual cities. See G. Strauss, *Nuremburg in the Sixteenth Century* (1976); C. R. Friedrichs, *Urban Society in an Age of War: Nördlingen, 1580–1720* (1979); and C. Pythian-Adams, *Desolation of a City* (1979), concerning Coventry, England. On urban women, see M. C. Howell, *Women, Production, and Patriarchy in Late Medieval Cities* (1986).

Art and Literature

On the art of the sixteenth century, see W. Friedländer, *Mannerism and Anti-Mannerism in Italian Painting* (1957). The works of Marlowe, Shakespeare, Lope de Vega, Cervantes, and Montaigne are available in numerous modern editions.

19

POLITICAL AND ECONOMIC CRISES: THE SEVENTEENTH CENTURY

The seventeenth century was the century in which modern European civilization took on recognizable form. Political, social, and economic upheavals almost as dangerous as those that had shaken medieval civilization in the fourteenth century convulsed Europe. In the 1640s, great rebellions weakened England, France, and Spain, the three most powerful European monarchies. The last wars of religion merged with wars to expand commerce or to overthrow or preserve the balance of power. Weather, famine, and plague compounded the ravages of war. In Germany and Spain, the Thirty Years' War (1618–48) and plague epidemics actually forced the population downward. Prolonged economic depression marked the middle decades of the century. Harvests repeatedly failed. Starvation and disease followed. The flow of silver from the New World that had stimulated the European economy dropped off sharply. After 1670, growth turned upward again, but only gradually. Poverty sharpened social unrest and inadequate revenues limited state power.

That unpromising environment nevertheless gave birth to a new Europe that was richer, controlled more of the world's commerce, and had more effective government in 1700 than in 1600. The troubles of the fourteenth century and the religious conflicts of the sixteenth century had slowed the process of building the sovereign territorial state begun in the thirteenth century. But it now proceeded rapidly. In the realm of theory, state-building required defining the concept of sovereignty. In the realm of practice, it meant concentrating supreme power in some organ of the state. And Europe simultaneously underwent an intellectual revolution, a sharp change in conceptions about humanity and the universe far deeper and broader in its consequences than the Italian Renaissance (see pp. 408–11).

FRANCE'S SEARCH FOR ORDER AND AUTHORITY, 1598–1661

The anarchy and religious violence that lasted from 1562 to the Edict of Nantes in 1598 deeply marked seventeenth-century France. Three feeble kings had allowed the unruly great nobles to challenge the monarchy. Civil wars had torn the fabric of trade that linked the merchants and manufacturers of the towns. The wanderings of ragged, undisciplined armies had savaged the peasantry. The population longed for security despite a continuing suspicion of any authority that might attack local privileges or increase taxes.

The lawyer Jean Bodin (*ca.* 1530–96), the most penetrating political thinker of the tragic years of the Wars of Religion, offered a theory that spoke to the universal yearning for order. Bodin's *The Republic* (1576) argued that a well-ordered state must give supreme power—sovereignty—to some organ of the state, preferably the monarchy. Bodin defined sovereignty as the essential characteristic of the state: the power of "giving laws to the people as a whole without their consent."

The laws of God and nature still bound Bodin's sovereign. But Bodin insisted that no human agency must limit the sovereign. Power must be "absolute," not divided, to be effective. Neither *parlements* (the highest French law courts) nor the Estates General should veto or modify decisions of the sovereign.

Bodin defined sovereignty far more clearly than previous theorists. He persuasively presented it as the only alternative to insecurity and civil war. The French absolute monarchy of the seventeenth century appeared to fulfill Bodin's prescription and became the model and envy of many of Europe's rulers.

Henry IV and Sully: Order Restored

Henry IV (r. 1589–1610), ex-Huguenot and victorious founder of the Bourbon dynasty, began the process of restoring royal power and French prosperity. He was a popular king—courageous, vigorous, humorous, tolerant, and sound in his judgment of subordinates. But he spent much time in pursuit of game and women and happily left the routine business of government to his chief minister, Maximilien de Sully, an austere ex-Huguenot artillery officer. Sully restored the monarchy's solvency by canceling some debts, avoiding expensive foreign wars, and patching up the inefficient, corrupt, and inequitable tax system.

The monarchy, like most early modern governments, "farmed" its taxes—that is, it granted the right to collect taxes to private contractors who paid the government a fixed sum and then extracted all they could from the population. The tax burden fell most heavily on the peasants, because nobles and the upper classes in the towns were exempt from major taxes. The nobility opposed attempts to redistribute the tax burden and helped to bring

---

Roots of the Modern State: Jean Bodin on Sovereignty

Political thinkers had recognized the fact *of sovereignty for some time, but Bodin was the first to express the* idea *in clear and uncompromising terms.*

Sovereignty is supreme power over citizens and subjects unrestrained by laws. . . . A prince is bound by no law of his predecessor, and much less by his own laws. . . . He may repeal, modify, or replace a law made by himself and without the consent of his subjects. . . . The opinion of those who have written that the king is bound by the popular will must be disregarded; such doctrine furnishes seditious men with material for revolutionary plots. No reasonable ground can be found to claim that subjects should control princes or that power should be attributed to popular assemblies. . . . The highest privilege of sovereignty consists in giving laws to the people as a whole without their consent. . . . Under this supreme power of making and repealing laws it is clear that all other functions of sovereignty are included.

From Jean Bodin, Six Books Concerning the Republic, *from the Latin version of 1586, trans. by F. W. Coker, in* Readings in Political Philosophy *(New York: Macmillan, 1938), pp. 374–77, 380.*

Triumphal Entry of Henry IV into Paris, a large sketch by the great Peter Paul Rubens (ca. 1630).

down the French monarchy in 1788–89 over that very issue (see pp. 584–85). Sully nevertheless did improve the system he inherited by attacking the crooked and inefficient tax farmers who as a rule pocketed as much as half the taxes collected before they reached the treasury. The reestablishment of internal order allowed agriculture and commerce to recover and increased the government's revenues, especially from customs duties. By the time a Catholic fanatic assassinated Henry IV in 1610, France's treasury contained a sizable surplus.

Richelieu and the Consolidation of the Monarchy, 1610–42

A few years of weakness at the center reduced the work of Henry IV and Sully to ruins. The regency of Henry's widow, Marie de' Medici, allowed rapacious courtiers the run of the treasury and permitted Spain to intervene once more in French affairs, sometimes in bizarre alliance with the Huguenots. Incompetence soon dissipated the financial surplus Sully had left and led in 1614 to a summoning of the Estates General of France to one of its rare meetings. But the deliberations of the Estates General soon produced deadlock over taxation and religious issues between the First and Second Estates (the clergy and the nobility) and the Third Estate (the middle classes of the towns, represented largely by provincial royal officers). The Estates General dissolved inconclusively, and did not meet again until 1789, on the eve of the French Revolution.

Fortunately for the monarchy, a minister far more powerful than Sully soon emerged. Henry IV's son, Louis XIII (r. 1614–43), assumed the throne and in 1624 appointed a brilliant young cardinal, Armand Jean du Plessis de Richelieu (1585–1642), as chief of the king's council. From then until his death Richelieu was the real ruler of France. The great Cardinal, rather than any member of the Bourbon dynasty, founded the French absolute monarchy.

The great cardinal: Richelieu, founder of the modern French state, painted by Philippe de Champaigne.

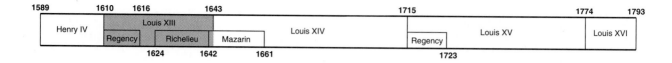

Richelieu had the clearest and most penetrating mind of any statesman of his generation as well as a largely deserved reputation for diabolical cleverness. He sought to establish beyond challenge the power and prestige of the French monarchy. He came to his task with a startling grasp of political and diplomatic possibilities, an infallible memory, and an inflexible will unconstrained by moral scruple. Richelieu admired Machiavelli (see pp. 412–14), and the heart of the Cardinal's political creed was *raison d'état,* "reason of state": the good of the state was the supreme good. That good justified the use of any means whatsoever—a stern creed that Richelieu nearly reconciled with his own religious conscience. He deemed it "essential to banish pity" when judging "crimes against the state," for mercy in the present only led to greater bloodshed in the future. He coolly sent innocent men to their death to terrify troublemakers. When Louis XIII expressed moral qualms, Richelieu beat the king's objections down with brutal frankness: "Man is immortal; his salvation is hereafter; the state has no immortality, its salvation is now or never."

Richelieu pursued four objectives: he sought to destroy the power of the Huguenots, crush the great nobles, exclude the Habsburgs from French internal politics, and decide in France's favor the Bourbon–Habsburg rivalry abroad that dated from the sixteenth century. The Edict of Nantes, the compromise of 1598 that ended the religious civil wars, had allowed the Huguenots to garrison about 200 towns. Richelieu persuaded Louis XIII that he would never be master in his own house until he had wiped out this "state within a state." A monopoly of force within its borders, then as now, was the essential characteristic of statehood.

Rumors that the government had de-cided to attack them provoked the Huguenots to rebel. Richelieu besieged and captured their chief stronghold at La Rochelle on the Atlantic coast. Despite his contempt for what he described as the "pretended Reformed religion," he nevertheless allowed the Huguenots to worship as they pleased once he had destroyed their political and military autonomy. He sought to conciliate Protestants abroad who might help him in war with Spain and Austria, and he hoped to make dependable citizens of the Huguenots. In that he was successful. The Huguenots served the crown in the war of 1635–59 against the Habsburgs and remained loyal in the great domestic crisis of the Fronde (see next section) that followed Richelieu's death.

Richelieu's attack on the nobility was less successful. Noble plotting threatened him until the end of his career. In response, he developed networks of spies, created a special tribunal to try noble lawbreakers, and sternly forbade duelling, a privilege that symbolized the nobility's freedom from ordinary restraints. The great nobles who had governed provinces almost by hereditary right gradually lost their powers to appointees of the crown called *intendants.* These temporary appointees came not from the old "nobility of the sword" but from the commons or the *noblesse de robe,* who were ennobled judicial officeholders of middle-class ancestry who had bought their offices from the crown. The economic and social privileges of the nobility survived Richelieu, but he curtailed its political power.

Richelieu was no financier and was no more interested in bettering the condition of the common people than were the rulers of other early modern states. He spent large sums to rebuild the armed forces and even more in wars against the Spanish and Austrian Habsburgs, Bourbon France's chief rivals for the leadership of Europe. He left the state's finances and the peasantry that supported those finances in worse condition than he had found them. But his subtle diplomacy and well-timed intervention in the Thirty Years' War (see pp. 489–91) made France instead of Spain the leading European power.

At his death in 1642, Richelieu left behind him the most powerful state in Europe. His success in establishing relative peace within France's own borders made economic growth possible, and France's steadily increasing power made Richelieu's creation the model for royal absolutism throughout the continent.

Mazarin, the Fronde, and the Coming of Louis XIV

Richelieu's death and that of Louis XIII in 1643 put the great Cardinal's work to a severe test. Louis XIV was a child of five when his father died, and his mother, Anne of Austria, became regent. She left the business of government to the man whom Richelieu had trained as his successor, the Italian Cardinal Giulio Mazzarini (1602–61), known in France as Mazarin.

Mazarin lacked his former master's relentless will and self-confidence. He sought to continue the war against Spain until the defeat of the Habsburgs, and to maintain the prestige of the monarchy that Richelieu had restored. But the nobility despised Mazarin as a foreign upstart, and the urban middle classes hated him for the high taxes that war demanded. The result was a movement known as the Fronde, the most serious rebellion against the monarchy before the Revolution of 1789.

The word *fronde* referred to a game of the unruly children of Paris, who threw dirt at passing coaches. The rebellion coincided with a period of severe harvest failures and lasted from 1648 to 1652. Like the children's game, it was annoying, but it ultimately failed to deflect the monarchy from its path. The Fronde's leaders were the judges of the *parlements,* or high courts; the chief financial officers who owned their offices and were thus heredi-

tary bureaucrats; and the nobility under the guidance of princes of the royal family. Each group hoped merely to increase its own influence, not destroy the French monarchy or upset the established social order.

They also failed to agree on a joint program beyond the purely negative policy of exiling Mazarin. The *parlements,* which began the struggle, stood for the privileges of the bureaucrats who controlled the courts and the ramshackle tax machinery. They wanted the king to rule with their advice rather than through councilors whom he could make or break at his pleasure. They insisted especially that he impose no tax without their consent. The nobles, who joined the rebellion later, had no intention of letting the *parlements* become dominant. They instead sought to abolish the upstart *intendants* and regain their old powers as provincial governors.

The result might have been different had any group dared to mobilize fully the deep-seated resentment of the lower classes—a resentment expressed throughout the century in urban riots and peasant rebellions against taxes and government. A few theorists, especially Huguenots, had argued that subjects possessed a "right of resistance" to unjust authority. But unlike the contemporary English rebellion, which asserted that right by defeating the king, the groups that led the Fronde were unwilling to unleash forces from below that might prove uncontrollable. Their conservatism, combined with the disunity of the rebels, eventually led to the Fronde's collapse.

Mazarin fled the country in 1651 and again in 1652–53 but returned to the saddle without difficulty, thanks to the support of Anne of Austria. By 1659, he had achieved victory over Spain. France gained two counties in the Pyrenees and the daughter of Philip IV of Spain as a bride for the young Louis XIV. That outcome symbolized the humiliation of Spain and the triumph of France as the leading power in Europe. The young king profited both from widespread revulsion against the disorders of the Fronde and from the prestige of foreign victories.

Cardinal Mazarin.

Fighting in Paris during the Fronde, 1648.

The morning after Mazarin's death in March 1661, Louis XIV announced to his ministers that he would henceforth be his own first minister. Richelieu had triumphed at last. The French monarchy had outlasted Huguenots and Fronde at home and Habsburgs abroad. Louis XIV henceforth ruled as an absolute monarch, endowed with a fuller sovereignty than any yet seen in the western Europe.

ENGLAND: IN SEARCH OF CIVIL AND RELIGIOUS LIBERTY, 1603–60

While Richelieu and Mazarin laid the foundations of absolute monarchy by divine right in France, England was slowly developing a constitutional, parliamentary system. The English groped toward a conception of sovereignty rooted in law and lodged in the hands of an assembly that represented the community—or at least its more wealthy and influential members. England was not alone in its resistance to absolute monarchy, but the result elsewhere tended to be anarchy and confusion as in Poland, or the victory of the crown as in France. In the end, the English example prevailed over absolutism. The "mother of parliaments" in London ultimately inspired parliamentary government in England's colonies and across modern Europe. But the road to constitutional monarchy in England was hard. It led through civil war and the execution of a king.

The Tudors: Crown and Parliament

England had always been peculiar. The strong monarchy of the Tudors (1485–1603) was part of a general European trend, but the survival and strengthening of Parliament under such a monarchy had no parallel elsewhere. While rulers on the Continent sought to abolish representative assemblies, the Tudors grudgingly used Parliament to legitimate laws and taxes. In the delicate area of religion, the Tudors found Parliament indispensable. Henry VIII had aspired to rule as an autocrat but had needed Parliament to break with Rome. Mary had asked Parliament to restore England to the Roman Church by statute. Elizabeth I had by statute once more broken with the Pope.

Elizabeth quarreled with her Parliaments, but the threat from Spain and the political good sense of both the queen and the parliamentary leaders had prevented a break. Both parties tacitly recognized that only Parliament could make a law or impose a tax. Parliament in turn recognized that making policy, especially foreign policy, lay within the sphere of "royal prerogative." Elizabeth's Parliaments tried more than once to reform the Anglican Church in a Puritan direction and to nudge the queen on foreign policy—presumptuous acts for which Elizabeth scolded them sharply. But she was too popular for Parliament to challenge her directly and too astute to demand a clear definition of her prerogative.

Under the Tudors, Parliament acquired a corporate feeling and a sense of being an integral part of government. The absence of provincial estates or privileges like those in France further increased its power. By the sixteenth century the lower house, called the House of Commons (see p. 363), represented both the landed gentry of the countryside and the richer merchants of the towns. The gentry also governed England at the local level as justices of the peace, for the English monarchy had failed to develop paid bureaucrats like the French *intendants*.

England was peculiar socially as well as politically. It lacked the Continent's rigid legal boundaries between social "orders." The gentry—baronets, knights, esquires, and simple "gentlemen"—were all commoners in the eyes of the law. Unlike its French counterpart, England's titled nobility was minuscule in numbers, a mere 121 English peers in 1641. The gentry included the younger sons of the nobility, who received neither land nor title thanks to the system of primogeniture that preserved noble estates by passing them in their entirety to the eldest son. Noble younger sons thus linked nobility and gentry; many pursued middle-class careers in the law or even commerce. At the same time, English merchants continually moved upward into the gentry by buying land. English society was hierarchical, but less so than continental societies. The comparative unity of England's gentry and nobility made the Parliament that represented them uniquely self-confident. That self-confidence was one source of the fateful clash between Crown and Parliament.

James I: Crown against Parliament

The Tudors had long ago put a stop to private wars waged by the high nobility. Under Elizabeth I, foreign and domestic

A formal meeting of Parliament in 1625. The Lords are seated; the Commons stand outside the bar.

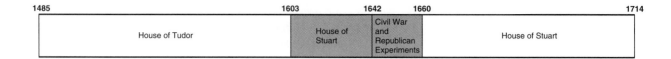

1485		1603	1642	1660	1714
House of Tudor		House of Stuart	Civil War and Republican Experiments	House of Stuart	

peril had rallied the Commons to the monarchy. But peace with Spain in 1604 and Europe's growing absorption in the Thirty Years' War after 1618 (see below) eliminated the danger of foreign invasion. The absence of threats inevitably lessened the authority of the Stuart family that succeeded Elizabeth, who was childless, in 1603.

James I (King of Scotland and of England, r. 1603–25) was the son of Mary, Queen of Scots. Well-meaning but pedantic, he failed to understand the political realities of the kingdom he had inherited from Elizabeth. The regents who ran Scotland after his mother's exile had raised him as a Protestant, but he had not relished that grim Presbyterian upbringing. His aims were entirely reasonable; he sought peace with Spain, toleration of England's Catholic minority, the union of England and Scotland, and a strong but benevolent monarchy.

But James, afflicted with a tendency to drool, preferred hunting, banqueting, and dalliance with male favorites to the sustained effort needed to govern. He failed to inspire confidence. And unlike Elizabeth, who often concealed her imperious will in ambiguous language, James made things dangerously clear. In a famous speech to the House of Commons in 1610, he proclaimed that "The state of monarchy is the supremist thing on earth; for kings are not only God's lieutenants upon earth, and sit upon God's throne, but even by God himself they are called gods." That lack of tact, his disorderly style of life, and the conspicuous financial corruption and bumbling foreign policy of the chief royal favorite, the Duke of Buckingham, offended many of the groups represented in Parliament.

The House of Commons began to attack the royal prerogative with arguments based on innovative readings of England's common law. The king in return denounced the parliamentary opposition.

The "country"—the nobility and gentry who ruled England at the local level and represented it in Parliament—attacked the "court party" of the increasingly friendless king. "Country" spokesmen denounced the court as secretly Catholic, influenced culturally by Spain and France, and financially and morally corrupt. The delicate Tudor balance collapsed.

Crown and Parliament clashed over three related issues: religion, money, and foreign policy. The Puritans and their sympathizers in the House of Commons wished to "purify" the Anglican Church of everything that still savored of Catholicism, from "Popish" ritual to the authority of bishops. James for his part knew from his youth in Scotland the Presbyterian system of church government that the Puritans sought. He was convinced that it would remove the church from royal control and threaten the monarchy itself. "No bishop, no king," he shouted in a moment of frustration.

Parliament continued to denounce the extravagance of the court and soon denied James the money needed to meet Elizabeth I's war debts and the rising cost of government in an age of inflation. James then raised money without parliamentary approval by increasing customs duties. Parliament contested his right to do so, but the courts ruled in the king's favor. The seeming subservience of the courts to the royal will further annoyed Parliament.

James I's foreign policy likewise exasperated his critics. He was too friendly with Catholic Spain for Puritan tastes, he did little to defend Protestants abroad against militant Catholicism, and he tried in vain to marry his son Charles to the daughter of the king of Spain. When James chided the House of Commons in 1621 for even discussing his foreign policy, the House bristled. It passed a unanimous Protestation defending its right to discuss "the arduous and urgent affairs concern-

The indolent James I.

ing the King, State, and defence of the realm, and of the Church of England." That was revolutionary talk. James tore the resolution from the Commons' *Journal* with his own hand, but he could not undo what the Commons had done. An aggressive and influential element among his subjects demanded rights and powers that he was unwilling to grant.

Charles I and the English Revolution, 1642–49

This crisis rapidly worsened after Charles I (r. 1625–49), second of the Stuarts, came to the throne. Charles tried to placate Parliament by attacking Catholic states. But Buckingham, the foppish favorite inherited from his father, failed to capture Cadiz in Spain or to save the French Huguenots besieged at La Rochelle. Parliament had urged war but had failed to grant sufficient taxes. Charles therefore levied a forced loan and imprisoned those who objected. In 1628 Parliament drew up a formal protest, the "Petition of Right," and compelled Charles to approve it. The Petition established that the king should henceforth levy neither taxes nor loans "without common consent by Act of Parliament" and that the government should imprison no one without showing cause. The king's subjects had begun to claim ever-broader rights against the state.

In 1629 Charles again roused the House of Commons to fury by asserting his full control of church and state. The Commons in reply declared that whoever introduced practices savoring of Catholicism into the Anglican Church was "a capital enemy to this kingdom and commonwealth," and that anyone who advised or submitted to taxation without parliamentary consent was "a betrayer of the liberties of England." The Commons thus raised the issue of the power to make law. Where did that power lie—in the king or in Parliament? The old answer, that it lay in the "king-in-Parliament," was no longer convincing. James I and Charles I between them had brought into the open the conflict between royal prerogative and the traditional "liberties of England" that descended ultimately from the *Magna Carta* of the barons (see pp. 311–12).

Charles, more stubborn than his father, ruled without Parliament from 1629 to 1640. In an attempt to duplicate Richelieu's absolutism, he chose advisers whose slogan was "thorough," such as Thomas Wentworth, Earl of Strafford, for political matters, and William Laud, Archbishop of Canterbury, for church affairs. Charles and his advisers devised new methods of taxation that did not require Parliament's approval and provided money enough to run the government so long as it stayed out of war. Laud challenged the Calvinist doctrine of predestination and sought to reestablish the authority of the bishops and reintroduce ritual into the Anglican service. The Puritans denounced him as a disguised Catholic. Up to 20,000 religious dissenters emigrated to the Netherlands or to bleak and distant Massachusetts. And Charles was unable to raise enough money to create the twin pillars of French-style absolutism—a royal administrative machine and a royal standing army.

Charles nevertheless prevailed until 1637–38. Then Laud tried to force the Anglican Book of Common Prayer on fiercely Presbyterian Scotland while Charles, with amazingly poor timing, alienated the Scottish nobility by seeking to reclaim from them the church lands they had acquired under Henry VIII. A fierce Scottish army was soon encamped in northern England. Charles and Strafford, unable to raise an army willing to fight, had to summon Parliament to vote money to buy the Scots off. The "Long Parliament" met in November 1640 and remained in session until 1653. It became a workshop of revolution. It sent Strafford and eventually Laud to the execution block. It dictated that the king must summon Parliament at least every three years. It outlawed all nonparliamentary taxation. It abolished the special royal law courts that had been the chief instruments of Charles's "Eleven Years' Tyranny." In less than a year (1640–41) Parliament destroyed absolute monarchy in England.

Charles secretly vowed revenge but acquiesced. He had no choice, for his government had alienated virtually all of the traditionally loyal groups whose cooperation he needed to rule England. Then the Catholics of Ireland decisively altered the

The autocratic Charles I.

situation by imitating the Scottish revolt and slaughtering Protestant settlers whom Elizabeth I and James I had planted in Ireland. Suppressing the Irish required raising an army once more—and Parliament distrusted the vengeful king too much to allow him to control that army. Simultaneously, the radical Puritans in Parliament abolished bishops in the Anglican Church. The inescapable issue of whether king or Parliament was to control army and church thereupon split England's upper classes. The growing political and religious radicalism of the House of Commons gave Charles what he had until then lacked—a royalist party that would fight to reassert his prerogatives. He attempted to arrest his parliamentary opponents in January 1642. By summer England was at war.

What was at first a confused struggle between factions of nobility and gentry soon turned into the English Revolution. Both Parliamentarians and Royalists claimed to support traditional English political and religious freedoms. London,

The English Revolution   1642–49

most towns, the middle classes, and the economically advanced southeast of England generally supported Parliament, although much of the population sought to remain neutral. Many rural areas and the backward northwest supported Charles. But the divisions between the parties did not correspond closely to England's economic, social, or regional divisions. Nobility, gentry, and artisans from all over England fought on both sides. The fierce religious and ideological issues at stake split many families, both noble and gentry.

Unlike the Fronde, in which narrow interest groups failed to proclaim programs with broad appeal, the English Civil War and Revolution offered dramatic alternatives to the established order—parliamentary monarchy instead of royal absolutism, and a Presbyterian Church with elected "presbyters," or elders, instead of an Anglican Church under crown-appointed bishops. Unlike the Fronde, the English Revolution produced radical movements that sought to abolish the monarchy, the established Church, and the landlords. "Levellers," "Diggers," and millenarian sects such as the "Fifth Monarchy Men" sought to inaugurate a new age of radical equality, or rule by "saints."

Parliament based itself in London, Europe's largest city, and proved more successful than the king at raising money and armies. Oliver Cromwell, a brilliant and ruthless cavalry officer, helped create a "New Model Army" drawn largely from his fellow Independents, strict Bible-reading Puritans who believed in democratically organized independent congregations with little or no church structure.

Cromwell and Parliament's numerically superior and ideologically motivated army ("Truly, I think he that prays best will fight best") defeated the king's forces decisively in June–July 1645. The king surrendered a year later. Then the army broke with the Presbyterians, who had dominated Parliament since the Anglicans had withdrawn in 1642 to join Charles I. Groups in Parliament and army with views ranging from social and religious moderation to extreme radicalism quarreled over the constitutional and religious settlement. The king sought to exploit the divisions among his opponents by devious negotiations. In November 1647 he escaped from custody to launch a brief second round of civil war.

The Independents in the army were now determined to root out all opposition. They purged Parliament of their Presbyterian rivals, defeated the king, and called the untrustworthy "Charles Stuart, that man of blood, to an account for the blood that he had shed." Cromwell, after initial hesitation, had Charles I executed in 1649, abolished the monarchy and the House of Lords, and set up a republic or "Commonwealth" with the "rump" of the Long Parliament as its government and with himself as its unchallenged leader. Parliament had tried a king ordained by divine right for treason against his own subjects, had cut off his head, and had abolished the very institution of kingship. England had set an example that was long remembered.

Cromwell's Dictatorship

Unlike later continental figures who seized command of a state through revolution, England's new dictator was a deeply religious man who did not initially seek supreme power. Yet power, and inevitable opposition to his will, brought out Cromwell's ruthlessness. He suppressed with fire and massacre the Irish rebellion that in 1641–42 had helped trigger the Civil War. He drubbed the Scots in two great battles when they intervened in favor of the son of Charles I. He presided over a naval war with the Dutch from 1652 to 1654. He wrathfully dissolved the rump of the Long Parliament in 1653, saying "You are no Parliament, I say you are no Parliament; I will put an end to your sitting." But he failed in his efforts to guarantee religious toleration to all Protestants except determined Anglicans and to find a satisfactory constitutional basis for government.

Cromwell attempted to rule with the consent of Parliament and through a written constitution, the "Instrument of Government"—the first such document in the history of a major state. He took the title of Lord Protector instead of king, but quar-

Democratic Radicalism in the English Revolution

With victory assured, Cromwell's army turned to politics. In 1647 a Council of the Army debated constitutional issues at Putney, outside London. Radicals and representatives of the common soldiers, influenced by the Levellers, pressed for political rights for all men. Gentry figures such as General Ireton, Cromwell's forceful son-in-law, countered with the claim that only ownership of land conferred the right to representation.

MAJOR RAINBOROUGH: I think that the poorest he that is in England hath a life to live, as the greatest he, and therefore truly, sir, I think it's clear, that every man that is to live under a government ought first by his own consent to put himself under that government, and I do think that the poorest man in England is not at all bound in a strict sense to that government that he hath not had a voice to put himself under.

GENERAL IRETON: Government is to preserve property. . . . The objection does not lie in the making of the representation more equal but in the introducing of men . . . in this government who have no property in this kingdom. . . .

SEXBY [a representative of the troops]: I see that though liberty were our end, there is a degeneration from it. We have ventured our lives to recover our birthrights and privileges as Englishmen, and by the arguments urged there is none. There are many thousands of us soldiers that have ventured our lives; we have had little property . . . yet we have had a birthright. But it seems now, except a man hath a fixed estate in this kingdom, he hath no right in this kingdom. I wonder we were so much deceived.

From Puritanism and Liberty, *ed. by A. S. P. Woodhouse (Chicago: University of Chicago Press, 1951), pp. 53, 62, 69.*

reled with Parliament as bitterly as had the Stuarts. In 1655 he installed an open military dictatorship to keep Parliament from disbanding his army and persecuting his coreligionists. Most Englishmen still rejected religious toleration, especially toleration of the religious and political radicals who made up a large part of Cromwell's army. And it became increasingly evident that England—like other states in the following centuries—could not break with history and set up a new regime simply by drafting a constitution. An unwritten "constitution" already existed, deeply ingrained in English political traditions.

Oliver Cromwell, by Samuel Cooper.

Cromwell's death in 1658 made General George Monck, his most important military subordinate, the most powerful figure in England. Monck recognized that Parliament was the only alternative to military dictatorship and that restoring Parliament also required recreating the monarchy. In 1660, a "Convention Parliament" under his protection invited the son of Charles I to return from France and take up the crown.

The Legacy of the English Revolution

The Civil War had made clear that England would not tolerate an absolute monarchy. Strafford and Laud had tried to do for Charles I what Richelieu and Mazarin had done for Louis XIV. But whereas the Frenchmen had died in their beds, the Englishmen had lost their heads to the executioner. The new Parliament confirmed many of the severe limits to royal power that the Long Parliament had set before the outbreak of the Civil War. The turmoil of the first half of the century left most Englishmen with half-expressed convictions that had lasting effects—a fear of too great a concentration of power, a deepened respect for government by law rather than by royal command, a reverence for Parliament as the defender of individual rights against royal despotism, and a fervent distaste for standing armies.

The restoration of King Charles II: the coronation in Westminster Abbey (from a contemporary print).

The early seventeenth century was a brilliant age in the history of English literature and thought. It included Shakespeare's mature work and the early years of the great poet John Milton. In 1611 the Authorized, or King James, Version of the Bible first emerged from the presses. Its sonorous cadences have influenced the writing of English to the present day. Statesmen and pamphleteers arguing for royalist, parliamentary, or radical principles likewise made this a formative period of modern political thought.

Thomas Hobbes's *Leviathan* (1651) distilled the political insights of the years of civil war. Under the influence of Thucydides' great history of the Peloponnesian War (see pp. 52–53), of which Hobbes wrote the first English translation, Hobbes saw in humanity "a perpetual and restless desire of power after power." Without some authority to enforce law, society would disintegrate into "a war of every man against every man." Life without government was "solitary, poor, nasty, brutish, and short." Hobbes, following Huguenot thinkers seeking to justify revolt against France's Catholic monarchy, postulated that humans set up sovereign powers through agreements or contracts.

But Hobbes drew from this "contract theory" of government conclusions opposite to those of the Huguenots, and of Cromwell and his army, who had declared "the king is king by contract" and had severed Charles I's head for violating that contract. For Hobbes, society agreed to obey the sovereign because the sovereign alone could maintain order. To ensure the maintenance of order, the sovereign's powers had to be absolute and unquestioned. Hobbes's contract therefore bound only the subjects, not the ruler. "There can happen no breach of the Covenant on the part of the Sovereign; and consequently none of his Subjects . . . can be freed from his subjection."

Hobbes thus took contract theory and transformed it into a justification of unfettered and arbitrary power. English political theorists during the remainder of the seventeenth century devoted much effort to finding some way to refute Hobbes— to subject political power to the restraint

of law and to the consent of the governed. But they, too, remained fearful of the ever-present threat of violence and chaos against which Hobbes had created his absolute sovereign.

GERMANY: DISINTEGRATION AND DISASTER, 1618–48

The consequences of the absence of sovereign power and the "war of every man against every man" were nowhere so visible as across the North Sea in Germany. While France built the mightiest monarchy

The title page of Thomas Hobbes's *Leviathan*, one of the fundamental works of Western political theory. Hobbes described the sovereign power of the state as "that great Leviathan, or rather (to speak more reverently) that mortal God, to which we owe under the Immortal God, our peace and defence."

in Europe and England underwent a crisis from which it emerged with new strength, the German-speaking peoples suffered the Thirty Years' War. It was in reality four successive wars that began in 1618 in Bohemia, spread to the rest of the Holy Roman Empire, and before its end in 1648 involved most major continental powers. It was a savage and demoralizing conflict that left central Europe poorer and weaker than the states to its west for the next 150 years.

The Causes of the Thirty Years' War

The war sprang from a complicated mixture of religious and political quarrels. The Peace of Augsburg (1555) had ended the previous round of religious war in central Europe (see p. 437) by dividing the German states between Catholic and Lutheran rulers. Each prince had received the right to determine the religion of his subjects. But in the following decades most Catholic bishoprics in north Germany had fallen into Lutheran or secular hands. The spread of Calvinism introduced a further source of friction, for the Peace of Augsburg had not recognized Calvinism nor assigned it any territories. Protestant successes caused increasing discontent in the Catholic camp.

In 1608, the foremost leader of the Catholics, Duke Maximilian of Bavaria, roughly disciplined the Protestant town of Donauwörth. That action led Frederick V, the Calvinist ruler of the Palatinate, a small state on the middle Rhine, to form a Protestant Union of German princes and cities. In reply, Maximilian organized a Catholic League with the support of German Catholic princes and the Jesuits. By 1609 the Holy Roman Empire had fractured once again into two hostile religious and military alliances. Protestant Union and Catholic League faced each other with hatred and suspicion, each determined to bar the other from further gains.

1. Revolt in Bohemia, 1618–20

These signs of anarchy and religious division within the Holy Roman Empire prompted the Habsburgs, who held the imperial title, to try to rebuild their authority. They began by seeking to consolidate their hold over their long-time family domains of Austria, Bohemia, and Hungary. The aging emperor Matthias secured the election of his heir-apparent, Ferdinand of Styria, as king of Bohemia in 1617.

Bohemia was a flourishing territory in which two chief nationalities (Germans and Czechs) and a variety of religions (Catholicism, Lutheranism, Calvinism, and remnants of the Hussite movement of the fifteenth century) lived in relative peace under Habsburg promises of toleration. But Ferdinand was a zealous Counter-Reformation Catholic. He had ruthlessly recatholicized Styria, and the Protestant majority in the Bohemian Estates rightly feared that he planned the same for Bohemia. In May 1618 the Bohemians therefore threw their imperial governors from the windows of Prague castle (an incident thereafter known as the "defenestration of Prague"). The Estates raised an army, declared Ferdinand deposed, and offered the crown of Bohemia to Frederick V of the Palatinate. Frederick's unwise acceptance extended the war from Bohemia to the Empire as a whole. His Protestant Union took the side of the Bohemian Estates, while Maximilian of Bavaria swung the Catholic League behind Ferdinand, who had been elected emperor.

The Bohemian phase of the war ended swiftly. In November 1620 the Imperial forces crushed the Bohemian rebels at the battle of the White Mountain near Prague. Frederick V fled, and Emperor Ferdinand proceeded to make Bohemia over at the cost of wrecking its economy and society. War and plague cut the population almost in half. The Czech nobility lost everything. Half the land in Bohemia changed hands through confiscation, and Ferdinand created a new nobility of adventurers from as far away as Ireland. The Jesuits, with Ferdinand's full backing, set out to reconvert the country to Catholicism by force. Within ten years they had stamped Protestantism out or driven it underground. The Czechs became a people without a ruling class and without a claim to an independent existence for two centuries. The Habsburgs and their Catholic allies had decisively won the first round of the great war.

2. Danish Intervention and Catholic Triumph, 1625–29

The fall of Bohemia terrified the German Protestants and elated the Catholics. The Spanish Habsburgs had also intervened against the Protestant states of north Germany, and the armies of the Catholic League were everywhere triumphant. But common danger failed to unite the Protestants. The Lutherans feared a Calvinist victory in Bohemia more than an Imperial triumph. The Lutheran kingdom of Saxony had actually helped Ferdinand put the Czechs down. And although Frederick V was the son-in-law of James I, Protestant England gave no help; James I and his successor Charles I were locked in their struggle with Parliament.

The king of Denmark joined his fellow Protestants in 1625, but his principal motive was greed for territory in north Germany. Within a year, the Catholics had beaten him back. Albrecht von Wallenstein, a brilliant military entrepreneur who had offered the emperor his services, crushed the Danes with an expert mercenary army that at its height numbered 125,000 men. Wallenstein's long-term aim was probably to secure central Europe for himself. His immediate goal was to build an Imperial Habsburg military machine that could eliminate the Protestants without the help of the Catholic League. By 1628 Wallenstein and the League were as much at odds on the Catholic side as Calvinists and Lutherans were on the Protestant. Religion slowly receded in significance as the war became a struggle between armies and states alone, a struggle for mastery in Europe.

The Habsburg and Catholic cause reached its high-water mark in 1629. Denmark withdrew, leaving Wallenstein's army supreme. The Catholic League and Jesuit advisers persuaded Ferdinand to issue an Edict of Restitution that restored to Catholic hands all church lands lost to Protestantism since 1552. Carrying out the edict meant yet more bloodshed to restore the dispossessed Catholic bishops of Protestant north Germany. That would also destroy both the rough religious balance between Catholicism and Protestantism in Germany and the power balance between the north German states on the one hand and Austria and Bavaria on the other. That threat finally roused Lutherans inside and outside Germany to action.

3. The "Lion of the North": Gustavus Adolphus, 1630–32

In 1630 Sweden, a country until now on the periphery of the European state system, intervened to check the Habsburgs. Its masterful king, Gustavus Adolphus, was the ablest ruler of his generation. Sweden had a population of roughly 1.25 million people, perhaps a fifteenth of the population of France. But Gustavus had cultivated rich copper and timber exports, a sophisticated iron and armament industry, and the most advanced army of the day. That army was not large, but it was the first in Europe recruited by universal conscription, and it possessed a high morale born of fierce patriotism. It also had the first uniforms, the first artillery light enough for battlefield maneuver, improved muskets, regular pay, and discipline, a rarity indeed in the Thirty Years' War. Its victories over Russia, Denmark, and Poland between 1611 and 1629 made the Baltic almost a Swedish lake.

Gustavus stepped into the great war in Germany to defend Sweden's Baltic interests, which Wallenstein appeared to threaten. But as the war continued, Gustavus began to toy with a broader aim— the creation of a federation of German Protestant states under Swedish leadership. He arrived too late to save the great city of Magdeburg from sack, massacre, and destruction by the Imperial forces in May 1631, an event that for generations symbolized the all-devouring brutality of this war. But in the fall of 1631 Gustavus shattered the Imperial armies at Breitenfeld in Saxony, and marched triumphantly to the Rhine.

That emergency compelled the Emperor to recall Wallenstein, whom he had dismissed at the insistence of the Catholic

League. Gustavus defeated Wallenstein decisively at Lützen in 1632, but paid for victory with his own life. Without Gustavus's leadership the outnumbered Swedes could not maintain their dominance in Germany. Swedish weakness in turn freed the Emperor from dependence on his over-mighty subject, Wallenstein, who perished by assassination at Ferdinand's orders. In the fall of 1634 the Imperial armies checked the Swedes at the battle of Nördlingen. Gustavus Adolphus had saved German Protestantism but had failed to decide the war.

4. France Intervenes, 1635–48

The most powerful state of all now acted, opening the fourth and final phase of the war. Since his appointment as chief minister in 1624, Richelieu had followed the war closely through his ever-present ambassadors and agents. His aim was to crush both Austrian and Spanish Habs-

burgs and to end Habsburg encirclement of France. Under his leadership, Catholic France accepted as allies all opponents of the Habsburgs regardless of religion. His first allies were the Protestant Dutch, who in 1621 had again gone to war with their ancestral enemy, Spain. Then Richelieu subsidized Sweden. But the Imperial defeat of the Swedes in 1634 forced him to choose between direct French intervention and Habsburg domination of Europe. In May 1635 he chose intervention; France declared war on Spain and allied itself with Sweden and Germany.

The Thirty Years' War had by then lasted for seventeen years. It continued drearily for a further thirteen years, for neither side had the strength to force a decision. French, Swedish, and Dutch armies slogged across central Europe pursuing or pursued by the Habsburg forces. The rebellions of Portugal and of the rich province of Catalonia in 1640 weakened Spain. In 1643, on the battlefield of Rocroi

The siege of Magdeburg in 1631 by Habsburg and Catholic forces, which ended with one of the bloodiest massacres of the war.

in the Netherlands, the French finally crushed the Spanish army and its legend of invincibility. Habsburg allies soon deserted the Empire, and the Swedes besieged Prague and menaced Vienna. The Habsburg attempt to roll back the Reformation in Germany and establish mastery over central Europe had failed.

Peace of Exhaustion: Westphalia, 1648

Habsburg defeat opened the way to the peace negotiated between 1644 and 1648 at the Congress of Westphalia. The gathering was Europe's first great peace conference and the first interstate meeting of importance since the Council of Constance of 1414–18 (see p. 427). But unlike Constance, the atmosphere and the business of the Congress that met at Münster in western Germany were entirely secular. The Congress was a meeting of sovereign states that recognized no earthly superior and only the most shadowy common interests. The unity of medieval "Christendom" had dissolved.

The Congress confirmed the importance of the sovereign state and set a framework for central European politics that lasted until 1801–06. In recognizing the right of the German principalities to make alliances and to declare war, the Congress accepted the disintegration of the Empire into more than 300 separate sovereignties. Switzerland and the Dutch Netherlands finally achieved recognition as independent states. France acquired ambiguous rights to Alsace, and Sweden gained strips of German territory along the Baltic and the North seas. The two German states of Brandenburg and Bavaria increased their territory and prestige.

As for religion, the Congress reaffirmed the principle of partition according to the religion of the ruler established in the Peace of Augsburg of 1555, and at last added Calvinism to Catholicism and Lutheranism as one of the recognized faiths. To prevent further dispute, the Congress froze the ownership of church lands as of 1624. North Germany remained Protestant and south Germany Catholic. Only France and Spain failed to reach

The Sack of Magdeburg   1631

For a generation after the destruction of this German city, the phrase "Magdeburg quarter" meant "no quarter."

Then was there naught but beating and burning, plundering, torture, and murder. Most especially was every one of the enemy bent on securing much booty. When a marauding party entered a house, if its master had anything to give he might thereby purchase respite and protection for himself and his family till the next man, who also wanted something, should come along. It was only when everything had been brought forth and there was nothing left to give that the real trouble commenced. Then, what with blows and threats of shooting, stabbing, and hanging, the poor people were so terrified that if they had had anything left they would have brought it forth if it had been buried in the earth or hidden away in a thousand castles. In this frenzied rage, the great and splendid city that had stood like a fair princess in the land was now, in its hour of direst need and unutterable distress and woe, given over to the flames, and thousands of innocent men, women, and children, in the midst of a horrible din of heartrending shrieks and cries, were tortured and put to death in so cruel and shameful a manner that no words would suffice to describe, nor no tears to bewail it.

From Otto von Guericke, in Readings in European History, *ed. by James Harvey Robinson (Boston: Ginn, 1906), Vol. II, pp. 211–12.*

agreement. Their war continued until Mazarin secured, in the Peace of the Pyrenees of 1659, the victory that Richelieu had sought.

The Consequences of the Thirty Years' War

The Thirty Years' War had been a terrifying demonstration of the anarchy that Europe's state-builders sought to avoid. It was one of the most destructive wars in recorded history. In Europe no later conflict matched it in ruthless devastation until the new "thirty years' war" of 1914–45. Armies pillaged, raped, and murdered their way across central Europe. The soldiery wiped towns off the map and reduced cities to a small fraction of their original populations. Cultivated land reverted to waste. Destruction of livestock even more than of crops crippled a primitive and mostly agrarian economy, for

Europe in 1648

Austrian Habsburg lands
Spanish Habsburg lands
Prussian lands
German states
Swedish lands
– – – Boundary of Holy Roman Empire
★ Major battle

plough and dairy animals were difficult to replace. Starvation and the massive plague epidemics that marched with the lice-ridden armies killed more than the sword.

The Holy Roman Empire (including Bohemia) lost an estimated 4 million out of roughly 21 million inhabitants. A few areas lost up to 80 percent of their population. The war also had deep psychological, social, political, and economic effects. The peoples of central Europe were soon happy to acknowledge any authority, however brutal, that promised peace. The fragmentation of the Holy Roman Empire

into small states quirkily divided by customs barriers hampered economic recovery. The war helped delay until the nineteenth century the emergence of a state called "Germany," and helped make its emergence an event that shook Europe and the world.

DUTCH UNREST AND SPANISH DECLINE

The political upheavals of the early seventeenth century touched many areas of

Europe other than France, England, and central Europe. Even distant Russia underwent an anarchic "Time of Troubles" before settling down uneasily under the rule of the first Romanov tsar in 1613. In the west, violent convulsions shook the Netherlands and Spain.

By 1609 the northern areas of the Netherlands had achieved effective independence from Spain and enormous economic success. An aggressively Calvinist party nevertheless pressed for renewed war against Spain in the southern Netherlands. Its leader was Maurice of Nassau, son of William the Silent, chief of the House of Orange and commander of the highly competent Dutch army. A second party, that of the merchant class, enjoyed the support of the religiously tolerant Arminians (those unwilling to accept Calvin's stern doctrine of predestination). It hoped to reestablish trade with Spain.

In 1619 Maurice of Nassau overthrew this "peace party" and had its leader executed after a political trial. The war with Spain resumed in 1621 and continued inconclusively until the Peace of Westphalia. Tensions between the House of Orange and the mercantile "regent class" continued throughout the century. For two decades after 1650 the "regents" dominated Dutch affairs. But when invasion—from France rather than Spain—came again in 1672, the old conflicts reopened. A mob in The Hague tore the leading regent, Johan de Witt, limb from limb and publicly sold his remains. The Dutch summoned the head of the House of Orange, the young Prince William, to lead them victoriously against overwhelming odds.

In Spain, religious-ethnic persecution marked the beginning of irreversible decline. In 1609 the monarchy and the Inquisition launched a campaign similar to the expulsion of Spain's 150,000 Jews after 1492 (see p. 459). In fanatical pursuit of religious uniformity and "purity of blood" *(limpieza de sangre),* the authorities deported to north Africa in 1609–14 as many as 275,000 Moriscos, the insufficiently converted descendants of the Moors who had given the Iberian peninsula much of its civilization. That savage persecution deprived Spain of a creative minority that it sorely needed. Plague and economic collapse reduced the population dramatically, from perhaps 8.5 million in 1600 to 7.5 million in 1650.

War, both foreign and domestic, also contributed to Spain's decline. The leading minister from 1621 to 1643, the proud Count-Duke of Olivares, committed Spain to war in Germany in 1620 and against the Netherlands in 1621. War with France as well in 1635 placed unbearable tax burdens on the Spanish monarchy's patchwork of provinces jealous of their traditional rights and liberties. Olivares struggled gloomily to establish a centralized administration with an effective system of tax collection. But as so often happened in early modern Europe, centralization—the creation of a modern state machine—provoked bitter revolt. In 1640 Portugal, forcibly united with Spain since 1580, made good its independence by force. The rich province of Catalonia attracted French support and defied the monarchy until 1652. Spain's Italian possessions also revolted.

Spain thus had to yield to France the position of leading power in Europe in 1659. Spain's political and military decline was in part a consequence of the over-ambitious policies of Olivares. But its deeper causes were economic and internal. Of all the powers, Spain suffered most from the crises of the European and world economy of the seventeenth century.

EUROPE'S POPULATION AND ECONOMY IN CRISIS

A suddenly hostile climate and a drastic fall in prices intensified the ravages that never-ending war inflicted on the societies of seventeenth-century Europe. Despite the slowly gathering force of commerce and industry, agriculture still dominated Europe's economy. The tyranny of the seasons in turn dominated agriculture. And during what historians have termed the "little ice age," the cold century and a half between the 1590s and the 1740s, that tyranny was harsh indeed. Usually ice-free rivers repeatedly froze over in winter. Springs and summers turned rainy and cold.

Even in the relatively warm fifteenth and sixteenth centuries, England had suffered one poor harvest in four, and one disastrous harvest in six. Between 1594 and 1597 rain and cold wrecked four harvests in succession from Ireland to east central Europe; the result was widespread famine. The harvests from 1647 to 1652–53 were similarly catastrophic, especially in France and Spain. The 1690s were the coldest decade in 700 years; in 1696–97 about a quarter of the population of Finland perished by famine. The "great cold" of 1709–10 produced a general crop failure in France. Beggars froze to death in the streets of Paris.

Human and animal epidemics inevitably accompanied famine, for malnutrition reduces resistance to disease. Spain lost perhaps a half-million dead from bubonic plague in 1647–52, and outbreaks were widespread until the early eighteenth century. The population of Europe dipped slightly (see Figure 19-1). Only after 1750 did a mellower climate, crop-rotation techniques pioneered in the Low Countries, New World crops such as the potato and maize, and dramatic improve-

ments in transport allow a new and sustained increase in Europe's population.

A second force intensified the effects of the seventeenth-century climate on Europe's fragile economy and population—the movement of prices. In the sixteenth century two trends had united to produce a "price revolution": the sudden and massive influx of New World silver and gold, and the rapidly increasing sophistication of Europe's merchants and bankers, who had multiplied the effective volume of money by speeding its circulation and by using credit far more extensively than in the past. In consequence, by 1600 prices had reached levels four to five times above those of 1500. That inflation, although modest by twentieth-century standards, had deeply unsettling effects on societies that still adhered to the medieval myth of a "just" price. The penetration of money ever deeper into the countryside brought with it price fluctuations that intensified the distress of the peasantry and ruined aristocrats who failed to adapt to the hard new age of profit and loss.

After about 1620 the influx of New World silver slowed as production in the mines of Mexico and Peru peaked. Loss of revenue helped cripple the policies of Olivares. Throughout Europe price inflation gave way to deflation, and hectic growth to stagnation. The wars and troubles after 1620, from the Thirty Years' War to the English Revolution and the Fronde, further intensified the economic depression. Only after 1670 did some northern areas of Europe, most notably England and the Dutch United Provinces, once more begin to enjoy a steady prosperity. In Spain, the pressure of taxes to finance Olivares' wars and the dead hand of his bureaucracy crushed what little independence and enterprise the middle classes of Castile had possessed. In the countryside, as in the Spanish New World, sheep replaced peasants. In France, the pressure of the monarchy's taxation, further intensified in the wars of Louis XIV after 1667 (see pp. 510–12), caused repeated revolts.

Yet Europe survived and grew—despite the "little ice age," deflation, and war—thanks above all to economic innovation. In industry—the production of

FIGURE 19-1   The Population of Europe, 1000–1700 (including Russia west of the Ural Mountains)

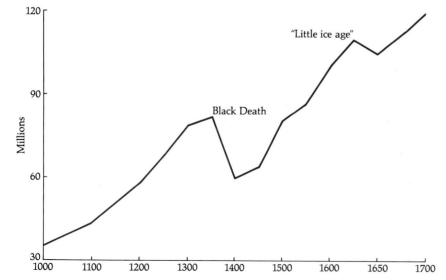

goods for market using specialized labor and machines—new techniques rapidly gained ground. In the 1580s, the Dutch introduced power saws worked by windmills. Water-driven power hammers for forging became common. Coal, at least in England, became the cheapest source of energy. Coal fueled London's growth from 200,000 inhabitants in 1600 to more than 550,000—Europe's largest city—by 1700. Coal made the English glass industry the most modern in Europe, and supplied London's shops with glass windowpanes at which visitors marveled.

All over Europe, commerce and industry began to break out from the medieval framework of town and guild monopolies. A new form of craft organization that bypassed the guilds, the "putting-out system," spread from the Low Countries. Traveling merchants supplied rural home workers with raw materials, then returned to collect the finished product. "Putting-out" was particularly effective in the greatest industry of early modern Europe, textiles. It was also well suited to an age in which techniques were simple and hand or animal power drove most industrial equipment. To the peasant family, it provided income that in years of crop failure might mean the difference between life and death. Putting-out slowly eroded guild restrictions, channeled money into the countryside, and dissolved the old peasant barter economy. It was a major source of Europe's economic growth.

In trade and finance, the century was one of continued rapid change. An ever-widening banking network spread across Europe, from Seville facing the New World to the grain and timber ports of the Baltic. A new institution apparently invented in Italy, the joint-stock company, made possible a far more widespread mobilization of capital than traditional family firms or partnerships. Individuals who were not necessarily traders could buy "shares" in great commercial enterprises such as the Muscovy Company (1553), the English East India Company (1600), and the Dutch East India Company (1602). The company directors then used the shareholders' money for their operations. Soon a vast market developed in the "shares" themselves, the ancestor of the modern stock exchange.

A further source of change was geographic. By the middle of the seventeenth century the westward and northward shift in Europe's economic center of gravity that had begun even before 1492 was complete. The Mediterranean and central Europe became backwaters. Venice, although victorious over the Turks at sea, suffered disastrous shrinkage both in its industries and in its trade with the eastern Mediterranean. The westward shift of trade to the New World and around the Cape of Good Hope helped destroy German banking dynasties such as the Fuggers of Augsburg. Then the Thirty Years' War completed Germany's economic ruin.

But even economies open to the ocean failed. Spain, thanks to religious persecution, rigid government controls, and high taxes, soon yielded much of its New World trade to Genoese and Dutch merchants. Antwerp, the great trading and banking center of northern Europe until the mid-sixteenth century, failed to assert its political independence from Spain. It lost its economic position as well to its Dutch neighbors to the north. The founding of the Bank of Amsterdam in 1609—the same year as the truce by which Spain recognized Dutch independence—symbolized the supremacy of the Dutch Republic as the center of Europe's economy, a supremacy that lasted throughout the seventeenth century. But the republic, with a tiny territory and a population that reached 2 million in 1650 but then remained essentially unchanged until 1800, was little more than a glorified city-state.

The future belonged to those powerful engines of growth, the modern "national markets" within the large territorial states, France and England. France seemed by far the richest, for it possessed the largest territory of any state west of Russia and a population greater than any other. But its agriculture suffered badly in the "little ice age." France's sheer size, the absence of good roads or navigable waterways, and the numerous customs barriers between provinces, and between towns and countryside likewise stunted growth. France's centralized war-making state crushed the peasants under a taxation that, along with dues to landlords, and Church, deprived them of roughly half their income.

Nor did the efforts of France's government to promote economic growth help. The great finance minister of Louis XIV, Jean-Baptiste Colbert (see p. 506) made an almost despairing attempt to promote the development of industry and commerce in the face of the economic depression that lasted through the 1680s. In the 1670s he founded many enterprises, including cannon foundries and textile mills staffed with Dutch experts. He strengthened the guilds as a means of ensuring the quality and uniformity needed to promote exports. He attempted to crush the Dutch with tariffs and with Louis's wars. Colbert was the most consistent adherent of a series of loosely linked notions, characteristic of a world of warring states, usually known as "mercantilism"—state intervention to promote industry and maximize

Ships bearing precious merchandise from the far side of the world: the front of the earliest headquarters of the English East India Company. Photo courtesy of the Granger Collection.

FRONT OF THE OLD EAST INDIA HOUSE.

The world's first stock exchange, at Amsterdam, in the mid-seventeenth century.

exports, protective tariffs to prevent imports, and strenuous attempts to create a trade surplus that would suck in gold and silver from competitors. Such methods long outlived the seventeenth century, but they did not help France. Most of Colbert's industries proved ruinously unprofitable, and his reinforcement of the guilds was a disaster for French industry. His tariffs damaged France more than the Dutch. France's commercial economy developed, but largely despite Colbert.

England was different. It too employed "mercantilist" practices, such as the Navigation Acts that after 1651 restricted all trade with England and its colonies to English ships, and channeled colonial products through English ports. England, too, fought wars with the Dutch over commerce in 1652–54, 1665–67, and 1672–74. But internally, England was already a large unified market; its guilds were decayed relics; its textile, coal, and iron industries were gradually expanding. By 1700 its economy, the least "mercantilist" and state-controlled in Europe, owed a third of its national product to commerce and industry, while the proportion in France was a fifth or less. In the long term, England's economy could not fail to have an impact on the wider world opened up in the age of discovery.

THE EUROPEAN EMPIRES

Europe's overseas expansion slowed briefly in the seventeenth century. Spain needed time to digest the conquered Aztec and Inca empires. In India, China, and Japan the Europeans faced ancient civilizations that still had the power to hold them at arm's length. Developing the North American wilderness required settlers in numbers unavailable until Europe's population growth resumed. And the extension to the outside world of the warlike competition between European states slowed Europe's economic penetration of the non-European world.

Trade and plunder had lured the Europeans overseas. Portugal persisted in that pattern, and its "colonies," with the exception of its early settlements on Madeira and its great land empire in Brazil, remained fortified trading posts that dealt in spices or slaves through native middlemen. The Dutch sought to follow the Portuguese example after 1600, when they seized control from Portugal of the Indian Ocean and China Sea. But in their Spice Islands south of the Philippines the Dutch soon found that maintaining exports required more than trading posts. As the Spaniards discovered during their feverish search for gold and silver in the Americas, trade and plunder led to rule and settlement.

The new model colonies of the seventeenth century were thus settlement colonies. The pattern dated from Portugal's settlement in the 1420s of the uninhabited Atlantic island of Madeira, and Spain had followed it in the Americas after the 1520s. The function of the settlement colonies was to produce raw materials essential to the mother country. That purpose required the export of European institutions, technology, plants, and animals to set up overseas societies on the European model. In Africa, malaria and yellow fever killed the vast majority of Europeans who attempted to penetrate inland, and Europe's military technology did not yet provide superiority over the natives on their own ground. Native middlemen and rulers continued to provide apparently inexhaustible supplies of slaves; the trading-post system persisted.

But in the New World, settlement was possible. And settlement meant production of the commodity most prized after gold and silver—sugar. Cultivating that addictive substance, first brought to Europe by the Crusaders, required back-breaking labor. As the Portuguese had demonstrated on Madeira, enslaved natives from the Canary Islands or from Africa most conveniently supplied that labor. Tobacco, coffee, and in East Asia tea and spices created similar patterns of cultivation and settlement. The riches that these products generated proved an irresistible source of conflict.

The Struggle for Mastery in the East

East of Africa and south of China the Portuguese soon lost the trading empire they had established after the voyages of Vasco de Gama. Dutch, English, and French interlopers appeared. Portugal was too economically and demographically weak and too technologically backward to hold empires both in the New World and in the East simultaneously, and its subordination to Spain from 1580 to 1640 exposed it to attack by Spain's enemy, the Dutch. Portugal's rivals founded powerful East India Companies: the English in 1600, the Dutch in 1602, the French in 1664. The Dutch proved the most ruthless, well-organized, and successful. Their seizure of the Cape of Good Hope in 1652 created the largest white community in Africa as a way-station for their shipping. Their massacre of English merchants on Amboina in 1623 and their control of Batavia on Java from 1619 and of the strategic Malacca strait after 1641 persuaded the English to concentrate on India. There England and France set up trading posts on the Portuguese model at Bombay, Madras, and Calcutta for England, and at Pondicherry for France. The Mughal empire that dominated South Asia barred the way inland. Only its collapse after 1707 opened the road by which Britain ultimately established its hegemony in the Mughals' place (see Chapters 22 and 27).

Sugar and Slavery in the Caribbean

In the Caribbean, the Dutch, English, and French competed for crumbs from Spain's overfilled table. After war between the Dutch and Spain resumed in 1621, the Dutch sought to damage Spain by seizing sugar-rich Brazil from Spain's dependency, Portugal. The Dutch failed, but they did take the Caribbean island of Curaçao as a base for raids on Spanish commerce. England settled Barbados in 1624 and gained Jamaica in 1655, while the French took Guadeloupe and Martinique. They had come for plunder like the Dutch, but they stayed to grow sugar. And sugar plantations required a ready supply of labor—

A tropical Amsterdam, complete with canals: the great Dutch port of Batavia, on Java (1682).

unfree labor. The Caribbean Indians were becoming extinct, thanks to smallpox, massacres, and slave labor exacted by Spain. The interloping powers therefore brought their own labor with them. On Barbados, white small farmers who cultivated tobacco gave way in the 1640s and 1650s to large, efficient plantations grouped around great sugar mills. At first white contract labor worked the plantations. These "indentured servants" worked off the price of their passage to the New World by years of servitude. But white labor could not compete with black slaves from Africa. Slaves were virtually unlimited in supply and cost less than whites—slavery was for life, not three, five, or seven years.

African rulers, Arabs, and Portuguese had pioneered the slave trade long before the discovery of the New World. The Portuguese had experimented with slave cultivation of sugar on Madeira. Extending that savage system to the New World required the transportation across the Atlantic of almost a million Africans in the course of the seventeenth century. Death rates ran as high as 20 percent during transport inside Africa and another 20 percent on the Atlantic crossing. Disease and

ill-treatment prevented the slave populations in the New World from reproducing enough to increase their numbers. Expanding the sugar economy thus required the import of ever-greater numbers of slaves. A triangular trade pattern developed—Europeans took goods such as weapons, rum, or tobacco to Africa, bartered them for slaves whom the kings of west Africa had seized from neighboring tribes and kingdoms, and exchanged the slaves in the West Indies for tropical goods that included molasses from which to make more rum. As the Portuguese slowly lost control of the west coast of Africa, the Dutch, English, and French stepped in to supply slaves to their own sugar islands and—through smuggling—to the plantations of Spain. Slavery, whether in the European colonies, the Islamic world, or Africa itself, had as yet attracted little attention as an institution of peculiar cruelty.

North America: The Dutch, the French, and the English

North of the sugar islands lay an immense waste of swamp and woodland: North America. Its only known resources were the codfish off Newfoundland and the furs and timber of its great forests. But three powers nevertheless attempted settlements there in the hope of breaking Spain's near-monopoly of the New World. The failure of Sir Walter Raleigh to found a colony in Virginia during the 1580s revealed some of the difficulties. Cold winters and poor soil made the creation of a tropical plantation economy difficult. Hostile natives were still relatively strong. Planting a permanent colony in North America required the transport of a large labor force and its support over many years until the settlement achieved self-sufficiency. That demanded capital, numerous emigrants, and unshakable determination.

The Dutch and French failed both demographically and economically. The Dutch explored the Hudson River in 1609 and had settled New Amsterdam on Manhattan Island by 1624. But their colony of "New Netherland" never became more than a center for trade and fur exports. The English seized it in 1664, immediately before the second of their wars with the Dutch (see p. 514).

The French excelled in the backwoods. Jacques Cartier discovered the St. Lawrence River in 1535 and Robert de La Salle coursed the Mississippi in 1682. France's explorers and fur-trading *coureurs de bois* ("wood runners") were more adventurous and France's Jesuit missionaries more determined than the New World representatives of any other European state except perhaps the Portuguese of Brazil. By 1605 French settlers had planted villages in Acadia, and in 1608 Samuel de Champlain founded Québec. By 1640 perhaps 3,000 French inhabited Canada, but the population had reached only 10,000 by 1700.

Growth was slow because the French government succeeded too well in imposing French absolutism and social patterns on its colonies. It regulated and stultified economic life while granting land in large blocks to a few proprietors under semifeudal conditions. Except under Colbert in the 1660s and 1670s, it gave French peasants little inducement to emigrate. For religious reasons it strictly barred from Canada all Huguenots, who took their economic talents to the English colonies instead. A cluster of French settlements spread across the St. Lawrence Valley, but the English settlers to the south far outnumbered the "New France" of lords and peasants.

England's constitutional and religious struggles spurred emigration. English governments, whether Stuart or Cromwell, encouraged colonizing projects but left great latitude to individuals or joint-stock companies in founding colonies. Above all, English governments allowed religious

The inhabitants of the New World, as seen in the 1580s by John White, one of the leaders of Raleigh's failed attempt to establish a colony on Roanoke Island, Virginia.

minorities to settle in English colonies. That speeded mightily the growth of an enterprising, independent, and rapidly multiplying population.

The Virginia Company planted England's first successful colony at Jamestown in 1607. It almost failed, but then the settlers discovered the rage in Europe for a native weed, tobacco. That cash crop paid for the manufactured goods they needed from England—and ultimately for African slaves to cultivate the tobacco. The small band of religious dissenters who landed at Plymouth in 1620 lost half their number during the first winter. But the Massachusetts Bay Company, which founded Boston, was able to profit by the Pilgrims' experience. In 1630 it transported 900 settlers across the ocean in a large and well-planned operation. Thanks in part to Laud's persecution of dissenters, the population of Massachusetts had swelled within ten years to about 14,000. By 1650 the population of "New England" was about 20,000. The settlers were soon shipping fur, fish, and timber to England.

By 1700 the English colonies held almost 200,000 settlers and dominated the continent. Twelve colonies existed, offshoots of the original settlements or created by royal grants. Georgia, the thirteenth, was founded in 1732. And unlike New France, which suffered under a royal central administration of Québec, the English colonies were in effect self-governing. Each colony acquired an elected representative assembly that passed its laws and controlled taxation. A royal governor appointed by London was in theory not responsible to the assembly. But because the governor generally depended on the assembly for his salary, his executive power and London's reach were in practice limited. In the 1660s Parliament did its best to impose mercantilist practices by requiring the export of some colonial goods exclusively to England in English or colonial ships. Those restrictions caused much complaint and smuggling. After the Glorious Revolution of 1688 (see p. 515) London gradually became less insistent on asserting its authority. The colonists accepted regulation of their trade so long as enforcement was lenient.

Unlike the colonial subjects of all other powers, the inhabitants of British North America thus became increasingly accustomed to self-government. Without conscious design, England had fashioned a new kind of empire. Armed trade had been the foundation of the Portuguese and Dutch empires. The empire of Spain placed a ruling class of soldiers, planters, and missionaries in command of large native populations. But the Protestant English felt none of the responsibility for the Indians that weighed upon the missionaries of Spain, nor could the English exploit the labor of the thinly settled Indian populations of North America. Instead, the English settlers and the Dutch of New Holland simply displaced the natives. England transferred an entire European population to a new environment and allowed it to blend institutions brought from home with innovations that new surroundings demanded. The result was a unique, unplanned experiment in economic, political, and religious freedom.

Russia Reaches the Pacific

While France and Britain were pushing westward across North America, the Muscovite state was pressing eastward from the Ural Mountains across Siberia toward the Pacific. Muscovy reached the Pacific first; no ocean separated its new dominions from the center of its power around Moscow. In 1581 groups of Cossacks—the "pioneers" or "frontiersmen" who had earlier pushed back Tartars and Turks and had settled the lower valleys of the Dnieper, Don, and Volga rivers—struck eastward from the Urals. Their fierce leader, Yermak, enjoyed the patronage of Tsar Ivan IV, the Terrible. Like the French in Canada, the Cossacks sought furs, particularly the incomparable sable. They therefore followed the pine forests and the northern tundra rather than the open plains to the south. The innumerable rivers and lakes of Siberia allowed the Cossacks, like the French *coureurs de bois,* to flow swiftly eastward, occasionally halting to found fortified outposts.

The Cossacks reached the Pacific in the early 1640s, three generations and

3,000 miles after their eastward movement began. Unlike America, no great mountain chains barred the way. Resistance from the small Tartar states and the numerically weak tribal peoples of Siberia was slight. The advanced civilization of China ultimately checked Muscovite expansion in the Amur River valley. In 1689, Russia and China concluded their first treaty at Nerchinsk, and Russia withdrew from the Amur basin for almost 200 years.

Like the English, the Cossacks sought freedom as well as furs. Their early communities in Siberia were as wild and lawless as the later towns of the American West. But like the French administration in North America, the despotism of the tsars soon reached out across vast distances to clamp its administration and taxes on the lucrative fur trade. By 1700 several hundred thousand Russians had settled Siberia. By the end of the century, Russian traders had ventured across the Bering Strait to Alaska and down the North American coastline in search of seals. Long before the English in America reached the Pacific, the Russians had through individuals daring and government backing staked a claim to the northern half of Asia and had reached out toward the Western Hemisphere.

The first half of the seventeenth century was thus a period of fierce turmoil both within Europe and in Europe's relations with the wider world. The French monarchy consolidated itself but remained vulnerable to its turbulent nobles. The English monarchy for a time collapsed. From 1618 to 1648 the states of central Europe—and outside powers from France to Sweden—fought the last and bloodiest of the wars of religion. European economic and population growth faltered under the battering of wars, epidemics, and the "little ice age." Yet Europe's expansion into the outer world continued ceaselessly, if less swiftly than in the sixteenth century. The rise of Europe's new territorial states continued; new theories and methods of statecraft and new economic techniques made them bastions of order and relative prosperity in a violent and anarchic world. Yet after 1600, one state rose so high that it threatened to overthrow the balance of power on which Europe's state system rested.

Suggestions for Further Reading

General

D. Ogg, *Europe in the Seventeenth Century* (1925, 1960), and G. N. Clark, *The Seventeenth Century* (1931), offer useful surveys. G. Parker, *Europe in Crisis* (1979), reflects recent work in the field. For a model comparative analysis of the upheavals that convulsed most early modern states, see P. Zagorin, *Rebels and Rulers, 1500–1660* (1982). M. S. Anderson, *War and Society in Europe of the Old Regime, 1619–1789* (1988), surveys one powerful force for change.

The Great Powers

For events in France, see the detailed survey of R. R. Treasure, *Seventeenth Century France* (1966). C. V. Wedgwood, *Richelieu and the French Monarchy* (1962), and C. J. Burckhardt, *Richelieu: His Rise to Power* (1964), are informative. P. Goubert, *The Ancien Regime: French Society, 1600–1750* (1973), is excellent on French social structure. On England, see especially C. Hill, *The Century of Revolution, 1603–1714* (1961); L. Stone, *The Causes of the English Revolution, 1529–1642* (1972); and C. V. Wedgwood, *The King's Peace, 1637–1641* (1955), and *The King's War 1641–1647* (1958). M. Ashley, *The Greatness of Oliver Cromwell* (1966), and C. Hill, *God's Englishman* (1970), deal in lively fashion with a central figure. P. Laslett, *The World We Have Lost,* 2nd ed. (1971), gives an enthusiastic introduction to England's seventeenth-century social history. S. Schama, *The Embarrassment of Riches* (1988), is entertaining on the culture and politics of the Dutch Republic. On events in central Europe, see especially R. W. J. Evans, *The Making of the Habsburg Monarchy* (1979); C. V. Wedgwood, *The Thirty Years' War* (1938); and G. Parker et al., *The Thirty Years' War* (1974).

The European and World Economies

On Europe's economic crisis, see especially C. M. Cipolla, *Before the Industrial Revolution* (1976); F. Braudel, *Civilization and Capitalism, 15th–18th Centuries* (1982); and *The Cambridge Economic History of Europe,* Vol. 4 (1967). C. McEvedy and F. Jones, *Atlas of World Population History* (1978), provides the best set of—admittedly speculative—population figures.

For relations between Europe and the world, see particularly J. H. Parry, *The Age of Reconnaissance* (1964), and J. H. Elliott, *The Old World and the New* (1970). A. W. Crosby, *The Columbian Exchange* (1972), and *Biological Imperialism: The Biological Expansion of Europe, 900–1900* (1986), provide elegant treatments of neglected but decisively important events.

20

ABSOLUTISM AND CONSTITUTIONALISM 1660–1715

The last half of the seventeenth century was the age of France. Its population of roughly 18 million in 1650 dwarfed the 7.5 million of Spain and the roughly 5 million of England. Its economy and its bureaucratic-military machine were the largest in Europe. Much of Europe imitated its culture, a subject treated more fully in the following chapter.

But French power had limits. Internally, high taxation, government regulation of the economy, religious persecution, and oppressive censorship stunted economic growth. Externally, Louis XIV's attempts to dominate Europe created a series of coalitions against France. In the two great worldwide conflicts of 1689–97 and 1701–15, England, the Dutch Republic, and Habsburg Austria compelled even the "Sun King" of France to recognize the law of relations between states: the law of the balance of power.

Other powers declined with giddying speed, or stagnated. Sweden, outclassed militarily thanks to its small population, ceased to be a great power. The Ottoman Turks mounted their last great threat to western Europe, and then began the decline that soon made their empire the "sick man" of the state system. The internal anarchy and external decline of Poland that led to its disappearance from the map between 1772 and 1795 became visible. Spain sank further. The Dutch settled down to enjoy their riches.

Winners emerged as well. Austria defeated the Turks and consolidated the Habsburg hereditary possessions into a state more centralized than anything before it in south-central Europe. England took command of the outer seas from the Dutch, as the Dutch had taken it from Portugal. Russia, until now a backward power outside the European system, suffered the first of the barbaric "revolutions

The Sun King's emblem.

from above" that transformed it into a military giant. And the uncouth electorate of Brandenburg, an obscure state on the eastern fringes of Germany, began its fateful rise to great power status.

THE FRANCE OF LOUIS XIV

Louis XIV, the "Sun King" (r. 1643–1715), was the living symbol of French military, political, and cultural domination. He was born in 1638 and took power decisively into his own hands the day after Mazarin's death in 1661. He died at the age of 77 and left the throne to his great-grandson. By temperament and training he incarnated divine-right monarchy—the notion that hereditary kingship was the only divinely approved form of government, that kings answered to God alone for their conduct, and that subjects owed absolute obedience to their king as the direct representative of God on earth. His education was sketchy, and he had little imagination and no sense of humor. But he had the qualities needed to rule—a willingness to work relentlessly, a commanding presence, and an imperious will.

Louis may not have spoken the famous words ascribed to him—"I am the state." But he practiced them. He sought to personify the concept of sovereignty. He took a deep interest in the elaborate etiquette and ceremonies of his court, for they dramatized his supremacy over the nobility. He also conducted the business of the state in person, as his own "first minister," from Mazarin's death in 1661 to his own in 1715, a dedication uncommon in monarchs. He set his preferred pastimes of hunting and womanizing aside when the state demanded it. "If you let yourself be carried away by your passions," he once remarked, "don't do it in business hours."

The administrative machine that served Louis XIV culminated in a three to five member "High Council" of great ministers that met with him almost daily. Professional "secretaries" at the head of bureaucracies then executed the decisions taken in council. In the provinces, the *intendants,* the royal administrative officers that Richelieu had created, received ever more power to enforce the king's will.

Three great ministers of middle-class origin—Jean-Baptiste Colbert, Michel Le Tellier, and his son, the Marquis de Louvois—directed the administration under the king's close supervision. Colbert, cold, gloomy, and fanatically precise, served as Controller General of Finance. He cut waste, streamlined the tax system, and gave France its first serious attempt at

---

Bishop Bossuet on Absolutism

Jacques Bénigne Bossuet was tutor to Louis XIV's son in the 1670s, and the most zealous and prominent theorist of the king's absolutism.

The royal power is absolute. With the aim of making this truth hateful and insufferable, many writers have tried to confound absolute government and arbitrary government. But no two things could be more unlike. . . . The Prince need render an account of his acts to no one. . . . Without this absolute authority the king could neither do good nor repress evil. . . . God is infinite, God is all. The prince, as prince, is not regarded as a private person: he is a public personage, all the state is in him; the will of all the people is included in his. As all perfection and all strength are united in God, so all the power of individuals is united in the person of the prince. What grandeur that a single man should embody so much! . . .

From Jacques Bénigne Bossuet, "Politics Drawn from the Very Words of Scripture," in Readings in European History, *ed. by James Harvey Robinson (Boston: Ginn, 1906), Vol. II, pp. 275–76.*

1589	1610	1616	1643		1715		1774	1793
Henry IV		Louis XIII		Louis XIV		Louis XV		Louis XVI
	Regency	Richelieu	Mazarin		Regency			

1624   1642   1661   1723

an annual budget. He sought to force France's economic growth by punitive tariffs against the Dutch, state-supported industrial projects, and colonial enterprises. He doubled the king's net income between 1661 and 1671. Le Tellier and Louvois, the ministers of war, then spent the proceeds.

The old French monarchy had imposed its authority through its law courts, the *parlements*. It had also frequently consulted provincial assemblies or the Estates General of France. The new monarchy that Richelieu had founded and Louis XIV perfected imposed its authority and its taxes by decree. Louis XIV checked the pretensions of the *parlements* and deliberately neglected to summon the Estates General. The new army paid for by Louis XIV's taxes mobilized French manpower and militarized French society to an unprecedented extent. It also provided the force to crush—often with mass hangings—the many attempts at tax rebellion in the provinces. Above all, the king completed Richelieu's work of destroying the political power of the French nobility.

The Domestication of the Nobility

The Fronde had forced Louis XIV to flee Paris three times, and had left him fiercely determined to break the turbulent nobility. His principal weapons were three: First, he denied the nobility its traditional share in the power of the state and sharply curtailed its independent power in the provinces. He chose his ministers almost exclusively from commoners, rotated *intendants* to prevent collusion with the local nobility, and treated *parlements* and provincial assemblies with contempt. Second, he cheapened the status of the nobility by increasing its numbers; the title of marquis soon became almost a joke. Finally, he required the high nobility to serve him at court.

That service was bound up with Louis XIV's deliberate display of himself as the symbol of the state. In 1683 he moved court and government from the Louvre palace in central Paris to Versailles, fifteen miles away. There he made his home in the formal gardens and ornate chateau that he had built on marshland, at great cost in lives and treasure.

Louis XIV on the Duties of a King

In the 1660s and 1670s, Louis XIV and his staff prepared notes to instruct his son in the art of ruling.

I have often wondered how it could be that love for work being a quality so necessary to sovereigns should yet be one that is so rarely found in them. Most princes, because they have a great many servants and subjects, do not feel obligated to go to any trouble and do not consider that if they have an infinite number of people working under their orders, there are infinitely more who rely on their conduct and that it takes a great deal of watching and a great deal of work merely to insure that those who act do only what they should and that those who rely tolerate only what they must. The deference and the respect that we receive from our subjects are not a free gift from them but payment for the justice and the protection that they expect to receive from us. Just as they must honor us, we must protect and defend them, and our debts toward them are even more binding than theirs to us, for indeed, if one of them lacks the skill or the willingness to execute our orders, a thousand others come in a crowd to fill his post, whereas the position of a sovereign can be properly filled only by the sovereign himself.

. . . of all the functions of sovereignty, the one that a prince must guard most jealously is the handling of finances. It is the most delicate of all because it is the one that is most capable of seducing the one who performs it, and which makes it easiest for him to spread corruption. The prince alone should have sovereign direction over it because he alone has no fortune to establish but that of the state.

From Louis XIV, Memoirs for the Instruction of the Dauphin, *ed. by Paul Sonnino (New York: Free Press, 1970), pp. 63–64.*

The medal on the left (1661) celebrates the young Louis's purported accessibility to his subjects. The one on the right (1685) extols the new discipline and professionalism of his armies.

The palace of Versailles (1686), with the king arriving by carriage.

Louis moved with impassive dignity through the innumerable court gatherings in the mirrored halls of Versailles. Years of self-conscious practice in kingship had given him a public façade—cool, courteous, impersonal, imperturbable—that fitted perfectly the artificiality of the small world of the court, as far removed from reality as Versailles itself was physically removed from the bustle of Paris. In that atmosphere, a ball seemed as important as a battle, and holding the basin for the king's morning ablutions became a task as coveted as the command of armies. Instead of competing in the provinces for political power against the monarchy, nobles squandered their fortunes in jockeying for prestige under the king's vigilant eye.

He left the nobility one other outlet—war. Military service harnessed the nobility's inborn aggressiveness to the purposes of the state. But that outlet also had a political cost. It created a noble "war party" at court that encouraged the king's own megalomania.

The Destruction of the Huguenots

The only potential challenges to Louis's absolutism besides the nobility were religious forces and groups. The king clashed with several popes who disputed his "Gallican" claim to control the Church in France. But those quarrels never led to a break with Rome, for in doctrine Louis XIV was strictly orthodox. And after 1680 he became increasingly concerned about the fate of his own soul. When his queen, Maria Theresa, died in 1683, he gave up all mistresses except the pious Madame de Maintenon, whom he secretly married. The king's growing piety naturally expressed itself politically. The wars of religion were over, but in the late seventeenth century religion and affairs of state remained tightly intertwined.

Louis XIV enthusiastically persecuted the Jansenists, an austere group of Catholic "puritans" who emphasized the teachings of St. Augustine on original sin, human depravity, and the need for divine grace. Louis, whose confessors were Jesuits, thought the Jansenists impertinent in their disapproval of his numerous mistresses, and subversive as well, for the pope had condemned them. In 1710–12 Louis razed their principal monastic center to the ground.

But it was the Huguenots, one of the most loyal and industrious groups in France, who felt the full force of Louis XIV's religious enthusiasm. Two religions under one prince was indeed, by seventeenth-century standards, an anomaly. And the French clergy had long insisted that the continued existence of Protestantism in France was an insult to the king's dignity and authority. After 1679 Louis apparently embraced the idea of atoning for his own numerous sins of the flesh—and his negotiations with the Otto-man Turks, enemies of Catholic Habsburg Austria—by crushing heresy in France.

He began by gradually tightening his interpretation of the Edict of Nantes, by which Henry IV had granted toleration to the Huguenots and ended France's religious civil wars in 1598. He forced Protestants to convert, destroyed their chapels, and quartered royal troops on their families. In 1685 he took the final step. At the urging of his Jesuit advisers, he announced that since all heretics had reconverted to Catholicism, the Edict of Nantes no longer served any purpose and was therefore revoked. The state closed all remaining Protestant churches and schools, and the Church baptized all Protestant children as Catholics. Louis enforced the revocation with imprisonment, torture, and condemnation to the galleys. Many Huguenots continued to practice their faith in secret. Perhaps 200,000, more than a fifth of the Protestant population of France, fled to England, the Dutch Netherlands, Brandenburg, and the New World. Their industry and skill contributed mightily to the rapid economic growth of their new homes.

The revocation of the Edict of Nantes was an act of religious intolerance that rivaled the Spanish expulsion of the Moriscos in 1609–14, the Habsburg ravaging of Bohemia after the battle of the White Mountain in 1620, or the systematic impoverishment and degradation of the Catholics of Ireland by English conquerors from Elizabeth I to Cromwell and his successors. But in those cases, unlike that of France, ethnic hatred had compounded religious savagery. The revocation of the Edict of Nantes was unique in the seventeenth century—a major act of barbarism that was *purely* religious in intention. It was the last such act in western Europe until Germany's attempt to exterminate the European Jews between 1941 and 1944.

Literature and Fashion: The Primacy of France

To dramatize his conception of kingship, Louis chose as his emblem the sun god, Apollo. The symbol of the sun, on whose rays all earthly life depends, became the theme of the architecture and sculpture of the new palace at Versailles. The "Sun King" patronized and presided over an "Augustan Age" of French culture. As befitted such a patron, the prevailing taste was classical. It emphasized form, order, balance, and proportion—the presumed ideals of reasonable individuals throughout history.

In 1636, Pierre Corneille (1606–84), the father of French classical tragedy, wrote *Le Cid,* the first of a series of powerful dramas that glorified willpower and the quest for perfection. Corneille was still active when Louis began his personal rule, but the dramatist's brilliant younger contemporary, Jean Racine (1639–99), soon eclipsed him. Racine wrote more realistically than Corneille about human beings in the grip of violent and sometimes coarse passions. He brought French tragedy to its highest perfection between 1667 and 1677. Then he underwent a religious conversion that caused him to renounce drama as immoral.

Some of the admirers of the tragedies of Corneille and Racine had little respect for the comic playwright Molière (1622–73), but his biting satirical drama became a model for future dramatists. From 1659 to his death he was the idol of aristocratic audiences at Versailles. All three playwrights concentrated on portraying types, not individuals—the hero, the man of honor violently in love, the miser, the hypocrite—embodiments of human passions and foibles that belonged to all times and places. Partly as a result, French classical drama of the age of Louis XIV was easily exportable. French literary standards influenced cultivated Europeans everywhere, although French literary creativity flagged in the later years of Louis XIV's reign, as religious persecution, political censorship, and economic exhaustion intensified.

In the other arts, and in social conventions, France likewise swayed the rest of Europe, although Louis XIV's growing religious intolerance and military aggressiveness prompted resistance to French culture, especially in Protestant republics

Engraving of a performance of Molière's last play, *Le Malade imaginaire* (1673). Molière died on stage on the fourth night of the performance.

such as the Dutch United Provinces, where middle-class art and manners flourished. French fashions in dress nevertheless spread across Spain, Italy, and much of Germany. The heavy French Baroque style, exemplified by Louis's palace at Versailles, broke the supremacy in architecture that Italy had enjoyed since the Renaissance. French became the language of diplomacy and polite conversation, and the court of the "Sun King" set the tone for countless smaller courts throughout Catholic Europe. As Florence had been the center of the Italian Renaissance, and Spain of the Counter-Reformation, so France in the late seventeenth century was the center of European politics, diplomacy, and culture.

France's Bid for the Domination of Europe

Richelieu and Mazarin had begun the process of creating a large, dependable standing army to replace the disorderly semi-mercenary, semi-feudal military system of the preceding century. Louis and his formidable ministers of war, Le Tellier and Louvois, completed the task. The ministers subordinated the aristocratic officer corps and the provincial private armies to royal authority, developed an efficient supply system, standardized the organization of infantry and artillery, and followed the example of Gustavus Adolphus by having the troops wear uniforms. The Seigneur de Vauban, the father of modern military engineering, invented the first effective bayonet and perfected the science of building—and smashing—fortifications in the age of gunpowder. Above all, Le Tellier and Louvois provided Louis with numbers. By the 1660s he possessed by far the largest and best-equipped army in Europe: 100,000 men in peace and up to 400,000 in war, numbers not seen in the West since the fall of Rome.

This unprecedented power inevitably brought the temptation to use it. War aroused the enthusiasm of the nobility and kept it occupied in ways that did not threaten the state. War exercised and justified the enormous and costly standing army. Above all, successful war enhanced the glory of the monarch, a glory that was Louis XIV's constant concern. Perhaps war would make him the arbiter not only of France but of Europe as well.

Louis XIV's first two wars (1667–68, 1672–79) were relatively limited in aim.

The decline of Spain and the collapse of the Holy Roman Empire left a power vacuum on France's eastern borders; Louis therefore sought to annex the Spanish Netherlands (later Belgium), Franche-Comté, and parts of western Germany and to reduce the Dutch to vassalage. In each of the two wars, alliances that at different times included the United Provinces, Sweden, and the Habsburg monarchy checked him after initial French victories. The Dutch held off his first onslaught in 1672 by opening their dikes and flooding the countryside. England simultaneously attacked the Dutch by sea but withdrew from the war in 1674. By 1678 Louis had gained only Franche-Comté and a few border fortresses in Flanders.

Thereafter, Louis briefly chose legal chicanery over musketry. He established French courts called Chambers of Reunion to "reunite" to France all lands on France's borders that had in the past been dependencies of French territories. That gave him control of the independent Protestant republic of Strasbourg in 1681, much to the indignation of the inhabitants and of Protestants throughout Europe. The revocation of the Edict of Nantes in 1685 provided further evidence of his arrogance.

In 1686 the Habsburg emperor, along with Spain, Sweden, and several German states, formed the defensive League of Augsburg. Habsburg victories in Hungary over the Turks, who were allied with Louis, shifted the balance in the West against Bourbon France. Louis replied with the most senseless atrocity since the Thirty Years' War—his armies systematically devastated the Palatinate, a rich region of western Germany, in 1688 simply to cow his enemies. That act instead helped weld them together. And French distraction in Germany allowed William of Orange, ruler of the Dutch Netherlands and Louis XIV's most implacable enemy, to claim the English throne in 1688–89. England and the Dutch, the two greatest economic and sea powers of the age, then joined the League of Augsburg and closed the circle around over-mighty France.

The participants' worldwide interests made this war the first *world* war, waged in India, the Caribbean, and North Amer-

The Conquest of Louis XIV   1661–1715

France before 1668

Acquisitions by the Treaty of Aix-la-Chapelle, 1668

Acquisitions by the Treaty of Nimwegen, 1678

Acquisitions by the Treaty of Utrecht, 1713

ica as well as in Europe. After ten years of fighting, France agreed to the Peace of Ryswick in 1697. Louis retained the gains made before 1678 but had to renounce nearly all conquests after that date except Strasbourg. England emerged from the war stronger than it had been in 1689, and France weaker.

The War of the Spanish Succession, 1701–14

The Peace of Ryswick lasted only four years. Louis had made peace in the hope of gaining a greater prize than any for which he had yet contended—the Spanish Empire. Charles II of Spain, bizarre end-product of generations of syphilitic degeneration and Habsburg inbreeding, and last of the Spanish Habsburg line that had ruled since 1516, was losing a 30-year struggle against numerous diseases. By 1697 he was close to death and had no direct heir. That raised an issue of vital

Officer and musketeer of the French Guard (late seventeenth century).

importance to all Europe: would the Spanish Empire fall to Emperor Leopold I of the Austrian Habsburg line, would it pass to the French Bourbon dynasty (for Louis XIV was both the son and the widower of Spanish Habsburg princesses), or would it be dismembered by its rivals?

England and the Dutch had obvious economic and strategic interests in preventing France from grasping Spain's colonial trade or the Spanish Netherlands. Louis seemed willing to compromise and twice concluded secret treaties that partitioned the Spanish dominions with the English and Dutch. But when news of the second treaty reached Madrid, the dying Charles II refused to see parts of his Catholic empire pass to Protestant powers. Instead, he made a will that left all his dominions to a grandson of Louis XIV. After the death of Charles II in 1699, Spain proclaimed that grandson King Philip V of Spain.

Louis XIV tore up the secret partition treaties, recognized the will of Charles II, and sent French troops to claim the Spanish Netherlands. In 1701 William of Orange formed yet another coalition against France. England, Holland, and Emperor Leopold I of Austria bound themselves to fight until they had ended the threat of Bourbon control of Spain and of the Spanish colonies. Louis had made his last and most far-reaching bid for the domination of Europe. But this time his enemies were as unyielding and powerful as he was.

Warfare had by now become thoroughly professional. In the long wars since 1618, innovators such as Gustavus Adolphus, Maurice of Orange, Le Tellier, and Louvois had replaced noble amateurs and independent military contractors with professional officers corps that bore the "king's commission." Ragged bands of freebooters yielded to disciplined ranks rigidly drilled in the new fire tactics. The combination of musket and bayonet united fire and shock in one weapon and drove out the clumsy combinations of pikemen and musketeers that had ruled the battlefield since the Spanish victory at Pavia in 1525. Commanders learned to coordinate infantry, the new mobile artillery, and cavalry. Sieges, thanks to Vauban, became scientific exercises.

In the new world war of 1701–14, the French soon found themselves outdone. Two commanders of genius led the Allied armies—England's John Churchill, first Duke of Marlborough, and the great Habsburg general and scourge of the Turks, Prince Eugene of Savoy. Marlborough's diplomacy held the ramshackle coalition together. His generalship smashed the great armies of Louis XIV in four battles of unprecedented slaughter that cost France up to 80,000 casualties—Blenheim (1704), Ramillies (1706), Oudenarde (1708), and Malplaquet (1709). England trounced the French at sea and seized Gibraltar, from which it thereafter dominated the western Mediterranean. An allied army even invaded Spain and several times took Madrid.

Louis XIV, with France exhausted militarily and in the grip of famine, sued for peace in 1709–10 on almost any terms. The Allies thereupon demanded that he send French troops to help expel his own grandson from Madrid. That was too great a humiliation. Louis XIV refused, and appealed with success to his subjects. Famine and economic crisis filled the French armies with new recruits, who preferred the risks of the battlefield to the certainty of starvation. An anti-foreign reaction in Spain helped drive the English and Austrian invaders out. In 1710 the English war party, the Whigs, gave way to the Tories, and a war-weary England recalled Marlborough. In 1712 the French severed Prince Eugene of Savoy's communications and forced him to retreat. It was the Allies' turn to seek peace.

The Peace of Utrecht, 1713–14

In theory, the Peace of Utrecht of 1713 and other treaties of 1714 that ended the war of the Spanish Succession gave France the prize that Louis had sought since 1701. Louis's grandson remained on the throne of Spain—but only on condition that no subsequent Bourbon should unite the crowns of Spain and France. And Louis gave up all conquests east of the Rhine and his bid for the Spanish Netherlands and Spain's colonial trade. France survived as the greatest single power. But the war had drained it of money and blood, and had made Louis XIV's government bankrupt and hated. When the great king died at last in 1715, France's common people reputedly "openly returned thanks to God."

England was the chief victor. It emerged from the war with the dominance of the seas that it held until the twentieth century. From France it took Newfoundland, Acadia (modern New Brunswick and Nova Scotia), and the Hudson's Bay Territory. It kept Gibraltar and Minorca, seized from Spain, and received the *Asiento*—the profitable privilege of supplying African slaves to the Spanish colonies.

The Austrian Habsburgs gained the Spanish Netherlands (which now became the Austrian Netherlands) and replaced Spain as the dominant power in Italy through the acquisition of Milan, Naples, and Sicily. Two new smaller powers, Brandenburg-Prussia and the Duchy of Savoy, increased their territories and prestige; they had chosen the winning side. The Dutch achieved their minimum war aim—they kept the Scheldt River closed, thus blocking the trade of Antwerp, the chief port of the Austrian Netherlands. But the long strain of fighting France for almost half a century had demoralized them. They could no longer compete at sea with England and soon slipped from the ranks of the great powers.

The Peace of Utrecht ended the first bid for European hegemony since the days of Philip II of Spain. Louis XIV's attempt to gain for France the domination of western Europe and the wider world had summoned up, through the workings of the balance of power, the coalition that had checked France. War had prevented the universal domination of one power. The European state system had survived a challenge to its very existence.

ENGLAND: THE EMERGENCE OF PARLIAMENTARY MONARCHY

While Louis XIV consolidated absolute monarchy in France, the English created a constitutional monarchy controlled by Parliament. The restoration of king, Parliament, and Anglican Church in 1660 had established a balance between Crown and Parliament. But that balance had remained unstable. Who was to exercise sovereignty—the king, or the gentry and merchants of Parliament? What would the religious settlement be, and who would make it? Who would control foreign policy? These questions had dominated the preceding forty years of turmoil and civil war. They still awaited answers.

Charles II and the "Cavalier Parliament"

Charles II (r. 1660–85), unlike his too stubborn father, was witty, attractive, worldly, a king of hearty sexual appetites and shrewd political sense. He had lived long in exile in France and took his cousin Louis XIV as his model. Charles was resolved not to risk exile or execution in the manner of his father. He instead hoped to restore England to Catholicism and to establish a French-style absolute monarchy through stealth, manipulation, and compromise. That ambition Charles II pursued through 25 years of court intrigue, party politics, and secret diplomacy that kept both Parliament and ministers guessing about his intentions.

The "Cavalier Parliament" of 1661–79 held a commanding position at the beginning of the reign. It was the preserve of the gentry, and of the aristocracy, now partly restored to its ancient influence in both local and national government. Both groups were for the moment strongly royalist and determined to stamp out all remaining political and religious radicalism. But they also had no intention of allowing the Crown to be financially independent of Parliament.

In place of the old idea that "the king should live of his own," Parliament now granted Charles a regular income from customs and excise duties. But it was not enough to meet even the ordinary expenses of government, let alone the expenses of Charles's wild doings at court or of his numerous mistresses and illegitimate children. And foreign war was unthinkable unless Parliament voted money. Charles therefore allowed Parliament, under the leadership of his father's adviser, Edward Hyde, Earl of Clarendon, to have its way for a time.

The House of Commons, on the Great Seal of England (1651).

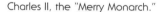
Charles II, the "Merry Monarch."

Parliament thus dictated the religious settlement. The Cavalier Parliament was as strongly pro-Anglican as it was pro-royalist. Between 1661 and 1665 it passed statutes known inaccurately as the "Clarendon Code"—Clarendon himself favored toleration—that excluded from local government Puritans who "dissented" from the established Church and purged Puritan ministers from the Anglican clergy. Later legislation barred dissenters from Parliament, from service in the army or navy, and from the universities at Oxford or Cambridge.

Puritanism and social radicalism appeared to be intertwined. The Cavalier Parliament was therefore determined to stamp out the first and discourage the second. But while the Clarendon Code lowered the social status of dissenters and narrowed their opportunities, it did not greatly decrease their number. Presbyterians, Congregationalists, Baptists, and Quakers formed persistent religious minorities that bitterly opposed both Anglicanism and Catholicism. Charles himself sought toleration as a first step to restoring Catholicism. In 1672 he issued a "Declaration of Indulgence" that suspended the operation of the Code against both Puritans and Catholics and appeared to assert—in the manner of Charles I—that royal prerogative could thwart acts of Parliament. Parliament forced him to withdraw the Declaration and imposed on him a Test Act that excluded non-Anglicans from civil and military office. To the Anglican gentry of Parliament, Puritans remained radicals and Catholics traitors.

Foreign Policy: The French Alliance

Two natural calamities, a fierce outbreak of bubonic plague that killed 60,000 of the 450,000 inhabitants of London in 1665 and a fire that destroyed much of the city in 1666, contributed to widespread unrest. Public opinion blamed the fire on an imaginary Catholic plot. Uneasiness increased as king and Parliament drifted apart over foreign policy. In 1665 Parliament forced Charles into a war with the Dutch over trade, but denied him the money needed to win. When swift victories did not follow, Parliament unfairly held Clarendon responsible and exiled him.

After Louis XIV began his attack on the Spanish Netherlands in 1667, English opinion began to see the military power of Catholic France as more threatening than the commercial rivalry of the Protestant Dutch. But Charles held to his connection with Louis, and in 1670 Charles allied England with France against the Dutch through the notorious secret Treaty of Dover. In the Treaty, Louis XIV offered money and French troops if Charles were to declare himself a Catholic and reconvert England to Catholicism.

Charles was probably unsure of how far down that road he meant to travel. He did acquire both a pro-French foreign policy and a French mistress who reported secretly to Louis XIV's ambassador. English forces also attacked the Dutch along with the French in 1672. Between 1675 and 1681 Charles concluded with Louis four additional secret agreements in which he undertook to thwart Parliament's anti-French moves in return for more French money. The existence of this close understanding with Louis inevitably leaked out and created fear of French domination and a return to Catholicism. The landed classes represented in Parliament were increasingly suspicious of Charles II and prone to panic.

London's catastrophic great fire of 1666.

Whigs and Tories: The Origins of Modern Party Politics

In 1678 these accumulated fears exploded in the lurid "Popish Plot." A disreputable former Anglican clergyman named Titus Oates concocted a story about a Jesuit plot to kill the king, to place his Catholic brother James, Duke of York, on the throne with French help, and to massacre England's Protestants. Parliament described it as "a damnable and hellish plot, for assassinating and murdering the king and rooting out and destroying the Protestant religion." A new civil war seemed about to break out.

The Earl of Shaftesbury, a great land-owner who had fought for Parliament in the Civil War, rallied a "Country Party" that campaigned fiercely to exclude James from the succession to the throne. In response, an Anglican and royalist "Court Party" assembled, although at first without much enthusiasm, to support Charles II and his brother. The Court Party denigrated the Shaftesbury group as "Whigs," a name hitherto applied to Scottish Presbyterian rebels. The Whigs in turn baptized their antagonists "Tories," a kind of Irish Catholic brigand.

The Whigs controlled the three brief Parliaments that followed the dissolution of the Cavalier Parliament in 1679. Shaftesbury and his associates merrily pressed the execution of some 35 Catholics for alleged complicity in the imaginary Popish Plot. But the Whig leaders overplayed their hand. Opinion swung back toward the king, and it was soon the turn of the Whigs to suffer. By 1681 Shaftesbury had fled abroad, the inventors of the Popish Plot were disgraced or executed, and Charles II was stronger than any monarch since the early days of James I. Until his death in 1685 Charles ruled without Parliament, with his brother James by his side and with the subsidies of Louis XIV filling his coffers.

These difficult years were nevertheless momentous for the West's tradition of political liberty. This struggle between the king and factions of the gentry in Parliament created the ancestors of modern political parties—groups organized for the purpose of electioneering and of controlling government through a representative assembly. Whigs and Tories were in part the descendants of the Parliamentarians and Royalists of the 1640s. But the great crisis of the 1680s produced, instead of civil war, the system of Parliamentary rule that England later passed on to its colonies and indirectly to the West as a whole.

The "Glorious Revolution" of 1688

James, Duke of York, succeeded his brother Charles II in 1685 as James II (r. 1685–88). He was a bigoted convert to Catholicism who lacked Charles's shrewdness and flexibility. Within three years he had infuriated almost every political and religious group of importance in England, and had provoked the revolution that Charles II had succeeded in avoiding.

Early successes made him overconfident. He introduced Catholics into the high command of both army and navy, and camped a standing army a few miles from London. He surrounded himself with Catholic advisers and attacked Anglican control of the universities. He claimed the power to suspend or dispense with acts of Parliament. In a vain attempt to win the support of Puritans as well as Catholics, he issued a Declaration of Indulgence along the lines of his brother's—thus further alienating the Anglican establishment. By revoking borough charters and browbeating sheriffs, he tried to ensure the election of a Parliament favorable to his policies. These measures, along with the example of Louis XIV's revocation of the Edict of Nantes in 1685, terrified England's Protestants.

The event that triggered James II's downfall was a happy one—the unexpected birth in June 1688 of a son to his Catholic queen. Until then, Protestants had consoled themselves with the thought that James II's two elder daughters by another marriage, Mary and Anne, were Protestants, and would succeed James. Now the existence of a Catholic male heir prolonged the Catholic absolutist threat indefinitely into the future. But unlike the events of 1641, the king had no "king's party." He had alienated Anglicans and

James II, who swiftly alienated even traditional supporters of the monarchy (engraved after a painting by Sir Godfrey Kneller, 1688).

dissenters, Tories and Whigs, aristocracy and commoners. The result was a bloodless "revolution," a rapid and fundamental political change that established the limited or parliamentary monarchy that has persisted to the present.

The agent of James II's downfall was William of Orange, *stadholder* and hero of the Dutch Republic, the man who had opened the dikes to halt the French invasion in 1672. In 1677, in pursuit of allies against France, he had married James II's eldest daughter, Mary, and had thus acquired a claim to the English throne. In June 1688 a group of prominent Englishmen, both Whigs and Tories, invited William to cross the English Channel and save the Protestant cause in England. That November William landed a Dutch army on the southern coast and marched slowly toward London. The countryside rose against James II, and William tactfully allowed the friendless king to flee to France. An improvised Parliament declared that James had abdicated the throne by flight and invited William and Mary to become joint sovereigns on condition that they ac-

cept a "Bill of Rights" that severely limited royal power.

This bloodless "Glorious Revolution" established at last the sovereignty of Parliament, which had made a king. William was strong-willed, but his priorities were continental and Dutch—the forging of an ever more powerful coalition against Louis XIV. He therefore grudgingly accepted Parliament's conditions. The "Jacobite" supporters of James II and his son invaded Ireland in 1690 and staged two bloody rebellions in the Scottish Highlands in 1715 and 1745, but all attempts at a second Restoration failed. Parliament had won. England had decisively rejected the French absolutist model of Louis XIV.

The Bill of Rights emphatically barred the king from suspending acts of Parliament or interfering with the courts. It furnished a base for the steady expansion of civil liberties in the generation after 1688. Parliament established religious toleration and freedom from arbitrary arrest. Censorship of the press quietly withered. The king had to summon Parliament annually, for he could neither pay nor control his

The speaker of the House of Lords offers William and Mary the English crown (from a contemporary engraving).

armed forces without parliamentary consent. Regular meetings of Parliament in turn strengthened the political parties and made the king dependent on their support. The monarch vetoed a parliamentary bill for the last time in 1707.

Hobbes Answered: John Locke and the Theory of Limited Government

The English Civil War and Glorious Revolution followed the Dutch revolt against Spain as the second of the Western revolutions that ended absolute monarchy and ultimately led to democratic representative government. Tradition demanded that English leaders in 1641–49 and 1688–89 deny that their acts were revolutionary. Parliament chopped off the head of one king and replaced another in the name of the *traditional* "liberties of England." But that half-fiction was unsatisfactory.

John Locke (1632–1704), a friend of the Earl of Shaftesbury who had founded the Whig party, provided a theoretical foundation for what Parliament had done and for the subsequent evolution of representative government. Locke probably wrote most of his *Of Civil Government: Two Treatises* while in political exile in Holland in 1683–89, but it emerged from the presses in 1690 as a belated rationale for the acts of Parliament during the Glorious Revolution. In it he at last answered Thomas Hobbes's justification of absolute sovereignty with a convincing theory of limited government.

Locke attacked the divine-right theory of monarchy and challenged Hobbes's claim that the only alternative to anarchy was absolute authority. Locke's first principle was that all individuals possess a natural right to "life, liberty, and property." That notion was revolutionary in an age of entrenched privilege. It remains revolutionary in our own, in which dictatorships or narrow oligarchies rule much of humanity. Locke derived the rest of his system from this premise of "natural rights," and from a more optimistic view of human nature than that of Hobbes. Like Hobbes and many predecessors and contemporaries, Locke argued that government was a contract in which humanity exchanged the anarchy of the "state of nature" for the security that government provided. But Locke's insistence that human rights were "natural" and prior to all government allowed him—unlike Hobbes—to limit the authority of government. The source of sovereignty, thanks to the natural rights of the governed, was the governed themselves: "The people alone can appoint the form of the commonwealth." It therefore followed, for Locke, that a government that acted without the consent of the governed dissolved the contract and gave the subjects a right to resistance or to revolution.

Locke also provided a principle for organizing government. Fearing concentration of power, he proposed a strict separation of powers that would allow the elected representatives of the people to check a tyrannical executive. Above all, he relentlessly emphasized property as the foundation of all freedom and the purpose of government itself: "The great and chief end. . . . of men's uniting into commonwealths and putting themselves under

John Locke (1632–1704), champion of "natural rights" and government by consent.

Locke on Government by Consent 1690

Compare with "Bishop Bossuet on Absolutism," page XXX.

Men being, as has been said, by nature all free, equal, and independent, no one can be put out of this estate and subjected to the political power of another without his own consent, which is done by agreeing with other men, to join and unite into a community for their comfortable, safe, and peaceful living, one amongst another, in a secure enjoyment of their properties, and a greater security against any that are not of it. . . . When any number of men have so consented to make one community or government, they are thereby presently incorporated, and make one body politic, wherein the majority have the right to act and conclude the rest. . . . Absolute, arbitrary power, or governing without settled standing laws, can neither of them consist with the ends of society and government, which men would not quit the freedom of the state of Nature for, and tie themselves up under, were it not to preserve their lives, liberties, and fortunes, and by stated rules of right and property to secure their peace and quiet.

From John Locke, Of Civil Government: Two Treatises (New York: Everyman's Library, 1924), pp. 164–65, 186.

government is the preservation of their property." Some twentieth-century commentators have denigrated what they describe as Locke's doctrine of "possessive individualism," his equation of property and liberty—but have failed to offer examples of societies that enjoy liberty without property.

In the eighteenth century, Locke's ideas were a powerful rationale for a society based on wealth rather than on inherited privilege and for a new kind of government, limited in its powers. Inalienable natural rights, government by consent, the right of revolution, and the sanctity of property seemed increasingly "self-evident" to Englishmen after 1688, and ultimately to the American colonists in 1776.

The Emergence of the Cabinet System

At the level of practice rather than theory, factional struggles in Parliament replaced struggles between king and Parliament after 1688. The Glorious Revolution made gentry and merchants the real masters of both central and local government in England. Generally speaking, aristocratic landowners, bankers, merchants, and most dissenters were Whigs, while the smaller gentry, the Anglican parish clergy, and some great lords were Tories. But parties were still loosely organized, and small cliques often held the balance of power.

Given the fluidity of parliamentary alignments and the monarchy's residual powers, it took more than a century for a smoothly operating system of constitutional government to emerge through the slow accretion of precedent. The ultimate answer was the "cabinet system."

Under Charles II, a "cabinet council," or inner circle of important ministers had taken shape. Gradually the members of this "cabinet" discovered that settling major issues among themselves and then presenting a united front to the king was the most efficient way to conduct business. A leader—the "prime minister"—inevitably emerged within the cabinet.

During the reigns of William and Mary (1689–1702) and of Mary's sister, Queen

Anne (1702–14), monarchs still considered their ministers responsible to the crown rather than to Parliament. But to gain Parliament's support in war or peace both William and Anne found it advisable to choose their ministers from the majority party in Parliament. By Queen Anne's death in 1714, real power in England was slowly falling into the hands of a cabinet of ministers who controlled a parliamentary majority, often by bribery, and who felt themselves ultimately responsible to the political interests of the landed and moneyed classes represented in Parliament. By almost imperceptible stages, the world's first—and most influential—representative parliamentary government was evolving.

The Religious Settlement

The Glorious Revolution also produced an unprecedented measure of religious toleration. The fanaticism unleashed in the Civil War had given religious intolerance a bad name, and both Anglicans and Puritans were now more afraid of Catholic France than of one another. In addition, King William, thanks to the Dutch Republic's unique tradition of toleration, insisted on a religious truce. The result was the "Toleration Act" of 1689, which allowed dissenters to worship as they pleased and to educate their clergy and laity in schools of their own. Most of the existing anti-Catholic statutes, along with the acts excluding dissenters from civil and military offices remained in effect, but after 1689 their enforcement lacked vigor.

The Act of Settlement of 1701 provided that the sovereign should always be an Anglican Protestant. That finally quieted fear that a Catholic might succeed to the throne. The act also settled the succession, in case James II's two daughters should die without children, on the descendants of the daughter of James I who had married the ill-fated Frederick V of the Palatinate before the Thirty Years' War. That provision brought the Elector of Hanover to the throne in 1714, when Queen Anne died without direct heirs and ended the Stuart dynasty.

Medal of Queen Anne (1702–14).

Ireland and Scotland: Coercion and Union

Civil War and Glorious Revolution also indirectly furthered the unification of the British Isles. England, Ireland, and Scotland had all had the same king from the time of James I's succession in 1603, but union went no further than the common crown. The two smaller kingdoms, especially Ireland, suffered greatly during the seventeenth century from involvement in England's religious and political struggles.

The native Irish were Catholic; Protestant England therefore despised them and feared them as potential allies of Catholic Spain and France. To cope with that strategic threat, James I had settled Protestant colonists in the northeastern province of Ulster. But the Ulster Protestants were Presbyterians and soon became anti-Stuart, while the Catholic Irish were generally loyal to the Stuart dynasty. In 1641 the Catholics revolted. Cromwell crushed them with fire and terror in 1649, and massacred the Catholic garrisons at Drogheda and Wexford (" . . . being in the heat of action, I forbade them to spare any that were in arms in the town."). In 1690, James II landed in Ireland with French troops and Catholic support, but William of Orange routed him at the Battle of the Boyne. The much-celebrated anniversary of that Protestant victory remains to the present day an occasion for religious bloodshed in Ulster. After the Boyne, English and Irish Protestant landlords systematically persecuted the Catholic Irish and their religion, while reserving both economic and political power for themselves.

The Scots, who had given England a king in 1603, had somewhat better fortune. Scotland had only a sixth of England's population, but its Protestantism, its long tradition of parliamentarism, its military power, and its poverty—which made it unrewarding as prey—enabled it to make a satisfactory bargain. Scottish resistance to the imposition of Anglicanism had triggered the crisis that ultimately led to Civil War in 1642. Nevertheless, much of Scotland, especially the Highlands inhabited by the turbulent and ruthless Catholic clansmen, remained strongly attached to the native Stuart dynasty. From 1650 to 1745, the clans provided a base for risings in support of the Stuarts. The Scots parliament accepted the Revolution of 1688 but refused the Act of Settlement of 1701. It threatened to choose a king of its own—possibly the exiled pretender James II—if James II's last daughter, Anne, died without producing an heir.

That threat frightened England into serious negotiation. In 1707 the Whig government and the Scots agreed to an Act of Union that eliminated the risk that Scotland might choose a separate monarch and created the kingdom of "Great Britain." Scotland retained its own laws and its Presbyterian state religion but surrendered its separate parliament in return for representation in London and full participation in the dynamic English economy. The loss of political independence and the coming of a money economy even to the wild Highlands caused disgruntlement, especially among the clans. But the Act of Union was successful, unlike England's difficult relationships with Ireland or with the colonies in America. Scottish merchants and administrators helped build the British empire. Scottish philosophers, economists, and historians contributed mightily to the widening of human knowledge in the eighteenth century known as the Enlightenment (see pp. 543–48).

The Growth of British Power

A final consequence of the Glorious Revolution, after parliamentary government, religious toleration, and the settlement with Scotland, was to unite crown and Parliament on foreign policy and to turn the energies of the next generations from domestic conflict to foreign war. Given England's fear of Catholicism, William of Orange had no difficulty bringing his new kingdom into the Grand Alliance against Louis XIV, who had given refuge to James II. Parliamentary monarchy soon demonstrated that it was more deadly to its enemies than Stuart absolutism. The government of William and his successors was able to raise money, the sinew of war, in ways that only the Dutch could match.

Anti-Catholic woodcuts showing the "prodigious cruelties" of religious warfare in Ireland (1689).

In 1694 William's Whig ministers created a Bank of England to mobilize England's growing commercial and financial power against France. Within a few days of its founding, the Bank had raised over a million pounds of investors' money, and it promptly lent the money to the government at 8 percent interest. The resulting permanent national debt was a revolutionary instrument. It financed the defeat of Louis XIV and provided the foundation for the subsequent commercial and maritime supremacy of Britain. Throughout the next century British wealth, transmuted into ships of the line, gave the island kingdom a striking power out of all proportion to its size and population. The Peace of Utrecht of 1713 gave British sea power a position without serious rivals. Britain's victory heralded the elimination of France as a colonial competitor and Britain's domination of the world outside Europe.

CENTRAL AND EASTERN EUROPE, 1648–1721

An imaginary line running north from the Adriatic Sea to the Elbe River that flows into the North Sea divided the economy

The Economic and Social Division of Europe

of early modern Europe into two sharply defined halves. West of that line, the towns and their trade were increasingly dominant. The majority of the population still lived on the land, but most peasants were free workers and many of them small landowners. Most serfs had become agricultural wage laborers in and after the crisis of the Black Death. Most nobles had become landlords who hired labor for wages, or simply lived on rents from tenants. Though still a minority, the urban middle classes were growing in influence.

East of the line, in Hungary, Bohemia, Poland, Prussia, and Russia, lay a land of lord and peasant. Towns were small, poor, and weak. Noble estates were larger and the landed nobility far more powerful politically than in western Europe. And in the sixteenth and seventeenth centuries, noble power was still growing. Grain prices rose with the price revolution of the sixteenth century, and the growth of the trading networks centered on Antwerp and Amsterdam offered export markets. That situation provided an economic rationale for the imposition of a "second serfdom" in eastern Europe. The nobles sought to lower labor costs by binding their peasants to the land and imposing on them two to five days a week of compulsory labor. The profits they earned on exports in turn further increased the nobles' power. And in politics, the states of eastern Europe encouraged and promoted noble domination. Either the state *was* the nobility, as in Hungary or Poland, or it made a tacit bargain that delivered the peasants to the nobility in return for noble service to the state, as in Brandenburg-Prussia and Russia.

As in western Europe, states were machines for power. They had to be, for the flat plains of central and eastern Europe offered no "natural frontiers" to check the invader. A state could remain a state only if it had an army. But the gunpowder revolution of the fifteenth century had so raised the costs of armies that only strongly centralized states with relentless tax systems could afford them. Few such states existed in central and eastern Europe in the seventeenth century. Most eastern rulers faced the same obstacles to centralized government that western rulers had faced two centuries or more before—a powerful landed nobility, a church that owned large portions of the land, a middle class too small to bear the weight of heavy taxation, desperately poor agriculture, limited commerce, infant industries, and a peasantry tied to the land and thus incapable of meeting the need of new industries for labor.

The Holy Roman Empire

The one large political organization that bridged eastern and western Europe was the Holy Roman Empire. But the Thirty Years' War had left it a political fiction. A Habsburg remained emperor and a Diet or deliberative assembly met "perpetually" at Regensburg after 1663. But the Empire had no common army, administration, taxes, laws, calendar, or tariffs. It included perhaps 1,800 political units and petty rulers, including free cities, free imperial knights, Church principalities, and the kingdom of Bohemia. The Peace of Westphalia had recognized the full sovereignty of the 300 or so larger units within the Empire and had accorded France and Sweden the right to take part in the Diet's deliberations. This Empire, as Voltaire (see p. 545) remarked in the mid-eighteenth century, was "neither Holy, nor Roman, nor an Empire."

The ruling families of a few large states—Bavaria, Saxony, Hanover, Brandenburg, and Austria—sought to expand their territories and prestige by war or marriage. Augustus the Strong of Saxony, in addition to fathering, according to legend, more than 300 children, secured election in 1696 as king of Poland. In 1701 the Elector of Brandenberg obtained the emperor's consent to style himself "king in Prussia." And in 1714 the Elector of Hanover became king of Britain. But only two great powers emerged from the wreck of the Holy Roman Empire—Austria and Brandenburg-Prussia.

The Habsburgs: Europe and Austria Defended

The attempt of Emperor Ferdinand II (r. 1619–37) to revive and strengthen the Empire under Habsburg control collapsed in the Thirty Years' War. The Habsburgs of Vienna thereafter turned to a policy that Ferdinand had also fostered. They sought to consolidate and expand their hereditary lands in Austria and the Danube Valley into a centralized monarchy that could hold its own against the states of western Europe. The chief architect of that policy was Emperor Leopold I (r. 1658–1705), with the help and occasional prodding of capable civil servants and a remarkable general, Prince Eugene of Savoy.

Achieving the Habsburg objective required the reduction of Austria, Bohemia, and Hungary to obedience. In the Duchy of Austria and neighboring Tyrol, Leopold's lawyers established his ascendancy over the nobility. Bohemia was even less of an impediment. The Emperor Ferdinand II had smashed its native Czech nobility after the Battle of the White Mountain in 1620, and in 1627 had made the previously elective crown of Bohemia a hereditary possession of the Habsburg family. Hungary, on the fiercely contested border between the West and Islam, was different. Although the Habsburgs had usually been the elected monarchs there since early in the sixteenth century, the Ottoman Turks directly or indirectly ruled almost two-thirds of the kingdom. The Hungarian Protestants were numerous and inclined to fear the Turks less than they feared the Catholic Habsburgs.

But the Ottoman Empire was no longer the power that had taken Constantinople in 1453, smashed the Hungarians at Mohács in 1526, and sought Mediterranean mastery at Lepanto in 1571. The Ottomans failed to keep pace with the West in technology, above all in the technology of war. Their metal-working, their cannon and handguns, remained those of the sixteenth century. Ottoman logistics and tactics likewise failed to match the growing professionalization that overtook war in the West during and after the Thirty Years' War. But Ottoman troops nevertheless remained fearsome in the attack and tenacious in defense. And after 1656, the Ottoman central government briefly revived under a vigorous line of grand viziers (first ministers to the Sultan), the

The crown of the Holy Roman Empire of the German Nation, used from 961 to 1792.

Prince Eugene of Savoy, who ended the Ottoman Turk threat to central Europe.

Köprülü family. In the 1660s the Ottomans began a new thrust up the Danube Valley against their Habsburg antagonists.

But Austria prevailed in the end. From July to September 1683 a Turkish army of more than 100,000 besieged Vienna after laying waste to everything in its path. Volunteers rushed to Austria's aid from all across the Continent. The greatest pope of the century, Innocent XI, proclaimed Europe's last crusade against Islam. A coalition army under the leadership of King John Sobieski of Poland descended from the heights outside Vienna upon the Turks and routed them. For the next sixteen years, Austria and its allies fought their way laboriously back down the Danube Valley. In 1697, Prince Eugene of Savoy at last broke the Turkish army at the battle of Zenta, near the present Serbian-Hungarian border. Turkey ceased to be a threat, and soon became a victim.

The resulting Peace of Carlowitz in 1699 gave the Habsburgs all of Hungary. The Emperor crushed the Hungarian Protestants and executed many of them for treason. The Hungarian nobility retained its serfs and privileges in return for recognizing the ultimate sovereignty of Vienna. But the Habsburgs imprudently left local administration to the nobility and failed to create a uniform, centralized system of administration for all their possessions. Eugene's victories nevertheless established a strong state in the Danube Valley where none had existed before. The Treaties of Ryswick in 1697 and Carlowitz in 1699 thus marked the emergence of the two new great powers that had risen to check the overbearing ambition of Louis XIV—Britain and Austria. And two further contenders for great power status had also begun their ascent—Brandenburg-Prussia and Russia.

The Curious Rise of Brandenburg-Prussia, 1614–1701

Prussia, the power that emerged from the obscure Electorate of Brandenburg, was the most improbable of all seventeenth- and eighteenth-century claimants to great—power status. The Habsburgs and even the primitive Grand Duchy of Muscovy had extensive territories. The Hohenzollern dynasty that created Prussia had been mere margraves—counts of a "mark," or frontier province—in Brandenburg since 1417. The one distinction of the small, sandy, barren principality around Berlin was that after about 1230 it was one of the seven "electorates" of the Holy Roman Empire, states whose rulers—at least in theory—voted to elect the emperor.

In the early seventeenth century, by the accidents of dynastic inheritance, the Hohenzollern family acquired two further territories of importance—the Duchy of Cleves and some neighboring lands on the Rhine in 1614, and the Duchy of Prussia on the Baltic coast to the northeast in 1618. The total population of all Hohenzollern possessions was perhaps 1.5 million. The provinces lacked defensible boundaries, standing military forces, and a central administration other than the household of the Elector. Each of the provincial estates jealously guarded its inherited privileges. Nothing suggested that these territories had the makings of a powerful state, especially after the Thirty Years' War had devastated Brandenburg. Berlin had lost more than half its population, and the Hohenzollern dominions as a whole had probably lost almost one-third of their people, a loss that took forty years to make up.

One man changed this situation. Frederick William of Hohenzollern, the Great Elector (r. 1640–88), was the first of the line of remarkable rulers that made Prussia. Born in 1620, he succeeded to power in 1640 after an education in Holland that had emphasized the latest in statecraft and technology. A devout Calvinist, he had learned toleration from the Dutch. In an age of fanaticism he respected the Lutheranism of his subjects. Above all, he learned from the helplessness of Brandenburg. "A ruler is treated with no consideration if he does not have troops and means of his own," he advised his son in 1667. "It is these, Thank God! which have made me considerable since the time that I began to have them."

Frederick William, the Great Elector, painted by his contemporary, Mathias Czwiczeic.

He inherited in 1640 a poorly equipped and mutinous army of 2,500 men. Before the end of the Thirty Years' War in 1648 his ceaseless efforts had increased it to 8,000 disciplined troops; by his death in 1688 he had a peacetime force of 30,000 that could expand to 40,000 in time of war. In the 48 years of his reign, the Great Elector built upon Brandenburg-Prussia's meager population the strongest military power in Germany, except for Austria.

That achievement rested on administrative centralization and the crushing of the provincial estates that largely controlled taxation. In Brandenburg he struck a bargain with the Estates in 1653 that provided a lump sum with which he raised further troops. The force in turn allowed him to collect taxes without further votes by the Estates, which—like Louis XIV— he never summoned again. In Prussia, far to the east, the townsmen were more stubborn than in Brandenburg, and the hard-bitten nobility, the *Junkers* (from *Jungherr*, "young lord"), proved unruly. The provincial opposition turned to Poland for support, but Frederick eventually crushed its resistance and executed its leaders. After campaigns against both Poland and Sweden, he also secured clear title to Prussia, which he had originally held as a fief from the king of Poland.

Despite some setbacks, Frederick nevertheless set up a tax system under civil servants of his own choosing that extended to all his territories. He deprived the nobility of the power it had exercised through the Estates and pressed it into state service as officers in the new standing army. In return, he confirmed and strengthened Junker control over the serfs. Power, not the betterment of the lowly, was the Great Elector's objective.

But against the background of the Thirty Years' War, the creation of the standing army and the order it brought was nevertheless a contribution to the welfare of the population. Devastation by foreign armies was even worse than Junker oppression. Moreover, Frederick William helped revive and improve agriculture after 1648 and encouraged industry and commerce. He made Brandenburg a haven for religious refugees—Lutherans, Calvinists, and large numbers of Huguenots after Louis XIV revoked the Edict of Nantes in 1685. These immigrants, together with Dutch, Swiss, and other newcomers, brought new skills in agriculture and industry, helped increase the population, and added considerably to the strength of the state. He welcomed even the more radical Protestant sects and the Jews but drew the line at the Jesuits, whom he considered too intolerant.

Frederick William's foreign policy was cautious. He sold his support to a succession of temporary allies in return for subsidies that helped pay for his army, while avoiding heavy fighting. The Swedes came close to Berlin in 1675, but he drove them off at the battle of Fehrbellin, a sign of Brandenburg-Prussia's rise and of Sweden's decline.

The recognition in 1701 of the Great Elector's son as Frederick I, "King in Prussia" (that is, in the province of Prussia, outside the boundary of the Empire), symbolized the appearance of a new power in Europe. In 1720, at the end of the Great Northern War that paralleled in eastern Europe the War of the Spanish Succession, the Hohenzollerns gained Pomerania and the vital port of Stettin from Sweden.

Prussia, as the Hohenzollern lands became known, had in eighty years transformed itself from a chance collection of feeble provinces into a state on the threshold of great power status. The weakness of its neighbors, rivals, or overlords—Sweden, Poland, Russia, and the Empire— gave it the opportunity. But this "Sparta of the North" rose primarily through its own efforts, through its army. All states in the fiercely competitive European system were machines for war, but Prussia devoted to its military relatively more of its population, resources, and energies than any other state. The army was the first institution common to all the Great Elector's lands, and its supporting bureaucracy was the model for Prussia's later organs of civil government. The nobility served the state in the army and bureaucracy and came to identify itself with state and army to an extent without parallel elsewhere.

That army, the army that conquered true great-power status for Prussia in the coming wars of the mid-eighteenth century, *was* the Prussian state.

Russia: Peter the Great's Revolution from Above

To the east of Prussia, Sweden, Poland, and the Ottoman Empire, no great power existed in the seventeenth century. The only contender was Muscovy, a state closer in constitution to the Ottoman Empire than to anything in Europe. As in the Ottoman Empire, India, and China, the Muscovite tsar "owned" his territory and his subjects, who enjoyed no rights against the state. That was no accident. Muscovy acquired its statecraft from Byzantium, and above all from the Mongols, its overlords from around 1240 until 1480 (see pp. 344–45).

The rulers of Muscovy were fully conscious of their uniqueness. They ridiculed the "limited" monarchs to the west as "men under contract" to their subjects and representative assemblies. In a letter addressed to Queen Elizabeth I of England in 1570, Tsar Ivan the Terrible had mocked her as no true sovereign but as one who had "men who rule beside you, and not only men, but trading boors." In Russia, even nobles lacked rights—even property rights—against the state; Ivan broke the hereditary nobility, or *boyars,* by torture, massacre, and wholesale confiscation of land in the 1560s and 1570s. He largely replaced them with a new "service nobility" that owed abject obedience to the autocrat. Scorn and hatred of foreigners characterized Muscovy's external relations. The alternation of despotism and anarchy marked its internal politics.

The unlamented death of Ivan the Terrible in 1584 indeed led to anarchy: a "Time of Troubles" that lasted until the coming in 1613 of the Romanov dynasty, which ruled Russia until 1917. Thereafter, religious strife compounded the weakness of the state. A reforming leader of the Orthodox Church, Patriarch Nikon, provoked a devastating schism in the 1660s by revising ritual and liturgy to bring them closer to the original Greek text of the Bible. That exasperated the traditionalist masses, to whom the Old Slavonic texts were sacrosanct. The Church split into a shallowly based state church and fiercely independent sects of "Old Believers" who braved execution and exile for their faith. As many as 20,000 may have burned themselves to death in the belief that the end of the world was at hand.

Abroad, Russia suffered defeats against Swedes, Poles, and Turks, and remained cut off from the Baltic and the Black Sea. English merchants made contact with Moscow in the 1550s by the icy route around Norway to the bleak port of Archangel on the White Sea. German merchants were also active in the capital. But Russia's chief import, then and later, was the West's technology, especially its military technology. Western culture—the Renaissance and Reformation—reached only as far as Catholic Poland.

In 1689, a new monarch, Peter I (r. 1682–1725), seized power at the age of seventeen in a palace coup. He was nearly seven feet tall, with inexhaustible energy and appetites, and a ferocious will. His insatiable curiosity led him to spend much time with the Dutch and Germans who lived in the "German Quarter" of Moscow. There he probably conceived the ambition of making Russia a great power by rapidly adopting Western technology, civil and military institutions, and customs. The partial realization of that ambition ultimately earned for him the title of Peter the Great.

Peter at first allowed others to rule for him. But in 1695 he ventured a first campaign against the Turkish fortress of Azov, where the Don River enters the Black Sea. The attack failed, but in 1696, with the help of Swiss, Dutch, and Habsburg experts, he built a fleet on the Don River, cut the fortress off from supplies and reinforcements, and stormed it. The lesson Peter I drew was that he needed additional Western experts to create a navy and to modernize his outmoded army.

In 1696–97, thinly disguised as a private citizen, Peter visited Holland, England, Germany, and Austria. There he learned how societies centuries ahead of

| 1462 | | 1613 | | | | | 1917 |

Grand Dukes of Moscow and First Tsars of Russia

House of Romanov

Peter I

Catherine II

1689   1725 1762   1796

Russia built ships, made munitions, and conducted government and diplomacy. He worked in the shipyards, eagerly questioned everyone he met about Western naval and military technology, and drank steadily through the night with his Russian companions. When he returned to Russia, he brought with him more than a thousand Western experts—seamen, gunners, shipwrights, engineers, mathematicians, surgeons.

An outburst of xenophobia at home cut short his European tour. The *strel'tsy*, a barbarous and undisciplined palace guard that he had thwarted in his seizure of power in 1689, remained a threat. In 1696, in league with the "Old Believers" and distrustful of Peter's increasingly obvious intention of introducing Western innovations, the *strel'tsy* marched on the Kremlin. Peter hastened back to Moscow to find that trusted aides had suppressed the revolt. He then made an example of the rebels that long haunted even the memories of his countrymen, accustomed to indiscriminate bloodshed. He executed a thousand *strel'tsy* to the accompaniment of torture on a scale not seen since Ivan the Terrible.

Peter also determined to use his autocratic sovereign power to "westernize" his subjects externally, by force if need be. In 1699–1700 he forbade the traditional long robes and the beards that his subjects wore in the belief that God was bearded and that man was made in his image. The tsar himself took a hand in the shaving of his courtiers. He fought the resulting antiforeign and Orthodox reaction with brutal repression. He also ended the seclusion of women and instituted Western-style social gatherings of both sexes at which polite conversation and ballroom dancing rather than strong drink were the chief entertainments. In his will to transform Russia, he brooked no opposition; when his son and heir Alexis showed himself a slothful dev-

otee of tradition, Peter I had him arrested, tortured, and put to death in 1618.

But Peter I's priorities were above all military. He sought first to imitate Western power, not Western civilization. Beginning in 1699, he set up a new army using German and other foreign experts as officers. An overwhelming defeat by the Swedes at Narva in 1700 only spurred him on; Russia either had to modernize its army or perish. The tsar encouraged the vital iron industry of the Urals, set up cannon foundries, and created schools for gunnery, navigation, engineering, and officer training. By 1709, the year of his great victory over Charles XII of Sweden at Poltava, Russia had a modern army of more than 100,000 troops. By the end of Peter's reign in 1725, that army had swelled to 210,000 regulars and 100,000 auxiliaries that included the dreaded Cossack cavalry. The navy had grown from nothing to 24 ships of the line. Those were powerful forces indeed for a state with a population of only 8 million.

The army, the largest in eastern Europe, had the chance to achieve results, for Russia was at peace only one year in all of Peter's long reign. In the south, Peter failed to hold Azov and had to leave the Turks to his successors. But in the Great Northern War, the tsar seized from Sweden the vital coastline on the Gulf of Finland. That gave him the "window on the sea," the direct contact with western Europe through the ice-free southern Baltic that was his primary geopolitical goal.

Peter's subjects, who bore the weight of his gigantic social engineering project, paid dearly for these military successes. The effect of Peter's sometimes haphazard social and fiscal legislation was to divide a relatively complex society with a variety of subtle status gradations into two great classes—the "service nobility," and the more or less enserfed peasantry. A century after Peter I, a Russian intellectual could

Contemporary cartoon of Peter cutting the beard of a Russian noble. Those who kept their beards had to pay a tax and carry a license *(below)*.

still quip bitterly that Russian society consisted of "slaves of the sovereign [the nobles], and slaves of the landlord [the serfs]; the former are called free only with regard to the latter."

Peter systematized the service nobility system he had inherited. All landowners owed service, and he decreed in 1714 the hated innovation of primogeniture, which forced noble younger sons off the land and into the army or navy. By instituting a fourteen-step "Table of Ranks" in 1722, Peter defined nobility in terms of one criterion alone, service. He made explicit what Louis XIV and the Great Elector could only practice—that service to the state, not birth, determined rank. In Russia, a lieutenant's commission now automatically brought noble status. That provided a career leading to ennoblement for the ambitious sons of commoners and helped divert them into state service and away from commerce and industry.

The peasantry, not the nobility, paid most heavily for Peter's innovations. In return for its service, the nobility gained a freer hand than ever before in dealing with serfs. A new tax census classified as a serf anyone whose position was doubtful. And the state demanded from the peasantry forced labor, military service, and taxes on an unprecedented scale. Supporting the new army required conscription, on the model of Sweden. After 1705 each twenty households had to furnish one recruit every year. The state provided the new military industries with serfs and convicts as labor, while a new head tax ("soul tax") tripled both state income and the tax burden. Forced labor and taxation, by one estimate, extorted from each household the equivalent of 125 to 187 days of labor each year. The ultimate result was depopulation, as peasants died of their privations or fled to the Don Cossacks to the southeast.

After 1709 Peter moved the seat of government from Moscow to a new city built on conquered territory on the Gulf of Finland: St. Petersburg, named for his patron saint. That change was the symbol of his aim to rival the West. The new city faced west, and its nearby naval base, Kronstadt ("royal city" *in German*),

claimed mastery of the Baltic. The methods that created the new capital, and its price, were also characteristic both of Peter's work and of that of later autocrats who sought to imitate him in Russia and in other backward states. St. Petersburg rose in an unhealthy marshland at the mouth of the Neva River and was a deliberate break with the Moscow-centered past. Peter compelled nobles and merchants to settle and build there. Construction proceeded rapidly through annual forced labor drafts of 20,000 peasants, many of whom perished from disease and exposure.

This new capital, founded on the bones of dead peasants, became the center of a new bureaucratic structure that Peter erected haphazardly over the primitive central administration he had inherited. The Western conception of "the state," as distinct from the private staff of the sovereign, now made its entry into Russian history. Peter set up provincial administrations, supervisory boards to coordinate the bureaucracy, and a "senate," or central administrative body to interpret his orders. He also created an organ, the *Preobrazhenskii Prikaz,* to ferret out "political crime," from tax evasion, to criticism of the tsar, to coup attempts. The deliberate vagueness of its charter, its sweeping authority, and its ruthless suppression of individuals for their political opinions rather than for their deeds made it the ancestor of the modern police state.

The new Russian state thus dominated its society in a way unknown even in Brandenburg-Prussia, much less in western Europe. The state mastered the Orthodox Church, already weakened by the great schism. After 1700 Peter neglected to appoint a patriarch and made the Church a mere department of his bureaucracy. The state defined the nobility by its service, and by demanding residence at St. Petersburg reinforced an already existing pattern of absentee landlordism that weakened the grip of the nobility on rural society. The state stunted the towns and ensured that the small and fearful middle classes that eventually emerged would be dependent on state employment and state contracts.

The bronze horseman: Peter the Great decrees the founding of St. Petersburg, Russia's window on the West.

The state then ordered its subjects to develop a consciousness, a public opinion. Peter was the first Russian sovereign to speak of "the common good." He founded Russia's first newspaper. He recognized that rivaling the West ultimately required voluntary collaboration from his subjects and the development of economic and intellectual initiative *from below.* But as his successors discovered, initiative from below was a deadly threat to the autocracy's own power. That tension, the result of grafting Western technology and military institutions onto non-Western social and political structures, was a pattern often seen later. Its consequence was a cycle of repression, "thaw," and further repression that has continued to the present.

But that ultimate consequence of Peter's work was far in the future when he died in 1725. What he left was a Russian great power, a military giant, irrevocably part of the European state system. And his example created a tradition of dynamic autocracy, of brutal revolutions from above carried through by pitiless force, that later Russian rulers sought to imitate or surpass.

The Losers: Sweden and Poland

While Prussia grew and Russia transformed itself, their Swedish and Polish neighbors declined. Sweden had burst on Europe as a military power of the first rank when Gustavus Adolphus swept into Germany in 1630–31. The Baltic virtually became a Swedish lake, with Swedish outposts that stretched from the Gulf of Finland to the North Sea. Copper, iron, and agriculture were Sweden's chief resources; superior cannon and muskets its chief military advantage. But Swedish power rested on shaky foundations. The country had a population of less than 2 million—not much larger than Brandenberg-Prussia or the Dutch Republic. The empire that Gustavus Adolphus had acquired was overextended; its enemies, from Russia and Poland to Prussia and Denmark, were hungry for revenge.

When young Charles XII (r. 1697–1718) came to the Swedish throne, a coali-

tion of Russia, Poland, and Denmark pounced on his Baltic territories. But Charles proved a greater commander even than Gustavus Adolphus. He crushed the coalition's forces in a series of lightning campaigns. Then success intoxicated him. In 1708–09 he launched Sweden into a foolhardy attempt to smash Russia and met devastating defeat at Poltava in the Ukraine. He subsequently escaped to Turkey, spent some years at the Ottoman court seeking allies, and died in the siege of an obscure Norwegian fortress in 1718. His meteoric career exhausted Sweden. In the peace settlements of 1719 to 1721 that ended this "Great Northern War," Hanover, Denmark, Prussia, and Russia divided up Sweden's Baltic empire. Sweden retired for good into the ranks of second-class powers.

Poland, an elective monarchy originally formed in 1386 through the union of the crowns of Poland and Lithuania (see p. 342), suffered a similar fate. Polish prosperity and culture had reached their peak

---

Peter the Great: The Bronze Horseman

The first and greatest modern Russian poet, Aleksandr Sergeyevich Pushkin (1799–1837), summed up Peter's place in Russian history in "The Bronze Horseman" (1833), named for the tsar's statue at St. Petersburg.

That square, the lions, and him—the one
Who, bronzen countenance upslanted
Into the dusk aloft, sat still,
The one by whose portentous will
The city by the sea was planted . . .
How awesome in the gloom he rides!
What thought upon his brow resides!
His charger with what fiery mettle,
His form with what dark strength endowed!
Where will you gallop, charger proud,
Where next your plunging hoofbeats settle?
Oh, Destiny's great potentate!
Was it not thus, a towering idol
Hard by the chasm, with iron bridle
You reared up Russia to her fate?

From Alexander Pushkin, Collected Narrative and Lyrical Poetry, *trans. by Walter Arndt (Ann Arbor: Ardis Publishers, 1984), p. 437.*

The Baltic: A Swedish Lake   1621–1721

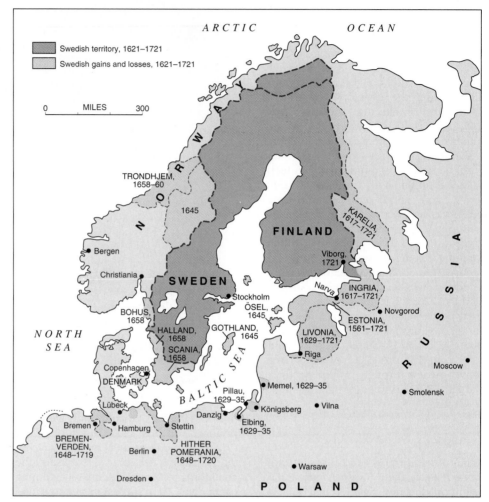

in the sixteenth century. Roman Catholicism had linked Poland to western Europe and had conveyed the influence of the Renaissance, the Protestant revolt, and the Counter-Reformation. But by the beginning of the seventeenth century Poland's economic and political decline had begun.

In France, Prussia, and Russia the state tamed the nobility. In Poland the nobility gradually became the state, thanks to the elective character of the monarchy. Until the 1570s the Polish nobility had usually elected the legal heirs of their monarchs. But thereafter they chose candidates who appeared to favor their own interests. By 1700 the nobility had deprived the monarchy of most of its powers.

Noble power had consequences. It sank the peasants as deeply in serfdom as anywhere else in Europe. It checked the small, weak towns, prevented the rise of urban middle classes, and froze the Polish economy in rural backwardness. Above all, it concentrated political power in the Polish Diet, which now represented only the nobility, since representatives of the towns no longer dared attend.

The Diet's procedure, tailor-made to preserve noble domination, was notorious—one negative vote, the "*liberum veto,*" could block any action. Moreover, the *liberum veto* allowed any member to "explode" a Diet session—to dissolve it and wipe out all legislation it had passed up to that moment. Of 57 Diets held in the century after 1652, all but nine "exploded." In one case a member cast a veto simply to see what would happen. And if by some accident legislation did emerge from the Diet, no machinery existed to enforce it against the provincial assemblies of lesser nobles or the private estate jurisdictions of the landed magnates. John Sobieski (1674–96), a native Pole of high integrity, was the last great king. He saved Vienna from the Turks but failed to save Poland from its nobility. After him, Poland declined into incoherence and eventual extinction at the hands of Austria, Russia, and Prussia between 1772 and 1795.

ABSOLUTISM, CONSTITUTIONALISM, AND THE BALANCE OF POWER

The half-century from 1660 to 1715 was thus a period of dramatic change. Internally, absolute divine-right monarchy reached its height in the France of Louis XIV. Powers from Madrid to St. Petersburg attempted to imitate the French model. Nevertheless, a few smaller peoples such as the Swiss had rejected monarchy in fa-

vor of republican government. The Dutch "Sea Beggars" had even shown that a republic could compete in the great-power arena. But it took England's Glorious Revolution and Marlborough's victories to demonstrate to Europe that even the greatest powers could choose alternatives to absolute monarchy.

Externally, relations between states and the workings of the balance of power almost completely superseded the religious-ideological conflicts that had rent Europe before 1648. France's bid for mastery after 1672 provoked the rise of England and Austria as great powers. Two great empires of the sixteenth century, Spain and the Ottoman Turks, continued their decline. Two peoples of limited resources and numbers, the Dutch and the Swedes, briefly claimed great-power status in the mid-seventeenth century but lacked staying power. Two new powers appeared in eastern Europe to join the balance—military Prussia and semibarbaric Russia. The rivalries of these states—Britain against France, France against Austria, Austria against Prussia, Austria and Russia against the Ottoman Empire—were the forces that moved European war and diplomacy after 1715.

Medals celebrating an abortive "Treaty of Eternal Peace" between Russia and Poland (1686). (*Above*) King John Sobieski, Poland's last great king. (*Below*) Personification of Poland and Russia.

Suggestions for Further Reading

Western Europe

J. Stoye, *Europe Unfolding, 1648–88* (1969), and J. B. Wolf, *The Emergence of the Great Powers, 1685–1715* (1951), provide useful introductions, but see also W. Doyle, *The Old European Order, 1660–1800* (1978). C. J. Friedrich and C. Blitzer, *The Age of Power* (1957), covers the general theme of this chapter. R. Hatton, *Europe in the Age of Louis XIV* (1969), is excellent on social history. P. Goubert, *Louis XIV and Twenty Million Frenchmen* (1970), wittily relates the career of the king to the

social history of France. See also J. B. Wolf, *Louis XIV* (1968), and W. H. Lewis, *The Splendid Century* (1954), an elegant account of the reign. On England, see especially C. Hill, *The Century of Revolution, 1603–1714* (1961). G. N. Clark, *The Later Stuarts, 1660–1714* (1934), is a fine synthesis. C. H. Wilson, *England's Apprenticeship, 1603–1763* (1965), covers England's emergence as a great power.

Eastern Europe

For the lands east of the Elbe, see especially S. H. Cross, *Slavic Civilization Through the Ages* (1948), and O. Halecki, *Borderlands of Western Civilization* (1952). On Germany, see H. Holborn, *A History of Modern Germany, 1648–1840* (1964). R. W. J. Evans, *The Making of the Habsburg Monarchy* (1979), and H. G. Koenigsberger, *The Habsburgs and Europe* (1971), are useful surveys. On Prussia, S. B. Fay and K. Epstein, *The Rise*

of Brandenburg-Prussia to 1786 (1937, 1964), is concise. See also F. Carsten, *The Origins of Prussia* (1954). B. H. Sumner, *Peter the Great and the Emergence of Russia* (1950), is a useful short account. For analysis, see especially R. Pipes, *Russia under the Old Regime* (1974), and J. Blum, *Lord and Peasant in Russia from the Ninth to the Nineteenth Century* (1961).

21

THE SCIENTIFIC REVOLUTION
AND THE ENLIGHTENMENT

ntil the seventeenth century the growth of knowledge about nature had been slow, fumbling, and frequently interrupted. Scholars had observed events in nature, had in many cases recorded them, and had sometimes derived useful generalizations from them. But "experiments" in the modern sense had been largely absent, and scientific inquiry was scarcely distinguishable from theological speculation.

That changed. By the eighteenth century, during the age of rapidly broadening and deepening knowledge that became known as the Enlightenment, the West had accumulated a large body of principles verifiable by experiment. Those principles in turn allowed the prediction and manipulation of nature. That type of knowledge has continued to accumulate, with revolutionary effect. The ever-accelerating understanding of and mastery over nature, for good or ill, was the achievement of the West, the first civilization in history to make a clear distinction between science on the one hand and religion or magic on the other.

THE SCIENTIFIC REVOLUTION

A new method of inquiry, later called the "scientific method," emerged from the universities of Western Europe in the late thirteenth and fourteenth centuries. After 1600 it achieved wide currency in western Europe. The new method was a combination of careful observation and controlled experiment with rational interpretation of the results, preferably using mathematics. That was the origin of modern science, an enterprise that a great twentieth-century mathematician-philosopher described as the "vehement and passionate interest in the relation of general principles to irreducible and stubborn facts."

The Medieval Universe

Precisely *why* the West took the lead in scientific speculation over the other great civilizations, China, Islam, and India, remains unclear. Even in the West, deep-rooted traditional assumptions about the nature of the universe dominated thought for centuries. Medieval learning dictated that the universe was a finite sphere with the earth at the center. Between the center and the outermost limit, nine transparent spheres supposedly carried stars, planets, sun, and moon in their daily revolutions about a motionless earth. The earth was the realm of change, decay, and original sin. The heavens were the realm of perfection and changelessness. Sun, moon, and heavenly bodies were perfectly spherical and moved in spherical tracks to the accompaniment of an ethereal "music of the spheres." The assumed dichotomy between heavenly perfection and earthly corruption demanded a sharp separation between the laws of heavenly and of earthly physics.

Even in the Middle Ages, not all scholars found this picture of the universe convincing. By the thirteenth and fourteenth centuries a small but increasing number had begun to question it, including Franciscan monks, perhaps inspired by their founder's sensitive feeling for nature. The study of the Greco-Arabic scientific texts that had reached the West stimulated a group of scholars at Oxford and Paris to apply mathematical reasoning to problems of physics and astronomy, such as motion and acceleration. Professors at the University of Padua continued these speculations in the fifteenth and sixteenth centuries. At Padua, a center of medical training for three centuries, scholars vigorously debated the proper method of studying nature in the course of arguments about Aristotle. The medieval universities kept interest in science alive and nurtured the first faint beginnings of the scientific revolution.

Most Europeans of 1500, however, did not question the Greek authorities, who had decreed that the normal state of everything in the universe was a state of rest. Aristotle had said that bodies moved only if a mover pushed or pulled them. Galen of Pergamum, in the second century A.D., had described the anatomy of the human body so convincingly that doctors still saw it through his eyes. In that same century, the Greco-Egyptian astronomer Ptolemy had compiled mathematical descriptions of the observed movements of the planets so ingenious that European authorities saw no need to discard them until after 1500. Ptolemy assumed that all motion in the heavens was circular and proceeded at a constant rate. But because the observed pattern of actual planetary motion in the heavens was not precisely circular, Ptolemy had invented the "epicycle," an additional small circle in which the planet moved while traveling around the circumference of its larger "sphere" around the earth. He and his successors needed eighty epicycles to force the observed motion of the planets to fit the theory, but in the end Ptolemy's system

The observatory of the Danish astronomer Tycho Brahe was the finest of the sixteenth century. Note the domes protecting the instruments.

explained what astronomers saw. Even more important, it permitted the prediction of lunar and planetary motion with some precision. At the close of the Middle Ages, few scholars saw much need to improve upon the observations and theories of the ancients.

The Background of Change

Nevertheless, forces in European society in the fourteenth, fifteenth, and sixteenth centuries prepared the way for a challenge to this orthodoxy. Artisans and craftsmen gradually adopted techniques more advanced than those of their medieval predecessors. Ever-smaller and more precise pocket watches took their place alongside the massive mechanical clocks of the medieval cathedrals. The development of the glass industry and the invention of the lens at some point before 1300, to take but one example, gave the promise of vastly extending humanity's ability to observe natural processes. Breakthroughs in shipbuilding and navigation (see p. 451) permitted the voyages of discovery, which in turn stimulated interest in nature generally.

The Renaissance, with its emphasis on literature and art and its veneration for the wisdom of the ancients, was in some respects hostile to the new science. But the Humanists were interested in Greek scientific texts as well as in Greek literature, and Renaissance patrons of artists were also patrons of inventors and technicians. Humanistic study revealed that ancient scientific authorities had differed among themselves on key issues, just at the moment when the authority of Galen and Ptolemy was becoming shaky for other reasons. Anatomical studies by the great Renaissance artists and the increasing practice of dissection suggested that Galen had made mistakes. Growing skill in mathematics exposed the clumsiness of Ptolemy's calculations. By the opening years of the sixteenth century, conditions were ripe for a dramatic shift in the West's underlying assumptions about the universe.

Vesalius and Copernicus: Observation and Calculation

In 1543 two notable scientific works heralded the end of medieval science. Andreas Vesalius, a Flemish anatomist at the University of Padua, published *On the Structure of the Human Body,* a marvelously careful description of human anatomy based on direct observation during dissection, and illustrated with accurate plates. Vesalius did not free himself completely from the authority of Galen, nor did his book offer much theoretical insight. But it was an influential example of the power of observation.

Even more powerful in its ultimate effect was the work of a Polish scholar, Mikolaj Kopérnik, better known as Copernicus. *On the Revolutions of the Heavenly Bodies* was a brilliant mathematical treatise that showed how to reduce Ptolemy's 80 epicycles to 34 by assuming that the earth turned on its axis once a day and moved around the sun once a year. Unlike Vesalius, Copernicus was not primarily an observer. During study at Padua in the early years of the century he had learned that some ancient authorities had held that the earth moved. That assumption made the motions of the moon and planets far simpler to explain mathematically than the medieval earth-centered theory. Copernicus, following the equally medieval notion that "nature always acts in the simplest ways," eventually discarded Ptolemy on grounds of logic, rather than from observation. His ideas gradually spread.

In 1600, the Inquisition tried a former monk named Giordano Bruno as a heretic and burned him at the stake in Rome. He had published works arguing that the universe was not a closed sphere but infinite in extent, that numberless suns and planets like our own filled it, and that God was equally present in every planet or atom in the cosmos. He also maintained that the existence of the infinite made it impossible to arrive at absolute truth, or find limits to the extent of knowledge. Copernicus had inspired him, although Copernicus himself believed in the finite

The Copernican revolution: the new sun-centered solar system.

sphere of the fixed stars and the uniqueness of the earth. Despite the fires of the Inquisition, Bruno's intuition of the infinity of the universe ultimately prevailed. It was the beginning of modern cosmology.

The Purposes and Method of Science: Bacon and Descartes

Two major prophets of the early Scientific Revolution, Francis Bacon (1561–1626) and René Descartes (1596–1650), followed Copernicus. Bacon, an English lawyer, statesman, and essayist, waged a vigorous scholarly battle against the deductive method of medieval scholasticism, which began with premises usually taken on authority and deduced from them their logical consequences. That might help to organize truths already known, argued Bacon, but it could never discover new truths. Only inductive reasoning, starting from direct observation of phenomena

and developing principles that explained them, could produce new truths.

Bacon set a practical goal for science, the "domination" of humanity over nature. He pictured an imaginary future society of scientists whose end was to benefit mankind by conducting hundreds of experiments that discovered useful facts. Bacon failed to appreciate the importance of mathematical models, and he found Copernicus unconvincing. Although he praised experimentation, he performed almost no experiments and collected his evidence in the traditional way, from books. His writings nevertheless dramatized the importance of empirical research. The founding in 1662 of the Royal Society of London, the first scientific society in England, owed much to Bacon's inspiration. He was the remote ancestor of the great laboratories and team-research projects of the twentieth century. His goal, the mastery of nature through rational analysis, has distinguished the West from the other historic civilizations.

Descartes, a French mathematician and philosopher, was an even more important figure than Bacon, but he lacked Bacon's intuitive understanding of the need for observation. To Descartes, the excitement of science lay in mathematical analysis and theory. In a famous autobiographical account, he told how the literature and philosophy that he had studied as a youth had left him unsatisfied because he reached no *certain* conclusions. By contrast, the precision and certainty of mathematics aroused his enthusiasm. He set out to discover a mathematical "method of rightly conducting the reason and discovering truth in the sciences."

In November 1619, in a moment of intuition, he saw the exact correspondence between geometry and algebra—the truth that equations and curves on graphs were interchangeable. That intoxicating vision suggested to him a new way of grasping ultimate truth. If humanity systematically doubted all notions based on authority or custom and started with clear and precise ideas known to be true, it might deduce systematically the entire universe from a few simple principles, just as he had derived curves from equations.

Descartes was one of the first to believe that science could save humanity. His enthusiasm was infectious and outran the knowledge available in the seventeenth century. He reduced the universe, including the human body, to a mathematically intelligible machine. Only the human intellect, he believed, resisted mathematical description. He therefore defined it as being outside the world of matter: The mind comprehended the world but did not exist in it. His generalizations in astronomy, physics, and anatomy were often premature, and his passion for system building went far beyond his capacity to confirm generalizations by experiment. He did important work in optics, but that in no way confirmed his far-ranging theories.

Nevertheless, Descartes' enthusiasm for scientific "method," his belief that mathematics could describe all phenom-

ena, and his insistence on systematic doubt of all earlier theorizing left a profound mark on the scientific thinking of the three centuries that followed. Descartes made it easier for his successors to reject old ideas, and they gradually came to accept his belief that mathematics must be the language of science.

Experiment and Mathematics

Bacon and Descartes were too optimistic. Bacon thought that a generation of determined experimentation would establish a solid structure of knowledge about the universe. Descartes expected that a few basic mathematical axioms would soon lead, by deduction, to a universal science. He also believed in a universe far simpler than it now appears. One of Descartes' pupils even described the world as a gigantic piece of clockwork.

Meanwhile, experimentation and mathematics were developing steadily in the hands of a growing host of scientists. William Gilbert (1544–1603), court physician to Elizabeth I, coined the word "electricity" and deduced that the earth itself was a huge magnet. His *De magnete* (1600) remained the foremost work on magnetism until the early nineteenth century. William Harvey (1578–1627), who had studied at Padua, argued in a work published in 1628 that the blood must circulate from arteries to veins to heart, then on to the lungs, back to the heart and back once more to the arteries. He did this by estimating the amount of blood the heart pumped in a minute and arguing that it must go somewhere. Later in the century the new microscope revealed the tiny capillaries that actually connect arteries to veins.

Evangelista Torricelli (1608–47), Blaise Pascal, and others investigated the ancient proposition, long believed by most scholars, that "nature abhors a vacuum." They created vacuums in test tubes, invented the barometer, and discovered that the pressure of the atmosphere varies between sea level and mountain top. They proved inherited wisdom false, and their work showed a growing precision in observation and an increasing skill in

Scientific revolutionaries of the seventeenth century: Francis Bacon (*above*) and René Descartes (*below*).

Harvey Discovers the Circulation of the Blood

Since calculations and visual demonstrations have confirmed all my suppositions, to wit, that the blood is passed through the lungs and the heart by the pulsation of the ventricles, is forcibly ejected to all parts of the body, therein steals into the veins . . . flows back everywhere . . . from small veins into larger ones, and thence comes at last into the vena cava and to the auricle of the heart; all this too in such amounts that it cannot be supplied from the ingesta [food] and is also in greater bulk than would suffice for nutrition.

I am obliged to conclude that in all animals the blood is driven around a circuit with an unceasing, circular sort of motion, that this is an activity of the heart which it carries out by virtue of its pulsation, and that in sum it constitutes the sole cause for the heart's pulsatile movement.

From C. C. Gillispie, The Edge of Objectivity *(Princeton, N.J.: Princeton University Press, 1960), p. 71.*

controlling experiments and in quantifying their results.

Mathematics likewise rapidly advanced. The invention of decimals and of logarithms early in the century made calculation easier. Pascal inaugurated the study of probability. At the end of the century Sir Isaac Newton and Baron Gottfried Wilhelm von Leibniz (1646–1716) crowned the work of many others by simultaneously but separately inventing the calculus, which provided the first mathematical method for describing accelerating or decelerating motion.

Kepler: The Foundations of Celestial Mechanics

Observational techniques and mathematical methods first united in astronomy and physics—producing results of a beauty and explanatory power that shattered for good all traditional notions of the place of science in human knowledge and of humanity in the universe.

The German astronomer Johannes Kepler (1571–1630) believed Copernicus's theory, but found discrepancies in it troubling. He worked from the observations of his master, the Danish astronomer Tycho Brahe (1546–1601), which were far more accurate than those available to Copernicus. Brahe's data ultimately caused Kepler to discard reluctantly the universal belief, which Copernicus had not challenged, that heavenly bodies moved in circles.

Kepler concluded that the ellipse, whose properties scholars had studied since the time of the Greeks, fitted Brahe's observations of Mars, the planet whose motion most contradicted the Ptolemaic and Copernican systems. The orbits of the planets, Kepler suggested, were elliptical, with the sun at one of the two foci of the ellipse. Further, he demonstrated that a line from the sun to a planet swept out equal areas of the ellipse in equal times and that the cube of the distance of each planet from the sun was proportional to the square of the time of its revolution. That was astounding proof of the intuition of Descartes and others that nature was in some mysterious sense mathematical. A geometrical figure, studied for centuries as an abstract form, "fit" the facts of nature. By implication, nature was perhaps itself a machine, intelligible to the careful observer equipped with mathematics.

The New Universe: Galileo

Kepler's work describing many of his findings appeared in 1609. During that same year a professor at Padua and Pisa, Galileo Galilei (1564–1642), turned on the heavens a newly invented instrument, the telescope. He soon published an account of what he saw. The changeless perfection and perfect sphericity of the heavenly bodies had dissolved before his gaze. He saw that the moon had craters and mountains, that spots moved on the sun, that rings encircled Saturn, and that Jupiter had four moons of its own. A bright new star—a supernova—had already appeared in 1572, and Brahe had noted it. In 1577 a new comet had cut a path through what should have been unchanging crystalline spheres. Now Galileo's telescope shattered forever the unchanging, finite, spherical universe of the Middle Ages. Thoughtful scholars suspected that Bruno had been right. Humanity was looking out into infinite space, at a sparse population of stars like the sun that might themselves have solar systems.

The medieval distinction between earthly and celestial physics was apparently dissolving. The moon and sun were not perfect globes and the stars were not changeless. Nor was the earth any longer the motionless center of the universe. The earth, like Mars and Jupiter, was a planet circling the sun against a backdrop of silent, infinite space. Perhaps the same forces and laws operated both on earth and in the heavens.

Such views soon attracted the wrath of the Church of the Counter-Reformation, which had denounced the Copernican theory in 1616. The Roman Inquisition condemned Galileo himself in 1632, threatened him with torture, and forced him to retract his theories. The legend soon arose that after repudiating his "heretical" view that the earth moved around the sun, he nevertheless muttered stubbornly under his breath "*Eppur si muove*"—"It *does* move." Nor could the Inquisition suppress Galileo's brilliantly written dialogues, which contributed mightily to the overthrow not only of Ptolemy in favor of Copernicus, but also of Aristotle in favor of a new physics.

The speculations of the fourteenth-century Franciscan monks inspired Galileo's physics, but he was far more thorough and accurate than they in developing mathematical formulas to describe motion. He worked out by experiment the law of falling bodies—the distance fallen increases as the square of the time. He saw that projectiles followed parabolic paths that were the resultant of the two forces acting upon the projectile—the initial impetus that launched it and the downward pull of the earth. That insight was the beginning of modern ballistics, the scientific foundation of the new warfare.

Galileo also came close to formulating the key concept of modern mechanics, the law of inertia: that bodies tend to remain at rest or to continue in motion in straight lines unless outside forces act upon them. That deceptively simple proposition—fundamentally opposed to Aristotle's concept of motion as the result of

some mover's action—was the source of the law of gravitation. Galileo prepared the way, but it was a man born in the year Galileo died who made that decisive breakthrough.

The Synthesis of Celestial and Terrestrial Mechanics: Newton

Sir Isaac Newton (1642–1727), the greatest figure of the Scientific Revolution, was the man who married Kepler's astronomy to Galileo's mechanics, broke down all distinctions between celestial and terrestrial physics, and accomplished at least part of Descartes' dream of establishing a "universal science." A fundamental intuition came to Newton while he was still a student in his twenties at Cambridge University: the force that bends the moon into its orbit about the earth must be the same force that pulls an apple from its branch to the ground. A reciprocal force of attraction between every body in the universe must exist, and that force—although as yet unexplained—must be calculable.

Newton's earliest calculations came close enough to mathematical proof to persuade him that the same force indeed operated on the moon and on the apple, and that this force varied "directly as the product of the masses" involved and "inversely as the square of the distance" separating those masses. For some time after formulating this "law" of gravitation in 1664–66 he seems to have lost interest. But twenty years later a friend, the astronomer Edmund Halley (who calculated the orbit of the famous comet), persuaded Newton to publish. Newton developed the necessary mathematics—the calculus—to prove his theory to his own satisfaction. He published his conclusions in 1687 in his *Philosophiae naturalis principia mathematica,* the "mathematical principles of natural philosophy." It was one of the most influential books in the history of human thought.

Newton's law of gravitation provided a simple and elegant explanation of a growing mass of data in astronomy and physics and laid the foundations of future research in both sciences. Newton also

The greatest scientific revolutionary of all: Sir Isaac Newton, painted by Kneller.

improved on Bacon and Descartes by giving the scientific method its classic formulation in his fourth "Rule of Reasoning":

In experimental philosophy [science] we are to look upon propositions collected by general induction from phenomena as accurately or very nearly true, notwithstanding any contrary hypotheses [theories] that may be imagined, till such time as other phenomena occur, by which they may either be made more accurate or liable to exceptions.

Newton's support of the experimental or inductive approach was aimed against the premature generalizing, the theoretical "system[s] . . . little better than a Romance," of Descartes and his followers. But Newton, unlike Bacon, was fully convinced of the necessity of mathematical theory. Newton combined at last both celestial and terrestrial physics on the one hand, and empirical observation and mathematical interpretation on the other.

Newton's Universe

News of Newton's work spread rapidly among laymen, thanks to popular scientific works that soon began pouring from the presses of London and Amsterdam. The new universe that Newton disclosed was far different from the cozy finite universe of the Middle Ages. Bodies moved through infinite space in response to predictable, universally operating forces. Mass, force, and motion were the key concepts, and mathematics made them intelligible.

The question "Why?" had obsessed the scholars of the Middle Ages, who had felt they understood a natural phenomenon once they had discovered its purpose. Seventeenth-century scientists limited themselves to asking "How?" The discovery of regular patterns in natural processes satisfied most of them. The world of Kepler, Galileo, and Newton was a vast machine, working according to laws expressible in mathematics, laws understandable by anyone who followed the proper experimental and mathematical

methods. The telescope continued to reveal an ever-larger portion of an apparently infinite universe. The new astronomy, after displacing the earth as the center of the universe, displaced the sun as well. The microscope, after the 1660s, began to reveal the wonders of the infinitely small foundations of life—bacteria, spermatozoa, cells, capillaries.

The question "Why?" nevertheless remained unanswered. What was the place of God and of humanity in this universe? That question did not become acute until the eighteenth century. No prominent seventeenth-century scientist thought that he was reading God out of the universe. Descartes considered himself a good Catholic and apparently did not see the theological dangers inherent in his sharp separation of the world of matter from the world of mind. Newton spent many of his later years absorbed in theological speculation and alchemy. The border between science and religion or magic was still fluid, and possible contradictions between faith and science were not clearly evident to most seventeenth-century scientists, or to their audience.

The French philosopher-scientist Blaise Pascal (1623–62), inventor of probability theory and of the first calculating machine, and contributor to fields as diverse as the calculus and the dynamics of gases and fluids, indeed attempted a synthesis between faith and the new sciences. For Pascal, "the whole visible world [was] only an imperceptible atom in the ample bosom of nature," and the universe "an infinite sphere, the center of which is everywhere, the circumference nowhere." "The eternal silence of these infinite spaces frightens me," he confessed. Yet to examine a mite, "with its minute body and parts incomparably more minute, limbs with their joints, veins in the limbs, blood in the veins, humors in the blood, drops in the humors, vapors in the drops," was equally astonishing. "What is man in nature? A Nothing in comparison with the Infinite, an All in comparison with the Nothing, a mean between nothing and everything." Pascal related the new universe explicitly to Christianity, to Christ's sacrifice on the cross, which made human-

Newton invented and built this first reflecting telescope.

ity, despite its apparent insignificance, the greatest presence in the universe beside God. Others soon saw less need to invoke Christianity.

By the later seventeenth century the hold of religious orthodoxy on Europe's intellectual elite was beginning to weaken. Religious authorities could no longer simply forbid scientific speculation or experiment. The burning or torture of "heretics" like Giordano Bruno slowly went out of fashion, except in Spain. And scientists themselves began to demarcate their activities sharply from questions of faith. The charters of the many scientific societies and academies that sprang up throughout Europe during the century usually contained clauses forbidding purely theological or political discussion and establishing that the group would not investigate "ultimate" or "final" causes.

The earliest history of the Royal Society of London, published in 1667, suggests that scientific discussions offered a peculiar attraction to thoughtful individuals during and after a fanatically bitter religious and civil war such as the English Revolution. Science, which by definition dealt with the empirically verifiable, might thereby become politically and theologically neutral and benefit humanity in practical ways. Scientific truth gradually emerged as an alternative to theological truth. It was not entirely accidental that modern science arose as religious warfare went out of fashion, amid general revulsion at the devastation that fanaticism had wrought.

Nevertheless, Newton's new "world picture" did not explicitly contradict religious feeling. Some indeed found in the mechanistic universe a source of religious awe. Baruch or Benedict Spinoza (1632–77), an Amsterdam lens grinder and philosopher descended from the Jewish communities that Spain had expelled, concluded that the new universe of mass, force, and motion, operating in strict obedience to inexorable laws, *was* God. Spinoza saw no need to consider God as above, behind, or beyond nature, as a "free cause" apart from natural law. God was not "Creator" or "Redeemer," but a "God *or* Nature" that included all being

and incarnated natural law: "God never can decree, nor ever would have decreed, anything but what is; God did not exist before his decrees, and would not exist without them." Humanity, like all else, was part of the natural order and thus of God, and wisdom consisted of contemplating that order with serenity and delight.

Both Jewish and Christian contemporaries considered Spinoza a dangerous atheistic radical, although he was the mildest, kindliest, and most optimistic of men. Most of his works emerged in print only after his death. Contemporaries pointed out that to claim that humanity was part of God made it difficult to explain evil. Later critics discerned in "Whatever is, is in God" a dangerous fatalism. But Spinoza's notion of religion was destined to have great influence in the eighteenth century.

THE CULTURE OF THE BAROQUE

The age of the scientific revolution was also, especially in the Catholic areas of the Continent, the age of the "baroque" style in the visual arts. The baroque sprang up in the later sixteenth century, reached its climax about the middle of the seventeenth, and came to its end around the middle of the eighteenth. Eighteenth-century critics invented the term *baroque* (French for "odd" or "irregular"), after tastes had again changed, to stigmatize seventeenth-century art as a grotesque corruption of Renaissance styles. But by the late nineteenth century critics had come to consider the baroque a great achievement. More than most styles, it is difficult to define because it reflected the contrasts and contradictions of seventeenth-century culture as a whole—religious ecstasy and worldly sensuality, credulity and rationalism, violence and respect for order.

Baroque painters and sculptors portrayed voluptuous women in repose, heroes in battle, and saints in ecstasy with equal skill and zest. In general, the dominant notes of the baroque were tension, conflict, the grandiose, and the dramatic. Renaissance painters and writers had been interested in humanity itself. Baroque artists depicted the conflicts of humanity against the universe, of man against man, and of man within himself on a tragic and heroic scale.

Instructive parallels exist between the thought-worlds of the baroque artists and those of the seventeenth-century scientists. Galileo and Newton studied bodies or masses moving through space under the influence of conflicting forces such as gravitation and centrifugal force. To the great French dramatists of the age—Corneille, Racine, and Molière—the objects of study were typical human beings torn between conflicting forces such as love and duty. Space intrigued baroque painters. The Dutch master Jan Vermeer (1632–75) portrayed figures in a space bathed in and suffused with light. The greatest of Dutch painters, Rembrandt van Rijn (1606–69), spotlighted figures in the midst of darkened space, while others pictured them floating through apparently infinite voids. To baroque artists the supernatural was natural. The scientists' concern with mass, force, and motion paralleled the painters' and poets' concern with individuals caught in the tension between elemental forces. The typical hero of baroque literature, critics have suggested, is Satan in John Milton's *Paradise Lost* (1667), the

only great epic poem in English. Swayed by colossal passions, Satan moves through vast three-dimensional spaces and bends the forces of the universe to serve his implacable will to domination: "To reign is worth ambition though in hell:/Better to reign in hell than serve in heav'n." But God frustrates Satan's designs in the end.

The most typical, although not usually the most beautiful products of baroque architecture were the great palaces: Versailles and the remodeled Louvre in France, Schönbrunn in Austria, or Blenheim, the regal residence in England that Marlborough received for his victories. The style of these buildings was fundamentally Renaissance-classical, but grander, more ornate, and above all larger, often to the point of excess. As with the many descendants of Versailles, the neo-classical official buildings of later centuries, excess served a political purpose. Sheer mass emphasized the power of the state. In this, as in much else, Louis XIV led the way. Even some baroque religious architecture, such as the massive elliptical colonnades that the great Giovanni Lorenzo Bernini (1598–1680) erected to frame St. Peter's in Rome, conveyed the majesty of God rather than his mercy.

The most original creation of the baroque were the operas that originated in Italy early in the seventeenth century. Drama set to music had existed in the West since the twelfth century. But the music had been essentially choral and polyphonic until around 1600, when a group of Florentine composers devised a "*dramma per musica*" (drama through music) in which the characters sang their parts as simple melodies without choral accompaniment. Opera immediately became, and has remained, a vast popular success. The grandiose and palatial stage settings, the dramatic conflicts of the action, and the emotional power of the music exactly suited the taste of the period. Italian composers led the way until the end of the seventeenth century—Claudio Monteverdi (1567–1643), Girolamo Frescobaldi (1583–1643), Alessandro Scarlatti (1660–1725), and the greatest master of Italian Baroque music, Antonio Vivaldi (1675–1741). But it was an Englishman, Henry

The glories of the baroque: altarpiece in St. Peter's, Rome, by the Italian master Giovanni Lorenzo Bernini (1598–1680).

Purcell (*ca.* 1658–95), who wrote the most moving opera of the century, *Dido and Aeneas* (1687).

ORIGINS OF THE ENLIGHTENMENT: SEVENTEENTH-CENTURY THOUGHT ABOUT HUMANITY

While the vast majority of the population of western Europe remained medieval in outlook, the most adventurous minds of the seventeenth century fashioned notions about humanity that rested on Renaissance ideas but pressed far beyond them. The rediscovery of the ancient world, the great overseas voyages, and the scientific revolution led seventeenth-century thinkers into new territory. Their efforts ultimately inspired the greatest break in the history of European thought since the collapse of the Roman Empire, the eighteenth-century flowering of modern conceptions of humanity known as the Enlightenment. The new ideas of the seventeenth century fall conveniently into three categories: individualism, relativism, and a rationalism tempered with empiricism.

Individualism

Radical thinkers of the seventeenth century were increasingly inclined to celebrate the individual. The most intense Christian piety of the period—whether it was the Catholic devotion preached by St. François de Sales, the stern conscience of the Puritans and Jansenists, or the warm inner conviction of the German Pietists—was highly individualistic. That trend was equally evident in political theory. The fashion was to start with the individual and then seek explanations of and justifications for the existence of societies and states.

    Supporters of the divine-right theory of kingship remained numerous, but by the middle of the seventeenth century the notion of an explicit or implicit "contract" between people and ruler was widespread. Hobbes and a few others, including Spinoza, argued that this contract, once made, was irrevocable and that it

Opera singers of the baroque: detail from an opera setting drawn by Ludovico Burnacinia, Vienna (1674).

bound the ruled but not the ruler. Others, like the Parliamentarians in the English Civil War and John Locke in political philosophy, argued for a right of rebellion against rulers who broke the terms of the contract by acting against the general welfare.

    The idea of a "social contract" soon took its place alongside the notion of the "political contract." Society, according to social-contract theorists, was itself the result of a voluntary agreement among individuals who had been absolutely independent in their original "state of nature." The two ideas mixed, somewhat confusedly, in the works of Locke and of later political philosophers. In both contracts, the individual with his rights and his "natural" independence logically came first; then came society or the state. The more radical thinkers of the seventeenth century thus came to think of society as an artificial organization of independent individuals that rested on their consent. That was a radical break with the medieval conception of society as an organism or a "body" of which individuals were mere "members," each with an assigned place.

Relativism

The greatest thinkers of the Middle Ages were confident that the peoples of Christendom were chosen by God, and that divine revelation gave humanity all necessary truths. But that self-assurance weakened during the sixteenth and seventeenth centuries, thanks to Humanism, to the voyages of discovery, and to the development of science.

Humanism had begun to reveal Greco-Roman civilization in some detail. Ancient literature, art, and historical writing brought alive a long-dead society that offered numerous alternatives to the medieval Christian system of belief. The Renaissance had first created the modern disciplines of history, archaeology, and philology. Seventeenth-century scholars broadened and deepened them. Thoughtful Europeans thus learned that other societies had existed in other times with values, beliefs, and institutions quite different from their own. That recognition was the origin of the concept of historical relativism, of the notion that value systems—including those of Christian Europe—were historical phenomena subject to change.

The age of discovery added to historical relativism a geographical counterpart. The discovery in America and Asia of other societies shattered European provincialism. The tribal hunter-gatherers of America and Africa, the urban civilizations of Aztecs and Incas, and the great empires of Asia with their advanced arts and amenities inspired study and reflection. Perhaps the "noble savages" of the New World were happier than the more cultured but "corrupted" Christians of Europe. Perhaps Persian sages and Chinese philosophers had something to teach Christians. Each society had different standards—was any value system grounded on anything more solid than custom? Doubts on these points affected increasing numbers of European thinkers in the seventeenth and eighteenth centuries. And scientific discovery likewise widened their vision of humanity's place in nature. European Christianity was not alone in time and space, and humanity itself might not be alone in the universe.

The work of Pierre Bayle (1647–1706), the great scholarly skeptic of the later seventeenth century, exemplifies the results of historical study, geographical exploration, and scientific discovery. Bayle was born a Huguenot, briefly converted to Catholicism, and then renounced all orthodox belief when his brother died

in a French dungeon during an attempt at forced conversion. Bayle took up residence in the relatively tolerant Dutch Netherlands and devoted the latter part of his life to a crusade against superstition, religious intolerance, and dogma of all kinds. In 1697 he published a huge rambling book, the *Historical and Critical Dictionary,* which had enormous influence on Enlightenment thought. Into the book he poured a relativism and skepticism acquired through extensive historical study, an amateur knowledge of science, and experience.

He defied convention by insisting that religion and political stability were not identical—atheists could be good citizens. He denounced religious conversions by force. He ridiculed astrology, a form of superstition even more current then than now. He derided tales of miracles. He distrusted all historical authorities, including the writers of the Old Testament, unless their account of events was inherently credible. An admirer of Descartes, his test of truth was "reason," and many scriptural accounts failed that test. Bayle was the most destructive critic of his generation. His war against traditional religion replaced, and in part derived from, the scarcely ended wars of religion.

Rationalism and Empiricism

The leading thinkers of the seventeenth century began a process that reached completion only in the eighteenth century: the replacement of the lost certainties of religious belief with a new object of worship—reason. It was the faculty that in theory distinguished humanity from the animal world. It was trustworthy; the triumphs of seventeenth-century science had proved that. An increasingly optimistic age concluded that reason gave humanity the *certain knowledge* of the world that religion no longer appeared to offer.

Reason also provided a law, "natural law," to replace the foundation that religious belief now failed to provide for human knowledge. The idea of a law of nature that served as a standard of behavior for all humans at all times was not new.

Greek philosophers such as Aristotle had enunciated a version of it, the Stoics had pressed it further, and Cicero had given the idea classic formulation:

> There is in fact a true law—namely, right reason—which is in accordance with nature, applies to all men, and is unchangeable and eternal. By its commands this law summons men to the performance of their duties; by its prohibitions it restrains them from doing wrong.

St. Augustine had then Christianized that law by identifying it with the law of God. The medieval scholastics had enthusiastically proclaimed that law to be the basis of earthly law and morality. During the Renaissance and the Reformation, the rediscovery of texts of the ancient Stoics and the work of Protestant scholars such as the father of modern international law, the Dutch jurist and diplomat Hugo Grotius (1583–1645), had secularized natural law once more, as a "law" inherent in the nature of humanity. Grotius, in *On the Law of War and Peace* (1625), attempted to find in natural law some basis for a "law of nations" that would transcend and moderate the religious fanaticisms of the Thirty Years' War. And the discovery of scientific "laws of nature," such as Kepler's laws of planetary motion, further reinforced the belief that natural laws of human behavior must also exist. Success in proving mathematical and scientific laws inspired faith that reason could discern "natural law" in human affairs.

The most influential example of that faith was John Locke's claim that every individual in the "state of nature," before the existence of organized societies, possessed certain "natural rights," most notably life, liberty, and property. From that premise it followed, as proof followed axiom, that humanity had formed societies and set up governments mainly to preserve those rights. Whereas Descartes had hoped to deduce the universe from a few central mathematical principles, Locke in his *Second Treatise of Government* (1690) assumed that he could deduce society and

government from a few simple axioms about humanity and natural law.

An undercurrent of empiricism, of respect for the evidence of the senses, nevertheless qualified that enthusiastic rationalism. Here too, Locke led the way in his *Essay Concerning Human Understanding* (1690), which many readers hailed as the counterpart in the study of humanity to Newton's work on the forces of nature. Locke argued that all human ideas came from the experience of the senses. The mind at birth was a *tabula rasa,* a clean slate, on which experience gained through the senses gradually imprinted conceptions. No "innate ideas" existed, and contrary to Descartes, no axioms were self-evident. Outside forces acting upon the mind explained all human ideas.

That was the purest empiricism. Locke hoped that it would provide a weapon for destroying the superstitions and prejudices of the past. It proved destructive of much else, including some of Locke's own doctrines. Locke's theory of the mind did away with original sin, for experience might mold the *tabula rasa* of the mind to do good rather than evil. It did away equally with the revelation on which Christianity rested and with mathematical axioms, for neither derived from the senses. Above all, it undermined Locke's own conception of "natural rights" that were innate and not based on experience.

The rationalism of Locke's natural-law theory of society clashed both with the empiricism of his theory of the mind and with the relativism in time and space that the Humanists and the great navigators had disclosed. The Enlightenment inherited this agonizing contradiction between rationalist faith in natural law and empiricist trust in sense-experience and in the evidence of comparative history.

THE EIGHTEENTH CENTURY: THE ENLIGHTENMENT

The task that the leading thinkers of the eighteenth century set themselves was to popularize the methods and principles of seventeenth-century natural science and to apply those methods and principles to God, humanity, and society. Scientific discovery continued, but the most brilliant writers of the age concentrated their effort on applying the new scientific method to long-festering human ills—economic, social, political, and ecclesiastical. Their concern was less to discover new truth about nature than to apply the methods of natural science to the transformation of society.

The eighteenth century's own name for this movement was "the Enlightenment"—*les lumières* in French. The term suggested the dawn of a new age of reason and knowledge after a long dark night of ignorance, superstition, intolerance, and despotism of kings and priests. That new light was the light of science, as the great English poet Alexander Pope (1688–1744) elegantly proclaimed:

> *Nature and nature's law lay hid in*
> *   night;*
> *God said, "Let Newton be," and all*
> *   was light.*

Correspondence, exchange of publications, and travel linked together a cultural movement that transcended state and religious boundaries. "Enlightened" writers and readers spanned Europe, from Russia to Spain, from Edinburgh to Naples, from the Philadelphia of Benjamin Franklin to the Virginia of Thomas Jefferson. But the center of the movement was indisputably Paris.

That was no accident. Most other countries were either too small or too backward to become major centers of Enlightenment thought and agitation. The major exception, England, had already fought its battles for religious toleration and political freedom. It had established after 1688 a freedom of thought and publication unprecedented elsewhere, even in the Dutch Netherlands. It had already had an Enlightenment, or "pre-Enlightenment," through Hobbes, Locke, and many others. By 1715, the England of gentry and merchants was too successful, both internally and externally, to provide much

nourishment for intellectual movements that fed on dissatisfaction with the existing order. Only the Scots, who delighted in stirring up their richer and duller neighbors to the south, were an exception. The philosopher and historian David Hume (1711–76) and the economist Adam Smith (1723–90) were major Enlightenment figures, and Edinburgh, the capital of Scotland, was one of the great centers of eighteenth-century European thought.

Three tendencies in French society united to make France the center of the Enlightenment. First, French government after the death of Louis XIV in 1715 became steadily more inept and ineffectual, both internally and in its wars and diplomacy (see pp. 563–64). Weakness at home and defeat abroad sapped the prestige of the existing order and of the Church that upheld it. Second, the aristocracy began to take its revenge on the monarchy that had reduced it to the role of courtly lapdog. In the realm of ideas, that revenge consisted of the articulation and eager propagation of potentially subversive ideas. Finally, the gradually increasing wealth that commerce and industry produced gave the growing urban middle classes an increasing consciousness of their own worth and importance. That consciousness led to rising social tension between the privileged and the less privileged. And that tension helped encourage an increasing body of literature that attacked the existing order at its weakest points: the obscurantism of the Church, the ineptitude of the noble-dominated royal administration, and the foolishness and arrogance of the nobility itself.

The weapons of the French Enlightenment writers were clarity, wit, and a deliberate ambiguity designed to ward off the wrath of officialdom. Government censors were often too slow-witted to catch hidden barbs aimed at Church or state, and after mid-century they often secretly agreed with the critics. Censorship stopped only the most blatantly subversive or obviously blasphemous attacks on the existing order. After the 1750s censorship was almost powerless against the flood of social criticism and satire that poured from the presses. The source of that flood was Paris, the center of the intellectual life of continental Europe. There the greatest intellectual figures of the age met and conversed in the *salons* or weekly gatherings that intellectual women of the aristocracy had begun to organize. The inhabitants of this world of ideas, whether commoner or noble, shared a common feeling that they were leading a revolution of ideas without precedent in European history, a crusade to end the absurdities and barbarities of the old order.

The "Philosophes": Voltaire, Montesquieu, Diderot

At first, London helped inspire Paris. The conventional date for the beginning of the Enlightenment as a movement was the visit to England in 1726–29 of a certain François Marie Arouet (1694–1778), better known by his pen-name, Voltaire. The French government had twice imprisoned Voltaire in the Bastille fortress in Paris for alleged or actual witticisms made at the expense of royal or noble personages. On the second occasion he had only achieved freedom by promising to leave for London. The man who came to personify the Enlightenment thus had good reason to hate the old regime.

In England, Voltaire read Newton and Locke, and relished the relative freedom of English society in comparison with his own. After returning to France he published *Philosophical Letters on the English* (1733), which passed on to his readers Newton's main principles and popularized Locke's theories of human nature and limited government. Voltaire skillfully contrasted the rationality of Newton's method and the tolerant reasonableness of the English way of life with the arbitrary and capricious realities of Church, state, and society in France.

Voltaire's English letters set the tone of Enlightenment propaganda in France for the next half-century. They were "philosophical" in the broad sense, because they reflected on the facts of human existence and attempted to discover their meaning, and because they searched for general principles useful to humanity as a whole. But the *philosophes,* as Voltaire

---

Voltaire on Superstition — 1776

Almost everything that goes beyond the adoration of a Supreme Being and submission of the heart to his orders is superstition. One of the most dangerous is to believe that certain ceremonies entail the forgiveness of crimes. Do you believe that God will forget a murder you have committed if you bathe in a certain river, sacrifice a black sheep, or if someone says certain words over you? . . . Do better, miserable humans; have neither murders nor sacrifices of black sheep. . . .

Notice that the most superstitious ages have always been those of the most horrible crimes. . . . The superstitious man is ruled by fanatics, and he becomes one himself. On the whole, the less superstition, the less fanaticism, and the less fanaticism, the fewer miseries.

From Voltaire, Dictionnaire philosophique *(Paris: Editions de Cluny, n.d.; reproduction of the edition of 1776), Vol. III, pp. 218–25.*

---

and kindred spirits became known, had little use for metaphysical speculation. They were less philosophers than popularizers, crusaders for the application of the best intellectual tools of the century to social problems. Voltaire was the greatest of them—the most prolific, the wittiest, the most readable, and perhaps the angriest. His preferred targets were bigotry, superstition, and despotism.

"*Écrasez l' infâme,*" cried Voltaire in his innumerable letters, pamphlets, stories, and satires: crush that "infamous thing," the Church. In the famous entry on "Religion" in his *Philosophical Dictionary* (1764), he described a vision he claimed to have had of a desert filled with piles of bones of "Christians with their throats slit by one another in theological disputes." He went on to report a philosophical conversation with the shades of Socrates and Jesus, who both deplored the spectacle he had just seen. And he attacked the religious intolerance of contemporary France as vigorously as the barbarism of the past. When he died in 1778, Voltaire was the most widely read author in Europe, the first writer to have made a fortune from the sale of his own writings. Paris buried him with a ceremony worthy of a king.

Voltaire, almost as skeptical as in life, by the master-sculptor Jean-Antoine Houdon (1781).

A second leading Enlightenment figure was the Baron Charles Louis de Secondat de Montesquieu (1689–1755), sometime president of the *Parlement* of Bordeaux. Montesquieu tried to create a "social science" by applying the methods of the natural sciences to the study of society. In his most famous work, *The Spirit of the Laws* (1748), he suggested that climate and other environmental factors helped determine forms of government, and he tried to discover what form of government best fitted a given set of environmental conditions. *The Spirit of the Laws* was not "scientific" by later standards, but it was the first serious attempt since the Greeks at tracing relationships between systems of government and the environment. In his popular *History of Civilization* (1756),

Voltaire took over and elaborated Montesquieu's concepts.

Montesquieu, like Voltaire, found Locke's theory of limited government persuasive. As a French noble he wished to limit the perceived excesses of royal absolutism. He followed Locke in concluding that the ideal political form called for the separation and balancing of powers within government. That conclusion later had great influence on the authors of the American Constitution (see p. 695).

A third major figure of the French Enlightenment was Denis Diderot (1713–84), co-editor of the famous *Encyclopédie,* an immense encyclopedia designed to sum up the totality of human knowledge. Despite Jesuit protests and cuts by timid printers, it appeared in 35 volumes between 1752 and 1780. Diderot was an enthusiast for science and saw the relationship between science and technology more clearly than most *philosophes.* The most remarkable feature of the *Encyclopédie* was the plates that show machinery and industrial processes. But Diderot was no mere compiler; he was a confident prophet of the Enlightenment's thisworldly religion of humanity. The entries and content of the *Encyclopédie* reflected the interests and enthusiasms of Diderot and his fellow *philosophes* and contained many of their most trenchant writings. The work was an immense success and became the bible of the "enlightened" everywhere. Through it ran faith in humanity's reason, pride in its accomplishments, and sublime confidence in its future.

Historical Relativism in Montesquieu: The Effects of Climate and Geography

In Asia they have always had great empires; in Europe these could never exist. Asia has larger plains; it is cut out into much larger divisions by mountains and seas . . . and the rivers being not so large form more contrasted boundaries. Power in Asia, then, should be always despotic; for if their subjugation be not severe they would soon make a division inconsistent with the nature of the country.

In Europe natural divisions form many nations of moderate extent, in which ruling by laws is not incompatible with the maintenance of the state: on the contrary, it is so favorable to it that without this the state would fall into decay. It is this that has formed a genius for liberty that renders each part extremely difficult to be subdued and subjected to a foreign power. . . . Africa is in a climate like that of the south of Asia and is in the same servitude. . . .

Monarchy is more frequently found in fertile countries and a republican government in those which are not so, and this is sometimes a sufficient compensation for the inconveniences they suffer by the sterility of the land. Thus the barrenness of the soil of Attica established a democracy there.

From Charles de Secondat de Montesquieu, The Spirit of the Laws *(Bohn Standard Library edition), Vol. I, Book XVII, Chs. 6, 7; Book XVIII, Ch. 1, pp. 289–91.*

The Enlightenment Faith

No intellectual movement is successful unless it has followers as well as leaders. The Enlightenment, like the Renaissance, produced its full quota of earnest hacks and disreputable scribblers. It also enjoyed a public, vast by previous standards, of silent supporters. Twentieth-century scholarship has shown that the *Encyclopédie* enjoyed astonishing sales in tiny provincial towns. Periodicals, libraries, book societies, and literary and scientific discussion groups spread knowledge, social criticism, and scandalous gossip. The main ideas of the Enlightenment took root all over Europe, and a new generation absorbed from them entirely new conceptions of human nature, society, and religion. Five words, each of which bore a heavy freight of meaning in the eighteenth century, sum up these ruling ideas: *reason, nature, happiness, progress,* and *liberty.*

The eighteenth century believed as passionately in reason as the seventeenth, but with a difference. The "reason" of Voltaire relied more upon experience and less on mathematics than that of Descartes. It was a weapon of skeptical inquiry based on observed facts—or on what Voltaire thought were facts—rather than a method of deduction from axioms. To the thinkers of the Enlightenment, reason was the alternative to superstition and prejudice. It was the only sure guide to the principles that governed humanity and nature. Reason could discover the fundamental rationality of the universe, and it could also make human societies more rational. The *philosophes* were less interested in "pure" science than in applied science, less concerned with intellectual system-building than with specific reforms. They regarded reason as a down-to-earth tool, applicable equally to agriculture, government, social relations, astronomy, and physics.

Nature was a second favorite word of the Enlightenment. The precise meaning the *philosophes* attached to "nature" was not always clear, but to nearly all of them "nature" or "the natural" was the proper standard for measuring God and humanity. A thing "according to nature" was reasonable and therefore good. Voltaire and his contemporaries brought the idea of natural law to the peak of its prestige. One of them devised the following definition of natural law:

The regular and constant order of facts by which God rules the universe; the order which his wisdom presents to the sense and reason of men, to serve them as an equal and common rule of conduct, and to guide them, without distinction of race or sect, towards perfection and happiness.

Order and law, then, ruled throughout the universe of the *philosophes*—laws of economics, of politics, and of morality as well as of physics and astronomy. Reason permitted the discovery of those laws. Humans might ignore or defy them but did so at their peril. To the "enlightened," the road to happiness lay in conforming to nature and nature's laws. The enlightened elite of the eighteenth century looked on those who "broke" nature's laws in the same spirit as the clergy of the Middle Ages had looked on heretics who broke God's laws: they were rebels against the order of the universe.

Happiness in this world, not salvation and eternal rejoicing in the next, was the end the *philosophes* had in view. The Enlightenment, like the Scientific Revolution, was a secular movement. When Thomas Jefferson (see p. 579) cited "the pursuit of happiness" along with life and liberty as inalienable human rights, he was expressing a general sentiment of the age. Medieval Christianity's toleration of misery in this life in the expectation of rewards in the next angered the *philosophes*. They demanded the realization of Christian ideals here and now. They abominated cruelty, judicial torture, slavery, and the callous treatment of the insane. An enlightened Italian civil servant of the Habsburgs, Cesare Beccaria (1738–94), was the first to suggest that savage penalties do not necessarily prevent crime and to propose a theory of penology. The *philosophes* were also cosmopolitan and even pacifist in temper. Voltaire penned some of the bitterest passages ever written about the "insanity" of war and the absurdity of blind patriotism.

Progress was an even more central constituent of the Enlightenment faith than happiness. The *philosophes* took the Christian idea of the spiritual progression of humanity from the Creation through the Incarnation to the Last Judgment, and secularized it. The progress of civilization, they believed, was now out of God's hands and in those of humanity, thanks to the discovery and use of nature's laws in government, economics, and technology. The *philosophes* were in general confident that both humanity and society were perfectible through human effort.

This was a major revolution in Western thought. The Middle Ages could not have conceived of progress that was unrelated to God. Renaissance thinkers still felt themselves inferior to the heroic Greeks and Romans. But even before a symbolic literary battle between "ancients" and "moderns" that began in 1687, some thinkers had suggested that the "moderns" were as good as, and probably better than, the "ancients." By 1750 a French *philosophe,* economist, and civil servant, Anne-Robert-Jacques Turgot, could suggest that the essential element in history was humanity's slow struggle upward toward the discovery of the scientific method.

In 1794 the Marquis de Condorcet, a mathematician and aristocratic reformer under sentence of death during the French Revolution, wrote a *Sketch for a Historical Picture of the Progress of the Human Mind* that summed up all the optimism of his century. He saw "the strongest reasons for believing that nature has set no limit to the realization of our hopes" and foresaw "the abolition of inequality between nations, the progress of equality within nations, and the true perfection of humanity."

Progress, Condorcet concluded, was now "independent of any power that might wish to halt it" and "will never be reversed." The scientific method was irrevocably fixed in the human mind, and scientific knowledge of natural laws would continue to accumulate. Progress was thus accelerating, irreversible, and infinite. The coming "perfection of mankind" was an intoxicating vision, a vision the majority of the enlightened shared despite the abundance of historical evidence suggesting that civilizations declined as well as rose. How Condorcet reconciled his vision of progress with his own status as fugitive from the executioners of the Revolution of "Liberty, Equality, Fraternity" is unclear.

Liberty, indeed, was yet another favorite word of the *philosophes.* They were acutely aware of the prevalence in France

of arbitrary arrest and restrictions on speech, religion, trade, and employment. Looking at England through lightly rose-tinted glasses, they envied Englishmen their economic, political, and religious liberties. Their concern for liberty was potentially the most explosive tenet of their faith, but few considered that violence was necessary to secure it. Liberty, for the *philosophes,* was inseparable from reason. Reason would soon reveal the true natural laws governing all things, from trade, to government, to religion. The artificiality and corruption of the present would become evident to all. A "benevolent despotism," an enlightened philosopher-king, would lead humanity into a new golden age—or so Voltaire and many other *Encyclopédie* authors hoped. But what if despotism was by its very nature not benevolent?

The Enlightenment and Religion

The new ideas inevitably had religious consequences. To the enlightened, religious fervor savored of the fanaticism of the wars of religion. The Enlightenment only prized enthusiasm for its new religion of reason, progress, and the "perfection of humanity." The fashionable form of belief common among the eighteenth century's educated elite came to be Deism, the belief in a God who is Creator but not Redeemer. The God of the Deists was a celestial watchmaker who had made the universe, wound it up, and then stepped aside to let it run according to natural law that he had laid down. God did not concern himself with humanity or act in or through human history.

The essence of religion, for the Deist, was thus awe and reverence before the rationality and perfection of the universe—a feeling reflected in the beautiful hymns of Isaac Watts still heard in many Protestant churches. To a Deist such as Voltaire, talk of revelation, miracles, or the special intervention of God in the natural order was false. Dogma and ritual were "superstition," for humanity needed only reason to see God. The heart of natural religion was a morality common to all mankind. "Light is uniform for the star

Sirius," Voltaire wrote, "and for us moral philosophy must be uniform."

Deism obviously tended to undermine orthodox Christianity and to substitute for it a rationalist belief in God as First Cause and in "natural law" as humanity's moral guide. A few *philosophes* such as Diderot went further and dared the censors by pushing beyond Deism to atheism. For Baron Paul Henri d'Holbach (1723–89), the universe contained nothing but matter, humanity itself was a conglomeration of atoms, and natural law determined all events. Holbach was the complete "materialist," an ancestor of much nineteenth-century thought.

Economics, Society, and Politics

The *philosophes* were interested in social and political issues, but they were reformers, not revolutionaries. Their formula for reform was simply to discover by reason and experience the natural laws that should operate in any given situation and to clear away all supposedly artificial obstacles to their operation. The result, "reason" indicated, would be "progress" toward happiness and freedom.

That outlook encouraged the beginnings of the modern discipline of economics. In 1758 François Quesnay published his *Economic Survey,* which proclaimed the existence of natural economic "laws" and urged an end to all restrictions, such as government control of grain supplies and prices, that prevented those laws from operating. But Quesnay and French economists of his school were too much the products of France's predominantly agricultural society. They saw agriculture as the source of all wealth and damned industry as "sterile" and commerce as parasitic. Adam Smith of Edinburgh saw more clearly. In *An Inquiry into the Nature and Causes of the Wealth of Nations* (1776), the first classic of modern economics, Smith extended the concept of "natural liberty" to commerce and industry.

He denounced all "mercantilist" practices, although he admitted that an age of warring states might make measures such as the Navigation Acts necessary for a time. In general, however, Smith maintained that state interference with the workings of the natural law of supply and demand decreased rather than increased national wealth. The "invisible hand" of natural law, Smith argued, was a self-regulating mechanism that automatically maximized the wealth and freedom of any society that respected it. To tamper with it was both dangerous and self-defeating.

In political theory, similar lines of reasoning led to three distinct schools of thought. The first rested on the notion of "enlightened absolutism." The *philosophes,* children of their age, were no democrats. Voltaire thought government should be for the people, but by kings: "The people, stupid and barbarous, needs a yoke, a cattle prod, and hay." Most *philosophes* hoped for a mellowing of divine-right monarchy into a benevolent "enlightened" philosopher-kingship that would govern—perhaps with well-rewarded *philosophe* advice—according to natural law rather than royal caprice. A second, smaller school believed that "reason" pointed in the direction of an English-style constitutional monarchy based on natural rights and on a contract that bound the sovereign to respect his subjects' liberties. And a very few advanced a third theory, still too radical to be of much immediate influence: the theory of democratic government. That school's foremost prophet was the eccentric Jean-Jacques Rousseau (1712–78), author of *The Social Contract* (1762).

Rousseau: Prophet of Democracy and Despotism

Rousseau, a native of Geneva, appeared in Paris in 1742 after a wandering youth. He came to know Diderot and other *philosophes* and for a time attempted to join them. But he was never easy in their company. He trusted reason but relied even more on emotion. He trusted nature, but to him nature was the unspoiled simplicity of the noble savage, of humanity before the coming of civilization. After a sudden vision experienced in 1749, he became convinced that humanity had lost more than it had gained by cultivating the arts and sciences. He lost all faith in progress.

An idealized view of Rousseau, misfit and social critic, from an eighteenth-century playing card.

The seeming artificiality of Paris society increasingly irritated him, and he broke with his former friends. Voltaire thought him insane, and in his miserable later years Rousseau indeed suffered from delusions of persecution.

Rousseau was the greatest social critic of the Enlightenment. By temperament he was a shy and sensitive misfit who desperately wanted to belong. He knew himself to be "good," on the model of the "noble savage." He therefore blamed his unhappiness, his failure to fit in, on the alleged artificiality of existing society. That society of kings, aristocrats, and priests—he felt—had "corrupted" and humiliated him. Consequently he imagined an alternative, not as a program for revolution—although many readers took it as one—but as a critique of existing societies.

Rousseau's utopia, described in *The Social Contract,* was a "direct democracy," a small and tightly knit community of free male citizens (like most men of the Enlightenment, Rousseau considered it part of "the order of nature that woman obeys man"). Government consisted of the citizens meeting face-to-face. From their de-liberations, Rousseau was confident, a "general will" would inevitably emerge. For humanity's essential goodness, in Rousseau's view, meant that a society that governed itself was immune from dissent and conflict. And by agreeing to form a community, Rousseau's citizens had in any case willingly sacrificed all individual rights to the group. Once the "general will" became known, all owed it absolute obedience.

Perhaps Rousseau had in mind an idealized image of Geneva as he wrote *The Social Contract.* In that city-state, citizens knew and trusted one another, and the minority normally accepted the majority's view with good grace, out of loyalty to the community. But it was Sparta, that least individualist and most austerely military of the Greek city-states, that recurred frequently in Rousseau's pages. It was his favorite model.

Perhaps Rousseau's knowledge of Sparta—of its relentless regimentation, its murderous *krypteia* or secret police, its ruthless enslavement of all surrounding cities—was imperfect. Perhaps, as some modern scholars assert, his proposals for a "progressive" education that would bring out the child's "natural" goodness and intellectual curiosity make Rousseau a prophet of individual freedom rather than Spartan uniformity. Perhaps his hostility to kings and aristocrats, indeed his aversion to all forms of authority, absolve him of responsibility for excesses committed after 1789 in the name of the "general will." But his theory of democracy was nevertheless a stunning illustration of the consequences—even the unintended consequences—of ideas.

Locke and Montesquieu had argued that the guarantee of political liberty was the separation of executive and legislative powers. Concentration of power threatened freedom. Their theory derived from an essential pessimism about human behavior, a long experience of human ambition and fallibility gained in the world of politics. Their theory of liberty was "negative"—liberty arose when institutional and legal checks limited the powers of government. That negative theory of liberty, of individual rights *against* government, was the foundation of modern representa-

Rousseau: The Despotism of the General Will

The problem is to find a form of association . . . in which each, while uniting himself with all, may still obey himself alone, and remain as free as before. This is the fundamental problem of which the Social Contract provides the solution: . . . the total alienation of each associate, together with all his rights, to the whole community. . . . Each man, in giving himself to all, gives himself to nobody. . . . Each of us puts his person and all his power in common under the supreme direction of the general will, and, in our corporate capacity, we receive each member as an indivisible part of the whole. . . . In order that the social compact may not be an empty formula, it tacitly includes the undertaking, which alone can give force to the rest, that whoever refuses to obey the general will shall be compelled to do so by the whole body. This means nothing less than that he will be forced to be free.

From Jean-Jacques Rousseau, The Social Contract *(New York and London: Everyman's Library, 1913), Book I, Chs. 6 and 7, pp. 14–18.*

tive democracies such as Britain and the United States.

Rousseau, an intellectual without worldly experience, took an entirely different view. For him humanity was "good" with the goodness of the noble savage. That goodness would express itself naturally in politics once the artificial restraints and corrupting influences of the old society fell away. Checks and balances, the separation of powers, the protection of specific rights would serve no purpose if "the people" governed itself. The "general will," by definition, could not will harm to itself! Rousseau's theory of liberty was "positive"—his liberty was the willing obedience to laws and decisions that the individual himself had helped to make. Rousseau's theory of liberty thus set no limit at all on what government could do if it expressed—*or claimed to express*—the general will. In a justly famous passage in *The Social Contract,* Rousseau even asserted that the community could force individuals to be free. That hard phrase was the precursor of an even harder reality after 1789.

Utopian visions like those of Rousseau, it later became clear, often originated among and appealed to intellectuals alienated from their societies. Utopianism flourished best under autocracies—like that of the successors of Louis XIV—that pursued policies sufficiently repressive to generate dissent, but not repressive enough to crush it. And the utopian search for a society without conflict, of which Rousseau was the greatest forerunner and prophet, could even lead to an attack on representative democracies whose "negative freedoms" appeared to foster doubt, unhappiness, and disunity. Rousseau died in 1778, but only chronology bound him to the Enlightenment. His true home was the post-1789 world of revolution, nationalism, and Romanticism that he helped to shape.

ARTS AND LETTERS IN THE EIGHTEENTH CENTURY

The art and literature of the later seventeenth and early eighteenth centuries reflected the belief of Enlightenment scientists and philosopers in the rationality, intelligibility, and order of the universe. Rationalism blended easily with classicism. The regularity and harmony of Newton's universe seemed to accord both with the balance, proportion, rationality, and restraint for which classical Greek architecture and Greek and Roman writers had striven. The dictators of literary and artistic taste at the close of the seventeenth century were classicists. When *philosophes* like Voltaire wrote dramas, they accepted classical standards as unquestioningly as had Corneille and Racine. The architects of the Georgian buildings of England and the beautifully proportioned Place de la Concorde in Paris accepted classical rules of balance and unity with equal zeal. Enthusiasm for classical antiquity reached its post-Renaissance climax after 1748, when Europe discovered the remains of the Roman city of Pompeii in startlingly well-preserved condition under the ashes and cinders from Mt. Vesuvius that had covered it in A.D. 79.

An Age of Prose

The "age of reason" was an age of prose. Essays, satirical tales, novels, letters, and histories were the characteristic literary forms of the eighteenth century. Authors bent their energies to description and narrative rather than to suggestion and imagination. The essays of Joseph Addison and Richard Steele, which began to appear in 1709, sketched a delightful picture of English rural society. Jonathan Swift's *Gulliver's Travels* (1726) and Voltaire's *Candide* (1759) offered biting social and philosophical commentary. As the century progressed, the novel emerged as the favorite form of literary expression; the most enjoyable example was perhaps Henry Fielding's *Tom Jones* (1749). Philosophy, economics, and history prospered alongside fiction. The eighteenth century's greatest monument of historical scholarship was Edward Gibbon's history of *The Decline and Fall of the Roman Empire* (1776–88), which in a luminous style that will forever delight its readers, sardonically described the "triumph of barbarism and religion" over the greatest empire of the ancient world.

Painting, especially fashionable portraits, well disclosed the elegant aristocratic flavor of eighteenth-century society. The delicate-featured and exquisitely groomed women who look coolly down on the observer, and the worldly, sometimes arrogant, faces of their husbands under their powdered wigs suggest the artificiality of aristocratic society, and sometimes the hardness of character of those who inhabited it. Opulent furniture and tableware, and the great town and country houses of nobles and wealthy merchants, reflect the same aristocratic elegance.

But not all books and art served the enjoyment of the aristocracy. The first newspapers written for a wide audience of educated readers emerged in the eighteenth century. William Hogarth (1697–1764) made engravings of his satirical sketches of English society and sold them by the thousands. Above all, novelists, dramatists, and musicians in London and Paris began to appeal to a middle-class audience. The Paris stage, with productions such as *The Barber of Seville* (1775) and *The Marriage of Figaro* (1784), by Pierre de Beaumarchais, turned a keen satirical edge against the aristocracy. The heroes and heroines of novels tended increasingly to imitate the middle-class origins of their audiences.

An Age of Music

But the greatest cultural achievement of the age was its music—above all, German music. Two great Germans dominated the musical world of the early eighteenth century: Johann Sebastian Bach (1685–1750) and George Frederick Handel (1685–1759). Handel in his oratorios for chorus and instruments and Bach in his richly varied works for keyboard instruments, chamber groups, orchestras, and choruses, realized all the dramatic and emotional possibilities of the baroque style. As the century drew on, the orchestra, which had originated in the seventeenth century, expanded and took in new instruments, the piano replaced the harpsichord, and music began to move from the aristocratic salon into the public hall.

Franz Joseph Haydn (1732–1809), who wrote both for chamber groups and for orchestras, developed the musical forms known as sonatas and symphonies. The other outstanding musical personality of the latter half of the century was Wolfgang Amadeus Mozart (1756–91), probably the most brilliant musician in history. Born at Salzburg in Austria, he began his career as a child prodigy, lived only 35 years, and died in poverty. But within that short span he produced over 600 compositions that included unequalled mas-

Eighteenth-century art for a popular audience: Hogarth, *The Village Fair*.

terpieces of invention and form—string quartets, sonatas, concertos, masses, symphonies, and operas such as *Le Nozze di Figaro* (The Marriage of Figaro, 1786), *Don Giovanni* (1787), and *Die Zauberflöte* (The Magic Flute, 1791).

THE LIMITS OF THE ENLIGHTENMENT: RELIGION, PHILOSOPHY, AND LITERATURE

The Enlightenment was the creation of a small elite, although many of its ideas circulated widely and penetrated far down the social scale. It was largely confined to western Europe and the English-speaking world. And countercurrents soon arose to challenge the supremacy of reason in philosophy and of rational structure and classical balance in art.

Contrary to the expectations of many Enlightenment figures, religion did not give way to Deism or wither away. Many Protestants found a compromise between Christian faith and the Enlightenment's rationalism, humanitarianism, and tolerance. The result was the nineteenth-century development of a liberal Protestantism. Others took the road of more intense piety. The cold rationality of Deism held no appeal for emotional natures, and only the educated could understand it. Hence the wide popularity of two warmly emotional Protestant movements, Pietism in Germany and Methodism in England and America. Both emphasized the importance of the inner religious experience of individual "conversion." Pietism was a second and milder Protestant Reformation that challenged not the pope, but the twin extremes of dogmatic orthodoxy and Deism that verged on unbelief. Individualist, tolerant, and indifferent to ceremonies, Pietism attracted followers among both Catholics and Protestants.

John Wesley (1703–91) was the leader of a somewhat parallel revival of a warm and personal Christian piety in England in the years following his conversion in 1738. When the Anglican clergy resisted his efforts, he took his message directly to the people. He addressed huge outdoor congregations and prayer meetings in remote chapels, taught his followers to sing their

Wolfgang Amadeus Mozart: the culmination of eighteenth-century music.

way to heaven with the hymns of his brother Charles, and deluged his congregations with streams of pamphlets from his printing presses. In the end, Anglican opposition forced Wesley to leave the established church and create a new denomination, Methodism, which took its name from the "methodical" piety of Wesley's followers that the orthodox had originally mocked. Methodism touched many thousands of Englishmen and women at home and in the colonies who found the dry intellectualism of much eighteenth-century Anglicanism repellent. Methodism's wide following, its emphasis on otherworldly concerns, and its conspicuous loyalty to existing political authority in this world made it a more effective buttress of the social order than Anglicanism.

Even philosophers saw reason's limits. David Hume, who along with Adam Smith was one of the greatest figures of the Scottish Enlightenment, started from a close study of the great French skeptic Bayle. Hume ended by denying the possibility of certainty. Only the experience of the senses, unverifiable by any independent means, kept the mind informed about external reality. And for Hume, sense-experience was a sequence of disjointed impressions, upon which the

John Wesley preaching.

mind—and the mind alone—imposed regularities, patterns, connections.

Hume's position, which has remained logically unassailable, cut at the root of the Enlightenment faith in the capacity of reason to discover laws in nature and human behavior. Hume did not doubt the validity of Newton's laws as a rule of thumb. What he denied was that anyone would ever be in a position to claim with certainty that Newton's laws applied to *all* times and in *all* places throughout the universe. Even observations that seemed to confirm those laws might not do so, for the evidence of the senses might be a snare. The sun *might* rise tomorrow; but then again it might not.

Hume was happy to concede that some kinds of knowledge were more certain than others. But he was the first philosopher to see the full depths of the

predicament into which the collapse of the medieval religious certainties had plunged humanity. In the philosopher's study, if not in practical affairs, certainty was unattainable. That was "the whimsical condition of mankind." The observer's point of view helped determine what the observer saw. Knowledge, like the human value-systems that varied through historical time and geographic space, was relative.

Hume's skepticism did not yet shake an optimistic age that sought to replace God with Newton's clockwork universe. But a few farseeing figures nevertheless understood what he had done. The greatest philosopher of the century, Immanuel Kant (1724–1804), took up Hume's challenge, although Kant never traveled more than a few miles from his native city of Königsberg in East Prussia. In his *Critique of Pure Reason* (1781), the most demanding of all the great works of Western thought, Kant saved scientific reason, at least in his own judgment, by limiting its domain to appearances, to the data of sense-experience.

The mechanical world of physics, Kant argued, *was* knowable with certainty, although only knowable to an observer equipped with concepts built into the mind, such as space and time, What was not knowable with certainty, for Kant, were the *true* natures of the "things-in-themselves" that humans perceived through their senses. Nor could reason deal with the domain of metaphysics and religion, the realm of things that transcended experience. To many thinkers, Kant's refutation of Hume merely confirmed the Scot's skepticism. Others reacted by taking Kant, who himself argued for the necessity of belief in God as one foundation of morality, as a point of departure for a renewed leap into faith in religion.

In literature, the slowly gathering revolt against the Enlightenment took the form of a celebration of emotion that defied classical notions of rationality and balance. French and English novelists cultivated extremes of sentimentality. Heroines suffered heartrending misfortune and mistreatment, while the author sought at every turn to arouse the reader's anger, pity, love, or terror. The most influential example was Samuel Richardson's 2,000-page tear-jerker, *Clarissa* (1748), which influenced Rousseau's *Nouvelle Héloise* (1761). The bizarre, grotesque, and fantastic returned to fashion. In both architecture and literature, critics began to revive the Gothic style, despised since the Renaissance.

In Germany, which had never fallen totally under the sway of the French Enlightenment, a "Storm and Stress" (*Sturm und Drang*) movement in literature emphasized the great elemental emotions and denied the supremacy of reason. Johann Gottfried von Herder (1744–1803) conceived a philosophy of history that emphasized the uniqueness of each nation or race, the individuality of its genius, and the falsity of any view that denied that uniqueness in the name of universal reason. Johann Wolfgang von Goethe (1749–1832) published at the start of his long literary career *The Sorrows of Young Werther* (1774), a morbidly sentimental tale ending in suicide. The "Age of Reason" thus summoned up its opposite and successor—the age of Romanticism. The new age prized fierce emotion over harmony and equilibrium, and celebrated individual and national peculiarity over the Enlightenment's universal reason.

The Scientific Revolution and the Enlightenment were the most decisive break in the history of Western thought. The world picture of fifth-century Greece and of the Old and New Testaments, preserved through the Middle Ages and Renaissance, now gave way to a distinctively "modern" cast of mind. The world of Luther and Loyola, of Charles V and Philip II, was still organically related to the Middle Ages. The world of Newton and Locke, of Voltaire and Rousseau, was unmistakably our own.

Suggestions for Further Reading

The Scientific Revolution

M. Ashley, *The Golden Century* (1968), offers a fine survey of seventeenth-century social and cultural history. A. R. Hall, *The Scientific Revolution 1500–1800* (1966), is the best recent account. H. Butterfield, *The Origins of Modern Science 1300–1800* (1949), is highly readable, but C. Brinton, *The Shaping of the Modern Mind* (1953), covers a longer period. T. S. Kuhn, *The Copernican Revolution* (1957), describes the transformation of astronomical thought and offers an influential interpretation of how science advances. On the social background of scientific development, see D. Stimson, *Scientists and Amateurs: A History of the Royal Society* (1948). G. de Santillana, *The Crime of Galileo* (1955), elucidates the most famous case in the history of freedom of thought.

The Enlightenment

P. Hazard, *The European Mind: The Critical Years, 1680–1715* (1935, 1952), offers a still-useful study of the transition from Scientific Revolution to Enlightenment. The most searching interpretation of the Enlightenment as a whole is E. Cassirer, *The Philosophy of the Enlightenment* (1932, 1951). C. Becker, *The Heavenly City of the Eighteenth-Century Philosophers* (1932), attacks the *Philosophes* as doctrinaires, while P. Gay, *The Enlightenment: An Interpretation,* 2 vols. (1966–69), defends them. N. Hampson, *A Cultural History of the Enlightenment* (1969), is a useful introduction. C. R. Cragg, *Reason and Authority in the Eighteenth Century* (1964), and D. Mornet, *French Thought in the Eighteenth Century* (1929), deal with England and France respectively. R. S. Westfall, *Never at Rest: A Biography of Isaac Newton* (1981), discusses some of the leading intellectuals of the period, but see also T. Bestermann, *Voltaire* (1969), and J. N. Shklar, *Men and Citizens: A Study of Rousseau's Social Theory* (1969). L. Krieger, *Kings and Philosophers, 1689–1789* (1970), relates thought to politics. On specific topics, see M. F. Bukofzer, *Music in the Baroque Era* (1947); A. Boime, *A Social History of Modern Art,* vol. 1, *Art in an Age of Revolution, 1750–1800* (1987); B. Semmel, *The Methodist Revolution* (1973); G. R. Craig, *The Church in the Age of Reason* (1961); and E. Fox-Genovese, "Women and the Enlightenment," in R. Bridenthal et al., *Becoming Visible: Women in European History* (1987).

22

THE TWILIGHT OF THE OLD REGIME, 1715–1789

The 75 years between the death of Louis XIV in 1715 and the outbreak of the French Revolution in 1789 were a period of relative stability, without religious wars or great rebellions, except for a desperate serf uprising in distant Russia and the revolt of Britain's North American colonies in 1776. Monarchy remained the prevalent form of government, but divine-right monarchy evolved into "enlightened absolutism."

Yet monarchy, as in the seventeenth century, rested on a compromise with the aristocracy. Even the republican or constitutional governments of the eighteenth century were aristocratic in tone. Whig aristocrats and merchants dominated the English Parliament. After the death of Louis XIV, French nobles prevailed in the royal councils, and reestablished the powers of the *parlement* law courts. Junkers commanded the armies of Prussia. Polish nobles made the Polish Diet a farce. The "service nobility" of Russia gradually escaped from its duties to the state after the death of Peter the Great. And small oligarchies based on wealth ruled the Dutch Republic and the German "free cities" of the Holy Roman Empire.

Throughout Europe, the aristocracies of birth, office, and wealth reclaimed powers, rights, and privileges lost to the centralizing absolute monarchies of the seventeenth century. Only monarchs or chief ministers of unusual ability succeeded in bending the revival of aristocratic influence to the purposes of the state. The undeclared war between monarch and aristocrat normally led to an unspoken compromise, an uneasy balance between centralization and decentralization, between absolute monarchy and aristocratic privilege. That balance was perhaps lacking in clarity and logic. But all remembered how fanatical adherence to principle had given birth to the bloody religious and civil wars of the two preceding centuries. Those who had the luxury of choice were therefore usually glad to accept the structure of society and government as they found it after 1715.

Abject poverty, injustice, and brutality remained widespread, but to the elite, the brilliant "civilization"—a word that first appeared in the 1750s—of the Paris salons and the London coffeehouses appeared to outweigh the tribulations of the poor. To those who looked back on the devastation of the Thirty Years' War or the fanaticism of the "saints" of the English Revolution, social stability and political equilibrium were worth a high price in injustice. That eighteenth-century equilibrium later seemed a lost golden age to the generation of aristocrats that witnessed 1789. A French noble spoke for his caste when he remarked that those who had not lived before the Revolution lacked all conception of the sweetness of life.

THE STATE SYSTEM

Balance was likewise the rule in relations between states. The defeat of Louis XIV's bid for mastery had cost much blood and treasure. The great powers after 1715—France, Britain, Austria, Prussia, and Russia—agreed on few things. But all were determined to preserve the "balance of

Frederick the Great of Prussia inspects his troops (1778).

power," to ward off domination by a single state. That proved easier in the eighteenth century than either before or after. In the sixteenth and seventeenth centuries religious hatreds had devastated the Continent. In the age of revolution after 1789, national and ideological hatreds were again to tear it apart. But between 1715 and 1789 only issues of power divided the states of Europe, and those issues were often calculable and negotiable.

Preserving the balance meant ceaseless diplomatic haggling over "compensation"—the principle that if one state were fortunate or daring enough to acquire new territory, the other powers would receive compensating advantages to preserve the power balance. Compensation often meant that small states suffered mutilation or suppression at the hands of the great. But the practice of compensation helped preserve the balance and sometimes preserved the peace.

Wars remained frequent but were uniquely limited in both means and ends—although that happy situation was not always apparent to the relatively small numbers of professionals who fought, suffered, and died in them. Eighteenth-century war affected the civilian population far less than did war before 1715 and after 1789. Armies avoided pillaging, even on enemy territory. To allow the troops to forage gave them a chance to desert, and the devastation of territory that the victor might later annex was bad business. Conscription fell out of fashion except in Russia, where most troops were serfs, and to a limited extent in Prussia. The troops, in the words of a British commander of a slightly later period, tended to be "the scum of the earth, enlisted for drink," or foreign mercenaries. Only esprit de corps, constant drill that made obedience in battle automatic, and a discipline based on flogging and hanging welded these forces together. The aim, in the view of Prussia's greatest king, was to make the troops more terrified of their own officers than of the enemy.

Warfare itself consisted of elaborate maneuver. Commanders normally avoided pitched battles, for trained troops were a precious investment. The 43,000

casualties of Malplaquet (1709) had shown all too well the vast slaughter that ensued when armies equipped with muskets blasted one another at ranges of fifty paces or less. Armies also moved slowly, for the knee-deep mud of Europe's roads did not allow swift movement of the artillery or of the thousands of wagons needed to transport food. In winter, war usually ceased. Campaigns generally centered on a single province or fortified strongpoint and ended indecisively. The dominant system of naval tactics had similar results. Fleets sailing in rigid battle lines blasted at one another from a distance. Engagements were rarely decisive, for commanders feared losing control of their fleets and avoided the bloody, confused close-range ship-to-ship duels that alone ensured annihilation of the enemy.

Limited objectives corresponded to these limitations in methods. The enemy of today might be the ally of tomorrow. Defeating any power too thoroughly might disturb the power balance and summon up unforeseeable complications. In these "cabinet wars"—decided in and directed from the royal cabinet or secretariat—statesmen and generals normally sought concrete political and economic objectives, not unconditional surrender or total destruction. Once a power attained its objectives or became convinced that they were unattainable, it concluded a truce or a peace. In spite of relentless competition—over prestige, land, population, colonies, and trade—the monarchs, bureaucrats, and aristocrats of the eighteenth century felt themselves part of a common civilization. The secret of the eighteenth-century equilibrium was the absence of the twin forces that drive inter-state conflicts to extremes—religious or ideological strife, and bids for universal domination by a single power.

Eighteenth-century statesmen were not unaware of the similarities between their system and Newton's picture of the universe—a stable order of perfectly balanced gravitational attraction and centrifugal repulsion in which every mass moved along predictable lines of force. Ministers took pride in their mastery of "political algebra," the exact calculation of the

The French nobility lampooned: *The Baron* (1785).

forces acting on state policy. Soldiers created elaborate geometrical systems to describe the century's art of war. Only after mid-century did French theorists, such as Pierre de Bourcet and François de Guibert, begin to create a new strategy, operations, and tactics of movement, flexibility, surprise, and annihilation—the methods of the new revolutionary armies after 1792.

The eighteenth-century equilibrium remained precarious, a balance between dynamic forces. Powers still rose and fell, sometimes with alarming swiftness and decisiveness, as in the case of Poland. Wealth and trade increased steadily, for revolutions in both agriculture and industry were slowly beginning. Europe's economy and diplomacy were becoming global rather than continental; the struggle for empire reached toward the farthest corners of the earth. For the first time, battles fought in America, Africa, and Asia affected the balance of power in Europe. And in trying to maintain its position, each state accentuated its own particular strengths. Britain relied increasingly on naval power and commerce. Prussia depended on its army and bureaucracy. Russia further intensified its reliance on serfdom. Austria compensated for weakness in Germany by increasing its power in southeastern Europe. France, the one power that refused to specialize, condemned itself to naval weakness, while its intellectual and cultural leadership masked but did not remedy its failure to overtake its British rival in commerce and industry. Inept generalship and financial weakness even prevented France from profiting from its greatest strength before 1715 and after 1789—its land power.

Intellectual and political change intersected with the inter-state, social, and economic rivalries that culminated in the great upheavals after 1789. The years between 1715 and 1789, the twilight of the "old regime," fall conveniently into three periods of roughly a quarter-century each: (1) a generation of peace and relative prosperity from 1715 to 1740; (2) a period of worldwide warfare from 1740 to 1763; and (3) an interval of enlightened absolutism, aristocratic resurgence, and domestic unrest from 1763 to 1789.

PEACE AND PROSPERITY, 1715–40

Governments and peoples were thoroughly weary of war by the time the treaties of 1713–14 and 1719–21 restored peace to both western and eastern Europe. The age that followed was unheroic and happily corrupt, as postwar periods often are. But peace allowed the restoration of order and of law, and stimulated an enormous expansion of trade, particularly in western Europe.

Commerce and Industry

Seaborne commerce was the most conspicuous source of Europe's wealth during the eighteenth century. Thanks to the enterprise of their merchants and the technical skill of their mariners, the volume of foreign trade in Britain and France multiplied itself by five during the century. In the British case, colonial trade led the increase. Britain therefore needed and acquired a larger merchant marine than its rivals and the strongest navy in the world. For France, trade with other European states was the greatest source of increase. In both cases the accumulation of wealth in the hands of the upper classes was spectacular. For the first time, the total wealth of Europe began to eclipse that of Asia. The two preceding centuries of exploration, conquest, and establishment of overseas trading networks now paid off handsomely. Sugar from the West Indies, wine from Portugal, and tobacco from Virginia might grace the tables of Liverpool merchants. Their wives might wear printed calico from India in summer and furs from Canada in winter. Their daughters might marry the heirs of aristocrats whose large and elegant Georgian houses were the visible evidence of the combined profits of land and mercantile investment.

The labor of slaves or serfs produced many of the commodities on which Europe's thriving trade rested. The plantations of the West Indies serviced Europe's ever-increasing craving for sugar. That demand in turn created an almost insatiable demand for African slaves. Liverpool and

Europe in 1715

London slave traders met much of that demand. The serfs who toiled without recompense for their landlords in the grain-producing regions of eastern Europe played an economic role similar to that of the slaves of the West Indies. Some of the European economy still rested, as had the economy of the ancient world, on servile labor.

Despite the immense increase in overseas trade, the vast bulk of European commerce was within the European states themselves. And in all states except the Dutch Netherlands and perhaps Britain, most of the national product still came from agriculture. Even Britain's vast foreign trade in the last third of the century only amounted to perhaps 10 percent of the growing British economy. And it was in Britain that the coming of revolutionary changes in industry became visible after mid-century (see pp. 619–22).

Boom and Bust: The Mississippi and South Sea Bubbles

European commercial capitalism, which had created the first joint-stock companies, stock exchanges, and state banks, continued to expand. The coming of peace in 1713–14 encouraged both financial speculation and wildcat commercial ventures. Those ventures in turn led in 1719 and 1720 to the first large-scale example of a typically modern phenomenon, a stock crash—or, as contemporaries described it, a "bubble."

The wars of Louis XIV burdened both French and British governments with debt. In the French case only bankruptcy appeared to promise relief. That plight offered opportunities to plausible figures such as the Scottish promoter John Law, who appeared at the French court after the death of Louis XIV and offered to solve the monarchy's financial woes. After his commercial bank in Paris began to prosper, he received in 1717–20 control of French taxes, the right to issue paper money, a virtual monopoly on foreign trade, and the office of Controller General of Finances. His Mississippi Company, chartered to trade with France's colony in Louisiana, soon mutated into a "Company of the Indies" and assumed France's state debt, which it paid off by promoting a boom in its own stock. Law's "system"—his reforms of government finances, his paper money, and his expansion of the credit available to merchants—stimulated the French economy. But when the price of his company's stock reached 36 times its original value, investors began to cash in their paper profits. The market collapsed, and Law fled.

A parallel episode occurred in London. Promoters organized a South Sea Company to exploit the trade with the Spanish colonies provided for in the Peace of Utrecht. It likewise took over much of the government's debt, and it too deliberately promoted a boom in its own stock. In 1720, a few months after Law's failure had shown the precariousness of stock booms, the South Sea "bubble" burst.

These twin financial catastrophes slowed the development of joint-stock companies and ruined many individual investors. But despite their speculative excesses, the bold experimenters in London and Paris had shown new ways to mobilize capital for commerce and industry and to support the public debt from as yet untapped sources. After reorganization, both companies made money for their investors for many years. However, the French government, by partially repudiating its debt in the wake of the crash, lost the confidence of investors. The French acquired a fierce distrust of credit, an attitude that constricted their economic growth. London did not make that mistake. The British government never again permitted private interests to assume responsibility for the state debt. Britain thus assured itself the credit that meant the difference between victory and defeat in a world of warring states.

The England of Walpole

The generation of peace abroad after the death of Louis XIV allowed England to consolidate peace at home. Under the Act of Settlement of 1701, the Elector of Hanover succeeded Queen Anne as ruler of England in 1714. The first two Hanoverian monarchs, George I (r. 1714–27) and George II (r. 1727–60), were dull-witted and spoke little English. Their only claim to distinction was their patronage of the great composer Handel, whom they induced to settle permanently in England. In politics, their chief contribution was petty interference in minor details of government; the "inner cabinet" of ministers therefore became increasingly responsible for framing policy. Although the king in theory remained free to choose his own ministers, Parliament's control over finances meant that he had to select men who could influence elections and command a majority. By custom, ministers usually accepted the leadership of the ablest or most powerful minister, who presented their policy to the king. Those who disagreed with the group's majority lost their offices. These informal practices foreshadowed the nineteenth-century "prime minister" and "cabinet system" that

1660	1689	1714		1917	
Restored House of Stuart	Wm. & Mary, Anne		House of Hanover		(House of Windsor)

later became almost universal in the representative democracies of western Europe and of the English-speaking world.

Robert Walpole, a country squire with family connections to both the landed gentry and commercial interests, was the first prime minister, although he did not accept that title. For some twenty years, from 1721 to 1742, he managed the Whig party in Parliament and led the government. The first two Hanoverians necessarily chose their ministers from the Whigs who dominated the House of Commons, for affection for the Stuarts tainted the Tories after the abortive Scottish Jacobite rising in 1715.

Walpole was a consummate manipulator who held his parliamentary majority together by tact, persuasion, patronage, and bribery. He kept George I's favor by passing generous budgets for the king's household through Parliament, and by an occasional donation to the royal mistress. His enjoyment of drink and off-color stories—as well as his steely ambition—helped him to manage the Whig merchants and landed gentry who controlled Parliament and ran local government as justices of the peace. But his principal appeal was that he offered to England a political stability unknown since Elizabeth I.

"Let sleeping dogs lie" was Walpole's motto. He sought to defuse religious conflict. He maintained the Test Act to reassure the Anglicans but conciliated dissenters by annual parliamentary votes that in effect suspended the Test Act temporarily and allowed dissenters to hold public office. His policy of "salutary neglect" left the colonies to grow in population and wealth by their own efforts. Above all, he did his best to avoid war; he maintained until the 1730s the alliance with France that his predecessors had concluded in 1716–17 to safeguard Hanoverian possessions in Germany.

Under Walpole's ministry, Britain and its colonies prospered; the credit of the government remained high; the ruling aristocracy of landed and commercial wealth governed in its own interests, but far less repressively than did other European ruling classes. Voltaire, after his visit to England between 1726 and 1729, somewhat idealized English society and government. He neglected to mention to his French readers the ferocity of eighteenth-century English law toward crimes against property. In theory it imposed death by hanging for over 200 offenses, including on occasion the theft of items worth as little as five shillings. In practice, "transportation" to the colonies usually took the place of hanging, and English laws guaranteed equality and individual freedom to an extent unknown on the Continent except perhaps in the Dutch Netherlands and Switzerland.

But Walpole's golden age of the gentry did not last. In 1739 the London merchants and their spokesmen in Parliament forced him into a commercial war with Spain. Within three years his majority collapsed, and he left office.

France: Louis XV and Cardinal Fleury

The peace that brought strength to Britain brought weakness to France. Louis XIV's great-grandson, Louis XV (r. 1715–74), became king at the age of five. The Duke of Orléans, the nephew of Louis XIV who governed as regent during the new king's minority, secured his own power by concessions to the powerful elements in French society that the Sun King had kept leashed. Nobles reappeared as royal ministers. The *Parlement* of Paris boldly reasserted its ancient claim to register and enforce royal legislation—or not—as it saw fit. The French monarchy in theory

". . . to be hanged by the neck until dead": eighteenth-century English law, applied here to a debtor convicted of defrauding his creditors.

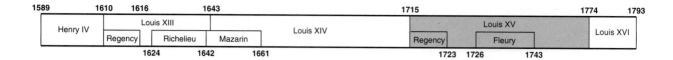

1589	1610	1616	1643		1715		1774	1793

Henry IV | Louis XIII | | Louis XIV | | Louis XV | | Louis XVI

Regency | Richelieu | Mazarin | | Regency | Fleury

1624 1642 1661   1723 1726   1743

remained as absolute as ever, but after Louis XIV it lacked the ruthless will needed to translate theory into practice. The resulting reinforcement of the privileges of the aristocracy infuriated the middle classes and in the long run condemned the royal government to financial ruin.

Cardinal Fleury, the leading minister from 1726 to 1743, halted the decline for a time. But Fleury was no Richelieu. He came to power at the age of 73, and his policy, much like Walpole's, sought to avoid expensive wars and to conciliate rather than confront powerful domestic interests. Fleury dissociated himself from the courageous attempt of another minister to tax the nobility. He nevertheless stabilized the currency, encouraged trade, and had considerable success in damping down the continuing struggle between Jansenists and Jesuits. In foreign policy his overriding goal was to prevent the renewal of the coalitions against France that had blocked Louis XIV. Fleury therefore sought to cooperate with Walpole in making the Anglo-French alliance work.

When Fleury died in 1743 at the age of ninety, Louis XV took Louis XIV as his model. Henceforth he sought to govern personally, without a first minister. But although Louis XV had inherited many of his great-grandfather's tastes—women and the hunt above all—he lacked the Sun King's relentless capacity for sustained work. The court frivolity with which Louis XIV had sought to corrupt the aristocracy had also corrupted his own successor. Given the centralized administrative machine that the Sun King had left behind, the sloth of Louis XV meant a fatal lack of coordination of the various branches of the bureaucracy and frequent paralysis. Louis XV did not govern in person, and from 1743 until his death in 1774 he largely prevented others from governing for him.

The aristocracy and the royal mistresses, of whom the Marquise de Pompa-dour (1745–51) and the Countess du Barry (1768–74) were the most notable, inevitably filled the resulting power vacuum. Louis XV was not unaware of the declining health of the state: "After me, the deluge" was his most famous—and justly remembered—remark. But France, thanks to its size, its population, and a growth rate in trade and industry as rapid as Britain's, remained potentially the most powerful nation in Europe.

Declining or Stagnant Powers

Elsewhere in Europe, with few exceptions, monarchical institutions likewise declined. In Spain a remarkable woman ruled: Elizabeth Farnese, the strong-willed Italian queen of Philip V of Bourbon (r. 1700–46), whom Louis XIV had put on the throne. With the help of her husband's chief ministers, Elizabeth Farnese beat back the claims of the nobility, encouraged trade and industry, and reestablished Spain's diplomatic status as a great power. But Spanish society and government failed to respond. Centralization that robbed subjects of all initiative, a taxation more crushing than anything west of Russia, absurd guild regulations, a pitilessly intolerant Church that was the single largest social institution, a sluggish nobility that amounted to 5 percent of the population, and a culturally rooted distaste for commerce and industry proved impossible to overcome. Spain's economy, colonies, army, and navy stagnated, while other powers pressed onward.

Austria remained an imperfectly united empire that linked the three kingdoms of Austria, Bohemia, and Hungary with two dependencies of entirely different cultures and traditions, northern Italy and the southern Netherlands. And the dynastic ties that bound together this bizarre assortment of territories were themselves open to challenge. The Habsburg Emperor Charles VI (r. 1711–40) had no son. He therefore spent almost thirty years persuading both his provinces and the powers to accept a "Pragmatic Sanction" that established his daughter Maria Theresa as heir to his scattered lands. By his death in 1740 he had secured the agreement on paper of all concerned. But in the absence of a strong Habsburg army and central bureaucracy, treaties were a fragile defense against the greed of neighboring monarchs and the restlessness of the Hungarian nobility.

Farther to the east, the Polish and Ottoman empires continued their decline. France and Spain fought a halfhearted and trivial war against Austria and Russia over the succession to the Polish crown between 1733 and 1738. The Russian candidate won. The losers received "compensation" in the form of scraps of territory elsewhere; Spain received Naples and Sicily from Austria. Simultaneously, Austria and Russia fought the Ottoman Turks, whose decline accelerated as Europe's technological lead continued to grow.

Russia after Peter I failed to make its full weight felt for a generation. His succession law, enacted after his mortal quarrel with his son Alexei, gave the autocrat power to choose his own successor. That in effect made Russia until after 1800 an elective monarchy—and the Guards regiments and court nobles did the electing, with bayonets. Between 1725 and 1741, palace coups gave the crown successively to women or children who reigned but did not rule. From 1741 to 1762 Elizabeth, a daughter of Peter I, ruled firmly after seizing power with the help of the Guards and eliminating her opponents in the customary fashion—by torture, execution, deportation, and confiscation of land.

German and particularly Prussian influence predominated at the Russian court. As in France, the nobility freed itself from many of the restrictions that a great monarch had placed upon it. The Russian nobility extended the power over the serfs that Peter I had given it, while gradually escaping its corresponding obligation to serve the state. In Russia, as in Hungary and Prussia during the eighteenth century, the peasants thus sank ever deeper into serfdom, while the government made re-

Habsburg domestic life, painted by Meytens: Empress Maria Theresa of Austria with her husband, Emperor Francis I, and their eleven children. The future emperor Joseph II stands at right center.

peated concessions to the nobility. Until the accession of Elizabeth, and especially of Catherine the Great in 1762, Russia lacked strong rulers. But the feebleness of Peter I's immediate successors showed the full extent of his greatness. Despite weakness at the center, Russia retained the great-power status that Peter had won for it.

Prussia: Sergeant King, Undisciplined Son

Prussia, as usual, was an exception to a general trend, for its monarchy became more rather than less absolute. King Frederick William I of Brandenburg-Prussia (r. 1713–40) was the most successful ruler of his generation. This strange, uncouth, and furious man, who smoked tobacco and drank beer in gargantuan quantities, was the second of the three great Hohenzollerns who made the poor and backward territories of Brandenburg-Prussia into a great power.

Frederick William followed in the footstep of the Great Elector, centralizing as a pathetic figure, unmilitary in habits and possessed of decadent tastes such as reading Voltaire and playing the flute. The irate father burned books, smashed flutes, and had Frederick beaten. When the prince attempted to flee the country with a friend in 1730, the king had the friend beheaded before Frederick's eyes, threatened Frederick himself with death for "desertion," and set him to work in the provincial bureaucracy. The experience rendered Frederick cold, dissimulating, and supremely cynical. But he also acquired a passion for administration and war, and a burning ambition to acquire glory and "establish his sovereignty like a rock of bronze." His opportunity came in 1740, the year in which both his hated father and Charles VI of Habsburg died.

THE WORLD WARS OF MID-CENTURY, 1740–63

Two great wars, the War of the Austrian Succession (1740–48) and the Seven Years' War (1756–63) punctuated the middle of the century. The wars were linked, and derived from two irreconcilable rivalries—Hohenzollern against Habsburg in central Europe, and Britain against France in North America, the West Indies, Africa, and India. Twice these separate conflicts became entangled, although the powers exchanged partners between the two wars. In the end, Britain and Prussia defeated France and Austria.

The War of the Austrian Succession, 1740–48

In 1740 Maria Theresa (r. 1740–80), a beautiful, strong-willed, courageous, but inexperienced woman of 23, succeeded her father Charles VI in the Habsburg dominions, as provided for in the Pragmatic Sanction. That gave Frederick II of Prussia his opportunity. Although he had published an anonymous pamphlet against the supposed immorality of Machiavelli's political precepts, he had learned the great Florentine's lessons well. In December 1740 he seized Silesia, Austria's rich prov-

Father and son: Frederick William I in a characteristic pose *(above)*, and the young Frederick II *(below)*.

his administration, paring civil expenditures to the bone, and working his subordinates remorselessly. The purpose of this drill-sergeant king was to build the most formidable army in Europe. He echoed Richelieu in demanding absolute obedience to the state: "Salvation is from the Lord, but everything else is my business." After 1733, he militarized the peasantry by imposing a form of conscription, the "Canton System." Peasants in the ranks served Junker officers who were the brothers or cousins of their Junker landlords in civilian life. Frederick William doubled Prussia's peacetime standing army to 80,000, nearly equal to Austria's theoretical total of 100,000 men. But he was careful not to use his blue-coated and precisely drilled army, for he loved his "blue boys" too much to expend them in war.

His son Frederick II (r. 1740–86)—the third great Hohenzollern—thus inherited a treasury surplus, a ruthlessly efficient civil bureaucracy, and an army that was the fourth largest force on the continent and the most relentlessly trained. Frederick had initially impressed his father ince to the northeast of Bohemia. Possession of Silesia, with its million inhabitants, its linen industry, and its iron ore, would finally make Brandenburg-Prussia a great power.

Frederick's thrust caught Maria Theresa off guard, and the success of his shameless aggression encouraged Bavaria, Spain, and finally France to join in the attack, in violation of their Pragmatic Sanction pledges. But Hungary, which resented Habsburg rule, ironically proved Maria Theresa's salvation. When she traveled to Budapest with her infant son and made an emotional appeal to the Hungarian Parliament, her bravery and tact inspired the Hungarian nobility to rise tumultuously to her support. An able minister, Count Haugwitz, centralized the Habsburg administration and reorganized the army during the wars that followed. Austria had been a helpless victim in 1740; now it became a formidable enemy. But Frederick's armies fought brilliantly, and at Hohenfriedberg in 1745 he achieved the first great Prussian victory due above all to his own generalship. The combined pressure of France, Bavaria, and Prussia— shaky though their alliance was—proved too much for Maria Theresa. In 1748, at Aix-la-Chapelle, she consented to a peace treaty that left Silesia in Frederick's hands.

The Anglo-French overseas rivalry intersected with the war on the Continent. Britain went to war with Spain in 1739 over Spanish maltreatment of English merchants smuggling goods to the Spanish empire. That "war of Jenkins' Ear" (named after an unfortunate English trader), and French intervention in Germany in support of a Bavarian claimant to the office of Holy Roman Emperor, made conflict between France and Britain almost inevitable. France and Spain, thanks to their Bourbon family ties, normally cooperated closely after 1700, and France had developed a large economic stake in the Spanish colonies, which it supplied with manufactured goods.

British and French interests also clashed in North America and India. The French military hold on Canada and Louisiana appeared to threaten the British colonies that stretched from Boston to Sa-

vannah. The fantastic rates of population growth of the British colonies on the eastern seaboard prompted a northward and westward expansion that seemed in turn to threaten the French. In the West Indies the British and French glowered at each other from their sugar-island strongholds. In India, where the Mughal empire had fallen into near-anarchy after the death in 1707 of the merciless Aurangzeb, its last strong ruler, the French and British East India companies sought to fill a power vacuum. From their respective bases at Pondicherry and Madras, each mobilized native rulers against the other. From Canada to the Carnatic Coast of India, France and Britain prepared for war, and British and French troops clashed in Germany as early as 1743.

In 1744 France declared war on Great Britain and merged the continental and overseas wars. In 1745 a force of American colonial militia with British naval support boldly seized the key to Canada, the great fortress of Louisbourg on Cape Breton Island in the St. Lawrence estuary. In 1746 the French seized Madras. But the overseas conflict was indecisive, because Britain failed to set clear objectives and establish priorities. In Parliament the "Patriot" partisans of overseas war denounced the British continental commitment as "Hanoverianism," a pandering to the interests of George II, who led a British army in Germany to defend his possessions as Elector of Hanover against France. The French defeated the British in a hard-fought battle at Fontenoy in the Austrian Netherlands in 1745, and in 1747 the British navy twice annihilated French fleets escorting West Indies convoys. George II's son, "Butcher" Cumberland, savaged the Highland clans after his victory over the last pro-Stuart rising, which had broken out with French encouragement in 1745.

Neither side pressed its successes far, except in Scotland. The War of the Austrian Succession was a typical "limited" war. The Anglo-French duel ended in stalemate. The French surrendered Madras, and the British government, much to the disgust of the American colonists, gave back Louisbourg. The French emerged from the war with increased prestige, an enlarged debt, and no concrete gains over either Britain or Austria. The British emerged with a clear sense of how to fight their next war with France.

The Overseas "War before the War," 1749–55

The peace of Aix-la-Chapelle did not end the overseas conflict between Britain and France. Joseph Dupleix, France's greatest colonial adventurer, sought after 1748 to make the French East India Company a political as well as a commercial power in India. By recruiting allies among the warring native states that contended within the hollow shell of the Mughal empire, he hoped to increase his company's revenue and ultimately drive the British from India. The English East India Company reinforced its outposts. Clashes ensued in which the British largely prevailed, thanks to their command of the sea and the brilliant leadership of the legendary Robert Clive. In 1754 the company directors, fearing that Dupleix had overreached himself, recalled him to France. The ensuing truce merely postponed the struggle for mastery in south Asia that Dupleix had begun.

In America, open warfare did not break out until 1752. The French in Canada used the interval of peace to build a chain of forts from the St. Lawrence down the Ohio to the Mississippi to block the westward thrust of Britain's American colonists. London countered, reinforcing the colonies with ships and troops. Britain held the advantage; 1.2 million British subjects, including slaves, faced about 60,000 French. The French sought to even the odds by an alliance with Indian tribes whose interest in preventing British westward penetration paralleled that of France. French raids in turn provoked in 1754 an unsuccessful attempt, under the leadership of Lieutenant Colonel George Washington of the Virginia militia, to capture the vital French base at Fort Duquesne, on the site of modern Pittsburgh. In 1755, near the same spot, General George Braddock and a force of British regulars discovered that rigid European tactics were poorly suited to war in the woods. The

French and Indian War, the final round of the Anglo-French struggle for North America, had begun.

The Climax of Old-Regime Statecraft: The "Diplomatic Revolution" of 1756

Overseas struggle was merely one prelude to a second round of war in Europe. The other prelude was a "diplomatic revolution" by which the chief enemies of the first general war of mid-century changed partners in preparation for the second. Britain had fought the War of the Austrian Succession in loose agreement with Austria, its traditional ally from the wars of 1689–97 and 1701–13. But London saw no British interest in fighting simply to restore Silesia to Maria Theresa. Bourbon France had fought against its traditional Habsburg enemy in a still looser alliance with Prussia; Frederick distrusted Paris and twice deserted it to make truces with Austria. By 1748, all four major powers were unhappy with their traditional allies.

The chief instigator of the ensuing revolution was Maria Theresa's chancellor, the wily Prince Wenzel Anton von Kaunitz. He began from the premise that the reconquest of Silesia—and the smashing of Prussia—was the prerequisite for Austria's resurgence as a great power. That aim prompted Kaunitz to think the unthinkable. He sought to replace the ancient antagonism between Bourbon and Habsburg with a Franco-Austrian alliance, possibly with Russian support, against Prussia. Even the battlefield genius of Frederick II, Kaunitz was confident, would be helpless against the three strongest land powers in Europe.

Kaunitz sought with success to win over the Marquise de Pompadour, the current mistress of Louis XV. But the king remained reluctant—until Britain and Prussia unintentionally convinced him. London had long feared that its Austrian ally lacked the will and ability to help Britain defend Hanover against France, and the outbreak of Anglo-French hostilities overseas increased British anxieties. In 1755 London therefore sought Russian help in the usual British way—subsidies

1701	1714		1740	1748	1756	1763		1789		1815
War of Spanish Succession	Walpole, Fleury, and Frederick William I		War of Austrian Succession	Diplomatic Revolution	Seven Years' War		Last Years of the Old Regime		Revolutionary Era	

that exchanged British gold for allied troops. That treaty alarmed Frederick II, for it raised the specter of a large Russian army encamped on his eastern border. He therefore approached London, and outbid Russia. By the treaty of Westminster of January 1756, Prussia itself agreed to defend Hanover, naturally in exchange for its own British subsidy.

The spectacle of Prussia, France's ally, contracting a quasi-alliance with Britain, a power already in conflict with France from the Ohio to the Carnatic, finally aroused the wrath of Louis XV. Bourbon France made a defensive alliance with Habsburg Austria. Kaunitz also enlisted Russia, and planned war for 1757. Frederick II judged that his only chance was to strike first. The Austrians had hoped for such a blow to weld Kaunitz's grand coalition together. Unfortunately for Kaunitz, Frederick II struck in August 1756, a year earlier than Vienna had anticipated. Unfortunately for Frederick, his aggression indeed did Kaunitz's work. It brought into play Austria's French alliance and created a grand coalition that almost destroyed Prussia.

The Seven Years' War, 1756–63

In the new war, the greatest worldwide conflict of the old regime, Britain thus fought for empire and Prussia for its life. After a feeble beginning, William Pitt became virtual prime minister of Britain. Pitt possessed a Roman nose, a talent for oratory, and a clear sense of Britain's global objectives. Convinced of his own indispensability ("I am sure I can save this country, and nobody else can") he pushed his way into the cabinet in spite of the disfavor of George II. From 1757 to 1760, he tirelessly directed Britain's war and drove his subordinates to their limits. In 1757, at Plassey near Calcutta, Robert Clive destroyed France's principal client, the Nawab of Bengal, and seized his rich province for Britain. That broke French power in India. Britain conquered France's chief slaving station at Gorée in Senegal and cut France's West Indian sugar islands off from their supplies of slaves and manufactured goods.

In 1759, the "year of miracles," Pitt conquered for Britain the domination of the outer seas that it held with only brief interruptions until 1941. A brilliant young general, James Wolfe, led an amphibious expedition up the St. Lawrence River. Outside the walls of Québec city he defeated France at the cost of his own life. That ended the French empire in North America. British fleets captured the rich West Indies sugar island of Guadeloupe and drove the French fleet onto the lee shore of Quiberon Bay in western France. Command of the sea was the key to Britain's triumphs.

On the Continent, Prussia survived only thanks to Frederick II and to his long-suffering troops, whom he drove toward

Britain's command of the sea in action: Wolfe takes Québec, 1759.

View of the Taking of Quebeck by the English Forces Commanded by Gen.ˡ Wolfe Sep: 13 1759.

the enemy with sarcastic wit: "You dogs, do you want to live for ever?" Prussia's "year of miracles" was 1757. At Rossbach in Saxony, Frederick with 21,000 troops decisively defeated a French army of 64,000 by attacking them in the flank. Having thus checked one of his three enemies, he hastened back to defend Silesia from Austrian invasion. A bare month after Rossbach, he smashed an Austrian army of 80,000 at Leuthen with a mere 36,000 Prussians.

But these great victories produced no decisive strategic result. Frederick was the supreme artist of eighteenth-century warfare, but his military instrument did not permit battles of annihilation. Pursuit, necessary to prevent a beaten enemy from re-forming to fight again, was impossible with troops that deserted once they were out of their officers' sight. And Prussia's desperate position, exposed to the French from the west, the Austrians from the south, and the Russians from the east, prevented the great king from finishing off any one of his adversaries. The war dragged on. Russia made its weight felt, and in 1759 an Austro-Russian army heavily defeated Frederick at Kunersdorf in Silesia.

Frederick thought despairingly of abdication. But dissension among his enemies saved him and Prussia. Kaunitz had not promised enough of the prospective spoils to France and Russia to inspire their all-out effort. Austria understandably feared that Russian troops, once invited into central Europe, would not leave. France's naval and overseas campaigns had exhausted its treasury, and the disgrace of Rossbach had shattered the monarchy's already low reputation at home. Pitt's lavish subsidies to the armies of German princelings, along with token British forces, pinned the French down in bloody fighting in western Germany.

In 1760 Frederick temporarily lost Berlin and by the end of 1761 he appeared close to total defeat, as 300,000 allied troops penned him into a fortified camp in Silesia. His British ally abandoned him. George III (r. 1760–1820), who had succeeded his grandfather, wished to prove himself thoroughly English, unlike the first

two Georges. He therefore withdrew from all involvement in German affairs and drove Pitt to resignation in October 1761. Lord Bute, George III's Scottish favorite, became chief minister and sought peace with France at almost any price, including the sacrifice of Prussia.

Then, on January 5, 1762, Elizabeth of Russia died. Her successor was the weak and eccentric Tsar Peter III, a German by birth and a fond admirer of Frederick the Great. He immediately withdrew Russia from the coalition. Only a crippled and sulking France now supported Vienna, and Maria Theresa and Kaunitz grudgingly abandoned their hopes of crushing the Prussian upstart. The long war was over.

Victory and Defeat: The Treaties of Hubertusburg and Paris, 1763

Two victors thus emerged from the treaties by which Prussia and Austria and Britain and France made peace in January– February 1763. At Hubertusburg, Austria conceded to Prussia the possession of Silesia and hard-won status as one of the five great powers of Europe. The Treaty of Paris almost eliminated France as Britain's overseas rival, although Britain did give back most of the economic outposts France had lost: trading stations in India, its slave-trade base at Gorée in west Africa, rich sugar islands in the West Indies, and two tiny islands off Newfoundland, St. Pierre and Miquelon.

But in the long run only the continents counted. Trading posts could flourish only if they controlled a large hinterland. Sugar islands produced great wealth in a few square miles but were incapable of defending themselves against a power, such as Britain, that controlled the sea. Failure at sea and the collapse of French land power in India and North America broke the first French colonial empire for good. France withdrew its troops from India and ceded to Britain all of Canada and of Louisiana east of the Mississippi, and Louisiana west of the Mississippi passed to Spain. Henceforth, the British had no serious rivals in North America except the colonists they had planted there.

ENLIGHTENED ABSOLUTISM, 1763–89

In the quarter century that followed the end of the Seven Years' War, the ancient institution of monarchy seemed briefly to take on new life. The major ideas of the Enlightenment—reason, natural law, happiness, progress, liberty—filtered through to the rulers. Some monarchs accepted the criticisms that *philosophes* had leveled at aristocratic and Church privileges, unequal taxation, and the degraded condition of the peasantry and the urban lower classes. In addition, the great wars of mid-century had strained the social fabric of most European states. The resurgence of the aristocracy forced monarchs to look to the middle classes for support. Only reforms could restore order, revive trade, refill the treasuries of Europe's monarchs, and check the pretensions of the nobility. The fusion of new ideas and practical needs produced the phenomenon that contemporaries described as "enlightened absolutism."

The concept of the enlightened absolutist inevitably fitted only a few rulers of the later eighteenth century. George III of England made no pretense to enlightenment, nor would his subjects have applauded if he had. English loyalty to the post-1688 status quo ran deep. In his last years, Louis XV of France showed unexpected resolution and zeal, but during most of his reign he was enlightened in few senses of the word. A few minor monarchs such as Gustavus III of Sweden (r. 1771–92) and Charles III of Spain (r. 1759–88) had some claims to the title. But the three rulers whom *philosophes* cited most often as enlightened absolutists were Catherine the Great of Russia, Frederick the Great of Prussia, and Joseph II of Austria.

The attack of the enlightened absolutists on irrational customs and vested interests, on aristocratic and Church power, and on town and provincial privileges was not new. It was in most respects a continuation of the centralizing drive of the seventeenth-century monarchies. What had changed was the climate of opinion in which monarchs acted. The ideas of the Enlightenment, the practical example of Britain, and the victorious struggle for self-government of the British colonies in North America after 1776 stripped of its persuasiveness the doctrine of the divine right of kings. Monarchs therefore had to appeal to their increasingly literate subjects with talk of following reason and of serving the public good. Frederick the Great described himself as "merely the first servant of the state." That monarchy now had to justify its existence was a sign of fatal weakness.

Russia: Catherine the Great

Catherine II (r. 1762–96), the most remarkable woman ruler of the century, was no Russian. Princess of the German line of Anhalt-Zerbst, she married the eccentric crown prince Peter in 1745. A woman of high intelligence, masterful cunning, implacable will, and a warm heart, she maintained a succession of lovers with lavish gifts of lands and serfs; as the poet Pushkin later remarked, "many were called, and many chosen." In her youth, Catherine survived the snake-pit of the St. Petersburg court by pretending to be frivolous, while

Catherine the Great looking the part.

finding allies and a lover among the officers of the crucial Guards regiments. Her husband Peter, after his coming to the throne as Peter III in 1762, alienated those same regiments by proposing to reform them along Prussian lines. He also appalled the pious by confiscating church lands. Within six months, Catherine seized power with the help of the Guards. Peter died under arrest, apparently at the hands of a relative of Grigori Orlov, Catherine's lover.

Catherine came to power with a genuine desire to improve the welfare of her subjects. She read the works of *philosophes* such as Montesquieu and advanced thinkers such as Beccaria. She corresponded with Voltaire, persuaded Diderot to visit her court, and proclaimed publicly her adherence to the Enlightenment. But as autocrat she could not afford too much enlightenment. Survival required independence from the faction that had brought her to power, and elimination of all potential rivals for the throne. She therefore sought to widen her political base by conciliating the nobility as a whole. She confirmed the most important act of her husband's brief reign, his release of the nobility from any obligation to serve the state. She made land ownership a monopoly of the nobility. She made promotion in the bureaucracy automatic, by seniority, a step that gravely weakened the power of her successors. In 1785 she granted the nobility a charter that conceded at last some rights against the state, some exemption from arbitrary arrest and from the barbaric punishments that Russian tradition demanded. But since the autocrat could still revoke noble status at any moment, the rights Catherine's charter granted were as much a matter of form as of substance.

In 1767–68 she even summoned a legislative commission to codify Russia's laws. Every social group except serfs sent representatives armed with statements of grievances. That was the autocracy's first open appeal to its subjects, its first attempt to give them a voice in Russia's central government. It was also the last before the twentieth century, when revolution forced the last tsar to concede a sham parliament.

Catherine dissolved the commission before it could suggest laws; its passing marked the waning of her "enlightened" phase.

She nevertheless drew from it a sense of what her subjects, especially the nobility, wanted. What they wanted and Catherine conceded was the strengthening of serfdom. As early as 1765 she gave landlords the power to condemn serfs to forced labor without legal formalities. In 1767 she banned serf complaints against landlords upon pain of hard labor for life and flogging with the dreaded Russian whip—the knout. The knout, now that the nobility was no longer obliged to do state service to justify their holding of serfs, was soon needed, for the freeing of the nobility in turn raised expectations among the serfs. When Catherine disappointed those expectations, the greatest of all Russian peasant revolts convulsed the Volga region from 1773 to 1775 under the leadership of the Cossack Emelyan Pugachev, who claimed to be Peter III. Catherine's army ultimately massacred the insurgents and brought Pugachev in an iron cage to Moscow. There, in time-honored fashion, Catherine had him broken on the wheel, beheaded, dismembered, and burned.

In the following years she sought to reorganize and strengthen local government to prevent further revolts, while extending the institution of serfdom to newly conquered provinces and to free categories of peasants. By the end of her reign, by one estimate, 34 million of the 36 million subjects of the Russian monarchy were serfs. By her encouragement of the nobility she furthered a process that never reached completion, the transformation of the service nobility into a Western-style aristocracy with rights against the state. In Russia, unlike western Europe, that process rested on the further enslavement of the peasantry. That left an explosive legacy.

Conquest, not reform, made Catherine II "the Great" in her own lifetime. Peter the Great had wrenched open a window to the West by driving the Swedes from the Baltic coast. Catherine pushed Russia's borders southward and westward against Poland and the Ottoman Empire.

Poland was her first victim, for its borders were a mere 200 miles from Moscow. In 1763 Catherine secured the election to the Polish throne of a former lover, Stanislaus Poniatowski. Thereafter, Catherine and Frederick II of Prussia worked to block constitutional reforms that might revive the fortunes of the Polish state. In 1772 the two monarchs joined to carry out a First Partition of Poland. Frederick took West Prussia, and thus secured a land bridge between Brandenburg and the province of Prussia. Catherine took a generous slice of northeastern Poland, with the pretext that Russian and Orthodox populations there were suffering under Polish rule. To preserve the balance of power, the two monarchs thought it wise to offer the province of Galicia, northeast of Hungary, to Maria Theresa. That gift distressed the pious empress, but reason of state triumphed over morality.

The First Partition shocked the Poles into a patriotic revival that swept up even Poniatowski, who forgot that he owed his throne to Catherine. In 1791, after the outbreak of the French Revolution, Poland enacted a remarkable reform constitution that abolished the *liberum veto* (see p. 528) and established a strong monarchy. Catherine gave a swift and ruthless answer. Early in 1792 she halted a promising war against the Turks, rushed an army to Poland, and restored the old anarchy. In 1793, in partnership with Prussia alone, she carried out a Second Partition that reduced Poland to a narrow strip wedged between Prussia, Russia, and Austria. The inhabitants of this rump-Poland, under the leadership of Thaddeus Kosciuszko, who had fought conspicuously in the American Revolution, rose in revolt against the partitioning powers. But Catherine's armies tracked down Kosciuszko and forced Poniatowski to abdicate. A Third Partition in 1795 wiped what was left of Poland off the map by dividing it between Russia, Prussia, and Austria. In the three partitions, Catherine secured almost two-thirds of Poland's original territory. A Polish state did not reemerge until the common ruin of the three partitioning powers in 1917–18.

Catherine's successes against the crumbling Ottoman Empire were almost

Russia's Drive to the West   1462–1796

as decisive. In wars in 1768–74 and 1787–92, Catherine secured most of the northern shore of the Black sea. By the Treaty of Kütchük Kainardji that ended the first war in 1774, Russia also received a vague right to protect Orthodox Christians in the Ottoman Empire, a right that later served as a perennial pretext for Russian intervention at Constantinople. Kütchük Kainardji marked the opening of the "Eastern Question"—the decay and partition of the Ottoman Empire—that bedeviled European diplomacy until its resolution by force in 1914–18. For the moment, the Ottoman Empire escaped the fate of Poland because of its size, its remoteness, and the mutual jealousies of its two European adversaries, Austria and Russia. But at Catherine's death in 1796, little seemed to stand between Russian power and Constantinople, the gate to the Mediterranean.

Maria Theresa on the First Partition of Poland

Frederick the Great, with his habitual cynicism, remarked that "Maria Theresa wept, but she kept on taking."

This unfortunate partition of Poland is costing me ten years of my life. . . . How many times have I refused to agree to it! But disaster after disaster heaped upon us by the Turks, misery, famine and pestilence at home, no hope of assistance from either France or England, and the prospect of being left isolated and threatened with war both by Prussia and Russia—it was all these considerations that finally forced me to accept that unhappy proposal which will remain a blot on my reign. God grant that I be not held responsible for it in the other world! I confess that I cannot keep from talking about this affair. I have taken it so to heart that it poisons and embitters all my days.

Excerpt from a letter to one of her diplomats, in Readings in Western Civilization, *ed. by Paul L. Hughes and Robert F. Fries (Paterson, N.J.: Littlefield, Adams, 1960), p. 134.*

Prussia: Frederick the Great

Frederick II of Prussia, who ruled until 1786, had better claims than Catherine to the title of "enlightened absolutist." The state he inherited, despite its narrow military traditions was unlike the "half-German, half-Tartar" autocracy that fell to Catherine II. Prussia's enserfed peasants suffered under the Junkers but had far more rights than the serfs of Russia. Prussia possessed a middle class and was a recognizably Western society capable of accepting gradual reform.

Frederick burnished his reputation for enlightenment by inviting Voltaire to Potsdam. They eventually quarreled over the merits of Frederick's rather awful poetry, but they agreed that the king's duty was to combat ignorance and superstition, to enhance the welfare of his subjects, and to promote religious toleration. The king welcomed all religious exiles, even Jesuits; only Jews remained hedged about with vexatious regulations. As a religious skeptic, Frederick found toleration easy.

In economic policy, Frederick was the most determined "mercantilist" since Louis XIV's minister Colbert. With his state-directed enterprises he sought to give Prussia self-sufficiency, above all in military supplies and equipment. He encouraged the new scientific agriculture that was slowly spreading from Holland. His policies induced 300,000 immigrants, including many skilled agricultural and industrial workers, to settle in Prussia. He also introduced Europe's first scheme for universal primary education, thus founding a tradition that in the nineteenth century became one of Prussia's greatest strengths. Finally, like other enlightened absolutists, Frederick rationalized laws and judicial procedures.

The Partitions of Poland

The Rise of Brandenburg-Prussia   1640–1795

Yet in many respects Frederick was less than enlightened. He believed firmly in birth and privilege. The Junkers served him well as officers in the most important organ of the state, the army. In return for that service he trusted the nobility far more than had his father or the Great Elector. Frederick improved the lot of serfs on his own estates but had little enthusiasm for emancipation. During his reign, noble estates expanded and the condition of the serfs worsened. His conception of society was static: nobles, townspeople, and peasants should remain at their respective posts. His preference for rigid caste lines over social mobility and for orders from above over economic initiative from below ultimately proved self-defeating.

Despite Frederick's enlightened pose, the discipline, efficiency, and ruthless centralization of the Prussian monarchy ultimately derived from a long Hohenzollern tradition entirely unrelated to the Enlightenment. The state that Frederick created in the wars between 1740 and 1763 and consolidated in peace from 1763 to 1786 was the most striking political achievement of his time. But without him, without

a genius at the helm, his economic and social policies doomed it to stagnation. Prussia's shattering military successes and Frederick's monopoly of diplomacy, strategy, and tactics put his officer corps to sleep. The coming storms of the revolutionary era almost destroyed Prussia. It survived only through the emergence of a "bureaucratic absolutism" in which the bueraucracy and army ran the state themselves, without much need for a monarch. That was Prussia's dangerous legacy to the German state that it ultimately created.

Austria: Joseph II

The monarch with the best claim to the title of enlightened absolutist was Joseph II of Austria (r. 1780–90). Although he professed contempt for the *philosophes,* he was more devoted to the main tenets of the Enlightenment and to the welfare of his peoples than any of his fellow monarchs.

Frederick II's conquest of Silesia in 1740 prompted a drastic reorganization of the Habsburg Empire that enabled it to survive until 1918. Maria Theresa, during her long reign (1740–80), developed an imperial bureaucracy that controlled from Vienna all provinces of the empire except Hungary. In 1775 that machine imposed a tariff union on the empire, except for Hungary. It compelled the nobles to assume some of the burden of taxation. It limited the amount of labor they could extort from the peasantry and curbed the power of private noble courts over the serfs, for whom Maria Theresa did more than any other ruler of her time.

Her son Joseph, who became emperor and co-regent after the death of her husband in 1765, took an increasingly energetic part in her efforts at reform. But

---

Joseph II, The Enlightened Despot   1783

The following extracts illustrate the paradox of enlightened absolutism; only autocratic methods made reform conceivable.

I have not confined myself simply to issuing orders; I have expounded and explained them. With enlightenment I have sought to weaken and with arguments I have sought to overcome the abuses which had arisen out of prejudice and deeply rooted customs. I have sought to imbue every official of the state with the love I myself feel for the wellbeing of the whole. . . .

The good of the state can be understood only in general terms, only in terms of the greatest number. Similarly, all the provinces of the monarchy constitute one whole and therefore can have only one aim. It is necessary therefore that there should be an end to all the prejudices and all the jealousies between provinces [and] all races which have caused so much fruitless bickering. [Circular letter of Joseph II, 1783.]

But given Austria's structure and traditions, only the monarch could dictate unity and the end of prejudices. The state needed a common language; Joseph II determined what it should be.

The German language is the universal tongue of my empire. I am the emperor of Germany. The states which I possess are provinces that form only one body—the state of which I am the head. If the kingdom of Hungary were the most important of my possessions, I would not hesitate to impose its language on the other countries. [Letter to a Hungarian noble, 1783.]

From T. C. W. Blanning, Joseph II and Enlightened Despotism *(London: Longman Group, 1970), pp. 131–32, and Louis Léger,* Histoire de l'Autriche Hongrie *(Paris, 1879), p. 373.*

Joseph sought to move farther and faster than his mother. Until her death in 1780 he chafed under Maria Theresa's compromises, particularly over religion. During the ten years that Joseph II ruled alone, thousands of decrees poured from the imperial chancellery in Vienna. He proclaimed religious toleration for all Christians and Jews. He dissolved monasteries that were devoted solely to religious contemplation and gave their revenues to the hospitals that in the next century made Vienna the medical center of Europe. He applied to everyone in the Habsburg dominions, regardless of rank or nationality, a system of equal taxation in proportion to income. He imposed one language for official business, German, on all parts of the empire, including Belgium, Italy, and Hungary. Above all, Joseph II abolished serfdom. Early in his reign he issued a number of decrees that gave all serfs in the Habsburg dominions personal freedom— freedom to leave the land, to marry as they pleased, to choose whatever job they liked. That act of Joseph II was permanent, even though his successors repealed other decrees by which he sought to make the peasants who remained on the land into property owners, free from forced labor obligations.

Through his policies of centralization and drastic reform, Joseph naturally made mortal enemies of the clergy, the landed nobility, non-German nationalities such as the Hungarians, and even peasants who failed to understand his intentions. In 1789, when revolution broke out in France, peasants in the Austrian Empire began to plunder and murder landlords to gain the rights Joseph had held out to them. By 1790 both Belgium and Hungary were in revolt against his rule, and the Church was bitterly hostile. Joseph lamented to his brother and successor Leopold: "I am the only one holding to the true course, and I am left to labor alone. . . . I am without any assistance whatsoever." Worn out, he died in 1790 after choosing a rueful epitaph: "Here lies Joseph II, who was unfortunate in everything that he undertook."

Joseph II, the "revolutionary Emperor," had built a structure stronger than he knew. It survived both the revolutionary era and the nineteenth century. The crippling limitations under which he labored stemmed above all from his position as a revolutionary without a party. His only supports were an unimaginative bureaucracy, a secret police that he had set up to combat opposition, and the Habsburg army. His brand of enlightened absolutism might have formed a bridge between divine-right monarchy and democratic politics. But his fate suggested that radical changes, at least on the Continent, demanded a broader base of popular support than he had been able to command.

BRITAIN, FRANCE, AND THE AMERICAN REVOLUTION, 1763–89

In France and British North America, revolution from below took the place of reform from above. Louis XV made a belated but vigorous attempt to quell internal opposition between 1770 and 1774. Thereafter the French monarchy drifted until its collapse after 1789 in the greatest of modern European revolutions. Overseas, the American colonists claimed their independence in the name of reason and natural rights. When Britain resisted, the colonists broke away by force.

France: The Failure of Reform, 1770–74

The Seven Years' War severely strained British and French finances. Louis XV proposed to cope by making permanent a temporary war tax that fell on nobles and commoners alike, and by levying a new tax on those who had bought judicial and administrative offices from the monarchy. Such measures were necessary if the monarchy hoped to avoid bankruptcy. But they raised a storm of opposition from nobility and middle classes alike. The *parlements,* which were narrow oligarchies of officeholders who had bought their positions, rationalized their privileges by borrowing from Locke. Any attack on their own tax exemption, they arrogantly proclaimed, violated the "fun-

Joseph II urging agricultural improvement on his peasants.

damental laws" of the kingdom and the "natural rights" of Frenchmen.

In 1770–71 Louis XV finally acted. His forceful ministers, the lawyer René de Maupeou for political affairs and the Abbé Joseph Marie Terray for finances, closed the *parlements,* exiled their most fractious members to distant villages, and reassessed taxes. Public opinion—except, significantly, for Voltaire—rose in outrage. But the king held fast and won. A new system of royal law courts replaced the *parlements.* Maupeou prepared to rationalize at last France's administration and finances. Then, in 1774, Louis XV caught smallpox and died. His son, Louis XVI (r. 1774–92), well-meaning and lamentably weak, was the monarchy's downfall. He dismissed Maupeou, acquiesced in the restoration of the *parlements,* and presided first over bankruptcy, then over the beginnings of the French revolution, described in the next chapter.

The Revolt of Britain's American Colonies

France's revolution did not begin until 1788–89, but events overseas furnished a powerful example. Britain's "salutary neglect" of its North American colonies did not survive the Seven Years' War. As in France, the financial strain of that war prompted a search for new revenues. Parliament in London naturally looked to its colonists. The colonies had in the past paid no taxes to Britain. They had paid only customs duties that Parliament had imposed—but only loosely enforced—to channel colonial trade to Britain. The colonists' tax burden was thus a mere 4 percent of the average Englishman's. And while the colonists had done little fighting, London had paid dearly to defend them against the French, against France's Indian allies, and against the 1763 uprising of the Ottawa chief Pontiac. But unfortunately for the British government, its entirely reasonable efforts to raise revenue coincided with the elimination of French power in North America. That freed the colonists of their dependence on Britain. The result, thanks to the traditions of government that the colonies had acquired from England itself, was an explosion that shattered the British Empire.

Salutary neglect had permitted a political experiment possible in no other European colonial empire. The thirteen colonies from quasi-theocratic Massachusetts, to anarchic Rhode Island, to Catholic Maryland, to Anglican Virginia, were in effect self-governing. The ministry in London appointed royal governors, but under the charters granted to the colonies, the colonial legislatures, not Parliament, paid the governors' salaries and voted—or refused to vote—the revenues needed to carry on government. Elections to those legislatures were far more democratic than those for Parliament or for other European representative bodies. And the colonists took seriously John Locke's theory of limited government and the practice of England's Glorious Revolution of 1688. They regarded the British Empire as a quasi-federal structure that rested on consent.

Parliament took a differet view. Beginning in 1765 it sought to impose both direct taxes and new customs duties on the colonists. The colonists replied with boycotts of British imports, smuggling, and the demand "that no taxes be imposed on them but with their own consent." By 1773 a chasm had opened between Parliament's conception of sovereignty and the colonists' conception of freedom.

In December 1773 a radical Massachusetts minority not unconnected to the smuggling trade took direct action. A crowd thinly disguised as American Indians boarded three British merchant ships in Boston harbor and dumped into the murky water thousands of pounds' worth of tea—on which London had expected the colonists to pay import duty. The "Boston Tea Party" was at once an act of defiance against Parliament's claim to impose taxes and a blow against the smugglers' British competitors.

Parliament reacted with fury. In 1774 it closed the port of Boston, deprived the Massachusetts legislature of much of its power, and ordered the deportation of offenders for trial in England. That drove the other twelve colonies to rally behind Massachusetts out of fear that Parliament would likewise revoke or amend their charters.

Worse still, Parliament passed an otherwise statesmanlike measure, the Quebec Act of 1774, that appeared to be a further attack on the English-speaking colonies. The act guaranteed the preservation of the French language and the Catholic religion in Canada and defined Canada to include all territory north of the Ohio River and west of the Allegheny Mountains. It banned American settlement beyond the mountains. That—and the act's toleration for "Popery"—enraged both rich and poor, land speculators and pioneers, in the English-speaking colonies.

Between them, the Quebec Act and the so-called "Intolerable Acts" against Massachusetts marked the point of no return. To George III and to a large majority of his English subjects, the American colonists had proved themselves childish and irresponsible rebels. To a majority of the colonials, Parliament was seeking to impose an unbearable tyranny of the kind they now argued they had sought to escape by emigrating to the New World. The government of George III succeeded in driving toward rebellion even sober, propertied men who feared unrestrained democracy as "the madness of the multitude." The colonists began to arm them-selves.

In April 1775, the British garrison at Boston sought to seize weapons and gun-powder that the colonists had assembled at Concord. The Massachusetts militia met the redcoats on Lexington green and fired the shots "heard 'round the world." Al-though the redcoats reached their ob-jective at Concord, American fire from behind houses and stone walls harried them back to Boston. A Continental Con-gress assembled at Philadelphia and for-mally declared the colonies independent of king and Parliament on July 4, 1776. Its ringing words were Lockean to the very marrow:

> *We hold these truths to be self-evident, that all Men are created equal, that they are endowed by their Creator with certain unalienable Rights, that among these are Life, Liberty and the Pursuit of Happiness. That to secure these rights, Governments are insituted among Men, deriving their just Powers from the Consent of the Governed. That whenever any Form of Government be-comes destructive of those ends, it is the Right of the People to alter or to abolish it, and to institute new Gov-ernment. . . .*

That was a call to revolution in the Old World as well as in the New.

The American War of Independence

The ensuing War of Independence was a civil war in both colonies and mother country. The colonists had sympathizers in both England and Ireland. A Whig fac-tion that included the founder of modern conservatism, Edmund Burke, in vain urged George III and his inept prime min-ister, Lord North (1770–82) to conciliate the colonists. A group of "radicals," under the inspiration of a boisterous and de-bauched demagogue, John Wilkes, at-tacked the king's influence in Parliament, urged the publication of parliamentary de-bates, and agitated for a democratization

Third of the Hanoverians: the unfortunate George III.

of parliamentary elections. Wilkes eventu-ally made his peace with the king, and the English radicals were too small a minority to carry much weight. But they neverthe-less proclaimed the political faith of the Declaration of Independence, that gov-ernment must rest on consent. Conversely, numerous "Tories" in the colonies, from Boston to the backwoods of North Caro-lina and Georgia, sympathized with or fought for the king. In the course of the war and its aftermath, some 80,000 fled or were driven out to Canada and their lands confiscated.

The war itself pitted the disorganized colonial militias and the small Continental Army under George Washington against a succession of seaborne British task forces. The Americans' strengths were Wash-ington's unique combination of daring and caution, sluggish British generalship,

George Washington, victorious at the battle of Princeton (1777), by Charles Wilson Peale.

smuggled muskets and powder that France supplied after 1776, and widespread popular support for the cause of independence. The British and their German mercenary troops rarely commanded more than the ground under their feet. Britain's assets were battlefield professionalism and command of the sea.

In October 1777, American forces cornered at Saratoga some 5,000 British troops that had descended from Canada. That victory, although it immediately followed Washington's loss of Philadelphia, ultimately decided the war. It induced Louis XVI and his ambitious foreign minister, the Comte de Vergennes, to intervene actively. French enthusiasts for American independence, including the Marquis de Lafayette, had joined Washington well

before France acted, but Vergennes, less idealistic than they, sought the humiliation of Britain. The French navy, improved since 1759, fought the British to a standstill in 1778 off Ushant, at the mouth of the English Channel. Across the Atlantic, it deprived Britain's forces of supplies and seaborne mobility until French defeat at the Battle of the Saintes (West Indies) in April 1782 restored Britain's naval supremacy.

That victory came too late for Britain in North America. At Yorktown in Virginia, a British force of 7,000, penned between the French navy and American and French troops, had surrendered on October 19, 1781. London, although it still occupied New York with 30,000 troops, recognized the futility of fighting on. In the Treaty of Versailles of 1783, Britain acknowledged the independence of the thirteen colonies and surrendered to them all of North America south of the Great Lakes, east of the Mississippi, and north of Florida. France gained revenge for the loss of Canada, some colonial outposts, and immense new debts that ultimately helped destroy its monarchy.

Yet independence did not settle the shape of the new American state. During the war most of the colonies had summoned conventions and drafted written constitutions with bills of rights. Between 1777 and 1781 the Continental Congress had united the former colonies in a loose federal union under the Articles of Confederation. In July 1787 Congress enacted the Northwest Ordinance, a momentous document that extended the principles for which the colonists had fought to the still unsettled western territories. When these territories became populated, they were to become not colonies or dependencies but "states," equal in status to the thirteen original members of the union.

Yet by 1787 it was clear that the Articles of Confederation failed to provide the necessary machinery for a common economic or foreign policy. The result was the summoning of a Constitutional Convention that hammered out a new federal constitution at secret meetings in Philadelphia. That document, which began with a characteristic flourish ("We, the People of the United States . . ."), has endured. The Constitution and the Revolution that created it founded the longest continuous tradition of democratic politics in history.

The American Revolution in History

The American Revolution had profound effects on Europe and eventually on the world. America was not the first "new nation"; the Dutch United provinces that had defeated Spain had that honor. But it was the only new nation of the Enlightenment. Its revolution was entirely secular and it claimed universal applicability for its principles. It had proclaimed and acted on Locke's theories of natural equality, unalienable natural rights, government by consent, and the right to revolution. Its state and federal constitutions demonstrated Montesquieu's theory of the separation of powers. Its constitutional conventions showed that a people could create a new government in an orderly fashion by formal contract, and that liberty need not mean anarchy. Its example showed that small political units could federate into a larger union. The American Revolution dramatized and propagated two of the West's principal political ideas—limited constitutional government and popular sovereignty, or democracy. The latter, but not the former, was destined to play a decisive role in the coming revolution in France.

By the last quarter of the eighteenth century, the tide of ideas and of politics was running strongly against the old regime. Aristocracy and enlightened absolutism were ceasing to command loyalty or even respect. The desire for equilibrium, whether social, international, or intellectual, no longer inspired educated Europeans. Balance and order in both art and politics were giving way to the thirst for emotion and change. The American Revolution accelerated that movement. After 1789, the greatest of European revolutions provided emotion, change, and violence enough for all.

Suggestions for Further Reading

General

For overviews, see especially G. Rudé, *Europe in the Eighteenth Century* (1972); L. Krieger, *Kings and Philosophers, 1689–1789* (1970); W. Doyle, *The Old European Order, 1660–1800* (1978); and I. Woloch, *Eighteenth-Century Europe* (1982). The relevant volumes of the *Rise of Modern Europe* series remain useful: P. Roberts, *The Quest for Security, 1715–1740* (1947); W. L. Dorn, *Competition for Empire, 1740–1763* (1940); and L. Gershoy, *From Despotism to Revolution, 1763–1789* (1944). O. H. Hufton, *The Poor of Eighteenth-Century France, 1750–1789* (1975), and L. Stone, *The Family, Sex and Marriage in England 1500–1800* (1977), are pioneering studies; A. Macfar-lane, *Marriage and Love in England: Modes of Reproduction, 1300–1840* (1986), reaches conclusions radically different from those of Stone. J. H. Parry, *Trade and Dominion: The European Overseas Empires in the Eighteenth Century* (1971); C. G. Robertson, *Chatham and the British Empire* (1948); and L. B. Wright, *The Atlantic Frontier: Colonial American Civilization, 1607–1763* (1947), provide useful discussion of overseas expansion. On economic and social change, see above all F. Braudel, *Civilization and Capitalism, 15th–18th Centuries* (1982).

The Major States

For discussions of developments within the major states, see especially J. Lough, *Introduction to Eighteenth-Century France* (1960); G. Holmes, *The Making of a Great Power. Late Stuart and Early Georgian Britain* (1993); R. Vierhaus, *Germany in the Age of Absolutism* (1989); and H. Rosenberg, *Bureaucracy, Aristocracy, and Autocracy, the Prussian Experience, 1660–1815* (1958). For biographies of leading figures, see J. H. Plumb, *The First Four Georges* (1957); G. Ritter, *Frederick the Great* (trans. 1968); C. L. Morris, *Maria Theresa: The Last Conservative* (1937); and G. S. Thomson, *Catherine the Great and the Expansion of Russia* (1950). On the American Revolution, see especially E. S. Morgan, *The Birth of the Republic, 1763–1789* (1956); R. M. Calhoon, *Revolutionary America: An Interpretive Overview* (1976); and R. W. Tucker and D. C. Hendrickson, *The Fall of the First British Empire: Origins of the War of American Independence* (1982).

23

THE FRENCH REVOLUTION AND EUROPE, 1789–1815

The French Revolution, along with the industrial revolution in England (described in the next chapter), changed the face of Europe and ultimately of the world. It was both political and social. Politically, it destroyed the older order first in France and then in much of western Europe. The French monarchy, which traced its traditions to Charlemagne, collapsed. Its successor, the French Republic, created a belt of satellite republics from Holland to Italy. Socially, the Revolution swept away the rigidly defined ranks of the old order. A new hierarchy, based at least in theory on talent and wealth rather than on birth, replaced the Old Regime's three-part division by "orders," the nobles, clergy, and common people.

Above all, the Revolution changed the ways in which the peoples of western Europe viewed themselves. It created new words for new things. "Citizens," "revolu-

tionary," "counter-revolutionary," "reaction," "guillotine," and the concept of the nation-state entered the West's political vocabulary. The Revolution gave birth to nationalism and mass politics. It opened the modern age of mass-based democracy and mass-based despotism in which we still live.

THE ORIGINS OF THE REVOLUTION

The collapse of the French monarchy in 1788–89 came suddenly. But like other great events, it had many causes. Underlying forces acting slowly over many years created a situation that made violent upheaval possible. Then the Revolution's immediate causes—the short-term forces and the events that detonated the explosion—came into play.

(Opposite) The Tennis Court Oath, by Jacques-Louis David, official painter to the Constituent Assembly and later to Napoleon. David did not complete this immense canvas, for most of those shown in it fell under suspicion during the Terror.

The Forces That Made Revolution Possible

Three underlying forces in French society prepared the way for revolution: population growth, the expansion of the middle classes, and the rise of an informed public opinion permeated with Enlightenment ideas that were subversive of monarchy and aristocracy.

As world climate grew warmer, France's population swelled from 22 to 28 million between 1700 and 1789. That dramatic increase made *la grande nation,* as France called itself, Europe's most populous state. Rapid population growth meant youth. In 1789, 36 percent of France's population was under twenty years of age. And population growth was precarious. It rested on improvements in the transport and distribution of food, not on major advances in food production. Drought, storm, or grain blight produced serious food shortages in 1770, 1774, 1778, 1782, 1784, and 1786. After 1770, increasingly violent swings in agricultural output and prices coincided with a decline in daily wages that resulted from the rise in population.

An increase and spread of wealth at the top of the social scale paralleled this increase in numbers below. France's middle classes grew from around three-quarters of a million in 1700 to 2.3 million, or between 8 and 9 percent of the total population, by 1789. The nobility's share of the total population remained static throughout the century at between 0.5 and 1.5 percent. Ever-greater numbers of wealthy commoners might hope to rise into the nobility, but only slowly, over several generations. Although nobles increasingly took an interest in trade and industry, land ownership remained the chief source of wealth and the badge of social rank. The lines between noble and commoner were gradually blurring, but too slowly to suit many wealthy commoners.

With the downward spread of wealth came the growth of a phenomenon new to France, although it had been visible in England since the Civil War in the 1640s: a reading public. By 1789 perhaps 37 percent of France's people could read and write. In 1700, France had three semi-official newspapers; by 1789, it had several hundred weeklies and dailies. Libraries and reading rooms sprang up even in the provinces. Nobles and commoners alike collaborated in spreading the ideas of the Enlightenment. The condemnation of ignorance, prejudice, and superstition by Voltaire and Diderot and the egalitarian creed of Rousseau reached a widening audience. The example of the American Revolution, carried back to France after 1783 by the Marquis de Lafayette, hero of Yorktown, and by other French officers, suggested that the enlightened could remodel institutions and society at will.

The new ideas divided nobility and middle classes alike. Only a small minority of either gave up their loyalty to Church and monarchy in favor of Deism and a "republic of virtue." But the new ideas had consequences. In place of the old certainties—original sin, redemption, and obedience to priests, nobles, and a God-ordained king—they offered new myths: the perfectibility of man and society and the supremacy of the "general will."

The Immediate Causes: Government Crisis, Revolt by the Nobility, Crop Failure

The long-term forces would surely have brought change. That they triggered an explosion was the result of the coincidence of three short-term factors. First, the unusual incompetence of the royal government destroyed its authority. Then the nobility, sensing weakness, attacked. Finally, in the spring of 1789, France's peasants and urban crowds, unhinged by the last and worst of a series of poor harvests, brought the entire structure crashing down.

The crisis began in finance and administration. War, the sport of kings and nobles and the test of the greatness of the state, had always imposed crushing burdens. Prosperity after 1715 had freed France only gradually from the immense war debts of Louis XIV. The Seven Years' War of 1756–63 again brought heavy deficits. Then France's intervention in the American Revolution once more reduced the royal finances to near-collapse.

Louis XVI, unlike his two immediate predecessors, kept no mistresses and lived a modest life, for a monarch. But he had neither the brains nor the ruthlessness needed to master events. Under his loose supervision, his ministers struggled against approaching bankruptcy. Jacques Necker, a pompous and vain Swiss banker, coped during the American war by borrowing at ever-higher rates while assuring king and public that the budget balanced. His successors as Comptroller-General of Finances, especially Charles Alexandre de Calonne, followed Necker's example.

By 1786 Calonne could borrow no more. He concluded that the only solution to the financial crisis was fundamental reform of what he described as "a Kingdom made up of lands with estates, lands without, lands with provincial assemblies, lands of mixed administration, a Kingdom where provinces are foreign one to another, where multifarious internal barriers separate and divide the subjects of the same sovereign, where certain areas are totally freed from burdens of which the others bear the full weight, where the richest class contributes least, where it is impossible to have either a constant rule or a common will. . . ."

Calonne proposed to rationalize France's ramshackle administration and impose a single uniform land tax. The tax would strike the tax-exempt nobility and clergy who held between a quarter and a third of France's major source of wealth, its land. Since by custom the monarch needed some sort of approval for new taxes, Calonne in 1787 put his reform proposals to a hand-picked assembly of the two orders he proposed to tax.

This Assembly of Notables predictably put a price on approving Calonne's proposals. It demanded public scrutiny of the budget. Since that would inevitably expose the monarchy's financial incompetence, Louis dismissed Calonne and replaced him with one of his critics, Loménie de Brienne, archbishop of Toulouse. Brienne tried to cajole the notables into accepting the taxes that he himself had formerly denounced.

They again refused, and demanded that the king convene the Estates General of France, which had not met since 1614. Only that body, the notables now claimed, could approve new taxes. The nobility thus opened the attack on the monarchy in the name both of reform and of its own historic privileges. It was the first of many groups that fished in troubled waters and was swept away.

Louis XVI sent the notables home. He told the *Parlement* of Paris, the court whose task it was to register new laws, that the new taxes were legal "because I wish it." Louis' energetic minister of justice then closed the *parlements*. Despite a petition from the dukes and peers of France, and riots in the provinces under the leadership of nobles and *parlement* lawyers, Louis held firm. For a moment it looked as if the government had won.

Then drought, hailstorms, and crop failures struck all of France's major agricultural regions at once, for the first time since the famine year of 1709. The projected government deficit soared: starving peasants paid no taxes, and starving cities demanded expensive imported grain. The bankers, friends of the still-ambitious Necker, capped the disaster by refusing to lend the crown any more money. That blow brought the government to its knees. In August 1788 Louis XVI called the Estates General to meet in May 1789, and allowed Brienne to resign. The king reappointed Necker, who brought with him fresh loans but no policy. The government had confessed its incompetence and its bankruptcy, and had appealed to its subjects for help. The French Revolution had begun.

THE REVOLUTIONARY BREAKTHROUGH, 1788–89

What sort of revolution it would be was still unclear. The nobles and clergy who had defied their royal master expected to dominate the Estates General. But the nobles' protests in the spring and summer of 1788, and still more the approaching meeting of the Estates General, drew into politics groups that had until now played no role.

The "Third Estate" and the Masses

The first of these was the middle classes. The reinstated *Parlement* of Paris had decreed in September 1788 that the Estates General vote by order, with nobility, clergy, and commons balloting separately, as in 1614. That arrangement would make the commons, or Third Estate, a permanent minority—although they represented 98 percent of the population of France. Political clubs, many of them led by nobles with enlightened views, urged the "doubling" of the Third Estate, giving it twice its traditional number of representatives so that it would equal the other two orders combined. The Abbé Emmanuel Sieyès, chief theorist of this movement, published in January 1789 the most famous pamphlet of the Revolution: *What is the Third Estate?* It began with three questions: "What is the Third Estate?—*everything*. What has it been until now in the political order?—

nothing. What does it seek? *To be something.*" Sieyès went on to demand the drafting of a constitution "which the nation alone has the right to do." That appeal to the *nation,* to popular sovereignty, meant the end of divine-right monarchy and ultimately of peace in Europe.

Initially Louis encouraged the commons as a counterweight to the nobility. He agreed at the end of December 1788 to double the Third Estate. His appeal to the privileged orders had begun the Revolution; his appeal to the Third Estaste led to the Revolution's breakthrough. But as the Estates General assembled at Versailles in May 1789, forces far more menacing to the established order than the lawyers, professional men, and bureaucrats of the Third Estate appeared on the scene—the peasantry and the urban lower classes. Their intervention converted a political struggle between elites, a conflict between the privileged and the merely rich or educated, into an upheaval that terrified nobles and Third Estate alike.

The motive force behind that upheaval was hunger, the result of the precarious balance between France's growing population and lagging agriculture. An extraordinarily hard winter followed the disastrous crop failures of 1788. The price of bread, the main food of the common people of Paris, rose by 60 percent between August 1788 and February 1789. Distress in the countryside depressed the demand for manufactured goods. Production of textiles, France's major industry, dropped perhaps 50 percent. Urban workers lost their jobs just as food prices soared.

The consequence was a rapid breakdown of public order in the spring and summer of 1789, before the new harvest arrived. The government had coped with past crises of this kind with price controls, emergency grain shipments, and police and army to enforce order. But now the royal administration itself was a wreck, the loyalty of the army's noble officer corps was shaky, and the revolt of the nobles and *parlements* had set a dangerous example.

Bread riots and disturbances broke out in the cities. In the countryside, the

Caricature of the French peasant supporting the clergy and nobility, while doves and rabbits, protected by the law for the sport of the nobility, eat the peasant's grain.

peasants stopped paying taxes. They also stopped paying the curious assortment of medieval obligations owed to landlords, local nobles, and the Church—money dues on land, tithes, and noble monopolies on flour mills, bakeries, wine presses, or law courts. These "seignorial dues," which a legal treatise of the day described as a "bizarre form of property," had long been the chief grievance of the peasants against what now, at one stroke, became the "Old Regime."

The peasants burned tax records and registers of dues. Where they could not find the registers, they burned the castles of the nobles to make sure. In late July 1789 rumors swept the countryside that "the brigands," the "English gang" (shades of the Hundred Years' War), or "the aristocrats" were approaching to slaughter and pillage. This "Great Fear," symptom of social breakdown, was both cause and consequence of peasant violence against the privileged orders.

From Estates General to Constituent Assembly, May–July 1789

When the Estates General met on May 23, 1789, the royal government, always indecisive, went back on the unspoken alliance with the Third Estate it had sought at the end of 1788. The king refused to allow the commoners to sit with the other two orders. He also rejected the demand of the Third Estate for voting "by head"—one delegate, one vote—which would have given the Third Estate a majority.

Under the leadership of Sieyès, the Third Estate reacted on June 17 by renaming itself the National Assembly—a new authority, independent of the monarchy and with an implicit claim to sovereignty. Liberal clergy and nobles joined the Third Estate. And when Louis ordered the Assembly's meeting-hall closed on June 20, it met at an indoor tennis court nearby. In the first of many scenes of drama and oratory that punctuated the Revolution, the representatives solemnly swore the "tennis court oath": not to disperse until they had given France a constitution.

Tom. I.   *Pag. 417.*

Emmanuel Joseph Sieyes.

Theorist of the "Third Estate": the Abbé Sieyès.

Louis, suddenly resolute, replied on June 23 with a defense of "his" nobility and clergy and with veiled threats to dissolve the Estates General. After he had left the hall, the leaders of the Third Estate erupted: "The nation in assembly does not take orders." "We will not move from our seats unless forced by bayonets." The resistance of the privileged orders crumbled. More and more nobles and clergy joined the Assembly, which soon officially took the title of Constituent Assembly and named a committee to write a constitution for France.

Paris Speaks: The Fall of The Bastille, July 14, 1789

Louis XVI wavered, then swung again toward resistance. Royal troops, many of them Swiss and German regiments, concentrated around Paris. Louis dismissed Necker. Counter-revolution seemed imminent. Then the removal of Necker set off an explosion in Paris that put the Constituent Assembly firmly in power. This city of 600,000, which dwarfed even the largest French provincial towns, was hungry. Crowds of shop owners, artisans, and housewives, with the backing of a rapidly growing ward organization independent of the royal authorities, attacked jails and barracks, seeking weapons. The police, a mere 2,000 backed by 3,500 royal troops, were powerless.

On July 14, 1789—whether coincidentally or not the day on which Paris bread prices reached the highest level of the century—the crowd attacked the royal fortress at the center of Paris, the Bastille. Helped by mutinous troops, the crowd took the fortress and butchered its commander. With royal authority utterly destroyed and with Paris in the hands of the insurgents, Louis XVI temporarily resigned himself to being a constitutional monarch.

The Fourth of August and the "Rights of Man"

The Constituent Assembly soon faced an emergency more serious than any menace from royal bayonets, or even from the Paris crowd. By the end of July the revolt of the peasants threatened not only noble property but all property in the countryside. Some members of the Assembly called for the restoration of order by force. Other more radical elements had begun to meet in a political club that later become known as the Jacobins. On the night of August 4, 1789, they took the Assembly by surprise. They induced the liberal—and landless—Vicomte de Noailles to propose the voluntary renunciation of privileges by the nobles and the Church.

In a frenzied meeting that lasted until two the next morning, the delegates renounced tithes, dues, the privileges of their orders, and the traditional rights of their towns and provinces. On sober second thought, the Assembly decreed in the following days that some of the dues be paid off in installments. That hardly impressed the peasants, and seignorial dues were dead even before their final abolition without compensation in 1793. The old order, in law as well as in fact, was gone. But the Assembly had achieved its immediate aim: disorder in the countryside subsided for the moment.

At the end of August, in its second major act, the Constituent Assembly adopted a preamble for the new constitution—the "Declaration of the Rights of Man and the Citizen." That document owed something to the Declaration of Independence, Constitution, and Bill of Rights of the new American democracy. It proclaimed liberty, and equality of rights, in stark contrast to the legal and social distinctions between orders current across the Continent. It led in 1791 to the emancipation of the Jews from the legal disabilities imposed on them in the Middle Ages. Even women, whom most revolutionaries, like Rousseau, sought to confine to the role of wife and mother, began to

Rebellious troops and citizens bombard the Bastille, July 14, 1789 (from a contemporary print).

demand equality on the basis of its principles. Olympe de Gouges, a woman writer in Paris, published in the summer of 1791 a widely discussed "Declaration of the Rights of Women."

But the Declaration's fundamental ideas were not those of Locke nor of the English common law that had molded the American Revolution. The Americans sought above all to prevent the executive or the legislature, even if elected by a majority, from trampling on individuals or on local state governments. The French, however, rashly subscribed to Rousseau's notion that the people, once freed of "ignorance, forgetfulness, or contempt for the rights of man," would spontaneously express a General Will that would in turn produce laws. That Will and those laws would by definition be incapable of oppression, except the presumably justified oppression of those whose actions or opinions violated their "duties" as citizens.

To these potentially dangerous notions the Declarations of the Rights of Man added an even more explosive element— the concept of the sovereign *nation*. In the United States, and even in a Britain that included Welsh and Scots, popular sovereignty meant little more than rule by elected representatives under law. In continental Europe, following the French example, it soon came to mean rule by one's own linguistic or ethnic group. The political definition of the nation found in the 1789 Declaration superseded the vague cultural notions of nationhood that had spread in the course of the eighteenth century.

This invention of the revolutionaries of 1789 later became known as national self-determination or *nationalism*. It ultimately meant war of all against all, and war of unprecedented intensity. Monarchies might occasionally bow to custom, religion, or law. But the new *nation-state* recognized no law other than reason—its own reason. When that reason came into conflict with the reason of others, force was the final arbiter. And the concept of nation made possible, for the first time in Europe, near-total mobilization. What other cultures had achieved only through the labor of slaves the French revolution-

---

The Declaration of the Rights of Man and the Citizen
August 27, 1789

The representatives of the French people, constituted as a National Assembly, and considering that ignorance, forgetfulness, or contempt for the rights of man are the sole causes of public misfortunes and the degeneration of governments, have resolved to set forth in a solemn declaration the natural, inalienable, and sacred rights of man so that this declaration, constantly kept in mind by all members of society, may unceasingly recall to them their rights and duties. . . .

1. Men are born, and remain, free and equal in rights. Social distinctions can only be founded on usefulness to society.

2. The aim of every political bond is the preservation of the natural and inalienable rights of man. Those rights are liberty, property, security, and resistance to oppression.

3. The source of all sovereignty is in essence the nation. No body or individual can exercise authority that does not derive expressly from it. . . .

6. Law is the expression of the general will. All citizens have the right to contribute, personally or through their representatives, to its creation. It must be the same, whether it protects or punishes, for all. . . .

From Archives parlementaires de 1787 à 1860, *première série, (Paris: Librairie Administrative de Paul Dupont, 1877), Vol. 9, p. 236 (translation by M. Knox).*

---

aries and their successors across Europe accomplished through the enthusiasm of citizens.

The Monarchy Humiliated: The October Days

All this was still in the future in the late summer of 1789. The Constituent Assembly had partially pacified the peasantry, but it still faced revolutionary Paris. The grain harvest of 1789 was good, but it had not yet reached the market. Supplies from the disastrous harvest of 1788 had run out. By late September Paris rang with cries of "When shall we have bread?" (as a pamphlet title put it). In this atmosphere, the arrival of a fresh regiment of royal troops at Versailles, greeted conspicuously by

Revolutionary propaganda:
"Frenchwomen become free."

Louis XVI's unpopular queen, Marie Antoinette of Austria, set off a new explosion.

An armed crowd with 6,000 militant Paris housewives at its head marched on Versailles. They overwhelmed the royal guards and triumphantly brought king, queen, and crown prince ("the baker, the baker's wife, and the little baker's boy") back to Paris. Alongside the royal coach, the crowd carried on pikes the heads of guards who had been killed defending their king. That was an unpromising beginning for constitutional monarchy.

THE FAILURE OF CONSTITUTIONAL MONARCHY, 1789–91

With the royal family virtual prisoners in the Tuileries palace in Paris, and with the Constituent Assembly in control of government, the Revolution seemed to have won. What remained was to recast France's society and administration. A new social pyramid based on property replaced the Old Regime's society of orders. The Constituent Assembly wiped from the map the Old Regime's quaint provincial and regional boundaries, and substituted 87 "departments" of roughly uniform size. Elected assemblies took over local government, a brief reversal of the Old Regime's drive toward centralization. France's first constitution, adopted in September 1791, set up a single-chamber Legislative Assembly elected only by men wealthy enough to pay taxes equivalent to three days' wages. That group made up perhaps 15 percent of the population. A further, steeper property qualification restricted membership in the Legislative Assembly itself.

The new regime faced three problems for which it had no answer: the financial crisis that had felled the monarchy, the continuing agitation in Paris, and above all the king's refusal to play the part the Revolution had assigned him. The nimble Marquis Charles Maurice de Talleyrand, bishop of Autun, hit on an expedient that promised to rescue France's finances. The state—like Henry VIII of England two and a half centuries before—would dissolve all monasteries and nunneries, and would seize and sell off the Church lands. The

profits would reduce the national deficit and give the parish clergy and bishops guaranteed salaries as state employees. The confiscation of Church land went smoothly, but the July 1790 "Civil Constitution of the Clergy" aroused widespread resistance. Priests all over France refused to swear the required oath of loyalty to the state, and the papacy in Rome soon backed them. The Revolution had gained a new and formidable adversary and had opened a quarrel with the Church that divided France until the twentieth century.

Nor did the seizure of Church lands solve the financial crisis. The *assignats,* the new currency backed by the proceeds of the land sales, fueled an inflation that guaranteed further urban unrest even when harvests were good. The lands themselves, sold at scandalously low prices, enriched only their middle-class and peasant buyers. The main benefit to the state of this massive transfer of property was indirect: along with the sale after 1792 of the property of nobles who had fled abroad, it tied powerful middle-class and peasant groups to the Revolution.

The Constituent and Legislative Assemblies also failed to master Paris. The middle- and lower-middle classes of the great city had by 1790–91 reached a state of political excitement unthinkable under the Old Regime. The revolutionary ward organizations or *sections,* made up of fiercely radical butchers, bakers, innkeepers, and artisans, held frequent noisy meetings. The Paris municipal government, or *Commune,* was soon in the hands of extremists. Around these organizations and around the frequent "Jacobin Club" meetings at the former Jacobin monastery there arose a unique revolutionary subculture. The *sans-culottes,* literally those "without knee breeches," scrapped the aristocratic dress code of the Old Regime. Wearing trousers and red caps, carrying pikes and muskets, they addressed one another as "citizen" and demanded equality of wealth as well as equality of political rights. Professional agitators and extremist journalists— Jacques Hébert, Georges Danton, Jean-Paul Marat, and Camille Desmoulins— rubbed shoulders with foreign hangers-on of revolution like the Prussian ex-baron and "orator of the human race," Anacharsis Clootz. With such leaders to spur it, revolutionary Paris was soon ready to turn its pikes and cannon even on the Assembly, should it suspect it of betraying the Revolution.

Those representatives gave Paris its chance soon enough, for the conduct of the king rendered all forms of moderation suspect. Louis had maintained secret contacts with royalist elements in the Constituent Assembly, with his many relatives who had fled abroad, and with Austria. In June 1791 he made a dash for the nearest friendly border, that of Austrian Belgium. But town authorities blocked the royal family's escape at Varennes, just short of safety. Once more France's king, queen, and crown prince returned to the Tuileries in humiliating captivity.

Louis' failed escape made the constitution practically useless even before its formal adoption in September 1791. The Constituent Assembly found itself with a monarch who had publicly demonstrated his disloyalty to revolutionary France. Louis continued to appoint ministers and approve legislation, but neither his throne nor his head was safe. Nor did the new Legislative Assembly, which replaced the Constituent Assembly in October 1791, prove capable of giving France stable government. Thanks to a proposal of Maximilien Robespierre, the Jacobin provincial lawyer who claimed to be the most high-principled of the revolutionaries, the Constituent Assembly had voted to bar its own members from running for the new legislature. That act of self-denial did not encourage the republican virtue it symbolized. Its main effect was to eliminate the modest store of parliamentary experience and political common sense acquired since 1789.

WAR, TERROR, AND DICTATORSHIP, 1792–94

Rather than govern, the Legislative Assembly went to war with all Europe. The dominant force in the new chamber proved to be a Jacobin group loosely associated with the commercial center of western France, Bordeaux. Collectively known as the "Gironde" after the name of Bordeaux's estuary, their leaders—Vergniaud, Isnard, and Jacques Pierre Brissot—were above all brilliant orators. The Girondin recipe for leadership was simple—war.

Playing cards of the Revolution: "Equality" and "Freedom of Religion" have taken the place of kings and queens.

FIGURE 23.1   France at War with Europe   1792–1815

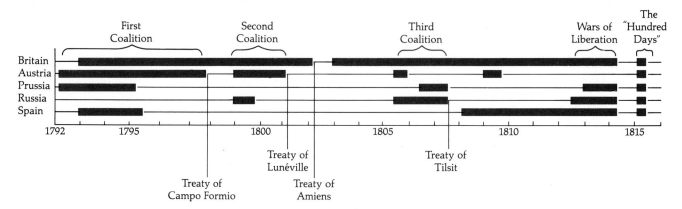

In August 1791, after the king's flight was blocked at Varennes, the emperor of Austria and the king of Prussia had proclaimed their intention to restore Louis XVI to his rightful place in full control of France. This "Declaration of Pillnitz" was a deliberately empty threat, for emperor and king had made Austro-Prussian action contingent on the improbable cooperation of the rest of Europe. Yet Aus-

Robespierre, "the Incorruptible."

trian and Prussian hostility, and the assembling of vengeful French refugee nobles in the German states along the Rhine, gave the Paris war party its chance. War, in Isnard's fervent words to the Assembly, was "indispensable for completing the revolution." At home, it would consolidate Girondin power. Abroad, a "crusade for universal liberty," a war "of peoples against kings," would smash the old order in Europe as the Revolution had done in France.

Robespierre, almost alone, made a stand against war. The enemies of the Revolution, he insisted in debate with Brissot at the Jacobin Club, were inside France. King, court, and aristocrats wanted war and French defeat in order to reverse the Revolution. But Brissot's promises of easy victory over an immense conspiracy of "kings against peoples" carried the excitable members of the Legislative Assembly. In April 1792 France declared on Austria a war that soon expanded to embrace all Europe. Except for a brief interval in 1802–03, the war lasted until France's defeat in 1814–15 (see Figure 23-1).

The Fall of the Monarchy: August–September 1792

The Gironde did not survive that long. The first act of the war galvanized Paris, and Paris destroyed first the monarchy and then the Gironde. The 1792 campaign began badly. Revolutionary indiscipline, lack of supplies, and the emigration of many aristocratic officers crippled the army. Prussian

May 1789	June 1789		Oct. 1791	Sept. 1792		Oct. 1795
Estates General	National Constituent Assembly		Legislative Assembly (Constitutional Monarchy)	National Convention (Republic)		

and Austrian forces advanced clumsily into eastern France. On July 25 the Prussian commander, the Duke of Brunswick, publicly proclaimed his intention of "delivering the King, the Queen, and the royal family from their captivity." That well-intentioned announcement seemed to the revolutionary extremists the final proof that Louis XVI and his Austrian queen were conspiring with the enemy. The result was the "second revolution," the Paris insurrection of August 10, 1792.

That day far surpassed Bastille Day in violence. The king fled the Tuileries palace before the attacking crowd and revolutionary troops closed in. While his Swiss guards died at their posts, he placed himself and his family under the protection of the Legislative Assembly. That body, itself facing the pikes and cannon of the Paris wards, voted to "suspend" the king. A temporary executive council took charge until the election of a new legislature by universal male suffrage. The equality of "one man, one vote" thus came to France, and to Europe, for the first time. With it came equality of another kind. The guillotine (p. 596), set up in a Paris square for the first time on August 13, extended to all the nobility's former privilege of death by decapitation.

The fall of the monarchy moved the Marquis de Lafayette, now commander of the French army in Belgium, to defect to the Austrians; the Revolution had no more room for moderates. The Austro-Prussians seized the key border fortress of Verdun. In Paris, the fiery orator Danton urged the nation to rise: "Gentlemen, we need boldness [*de l'audace*], boldness, always boldness, and France is saved." On September 20, 1792, at the battle of Valmy, the revolutionary armies held, to the cry of "*Vive la Nation!*" The Old Regime's artillery, the best in Europe, persuaded the Prussians to withdraw.

Revolutionary Paris, without help from either Brissot or Robespierre, had again imposed its will on France on August 10. But it was not yet finished. Two hours after Danton's passionate plea for boldness, the Paris *Commune* summoned the crowds to arm themselves against Prussians and counter-revolutionaries. Deranged rumors of a plot—to release imprisoned aristocrats to slaughter the wives and children of patriots—inspired mobs to attack the Paris prisons. Brutal and sometimes drunken crowds massacred between 1,100 and 1,400 aristocrats of all ages and both sexes, along with priests and other prisoners. Robespierre immediately justified these "September Massacres": "Do you want a Revolution without revolution?" He and his Jacobin associates now sought to turn the fury of Paris against their Girondin rivals.

The Convention Executes the King

The new French Republic appeared to be the culmination of the Revolution. Within a year its partisans had remade even the calendar. September 22, 1793 became the first day of Year I, and Sundays disappeared. The red, white, and blue tricolor of France replaced the Bourbon family's white banner with lilies. The *Marseillaise,* rousing and bloodthirsty marching song of a battalion from Marseille called to Paris during the August 10 uprising, became the national anthem.

The new assembly, the National Convention, was the most revolutionary of France's many legislative bodies after 1789. For good reason. Public voting under the scrutiny of the revolutionaries, not secret ballot, had been the preferred method of election. Only 10 percent of France's eligible population was brave enough or friendly enough to the Revolution to vote. Brissot and his Girondin

Louis XVI in prison after the August 1792 insurrection, by Joseph Ducreux.

companions returned, reelected in the provinces and outnumbering Robespierre and his partisans.

But Robespierre took the initiative at home while the French armies, buoyed up by a fierce national pride, invaded Belgium and crossed the Rhine. In late November the revolutionaries discovered in the Tuileries palace a safe containing Louis XVI's secret correspondence with the refugee nobles. Robespierre and his terrifying young associate, Louis Antoine Saint-Just, demanded the Louis' execution without trial: he was guilty not merely of treason, but of being a king. The Convention nevertheless decided to try the case itself.

The trial desperately embarrassed the Gironde, which despite its hostility to the monarchy shrank from killing the king. Others were more resolute. Revolutionary conviction—and fear of Robespierre, the Jacobin extremists, and the Paris crowd—spurred the Convention to convict Louis XVI of treason and other crimes. He died under the guillotine on January 21, 1793. Now at last there was no going back. The Revolution had killed a king who had ruled by divine right. A week later, the French Republic declared war on Great Britain and its ally Holland.

The "Despotism of Liberty": The Committee of Public Safety

Internal crisis and external defeat again combined to drive the Revolution to extremes. Food riots in February and March 1793 kept the pressure on the Convention. In March, the military conscription decreed in revolutionary Paris provoked the Catholic peasants of the Vendée, in the backward far west of France, to revolt under royalist leaders. That guerrilla war dragged on for years and cost the young Republic dearly. The commander of the French army in the low countries, Charles Dumouriez, defected after losing decisively to the Austrians at the battle of Neerwinden. The supposedly oppressed peoples on France's borders fought against the French "crusade for universal liberty" rather than for it. The second city of France, Lyons, rose in May 1793. In June and July much of the south, including

Marseille, followed. Royalists handed over to a British fleet the great Mediterranean naval base of Toulon.

The Convention proved equal to these challenges. In March it established a revolutionary court and "surveillance committees" to crush dissent and counter-revolution. In April it gave France an executive, the Committee of Public Safety. To pacify Paris, it temporarily imposed price controls (the "maximum") on grain and flour, and sent rapacious foraging parties into the countryside. Danton and Robespierre attacked the Gironde for alleged complicity with the traitor Dumouriez. The Convention, surrounded by the crowds of the Paris wards armed with 150 cannon, decreed the arrest of the Gironde for treason in June 1793. In July, Robespierre and Saint-Just joined the Committee of Public Safety. France, for the first time since Louis XIV, had a government determined to rule.

The Committee included Lazare Carnot, the "organizer of victory," for the army, Lindet for food supplies, Barère for relations with the Convention, and the men of blood, Billaud-Varenne and Collot d'Herbois, for hunting down the Revolution's internal enemies. Ideological leadership rested with "the incorruptible," Robespierre, and with his associate Saint-Just. Although it was responsible in theory to the Convention, in practice the Committee of Public Safety ruled France alone for the next year. Its rule, which the revolutionary martyr Marat hailed as the "despotism of liberty," was more absolute than that of the Old Regime, and infinitely more effective.

Against the external enemy, the Committee ordered in August 1793 the mobilization of the entire population by the famed *levée en masse*. By 1794 850,000 men were under arms, far outnumbering the armies of the kings France faced. Against the peasant guerrillas of the Vendée, the Committee sent General Kellermann, victor over the Prussians at Valmy, with orders to deport noncombatants and seize crops and livestock. After the army reconquered Lyons, Collot d'Herbois and Joseph Fouché, emissaries of the Committee, killed thousands in reprisal for the revolt. The Convention changed the very name of Lyons to *Ville-Affranchie* ("Freed-City"). At Toulon an artillery major of Corsican birth, Napoleon Bonaparte, found the key to driving the British fleet from the harbor and retaking the city. His reward was promotion to brigadier general at the age of 23. By the end of 1793 the emergency in the south was over.

The Great Terror, 1793–94

The Committee and its lesser ally, the Committee of General Security, also moved to monopolize terror. That instrument was too important to leave to the Paris agitators and crowds to whom the Convention and the Committees owed their power. The Committee and the Convention damped down the Paris ward meetings, muzzled the press, and arrested some leading extremists in September 1793.

But the Committee of Public Safety's chief business was with those who were not extreme enough. "The gods," wrote the Robespierrist journalist Desmoulins, "are thirsty"—for blood. Marie Antoinette, tried for treason and on fraudulent charges of immorality, died bravely in October. The Gironde went to the guillotine in November. Aristocrats, monarchist politicians, failed generals ("to encourage the others") followed. In the provinces, the traveling representatives of the Committees dispensed death to priests, aristocrats, and moderates by portable guillotine, firing squad, grapeshot, and "vertical deportation" (drowning). Perhaps 20,000 men and women perished in the Great Terror of 1793–94. Although that was a small number by the standards set by twentieth-century revolutions, the Terror left memories in France that long endured.

Yet even after the elimination of the Girondins, Robespierre was unable to rest. The theories of the Enlightenment decreed that society, freed of the chains of the Old Regime, would spontaneously express a General Will. Yet Robespierre bitterly recognized that the Revolution had failed to produce "one will, *one*." The fault therefore had to be that of the remaining evil men—plotters, traitors, Parisian ward extremists, lukewarm Jacobins, and counter-revolutionaries. It was not simply war and

The Modern State Mobilizes Its Citizens: The Levée en Masse

Barère to the Convention, August 23, 1793:

From this moment, until our enemies have been driven from the territory of the Republic, the entire French nation is permanently called to the colors. The young men will go into battle; married men will forge weapons and transport supplies; women will make tents and uniforms, and serve in the hospitals; children will make old cloth into bandages; old men will have themselves carried to the public squares to rouse the courage of the warriors and preach hatred of kings, and the unity of the Republic.

From Archives parlementaires de 1787 à 1860, *première série (Paris: Librairie Administrative de Paul Dupont, 1907), Vol. 72, p. 674 (translation by M. Knox).*

The Spirit of the Terror: Sayings of Saint-Just

This man [Louis XVI] must reign or die.... All kings are rebels and usurpers.

To the Convention, November 1792

The French people votes the liberty of the world.

Draft constitution, April 1793

The people and its enemies have nothing more in common except the sword.... *We must oppress tyrants.*

To the Convention, October 1793

Spare the aristocracy, and you will give yourselves fifty years of troubles. *Dare!* That one word summarizes the entire politics of our Revolution.

To the Convention, February 1794

There is something terrifying in the sacred love of one's country. It is so all-exclusive that it sacrifices everything, without pity, without fear, without regard for humanity, to the public interest.... You cannot make a republic with compromises, but only with ruthless severity, inflexible severity, toward those who have betrayed.

To the Convention, for the Committee of Public Safety, demanding the heads of Danton and others, March 1794

From Louis-Antoine de Saint-Just, Pages Choisies *(Paris: Éditions du Point du Jour, 1947), pp. 121, 123, 162, 199, 206, 223; and Denis Roche, ed.,* La liberté ou la mort *(Paris: Tchou, 1969), p. 49 (translation by M. Knox).*

Queen Marie Antoinette resolutely faces the guillotine (sketched from life by David).

internal threat that drove the revolutionaries to shed ever more blood. It was their faith in the perfectibility of humanity and their claim to embody the General Will.

The leaders of the Paris crowd, Hébert and the *Enragés,* or "wild men," were even more radical than the Committee of Public Safety. In March 1794 they tried to lead yet another Paris revolt. They failed and perished under the falling blade. Those more moderate than Robespierre—Danton, Desmoulins, and their allies in the center of the Convention—helped him against the Paris extremists. Then the moderate Jacobins began to plead for a relaxation of the Terror, for freedom of the press, and even for peace—for the spring of 1794 was a spring of French victories. Within a week of the decapitation of Hébert, the Committee arrested Danton and his allies. Saint-Just accused them of treason before the Convention. They too died.

With these blows against Hébertists and Dantonists, the Committee created a

wasteland around itself. The execution of the "wild men" destroyed its support in the Paris wards. That of the Dantonists weakened the Committee's hold on the center of the Convention, the moderates from the provinces who held the parliamentary balance. The Committee now ruled by terror alone. The pace of arrests and executions swiftly increased. More than 1,400 perished in Paris alone in June and July 1794.

The Revolution Ends: Thermidor, July–August 1794

Victory sealed the fate of Robespierre, as defeat had that of the Gironde. French troops, ever more experienced and more numerous, flooded once more across Belgium. The military emergency that had justified terror was over. The associates of Robespierre began to think of their own survival. Relative moderates such as Carnot joined with jealous members of the Committee of General Security. The bloodiest-handed of all, Collot d'Herbois and Billaud-Varenne, hoped the elimination of Robespierre would provide their own ticket to respectability. The center of the Convention secretly offered support.

An ominous speech in which Robespierre threatened unspecified enemies spurred the plotters to act before it was too late. On July 27, 1794—9 Thermidor by the revolutionary calendar—the plotters bodily prevented Robespierre from speaking to the Convention. Then they rushed through a decree for the arrest of the Robespierrists. The Paris wards, summoned to the rescue, responded poorly; they too had suffered under the Committee's dictatorship. The next day, 10 Thermidor, Robespierre, Saint-Just, and company went to the guillotine to which they had sent so many others. The Revolution had "iced over," Saint-Just wrote shortly before his arrest. The Robespierrists themselves, by their elimination of Hébert and the Paris ward agitators, had halted the seemingly unstoppable movement toward ever greater extremes. The Revolution was over, except for the endless war it had launched.

Here Lies All of France: cartoon of Robespierre executing the last Frenchman—the executioner.

FRANCE FROM THE CONVENTION TO THE DIRECTORY, 1794–99

The "reaction" of Thermidor, as it soon became known, produced a widespread sense of relief at the end of terror and of revolutionary attempts to remold human nature. French society, no longer cowed by terror and censorship, reasserted itself. The urban middle classes that had profited from the Revolution now sought to enjoy themselves in a frenetic round of banquets and dances. The *salons* reappeared, now led by educated women from the middle classes instead of the aristocracy. In their drawing rooms former terrorists drank champagne with former aristocrats and with the Revolution's new rich, the land speculators and army contractors. The "gilded youth" of the better-off quarters of Paris equipped themselves with clubs, and went to hunt Jacobins. In the provinces, a royalist "white terror" against republicans reenacted the horrors of the terror of the revolutionary Committees.

The relaxation of the price controls which the Robespierrists had imposed led to new Paris food riots in April and May 1795. But the Convention suppressed them, along with the last large-scale Paris revolt in October. In the last case, the young General Bonaparte mowed down the crowd with field artillery. Grapeshot, scientifically employed by loyal and experienced troops, had made 1789–style urban insurrection obsolete.

What Thermidor failed to provide was a stable government responsive to the new society, organized by wealth rather than rank, that was emerging from the Revolution. Ending the dictatorship of the revolutionary executive automatically meant increasing the danger of a restoration of the monarchy. The Convention nevertheless weakened the Committee of Public Safety by rotating its members and reducing its powers. In 1795, the Convention drafted and adopted yet another constitution, which remained in effect until the end of 1799. It replaced the Committee with a Directory of five members and supplanted the Convention itself with a new legislature, the Five Hundred. Wealth once more became a prerequisite for voting.

The five directors included Carnot, the Vicomte de Barras, and Jean-François Reubell, an Alsatian who believed that the Rhine was France's "natural frontier." Two-thirds of the Five Hundred were to come by law from the outgoing Convention—the so-called "perpetuals." The Convention intended this measure as a guarantee against royalist agitation in the provinces. It helped achieve that goal, but at the price of discrediting the new regime's claim that it represented the nation.

The remaining threat from Paris soon subsided. A poor harvest and an unprecedentedly severe winter in 1795–96 reduced the poor to near-starvation. Survival, not revolt, became the chief concern of the remaining *sans-culottes*. The last major attempt to mobilize Paris was the so-called "Conspiracy of the Equals" in the spring of 1796. The "Equals," especially Gracchus Babeuf and the Italian revolutionary Filippo Buonarroti, confusedly advocated extreme egalitarianism and a primitive agrarian communism. Their plot failed, but left an ideological legacy for the future.

It was the royalists who threatened the middle-class republic of 1795–99. But fortunately for the Directory, the young son of Louis XVI died in prison in June 1795. His uncle, in exile, took the title of Louis XVIII and announced his intention of restoring the Old Regime in its entirety. That program inevitably alienated both the constitutional monarchists and the powerful middle-class and peasant groups that had done well during the Revolution. A royalist uprising in the west of France poorly coordinated with a British and royalist landing at Quiberon ended in failure and massacre in 1795. Royalist deputies nevertheless did well enough in elections in 1797 and 1798 to force the Directors to undertake a series of coups d'état and purges to maintain control of the Five Hundred.

Stability and representative government had been impossible under the Convention because of the strength of the disloyal opposition and the exaggerated expectations of unity of ideologues such as Robespierre. They were likewise impossible under the Directory. By the end, by December 1799, the regime rested only on the army.

SON OF THE REVOLUTION: BONAPARTE, 1799–1815

That army had in the hard years since 1792 acquired matchless experience and prestige. The Old Regime had left it the most mobile and powerful artillery in Europe, and the innovative tactical and strategic theories of Guibert and Bourcet. The Revolution's war "of peoples against kings" had unleashed the energies and loyalties needed to use those theories to the fullest. The result was a new kind of warfare.

The man of destiny: the young Napoleon, by David.

Under the Old Regime, the eagerness of troops to desert and the inadequacy of the supply services had restricted the size and mobility of armies. No commander could easily control, feed, and move more than 70,000 men. But the new French armies, filled with nationalist fervor, deserted less often and showed a fierce initiative on the battlefield. Their leaders could trust them to fight as skirmishers, tormenting the rigid ranks of the Old Regime's armies as the American revolutionaries had tormented the British redcoats. The new armies could march dispersed, in self-contained "divisions" of 8,000 to 10,000 infantry equipped with their own artillery for support. This style of movement helped prevent bottlenecks and allowed the troops to feed themselves by looting the countryside as they passed. The division, and still more the next largest unit, the *army corps* of perhaps 30,000 men, had unparalleled offensive and defensive power. Corps could and did hold against an entire enemy army—until other French corps arrived with crushing effect on the flank or rear of the enemy. Concentration of forces on the move, on the field of battle itself, repalced the Old Regime's rigid and time-consuming deployments. The new system of warfare, the ruthlessness of the French revolutionary commanders, and the numbers, fervor, and readiness for sacrifice of the troops overwhelmed their traditionalist opponents.

The supreme master of the new techniques, and the ultimate beneficiary of the army's role as the Directory's sole support, was the young General Bonaparte. He had proved his usefulness to the Directory by crushing the Paris crowd in October 1795. After marriage to the fascinating Joséphine de Beauharnais, the former mistress of the Director Barras, Bonaparte received command of the Army of Italy in the spring of 1796. He was 27 years old.

The Directory's chief war aim was to secure the west bank of the Rhine; Italy was a sideshow. But Bonaparte made it the main theater. He began the fateful extension of French conquest far beyond the "natural frontiers" supposedly sought by Louis XIV. In the brilliant campaign of

1796–97, he smashed first the Piedmont-ese allies of the Austrians, then the Austrians themselves. Increasingly independent of the Directory, he ruled and looted north Italy as he pleased. In 1797 the Austrians sued for peace. By the Treaty of Campo Formio they relinquished their claims to Belgium and to the rich north Italian plain. In compensation they received from Bonaparte and the Directory a cynical gift, the once-proud republic of Venice.

By late 1797 France thus dominated Europe from Holland to north Italy. Prussia, busy seizing its share of the third and final partition of Poland, had made peace as early as 1795. Only Britain, surrounded by the seas and its fleet, fought on. The First Coalition against Revolutionary France had collapsed.

Bonaparte, the Revolution and Europe

For Bonaparte, the Revolution was "an idea that has found bayonets." France's ever-broadening rule indeed meant more than the rights of man. Intellectuals in lands as different as Britain, Germany, and Italy had initially greeted the Revolution with delight. "Bliss was it in that dawn to be alive / And to be young was very heaven," the English poet William Wordsworth wrote of 1789. Others were less optimistic. As early as 1790 the passionate Anglo-Irish parliamentarian and political philosopher Edmund Burke prophesied, in his *Reflections on the Revolution in France,* that the uprooting of historic institutions would lead to the rule of "some popular general."

The common people on France's borders soon found that occupation by the republic's armed hordes brought pillage and rape, the systematic exactions of French officialdom, and attacks on the Church. Even the "rights of man" offended deeply held popular prejudices such as those against the Jews. That liberty and equality came to much of Europe by French conquest was ominous: the counter-nationalisms that French ideas and French bayonets summoned up might eventually oppose democracy at home. For the moment, sporadic urban revolts and guerrilla struggles

CANONNIER.

"Great battles are won by artillery," wrote Napoleon of his favorite weapon.

did no more than annoy the victorious Republic.

A New French Empire in the Middle East?

Fearing inactivity, and wary of premature involvement in the intrigues around the Directory, Bonaparte sought the leadership of a French expedition to Egypt in 1798. That dependency of the Ottoman Empire, the Directory thought, had potential as a French colony that would help make up for the empire lost in 1763. It might also threaten Britain's road to India.

That French ambition did not survive the destruction of the French fleet at the battle of the Nile in August 1798. Horatio Nelson, Britain's greatest naval leader, cut Bonaparte's sea communications and marooned him and his 40,000 troops. After a year of difficult campaigning against

Egyptians, Turks, and British, Bonaparte slipped stealthily back to France. His abandoned army ultimately surrendered to the British.

Strategically, that outcome was no surprise. French domination, then and later, ended at the high-tide mark. But in cultural terms the Egyptian expedition gave an immense impulse to Western historical and linguistic studies. Bonaparte, a man of the Enlightenment, had taken with him to Egypt teams of experts to study the monuments and to loot the artifacts of one of the oldest civilizations in continuous existence. In the booty the French swept up and the British later captured was a stone slab found at Rosetta in the Nile delta (and now in the British Museum in London). On it are three inscriptions of the same text: one in ancient Greek, one in phonetic Egyptian script, and one in Egyptian hieroglyphics. The "Rosetta stone" provided the key with which a brilliant young scholar, Jean-François Champollion, deciphered the hieroglyphics in 1821–22. That achievement opened the road to the reconstruction of three millennia of Egyptian history. The Egyptian expedition symbolized more than European colonial greed. It also demonstrated the West's voracious curiosity, which in the coming century blossomed into a series of new disciplines aimed at understanding other cultures—comparative history, philology and linguistics, anthropology, and sociology.

From First Consul to Emperor, 1799–1804

Bonaparte timed his return to France in October 1799 perfectly. A Second Coalition against France had replaced the first. The Egyptian expedition had drawn Russia into the war, for Tsar Paul resented non-Russian attempts to bully the Turks. The Austrians also resumed fighting. A short but nasty Russian incursion into Switzerland and north Italy thoroughly alarmed French opinion. The Directory, its members at odds, was utterly discredited. Restoration of the monarchy threatened once more.

Sieyès, the propagandist of the Third Estate who had helped launch the Revolution, had survived the Terror by being discreet. In May 1799 he reemerged to join the Directory. He sought one last coup d'état to stabilize the rule of the beneficiaries of the Revolution, the Third Estate. For that he needed "a saber," a tame general. Sieyès approached Bonaparte, who accepted the role but with a difference: he would make this coup for himself.

And so, on November 9 and 10, 1799—18 Brumaire of the soon-to-be discarded revolutionary calendar—Bonaparte struck. With the help of his politician brother Lucien, Sieyès, and army bayonets, he cowed the legislature and assumed power as "First Consul." Sieyès found himself shunted off into gilded retirement. Much of French opinion had hoped for and expected a monarch. Instead, France got a dictator.

To consolidate his power, Bonaparte fell back on the technique of which he was the unparalleled master: battle. In the spring of 1800 he once more led a French army across the Alps, and attacked the Austrians in the rear. A close and bloody French victory at Marengo, and another on the German front, forced Austria to negotiate. The Second Coalition, as disunited as the first, collapsed. By the Treaty of Lunéville (February 1801), Austria conceded hegemony in Italy and the Rhine frontier to France. Russia, under the mad tsar Paul, had already withdrawn from the war. In March 1802, even Britain negotiated a grudging peace, the Treaty of Amiens. Britain's merchant elite was willing to try coexistence with the "Corsican tyrant," although continuing French control of Holland and Belgium was a far greater threat to British security than any conquest of Louis XIV.

Victory and peace enabled Napoleon, as he now began to style himself, to strengthen his grip on France. In 1802 he had himself proclaimed "First Consul for Life" and in 1804 "Emperor of the French." The pope, with whom Napoleon had signed in 1801 a treaty that partially bridged the gap between France and the Church, presided at the imperial coronation. But in an act contrary to custom that symbolized his will to power, Napoleon crowned himself.

1789	1795	1799		1814
Revolutionary Governments	Directory	Consulate	First Empire	

Napoleon

1804

Napoleon's rule brought France more than a new Bonaparte dynasty, complete with an improvised aristocracy of generals and Corsican relatives. For it was Napoleon, the former revolutionary, who at last brought enlightened absolutism to France by completing the Old Regime's drive toward centralization. In 1800 the Revolution's departments received permanent administrators sent from Paris. These "prefects," powerful successors to the Old Regime's *intendants* as the representatives of the central will in the provinces, long outlasted Napoleon. His model of the modern, centralized, bureaucratic state was one of the most powerful legacies of the Revolution. It swiftly found imitators throughout continental Europe and—much later—the non-Western world.

Along with centralization came legal uniformity. Napoleon's second major innovation in government was his law code, eventually known as the *Code Napoléon.* It replaced with a single national code the Old Regime's patchwork of customary and Roman law. It proclaimed equality before the law, reverence for property, and the supremacy of the male head of the family. The Code, like the prefects, was a much-imitated model. French bayonets imposed it in the ever-larger areas of Germany, Italy, and the Netherlands that Napoleon annexed. Its example moved French satellites and even enemies to institute legal reforms. Eventually only England, with its constitution formed through the slow accumulation of custom and precedent, remained untouched.

Napoleon's Conquest of Europe, 1803–07

Works of peace did not satisfy Napoleon's ambition for long. Starting in late 1802, he dispatched agents to the Middle East and prepared to stir up trouble for Britain in India. In Germany, after Lunéville, Napoleon oversaw a "princes' revolution" by which the larger states gobbled up lesser princes and Church rulers. That display of French power offended Austria, which still held token overlordship over the now crippled Holy Roman Empire.

The British, confident that a new coalition would soon form, resumed the war in May 1803. At first London stood alone, and Napoleon concentrated 400,000 men of his newly reorganized *Grande Armée* along the Channel coast. Southern England was virtually defenseless by land. "If we can be the masters of the narrows for six hours, we shall be masters of the world," Napoleon wrote to one of his admirals. But like Philip II of Spain and Louis XIV, Napoleon found the British fleet blocking his path to universal domination.

Thwarted at sea, Napoleon turned in 1805 to a land campaign in Germany. There he could bring his skill and France's power to bear. His coronation as emperor, with its overtones of a claim to the legacy of Charlemagne, had alarmed the Austrians. His crowning in May 1805 as "emperor" of the satellite kingdom of north Italy—where Charlemagne had also ruled—proved the final act that brought a new coalition into being. Austria and Russia now joined England. Irresolute Prussia, intent on absorbing the fat, English-ruled German state of Hanover, remained neutral.

Napoleon flung the *Grande Armée* from the Channel coast into south Germany before the Austrians and the Russians could join forces. One Austrian army, under the inept General Mack, found itself surrounded and forced to surrender at Ulm on October 20. But the next day, in the distant seas off Spain, the British navy reversed Napoleon's run of luck. At Cape Trafalgar Nelson captured or sank more than half the combined French-Spanish fleet. He paid with his life, but made sure that Napoleon could never repeat the invasion threat of 1803–04. Britain's victory at Trafalgar and the arrival of Russian armies in central Europe propelled Prussia slowly toward the coalition.

To free himself from this growing threat, Napoleon characteristically chose battle. He lured the combined Austro-Russian forces to attack him prematurely. On December 2, at Austerlitz north of Vienna, he faced 90,000 Austrians and Russians with 70,000 French, and broke the enemy line with an unexpected thrust. The Austro-Russians lost 27,000 dead and prisoners to Napoleon's 8,000 casualties, and Austria left the war. It was Napoleon's most brilliant victory.

Austria's collapse made Napoleon master of Germany, which he had already helped to remodel after Lunéville. Now Napoleon imposed a second round of revolution from above. The decrepit Holy Roman Empire died unlamented. Napoleon replaced it with a league of satellite states, the Confederation of the Rhine.

Napoleon's claim to universal domination: the emperor on his throne, by Ingres (1806).

Germany's remaining small states fell prey to their more powerful neighbors. In 1801 Germany had more than 1,800 separate political units. By the end of 1806 fewer than forty remained. Centralization was convenient for Napoleon's tax collectors, and for the Bonaparte relatives who received German states as gifts. But it also proved a mighty step toward the German nation-state that within a century came to dwarf and humiliate France.

Only Prussia, afraid that Napoleon would make peace with London and force it to give up Hanover, remained outside Napoleon's new German alliance. In October 1806, alone except for promises from distant St. Petersburg, Prussia went to war. Within a week Napoleon had launched the *Grande Armée* around the flank of the rigidly old-regime Prussian army. On October 14, 1806, converging French corps annihilated the Prussians at the twin battles of Jena and Auerstädt.

Within weeks Napoleon was in Potsdam with his generals, paying homage at the tomb of Frederick the Great: "Hats off, gentlemen; if *he* were still alive, we would not be here." But unlike Austria the year before, Prussia did not quit at once. Europe's resistance to Napoleon's increasingly open claim to universal domination was gradually stiffening. In cooperation with their Russian allies, the Prussians fought on in Poland. There, unlike the green lands of western Europe, the French found little to eat. The few roads were ice-covered bogs. The Russians appeared in force, and in the great slaughter at Eylau in February 1807 proved dogged though unimaginative foes. The coming of summer allowed the French to maneuver. At Friedland in June Napoleon finally crushed the Russians with a victory he proclaimed "as decisive as Austerlitz, Marengo, and Jena."

Tsar Alexander, the erratic grandson of the great Catherine and son of the madman Paul, whose murder in a palace coup in 1801 he had secretly welcomed, offered negotiations. Alexander met Napoleon at Tilsit on their common border, and totally reversed Russian policy. Not for the last time, Russia agreed to divide Europe into western and eastern spheres of influence.

Napoleon kept Germany, including Alexander's Prussian ally. To Russia fell Finland, Sweden, and Turkey. Alexander in return secretly promised to declare war on England and to help the French close the Continent to British trade.

That trade boycott, given the loss of much of the French navy at Trafalgar, was Napoleon's only weapon against Britain. In the Berlin Decree, issued in November 1806, he had declared a "blockade" against British exports to the Continent, confident that state bankruptcy and revolts by factory workers thrown suddenly out of work would force London to make peace. But this "Continental System" had leaks. Along the coastline that stretched from Spain to Russia, smugglers plied a roaring trade with the British, with corrupt French officials as accomplices. And Britain managed to keep its other markets open. Until 1812 it avoided war with its most powerful seagoing trading partner, the United States, despite bitter conflict over British searches and seizures of U.S. vessels. And in 1812–15, when the United States did go to war with Britain, Na-

poleon's break with Russia once again opened Scandinavia and Russia to British exports.

Europe Begins to Fight Back, 1808–12

The failure of the Continental System was only one sign that Napoleon's power had begun to wane after the agreement at Tilsit. More serious was rising resistance on the Continent. Revolutionary France had invented modern nationalism, and through it had tapped unprecedented military power. Now others, in Prussia and even in Austria, began to follow France's example. But Napoleon's first major setback on land came in a country scarcely touched by modern ideas—Spain.

There, in 1808, a savage guerrilla war broke out against the French troops Napoleon had sent to put his brother Joseph on the throne of the Spanish Bourbons. In scenes fixed forever in historical memory by the genius of the Spanish painter Francisco Goya, the French shot, hanged, and impaled the guerrillas, who in return

A Goya sketch of "The Disasters of War": A French dragoon contemplates Spaniards he has hanged.

hacked at the French with improvised weapons. Nobles, priests, and brigands led the masses, for the revolt was as much a reaction against the Enlightenment ideas the French brought as against the French themselves.

Unaided, the Spanish revolt might eventually have petered out, but Britain soon sent armies to Spain and Portugal. On the outskirts of Europe, sea communications were more efficient than the appalling Spanish roads that linked the French armies to Paris. The Duke of Wellington, a skillful commander already proven in India, found a secure base at Lisbon. The "Spanish ulcer" resisted treatment by Napoleon in person in late 1808. Thereafter he left Spain to less competent subordinates, and Wellington's army gradually wore the French down.

In Germany, the Tilsit settlement failed to stamp out the embers of a modern nationalism that eventually proved more terrifying than that of the French. Germany's sense of nationhood was at least as old as Luther's German Bible. The cultural revival of the late eighteenth century had given Germans a justified pride in their literature, which by the 1790s had begun to rival that of France. But it was French conquest that brought German nationalism into politics, while making it peculiarly militant. And the imposition of the "rights of man and the citizen" and of the *Code Napoléon* on Germany by an outside force helped make German nationalism potentially antidemocratic. In France, nationalism was subversive of the Old Regime. In Germany and farther east, nationalism might serve to reinforce it.

That was certainly the lesson that Prussian soldiers and bureaucrats drew from their defeat in 1806–07. King Frederick William III, with his territories halved after Tilsit, was even willing to appeal to his people in order to survive. He gave power to a cadre of unconventional civil servants and generals: Karl vom und zum Stein, Karl August von Hardenberg, August von Gneisenau, Gerhard von Scharnhorst. To defeat the French, Prussia needed what Hardenberg described as a "revolution in the good sense," an authoritarian "revolution from above." The reformers abolished serfdom, although dogged resistance from the nobility prevented full implementation. They gave towns and cities limited self-government in order to bring the population into politics in support of the Prussian state. They abolished most of Frederick the Great's restrictions on freedom of commerce and industry, and opened land ownership to non-nobles. Above all, they laid the basis for universal military service—decreed in 1814—and for the recruitment of non-noble officers. Their military-bureaucratic revolution from above sought to shore up enlightened absolutism with popular sup-

Prussia Responds: Revolution from Above

Baron von Hardenberg to King Frederick William III, "On the Reorganization of the Prussian State," September 12, 1807:

The French Revolution, of which the present wars are the continuation, has given the French amid bloodshed and upheaval entirely new energies. . . . Neighbors and conquered have been carried away by the flood. All barriers created to dam it up have proved feeble. . . .

The illusion that we could withstand the Revolution most effectively by holding fast to the old . . . has itself resulted in the promotion and ever greater extension of the Revolution. The power of its principles is so great, they are so generally recognized and widely spread, that the state that fails to take them up voluntarily will either suffer destruction or be compelled from outside to accept them. . . .

Therefore, our goal, our guiding principle, is a revolution in the good sense, leading straight to the great purpose of the ennoblement of humanity through the wisdom of those in authority, rather than through a violent upheaval from below or without. Democratic principles in a monarchical government: that seems to me the form appropriate to the current spirit of the age. . . .

In other, but similar circumstances, although under an entirely different spirit of the age, Elector Frederick William the Great revolutionized . . . his state and laid the foundations for its later greatness.

From Georg Winter, ed., Die Reorganisation des Preussischen Staates unter Stein und Hardenberg *(Leipzig: S. Hirzel, 1931), Vol. I, pp. 305–306 (translation by M. Knox).*

port. Its ultimate consequence was "bureaucratic absolutism," a power-state that bureaucrats and officers ruled under a thin veneer of royal authority.

For the moment, the Prussian reformers could only hope that Napoleon would somehow falter. Austria, in April 1809, took Napoleon's Spanish defeats as a signal to renew the war. The Habsburgs incited the Tyrolean mountaineers, whom Napoleon had separated from Austria, to a desperate guerrilla revolt. Dynastic Vienna appealed publicly to "the German nation." The old regime was learning new tricks. The Habsburg Archduke Charles, one of the most talented of Napoleon's opponents, fought him to a standstill at Aspern, near Vienna. Then Napoleon triumphed in a grueling two-day struggle at Wagram on July 5–6, 1809. Victory was becoming more difficult. The rest of Europe had begun to imitate the Revolution.

Austria nevertheless sued for peace after Wagram. Its new foreign minister, Clemens von Metternich, bought Napoleon's good graces with the marriage offer of a Habsburg archduchess, Marie-Louise. Napoleon was happy to accept, and to discard Joséphine Beauharnais. A marriage alliance with the oldest major ruling house of Europe would give the upstart Bonaparte dynasty much-needed legitimacy.

The End: From Moscow to Saint Helena, 1812–15

Yet Napoleon's power still rested on force, and with defeat in Russia in 1812, that force melted away. Until the end of 1811 Napoleon had expected to hold Tsar Alexander to the Tilsit bargain with threats. But Russian cooperation with the Continental System against Britain had always been

Napoleonic Europe   1812

weak, and Alexander had secretly approached Prussia and Austria with proposals for a new coalition. In the spring of 1812 Napoleon broke relations with St. Petersburg and launched what he himself described as "the most difficult enterprise I have ever attempted," the invasion of Russia.

The vanguard of the largest army ever seen, more than a half-million men of whom 250,000 were French, crossed the Russian border in June 1812. The immense distances, the absence of roads, and shortage of food and fodder devoured Napoleon's *Grande Armée*. Russian resistance, compounded of equal parts courage, stubbornness, and vodka, stunned the French with its bitterness. As in Spain, guerrillas attacked French communications. Napoleon failed to force the ever-retreating Russian armies into a decisive battle. The immense slaughter at Borodino (almost 70,000 casualties) and the capture of Moscow in September 1812 were not victories. The Russian governor put the city to the torch. Tsar Alexander, perhaps fearful of being strangled like his father if he showed weakness, obstinately refused to negoti-

ate. After a fatal month of hesitation, Napoleon began an improvised withdrawal. The Russian winter and the pursuing Cossack cavalry did the rest. Perhaps 10,000 men out of the entire *Grande Armée* escaped from Russia in any condition to fight.

As Napoleon sprinted for Paris to raise a new army, Germany turned against the French. Princes, literati, and the middle classes united in an outpouring of national feeling. A mutinous Prussian general joined the advancing Russians with his army corps on New Year's Day, 1813. The Prussian state soon followed. Austria too joined the new coalition after Metternich vainly pressed Napoleon to settle for an empire confined to France and a return to the pre-1789 balance of power. Napoleon replied that any settlement short of victory would deprive him of the prestige he needed to rule France itself. It was that necessity, as well as his own immense ambition, that had spurred him toward universal empire.

Napoleon's dogged refusal to compromise thus created the coalition that finally brought France down. By August

The *Grande Armée's* flight across the icy Beresina River (late November 1812).

1813 the alliance was complete. Its forces caught and destroyed Napoleon's new and inexperienced army at Leipzig in October. The Allies had discovered how to defeat Napoleon—by coordinating their movements, giving battle only when united, and smashing Napoleon's less-talented subordinates separately before closing in on the Emperor himself.

With Germany gone and with Wellington advancing across the Pyrenees from Spain, Napoleon fought a last brilliant campaign to the north and east of Paris in the spring of 1814. He himself now suffered from a variety of ailments, his troops were green and badly outnumbered, his generals weary, and his subjects despairing from never-ending war. But he proved as dangerous as ever on the battlefield.

The coalition nevertheless held. Viscount Castlereagh, the British Foreign Secretary, welded together the unlikely allies—Britain, Austria, Russia, Prussia—with the Treaty of Chaumont (March 1814). That Quadruple Alliance pledged to fight to restore the balance of power and confine France to its traditional boundaries, and to remain united for twenty years after war's end. The Allies drove toward Paris and ignored Napoleon's last bold attempt to cut their communications. Military defeat, the plotting of his former foreign minister, Talleyrand, and the defection of key generals finally brought Napoleon down. In early April 1814 he abdicated and received from the Allies the Tuscan island of Elba for his retirement.

Louis XVIII, his relatives, and their court returned to France in the baggage trains of the victorious allied armies, and rapidly made themselves unloved. When Napoleon escaped from Elba and landed

The end, 1815: Napoleon and his staff, bound for exile on St. Helena.

in southern France in March 1815, the army rallied to him and joyous crowds carried him up the steps of the Tuileries palace.

The Allies were less delighted. Wellington and the Prussian commander, Blücher, rapidly concentrated their armies in Belgium. Napoleon, intent on one last throw of the dice, advanced to meet them. After drubbing the Prussians at Ligny he tried on June 18 to overwhelm Wellington at Waterloo before Blücher could join him. Wellington, as he freely if ungrammatically admitted, had been "never so near to being beat." Then Napoleon's Imperial Guard recoiled from the thin red line of British infantry and the Prussians attacked Napoleon's flank. Napoleon's last "Hundred Days" in power and France's career of conquest were over.

The Bourbons once more returned. Napoleon surrendered to the British, who shipped him off to the desolate South Atlantic island of St. Helena. There he occupied himself until his death in 1821 with the construction of the Napoleonic myth: that his empire built on force had been "a kind of republic" and that he himself had championed the principle of national self-determination for nations other than France.

The wars of the Republic and of the Empire had cost the *grande nation* perhaps 1.3 million lives—or one Frenchman in ten. The rapid population growth of the eighteenth century subsided as France's peasants concentrated on enjoying and conserving. France henceforth lacked the will for a serious bid to overturn the balance of power. But the Revolution and its wars had set loose in Europe ideas and forces that the victors could not still. It had unleashed, through the concept of the nation-state, new energies within and new conflicts without. It had demonstrated that a society could discard its rulers and freely adopt new myths and institutions. It had established the pattern of the modern bureaucratic state. And it had shown that popular sovereignty unlimited by law might produce a "despotism of liberty" instead of democracy. These were powerful lessons for the future.

Suggestions for Further Reading

The French Revolution

The best recent interpretive surveys are W. Doyle, *The Oxford History of the French Revolution* (1989), and D. M. G. Sutherland, *France 1789–1815: Revolution and Counter-Revolution* (1985). A. Cobban, *A History of Modern France*, Vol. I, *1715–1799* (1957), still offers a fine introductory summary. For the "classic" French Marxist view, see G. Lefebvre, *The French Revolution* (1962–64), and A. Soboul, *The French Revolution: 1787–1799* (1971). R. R. Palmer, *The World of the French Revolution* (1971), places the Revolution in its broader European context, as does E. J. Hobsbawm, *The Age of Revolution, 1789–1848* (1962), brilliantly, from a Marxist viewpoint. F. Furet and M. Ozouf, *A Critical Dictionary of the French Revolution* (1989), offers incisive discussions of key topics.

R.W. Greenlaw, ed., *The Social Origins of the French Revolution* (1975), and T. C. W. Blanning, *The French Revolution: Aristocrats versus Bourgeois?* (1988), offer useful introductions to the fierce debate over whether the Revolution was a class struggle. A. Cobban, *The Social Interpretation of the French Revolution* (1964), wittily attacks Lefebvre and Soboul. J. Talmon, *The Origins of Totalitarian Democracy* (1952), F. Furet, *Interpreting the French Revolution* (trans. 1981), and C. Blum, *Rousseau and the Republic of Virtue* (1986), stress ideology rather than class as the Revolution's driving force. F. Aftalion, *The French Revolution: An Economic Interpretation* (1990) explores the role of inflation. On the masses, see G. Rudé, *The Crowd in the French Revolution* (1959), and R. Cobb, *The Police and the People* (1970) and *The People's Armies* (1987). T. C. W. Blanning, *The Origins of the French Revolutionary Wars* (1986), is excellent on the Revolution's relations with Europe. The following also stand out: W. Doyle, *The Origin of the French Revolution* (1980); N. Hampson, *The Life and Opinions of Maximilien Robespierre* (1974); R. R. Palmer, *Twelve Who Ruled* (1941); A. Soboul, *The Parisian Sans-Culottes and the French Revolution* (1964); C. Tilly, *The Vendée* (1964); M. Lyons, *France under the Directory* (1975); A. Forrest, *The French Revolution and the Poor* (1981); L. A. Hunt, *Politics, Culture, and Class in the French Revolution* (1984).

Napoleon

G. Bruun, *Europe and the French Imperium, 1799–1814* (1938), and G. Bergeron, *France under Napoleon* (Princeton, 1981) offer useful surveys. G. Lefebvre's two-volume *Napoleon* (1969) is masterful and comprehensive. R. Holtman, *The Napoleonic Revolution* (1967), is useful on Napoleon's domestic policy; for the impact of Napoleonic France on Europe, see especially S. J. Woolf, *Napoleon's Integration of Europe* (1990). D. Chandler, *The Campaigns of Napoleon* (1966), offers a thorough treatment of Napoleon's wars, with good maps; for a shrewd contemporary's reflections on what those wars meant, see C. von Clausewitz, *On War* (1976), eds. M. Howard and P. Paret.

·24·

THE DEMOGRAPHIC AND INDUSTRIAL REVOLUTIONS 1750–1914

*H*istorical forces move at varying rates. The French Revolution transformed the politics of Europe in the two decades after 1789. But by then other even more powerful forces had begun to revolutionize the entire world: the leap from agriculture to industry and the continuing explosion of human knowledge ignited by the scientific revolution and the Enlightenment.

Those forces gathered strength only gradually in the course of the nineteenth century. And they are still at work. Understanding their origins, development, and consequences requires isolating them from other events and following their course through the long and relatively peaceful century from 1815 to 1914. That is the purpose of this chapter, which traces the coming of industrialization and the massive modern growth in population—

and of the next, which explores the movement of ideas. Both deal with the sweeping long-term forces that shaped both the nineteenth century and our own world.

The coming of the machine—the substitution of mechanical precision and power for human skill and human or animal strength—was the greatest single change in human existence since the agricultural revolution of the New Stone Age. In the late eighteenth century, the British economy began for the first time in history to generate an ever-increasing surplus of food and goods. Western Europe, the United States, and one non-European power, Japan, soon followed Britain's lead.

The coming of sustained and self-sustaining economic growth in Europe intersected with the "demographic revolution," the swift growth of population that began in the 1740s with the end of the

(Opposite) The face of the Industrial Revolution: "Fritz," a gigantic steam-hammer installed at Essen in the Ruhr by the firm of Krupp (1861).

"little ice age" (see p. 493). These two revolutions together laid the physical foundations of the societies of our own era, societies far larger, richer, and more powerful than any before. Machinery and population growth together also drove toward culmination the Europeanization or "Westernization" of the world that had begun in 1492.

THE STARTING POINT: THE BIOLOGICAL AND ECONOMIC "OLD REGIME"

Before the eighteenth century, the lives of all except kings, large landowners, upper clergy, and small merchant and professional classes tended to be "nasty, brutish, and short." In most of Western Europe farming was primitive and had changed relatively little from the eleventh century to the seventeenth. Nobility, clergy, and warring states devoured the small surpluses left after the people were fed. A precarious existence depended above all on two factors: favorable weather and the absence of disease. Drought or downpour, hail or frost—any whim of the climate might spell famine and death. Plant or animal diseases might cause disaster in small areas or across the continent. By one count, France suffered 13 general famines in the sixteenth century, 17 in the seventeenth, and 16 in the eighteenth.

Human epidemics were even less forgiving than those of the plant and animal world. The Black Death of the fourteenth century remained a serious threat, striking Amsterdam and Paris repeatedly and killing as much as a seventh of London's population in 1664–65. Columbus's discovery of America also contributed. It introduced smallpox to the Indians and syphilis to the Europeans. After 1493 syphilis spread with fierce virulence from Spain across the Continent. A new form of tuberculosis, more dangerous than its predecessors, arrived in Europe from India in the eighteenth century. As late as 1831–32 cholera from India produced a terrifying epidemic.

And along with the great diseases came the lesser endemic ones. Smallpox infected perhaps 95 percent of the inhabitants of early modern Europe—and roughly one in seven of those infected died. Malaria lessened life expectancy by perhaps a third. Before the eighteenth century it was endemic in marsh areas as far north as England. Typhus, typhoid fever, and many no longer identifiable but often fatal diseases were equally widespread.

Death was thus ever-present under the "biological old regime." The death rate exceeded the birth rate—population actually decreased—in times of famine and epidemic. Although a rapid rise in births followed each disaster, infant mortality was an even greater scourge than in today's Third World. In one prosperous French province in the seventeenth century infant deaths ran between 25 and 33 percent of all newborns in their first year. Only half of all newborns lived to the age of twenty.

Accompanying the familiar presence of death was an overwhelming dreariness of life. Since the industrial revolution it has been fashionable to lament, on well-filled stomachs and in the comfort of well-heated houses, the purity and authenticity of "the world we have lost." But the inhabitants of pre-industrial Europe did not live in picturesque rural bliss. They fought a grim and often losing struggle for survival amid squalid poverty without equivalent today except in the "Third World."

The vast majority of Europe's inhabitants lived through backbreaking toil in fields and cottage workshops. Children worked for their parents from the moment they were able. Those who did not work starved—as did many of those who did work. Agriculture followed the tyranny of the seasons: too little work in winter, and too much at ploughing and harvest time. Food had a desperate sameness. In the aftermath of the Black Death, population shortage and high wages had made meat a frequent food of the common people. But by the seventeenth century the population was again pressing against the limits of subsistence, and the vast majority of Europeans ate little but cereals. Wheat was the staple food, at least in western Europe. Rye, barley, or oats—"in England a food for horses, in Scotland for men"—prevailed in outlying areas of the east and north. Rice was an exotic eastern import until the creation of broad malarial rice-fields in northern Italy after the fifteenth century. In the seventeenth and eighteenth centuries the New World crops, especially maize (corn) and potatoes, began to spread slowly but without changing the underlying pattern of the European diet. The population ate peasant bread baked a few times a year and stored like bricks. Ergot fungus, which causes hallucinations and convulsions, often contaminated rye. Too exclusive a diet of cornmeal mush (the Italian *polenta*) caused pellagra, a devastating vitamin deficiency disease. Only the rich, and the small populations in the mountains and wastelands given over to sheep and cattle, ate much meat.

As for shelter, the common people, until very late, lived in thatched hovels with dirt floors and one or two pieces of furniture. In many cases, the peasants shared the roof with their animals, as well as with bedbugs, fleas, and lice. Clothing was scarce, expensive, and rarely washed.

Isolation added to the monotony of work, food, and lodging. Few peasants journeyed beyond their native valleys. Peasant villages and even small towns were tight little societies torn by small hatreds and fiercely antagonistic toward outsiders. Only the rare visits to local market towns or fairs, or the brief village religious festivals with their ritualized overeating and drunkenness, punctuated a bleak existence. Small wonder that the peasants of the French Alps described the height of happiness in such macabre terms as "happy as a dead'un." Misery seemed tolerable because it was familiar; no alternative had ever existed except for the privileged few who lived above subsistence level.

The demographic and economic "old regime" began to give way to the new age in the course of the eighteenth century. The population of Europe had increased before, from 1100 to 1350; the Black Death had then reduced it by up to a third. Growth had resumed from 1450 to 1630, until the stagnation of the "little ice age."

Now, after 1750, Europe's population began to increase with unprecedented and apparently uncheckable speed.

The pattern was not unique. The populations of China and India, although statistics are sketchy, apparently grew at a similar rate and with a similar cause (see Figure 24-1). The most likely source of the general upturn after 1750 was a change in weather patterns. After the "little ice age" in the seventeenth and early eighteenth century, world climate appears to have warmed significantly. Agricultural production and nutrition improved. The death rate slowly declined and the birth rate rose. Population growth resumed at a rapid rate.

Two things that had little or no effect on the initial upturn of the population curve, despite the contrary impressions of contemporaries and historians, were modern medicine and sanitation, and industrialization itself. Medicine and sanitation, with the possible exception of vaccination for smallpox, introduced in 1796, played little role before the 1850s, and then primarily in England, the most advanced nation. The widespread draining of marshes, removal of rotting refuse from villages and towns, increased use of soap, baths, and cotton (and hence washable) underclothes probably cut the insect population of Europe. Malaria, transmitted by mosquitoes, and flea- and louse-borne plague and typhus did decrease. But the marshes were drained to reclaim land for farming, and the other changes served comfort, not medicine. Conscious efforts against disease had to await the discovery of its causes and carriers in the nineteenth century.

As for industrialization, it affected Britain first, and mainly after 1760. The 1780s was the decisive decade in which British economic growth turned sharply upward. Industry, in other words, did not itself cause the demographic revolution. Nor does industry's existence or absence fit neatly with population growth. Western Europe, which industralized, grew 280 percent between 1680 and 1900 (71.9 million to 201.4 million), whereas China, which did not industralize, grew at a roughly similar rate (150 million to 450

FIGURE 24.1   **World Population**   **1000–2000**

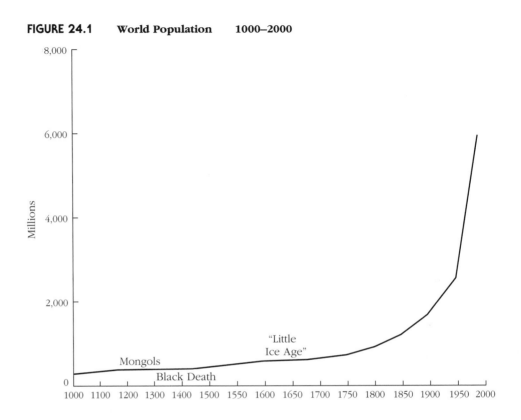

England, Europe's most dynamic society: the port of London on the eve of the Industrial Revolution (1757).

million). The peak growth rates of industrializing regions within Europe did outstrip most other areas. The presence of work encouraged both migration and earlier marriages that produced more children. England's population grew by a staggering 133 percent (from 4.93 million to 11.5 million) between 1680 and 1820, and 86 percent of that increase took place after 1760. But population also grew rapidly in nonindustrial areas. The population of England and Wales grew by 48 percent between 1751 and 1801; Ireland's grew by 75 percent.

Whatever its sources, the consequences of growth were startling. The total population of Europe west of the Ural Mountains grew from perhaps 140 million in 1750 to 390 million in 1900. England and Russia, at opposite ends of the Continent and of the scale of social and economic development, led the way (see Figure 24-2). In central Europe the populations of Germany and Austria-Hungary approximately doubled. Italy, thanks to massive emigration to the New World in the last quarter of the century, grew only 87 percent. France, whose career as *la grande nation* was ended demographi-

cally as well as militarily, increased only 65 percent.

Ireland, the classic European example of the consequences of unchecked population growth without industrialization, suffered catastrophe. Its population doubled in the seventeenth century, then more than doubled in the eighteenth century at the steepest rate in all Europe. That rise continued, from 5.25 million in 1800 to 8.5 million in 1845—of whom perhaps a quarter were unemployed. Then a potato blight and catastrophic famine in 1845–48 killed perhaps a million Irish, and flight to the New World cut population to around 4.5 million.

What prevented further demographic catastrophes of the kind that afflicted Ireland, or China in the 1850s and 1860s, when perhaps 20 million died in famines? As in Ireland and China, Europe's death rates gradually declined in the course of the century. Although birth rates also dropped, the spread between the death-rate and the birth-rate curves rapidly opened, and the population leapt upward. But unlike the outcome in Ireland and China, industrialization and medicine sustained Europe's increase. Only after the

FIGURE 24.2   Population Increase by Country   1700–1900

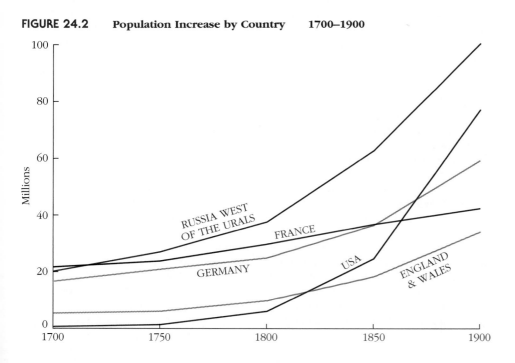

turn of the century did most of Europe pass through a "demographic transition" to a new pattern of lower birth rates. That transition was one symptom of the maturing of Europe's new industrial societies.

THE INDUSTRIAL REVOLUTION: CAUSES

The World Primacy of the West

Why did industrialization happen? Or, rather, why did it happen in the West? And why in Britain? Two other contenders, the Islamic world and China, might have led the way. They did not, although (as described earlier) in the early Middle Ages Islam had provided the then-backward West with lost Greek texts and vital concepts such as decimal numbers and algebra. And in 1078 China had briefly achieved a level of coal-smelted iron production (125,000 tons) that Britain did not match until 1796.

But the Islamic world and China shared common misfortunes. The savage waves of nomads from Central Asia hit them harder than they did Europe. Nomads conquered China's major iron-producing provinces. The Mongols sacked Baghdad and ruled China as the Yuan dynasty. The Ottoman Turks overran and held the core lands of Islamic civilization. In China a second "conquest dynasty," the Manchus, proved as disruptive as the Mongols.

Even more serious than invasion and foreign rule was a loss of impetus, an intellectual turning inward. In the Islamic world, that tendency may have had doctrinal roots. *Islam* means "submission"— to the will of God. From the beginning, Islam's thrust toward a life totally devoted to God meant potential hostility to nonreligious knowledge. In the tenth century, the "gates of independent judgment" about the Koran began to close. Further speculation about either theology or the physical world became increasingly suspect, and slowed dramatically (see pp. 217–18). As for China, the Ming dynasty's great trading and war fleets of 1405–33 dominated the South China Sea

and the Indian Ocean, and were technologically superior to those of the Portuguese who followed less than seventy years later. But China's confident ethnocentrism and the nomad threat to its northern border turned it inward for good.

Political disadvantages multiplied the disadvantages of circumstances and culture. The Islamic world and China shared a similar form of government—centralized despotism. Caliphs, Ottoman sultans, and emperors of China in theory *owned* their territory and its inhabitants. Human inefficiency, frequent struggles over the succession of the throne, and the need to rely on elites, such as China's scholar-gentry, that might in time become independent, often tempered that absolute power. But the claim to total power remained. All property in theory belonged to the ruler. He merely lent it to his subjects and could tax or reclaim it when he chose.

Europe—except for the Russian state (see pp. 343–47)—was different. After the assimilation or defeat of the Viking and Magyar raiders in the tenth century, Europe suffered relatively little from outside invasion. Mongols and Turks devastated only fringe areas such as Muscovy, Hungary, and the Balkans. And far from relapsing into self-satisfaction, Europeans developed that uniquely inquiring cast of mind already described in discussing the Renaissance and the scientific revolution. Theological speculation separated from inquiry about the physical world. Slowly and haltingly, the West crossed the divide between magic and science. And after 1100, Europe's science and technology slowly overtook and surpassed even those of China. The Western obsession with clocks, with the mechanical measurement of time, was symbolic of far more—the application of rationality, calculation, and step-by-step problem-solving to broader and broader areas of life.

Politics also helped. Despite the efforts of popes and emperors, Europe remained divided into warring states and principalities. Charlemagne, Gregory VII, Charles V, Philip II, Louis XIV, and Napoleon all failed to establish universal empires. Europe also lacked the identification of government and religion seen in both

Islam and China. The Investiture Conflict and the Protestant Reformation guaranteed that Caesar and God would remain distinct. That left space, however small at first, for freedom.

Finally, political fragmentation allowed subordinate groups and individuals to claim *rights,* even against their rulers—a concept almost unimaginable elsewhere. From the security of their fortified walls, medieval towns could defy their overlords. The barons extorted the *Magna Carta* from the English monarchy. The right of resistance to oppression became a stable principle of poltical thought in Europe, and nowhere else. Relative freedom under laws, however limited in practice, persisted and widened over the centuries.

And the close connection between political freedom and the free enjoyment of property allowed wide latitude and security for economic activity. In western Europe, and in western Europe alone, great bankers like the Medici and the Fuggers could deal almost as equals with emperors and kings. The straightjacket of the European mercantilist state was a small impediment to growth compared to the punitive taxation or confiscation that awaited Moslem or Chinese merchants whose economic success made them conspicuous. Relative freedom from devastation by nomads, the preeminence of curiosity and rationality, political pluralism and division between religious and secular power, and the concept of rights against the ruler propelled Europe past its rivals.

The Primacy of Britain in Europe

Within Europe, Britain led the way after the seventeenth century. Even more than the rest of Europe, it enjoyed freedom from external threat. The last successful invasion had been the Norman conquest in 1066. Internal turmoil, from the Wars of the Roses to the Civil War of the 1640s and the Highland clan risings of 1715 and 1745, was superficial and short-lived compared to the great wars that tore the Continent. An inquiring cast of mind had long distinguished the English, who contrib-

uted more than any other people to the scientific revolution. The Reformation and the breaking of the religious monopoly of the Anglican Church in the Civil War meant that religious restraints on speculation and on the free flow of knowledge were largely absent.

Finally, English politics and society helped establish England's primacy over rivals such as France, just as the nature of European politics and society gave Europe the lead it had acquired by 1700. The remnants of English feudal institutions and land tenure had disappeared by the sixteenth century. England had ceased to have serfs or even a hereditary peasantry. After the mid-sixteenth century even mining rights, except in gold and silver, belonged to the landowner and not to the king—a situation unique in Europe. When the Civil War of 1641–48 pitted the Crown against England's landowners organized in Parliament, the landowners had won, and had completed the process begun with the *Magna Carta*. Rights of property became absolute, dependent neither on service nor on the claims of overlords, tenants, or church. The purpose of government itself, as John Locke had spelled it out in 1690, was simple: "The great and chief end . . . of men's uniting into commonwealths and putting themselves under government is the preservation of their property." That concept of property was far more absolute than that prevailing even in old-regime France, much less in lands east and south of France.

By the eighteenth century, the inhabitants of England thus enjoyed guaranteed rights and a social mobility undreamed of on the continent. "All are accounted gentlemen in England who maintain themselves without manual labor," remarked an eighteenth-century traveler's handbook. In this relatively "open aristocracy," wealth bought status with a speed and directness not visible in France. That was an immense stimulus to the pursuit of wealth. Britain's upper classes were far less fastidious than their continental counterparts about how to acquire that wealth. The barriers against nobles engaging in trade and industry that were slowly breaking down in old-regime France scarcely existed in eighteenth-century Britain. And the guild restrictions that still hobbled industry on the continent had long vanished.

British family structure and inheritance customs also promoted mobility and growth. Unlike the practice in France, where all children of the nobility inherited their parents' status, the younger sons of the great English families received neither land nor title. On the Continent, caste-bound younger sons had to make do with careers in church or army. In Britain, younger sons went out into the world to earn money. These features made Britain into Europe's most dynamic society. It was the first to industrialize because it alone was ready.

Other factors help explain why Britain industrialized when it did. First among them was the gradual but impressive growth of English agriculture, which between 1700 and 1800 increased its output per acre by 44 percent. New timetables for ploughing, new methods of field rotation with crops such as clover or turnips that returned nitrogen to the soil and supplied fodder, larger numbers of sheep and cattle eating that fodder and manuring the fields, selective breeding of livestock—all contributed to growth. The absence of a hereditary peasantry allowed landowners, whether "gentlemen" or merely prosperous farmers, to consolidate the common lands of the medieval village into "enclosed" fields, either by agreement with the villagers or by act of Parliament. Consolidation of holdings was virtually complete by the first decades of the nineteenth century, and made England a land of economically efficient large and medium-sized farms, far different from the patchwork of open-field strips and small peasant holdings still found on the Continent.

This "agricultural revolution" had three major consequences for British industrialization. Contrary to widespread opinion, enclosure apparently did not contribute to industrialization by driving laborers off the land and into the new industrial labor force. The enclosed fields with their livestock and multiple crops required more, not less labor than the old system. It was the increase in the rural population, not enclosure, that filled the new industrial cities. But agriculture did help to keep the new urban population fed, while enclosure freed land for industry or mining. And agricultural prosperity increased the market for industrial products.

But agriculture only provided a foundation for growth. On that foundation a rich commercial and industrial economy arose that as early as 1700 was supplying a third of England's national product. By comparison, at that date commerce and industry made up a fifth or less of the French economy. And England's commerce, unlike that of France, had by 1700 already created a national market that matched goods with buyers. A cash economy centered on London reached to the far corners of the island. Barter, still prevalent in backward areas of France, was relatively rare. The internal customs barriers that bedeviled French merchants and the inter-state ones that cut eighteenth-century Germany into incoherent dwarf economies did not exist in England.

Even geography favored the creation of a national market. No part of Britain is more than seventy miles from the sea. Navigable rivers—the Thames, Severn, Tyne, Humber—improved with dredging and locks, made possible the economical transport of bulk cargoes such as coal, of which London was already consuming 100,000 tons a year by the early seventeenth century. Especially after the 1760s, entrepreneurs promoted a massive expansion of canals that linked the major rivers into a national transport network. Similar private companies made British roads the best in Europe by the end of the eighteenth century (see Figure 24-3). Nor did the British market end with Britain itself. England's export trade, which grew sixfold during the eighteenth century, offered a further incentive for firms to expand production relentlessly.

Thus England was already rich, and its people, along with those of Holland and the United States, enjoyed the world's highest standard of living by the late eighteenth century. That wealth made it the only country in Europe that possessed the makings of a true mass market, a public

FIGURE 24.3   **The Transport Revolution in Britain**

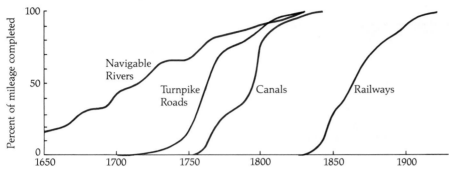

capable of buying large quantities of inexpensive goods. The pull of that market at last harnessed the West's love of gadgets and its willingness to search for practical results by trial and error to economic purposes. The pull of that market prompted the emergence of a cluster of technological innovations that propelled Britain into spectacular growth. For the first time in history, an economy expanded not primarily by increasing its labor input, but by replacing labor with machinery.

THE FIRST INDUSTRIAL REVOLUTION, 1750–1850

The innovations of this "first industrial revolution" affected above all three key industries: cotton, coal, and iron. Cotton, the miracle fiber from India, the Middle East, and the slave economies of the Caribbean and American South, led the way. Cotton was durable, lighter than linen, and easily washed, dyed, printed, and worked by machine. It was also in insatiable demand: As a London magazine put it in 1783, "every servant girl has her cotton gown and her cotton stockings."

In the 1730s the first of the major innovations, John Kay's flying shuttle, dramatically speeded up the weaving of cotton cloth. That increase created a bottleneck in spinning the raw fibers into thread. By the 1750s the flying shuttle was in general use, and tinkerers and entrepreneurs bent to the task of mechanizing spinning. James Hargreaves's "spinning jenny" of 1765, Richard Arkwright's larger and more pow-

erful "water frame," and Samuel Crompton's "mule," a hybrid with features from its two predecessors, filled the gap.

The new devices produced cotton thread in previously unimaginable quantities, and of a strength and fineness that hand spinners could not match. A twelvefold leap in cotton production and consumption between 1770 and 1800 in turn created further imbalances. The tiny chemical industry found itself pressed for vast quantities of soaps and bleaches for processing textiles. And the flying shuttle of the home weavers could no longer keep up with the output of thread. The answer was Arkwright's power-loom, invented in 1787. By 1833 one man with a twelve-year-old boy as helper could produce as much as twenty hand-weavers. Annual production of cotton cloth skyrocketed from perhaps a million pounds a year in 1730 to 100 million in 1815.

That expansion created an entirely new institution, the factory. The grouping together of workers in large workshops was not new. It had existed in the ancient world and in Europe before the Industrial Revolution. But in all except the heaviest metal industries, large workshops had little or no competitive advantage over cottage industry. In 1770, the date of Arkwright's first large factory, the vast bulk of production still took place at home under the "putting-out" system. The entrepreneur provided raw material to home workers (his subcontractors) and then collected and sold the finished product. The coming of power-driven machinery that was swifter, more efficient, and larger and

A replica of Arkwright's water frame, patented in 1769.

The factory: steam power and long rows of iron-framed machines. A cotton mill in the mid-1840s.

The Coming of Steam: A View from the Bottom   1818

When the spinning of cotton was in its infancy, and before those terrible machines for superseding the necessity of human labour, called steam engines came into use, there were a great number of what were then called *little masters;* men who with a small capital, could procure a few machines, and employ a few machines, and employ a few hands men and boys (say to twenty or thirty). . . . A few years however changed the face of things. Steam engines came into use, to purchase which, and to erect buildings sufficient to contain them and six or seven hundred hands, required a great capital. The engine power produced a more marketable (though not a better) article than the little masters could at the same price. The consequence was their ruin in a short time; and the overgrown capitalists triumphed in their fall.

Black Dwarf, *September 30, 1818, pp. 623–24, quoted in Theodore Hamerow,* The Birth of a New Europe *(Chapel Hill: University of North Carolina Press, 1983), p. 13.*

more expensive than anything possible in the home or in small workshops forced the concentration of industry into ever-larger units, into *factories* built around their machines and power sources. The "factory system" was an organizational and logistical leap comparable in importance to the technological advances that made it necessary and possible.

The take-off of the cotton industry, with its pattern of new machines perpetually challenging entrepreneurs to further mechanize the slower phases of the pro-

duction cycle, encouraged other industries as well. Coal and iron, the other two sectors of this first industrial revolution, felt the stimulus. Water power, which drove the early factories, was proving inadequate by the 1790s. Its force varied with the seasons and it was found only on suitable streams, often far from markets or sources of raw materials. The solution was to tap an inanimate source of power whose supply seemed almost unlimited—coal.

The machine that turned the energy of coal into rotary motion to drive the new textile machines was the steam engine, the very symbol of the Industrial Revolution. Playthings such as the rotating kettle powered by a steam jet had existed since antiquity. But the first practical steam engine was Thomas Savery's "fire engine," or steam-powered pump, of 1698. Seven years later Thomas Newcomen, a blacksmith of Dartmouth in southern England, built the first true steam engine. It moved a crossbeam connected to a pump cylinder. Less than 1 percent of the energy released from its fuel did useful work. But that was enough. The machine was tireless and could be almost any size needed. It served at first to pump out and ventilate coal mines. It allowed the rapid expansion of coal production from ever-deeper seams, although its inefficiency prevented its use any distance from cheap coal.

Then, in the 1770s, James Watt invented an improved engine four times as efficient. That breakthrough created the "age of steam." The seemingly unlimited coal deposits of northern England could now power ever-larger spinning and weaving machines. Watt's partner was understandably immodest about their achievement: "I sell, Sir, what all the world desires to have—power."

Steam for pumping had permitted the expansion of coal production. Steam for industry in turn increased demand for coal. Steam power, coal, and the demands of war with France after 1793 between them revolutionized the iron industry. The English by 1740 already consumed ten or eleven pounds of iron per capita each year, far more than the French (although as late as the 1780s France's iron produc-

Watt's design drawing for his steam engine (1769).

tion was in absolute terms larger than Britain's). But English metallurgy soon came up against a seemingly unbreakable bottleneck: fuel. The supply of wood to make charcoal for smelting iron ore into pig iron was limited. Coal, in its charred form, coke, normally contaminated the iron with impurities that rendered the finished product unusable.

After long experiment, Abraham Darby successfully smelted iron ore with coke (as the Chinese had centuries before him) in 1709. But not until the 1750s did the technique become widespread. The triumph of coke smelting and further innovations, such as the steam-powered forced-blast furnace and the preheated air blast, drove British production of pig iron upward from 17,350 tons in 1740 to 2.7 million tons in 1852. That vast increase called forth further innovations elsewhere in the production cycle. The decisive breakthrough in the processing of pig iron (from 2.5 to 5 percent carbon) into wrought iron (less than .1 percent carbon) came in the 1780s with Henry Cort's "puddling" and steam-powered rolling process. Crude standardized shapes such as iron beams, bars, and rails became possible for the first time. Britain's iron industry left France's in the dust.

As iron became ever cheaper, new sources of demand appeared. Weapons had traditionally been the largest single use of iron, and remained so until after 1800. Royal Navy orders ensured the success of the Carron Company, Scotland's first major ironworks (1759). A new precision process for boring cannon from solid castings speeded production and made weapons more accurate. The steam engine's leaky cylinders also benefited from the new boring techniques. Iron beams began to appear in buildings and bridges in the 1770s, and the first practical iron-hulled ship emerged in 1815. Iron frames, rollers, gears, and pushrods replaced wood in the new generation of steam-powered textile machines, cutting vibration and permitting ever higher operating speeds.

The culmination of the age of steam was the application of coal power to transport—the railroad and the steamship, the

The new metallurgy: smelting iron with coke in Upper Silesia, 1841.

first self-moving vehicles in world history. The first practical steamships were the creation of a French marquis, Claude Jouffroy d'Abbans, in the late 1770s and early 1780s. Americans and British developed the innovation further, and the first partially steam-powered Atlantic crossing came in 1819. The railroad was a combination of the steam engine with the rail-wagons used since the late sixteenth century in mines and quarries. In the late 1750s iron rails had begun to replace wood. Then, after 1800, inventors sought to power a vehicle to run on those rails. In 1801–04 Richard Trevithick, developer

Iron ships: The huge *Great Eastern* (1858), built by Isambard Kingdom Brunel (1806–1859), one of Britain's greatest engineers.

The opening of the world's first freight and passenger rail line, the Stockton-Darlington Railway, on September 27, 1825. Photo courtesy of the Mansell collection.

of a high-pressure engine more efficient than Watt's, succeeded. After the mid-1820s the first railways began to spread across Britain and the United States.

Railroads and steamships drove forward the transport revolution begun with roads and canals. Rail immensely expanded the internal market, while the steamship widened the international one. Together they created a demand that stretched the iron industry, as the widening consumer market had stretched the cotton industry. Each mile of railway track required three hundred tons of iron. By 1851, the year of the Great Exhibition at London that measured Britain's achievements against those of its European rivals, Britain had more than 9,000 miles of track. Rails covered Britain like a web, linking mines, factories, ports, and huge new cities. The railroad was the last of the cluster of technologies of that first industrial revolution that made Britain the "workshop of the world."

THE SECOND INDUSTRIAL REVOLUTION: FROM THE NINETEENTH CENTURY TO THE TWENTIETH

By the time of the Great Exhibition, the Industrial Revolution was spreading rapidly. Societies on the Continent that were socially and economically ready to follow Britain's lead now began to close the gap. Britain's share of world industrial production dropped steadily as its rivals caught up (see Figure 24-4). And new rivals beyond the seas, in America and ultimately in Japan (see pp. 706–08), rose to challenge both Britain and Europe.

These "followers" suffered from one major disadvantage: their infant industries, especially in textiles, faced the competition of low-cost mass-produced British goods. But the followers also benefited from Britain's pioneering. After Britain, industralization would never again be unforeseen and unplanned: the followers

FIGURE 24.4   **Leader and Followers: Relative Shares of World Industrial Production**

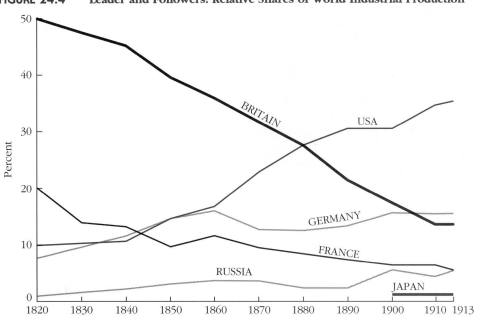

had a model. They could study and seek to avoid some of that model's shortcomings. They could adopt technology already pioneered in Britain, and save development costs. Finally, their industralization coincided roughly with a new wave of innovations, the "second industrial revolution," that appeared between 1850 and 1880. The followers could enter the new industries of this second wave without the burden of investment or labor force tied up in older industries. In the new industries the followers could in some cases compete on equal terms.

Four new technologies of the second industrial revolution propelled the world into the twentieth century: steel, chemicals, electricity, and the internal combustion engine. Steel was at first the most important. An alloy of iron known since antiquity, steel contains between .1 and 2 percent carbon. It combines strength, hardness, and elasticity in unique proportions. It holds under stresses that snap brittle pig or cast iron (2.5 to 5 percent carbon) and spread soft wrought iron (less than .1 percent carbon) like butter.

Until the 1850s no process existed for making steel cheaply and in quantity. The oldest technique involved baking wrought iron bars at high temperature in a bed of carbon to diffuse the carbon into the iron. Then a blacksmith laboriously reheated, folded, and hammered the iron bars into themselves by hand to distribute the carbon throughout the iron evenly. In the

Rolling steel in a mill.

Steel for a new age: the
Bessemer process.

1740s, along with the other metallurgical
discoveries of the early industrial revolution, came a process, long known in China
and South Asia, for making steel in small
melting pots, or crucibles. This crucible
process was small-scale and expensive,
but it produced the hardest and most uniform steel yet made in any quantity. And
it made possible for the first time the cast-
ing of large steel objects such as drive
shafts, railroad wheels or axles, and huge
shell-firing cannon.

Then came two breakthroughs. In the
1850s Henry Bessemer, an armaments
designer, discovered that blowing air
through a crucible filled with molten pig
iron rapidly burned off the excess carbon
and in the process generated the heat
needed to keep the iron molten. This "Bessemer converter" eliminated the laborious
intermediate steps required in earlier
processes. Amid spectacular showers of
sparks, it accomplished in ten to twenty
minutes what before had taken 24 hours
and immense quantities of coal. The
slightly later Siemens-Martin open-hearth
furnace, which recirculated superhot
combustion gases to create ever-higher
temperatures, also produced steel that
was as cheap as wrought iron. These
breakthroughs made the age of steel, an
age only now ending (see Figure 24-5).

In chemicals, another series of breakthroughs created entirely new industries.
Until the mid-nineteenth century chemical
production had mostly catered to the expanding textile industry's appetite for
soaps and bleaches. Then, thanks to Brit-

ish and French laboratory work on organic
chemicals derived from coal, came synthetic dyes. There followed mineral oils,
mineral oil derivatives, the anesthetic
chloroform, nitrated high explosives and
fertilizers, celluloid, cellulose fiber textiles
such as rayon, and the first primitive plastics. Alfred Nobel, Swedish inventor of stabilized nitroglycerine, the first practical
high explosive, felt such remorse at the
military uses of his product and the wealth
he gained from it that he established
the prizes—ironically including one for
peace—that bear his name.

Electricity, the third key technology,
came into its own by the 1880s. Its first
practical use, the telegraph, dated from
1837–38. Undersea telegraph cable linked
Britain and France by 1851 and spanned
the Atlantic by 1866. The telegraph, Alexander Graham Bell's telephone (1876),
and Guglielmo Marconi's radio (1897–
1901) revolutionized communications.
But electricity's most important use was
as a source of power, after a series of
inventions—generators, alternators, trans-
formers—from the 1860s to the 1880s.
Electricity lighted the new industrial cities,
replacing the coal gas lighting pioneered
in Britain around 1800. It also provided

FIGURE 24.5   **The Age of Steel**

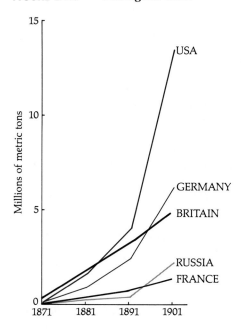

cheap, portable power in the factory, and ultimately replaced dangerous and unreliable webs of transmission belts with compact, powerful electric motors.

Last came the internal combustion engine. By the mid-nineteenth century the limitations of steam were apparent. Steam engines were heavy. Their usual fuel, coal, was equally so, and required legions of sweating stokers to feed the boilers. Consequently, steam was unsuitable for powering small vehicles. A German, Nicolaus Otto, provided the answer in 1876 with the first really practical internal combustion engine, which ran on coal gas. When converted to gasoline, it provided the motive power for the first automobiles in the 1890s, and for powered flight in 1903.

The technologies of the second industrial revolution in turn encouraged further changes in the methods and organization of production. Cheap steel and the machine tool industry it encouraged allowed the production for the first time of machines with interchangeable parts. That innovation, despite the claims of Samuel Colt for his early revolvers, remained more aspiration than reality until the 1870s. But after that, high-speed cutting steels, precision gauges, and a drive toward discipline and standardization in sizes and screw threads made possible the mass production of ever more intricate machines.

The new techniques of mass production with interchangeable parts found early application both in small arms and in the sewing machine. The American firm of Isaac Singer marketed this first domestic appliance on a worldwide scale after the 1850s. The same techniques, further rationalized, made possible in the twentieth century the production of automobiles on assembly lines. Mass production, in the proud words of the pioneer Henry Ford, was "the focusing upon a manufacturing system of the principle of power, accuracy, system, continuity, and speed."

The technology and organization of the second industrial revolution was different from that of the first. The new technologies required far greater amounts of capital than early textile innovators or even the eighteenth-century ironmasters had required. Until the coming of the railroads, entrepreneurs had tended to form closed partnerships that expanded by ploughing back profits into the enterprise. The scale of the new industries placed family firms and partnerships at a disadvantage, except for a few giants such as the firm of Friedrich and Alfred Krupp, the "cannon kings" of the Ruhr Valley. The solutions to this financial bottleneck, especially after mid-century, were the joint-stock company and large-scale bank loans to industry. Giant enterprises, bank financing, and close connections to the state became and remained conspicuous charcteristics of German industry, and of those of many other followers. Britain, by contrast, resisted concentration. It increasingly missed out on the economies of scale from which giant enterprises usually profit.

The second characteristic of the new technologies was their close connection to science. The inspired tinkerers that led the first industrial revolution shared the analytical, problem-solving, empirical cast of mind that had made the scientific revolution. But their discoveries had originated in workshop and forge, not in the laboratory. And their achievements were those of individual brilliance, not of teamwork. The new metallurgical, chemical, and electrical industries were different. From the beginning, the contribution of scientific theory to practice was great and ever-growing. Science-intensive industries in turn required ever-larger numbers of scientists and trained technicians. The sheer size of the new enterprises required a group effort of management, scientists, and technicians.

In France, state institutions such as the *École Polytechnique* and lesser provincial institutes supplied the necessary experts. But it was the reforming bureaucrats of Germany who triumphed in the new world of applied science and teamwork. Universal primary education and a widespread network of technical schools in many German states from the 1820s had no parallel on the Continent or anywhere else, except perhaps the United States after mid-century. Britain, where primary education did not become compulsory until 1880 and where the elite studied

Latin and Greek but not chemistry, suffered accordingly. By 1872 the University of Munich alone had more graduate research chemists than all English universities combined. And German and American management proved remarkably skillful at the large scale organization of research, development, and production.

The followers developed at different rates and achieved widely varying results. Belgium and France started first, in the 1820s. Belgium was probably the first society after Britain whose industry produced more by value than its agriculture. But it lacked the population and resources to be more than a minor industrial power. France was a potential rival to Britain, but it suffered from major constraints. Until the railway boom of the 1850s its communications were poor. Its large peasantry acted as a drag on the rest of the economy, lessening demand. Above all, old habits of mind died hard. The French entrepreneur, with some exceptions, bowed to the social pressures of a society that despite Revolution and Terror remained less competitive and more hierarchical than Britain's. The French and even the Germans tended until quite late to see business as a zero-sum game in which victory came only at the expense of others—who also had the right to a "fair" living. Robber-baron success seemed antisocial. The French economy grew steadily, but industry's share of the national product did not surpass that of agriculture until 1909.

Germany and the United States took up the British challenge most fully. By the end of the century, thanks to the coal and iron of the Ruhr Valley and to economic unity bloodily achieved in 1866–71 (see pp. 674–81), Germany had surpassed Britain. Pig-iron output increased twenty-fold between 1850 and 1870. Giants such as Krupps and the Borsig engineering works in Berlin dominated the production of locomotives, machinery, and engines of destruction. In chemicals, great firms such as AGFA, Höchst, and BASF had captured 90 percent of the world market for synthetic dyes by 1900. AEG and Siemens, the electrical giants, achieved positions in the world market that only their counterparts in the United States rivaled.

The economic development of the United States was if anything even more spectacular than Germany's. Growth rested on several factors. Land, once violently cleared of Indians, was "free." Vast mineral resources, from Appalachian coal to the Mesabi iron range to the gold of California, fueled development. The highest birth rate in the West and the immigration of 30 million people between 1845 and 1914 provided enough labor to meet needs, but not enough to depress wages or to discourage the introduction of labor-saving machinery. Relatively high wages in turn promoted consumer demand.

Mechanization began in textile production, as in Britain, in the 1770s in the water-powered mills of New England. Eli Whitney's cotton gin (1793), which separated fibers from seeds quickly and cheaply, helped create a boom in the slave South. Cotton shipments to the mills of Massachusetts and Lancashire leapt upwards. By 1840 the United States had already passed Britain in steam-engine horsepower. The Erie Canal, opened in 1825, cut across the Appalachians and connected the industry of the East with the grain of the Midwest. After 1830 railroads opened up sources of coal and iron and fed ever larger cities. Large farms and a relative shortage of labor encouraged the mechanization of agriculture on a scale undreamed of elsewhere. Cyrus McCormick's reaper (1831), the railroad, and the steamship allowed grain from the Great Plains to undersell European grain in European markets by the 1870s. Refrigeration, invented in the 1830s, made possible the mass distribution and export of meat by the 1880s. And in heavy industry, the United States created a zone of huge coal and steel firms, like those of Germany's Ruhr Valley, that stretched from Pittsburgh to Chicago and outclassed all rivals. By 1914 the industrial output of the United States was almost 80 percent of that of all Western Europe.

Last of the early followers came Italy, Russia, and Japan. Italy broke into rapid growth in the first decade of the twentieth century, but its depressed agriculture and lack of coal or oil held it back until after 1945. Russia and Japan were the first cases of a phenomenon increasingly familiar later in the new century—the industrialization of societies that were either partially (Russia) or wholly (Japan) non-Western in politics and culture. Economic growth in both cases was spectacular. But political and cultural traditions did not always encourage the sober use of the power that industrialization brought.

The second industrial revolution and the industrialization of the followers made a true world market. Before the wars of the French Revolution, Europe's mercantile world economy had shown some signs of the now familiar boom and bust pattern of the business cycle. The depression that followed the wars of the French Revolution had been unusually severe and widespread. By mid-century, transport and communications had begun to weld the world together. The California gold strike in 1848 and an outbreak of railway fever fueled an American, European, and world boom that broke in the first true world depression, the panic of 1857. Further growth culminated in a second collapse in 1873. That crash inaugurated a twenty-year period of falling prices known misleadingly as the nineteenth century "great depression." The term is a misnomer, because this was a period of unparalleled growth in output for the followers, especially Germany and the United States. Falling prices caused dislocation, especially in European agriculture. But they were a sign of health, a sign of the abundance that the mechanization of industry, agriculture, and transport made possible. And after 1896 a new boom lifted the world economy, with a brief interruption in 1907, until 1913.

THE INDUSTRIAL REVOLUTION: HUMAN AND SOCIAL CONSEQUENCES

The Industrial Revolution transformed every society it touched—in standard of living and life expectancy, the location and occupations of the population, the structure of the social hierarchy, and the character of the basic human unit, the family.

The Rise in Living Standards and Life Expectancy

England, along with Holland and the infant United States, already enjoyed the world's highest living standard in the eighteenth century, before industrialization. Britain preserved that lead throughout the nineteenth century except compared to the United States. Advance was nevertheless far from smooth; Britain, in particular, paid the price of pioneering. From the 1790s to the 1840s English real wages (wages adjusted for the cost of living) appear to have stagnated. The peak of Britain's birth rate coincided with the triumph of the factories over domestic handicrafts. Moreover, after the 1790s women and children made up an increasing proportion of the work force in factories and mines. Entrepreneurs could pay them less and dominate them more effectively than they could men. Factory work and the filth of the improvised industrial cities dragged urban life expectancy down below that of most rural areas.

The workers of the early industrial revolution also suffered less tangible losses. They exchanged the familiar if poverty-racked countryside or small-town workshop for filthy slum streets and "dark satanic mills" enveloped in clouds of coal soot. The "Black Country" around Birmingham came by its name honestly. The workers exchanged the tyranny of the seasons and of crop blights for the domination of the tireless machine. Breaking the new industrial labor force to the discipline of the clock was one of the major challenges facing the early entrepreneurs. Workers long resisted the habit of arriving for work on Mondays or arriving sober on Tuesdays. And the tyranny of the business cycle replaced that of nature. Overproduction or disruption of normal trade patterns could spell unemployment and massive distress for entire regions. The "cotton famine" that resulted from the U.S. Civil War (1861–65) caused near starvation in the mill-towns of Lancashire. In the new cities, overcrowding, poverty, and the sudden release from the traditional religious and social restraints of the tight rural community led to widespread illegitimacy, alcoholism, and prostitution.

But after 1840 conditions slowly improved. Between 1851 and 1878, British per capita real income increased by a startling 30 percent. Until 1900 it continued to rise at the unprecedented rate of between 17 and 25 percent per decade. And workers worked less; the average (estimated) workweek in British industry declined from almost 60 hours in the 1860s to around 53 hours in 1900. In Europe as a whole the estimated average workweek dropped from an appalling 84 hours in 1850 to 60 hours in 1910.

A dramatic increase in life expectancy reflected and paralleled the rise in real income. The crucial factor was a decline in infant mortality. The death rate of infants less than one year old dropped in England from 36 percent in 1751–60 to 11.7 percent in 1906–10. France's infant mortality after the turn of the twentieth century was slightly higher than Britain's, and Sweden's was somewhat lower. Russia's remained at 25 percent as late as 1900–09. Adults also lived longer. The decrease in infant mortality and greater longevity together raised life expectancy in western Europe from less than forty years in 1840 to the mid-50s by 1900. That rapid change was unparalleled in human history.

What did this mean for the bulk of the population? For the first time, appreciable numbers of people began living significantly above subsistence level and consuming an increasing variety of goods. Already in the 1780s English workers had come to expect tea, coffee, sugar, and inexpensive cottons. After 1850 workers paid a steadily decreasing proportion of their wages for food and lodging. They began to have money and time to spend on leisure and entertainment.

Industrialization naturally did not distribute its benefits equally. The elites had always lived better and longer than those at the bottom of the social pyramid. And industrialization opened further the gap between rich and poor: the rich grew richer faster than the poor. The concentration of wealth therefore increased. The immense fortunes of the entrepreneurs generated envy in the increasingly politically conscious workers and fear in the landowning elites which had until now dominated society.

Urbanization and Emigration

The new age also brought migrations unprecedented since the fall of the Roman Empire. Population growth dictated movement. The agricultural countryside simply could not support the increase in numbers after 1750. The growth of industry encouraged movement by providing jobs. After 1850 the revolution in transportation, the railroad and the steamship, made movement on an unprecedented scale possible. The result was urbanization and emigration.

Urbanization, the concentration of the population in cities, was most conspicuous in Britain, where the monster city, London, had long been the largest in Europe. In 1800 it contained about 12 percent of Britain's total population. By 1890 more than 60 percent of the British lived in cities of 10,000 or more. German and Belgian figures were in the 30 percent range, and France's only 25 percent (see Figure 24-6). Where sheep had grazed a generation or two before stood the largely unplanned cities of Manchester and Birmingham and the mine tailings and slag heaps of the Ruhr and of northeastern France. Not until after mid-century did the new cities gradually receive sewage systems, relatively clean water supplies, and housing that even remotely approximated the population's needs.

Emigration was the alternative to the cities. It tended to affect all countries with high rates of population increase, whether they led or followed industrially. Britain grew from 8.9 million in 1801 to 32.5 million in 1901, even while giving up millions of emigrants. Germany, between the "hungry forties" and the maturing of its industrial economy by 1900, gave up perhaps 5 million emigrants. France, with its stable peasant economy, low birth rate, and slow industrialization, showed a unique pattern of low emigration.

Predominantly agricultural countries also participated in this continent-wide

The new industrial city, crowded and sooty: London by Gustave Doré.

migration. Ireland, after the famine, gave up roughly 3 million emigrants before 1900. Scandinavian emigration peaked in the 1880s. Emigration from relatively backward areas such as Russia, Spain, and Italy continued to increase until World War I cut it short in 1914. Italy, with its overpopulated South and late industrialization, gave up an unprecedented 880,000 emigrants in 1913. The recipient of most of this great migration was the United States, which received 82 percent of all transatlantic emigration in 1866–70 and received still 61 percent in 1896–1900.

The combined effect of urbanization and emigration was to open up the old rural societies and to create new social relationships in the new cities and lands across the oceans. Returnees from the cities and even from the New World (10 million people *returned* to Europe between 1886 and 1915) brought new ideas into the narrow agricultural communities from

FIGURE 24.6   **The Urbanization of Europe**

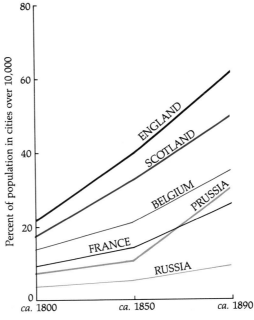

which they had escaped. Compulsory military service, which became almost universal after 1870, had similarly broadening effects. The knowledge that better or at least profoundly different patterns of life existed elsewhere helped dissolve what remained of the old order.

Social Structures

The industrial revolution weakened old social groups and created new ones. The rapid rise of a new business elite undermined the social power of the nobility far more than the events of 1789 had done. In Britain the aristocracy controlled perhaps 20 percent of the national product in 1820. By 1850 that proportion had sunk to 10 percent. A decline in the role of agriculture paralleled that of the nobility, the elite that defined itself by ownership of land. Britain's case was extreme: decline was so precipitous that by 1901 less than 5 percent of the population actually worked in agriculture or fishing. France, as usual, resisted the trend. Simultaneously, the industrial population and the proportion of the national wealth that industry produced swiftly increased

throughout western Europe (see Figure 24-7). Industry's proportion of the national product passed agriculture before 1820 in Britain, around 1890 in Germany, and in the first decade of the new century in France.

In the new cities, the middle classes expanded rapidly. By the end of the century they made up a far larger proportion of the total population than ever before—from perhaps 20 percent in northwestern Europe to 5 percent in the south and east. The middle classes consisted first of all of the entrepreneurs, the driving force and chief beneficiaries of the new age of cotton, coal, and steam. Then came the professional middle classes, the growing ranks of lawyers, doctors, higher bureaucrats, professors, and professional intellectuals. The nineteenth century was theirs as no other century has been, for the nobility had lost its monopoly of power and the masses were as yet hesitant in pressing their claims.

Below the entrepreneurial and professional middle classes, new groups proliferated. Increasing specialization of work paralleled and influenced the increasing number of subtle gradations in

FIGURE 24.7   **The Triumph of Industry over Agriculture: Germany and Britain**

Women in the industrial work force: slitting pen nibs in a Birmingham factory (1851).

the social hierarchy. The artisans and home handicraft workers, victims of the machine, dwindled. Only the continued existence of trades difficult to mechanize fully, such as clothing manufacture, guaranteed their continued existence. Alongside this "old lower-middle class" of distressed artisans, there grew a "new lower-middle class" of white-collar workers in government or business bureaucracies. This group was as characteristic of the new industrial age as were the industrial workers below it.

The lower classes divided into numerous subcategories. Peasants and landless rural laborers stood at the bottom of the hierarchy in the countryside. A large class of domestic servants made possible the leisured existence of the new middle classes. The industrial workers themselves were anything but uniform. They ranged from the "labor aristocracy," skilled iron and steel workers, machinists, and foremen, to unskilled or semiskilled workers at starvation wages. Below the working classes was an underclass of pickpockets, prostitutes, and beggars, sometimes organized, but often anarchic and always violent.

The lines between groups remained far more fluid than under the old society

of orders on the Continent. Becoming an entrepreneur was relatively easy at first, at least in Britain, but class lines hardened as the century wore on. The amount of capital needed to enter industry increased dramatically with the coming of the steam engine and still more with the second industrial revolution. The new cities, unlike the old, were segregated by class. In the pre-industrial past, workers had lived in attics and cellars, above and below the rich. But in new industrial cities such as Manchester and Birmingham, the new rich instead retreated to villas in the countryside, leaving the pestilent city centers to the poor. And the growth of an independent working-class culture and ideologies in response to the Industrial Revolution (see pp. 652–53) acted as a barrier to mobility. Those who did rise socially risked ostracism for "betraying their class."

From Traditional to Nuclear Family

Finally, the processes of industrialization and urbanization affected the very structure of the family and the role of women. Even before industrialization, the early modern family, with its extended networks of kin and its family ties based on subordination and respect, had begun to give way to the nuclear family of parents and children. Nuclear families of parents and children, based at least in theory on love, may have existed in England since the late Middle Ages. They had in any case conquered the English middle classes by 1800. Family and workplace separated. The family became a private realm. The increasing fashion for romantic love as the chief reason for marriage undermined the old role of the father as a monarch in miniature. Once children chose their own mates, the authority of the father was under attack.

Similar developments, with a considerable lag, penetrated the urban areas of the Continent as well. First the upper middle classes adopted the new style, then the nobility. Finally it trickled down the social scale as the nineteenth century drew on. Increasing affluence, literacy, and longer lives encouraged the transition. Unlike the biological old regime, when plague or famine might at any moment strike down a spouse or child, affection was now a sounder emotional investment.

The new family structure hardly liberated women, but it did improve their status. The social conventions of romantic love ultimately sapped the Code Napoléon's attempts to bolster the power of the father and eroded the dominance of the

bewhiskered patriarchs of nineteenth-century Britain or Germany. A man could only with difficulty combine the roles of master, companion, and lover. And the separation of work from the home and the profusion of domestic servants meant that middle-class women had more leisure than before industrialization. A British male commentator noted in the 1850s that "the day is thrown idle on woman's hand. The thousand exciting events and undertakings that . . . stretch the faculties of man, are reckoned beyond her sphere." That leisure gave more and more educated women opportunity to reflect on their condition and eventually to revolt against it.

By 1914 most of western Europe had passed through the fires of industrialization. Britain, Germany, and France had become industrial great powers. The United States had outstripped all rivals. Russia and Japan were beginning to overtake Western Europe. Industrialization had transformed the ways of life of the peoples and classes it had touched. Some groups had lost; many more, despite the bitterness of the struggle, had won. And industrialization, along with that other revolution in France, had also helped transform the ideas and categories through which the West understood the world and sought to change it.

Suggestions for Further Reading

The Pre-industrial World

On the world before industrialization, see the analysis of C. Cipolla, *Before the Industrial Revolution* (1975); for England, P. Laslett offers a quasi-nostalgic view in *The World We Have Lost* (1971). For the adventurous, F. Braudel, *Civilization and* *Capitalism, 15th–18th Centuries* (1982), provides an unparalleled guided tour of the pre-industrial world economy. C. McEvedy and F. Jones, *Atlas of World Population History* (1978), is first-rate.

Why the West, and Why Britain?

On the West's primacy and its causes, see especially D. Landes, *The Unbound Prometheus* (1972); E. L. Jones, *The European Miracle* (1981); W. O'Neill, *The Pursuit of Power* (1982); and N. Rosenberg and L. Birdzell, *How the West Grew Rich* (1986). For England's peculiarities, see the contrasting accounts of A. Macfarlane, *Marriage and Love in England* (1986), and L. Stone, *The Family Sex, and Marriage in England 1500–1800* (1977), and the summary of recent demographic research in E. A. Wrigley, "The Growth of Population in Eighteenth-Century England," *Past and Present* (February, 1983), pp. 121–50. H. Perkin, *The Origins of Modern English Society 1780–1880* (1969), offers an excellent synthesis of the social causes of British industrialization.

The Industrial Revolution

On the interrelationship of technological change and economic growth, see above all D. Landes, *The Unbound Prometheus,* and J. Mokyr, *The Lever of Riches: Technological Creativity and Economic Progress* (1990). P. Deane, *The First Industrial Revolution* (1965), and E. Pawson, *The Early Industrial Revolution* (1979), are useful on Britain, as is T. S. Ashton, *The Industrial Revolution* (1970). On the industrialization of the followers, see T. Kemp, *Industrialization in Nineteenth-Century Europe* (1969), and C. Trebilcock, *The Industrialization of Continental Europe* (1981). B. Mitchell, *European Historical Statistics* (1981), is a useful source, and Paul Bairoch, "International Industrialization Levels from 1750 to 1980," *Journal of European Economic History 2,* no. 2, provides indispensable data on shifts in the economic balance of power. T. Hamerow, *The Birth of a New Europe* (1983), is a fine survey of the social and political consequences of industrialization.

THE NINETEENTH-CENTURY
REVOLUTION OF IDEAS

he twin revolutions in France and in the mills and foundries of Britain generated new ideas and modified old ones. Yet the movement of ideas, like industrialization, was in part independent of other forces. Like industrialization, it was a continuous, expanding process operating throughout the relatively peaceful century that followed 1815. And like industrialization, it is best understood as a whole. This chapter therefore sketches the nineteenth century explosion of knowledge about nature and about humanity in its entirety. Then Chapters 26 and 27 introduce the political events of 1815–71 and European expansion into the wider world.

All across Europe, the old religious certainties, whether Catholic or Protestant, remained valid for the great mass of the population throughout the nineteenth century. But religion gradually became central to fewer lives. Science and scholarship appeared to undermine it. Urbaniza-

tion and the decay of the traditional village community lessened its grip. In the realm of culture, a new movement, romanticism, fiercely attacked both the ideas and the style of the Enlightenment. In philosophy, two generations of Germans laid the foundations for much of nineteenth-century political thought. In politics, a "counter-Enlightenment" in some ways parallel to romanticism developed: conservatism, the ideology of opposition to revolutionary France and to all revolution. The adversary of conservatism was the ill-assorted conglomerate of economic and political doctrines known as liberalism. And beyond liberalism but related to it and locked in struggle with it came socialism, a political faith for the new industrial workers. Last of all, the French revolution's most powerful legacy, nationalism, spread eastward across Europe.

In the realm of practice, as opposed to that of ideas, new forces and tendencies modified European intellectual and social life. State bureaucracies hesitantly developed an interest in the education and welfare of their populations. Rising literacy and wealth led to the appearance of a new force that increasingly made rulers tremble: public opinion. Submerged social groups and categories, women and workers, began for the first time to make themselves heard.

THE FORCE OF IDEAS

Science and Scholarship

The nineteenth century opened new and unsuspected vistas. Mathematics, the discipline seemingly most remote from experience, equipped itself with the tools needed to inspire and describe the discoveries of twentieth-century physics. The creation of the first non-Euclidian geometry by a Russian, Nikolai Ivanovitch Lobachevsky (1793–1856), led to the invention of topology by Georg Friedrich Riemann (1826–66) of Göttingen. That, and the tensor calculus of Gregorio Ricci (1853–1925), in turn made possible the twentieth-century mathematics of space-time and gravity.

In physics, electricity and heat were the phenomena that nineteenth-century science explored most successfully. The discovery of electric current in 1786 led to Alessandro Volta's battery in 1799, to Hans Christian Oersted's discovery of a connection between magnetism and electricity in 1819, and to Michael Faraday's theory of electromagnetic induction in 1831. Ultimately James Clerk Maxwell, in *Electricity and Magnetism* (1873), provided a mathematical synthesis suggesting that light was also an electromagnetic phenomenon.

With electricity, advances in the laboratory created new industrial technologies. The reverse occurred with the steam engine. It inspired Sadi Carnot, son of the Carnot of the revolutionary Committee of Public Safety, to formulate in the 1820s the generalizations that later physicists codified as the first and second laws of thermodynamics.

The advance of chemistry was even more spectacular than that of physics. John Dalton's sketch of an atomic theory in the first decade of the century opened the way for the study of chemical compounds and structures. The synthesis in 1828 of urea, a compound found in nature, opened the study of organic chemistry, the chemistry of carbon. By the 1860s, chemists had begun to explore the molecular structure of simple carbon compounds such as benzene. In 1869 Dimitri Ivanovitch Mendeleev formulated a periodic law and table of elements that for the first time gave scientists a sketchy notion of some of the basic building blocks of the universe. The periodic table predicted the existence of elements as yet unknown; researchers using Mendeleev's theory isolated gallium (1871), scandium (1879), germanium (1886), and helium (1895).

But not until the end of the century did breakthroughs on the boundary of chemistry and physics revolutionize science's picture of the world and place the old Newtonian certainties in question. Wilhelm Roentgen's discovery of X rays (1895) soon led to the unearthing of radioactive elements that apparently emitted particles smaller than the atom. By the turn of the century, the theoreticians Max Planck and Albert Einstein had begun to lay the foundations for a non-Newtonian physics that unified the universe of subatomic particles with that of space-time and predicted the convertibility of matter into energy.

Biology, essentially a creation of the nineteenth century, developed practical uses after mid-century. The explorations of the world of bacteria by Louis Pasteur (1822–95) and Robert Koch (1843–1910) opened the door to an understanding of many diseases and aided Joseph Lister (1827–92) in the development of sterile surgical procedures.

But the greatest biological questions were theoretical. What caused the unparalleled diversity of life forms that eighteenth- and early nineteenth-century naturalists had classified? How had humanity originated? Studies in embryology in the 1820s implied that embryos, during their growth, might be recapitulating their species history, for bird embryos developed gill-slits. The study of fossils, still in its infancy, suggested change and development over immense periods of time. The discovery in 1856 of an apelike but large-brained skull at Neanderthal near the Ruhr (see p. 3) implied that humanity might have nonhuman ancestors.

Geology, an entirely new science, appeared to offer corroboration. Charles Lyell's *Principles of Geology* (1830–33) provided the first satisfactory explanation of the Earth's physical features and their origins. A variety of speculative thinkers suggested that life—including human life—might also be the result of evolutionary processes. But the mechanism by which that evolution occurred was still a mystery. Jean Baptiste Lamarck, who invented the term "biology," proposed in 1809 that creatures acquired characteristics in response to changes in their environment and subsequently passed those "acquired characteristics" to their offspring. That would account for diversity and change—if it were true.

It was Charles Darwin (1809–82) who most cogently suggested, after long investigations on the isolated Galápagos islands off Ecuador and elsewhere, that species evolved through a savage "struggle for life." Darwin announced that conclusion in 1858, after a fellow biologist, Alfred Russel Wallace (1823–1913), had sketched out a similar theory. The following year, Darwin published his path-breaking synthesis, *The Origin of Species by Means of Natural Selection, or the Preservation of Favored Races in the Struggle for Life.* Darwin argued, with a crushing weight of examples drawn from field research, that scarcity of food produced a fierce competition that killed off "unfit" variants of a given species before they could reproduce. "Sexual selection," or the triumph of the "fittest" males in competition for females further reinforced that mechanism. "Natural selection," working over immense spans of time, had produced the rich diversity visible in nature.

Darwin, although he recoiled from controversy with the religious establish-ment, ultimately extended his logic to humanity itself in *The Descent of Man* (1871): "Thus from the wars of nature, from famine and death, the most exalted object which we are capable of conceiving, namely the production of higher animals, directly follows." That claim, popularized in innumerable works by other "Darwinists," accomplished the most far-reaching revolution in the West's conception of itself since Copernicus had suggested that the Earth was not the motionless center of the universe. Darwin's explanation of humanity's place in the new world that science was uncovering made him the most widely influential scientific thinker of the century.

His theories also made him the father of modern biology. His single powerful generalization accounted for all the diversity of life. But Darwin's theory of evolution nevertheless had a major weakness: it accounted only for the change of *entire* species over time. Darwin could not find a convincing physical cause for the all-important variations between *individuals* that apparently drove those species changes. He fell back in part on Lamarck's untenable theory of the inheritance of acquired characteristics. Not until later did the long-neglected work of the Bohemian monk Gregor Mendel (1822–84), the father of genetics, provide the answer. In 1901 Hugo De Vries drew on Mendel's work to formulate a theory of genetic mutation by sudden random leaps. Later experiments using the fast-multiplying fruit fly laid the groundwork of modern genetics, which explained individual variation and provided Darwin's basic insights with powerful support.

In the social sciences, the nineteenth century likewise opened a new age. The eccentric Auguste Comte (1798–1857) invented the word sociology, if not the discipline it describes. A revolution in sources, methods, and subjects transformed history from a literary pastime into a scholarly profession. The German scholar Leopold von Ranke (1795–1886) laid down the doctrine that historians must first of all investigate and cross-check primary source materials, the evidence the histori-

Charles Darwin, father of modern biology and greatest scientific mind of the nineteenth century.

cal actors themselves had left. Ranke's notion that the historian's duty was to reconstruct events "as they actually happened" was not new. Thucydides the Athenian had suggested something of the sort in his fifth-century B.C. history of the Peloponnesian War (see pp. 56–57). But now, in the early nineteenth century, it was at last possible to attempt to translate that conception of history into systematic practice. In England, France, and Germany governments and private groups founded institutions such as London's Public Record Office for the collection and publication of historical source documents.

Vast multivolume national histories began to appear, monuments to the industry and learning of their authors, though, alas, not always readable. The Prussian professor of law, Karl von Savigny (1779–1861) founded a historical school dedicated to explaining the evolution of law. He proclaimed the superiority of Germanic law, which had grown by the slow accretion of precedent, over the artificial law codes of the French.

Historical scholarship even touched Scripture. David Friedrich Strauss's *Life of Jesus* (1835) examined the Gospels as historical documents and expressed skepticism about the divinity—and existence—of their subject. The French intellectual Ernest Renan provoked outrage in the 1860s by describing Christ as "an incomparable *man*." His biography of Christ was a popular success.

Finally, historians and philologists began investigating the diversity of human languages and deriving general laws. In 1835, a British scholar, Sir Henry Rawlinson, followed up Champollion's 1822 decipherment of hieroglyphics by reading the cuneiform inscriptions of the ancient Persians. German scholars studied the shifts of consonants in numerous languages over many centuries, and deduced laws governing the evolution of languages. They demonstrated that the Indian language Sanskrit and most European languages shared a common Indo-European origin. That discovery helped open up the study of the prehistory of Europe and of South and Central Asia (see pp. 8–10).

Religion

Religious skepticism had become commonplace among educated Europeans in the course of the eighteenth century. In the nineteenth century, that detachment from religion began to spread to the masses. That was partly a consequence of politics. The American and French revolutions, unlike the English Revolution of the 1640s, had been secular upheavals. Many French revolutionaries had been overtly anticlerical. Urbanization and its consequent social dislocation likewise undermined religion. In the jerry-built industrial city of Birmingham in 1851 the churches could hold less than a third of the population. And many of the new industrial workers resented the churches' defense of the social status quo. Finally, the retreat from religion was in part a consequence of the same process of scientific advance that had inspired the deists and skeptics of the Enlightenment.

But the science of the nineteenth century appeared far more powerful, and less compatible with traditional religion, than that of the eighteenth century. Lyell's geology and Darwin's evolution placed in question the biblical account of creation. That above all affected Protestants (and to a lesser extent Jews), given the central place of the biblical texts in their beliefs. Darwin's work provoked a veritable "warfare of science and theology." The Archbishop of Canterbury, in a furious debate in 1860, sarcastically asked "Darwin's Bulldog," the biologist Thomas H. Huxley, which side of his family descended from apes. A minority of "fundamentalist" Protestants, especially strong in the United States, continued to assert the literal truth of the biblical account of creation. The majority, thanks to Protestantism's emphasis on the individual's freedom and direct relationship with God, made a variety of compromises between faith and reason.

Strong forces nevertheless counteracted the decline of religion. Women of the lower classes, submerged by custom and illiteracy, tended to retain their traditional piety. The rural masses held to their faith whether they stayed at home or emigrated, as did so many Irish and Italians. Governments, whether of kings or liberals, continued to prize religion as a foundation for social order. Above all, religion itself showed continued vitality and expansive force.

In England and the United States the nineteenth century was a time of intense religious ferment. The impetus of German Pietism and of John Wesley's Methodism (see pp. 553–54) was far from spent. Other Protestant sects expanded with equal rapidity. Waves of religious enthusiasm swept over South Wales, for instance, in 1807–09, 1828–30, 1839–48, 1854, and 1859. In America after 1800 a "Great Revival" moved westward with the frontier.

The politics of Wesley, the Pietists, and their offshoots tended to bolster the social order. In the words of the *Statutes of the Wesleyan Body* (1792), "the oracles of God" commanded obedience to government. That attitude permeated English and American popular religion. Along with the early spread of democratic politics in those societies, it limited the appeal of the socialist panaceas for the ills of *this* world so popular in continental Europe, and described later in this chapter. And the spread of democracy helped the churches by providing a widely popular and defensible status quo.

European Catholicism was even more closely intertwined with the existing order than Protestantism, and after 1789 that order was under attack. Some advanced Catholic thinkers foresaw the need for the Church to distance itself from monarchy lest it perish in the monarchy's ruin. Félicité de Lamennais, a formerly ultraconservative French cleric, published *Words of a Believer* after the 1830 Paris revolution (see p. 662). He appealed for equality and democracy, and denounced "the passion to acquire and to possess." Rome damned Lamennais in two thundering encyclicals.

Pope Pius IX (r. 1846–78) appeared briefly as a champion of change. Then the revolutions of 1848 (described on pp. 666–69) dissuaded him. His encyclical *Quanta cura* of 1864, with its appended *Syllabus errorum,* or "listing of errors," denounced the notion that "the Roman Pontiff can and ought to reconcile himself to and agree with progress, liberalism, and modern civilization." The reforming Pope Leo XIII (r. 1878–1903) reversed that uncompromising stance in a path-breaking encyclical of 1891 entitled *Rerum novarum* ("Of New Things"). The gradual dechristianization of the urban masses and the challenge of socialism had led to a rethinking. *Rerum novarum* was the charter of a new social and reforming Catholicism that condemned both capitalist greed and socialist denial of God. Leo XIII's successor, Pius X (r. 1903–14), reverted to rigid defense of received doctrine and purged the Church of "modernists" who sought to reconcile science with theology. But in the end it was Leo XIII's policy of adaptation to the new age that triumphed.

Romanticism

A new style, opposed to the rationalism and classicism of the Enlightenment (see pp. 543–48), emerged toward the end of the eighteenth century. The stormy young German writers of the *"Sturm und Drang"* movement of the 1780s, in particular, had defied convention and celebrated emotion. By 1800 German critics had coined the distinction between "classical" and "romantic," although "romantic" has no tidy definition.

Some romantics, such as the great English poet George Gordon, Lord Byron (1788–1824), thought of themselves as revolutionaries: "I have simplified my politics into a detestation of all existing governments." The French poet, dramatist, and novelist Victor Hugo (1802–85) could write that "romanticism is liberalism in literature." Byron's friend Percy Bysshe Shelley (1792–1822) proclaimed that "poets are the unacknowledged legislators of the world." Heinrich Heine (1797–1856), and last major German romantic poet and the greatest German lyric poet of the century, was a lifelong radical democrat. The French painter Eugène Delacroix (1798–1863) could paint, in *Liberty Leading the*

People (1834), the ultimate romantic vision of the triumph of revolution (see p. 656).

Other romantics, such as the English lyric poets William Blake (1757–1827) and William Wordsworth (1770–1850), outdid one another in their rejection of the "dark satanic mills" of the new industrial age. In politics, Wordsworth's original enthusiasm for the French Revolution gave way to bitter opposition even to modest Parliamentary reforms in England (see p. 660). Especially in Germany, romanticism turned increasingly into a celebration of the Middle Ages, which were supposedly more authentic than the Renaissance or the alleged artificiality and frenchified rationalism of the detested eighteenth century. The eerie landscapes of Caspar David Friedrich (1774–1840), painted from imagination rather than life, illustrated the romantic vision of the Middle Ages. In England, the medieval historical novels of Sir Walter Scott, the paintings of John Constable and Joseph Turner, and the revival of Gothic as an architectural style embodied similar tendencies.

But the romantics, however varied their politics and aesthetics, tended to share four things. First, they rejected the eighteenth century's "classical" limitations on form and structure in art. In music, romantics from the greatest master of the symphony, Ludwig van Beethoven (1770–1827) to the dogmatic theorist and practitioner of "total opera," Richard Wagner (1813–83), gleefully disregarded inherited conventions of form, and of orchestra size and make-up. Poets such as Wordsworth deliberately chose a vocabulary closer to spoken English than to the measured couplets of predecessors such as Alexander Pope. Continental dramatists discarded for good the restrictions on subject, time, and place that classical theories of drama had imposed.

Second, the romantics prized emotion, the stronger the better. That led even former fellow-travelers such as the great German poet Johann Wolfgang von Goethe (1749–1832) to conclude that "classic is that which is healthy, romantic that which is sick." The line between emo-

Cloister Graveyard in the Snow (1810) by Caspar David Friedrich.

tion and morbid self-preoccupation was a narrow one. But the romantic emphasis on the creative power of the individual imagination was a liberating force. If combined with craftsmanship and self-discipline it could produce masterpieces.

Third, the romantics tended to celebrate nature. Their nature was not the manicured eighteenth-century ornamental garden, but the craggy uplands of Wordsworth's imagination:

> Once again
> Do I behold these steep and lofty cliffs
> That on a wild secluded scene impress
> Thoughts of more deep seclusion;
>   and connect
> The landscape with the quiet of the
>   sky.

Rousseau, with his mystical *Reveries of a Solitary Wanderer* (1776–78) had shown the way. Nature, the "nature or God" of Spinoza (see p. 539) brought humanity—or at least skeptical intellectuals—closer to an otherwise unknowable God. The popularization of this "natural supernaturalism," as the English philosopher-historian Thomas Carlyle (1795–1881) called it, was one of the major legacies of romanticism.

Finally, the romantics both celebrated and embodied the cult of the solitary, youthful, misunderstood genius who defied convention and perhaps suffered persecution for political radicalism or, like Byron, for sexual peccadillos. Like Shelley, the genius might be dead by thirty; tuberculosis was as much the romantic disease as morbid introspection. The cult of the artist as misfit was in part an extension of the romantic emphasis on imagination, on the creative powers of the individual. The collapse of aristocratic art patronage after 1789 may also have contributed, for the middle classes were not yet rich enough to step in. Age, respectability, and middle-class patrons nevertheless tamed those romantics who survived. Although the movement did not outlast mid-century, it broke Enlightenment formalism for good. Art was henceforth what the artist, the individual as towering genius, decreed it to be.

The Revolution in German Philosophy: From Kant to Hegel

Parallel to romanticism and not unrelated to it came an explosion of creativity in German philosophy. Misty speculation, including opposition to Newton's mathematically precise account of matter and motion, had long been a German specialty. Immanuel Kant (see p. 554) had sought to rescue reason from the skepticism of Enlightenment philosophers such as David Hume, who refused to accept as certain the evidence of the senses. Kant saved reason by limiting its domain. He postulated that the human mind was capable of limited knowledge of the world around it, but only on the basis of categories such as space and time, categories already built into the structure of the mind itself. Humanity could not perceive "things in themselves," things as they really were, except through those categories.

Kant's second main contribution was related to his theory of knowledge. Moral judgment was similar to the mind's inborn mechanism of perception, Kant argued. Morality was the result of a universal law found within ourselves. And for Kant, freedom was obedience to that law. The poet Heine rightly remarked that as a revolutionary, Kant put Robespierre in the shade. Kant's notion of morality, in particular, opened the way for individuals to discover moral standards *for themselves.* Kant was a loyal supporter of the Prussian state, but his doctrine struck at the root of any claim to authority that individuals chose not to accept.

Kant's theory of knowledge provoked his successors, especially Johann Gottlieb Fichte (1762–1814) and Georg Wilhelm Friedrich Hegel (1770–1831), to a decisive step. Fichte saw the implausibility of saying that things-in-themselves existed but that the mind could not know them. If the mind knew about them, they must exist. Rather than falling back into Enlightenment rationalism, Fichte and Hegel took a leap of faith even greater than Kant's. Both things-in-themselves and the mind must be part of a larger whole, a universal consciousness, an all-encompassing "world spirit" that was a descendant of Spinoza's "nature or God."

Hegel, the most influential philosopher of the century, proclaimed that history was the process of the upward evolution or self-realization of that world spirit. History thus had a goal. It also had a mechanism, the "dialectic," a step-by-step progress through a series of reversals or negations. It had already passed through three stages: the oriental, in which the despot alone was free; the ancient world, in which a few men in Greece and Rome had been free; and the Christian-Germanic civilization of northern Europe, which had at last recognized that humanity itself was or could be free.

In this process, this ever-upward striving toward the self-realization of the world spirit, the role of the individual was clear. Kant's self-determining individual would inevitably will an ever-closer identification with Hegel's world spirit. And Hegel, as befitted a professor of philosophy at the University of Berlin, came to identify the world spirit with the Prussian power-state: "The State is the divine Idea as it exists on earth." Others took Kant's notion of self-determination, and Hegel's goal-oriented theory of history and put them to uses that their originators could hardly have foreseen.

Conservatism

Although Hegel's ideas helped to shore up the royal Prussian status quo, the doctrines later called conservatism had entirely different sources. First and most important was the Anglo-Irish Tory, Edmund Burke (1729–97). His inspired diatribe of 1790, *Reflections on the Revolution in France,* was uncannily prophetic (see p. 599). It still reads as if written in 1793–94, against the background of war and Terror. Burke denounced the doctrinaire logic of the French revolutionaries, whose "rage and frenzy will pull down more in half an hour than prudence, deliberation, and foresight can build in a hundred years." His model was the English constitution, that agglomeration of custom and precedent that over many centuries had created what freedom existed in Britain. Organic growth, not

radical panaceas, was the only sound basis for a political system. Change was admissible, although "when I changed it should be to preserve." Even revolution, as in 1688 and 1776, might be acceptable if it reasserted a historic tradition. But plans for change should not assume human perfectibility. They should postulate, on the basis of long sad experience, the "ignorance and fallibility of mankind."

Burke's commitment to individual liberty, which had led him to sympathize with the complaints of the American colonists, did not survive translation into French and German. Burke the militant, the Burke who wrote in 1796 of the French Revolution that "it is with an *armed doctrine* that we are at war," was the Burke who inspired continental conservatives to create their own armed doctrines of counterrevolution. Joseph de Maistre (1754–1821), the most lively of the conservative theorists, acknowledged Burke's influence. But de Maistre's doctrine had little place for freedom: "All power, all discipline, are based on the executioner. He is at once the horror of human society and the tie that binds it together. . . ." In Germany, admirers of Burke invoked his name to support notions of a return to divine-right monarchy and medieval Christianity. That was not conservatism, but "reaction," an attempt to erase everything after 1789.

Liberalism

Conservatism, or reaction, was the ideology of what became, from its place in the seating arrangements of the post-1815 French assemblies, the "Right." Liberalism was the creed of the "Left." Like most "isms," the term is exceedingly vague. It has so broadened in the twentieth century that it now conveys a mood rather than a body of ideas.

Nineteenth-century liberalism was narrower. It meant, first of all, a body of economic thought that preached *laissez-faire,* the removal of all artificial restraints on the market. In politics, nineteenth-century liberalism stood, more or less squarely, for individual freedom and for equality of opportunity but not of outcome. Political liberalism—like Locke, its founding father—identified liberty with property; that identification was the link between political and economic liberalism. Liberalism was an optimistic creed that united capitalism and individualism under the banner of "progress," the faith of the Enlightenment. Liberalism was the creed of the middle classes, to whom the explosive growth of industry and trade gave increasing self-confidence.

The "classical economists," of whom the three most important were Adam Smith (1723–90), Thomas Robert Malthus (1766–1834), and David Ricardo (1772–1823), asked many of the questions that still occupy economists. Smith and Ricardo in particular argued that only the market could allocate resources efficiently. The "hidden hand" of supply and demand, by a self-operating law, would maximize the increase in wealth.

In his *Essay on the Principle of Population* (1798, revised 1803), Malthus explored the relationship between population and food. He concluded gloomily that "population, when unchecked, increases in a geometrical ratio. Subsistence only increases in an arithmetical ratio." Malthus' generalization that population—"when unchecked"—tends to outrun food made nineteenth-century economics the "dismal science." It also provided Darwin with his principle of the "struggle for survival" in the face of inevitable scarcity.

But Malthus qualified his theory in an important way that escaped many later critics. A "preventive check" on population increase existed: the tendency in Europe and especially in Britain for men and women to marry late, and hence have fewer children than their biological maximum. Malthus theorized that "moral restraint" or a growing taste for consumer luxuries might lead individuals to limit their families. Such tendencies could lead eventually to a shortage of labor, and "in the natural course of things" to a rise in wages. Malthus was a prophet of affluence as well as of doom.

His contemporary Ricardo had less foresight. In his *Principles of Political Economy and Taxation* (1817), the last great work of classical economics, Ricardo

proclaimed what soon became known as the "iron law of wages." Since population and hence labor supply supposedly increased geometrically, wages would always remain just above starvation level. Raising wages above that level would merely encourage overpopulation. That would in turn increase the supply of labor until wages once more dropped. Generosity toward the workers was thus futile, even pernicious. Ricardo's misunderstanding of Malthus was highly convenient to the early textile mill owners, hard men reared in a hard school. They enthusiastically embraced his doctrine. Economic science had shown conclusively, Ricardo's popularizers trumpeted, that poverty was inevitable and that efforts to avert it would produce ever more poverty.

Ricardo's other major contribution was to clarify a concept found in Adam Smith's work that had profound political implications. That was the "labor theory of value," the notion that the "value" of a manufactured article was proportional to the amount of labor required to make it. Ricardo used the theory to explain where profits came from. For him they were the difference between the cost of labor per article to the industrialist and the selling price of the article, after the deduction of the industrialist's overhead costs. Ricardo applauded profit; socialists later used his work to argue that profits were "surplus value" stolen from the workers.

The political ideas of nineteenth-century liberalism in part contradicted the "dismal science." The English philosopher and reformer Jeremy Bentham (1748–1832), the key figure in the transition from Enlightenment to nineteenth-century liberal thought, rejected the Lockean tradition of natural rights. Instead, as befitted an age of machinery, Bentham postulated that "utility" must guide humanity. Bentham's utility dictated the search for "the greatest happiness of the greatest number," and he defined happiness merely as "pleasurable feelings and . . . freedom from pain." For Bentham and the "Utilitarians," as his followers became known, the best government delivered the most pleasure and the least pain to the most people. Utility, in Bentham's view, replaced

Thomas Robert Malthus, pioneer of the study of population growth.

Locke's natural rights as the philosophical foundation of liberal democracy. But utility could also justify social engineering that trampled on those rights. For in Bentham's view, utility demanded the regimentation of the poor for their own supposed good.

Bentham's most influential successor, John Stuart Mill (1806–73), drove Benthamite liberalism to one possible logical conclusion, and inevitably made himself unpopular. Mill's *On Liberty* (1859) proclaimed utility as "the ultimate appeal in all ethical questions." Government was suspect: "That government is best that governs least." Mill asserted that "the only purpose for which power can rightfully be exercised over any member of a civilized community, against his will, is to prevent harm to others."

Mill, like Bentham, deduced that utility demanded democratic government. But what if that government, faced with the horrors of the early nineteenth-century factory system and with the plight of the poor, demanded limits on the economic freedom of the entrepreneur? Mill ultimately concluded that the state must intervene to protect children and improve living and working conditions. He also attacked the domination of men over women. After urging votes for women in Parliament in 1867, he published *The Subjection of Women* (1869). The work largely derived from ideas that his wife, Harriet Taylor Mill, had already put forward. It scandalized British middle-class opinion by insisting that women, too, should enjoy liberty. That demand followed from Mill's premises and from those of nineteenth-century liberalism generally. But few accepted that logic in the 1860s.

On the Continent, liberalism was more cautious than in Britain, thanks in part to the relative weakness of the middle classes there until industrialization was well under way. In politics, constitutionalism before liberty was the preference of Benjamin Constant (1767–1830), France's answer to Bentham. Constant proclaimed liberty as "the object of all human association" but resisted extension of France's limited franchise. German liberals (see p. 670) tended to confuse national self-

assertion with liberty. And in economics, French and German thinkers resisted the full force of *laissez-faire*, with its tendency to dissolve all traditional social ties. Some German economists challenged liberal orthodoxy frontally. The influential Friedrich List (1789–1846) argued that industrialization in the face of British competition required a neo-mercantilist planned economy, protective tariffs, and state-supported railway construction.

Socialism

Despite its internal contradictions, economic and political liberalism was a thumping success as a secular religion of progress for the middle classes. But it inevitably summoned up a counter-ideology, "socialism." The term, almost as indefinable as liberalism, implies concern for the good of society as a whole, in opposition to liberalism's focus on individual liberty, property, and profit. Socialism and its overlapping but more extreme companion, "communism," had a pedigree going back at least to the abortive Paris rising of Gracchus Babeuf and the "Equals" in 1796 (see p. 597). But after 1815, as industrialization gathered force, it acquired new meaning.

Middle-class thinkers began to postulate an irrepressible conflict between workers and industrialists. Ricardo's economics, with its emphasis on inherent conflicts of interest between labor, capital, and landed wealth, provided tools for a radical attack on existing society. In England, a successful entrepreneur, Robert Owen (1771–1858), presented an alternative vision. Abolition of the profit motive and its replacement by "cooperation" would remake humanity, which Owen in Enlightenment fashion saw as a product of its environment. Across the Channel, Charles Fourier (1772–1837) pressed similar notions, which included the foundation of "phalanxes," or self-sufficient model agrarian communities. Owen demonstrated the fallacy of Ricardo's "iron law" by raising wages and providing housing for the workers in his model factories at New Lanark, Scotland, while at the same time increasing output and profits. His

John Stuart Mill, the conscience of nineteenth-century liberalism.

Robert Owen's vision of New Harmony, his utopian community in the Indiana wilderness.

later attempt to found a utopia at New Harmony, Indiana, was less successful.

A sterner prophet than Owen or Fourier was the French Count Henri de Saint-Simon (1760–1825). Although frequently classed with the "utopian" socialists Owen and Fourier, Saint-Simon was no enthusiast for model communities. He was the first to conceive of socialism as the outcome of an inexorable historical process that affected the whole of society. He prophesied that in the new society "rule over men" would give way to "the administration of things." His brave new world would be an earthly paradise in which *École Polytechnique* technocrats tamed nature for good with immense engineering projects. He was thus not only a father of socialism but also the inspiration of the heroic age of French engineering that produced the Suez Canal (1869) and the first railroad tunnels through the Alps.

The theory that came to dominate European socialism owed something to Saint-Simon but derived above all from a strange marriage between the misty realms of Hegelian philosophy and the apparent rigor of classical economics. Karl Marx (1818–83), a German Jew from the Prussian Rhineland, and Friedrich Engels, the scholarly son of a prosperous Rhineland industrialist, were its fathers. Marx became interested in philosophy while studying law at the University of Berlin. Following the example of Kant and Hegel, he set out to create a system.

By 1844–46, Marx had arrived with Engels' help at a preliminary synthesis. He kept Hegel's dialectical mechanism and goal-oriented stage-theory of history. But he replaced Hegel's mystical world spirit with humanity as a species. From the rigorous materialist Ludwig Feuerbach ("Man is what he eats"), Marx took the notion that the essence of the human species was work. Human nature was to be a "free producer."

Under capitalism, as Ricardo had seemingly demonstrated, humanity lost the product of its labor through the capitalist's confiscation of "surplus value." Under capitalism, Marx added, private property and specialization of work (the "division of labor") had "alienated" humanity from its true nature as "free producer." This was a sophisticated Hegelian

Karl Marx, the bourgeois patriarch (*right*), with his wife, two daughters, and Friedrich Engels in the 1860s.

Marx the Determinist Philosopher of History

In the social production of their existence, men enter into definite, predetermined relationships that are independent of their will. Those relations of production correspond to a given stage of the development of material productive forces. The totality of those relations of production forms the economic structure of the society, the real base, upon which a juridical and political superstructure rises, and to which given forms of social consciousness correspond. The mode of production of material life conditions the social, political, and intellectual life process itself. It is not the consciousness of men that determines their existence, but rather the reverse: their social existence determines their consciousness.

From Karl Marx, preface to A Contribution to the Critique of Political Economy *(1859; translation by M. Knox).*

version of the romantic and utopian socialist attack on early nineteenth-century industrial society.

But for Marx, unlike his "utopian" predecessors, history was destined to remedy the ills of past and present. He translated into economics Hegel's dialectical upward struggle of the world spirit toward self-realization. He joked that he had stood Hegel "right side up," and discovered the "rational kernel within the mystical shell." Work, not the Hegelian world spirit, powered history. Successive "modes of production," following one another dialectically, created new modes of consciousness, new stages in the upward progress of the human species. Instead of Hegel's oriental, ancient, and Germanic-Christian stages of history, Marx saw a progression of "modes of production," from ancient slave society, through "feudalism," to industrial capitalism, to a final stage: communism.

For the dialectic expressed itself politically as the struggle between economic classes: "The history of all existing society is the history of class struggle." That struggle now pitted the new industrial working class, the "proletariat" born of the Industrial Revolution, against the capitalist class or "bourgeoisie." That struggle, Marx con-

fidently predicted, would end with the victory of the proletariat, since capitalist industrialization would create ever-larger numbers of ever-poorer proletarians. And the proletariat's victory would bring the end of history—or rather the end of what Marx called "the pre-history of human society." For the proletariat, the class supposedly more alienated than any other in history from humanity's essence as "free producer," had a historic mission. Its revolution would be the last, and would turn philosophy into reality: "The government of persons is replaced by the administration of things, and by the conduct of the processes of production. The state is not 'abolished.' *It withers away.*"

Marx had worked out the main lines of his vision even before writing the famous *Communist Manifesto* with which he and Engels sought unsuccessfully to influence the 1848 revolutions described in Chapter 26. Marx spent the next thirty-five years as an exile in London, the center of world capitalism. There, drawing on the immense resources of the hospitable British Museum library, he fitted out his Hegelian framework with economic evidence that he believed proved its validity.

In *Capital,* the great unfinished work that began to appear in 1867 and set forth his system in its most elaborate form, Marx analyzed and damned the "capitalist mode of production." Its essence was greed: the capitalist was ". . . capital personified. His soul is the soul of capital." Capital was "dead labor, which, vampire-like, lives only by sucking living labor, and lives the more, the more labor it sucks." That demonic vision of capitalism appeared to derive from Marx's views on Judaism, as set forth in his notorious *On the Jewish Question* (1843). There, in pathological language, he had proclaimed that "money is the jealous God of Israel" and demanded an end to "the *empirical* essence of Judaism—huckstering."

Marx's system was at least three things: a philosophy of history, an economic theory and analysis of society, and a call to revolution. Logic and events have dealt harshly with the first two. His philosophy of history claimed scientific knowledge of the human future, and of the meaning of human history as a whole. But the whole past and the future are unknowable; statements about the meaning and destination of something largely unknowable are not science but a sort of religion.

And capitalism did not collapse. Capitalist industrialization did not polarize societies into ever-larger masses of increasingly degraded proletarians and ever-smaller groups of ever-richer capitalists. Revolution did not come to the most advanced capitalist countries, as Marx assumed it would. Instead, as described in Chapter 24, capitalist industrialization led to relative affluence and to an ever-broadening number of social groups. In the most advanced countries it was the industrial proletariat, not the state, that eventually withered away. And Marx's prediction of an ever-falling rate of profit under capitalism ignored the "dialectical" driving force of science and technology. New technologies create industries that are vastly profitable until they saturate their markets; then still newer technologies supersede them.

Marx's call to revolution proved to be the most powerful and durable part of his system. From the 1860s on, it made him the unchallenged intellectual leader of European and world socialism. But Marx's massive works concealed an underlying contradiction. His philosophy of history seemed to predict the almost automatic extinction of capitalism once economic conditions had ripened. That comforting thought might lead socialists to await the great day passively, a conclusion Marx and many later Marxists rejected. Marx left unresolved the tension in his writings between determinism and "voluntarism," between the temptation to await what was foreordained and the urge to force the pace of history through revolution.

Marx's endorsement of revolutionary terror and of the "dictatorship of the proletariat" also threatened his proclaimed goal of human freedom. Marx celebrated Jacobin-style violence as the midwife of history: under some circumstances there was "only one means to *curtail,* simplify and localize the bloody agony of the old society and the bloody birth-pangs of the new, only one means—the revolutionary ter-

ror." But he also recognized that humanity made its history not "as it please[d] . . . but under circumstances directly found, given, and transmitted from the past." Revolutionary terror would therefore constitute part of his new society's "past" and might influence its future in directions other than liberation.

And what if the "dictatorship of the proletariat" refused to wither away? Marx

Marx the Revolutionary Prophet

The history of all hitherto existing society is the history of class struggles.

Freeman and slave, patrician and plebeian, lord and serf, guildmaster and journeyman, in a word, oppressor and oppressed, stood in constant opposition to one another, carried on an uninterrupted, now hidden, now open fight, a fight that each time ended, either in a revolutionary reconstitution of society at large, or in the common ruin of the contending classes. . . .

The modern bourgeois society that has sprouted from the ruins of feudal society has not done away with class antagonisms. It has but established new classes, new conditions of oppression, new forms of struggle in place of the old ones.

Our epoch, the epoch of the bourgeoisie, possesses, however, this distinctive feature: it has simplified the class antagonisms: Society as a whole is more and more splitting up into two great hostile camps, into two great classes directly facing each other: Bourgeoisie and Proletariat. . . .

All previous historical movements were movements of minorities, or in the interests of minorities. The proletarian movement is the self-conscious, independent movement of the immense majority, in the interests of the immense majority. . . .

The advance of industry, whose involuntary promoter is the bourgeoisie, replaces the isolation of the laborers, due to competition, by their revolutionary combination, due to association. The development of Modern Industry, therefore, cuts from under its feet the very foundation on which the bourgeoisie produces and appropriates products. What the bourgeoisie, therefore, produces, above all, is its own grave-diggers. Its fall and the victory of the proletariat are equally inevitable.

From Karl Marx and Friedrich Engels, The Communist Manifesto *(1848).*

doggedly refused to take that question seriously, even when his rival in the international socialist movement, the eccentric Russian aristocrat Mikhail Bakunin (1814–76), attacked him publicly. Bakunin's anarchist answer to oppression was improbable: smashing the state would return humanity to a state of nature in which its essential goodness would at last prevail. But on the likely consequences of a transitional revolutionary dictatorship, Marx was the utopian and Bakunin the realist: "no dictatorship can have any other aim than to perpetuate itself."

Marx's vision conflicted in other ways with his goal of liberation. His claim to

Bakunin the Anarchist Foresees a Dictatorship over the Proletariat

In 1874–75, Marx copied into his notebooks long passages from Statehood and Anarchy, *a work of his anarchist rival Mikhail Bakunin, and adorned them with furious comments (printed in brackets).*

(Bakunin) . . . the so-called people's state will be nothing other than the quite despotic administration of the masses of the people by a new and very non-numerous aristocracy of real and supposed learned ones. The people is not learned, so it will be entirely freed from the cares of governing, wholly incorporated into the governed herd. A fine liberation! The Marxists sense this [!] contradiction and, realizing that the regime of the learned [*quelle reverie!*], the hardest, most offensive, and most contemptuous in the world will in fact be a dictatorship in spite of all the democratic forms, console themselves with the thought that the dictatorship will be temporary and short-lived.

(Marx commentary) [*Non, mon cher!* The *class domination* of the workers over the resisting strata of the old world must last until the economic foundations of the existence of classes are destroyed.]

(Bakunin). . . . They say that such a state yoke, a dictatorship, is a necessary transitional means for attaining the most complete popular liberation. So, to liberate the masses of the people they first have to be enslaved. Our polemic rests and is founded on this contradiction. They maintain that only a dictatorship, their own naturally, can create the people's will; we answer: no dictatorship can have any other aim than to perpetuate itself. . . .

From Robert C. Tucker, ed., The Marx-Engels Reader, *2nd ed. (New York: W. W. Norton, 1978), pp. 546–47.*

possess the meaning of history encouraged intolerance. If Marx, in Engels' famous words, was the Darwin of human society, if he had "discovered the fundamental law that determines the course and development of human history," then those who stood against him stood against history. Marx and his successors were not slow to point that out.

And as later critics have suggested, Marx's ideas contained implications for revolutionary regimes that went far beyond his advocacy of terror and temporary dictatorship. Since Marx claimed that all human conflict stemmed from the class struggle, conflict after the revolution could only be a result of resistance by the old ruling classes. Anyone who disagreed with the new regime thus became a legitimate target for further liberating violence. And if freedom meant social unity, as Marx—following thinkers as otherwise different as Rousseau and Hegel—assumed, then the more unity the more freedom. That belief could likewise point the way to the elimination of all who failed to fit in. And if, as Marx suggested, communism would enable humanity to control the conditions of its existence, then a regime that described itself as communist could do *anything it liked*. Nothing on earth, no law either economic or moral, need restrain it.

Marx's legacy was thus ambiguous. He made economics part of history. Economic forces, "modes of production," and social classes were henceforth objects of historical study alongside kings and battles. He offered a fierce critique of capitalism, although the credibility of that critique diminished as the brutal conditions of early British industrialization gave way to rising living standards. Above all, Marx created a messianic faith in revolution. That faith arrived on the scene too late in the nineteenth century to preside over a genuine revolution. The twentieth century offered new opportunities.

Nationalism

From the beginning, socialism found itself competing with an even more powerful force: nationalism. The political idea of the nation-state, born in the French Revolution and spread by its wars, created deeper divisions than any between labor and capital. Two great forces, one political and one economic, acted throughout the nineteenth century to transmit nationalism eastward across Europe.

The first was the example of France's crushing military successes after 1792. Once French revolutionary nationalism had tapped the power of France's entire population, Europe's other peoples had to follow or go under. The second force was the Industrial Revolution. Once Britain showed the way to wealth and power, others had to follow. And survival, whether on the battlefield or in the cold marketplace world of profit and loss, demanded literate populations. Europe's states, as described in the next section of this chapter, responded by introducing compulsory schooling for their subjects. The new schools in turn had to teach a national language, for the days of medieval Latin as the universal language of western and central Europe were long past. National languages and state schools brought with them national cultures, complete with nationalist myths and historic grievances against neighbors.

This age of increasingly rapid change created emotional as well as political and economic needs. As money and goods and mass migrations dissolved Europe's traditional village communities, nationalism offered a new sense of belonging, a new anchor for popular loyalties. It offered that same sense of belonging—along with careers and power—to Europe's intellectuals. Yet the forces that spread nationalism did not determine and do not explain its ultimate effect, which was to tear Europe apart. Only the content of nationalist ideas can explain nationalism's consequences.

The nationalisms of nineteenth-century Europe were compounds of four major elements. First was the theory of the social contract and general will that the French Revolution had attempted to translate into reality. When the nation of king and nobles gave way to the nation of freely associating citizens, nothing except the "general will" limited the nation's ac-

tions. Second was Kant's doctrine of the moral autonomy of the individual. When extended to nations, that autonomy, that "self-determination," meant that nations needed to acknowledge no law they had not themselves chosen. Third was Hegel's notion of the state as the moral force in a history that was proceeding through struggle toward a goal. Hegel was no German nationalist; he had hailed Napoleon as a historic individual whose conquests advanced the self-realization of the world spirit. But his deification of the Prussian state had nationalist uses.

The fourth and most dangerous element of European nationalism was the ethnic concept of the nation. That too was above all a German contribution. Johann Gottfried von Herder (1744–1803), a prominent exponent of *Sturm und Drang,* had worked out in the 1770s and 1780s a philosophy of history that justified German resistance to the cultural domination of France. For Herder each nation, each *Volk,* was equally close to God. Each therefore had the duty to cultivate its own peculiarities: "Spew out the ugly slime of the Seine / Speak German, O you German!" Herder rejoiced in human diversity. Like Hegel, he was no nationalist. But once again, his ideas had nationalist uses.

German philosophers such as Fichte were soon proclaiming the *superiority* of the national language. The French, wrote Fichte after Napoleon's conquest of Germany in 1806, were a Germanic people who had foolishly abandoned their native tongue for a language derived from Latin. That had infected them with a "lack of seriousness." Herder's successors thus established a new test for nationhood: language. They made language the standard for drawing or redrawing boundaries. They made it what it had rarely been before: a matter of life and death.

In the decades after 1815, the French revolutionary conception of the general will, the notion of self-determination, the concept of the state as the moral force in history, and the ethnic-linguistic concept of the nation fused. The result was a uniquely European invention, *the secular religion of the nation-state.* For the nationalist, individual freedom and self-

Mikhail Bakunin, aristocrat and professional revolutionary.

The invention of national traditions: German peasant costume, as imagined by Ludwig Emil Grimm (1828).

Giuseppe Mazzini, prophet of the religion of the nation-state.

fulfillment lay only in service to such a state. That peculiar belief distinguishes nationalism from patriotism, the instinctive loyalty to homeland, and from xenophobia, the traditional and unthinking hatred and contempt for foreigners. Patriotism and xenophobia have existed throughout history; nationalism was an invention of the decades immediately after 1789.

It first spread in and through literature. Herder had provided a rationale for cultivating the language and culture of one's own *Volk*. The brothers Jakob and Wilhelm Grimm collected folk tales and Germanic mythology, and explored the roots of the German language. Poles, Czechs, Hungarians, and Balkan nationalities followed. Dictionaries and editions of medieval epic poems appeared, monuments to the peculiarities of each nation's history. Poets like Sándor Petöfi (1822–49) in Hungary and Giacomo Leopardi (1798–1837) in Italy wrote verse celebrating the national spirit and demanding national liberation.

Politics followed poetry. The defeat of revolutionary France did not remove nationalism from politics. Italy, which remained under Austrian domination after 1815, set the example. The conspiratorial sect of the *carbonari* ("charcoal-burners") had originated in south Italy as a protest against French rule. Although lacking a discernible program, it served as a magnet both for police spies and for youth hostile to the status quo. One such youth was Giuseppe Mazzini (1805–72), the greatest prophet of nineteenth-century nationalism.

Mazzini joined the *carbonari* in 1827 in his home town of Genoa and spent time in jail in 1830 for subversive activity. In exile in 1831 he founded a new type of conspiratorial organization: *Giovine Italia,* or "Young Italy." The movement had little practical success but its romantic emphasis on youthful enthusiasm set a powerful example. Mazzini proclaimed liberty, but his liberty was the liberty of the individual to serve the national idea. Nationalist politics was a *fede,* a faith, a political religion.

Mazzini proclaimed the liberty and equality of all nationalities and their inevitable brotherhood once Europe became a "Europe of the Peoples." But he also insisted it was Italy's mission to provide "a new and more powerful Unity to all the nations of Europe." Italy had given Europe unity under the Roman Empire and the papacy. Now the "Third Rome," the "Rome of the Italian people," would fulfill that same universal mission. It would create a "third and still vaster Unity." That was no small claim, and it helped set a widely imitated pattern of nationalist megalomania. Nor did Mazzini address the decisive question: when the claims and "rights" of nationalities conflicted, who or what would decide?

Nationalist visionaries who followed Mazzini had less respect than he for liberty. As the century drew on, they increasingly emphasized the least tolerant strand of nationalism, its ethnic-linguistic element. Language and culture could nevertheless still be learned by outsiders. Nationalisms that retained them as the test for citizenship, as did France or Italy, remained relatively benign. But in Germany, where the ethnic-linguistic theory of the nation had originated, nationalism after the 1870s fused with a misunderstood Darwinism (see p. 729). By 1900 the German test for membership in the *Volk* was on its way to becoming implacably pseudo-biological. That leap from mother-tongue to "blood" and "race" was a crucial step toward the nationalist wars and genocides of the twentieth century.

IDEAS AND SOCIAL REALITY: THE STATE, WORKERS, AND WOMEN

Without a public capable of receiving them, ideas have little practical effect. In nineteenth-century Europe the gradual widening of literacy and of leisure created that public. States began to take responsibility for their subjects' welfare and education. And submerged groups such as workers and women reacted to new ideas and new conditions with broadening demands for social and political rights.

The Role of the State

States had traditionally been machines for power, not welfare. Yet in the seventeenth and eighteenth centuries, the states of western Europe began to recognize that the prosperity and education of their inhabitants might increase that power (see pp. 571–77). In the nineteenth century the industrial revolution further intensified the apparent need for states to supervise the education, health, and wealth of their citizens. Power, necessary for survival, remained the state's ultimate purpose, but alongside it there gradually emerged the modern bureaucratic "welfare state."

The states of the nineteenth century, as befitted the age of *laissez-faire,* removed economic restraints that appeared to impede the creation of wealth. By the 1860s, the centralizing bureaucracies of the German states had overcome the fearful rear-guard action of small-town Germany, with its xenophobic guilds and restrictions on free competition. In Britain, a militant middle-class movement institutionalized *laissez-faire.* In 1846 Parliament abolished the grain tariffs or "Corn Laws" that Britain's landed interests had imposed in the post-1815 slump. That step marked the political triumph of Britain's all-conquering industries over agriculture.

The state also intervened in the economy. Especially on the Continent, it took the lead in the creation of national markets and industrial economies. The obvious abuses of the factory system and the wretched sanitary conditions in the new industrial cities also provoked outcry and government action. In Britain, legislation as early as 1802 had attempted to regulate working hours for apprentices. In 1819 Parliament passed the first of a series of Factory Acts, forbidding the employment of children under nine and limiting the work day of children over nine to twelve hours. An act of 1831 forbade night work by those under 21; an act restricting the work day to ten and a half hours passed in 1850. The first Factory Acts applied only to cotton mills, but by the 1860s legislation covered most industries. Acts in 1841 and 1855 banned the employment of women and children in mining. Parliament also sought to regulate city sanitation and standards for wholesome food and drink, beginning with the Public Health Act of 1848. France and Prussia passed similar laws. Despite a long

record of poor enforcement and of collusion between factory inspectors and manufacturers, working and living conditions gradually improved.

In the face of British industrial competition, the continental states adopted protective tariffs. Prussia, in particular, made tariff policy an instrument of state power. Beginning in 1818, reforming Prussian bureaucrats aggressively pressed customs unions upon their smaller neighbors. In 1833, Prussia succeeded in creating a *Zollverein,* or customs union, that eventually covered all important German states except Austria. Prussia's bureaucracy and military also took the lead in the expansion of the railroad network. After mid-century, the army began gearing the railroads to its ever-faster mobilization system. Only the Russian state, in the period of its industrial "take-off" after 1880, surpassed the role of the Prussian state in economic development.

Prussia led in a second, absolutely decisive area: its school system pioneered mass literacy. That was a daring step. The value of widespread literacy in the eighteenth century was far from obvious, at least to the European upper classes. Catherine the Great neatly summarized their attitude in a letter reputedly sent to a subordinate: "We must not in any way provide instruction for the lower class of people. If they knew as much as you or I . . . they would no longer want to obey us. . . ." Even after 1800, members of the British Parliament railed against the democratization of knowledge; it might render the lower orders "insolent to their superiors."

The Prussian bureaucracy, ruling over what a French intellectual in the 1830s described as the "classic country of barracks and schools," had no such qualms. Prussia, after 1819, became the first state in history to enforce universal school attendance. A literate subject was a better soldier and a more productive subject. France followed in 1833 by requiring villages and towns to maintain schools. The Habsburg monarchy followed in the 1860s. Britain, in the spirit of *laissez-faire,* neglected its schools, and paid dearly. It made universal primary schooling compulsory only in 1880.

The coming of literacy worked yet another revolution. Throughout most of history, only very small elites had been able to read or write. At the beginning of the nineteenth century slightly more than half of all adult males in England and France and perhaps one in three or four women could write their own names. A century later, literacy in the developed countries of western Europe was well above 95 percent of both men and women (see Figure 25-1). The Industrial Revolution made mass literacy possible. But it was the state that turned that potential into reality.

Workers

Mass literacy, among its many side effects, made the claims of the outsiders increasingly difficult to ignore. In politics, both workers and women participated in the revolutionary ferment that culminated in the Europe-wide uprisings of 1848, described in the next chapter. In the workplace, workers by that point had long since begun to organize against what they perceived as oppression. The introduction of machinery led to widespread artisan protest and machine-breaking both in England and on the Continent. From 1811 to 1816 English rioters rose repeatedly to smash knitting machines and power looms in the name of a mythical "King Ludd." Agricultural workers imitated the "Luddites" in 1830–32 by smashing threshing machines and burning barns.

But incoherent protest and anarchic violence had little chance even against the decentralized British state. Workers explored other paths, beginning in the 1820s. With the Combination Acts of 1799 and 1800 Parliament had ended early attempts by workers to organize rudimentary labor unions under the inspiration of the French Revolution. But in 1824–25 Parliament weakened the Acts in response to continued unrest and to the pleas of middle-class reformers for toleration of working-class "cooperation." Strikes remained illegal but unions could now organize. In 1829 Robert Owen presided over the founding of a Society for Promoting Co-operative Knowledge that in 1831 became the National Union of the Working Classes, the first true British trade union.

It turned out that regional and craft loyalties were stronger than working-class solidarity. Yet recurrent economic crises and the pressure of population growth kept unrest alive. In 1838 a leading workers' group, the London Working Men's Association, initiated a nationwide campaign to urge Parliament to adopt universal male suffrage and other reforms listed in a "People's Charter." Chartist agitation, under the leadership of the fiery journalist and speaker Feargus O'Connor, continued sporadically for the next ten years but failed to influence Parliament.

Chartism's internal rivalries and its political failure did not inhibit other working-class efforts. A national Association for the Protection of Labour emerged in 1845 and by 1859 was able to persuade Parliament to legalize peaceful picketing.

FIGURE 25.1   **The Decline of Illiteracy**

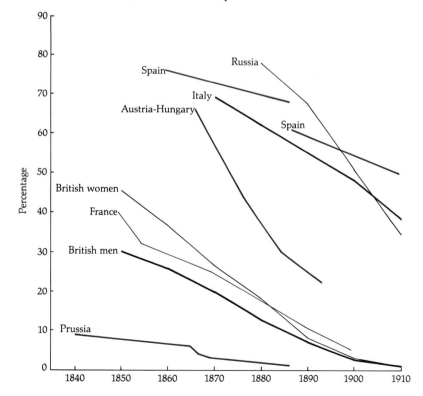

In 1868 a Trades Union Congress that represented more than 100,000 workers met at Manchester. By 1875 British trade unions had won the right to strike and picket.

On the Continent, working-class organization inevitably lagged, given the gap in development between Britain and its followers. Belgium prohibited labor unions until 1868. Revolutionary France had forbidden unions and strikes, and Napoleon's law code had confirmed that ban in 1803. Socialist underground secret societies, and uprisings such as those of the impoverished silk workers of Lyon in 1831 and 1834, merely provoked savage repression. Not until after 1871 did the French working classes organize effectively. In Germany, revolutionary sects such as the tailor Wilhelm Weitling's League of the Just emerged a generation before the creation of an organized German labor movement in the 1860s.

Despite rivalries between regions and crafts, home artisans and factory workers, highly skilled "labor aristocrats" and simple laborers, the European working classes were by the 1870s nevertheless well on their way to creating stable organizations to represent their interests. In England the ideological glue that held them together was frequently the piety of the Protestant sects. On the Continent, most of them adopted orthodox Marxism under the guidance or inspiration of the "First International," the "International Working Men's Organization" that Marx and Engels helped found in 1864. Workers' organizations soon made increasingly effective demands for change and gave birth to the first workers' political parties.

Women

The French and industrial revolutions made relative freedom for women possible, but did not produce it. As with workers, only struggle could do that. In revolutionary Paris, Olympe de Gouges had pointed out the inconsistency of proclaiming the Rights of Man while denying those same rights to women. In her pathbreaking *Vindication of the Rights of Women* (1792), the English writer Mary Wollstonecraft demanded equality, and freedom for women to employ their talents. The romantic poet Shelley, son-in-law of Mary Wollstonecraft, put the issue succinctly in 1817: "Can man be free if woman be a slave?"

That question passed through three overlapping phases in the course of the nineteenth century: literary self-assertion, theoretical elaboration, and political action. In the first phase, women intellectuals began to write with a frequency and eloquence that eventually won them grudging respect. Germaine de Staël, daughter of the banker Necker and France's leading woman writer until her death in 1817, took on Napoleon in print and had to take refuge in exile. Her novels *Corinne* (1804) and *Delphine* (1807) attacked conventional views of marriage and of women's education. She also played a decisive role in explaining German romanticism to the rest of Europe. Napoleon had the first edition of her *De l'Allemagne* (1811) burned as "un-French."

The French romantic novelist and social critic George Sand (Amantine-Lucile-Aurore, Baroness Dudevant, 1804–76) was an adherent of Fourierist utopianism who scandalized French polite society by wearing men's suits and smoking in public. Fleeing a provincial marriage of convenience, Sand went to Paris and wrote some eighty popular novels. She supported herself and her two children on the proceeds, an achievement almost without precedent. She also advocated and practiced "free love," by which she and other Fourierists and Saint-Simonians meant living together or marriage based on equality of the sexes and on sexual or emotional bonds rather than social convention. Sand, despite her deliberate unconventionality, was a prototype of the successful professional women who became common later in the century.

By midcentury, women authors were emerging whose achievements were unrivaled. Charlotte Brontë, in her novels *Jane Eyre* (1847) and *Shirley* (1849), presented strong women heroines in quest both of love and of independence. Her sister Emily, before her death of tuberculosis,

George Sand (1838).

produced the violent and terrifying *Wuthering Heights* (1847), one of the greatest of English nineteenth-century novels.

By that time both men and women had begun to explore the question of woman's role. Their views fall into three rough categories: those who reaffirmed woman's traditional subordination to man, those who argued that women were equal but different, and those who insisted on an absolute legal and political equality that would allow women to be like men if they chose.

Most males inevitably argued for woman's subordination. And many women still agreed. Woman's role was to obey, help, and comfort man the breadwinner, to bear and raise his children, and to preside over the home, a warm sanctuary in the cold and increasingly competitive new industrial world. That was the prescription of Sarah Stickney Ellis, an English writer of women's handbooks from the late 1830s on, and of numerous continental theorists from reactionaries such as De Maistre to liberals of all stripes.

The "equal but different" tradition was most prominent on the Continent. The title of a French tract of the 1830s sums up its message: *The Education of Mothers; or the Civilization of Mankind by Women.* Woman's first role was as mother. The mother's calling was to be the educator, the bearer of culture, the civilizer of the drunken, destructive, childlike male. As Jeanne Deroin (1805–94), the foremost French woman's advocate of midcentury, put it in the newspaper she published during the 1848 revolution, woman's "sublime humanitarian maternity" had the duty to "teach everyone how fraternity should be practiced." The world of politics and of relations between states should conform to the standards of the well-ordered home.

Nor should women seek to imitate men, insisted Louise Otto (1819–95), Deroin's foremost German counterpart. "True womanliness" was the goal. "Georgesandism" outraged Otto as much as it did any defender of the old order. Emancipation must not "[devalue] woman to become a caricature of a man." This tradition had appeal not only in Germany

and France, but even in England and the United States. There it contributed not only to the assertion of women's rights but also to the temperance movement that gathered force as the nineteenth century drew on. And the notion of the mother as educator appealed to female theorists of eastern European nationalism. It gave woman a decisive role in the national struggle. Man's vocation was to fight; woman's was to transmit the *Volk* language and nationalize the minds of the young.

The third tradition that emerged in the course of the nineteenth century drew its ultimate inspiration from Locke. Men enjoyed autonomy and self-determination by natural right. To deny that same right to women was neither just nor civilized. Women must receive the same autonomy and education as men, even if that meant painful social readjustment. Wollstonecraft gave first expression to such views. John Stuart and Harriet Taylor Mill's *The Subjection of Women* (1869) provided the tradition's basic text. Its ideas were particularly influential in Britain and the United States, where they meshed with the Lockean political culture from which they derived.

Theorists of the "equal but different" tradition—and male supremacists—inevitably attacked the Mills for inciting women to what they described as antisocial self-indulgence. Ruthless individualism, the critics claimed, was no answer to the biological and social imperatives that governed women's conduct. Emancipation could not and must not mean emancipation from children, or from marriage, the building block of society. Women's biological role demanded special legal protection for the family, not the cold comfort of strict equality with men.

The issues at stake were so intractable and emotion-laden that the argument between the two schools has continued to the present. But regardless of theoretical differences, by the 1860s and 1870s a broadly based movement of women, primarily of the middle classes, had arisen both in Europe and in the United States. It increasingly turned to political action to secure women's rights (see pp. 727–29).

The new age of ideas after 1789 was both a continuation and a repudiation of the Enlightenment. Faith in "progress" and in the perfectibility of humanity swelled with the advance of science, the coming of steam-powered industry, and the spread of liberalism and socialism. Submerged groups found voices; states began to act as machines for welfare as well as for power. Yet strong countercurrents persisted. Conservatism or "reaction" inspired both nobles and intellectuals. Peasants and many in the middle classes still held to traditional community and dynastic loyalties. Romanticism damned the new industrial age but also undermined the remains of the old order through its stormy cult of the individual. And nationalism, which many conservatives mistook for liberalism, soon revealed itself as the overriding political faith of the nineteenth and twentieth centuries, the force that transmuted "geographical expressions" into nation-states.

Suggestions for Further Reading

Science, Religion, and Culture

For overviews that place nineteenth-century thought in its political and social setting, see E. J. Hobsbawm, *The Age of Revolution, 1789–1848* (1962), and *The Age of Capital, 1848–1875* (1975). F. L. Baumer, *Modern European Thought: Continuity and Change in Ideas, 1600–1950* (1977), offers a useful general survey of the movement of ideas. For the fate of religion, see O. Chadwick, *The Secularization of the European Mind in the Nineteenth Century* (1975). On the impact of Darwin and geology, see especially W. Irvine, *Angels, Apes, and Victorians* (1955); J. C. Greene, *The Death of Adam* (1959); and C. C. Gillispie, *Genesis and Geology* (1951). For romanticism, see especially J. Barzun, *Classic, Romantic, and Modern* (1961); J. B. Halstead, ed., *Romanticism* (1965); J. Clay, *Romanticism* (1981); and M. le Bris, *Romantics and Romanticism* (1981). On German philosophy, R. N. Stromberg, *European Intellectual History After 1789* (1981); R. Scruton, *From Descartes to Wittgenstein* (1981); K. Löwith, *From Hegel to Nietzsche* (1964); and G. D. O'Brien, *Hegel on Reason and History* (1975) are useful.

Social, Economic, and Political Thought

The best introduction to conservatism is still E. Burke, *Reflections on the Revolution in France;* K. Epstein, *The Genesis of German Conservatism* (1966), describes some of conservatism's continental ramifications. For liberalism, both economic and political, the classic texts are A. Smith, *The Wealth of Nations;* T. R. Malthus, *An Essay on Population;* and J. S. Mill, *Autobiography* and *On Liberty.* On Mill and his fellows, see especially J. Hamburger, *Intellectuals in Politics: John Stuart Mill and the Philosophic Radicals* (1965). G. Lichtheim, *The Origins of Socialism* (1969), and P. Singer, *Marx* (1980), offer concise introductions to socialism. R. Tucker, ed., *The Marx-Engels Reader* (1972), provides a selection of the essential texts. L. Kolakovski, *Main Currents of Marxism,* Vol. 1 (1978), lucidly analyzes the intellectual development of Marx and Engels, explains their debts to earlier thinkers, dissects the weaknesses of their system, and suggests some of the potential consequences of their ideas—but see also D. Conway, *A Farewell to Marx* (1987). E. Kedourie, *Nationalism* (1966), and Ernest Gellner, *Nations and Nationalism* (1983), offer complementary interpretations of a subject of overriding importance.

Consequences of the Industrial Revolution

For the intellectual and social impact of the industrial revolution, see especially the broadly conceived work of T. S. Hamerow, *The Birth of a New Europe* (1983). A. Briggs, *The Age of Improvement, 1783–1867* (1959), and E. P. Thompson, *The Making of the English Working Class* (1963), offer differing perspectives on English workers; L. Chevalier, *Working Classes and Dangerous Classes in Paris During the Nineteenth Century* (1971) and B. Moss, *The Origins of the French Labor Movement* (1976), cover France. R. Bridenthal et al., *Becoming Visible: Women in European History* (1987), offers a useful introduction to the changing status and aspirations of nineteenth-century women.

26

THE BREAKTHROUGH OF THE
NATION-STATE, 1815–1871

While population growth, industrialization, and the spread of literacy and new ideas were transforming Europe after 1815, the Continent enjoyed a century of relative peace. Four general wars and innumerable minor conflicts had punctuated the eighteenth century. Prussia and Russia had become great powers. Sweden had ceased to be one. Poland had ceased to be. But from 1815 to 1914 only three major conflicts—the Crimean War (1854–56) and the wars of Italian (1859–60) and German "unification" (1864, 1866, 1870–71)—affected even parts of Europe. And the nineteenth-century conflicts, unlike the great world wars of 1701–14, 1740–48, 1756–63, and 1792–1815, were short and involved only a few of the great powers.

Peace and stability were the result of both ideology and the structure of international politics. Conservative fear of "the Revolution" had welded together the final coalition that brought Napoleon down. That fear inspired a settlement in 1814–15 that bound the powers together in a network of treaties and mutual obligations. Treaties, custom, and the consolidation of neutral buffer states separating the great powers made it harder than before for one power to challenge the rest. And fear of revolution, intensified by the three waves of unrest that convulsed the Continent in 1820, 1830, and 1848, continued to hold the great powers back from foreign adventures until after mid-century.

Then the collapse of the revolutionary myth in 1848 ushered in a brief era of almost unrestrained rivalries between states, pursued under the banner of nationalism. The consequence was the breakthrough of the nation-state in central Europe: the creation of Italy in 1859–60 and of Prussia-Germany in 1866–71. Those "revolutions from above," especially the German one, destroyed the small and intermediate buffer states that had been a key restraining element in the 1814–15 settlement. Nevertheless, thanks to the weakness of the new Italian state and the temporary self-restraint of the German one, the main lines of the 1814–15 settlement survived the wars of midcentury. Only after 1890 did a new challenge to the balance of power end the "long peace" and inaugurate a new century of world wars.

UNDER THE SHADOW OF REVOLUTION: THE CONGRESS OF VIENNA AND AFTER, 1814–48

The powers that had defeated Napoleon faced two intertwined tasks—the restoration of an international balance of power and of internal stability in the wide areas of Europe that France had conquered. As Britain's foreign secretary, Castlereagh, remarked, the victors needed to return Europe to "peaceful habits." The diplomats redrew the map in 1814–15 in ways that bore little relationship to the wishes of Europe's populations. Internally, the "re-

action" that followed the restoration of many of Europe's ruling houses was undeniably oppressive. But by the standards set in later peace settlements, the treaties of 1814–15 were both humane and durable.

Europe—or rather the five great powers—met at the Congress of Vienna in September 1814 to draw up the settlement. The four decisive figures in this first general European settlement since the Peace of Westphalia in 1648 were Tsar Alexander of Russia, Talleyrand for Bourbon France, Castlereagh for Britain, and the host, Chancellor Prince Metternich, for Austria. Frederick William III of Prussia and his ministers cut lesser figures. Around the principals danced the nobility of Europe and their innumerable hangers-on, while Metternich's secret police searched wastebaskets and boudoir drawers in search of diplomatic correspondence.

The two overriding issues were the settlement with France and the division of the booty in central and eastern Europe. The allies at first tried to exclude Talleyrand from their deliberations. But Russia's unpredictable ruler soon provoked a crisis that reversed the powers' roles. If France was the threat of yesterday, Alexander, with his insistence on entering Paris as a conqueror, might be the threat of tomorrow. His demand that the Congress confirm his control of most of Poland alarmed his allies, since a Russia that close to central Europe would be an over-mighty neighbor. Even Alexander's promise to equip his Polish territories with a constitution seemed a fig-leaf for the voracious expansionism of the Russian state. Metternich was in any case no lover of constitutions.

The tsar's Prussian ally also gave the impression that it might some day threaten the European balance. The Prussian military reformers, intoxicated with their victory over Napoleon, now demanded the annexation of Saxony, whose king had changed sides too late in 1813. (In revolutionary times, as that expert at well-timed shifts of allegiance, Talleyrand, remarked, treason was "a question of dates.") The upshot was deadlock. Russia and Prussia

The Congress of Vienna: the official view, by Jean-Baptiste Isabey.

Europe in 1815

faced England and Austria, while the Prussian generals muttered threateningly. To defend the balance, Castlereagh and Metternich brought a willing Talleyrand into play. A brief triple alliance of the old enemies, France, Britain, and Austria, persuaded the Prussians and the tsar to back down.

France remained a great power, and preserved its pre-1789 borders almost unchanged. Russia gave up some Polish territory. Prussia kept some of Poland and secured only half of Saxony. In compensa-

tion, it gained the formerly Napoleonic territories in northwestern Germany. Castlereagh and Metternich placed a reluctant Prussia on the Rhine, in the front lines against a possible renewal of the French threat to the balance of power. England and Austria thus also unwittingly gave Prussia the immense coal and iron deposits of the Ruhr Valley, with economic and political consequences immeasurably important for the future of Prussia, Germany, and Europe. The separation of post-1815 Prussia into eastern and western halves generated additional pressure, if the Prussian power-state needed pressure, for further expansion—the annexation of the smaller states in between.

Other issues at Vienna generated less tension than the Poland-Saxony deadlock. In principle—as proclaimed by Talleyrand and Metternich—"legitimacy," or tradition, was to guide the settlement. That slogan was convenient for Bourbon France and Habsburg Austria. But it had less to do with the actual shape of the settlement than with the need for stability and balance that all felt deeply after almost 25 years of revolution and war.

The Bourbons returned to the thrones of France, Spain, and eventually Naples. The Pope reclaimed the Papal States, stretching across central Italy. Switzerland, released from its status as a satellite of revolutionary France, received a guarantee of perpetual independence and neutrality. But at British insistence, Holland received the former Austrian territory of Belgium to strengthen it as a barrier against France. Piedmont-Sardinia likewise and for the same reason received the former republic of Genoa. Austria kept Venetia and Lombardy.

In Germany expediency and the quest for stability triumphed. The surviving princes, whose territories had grown fat in the princes' revolution of 1801–03 and in Napoleon's redrawing of the map in 1806 and after, were poor examples indeed of "legitimacy." The deliberations of the German states at the Congress gave birth to a loose league, a German "united nations" of 39 states and mini-states, with an assembly sitting at Frankfurt. Austria held the presidency of this German Confederation with Prussia as its sometimes reluctant second. The Confederation's two-fold function was to give the awakening German nation a political home now that the Holy Roman Empire no longer existed, and to serve as a defensive barrier against a resurgent France or an aggressive Russia. The Confederation's principal weaknesses were the built-in split between Austria and Prussia and the egotism of its lesser princes. Both conspired against the greater unity that German nationalists were already demanding.

The inconsiderate and violent return of Napoleon during the "Hundred Days" of 1815 emphasized further the need for continuing great-power solidarity. The allies renewed the Quadruple Alliance for twenty years, and confirmed the principle established at Vienna that the great powers in concert would decide all major international questions.

But once the powers began to discuss the internal regimes of Europe's states, their ways parted. The symbol of the divergence between Britain on the one hand and Russia, Prussia, and Austria on the other was Tsar Alexander's treaty of the "Holy Alliance" of September 1815. This "piece of sublime mysticism and nonsense," in Castlereagh's scathing phrase, pledged the three eastern monarchies to conduct their policies in accordance with the principles of the Christian religion. Those principles, as interpreted by the eastern monarchies, apparently included the suppression of liberalism and revolution everywhere. Although the Holy Alliance itself had little practical effect, it gave its name to an era of obscurantism, arbitrary imprisonment, and muzzling of the press.

In Spain and Naples the restored Bourbons abolished the constitutions they had granted in 1812. Pope Pius VII reestablished his authority in the Papal States by again confining the Jews to ghettos, by reviving the Inquisition, and by abolishing the reforming law codes the French had brought. In Germany, Metternich attacked freedom of expression. In 1819 Prussia and the German Confederation adopted his repressive "Carlsbad Decrees" and suppressed liberal and nationalist agitation in Germany for a decade.

Even England passed through a brief repressive phase. The inevitable post-war economic slump in 1815, combined with population growth, brought widespread poverty and unemployment. Unlike their counterparts on the Continent, middle-class radicals called not for revolution but for reform of the corrupt parliamentary voting system. The Tory (Conservative) government nevertheless replied with ill-considered force in 1819. British troops routed a peaceful crowd of demonstra-

Cavalry disperses the crowd at the "Peterloo Massacre" (1819).

tors with considerable loss of life in the so-called Peterloo Massacre. Parliament passed the notorious "Six Acts" that made the expression of unorthodox political opinions a crime. But neither Britain nor the continental monarchies had the bureaucratic machinery or propaganda techniques needed to remold their subjects' thoughts; that was reserved for the despotisms of the twentieth century.

The "concert of Europe," for which the Quadruple Alliance had prescribed regular meetings, soon broke up. In 1820, the first of a series of disturbances in southern Europe posed the question of whether the great powers should intervene. A revolt to force parliamentary government on the Spanish Bourbons triggered disturbances in Naples, Piedmont, and Portugal. Castlereagh refused to attend the Congress of Troppau (1820) at which the three eastern monarchies declared their readiness to act. The ensuing Congress of Laibach (1821), over British protests, authorized Austrian military action to restore the Bourbons in Naples and Sicily. In October 1822, at Verona in north Italy, the last congress met to discuss intervention in Spain. Britain refused its con-

sent and withdrew: "Every nation for itself and God for us all," quipped George Canning, Castlereagh's successor.

Despite British disapproval, a royal French army crossed the Pyrenees to restore the Spanish Bourbons. Unlike 1808, no guerrilla resistance resulted. France was intervening for rather than against the Bourbons, the Church, and Spain's landowning nobles. The custom of consultation between great powers established at Vienna continued, though less formally than in the congress period.

If Britain's departure from Verona marked the effective end of the Quadruple Alliance, the Greek war of Independence (1821–29) soon crippled the Holy Alliance as well. The war was a major step in a process soon drearily familiar to European statesmen: the "Eastern Question," the breakup of the Ottoman Turk empire under the pressure of hostile great powers without and of nationalism within. Russia had humiliated the Turks in Catherine the Great's wars. The Serbs, under their chieftain "Black George," had set the example of national—or tribal—revolt against Constantinople in 1804. By 1817 the embryo of a Serb state had emerged, although it remained for the moment under Turkish overlordship. The Greeks followed in 1821 by massacring all Turks in the Peloponnese—a massacre the Turks repaid with interest.

The Greek cause attracted support among Western admirers of ancient Greece. Flamboyant figures such as the brilliant and dissolute English romantic poet Lord Byron flocked to Greece. Russia, always hostile to Turkey and now solicitous of its Slav "little brothers" under Turkish rule, broke with Metternich and lent aid to "the Revolution." A bizarre alignment of Britain and France with the Russia of Alexander's successor, the reactionary Tsar Nicholas I, annihilated the Turkish fleet at Navarino in 1827. In 1832 independent Greece received from Europe the quaint gift of a Bavarian prince as a ruler.

From 1830 Revolutions to 1840 Crisis

The second wave of revolutions, in 1830–32, was a more serious affair than the first. The breakdown of the Holy Alliance over

King Louis Philippe courts the public, in a contemporary cartoon.

the Greek war and the fading of the memory of revolutionary turmoil—but not of revolutionary achievements—contributed to its force. And, far more than in 1820–21, nationalism drove events. Finally, as in 1789, Paris set the example that had been missing in 1820. Louis XVIII, who had accepted a degree of constitutionalism after 1814, died in 1824. His successor, Charles X, considered himself king by divine right. He muzzled the press and defied the liberal majority in his Chamber of Deputies. His appointment of an ultra-monarchist ministry in 1829 brought deadlock in the middle of a series of poor harvests.

When Charles X attempted in July 1830 to dissolve the Chamber and reduce the already small electorate to a mere 25,000 wealthy men, Paris responded with the well-tried methods of July 1789. Charles, amazingly unprepared to crush the bloody revolt he had provoked, abdicated. Moderate liberals, with the help of that hardy perennial of Paris revolutions, the Marquis de Lafayette, took control. Their candidate, Louis Philippe of Orléans, son of a renegade cousin of Louis XVI who had helped unleash the revolution of 1789 and had taken the name "Philippe-Egalité," ascended the throne as first and last of the Orléans dynasty. This new "July Monarchy" promised France an end to experiments in absolutism.

News of the Paris revolution swept across Europe and ignited further outbreaks. But these, with the exception of stirrings in Britain and the overthrow of a number of unpopular German princelings, were of a different pattern than events in France. In Belgium, north-central Italy, and above all in Poland, the 1830 revolutions were nationalist revolts against foreign domination. The Catholic and French- or Flemish-speaking Belgians given to Holland in 1814–15 chafed increasingly under Protestant Dutch rule. Their revolution succeeded because Britain, France, and Prussia restrained the Dutch from attempting reconquest. In 1839, the five great powers gave Belgium the same guarantee of perpetual independence and neutrality that Switzerland had received in 1815. In Italy, revolutionaries seeking a unified Italian state, and cooperating more effectively than in 1820–21, took over Modena, Parma, and much of the Papal States. Then Metternich's armies marched south once more and restored the "legitimate" rulers.

The most tragic events of 1830 occurred in Poland. There intellectuals and patriots rose against the mild form of Russian rule experienced under Tsar Alexander's 1815 constitution. The Russian authorities initially showed the same unpreparedness and indecision as Charles X and the Dutch. But they soon corrected their mistake. The Russian reconquest, aided by dissension among the Poles, brought mass executions and imprisonment, military rule, and brutal attempts to Russify the population. A generation of Polish intellectuals died or emigrated.

In Germany, minor disturbances led to the granting of constitutions in some of the mid-sized states. In 1832, a nationalist mass movement staged a *Nationalfest* at Hambach near Frankfurt. A crowd of 30,000 heard speakers demand wider voting rights and a national state. Metternich replied with new Carlsbad-style decrees. Silence again descended in Germany.

Finally, the July Revolution of 1830 had repercussions even in Britain. The Conservative regime responsible for the Peterloo Massacre had slowly mellowed. In 1829 the Duke of Wellington's cabinet allowed Parliament to revoke Britain's longstanding discriminatory laws against Catholics. But the scandalous inequities of the electoral system persisted. The absence of any mechanism for redistricting meant that the new industrial cities such as Birmingham and Manchester had no representation in Parliament, while "pocket boroughs" and sleepy villages dominated by one or two great landowners did.

When the Conservatives balked at reform, elections in 1831 gave a majority to the opposition Whigs, or liberals. In 1832, after the House of Lords had tried and failed to block reform, the Reform Bill became law. It eliminated the worst abuses and extended the vote to one adult male in five, compared to one in twenty in Louis Philippe's France. Gradual reform, however grudgingly granted, helped Britain escape the Continent's cycle of bloody repression and bloodier revolution.

In international politics, the 1830 revolutions restored the solidarity between Russia, Prussia, and Austria that had collapsed during the Greek war. Each of the three occupied a part of Poland—and fear of their Polish subjects brought them together at Münchengrätz in Bohemia in 1833, where they concluded agreements against revolution in the spirit of the Holy Alliance that lasted until 1848 and after. Russia and Austria pledged to resist any threat to their Polish lands. They also agreed to oppose further changes in the status quo in Turkey and to act together if a change seemed unavoidable. This last agreement was a symptom of the continuing importance of the Eastern Question, which was to drive Austria and Russia apart repeatedly until the final crisis of 1914.

After the end of the Greek affair, Russia had moved to assume the position of "protector" to and eventual heir of the declining Ottoman Empire. A few months before Münchengrätz, Russia had landed troops at Constantinople to protect the Ottoman sultan from attack through Syria by his rebellious Egyptian vassal, the former Albanian bandit chieftain Mehemet Ali. This Russian protectorate of Turkey inevitably aroused Britain, whose strategic interest in maintaining a Mediterranean route to India required that Russia remain locked in the Black Sea.

But not until Mehemet Ali's second war with Turkey in 1839–40 did the British have an opportunity to act. The boisterous Lord Palmerston, a fit successor to Castlereagh and Canning as foreign secretary, made full use of British power, which thanks to industrialization was now reaching its zenith relative to its continental rivals. When Mehemet Ali's forces drove into Lebanon on their way to Constantinople, Palmerston persuaded Austria and Russia to support efforts to block him. The Royal Navy bombarded Beirut and a landing force cut the Egyptians to shreds. Mehemet Ali retreated; the Ottoman Empire for the moment survived.

THE REFORM BILL.

The Reform Bill of 1832, dramatized in a contemporary cartoon. Pocket boroughs go into the "Reform Mill" and a triumphant Britannia emerges.

The only opposition came from Louis Philippe's France. Nostalgic for the Egyptian colony that Napoleon had failed to bequeath, France broke with its "liberal" partner, Britain. In 1840 Paris briefly challenged all of Europe. Then British naval supremacy and a sudden blaze of hostility to France across the Rhine in Germany brought Louis Philippe's ministers to their senses. As the crisis subsided, Britain took Russia's place as chief "protector" of Turkey. The Turkish Straits, by an 1841 treaty between the great powers, were now closed to warships in time of peace. Russia was caged. If war came, Palmerston was confident Russia would remain caged, for Turkey and Britain would be allies and Russia's Black Sea coasts would lie open to bombardment by the Royal Navy.

In Europe itself, the chief importance of the 1839–40 crisis was as a warning for the future. Germany had reacted in kind to France hostility. Nationalist sentiment reached heights not touched at Hambach in 1832. Anti-French songs celebrating "the free German Rhine" enjoyed a fierce popularity. The marvelous Habsburg anthem of the great composer Haydn received new German-national words: "Germany, Germany, before everything, before everything in the world." The lack of moderation of *Deutschland über Alles* was symptomatic. Also symptomatic was Prussia's role in the crisis. As Germany's bulwark on the Rhine against France, the Prussian power-state gained a new prestige with German nationalists.

THE END OF REVOLUTION IN WESTERN EUROPE, 1848–50

Fear of revolution, the chief restraint on the great powers after 1815, still held German nationalism in check. Before the way was clear for attempts to redraw the borders established at Vienna, Europe had to pass in 1848–49 through a third and culminating round of the revolutions that had shaken it since 1815. These new upheavals combined features of 1789, 1820, and 1830.

The underlying conditions that made revolution possible in 1848 were similar to those of 1789 and 1830. Mainly agrarian societies with rapidly expanding populations and slowly increasing productivity faced a food crisis. The population of most European states had risen by 30 to 40 percent in the thirty years from 1815 to 1845. Urban workers spent between 60 and 70 percent of their wages on food. And in the previous fifty years, the working classes had come to depend disproportionately on one crop, an innovation from the Americas—the potato.

When a fungus rotted potato crops and grain blights struck most of Europe in 1845–47, the result was unrest from Ireland to Poland. Agricultural collapse, as in 1788–89, also generated a downturn in commerce and industry; food prices and unemployment rose together in the cities, with grim consequences. Grain prices peaked in early 1847 and then declined, but the business slump and unemployment continued (see Figure 26-1). And this temporary crisis sharpened the impact of a deeper structural change: by 1848 the introduction of machinery had begun to impoverish or drive from business many of the artisans who formed the majority of the population of Europe's cities. These conditions, in combination with the political myth of the Great Revolution of 1789, produced a chain reaction in the spring of 1848: western and central Europe's last 1789-style revolutions from below.

But 1848 was not 1789. Four essential differences made the Europe-wide movement of 1848–49 wider but far shallower than 1789. First, the example of the Terror of 1792–94 deterred the moderate liberals who led most of the revolutions from pushing too hard against the old order. A seasoned observer and participant in the events (Alexis de Tocqueville, whose *Democracy in America* is among the two or three greatest nineteenth-century works on politics) put it well: "We sought . . . to warm ourselves with the passions of our fathers, without quite managing it; we imitated their gestures and poses as we had seen them on the stage, since we could not imitate their enthusiasm or feel their rage."

Second, this absence of passionate leadership from above found a counterpart below, at least in the countryside. The

FIGURE 26.1   France, 1848: Economic Forces and Revolution

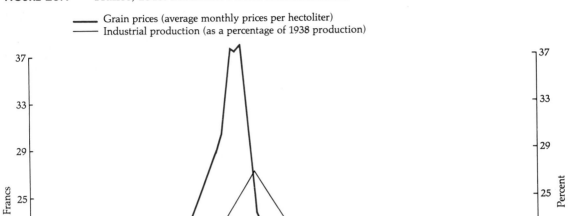

From Maurice Aqulhon, 1848 ou l'apprentissage de la République *(Paris: Editions du Seuil, 1973), pp. 100–01.*

peasants of central Europe sacked a few manor houses and attacked Jewish moneylenders. But the old order in the countryside did not collapse as it had in France in the Great Fear of 1789. The ingredient that had helped convert noble and urban revolt into the destruction of the old order was largely absent in 1848.

In France the peasants had profited from 1789 and were now indifferent or hostile to the revolutionaries in Paris. In Germany and Austria, both royal bureaucrats and liberals moved swiftly to bribe the peasants into passivity. Officials and parliamentarians rather than revolutionaries abolished most of the remaining peasant obligations to landowners. In Austrian Poland, in one of the earliest incidents in the wave of unrest that preceded 1848, the authorities even crushed a nationalist rising by inciting non-Polish peasants to massacre their Polish landlords.

The revolutions of 1848 were thus essentially urban, except where, as in Hungary, the rural upper classes helped lead a national insurrection. And the revolutions came mainly from two groups: the intellectuals and the artisans. The intellectuals often hated the old regime for its failure, as they saw it, to recognize their talents. Hunger or fear of hunger moved the artisans. The intellectuals demanded political or national rights; the artisans economic ones. The intellectuals for the most part called for free competition, for industry, for "progress." The artisans aspired to return to the cozy world of guild restrictions, or, at a minimum, to a job guaranteed by the state. The intellectuals feared "the mob." The artisans in turn soon recognized how little the intellectuals offered them. This mutual hostility of the two main revolutionary forces (forces that had been briefly allied in 1793–94 under Robespierre) was the third major reason for the collapse of the 1848 revolutions.

The fourth and most important difference between 1848–49 and 1789–94 was the absence of war, which had spread the revolution of 1789 across Europe while requiring and justifying radicalization at home. In 1848 the moderate liberals riding the wave of Parisian radicalism soon showed unexpected caution. The new French foreign minister, the poet Alphonse de Lamartine, took a sober line in the face of Parisian radical demands for yet another crusade of peoples against kings: "We love Poland, we love Italy, we love all oppressed peoples, but we love France above all else. . . ." France's middle classes and peasantry, the beneficiaries of 1789, had lost all desire to export revolution. France once again became a republic, but continued to support the international status quo. Further east, German radicals and even moderate liberals yearned for a great war—but the Prussian monarchy refused to oblige. And without a great revolutionary war to throw central and eastern Europe into the melting pot, the old order was bound to recover.

The Vienna crowd mounts the barricades, March 1848.

1848–49: From Outbreak to Collapse

The year of revolutions opened with a Sicilian uprising against the Bourbons of Naples: an antitax revolt, mixed with brigandage and Sicilian separatism. But it was the overthrow of the king of the French, Louis Philippe of Orléans, on February 22–24, 1848, that roused Europe. The liberal opponents of Louis Philippe staged banquets featuring speeches in favor of wider voting rights. When the government banned further banquets, the result was the now-customary explosion of violence in Paris. After fighting that produced fewer than 400 dead, Louis Philippe fled for London. Lamartine and other moderate republicans proclaimed the second French republic.

News traveled rapidly. On March 13, crowd violence in Vienna led to panic at the Habsburg court, which proceeded to dismiss Metternich. The symbol of the reactionary Holy Alliance departed ignominiously for exile—in liberal London. Metternich's replacement by a cabinet of indecisive bureaucrats was the signal for further revolutionary outbreaks. The city of Milan, in the first mass example of Italian nationalism, revolted against Austria. In five days of bitter fighting in March, the Milanese, armed with a few muskets and with pikes from La Scala opera house, harried the Austrian garrison. Field Marshal Joseph Radetzky, veteran of the wars against Napoleon, withdrew in defeat. The Hungarians, the principal subject nation of the Habsburgs after the Germans, demanded and received the right to domestic self-government. To the north, news of Metternich's fall emboldened street demonstrators in Berlin and other German cities. In Berlin, after his troops fired on the crowd on March 18, the eccentric King Frederick William IV panicked and virtually surrendered. Military Prussia received a ministry of moderate liberals and a parliament.

The revolution seemed to have swept all before it. Only the two great powers at the opposite ends of Europe and of the scale of political, social, and economic development were exempt: Britain and

Russia. In Russia only the nobility was as yet politically conscious. In Britain the Chartist League's agitation for universal manhood suffrage never passed beyond the stage of peaceful mass meetings.

But even in Paris, Vienna, and Berlin appearances were deceptive, for the armies remained intact. France unexpectedly took the lead in reining in the revolution. In April 1848 the new republic held the first free elections under universal manhood suffrage of any major European power. The results were a stinging repudiation of revolutionary Paris. Peasants and provincial middle class voted for moderates and monarchists.

The new national assembly, faithfully representing the views of the majority of the electorate, soon began to dismantle the most striking gain the Paris crowd had achieved in the February revolution: the "national workshops" that gave work to the unemployed at government expense. The unemployed and the revolutionary artisans of Paris reacted. Without political leadership, without coordination, but with the tenacity of despair, they rose on June 22. The army and the paramilitary National Guard, under Eugène Cavaignac, a republican general who had learned his trade in colonial Algeria, fought back pitilessly. Perhaps 5,000 died in the Paris "June Days" of 1848; at least 3,000 were insurgents shot after resistance had ceased.

The republic, with its moderate republican and monarchist assembly, then faced the need to find a monarch. Bourbons and Orléans had in turn proved themselves unsuitable. As in 1799, a Bonaparte stepped in to fill the vacuum. In December 1848 the votes of moderate republicans and of France's conservative peasantry elected the eccentric Louis Napoleon Bonaparte—nephew of the great Napoleon and leader of failed conspiracies against the July Monarchy—to the presidency of the republic. Revolutionary universal suffrage had proved remarkably conservative in practice.

In central Europe as well, the revolutionary wave crested and began to recede in the summer of 1848. Prince Alfred Windischgrätz, commander of the Habsburg forces in the Czech lands, crushed a quasi-insurrection in Prague in mid-June and dispersed the Slav Congress that had met to call for Czech rights. A man "equally devoid of fear or pity," he hit upon the simple expedient of withdrawing his troops from the rebellious city and bombarding it into submission with artillery.

In Italy, the Habsburgs also recovered rapidly. Charles Albert of Piedmont-Sardinia followed up the victorious insurrection of the Milanese by declaring war on Austria. Italy, he proclaimed grandly, would "do it itself": Piedmont alone would defeat Austria and seize north Italy. But his poorly led army ran afoul of the canny Radetzky at the battle of Custoza in July. Charles Albert's attempt to reverse that verdict the next spring led to a second defeat at Novara and his own abdication. His principal legacy was the constitution he had grudgingly granted in March 1848. Further south, the visionary Mazzini and the greatest soldier of Italy's wars of independence, Giuseppe Garibaldi, led an epic defense of a Roman republic proclaimed by radical democrats in February 1849. French troops that Louis Napoleon sent—in a bid for French Catholic support—ultimately prevailed.

Victory at Prague and Custoza emboldened the Habsburg court. The addled young emperor Ferdinand ultimately abdicated in favor of his military-minded nephew Francis Joseph. Revolutionary Vienna received the Windischgrätz treatment, complete with executions of democrats. By late fall 1848 only Hungary, against which the Habsburgs had mobilized smaller nationalities such as the Croats, still asserted autonomy. In April 1849, after victories over invading Habsburg armies, Hungary's most radical leader, the fiery Lajos Kossuth, proclaimed Hungarian independence within "historic" borders that included large numbers of Slavs and Rumanians. Revolutionary greater Hungary proved more than a match for the Habsburgs and their Croat and Rumanian allies. But Russia, fearing that Austria's collapse would mean revolution throughout central Europe and confident by now that France would not launch a war over Poland, intervened massively. By August 1849 Russian troops

The adventurer: Napoleon III.

Nationalities of the Habsburg Empire

had bloodily restored Hungary to Habsburg control.

Far to the north, the German revolution also collapsed. In the spring of 1848 leading liberals such as Max von Gagern of Hesse-Darmstadt urged on Frederick William IV of Prussia a revolutionary German-nationalist war against Russia. Restoring Poland was to be the pretext, German unity and German domination of central Europe the real goal. But Frederick William, indecisive in many things, was firm about monarchical solidarity. He angrily rejected German liberalism's war: "By God, never, never shall I draw the sword against Russia."

The movement of German intellectuals that culminated in an all-German Parliament at Frankfurt in May 1848 therefore faced an insoluble dilemma. The war that nationalists yearned for to achieve unity required the cooperation of the very dynasties and princely armies that stood in the way of unity. The Frankfurt Parliament of lawyers and professors did succeed in launching a brief war against Denmark in April 1848, after the disputed but overwhelmingly German-speaking border duchies of Schleswig and Holstein had revolted against Denmark. But the Prussian troops who did most of the fighting stopped on Frederick William IV's orders when the king found he faced British, French, and above all Russian disapproval.

Inside Prussia itself the army and bureaucracy took heart after Windischgrätz's reduction of Vienna. Frederick William appointed a general as prime minister in November 1848. Then he closed parliament and imposed a conservative constitution to match his new government. In spring 1849 Prussian troops moved south to crush short-lived democratic republics in Saxony, the Bavarian Palatinate, and Baden. The democrats who had overthrown the grand duke of Baden fought with particular tenacity against a Prussian army under Frederick William IV's brother and eventual successor William. William in turn had a number of captured revolutionary leaders shot.

The end of revolution did not immediately restore stability to Germany. Frederick William had refused the crown of a united Germany that the discredited Frankfurt Parliament had offered him in April 1849. But his disdain for this "crown smelling of the gutter" did not prevent him from aspiring to a similar offer from his fellow princes. Embarrassment in Hungary might yet persuade Vienna to accept Prussian domination of Germany. By summer 1849 Frederick William had recruited most of the German princes for his "Prussian Union." Then Austria moved to reconstitute the German Confederation of 1815. Both powers appealed to Russia. In November 1850 a standoff nearly led to war when Austria and the Confederation challenged Prussia's control of the vital military roads across Hesse that linked the Prussian Rhineland to Berlin. Austrian and Prussian patrols traded shots for the first time since 1778. Prussia mobilized. Russia, seeking to restore the pre-1848 status quo and unenthusiastic about the emergence of a powerful united Germany, backed Austria. Some Prussian generals were confident of victory, but Frederick William was no more willing to fight Russia than he had been in 1848. By the treaty of Olmütz (November 1850), Prussia agreed to dismantle the Prussian Union and to demobilize. After long negotiation, Berlin also consented to restore the German Confederation of 1815. That agreement, which Prussian chauvinists denounced as the "humiliation of Olmütz," put off the struggle for mastery in central Europe for a generation.

From Revolution to Nationalism: The Consequences of 1848

The failure of revolution in 1848 meant the end of an era dominated by the example of 1789. The old pattern of repeated agricultural crises, urban and rural revolt, middle-class radical leadership, and government ineptitude had shown its limitation—at least in the absence of a continent-wide war. Railroads soon brought cheap food to urban markets and industrialization supplied work for impoverished and displaced former artisans. Middle-class intellectuals feared the masses they claimed to lead more than the old order they hoped to overthrow. And after the first shocks of March 1848, governments had swiftly recovered their nerve. The brilliant generalship of Radetzky and the successful brutality of Cavaignac, Windischgrätz, and Prince William of Prussia showed that the triumph of "the Revolution" was far from inevitable. Governments even began to imitate Britain in co-opting the lower orders.

The freedom from fear of revolution that Europe's statesmen now enjoyed liberated them from some pre-1848 restraints on the vigorous pursuit of power in the international arena. The year 1848 also changed the definition of those interests by revealing the full power of the revolution's child, nationalism. From the Turkish Balkans to Schleswig-Holstein, awakened nationalities clamored for self-determination. History and reason, their nationalist intellectuals claimed, gave them "historic rights."

Under the old dynastic order, ethnicity and language had only sometimes been a matter of life or death. Now they became the most powerful source of bloodshed in Europe. For each nationality defined "history" and "reason" according to its own convenience. And the ethnically mixed settlement pattern of central Europe ensured that right conflicted with right. The only remedy, as Kossuth had explained to the Serbs in 1849, was naked force: "The sword shall decide between us." That sword, the sword of nationalism, was to cleave first Europe and then the world.

In 1848—this too was a portent for the future—the most powerful of European nationalisms showed its cards. The Frankfurt Parliament was short on deeds and long on talk, but it had one great merit. Its discussions registered faithfully in cold print the aims of the German national movement. The Parliament debated the claims of the Poles in Posen, the activities of the Slav Congress in Prague, the rights of the Danes in Schleswig. Voices of moderation stood little chance in the face of calls for "healthy national egotism," of ex-

hortations to resist "the attempts of the puny little nationalities to set up housekeeping in our midst, and like parasites to destroy our own existence," and of proclamations that Germany's final mission was to wrest world mastery from Britain. The unanswered long-term question was whether Europe could tolerate such a Germany.

THE MAKING OF ITALY AND GERMANY, 1851–71

In the aftermath of the year of revolutions, the Holy Alliance alignment that had maintained stability since 1815 appeared restored. Russia had underwritten Austria's survival and had shepherded Frederick William IV back into the conservative fold. Appearances were deceptive: the stability of the Metternich era did not return.

The Concert of Europe Destroyed: The Crimean War

The chief agent of upheaval, for the last time in Europe's modern history, was France—or rather a Bonaparte. Louis Napoleon, political speculator and gangleader of the conspirators who had helped him to power, had none of the genius of his uncle and namesake, Napoleon I. What he did have was a mystical belief, derived from a naive reading of his uncle's cynical propaganda, in national self-determination. Even before taking power, he had conceived vague schemes for the reorganization of Europe. A coup d'état—in imitation of his uncle—made him First Consul in December 1851; a year later he proclaimed himself Napoleon III, Emperor of the French. Then he began his search for a way to tear up the 1814–15 settlement and redraw Europe's borders.

Russia's backing for Austria and for the status quo barred the way in central Europe and Italy. The Eastern Question therefore seemed to offer the best opening. A struggle over the Ottoman Empire might force Russia to abandon its role as protector of Austria, while giving Napoleon III the military prestige he needed to consolidate his rule at home. In 1851–52 he challenged Russian claims to a protec-

---

German Nationalism Speaks: 1848
Voices from the Frankfurt Parliament

To want to resurrect Poland merely because its downfall fills us with justified regret, I call moronic sentimentality. . . . Our right is none other than the right of the stronger, the right of conquest. . . . The German conquests in Poland were a necessity of nature. The law of history is not the same as that in the law books. History knows only the laws of nature, one of which tells us that a people does not gain the right to political independence through mere existence, but only through having the power to assert itself as a state among other states.

Wilhelm Jordan (Berlin), a member of the center-left, in the debate on Posen, July 25, 1848.

. . . but it is our aim to found a giant empire [Reich] of 70 million, and if possible of 80 or 100 million, and plant the standard of Arminius [a famous Germanic chieftain who had smashed three Roman legions in A.D. 9] in that Reich, to stand there armed against east and west, against the Slavic and Latin peoples, to wrest mastery of the seas from the English, and to become the most powerful nation [Volk] on this earth—*that* is Germany's future! With that prospect in view, petty debates over the drafting of our constitution, all petty debates, [must] retreat into the background. . . .

Count Friedrich Deym, a liberal Austrian noble, in the debate of October 27, 1848.

Stenographischer Bericht über die Verhandlungen der deutschen constituirenden Nationalversammlung zu Frankfurt am Main *(Leipzig: Teubner, 1848–49), Vol. 2, pp. 1144–46; Vol. 4, p. 2882 (translation by M. Knox).*

A CONSULTATION ABOUT THE STATE OF TURKEY.

A Consultation about the State of Turkey, a mid-nineteenth-century cartoon. The "Sick Man of Europe" (Turkey) is threatened by Death (Russia), while the physicians (France and England) hold their consultation.

torate over the Christian holy sites in the Ottoman Empire, which included Palestine. That gambit triggered a diplomatic chain reaction—and a war that divided the great powers and left the road open, as Napoleon III had hoped, to further adventure.

Russia responded by putting pressure of its own on Turkey. That provoked France and Britain to send their fleets to Constantinople, and that in turn encouraged the Turks to declare war on Russia in October 1853. A crushing Russian victory over the Turkish navy—the so-called "Sinope massacre"—then brought into play a new factor in international politics: British public opinion. Liberal abhorrence of Russia—acute since its bloody intervention in Hungary in 1849—and the fiery Palmerston propelled Britain into a war to destroy for good Russia's power to threaten Turkey. Napoleon III also fought—to stir up trouble. Austria mobilized, but took only diplomatic steps against Russia. Austrian

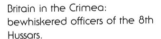
Britain in the Crimea: bewhiskered officers of the 8th Hussars.

The balance of power, by the French artist and caricaturist Honoré Daumier.

the right to have a Black Sea fleet, as Britain desired. But the war had other consequences London had neither bargained on nor greatly welcomed. Under Nicholas I's successor, Tsar Alexander II, Russia turned inward for a generation. Russian power no longer threatened Turkey. It also no longer upheld Austria. Indeed, Russia now sought revenge for the Austrian "ingratitude" that had repaid Russia's aid against Hungary in 1849 with a tilt toward the western powers in 1853–56.

France profited most from this breakdown of the conservative alignment. Napoleon III presided imperially over the 1856 Paris peace conference. Much to the disgust of the British, he was soon intriguing for a bargain with Russia that would help him to redraw the map of Europe. He was not alone.

The Making of Italy, 1858–60

In the last stages of the Crimean War, the "Italian Question" had reemerged from the limbo into which Radetzky's victories had thrust it in 1848–49. Charles Albert's successor, the fierce and erratic Victor Emmanuel II, had insisted on a war to restore the prestige tarnished by Piedmont's defeats at Custoza and Novara. His liberal prime minister, Count Camillo di Cavour, sent 15,000 troops to the Crimea as allies of Britain and France—and thus gained access to the Paris peace conference, at which he embarrassed the Austrians by criticizing their support of corrupt regimes in the Papal States and Bourbon Naples.

Dictatorial in temperament but an admirer of the British Parliament, Cavour was an unparalleled master of political improvisation, a "Piedmontese Machiavelli." His chief weakness was his tendency, striking even in the age of the deceitful and vacillating Napoleon III, to flagrant untruths that diminished his credibility: "If we did for ourselves what we are doing for Italy, we should be real scoundrels." His goal was to expand Piedmont, not to create an Italian nation-state. He also labored under severe constraints. National revolution, if encouraged too much, might yet turn into barbaric peasant revolt. And only north Italy appeared suitable for annexation to Piedmont. The South was a

fear of an all-out land war that it might lose, coupled with the neutrality of Prussia and the lesser German states, prevented a general European war.

Austrian and German passivity also meant that Britain and France could only strike Russia from the sea. In September 1854 the two allies therefore landed forces on the Crimean peninsula to attack Russia's principal Black Sea naval base, Sebastopol. Bitter Russian resistance and the immense effort of supplying large armies by sea made the expedition a predictable fiasco. Britain and France took Sebastopol only after a year of bloody fighting; industrial firepower was already beginning to make movement on the battlefield difficult. The Crimean War cost at least three quarters of a million dead, of whom 80 percent died of cholera, dysentery, or typhus.

The war's main consequence was disruption of the European state system, a disruption that ultimately permitted the wars that created Italian and German nation-states in 1859–60 and 1866–71. Russia indeed suffered a decisive check. It lost world centuries behind Lombardy and Piedmont; great landowners and gangs—*Mafia, 'Ndrangheta,* and *Camorra*—dominated a downtrodden peasantry under the distant overlordship of pope and Bourbons. Above all, Cavour faced the unbroken power of Austria. The lesson of 1848–49 was that Italy could *not* do it itself.

Not all Italians agreed. Mazzini held to his vision of an Italy created through spontaneous uprising from below by the—nonexistent—nationalist masses. An Italian National Society came into being in 1857 with a more practical goal: support for a renewed Piedmontese bid for expansion. Garibaldi, revealed in 1848–49 as a great military talent, waited for his chance. The creation of an Italian state was ultimately the product both of a "royal war" of Cavour, king, and Napoleon III, and of pressure from below from Mazzini's ideas and Garibaldi's freebooters.

Initially everything depended on Napoleon III. In January 1858 the explosion of an Italian revolutionary's bomb outside the Paris Opera reminded Napoleon that he had yet to do "something for Italy." He soon approached Cavour. The two met in secret at Plombières near the Piedmontese border in July 1858 and agreed on a program. A French-Piedmontese war against Austria would seize Lombardy, Venetia, Parma, and Modena for Piedmont. In return for committing 200,000 troops, Napoleon would receive Savoy, an Italian satellite state, and the domestic prestige of a Napoleonic Italian campaign. The pope would lose territory but become head of an Italian confederation of states. Napoleon III gave to Cavour the task of provoking Austria into war without himself appearing the aggressor, and of providing 100,000 troops.

To present this French-Piedmontese war of conquest to international opinion as justified self-defense required all of Cavour's genius. At the end, in April 1859, Austrian recklessness saved him. Vienna's bullying ultimatum demanding that Piedmont demobilize destroyed what little was left of Austria's international backing. England, despite misgivings about Napoleon III, stood aside; the aftermath of the 1857 Indian mutiny (see pp. 689–90) had absorbed most of Britain's limited land power. Russia watched Austria's humiliation with satisfaction. Only Prussia, Austria's other rival, offered aid. But its price was the reversal of Olmütz: Prussian supremacy in north Germany.

The war itself was swift, for Napoleon III and Cavour had isolated their opponent. The Piedmontese army scraped together only 50,000 men instead of the 100,000 Cavour had promised, but this time it faced no Radetzky. Piedmont fought a creditable holding action until the French arrived, partly by rail. In two bloody battles of June 1859 at Magenta and Solferino, the French drove the Austrians back with furious charges.

Then Napoleon III, appalled at a carnage for which he lacked his uncle's strong stomach, angry at the meagerness of his allies' contribution, disquieted by signs that Cavour coveted central as well as north Italy, and unnerved by a Prussian

The Making of Italy

The makers of Italy: Count Camillo di Cavour (*top*) and Giuseppe Garibaldi (*bottom*).

threat on the Rhine, called a halt. By the July 1859 armistice of Villafranca with Emperor Francis Joseph, Napoleon III abandoned Cavour. Piedmont would receive only Lombardy. Cavour, when he heard that Victor Emmanuel II had agreed without consulting him, resigned in fury. He seemed to have lost.

But Cavour had proved his indispensability, and Victor Emmanuel II recalled him in January 1860. Cavour soon engineered the annexation of Tuscany, Romagna, Parma, and Modena to enlarged Piedmont. Rigged plebiscites, a favorite Napoleonic device, seemingly confirmed the unanimity of popular sentiment for Piedmontese annexation. Napoleon III, outwitted in his attempt to confine Piedmont to the north Italian plain, now demanded his price: Savoy, which was French-speaking, and the city of Nice, which was not. Cavour agreed, to the fury of Piedmontese public opinion. Garibaldi bitterly resented the loss of Nice, his home town, but he soon had his revenge. Despite Cavour's halfhearted attempts to stop them, Garibaldi and a volunteer "thousand" left Genoa for Sicily in early May 1860. Against Cavour's expectations and hopes, Garibaldi's ill-equipped troops routed the Bourbon army, roused the Sicilian peasantry to revolt, crossed to the mainland, and took Naples.

The epic campaign of Garibaldi's "Thousand" made Italy. To derail the social revolutionary elements of Garibaldi's program and to rescue the prestige of Piedmont, Cavour and Victor Emmanuel II had to act. The Piedmontese army invaded the Papal States and moved on Naples. Garibaldi, a monarchist at heart, unlike the fiercely republican Mazzini, yielded his conquests to the new Kingdom of Italy. He received little thanks from Cavour or from the Piedmontese army.

Italy was complete except for Venetia, which the new state received in 1866, Rome, which it took in 1870, and Trento and Trieste, which it did not conquer until 1918. As a colleague and rival of Cavour remarked, the process of "making Italians" remained. Cavour's representatives in the South soon made themselves more hated than the Bourbons. The brutal imposition of Piedmont's French-style prefects, military conscription, and high taxes triggered a guerrilla war in the South that lasted more than five years and cost more dead than the wars of 1848–49 and 1859–60. Italy's *Risorgimento,* its "resurgence" and political unification, had come so swiftly and had joined areas so different in culture and traditions that "making Italians" took generations. Cavour, perhaps fortunately for his reputation, died of malaria and inept doctors in mid-1861. Time alone would tell if the foundations of the Italian nation-state that he and Garibaldi had created were sound.

The Struggle for Mastery in Germany: Prussia against Austria, 1862–66

Austria's international isolation had made a united Italy possible. That same isolation was the prerequisite for a far greater revolution in the state system than the birth of Italy, "least of the great powers." That revolution was the creation of a Prusso-German nation-state.

The Prussian military monarchy at first seemed an unlikely ally for the German nationalism it had rejected in 1848. But German unity, if it came at all, clearly had to come through one of the two German great powers, Prussia and Austria. And by the early 1860s Prussia possessed advantages Austria could not match. First, except for its Polish provinces, it was wholly German. Second, its Ruhr Valley coal and iron and its leadership since the 1830s of a German Customs Union, the *Zollverein,* had already made it the economic nucleus of any conceivable German nation-state. Third, its role as military bulwark against France and if need be Russia gave even its dynastic military establishment a certain national aura. Fourth, that military establishment soon proved that it had learned from Jena and Auerstädt. In its technique if not in its politics, the Prussian army was by 1860 the most innovative armed force in the world. Finally, after September 1862 Prussia had a leader as indispensable as Cavour—Otto von Bismarck.

Bismarck was a Pomeranian Junker by birth ("I am a Junker, and I mean to profit by it"). But his deep understanding of historical forces and political tactics far surpassed the blinkered outlook of his caste. He combined apparently genuine Pietist religious convictions with a total absence of political scruple. But like Cavour and unlike their successors in both countries, Bismarck recognized limits. Politics was "the art of the possible." Statesmen could exploit great historical forces but could not stand against them: "the stream carries you, but cannot be ruled" ran his favorite Latin motto. Bismarck's political technique—like that of the great Napoleon in warfare—was to aim at a range of alternative goals and to be prepared to achieve them by a variety of means, always leaving for himself a fallback position in the event of failure. When Bismarck gambled on war, it was only after exploring and ruling out less risky alternatives and after reducing incalculable dangers as far as possible. And once war had achieved his goals, he became as fierce a defender of the new status quo as he had been an opponent of the old.

Bismarck, like Cavour, did not set out to found a nation-state. His early career as fiery opponent of liberalism and nationalism in the Prussian Chamber in 1848 had branded him, in words that Frederick William IV had perhaps meant as a compliment, as a "red reactionary, smells of blood." But Bismarck's appointment as Prussian ambassador to the German Confederation in 1851 led to a slow change in his outlook. He came to recognize two things: that Austria's claim to leadership of the Confederation was incompatible with Prussia's dignity and security, and that Prussia's natural ally in the struggle for mastery in Germany was German nationalism. Monarchical solidarity abroad and unbending conservatism at home were contrary to Prussia's interests as a state: "Prussia's mission is to extend itself." Prussia must not tie its trim frigate to the "moth-eaten Austrian galleon." In 1859 he had urged Berlin to "let Austria get thoroughly bogged down in its war with France and then break out southwards with our entire army, taking our border posts in our knapsacks and planting them either on [the Swiss border] or wherever the Protestant religion ceases to predominate. . . ."

Berlin ignored that shocking advice. What catapulted Bismarck into power as prime minister and foreign minister in September 1862 was not his ruthless approach to foreign affairs. It was rather the deepening deadlock between the Prussian lower house and the new king, William I, who had succeeded his incapacitated brother Frederick William IV as regent in 1858 and as king in 1861. The military-minded new king sought to more than double the strength of the army's line units to half a million men and to reduce the role of the reserves, which had middle-class officers. This reorganization and the accompanying increase of compulsory military service from two years to three would drastically increase the weight of the army within Prussian society. It would also dramatically increase Prussia's external striking power. But the liberal majority in the Prussian Chamber repeatedly blocked funding of these plans. William, determined to have his way on grounds both of military efficiency and of monarchical authority, mournfully contemplated the English precedent, the struggle between Crown and Parliament in the 1640s. In this impasse the king turned to Bismarck as the one man steadfast enough to dominate the Chamber and see the king's will done.

Bismarck immediately sought to defuse the constitutional conflict by playing the card of German nationalism. In a speech that mixed insults with tempta-

"Mad Junker" and maker of Prussia-Germany: Otto von Bismarck.

Bismarck Takes Office: 1862
"Iron and Blood"

Germany looks not to Prussia's liberalism, but to its power; Bavaria, Württemberg, and Baden may indulge in liberalism, but Prussia's role is not for them. Prussia must concentrate its power and hold it concentrated for the favorable moment that we have already several times missed. Prussia's borders as drawn in the Vienna treaties do not favor a healthy state existence; the great questions of our time are not decided through speeches and majority votes—that was the great error of 1848 and 1849—but through iron and blood.

Bismarck, to the Prussian Chamber's budget committee, September 30, 1862.

From Bismarck: Die gesammelten Werke *(Berlin: Otto Stollberg Verlag, 1928), Vol. 10, p. 140 (translation by M. Knox).*

The new model Prussian army, 1861.

tions, he announced that "iron and blood" would settle the German question. The liberals professed to be shocked. Bismarck's first bid for liberal cooperation had failed, although some liberals had long called for "a great genius or mighty tyrant . . . capable of decisive action."

The "iron and blood" speech also appalled the king. But Bismarck put the issue to him in military terms: he could fight for his throne or tamely surrender. The fight involved muzzling the press, disciplining liberal sympathizers in the bureaucracy, and spending money that the Chamber had not appropriated on an army reorganization that it opposed. To the Chamber Bismarck impudently proclaimed his "loophole theory" of the constitution: when king and parliament disagreed, the king's latent powers entitled him to act for the general welfare. The conflict deepened. New elections returned the latest in a series of ever-larger liberal majorities. Thanks to the "three-class" Prussian election law, which weighted votes by wealth, those majorities represented only middle-class opinion. But Bismarck's fellow Junkers would not yet let him play the masses against the liberals.

Foreign policy ultimately offered a way around this stalemate, as Bismarck had hoped. A new Polish revolt, even more tragic than that of 1830, convulsed Russian Poland in 1863. Russian repression of the Poles alienated Napoleon III, whose alignment with Russia had underwritten the Italian war. Now *each* of the European great powers was isolated from the others—except Prussia, which maintained its "line to St. Petersburg." In this open situation, Bismarck soon found a cause that would allow him to undermine the status quo while claiming conservative intentions acceptable to Russia and Austria. In 1863 the Danish monarchy moved to incorporate Schleswig, with its minority of Danes and majority of Germans, into Denmark. That step was a flagrant breach of the 1852 Treaty of London that had ended the German-Danish fighting in 1848–49 and had confirmed the continued membership of the duchies of Schleswig and Holstein in the German Confederation. In January 1864 Bismarck therefore secured an alliance with Vienna to restore

the status quo, by force if need be. He secretly aimed at annexing the duchies to Prussia as the first step toward Prussia's long-sought domination of north Germany.

The Danish war of 1864 was swift and decisive, and British protests to Berlin and Vienna were halfhearted. Britain had tilted too close to the Confederacy in the U.S. Civil War (described in Chapter 27). By 1864, it found itself facing the eventual prospect of a million battle-hardened Union veterans on Canada's indefensible borders. It had no troops to spare to rescue Denmark. When the Danes foolishly rejected Bismarck's offer of a compromise, the Prussians stormed the key Danish position at Düppel in April 1864. In August a Prussian amphibious threat to Copenhagen forced the Danes to surrender both Schleswig and Holstein to Prussia and Austria.

That triumph demonstrated the power of the newly reorganized Prussian army and lessened pressure on Bismarck at home. Influential liberal publications soon came around to the view that Prussian state interest and German nationalism ran parallel: Prussia should annex the two duchies. Bismarck himself settled for a policy of gradual encroachment on his Austrian partner. He would "try all roads, the most dangerous road, last." If Austria would concede Schleswig and Holstein and the mastery of north Germany to Prussia, Prussia would perhaps underwrite Austria's survival. If Austria proved obstinate, force would decide.

The Austrians claimed to be shocked at Bismarck's suggestions of Prussian annexation of their joint property, the duchies. Vienna had joined Bismarck's Danish war in hopes of a conservative partnership to cement the status quo in central Europe. Too late it discovered that its partner had other ideas. But Bismarck was not ready for a new war in 1865, although the chief of the general staff, Helmuth von Moltke, was confident. Prussian and Austrian leaders met at Bad Gastein in August 1865 and "papered over the cracks." Prussia would administer Schleswig, Austria Holstein, and the partners would reject the claims to the Duchies of the German-national candidate, the Duke of Augustenburg.

The Gastein agreement lasted only a few months. Vienna was dimly aware that it could preserve its position in the German Confederation only with the support of the lesser states. It therefore broke the Gastein agreement and courted Augustenburg, the candidate of those states and of non-Prussian liberal opinion. Bismarck for his part sounded out Napoleon III in October 1865; the Emperor did not object to Prussian expansion. He presumably expected a long and indecisive Austro-Prussian war that would give France opportunities to intervene and demand its price. By February 1866 Bismarck was sure of his course. He put Austria's violations of the Gastein agreement to a Prussian crown council. William I, convinced of Austrian disloyalty, agreed that Prussia must prepare for war. The issue was simple: who was to be master in Germany.

Yet Bismarck still had to secure allies, and overcome William I's lingering scruples. Italy was happy to sign a three-month offensive alliance in April, thus performing the essential function of tying down large Austrian forces in Venetia. Bismarck, the conservative statesman, also conspired with Hungarian revolutionaries, justifying himself with a favorite quotation from Vergil: "If I cannot prevail on heaven, I shall mobilize hell." And he again appealed to German nationalism. Prussia promised after victory a German parliament elected under universal manhood suffrage.

Securing allies was easy compared to the frustrations of managing the king's conscience: "I have brought the horse to the ditch; he must jump!" Then, as in 1859, Austria rescued its enemies with an ill-timed gesture that appeared provocative. Vienna's slow and cumbersome mobilization system meant that it could not wait if war seemed inevitable. And Austrian mobilization, along with warnings from conservative aides against a "second Olmütz," finally induced William I to jump. On June 7, 1866, Prussian troops attacked the Austrians in Holstein and began to concentrate on the borders of Bohemia.

The "Seven Weeks' War" was a startling demonstration of Prussia's efficiency and might. Moltke used telegraph and railroad, proven in the U.S. Civil War (see pp. 699–702), effectively for the first time in a European conflict. Three Prussian armies detrained on the Bohemian border and converged with unexpected speed on the Austrian forces east of Prague. On July 3, 1866, two of the Prussian armies attacked the Austrian positions at Königgrätz (Sadowa). The firepower of Prussia's Dreyse breechloading rifle shocked the Austrians: it fired five rounds a minute to the Austrian muzzle-loader's one and a half. And unlike troops using muzzle-loaders, the Prussians could reload and fire while lying down. The Austrians held with counterattacks and heavy artillery fire. Then, in mid-afternoon, the third Prussian army, under Crown Prince Frederick, arrived on the Austrian flank and decided the fate of Germany. The Austrians lost 25,000 dead and wounded and 20,000 prisoners.

Bismarck stepped in to check the enthusiasm of king and generals for a push on Vienna. Further fighting would only provoke French intervention, without serving any useful purpose. Bismarck insisted that Protestant Prussia could not

Bismarck Demands War   February 1866

The Minister President spoke . . . [to the Prussian crown council] in the following terms: Prussia is the only workable political unit that has emerged from the ruins of the old German *Reich* [the Holy Roman Empire], and that is why Prussia had been called to lead Germany. Austria in its envy has always resisted the natural and entirely justified efforts of Prussia toward that goal; it has refused to concede to Prussia the leadership of Germany that it is incapable of exercising itself. . . . Austria has granted Prussia neither the influence due it in Germany, nor the secure position in the [Schleswig-Holstein] duchies necessary to both Prussia and Germany, nor the fruits of [Prussia's] victories. . . . It would be a humiliation, if Prussia now withdrew. Any such humiliation must be avoided at all costs. But in that case a break with Austria is probable. We must therefore discuss and decide the question of whether Prussia should pull back in fright from this obstacle—a break and possible war with Austria. . . . The whole historic development of German affairs and the hostile attitude of Austria drive us toward war. It would be an error to seek to avoid it now. . . .

From the Prussian crown council minutes, February 28, 1866, in Die auswärtige Politik Preussens 1858–1871 *(Berlin: G. Stalling, 1939), Vol. 6, pp. 611ff (translation by M. Knox).*

successfully absorb the Catholic German populations that the total destruction of the Habsburg Empire would give it. The king and Moltke grudgingly gave in. By the treaties of Nikolsburg and Prague (July–August 1866) Austria renounced any role in north Germany, accepted Prussia's absorption of Schleswig-Holstein, Hanover, Hesse-Cassel, and Frankfurt, and agreed to the dissolution of the German Confederation of 1815 and the creation in its place of a North German Confederation under Prussia. To avoid French intervention, Bismarck left nominal independence to defeated Baden, Württemberg, and Bavaria. But he fastened upon them military alliances that in wartime made their armies mere appendages of Prussia's.

Domestically, the war of 1866 ended the Prussian constitutional conflict. Elections, held on the day of Königgrätz, returned a conservative majority. Victory intoxicated the remaining liberal deputies; they gladly accepted Bismarck's promises that he would in future respect the Chamber's budget rights. With the liberals as allies, Bismarck now molded the North German Confederation, the pattern for the German nation-state. He personally supervised the drafting of the new constitution, which played off a universal male suffrage *Reichstag* or lower house against representatives of the princes in the upper house. Bismarck, as Prussian prime minister and foreign minister, and as chancellor of the new Confederation, held the balance. Prussia had conquered Germany, and Bismarck had conquered Prussia.

The Struggle for Mastery in Europe: Germany against France, 1867–71

Yet the North German Confederation was not the Germany that the German national movement dreamed of. Bismarck himself, while no nationalist, aimed from the beginning to draw the south German states into his greater Prussia. Unfortunately the economic attraction of the Prussian *Zollverein,* of a unified national market with uniform tariffs, weights, measures, and law codes, was not enough to overcome south German separatism. "Württemberg

wants to remain Württemberg as long as it has the power," said that state's chief minister—a sentiment heartily echoed in Bavaria and even Baden.

Bismarck therefore once more fell back on foreign policy to drive domestic affairs. Napoleon III offered the occasion. Disgruntled over his 1866 miscalculation, smarting over the 1867 defeat of his harebrained scheme for an empire in Mexico (see p. 694), and under increasing pressure from a liberal public opinion he had helped create by loosening his control of press and politics in the early 1860s, Napoleon III too sought a foreign victory. An initial public clash with Bismarck in early 1867 over a French plan to buy Luxemburg from its ruler, the king of Holland, ended in humiliation for Napoleon. Both France and Prussia came to consider war inevitable as soon as frantic French military reforms were complete.

War came in 1870. The candidacy of a junior member of the Prussian royal house for the vacant throne of Spain offered the occasion. Bismarck had pressed the plan in secret, as one more small diplomatic blow against France, but he could not have known from the beginning that it would lead to war. When the candidacy prematurely became public, the French ambassador visited William I at the summer watering place of Ems and impertinently demanded that Prussia renounce the candidacy "forever." William I, miffed, cut the interview short. When Bismarck received the foreign office telegram describing the interview, he asked Moltke if the army was ready. The chief of the general staff replied that the sooner war came, the greater Prussia's relative strength would be. Bismarck then edited the "Ems telegram" for release to the press. The edited version implied that William I had curtly refused the French demand and had ruled out further negotiation, thus handing France a major diplomatic humiliation.

In Paris, Napoleon III's ministers and supporters reacted as Bismarck had expected. Hysterical at the visible loss since 1866 of France's leading role in Europe, they erupted: "To Berlin!" France declared war on July 19, 1870, without allies. Austria had no stomach for a rematch with Prussia. Italy wisely chose to remain neu-

The Making of Germany

tral, despite the childlike enthusiasm of Victor Emmanuel II for war, any war. Russia's only thought was to free itself of the degrading Black Sea naval disarmament imposed after the Crimean War. Britain, without a mass army or a policy, watched impotently.

Moltke's mobilization timetables once again delivered three superlatively equipped Prussian and south German armies, now totalling 380,000 men, to their railheads. The French muddled about in tragic disorder. They now had a better breechloading rifle than the Germans, the Chassepot, and a secret weapon, the *mitrailleuse*, a primitive machine gun. But the cast-steel artillery of Krupp outclassed anything the French could field, and French logistics were chaotic.

The Germans drove across the border and pushed the French back in a series of punishing battles. At Gravelotte-St. Privat, on August 18, the elite Prussian Guard corps attacked uphill across open ground. French firepower killed or wounded 8,000 Prussians, most of them in the space of twenty minutes. Fortunately for the Germans, the ineptly led French then fell back on the fortified city of Metz. Leaving a force to screen the city, the German armies pressed on to squash Napoleon III's reserve army against the Belgian border. Desperate breakout attempts by French cavalry failed in a hail of Prussian rifle fire. The French charges were magnificent, but no longer a serious form of war. The armies of Europe were beginning to discover that industrial firepower killed. On

September 2, 1870, Napoleon III surrendered his army at Sedan.

Unlike Königgrätz in 1866, Sedan did not end the war. This last of Bismarck's wars was no "cabinet war" but rather the first of three Franco-German national wars that tore Europe apart and destroyed its world position. Paris, besieged, resisted under increasingly radical leadership. A French republic based on Tours and then on Bordeaux raised new armies in the style of 1793. Guerrillas, including the intrepid Garibaldi, harassed Prussian patrols and rail lines. The Prussians replied by executing civilians and burning farms and villages.

Finally, after much death, destruction, and bitterness, the French agreed to an armistice in January and signed a peace treaty at Frankfurt on May 10, 1871. The war had cost perhaps 190,000 lives. Bismarck exacted an indemnity equivalent to a billion dollars and annexed Alsace-Lorraine, whose inhabitants mostly spoke indeterminate dialects but considered themselves French. That least moderate of his peace settlements was the consequence of the nationalist furor Bismarck

had helped stir up—to force the south German states to put their weight behind the war effort and to acquiesce in greater unity. And Bismarck achieved that last objective even before the end of war with France. With bribes from the funds of the dispossessed house of Hanover, Bismarck overcame the scruples of the king of Bavaria, the last and most powerful holdout. On January 18, 1871, in Louis XIV's Hall of Mirrors in the Versailles palace, Bismarck had William I proclaimed German Emperor, or *Kaiser*.

Bismarck had said in 1866 that "If there is to be revolution, we would rather make it than suffer it." He had made it. His "revolution from above" had produced a German national state that dwarfed its neighbors militarily and was soon to do so economically. Internally, Bismarck had struck a compromise with middle-class national liberalism, a compromise that preserved Junker power far into the twentieth century. What he deliberately did not do was to fulfill all the aims of the German national movement.

Except for the annexation of Alsace-Lorraine, Bismarck had struck compro-

Europe in 1871

mises with the defeated. He had accepted limits. He had left the Catholic Austrian Germans outside his Protestant-dominated "lesser Germany." The unsatisfied aspiration of many German nationalists for a "greater Germany" spanning the Continent from Schleswig to Trieste and from Strasbourg to Riga might yet undo Bismarck's work.

Western and central Europe had traveled a long road since 1815. Revolution against the old order, the legacy of 1789, was played out. A final despairing outbreak, the "Paris Commune" of March–May 1871, gave in to the troops of the French republic soon after France's peace with Germany. The republic shot 20,000 insurgents and deported another 10,000 to a tropical death in French Guyana. The myths and realities of the new nation-state—flag-bedecked ceremonies, military conscription, compulsory schooling, elections, bureaucracies, and railroads—filled the place of revolution. The power of the nation-state held great potential for good, for the prosperity and freedom of its citizens, but also for evil.

Suggestions for Further Reading

General

A brilliant introduction to the period up to 1848 is E. J. Hobsbawm, *The Age of Revolution, 1789–1848* (1962). For more detail, see F. A. Artz, *Reaction and Revolution, 1814–1832* (1934); W. L. Langer, *Political and Social Upheaval, 1832–1852* (1969); and J. Droz, *Europe between Revolutions, 1815–1848* (1968). For the various powers, see especially A. Briggs, *The Making of Modern England* (1959); A. Cobban, *A History of Modern France,* Vol. II (1957); T. S. Hamerow, *Restoration, Revolution, Reaction: Economics and Politics in Germany, 1815–1871* (1958); A. J. P. Taylor, *The Habsburg Monarchy, 1809–1918* (1948); and the sardonic and brilliant R. Pipes, *Russia under the Old Regime* (1975).

Europe to 1848

On international politics before 1848, H. Nicolson, *The Congress of Vienna: A Study in Allied Unity, 1812–1822* (1946), and H. G. Schenk, *The Aftermath of the Napoleonic Wars* (1947), remain serviceable. The most successful overviews of 1848–49 are P. Robertson, *Revolutions of 1848: A Social History* (1952), and P. Stearns, *1848: The Revolutionary Tide in Europe* (1974). T. S. Hamerow, *Restoration, Revolution, Reaction* (1958), is outstanding on Germany. L. Namier, *1848: The Revolution of the Intellectuals* (1964), stresses the emergence of savagely competing nationalisms; see also, in general, E. Kedourie, *Nationalism* (1960).

Europe after 1848

The best survey of the post-1848 period is again E. J. Hobsbawm, *The Age of Capital, 1848–1875* (1975). A. J. P. Taylor's brilliant *The Struggle for Mastery in Europe, 1848–1918* (1954) is still the best synthesis of nineteenth-century international politics. M. S. Anderson, *The Eastern Question* (1966), expertly chronicles the decay of the Ottoman Empire and its consequences. On the Crimean War and after, see both W. E. Mosse, *The Rise and Fall of the Crimean System, 1855–1871* (1967), and P. W. Schroeder, *Austria, Great Britain and the Crimean War* (1979). For France after 1848, see J. M. Thompson, *Louis Napoleon and the Second Empire* (1955). D. Mack Smith, *Cavour and Garibaldi, 1860: A Study in Political Conflict* (1954); *Victor Emmanuel, Cavour, and the Risorgimento* (1971); and *Cavour* (1985), are excellent on the creation of the Italian state. On Bismarck's revolution from above, see especially O. Pflanze, *Bismarck and the Development of Germany: The Period of Unification 1815–1871* (1963), and L. Gall, *Bismarck* (1986); T. S. Hamerow, *The Social Foundations of German Unification, 1858–1871* (1969), supplies the domestic background. On the military events, D. E. Showalter, *Railroads and Rifles: Soldiers, Technology, and the Unification of Germany* (1975); G. Craig, *The Battle of Königgrätz* (1965); and M. Howard, *The Franco-Prussian War* (1961) are excellent. H. Strachan, *European Armies and the Conduct of War* (1983), provides a useful overview.

27

EUROPE AND THE WORLD IN THE NINETEENTH CENTURY

he forces that transformed the societies of Europe in the nineteenth century also propelled them outward, in a movement that flowed irresistibly and continuously throughout the century. In 1800 Europeans occupied or controlled a mere 35 percent of the world's land surface; by 1914 they controlled a staggering five-sixths of it.

Britain and its colonists led the way. British superiority at sea after Trafalgar (1805) ensured that the peace outside Europe would be a *pax Britannica*. Britain's growing industrial might and swiftly expanding population led to an expansion, virtually constant throughout the century, of the area under the British flag. By 1900 the British Empire ruled 23 percent of the world's land surface and 20 percent of its population. It was Britain that for the first time in history united most of humanity in a world market that pulsed with the erratic rhythms of the business cycle. The force of that market, more than anything else, drove to its culmination the Western conquest of the world begun in 1492.

But Britain's effortless superiority in the first decades after 1815 did not last. Its economic lead slackened as "followers" such as France and Germany industrialized, with political consequences in the wider world. By the 1840s and 1850s the power of Britain's offspring, the United States, was beginning to make its weight felt in North America and the Caribbean. As early as the 1850s America's naval reach touched Japan. Northern victory in the U.S. Civil War meant that Britain faced a unified industrial giant that it could not match in the long run. And by the 1880s European rivals were appearing in strength in Africa and East Asia: France in West Africa, Indochina, and China; Germany in Africa; and Russia in north China.

(OPPOSITE) THE IMPACT OF WESTERN POWER ON THE WIDER WORLD: A BRITISH WARSHIP ANNIHILATES A FLEET OF CHINESE WAR JUNKS DURING THE FIRST OPIUM WAR (1841).

By the end of the century a non-European power, Japan, had risen to dominate northeast Asia. That rise was a sign of the impermanence of the garish empires British and Europeans had patched together. For along with the world market, along with gunboats, rifles, rum, and Bibles, the Europeans brought nationalism to the wider world.

THE BRITISH WORLD EMPIRE

The 1815 Peace Settlement outside Europe

Britain had consolidated its first empire in the Seven Years' War in the mid-eighteenth century. The loss of the American Colonies and the inconclusive war of 1812, embarrassing to both parties, had given the British "official mind" a sharp lesson in the limitations of British power in North America. But elsewhere Britain was unchallenged. Wars in India after 1798 confirmed the verdict of the battle of Plassey (1757): Britain was paramount on the subcontinent.

That immense land empire in South Asia provided both the troops and the commercial and strategic motives for further British colonial annexations throughout the century. By 1819 the British had secured their route to India and their command of the Mediterranean, Atlantic, and Indian Oceans with a net of bases that stretched from Gibraltar and Cape Town to Singapore and Australia.

British naval supremacy had far-reaching effects. It largely ended piracy, from the Caribbean to the seas off Borneo. It also gradually cut off the African slave trade. Britain had controlled half of that trade by 1800 but had outlawed it by an act of Parliament in 1807, thanks to the pressure of crusading idealists such as William Wilberforce (1759–1833). The United States, despite fierce objections from its slave states, had followed suit the next year. In 1814–15, Castlereagh had extracted pledges from the powers at Vienna to work toward the end of the trans-Atlantic slave trade. In the following decades, Britain backed up that ban with Royal

Navy patrols. That did not end the vast forced migration to the New World of perhaps 11.7 million Africans, of whom 1.9 million died on the crossing; only the closing of the slave markets in New Orleans, Havana, and Brazil could do that. But it was a start. And Britain was the first major power in history to abolish the institution of slavery itself, in 1833. For the moment, most other powers failed to imitate that example.

The Forces Driving British Expansion

Britain soon pressed on beyond the limits of 1815. The forces behind that expansion came not from the government in London but from the mills and foundries of the Midlands and North, the slums of Birmingham and Liverpool, and the crumbling peasant societies of Scotland and Ireland. Britain imported raw materials and food, especially after the repeal of the Corn Laws in 1846, from the far side of the globe. It exported both goods and people. First came the adventurers, in search of booty or high-profit trade, and the missionaries, intent on imposing Christianity and "progress" on "the heathen." Then came the trading companies with systematic plans for development. To states that were capable of aspiring to follow the West's lead—the Ottoman Empire, Egypt, and some societies in Latin America—bankers happily extended loans. Finally, in areas where "white" settlement appeared promising, increasing numbers of emigrants set up societies on the British and North American pattern.

The motive forces behind imperial expansion—economics and demography—remained virtually constant over the century except for a gradual decline in Britain's rate of population increase and economic growth. What changed, and what accounts for the changes in the forms that expansion took, was the available means. Western expansion had always faced constraints: distance and natural obstacles, disease, the resistance of native societies, and the unwillingness of European governments and peoples to make major sacrifices for empire. These limits

The British Empire in the Nineteenth Century

British possessions

British protectorate

Labeled islands are British possessions or protectorates

CHRISTMAS IS.

DOMINION OF CANADA

PACIFIC OCEAN

BR. HONDURAS

BERMUDA IS.

NEWFOUNDLAND

BAHAMA IS.

JAMAICA

GREAT BRITAIN

ATLANTIC

BARBADOS

TRINIDAD

BRITISH GUIANA

GIBRALTAR

OCEAN

MALTA   CYPRUS

EGYPT

ADEN

SIERRA LEONE

SUDAN

GOLD COAST

NIGERIA

FALKLAND IS.

ASCENSION

ST. HELENA

RHODESIA

BECHUANALAND

CAPE COLONY

TRISTAN DA CUNHA

Cape Town   CAPE OF GOOD HOPE

KENYA

ZANZIBAR

SOCOTRA

BRITISH SOMALILAND

KURIA MURIA IS.

SEYCHELLES

INDIAN

OCEAN

MAURITIUS

GILBERT IS.

ELLICE IS.

PACIFIC OCEAN

WEIHAI

HONG KONG

BR. N. BORNEO

SARAWAK

BURMA

MALAYA

NICOBAR IS.

BRITISH   SINGAPORE

INDIAN EMPIRE

LACCADIVE IS.

CEYLON

MALDIVE IS.

COCOS IS.

SOLOMON IS.

BRITISH NEW GUINEA

FIJI IS.

AUSTRALIA

NEW ZEALAND

TASMANIA

Singapore, One of Britain's far-flung outposts, in 1830.

had not prevented the conquest of most of the New World after 1492. But between them they had limited European penetration before 1815 to the maritime fringes of Asia and Africa. On the Asian mainland only India had succumbed, after drawing the British in through its constant internal strife and rich commerce.

After 1815 the means of expansion—transport, tropical medicine, and weaponry—available to the Europeans and particularly to the British changed dramatically, thanks to the industrial revolution. First came steam. From the mid-sixteenth century, European sailing ships with their heavy cannon had outmaneuvered and outfought Arab dhows and Chinese junks on the high seas. But inshore, European square-riggers were clumsy and vulnerable to grounding or shifting winds. They could not move up narrow winding rivers against the current, and towing by rowers in ships' boats was pathetically inefficient. European naval power thus ended at the high-water mark except where the prize ashore was worth landing a substantial ground force.

Steamboats opened up the Asian and African coastal waters and at last allowed European trade and power to penetrate the interior with little effort. The British East India Company gave the first demonstration of the potential of a steam-powered "river war" in an 1824–26 conflict with India's eastern neighbor, the kingdom of Burma.

Iron-hulled steam vessels were the next step. They demonstrated their worth in the 1839–42 "First Opium War" between Britain and China. Chinese defenses and war-junks had been adequate against wooden-hulled sailing ships unable to maneuver on rivers. Against iron-hulled steamboats they were powerless. The war ended when the British steamed up the Yangtze River and cut the Grand Canal, which supplied Beijing (Peking) with rice. Steam played a decisive role in Commodore Matthew Perry's opening of Japan to American and European trade in 1853–54, and in the French conquest of Indochina in the 1870s and 1880s.

The second major innovation that made British and European expansion possible was quinine. Of all the major tropical diseases—dysentery, yellow fever, dengue, and the numerous nameless fevers—the African falciparum strain of malaria is the most consistently deadly. A few lucky individuals, such as the Scottish surgeon Mungo Park, who explored the river Niger in the 1790s, managed to survive it. But the first attempt to navigate the Niger by steam, in 1832, ended with the death of 40 of the 49 whites on the expedition. Between 1817 and 1836 British garrisons on the Gold Coast lost 66 percent of their strength each year.

The antimalarial properties of the bark of a South American tree, the chinchona, had long been known or suspected. But not until 1820 did two French chemists isolate the alkaloid, quinine, that accounted for those properties. By the 1830s production of quinine in quantity had begun; experience soon suggested that it worked best when taken regularly as a preventive. In 1854 a Niger expedition returned without casualties. The way lay open at last for trade far in the interior and ultimately for the extension of European power into all of sub-Saharan Africa.

The final factor that permitted the British and European conquest of the world was a revolution in weaponry. Until the 1840s, the chief advantages of the Europeans were their logistical organization, trained leadership, and cohesion under fire. The bayonet remained as important as fire from the one-round-per-minute musket, a weapon that some native societies could copy. Skilled enemies with muskets, such as the Algerians or Afghans who resisted the French and British in the 1830s and 1840s, could turn colonial conquest into an expensive, long-drawn-out, and exceedingly grim business—or block it altogether. The greatest European advantage in weaponry was artillery, which was hard to transport except by river and little help against guerrillas.

Then came the first effective muzzle-loading rifles, followed by breechloaders like the Sharps, Dreyse, and Chassepot. From the 1840s to the 1870s the range and rate of fire of European small arms increased at least fivefold—and no native blacksmith could copy the new industrially produced weapons or their ammunition. By the 1880s the box-magazine breechloading rifle and the first easily portable machine gun, the Maxim gun, enabled even small European forces to destroy native armies many times their size. In the climactic 1898 battle against the forces of the *Mahdi,* the Islamic prophet who had raised the Sudan against the unbeliever, the British lost 48 men. The *Mahdi's* armies lost 11,000. The Maxim gun made possible a brief age of military tourism.

The mid-nineteenth-century revolutions in transport, tropical medicine, and weaponry made colonial conquest far easier than before. They did not make it more orderly, however; Britain's steady expansion in particular was hardly a process planned or directed by London. The government from the beginning held to the utilitarian principle that the best government governed least. Until the 1860s those who made British policy were supremely confident that free trade would benefit the world as well as Britain. Palmerston had summed up that credo in a parliamentary speech in 1842, the year of the British victory that opened China. Commerce would lead "civilization with the one hand and peace with the other"; it would render mankind "happier, wiser, better." Free trade, one of its spokesmen announced in 1846, would make "foreign nations . . . valuable Colonies to us, without imposing on us the responsibility of governing them." The British formula, as two later historians have described it, was "informal empire"—"trade with informal control if possible; trade with rule when necessary."

As the century drew on, trade with rule seemed more and more necessary, despite the laments of a central bureaucracy bent on sparing the taxpayers. Trade might make humanity "better"—more like the British—but not in the short term. Trade, and the inevitable missionaries and settlers (where appropriate), invariably required the protection of the flag. Trade required enforceable contracts and security for money and goods. Trade frequently conflicted with the customs, laws, or policies of those it touched, from the tribal empires of Africa to the long-estab-

"Whatever happens we have got The Maxim Gun, and they have not," wrote the British satirist Hilaire Belloc (1870–1953) of this essential tool of empire.

lished states of China and Japan. Trade and loans in Latin America, the Ottoman Empire, and Egypt in many cases destroyed the authority of those who accepted them.

Trade, loans, missionaries, and settlers thus generated a variety of unstable mixtures of resistance and collaboration in the native societies they affected. The interaction between the outward thrust of Britain and its European imitators, and the resistance or lack of it in non-Western societies, was the mechanism that created the British Empire and extended Western domination throughout the world.

Resistance took many forms. Tribes from the Afghans northwest of India to the Kaffirs and Zulus of Africa raided British possessions on the innumerable turbulent frontiers of empire. Religious or proto-nationalist groups—the Mahdists of the Sudan, the Egyptian army, and the Boer farmers of South Africa—rose against the British or against rulers who collaborated with them. And states such as China and Japan refused to open their markets or provide security for the persons and property of British merchants. Resistance or defiance normally called forth a British response. Typically, London or its agents on the spot intervened militarily to protect what they perceived as existing British interests. The security of India's borders, of the China trade, of the Suez Canal or the Cape of Good Hope demanded increasingly strenuous action. That mechanism explains the patchwork character of expansion. Britain did not obey a grand design; it responded when action seemed unavoidable.

Collaboration by native societies also helped govern the timing, extent, and ultimate collapse of British and Western dominance. One corollary of London's belief in free trade and in a minimum of government intervention was the need for native auxiliaries. Princes and tribal rulers, native troops, and Western-educated natives might all serve as more or less willing collaborators with Britain's informal empire. The collaborators found themselves caught between two worlds: the British world market and their own societies. If the market pressed too rapidly and disruptively against the native economy, institutions, or religious and cultural traditions, collaborators might fumble and collapse in the face of antiforeign revolt. That presented Britain with a difficult choice: to get out, or to go in—at great and continuing expense—and rule directly. And to establish and maintain direct rule required the collaboration of the conquered. When that collaboration faltered or ceased, the European empires ultimately collapsed.

Britain's "White" Colonies: Canada, Australia, and New Zealand

The ideal collaborators were of course Britain's own colonists. The societies they created, with the exception of those of the French Canadians and Dutch-descended Boer farmers that London acquired in 1763 and 1814, were replicas of Britain. Britain's demographic expansion drove them onward. The satellite economies of Australia, New Zealand, and eventually Canada in turn contributed wool, grain, meat, and markets to British economic expansion. Along with the United States and Argentina, they also received most of Britain's immense overseas investments.

London, after its sad experience with the thirteen American colonies, did its best to defuse colonial discontent by conceding self-government as soon as possible. Canada, the most heavily populated and turbulent, came first. Conquest in the Seven Years' War and the subsequent ar-

rival of large numbers of American loyalists after 1775–83 had disquieted the deeply rooted Catholic society of Norman peasants that France had planted in Québec. Britain's effort, in the Constitutional Act of 1791, to give each nationality its own province failed to quiet unrest.

In 1837 the suppression of a Québec rising and a revolt in the English-speaking province of Upper Canada (now Ontario) required British troops. In the aftermath, the Earl of Durham, one of the authors of Britain's 1832 Reform Bill, became governor-general. He recommended that Britain give Canada representative self-government as a unified province in which English-speakers would outnumber the French. London adopted his recommendations in the 1840s, but the French-English conflict inevitably persisted. By the time of the U.S. Civil War, the need for strong central government to promote internal cohesion, defense, and railway development was obvious. In 1867, after long negotiation between Canadian leaders, Parliament in London passed the British North America Act. Québec once again received its own administration within the "Dominion of Canada," a federation that included the maritime provinces. Britain happily gave the colonials management of their own affairs, including defense against rebellion and Indian raids.

Britain's invention of the self-governing "dominion" was decisive for Australia and New Zealand. The various territories of Australia, which had served from 1788 as a dumping ground for English convicts, received representative self-government in 1851–55. By then free immigrants far outnumbered the descendants of deported prisoners. In 1901 London conceded dominion status to the Commonwealth of Australia, a continent spanned by railroads and rich in wool, grain, and gold. The independence of New Zealand was a slower process, largely because of a series of unpleasant land wars with the native Maoris, a fierce and tenacious Polynesian warrior people. The land-hungry British settlers refused to dispense with London's protection until

British troops had broken Maori resistance. Self-government nevertheless came in 1876 and dominion status in 1907.

Britain's Indian Empire

In India the British, alone of the colonial powers, took steps in the nineteenth century to prepare the way for the ultimate independence of the non-European peoples they had conquered. The process was neither swift nor peaceful. To protect and extend its trade, the East India Company had succeeded the Mughal emperors as the paramount power on the subcontinent. In the Third Mahratta War of 1817–18 the Company broke for good the power of the Hindu warrior states. By that point the Company itself had ceased to be a private entity with a monopoly on India's trade. As early as 1773 the Crown had taken for itself the power to appoint a governor-general. In 1784 London had assumed control of the Company's political activities. In 1833 the Company lost its trading function entirely; henceforth its only mission was to govern India through the elite Indian Civil Service.

The end of the Company trade monopoly and the extension of British direct rule intensified pressure on the native societies of the subcontinent. The Company had usually been content to leave Indian social and religious custom undisturbed. But once it lost its monopoly, the way was open for the ever-intensifying penetration of independent British merchants and missionaries. Pressure in Parliament and in the British press for the reform of Indian society along British lines mounted.

By the 1830s the reformers had won. As true disciples of Jeremy Bentham (see p. 643), they felt passionately that India was theirs in trust, to Westernize and prepare for self-government at some point in the far distant future. The great British historian Thomas Babington Macaulay, one of the reformers, spelled out the goal: to create "a class of persons Indian in colour and blood, but English in tastes, opinions, and intellects." And Karl Marx celebrated in newspaper articles the creation in India of "a fresh class . . . endowed with the requirements for government and

imbued with European science." Britain's mission, he triumphantly announced, was "the annihilation of the old Asiatic society, and the laying of the material foundations of Western society in Asia." Old East India Company hands had misgivings about this revolution from above and the blind self-confidence that drove it. "Englishmen are as great fanatics in politics as Mohommedans in religion. They suppose that no country can be saved without English institutions," fumed a former governor of Madras.

The reform effort culminated with the 1848–56 administration of governor-general Lord Dalhousie, the very personification of utilitarian enterprise and "progress." Dalhousie introduced the telegraph, built the famous Grand Trunk Road across northern India, and planned the railways that by 1905 were the longest and best in Asia. His irrigation canals made vast areas of northern India fertile.

In politics, a less tidy field than engineering, Dalhousie's messianic faith in the benefits of Western civilization made him an annexationist. He completed the conquest of the Sikhs of the Punjab, seized Sind in the west and lower Burma in the east, and gradually annexed Indian states whose thrones fell vacant. British rule now brought ever-increasing missionary activity, equality before the law that disrupted these societies of rigidly demarcated castes, and interference with Hindu religious customs such as *sati,* the ritual burning of widows on their husbands' funeral pyres.

By 1857, the strain on native society had grown intolerable. Over wide areas of northern India the population, from lord to peasant, had grown convinced that Britain's ultimate purpose was to abolish Indian society and religion, whether Hindu or Moslem. The occasion but not the cause of the ensuing explosion was the foolish introduction into the Company's Indian army of new rifles that took paper cartridges waterproofed with tallow Loading required biting the cartridge open. And when rumors, later confirmed, flew that the manufacturers had used tallow made from a blend of pig and cow

1756 1763		Great Mutiny 1857		Indian Independence 1947
Seven Years' War	British East India Company Control (Mughals keep imperial title)		Direct Rule by British Government	

fat, the *sepoys*—the Company's native soldiers—faced an appalling dilemma. The cow was sacred to Hinduism, the pig forbidden to Moslems. The troops could bite the cartridge and suffer loss of caste if Hindu or defilement if Moslem. Or they could betray their deeply felt oath to the army.

Many chose mutiny and rose against the British with the support of much of the population of the dusty plains around Delhi. Native leaders harked back to the proud days of Mahrattas and Mughals, and sought to drive the British from India. The *sepoys* committed numerous atrocities against British prisoners, women, and children. The British, isolated and fearful amid an immense and largely hostile population, fought a pitiless race war. They celebrated the reconquest of Delhi by lashing *sepoy* prisoners across gun barrels and blasting them to shreds. London dissolved the East India Company, drastically reorganized its Indian army, made India a possession of the Crown, and publicly disclaimed any intention of tampering with its subjects' religions.

The Great Mutiny of 1857–58 was a shock not only to the British rulers of India but to British imperial self-confidence. It drove home the obvious: non-Western societies did not automatically take to Western values. It revealed that the reformers' "fresh class" of English-educated collaborators lacked roots in the Indian population. The English henceforth proceeded with greater caution and far lower expectations. Stability, not social revolution became their goal. Creeping annexation ceased. The Indian subject princes, who for the most part had remained loyal, preserved their territories into the twentieth century. Britain now confined its activities primarily to administration, engineering, and the defense of India's borders.

Nevertheless, the reformers succeeded in the long term. The Great Mutiny was the last sizable traditionalist Indian revolt. English-educated Indians took an increasing role in the junior ranks of the administration, in the new English-speaking law courts, and in the creation of textile, coal, and steel industries. By the 1880s a modern Indian public opinion, both Hindu and Moslem, had come into being. The founding, with help from British liberals, of the Indian Congress party in 1885 marked the birth of the force that ultimately succeeded the British. The Indians whom Britain had educated in turn invented Indian nationalism.

A scene from the Great Mutiny, 1857: British firepower and discipline halt a sepoy attack during the siege of Delhi.

Britain in Africa to the 1880s

Except for the Cape Colony and a few fever-ridden trading stations on the west coast, Britain in 1815 had little use for Africa. That changed. The penetration of British palm-oil traders, missionaries, and antislavery reformers, especially after midcentury, brought increasing clashes with

The Scramble for Africa   1884/1914

But the extension of British rule to much of Africa followed from two great crises in the 1880s and 1890s, both connected with the security of the routes to India. In North Africa the stake was the great canal across the Suez isthmus that the Saint-Simonian engineer and promoter, Ferdinand de Lesseps, had completed in 1869. In 1876 the Egyptian Khedivate, the regime of the successors of Mehemet Ali (see p. 663), collapsed in

native forces. In West Africa, the warlike Ashanti kingdom in the hinterland of the Gold Coast was the main barrier. A British punitive expedition in 1874 checked its power, but Britain did not finally annex the kingdom until 1896. In East Africa, British attempts to put down the slave trade destroyed the authority of Britain's client, the Sultan of Zanzibar. That drew London ever deeper into the affairs of East Africa.

The strategic Suez Canal, in the 1890s.

bankruptcy; it had attempted to modernize Egypt on European credit. The French and British governments took command of Egyptian finances and taxation to see their bondholders paid.

That intrusion was the latest of a long series of defeats at the hands of unbelievers since Bonaparte. It generated a radical response; unlike the Indian Mutiny, that response was recognizably modern. In 1882 a movement in the partially Westernized Egyptian army overthrew its own government and defied the West. The movement's ideological basis was a modernizing current of Islam; its program, Egypt for the Egyptians; its leader, the charismatic Colonel Ahmed Arabi Pasha.

That situation, now all too familiar, took Britain and France aback. A naval show of force of the traditional sort merely provoked a massacre of foreigners at Alexandria. The British responded with cannon fire. That was the point of no return: British prestige was committed, the prestige required to hold India. The pacific Liberal cabinet of William Ewart Gladstone (see p. 712) unhappily landed an army to restore a cooperative Egyptian government. The French had no need of a route to India, and refused to follow.

The British convincingly crushed Arabi's army, and found themselves ruling Egypt. To Gladstone's dismay, the old techniques of informal empire no longer served. British interests appeared too great, Egyptian resistance too fanatical. If Britain withdrew, its discredited clients would again collapse, leaving Canal and debt at the mercy of anti-Western forces. Britain therefore stayed, despite the increasing hostility of the French, who illogically concluded that the British had slyly usurped the Egyptian empire that Bonaparte had failed to bequeath to France.

Worse, Egypt was not self-contained: the mighty river Nile upon which its agriculture depended rose in the Sudan, far to the south. That province was in theory Egypt's, held through isolated garrisons. But in 1881 an Islamic figure even more charismatic than Arabi had arisen there and had begun to weld the region's Dervish religious orders into an army and a state. The *Mahdi,* Mohammed Ahmad, swept the Egyptian garrisons out of the Sudan in 1883. In 1885 he destroyed a British-led force under an eccentric soldier of fortune, General "Chinese" Gordon.

Gladstone, lamenting his "Egyptian bondage," left the *Mahdi* for later British governments to deal with. But British occupation of Egypt had unleashed French ambitions in West Africa. Other powers also took a hand. The resulting "scramble" for protectorates and annexations divided up the African continent, at least on paper, in the 25 years after 1882. In West Africa Britain left much to the French but kept Nigeria and a number of smaller river colonies. In East Africa the British were less generous to their rivals. Proximity to India impelled them to keep most of the coast, except for areas conceded, graciously or not, to Italians and Germans.

And a second great crisis far to the south drove Britain to extend its control still further. Britain's principal stake at the Cape of Good Hope was also originally strategic. The Cape was an indispensable base, "the true centre of the Empire . . . clear of the Suez complications, almost equally distant from Australia, China, India, Gibraltar, the West Indies, and the Falklands," as a Colonial Office official pointed out in the 1870s. Unfortunately, the Cape had a land frontier. It also had non-British white inhabitants: the settlers whom the Dutch East India Company had planted in 1652 to provide supplies for its shipping.

British relations with the Cape Dutch after annexation were friendly; the colony received representative self-government in 1872. Dealings with the Boer ("peasant") farmers of the inland frontier were less satisfactory; British humanitarians frowned on the Boer habit of enslaving the Africans. Between 1835 and 1844, hungry for land and determined to preserve a white supremacy they felt God had ordained, the Boers streamed north across the Vaal River and out of British control. The climax of that "Great Trek" came at the battle of Blood River in 1838. A Boer wagon train defeated the onslaught of the Zulu king Dingaan, heir of the great Shaka, who had created the mightiest army south of the Sahara. To the *Trekboers,* reared in the stern Old Testament faith of the Dutch Reformed Church, victory at Blood River proved that God had chosen them.

The Trekboers founded twin republics, the Orange Free State and the Transvaal—states that in their very origins represented an almost tribal reaction against Britain. When London sought in the 1870s to force them into a Cape federation that would eventually become a dominion, Transvaal Boer rifles replied. A British defeat in 1881 persuaded Gladstone to recognize Boer independence, subject only to a vague right of veto over Boer relations with foreign powers. Unlike the situation in Egypt, the stakes were not high enough to warrant a major British commitment, and Boer nationalism was clearly too tough to take on lightly.

Gladstone's retreat postponed the struggle for mastery in South Africa. That development, like the climax of the British-French struggle for the Nile and the crises in East Asia around the turn of the century, is best left for discussion in its international context (see pp. 750–53). But even before the second round against the Boers, and despite doubts and hesitations in London, Britain had annexed most of a new empire in Africa. Egyptian revolt, the fanaticism of the *Mahdi,* and Boer proto-nationalism had marked the limits of informal influence. Africa's resistance drove Britain to defend by ever-broader annexations what Britain already held. And the growing rivalry from the other European powers increasingly confirmed the British on the path they had chosen.

BRITAIN'S RIVALS: FRANCE, GERMANY, ITALY, RUSSIA

The other European powers inevitably sought to imitate Britain. But each power did so in its own way. And they ultimately did so at Britain's pleasure, for neither separately nor together could they challenge British naval supremacy.

France

French imperialism, which created the second largest nineteenth-century European empire, was primarily military in inspiration. It began in 1830 with an attack on the pirate kingdom of Algiers. The dying Bourbon dynasty sought the prestige of conquest; Louis Philippe inherited some coastal outposts and a hinterland that resisted fiercely. The French army, in almost twenty years of bloody campaigns and hair-raising atrocities, prevailed by 1847 against the canny resistance leader Abd-el-Kader.

The Algerian outpost provided security for French Mediterranean shipping. Its conquest produced and gave a home to that quintessential French colonial force, the Foreign Legion. It offered a training ground for generations of colonial officers. And thanks to French and European immigration and agricultural settlement, Algeria almost began to pay for itself after the suppression of a further Moslem uprising in 1870.

But Algeria was no product of trade and industry, the forces behind British expansion. And even if the French had aspired to an informal commercial empire in North Africa, Moslem resistance would have thwarted them. The French empire did have economic functions. But its reason for existence lay above all in the belief of successive French governments before 1870 that France's claim to European primacy required colonial possessions. And the loss of that primacy in 1870 made colonial self-assertion a necessary compensation for European humiliation.

Under Napoleon III, General Louis Faidherbe made Senegal, France's most important West African outpost, a major source of native troops. In 1858–59 Napoleon seized Saigon and Da Nang in Vietnam as a reprisal for native killings of French missionaries. In the 1860s France annexed the southern areas of Vietnam. Napoleon III exploited the U.S. Civil War to impose the Austrian Archduke Maximilian as Emperor of Mexico, with the support of Foreign Legion bayonets. Union victory and Mexican resistance brought French withdrawal and the Archduke's death by firing squad in 1867.

The Franco-Prussian war inevitably imposed a pause. But by the early 1880s France had again begun to expand. It forced a protectorate on Tunis, Algeria's difficult neighbor, in 1881. After humiliation in the Egyptian crisis of 1882, French consuls and officers on the West African rivers began feverishly staking claims that Paris until then had been unwilling to back. Collision with a series of unbending Moslem theocracies in the West African interior compelled the French to make good their paper claims with Maxim guns. The colonial army and France's formidable naval infantry happily bent to that task. By 1902 the French empire extended from Algeria to the Gulf of Guinea, and France had annexed Madagascar on the Indian Ocean side of the Cape of Good Hope.

Germany and Italy

The German and Italian empires had even less economic function than the French; as latecomers, Germany and Italy could only seize territories so worthless that Britain and France had passed them by. Bismarck had utter contempt for the German colonial enthusiasts who had emerged after 1871. He nevertheless set them loose in 1884–85 to claim Togo, Cameroons, South-West Africa, and German East Africa to create artificial friction with London. At the 1884–85 Berlin colonial conference he also helped give the brutal King Leopold II of Belgium control of the Congo basin; British-French rivalry benefited other powers besides Berlin.

Bismarck's purposes in picking a colonial quarrel with Britain were diplomatic and domestic, not colonial: rapprochement with France, a thumping German

nationalist vote in the 1884 elections, and reinsurance against dismissal by the mildly liberal and pro-British Crown Prince Frederick when William I ultimately died. Those passing needs saddled Germany with expensive and useless African territories and an assortment of Pacific islands. Bismarck's successors acquired a Chinese port. That unsatisfactory empire did not disillusion German opinion; it whetted its appetite for larger things.

Italy, as the least of the great powers, found even slimmer pickings than Germany. It acquired the Red Sea port of Assab in 1882 and asserted a protectorate over the Coptic Christian kingdom of Ethiopia in 1889. The Amhara rulers of Ethiopia appeared to accept, but then resisted further Italian encroachment. Menelik, the emperor, acquired European rifles and French military experts. On March 1, 1896, at Adowa he dealt the Italians the worst defeat inflicted upon a would-be European colonizer in the nineteenth century. In the face of an enemy that outnumbered them by five to one, the Italians had divided their forces and had struck out on divergent routes across unmapped mountains. They lost 6,000 dead and 4,000 wounded or captured; political chaos at home prevented a renewal of the war. Italy made do for a generation with the coastal enclaves of Eritrea and Somalia.

Russia in Asia

Finally, Russia rounded out an empire in central and east Asia in the course of the nineteenth century. That process was like French expansion in that it was military, and like that of the United States in that it pursued geopolitical "manifest destiny." The Crimean War checked Russia in Europe but sharpened its appetites elsewhere. In 1853–54 it annexed large areas around the Aral Sea. In the next twenty years it methodically crushed the central Asian nomad peoples and the surviving Tartar khanates of Bukhara, Khiva, and Kokand. By 1884 Russia had reached the Afghan border. Farther east, it pressed into Mongolia. And in 1858 and 1860, by the army's bayonets and the treaties of Aigun and Beijing (Peking), Russia seized from

Colonial troops: An Algerian officer in the French army of the 1880s.

the Chinese the Amur and maritime provinces opposite Japan. At the southern tip of the maritime province it founded a naval base with a name that was a program: Vladivostok, "Ruler of the East." And from 1891 Russia began pushing a railroad across Siberia toward the Pacific at Vladivostok, to make that program reality.

BRITAIN'S LEGACY IN NORTH AMERICA: THE EXPANSION OF THE UNITED STATES

The Young Republic

By the 1890s an entirely different sort of state had reached the Pacific shores of the New World. The United States that emerged from the Revolutionary War of 1775–83 and the Constitutional Convention of 1787 was a unique experiment. It was a new state, not founded through the slow processes of dynastic and military-bureaucratic consolidation that had made the states of Europe. Its sovereign people—"We the people of the United States"—did not claim to be a "nation," a political unit preordained by language, culture, and historic boundaries. America's language and culture were initially British, and its territorial boundaries were lost in the endless forests of the Appalachians and the swamps of southern Georgia. The foundation of the new state was its principles: "We hold these truths to be self-evident, that all Men are created equal, that they are endowed by their Creator with certain unalienable rights, that among these are Life, Liberty, and the Pursuit of Happiness. . . ." The securing of those natural rights was the purpose of American government, the unity of the thirteen colonies was the means.

Hard experience in town and county meetings, state assemblies, and the Revolutionary War had given the framers of the Constitution a realism—or a pessimism—about human nature that contrasted sharply with the Rousseauite optimism of later European revolutionaries. As James Madison of Virginia, one of the Constitution's principal architects, observed: "If men were angels, no government would

Tocqueville Foresees the World Domination of Russia and America   1835

There are at the present time two great nations in the world, which started from different points, but seem to tend towards the same end. I allude to the Russians and the Americans. . . . All other nations seem to have nearly reached their natural limits, and they have only to maintain their power; but these are still in the act of growth. . . . These alone are proceeding with ease and celerity along a path to which no limit can be perceived. The American struggles against the obstacles that nature opposes to him; the adversaries of the Russian are men. The former combats the wilderness and savage life; the latter, civilization with all its arms. The conquests of the American are therefore gained by the plowshare; those of the Russian by the sword. The Anglo-American relies upon personal interest to accomplish his ends and gives free scope to the unguided strength and common sense of the people; the Russian centers all the authority of society in a single arm. The principle instrument of the former is freedom; of the latter, servitude. Their starting-point is different and their courses are not the same; yet each of them seems marked by the will of Heaven to sway the destinies of half the globe.

From Alexis de Tocqueville, Democracy in America *(New York: Vintage Books, 1953), Vol. I, p. 434.*

be necessary." Majority will unchecked by law meant tyranny over both individuals and states. Madison and others therefore built into the Constitution what a great American historian has described as a "harmonious system of mutual frustration": the separation of powers.

Legislature, executive, and judiciary checked and balanced one another, as did the new federal government and the thirteen states. Within Congress, the indirectly elected Senate moderated the impetuous House of Representatives. Neither majority whim in Congress, nor the authority of that elected monarch, the president, nor any caprice of the Supreme Court's judges could prevail for long without the cooperation of the other branches. That system, so cumbersome in theory, in practice usually forced the deliberate creation of the compromise and consensus without which democratic polities fall into chaos or despotism. The Constitution did not guarantee the success of the American experiment. That depended above all on the common sense, civic spirit, and political experience of the citizenry. But it did provide a framework that used those qualities to advantage.

The Constitution was above all a democratic document, although its framers were men of property and social distinction and although it made allowances for the South's "peculiar institution," slavery. To secure the agreement of the southern states, the framers counted each slave, for purposes of apportioning representatives, as three-fifths of a white citizen. Despite that concession to inequality, the Constitution swiftly developed in the direction of still greater democracy. To overcome opposition to its adoption, Madison and others put forward a further series of guarantees that the new federal government would not imitate the "tyranny" of George III. The first ten amendments, or Bill of Rights, adopted in 1789–91, placed the rights of the individual against the state at the center of the new political system. Those rights gradually grew as the country expanded and the political weight of the socially stratified east coast states decreased. Most states that had restricted voting through religious tests or property qualifications had enacted universal male suffrage by the 1820s.

The founders gradually passed from the scene, leaving a vacuum that political parties ultimately filled. The first grouping of importance was the Federalists, whose advocacy of a strong central government helped push the Constitution through. Their leading light was Alexander Hamilton, first Secretary of the Treasury and prophet of the economic development of the United States. Their program implied the supremacy of industry and commerce over agriculture and of the cultivated elite over the masses. Thomas Jefferson and Madison of Virginia formed a Democratic-Republican party that opposed Hamilton with a vision of an egalitarian farmers' republic. Great cities, Jefferson wrote, were "pestilential to the morals, the health, and the liberties of man."

That conflict of ideologies and interests persisted throughout the century and beyond. It soon became at least in part a regional division. The egalitarian frontier triumphed in the 1828 election, the first fought by recognizable national parties. Andrew Jackson, "the People's Choice" against the eastern elites, was ironically a Kentucky landowner. But his overwhelming popular-vote victory at the head of the Democratic party was a mighty step toward the emergence of the system of two national parties, powerful engines of consensus, that still exists.

By 1828 the United States was well on its way to territorial consolidation. Jefferson, as president in 1803, had bought from Napoleon the Louisiana territory that commanded the mouth of the Mississippi and stretched west to the Rocky Mountains and north to the still unmarked Canadian border. In the aftermath of the War of 1812, Britain and the United States agreed to demilitarize the Great Lakes and establish the 49th parallel as their mutual border as far as the Rockies. In 1819 Spain sold Florida to the United States. By 1837 the original thirteen states had doubled in number. Jackson encouraged and speeded the "removal" by force of most of the remaining Indian tribes east of the Mississippi. Only Mexico to the south was now a potential rival.

The United States even began to interest itself in Latin American affairs. Napoleon, by deposing the Bourbons in 1808, had cut adrift the Spanish Empire in Latin America. The revolts against Spain that followed had produced by the early 1820s a collection of weak and internally divided states. After France's 1823 invasion of Spain to restore the Bourbons, French backing for Spanish efforts at reconquest appeared to threaten what Britain considered a promising market. George Canning, Castlereagh's successor as British Foreign Secretary, suggested a joint British-United States declaration to ward off European intervention.

But President James Monroe preferred to act unilaterally. With a characteristically American statement of republican principles, the Monroe Doctrine, he an-

"Old Hickory": Andrew Jackson (1767–1845)

nounced to Congress in December 1823 that the United States would regard attempts to establish or reestablish European control in the western hemisphere as signs of "an unfriendly disposition towards the United States." Canning could boast to Parliament that he had "called the New World into existence to redress the balance of the Old." But it was the Royal Navy, not the still minuscule seapower of the United States, that initially backed the Doctrine with force. Until the very end of the century the Royal Navy, in Britain's own interest, served as ultimate guarantor of the maritime security of the United States.

Expansion and Disunion: The Origins of the Civil War

Economic and territorial expansion soon strained both the principles and the political fabric of the Republic. The trading Northeast, which acquired a merchant marine second only to Britain's, industrialized rapidly (see p. 626). The Erie Canal and the railroad opened the Midwest to settlers, and gave those settlers new markets in the East for their grain.

The South, despite the misgivings of figures such as Jefferson ("Indeed I tremble for my country, when I reflect that God is just"), further refined the slave economy established in the seventeenth century. Tobacco was less and less profitable, but after 1793 the cotton gin, a machine invented by the Yankee Eli Whitney, made the short-fiber cotton that grew in the South into a fabulously profitable plantation crop. The slave economy spread rapidly westward, creating a "Cotton Kingdom" from Savannah to Mobile and New Orleans. By the 1820s the South was shipping 60 million pounds of raw cotton annually to the mills of Europe.

Old divisions between states blurred. Divisions between Puritan trading New England, the religiously and socially varied central Atlantic states, and the Anglican slave South had been less important than the gulf between the settled and hierarchical societies of the coastal plains and the egalitarian frontiersmen of the Appala-

The mechanization of the slave economy: Eli Whitney's cotton gin.

chians and beyond. Now canal, railroad, and river steamer riveted North and South firmly to their respective hinterlands. Free labor spread across the northern backcountry, slave labor across the South.

Economic and territorial expansion brought to a head the fundamental conflict of principles: could a system founded on individual freedom ultimately tolerate slavery? By the 1830s stern New England voices had begun to attack the Cotton Kingdom at its most vulnerable point—its principles. Agitators such as William Lloyd Garrison and Wendell Phillips ceaselessly pounded at the irreconcilability of black slavery and white freedom. Garrison denounced the Constitution itself as "a covenant with death and an agreement with hell," for it permitted slavery. The Southern response was increasingly implausible and hysterical. John C. Calhoun, the South's greatest national political figure, told the Senate in 1837 that slavery was no evil, "but a good, sir, a positive good." The Abolitionists were and remained a tiny though noisy minority, but they inspired a persecution mania in the South that in the end drove it to revolt and ruin.

Economic issues also helped strain relations between the two regions. The South, as befitted a satellite economy of Britain, demanded free trade; the industrializing North with its Midwestern markets sought protective tariffs. In 1832 that conflict led to a great crisis. The "sovereign state" of South Carolina, under Calhoun's leadership, "nullified" a protective tariff that Congress had passed. President Jackson prepared to use force: "The laws of the United States must be executed." Since the issue was not slavery itself, the other Southern states were not prepared to back South Carolina. A compromise deferred until later the issue of "states' rights." The rebellious state withdrew nullification and Congress agreed to reduce tariffs. Nor did economics always pull the sections apart. Northern industry's dependence on Southern cotton led the South to bet heavily though in vain upon the existence of an implicit alliance between plantation chattel slavery and factory "wage slavery," between the "lords of the lash and the lords of the loom."

The relentless territorial expansion of the United States, by constantly raising the stakes in the competition between two irreconcilable systems, ultimately brought war. Admitting new states created a series of ever-greater crises. Missouri's admission as a slave state was possible only as part of an 1820 compromise that established latitude 36° 30', Missouri's southern border, as the future boundary between slave and free territories.

Then, in the 1820s and 1830s, settlers, including planters and their slaves, flocked into the Mexican territories west of Louisiana, ironically at the invitation of the Mexican government. Attempts to reassert Mexican control led to revolt by the settlers in 1835–36 and the proclamation of a "Republic of Texas." Eight years later the Democratic party under James K. Polk carried the presidential election by promising to annex Texas, which had asked to join the Union. Mexico's warnings that it would fight what it regarded as aggression, and clashes with Mexican patrols on the Rio Grande, brought war in 1846–48. The minuscule U.S. Army outclassed its adversary. It captured Mexico City and seized by force the entire Southwest from Texas westward to California.

This extension of U.S. power, and Polk's compromise with the British to extend the 49th parallel border with Canada westward to the Pacific across the Oregon territory, created a far greater North-South crisis than had Missouri. Polk had promised the northern states an Oregon-Canada border ("Fifty-four forty or fight!") far to the north of the one he ultimately secured. Northern leaders retaliated by demanding that Congress exclude slavery from the territories seized from Mexico. The South, which had contributed disproportionately to victory, replied with threats of secession from the Union.

The Compromise of 1850 failed to paper over the cracks. It admitted California as a free state but left the status of the lands between California and Texas to the choice of their eventual inhabitants. It also pledged the North to return fugitive slaves, thus forcing northern authorities to choose between conscience and federal law. And Harriet Beecher Stowe's popular novel, *Uncle Tom's Cabin* (1852), dramatized the nature and consequences of slavery for the Northern public. The conflict deepened.

Congress and the Southern-dominated Supreme Court tore up the Missouri Compromise in the Kansas-Nebraska Act of 1854 and the Dred Scott decision of 1857. All territories, even those previously covered by the Missouri Compromise, could now choose to be free or slave. The consequence was a savage guerrilla struggle punctuated by mob violence in "bleeding Kansas," west of Missouri but north of the Missouri Compromise line.

Quasi-war over Kansas opened the door to the men of blood on both sides. There an Abolitionist extremist, John Brown, made a name for himself with a series of unsavory killings. In October 1859, impelled by visions of arming the slaves and provoking an immense revolt, he and a band of followers seized the federal arsenal at Harpers Ferry, Virginia. Colonel Robert E. Lee, U.S. Army, swiftly turned him out. Virginia as swiftly hanged him. Brown provided Abolition with a martyr and convinced the increasingly deluded South that it stood alone, for "states' rights" and slavery, against the rest of the Union.

The election of 1860 showed that North-South polarization was complete. Abraham Lincoln of Illinois ran for the new Republican party ("free soil, free men") that represented the North and Northwest. He carried seventeen of the

Slave States and Free States   1861

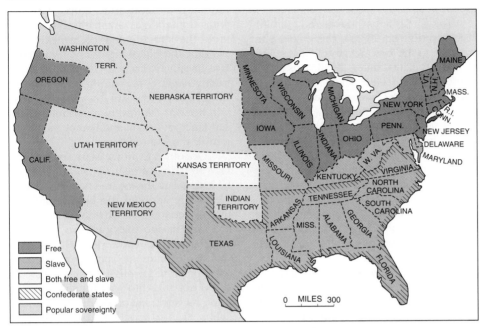

eighteen free states. The fifteen slave states overwhelmingly opposed him. Lincoln sought to preserve the Union with conciliatory gestures. He abhorred slavery but was a practical politician, not a zealot. The fire-eaters of the South, trusting in the economic power of "King Cotton" over both New England and Lancashire, and in their military spirit and talent as a planter aristocracy, decided for secession. On April 12–14, 1861, South Carolina bombarded and took Fort Sumter, the federal outpost in Charleston harbor. The "irrepressible conflict" had begun.

The Second American Revolution, 1861–65

The slave South's appeal to arms unleashed the world's first industrialized war, the longest, bloodiest, and most consequential struggle in the Western world between 1815 and 1914. The Crimean War had come too early and Bismarck's wars were too short to show what happened when industrialized powers collided. The U.S. Civil War was different. It was the first conflict between Western powers un-

limited in aims since the Wars of Religion. To the South's limited war to assert the "right" of states to preserve slavery, the North replied with *unconditional surrender*—a war aim the French revolutionaries had hinted at but which even Napoleon had hesitated to pursue. Reestablishment of the Union ultimately demanded the total destruction of the South's military power, the elimination of slavery, and the remaking of Southern society through a second American Revolution.

Neither side possessed at the outset a serious military establishment by European standards. The 16,367 officers and men of the peacetime U.S. Army split. A quarter of the 1,066 regular officers went South, including Colonel Lee, who stood with Virginia when it seceded to join the Confederate States of America. The Confederacy used these defectors wisely, to train and lead the state militias that became its army. The Union inherited the regular army, and kept its officers with regular army units. The Northern militias, sketchily trained and led by political appointees and elected officers, paid in blood for that mistake. Not until 1863–64 did Union battlefield effectiveness begin to rival that of the "rebels."

The Confederacy faced a daunting task. It produced 26,000 tons of pig iron annually to the Union's 160,000 tons. The Union had 22,000 miles of railroads to the Confederacy's 9,000. The Union had a population of 22 million; the Confederacy's whites were 6 million, with 3.5 million slaves. Weight of numbers and an almost infinitely expandable productive capacity were thus the Union's greatest assets. Yet the Confederacy coped in the short term. It improvised military-run war industries virtually overnight in Birmingham, Selma, Atlanta, Richmond. And the new rifled fire-power provided by the industrial revolution favored the tactical defensive.

Union morale was also anything but firm; the Confederacy's will to resist, at least in the early years, was unconditional. "Peace Democrats"—or "Copperheads" to the supporters of the Union cause—sought with considerable success to undermine Lincoln. In the border states partisans of the Confederacy intrigued, plotted, and spied. The 1863 introduction of a draft in the North caused an insurrection in New York City; mobs burned government offices and killed blacks as scapegoats for the war. Putting these "draft riots" down required a Union army corps. To cope with Confederate sympathizers Lincoln took the drastic step of partially suspending the Bill of Rights and trying civilians in military courts. The Confederacy's purely negative war aim gave it a further advantage. A few striking victories might win the war. Northern opinion might desert Lincoln; Britain and France might recognize the Confederacy.

Lincoln had no military experience. Like so many of his troops and generals, he learned on the job and he learned well. He swiftly adopted the key elements of the "Anaconda plan" that the aged generalissimo of the Mexican war, Winfield Scott, had proposed. The Union navy would blockade the Confederacy's coasts and dominate the Mississippi. But Lincoln could not afford to wait for strangulation to do its work; Union opinion demanded action. He also soon concluded that strangulation alone could not produce unconditional surrender. Union armies had to penetrate the heart of the Confederacy and destroy it.

The Confederate armies in northern Virginia dominated the first phase of the war, which lasted until mid-1863. They repeatedly threw back inept Union

Industrial fire-power: "The Dictator," a Union 13-inch mortar.

attempts to seize Richmond. But Lee failed to exploit the inexperience of the Union armies to deliver the crushing counteroffensive blow needed to unseat Lincoln.

The Confederacy's two major attempts to invade the North ended in disaster. The first, in September 1862, led to the appalling bloody draw at Antietam Creek in Maryland. The Union won a strategic victory, for Lee had to retreat. That gave Lincoln the platform to launch the political offensive that secured his place in history. On September 23, 1862, he announced that after January 1863 all slaves in states still in rebellion would be free. And on New Year's Day he issued the Emancipation Proclamation, which made the war a crusade to end slavery. It captured for the Union the support of European liberal opinion. It threatened the cohesion of the Confederacy's home front. It gave the Union armies, by the end of the war, almost 180,000 black soldiers, an eighth of their strength.

Lee's second invasion of the North, in June–July 1863, ended at Gettysburg, the largest battle fought in North America to this day. Lee's instinct for the Napoleonic tactical offense betrayed him. The artillery and rifle fire of the new industrial age shredded the ten brigades he launched at the Union center. His army, reduced by more than 20,000 dead, wounded, or missing, retreated through rain and mud to defend Virginia.

The Union had not merely halted Lee's last offensive. In the neglected western theater Lincoln had found a winning strategy and two generals equal to any who fought for the Confederacy. Ulysses S. Grant, a whisky-sodden failure in peace, had shown himself in 1861–62 to be a brilliant strategist and dogged tactician. On July 4, 1863, the day after Gettysburg, the Confederate citadel at Vicksburg in Mississippi fell to Grant and his subordinate William Tecumseh Sherman after a long amphibious campaign. The greatest river of the continent belonged to the Union from Ohio to New Orleans; the Confederacy was cut in two. After Grant and Sherman took Chattanooga at the end of 1863, the way was open for a Union

The South in ruins: Richmond, 1865.

drive through the Appalachians to cut the South in three and tear out its heart.

That task fell to Sherman, who practiced to the fullest his insight that "War is hell." He marched on Atlanta, the hinge of the rail system that linked the arsenals of Alabama with the Richmond front. He took and burned Atlanta and its factories. Then he discarded his rail supply links and marched to meet the Union navy at Savannah, cutting a fifty-mile-wide swath of scorched earth across Georgia's richest plantations. Sherman's victories gave Lincoln the decisive edge against Democrats and Copperheads in the hotly contested 1864 election.

To the north, Grant had become commander-in-chief under Lincoln. He methodically ground Lee's forces down in a year of staggeringly bloody battles of attrition around Richmond. Lincoln had at last found the method appropriate to the Union's unlimited war aim. As a Union general remarked to the Prussians while observing their 1870–71 campaign, the aim was to leave enemy civilians with "nothing but their eyes to weep with over the war."

The end came in March–April 1865. While Sherman savaged the Carolinas on his way north toward Lee's rear, the Confederate armies began to melt. Sherman's destruction of the South's farms and livestock created an irresistible urge to desert. And the pressure of Grant's will and of the Union's immense manpower on the

The strain of war: Abraham Lincoln, April 1865.

Confederate trenches at Petersburg near Richmond ultimately forced Lee out. Cornered in the open at Appomattox Court House, he surrendered to Grant on April 9, 1865. Five days later, a Confederate sympathizer assassinated Lincoln.

Reconstruction, the process of reintegrating the South into the Union, would have to go forward without the political genius of this greatest of presidents. The North faced a choice: it could simply return the South to the rule of the unrepentant planters in return for promises not to repeat the experiment of secession. Or it could attempt to reconstruct the South on a Northern pattern, ensuring that the newly freed slaves would receive the equality that blacks and many Northern whites had fought to achieve.

Lincoln's successor Andrew Jackson took the first path. It led to his impeachment at the hands of the Republican majority in Congress, which imposed the second alternative, "radical reconstruction." But martial law and federal aid for the ex-slaves were not enough to break the united resistance of planters and poor whites. The South's commitment to victory was as fierce after 1865 as before, and the North's staying power was limited.

Within twelve years, Ku Klux Klan terrorism and the more subtle opposition of the South's ruling class had won. To win the disputed election of 1876 the Republicans in Congress agreed to end Reconstruction. Henceforth the white South, in return for being left alone, gave the Democratic party a bloc of safe congressional seats. Blacks in effect lost the guarantees of life, liberty, property, and the vote given them in the thirteenth through fifteenth amendments of 1865–70. Compulsory labor, sharecropping, and debt bondage to the landlord replaced the old slave order and guaranteed a future of poverty. Sharecroppers and their masters do not innovate, nor do they give industry the markets needed to support growth. And in the course of the war Egyptian and Indian cotton had conquered the South's export markets. Low cotton prices further slowed recovery from the devastation of war.

Despite its immense cost—roughly 359,000 Union and 258,000 Confederate

dead and a legacy of resentment and economic stagnation in the South—the Civil War had decided issues as vital as those decided in the Revolutionary War. The United States would remain united, rather than splitting into rival assortments of squabbling states; Napoleon III had to end his Mexican escapade or face war. Slavery was dead; the United States would be a predominantly industrial society of free men and women. And Reconstruction was a battle better fought and lost than not fought at all.

Toward an Industrial Society

In the North and West, the years after the war were a time of unprecedented expansion and change. William H. Seward, secretary of state to Lincoln and Johnson, bought Alaska from Russia in 1867 for $7.2 million. He also annexed the island of Midway, halfway across the Pacific. The completion of the first transcontinental railroad in 1869 welded California to the East. The Great Plains went under the new steel plows or suffered division by barbed wire. By 1890 the frontier was passing.

The new age brought to the North and West the usual social conflicts of industrialization. The towns and cities, in which more than one-third of the North's population already lived in 1860, asserted their power over the countryside. Railroads and banks dominated the farmers of the plains, setting freight rates and conceding credit on whatever terms they pleased. "Trusts," vertically integrated monopolies such as John D. Rockefeller's Standard Oil, and giant corporations, such as Andrew Carnegie's U.S. Steel, replaced old-style family firms. Wall Street buccaneers such as Jay Gould and Jim Fisk left behind them trails of looted companies.

Industry demanded and received the highest protective tariffs in the world from the most uproariously corrupt Congresses in U.S. history. But a reaction against monopolies eventually set in. The Interstate Commerce Act of 1887 sought to regulate the railroads in the interests of the farmers. The Sherman Antitrust Act of 1890 made a gesture toward controlling the trusts. And in national politics, farmers organized. From the National Grange of 1867 through the Farmers' Alliance of the 1880s to the People's party, or Populists, of 1891, they sought to defend the Jeffersonian vision of a farmers' republic. They stood against banks, cities, and the ever-growing masses of immigrants. The "prolific womb of governmental injustice," the Populists thundered, was breeding "two great classes—tramps and millionaires."

In the 1896 election the Populists coalesced with the Democratic party under the leadership of William Jennings Bryan, later famous as an opponent of the teaching of Darwinism. His florid oratory failed to carry the Northeast and Midwest against the Republican and industrial candidate, William McKinley. Industry, which had already surpassed agriculture's share of the national product in the 1860s, had defeated agriculture for good.

In the cities that the Populists so abhorred, new forms of organization were emerging. The Knights of Labor, formed in 1869, had more than 700,000 members at its height. An 1886 episode of European-style anarchist bomb violence at the Haymarket in Chicago helped discredit the Knights, although they were not involved. The American Federation of Labor (AFL), an organization of skilled craft unions under the reformist Samuel Gompers, replaced them. The first major union actions inevitably brought defeat. Andrew Carnegie and his partner Henry C. Frick called in troops to crush AFL opponents in the great 1892 Homestead steel strike in Pittsburg. Eugene Debs' American Railway Union likewise failed in its bitter confrontation with the Pullman Company in 1894. But the unions survived.

In politics, the industrial cities of the Northeast and Midwest were the scene of a vast social experiment—the creation of Americans out of speakers of languages other than English. This was relatively new, for until the 1870s the only non-English-speakers to arrive in large numbers had been Germans. The waves from eastern and southern Europe after 1870 learned swiftly. Their children grew up as Americans, thanks to compulsory elementary schooling. Their political participation, with the hearty encouragement of the big city machines ("Vote early and often"), gave new meaning to the liberties proclaimed in the Constitution. A country as empty and short of labor as America, a country founded on principles rather than on notions of ethnic identity, was open to anyone willing to subscribe to those principles—except for the Chinese and Japanese, excluded by racist public opinion in 1882 and 1907 respectively. Industry and immigrants together transformed the United States from farmers' republic into cosmopolitan industrial empire, another Europe in size, ethnic variety, and power.

THE NON-WESTERN WORLD: RESISTANCE AND EMULATION, FAILURE AND SUCCESS

Others were less fortunate. The major non-European states of the nineteenth century responded to the Western challenge in a variety of ways. Some vegetated. Some collapsed. Some attempted to adapt Western technology while rejecting the ideas that had created it. And one, the empire of Japan, carried out a revolution from above that in forty years, from the 1850s to the 1890s, transformed it from victim into conqueror.

Latin America: Anarchy and Dictatorship

The states that emerged from the collapse of Spain's New World empire between 1808 and 1824 suffered serious disabilities. Spain had created societies stratified by blood. First came the Spanish administrators, then the Creoles—native-born of Spanish blood—then the *mestizos*—those of mixed Indian and Spanish descent. At the bottom were the Indians and the African slaves or ex-slaves of the Caribbean and Brazil. These societies had no tradition of self-rule; the jealous centralization of Spain, which distrusted the Creoles, had seen to that. And racial stratification meant weak states in which the masters had more in common with their counterparts in neighboring states than with their own peasants.

Repeated Creole revolts against Spain produced an unstable collection of fifteen

Hero of the independence struggle against Spain: Simón Bolívar, el Libertador.

Sultan Abd al-Hamid II, known for his cunning and cruelty.

states. Only Brazil, which achieved independence under the heir to the Portuguese throne, escaped a major upheaval. The new states oscillated between anarchy and the rule of narrow landowner oligarchies or despotic *caudillos*. Simón Bolívar (1783–1830), liberator of half the continent, despaired: ". . . America is ungovernable." By 1826 he already foresaw the future: "Many tyrants will rise upon my tomb."

The inland state of Paraguay provided the most spectacular example of those tyrants. Three men ruled it mercilessly between 1811 and 1870: José Gaspar Rodríguez de Francia (1811–40), Carlos Antonio López (1840–62), and his son, Francisco Solano López (1862–70). Francia created a police state cut off from the outside world and an army that under his successors became the most powerful in Latin America. In 1864 López junior took that army to war against all three of Paraguay's neighbors: Brazil, Argentina, and Uruguay. By the end, in 1870, the population of Paraguay had fallen from more than half a million to less than a quarter; almost all adult males were dead.

A few states, especially after midcentury, began to develop economically, as part of the British informal empire—Argentina, Brazil, Chile. Increased European immigration, especially to Argentina, speeded the pace of change. Elsewhere, savage struggles between peasants, rancher oligarchs, and the immensely powerful landowning Church produced repeated civil wars. Mexico changed chief executives 46 times in its first thirty years. It suffered a massive civil war and French intervention in mid-century, and the quasi-dictatorship of Porfirio Díaz from 1877 to 1911. Much of Latin America ended the century further behind the West in economic and social terms than it had been in 1800.

Egypt and the Ottoman Empire: Collapse and Survival

Closer to Europe, the Islamic world faced the full force of Western power. Algeria, Tunisia, and Morocco (in 1911) succumbed to French military colonialism.

Persia and the weak states of the Persian Gulf fell under the protectorate of Britain's Indian Empire. Only Egypt and Turkey were strong enough to have a chance at survival.

Egypt failed. The cotton boom of the 1860s encouraged the successors of Mehemet Ali to launch ambitious public works such as the reconstruction of Cairo in the image of Napoleon III's Paris. By the 1870s the Khedive Ismail was spending twice Egypt's revenue annually and plugging his deficit with European loans. Bankruptcy and the fierce reaction of Egypt's partially Westernized elites to the Khedive's subservience to Britain and France produced the explosion that led an unhappy Gladstone to occupy Egypt. The country's vital strategic importance to Britain, its easily controlled terrain, and its still largely peasant society doomed it.

The Ottoman Empire was both more fortunate and less digestible than its sometime vassal Egypt. It faced stirrings of nationalism, reinforced by religion, among its Balkan peoples. Russia, despite defeat in the Crimea, remained a major threat. Bankruptcy and foreign financial controls, as in Egypt, followed upon rash borrowing and frivolous expenditure in the 1870s. But the empire's international situation and military tradition saved it from dismemberment in the nineteenth century. Britain propped it up to keep Russia away from the Middle East. Austria supported it lest the demise of the Ottoman multinational empire free Balkan nationalities to turn against the multinational Habsburg empire. Germany supported it to stabilize Austria and as a field for German "informal empire." France supported it because France held much of the Ottoman debt. The powers would not tolerate one of their numbers monopolizing the Ottoman Empire, nor could they agree on how to divide it. Its poor but warlike peoples and its mountainous terrain made it an unpromising conquest.

Under the stubborn and wily Abd al-Hamid II ("the damned"), who ruled from 1876 to 1908–09, the Empire survived war with Russia in 1877–78 (see p. 745). It received military equipment and training from Prussia-Germany. In 1908–09 a

1368		1644	Revolution 1911
	Ming Dynasty		Qing (Manchu) Dynasty

group of Westernized "Young Turk" officers on the pattern of Arabi made the sultan a figurehead. In the following years they proved that the Ottoman warrior tradition could inspire a twentieth-century fighting force. That force ultimately upheld Turkish independence.

China: Resistance and Decline

The China that faced the Europeans in the middle decades of the nineteenth century was the most populous state on earth, with a historical tradition that stretched back three millennia. To the Manchu aristocrats of the Qing (Ch'ing) dynasty (1644–1911) and to the Confucian scholar-gentry who ruled China, the "Middle Kingdom" was the center of the universe. The overseas "barbarians" who had first appeared along China's coasts in the sixteenth century seemed no different than the nomads of central Asia or the tributary kingdoms of Vietnam, Korea, and Tibet. Barbarians

China in the Nineteenth Century

could enter into relations with China only by bringing tribute and prostrating themselves before the emperor. The dynasty kept them in their proper place in the eighteenth century by restricting them to the single trading port of Canton.

But China proved less and less capable of imposing Chinese norms on the seaborne barbarians or on the Russian land power to the north. The barbarian technological lead lengthened decisively with the coming of steamships and shell-firing cannon. And the Qing dynasty appeared to be following the law of cyclical rise, crisis, and decay that had long shaped Chinese thought about history and politics. By 1800 the dynasty had passed its peak and was descending, amid secret-society agitation, peasant rebellions, massive overpopulation, and immense natural catastrophes that took millions of lives. The sheer size of the empire, along with administrative inefficiency, corruption, and the inherent conflict between Manchu and Chinese, crippled efforts at reform.

The end of the East India Company's monopoly of the China trade in 1833 stimulated a rush to Canton by private British merchants, and led to the opening of China by force. British traders developed a profitable black market in China for the Indian-grown opium that paid for the West's imports of tea, silk, and the gleaming ceramics that had inspired envy and imitation in eighteenth-century Europe. When the Peking government made a desperate attempt to close down the opium trade for both fiscal and health reasons, the British replied with gunboats. The first and second Opium Wars of 1839–42 and 1856–60 flattened the dynasty's armed forces, opened numerous ports to European trade, delivered Hong Kong to Britain and vast northern territories to Russia, and gave foreigners immunity from Chinese law, with its custom of judicial torture. Traders, missionaries, and diplomats flocked in, rousing xenophobia. Killings of foreigners and frequent gunboat reprisals were the predictable result.

Internally, defeat in the First Opium War and the strains of dynastic decline unleashed an immense civil war. Hong Xiuquan (Hung Hsiu-ch'üan), the princi-

pal leader of the "Taiping Rebellion" that conquered south-central China in the 1850s, believed that he was the younger brother of Jesus and that his mission was to exterminate the Manchus. Hong's unstable blend of Western religious ideas and Chinese peasant millenarianism attracted a wide and fanatical following. But its foreign elements made it suspect to the Confucian provincial gentry. Eventually the dynasty rallied, thanks to armies that the gentry raised and led. With help from foreign military experts such as "Chinese" Gordon, they crushed the Taiping rebels by 1864. The European powers, in the end, preferred the Qing to chaos. Twenty million peasants perished in the war and its accompanying famines.

Qing survival now required drastic measures—not merely the adoption of Western techniques, but of the ideas on which they rested. The dynasty made a start in the late 1860s under the leadership of the Manchu Prince Gong (Kung). But Gong lost a series of palace struggles to the pitiless Empress Dowager Ci Xi (Tz'u Hsi), who henceforth dominated court and central administration until her death in 1908. Her hostility to anything she did not control paralyzed the regime. And to a true Confucian, the West's material and military success was irrelevant; tradition and virtue were their own reward. China's "self-strengthening" program grudgingly acquired armament plants, railways, and a military academy, but it lacked conviction. Neither dynasty nor scholar-gentry created the leadership and institutions required to save China from further dismemberment by the Europeans and Japanese.

Japan: From Victim to Great Power

Japan, until the arrival of Commodore Matthew Perry of the U.S. Navy in 1853–54, was even more closed than China. The great lord Tokugawa Ieyasu (1542–1616) had unified it in a series of wars that lasted until 1600. He and his successors imposed peace, exterminated or forced underground the Christian communities that the Jesuits had founded, and recognized only

The Empress Dowager Ci Xi (Tz'u Hsi), r. 1861–1908, whose fierce resistance to change helped doom the Qing dynasty.

A Japanese view: Commodore Matthew C. Perry, charged by President Millard Fillmore with opening Japan to Western trade, parades through the streets of Yokohama (1854).

the Dutch—limited to one port and one ship a year—as trading partners. The Tokugawa discouraged and occasionally persecuted Japanese who pursued "Dutch learning," the new European knowledge.

The Japanese system after 1600 was nevertheless quite different from anything in China. Both Western scholars and their twentieth-century Japanese counterparts have frequently described it as "feudal," for its basis was some 250 domains, or *han*, whose lords were dependents or vassals of the Tokugawa family. But a key element in European feudal institutions, the rights of the vassal against the lord, was lacking. And the system was infinitely more centralized than anything in medieval Europe. Most of Japan's hereditary warrior caste, the samurai, did not even own land, but received allowances in rice from their *han*. Their ethos stressed above all service to their lord.

Japanese politics were thus far different from those of China. The Tokugawa ruled, at least in theory, as deputies (*Shō-gun*) of the imperial house, which had reigned, although rarely ruled, from time immemorial. The emperor was both a figurehead for the Tokugawa and the most powerful symbol of Japanese unity. He might become a figurehead for others, legitimizing revolution. And the division of Japan into domains offered regional bases for movements to overthrow the Tokugawa.

Culturally, Japan had a tradition of borrowing. It acquired Confucianism and Buddhism from China and sixteenth-century guns from the Portuguese. The early curiosity of Japanese scholars about the outside world had few parallels in China. And the practical warrior ethos of the samurai took precedence over Confucianism. On the battlefield virtue was irrelevant; the issue was victory or defeat. A leader in "Dutch learning," Sakuma Shōzan (1811–64), compiler of foreign-language dictionaries and cannon-foundry master, commented caustically: China had lost the First Opium War "because foreign learning is rational and Chinese learning is not."

Structurally, Japan was small and ethnically homogeneous, with a fierce sense of distinctness. During the long Tokugawa peace, it had developed a flourishing agricultural economy and a large and growing merchant class. The Tokugawa, although still in control in 1854, were losing their grip on an increasingly rich and diverse society. Like eighteenth-century Britain, Japan had the cultural and social potential for a vast leap in productivity.

Finally, Japan's economy, although dynamic, was—unlike China's—not conspicuously rich enough to attract Western greed immediately. The opening of Japan was an afterthought. That was why Perry got there before the British. And the Japanese, in framing their response to Perry's peremptory demands for trading ports, had the advantage of knowing what had happened to China. Collaboration, not resistance, was clearly wisest until Japan was stronger.

Perry's arrival created a revolutionary situation. The Tokugawa shogunate grudgingly opened Japanese ports and accepted "unequal treaties." Xenophobic "men of spirit" among the lower samurai replied by assassinating foreigners and the Tokugawa officials who collaborated with them. In 1863 Britain bombarded the city of Kagoshima in reprisal. The shogunate's impotent collaboration with the West, like that of the khedivate in Egypt, deprived it of the legitimacy needed to rule.

But Japan took a different path than Egypt or China. The shogunate avoided open war with the West. And in the outer *han* of Satsuma, Chōshu, Tosa, and Hizen, middle and lower samurai with some understanding of the outer world offered an alternative to supine acquiescence or self-destructive fanaticism. In 1868 they persuaded their lords to revolt in the name both of tradition and modernity. The Tokugawa shogunate fell after a brief but bloody civil war.

The insurgents "restored" the emperor, who took the reign-title of Meiji. The new leaders were ruthless and clear-sighted. Backed by imperial authority and

the newly invented tradition of the Shinto state religion, they swiftly swept away all perceived obstacles to a "rich country, strong army." Loyalty previously given to "feudal" superiors proved readily transferable to emperor and nation.

The Meiji oligarchs pensioned off the domain lords in 1871. In 1873 they began the creation of a Prussian-style conscript army, breaking the "feudal" samurai monopoly of arms. The oligarchs abolished their own caste, the samurai, to mobilize all energies in a race against time to preserve Japan's independence. In 1877 their new army pitilessly crushed a last great rising of dissident samurai under a former comrade. The oligarchs created state enterprises with Western machinery, and sold them off to a merchant class that rose eagerly to the challenge of creating an industrial economy. The oligarchs imposed Western-style code law and compulsory education to reinforce Japan's existing traditions of learning, hard work, and respect for authority. They secured French, Prussian, and British advisers for army and navy. They created a military-bureaucratic absolutism with a Bismarckian constitution (1889) as fig-leaf. And in foreign affairs, they succeeded in appearing meek until Japan was strong enough to face the West on equal terms. The oligarchs of the Meiji Restoration created a mighty modern state, a powerful engine of change and conquest, the first modern non-Western great power. Its chief defect, it later emerged, was a lack of brakes.

Early in Britain's century, its seapower and its industrial lead had allowed it to dominate the wider world without apparent effort. Non-European peoples and states, from Latin America, to Egypt, to Burma, to China failed to rise to the challenge and suffered colonial occupation or "informal" domination through gunboats and treaties. When Africa went under the knife, divided by diplomacy and the

Maxim gun in less than twenty years, Britain took the lion's share. But ultimately both Britain's European "followers" and the two new non-European great powers proved dangerous rivals. The United States, thanks to swift demographic and economic growth and Northern victory in the Civil War, was by the 1890s poised to dominate the Americas. And Japan was about to create an empire that foreshad-owed the collapse of European domination in Asia. As the century ended, the world hegemony of Britain and of Europe rested precariously on narrow demographic foundations, on the grudging collaboration of the non-European peoples, on the toleration of the new non-European great powers, and on the long but increasingly fragile peace in Europe itself.

Suggestions for Further Reading

British and European Expansion

For much of the conceptual framework of this chapter, see the essays of J. Gallagher and R. Robinson in W. R. Louis, ed., *Imperialism* (1976), and D. Headrick, *Tools of Empire: Technology and European Imperialism in the Nineteenth Century* (1981). B. Porter, *The Lion's Share: A Short History of British Imperialism, 1850–1983* (1984), is useful on Britain. D. K. Fieldhouse, *The Colonial Empires* (1966), and *Colonialism, 1870–1945* (1981), offers a comparative perspective, as do S. K. Betts, *Europe Overseas* (1968); the sardonic V. Kiernan, *From Conquest to Collapse: European Empires from 1815 to 1960* (1982); and W. Baumgart, *Imperialism: The Idea and Reality of British and French Colonial Expansion, 1880–1914* (1982). For Britain's "white" colonies, see D. G. Creighton, *Canada's First Century* (1970); E. McInnis, *Canada: A Political and Social History* (1947); and C. H. Grattan, *The Southwest Pacific to 1900* (1963). On India, see J. M. Brown, *Modern India: The Origins of an Asian Democracy* (1985), and S. Wolpert, *A New History of India* (1982). R. Robinson, J. Gallagher, and A. Denny, *Africa and the Victorians: The Climax of Imperialism* (1968), is delightfully provocative on the "scramble for Africa."

The United States

The literature on the United States is distressingly vast; J. M. Blum et al., *The National Experience: A History of the United States,* 8th ed. (1993), is an excellent introductory survey with detailed bibliographies. On the pre-Jacksonian period, see G. Dangerfield, *The Awakening of American Nationalism* (1965); J. C. Curtis, *Andrew Jackson and the Search for Vindication* (1976), covers the "Age of Jackson." For the road west, see R. A. Billington, *Westward Expansion* (1967). On slavery, see especially E. D. Genovese, *Roll, Jordan, Roll: The World the Slaves Made* (1974). J. M. McPherson, *Battle Cry of Freedom: The Civil War Era* (1988), describes the greatest crisis in America's history; C. Royster, *The Destructive War* (1991), analyzes its peculiarly violent character; C. V. Woodward, *Origins of the New South, 1877–1913* (1951), covers its long-term impact.

Latin America, the Islamic World, and East Asia

For general surveys of Latin America, see J. F. Rippy, *Latin America: A Modern History* (1958, 1968), and T. H. Skidmore and P. H. Smith, *Modern Latin America* (1984); J. Lynch, *The Latin American Revolutions, 1810–1826* (1973), describes the initial upheaval that brought independence. For the fates of Ottoman Turkey and Egypt, see respectively B. Lewis, *The Emergence of Modern Turkey* (1968), and J. C. B. Richmond, *Egypt, 1798–1952* (1977). On China and Japan see C. Schirokauer, *A Brief History of Chinese and Japanese Civilizations*, 2nd ed. (1989); J. K. Fairbank, *The Great Chinese Revolution, 1800–1985* (1986), *The Cambridge History of China*, Vols. 10 and 11 (1978, 1980); and W. G. Beasley, *The Modern History of Japan* (1981), and *The Meiji Restoration* (1972).

28

EUROPE IN THE LONG PEACE
1871–1914

The years between 1871 and 1914 were the longest period of uninterrupted peace in Europe since the "five good emperors" of the first and second centuries A.D. Only minor Balkan conflicts disturbed the peace. The workings of the balance of power and especially the self-restraint of the new Germany prevented war between the great powers. Only after 1890 did a German bid for European domination and world-power status (see pp. 757–67) lead to a new age of world wars.

Monarchy and its attendant aristocracy remained the preeminent form of government. Landed wealth still dominated state administrations, diplomatic services, and standing armies. Revolution was no longer practical politics in western Europe, although faith in it persisted and even broadened. The demands of the working classes had little political weight until after 1900. The welfare state, with its bureaucracies, regulations, and taxes

was still in its infancy. These conditions, along with the immense strides of industry and commerce, made these decades the golden age of the middle classes. Money was now the foremost badge of social status, although those with money still sought to climb socially by marrying into the aristocracy. The middle-class citizens of Europe, thanks to steam, electricity, and the absence of government restrictions on movement, could travel as never before or after. Letters of credit and British banknotes took the place of passports.

This golden age was short. Both liberal principles and the preservation of domestic peace after the coming of mass education and the second industrial revolution seemed to demand an ever-wider expansion of the vote. Universal male suffrage in turn created the first workers' parties and encouraged women to demand the vote for themselves. In the realm of ideology and culture, a confident middle-class materialism compounded of

(OPPOSITE) THE GOLDEN AGE OF THE MIDDLE CLASSES: *A SUMMER SUNDAY AFTERNOON ON THE ISLAND OF LA GRANDE JATTE,* BY THE INNOVATIVE PARISIAN PAINTER GEORGES SEURAT (1884–86).

Darwin, steel, and electricity provoked a response: outright hostility to the gospel of science and "progress." The very rapidity of change created immense tensions, psychological as much as political and intellectual. Those tensions ultimately discharged in spontaneous rejoicing among the urban masses at the coming of war in August 1914.

EUROPEAN POLITICS AND SOCIETY

England: The Limits of Gradualism

By the 1860s Britain's spurt of dramatic economic growth was ending. From the

1870s its rivals began pressing ever more insistently at its heels. Yet as late as 1914 London remained the center of the world economy. Britain's money market was the largest, although upstart New York increasingly rivaled it. Britain dominated insurance and financial services, and controlled the world's largest merchant marine. Britain's overseas investments more than doubled between 1870 and 1900; in 1914 they still dwarfed those of other powers and underwrote economic growth on every continent. Britain's export of knowhow and import of interest and insurance premiums increasingly rivaled its trade in goods. But financial dominance proved a poor substitute for the mastery of world manufacturing that was passing to others (see Figure 24–4, p. 623).

Politically, the Britain of Queen Victoria (r. 1837–1901) was a time of gradual adjustment. The temperamental Palmerston had dominated shifting factional alignments in Parliament until his death in 1865. Parties remained incoherent collections of notables, without central machinery or discipline. The Queen was thus able to assert considerable power as constitutional monarch. But under Palmerston's two great successors, Benjamin Disraeli and William Ewart Gladstone, Liberals and Tories (Conservatives) took on their modern shape, following a pattern also visible in the United States. The monarchy's influence receded as the mass electorate and mass parties advanced.

The parties alternated in power, spurring each other to enlarge the franchise and appeal to the new electorate. Gladstone, "the People's William," took the initiative on the franchise in 1866. But it was Disraeli, son of a converted Jew, author of novels about the social question, and radical Tory, who shot ahead of his rival

Queen Victoria on the Prerogatives of a Constitutional Monarch   1850

She requires: 1. That he [Lord Palmerston, the Foreign Secretary] will distinctly state what he proposes in a given case, in order that the Queen may know distinctly to *what* she has given her Royal sanction. 2. Having *once given* her sanction to a measure, that it be not arbitrarily altered or modified by the Minister: such an act she must consider as failing in sincerity towards the Crown, and justly to be visited by the exercise of her Constitutional right of dismissing that Minister. She expects to be kept informed of what passes between him and the Foreign ministers before important decisions are taken . . . ; to receive the Foreign Dispatches in good time, and to have the drafts for her approval sent to her in sufficient time to make herself acquainted with their contents before they must be sent off.

From Queen Victoria to Lord John Russell (the Prime Minister), August 12, 1850, The Letters of Queen Victoria, ed. by A. C. Benson and Viscount Esher (London: John Murray, 1907), Vol. II, p. 315.

with a Second Reform Bill of 1867 that almost doubled the electorate. Gladstone, during his governments of 1868–74 and 1880–85, then introduced the secret ballot in 1872 and a Third Reform Bill in 1884 that gave most adult males the vote.

The consequences of the coming of democracy to Britain were at least three. First, it created the modern machinery of mass parties. In the 1874 election Disraeli pioneered the use of grass-roots committees coordinated from the center. Gladstone replied in 1880, attacking Disraeli's foreign policy in Britain's first populist stump speeches by a major political leader. Gladstone's tactics had once prompted Disraeli to describe his rival as an "unprincipled maniac, and with one commanding characteristic—whether preaching, praying, speechifying or scribbling—never a gentlemen." The day of the gentleman in politics was indeed passing. The Liberal party machine, under "Radical Joe" Chamberlain, self-made businessman and reforming mayor of Birmingham, improved on Disraeli's 1874 example and converted Gladstone's "speechifying" into victory. Appeals to and organization of the new mass electorate replaced social standing as the key to political success.

The second major consequence of democracy was to raise the problem of Ireland, Britain's earliest colony. Elizabeth I, James I, and Cromwell had imposed Protestant landlords on Ireland's Catholic peasants. An Irish nationalist revolt in the 1790s had failed. The famine of the 1840s had cut the population by a third, but peasant resistance to the landlords remained strong. A "Fenian Brotherhood" founded in 1858 in New York pressed the Irish cause with intermittent terrorism. And the Second Reform Bill and the secret ballot between them brought more than fifty Irish nationalist members to Parliament. There they obstructed proceedings with long speeches demanding rights for the peasantry and autonomy within the British empire—home rule—for Ireland. Gladstone's first administration (1868–74) made an inadequate start on the peasant question; his second (1880–85) settled it with the Land Act of 1881. But he was already too late. Exorbitant rents, arbi-

Queen Victoria, symbol of an era (r. 1837–1901).

trary evictions, peasant boycotts, violence against landlords, and Irish nationalist assassinations of high British officials had unleashed the extremists on both sides. Gladstone's conversion to Irish home rule and his attempts to implement it in 1886 and during his tragic last government in 1892–94 were in vain. Home rule meant placing Protestant landlords and the Presbyterian Scottish settlers of Ulster under the "Rome rule" of the Catholic majority.

To the delight of the Tories, who as a result gained uninterrupted power from 1895 to 1905, home rule split Gladstone's party. "Radical Joe" Chamberlain and the imperialist wing of the Liberals joined the Tories. The Irish question, which had now become a religious-national conflict between Protestant Ulster and the Catholic south and west, festered. On the eve of World War I, the Liberals made a final attempt to impose home rule. The Protestants of Ulster, armed to the teeth, defied London. The army officer corps, as closely connected to Ulster as its Prusso-German counterpart was to Prussia's Polish borderlands, resisted government policy in a fashion not seen since Cromwell. Then war in Europe postponed civil war in Ireland.

The great antagonists: Disraeli (*above*) and Gladstone (*below*).

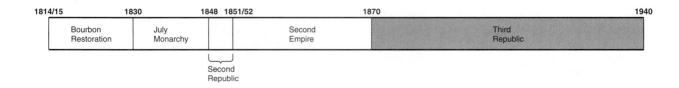

1814/15	1830		1848	1851/52		1870		1940
Bourbon Restoration	July Monarchy			Second Empire			Third Republic	

Second Republic

The expansion of the vote had brought the Irish question, which seemingly had no peaceful solution, to a head. Ballot and Irish question together introduced the third major consequence of democracy in Britain: the rise of a workers' party. Until the 1890s the working-class movement had confined itself to trade unionism. Craft unions had organized the Trades Union Congress in 1868; unskilled workers won their first major victory in the great London dock strike of 1889. But Gladstone and Liberals to his left on social issues, such as Chamberlain, held the working man's vote—until the party split over home rule.

Chamberlain's defection to the Tories created the political space for a working-class party. Keir Hardie, Scottish leader of the miners, organized the Independent Labor Party (ILP) in 1893. In 1900 the ILP, the gradualist middle-class "Fabian Socialists" of Sidney and Beatrice Webb, and a variety of other groups coalesced to form what became the Labour Party. In the 1906 election it won 29 seats. Although the Liberals won the election of 1906, they now had to reckon with an increasingly formidable force to their left. That strengthened the Liberal commitment to expensive social reforms such as old-age pensions (1908) and unemployment and health insurance (1911) under the leadership of the "Welsh magician," David Lloyd George.

When the unrepresentative Tory majority in the House of Lords balked at Lloyd George's "People's Budget," the Liberals rammed through a Parliament Act in 1911 that stripped the Lords of their veto over money bills. But the Liberals did not recapture Labour. Indeed, a wave of strikes after 1911 culminated in the ominous 1914 "Triple Alliance" of railwaymen, transport workers, and miners. Here also the coming of war rescued the Liberals from

crisis—but that rescue proved only temporary.

France: The Third Republic under Siege

France entered the long peace with a difficult legacy. Since 1789 three constitutional monarchies (1789–92, 1815–30, 1830–48), two republics (1792–99, 1848–51), and two Bonaparte dictatorships (1799–1815, 1851–70) had tried to rule it. All had collapsed within twenty years. Savage disputes divided Bourbon Legitimists, Orleanists, and Bonapartists, moderate "opportunists" and radical republicans, clericals and anticlericals. War, defeat, and the crushing of the Paris Commune in 1871 (see p. 681) had created lasting bitterness. Yet by 1879 France had established a regime that weathered one world war and collapsed only after crushing defeat in a second.

The Third Republic would have gladdened the heart of Edmund Burke. It represented the triumph of the provinces over radical Paris. Thanks to its middle-class leadership and its peasant voters, it proved remarkably conservative.

Its origin was Bismarck's demand for a French regime with a popular mandate to make peace. The universal male suffrage elections of February 1871 produced a chamber of monarchists, because the republicans had discredited themselves by preaching war to the bitter end. But the monarchists did not restore the monarchy. The Legitimist claimant, the childless Count of Chambord, refused to abandon the white flag with lilies of his royal forefathers. The country would not give up the Revolutionary and Napoleonic tricolor. Nor while Chambord lived would the Legitimists support the more flexible Orleanist claimant, the Count of Paris.

David Lloyd George (1863–1945), last of the great Liberal Party reformers and war prime minister, 1916–22.

The monarchy's moment soon passed. The monarchists had brought peace, but the peasantry feared that if they stayed in office they would restore the pre-1789 old regime. Elections gradually tipped the parliamentary balance toward the republicans. In 1877 they captured a majority in a hotly contested election called by the monarchists' figurehead president. Marshal MacMahon. In 1879 MacMahon resigned and Jules Grévy became the Third Republic's first republican president.

The president, however, was not to be the Third Republic's executive. A strong presidency might fall to another Louis Napoleon or MacMahon. Prime minister and cabinet, ever-changing according to the Chamber's whims, ruled France. The Third Republic spread power so widely that paralysis sometimes resulted.

Yet it could act decisively. Under the stern leadership of Jules Ferry, minister of education from 1879 to 1881 and prime minister in 1880–81 and 1883–85, the Republic created a national educational system independent of the implacably hostile Church. The mission of France's new schoolteachers was to nationalize and republicanize the rural masses, and to make France competitive with Prussia-Germany. In the villages, the "schoolmaster's party" now faced the "priest's party." Railways, another priority of Ferry and of his colleague Charles de Freycinet, likewise opened up the countryside to new ideas. The Republic finished the rail network that Napoleon III had begun, and at last consolidated France as a national market.

Its successes did not save the Republic from two major internal crises before the turn of the century. Despite the collapse of the royalists and the extinction of Bonapartist hopes with the death of Napoleon III's son in 1879, the Right remained hostile. The agricultural downturn of the 1880s, the phylloxera vine blight that almost destroyed France's historic wine industry, and a slowdown in industrial growth sapped the regime's popularity. After 1885 the moderate "opportunist" republicans who had presided over the establishment of the Republic no longer

had a majority. Three groupings of roughly equal size, the Right, the Opportunists, and the radical republicans, faced one another.

In this tense situation the chief figure among the Radicals, Georges Clemenceau, imposed his protégé, General Georges Boulanger, on the cabinet as minister of war. Boulanger, an impressive figure on horseback, cultivated popularity with the troops and made hostile remarks about Germany, remarks Bismarck gleefully exploited. When the government fell in 1887, Boulanger intrigued with both Catholic Right and extreme Left. In his support the ferocious anti-Semite Edouard Drumont joined the demagogue Paul Déroulède, one of the first of those nationalist extremists, common in the twentieth century, whose politics failed to fit the classic nineteenth-century categories of Left and Right. Boulanger began posing as a potential Bonaparte—until a resolute Opportunist government frightened him into exile in 1889. There he committed suicide on the grave of his mistress.

The Republic survived, despite continuing depression and a series of scandals that included revelations that de Lesseps' Panama Canal company, which had failed to repeat his triumph at Suez, had paid off numerous deputies. The Republic's second major crisis came from a different direction. In 1894 army intelligence recovered from a wastebasket at the German embassy a document suggesting that a member of the French general staff was selling war plans to Germany. The army immediately fixed upon a culprit, Captain Alfred Dreyfus, the only Jew on the staff. It court-martialed him without a shred of evidence, stripped him of his rank, and condemned him to imprisonment on Devil's Island off French Guyana. His family protested but failed to gain a hearing until evidence emerged that the leaks to Germany were continuing.

In 1898 the flamboyant novelist Émile Zola wrote an open letter to the president of the Republic entitled "*J'accuse!*" He accused the army of unjustly condemning an innocent man and of covering the real traitor. He challenged the authorities to sue him for libel. The "*Affaire Dreyfus,*"

Statesman of the Third Republic: Jules Grévy, president, 1879–87.

The young Georges Clemenceau, "Tiger" of the Radicals and war prime minister, 1917–20.

The French army, determined to brand Dreyfus as a traitor, provides him with a "guard of dishonor" whose backs are turned (1899).

or simply "the Affair," split France into warring camps. The clericals, who had in 1892 refused a pressing invitation from the reforming Pope Leo XIII to "rally" to the Republic, stood with officer corps, monarchists, anti-Semites, and the radical Right of the streets. For them, Dreyfus was guilty; he must be guilty—for his innocence meant the guilt of army, aristocracy, and Church. The Left stood in general for Dreyfus, although nationalism led many Opportunists and Radicals to support the army.

The government, which had foolishly claimed in 1897 that "there is no *Affaire Dreyfus*," collapsed. The suicide of the officer who had forged the cover-up evidence and the flight of the real traitor, a Lieutenant Esterhazy, led to a succession of new trials and Dreyfus's eventual rehabilitation. A Déroulède coup attempt in 1899 failed. Anticlerical Radical governments dissolved religious orders that had attacked the Republic, took the Church off the state payroll, and purged the army. The Republic won its confrontation with the Right and carried to completion the process of secularization begun with the Civil Constitution of the Clergy of 1790 (see p. 590).

Finally, the Republic even deflected or absorbed the workers' movement. The elections of 1893 brought almost fifty socialists into the Chamber. The economic upturn after 1896 eased France's domestic

distress and encouraged socialist and trade-union struggles. The General Confederation of Labor (CGT) and the socialist groups that coalesced in 1905 to form a united Socialist Party gave France a workers' movement second only to that of Germany. Marxism, which the austere Jules Guesde had introduced into the French labor movement in the late 1870s, prospered. Yet the greatest of all French Socialists was a Marxist only by courtesy. Jean Jaurès, the man who unified the movement's quarreling sects, had concluded that capitalism did not necessarily lead to revolution. By temperament he preferred conciliation to violence. And in the advocacy of violence the Marxists had a powerful rival—the anarchist myth of the revolutionary general strike, creation of the eccentric Georges Sorel, author of *Reflexions on Violence* (1908). Militants influenced by Sorel captured the CGT amid violent strikes in 1905–06. Clemenceau and Aristide Briand, prime ministers in 1906–10, ruthlessly suppressed them. But the Republic demonstrated that it could absorb as well as repress hostile forces. To the left of the now-respectable Radicals an exotic new hybrid, the "Radical-Socialists," sprang up. A genuine though non-Marxist Socialist joined a French government for the first time in 1899. Others eventually followed.

The Republic, to the surprise of all, far outlasted its predecessors. It proved strong enough to face war squarely in 1914. As international tension mounted after 1911 the Chamber swallowed its qualms about leadership. It appointed as president Georges Poincaré, a dour, forceful, and uncompromising Alsatian. It increased compulsory military service from two years to three to compensate partially for Germany's population advantage. When war came, even the Socialists marched.

Germany: Bismarck and After

The new German Reich of 1871 was a hybrid—partly centralized and partly federal, part military dictatorship and part constitutional monarchy. The King of Prussia and German Emperor (Kaiser), as

"Supreme War-Lord," personally controlled the German army. The Emperor appointed and dismissed the Reich chancellor without reference to the Reich's legislature. Prussia, which made up more than three-fifths of the Reich, dominated the upper house of that legislature, which consisted of representatives of the German princes. The lower house, or *Reichstag*, elected under universal male suffrage, had the indispensable right to approve or disapprove the budget; that much the Prussian Liberals had won in the constitutional conflict of 1862–66. Nor could the Reich government levy direct taxes. The states retained that right, and made occasional contributions to Reich finances at their pleasure. Finally, the constitutions of the states, especially the inequitable "three-class" franchise law of Prussia, which weighted votes by wealth, balanced the universal suffrage of the *Reichstag*.

This was a system of checks that only Bismarck could balance. Its complexity was in part a result of his desire to make himself indispensable, and in part a reflection of the strength of the various mutually hostile forces with which he had to deal. The "National" Liberals, who had chosen to cooperate with Bismarck after 1866, at first controlled the *Reichstag*. The Conservatives, thanks to the weighting of votes by income in the Prussian elections, held Prussia. The states retained the power to paralyze Reich finances.

All three forces were losers in the long term. The National Liberals failed to make the leap from mid-nineteenth century party of notables to mass party that British Liberals and Tories had made between 1868 and 1880. That failure doomed the German liberals to long-term decline. The Conservatives, despite an increasingly populist style from the 1890s on, survived because of the three-class franchise in Prussia and the votes of the landless peasants of the great estates of eastern Germany. Conservatism lost whatever Pietist ethical content it may have once had, and became the party of Junker "agribusiness." And the states lost vitality as national integration proceeded. That left a vacuum into which other forces gradually moved.

First of those forces were the German Catholics, who made up more than 30 percent of the Reich's population. They responded to Bismarck's Protestant "Greater Prussia" with a national Catholic political party, the Center. When Bismarck and the National Liberals attacked them in the

The Dreyfus Affair: Zola Accuses — January 1898

I accuse Lieutenant Colonel Du Paty de Clam [the investigating officer] of having been the diabolical author of the [original] judicial error—unknowingly, I may hope—and of thereafter defending his evil work, for the last three years, by the most bizarre and reprehensible machinations.

I accuse General Mercier [the former Minister of War] of having become the accomplice, at best through weakness of intellect, of one of the greatest iniquities of the century.

I accuse General Billot [the present Minister of War] of having had in his hands the indisputable proofs of the innocence of Dreyfus, and of having suppressed them. . . .

I accuse General de Boisdeffre and General Gonse [chief and deputy chief of staff of the army] of having become accomplices in that same crime. . . .

I accuse the first court martial [of Dreyfus] of having violated the law by condemning the accused on secret evidence, and I accuse the second court martial of having covered up that illegality, on orders from above. . . .

In making these accusations, I am not unaware that I am placing myself in jeopardy under articles 30 and 31 of the press law of July 29, 1889, which punishes the crime of defamation of character. I do so voluntarily. . . .

I have only one passion, that of enlightenment, in the name of humanity, which has suffered much and has a right to happiness. . . . Therefore let them dare to take me to court, and may the investigation take place in the light of day!

I am waiting.

From Émile Zola, Oeuvres Complètes *(Paris: Cercle du Livre Précieux, 1969), Vol. 14, pp. 930–31 (translation by M. Knox).*

early 1870s as "enemies of the Reich" who took their orders from Rome, Catholics rallied to the Church and the Center party. This *Kulturkampf* or "cultural struggle" between the Prusso-German state and the Catholic Church consolidated German political Catholicism as a party holding as much as a quarter of the popular vote. The Center's electorate, precisely because its bond was religion, came from all classes, although it was concentrated regionally in the Catholic south and west of Germany.

The second German mass party was that of the workers. Various workers' parties had emerged in the course of the 1860s, and in 1875 they coalesced to form the Social Democratic Party of Germany (SPD). Like the Center, the SPD suffered a preemptive attack by Bismarck. In 1878–79, in the course of a major policy change that involved alliance with Vienna, heavy protective tariffs, and the deliberate splitting of his National Liberal allies, Bismarck persuaded the *Reichstag* to outlaw SPD propaganda and mass meetings. He and his successors attempted to wean the workers away from the SPD with factory legislation and with the world's first state sickness and accident insurance (1883–84) and old-age and disability pensions (1889). Neither stick nor carrot checked the SPD's growth. The masses flooding into the new industrial cities voted, and voted Socialist.

By 1891, affiliated with highly disciplined trade unions and equipped with a Marxist program, the SPD was poised for expansion. By the Reich's last election in 1912, it had conquered 29 percent of the vote, the largest of any single party—and the largest vote for any workers' party in the world. This massive bureaucratic organization, with its women's and youth affiliates, its social clubs and workers' libraries, its newspapers and periodicals, was the mainstay of the international working-class movement, the "Second International" that emerged in 1889 after the collapse of Marx's "First International."

Despite its verbal commitment to revolution, its "proletarian internationalism," and its hostility to "militarism," the SPD was a working-class copy of the organization, sobriety, and discipline of the Prussian army. But it was not monolithic. The "revisionists" of its center and right, under the leadership of Edouard Bernstein, proposed to "revise" Marx. Like Jaurès in France, Bernstein believed that revolution was neither inevitable nor necessary, for the standard of living of the workers was rising. Social reform should come through ballot box and trade union. The SPD left, whose leading theoretician was the formidable Rosa Luxemburg, replied with insults. Reform was a "bourgeois swindle" and the revolutionary general strike was the just and necessary weapon of the "proletariat." That split increasingly threatened to crack the party open.

Failure to strangle the SPD at birth was the greatest of Bismarck's domestic defeats, but not the only one. His turn to protective tariffs in 1878–79 missed its two main goals. It did not provide the Reich with adequate revenues independent of the states. Nor did it give the government a stable *Reichstag* majority. The often stormy alliance between right National Liberals and Conservatives, industry and agriculture, "iron and rye" that Bismarck created around protective tariffs gained an absolute majority only once, in the 1887 elections. Without a Boulanger, without an emergency real or imagined with which to rouse the electorate with cries of "the Fatherland in danger," neither Bismarck nor his successors were able to dominate the universal-suffrage *Reichstag* he had created.

Ultimately Bismarck was unable to dominate the Kaiser either. The dependable William I died in 1888 at age 91. His successor, the reputedly liberal Frederick III, died of throat cancer shortly after ascending the throne. Instead, William I's brilliant but unstable grandson became Kaiser William II. His mother, Queen Victoria's daughter, voiced private forebodings: "My son will be the ruin of Germany."

William II did not merely lead the new German industrial military monarchy forward, as he put it, "toward glorious times." He personified its blend of manic self-confidence and inward self-doubt, of fear and aggression. He soon quarreled with Bismarck—who, to render himself indis-

Frederick III

| 1871 | 1888 | 1918 | 1933 |

William I

Bismarck

William II

Weimar Republic

1890

Imperial Germany

pensable, wrecked the *Reichstag* coalition of 1887 and proposed to suppress the SPD with Maxim guns. In March 1890, after an exchange of insults, the Kaiser sent Bismarck into vengeful retirement.

William II then tried to rule in person. But he failed to fill Bismarck's heroic role, and he and his subjects increasingly lacked Bismarck's sense of limits. The Kaiser's frequent "oratorical derailments" created chaos in both foreign and domestic affairs. By 1897 he did acquire a team capable of translating his enthusiasms into coherent policy: the 78-year-old Prince Chlodwig von Hohenlohe-Schillingsfürst as figurehead chancellor, the slippery Bernhard von Bülow as foreign secretary, and the supremely devious Admiral Alfred von Tirpitz as chief of the navy that was to make the new Germany a world power (see pp. 757–59). But William's short attention span and failure to resist the influences of the fire-eating young Guards officers who surrounded him guaranteed further crises.

In 1908, after a series of scandals at court had undermined the monarchy's reputation, William gave an interview to the British *Daily Telegraph* in which he offended both British and German public opinion at once. The ensuing outcry gave him a nervous breakdown. After 1908, his interventions in Reich policy were less frequent, although his fear of being thought weak played a fateful role in 1914.

German nationalism increasingly took the monarchy's place and filled the political vacuum left by the failure of the National Liberals. The Liberals themselves promoted a growing Bismarck cult to combat regionalism. On the far right a variety of groups emerged with more extreme visions. The Farmers' League, a rabble-rousing spin-off of the Conservatives, began in the 1890s to mobilize the rural masses with anti-Semitism. Jews, money, machinery, cities, the SPD, modernity—all were allegedly ruining the world of authentic German values and destroying the *Volk* community.

This sort of racist "cultural pessimism" was not unique to Germany. French racist fanatics such as Count Arthur de Gobineau (*On the Inequality of Human Races*, 1859) and Drumont had thought up or spread many of the notions that became current in Germany in the 1880s and 1890s. But France was industrializing less rapidly than Germany and was thus under less intense social strain. Above all, its political tradition since 1789 had stressed equality and rights. In Germany, once religious anti-Semitism met Darwin's ambiguous legacy in the 1880s, restraints collapsed. The Conservatives made anti-Semitism socially respectable, part of the ideological armory of the new nationalism.

Other groups, such as the Navy League to which Tirpitz played sorcerer's

William II, king of Prussia and emperor of Germany, 1888–1918, in a favorite uniform—that of the Death's Head Hussars.

apprentice and the Pan-German League founded in 1890, put forward megalomaniacal foreign policy programs with domestic implications. Their more extreme members created a grass-roots right-wing politics of a new kind, independent of the parties and the government. This loose movement was increasingly divorced from the monarchy and from the nobility, whom the new nationalists saw as castebound and inadequate. Erich Ludendorff, non-noble general staff officer and anti-Semite, personified the new outlook. While his seniors still looked to the Kaiser, Ludendorff pledged his loyalty to the "Fatherland." All that such people lacked was a vehicle and an occasion for mobilizing the masses. The coming great war gave them that and much else.

Russia: Despotism and Revolution

"Russian government is an absolute monarchy tempered by assassination," wrote a French observer in the 1830s. Despite Catherine the Great's concessions to the nobility, the tsar, thanks to the Tartar autocratic tradition of the Russian state, remained a ruler more absolute than any eighteenth-century Western monarch. Preserving autocracy as the nineteenth century drew on required ever-sterner measures.

Nicholas I succeeded the neurotic Alexander I in December 1825. Confusion over the succession led dissident noble officers under the influence of half-understood French liberalism to attempt a palace coup. After its failure, Nicholas had personally interrogated the surviving "Decembrist" leaders. He also vowed to prevent a recurrence. His remedy was an ever more extensive and powerful secret police and laws against what the next century came to call "thoughtcrime." The tsarist criminal code of 1845 was unique in Europe. It devoted 54 pages to "crimes against the state" and decreed savage penalties for merely raising "doubts" about the authority of the tsar.

Like his predecessors since Peter the Great, and like many non-Western regimes in both the nineteenth and twentieth centuries, the Russian autocrat faced an impossible choice. His power rested on external success. Yet the bayonets of conscripted serfs were no longer enough; defeat in the Crimea in 1854–56 had proved that. Success, and thus autocracy, in the machine age required a society capable of economic growth. But growth in turn created demands for political participation that threatened autocracy.

The successor of Nicholas, Tsar Alexander II (r. 1855–81), chose economic growth, but with what he hoped were safeguards. In 1861, following the example of Peter the Great, he imposed on Russia a revolution from above: the freeing of the serfs. The end of serfdom would permit universal military service, raise agricultural productivity, free labor for industrialization, and galvanize society into a prosperity that would restore Russia's threatened power position. Alexander's great Emancipation Edict of 1861 freed from the rule of their landlords the 22.5 million serfs who made up almost 38 percent of the Russian empire's population. What it did not do was free them from the land. To aid tax collection and to retain control of the peasantry, the autocracy kept the peasants bound to their village community, the *mir*. The landowners retained two thirds of the land and the former serfs received only a third, for which they had to pay by installments over the following 49 years.

Land redemption debt, the stifling effects of the *mir* on peasant enterprise, and massive population growth ensured that emancipation merely turned a serf problem into a peasant problem. The rural population leapt upward from 50 million in the early 1860s to 82 million in 1897. Competition from newly created industries in the cities lessened peasant income from traditional village handicrafts. Peasants who stayed on rather than migrating to mines and cities waited expectantly for a final redivision of the land that would wipe the landlords out.

More immediately damaging to the autocracy than the growing possibility of rural revolt was a loss of control over educated society. Russia had few cities and no middle class of any size in 1800. It developed them hesitantly, with the support of the autocracy's effort at industrialization. What it developed above all was an *intelligentsia,* a minority defined first by its education and then by its opposition to the autocracy. That minority produced some of the nineteenth century's greatest literature, from the poetry of Pushkin to the novels of Turgenev, Tolstoy, and Dostoyevsky. But thanks to the autocracy that prevented it from acquiring political experience, the intelligentsia also developed, like the thinkers of Enlightenment France, a variety of dangerous utopias.

The generation that followed the Decembrist plotters of 1825 took their inspiration from Hegel rather than from liberalism. They asked how Russia might contribute to the self-realization of the world spirit. In the 1840s and 1850s their dominant school, the "Slavophiles," argued that Russia's very differences from the West were Russia's strength. The Westernizing experiment of Peter the Great, they insisted, had been a disastrous mistake. But thanks to Orthodox Church and *mir,* Russia had not succumbed to rationalism, individualism, alienation. Russia's mission, they proclaimed, was therefore to give humanity back its soul. A variety of critics, often called "Westerners," pointed out that the *mir* was primarily an invention of the autocracy's tax collectors, and suggested that talk of Russia's soul was utopian glorification of backwardness. But Slavophilism persisted, and furnished much of the substance of Muscovite "Great Russian" nationalism.

The generation that followed the emancipation of the serfs argued more about politics than about Russia's soul. By the 1860s non-nobles had reached the universities in numbers. The learned professions were beginning to multiply, providing political radicalism with a social base. A Left emerged that mocked the reforms of the 1860s as insufficient and dedicated itself to overthrowing the autocracy. In 1874 several thousand students went "to the people" to create a peasant revolutionary movement. Peasants reacted to these "populists" with suspicion, and revealed a deep interest in private property that shocked students brought up on Slavophile visions of peasant communism.

Defeat in the countryside and mass arrests impelled some radicals toward terrorism. A tiny conspiratorial group, with the boldness characteristic of those who believe they possess the absolute truth, named itself "The People's Will" (*Narodnaya Volya*). It hunted down the tsar himself and killed him in March 1881. The new tsar, Alexander III (r. 1881–94), crushed *Narodnaya Volya* and created the dreaded *Okhrana,* a secret police even more powerful than its predecessors. Repression froze what little political life Russia possessed. An anti-Semitic radical Right grew, with government support, to oppose the revolutionary intelligentsia. Slavophilism mutated into Russian nationalism and Pan-Slavism, the claim that the Russian state was the patron of Slavs everywhere. Right-wing opinion, as in Imperial Germany, began to place limits on the autocracy's flexibility in foreign affairs.

At home, after the defeat of *Narodnaya Volya,* the radicals turned increasingly to the "scientific" certainties of Marxism. But Marxism was a theory of revolution for advanced countries. It hardly fitted Russia, which still awaited both a "bourgeoisie" and a "bourgeois revolution." Vladimir Ilyitch Ulyanov, brother of a hanged member of *Narodnaya Volya* and son of an imperial bureaucrat, found the answer. Under the alias of V. I. Lenin, he embraced the voluntarism, the faith in the primacy of the human will, that was one part of Marx's legacy. It was the task of Russian Social Democracy, Lenin announced, to force the pace of history. It must take command of Russia's small but growing industrial working class and overthrow the autocracy.

For that task, Lenin created a new kind of organization, the embryo of the twentieth-century one-party state. The history of Europe after 1848, Lenin saw, demonstrated that Marx had been wrong. The proletariat under capitalism was not revolutionary. "The working class, exclusively by its own effort, is able to develop only trade-union consciousness," he wrote with contempt. Logically enough, Lenin recognized that the vehicle of socialist revolution was not the working class

The professional revolutionary: Vladimir Ilyitch Lenin (*center*) with associates (1895).

but the "bourgeois intelligentsia: contemporary socialism was born in the heads of individual members of that class." Only the mobilization of that "class" could bring revolution. In 1902 he spelled out what was needed in a famous tract, *What Is to Be Done?* An organized minority of "professional revolutionaries" must serve as vanguard to the childlike masses. "Give us an organization of revolutionaries," wrote Lenin, "and we will overturn Russia!" Lenin's splitting of the Russian Social Democratic party at its conference in London in 1903 created that organization. His faction claimed for themselves the title of "men of the majority," or *Bolsheviki,* and imposed on their irresolute opponents the demeaning title of *Mensheviki,* or "men of the minority." Lenin's narrow sect ("better fewer, but better") slowly grew.

Imperial Russia's first revolution owed nothing to the Bolsheviks. The autocracy sought reinforcement by "a victorious little war" against Japan in 1904 (see p. 756). Defeat instead led to urban and rural revolt. Russia after 1890 had begun to industrialize at a startling rate under the impulse of French loans and of bureau-

crats such as Sergei Witte, creator of the Trans-Siberian Railway. The opening up of the coal and iron of the Donetz Basin and the oil of the Caucasus made Russia an industrial world power. In the cities of northern Russia, textile and mechanical industries grew feverishly. And an industrial work force torn from its villages and as yet largely unprotected by factory legislation proved far more radical than Lenin had expected.

The shooting in front of the Winter Palace of an unarmed crowd petitioning the tsar on January 22, 1905, "Bloody Sunday," touched off widespread anarchic revolt in the cities. But that spontaneous popular insurrection failed to find leaders. The Mensheviks lacked the will; they expected that in the fullness of time a "bourgeois revolution" would pave the way for their own socialist one. The Socialist Revolutionaries, heirs to the Populists, expected peasant uprisings and were unprepared to lead the workers. The Bolsheviks were too few and naturally distrusted this spontaneous expression of the popular will. The last tsar, the fatuous Nicholas II (r. 1894–1917), was thus able to end the Revolution of 1905. He gave his subjects a legislature, or *Duma,* while loyal troops, bureaucrats, and police gradually suppressed the revolutionary workers' councils, or *Soviets,* that had given the revolution what little organization it possessed. The far Right, organized with official approval in the "League of the Russian People," or Black Hundreds, massacred Jews and opponents of the autocracy.

Constitutional experiments soon ended. Two successive *Dumas* defied the government, demanding civil rights and reforms. Nicholas refused to surrender his autocratic power. Restriction of the franchise produced a Third *Duma* (1907–12) of "masters, priests, and lackeys" that proved more obedient. Under its last strong minister, Peter Stolypin, the autocracy attempted belatedly to finish the emancipation of the peasants from the *mir,* while suppressing all opposition. Stolypin died by assassination in 1911. More despotism bred further extremism and pushed Russia's few Liberals to believe naively that the far Left was preferable to the autocracy. As a new war approached in 1914, waves of massive strikes con-

Lenin Invents the Dictatorship of the Vanguard Party   1902

I assert:

1. that no revolutionary movement can endure without a stable organization of leaders maintaining continuity;

2. that the broader the popular mass drawn spontaneously into the struggle, which forms the basis of the movement and participates in it, the more urgent the need for such an organization, and the more solid this organization must be (for it is much easier for all sorts of demagogues to side-track the more backward sections of the masses);

3. that such an organization must consist chiefly of people professionally engaged in revolutionary activity;

4. that in an autocratic state, the more we *confine* the membership of such an organization to people who are professionally trained in the art of combating the political police, the more difficult it will be to unearth the organization.

From Vladimir Ilyitch Lenin, What Is to Be Done? Burning Questions of Our Movement *(New York: International Publishers, 1969), p. 121.*

Bloody Sunday, January 22, 1905. Tsarist troops fire on a procession of workers, killing 70 and wounding 240.

vulsed urban Russia. Tsarism desperately needed victory, but victory might not be enough to save it.

Austria-Hungary: Dynastic Empire in an Age of National States

For Austria, 1866 was not merely a military defeat, but an omen. The breakthrough of the national state in central Europe threatened the breakup of the Habsburg empire itself. Austria survived because Bismarck needed it. "If you ask me what we have promised Austria in return for her friendship, I should answer 'life,'" remarked Prussia's ambassador in Vienna to his Russian colleague in the fall of 1870. Austrian collapse would saddle Protestant Prussia with the Catholic Austrian Germans and with Austria's Balkan quarrels with Russia.

But German goodwill alone could not ensure Austria's long-term survival. That required an ideology, an "Austrian Idea," to counter the nationalism of the empire's subject peoples. The economic integration of the Danube Basin, the ties of agrarian Hungary to industrial Vienna and Bohemia, was not sufficiently inspiring. Good government from the most efficient bureaucracy of east central Europe was likewise no answer to the growing clamor of the nationalities for rule—or misrule—by their own. And Austria's substitute for colonial expansion, its "civilizing mission" in the Balkans, encouraged the same sort of nationalist reaction that bedeviled the European powers in Asia and Africa.

Emperor Francis Joseph (r. 1848–1916) and his ministers faced a paradox. Preserving Habsburg freedom of action, as always, required playing off the empire's provinces and nationalities against one another. But in the age of nationalism, that strategy could only encourage the nationalities to greater and greater mutual intolerance, and tear the monarchy apart. And if, by some miracle, the monarchy should successfully promote compromise between the nationalities, they would then be free to combine against the monarchy itself.

The dynasty therefore played for time. In 1866–67 Francis Joseph grudgingly struck a bargain with Hungary to prepare the way for a war of revenge against Prussia. That "*Ausgleich,*" or compromise of 1867, gave the Hungarians what their moderates had sought in 1848: full control of affairs within the far-flung borders of a "greater Hungary" that included millions of Rumanians, Serbs, and Croats. The only institutions of importance that Hungary shared with the rest of the monarchy after 1867 were the emperor and the ministries of foreign affairs and war. And Hungary received, in effect, a veto over Habsburg foreign and military policy.

When Austrian revenge on Prussia seemed possible in alliance with France in the war of 1870, the Hungarians exercised that veto. Prussia had made the *Ausgleich* possible; a Habsburg reversal of the verdict of 1866 would automatically place Hungary's hard-won autonomy in question. The revolutionary alliance with Hungary against Vienna that Bismarck had toyed with in 1866 thereby became a tacit German-Magyar agreement to preserve the new status quo. Thus the provisional became permanent. The *Ausgleich* made Austria the "Dual Monarchy" of Austria-Hungary until 1918. In Hungary, the gentry ruthlessly Magyarized the subject nationalities and dominated the voteless and voiceless Hungarian peasantry. In the rest of the empire, the German "ruling *Volk*" fought a losing battle against the rise of the Czechs.

After a series of unsatisfactory German liberal ministries, Francis Joseph turned in 1879 to an aristocrat of Irish extraction, Count Eduard Taafe. Taafe's formula was simple and for a time effective. In the *Reichsrat,* the legislature of the non-Hungarian parts of the empire, he created a government bloc of loyal Poles, clericals, and Czechs, the so-called "iron ring." With that support, and with the aim of keeping "all the nationalities of the empire in a balanced state of mild dissatisfaction," he kept the peace until his fall in 1893.

The German-Czech conflict over rich and rapidly industrializing Bohemia destroyed Taafe's framework. Since 1848 the Czechs had developed a high culture, complete with composers such as Bedřich Smetana and Antonín Dvořák, that put to shame German claims of cultural superiority. The Czechs had nationalized their masses with schooling in Czech and with a university at Prague. They were developing an industrial middle class. And their most advanced politicians, the "young Czechs" (shades of Mazzini) refused to subscribe to Taafe's proposed arrangement for sharing power with the Germans in Bohemia.

The Germans were equally obstinate. In Vienna, that cosmopolitan city of art and vice, a variety of anti-Slav and anti-Semitic demagogues arose. The fanatical Georg von Schönerer preached that "religion is irrelevant, *race* is the source of the swinishness" that he ascribed to the Jews. The mayor of Vienna, Karl Lueger, organized a "Christian Social" party that mixed populist clericalism with an anti-Semitism less crude than that of Schönerer; its descendants still give Austrian politics their peculiar tone. Even Austrian social democracy divided into German and Czech national socialisms. Language and culture proved, there and elsewhere, more powerful than class.

In 1897 the dynasty tilted decisively toward the Czechs. It pushed through a decree requiring that state officials in Bohemia be bilingual in Czech and German. Since no German would stoop to learn Czech, the decree in effect excluded the Germans from state employment and from power. The Germans rioted. Schönerer thundered at the dynasty's betrayal of Germandom. He and other lesser fanatics looked to Prussia-Germany against a Habsburg state that they accused of submerging the Austrian Germans in Slavs and Jews.

In the short term the Germans won. The monarchy dismissed Count Casimir Badeni, responsible for the language decree, and retracted the decree itself in 1899. Naturally the Czechs rioted in response. Slovenes and Italians fought in Trieste. Some Croats began to feel the pull of the notion of a "South Slav" (Yugoslav) state of Croats, Slovenes, and Serbs across the border. The "South Slav" idea had little basis in history, culture, or religion, for Slovenes and Croats were Catholic and Western in orientation, and Serbs were

Orthodox and Balkan. But it gradually spread; fear that independent Serbia might prove the "Piedmont of the South Slavs" provoked hysteria in Vienna.

In 1906–07 the dynasty at last fell back on universal suffrage, hoping to submerge the competing nationalisms in a flood of loyal peasant votes. But universal schooling had made the peasants into Germans, Czechs, Croats, and Slovenes. After 1909, Francis Joseph and his ministers ignored the *Reichsrat* and ruled by decree. Reformers floated a variety of federal or "trialist" plans to give Slavs equality with Germans and Magyars. But Germans and Magyars preferred to wreck the monarchy rather than suffer diminution of their "historic rights." In the face of ever-intensifying internal conflict, Austria-Hungary's "idea" remained Church, dynasty, bureaucracy, and army. By 1914 those institutions were strong but wasting assets.

Italy: Least of the Great Powers

The weight of Italy's historic greatness almost crushed the new Italian national state. Nationalists from the radical Mazzini rightward insisted that the new Italy must be and act as a great power. The legacy of the Roman Empire and of Italy's economic and cultural primacy in the Renaissance demanded no less.

Italian reality was ill-equipped to live up to such expectations. The South, where the landlords' horses lived better than the peasants, was two centuries or more behind the North. At unification in 1861, illiteracy ranged from 54 percent of the population over six years of age in the North to 89 percent in the South and the islands. Even the relatively prosperous North lacked an industrial base, for Italy had little iron and almost no coal.

The new state also had a narrow political base. In part, this was deliberate. Cavour and his heirs feared the masses with their potential for anarchic radicalism or Bourbon-clerical revolt. Until 1882 the electoral law gave 2 percent or less of the population the vote; after that date 7 to 9.4 percent could vote. In part, narrowness was unavoidable. The illiterate, until the coming of conscription, had little idea that they even belonged to a national state. And after 1870, furious at his loss of Rome, Pope Pius IX had locked himself in the Vatican and ordered a Catholic boycott of Italian politics. That was no small loss for a state with a population that was nominally 99 percent Catholic.

Finally, the later stages of unification were demoralizing. War in 1866 brought Venetia into the state, but only because Prussia won at Königgrätz; Italy itself suffered humiliating defeats by land and sea. The taking of Rome from the Pope in 1870 was inglorious. The petty spectacle of parliamentary politics provoked the scorn of the aged Mazzini and of nationalists such as the poet Giosuè Carducci: "Oh for the days of sun, of liberty and glory in 1860. . . . Oh for the struggles of titans between Cavour and Garibaldi in 1861!" "What have we become?" asked Carducci despairingly.

What Italy had become was a moderately successful parliamentary regime under a series of centrist coalitions resembling those of France's Third Republic. Defeat in 1866 at least prevented any revival of royal absolutism. Victor Emmanuel II and his army lacked the prestige for Bismarckian solutions. Under Cavour's heirs, the moderate liberal *Destra,* or Right, Italy paid the immense debts of the wars of unification and balanced the budget. The money came mostly from the hard-pressed peasantry, but at least Italy did not follow Egypt and Turkey into debt bondage. The *Destra* reformed the army, although that institution still lacked the prestige needed to attract first-rate officer material. Finally, the *Destra* gave Italy some small voice in the councils of the great powers.

In 1876 a motley coalition of northern left-liberals and southern landowners henceforth known as the *Sinistra,* or Left, ousted the *Destra.* The *Sinistra* extended the franchise and made elementary education free and compulsory in law if not yet in fact. It also created a parliamentary tradition that outlasted the century, for the southern landlords, in return for patronage jobs and public works, gave the government of the day their votes. That

bargain, rather like the tacit agreement that ended Reconstruction in the United States, helped stabilize parliament at the price of social and political stagnation in Italy's south.

By the 1890s new forces pressed against the system. The steamship brought in cheap grain and ruined southern agriculture, then bore away the resulting emigrants. Peasant unrest in Sicily unnerved the governments of the early 1890s. A socialist movement, anarchist in the 1870s and Marxist by the 1890s, gained ground. And unlike their counterparts elsewhere, the Italian socialists successfully organized parts of the countryside. By the first decade of the new century, the unions of the landless agricultural laborers of the rich Po Valley in north Italy were strong enough to stage bitter province-wide strikes.

Even Catholicism began to stir politically. Leo XIII (r. 1878–1903) weakened his predecessor's prohibitions on Catholic political participation in Italy, just as he had urged Catholics to rally to the Third Republic in France. Then his successor Pius X (r. 1903–14) revived some of Pius IX's denunciations of modernity. The entry of organized Catholicism into Italian politics was thus slow. But by the 1913 election, it was an accomplished fact.

The *Sinistra* had its last incarnation under the charismatic Sicilian and former Mazzinian, Francesco Crispi (prime minister, 1887–91, 1893–96). It fell resoundingly after catastrophe at Adowa ended Crispi's bid for a vast East African empire. Riots against the African war and hard times at home inaugurated a period of bayonets in the streets and right-wing governments. The king, Victor Emmanuel II's son Umberto I, imposed a general as prime minister before his own assassination by an anarchist in 1900. Parliament fought back and won decisively.

With the new century came economic takeoff and political stability under the greatest of Cavour's successors, Giovanni Giolitti (prime minister 1903–05, 1906–09, 1911–14). Giolitti despised rhetoric; that won him respect but no fanatical followers. He knew well that Italy's uneven economic and social development had produced bizarre political effects—including his own need to pay southern deputies for their support. If you cut a suit for a hunchback, he once remarked, you get a hunchbacked suit.

What he attempted was gradual reforms that would integrate the new mass forces, the Socialists and Catholics, into the Liberal parliamentary system without destroying it. He refused to persecute the Socialists. To the horror of Italy's industrialists, he did his best to keep the state neutral in labor disputes. His greatest monument was the enactment in 1912 of virtual universal male suffrage, which expanded the electorate from 3.3 million to 8.6 million. It was also his downfall.

The Catholics proved difficult and demanding allies. On the Left, extremists that included a certain Benito Mussolini (see pp. 834–38) captured the socialist party-leadership and closed off any chance of cooperation with Giolitti. The prime minister's own supporters in parliament resented concessions he had made to the Catholics and overthrew him in March 1914. "Red Week," an immense wave of riots led by Anarchists and Left-Socialists that swept north Italy in June 1914, soon made Giolitti's sober common sense and conciliation look outdated and naive.

Intellectuals of all stripes had long railed against his lack of charisma. The young literary firebrands of the Italian Nationalist Association lamented that Italy "had been too much made with diplomatic intrigues and foreign arms." They and others forcefully revived a myth widespread since the anticlimax of the *Risorgimento* in the 1860s. "Making Italians," the completion of national integration, required a great war. Giolitti's right-Liberal successor Antonio Salandra was soon to find that war, and with it destroy Liberal Italy.

BATTLES FOR WOMEN'S RIGHTS

The coming of mass politics for men inevitably raised the question of the rights of women. It opened an arena in which large numbers of women could for the first time

Facts, not rhetoric: Giovanni Giolitti (1842–1928), five times prime minister of Italy.

press their case not merely for the vote but for equality between the sexes. That was a question that went far beyond politics.

Male domination of women has taken many forms. Its foremost mid-nineteenth-century version was middle-class woman's role as pedestal-mounted "angel in the house." That notion was in part a consequence of the separation of life into work and home, male and female domains, that came with industrialization. But it also had pseudoscientific underpinnings. Learned doctors discoursed on women's presumed lack of sexual passion and on the alleged "gigantic power and influence of the ovaries" over a women's whole being. For such pundits, women's position was biologically determined. "What was decided among the prehistoric Protozoa, cannot be annulled by Act of Parliament." Even liberals could claim that the scientific wisdom of the day freed them from having to give women the same natural rights as men.

Religion contributed as well to the myth of women's domestic nature. In the 1820s the churches took to insisting that women, who were proving more resistant than men to the temptations of religious skepticism, were also "purer" than men.

Preservation of that purity required their continued confinement to the home.

By the 1860s, especially in Britain, these notions were under attack. Women had penetrated previously male citadels such as hospitals and schools. Florence Nightingale made nursing a profession for women by her crusade against the British army's grotesque mismanagement of medical services in the Crimea. Soon a broad women's movement pressed for higher education and careers for single middle-class women. In the 1870s Girton and Newnham Colleges at Cambridge began granting degrees to women. Pioneers opened up medicine and the law. Agitation led to reforms in the 1870s and 1880s of Britain's crude laws governing marriage, divorce, and the age of consent. Women's bodies and property ceased to belong to their husbands in a literal, legal sense.

The British "feminists"—the French word became current in the 1890s—also attacked the legal double standard in a more spectacular way. They crusaded successfully against the Contagious Diseases Act (repealed 1886) that required veneral disease examinations and quarantine for prostitutes—but not soldiers—in garrison towns. The acts, they insisted, were government endorsement of the creation of "a *slave* class of women to minister to lust."

Crusader for hospital reform: Florence Nightingale (1820–1910).

The crusaders sought to do more than raise the status of women. They proposed to reform men and revolutionize the relationship between the sexes.

When the Liberals came to power in the 1906 election, the women's movement tried to hold them to liberal principles. But the evasive Herbert Asquith (prime minister, 1908–16) and the even more slippery Lloyd George torpedoed women's suffrage legislation in 1910. The Women's Social and Political Union (WSPU), under the leadership of Emmeline Pankhurst and her daughter Christabel ("Votes for Women, and Chastity for Men"), then declared war on government, Parliament, and men. "Suffragette" activists attempted to break police cordons in Parliament Square; the police and male bystanders replied with violence and sexual abuse. Christabel Pankhurst orchestrated a campaign of window-smashing, burning of country houses, attacks on art galleries, and bombs in Westminster Abbey. To trial and imprisonment, the WSPU replied with hunger strikes. The government countered with forced feeding. Opinion, including opinion among women, was overwhelmingly against WSPU defiance of the law. But WSPU tactics provoked the government to acts that weakened its position.

Finally, in June 1914, Asquith agreed to receive a delegation of working women under the leadership of Sylvia Pankhurst, Christabel's sister and a labor activist. The specter of a potential mobilization of working-class women into a genuine mass movement apparently made Asquith quail. He lost all stomach for further warfare between the sexes and undertook to support a women's suffrage bill. The war delayed it until 1918 but eased its passage. The contribution of women to the war effort made it impossible to deny them the vote.

Continental feminists faced societies far less tolerant than Britain (or than the United States, where suffrage agitation was intertwined with evangelical religion and the temperance movement). And like continental liberalism, continental feminism tended to be far less radical than its British counterpart. In France and Germany, middle-class feminists inclined toward the "equal but different" school. Woman's role as mother and her right to control reproduction was the focus of the work of widely influential figures such as Ellen Key (1849–1926) of Sweden and Nelly Roussel (1878–1922) of France. The most radical continental women tended to gravitate to the women's affiliates of the socialist parties, which took more interest in woman's presumed oppression by capitalism than her domination by man. Nevertheless, the socialist parties of the Second International were the first continental political parties to endorse women's suffrage. By the end of the great war that began in 1914, much of western Europe was ready to follow them.

A policeman carries Emmeline Pankhurst bodily off to jail during a 1911 suffrage demonstration.

RISE AND FALL OF THE CULT OF SCIENCE

The waning of traditional forms of religious belief helped open space for a variety of other faiths. Nationalism and socialism gave their adherents many of the consolations that earlier generations had gained from religion. After mid-century a misunderstood science provided a third secular religion: the "cult of science."

The furious attacks of religious figures on Darwin and Lyell were misplaced; the rise of science did not challenge religion in any direct, logical sense. God is not subject to empirical proof or disproof. But the new science did provide a semblance of empirical underpinning for statements of faith—in science. The source of the cult was the Enlightenment vision of a machine-like universe in which everything was in principle knowable. The cult's nineteenth-century founder, Auguste Comte (1798–1857), attempted from the 1820s to the 1850s to systematize all of human knowledge. He postulated—like Hegel and Marx—a series of stages. For Comte, humanity's road led from theology to metaphysics and from metaphysics to science, which was the domain of what Comte called "positive" or empirically verifiable knowledge. The "Positivism" of Comte and successors enshrined science as the new diety. Comte was confident

that even the messy affairs of humanity would eventually yield scientific general laws in the form of a discipline of "sociology."

That discipline has still to yield general laws. That did not stop Comte's most conspicuous successor, the indefatigable Herbert Spencer (1820–1903) from following in his footsteps. Spencer's *Synthetic Philosophy* (1862–96) attempted in ten volumes what Comte had attempted in six, the compression of all of human knowledge into a positivist framework. Darwin was the centerpiece of Spencer's work, but a Darwin misapplied to social phenomena. Darwin himself was in part responsible for this misunderstanding. In *The Descent of Man* he incautiously speculated that "the wonderful progress of the United States, as well of that character of its people, are the results of natural selection; the more energetic, courageous, and restless men from all parts of Europe having emigrated during the last ten or twelve generations to that great country. . . ."

Alongside Spencer a wide variety of "social Darwinists" proliferated. Most argued (in the words of Walter Bagehot, high priest of the English constitution) that "the majority of the groups which win and conquer are better than that majority which fail and perish." That was a wonderfully convenient rationalization for "might makes right" among nations, social groups, and individuals. The oil king John D. Rockefeller trumpeted that business was "merely the survival of the fittest . . . the working out of a law of nature and a law of God."

In Germany the task of propagating and popularizing Darwinian biology fell to Ernst Haeckel (1834–1919). He followed in the footsteps of Feuerbach (whose materialism had influenced Marx) and of the best-selling crank Ludwig Büchner (1824–99). Büchner's *Force and Matter* (1852) confidently asserted that since matter and energy were eternal, it was "impossible that the world can have been created. How could anything have been created that cannot be annihilated?"

Haeckel, simultaneously Darwinist and social Darwinist, defied 25 centuries of Western thought by abolishing any distinction between humanity and nature; he called the cult he founded and led "Monism." In his international best-seller of 1899, *The Riddle of the Universe,* he mocked theological and metaphysical speculation. Questions without empirical answers were not questions. And "Monism" meant that upon pain of degeneration humanity must live in harmony with "the laws of nature." Chief of those laws was natural selection. When Haeckel's notion of nature as legislator for man met the ideas of racist cranks such as Gobi-

neau, the results were intellectual high explosive. Marx had abolished all theoretical restraints on revolutionary dictatorship and on the elimination of the "class enemy." Haeckel, Gobineau, and Kaiser William II's friend, the racist–social Darwinist Houston Stuart Chamberlain (*The Foundations of the Nineteenth Century,* 1899) similarly abolished intellectual and moral restrictions on the liquidation of the "racial enemy."

The Revolt against Positivism

The domination of the positivist cult of science was shortlived, although its influence persists to our own day. In philosophy, a commanding figure soon emerged who denounced almost every aspect of the present, science and its worshipers included. Friedrich Nietzsche (1844–1900), son of a Protestant pastor, was the last great German philosopher of the nineteenth century. He was the antithesis of system-building predecessors such as Hegel, whose work he ridiculed. From 1872 until his final collapse into syphilitic madness in 1889 he bombarded his growing public with at least one work each year. One of the greatest masters of the German language, he leapt from one striking aphorism to the next. He frequently contradicted himself, and always contradicted others. He damned the smugness of the age.

Nietzsche's message was at bottom consistent. Contradiction was life. Philosophy was not systemic, but perpetual question and experiment. Morality—for Nietzsche in his eccentric way was the last great moralist—took precedence over knowledge. Scientific truth was valuable only insofar as it contributed to "life." And to Nietzsche the law of the modern world was not the survival of the fittest, but the inevitable triumph of mediocrity. Darwin had it backwards. In reality "happy accidents are eliminated, the more highly evolved types lead nowhere, it is the average and below average types which ineluctably ascend to power." Women's emancipation was "one of the worst developments of the general *uglification* of Europe." Nationalism was unbearably crass:

The Thinker: Friedrich Nietzsche, the last great German philosopher.

the new Reich of 1871, bristling "hedge-hog-fashion" with arms, was "the most stupid, the most depraved, the most mendacious form of 'the German spirit' that ever was." Nietzsche likewise denounced anti-Semitism and the Germanic tribal cult of the composer Richard Wagner, whom he had originally admired.

Christianity, for Nietzsche, was worst of all. It stifled "life" and dragged down the exceptional individual with its "slave morality" of meekness and compassion. Nietzsche consoled himself by contemplating what he described as "the greatest event of recent times—that 'God is dead,' that the belief in the Christian God is no longer tenable." Nietzsche's morality was that of the isolated exception, the aristocratic *Übermensch*, or "superman," living "beyond good and evil" and outside society and politics. "Life," the *will to power*," was supreme over all else.

That proved a dangerous legacy. In the short term, Nietzsche appealed to socialists, anarchists, and outsiders. His denunciations of German nationalism infuriated the pan-Germans. But the spread of Nietzsche's ideas, which ironically accelerated immediately after his descent into madness, ultimately made "the will to power" and the "superman" into myths of the new populist Right. "Everything is permitted" became a credo for political "supermen" riding the coming wave of war and revolution.

Other late nineteenth- and early twentieth-century philosophers, especially the Frenchman Henri Bergson (1859–1941), shared Nietzsche's horror of rationalist system-building. But it was the world of medicine and scholarship that offered the most decisive rejection of positivism. In the mid-1890s a Vienna medical figure, Sigmund Freud (1856–1939), launched the first serious medical—rather than philosophical—attempt to understand the human mind. Freud, like Nietzsche, saw that secretive, cunning, savage forces dominated the mind. But where Nietzsche saw *power* as the central human lust, Freud merely saw sex—a more comforting conclusion, although still shocking to a prudish age. In treating his patients, Freud tapped the uncon-

scious mind with novel techniques: hypnosis, dream interpretation, and free association. What Marx did for economics as a historical force, Freud did for the unconscious.

Unfortunately for the further development of his new discipline of psychoanalysis, it soon emerged that Freud's elaborate theoretical structure was metaphor rather than a verifiable scientific

Nietzsche Speaks

Truths are illusions that one has forgotten *are* illusions.

Nothing is true, everything is permitted.

Why morality, when life, nature, and history are "unmoral"?

The common man alone has the prospect of carrying on, of propagating himself—he is the man of the future, the only survivor; "Be like him! Become mediocre!" is now the only morality that still has a meaning or an audience. But it is hard to preach, this morality of mediocrity.

Objection, evasion, gleeful mistrust and irony are signs of health. Everything absolute belongs to pathology.

In individuals, insanity is rare, but in groups, parties, nations and epochs, it is the rule.

The thought of suicide is a powerful consolation; with it one can get through many a bad night.

Man must be trained for war and woman for the recreation of the warrior: anything else is silliness.

I have only rarely the courage of what I know.

Dear Professor, in the end I would have much preferred being a Basel professor to being God. But I did not dare carry my private egotism so far as to omit—for its sake—the creation of the world. . . . [Nietzsche's last letter, to the Basel historian Jacob Burckhart, January 1889]

From Friedrich Nietzsche, Werke in Drei Bänden, *ed. by Karl Schlechta (Munich: Karl Hanser Verlag, 1954–56), 3:314, 2:889, 2:645, 2:737, 2:637, 2:328, 3:1272, 3:1351 (translation by M. Knox).*

Sigmund Freud, explorer of the
unconscious mind.

theory. Freud warred with prominent disciples such as Carl Gustav Jung (1875–
1961) and Alfred Adler (1870–1937) over
key points of interpretation. Even more
than Marxism, Freudianism and the larger
psychoanalytic movement that it created
relished the hunt for error and deviation.
That placed in question its claim to be
science; for good or ill science is about
empirical proof. And Freud's attitude toward women, whom his odd theory of
"penis envy" consigned yet again to biological inferiority, has not gone unchallenged. But Freud was in some ways a
good prophet of the twentieth century,
thanks to his experience of Austria-
Hungary's vicious ethnic quarrels and to
his membership in Vienna's most conspicuously persecuted minority, the Jews. Humanity, Freud asserted, was incurably
predatory.

A final challenge to positivism
emerged in the social sciences. The man
who actually founded the "sociology" that
Comte had named was Max Weber (1864–
1920), Prussian reserve lieutenant and
professor. Weber, the "bourgeois Marx,"
was a realist: "All ideas aimed at abolishing

the dominance of men over men are 'Utopian.' " He began by asking a question that
Marx had neglected: how did capitalism
originate? Weber hit upon religion as the
key variable that distinguished societies
that had industrialized from those that
lagged. And within Western society he
found a close historical association between the "Protestant ethic," especially
that of Calvinism (see p. 439), and the
joyless drive to accumulate ever-greater
masses of capital. This "Weber thesis" has
proved a fruitful source of argument from
his day to the present, although critics
have pointed out that the earliest European capitalism—in the Italian city-
states—was Catholic.

Weber's other major contribution was
his attempt, in a massive unfinished work
entitled *Economy and Society,* to make
sense of the relationships between economics and social and political institutions. But unlike many later sociologists,
Weber rejected the Comtean notion that
the social sciences, like the natural sciences, must formulate general laws. In the
human sciences, Weber pointed out, verification through controlled experiment
was unfeasible. The researcher's own
value system inevitably intruded on the
results. Truth was only possible within
narrow limits. Weber's work on method
demolished the positivist approach to society and history. Humanity would have
to make do with lawlike hypotheses like
the "Protestant ethic."

Finally, Weber was in his way a
prophet, although a self-limiting and modest one. Like Marx but without Marx's dogmatism, he saw goal-oriented movement
in history: the "disenchantment of the
world," the decay of traditional religious
and social certainties in the face of ever-
increasing rationalization and bureaucratization. Weber feared that in the new
century that process would end with humanity bound in a static "iron cage of serfdom" under immense self-perpetuating
state and capitalist institutions. His prophecy ignored both the growing freedoms of
the West's democratic societies—of which
Weber the Prussian lieutenant had little
understanding—and the dynamism of

technological change. But Weber's "iron cage" metaphor proved less off-center than the prophecies of Marx.

ART IN AN AGE OF SCIENCE

In the realm of culture, the last half of the nineteenth century was a period of crisis. Romanticism had broken all restraints on form and content. Everything was permitted. A bewildering variety of styles and radical disagreement about the purposes of "art" were the result. The notion that art should imitate reality or nature, the central idea of Western art since Plato and Aristotle (see pp. 57–58) was passing.

Architecture and design were the principal exceptions to this growing confusion of styles. The fragmentation of architecture had begun well before that of literature and the visual arts. In the late eighteenth century, a profusion of "revivals" had followed the dying Baroque. As the nineteenth century drew on, Greek temples mutated into churches, museums, and banks; Gothic cathedrals provided models for hideous town halls in grimy industrial cities; Romanesque arches adorned the massive temples of science at the universities. Furniture became steadily heavier, more overstuffed, and more hideously carved. But by the end of the century a reaction had set in.

In design, the opening of Japan in 1854 was as important to the nineteenth century as the influence of Chinese art had been to the eighteenth. The geometric shapes and absence of ornament of Japanese interiors were a revelation to European designers and architects. Simultaneously, the machine age stimulated new thought. Some, such as England's William Morris (1834–96), revolted against mass production. Morris's politics were a romantic socialism, his taste an attempt to relive a lost golden age of craftsmanship now submerged in shoddy machine-made furniture. His "Arts and Crafts Movement" created a spare geometric style that was the beginning of modern home furnishing. German designers in the *Werkbund,* or Craft League, that flourished from 1907 to 1914 pioneered a style that in some ways resembled Morris's—but they did not share his hostility to the machine.

Architecture developed in a like manner. Steel and glass were its materials. The Crystal Palace of the 1851 Great Exhibition, the immense canopy of St. Pancras station in London (1863–65), and the Eiffel Tower (1889) pioneered their use. But it was America, thanks to sheer technological exuberance and to the high property costs in its new city centers, that invented the steel-framed skyscraper in the 1880s. The Americans Louis Sullivan (1856–1924) and his pupil Frank Lloyd Wright (1869–1959) gave the new architecture its slogan: "form follows function." Sullivan did not disdain ornament, although he aspired to buildings that would be "comely in the nude." After 1890, his buildings took on a geometric grid-like pattern. German architects associated with the *Werkbund,* especially Walter Gropius (1883–1969) and Bruno Taut (1880–1938), had also begun before 1914 to design functional steel and glass buildings. The "international style" of the twentieth century, the first unified style in Western architecture since the Baroque, had arrived.

The fate of literature and the visual arts was entirely different. Old conventions of form and substance collapsed, but fragmentation instead of unity was the consequence. The novel, the nineteenth century's foremost art form, passed from the psychological "realism" of Gustave Flaubert (1821–80) to the pseudopositivist "naturalism" of Émile Zola (1840–1902). Flaubert, in his great *Madame Bovary* (1856), dissected the consciousness of a small-town doctor's wife whose dreamy reading of romantic novels leads her to adultery and destruction. Both subject and technique scandalized contemporaries. The far less talented but more prolific Zola churned out a sequence of twenty novels between 1871 and 1893 that traced "the social and natural history of a family" during the Second Empire. Zola kept careful track of his "facts" and propounded laws of human nature. But his sometimes lurid style suggested the opposite of scientific detachment. His Naturalism was above all social criticism; his intervention in the Dreyfus case and brief exile to escape prison were the high point of his career.

The work of the great Russians, Count Leo Tolstoy (1828–1910) and Feodor Mikhailovitch Dostoyevsky (1821–81), showed a similar tension between psychological observation and social and political commitment. Tolstoy eventually repudiated his greatest works, *War and Peace* (1869) and *Anna Karenina* (1871), and turned his back on Russian society in favor of a mystical New Testament faith and pacifist "nonresistance to evil." Dostoyevsky migrated from advanced revolutionary beliefs to a mystic Slavophilism. In *The Possessed* (1871–72) he drew on his youthful experiences and his deep psychological insight to suggest the demonic nature of revolutionary messianism—just as much of the Russian *intelligentsia* embraced that messianism.

One conspicuous exception to this pattern of ideological commitment was the American expatriate, Henry James (1843–1916). His many novels, novellas, and short stories combined Flaubert-like psychological observation with penetrating commentary on the contrast between European and American manners and morals. James's European-style novels earned him an international reputation; his most conspicuous American contemporaries, Herman Melville (1819–91) and Mark Twain (1835–1910), remained curiosities to Europeans. Melville's symbolic epic of whaling and the struggle between evil and good, *Moby Dick* (1851), derived from the Protestant biblical tradition, not the European novel. Twain achieved the impossible. In *The Adventures of Huckleberry Finn* (1884) he rendered backwoods dialect—or rather a carefully contrived illusion of dialect—into art, in a comic yet often grim tale of life on the Mississippi against the ominous background of the slave South. Twain was deliberately and aggressively provincial; he frequently spoofed European social and linguistic snobbishness.

While Flaubert, James, and the Russians between them seemingly exhausted most of the novel's possibilities, the Norwegian Henrik Ibsen (1828–1906), the Swede Johan August Strindberg (1849–1912), and the Russian Anton Pavlovitch Chekhov (1860–1904) did the same for drama. Ibsen mercilessly attacked social pretension and the oppression of women. He depicted the quest of the modern individual for self-understanding. The truth, he suggested, could destroy as well as free. But humanity was not irredeemable; love was still conceivable. Not so for Strindberg, who created increasingly dreamlike plays in which unlovely characters, "bound together by guilt and crime," inexorably destroyed one another. Chekhov, who depicted symbolically the dissolution of Russian aristocratic society, pioneered a drama that turned its back on conventional notions of plot. He gave artistic form to the anarchy of life. Chekhov's characters speak in seemingly disconnected remarks, dramatic development occurs within the characters themselves, and action is inconclusive.

It was in poetry, music, and painting that the breakthrough to the artistic fragmentation of the twentieth century was most dramatic. In poetry, late Romantic lyricism dissolved into Symbolism. Intended for a few initiates rather than for a mass audience, Symbolism was in part a reaction to the dreary Naturalist notion that art should serve social and political betterment. Symbolism's predecessor was the dissipated "accursed poet," Charles Baudelaire (1821–67), and its banner "art for art's sake." The Symbolists, above all the schoolboy prodigy Arthur Rimbaud (1854–91), Stéphane Mallarmé (1842–98), and Paul Verlaine (1844–96), wrote a poetry of deliberate obscurity and musical effects. Their style influenced the two greatest German poets of the new century, Rainer Maria Rilke (1875–1926) and Stefan George (1868–1933). It furnished the basis for much twentieth-century poetry.

In music, Richard Wagner's "total work of art," his four-evening-long *Ring of the Nibelungen* opera cycle (1853–74), was the end of romantic music as well as one starting point of the new German Reich's political mythology. Gustav Mahler (1860–1911) and others continued

Wagner's tradition of orchestral excess and startling effects, but with less conviction. In France, Claude Debussy (1862–1918) and Maurice Ravel (1875–1937) pioneered a new style that deliberately paralleled Symbolist poetry. The irregular rhythms and harsh dissonances of Igor Fëdorovitch Stravinsky's *Rite of Spring* caused a riot at its Paris premiere in 1913. Arnold Schönberg (1874–1951) and his pupils created a new "atonal" music that defied traditional notions of melody.

In painting, an entire epoch in Western art ended with the school known as the Impressionists. Claude Monet (1840–1926) and Auguste Renoir (1841–1919) were its originators and masters. They discarded the age-old attempt to render reality on canvas literally. Photography, invented in the 1820s, had by the 1860s rendered realism seemingly superfluous. Instead, the Impressionists sought to use the play of light, represented with dabs of color, to show scenes as they appeared to the mind's eye. Their paintings shocked contemporaries accustomed to increasingly sterile imitations of ancient or Renaissance models. But the Impressionists were not revolutionaries; they were the brilliant end of a long tradition.

After them came Paul Cézanne (1839–1906), proclaiming both in words and on canvas that "all of nature is formed by the cylinder, the sphere, and the cone." Vincent van Gogh (1853–90) reproduced a tortured life in violent colors and swirling shapes. Georges Seurat (1859–91) composed stiff, flat figures out of thousands of tiny colored dots. And after 1900 Pablo Picasso (1881–1973), Wassily Kandinsky (1866–1944), the "Cubists," and Italy's fiercely irreverent "Futurists" began to cut painting's links with visual reality. The art of the twentieth century was to be an art of increasing abstraction and of proliferating schools and slogans.

It was also increasingly an art for the few rather than the many. Until the nineteenth century Western art had always spoken to a unified audience, a cultivated and largely aristocratic elite. Mass literacy and mass market ended that. Wood-pulp paper and the machine-driven rotary press

Thickly applied paint and new ways of representing light: *van Gogh's Chair* (1888).

made possible the first truly cheap newspapers, the first modern "mass media" based on advertising. Great press barons arose, profiteers of ignorance with a secret

---

The "Yellow Press": A Novelist's View

In New Grub Street *(1891), the English novelist George Gissing presented through the mouth of his fictional editor, Whelpdale, a view of the mass media's conception of its audience that is still surprisingly up-to-date.*

No article in the paper is to measure more than two inches in length, and every inch must be broken into at least two paragraphs. . . . Let me explain my principle. I would have the paper address itself to the quarter-educated; . . . the young men and women who can just read, but are incapable of sustained attention. People of this kind want something to occupy them in trains, and on buses and trams. . . . What they want is the lightest and frothiest of chit-chatty information—bits of stories, bits of description, bits of scandal, bits of jokes, bits of statistics, bits of foolery. Am I not right? Everything must be very short, two inches at the utmost; their attention can't sustain itself beyond two inches.

From George Gissing, New Grub Street *(London: Eveleigh Nash & Grayson, 1927), p. 419.*

contempt for their public. Alfred Harmsworth (later Lord Northcliffe) of the London *Daily Mail* first achieved a daily circulation of more than a million, with a paper that combined gossip and crude xenophobia in equal proportions. Publishers churned out vapid "best-sellers" by the hundreds of thousands. The mass press was not responsible for its readers' lack of sophistication, but it worked hard to perpetuate it. That narrowed the market for genuine art and gave it a snobbish exclusiveness that further deepened the gap between high and low culture characteristic of the twentieth century.

Like the aristocrats who after 1789 lamented a lost golden age, the middle classes of Europe were soon to mourn the long peace. The years from 1871 to 1914 were the peak of Europe's power and wealth relative to the other continents. The cultural brilliance of Europe's capitals, above all Paris and Vienna, made the last decades of peace a "*belle époque*," a delectable era. But powerful forces were working against equilibrium and tolerance. Those forces, above all the force of nationalism and the growing economic power of the new Germany, slowly undermined the stability of the European state system. That shift, invisible to peoples absorbed in their everyday lives, in the end proved a matter of life and death for millions of Europeans.

Suggestions for Further Reading

General

E. J. Hobsbawn, *The Age of Capital, 1848–1875* (1975), and *The Age of Empire, 1875–1914* (1987), are outstanding works of synthesis. Readable surveys include N. Rich, *The Age of Nationalism and Reform, 1850–1890* (1977), C. J. H. Hayes, *A Generation of Materialism, 1871–1900* (1941), and O. J. Hale, *The Great Illusion, 1900–1914* (1971).

Domestic Affairs

On Britain, see above all A. Wood, *Nineteenth Century Britain* (1960); G. Dangerfield, *The Strange Death of Liberal England, 1910–1914* (1935); and F. Bédarida, *A Social History of England, 1851–1975* (1979). The most accessible discussions of France are A. Cobban, *A History of Modern France*, Vol. 2 (1957), and R. D. Anderson, *France, 1870–1914: Politics and Society* (1977); E. Weber, *Peasants into Frenchmen: The Modernization of Rural France* (1976), is full of wonderful material. For Germany, H. U. Wehler, *The German Empire, 1871–1918* (1985), is short and provocative, but the relevant portions of G. Craig, *Germany, 1866–1945* (1978), are a better guide to what actually happened. For Russia, see R. Pipes, *Russia under the Old Regime* (1974); H. Seton-Watson, *The Russian Empire, 1807–1917* (1967); A. Ulam, *Lenin and the Bolsheviks* (1966); and the intelligent popular account of E. Crankshaw, *The Shadow of the Winter Palace; Russia's Drift to Revolution, 1825–1917* (1976). On Austria-Hungary, C. A. Macartney, *The Habsburg Empire* (1969), is lucid and balanced; A. J. P. Taylor, *The Habsburg Monarchy, 1809–1918* (1948), is one-sided and entertaining. On Italy, the best treatment is C. Seton-Watson, *Italy from Liberalism to Fascism, 1870–1925* (1967), but see also the pertinent portions of D. Mack Smith, *Italy, a Modern History* (1959–   ), and M. Clark, *Modern Italy, 1870–1982* (1984). J. A. Thayer, *Italy and the Great War: Politics and Culture, 1890–1914* (1964), describes the fatal fascination that a last great war to achieve national integration exercised over Italy's elites.

Society and Culture

On the rise of feminism, see especially R. Bridenthal et al., *Becoming Visible: Women in European History* (1987), and S. K. Kent, *Women and Suffrage in Britain, 1860–1914* (1987). The best introductions to Nietzsche are J. P. Stern, *Nietzsche* (1978); W. Kaufmann, *Nietzsche: Philosopher, Psychologist, Antichrist* (1956); and R. Heyman, *Nietzsche: A Critical Life* (1980). On Freud and his legacy, see especially R. Wollheim, *Sigmund Freud* (1971); the critical treatment of H. J. Eysenck, *The Decline and Fall of the Freudian Empire* (1984); and Ernest Gellner, *The Psychoanalytic Movement* (1985). On Freud's environment, see above all C. Schorske, *Fin-de-Siècle Vienna: Politics and Culture* (1980). W. J. Mommsen, *The Age of Bureaucracy* (1974), offers an excellent short introduction of Max Weber and his ideas. E. Wilson, *Axel's Castle: A Study of the Imaginative Litera-*ture of 1870–1930 (1931), is still the best introduction to literature from the Symbolists onward. R. Raynal, *The Nineteenth Century: New Sources of Emotion from Goya to Gauguin* (1951), with fine illustrations, and F. Mathey, *The World of the Impressionists* (1961), remain excellent introductions to the new painting.

29

Europe from Balance to Breakdown, 1871–1914

In international politics, the long peace between Bismarck's wars and the First World War was the classic age of the European balance of power. Fear of revolution and the solidarity of the great powers, which had damped down rivalries after 1815, were gone. The princes and their standing armies had defeated revolution in 1848–49, and the Crimean War had destroyed the European concert. Europe, Bismarck scoffed, was a mere "geographic expression": "I only hear a statesman use the word 'Europe' when he wants something for himself." The long peace after 1871 rested almost exclusively on the balance of power, a mechanism seemingly as self-operating as the free market. Threats by one power automatically led the others to combine and force it to retreat.

But by the 1890s the European system was no longer self-contained. The rise of two great powers outside Europe, the United States and Japan, made it for the first time a world balance. That undermined the balance on the European continent itself—just as industrialization tilted that balance toward a single mighty state. That state was Germany, whose industry surpassed Britain's between 1900 and 1913. And Germany, already the greatest land power, also challenged Britain after 1897 for world mastery at sea. New technologies of war and transport improved the position of the great continental powers and increasingly threatened Britain's ability to bring its seapower to bear. The shift of the balance in Germany's favor, and Germany's ill-advised attempts to exploit that shift, eventually drove Britain to ally itself with France and Russia, Germany's neighbors. Germany answered with war.

THE FORCES BEHIND DIPLOMACY

The industrialization and democratization of Europe also meant the industrialization and democratization of war and foreign policy. Generals, admirals, and diplomats resisted but could not reverse those forces. The war of 1866 was the last "cabinet war." After that, victory required and nationalism inspired the participation of the masses. The expansion of literacy and the extension of the vote also meant that the masses began to influence foreign policy as well.

Toward Mass Armies and Industrial War

Until 1871 only Prussia had a genuine mass army based on universal military service. The other powers followed the lead of post-1815 France in preferring long-service professional armies. Then the Prussian army, created in 1814 and doubled in size by William I's military reforms in the 1860s, crushed the Austrians in 1866 and the French in 1870. That forced the others to imitate Prussia—and conscript much of their male population—if they hoped to remain or become great powers. Austria-Hungary introduced universal ser-

The French 75mm field gun.

vice in 1868; France, Italy, Russia, and Japan had followed by the 1880s. Only Britain and the United States, which faced no land threats, could afford the luxury of volunteer armies.

Military power thus rested more than ever on demographic strength. That weakened the position of France even more than had defeat in 1870, for France's population almost ceased to grow after 1840, while Germany's increase continued (see p. 615). Of the great powers, only Russia and the distant United States surpassed Germany in total population. And Russia's economic weakness and political fragility meant that numbers were its only great asset.

An accelerating revolution in destructiveness of weapons paralleled the revolution in the size of armies. Alfred Nobel's nitrated explosives, ever-tougher steels, precision manufacturing, and advances in optics vastly increased the range and power of small arms and artillery. Between the 1860s and 1914 the battlefield of the twentieth century—empty because all visible movement draws fire—took shape. A hail of shell splinters and machine-gun bullets reversed the advantage that the attack had enjoyed in the days of the great Napoleon. Only crushing superiority of fire and manpower could now break a determined defense, and success might extend only so far as the next belt of enemy positions.

By 1900 the railroad had also worked a revolution, by vastly increasing the strategic mobility of land powers. In the Napoleonic wars, Wellington's sea communications proved better than the road links of the French. The railroad changed that; land powers could now meet amphibious threats rapidly and with overwhelming force. And the new mass armies could mobilize with unheard-of rapidity. Mobilization and concentration for battle became a single continuous operation. Speed, as the Prussians had demonstrated in 1866 and 1870, was all-important. The state that mobilized first and fastest, the general staffs of Europe concluded, would win.

What the staffs failed to see was that industrialization and industrial firepower

FIGURE 29-1   The Balance Shifts: Total Industrial Potential of the Great Powers

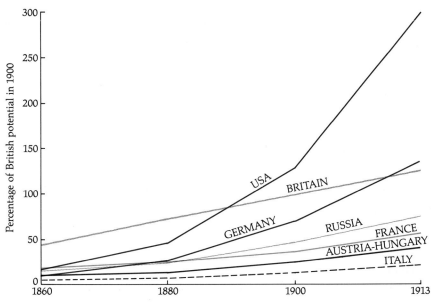

And in total industrial potential, by 1913, one power had surpassed all others except the United States: the Germany of Kaiser William II (see Figure 29-1). That was a fateful shift in the balance of power.

made a swift decision increasingly unlikely. Prussia's victory in 1870 had been a fluke, a consequence of France's disorganized mobilization and ineptitude in the first battles. War between industrial powers, as the U.S. Civil War had shown, could easily become an immense struggle of attrition. The outcome of a protracted war between industrial powers depended less on rifle strength in the first battles than on industrial might and financial stamina.

Technology also revolutionized war at sea—and likewise threatened Britain's position. France and the contenders in the U.S. Civil War had pioneered steam-powered armored warships. By the 1880s steel cannon, turrets, and armor had out-

The first duel between armored warships: the *Monitor* against the *Merrimac* (renamed *Virginia*) at Hampton Roads, March 1862.

classed and replaced the wooden ships that had won at Trafalgar. By 1900 a battleship mounted four 12-inch guns, displaced 14,000 tons, and was capable of 18 knots. Then the British, to outrace all rivals, introduced the first all-big-gun ship, H.M.S. *Dreadnought,* in 1904–05. With its ten 12-inch guns and 21-knot speed, it could stand off at long range and batter older battleships into flaming scrap.

Fleet size was as vital—and as much a matter of international competition—as warship design. Growing threats moved the British in 1889 to launch a crash rearmament program, the Naval Defense Act. London adopted the "Two-Power Standard" as a yardstick of naval strength: British strength had to equal that of the two next-ranked naval powers. But Britain's rivals continued to build, and by 1912 every great power had fleets of Dreadnoughts. And other weapons challenged the supremacy of the battleship. Torpedoes, mines, submarines, and eventually aircraft evened the contest between Britain and its rivals, between the greatest sea power and the land powers.

Technology inevitably raised the cost of warfare and of preparation for war. Britain's defense expenditure more than dou-bled between 1890 and 1914. Germany's almost quadrupled. But since their economies were also expanding, the burden of military expenditure as a percentage of gross national product did not increase as sharply as did the absolute amounts spent. What many contemporaries saw as an uncontrolled upward-spiraling "arms race"—a metaphor that gained currency in the decade before 1914—was in reality a slow climb. Nevertheless, the weaker or slower-growing powers—Italy, Austria-Hungary, Russia, and France—found it harder to become or remain great powers than did the economic giants. In a long war, those that had difficulty keeping up before 1914 might well go under.

Public Opinion and Foreign Policy

Educated opinion first began to affect foreign policy in Britain and the United States. Public opinion made the Crimean War, and destroyed the British Cabinet that bungled it. Public opinion was decisive in making and—under Lincoln's inspired leadership—in deciding the U.S. Civil War. Gladstone mobilized public opinion against Disraeli's foreign policy in the 1880 election; his own command

The ten 12-inch guns of the H.M.S. *Dreadnought* (launched 1906), outclassed all previous warships.

of Parliament crumbled after the public discovered that his muddling had sent Gordon to his death at Khartoum in 1885.

As public opinion broadened to include an ever-larger segment of the population, it began to affect policy in four principal ways. First, its often confusing message increasingly aggravated—or excused—the indecision of policy-makers. As Gladstone's Conservative successor Lord Salisbury lamented in 1895, "When the great oracle speaks, we are never quite certain what the great oracle said." Public opinion, it often seemed, wanted no foreign policy at all.

Second, public opinion made it increasingly difficult to maintain consistency and continuity in policy. Democracy, as Tocqueville pointed out in the 1830s, "can only with great difficulty regulate the details of an important undertaking, persevere in a fixed design, and work out its execution in spite of serious obstacles. It cannot combine its measures with secrecy or await their consequences with patience." The British foreign office made the fickleness of Parliament and public into a virtue, a ready excuse when other powers pressed for inconvenient British commitments. The French Chamber destroyed its government for attempting to cooperate with Britain in Egypt in 1882, then held a grudge against the British for going ahead alone. In 1885 the Chamber suddenly overthrew Ferry after a minor defeat in Indochina. Italian governments fell for "losing" Tunisia to France in 1881 and for losing to the Ethiopians at Adowa in 1896. The coming of democracy confronted the makers of foreign policy with entirely new pressures and limits.

Third, Liberal opinion in Britain and Socialist opinion on the Continent tended to confuse morality with policy, to the dismay of self-proclaimed realists such as Disraeli or Bismarck. The interest of the state often appeared to require actions (such as the threat of war) or allies (such as the Turks), that were distasteful to an electorate influenced by Gladstone-style moralizing. Extreme moralists rejected the rules of the international game altogether. Richard Cobden and John Bright, middle-class crusaders against Britain's Corn Laws, denounced the Crimean War and lost their seats in Parliament. They shared a faith that free trade would act "on the moral world as the principle of gravitation in the universe—drawing men together, thrusting aside the antagonism of race, and creed, and language, and uniting us in the bonds of eternal peace." Free trade triumphed, but eternal peace did not appear. Cobden and Bright blamed that "foul idol," the balance of power, and the aristocracy, a historical fossil for which the British diplomatic service allegedly served as a gigantic welfare system.

Socialist opinion saw a different villain. Capitalism, the root of all evil, must also be the cause of war, not its cure (as Cobden and Bright had claimed). Rosa Luxemburg and Lenin clashed over whether party leadership or spontaneous risings by the masses were the key to revolutionary struggle, but they fervently agreed that imperialism and war were the inevitable result of capitalism. They and others in the revolutionary wing of the Second International insisted that capitalist-imperialist war would and must lead to socialist revolution. Thinkers less committed to Marxism merely deplored armaments spending. Countess Bertha von Suttner, an Austrian writer, gained wide success with her pacifist novel, *Lay Down Your Arms!* (1889). She helped inspire the guilt-ridden Alfred Nobel to establish the peace prizes that bear his name, and in 1905 she was the first woman to receive one.

Some states even courted pacifist opinion. Nicholas II of Russia, fearing that his ramshackle finances would not support re-equipping his army with new artillery, proposed a ten-year "holiday" on armaments in 1898. But the disarmament conference held the following year at the Hague in Holland failed. So did a second in 1907; its only results were agreements on the treatment in war of neutrals, prisoners, wounded, and noncombatants, the stipulation that small-arms bullets must have full metal jackets rather than the far more lethal expanding lead tip, and a World Court incapable of resolving major disputes. Most rulers and military figures were secretly grateful to William II for sab-

Bertha von Suttner (1843–1914), recipient of the 1905 Nobel Peace Prize.

otaging the conferences. The Kaiser scoffed rudely in private and proclaimed his reliance "on God and on my sharp sword." Sir John ("Jacky") Fisher, the reforming admiral responsible for the *Dreadnought,* was equally forthright: "The essence of war is violence. Moderation in war is imbecility." What counted was winning, and winning required the swift application of overwhelming force.

William II and Fisher need not have worried. In an age of nationalism, the more democracy, the more nationalism. That was the fourth major consequence of the growing power of public opinion. Pacifism remained the faith of small minorities. The principal pre-1914 leader of the German Social Democrats, August Bebel, admitted in 1892 that even his own party was "a sort of preparatory school for militarism." In Britain and France, "jingoism" and Boulangism (see pp. 745 and 715) showed that universal male suffrage did not necessarily bring peace.

Even authoritarian regimes had to consider the views of their publics and their officer corps. Nationalist opinion had driven Napoleon III, against his better judgment, to war and his doom in 1870. Nationalist opinion, originally unleashed with government support, helped drive Imperial Germany after 1905 to make a violent bid for the mastery of Europe. By the 1870s, Slavophilism had mutated into Russian nationalism and "pan-Slavism." Russia was the patron and protector of its Slav "little brothers" everywhere—a sacred duty that extended the Russian state's potential claims far into central Europe and the Balkans. Journalists like Nikolai Katkov of the *Moscow Gazette* preached that duty and those claims in a manner that the tsars, given Russia's tradition of assassination, found hard to ignore. Even in Japan, the Meiji oligarchs and their successors were responsive to opinion, especially military opinion. Assassination sometimes struck down Japanese statesmen who appeared insufficiently resolute in defending Japan's security and rights.

BISMARCK THE CONSERVATIVE, 1871–90

Disraeli had greeted with dismay Germany's victory over France in 1870: "The balance of power has been entirely destroyed. . . ." That prophecy came thirty years too soon. In the 1860s Bismarck had harnessed German nationalism to the purposes of the Prussian state; after 1871 he kept it harnessed. The new Germany, he repeatedly declared, was a "satiated" power. Bismarck merely sought to preserve the dominant position in Europe that he and Moltke had won.

That meant keeping the peace. In a future great war the powers whose mutual hostility had neutralized them in 1866 and 1870 might yet combine against Germany. France, which had refused to accept the loss of Alsace-Lorraine in 1870–71, was the chief threat. If France found allies, Germany would face a dangerous coalition. And if Russia's traditional friction in the Balkans with Austria-Hungary led to open conflict, Germany might have to support Vienna. Russia would then bid for French support. Bismarck's annexation of Alsace-Lorraine meant that any open conflict between Austria and Russia would almost

Bismarck the conservative.

certainly become a general European war in which Germany would have to fight on two fronts.

Bismarck therefore encouraged the mutual tensions of the powers to keep them dependent on Berlin. He exploited any colonial rivalry that might divert the attention of his neighbors from Alsace-Lorraine. Bismarck's policy, as much as Germany's strength, made Berlin the center of European diplomacy for a generation. To freeze the status quo, Bismarck also attempted to restore the unity between Vienna, St. Petersburg, and Berlin that had guaranteed stability before the Crimean War. The aim of his German-Russian-Austrian "Three Emperors' Leagues" of 1872–73 and 1881 was to prevent Austria-Hungary and Russia from clashing in the Balkans. Bismarck was less successful than Metternich; the three eastern monarchies were now incapable of marching in step for long.

Bismarck himself unintentionally fractured the first Three Emperors' League in early 1875, when he tried to bully a fast-reviving France with newspaper warnings ("Is War in Sight?") and private threats of war. Those threats led Russia, for the first time since Prussia's thrusts against Denmark in 1848–49, to join Britain. When the Tsar and Disraeli jointly warned Berlin that they would not permit Germany to crush France again, Bismarck retreated. The balance of power, the mechanism that thirty years later was to bring Britain, Russia, and France together against Germany once more, had shown Bismarck his limits. Germany was the single most powerful continental state, but it was not the master of Europe—yet.

The First Great Eastern Crisis and the Congress of Berlin, 1875–78

The "war-in-sight crisis" of 1875 passed quickly, despite its menacing undertone for Germany. It was the Balkans that ultimately wrecked Bismarck's attempts to keep Germany, Russia, and Austria-Hungary together.

The two great Balkan crises of 1875–78 and 1885–87 were entirely different from their predecessor, the Crimean War.

Balkan nationalism had come of age; the Balkan nationalities, not the great powers, were now the main threat to the Ottoman Empire. The Christian Slavs of Bosnia triggered the first and greatest of the two crises by rising in revolt in July 1875. When the revolt spread to the province of Bulgaria, the Turkish overlords replied with massacres. Tsar Alexander II, under pressure from pan-Slav opinion, prepared to rescue Russia's Balkan "little brothers" from the Turks—and seize Constantinople.

But this time, unlike 1854–56, France did not move. Britain was paralyzed: Gladstone used the Turkish massacres to undermine the government of his rival Disraeli and to attack Britain's traditional policy of supporting Turkey to bar Russia from the Mediterranean. Austria-Hungary also stood aside, fearing that any victory by the Balkan peoples over Turkey would make Austria-Hungary itself the next "sick man" of Europe. The Russians offered Ottoman territory to Vienna as compensation for eventual Russian and Slav gains, and promised not to create a "large compact Slav state" that would threaten the Habsburg monarchy.

To everyone's surprise, the Turks fought well when Russia went to war in April 1877. At the entrenched camp of Plevna on the main road to Constantinople, their British rifles stalled the ill-equipped Russians until December 1877. That victory gave the Ottoman Empire another forty years of life. Britain's fickle public opinion swung decisively: the Turks were no longer the Moslem butchers of Christian Slavs, but the plucky defenders of Plevna. That freed Disraeli to send the British fleet to face Russia at the Turkish Straits. And it gave the world a new word for populist aggressiveness, "jingosim":

> We don't want to fight,
> But by Jingo, if we do,
> We've got the ships,
> We've got the men,
> We've got the money, too.

Russia, exhausted by Turkish resistance, was soon in no condition to fight

The Treaty of San Stefano   1878

The Congress of Berlin   1878

had promised, led Austria-Hungary to join Britain. Then Bismarck stepped in as "honest broker" and convened an international "Congress of Berlin" in June–July 1878. The location of the meeting symbolized the new Germany's decisive role in Europe.

Russia backed down, and grudgingly divided the great Bulgaria of San Stefano into three: Bulgaria, an "Eastern Rumelia" technically under Turkish overlordship, and a "Macedonia" that reverted to Turkey. In compensation, Austria-Hungary received the Serb-inhabited provinces of Bosnia and Hercegovina to administer as a sort of trust. Serbia officially became independent of Turkey, although in 1881 Austria-Hungary made it a client state for a generation. Disraeli returned from Berlin triumphant, with Turkish Cyprus as a sort of payment for saving Constantinople from the Russians. The Congress of Berlin had patched up a map of the Balkans that lasted with only minor modifications until 1912. Russia turned to expansion in central Asia.

Bismarck's Alliance System, 1879–83

In the aftermath of the first great eastern crisis, Bismarck took the very step for which he had reproached the Prussian governments of the 1850s: he tied the "trim Prussian frigate" to the "moth-eaten Austrian galleon." In September 1879 he signed at Vienna a defensive military alliance against Russia that lasted until both Austria-Hungary and Germany collapsed in 1918.

With this Dual Alliance—the first peacetime alliance between great powers since the eighteenth century—Bismarck pursued three fundamental goals. It would reassure Austria-Hungary about its security. It would restrain Austro-Hungarian aggressiveness in the Balkans and against Russia—for Bismarck could at any time point out that the alliance was defensive, and threaten to leave Vienna to its fate if it provoked a war. Finally, the Dual Alliance would give German nationalism a surrogate for the "greater Germany" from the Baltic to the Adriatic that Bismarck had

Britain. But the Tsar's peace treaty of San Stefano with Turkey (March 1878) nevertheless went too far. It created a great Bulgaria covering the entire eastern Balkans. That "large compact Slav state," and Russia's failure to offer the compensation it blocked by creating his greater Prussia in 1866–71.

Bismarck's new policy held great dangers. Berlin's promise of support in fact increased rather than decreased Vienna's aggressiveness. And the German public's vocal support for the Germans of Austria-Hungary made it less and less possible for Bismarck to threaten to leave Vienna in the lurch. His successors felt themselves bound to Vienna by German nationalist "*Nibelung* loyalty"—a doom-laden Wagnerian tune repeatedly sounded as both empires went down in 1914–18. Finally, the Dual Alliance tied Alsace-Lorraine and the Eastern Question together even more tightly than before. Germany, bound to Austria-Hungary by alliance and divided from France by an insoluble quarrel, was the link between East and West. No matter how a great-power war started, Germany and Austria-Hungary would now face both France and Russia.

To put off that day, Bismarck followed the Dual Alliance with a second Three Emperors' League in 1881. Russia agreed for the moment not to join France in a war against Germany, and the three powers agreed to take no action in the Balkans except by mutual agreement. The second League rested on even weaker foundations than the first. Alexander III, now in power thanks to his father's assassination in 1881 (see p. 721), was a narrow autocrat of nationalist instincts. The solidarity between monarchs of the age of Metternich meant little to him, and still less to Vienna, which Bismarck had to pressure into signing the three emperors' agreement.

To compensate Vienna for this forced cohabitation with Russia, Bismarck made yet another treaty. In 1882 he roped the Italians into a Berlin-Vienna-Rome triangle, the Triple Alliance. Rome, humiliated over France's seizure of Tunisia in 1881, was delighted at this recognition of Italy's importance, however insincere. Vienna received an unconvincing Italian promise not to seek Trento and Trieste, the Dual Monarchy's remaining Italian-speaking areas, if Russia attacked Austria-Hungary. Bismarck paid the bill by promising to

support Italy against French attack, an event he thought unlikely.

In 1883 Bismarck added Rumania to this increasingly bizarre treaty structure. That action ran directly counter to assurances he had given Russia that he had underwritten Austria-Hungary's survival but not its Balkan interests. Secret pledges that Berlin and Vienna would defend Rumania against attack in effect blocked Russia's land route to Constantinople. The Balkans, as Bismarck had told the *Reichstag* in 1876, contained no German interests worth the "bones of a Pomeranian musketeer." Yet Bismarck had now committed Germany to defend the eastern Balkans against Russia.

The Second Eastern Crisis and the Reinsurance Treaty, 1885–87

Bismarck's diplomacy more and more resembled an elaborate juggling performance. The second of the great Balkan crises, which arose in 1885, tested his genius to the fullest. The issues this time were fortunately less explosive than in 1877–78. Russia's principal goal was now security against British naval attack in the Black Sea and free passage through the Turkish Straits for its growing grain exports from the Ukraine.

Russia nevertheless quarreled with Britain in 1885–87, first by encroaching on Afghanistan, India's vital buffer, then over Bulgaria, the gateway to the Turkish Straits. Ultimately, both issues led to standoffs; Russian ambitions turned toward East Asia. But the crisis also drove Britain, under Gladstone's Conservative successor, Lord Salisbury, toward the Triple Alliance. In two "Mediterranean Agreements" of 1887, Salisbury joined Italy and Austria-Hungary in guaranteeing—against Russia and France—the territorial status quo in the Mediterranean and Black Sea. Britain, France, and Italy thus blocked Russia at Constantinople, with Bismarck's blessing.

Bismarck added the final touch to this eccentric combination by negotiating a secret agreement with the Russians to replace the collapsed Three Emperors' League. The three-year "Reinsurance Treaty" of June 1887 seemed to pledge

German support for Russian action against Constantinople if the Turks allied themselves with the Western powers. Germany and Russia also promised each other neutrality should war come, except if Germany attacked France or Russia attacked Austria-Hungary.

That secret pledge contradicted the spirit if not the letter of the Dual Alliance that linked Berlin and Vienna, and the German alliance with Rumania as well. And by promising Russia support at the Turkish Straits, the Reinsurance Treaty also ran counter to the second Mediterranean Agreement that linked Bismarck's Italian and Austro-Hungarian allies with Britain against Russia. Bismarck had created a system of mutually contradictory commitments that froze the Austro-Russian quarrel while keeping Germany's "line to St. Petersburg" open. But if treaties alone could not keep the Balkans quiet, he would have to choose sides. Germany could only choose Austria-Hungary, and a clash with Russia.

The Collapse of Bismarck's System, 1887–90

This astounding performance taxed even Bismarck. It also had unforeseen effects. France, weary of diplomatic isolation, reluctantly drew closer to Russia. The tsar, annoyed at Bismarck's closing of the Berlin loan market during the Bulgarian crisis and his continued backing of Austria-Hungary, swallowed his royal doubts about accepting the French Republic's money. The Russians gained their first sizable French loan in October 1888. In January 1889 they ordered large quantities of French rifles after promising not to use them against France.

Bismarck was no longer sufficiently in control in Berlin to counter this threat. The new Kaiser, William II, had fallen under the influence of Moltke's successor, Count von Waldersee, who insistently urged "preventive" war against Russia before Russia became too strong. In fall 1889, without Bismarck's approval, William II assured Vienna that whatever the source of the quarrel, Germany would mobilize its forces alongside Austria-Hungary. Ger-

many was abandoning its Russian connection.

Then, in March 1890, Bismarck and the young Kaiser quarreled over domestic policy. When the Russians anxiously suggested a renewal of the Reinsurance Treaty, Bismarck was gone. His successor was a conscientious but limited general, Count Leo von Caprivi, who found Bismarck's foreign policy too complex and self-contradictory. He feared that St. Petersburg might leak word of Germany's promise to support Russia at the Turkish Straits. That would destroy Germany's ties to Russia's enemy, Britain. Nor would German opinion or the Vienna government take kindly to Germany's sins against the nationalist loyalty-unto-death supposedly enshrined in the Dual Alliance.

Germany therefore turned down the Russian offer and drew temporarily closer to Britain with an 1890 agreement over colonial issues. The end of the Reinsurance Treaty and Germany's wooing of Britain accelerated a process already under way: Russia's move toward France. In July 1891 a surly Tsar Alexander III stood at attention for the playing of the *Marseillaise,* hymn of revolution, during a visit by the French fleet. Bismarck had deliberately isolated France; William II and Caprivi had left Russia isolated. In August 1891 France and Russia agreed to coordinate their foreign policies. Both sought the independence from Berlin that Bismarck had denied them.

By 1892 French and Russian negotiators had hammered out a military pact that pledged France to attack Germany if Germany attacked Russia, and Russia to attack Germany if Germany attacked France. If Austria-Hungary alone mobilized, France pledged to mobilize too. That promise broke with France's previous reluctance to enter Balkan quarrels. But Paris agreed because it desperately wanted security against Germany and did not expect Austria-Hungary would ever act alone. The Franco-Russian alliance was intended to last as long as the Triple Alliance of its adversaries.

The ratification of the alliance in December–January 1893–94 did not, as is often claimed, make a general war proba-

Tsar Alexander III, the French Republic's grudging alliance partner.

Alliances and Alignments before 1914

——— Austro-German (Dual) Alliance, 1879	—··—··— Franco-Russian Alliance, 1894
——— Triple Alliance, 1882	—·—·— Triple Entente, 1904/07
·········· Reinsurance Treaty, 1887–90	—··—··— Anglo-Japanese Alliance, 1902
	———— Franco-Italian Agreement, 1902

ble. The annexation of Alsace-Lorraine and Bismarck's Dual Alliance had already done that. What the Franco-Russian alliance did was to reassert the European balance of power and end the German political domination of Europe that Bismarck had established. As late as 1892 the young Kaiser could confide to associates his vision of establishing "a sort of Napoleonic supremacy" in Europe "in the peaceful sense." But after the Franco-Russian alliance, a German "Napoleonic supremacy" could come only through war.

THE BREAKTHROUGH TO WORLD POLITICS, 1890–1904

Europe nevertheless enjoyed peace for another twenty years. The Franco-Russian alliance gave France and Russia security in Europe. Russia and Austria-Hungary remained calm when a new Near Eastern crisis erupted in 1895 over Turkish massacres of Armenians, and in 1897 they agreed to put the Balkans "on ice." For a generation Europe turned its attention to Africa and East Asia. And for the first time non-European great powers, Japan and the United States, made their presence felt. That made the European balance a world balance of power, dwarfing powers like France that were merely European in scale.

Theories of World Politics

Theorists such as Sir John Seeley (1834–95) had long noticed that even the British Empire lacked the vast territorial and demographic base of continent-spanning powers like the United States and Russia.

Britain could compete, argued Seeley in the 1880s, only if it welded its white colonies and home islands into a world-spanning trans-national federation, a "Greater Britain." That remedy appeared less and less plausible: the white colonies, like the thirteen colonies before them, were developing away from Britain, not toward it. Particularly after 1900, informed British opinion feared the disintegration of the empire.

In Germany, nationalist professors provided a conceptual framework suitable for a "rising" power. From the summit of the German historical profession, the liberal Johann Gustav Droysen and the far less liberal Heinrich von Treitschke declared that unity under Prussia was the culmination of all previous German history. Droysen's fourteen-volume *History of Prussian Policy* (1853–86) and Treitschke's five-volume *History of Germany in the Nineteenth Century* (1879–94) portrayed the past, in good Hegelian fashion, as the upward struggle of a Prussian state embodying the world spirit. They also looked forward to higher things: Germany's mission in the world paralleled Prussia's mission in Germany. An entire generation absorbed their outlook.

The sociologist Max Weber suggested in a famous 1895 speech that the achievement of German unity had been a waste of time unless it was to serve as prelude to a "German world-power policy." The founder of the odd quasi-discipline of geopolitics, Friedrich Ratzel, suggested in his *Political Geography* (1897) and other publications that national borders were fluid and ever-changing. Organization and numbers were the key elements in an eternal struggle for "living space." Political pressure groups like the Pan-German League, founded in 1891, agitated fervently for more "space" for Germany. Britain's decline, the Germans argued, was Germany's opportunity to break through into the charmed circle of true world powers alongside Russia and the United States.

In Russia, figures like Katkov temporarily set aside pan-Slav fantasies for a Russian nationalist "manifest destiny" in East Asia. Russia in Asia, Katkov argued, was

"as much at home as in Moscow." As the trans-Siberian railroad crept eastward, the Tsar and his subordinates began to look to control of northeast Asia as the foundation of Russia's world power status.

In the United States, pundits urged a search for new frontiers beyond the seas to replace the land frontier that was passing. "Manifest destiny," a phrase coined by a Southern journalist in 1850, appeared to extend beyond the Pacific shores to "universal empire." But America's most influential prophet of empire was more modest. When Captain Alfred Thayer Mahan of the U.S. Naval War College published *The Influence of Seapower Upon History, 1660–1783* in 1889, it enjoyed instant success.

Mahan derived two simple laws from the great age of British naval power. One he merely implied: power, from the Roman empire to the British empire, meant *sea* power. The second he stated baldly: sea power meant a battle fleet. These notions made Mahan's book the bible of the U.S. Navy and of its great-power rivals, for he offered a recipe for success in the new age of world politics: build battle fleets and seize overseas bases and colonies to protect and foster an ever-expanding commerce. Ironically, Mahan achieved prominence just as technology—railroad, torpedo, mine, and submarine—was evening the contest between land power and sea power, and just as non-European nationalism was making colonies an increasingly doubtful investment.

The Struggle for Mastery in Africa, 1895–1902

The rivalries of the new age of world politics unfolded in two main theaters of action. In Africa, Britain and France confronted each other at the climax of the "scramble" for territory that had begun with the British occupation of Egypt in 1882. In East Asia, China's failure to keep pace with Japan or with the European powers led to a decade of bitter conflict.

France's refusal to accept British control of Egypt led it into dangerous paths in Africa. In 1897 Paris sent a small expedition under a Captain Marchand to stake a claim on the Upper Nile, the key to Egypt's water supply. But London, after Salisbury and the Conservatives returned to power in 1895, had decided to avenge the Mahdi's defeat of Gordon at Khartoum (see p. 692). Britain's security in Egypt demanded command of the Sudan.

A British army under Sir Herbert Kitchener ascended the Nile by steamer to face the army of the Mahdi. That made the issue between Britain and France one of power alone. At Omdurman, in September 1898, Kitchener crushed the Mahdists. Three weeks later, Kitchener found Marchand and his small force at Fashoda on the Upper Nile. To make good its territorial claims, France would now have to go to war. Salisbury refused to negotiate: "We claim the Sudan by right of conquest. . . ." The Dreyfus affair had crippled Paris politically, and France suddenly remembered that Britain still held the naval control of the Mediterranean that Nelson had won in 1798 at the Battle of the Nile. Marchand withdrew.

The Fashoda crisis was not the end of Britain's African woes. The great conflict with the Boers that Gladstone had postponed by retreating in 1881 finally erupted in the 1890s. The discovery of gold on Boer territory in 1886 made the Transvaal republic the greatest power in southern Africa. British entrepreneurs rushed in to exploit the Transvaal mines—but every ounce of gold they extracted increased the wealth and power of the Boers. After 1894 a railroad through Portuguese East Africa gave the Transvaal an independent link to the outside world. German political and economic influence flowed in, to the alarm of the British.

Most alarmed was Cecil Rhodes, the great robber baron of the Transvaal diamond mines and gold fields, and Britain's governor of the Cape Colony. In 1895 Rhodes decided to destroy Boer independence before Britain lost control of the Cape—and before his own mining interests suffered. With the secret help of the former Liberal Joseph Chamberlain, now Salisbury's secretary for colonies, Rhodes planned a raid against the Transvaal in support of a promised uprising of British

settlers and miners inside the Boer Republic itself. But these "Uitlanders," as the Boers called them, failed to move when Rhodes's raiders, under the leadership of a Dr. Jameson, struck in January 1896. The mounted infantry of the Boers neatly trapped the attackers, humiliating both Rhodes and Britain.

The main consequence of this "Jameson raid" was to provoke the unpredictable German Kaiser, William II, to send a foolish telegram of congratulation to the president of the Transvaal, the bearded patriarch Oom Paul Kruger. That gesture, which seemed to foreshadow further German meddling in southern Africa, made British action more urgent. Chamberlain, convinced that Britain must fight for its position at the Cape before it was too late, began preparing British public opinion for war. Salisbury, the prime minister, was unhappy: "I see before us the necessity for considerable military effort, and all for people whom we despise and for territory which will bring no power and profit for England." Yet Chamberlain and his deputy at the Cape, Sir Alfred Milner, had their way. In October 1899 Milner at last provoked the Boers into declaring war.

Contrary to expectation, the Boer War was no walkover. Britain controlled the sea; despite European disapproval and violent pro-Boer agitation in Germany, Britain's European rivals were helpless. But the Boers were not. Unlike Mahdists or Zulus they did not obligingly charge into British machine guns. Instead, they allowed the British to attack, and sent them reeling with German-supplied rifles and

Architects of empire, and of the Boer War: Joseph Chamberlain (*above*) and Cecil Rhodes (relaxing in the bush during the Matabele war, 1896).

Three generations of defiant Boers, with their Mauser rifles.

field guns. Boer knowledge of the country made their swift-moving mounted infantry hard to find as well as hard to defeat. Not until June 1900 did a huge and clumsy British army conquer the Boer capital, Pretoria. To defeat a few thousand backwoods farmers, Britain ultimately had to commit 450,000 men.

The conquest of Pretoria did not give Britain control of southern Africa. The Boers fought on in a bitter guerrilla struggle. The British replied with savage reprisals and "concentration camps": barbed-wire open-air prisons for the Boer civilians and their African dependents, to keep them from supplying the guerrillas. Roughly 20,000 Boers and 12,000 Africans died in the camps from disease and British

Asia in 1880

mismanagement. The Liberal opposition in London attacked the Conservative government for defending civilization with the "methods of barbarism." Soon all except the most determined "jingoes" were heartily tired of the brutality and sacrifices that empire required.

Attrition and Britain's increasing use of Boer turncoats and African volunteers finally persuaded the Boers to give up in May 1902. The greatest colonial war of the nineteenth century was over. But the fierceness of Boer resistance forced concessions from London as well. In 1910, Britain gave dominion status to a Boer-dominated Union of South Africa. The Boers had won in all but name.

The Struggle for Mastery in East Asia, 1894–98

African struggles were still part of the old framework of European and colonial rivalries. East Asia was different. There a new power, Japan, burst upon the scene by attacking China in September 1894. In the 1870s the Meiji oligarchs had restrained Japanese extremists who had urged a war with China's dependent kingdom, Korea. Now Japan was ready, and friction over Korea provided the occasion. Japan's new European-style army drove the Chinese from Korea and invaded Manchuria. Japan's new navy battered the poorly trained Chinese fleet off the mouth of the

Asia in 1914

Yalu River. Japan seized the vital base of Port Arthur on the Liaodong peninsula. By the Treaty of Shimonoseki of April 1895, Japan forced China to give up Port Arthur to Japan and to recognize Korean independence—but independence from China, not from Japan.

Then disaster struck. Russia and its French ally intervened diplomatically, posing as China's protectors. Their adversary in Europe, Germany, joined them in the hope of regaining favor with the Russia it had estranged in 1890. The three powers "advised" Japan against keeping Port Arthur and the Liaodong peninsula. The resentful Japanese agreed to give them up. Japan's main prizes were Taiwan, which it took as a colony, and an unstable joint overlordship with Russia over Korea.

Japan's victory over China opened a new scramble for concessions and ports that seemed to foreshadow the final collapse of the decrepit Chinese empire. Russia now made its bid for control of north China. It plied China with loans and gained the right to build a spur of the trans-Siberian railway directly across Manchuria to Vladivostok (see the map on p. 753). In December 1897 the Russians seized the prize the Japanese had sought, the ice-free naval base of Port Arthur, and secured from China the right to connect it to their railroad. In 1897–98 Germany and Britain also seized ports on the Shandong peninsula, opposite Port Arthur. Italy demanded a port, but China understood Europe well enough to know that it could safely refuse. The powers divided China into spheres of influence: Manchuria to Russia, southwest China to France, the great Yangtse Valley in the center to Britain, and Shandong to Germany.

The United States as a World Power: 1898

While the European powers and Japan were stripping China to the bone, a power greater than any of them began to develop a foreign policy of its own. That was a novelty, and not always a welcome one, for the United States. Thanks to its ocean boundaries and to the British fleet—which had barred European interference in the

New World in Britain's own interests—the United States had largely ignored the European balance throughout the nineteenth century. But a new assertiveness emerged in the 1890s, as industrial America reached maturity. In 1895 President Grover Cleveland's secretary of state intervened in a boundary dispute between Britain and Venezuela with the brash claim that "the United States is practically sovereign on this continent, and its fiat is law. . . ."

In 1898 the second of two Cuban revolts against Spain tempted the United States to make good that assertion. The battleship *Maine*, sent to Havana as a symbol of U.S. support for the revolt, exploded and sank in harbor, probably by accident. But the jingoist press of William Randolph Hearst claimed a Spanish plot: "Remember the *Maine*!" That agitation and the coming election moved President William McKinley to strike.

The shining new U.S. Navy, built up since the early 1890s on Mahan's theories, swept Spain's antiquated fleet from the seas. A hastily improvised landing on Cuba eventually defeated the Spaniards despite sketchy training and logistical chaos. Theodore Roosevelt, soon to be McKinley's successor, made a name for himself as leader of the dashing "Rough Riders." The navy too reached out across the Pacific: Commodore George Dewey crushed the Spanish fleet in the Philippines at the battle of Manila Bay. He then challenged a German squadron that was loitering nearby in hopes of snapping up a coaling station. The Germans wisely refused Dewey's challenge.

The Filipinos proved more difficult than Spain or the Germans. Already in revolt against Spain, they failed to see the charm of United States domination. It required up to 70,000 troops, three years, and all the U.S. Army's Indian-fighting skills to defeat the insurgency of Emilio Aguinaldo. Anti-imperialists at home fervently denounced the war. Ultimately the United States pacified the Philippines and stabilized its relationship with a nominally independent Cuba through an unspoken bargain. In return for the loyalty of the planter oligarchy that Spain had created,

Theodore ("Teddy") Roosevelt, Rough Rider and future president, 1898.

the United States promised to maintain order. That guaranteed short-term stability, but offered no long-term release from the fierce conflicts within these sharply stratified colonial societies.

The United States rounded out its new overseas empire by annexing Guam, Puerto Rico, and Hawaii. It also intervened diplomatically—mixing moralism and American interests in the style of the Monroe Doctrine—in faraway China. In 1899 McKinley's secretary of state, John Hay, urged the powers to preserve an "Open Door" to trade and to respect China's territorial integrity, rather than dividing China into exclusive spheres. The powers humored the newcomer and agreed. Paper promises were cheap, and easy to disavow.

Closer to home, the United States also made good the claim to the exclusive Latin American sphere of influence, free of European interference, first implied in the Monroe Doctrine in 1823. Britain in effect conceded United States domination of the Caribbean in the Hay-Pauncefote treaty of 1901. Under Theodore Roosevelt and his successors William Howard Taft (1909–13) and Woodrow Wilson (1913–21), the United States engineered the secession from Colombia of a new state—"Panama"—and between 1904 and 1914 carried through the Panama Canal project that had defeated de Lesseps. U.S. Marines brought imperial order to Central America and the Caribbean while diplomats sought, in Wilson's words, to teach the inhabitants "to elect good men." A navy of Dreadnoughts, with bases stretching from Manila Bay to Norfolk, Virginia, assured the security of the new empire and of America's growing trade. And America's immense and still-growing share of the world's industrial production reinforced its claims as a power.

The Struggle for Mastery in East Asia and the European Balance, 1899–1905

Meanwhile Western intrusion into China after 1897 triggered the largest spontaneous anti-Western rising since the Indian Mutiny of 1857–58. The "Righteous and Harmonious Fists," or "Boxers," had originated as an anti-dynastic secret society. They claimed that Taoist magic powers protected them from Western bullets. In 1898–99 the society spread across north China as a mass movement to "expel the foreign bandits and kill the Christian converts." The Dowager Empress and her conservative advisers in Beijing (Peking) quietly encouraged the Boxers, who obligingly ceased opposing the Qing dynasty itself.

International intervention to protect missionaries triggered a Boxer-led rising that besieged the Westerners in Beijing. Boxers assassinated the German minister. The Qing declared war on the European powers. As an Italian nationalist cynically remarked a year or two later, only an invasion from Mars could unite humanity. China briefly had the same effect; Europe, Japan, and the United States momentarily forgot their quarrels. William II dispatched Field Marshal Waldersee to lead the conquest of north China, sending the troops off with an impromptu speech that urged them to take no prisoners and to rival the fearsome reputation of Attila and his Huns. That was a phrase that Germany's enemies later remembered.

Even before Waldersee's arrival, Maxim guns had defeated Taoist magic. The powers imposed a stiff settlement but preserved the dynasty with the fiction that the Boxers had been an anti-Qing rebellion. The dynasty staggered on; the death of the Empress Dowager in 1908 and a revolution of provincial armies and Westernized intellectuals in 1911 ultimately destroyed it.

In the present, Russia's occupation of Manchuria and of Beijing itself worried Britain. London now felt little need for allies in Europe, for by the mid-1890s Salisbury at last felt strong enough to quietly abandon Britain's commitment to defend the Turkish Straits. The revival of British naval power and Britain's possession of Egypt had made "splendid isolation" practical. But to resist Russia in China, Britain needed a land power as an ally. That led Chamberlain to seek an agreement with Germany between 1899 and 1901. The Germans proved slippery, for good

The Western Powers line up for their slices of China (from a German cartoon, 1900).

churia. Russian machine gun and artillery fire exacted a terrible price from the attackers, but Port Arthur ultimately fell in January 1905. By March the Japanese had worn the Russians down in great battles of attrition in Manchuria. The trans-Siberian railway was still single-tracked, and Russian supplies and reinforcements were precarious. The Russians retreated northward.

At the end of May 1905 the Russian Baltic fleet, sent halfway around the world to rescue Port Arthur, met the Japanese off the island of Tsushima, south of Korea. The Japanese "crossed the T" of the advancing Russian fleet, sweeping the leading Russian ships with the long-range broadsides of their entire force. The annihilation of that last Russian fleet and the revolution that had broken out in European Russia in January 1905 (see pp. 722–23) forced Russia to cease fighting. "Teddy" Roosevelt, trying out America's new status as a Pacific great power, stepped in to mediate and to preserve a balance that would keep China alive. His Treaty of Portsmouth (New Hampshire) of September 1905 recognized Japan's "paramount interests" in Korea, forced Russia to return Manchuria to China, and gave Port Arthur, its railway, and the southern half of Sakhalin island to Japan (see the map on p. 753). Within five years Japan had annexed Korea. A non-European power had for the first time defeated a European great power. That set a powerful example for all non-Western peoples.

The Russo-Japanese war also decisively altered the European scene. The approach of war in Asia had caused the French deep anxiety: would Russia's war with Japan, a British ally, drag France into war with Britain? Théophile Delcassé, France's crafty foreign minister, therefore turned toward Britain. The British, equally intent on avoiding a clash, turned toward France. Queen Victoria's successor, the high-living Edward VII, wooed French opinion with a state visit in 1903 and with less official gastronomic and amorous cross-Channel excursions. By April 1904 the British and French had settled the colonial disputes that had divided them since the occupation of Egypt in 1882. France

reason. British goodwill and Germany's small stake in China were not sufficient cause for Germany to alienate Russia further. Germany shared European borders with Russia and with Russia's French ally; Britain did not.

In January 1902 Britain therefore found a different partner, that other "island empire," Japan. Tokyo and London pledged to go to war if either of them faced *two* great powers in East Asia. That meant that Britain and Japan would fight side by side only if France intervened alongside its Russian ally. Britain's role was to keep the French neutral while Japan, if necessary, stood up to Russia.

Russian recklessness soon made that necessary. In March 1903 the first train across the trans-Siberian railway reached Port Arthur. With their supply line apparently secure, the expansionists in St. Petersburg could look forward to ousting their Japanese partners and seizing Korea—and the domination of northeast Asia—for themselves. But Korea, as a Prussian general staff adviser had taught his Japanese pupils, was "a dagger pointed at the heart of Japan," a position of supreme geopolitical importance. Yamagata Aritomo, founder of Japan's modern army and the most Prussian of the surviving Meiji oligarchs, demanded war to stop Russia before it was ready to move.

When Russia refused to accept Japanese predominance in Korea in return for Japanese recognition of Russian control of Manchuria, Japan chose war. On January 8, 1904, the Japanese navy surprised and crippled the Russian fleet at Port Arthur. Command of the sea enabled Japan to lay seige to Port Arthur and to invade Man-traded its useless claims in Egypt for a British promise to support the eventual French annexation of Algeria's western neighbor, the decrepit Sultanate of Morocco. This Anglo-French *Entente Cordiale* was thus East Asian in origin and colonial in nature. But it soon became an alliance in all but name, facing the greatest European power, Germany.

That fateful development was a consequence of a second major effect of Russia's defeat by Japan: the disruption of the European naval and military balance. Until Russia recovered, Germany was supreme on the Continent. Its naval buildup, of which more below, soon outpaced the fleets of the Franco-Russian alliance and threatened to outpace that of Britain. Its land forces, freed temporarily from the two-front threat, held France hostage. And its efforts to reduce France to vassalage moved Britain, for the first time since Waterloo, to think of committing British forces to a land war in western Europe.

GERMANY ON THE LOOSE, 1905–14

Perhaps Germany's ever-greater industrial power should have inspired its leaders to *buy* Europe rather than conquer it. But German nationalist prophets, from the Liberals of the Frankfurt Parliament in 1848 to the Pan-Germans of the 1890s (see pp. 670 and 720), dreamt of "wrest[ing] mastery of the seas from the English, and . . . become[ing] the most powerful *Volk* on this earth." That was a goal only force could achieve.

Germany Challenges Britain, 1897–1905

Once the Franco-Russian alliance had barred the road to "Napoleonic supremacy" on land, the Kaiser looked seaward. Personal rivalry with his English royal cousins, an amateur interest in naval technology, and identification with the world-spanning goals of German middle-class nationalism made him from the early 1890s the chief advocate of enlarging Ger-

many's coastal defense navy into something far more impressive. In 1894 the Kaiser read the *Influence of Seapower Upon History* and became a convert to Mahan's gospel of the battle fleet. But not until 1897 did he find the team capable of translating his wishes into budgets and battleships: Bernhard von Bülow at the foreign office and Admiral Alfred Tirpitz at the Reich naval office.

Bülow provided the foreign policy cover for the fleet program. Germany was to avoid entanglement with either England or Russia while it created a fleet that would alter the world balance of power. It was the task of Tirpitz, with a formidable bifurcated beard and the wiliest political mind in Germany, to provide that fleet. To convince the *Reichstag* of the need for a battleship navy, he mounted Germany's first modern advertising campaign; the admiral's enemies did not call him "the Father of the Lie" for nothing. Charts showing Germany's comparative naval strength appeared in dentists' waiting rooms all over Germany. Schoolchildren chipped in pennies to pay for the fleet. Professors and industrialists spoke and wrote fervently of Germany's "sea interests" and world mission. In 1898 the *Reichstag* passed a first naval law providing for 19 battleships, and in 1900 accepted a second that doubled the fleet to 38 battleships and stepped up the building tempo to 3 ships each year.

To justify the enormous expense and *Reichstag* advance appropriations stretching over decades, Tirpitz claimed that Germany's increasing foreign trade and colonial empire required a fleet for its security. Only a fleet capable of placing "the greatest naval power" at serious risk would provide that security. Tirpitz's so-called "risk theory" appeared on the surface to be defensive, a strategy of deterrence. But no power threatened Germany's commerce or its largely useless colonial empire. Nor was deterrence Tirpitz's aim. In private memoranda for the Kaiser and others, he preached decisive battle "between Helgoland [an island off the German coast] and the Thames." For the "greatest naval power," the opponent Tirpitz had chosen, was Britain.

Admiral von Tirpitz, who built the fleet against Britain.

Germany's World Mission in the Words of Its Leaders

Even before 1900, the Kaiser's frequent "oratorical derailments"—as an aide privately described them—and the more cautious remarks of his chief foreign policy assistant, Bernhard von Bülow, had suggested the magnitude of Germany's ambitions:

Germany is gradually growing out of its children's shoes, and entering its youth. . . . We are bound for great things, and I shall yet lead you into glorious times.

The Kaiser, February 24, 1892 [speech in Berlin]

The German Empire has grown into a world empire. . . . German goods, German know-how, [and] German enterprise span the oceans.

The Kaiser, January 18, 1896 [speech in Berlin]

We do not seek to put anyone in the shade, but we demand our place in the sun! (Bravo!)

Bernhard von Bülow, December 6, 1897 [to the Reichstag]

If we look around us, we can see how the face of the world has changed in the last few years. Old world empires are passing away and new ones are coming into being.

The Kaiser, October 18, 1899 [speech in Hamburg]

Some have said . . . that in each century a conflict, a massive settlement of accounts redistributes influence, power, and possessions around the globe. In the sixteenth century the Spaniards and Portuguese divided the New World. In the seventeenth century the Dutch, French, and English entered the race while *we* were beating in each other's heads [in the Thirty Years' War] (merriment). In the eighteenth century the Dutch and French lost most of what they had gained to the English. In our own nineteenth century England has ceaselessly extended its colonial empire, the mightiest the world has seen since the days of the Romans, while the French have planted themselves firmly in North and East Africa and have created a new empire in Indochina, and Russia has begun a mighty procession of victories in Asia that has carried it to the high plateau of the Pamirs and the shores of the Pacific. . . . Are we once again facing a new division of the world, as the poets fancied a century ago? I think not, or rather I do not think it yet. But in any case we cannot permit any foreign power, any foreign Jupiter, to say to us: "Hard luck. The world had already been given away." We do not seek to injure other powers, but we also seek to keep other powers from kicking us around (Bravo!). . . . In the coming century the German people will either be a hammer or an anvil.

Bernhard von Bülow, December 11, 1899 [to the Reichstag]

From Michael Behnen, ed., Quellen zur deutschen Aussenpolitik im Zeitalter des Imperialismus 1890–1911 *(Darmstadt: Wissenschaftliche Buchgesellschaft, 1977), pp. 63, 146, 166, 225, 230–31 (translation by M. Knox).*

Victory over Britain, Tirpitz calculated, depended on four assumptions. Rivalry with France and Russia would tie up the British navy in China and the Mediterranean, leaving Britain weak in the North Sea. The feeble British would neither pay for nor be able to man the additional ships needed to keep pace with the German buildup. Technology, Tirpitz assumed, would remain static; German battleships built in 1900 would be roughly equivalent to British and German ships commissioned later. Finally, in the event of war the British fleet would charge into Germany's mine- and submarine-infested waters to mount its traditional close blockade of enemy ports, as in the days of Nelson. That would give the Germans their opportunity to fight close to their bases on advantageous terms.

The Kaiser was enthusiastic. The fleet would assure him his place in Prusso-German history. Just as his grandfather William I—thanks to Bismarck—had used the Prussian army to give the new Germany a dominant position on the Continent, so he himself would use the navy to break through into the circle of authentic world powers. And just as William I and Bismarck had defeated Prussian Liberalism by victory abroad in 1866–71, so he and his "second Bismarck," Bülow, would defeat Social Democracy. And the Kaiser's fleet, thanks to provisions in the naval laws that automatically replaced over-age ships without the need for further *Reichstag* votes, would ultimately become independent of the hated legislature.

The British were not amused. Britain by 1900 was closer than Germany to being an industrial society; more than half of Britain's food was imported, and those imports came by sea. Naval supremacy in home waters was no luxury for Britain, but a matter of survival. The British navy scrapped its Chinese river gunboats and its Caribbean squadron to free manpower for the North Sea. After 1903 it created new naval bases facing Germany at Rosyth in Scotland and at Scapa Flow in the Orkneys (see map, p. 770). Admiral "Jacky" Fisher, as Admiralty chief after 1904, supervised Britain's technological leap to the all-big-gun ship, the Dreadnought. He also urged destruction of the German fleet in harbor before it was strong enough to challenge Britain. Finally, Britain sought allies against Germany: France and eventually Russia. By 1905, the principal assumptions of Tirpitz's plan were all proving false. Germany had challenged Britain to a naval race that the British dared not lose, and had isolated itself diplomatically except for its alliance with an increasingly ramshackle Austria-Hungary.

The First Morocco Crisis and the Anglo-Russian Entente, 1905–07

Germany might have sought to loosen by good behavior the "encirclement"—as Germans now began to call it—that Germany had created around itself. Britain, France, and Russia were an odd assortment: two parliamentary regimes, one brutal autocracy. Britain and Russia might still clash anywhere from China to Persia, if Germany lay low. But Bülow and the chief brain at the German foreign office, the secretive Friedrich von Holstein, chose to break "encirclement" with threats. Japan's defeat of Russia in 1904–05 had temporarily paralyzed France's continental ally. Bülow and Holstein, seeking to exploit that weakness, picked a quarrel with France in the expectation that Britain would abandon France to German domination.

As a pretext the Germans chose French encroachment on the decaying Sultanate of Morocco. But this "First Morocco Crisis" was in reality not a colonial quarrel. It was rather a crisis of the European balance of power. In March 1905, with Russia in revolutionary chaos, Bülow and Holstein diverted to Tangier the Kaiser's habitual Mediterranean cruise. There William II blusteringly asserted Germany's nonexistent "great and growing interests in Morocco" against France. Tension mounted as summer, the season for war, drew near. In June the French cabinet's nerve cracked, and Paris accepted the humiliating German demand that Delcassé resign as foreign minister.

Germany seemed to have won; William II made Bülow a prince. And in July William II succeeded in persuading his cousin "Nicky"—Tsar Nicholas II—to sign an alliance with Germany at a meeting of their yachts off the Finnish island of Björkö. Nicholas agreed, hoping that German backing would help him get better peace terms from Japan. Germany had apparently broken the Franco-Russian alliance and had achieved supremacy on the Continent.

But Russia in defeat and revolution needed French money more than ever before. And France would only supply that money if Russia abandoned the Björkö agreement—which the Russians in any case no longer needed once they had made peace with Japan in September 1905. The Germans also made a fatal error. Instead of working out a private bargain with France over Morocco, they called for an international conference.

The representatives of the powers met at Algeciras, opposite Gibraltar, in January 1906. Germany found itself isolated except for Austria-Hungary. Even its Triple Alliance partner Italy stood alongside France. In 1900 Italy had secured secret French agreement to its eventual annexation of Libya in return for its support of France in Morocco. In 1902 Rome had even sinned secretly against the Triple Alliance by promising France that Italy would remain neutral if Germany "provoked" France to declare war. The Algeciras conference therefore handed Germany a major diplomatic defeat. And Britain had already taken secret steps to bolster the French. In December 1905, as the Liberals took office, talks had begun between the British and French army staffs over the commitment of a British army on the left wing of the French if Germany attacked.

The crisis Germany had provoked had mightily reinforced the ring forming around Germany. By their actions, Bülow and Holstein had converted the Anglo-French colonial agreement of 1904 into a quasi-alliance against Germany to preserve the European balance of power. And on August 31, 1907, Russia and Britain, the two most persistent great-power enemies of the nineteenth century, signed an agreement settling their long-standing disputes in China, Tibet, and Persia. The

"Triple Entente" of Britain, France, and Russia now faced the Triple Alliance of Germany, Austria-Hungary, and Italy.

Naval Race and Bosnian Crisis, 1907–09

The Germans learned little from this First Morocco crisis. The noisy diplomacy of Bülow and Holstein had contradicted Tirpitz's need for quiet in which to build a fleet against Britain; now the building of Tirpitz's fleet thwarted Germany's far greater need to lie low. By 1908 Tirpitz could see that he might fail. The Liberals in Britain, despite their loathing of "great armaments" and their desire to increase social-welfare spending, refused to give up Britain's lead over the German fleet. Tirpitz, amid noisy anti-British propaganda from the German Navy League, therefore pushed a third naval law through the *Reichstag* that raised the German building tempo to four Dreadnoughts per year.

Britain replied by proposing a one-year halt in building, a "naval holiday." Berlin refused. Except for the pacifist Cobdenite wing of the Liberals, British public opinion was now unanimous. Britain must keep its naval lead whatever the cost. "We want eight [Dreadnoughts] and we won't wait!" thundered the popular press. In 1909–10 Britain began construction of ten battleships and battle cruisers. When the time came to pay the bill, the Liberals raised the income tax, slapped on inheritance taxes, and overrode aristocratic protests in the House of Lords; the knowledge that naval superiority was a matter of life or death strengthened British resolve. In Germany, Bülow's attempt to raise taxes to cover the vast increases in fleet costs led to the defection of the *Junker* Conservatives, the collapse of the government's *Reichstag* majority, and ultimately to Bülow's own dismissal.

As Anglo-German tension mounted, Germany's ally Austria-Hungary made its own contribution to the growing European crisis. For a decade it had held to its 1897 agreement with Russia to keep the Balkans quiet. But in 1903 a group of fanatical Serb officers slaughtered Vienna's clients, King Alexander and Queen Draga

Obrenovitch of Serbia. As Austria-Hungary's relations with Serbia deteriorated, France offered Serbia economic support. By 1908 the Austro-Hungarian foreign minister, Count Aehrenthal, had concluded that Vienna's prestige was at stake.

In October 1908, as a blow against Serbia, he announced Austria-Hungary's formal annexation of Bosnia and Hercegovina, the largely Serb-inhabited provinces bordering Serbia that the Congress of Berlin had allowed Austria-Hungary to occupy in 1878. Aehrenthal's Russian counterpart, Count Isvolsky, had secretly agreed—but only if Austria-Hungary helped toward a long-standing Russian goal, the opening of the Turkish Straits to Russian warships. Aehrenthal's announcement thus caught the Russians before they had secured their reward. Austria-Hungary kept Bosnia and Hercegovina, while Russia grumbled and threatened and Serb crowds demanded war against Austria. Eventually William II appeared, as he himself put it, "in shining armor" at Austria-Hungary's side. Berlin demanded that Russia and Serbia accept the annexation, or else. The Russians gave in; they had not yet recovered from war with Japan. But what seemed to Berlin a triumphant reassertion of German and Austro-Hungarian prestige struck the other powers as dramatic evidence of German aggressiveness. Bülow later claimed that he had warned the Kaiser—when William dismissed him in summer 1909 after a personal clash—not to "repeat the Bosnian affair." It was sound advice.

The Second Morocco Crisis, 1911

Bülow's successors, Chancellor Theobald von Bethmann Hollweg and foreign secretary Alfred von Kiderlen-Wächter, did not act on it. Instead, Kiderlen tried once again to use Morocco as a pretext for bullying France, in the hope of breaking the Triple Entente and riding German nationalist enthusiasm to a government victory in the 1912 *Reichstag* elections. In May 1911 the French occupied Fez, the capital of Morocco, after rebellion and anti-foreign riots like those in Egypt in 1882. Kiderlen reacted by dispatching a gunboat, the *Pan-*

ther, to the Moroccan Atlantic port of Agadir on the pretext of protecting German lives—which were not threatened. The German press was ecstatic: "Finally, a Deed!"

Kiderlen also secretly threatened Paris with war, while offering to settle for the entire French Congo in compensation for France's seizure of Morocco and as a symbol of France's vassalage to Germany. But the French and Russian armies were now stronger than they had been in 1905. Lloyd George, whom the Germans had taken for a pacifist Liberal, stiffened the French with jingo oratory promising British support.

Bethmann Hollweg shared what his private secretary described as "the authentic and fitting German idealist conviction that the *Volk* needs a war." But the Kaiser was less enthusiastic. Germany ultimately settled for several strips of swamp in the French Congo. France retained its independence. The Pan-Germans, whose backing Kiderlen had courted throughout the crisis, vented their fury on the Reich government for this "new Olmütz" (see p. 669). And Britain made further secret commitments to France. London reaffirmed its decision to send a British Expeditionary Force (B.E.F.) to France in the event of German attack. Sir Edward Grey, the foreign secretary, authorized further military discussions with the French while keeping the cabinet's pacifist Liberals in the dark. And Sir Winston Churchill, civilian chief of the navy after 1911—and a distant descendent of the great Duke of Marlborough who had halted the France of Louis XIV—called the Mediterranean fleet home to the North Sea to face the Germany of William II. The French took over Britain's Mediterranean responsibilities in return for a secret British pledge to protect the coasts of northern France against the German fleet. That was Britain's most far-reaching commitment against Germany to date.

Germany Prepares for War, 1912–13

The German response to defeat in the Second Morocco Crisis was retrenchment—of a sort. Tirpitz lost the unchallenged right to funding that his navy had enjoyed since 1897; in 1913 and 1914 the German building tempo fell to two battleships a year. Berlin at last recognized that it must secure its continental position before taking on Britain. The Kaiser and Bethmann Hollweg now gave the army priority. Radical nationalists on the general staff such as Erich Ludendorff broke *Junker* resistance to expanding the army and thus bringing more and more non-nobles into the officer corps. In 1912 and 1913 two army bills increased the army's size by a quarter, and the *Reichstag* paid the bill by passing an inheritance tax over Conservative objections. Tirpitz's only consolation was the Kaiser's rejection of another British proposal for a "naval holiday."

The increase in the size of the army was necessary, if Germany was to implement its chosen strategy in war. Waldersee's successor as Chief of the Great General Staff, Count Alfred von Schlieffen (1891–1905), faced the same nightmare of a two-front war as his predecessors. But his answer was different. Instead of attacking Russia and defending in fortified Alsace-Lorraine, as both Moltke and Waldersee had proposed, Schlieffen planned to strike France first. France, he reasoned, was vulnerable to a swift decisive blow, whereas the Russians could always retreat into their limitless spaces as they had in 1812.

Schlieffen had studied military history, classifying battles as an entomologist does insects. Decisive battles, he concluded, were all envelopments. The most perfect was Hannibal's crushing double envelopment of the Romans in 216 B.C., at Cannae in south Italy (see p. 78). But mountains, French fortifications, and the absence of space for Germany's million-man army would not permit the attack across the Franco-German border needed for a double envelopment. Instead, Schlieffen planned a holding action there to distract the French. Meanwhile an immense right wing, three-quarters of the entire German army, would swing down through neutral Belgium and attack the unfortified and undefended French rear.

Timing was everything: if Germany did not mobilize in time, or if it failed to knock France out immediately, the

Schlieffen's Plan

"Russian Steamroller" would crush Germany's skeleton forces in East Prussia and drive on Berlin. And Schlieffen, in his admiration of Hannibal, had forgotten one vital fact. In the end, Rome had defeated Hannibal and destroyed Carthage through attrition and through its command of the sea.

Schlieffen's plan had at least two fatal strategic flaws. It required that any German war, even one stemming from a Bal-

"War the sooner the better": Helmuth von Moltke the younger, Prussia-Germany's chief of staff, 1906–14.

kan quarrel, must begin with an attack on France that staked Germany's future on a single card. And the violation of Belgium, whose neutrality Prussia and the other great powers had guaranteed in 1839, virtually ensured that Britain would join Germany's enemies. To Schlieffen that seemed unimportant. Britain had no mass army, and the war would be over—*must* be over—before it had time to raise one. Those were dangerous illusions.

Schlieffen retired in 1905 and died in 1913, leaving his plan to Helmuth von Moltke the younger, the high-strung and indecisive nephew of the great Moltke. The new chief of staff had doubts about Schlieffen's "infallible recipe for victory," but kept them to himself. And at the end of 1912 the German leaders apparently decided to act. A British warning that Britain would stand by France in the event of war enraged the Kaiser. On December 8, 1912, he presided over a conference of his military advisers at Berlin. Moltke urged war "the sooner the better," to crush Germany's adversaries before they grew too strong. New Russian railways in Poland and rearmament of the Russian army with modern weapons would make the Schlieffen plan impractical by 1917. Tirpitz advised restraint for the moment; the navy was not ready. The conference, without consulting Bethmann Hollweg, decided to mobilize the press to prepare the public for war. With government encouragement, newspaper stories increasingly hostile to Russia began to appear.

At the general staff, Moltke and his assistant Ludendorff made two fateful decisions in 1913. First, they discarded Germany's one remaining alternate plan, which had provided for an offensive against Russia and defense against France. Second, Ludendorff added to the Schlieffen plan an immediate thrust through neutral Luxembourg and Belgium, starting the moment the German army mobilized, to seize the key rail junction of Liège. If danger threatened, Germany—unlike the other powers—could not mobilize and wait to see what happened. It planned to violate Belgium in the process of mobilizing its army, and to attack France regardless of what triggered the crisis.

The Balkan Wars, 1912–13

While the Germans prepared, the great powers lost control of the Balkans. France's seizure of Morocco had set off a chain reaction. Giovanni Giolitti of Italy feared that the French—now that they had secured Morocco with Italian approval—would forget their earlier promise to support Italy's claim to Libya. In September 1911, Giolitti therefore declared war on Turkey, Libya's nominal overlord, and sent a fleet to Tripoli. A hastily improvised landing failed to subdue the warlike Arabs of Libya or their Turkish advisers. Italy then seized Turkish islands in the Aegean and attacked the Turkish Straits. Not until October 1912 did the Turks give up a still unpacified Libya to Italy.

The Italian example encouraged the Balkan states. Serbia and Bulgaria, with Russia as godfather, signed an alliance in March 1912. Greece and Montenegro joined them. The Russians thought of the new alliance as defensive; the Balkan states had other ideas. In September 1912 this Balkan League attacked and swiftly divided up the remaining Ottoman territories in the Balkans. Then the victors quarreled over the booty. Bulgaria attacked Serbia in the hope of seizing Macedonia, claiming that the powers had defrauded it of that province in 1878. Serbia, Greece, Montenegro, Rumania, and Turkey repelled the Bulgarians.

In the aftermath of the two Balkan Wars, the great powers worked together under the leadership of Sir Edward Grey of Britain to calm the triumphant Serbs and stabilize the new Balkan order; an independent Albania that barred Serbia from the Adriatic was one result. But the Balkan Wars were clearly not the last Balkan crisis. The collapse of the multinational Turkish empire in Europe made Austria-Hungary, the new "Sick Man" of Europe, increasingly desperate to reassert its shrinking prestige against the growing

The Dissolution of the Ottoman Empire to 1914

The Balkan Wars: Turkish infantry moves up.

power of Serbia, the self-proclaimed "Piedmont of the South Slavs."

FROM BALKAN CRISIS TO GERMAN WAR: JULY 1914

On June 28, 1914, at Sarajevo in Bosnia, a Bosnian Serb terrorist assassinated Archduke Franz Ferdinand, heir to the throne of Austria-Hungary. The terrorists, following a pattern common later in the century, were associated with a secret society—the "Black Hand"—sponsored by Serbian military intelligence. Although Vienna did not know that, it reacted with predictable fury. The chief of staff, Conrad von Hötzendorff, longed for a war to restore Habsburg prestige and crush Serbia for good. Austria-Hungary's frivolous foreign minister, Count Leopold von Berchtold, concurred. Only the Hungarians, whose privileged position within the monarchy might suffer if Vienna annexed yet more Slavs, urged caution.

Berlin broke the deadlock in Vienna. When Berchtold's envoy met the Kaiser on July 5, 1914, the Kaiser urged an immediate attack on Serbia, regardless of Russia's reaction. He repeatedly assured a friend, Krupp von Bohlen, that "this time I will not chicken out [*Diesmal falle ich nicht um*]." Bethmann Hollweg told his closest confidant on July 8 that Germany would probably win a general war. If Russia shrank from a war, Germany would nevertheless split the Entente and achieve a decisive diplomatic and strategic victory. In Vienna, Berchtold used Berlin's so-called "blank check"—in reality a virtual order to act—to break the Hungarians' opposition to war. Hungary owed its autonomy after 1866 to Berlin; it could not refuse Berlin's command.

But partly from Viennese sloth and partly from calculation, Berchtold did not deliver his ultimatum to Serbia until July 23. That long delay and the ultimatum's contents made Berchtold's actions seem coldly premeditated, and weakened Austria-Hungary's position. One senior German diplomat could not believe that Vienna had drafted the ultimatum; its brutal tone was "Prussian to the very bones."

Berchtold made the deliberately humiliating demand that Austro-Hungarian police be permitted to enter Serbia and join the hunt for the terrorists and their accomplices. He also announced that Vienna would treat refusal of any single condition in the ultimatum as a total rejection. The Serbs returned a conciliatory answer. But they refused to accept Austro-Hungarian intervention inside Serbia itself.

For Vienna, that was pretext enough for war. And for Berlin, where the leadership, in the words of a participant, "worried only that the Serbs might swallow the [Austro-Hungarian conditions]." Bethmann Hollweg sabotaged efforts by Britain to arrange a conference of the kind that had prevented the Balkan Wars from growing into a great-power conflict. On July 28, with strong German encouragement, Austria-Hungary declared war on Serbia. Vienna's mobilization was too slow to permit an invasion for several weeks, but Vienna and Berlin were determined to present the other great powers with a violent *fait accompli*. Austria-Hungary therefore shelled Belgrade, the Serb capital.

Now Russia had to respond or suffer a humiliation far worse than the Bosnian crisis. On July 28, Nicholas II and his foreign minister, Sergei Dimitrievich Sazonov, tried to deter Vienna by ordering mobilization of the four Russian military districts opposite Austria-Hungary. But then the Russian generals reported that their cumbersome mobilization system permitted only a general mobilization. On July 31 Russia published the order for general mobilization. That was the point of no return, although the Russian purpose was still deterrence, not war.

In Berlin, the news of Russian mobilization was welcome indeed. The Kaiser had begun to waver, and Moltke was pressing Bethmann Hollweg with increasing fierceness to mobilize before Russia could. Bethmann Hollweg himself feared the domestic consequences of being first to mobilize; his task was to keep the German Social Democrats loyal to the coming war effort. Consequently, Russia's mobilization appeared heaven-sent. "The mood is brilliant," wrote the Kaiser's chief naval

Sarajevo, June 28, 1914: The arrest of the assassin, Gavrilo Princip.

aide in his diary on August 1. "The government has succeeded very well in making us appear as the attacked." Germany dispatched an ultimatum to Russia summoning it to demobilize. Russia refused.

On August 1 Germany declared war on Russia and ordered mobilization. France honored its alliance obligations to Russia by mobilizing also, in defiance of a German ultimatum to Paris demanding French neutrality in a Russo-German war. The ultimatum was for show only; German strategy dictated an attack on France. If France dared to upset the Schlieffen plan by abandoning its Russian ally and

Conrad von Hötzendorff, Austria-Hungary's chief of staff, contemplates war on three fronts (1914).

The Kaiser Spurs Vienna On   July 5, 1914

The Kaiser's message, as reported by Austria-Hungary's ambassador, Count Ladislaus Szögyény, was no simple "blank check" or assurance of support. It was an incitement to war.

After lunch, when I once again underscored with the greatest emphasis the seriousness of the situation, His Majesty [Kaiser William II] authorized me to report to our most gracious Majesty [Emperor Francis Joseph] that in this case as in others we could count on Germany's full support. . . . He (Kaiser William) was of the opinion that this action must not be delayed. Russia's attitude will in any event be hostile, but he had been prepared for that for years, and should it come to a war between Austria-Hungary and Russia, we could be assured that Germany would stand by our side with its usual faithfulness to its alliances. . . . He understands full well that His royal and imperial Apostolic Majesty [Emperor Francis Joseph] would be reluctant, given his well-known love of peace, to march into Serbia. But if we had really become convinced of the necessity of military action against Serbia, he (Kaiser William) would regret it if we allowed the present highly favorable moment to pass unused.

From Imanuel Geiss, ed., Julikrise und Kriegsausbruch 1914 *(Hannover: Verlag für Literatur und Zeitgeschehen GmbH, 1963), pp. 83–84 (translation by M. Knox).*

remaining neutral, the German ambassador in Paris was to ask provocatively for the surrender of French border fortifications. That would force France to fight. In the event, France did not accept Berlin's ultimatum. On August 2 Germany invaded Luxembourg and demanded that Belgium give free passage to German troops. Belgium refused. On August 3 Germany declared war on France. On the morning of August 4 German troops entered Belgium—and pushed the indecisive British cabinet into war. The violation of Belgium allowed the Liberals to feel moral about a war to defend British security and the balance of power; the Cobdenite pacifist Liberals resigned, and Britain dispatched an ultimatum demanding that Germany withdraw from Belgium. At midnight on August 4, that ultimatum expired, and all the European great powers were at war. As the Kaiser addressed the *Reichstag* amid stormy applause, the Prussian war minister, Erich von Falkenhayn, was over-

come by emotion: "Even if we end in ruin, it was beautiful." That was a fitting epitaph for Imperial Germany and for the long peace.

"War Guilt," War Causes

After 1918, it became fashionable to dispute Germany's preeminent responsibility for the war of 1914–18. German scholars rallied around their foreign office and accused Russia or Britain. Anglo-Saxon "revisionists" charged Vienna, St. Petersburg, Paris, and even London with "war guilt." Guilt is a notion best left to psychoanalysts—but causes and responsibilities are the historian's business.

The long-term causes of the war were two: Austria-Hungary's decline and—above all—Germany's rise. Balkan nationalism threatened an Austria-Hungary entangled in a perennial struggle with Russia. After 1890, German nationalism proved not at all "satiated"—and the transition to a world balance-of-power system excited it still further. Bismarck, with his alliance with Austria-Hungary in 1879, had tied together these two principal sources of European conflict. After 1905 they interacted explosively. Balkan nationalism undermined Austria-Hungary just as the growing German threat drove Britain, France, and Russia to coalesce against Germany.

In the final crisis, responsibility was unevenly divided. Britain intervened only when the Germans invaded Belgium. France merely accepted a war that Germany forced on it. The Serb government did not seek war, although its army had nurtured the terrorists. Russia had backed Serbian expansion in the Balkan Wars, and in July 1914 it may have encouraged the Serbs to refuse the most humiliating of Austria-Hungary's demands. Russia had also been the first to mobilize, although it aimed not at war, but at getting Vienna's attention.

The responsibilities of Austria-Hungary were more serious. It sought war with Serbia, made sure that its ultimatum would lead to war, and shelled Belgrade. But Berlin took the key decision: without German pressure, Austria-Hungary would never have acted, and the crisis would have fizzled out. Since late 1912 Germany's leaders had looked forward to a general war, given a suitable occasion. Moltke actively sought war "the sooner the better." His purpose was to strike down Germany's *potential* enemies before they became too strong—a goal little different from outright aggression. Bethmann Hollweg, obsessed with the ever-growing—though hollow—Russian colossus, and optimistic about German chances of victory if general war came soon, was willing to risk it. All trusted in a "fresh and joyous war" (in the phrase of the Kaiser's boisterous son, Crown Prince William), victorious in the style of 1870.

Germany's minimum goal was a small Balkan war to shore up a flagging Austria-Hungary and split the Triple Entente. Its maximum goal was to destroy the balance of power and make Germany supreme in Europe. And the Schlieffen plan—after 1913 Germany's *only* war plan—guaranteed that any German war against Russia would begin with an attack on Belgium and France. That assured British intervention. Germany unleashed a Balkan war, then turned it into a general war that destroyed Europe's world position.

Suggestions for Further Reading

The European Balance

The relevant chapters of A. J. P. Taylor's indispensable *The Struggle for Mastery in Europe* (1954) give a detailed and brilliant general account, but see also N. Rich, *Great Power Diplomacy, 1814–1914* (1992), and P. Kennedy, *The Rise and Fall of the Great Powers* (1987). W. L. Langer, *European Alliances and Alignments, 1871–1890* (1950), is still useful on Bismarck's conservative phase. M. Hurst, ed., *Key Treaties for the Great Powers, Vol. 2, (1871–1914)* (1972), gives English texts of key agreements such as the Triple Alliance. Among the many accounts of the policies of the various powers, see especially G. Bourne, *The Foreign Policy of Victorian England* (1970); B. Porter, *The Lion's Share* (1984); and D. Geyer, *Russian Imperialism* (1987). On military affairs, see the relevant chapter in H. Strachan, *European Armies and the Conduct of War* (1983).

World Politics

The chapter on international affairs in G. Barraclough, *An Introduction to Contemporary History* (1964), remains the best short introduction to the rise of "world politics." W. L. Langer, *The Diplomacy of Imperialism* (1950), covers the 1890–1902 period in informative detail. H. W. Morgan, *America's Road to Empire* (1965), conveniently summarizes America's entry into world politics; see also C. S. Campbell, *The Transformation of American Foreign Relations, 1865–1900* (1976), and H. K. Beale, *Theodore Roosevelt and the Rise of America to World Power* (1956). R. Van Alstyne, *The Rising American Empire* (1960), offers a jaundiced view of U.S. motives. T. Pakenham, *The Boer War* (1978), and I. Nish, *The Anglo-Japanese Alliance* (1966), are excellent.

The Road to the First World War

The best single work on the origins of the First World War remains L. Albertini, *The Origins of the War of 1914* (1952). P. Kennedy, *The Origins of the Anglo-German Antagonism, 1860–1914* (1980), is a model of analysis. V. Berghahn, *Germany and the Approach of War in 1914* (1973), and Z. Steiner, *Britain and the Origins of the First World War* (1977), offer parallel accounts that emphasize German responsibility. On France, Russia, Austria-Hungary, and Italy, see J. Keiger, *France and the Origins of the First World War* (1983); D. Lieven, *Russia and the Origins of the First World War* (1983); F. R. Bridge, *From Sadowa to Sarajevo: The Foreign Policy of Austria-Hungary, 1866–1914* (1972); and R. Bosworth, *Italy and the Approach of the First World War* (1983). V. Dedijer, *The Road to Sarajevo* (1967), throws some light on Serb machinations. G. Ritter, *The Schlieffen Plan* (1958), and P. M. Kennedy, ed., *The War Plans of the Great Powers, 1880–1914* (1979), are useful on military planning. For the final crisis, I. Geiss, ed., *July 1914* (1967), is indispensable. F. Fischer, *Germany's Aims in the First World War* (1967) and War of Illusions (1975), make a strong case for a premeditated German war of aggression. G. Schöllgen, ed., *Escape into War? The Foreign Policy of Imperial Germany* (1990), summarizes the resulting "Fischer debate."

30

WAR AND REVOLUTION
1914–1929

The war that began in August 1914 smashed nineteenth-century Europe beyond repair. Contrary to almost universal expectation, the first battles did not decide the war. Instead, as in the U.S. Civil War, industrialized states summoned up their full reserves of human and machine power and battered each another into collapse. In the process, Europe lost its world economic leadership, already threatened by the growth of the United States. The nationalism of the colonial peoples received powerful reinforcement. The four great empires of Europe and the Middle East perished. One of them, Russia, suffered a revolution utopian in its aims and unparalleled in its ferocity, the first Marxist revolution. The European balance of power collapsed, and only the intervention of an outside power, the United States, brought Germany's defeat. Then the swift withdrawal of the United States after 1919 left the exhausted victors, Britain and France, face to face with a vengeful Germany that refused to accept the outcome. The Great War of 1914–18 was merely the *First World War*.

THE WAR OF MOVEMENT, 1914

The German Gamble Fails

On August 4, Schlieffen's great right wing—a million men in four German armies deployed in northwestern Germany—began to swing across Belgium. The French obligingly attacked the fortifications of the German left wing in Lorraine, and plunged deeper into the trap. The Lorraine offensive cost France 300,000 dead, wounded, and missing.

But Schlieffen and Moltke the younger had made no allowance for enemy reaction. Nor had they given enough thought

(*Opposite*) TOTAL WAR: WOMEN, STEEL, AND HIGH EXPLOSIVES AT A BRITISH MUNITIONS PLANT, 1917.

The First World War   1914–18

to "friction," the forces of accident, error, and confusion that make even the simplest plans in war heartbreakingly difficult to carry out. Belgian civilians sniped at German troops, despite German massacres in reprisal. The Belgians wrecked their railroads to keep supplies from reaching the German armies. And the long marches exhausted the German reservists. By September, wrote an officer on the far right wing, "the men stagger forward, their faces coated with dust, their uniforms in rags, looking like living scarecrows. They march with their eyes closed, singing in

chorus so as not to fall asleep. . . . It is only the delirium of victory that sustains our men."

Delirium soon receded. As the Germans neared the Franco-Belgian border, they met both the French and the 120,000 professionals of the British Expeditionary Force. The Kaiser spurred his commanders to "exterminate the treacherous English" and to walk over their "contemptible little army." The B.E.F. replied with shockingly accurate and rapid rifle fire. German numerical superiority finally forced the British and French to withdraw southward, but the price of German victory was high. That price rose further as the French commander in chief, the unflappable "Papa" Joseph Joffre, gave up his offensive in Lorraine and switched forces by rail to face the main German attack as it swept down from Belgium. Schlieffen had simply assumed that the French would be too paralyzed to strike back; the French decided otherwise.

The Germans, footsore in the August heat, found by the end of the month that they lacked enough troops to swing west and north of Paris, as Schlieffen had originally planned. And as the outermost German army swung south and east of Paris, it exposed its flank and rear to French forces in the city. Joseph Galliéni, conqueror of Tonkin and Madagascar, threw his troops against the German weak point, and marshaled the taxis of Paris to bring up reserves. The German commander on the spot frantically turned back to the northwest to counter Galliéni, and opened a fatal gap between his army and its neighbor. On September 8–9, spurred on by fierce demands from Joffre ("the honor of England is at stake"), the battered B.E.F. staggered northward across the Marne River into the gap between the two German armies. That break in the German line threatened disaster; Moltke's liaison officer and commanders on the spot panicked. On September 9 the exhausted Germans withdrew northward. Moltke suffered a nervous breakdown. France's defensive victory on the Marne meant that Europe faced a long war.

Moltke's replacement, the moody Erich von Falkenhayn, dissipated German reserves in a series of piecemeal attacks north of Paris. The B.E.F. and the French held with difficulty, but they held. This "race to the sea" ended in October–November 1914 with a huge slaughter in Flanders. At Langemarck, near Ypres, Falkenhayn committed scarcely trained volunteers, fresh from school or university, against the remnants of the B.E.F. It was a "massacre of the innocents." Little remained of the volunteers, of whom Germany had much need later, or of the B.E.F., the only source of experienced leaders for Britain's coming mass armies.

In mid-November Falkenhayn admitted to Bethmann Hollweg that the Imperial German Army was "a broken instrument," incapable of forcing a decision. By year's end Germany had lost almost a million dead and wounded, and France at least 900,000. Trenches and barbed wire stretched from the Channel to Switzerland. Until early 1918 the lines on the western front scarcely moved, despite unparalleled carnage.

In the East the Germans had better luck. The "Russian Steamroller" rolled into East Prussia, and then broke down. When the outnumbered German defenders wavered, Moltke dragged a senior general, Paul von Hindenburg, out of retirement and gave him Ludendorff as chief of staff. Ludendorff, with the help of intercepted Russian radio communications, concentrated his forces against one of the two Russian armies and crushed it at Tannenberg by August 29. Russia lost 92,000 men and 400 guns. Then Ludendorff turned on the other Russian army and drove it back in disorder. Hindenburg and Ludendorff emerged as much-needed symbols of German invincibility.

Germany's ally fared less well. Austria-Hungary's first invasion of Serbia was a fiasco, and the main Russian attack in Galicia drove Conrad von Hötzendorff's

Victors on the eastern front: Hindenburg (*left*) and Ludendorff.

armies back in confusion. But by the end of the year German troops had retrieved the situation. In the vast spaces of eastern Europe, movement was still possible, although here too siege warfare around key fortresses and rail junctions was frequent.

The War Spreads beyond Europe

To the south, one member of the Triple Alliance did not go to war in August 1914: Italy. Its grounds were entirely reasonable, for the alliance did not require it to share a war of aggression about which Berlin and Vienna had failed to consult it in advance. But Italian neutrality did not prevent the spread of the war beyond Europe. A German Mediterranean force, the battle cruiser *Goeben* and the cruiser *Breslau,* evaded an inept British pursuit and sought refuge at Constantinople in August 1914. The Turkish government then gambled on the victory of Germany, its longtime patron, over Russia, its perpetual enemy. When *Goeben* and *Breslau* bombarded Odessa in October, Russia declared war and attacked Turkey by land in the distant Caucasus. The entry of Turkey extended the war to the Middle East, from the Caucasus to Suez to the Persian Gulf.

Farther afield, British sea power was supreme. Britain swept the seas clear of German surface raiders by the end of 1914. And Britain's Grand Fleet did not charge into the mines and the submarine ambushes off the German fleet base of Wilhelmshaven, as Tirpitz had expected. Instead, it established blockade lines at the Channel and from Scotland to Norway, a "distant blockade" outside the reach of the fleet that Tirpitz had built. Britain, thanks to its geographic position, could cut Germany off from the outer world without fighting the fleet action on German terms for which Tirpitz had planned.

Thanks to sea power, the Dominions were free to join Britain, and the German colonies were easy prey. Even the Boer leaders cooperated with London. French and British forces seized Togo, Cameroons, and South-West Africa. Only in and around German East Africa (now Tanzania) did the Germans hold out. There,

until 1918, Paul von Lettow-Vorbeck and his native *askaris* repeatedly made fools of their British, Indian, British-African, and Boer pursuers. The "war of the white tribes" of Europe and the sight of Lettow-Vorbeck's *askaris* defeating whites proved a major stimulus to African nationalism.

In Asia the war gave Japan its opportunity to reverse the verdict of 1895, when the powers had forced it to give up its gains in China. Tokyo enthusiastically offered Britain its support in August 1914. It gobbled up the German outpost in Shandong, and the German island possessions in the Pacific that Australia did not. In January–May 1915 it imposed on China the "twenty-one demands," which included recognition of Japan's possession of Shandong and of its claims to southern Manchuria, Inner Mongolia, and an industrial region in central China. Britain persuaded Japan to "postpone" its most extreme demands, such as a right to impose advisers on China's central government. But diplomacy was an increasingly flimsy barrier against Japan's growing threat to China—and to Europe's domination of Asia and the Pacific.

THE INDUSTRIAL AND GEOGRAPHIC BALANCE

The reasons for the stalemate after September 1914 are clearer now than they were then. Railroads allowed the mobilization and movement to battle of immense armies. The size of those armies allowed the occupation of ever-wider defensive frontages. Finding an enemy flank against which to launch a decisive attack, as the 1914 "race to the sea" demonstrated, was almost impossible. And on the battlefield itself, the storm of steel and lead, the ever-thicker coils of barbed wire, and the absence of transport for troops, ammunition, and food immobilized the mass armies. Cars, trucks, and motorcycles were neither bulletproof nor available in adequate numbers. The defenders' reserves, thanks to railroad, telephone, and radio, could always reach a threatened point faster than the attackers could break through on foot. And air reconnaissance and air photography enabled defenders to detect offensive preparations. Strategic mobility checkmated tactical decision, firepower crushed movement, communications and air reconnaissance removed surprise.

Two other factors made the war of 1914–18 an unprecedented struggle of attrition. First, although the general staffs of Europe had largely ignored it, the U.S. Civil War had demonstrated that wars between industrial powers could last for years even when one contender was far stronger industrially than the other. In the absence of striking military ineptitude of the sort the French had displayed in 1870, only attrition could decide the outcome. And the coalition nature of the 1914–18 war likewise prolonged the struggle. As in the world wars of the eighteenth century but unlike 1859, 1866, and 1870–71, the belligerents of 1914–18 had great-power allies. When the weak faltered, their allies usually sustained them. And although Russia collapsed in 1917, the United States simultaneously intervened to shore up a flagging France and Britain with money, food, munitions, and troops.

The keys to victory in this world struggle were industrial might, geographic position, and access to raw materials. The three Allied powers, Britain, France, and Russia, had in 1913 a total industrial potential a third greater than that of the Central Powers, Germany and Austria-Hungary. But the Central Powers were superior to France and Russia alone and after 1914 probably also to Britain and France combined. The Schlieffen Plan had at least deprived France of a fifth of its wheat, half of its coal, and two-thirds of its iron production. Only U.S. intervention in 1917 gave the Allies the better than two-to-one margin in total industrial power that brought victory.

In geographic position, the Central Powers enjoyed one major advantage and one serious but not insuperable drawback. The advantage was the result of Germany's two-front predicament; German possession of "interior lines" allowed swift transfer of forces from west to east to meet successive threats. Given the stalemate at the tactical level, that was no small advantage. The Allies, conversely, were unable to link Russia, their major source of manpower, with the weapons and ammunition produced in the West.

But "encirclement" was also a major disadvantage for the Central Powers: it cut them off from the world market. Shortages of vital materials such as nitrates, rubber, and copper set in immediately. The Germans at first coped. Holland and Scandinavia served as channels for German imports and exports. A German Jewish research chemist, Fritz Haber, broke the nitrate bottleneck with his nitrogen-fixation process, perfected in 1913: the inexhausible nitrogen available in the atmosphere gave Germany the explosives it needed to continue the war.

In the long run, Germany suffered. Command of the sea enabled Britain and France to draw on munitions made in the United States and on loans to pay for them. The United States, at least at first, would have gladly done business with the Germans as well. But German shipping remained locked in the Baltic and North Sea. The loss of overseas food and fertilizer imports, the forced slaughter of livestock to save fodder, and farm labor shortages crippled German agriculture. First potatoes and then turnips became the staple of the German diet. The British blockade failed to paralyze German industrial production, but it did slowly sap civilian morale.

On balance, the Germans had the advantage until 1918. German possession of northern France forced the Allies to take the offensive. Given the devastating effects of defensive firepower and the dogged ineptitude of most Allied generals, that meant immense slaughter for no gain. Geography isolated Russia and political and industrial weakness made it increasingly vulnerable. Finally, the quality of German leadership at the tactical and operational levels compensated for the Central Powers' two-to-three disadvantage in total potential against the Triple Entente. Germany, by 1917, had virtually won the war it had started. It went under only because it started another war—with another continent, the United States.

POLITICS, SOCIETY, AND THE "HOME FRONT"

All the powers, except perhaps Italy and Rumania, entered the war with the certainty—in some cases bogus—that they were victims of unprovoked aggression. That conviction—and the sense of sudden release from the cares, frustrations, and social tensions of Europe's rapidly changing yet narrowly class-bound societies—brought widespread rejoicing. Especially in the cities, reservists marched to the stations through crowds waving flags and pelting them with flowers. As the trains rolled, the troops chalked "To Paris!" or "To Berlin!" on the boxcars. They expected to be home before the autumn leaves fell.

That those who lived through the August days never forgot the spontaneous outpouring of a national enthusiasm that momentarily abolished social distinctions. An assistant to Bethmann Hollweg noted with wonder on August 14: "War, war, the *Volk* has risen! . . . All deeply joyful, to live, for once, caught up in a great cause." And a recent immigrant to Munich from Austria-Hungary named Adolf Hitler later wrote in his memoirs that "overpowered by stormy enthusiasm, I fell down on my knees and thanked Heaven from an overflowing heart for granting me the good fortune of being permitted to live at this time." Then as later, he expressed a widely felt emotion.

That emotion guaranteed national cohesion across class and party lines. The socialist Second International collapsed amid mutual recriminations by its members. In Germany, the government declared a political truce, the *Burgfrieden* ("peace inside the fortress"). Even revolutionary Social Democrats, at the request of the SPD leadership, voted for the first war appropriations. Good Marxists could not refuse a seemingly defensive war against tsarist Russia, the European state Marx had hated above all others. But Germany's unity was short-lived.

For the Reich, despite its public claims, fought to create an immense central European empire as the basis for German world domination. In September, as the German armies began their retreat from the Marne, Bethmann Hollweg drafted a confidential memorandum setting forth Germany's aims: annexations in France and Belgium that would reduce those nations to vassalage, the absorption of Luxembourg, and the creation of a central European customs union that would guarantee Germany's economic as well as military supremacy on the Continent. German war aims in eastern Europe were even more voracious. And the leaders of the Reich looked beyond Europe to vast African annexations and to a victory that would give Britain's world position to Germany. The war, as the chancellor's assistant noted in his diary in mid-1916, was in part a "struggle with England for world mastery."

Public discussion of Germany's aims, despite the attempts of Bethmann Hollweg to still it, increasingly broke into the open. By 1915 politicians, business figures, and pan-Germans were vying with one another to claim ever-larger areas of Europe and ever-tighter control over the small states, Germany's vassals-to-be. Racist pan-Germans urged the removal of inconvenient Poles from the annexed lands. Much of the Left soon concluded that the war was a war of conquest. The Right coupled demands for total victory and immense annexations with refusal to reform the inequitable Prussian franchise, which weighed votes according to wealth. Germany's lack of cohesion at home was its weak point. But only military defeat could transform weakness into collapse.

In France, all political forces joined a *Union Sacrée* against the German invader. In Britain, German aggression against Belgium utterly discredited the Cobdenite pacifist Liberals. Volunteers swamped the British army. In Austria-Hungary, quarreling nationalities loyally answered the call to the Habsburg colors. Even the Russian autocracy gained a brief reprieve: the prewar wave of strikes subsided and the peasant reservists marched. Only Italy, which chose intervention in 1915 without disguising it as national defense, faced from the beginning an internal struggle against those who failed to see the necessity of war.

Parliamentary regimes showed greater staying power than their autocratic counterparts. Warfare in the age of the masses required popular support and only political participation guaranteed that support. That was one secret of France's survival, despite the death or wounding of 60 percent of all Frenchmen who reported for duty between 1914 and 1918. Britain, with amazing unanimity, abolished cherished traditions of *laissez-faire*. When volunteers began to fall short in 1916, the British cabinet took the radical step of conscription. Conversely, once the war turned sour in 1915–16, internal social and national tensions placed Austria-Hungary, Russia, Italy, and even Germany at risk.

Parliamentary regimes also proved surprisingly successful at directing their war efforts. At first the soldiers dominated in Britain, France, and Italy, thanks to their alleged professional wisdom. But much of that wisdom proved wrong. When the generals failed to force a decision, the civilians took a hand. In December 1916 the feeble—or too humane—Asquith gave way to a Liberal-Conservative-Labour coalition under Lloyd George, a man known to have "fire in his belly." Lloyd George asserted, not always successfully, London's control over Britain's obstinate commander on the western front, Sir Douglas Haig. The French Chamber made Joffre a figurehead in December 1916. The national emergency of 1917 made the cynical and iron-willed Clemenceau, "the Tiger" of the Radicals, prime minister and virtual dictator by consent of the Chamber and the nation. Vittorio Emanuele Orlando, a less compelling figure, assumed some of the same powers in Italy's dark winter of 1917–18.

The autocracies took two paths. In Russia and Austria-Hungary, the monarchies held jealously to power, while inefficiency and defeat sapped their store of prestige and public trust. The essential question on the eastern front until 1917 was which of the two great empires would win the race to military collapse and political disintegration. Germany traveled another road. The Kaiser's bloodcurdling speeches and blustering orders of the day imperfectly concealed his weak nerves.

By 1916 he had become a figurehead for Hindenburg and Ludendorff.

Socially, the war marked the real beginning of the "century of the common man." Until 1914 aristocrats and landowners had dominated the bureaucracies, diplomatic services, and officer corps of Europe. The war did not end that domination everywhere, but it made a mighty start. The military aristocracies paid in blood for their privileges. Pomeranian Junkers, Ulster landowners, Russian nobles, Hungarian gentry, and the impoverished aristocracy of France led their peasant soldiers from in front, and suffered accordingly. Noble families without daughters died out, their sons fallen on the Marne, in Galicia, or in the great 1915–16 battles of attrition in the West. By 1916 most of the professional officers of 1914 were dead or disabled. Those who survived graduated gratefully to staff jobs and high commands.

The middle classes took their place as company and battalion officers. The lower middle classes, which in peacetime had rarely aspired to ranks higher than sergeant, suddenly became lieutenants. These "temporary gentlemen" suffered the sneers of the officers' mess at their accents and bearing. The Germans created a special indeterminate rank of "officer substitute" to avoid giving deserving sergeants

Britain recruits a mass army, 1915: the appeal (*above*), and the result (*below*).

commissions. But the new men proved themselves in battle. The Great War, along with death and bereavement, brought social promotion to an entire class. That sudden increase in social mobility, along with the classless society of shared danger at the front, was the origin of powerful myths. Finally, the war integrated the peasantry into the nations of the middle and upper classes far more effectively than universal schooling or even peacetime military service had done. Enforced travel, mixing with men from different regions and backgrounds, and above all the experience of fighting together for the national cause made Pomeranian, Swabian, or Bavarian peasants into Germans and made Bretons, Normans, or Gascons into Frenchmen.

At home, industrial mass warfare dictated a new sort of labor force. With men at the front, women and unskilled adolescents joined the work force in numbers not seen since the early industrial revolution in Britain. Almost a quarter of the workers in France's war industries were women, as were 60 percent of the workers in Britain's munitions plants. British craft unions fought jealously against this "dilution" of the work force, but lost. War work expanded women's horizons and gave them a new sense of confidence and competence.

Industrial mass warfare also dictated an unprecedented intensity and extent of state action. The autocracies already had strong traditions of "state capitalism." The democracies mobilized their economies with similar and often more drastic methods: a bewildering variety of war-production and raw-materials allocation boards and bureaucracies, and close coordination between the state, the labor unions, and the military. The wartime industrial state seemed to confirm Weber's depressing vision of the "iron cage" of bureaucracy and furnished the model for the welfare state of the later twentieth century.

Finally, mass warfare dictated the mobilization of mass opinion. German propaganda damned the barbaric British "hunger blockade" and stressed the German world cultural mission that over-rode the rights of "parasitic" small nations such as Belgium. British, French, and (after 1917) U.S. propaganda dwelt on examples of "Hun" barbarism that included poison gas and Zeppelin or submarine warfare against noncombatants and neutrals. Opinion was as powerful as high explosive, and both sides sought to exploit it to the full.

ATTRITION, 1915–16

Deadlock, 1915

Throughout 1915 the powers made confused attempts to break the unexpected stalemate. The Germans were most successful. In the West, Falkenhayn stood on the defensive. He remained so until 1916, except for a brief experiment of Fritz Haber's with chlorine gas near Ypres in April 1915. The German command failed to mass reserves to exploit the unexpected gap the gas opened in the Franco-British lines. Introduction of this new and apparently barbaric weapon profited the Germans nothing and mightily helped the Allies in the battle for neutral opinion.

For most of the year, Britain and France attacked. Their strategic goal was to drive Germany out of France and win the war; that dictated the offensive. But their generals had no better method for restoring movement to the battlefield than steadily increasing weights of high-explosive shell to blast the German wire flat and silence the machine guns. At Neuve Chappelle, and Loos, and in the repeated French "pushes" in Artois and Champagne, and Allies suffered repeated bloody reverses and gained virtually no ground. The Germans became ever cannier at sheltering their troops in dugouts and in positioning reserves and artillery in depth. In 1915 the French lost 1,500,000 dead and wounded, Britain 300,000, and the German defenders perhaps 875,000.

In eastern Europe, Generals August von Mackensen and Hans von Seeckt broke through the Russian front in Galicia. By September 1915 they had sent the tsar's armies reeling back 300 miles with a loss of 1.7 million dead, wounded, and captured. Yet Falkenhayn still did not believe that the eastern front offered a chance of decisive victory. He halted his advance, although the immense defeat of 1915 had opened wide the fractures between Russia's rulers and their subjects that the German declaration of war had temporarily closed in 1914. The Germans, totally discarding what little remained of European traditions of monarchical and noble solidarity, attempted to widen those fractures by covert action. SPD leaders with ties to their Russian counterparts funneled large sums into Russia to create unrest among the Russian Empire's workers and border nationalities. And in the Middle East, German agents based in Turkey sought with some success to raise Islam against the Allies.

Far to the southeast, new fronts opened. Britain, thanks to the genius for war of the impulsive young Winston Churchill at the Admiralty, attempted to seize Constantinople and open a year-round warm-water supply route to Russia. But the muddled British high command was unequal to the task of coordinating a simultaneous land and sea assault. The British navy, using expendable pre-Dreadnought battleships, failed to force its way past the shore batteries and mines defending the Dardanelles in February–March 1915. The Turks ran out of ammunition just as the British navy pulled back. Then it was the turn of the army. British and Australian landings on the Gallipoli Peninsula in April soon bogged down; the Turks proved unexpectedly stubborn and skillful. The only British success was the brilliantly planned and coordinated evacuation of the failed beachheads by January 1916; France and Britain retained a toehold at Salonika in Greece.

The Gallipoli landings, before British bungling became apparent, moved the least of the great powers to take a hand. In October 1914, Salandra, Italy's prime minister, had incautiously announced that henceforth "holy national egoism"—*sacro egoismo*—would guide Italy's course. In winter–spring 1914–15 he proved as good as his word. Salandra and his foreign minister, Sidney Sonnino, secretly auctioned Italy to the two groups of powers. The Allied bid was the higher: Trento,

Trieste, and Dalmatia (where Italian-speakers were a tiny minority) from Austria-Hungary, a piece of Turkey, and unspecified colonial gains. On May 24, 1915, Salandra, Sonnino and King Victor Emmanuel III took Italy to war against the will of its parliament. Italy's armies crossed the Austro-Hungarian border and ran headlong into long-prepared defenses on the Isonzo River. There the Italians stalled, despite repeated bloody offensives.

And in fall and winter 1915 the Germans confirmed the verdict of Gallipoli. Bulgaria joined the Central Powers after an auction similar to that in Rome. German, Austro-Hungarian, and Bulgarian armies attacked Serbia from three sides. By luring Bulgaria into the war and by smashing Serbia, Germany had secured its communications through the Balkans to Turkey. Russia would receive no Allied aid through the Straits. Only the icy sea route to Murmansk and Archangel and the single track of the Trans-Siberian Railway linked Russia to the West.

Yet by December 1915 Falkenhayn was not satisfied. Germany's immense losses had brought it no closer to its goal: a strategic decision over one of its three adversaries. In his 1915 "Christmas Memorandum," Falkenhayn concluded that Britain was the keystone of the enemy

Between the Turks and the sea: Gallipoli, 1915.

Pétain of Verdun.

alliance. To strike it required the intensification of submarine warfare against British and neutral merchant shipping, which the Germans had introduced in February 1915, and of terror attacks on British civilian targets with Zeppelin airships.

Falkenhayn identified French morale as Germany's second, and most promising, target. The collapse of France would "strike England's best sword from her hand." The method he chose was attrition, and he sought an objective "for the retention of which the French leadership will commit their last man. If they do this, France's strength will be bled white, since once committed to such a course there is no alternative for them, whether we reach the objective itself or not." Limited German infantry attacks would pin the French defenders under a giant mincing machine: the German artillery. Falkenhayn baptized

his brainchild Operation GERICHT—"execution place."

1916: Verdun and the Somme

On February 21, 1916, the army of the German Crown Prince attacked the fortified city of Verdun at the hinge of the French line. More than 2,000 German guns tore the French to pieces with the heaviest artillery fire so far seen. As the French gave way, Joffre appointed Henri Pétain, a master of the defensive, to command Verdun. "Courage! We'll get them!" was his watchword. In the course of the next eight months, over three-quarters of the French army passed down the muddy truck route to Verdun and emerged shattered.

Yet France held. By May 1916, despite German innovations such as flame-throwers, phosgene gas shells, and masses of fighter aircraft, Falkenhayn himself was caught fast in the snare he had rigged for the French. The Germans had themselves invested so much prestige, morale, and blood at Verdun that they had to take the city. The French fought them to a standstill by July, then counterattacked in October, November, and December to regain the lost ground. Verdun cost the French 377,000 dead, wounded, and missing and the Germans at least 337,000. Neither army, but especially that of France, was ever the same again.

The agony of France had repercussions. As in 1914, Russia sought to help its ally. Russia's most brilliant general, Alexei Brusilov, launched a surprise offensive in the Ukraine in June. Austria-Hungary's eastern armies collapsed; the Russians took 200,000 prisoners. Conrad von Hötzendorff had to break off a promising "punitive expedition" against his favorite victim, Italy. Falkenhayn loosened his grip at Verdun and sent divisions eastward to prop up Austria-Hungary.

Then, on July 1, 1916, Sir Douglas Haig attacked the German defenses north and south of the Somme River. On a day of "intense blue summer beauty," after a seven-day bombardment of unprecedented weight, the infantrymen of Britain's volunteer "New Armies" climbed

Verdun 1916: The Return from the Front

I have never seen anything more heart-rending than the passage of the two regiments of the brigade that flowed past me on that road [from Verdun] the whole day long. . . .

First came skeletons of companies, sometimes with a surviving officer in front, propping himself up with a cane; all walked or rather moved with short steps, bent knees forward, folded into themselves, staggering as if gripped by drink. Then came groups that were perhaps squads, or even platoons; there was no telling. They advanced, head down, staring blankly, crushed under their rucksacks, holding by the slings rifles red with mud. The color of their faces scarcely differed from that of their over-coats. Mud had covered everything and dried, then more mud had covered them once more. . . . Cars thundered past in close-packed columns, scattering this pitiable flotsam, survivors of the great slaughter. But [the troops] said nothing, made no sound. They had lost even the strength to complain. . . .

Some reservists, from the roadside, looked on somberly. . . . I heard one saying: "It's not an army; it's corpses!". . . . Two of the reservists cried silently, like women.

From Georges Gaudy, Les trous d'obus de Verdun (février-août 1916) *(Paris: Plon, 1922), pp. 233–34 (translation by M. Knox).*

from their trenches. Loaded with a minimum of 66 pounds of gear per man, aligned in rigid formations, they walked toward the German wire, which in most areas the British artillery had failed to cut. As the British bombardment lifted, German machine-gunners scrambled unhurt from their deep concrete-lined dugouts and massacred the British infantry. German artillery observers had never before seen such tempting targets. The French, further south, advanced in small groups, taking cover wherever possible. They did rather better.

Haig's army lost 57,470 dead and wounded—nearly half the men engaged—on the first day. But Haig, "brilliant to the top of his army boots" (as Lloyd George later put it) remained convinced that German losses were so severe that the enemy was bound to crack. Using the same unimaginative tactics, he persevered until the battlefield became a sea of icy mud in November. The maximum British penetration was less than six miles. British losses were 419,000, those of the French, over 200,000. The German defenders lost more than half a million.

As Brusilov's push petered out and the British pressed on the Somme, a sudden emergency led to Falkenhayn's downfall. Rumania, like Italy, had been associated with the Triple Alliance; it had likewise chosen neutrality in 1914. Now, in August 1916, Brusilov's success moved the Rumanians to join the Allies. Their timing was remarkably poor. The Kaiser dismissed Falkenhayn as chief of staff but gave him Rumania as a consolation prize. Falkenhayn, Mackensen, and Seeckt rolled up the inept Rumanians within four months.

At German supreme army headquarters, a new team took control—Hindenburg and Ludendorff. Hindenburg, the "wooden Titan," was content to be a symbol of national resistance. Ludendorff, the dominant partner, brought a new ethos to the supreme command, the ethos of the pan-German "right opposition." He despised the Kaiser as a weakling. His devious aide, Colonel Max Bauer, cultivated pan-Germans and right radicals. The Kaiser feared his nominal subordinates;

Hindenburg and Ludendorff alone commanded the confidence of the masses. Once he had appointed them, the Kaiser could remove them only at the risk of his throne.

The new team had two recipes for victory. First, total war demanded total mobilization. Under the "Hindenburg Program," Germany planned to double its production of munitions and treble that of artillery and machine guns. The army, with the assistance of the SPD unions and of the industrialists, applied compulsory service to the work force. Substitute—*ersatz*—materials would make up for shortages. Germany, by a supreme effort of will, would submerge its opponents in fire and steel. The new team's second innovation was to stake Germany's future on one card, in the manner of Schlieffen. That card was the submarine.

THE WAR IN THE BALANCE, 1917

Germany Challenges America

The U-boat question had been long in ripening. Tirpitz had realized by late 1914 that the British distant blockade had neutralized his battle fleet. He therefore pressed for the use of submarines, which he had neglected before 1914, against British merchant shipping. But submarines were effective only if used from ambush. Attempts to board and search merchant ships before sinking them, as international law required, might expose the surfaced submarine to deadly fire from camouflaged guns on the merchant ship. The Germans therefore adopted in February 1915 a policy of "sink on sight" around the British isles. On May 7, 1915, Germany's U-20 sank the British liner *Lusitania* off the southern tip of Ireland and killed 1,198 people, of whom 128 were U.S. civilians. The Germans struck a medal to commemorate their feat.

President Woodrow Wilson, a grim former academic of messianic bent, had no intention of leading the United States into war. Unlike his rival, "Teddy" Roosevelt of the Rough Riders, Wilson was proud of being "too proud to fight." He

U-boat warfare: Germany warns
neutral travelers that it will sink
the Lusitania if it can (above).
U-boats at sea in the
Mediterranean (below).

was soon to run for reelection in 1916 on the slogan "He kept us out of the war." But the *Lusitania* outrage prompted even Wilson to bombard Berlin with stern summonses to obey international law.

The United States had long been suspicious of Imperial Germany. Germany's treatment of Belgium and use of poison gas had appalled American opinion. The *Lusitania* sinking swung America heavily against the Central Powers. Bethmann Hollweg persuaded the Kaiser and the navy to retreat and postpone confrontation. Then Falkenhayn, in his "Christmas Memorandum," urged the renewal of unrestricted U-boat warfare. In February 1916, the Germans synchronized "intensified" submarine warfare around Britain with their attack at Verdun. A further sinking involving U.S. citizens followed inevitably in March, and Wilson's typewriter clattered threateningly once more. The Germans again retreated. Bethmann Hollweg, at least, was now aware that further sinkings might goad Wilson into "a sort of crusade against Germany."

The German navy tried to make do with surface action. On May 31, 1916, Admiral Reinhard Scheer took the German High Seas Fleet out. But the British had intercepted Scheer's radio messages, and Admiral John Jellicoe's Grand Fleet was waiting off Jutland. The German Dreadnoughts and their British rivals faced one another for less than thirty minutes, until the outnumbered Scheer frantically turned away into clouds and smoke and ran for Wilhelmshaven. The Germans lost fewer ships, and claimed victory. But the British were the strategic victors, for they still controlled the exits from the North Sea. And the Germans concluded from their narrow escape that surface action could not break the blockage.

Thus when Hindenburg and Ludendorff arrived on the scene in August 1916, they found the navy once more pressing for a decision to unleash the submarines. Tirpitz had resigned over the issue in March and had raised a fanatical public outcry for U-boat war. To buy time and to preempt a mediation attempt by Wilson, Bethmann Hollweg launched a Central Powers "peace offer" in mid-December 1916. The offer failed to mention the freeing of Belgium, and was thus unacceptable to the Allies. Its inevitable rejection, Bethmann Hollweg apparently hoped, might turn Wilson's wrath on Paris and London. That would give Germany a convincing pretext for launching unrestricted submarine warfare.

At the Castle of Pless in Silesia, on January 9, 1917, the Germans took the decision that doomed them. The navy sang its usual tune: U-boats would bring Britain "to its knees" in a few months. Hindenburg and Ludendorff argued fiercely for action, regardless of consequences. They made the same error with the United States that Moltke had made with Britain in 1914. Because their new enemy had no mass army, they assumed that it was safe to defy it. Germany's U-boats received orders to sink all shipping around Britain after midnight on January 31, 1917. Wilson broke relations with Germany but still hoped to keep the United States neutral in order to mediate a "peace without victory."

But by 1917 the powers had invested too much blood and money to settle for any peace short of victory or defeat. Nor, thanks to the Germans, could Wilson remain neutral for long. The Reich foreign secretary, Arthur Zimmermann, proved that the stresses of total war had caused Berlin to take leave of its senses. Using the telegraph channel that Wilson had thoughtfully provided the Germans for possible peace negotiations, he secretly cabled the German ambassador in Mexico City. The message offered the Mexicans a military alliance and the recovery of Texas and the Southwest. The British intercepted it, deciphered it, and delivered it to Wilson along with proofs of its authenticity. It arrived in Washington at the end of February, along with news that a U-boat had sunk the British liner *Laconia* with the death of three Americans, two of them women.

Wilson gave the Zimmermann telegram to the press on March 1. Zimmermann compounded his amazing blunder by admitting that the telegram was genuine. Even voices of the isolationist Midwest, such as the Chicago *Tribune* and the Cleveland *Plain Dealer,* accepted war. A Germany that encouraged Mexico to attack the United States was intolerable. On April 2, Wilson, to repeated applause, addressed Congress: "The world must be made safe for democracy." The United States declared war on Imperial Germany. The New World was coming belatedly to restore the balance of the old.

The Russian Revolutions:
February and October

While Wilson debated his course, events in eastern Europe disclosed the full magnitude of Germany's blunder in provoking the United States. Russia now ceased to count as a belligerent, and Germany faced only a weakening France and Britain. In 1916 munitions strikes paralyzed industry in Moscow and Petrograd (the new non-German name given to St. Petersburg in 1914). Russia's railroads broke down. Refugees and wounded soldiers swamped Russia's ramshackle administrative machinery. Food ran short in the cities; conscription and government purchases of food at artifically low fixed prices alienated the peasantry. The failure of the Brusilov offensive to decide the war and the antics of the tsarina's favorite, the faithhealing charlatan Grigorii Rasputin, lost the autocracy what little public support it still possessed. Strikes and food riots by workers and housewives in Petrograd

---

The Zimmermann Telegram   January 19, 1917

[To German Ambassador, Mexico City]
Top Secret—Decipher Personally

We intend on 1 February to begin unrestricted U-boat warfare. We shall nevertheless attempt to keep America neutral. Should that not succeed, we propose to Mexico an alliance on the following basis. Joint conduct of the war. Joint peace settlement. Lavish financial support and agreement on our part that Mexico should reconquer its lost territories in Texas, New Mexico, and Arizona. We leave settlement of the details to your Excellency.

Your Excellency should disclose the above offer in the greatest secrecy to the President [of Mexico, Don Venustiano Carranza] as soon as outbreak of war with the United States seems certain, and add the suggestion that he should on his own initiative invite Japan to join the alliance, and [that he should] simultaneously mediate between Japan and ourselves.

Please call to the President's attention the fact that merciless use of our U-boats now offers the prospect of forcing England to make peace within a few months.

Acknowledge receipt.

                                                                    Zimmermann

From Herbert Michaelis, Ernst Schraepler, eds., Ursachen and Folgen vom deutschen Zusammenbruch 1918 und 1945 *(Berlin: Dokumenten-Verlag Dr. Herbert Wendler, 1958), Vol. 1, pp. 151–52 (translation by M. Knox).*

---

challenged the autocracy in early March 1917 (February by the "old style" Julian calendar that symbolized Russia's isolation from Europe). The peasant soldiers deserted the autocracy on March 12; it fell without a struggle.

A provisional government of liberals, of Lenin's Menshevik rivals, and of Socialist Revolutionaries attempted to fill the vacuum this "February Revolution" had left. But in Petrograd the Soviets, or councils of workers, soldiers, and sailors, now controlled the streets. On March 14, 1917, the central Petrograd Soviet addressed to the war-weary world a proclamation that blamed "monarchs, landholders, and bankers" for the war and demanded an immediate end to the "horrible slaughter."

"The Russian Ruling House": a contemporary cartoon of Rasputin manipulating Tsar Nicholas II and Tsarina Alexandra.

The new master: Lenin in Moscow, 1917.

Similar appeals in 1915 and 1916 from the wrangling representatives of the parties of the socialist Second International had lacked resonance. The call of the Petrograd Soviet was different: it came from a body with power. And its claim to world ideological leadership conflicted with the call for "war to end war" that Wilson was soon to issue from Washington.

Soon after the Petrograd Soviet's peace message, the Germans made a further contribution to the disruption of Russia. They shipped Lenin and a few chosen Bolsheviks home to Russia from their place of exile in neutral Switzerland in a sealed boxcar ("like a plague bacillus," as Winston Churchill later observed). Lenin arrived at Petrograd's Finland Station on April 16, 1917, and dictated to his party a few simple policies: support of the Soviets, implacable hostility to the provisional government, and an immediate end to the war.

In June 1917, Lenin launched a slogan of vast appeal to the peasantry, which made up 80 percent of Russia's population, and to the overwhelming majority of Russia's 7 million troops: "Bread, Peace, Land." His aim was as simple as his slogan. He proposed to seize power and hurl backward Russia directly into socialism. Revolutionary breakthrough in Russia would then trigger the revolutions in western Europe and the world without which a socialist Russia, isolated, would inevitably perish.

The provisional government was divided and inexperienced, thanks to the stifling effect the autocracy had had on Russian political life. It shared power uneasily with the Petrograd Soviet while seeking to continue the war against Germany. The government's most conspicuous personality, the Socialist Revolutionary Alexander Kerensky, identified himself with a final bungled offensive in July 1917. Bolshevik appeals spread through the army and undermined what little discipline remained. Peasant soldiers, weary of war and obsessed with the notion that revolution meant the long-awaited final redivision of the *mir* land (see p. 720), "voted with their feet." Many

went home; those that stayed demanded an end to the fighting.

A Petrograd insurrection against the provisional government in July showed that the Bolsheviks were gaining ground. Their unyielding utopian radicalism was better attuned to the mood in the cities than their more responsible or faint-hearted opponents. Kerensky arrested some Bolsheviks but lacked the ruthlessness or perhaps the power to suppress them outright. Then, in August, General Lavr Kornilov, Kerensky's army commander in chief, marched on Petrograd to restore order. Workers and mutinous troops from the capital persuaded Kornilov's forces to defect.

Kornilov's failed coup from the Right further weakened Kerensky and his allies. Mensheviks and Socialist Revolutionaries, by their association with the provisional government and the continuing war, lost much of the popular support they had enjoyed in Petrograd in the spring. The Bolsheviks painted the disintegrating provisional government and its parties as Kornilov's accomplices; Bolshevik numbers swelled.

On November 6–7 (October 24–25 by the Russian calendar), Lenin and his dashing ex-Menshevik associate, Leon Trotsky, launched their own coup from the Left. The Military Revolutionary Committee of the Petrograd Soviet, of which Trotsky had gained control, seized key points with picked troops. On the evening of November 7 (October 25), the provisional government's last stronghold, the tsar's Winter Palace, fell. Kerensky fled. The Bolsheviks had acted in the name of the Soviets against the provisional government. The Bolsheviks soon infiltrated or cowed the Soviets while taking for themselves the mantle of legitimacy that the Soviets provided. And in January 1918 Bolshevik bayonets dispersed Russia's first and only democratically elected parliament, the Constituent Assembly.

The Bolsheviks had won less than 25 percent of the seats in the Constituent Assembly. But they had guns and organization, and they briefly commanded a popular majority in Petrograd and Moscow. Above all, they moved swiftly to institutionalize terror. In December 1917 Lenin's security officer, the fanatical Pole Feliks Dzerzhinsky, became chief of a new organization, the "All-Russian Extraordinary Commission for the Struggle Against Counterrevolution and Sabotage," known by its acronym of CHEKA. Its task was to exterminate the enemies of the revolution; their place, in Lenin's words, was "against the wall."

In January 1918 the Socialist Revolutionaries, whose peasant loyalists had given them more votes than any other party, fought back against the dissolution of the Constituent Assembly. They rose against Bolshevik dictatorship—and Lenin and Dzerzhinsky massacred them. In July 1918 the Bolsheviks likewise shot—with Lenin's approval—the ex-Tsar Nicholas II and his entire family. By that point Lenin and his CHEKA had discarded the concept of individual responsibility for actions, the basis of Western and even tsarist law. The CHEKA defined its enemies by class, and killed them not as individuals but as members of a category. The bourgeoisie was "objectively"—by its very existence—guilty of counterrevolution. That was a logic not seen in action in the West since the September massacres of 1792 and the Jacobin Terror of 1793–94. It was the logic of genocide.

Terror worked well internally. Externally, Lenin faced an immediate crisis. The German masses did not overthrow their rulers in response to the "Decree on Peace" that Lenin and Trotsky published immediately after the October Revolution. Instead, Russia's peasant armies continued to melt, while the Germans advanced toward Petrograd. Lenin therefore sought a breathing space for the Revolution, to give time for the western European and world revolution he unrealistically expected; he had predicted in September 1917, before taking power, that "to secure an armistice means *to conquer the world.*"

Lenin secured that armistice from the Germans in December and began negotiations at Brest-Litovsk in Poland for a Russo-German peace. But the Bolshevik negotiators soon found that self-determi-

The Logic of the Red Terror   1918

M. Y. Latsis, the terrifying Latvian who was Dzerzhinsky's chief subordinate at the CHEKA, spelled out in a 1918 newspaper article the logic under which his organization acted.

We are not carrying out war against individuals. We are exterminating the bourgeoisie as a class. We aren't looking for evidence or witnesses to reveal deeds or words against the Soviet power. The first question which we ask is—to what class does he belong, what are his origins, upbringing, education, or profession? These questions define the fate of the accused. This is the essence of Red Terror.

Quoted in Harrison Salisbury, Black Night, White Snow: Russia's Revolutions, 1905–1917 *(Garden City: Doubleday, 1978), p. 565.*

nation, as the Germans interpreted it, meant stripping away the conquests of all tsars since the seventeenth century. The border peoples, from Finland through the Ukraine to the Caucasus, were to become independent under German "protection." When the Bolsheviks refused, the Germans resumed their effortless advance on Petrograd. Lenin then dragooned his wavering comrades into signing; the Revolution had to swallow the German terms if it hoped to survive. On March 3, 1918, the Bolsheviks signed the treaty of Brest-Litovsk, which deprived Russia of a quarter of its European territory, a third of its population, more than half of its coal and iron, and a third of its industry. But it left the Bolsheviks in power.

The Crisis of the Allies, 1917

The collapse of Russia came close to wrecking the Allies. The October Revolution, which took Russia out of the war for good, followed a series of catastrophes. Germany's submarines almost throttled Britain's Atlantic supply line between March and August 1917. British food stocks, despite rationing, fell to a mere two months' supply. But the German navy soon found that it was unable to sink ships faster than the United States could build them. Lloyd George stormed into the Admiralty and compelled it to set up convoys, which it had originally despised as a "defensive" and therefore inferior form of war. Mine barriers partially closed the exits from the North Sea even to U-boats. The U.S. Navy, with its eight Dreadnoughts and its indispensable escort craft, reinforced the British.

As the U-boats battered Britain, France faltered. Joffre's replacement, Robert Nivelle, was convinced that he had found the secret of victory: surprise. The discovery was not original, and both sides could use it. In Operation ALBERICH, named after the malevolent dwarf in Wagner's *Ring of the Nibelungen,* Ludendorff secretly withdrew to a new line 12 to 25 miles behind the original front. The Germans had a further surprise for the French: flexible defensive tactics far superior to the thin and brittle trench lines of 1914–16. The German "defense in depth"—deep belts of strongpoints interlocked by fire, coordinated artillery barrages, and swift and terrifying counterattacks—broke Nivelle's offensive of April 1917, and inflicted 200,000 casualties. The French army had believed in Nivelle; now its morale cracked. From the end of April until June 1917, units mutinied. Some waved red flags; the example of the Petrograd Soviet, with its call for immediate and unconditional peace, was contagious.

Fortunately, German intelligence was characteristically poor. Had Ludendorff known of the mutinies, he might have driven France from the war. Instead, Pétain, who had saved France at Verdun, now had time to save it once more. He suppressed the mutinies with a judicious combination of firing squad and conciliation. He listened to the troops and gave them what they wanted: home leave, better food, and no more offensives. The French army would do its part in defense, but others would have to break Germany.

The mutinies gave Haig what he thought was his opportunity. In the third battle of Ypres, from July to December 1917, he threw his troops again and again at the German lines as heavy artillery and rain churned the soil of Flanders into "a porridge of mud." As in 1916, Haig suf-

fered from the delusion that the Germans were about to crack. The maximum British and Canadian penetration was about five miles around the village of Passchendaele; the cost, perhaps 400,000 dead and wounded. By the end of the year British morale was scarcely higher than that of the French.

Finally, far to the south, the Germans showed that they were developing a tactical answer to the riddle of the trenches. On October 24, 1917, after a brief surprise bombardment, an Austro-German army crashed through the Italian defenses on the Isonzo River around the village of Caporetto. The Germans moved in small, stealthy groups equipped with light machine guns. Instead of advancing on a broad front and slowing to tidy their flanks, they pushed rapidly through weak points and on into the Italian rear, sowing alarm and despondency. Positions too difficult to take they simply bypassed.

The Italian army crumbled and withdrew almost to Venice. Then, to the surprise of Germans and Austrians, it held on the Piave River even before British and French troops arrived to prop Italy up. Caporetto and the resulting loss of most of Italy east of Venice had at last made the unpopular war of 1915 a war of national defense.

On the home front, 1917 was equally disastrous for the Allies. Commodity shortages and the indiscriminate printing of money to finance the immense war expenditures drove prices steadily upward. Inflation and scarcity generated popular discontent (although troops on leave found civilian complaints about rationing tiresome—the civilians were safe from shellfire). The extreme left of the European socialist parties took up with enthusiasm the slogans of the Petrograd Soviet and of the Bolsheviks. Shortly before Caporetto, a workers' revolt convulsed one of Italy's principal industrial centers, Turin. Civilian disturbances and demonstrations accompanied the French army mutinies. Even Britain experienced unrest.

Nevertheless, the outlook was not totally bleak either on the western front, in the Middle East, or in central Europe. In

November 1917, at Cambrai, Haig for the first time committed en masse that bizarre British invention, the tank. The British high command had failed to find a tactical answer to the trench deadlock, but a few innovators, among them Winston Churchill, had found a technological one. The combination of the internal combustion engine, caterpillar track, armor, and machine guns or cannon might yet restore mobility to the battlefield. Unfortunately, Haig had squandered surprise by using a few isolated tanks on the Somme in 1916. At Cambrai, the 400 tanks that Haig committed overwhelmed the terrified Germans. But the usual British failure to coordinate infantry, artillery, and reserves left the tanks exposed to a German counterattack that regained most of the ground lost.

In the Middle East, Turkey was beginning to crumble, despite its victory at Gallipoli and an appalling series of British blunders in Mesopotamia in 1914–16. Sir Edmund Allenby, perhaps the most imaginative British commander of the war, took Jerusalem in November 1917 after a push northward from Egypt into Ottoman Palestine. Simultaneously, Britain issued the Balfour Declaration, which appeared to promise "the establishment in Palestine of a national home for the Jewish people." London sought to mobilize Zionist—Jewish nationalist—support in Europe and to create a buffer between the Suez Canal and the postwar sphere allotted to the French in Syria. With the aid of Arab irregulars led by the eccentric T. E. Lawrence (later "Lawrence of Arabia"), Allenby pressed on for Damascus and Constantinople.

Finally, Austria-Hungary too was beginning to crumble. Allied statesmen had reluctantly dabbled in the subversion of Austria-Hungary as early as 1916. The "old Kaiser," Francis Joseph, who had reigned since 1848 and had become the symbol of the Dual Monarchy, died that November. His death deprived Austria-Hungary of its essential symbol of unity. In 1917 the Petrograd Soviet and the Bolsheviks, among their many slogans, launched that of "self-determination." Wilson took it up to prevent the Bolsheviks from monopo-

LETTING DOWN A LADDER

The Kaiser and Wilson's Fourteen Points (an American view).

lizing it. In his statement of American war aims of January 1918, the famous "Fourteen Points," he demanded "autonomous development" for the peoples of Austria-Hungary and the resurrection of the Polish state destroyed in 1795. Self-determination was a powerful political weapon in the hands of the Allies. But it was a weapon of desperation that might well destroy any prospect of postwar order in central and eastern Europe.

As the year 1917 closed, the Allied leaders contemplated their position with alarm. Russia had dissolved. Britain, France, and Italy had each in turn come close to collapse. Germany was victorious in eastern Europe and in Italy. It seemed poised to attack in the West. The home front was wavering. The "Yanks," Allied propaganda insisted, were coming. Would they come in time?

GERMANY'S LAST THROW, 1918

"Michael"

Ludendorff might have played for time and trusted to his army's defensive skill to blunt Allied offensives in 1918. But time appeared to be working against Germany. Since the "turnip winter" of 1916 the British blockade had bitten deeper and deeper into German civilian morale and health. Austria-Hungary, Bulgaria, and Turkey were on the verge of collapse. Time would allow the Americans to mobilize a mass army and would fortify the Allies with U.S. food and munitions. Ludendorff also rejected a political solution that the war-weary Allies might have had to accept in the dark winter of 1917–18: German withdrawal from Belgium and northern France in return for a peace that left to Germany its immense gains in eastern Europe—and thus the mastery of the Continent.

With defense and negotiation ruled out, the remaining solution was attack. Russia's collapse freed enough German forces to give them rough equality in France by March 1918—although Ludendorff's megalomania nevertheless kept a million Germans in eastern Europe to bring in the grain of the Ukraine and to seize the oil of the Caucasus. Ludendorff planned to use the reinforcements and the methods proven in Russia and at Caporetto to "hack a hole" in the western front. The rest, Ludendorff insisted, would "take care of itself." The great German offensive, in the words of a member of his staff, "would not be a battering ram, pounding head-on against a wall, but rather like a flood of water, flowing around obstacles, isolating them, and following the path of least resistance deep into the enemy's territory." Throughout the winter the German staffs pulled divisions out of the line, formed assault battalions (*Stosstruppen*), trained them in the new "infiltration" tactics, and rested them for a last supreme effort. Ludendorff knew the risks. When a politician asked him what would happen if he failed, he was frank: "Then Germany is finished."

The German objective of dominating Europe, the German style of all-or-nothing gambles, and the immense expectations that victory over Russia had aroused in the German public all dictated action. No political check on Ludendorff existed. In January 1917 Bethmann Hollweg had given up his small remaining authority by agreeing to unrestricted submarine warfare. In July 1917 Hindenburg and Ludendorff forced Bethmann Hollweg's resignation by threatening their own. The intimidated Kaiser appointed an unknown bureaucrat as chancellor. Tirpitz organized the political underpinnings of the Hindenburg-Ludendorff regime. On Sedan Day, September 2, 1917, a "Fatherland Party" (*Vaterlandspartei*) emerged, proclaiming pitiless war until final victory over both Allies and SPD, and massive annexations in east and west to secure that victory for all time. Germany's mission, Tirpitz announced, was to lead Europe against the "all-devouring tyranny of Anglo-Americanism." The *Vaterlandspartei* soon had more members than the SPD. It was the first—but not the last—fanatical mass party of German nationalism. Its spirit momentarily galvanized the home front in the expectation of final victory.

On March 21, 1918, the first of Ludendorff's offensives, baptized MICHAEL, struck the British line between St. Quentin and La Fère. The British defenders massed in their forward trenches, where German high explosive and gas shells massacred them. Haig had failed to learn from the German defense-in-depth that had cost the Allies so dear in 1917. Then the new German offensive tactics—attack in depth—tore a hole through the British lines thirty miles deep. It was the greatest gain on the western front by either side since 1914. The French prepared to withdraw to defend Paris.

But the British ultimately held. Ludendorff broke his own rule of always bypassing resistance, and shattered his reserves against the stubborn British defense of Arras. In April a second German offensive in Flanders took back the gains Britain had achieved at heartbreaking cost in the 1917 Passchendaele offensive. A third attack, in May–June 1918, drove the French back to the Marne and came within forty miles of Paris. Each time, Ludendorff achieved operational freedom but failed to translate it into a strategic victory that would force the Allies to make peace before the Americans appeared in force.

The Yanks Arrive

And on the Marne, U.S. Army and Marine Corps units at last joined the French in counterattacks at Belleau Wood and Château-Thierry. The Americans lacked experience. But they were willing to die in a manner not seen since 1914–16, the manner of Langemarck and the Somme. That spirit, and American numbers and weight of artillery terrified the Germans even as they shot the Americans down in droves.

Ludendorff's fourth and fifth offensives failed miserably, at great cost. Ludendorff had bled the German army to death. In March his forces in the West had numbered 3,800,000. By July they had suffered almost a million casualties. German troops shipped in from Russia as replacements began to vote with their feet, jumping from the slow-moving troop trains before they reached the western front. Yet in the face of hunger, desertion, demoralization, and defeat, Ludendorff still refused to allow negotiations with the Allies.

In July, August, and September, the Allies began to counterattack in a series of carefully limited operations. An inter-Allied high command under the hard-driving Marshal Ferdinand Foch of France at last began to coordinate Allied actions effectively. Allied infantry, often with tank support, would break into the German lines until German reserves arrived and resistance stiffened. Then the Allies would shift to another sector.

These attacks slowly nibbled away the German gains of the spring and further demoralized the Germans. On August 8, the "black day of the German army," whole German units surrendered for the first time to British tanks and infantry. In September, Haig broke through the strongest German defenses in the West, the "Hindenburg Line." By now the U.S. Army in France was 1,500,000 strong and under its own commander, John "Black Jack" Pershing. It pinched out the St. Mihiel salient east of Verdun and prepared for a massive drive into Lorraine to roll up the German front and meet the British in central Belgium.

March 21, 1918: Germany Attacks

Ernst Jünger, winner of Germany's highest decoration, the Pour le Mérite, *and of its foremost literary award, the Goethe Prize, led a* Stosstrupp *in the 1918 offensives. His vision of war, set forth in postwar memoirs such as* Storm of Steel, *was widely popular in 1920s Germany, and very different from the laments over war's futility and waste frequently found in British and French war writing.*

Here Jünger describes Ludendorff's stunning opening bombardment and the initial German assault.

The minute hand moved closer and closer; we counted off the last minutes. Finally it stood at 0505. The hurricane broke loose.

A fiery curtain rose high in the air, supported by sudden, unceasing upwellings. A raging thunder, into which even the heaviest shell-bursts merged, shook the earth. The gigantic eruption of annihilation from the innumerable [German] cannon [firing overhead from] behind us was so frightful, that the greatest of the battles we had passed through before this seemed like children's games. . . . The enemy artillery remained dumb; it was flattened as if by a single blow from a giant's club. . . .

It had become day. Behind us the immense din still grew. Before us rose an unpierceable wall of smoke, dust and gas. Men ran through the trench and yelled joyfully in one another's ears. Infantry and artillery, combat engineers and field telephone linemen, Prussians and Bavarians, officers and men, all were overmastered and gripped with enthusiasm by this elemental outpouring of our power, and were burning for the assault at 0940. . . .

The great moment had come. The barrage rolled across our first line. We attacked. . . . The overpowering desire to kill gave my feet wings. Rage squeezed bitter tears from my eyes. The immense desire to destroy and annihilate that hovered over the battlefield thickened our minds and dipped them as if in a red haze. We called to each other stumbling and stammering disjointed phrases, and an outside observer might perhaps have believed that we were overcome by an excess of joy.

From Ernst Jünger, In Stahlgewittern *(Berlin: E. S. Mittler, 1941 [1st ed., 1920]), pp. 253–57 (translation by M. Knox).*

At the end of September, Ludendorff's fears about Germany's allies at last proved correct. The Franco-British army at Salonika broke the Bulgarians and drove north through the Balkans, threatening

The Yanks arrive: General John J. ("Black Jack") Pershing (*right*) meets Haig.

Austria-Hungary and Germany's southern border. Ludendorff panicked and demanded the appointment of a German civilian government to take the blame for the approaching defeat. He insisted that Germany seek an armistice from Wilson before total collapse ensued. The Fourteen Points, Ludendorff slyly assumed, would allow Germany to keep at least some of its gains. Pershing foresaw that the Germans would deny they had lost unless the Allies dictated peace in Berlin. Wilson, less far-sighted, entered negotiations in October.

Then events took command. Italy attacked on October 24 and reached Trieste by November 3. Austria-Hungary collapsed into a chaotic mass of seething nationalities, each attempting to carve out its own state. The German naval command, knowing the war was lost and hoping to create a suitably Wagnerian legend for the future, attempted to send the High Seas Fleet on a death ride down the English Channel. The sailors understandably mutinied and seized Kiel naval base. Revolution spread to Munich and Berlin. The SPD leaders in Berlin proclaimed a German Republic on November 9; the Kaiser abdicated and fled to Holland. And the Allies, under pressure from Wilson and from their own war-weary public opinion, permitted

the Germans an armistice while Germany still occupied most of Belgium and some French territory.

On the "eleventh hour of the eleventh day of the eleventh month" of 1918, silence at last descended on the western front. As the armistice terms commanded, the Germans withdrew to the Rhine, demobilized, and sailed their fleet to the British fleet base at Scapa Flow. The war had cost at least 20 million lives. Germany suffered approximately 2 million military dead, Russia 1.7 million, France 1.3 million, Austria-Hungary 1.1 million, Britain and its empire 750,000 and 250,000 respectively, Italy about 500,000, Turkey somewhat less, and the United States 114,000. Civilian casualties included 100,000 killed by U-boats and air raids, 30,000 Belgians killed by German forced labor, reprisals, or artillery fire, and at least 1.5 million Armenians whom the Turks had massacred in 1915. A further 20 million died in the great influenza pandemic that struck the world in 1918.

TREATIES WITHOUT PEACE, 1919–22

The first general European peace conference since Vienna in 1814–15 met at Paris in January 1919. It faced a more difficult task than Metternich and Castlereagh (see pp. 000–00). They had merely attempted to return the world "to peaceful habits" and reestablish a balance of power that France had upset. The peacemakers at Paris in 1919 faced similar requirements, and far more.

Scores of outraged nationalities, mercifully silent at Vienna, now clamored for self-determination and "rights"—including the right to oppress minorities or neighboring nationalities. Public opinion, mobilized to hate for four long years and politically potent thanks to universal suffrage, made moderation difficult. Bolshevism, a revolutionary threat without parallel in 1814–15, appeared to menace central Europe. War and the new national boundaries had disrupted complex industrial economies; the permanence of peace might depend in part on

The Peace Settlements in Europe   1919–20

Legend:
- Boundaries of German, Russian, and Austro-Hungarian empires in 1914
- Areas lost by Austro-Hungarian Empire
- Areas lost by Russian Empire
- Areas lost by German Empire
- Areas lost by Bulgaria
- Demilitarized Zone
- Boundaries of 1926

0   300 MILES
0   300 KILOMETERS

the economic solutions the peacemakers found. And Wilson, who insisted on attending the conference in person, rejected a French proposal for drafting a clear agenda and order of business. The "Big Four," Wilson, Lloyd George, Clemenceau, and Orlando, leapt from issue to issue. From confusion they created chaos.

The Big Four at Paris, 1919:
Orlando makes a point to Lloyd
George, while Clemenceau
(*center*) and Wilson (*far right*)
look on.

Germany and the Versailles "Diktat"

Germany's fate was the chief issue facing the conference, and its chief failure. In the abstract, two courses were available that might have prevented Germany from attempting again the experiment of 1914. The Allies and the United States could conciliate the new German republic by offering a lenient peace. Or they could fasten on Germany a genuinely Carthaginian peace that would undo Bismarck's work and divide Germany into two or three: Prussia, Catholic south Germany, and an independent Rhineland. Clemenceau, who had seen two German invasions of France in his lifetime, naturally preferred the second alternative. But neither Lloyd George nor Wilson was a neighbor of Germany. Britain already controlled the German fleet; it could afford to scoff at Clemenceau's fears and reject the open-ended military commitment needed to enforce his drastic solution. And Germany was an economic unit essential to European and British prosperity, as well as the only remaining counterweight to Bolshevik Russia in eastern Europe.

The Big Four therefore compromised. Bismarck's Reich remained in existence, and Britain and the United States calmed France with the offer of an Anglo-American security guarantee, a military al-liance against German resurgence. But having decided to preserve Germany, the Allies failed to adopt the corollary of that decision, a peace as lenient as that offered to Bourbon France in 1814–15. Allied public opinion, even in Britain, shouted "Hang the Kaiser!" The disorderly procedure of the Paris conference meant that demands on Germany accumulated piecemeal and found their way into the peace treaty without any weighing of their cumulative effect. And their own disunity prevented the Big Four from inviting the Germans to help draft the treaty, as the French had in 1814.

The treaty that the German delegation grudgingly signed in the Hall of Mirrors at Versailles on the fifth anniversary of Sarajevo (June 28, 1919) was relatively lenient—compared to Brest-Litovsk. Germany lost only 13.5 percent of its 1914 territory, mostly areas inhabited by Poles, Danes, and French. The Allies piled on (1) financial "reparations"; (2) disarmament to an army of 100,000 men without heavy equipment, aircraft, or general staff, and a navy of 15,000 manning obsolete battleships; (3) temporary Allied occupation and permanent demilitarization of the Rhineland; (4) loss of the Silesian coalfields and most of Posen and West Prussia to Poland, with the German-inhabited port of Danzig in West Prussia becoming a self-governing "Free City"; (5) loss of Memel in East Prussia to Lithuania; (6) temporary cession to France of the Saar; (7) loss of Germany's useless overseas colonies; and (8) a prohibition on union with the Germans of Austria. The core of Bismarck's Germany nevertheless remained intact.

Yet compared to German expectations, the "*Diktat*" or dictated peace that the Germans received at Versailles was a nightmare. For four years German propaganda had told the German people that a savage ring of aggressors had attacked Germany out of Cossack bloodlust, French thirst for revenge, and British "trade envy." Germany's leaders had assured their public that victorious occupation of Belgium, northern France, and vast stretches of Russia guaranteed Germany a victorious peace. And the Germans had also, quite without justification, expected a Wilsonian "peace without annexations or indemnities" as their reward for proclaiming a republic. They had evidently not read Point thirteen of Wilson's Fourteen Points, which specified the creation of a Poland with access to the sea, inevitably across German territory.

The abrupt transition in 1918 from the expectation of victory to the reality of defeat, territorial loss, and national humiliation lessened the German public's already tenuous grip on reality. Germany, its political leaders at its head, denied the obvious. Germany, they claimed, had not provoked the war—although numerous German documents soon emerged indicating that it had, and few could deny that Germany had attacked Belgium without provocation. The Germans damned as a "war-guilt lie" the Allied attempt, in Article 231 of the Versailles Treaty, to establish the financial responsibility of Germany and its allies for "loss and damage" resulting from the war imposed on the Allied Powers "by the aggression of Germany and its allies." The Germans, from the beginning, furiously denied the Treaty's moral validity.

Nor had Germany suffered military defeat, according to most German leaders, including the new SPD president of the republic, Fritz Ebert. Through the mouth of Hindenburg, the German Right added the crucial corollary. If the Allies had not defeated Germany, the culprits could only be the "November Criminals" of the SPD, whose Revolution had allegedly stabbed the heroic troops "in the back." The twin legends of Allied victory through trickery and German defeat through a "stab-in-the-back" ensured that Germany would have the will to reverse the verdict of 1914–18.

And the Versailles Treaty's relative lenience ensured that Germany would have the means. For east-central Europe was now a power vacuum. The collapse of Austria-Hungary brought into being five miniature Austria-Hungaries: rump Austria, a diminished Hungary, Czechoslovakia, Poland, and a Serb-dominated kingdom of Serbs, Croats, and Slovenes that later took the name of Yugoslavia. Rumania, which now absorbed both the Hungarians of Transylvania and the Rumanian-inhabited ex-Russian territory of

Bessarabia, formed a sixth weak state between Germany and Russia. Italy, by seizing Trento and Trieste, became the seventh "successor state" of the defunct Habsburg empire.

With Russia in eclipse and German economic and demographic power virtually intact, only the United States could balance Germany once it began to revive.

National Minorities in Central Europe   1919

Polish
German
Russian
Serbian
Croatian
Slovenian
Bosnian
Macedonian
Bulgarian
Hungarian
Rumanian
Albanian
Czechoslovakian

0   MILES   200

The war, despite Germany's defeat, had paradoxically made Germany potentially stronger *relative to the rest of Europe* than in 1914. The states of eastern Europe, the Germans correctly judged, were *Saison-staaten,* "states for a season" destined to wilt under the hot sun of renewed German greatness.

Wilson, the League, and the U.S. Commitment to Europe

Wilson soon hastened the sunrise by destroying any chance that the United States would underwrite a new European balance. In the course of 1917–18 the notion of a "League of Nations," brainchild of British pacifist Liberals, had captivated the President. He saw in the League an alternative to the alleged evils of the balance of power and of secret treaties that Cobdenite mythology blamed for the war.

In the Paris negotiations Wilson therefore devoted an increasing portion of his energy to writing the League's "Covenant" into the Versailles Treaty, thus confusing further the process of settlement with Germany. The League, Wilson came to hope, would remedy imperfections in the Treaty, bind the potentially isolationist United States to Europe, and ensure the perpetual peace that he had promised would come out of this war to "make the world safe for democracy."

In pursuing the mirage of the League, Wilson destroyed any chance that the United States would underwrite European stability by a permanent commitment of its power, the power that had defeated Germany. The Republicans took control of the Senate in the fall 1918 elections. They balked at the open-ended global commitments that League "collective security" entailed. Their leader, Henry Cabot Lodge, was no isolationist; he favored a continued commitment of American power to prevent Germany from renewing its "war of world conquest." But Wilson rejected Lodge's offer to ratify the Treaty with reservations. Wilson—dogmatic about presidential prerogatives, always rigid of character, and now increasingly ill—defied an essential feature of the Constitution: the requirement that the President lead rather than command the Congress.

Wilson's reward, after he had suffered nervous collapse and an incapacitating stroke while taking his case to the people, was Senate rejection of the Treaty in March 1920. The British economist John Maynard Keynes influenced the Senate with his merciless pamphlet against Wilson and the Treaty, *The Economic Consequences of the Peace.* Wilson himself ensured rejection by ordering his loyalists to vote against the amended version the Republicans proposed. And the wreck of Wilson's policy and presidency destroyed any prospect of any Anglo-American security guarantee for France. The Republican presidential candidate, Warren G. Harding, summed up the rising national yearning for a return to the womb with a word of his own invention: America needed "normalcy." Harding carried the 1920 election. The United States retreated into resentful isolation, except for its petulant demands for repayment of Allied war debts.

Peace in the Pacific? The Washington Conference, 1921–22

The Pacific proved the one area in which the United States continued to play a great-power role. Wilson had sought unsuccessfully at Paris to lever the Japanese out of Shandong and compel them to retract the "twenty-one demands" they had forced on China in 1915. U.S. opinion also looked unkindly on the Anglo-Japanese alliance, and U.S. admirals saw it as a two-ocean threat that demanded a fleet larger than the navy "second to none" projected in 1916, after the first submarine outrages. The United States, with the help of Canada, forced Britain to choose between its alliance with Japan and its friendship with the United States. Britain, in no condition to engage in a naval "race" with the United States, acquiesced. Britain had abandoned the "Two-Power Standard" (see p. 742) to face the German challenge; now it abandoned its alliance with Japan and accepted formal parity with the greatest naval power, the United States.

At the Washington Conference on arms limitation and Pacific affairs in 1921–22, the powers laid down a new naval and East Asian order. The Washington Naval Treaty of February 1922 apparently froze the world ranking of naval power. It decreed a ten-year "holiday" in battleship construction and limited total tonnage of capital ships to 525,000 each for Britain and the United States, 315,000 for Japan, and 175,000 each for France and Italy. The powers relieved China of most Japanese encroachments and reaffirmed the "Open Door." The Anglo-Japanese Alliance dissolved into a meaningless Four-Power Treaty in which Britain, France, Japan, and the United States pledged to preserve the Pacific status quo. Japan agreed to the Washington settlement in return for British and American pledges not to build fortified bases north of Singapore and east of Hawaii. Tokyo retained naval supremacy in northeast Asia, along with Hong Kong and the Philippines as hostages to ensure British and American good behavior. The Washington treaties seemed to promise an era of peace. Their real results were a perilous complacency in the democracies and the cutting loose of Japan from the restraining influence of its alliance with Britain.

WARS AFTER THE WAR, 1919–23

Meanwhile, U.S. withdrawal left Europe on its own. Peaceful habits did not return. Social and national struggles convulsed Europe until 1923. The League of Nations generated immense masses of paper and gave small nations a forum for interminable talk. But it was impotent whenever it faced a great power. Even Italy defied the League in 1923 over an incident with Greece.

Civil Wars in Germany, Italy, and Russia

In Germany and Hungary, short-lived Left-extremist uprisings or regimes perished when faced with ruthless force from the Right. The SPD government of the German republic, unable to impose order with the debris of the Imperial German Army, authorized the recruitment of right-wing freebooters, the *Freikorps*. These units appealed to Germans of the Ernst Jünger type, who had enjoyed the Great War and were reluctant to give it up, and to nationalist students too young to have fought in 1914–18. In January 1919, after an abortive Communist ("Spartacist") coup in Berlin, the *Freikorps* shot Rosa Luxemburg and other leaders of the far Left "while attempting to escape." That was a euphemism much used later. A *Putsch,* or military coup, by *Freikorps* elements and a Communist uprising in the Ruhr almost destroyed the German republic in 1920.

In Italy, the Liberals lost control of the mass political forces that Giolitti had unleashed with universal male suffrage in 1912–13. The delusion that Italy was Russia gripped the Italian socialists. Their verbal threats of revolution and occasional violence against landowners and veterans soon provoked a virtual civil war, which the socialists inevitably lost (see p. 834).

Further east, Bolshevik Russia fought for survival. The 1918 Armistice had forced Germany to give up the gains of Brest-Litovsk. But the Bolsheviks continued to

Postwar wars: street fighting in Berlin, 1919.

proclaim the goal of world revolution, without which they expected a Communist Russia to succumb to "capitalist encirclement." Lenin and his associates split the European socialist parties by founding their own Third ("Communist") International in March 1919. They also appealed to the colonial peoples, furthering the disruption of the European empires that the war had begun.

Trotsky raised Bolshevik armies and fought with increasing success against "White Russian" forces under former tsarist generals who sought to restore the old regime. The Allies landed troops in 1918 at Vladivostok and Murmansk to secure the supplies they had sent to the tsar and to support the Whites. Except for the eager Japanese, who remained at Vladivostok until 1922, the Allies soon withdrew. By 1920 the Red Army had defeated the Whites, but the Poles made the error of attempting to seize the Ukraine. In July 1920 the Red Army drove into Poland with hopes of continuing westward. Then the Poles under Marshal Josef Pilsudski held at Warsaw. Russia's borders stabilized. Finland, Estonia, Latvia, and Lithuania kept their newly acquired independence; Rumania kept Bessarabia. In other respects Bolshevik Russia preserved the territories of the tsarist empire.

Eastern Europe and the Balkans

In the vacuum between Germany and Russia, the successor states quarreled. The diplomats at Paris did their best to draw new borders for Germany's former allies by the treaties of St. Germain (September 1919) for Austria, for Neuilly (November 1919) for Bulgaria, and of Trianon (June 1920) for Hungary. These frontiers, although much criticized as a source of conflict, in most cases merely ratified what the nationalities of eastern Europe had already done in pulling Austria-Hungary down. The great powers thereafter failed to moderate the squabbles of the small. Poland and Czechoslovakia disputed the border town of Teschen. Lithuania quarreled over its borders with Poland and Germany. Hungary claimed territory from all three of its neighbors—Rumania,

Czechoslovakia, and Yugoslavia. Those powers sought security through alliances with one another, a combination the Hungarians mocked as the "Little Entente." France, seeking an eastern ally to replace Russia, contracted alliances with Poland and Czechoslovakia, and entered into consultative pacts with Rumania and Yugoslavia.

Germany and Bolshevik Russia, the pariahs of the international scene, sought comfort together. In 1922, at Rapallo, they publicly canceled their mutual debt and reparations claims. Secretly, Red Army and German *Reichswehr* contracted a profitable bargain. Germany gave the Bolsheviks modern military technology and in return received an opportunity to secretly experiment in Russia with weapons such as gas and aircraft which were forbidden under the Versailles Treaty.

Far to the south, the Turks reacted to the collapse of their empire by creating a national state, under the leadership of the victor of Gallipoli, Mustafa Kemal Pasha. A foolhardy Greek advance into Turkey in pursuit of the "Great Idea" (*Megali Idea*) of a Greek empire from the Adriatic to the Black Sea led to disaster in 1922. The Turks then massacred or expelled the 1.35 million Greeks in Asia Minor whose ancestors had lived there for three millennia. The Greeks in turn drove almost half a million Turks from Greek Thrace. This "exchange of populations," as League bureaucrats euphemistically described it, still appeared barbaric in the 1920s. Unfortunately it did not appear so for long.

After a confrontation with British troops at Chanak near Constantinople that brought down Lloyd George's government in October 1922, the Turks permitted the Allies to leave them alone. The 1923 Treaty of Lausanne recognized the independent Turkish state. Kemal, who later took the name Atatürk ("father of the Turks"), abolished the Ottoman sultanate and ruled ruthlessly until his death in 1938. The Eastern Question was closed. Its worthy successors were the merciless struggles throughout the Middle East between the Ottoman Empire's former subjects.

The Final Battle of World War I: The Ruhr

Meanwhile, France and Germany fought a deadly although largely bloodless struggle. The issue was simple: would Germany accept its apparent demotion to second-rate power? The Germans refused to accept as final the loss of Posen, West Prussia, and Upper Silesia to Poland. Above all, Germany refused to pay promptly and fully the reparations that the Allies had fixed in 1921 at a theoretical total of $32 billion dollars (although they seem to have expected the Germans to actually pay only $12.5 billion).

The French faced immense expenses to repair the devastation wrought by the war and by the Germans, who had systematically wrecked French territory as they retreated in 1917 and 1918. France also hoped that heavy reparations would make it harder for Germany to rearm, and was confident that $12.5 billion was well within the German capacity to pay. It therefore did its best to hold Germany to the Allied payment schedule.

When the Germans defaulted massively in late 1922, France and its ally Belgium acted. Poincaré sent French troops into the Ruhr Valley to seize Germany's mines and factories. Mining coal with bayonets was expensive, but the French made a modest profit. The German government of Wilhelm Cuno ordered passive resistance. Cuno began printing marks feverishly, fuelling the inflation already under way as a result of Germany's immense internal war debt. Cuno wrecked Germany's currency to prove that Germany could not pay. What he proved was that Germany would not pay.

In August–September 1923 Cuno and passive resistance collapsed as the mark rose from 4 million to 160 million to the dollar. Gustav Stresemann, a crafty former National Liberal with an extreme annexationist past, took power as chancellor. He mastered internal disorder, which included a radical nationalist uprising in Bavaria under the leadership of a fanatical ex-corporal and winner of the Iron Cross, Adolf Hitler (see pp. 838–39).

France occupies the Ruhr Valley, 1923.

Stresemann sought a compromise with France that would give Germany a breathing space. Britain and the United States, concerned over the economic repercussions of chaos in Germany, helped. They threatened economic reprisals if Poincaré did not withdraw from the Ruhr. By spring 1924 Stresemann had stabilized the currency by introducing a new mark. Poincaré gave way to a left-wing coalition in the May 1924 French elections. His successor, Aristide Briand, was a weaker and more conciliatory man. An emissary of the United States, Charles G. Dawes, patched together a temporary reparations settlement, the Dawes Plan. It lowered payments to a level Germany consented to pay and underwrote Germany's solvency with a U.S. loan, the first of many. U.S. credit to Germany after 1924 indirectly furnished the sums Germany paid as reparations. The last French troops left the Ruhr in August 1925. France had lost a great trial of strength.

THE ILLUSIONS OF LOCARNO, 1925–29

From the French viewpoint, worse followed. Austen Chamberlain, Britain's

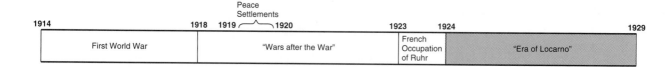

1914		1918	1919	Peace Settlements	1920		1923	1924		1929

First World War	"Wars after the War"	French Occupation of Ruhr	"Era of Locarno"

The god of war scoffs at the Kellogg-Briand Pact (a Dutch view).

A DUTCH JAB

Mars: "If your disarmament talkers don't stop, I'll die laughing."

foreign secretary, hoped to prevent a repetition of the Ruhr occupation by giving France security against Germany in an Anglo-French pact that would replace the failed 1919 Treaty of Guarantee. Stresemann got wind of the project and slyly preempted it with an offer of a general western security pact that Germany would also sign.

Instead of a revival of the Anglo-French Entente Cordiale, the French received the multilateral Treaty of Locarno (October 16, 1925). France, Germany, and Belgium pledged to respect their mutual borders, as drawn in the Versailles Treaty, and to preserve the demilitarization of the Rhineland. Britain and Italy acted as outside guarantors against "unprovoked attack," a vague and elastic phrase. And France could now respond militarily only to "flagrant" violations of the demilitarization of the Rhineland. Locarno thus significantly weakened a key provision of Versailles.

Despite Stresemann's claims of conversion to being a "good European," Locarno was an immense German victory. It prevented a repetition of the Ruhr: if France sought to use force to uphold the Versailles Treaty, Britain might be treaty-bound to fight France! Locarno also ruled out Anglo-French staff talks on the pre-1914 model, much to the relief of the British army and government. And Locarno covered only the West. Germany retained freedom to redraw, by force if necessary, its eastern borders.

A brief Indian summer of illusion, the "era of Locarno," followed the treaty. France and Britain repeatedly ignored massive German violations of the Versailles Treaty's disarmament provisions, and soon gave up their right of on-site inspection. Germany entered the League of Nations. In 1929, in a second reparations settlement (the "Young Plan") negotiated under U.S. auspices, Germany

agreed to make modest payments until 1988. France in turn undertook to evacuate its Rhineland occupation zone by summer 1930, five years ahead of the Versailles Treaty schedule.

Western public opinion demanded forgetfulness and illusion from its political leaders, and it received them. The Great War, much of the public concluded, had been an exercise in criminal futility that must never be repeated. Alliances and armaments—not German aggression—had caused the war. Therefore alliances and armaments (except semiclandestine German armaments) were evil. Enlightened international public opinion, working through the League of Nations, would prevent war.

Illusion reached its height with the famous pact "outlawing war" that Aristide Briand and Frank B. Kellogg, the U.S. secretary of state, drafted in 1928. Briand hoped the pact would bind the United States, however sketchily, to Europe. But the Kellogg-Briand Pact, which 62 nations happily signed, contained no enforcement provisions whatsoever. It also included an escape clause wide enough to accommodate entire tank armies: signatories could still fight in self-defense. The pact had all the force of a pious declaration against sin.

Fifteen years of war and revolution broke for good the "peaceful habits" acquired in the nineteenth century. For four years millions of men had killed one another in mud holes while Europe had transformed its vast accumulated wealth into steel and high explosives. Those who returned from the front carried the language and habit of violence into politics. In the East, a pitiless utopian sect had taken control of a great power of immense economic and military potential. In central Europe, the greatest European power of all had emerged from the war unreconciled to defeat. The victors had checked at heartbreaking cost the German bid for European and world mastery but had left Germany capable of repeating that bid. Soon—with the onset of the Great Depression in 1929—the world economy collapsed. That collapse enfeebled the democracies and unleashed voracious "have-not" powers first in Asia and then in Europe. As the Great War receded into memory, another even greater war took its place.

Suggestions for Further Reading

General Works

No up-to-date one-volume history of the war exists. M. Ferro, *The Great War, 1914–1918* (1973), A. J. P. Taylor, *The First World War* (1972); and C. R. M. F. Cruttwell, *A History of the Great War, 1914–1918* (1934/1991), offer intelligent surveys. M. Eksteins, *Rites of Spring: The Great War and the Birth of the Modern Age* (1989), probes its cultural significance with exceptional insight. Z. Zeman, *The Gentlemen Negotiators* (1971), and D. Stevenson, *The First World War and International Politics* (1988), cover diplomacy and strategy with style. P. Kennedy, "The First World War and the International Power System," *International Security*, 9 (1984), analyzes the relative strength of the powers. A. Offer, *The First World War: An Agrarian Interpretation* (1989), offers a new look at economics, strategy, and the nature of the contending societies. For life and death on the western front, see particularly the chapter on the Somme in J. Keegan, *The Face of Battle* (1976).

War and Revolution

For Germany's war, see F. Fischer, *War of Illusions* (1975), and *Germany's Aims in the First World War* (1967); H. W. Gatzke, *Germany's Drive to the West* (1950); T. Lupfer, *The Dynamics of Doctrine: The Changes in German Tactical Doctrine During the First World War* (1981); and J. Kocka, *Facing Total War: German Society, 1914–1918* (1984). On Britain, E. L. Woodward, *Great Britain and the War of 1914–1918* (1967), is unsurpassed, but see also A. Marwick, *The Deluge. British Society and the First World War* (1965). For France, see especially P. Bernard and H. Dubief, *The Decline of the Third Republic, 1914–1938* (1985), and A. Horne, *The Price of Glory; Verdun, 1916* (1962). S. Fitzpatrick, *The Russian Revolution, 1917–1932* (1982), gives a useful overview; A. Ulam, *Lenin and the Bolsheviks* (1965), and R. Pipes, *The Russian Revolution* (1990), are more detailed; L. Trotsky, *History of the Russian Revolution* (1936), is an unparalleled history-memoir by a key participant. On United States intervention, see especially B. Tuchman, *The Zimmermann Telegram* (1958); E. May, *The World War and American Isolation, 1914–1917* (1959); and D. Smith, *The Great Departure: The United States and World War I* (1965).

Settlement and Aftermath

On the power consequences of the war, see Kennedy, "The First World War" (above); G. Weinberg, "The Defeat of Germany in 1918 and the European Balance of Power," *Central European History*, 2 (1969); and H. Holborn, *The Political Collapse of Europe* (1954). P. Birdsall, *Versailles Twenty Years After* (1941), remains the best treatment of the peace conference, but see also K. Schawbe, *Woodrow Wilson, Revolutionary Germany, and Peacemaking, 1918–1919: Missionary Diplomacy and the Realities of Power* (1985). On the aftermath, S. Marks, *The Illusion of Peace. International Relations in Europe, 1918–1933* (1976), is unsurpassed. C. A. Macartney and A. W. Palmer, *Independent Eastern Europe* (1962), is excellent. S. Marks, "The Myths of Reparation," *Central European History*, 11 (1978), demystifies a widely misunderstood issue.

31

THE WORLD BETWEEN THE WARS, 1919–1939

*T*he virtual withdrawal of the United States and Russia from world politics created a fleeting illusion: that Britain and France, the victors in 1914–18, dominated Europe and the wider world as in the early nineteenth century. But France's failure to coerce even a disarmed Germany and Britain's economic and imperial troubles soon revealed the hollowness of appearances. Germany enjoyed a brief prosperity after 1924, thanks to U.S. credit. But political stability eluded it. Few of the new states of central and eastern Europe found either stability or prosperity. The United States enjoyed an unprecedented economic boom—in isolation.

Then, in 1929–30, came the Great Depression. It extinguished the few surviving parliamentary regimes between Germany and Russia. It almost destroyed world lending and trade. It mortally wounded the great democracies, confirmed the United States in its isolationism, and freed "have not" powers to attack the West both in Europe and Asia. Fascist Italy under Benito Mussolini, a racist Germany under Adolf Hitler, and a militarized Japan destroyed the order established in the Versailles and Washington treaties, while Lenin's implacable successor, Joseph Stalin, sought to profit from the resulting chaos. Britain, France, and the United States met these global challenges demoralized and disunited. France went under; Britain nearly perished; the United States paid dearly for its irresponsibility after 1919.

THE TWENTIES: A GOLDEN AGE?

Britain: Stability and Stagnation

War and its aftermath broke the Liberals. In 1916 Asquith gave way to Lloyd

George, and then, in May 1918, attacked him in the House of Commons and split the Liberal party. In the "khaki election" of December 1918 Lloyd George led his wartime Liberal-Conservative coalition to a crushing victory over both Asquith and Labour. That victory condemned the divided Liberal party to permanent opposition and decline.

But the Conservatives soon found Lloyd George's leadership irritating. His brinkmanship in the Chanak crisis with Turkey in October 1922 gave the stolid foot soldiers of the Conservative party their opportunity. The comfortable, avuncular, pipe-smoking Stanley Baldwin rose up and denounced Lloyd George as "a great dynamic force"—"a very terrible thing." By 1923 Baldwin, whose enemies mocked him as "a man of the utmost insignificance," was prime minister.

He remained until 1929, except for a brief Labour minority government in 1924. Baldwin was the tweedy personification of a largely extinct rural England. A master of conciliation, of fudging issues, he defused social conflict with the soothing syrup of his "fireside chats" on that new

medium, the radio. He found foreign policy boring. The Locarno treaty seemed to make foreign policy unnecessary; Baldwin did his best to have none.

The British mass army that had broken the Hindenburg Line in 1918 shrank to an insignificant imperial police force. The new Royal Air Force remained a hollow shell. The navy vegetated. In 1928 Britain adopted as permanent a 1919 budgetary invention of Lloyd George— the "ten-year rule." All defense expenditure and planning was to rest on the assumption that Britain would not fight a great power for at least ten years. That assumption was in effect a rationalization for Britain's unilateral disarmament.

In 1926, Baldwin's government weathered the general strike feared since the miners, dockers, and railwaymen had formed a "triple alliance" in 1914. The Polish and German mining industries had recovered from war and disruption and had forced coal prices down. Britain's miners struck to protest the resulting pay cuts. Transport and other workers joined the miners in sympathy. But the government did not need the armored cars that

The General Strike, 1926: London police protect delivery workers from possible reprisals by strikers.

Churchill, by then a defector to the Baldwin cabinet from the dying Liberals, gleefully displayed in Hyde Park to intimidate the strikers. Baldwin supervised a conciliatory settlement for the transport workers; the miners eventually surrendered.

The General Strike of 1926 left a legacy of bitterness, especially among the miners. But Baldwin's tranquilizing manner nevertheless preserved Britain's traditions of gradualism and social peace, despite the rise of Labour and the strain of unemployment in declining areas and industries that idled more than 10 percent of Britain's labor force in every year except 1927. But Baldwin was certainly no "dynamic force." Neither he nor his Labour successor of 1929–31, Ramsay MacDonald, was the man to counter the decay of Britain's heavy industry or arrest Britain's military decline.

France: Instability and Resilience

France, at least superficially, contrasted sharply with Britain's orderly alternation between Conservatives and Labour. France went through seventeen governments between 1920 and 1929. Once the war emergency was past, the Chamber reasserted its dislike of leaders. It did away with Clemenceau in 1920. The Ruhr crisis with Germany over reparations brought Poincaré to the fore in 1922–24. Then *"Poincaruhr"* departed when the May 1924 victory of the moderate left *Cartel des Gauches* displaced the nationalist chamber elected in the enthusiasm of 1919. The Cartel, in turn, was politically incoherent. Radical-Socialists and Socialists squabbled. The Communists, who had captured from the Socialists most of the members of the largest union, the General Confederation of Labor (CGT), gleefully attacked the Cartel from the left. Moscow demanded then and later that all Communist parties concentrate their fire not on the Right but on their Socialist rivals. A "cascade" of short-lived Cartel ministries proved incapable of governing in 1925–26, as the franc declined catastrophically after the Ruhr crisis. Poincaré returned in July 1926; his authority saved the franc.

Remarkably, he remained—and retired voluntarily in 1929.

The appearance of chaos, except under Poincaré, was deceptive. The Third Republic rebuilt the war-devastated areas by the end of the 1920s. The coal and iron of Lorraine, now liberated from Germany, fueled a sharp rise in steel production. André Citroën pioneered the mass production of automobiles in Europe, an innovation the British were slow to follow. Hydroelectric power and bauxite deposits in southern France made it a major producer of that new light metal, aluminum. While unemployment was laying waste to Britain's mining and shipbuilding areas, France was suffering a labor shortage. Prosperity and the immense wartime losses created job openings that 1.5 million immigrants from eastern Europe and the colonies filled.

But France's position was precarious; it rested above all on German disarmament. For as in 1914, France's industrial economy was about half the size of Germany's, and three Germans of military age still faced every two Frenchmen. After the Ruhr fiasco and the Locarno treaty, which barred France from invading western Germany, the French sought security in defense and implicitly abandoned their allies in eastern Europe. In 1929, the government initiated a gigantic engineering project to seal France's eastern borders and protect its vital industries from a repetition of 1914. The Maginot Line, named for the minister of war of the moment, André Maginot, was an immensely strong crust of obstacles and fortresses linked with tunnels and underground railways. It had one weakness: it did not cover the Belgian border. Belgium was a French ally and had its own fortifications facing Germany. If Belgium ceased to be an ally, both the Maginot Line and France might fall.

Germany: Republic without Republicans

Germany's new democracy showed neither British stability nor French resilience. The SPD, Center, and German Democratic (left-Liberal) parties received 75 percent of the vote in the January 1919 elections,

| German Empire ("Second Reich") | Weimar Republic | Hitler ("Third Reich") |

thanks to Germany's need to appear democratic for the Paris peace conference. The new legislature convened under their leadership in the provincial town of Weimar, safe from the Spartacist radicals in Berlin, and drafted the most democratic constitution conceivable. It gave the vote to both sexes at age twenty and employed an extreme form of proportional representation that measured, like a delicate seismograph, every quirk and blip of public opinion. Any party that could collect 60,000 votes in all of Germany could have a *Reichstag* seat. That was an invitation to political fragmentation; by 1928 Germany had at least 45 parties.

The Weimar constitution had a further weakness that in the end proved fatal. Max Weber, who helped draft the constitution, believed that a strong American-style presidency would ward off what he took to be democracy's tendency toward incoherence. Thanks to Weber and to Germany's monarchical tradition, the Republic received *both* a chancellor responsible to the legislature *and* a popularly elected Reich president. And the Reich president had something his American counterpart did not have, although Lincoln at war had in practice claimed it: emergency powers to make law by decree.

Underground in the Maginot Line.

The Weimar constitution failed to work because its drafters superimposed it upon a state and an electorate that were anything but democratic. The officer corps, core of the old Reich, saved itself in 1918–19 by cooperation with the SPD. Thereafter, under General von Seeckt, it supported the Republic grudgingly so long as the Republic tolerated the army's semi-independent status as a "state within the state." As for the electorate, it voted its convictions in the 1920 election and placed the founding parties of the Republic in a permanent minority. Democracy had failed as a means of ensuring a lenient peace. Middle-class Germans had no natural love of democracy for its own sake, and therefore deserted the German Democratic party for the Right. Even the SPD and Center parties were scarcely democratic by vocation. The SPD had to retain its Marxist rhetoric to prevent further defections to the increasingly vocal Communists to its left; the Center had a built-in authoritarian bent.

That the Republic survived as long as it did, and that it provided the backing for Stresemann's moderate foreign policy from 1923 to 1929, was almost miraculous. This was a political system unable to reach agreement on the colors of the national flag; a cabinet fell over that issue in 1926. Coalitions, to command a *Reichstag* majority, had to extend so far left or right that they were prone to break down at any moment.

Nevertheless, three factors preserved the Republic. No alternative existed. The monarchy was politically dead; Communist risings failed in 1919, 1920, and 1923; *Putsches* from the Right collapsed in 1920 and 1923 because Seeckt and his army were neutral or hostile. Second, the Republic acquired an unexpected respectability in 1925. Tirpitz, in his last contribution to German politics, persuaded Field Marshal von Hindenburg to run for Reich president. Hindenburg's triumphant election compelled the old Right to moderate its hatred for the Republic. Finally, Germany after 1924 began to recover its pre-1914 prosperity, thanks primarily to U.S. short-term loans. But if a political alternative arose, if Hindenburg disappeared, if the army turned against the Republic, or if prosperity ended, Weimar might end as well.

The Habsburg Successor States: Democracies and Dictatorships

German democracy, however precarious, was an earthly paradise compared to conditions further east. The states of eastern Europe greeted 1919 clothed in Wilsonian democratic garb. Within a decade, the absence of native parliamentary traditions and the pressures of nationalism and peasant-landlord conflict had turned most of them into dictatorships.

As Austria-Hungary collapsed, its peoples had erected national states. Inevitably, given central and eastern Europe's mixed pattern of settlement, the new borders included large national minorities. Rumania forcibly incorporated the 1.5 million Hungarians of Transylvania, and returned with interest harsh Hungarian treatment of the minorities of pre-1914 greater Hungary. The Poles sometimes dealt arrogantly with their German minority, despite the danger of provoking the German state. In Yugoslavia, Orthodox Serbs lorded it over Catholic Croats and Slovenes, former subjects of Austria-Hungary. Virtually all states and peoples mistreated the Jews. League of Nations safeguards for ethnic minorities proved mere scraps of paper.

Social oppression was almost as pervasive as national oppression. Except in industrial Czechoslovakia and in post-1918 Austria (which consisted of Vienna and an assortment of Alps), the chief class was the peasantry. It ranged in size from 80 percent of the population in Bulgaria to 55 percent in Hungary. Controlling it was the chief preoccupation of eastern Europe's landholding ruling classes. In the Baltic states of Estonia, Latvia, and Lithuania, the landlords were predominantly Russians, Germans, or Poles; the new nationalist governments happily took their

Seeckt, planner of German victories over the Russians and Romanians in 1915–16, made Germany's postwar 100,000-man force an elite "army of leaders," cadres for a future mass army.

land. Elsewhere, peasant land hunger and landlord resistance contributed mightily to political instability.

By 1930, Hungary, Poland, Lithuania, Yugoslavia, Bulgaria, and Rumania were all essentially dictatorships. Hungary went first. From March to November 1919 it suffered the Bolshevik dictatorship of Béla Kun, Rumanian invasion, and finally a bloody reconquest by the Right under the

The dreariness of Weimar, depicted by Georg Grosz, an artist of the Left who bitterly attacked the Republic.

"Strong men" of eastern Europe:
Horthy of Hungary (*above*) and
Pilsudski of Poland (*below*).

leadership of Austria-Hungary's greatest naval leader, Admiral Nicholas Horthy. The result was a gentry-controlled sham parliament under a narrow oligarchy with Horthy at its head. A nationalist dictatorship of the peasant Right emerged in Lithuania in 1926. Poland's parliamentary interlude yielded to a 1926 coup by an ex-socialist "man on horseback," Marshal Joseph Pilsudski. In Yugoslavia, the assassination in parliament of the chief Croat leader in 1928 rendered the country ungovernable. King Alexander imposed a royal dictatorship supported by Serb bayonets. Some Croats replied with terrorism. And in Bulgaria, a military coup in 1923 displaced the ruthless peasant leader, Alexander Stambolisky, who had ruled since 1919. Stambolisky and some 10,000 of his followers perished in ensuing uprisings and massacres. In 1925 a Communist bomb dropped the roof of Sofia cathedral on the representatives of the Right. Enough survived to massacre the Left and impose a royal and military dictatorship with parliamentary trimmings. In 1930 the dissolute King Carol of Rumania returned from exile and adopted a similar solution.

There were two exceptions to this pattern. Austria, despite the economic ruin of separation from Hungary and Bohemia and a built-in cleavage between "Red Vienna" and the *Freikorps*-like hearties of its Alpine valleys, managed to last out the decade as a parliamentary regime. Czechoslovakia, although a veritable patchwork of nationalities, was an island of relative freedom and prosperity under the enlightened leadership of its Czech founders, Thomas Masaryck and Eduard Beneš. But no eastern European state was equipped to face the coming storm.

The United States: The "Roaring Twenties"

Unprecedented domestic prosperity appeared to reward the international irresponsibility of the United States. The economy grew steadily after the brief worldwide slump of 1920–21. By 1929 the real per capita income of the average American had improved by more than a third compared to 1921. The automobile

came into its own as the engine of growth and symbol of the "American way of life." By 1926, Henry Ford had sold 16 million Model T's, the first true mass-production automobile. By 1929, the United States had one car for every five people; European automobile production was a mere 13 percent of the U.S. level. The U.S. electrical industry followed suit: radios, refrigerators, and vacuum cleaners deluged a public that displayed an apparently insatiable appetite for consumer goods.

Politically, the 1920s were a placidly Republican decade. President Harding died suddenly in 1923 during the revelation of financial scandals involving his associates. His Vice President, Calvin ("Silent Cal") Coolidge, then presided in masterful inactivity until 1928. A man of few words but pithy ones, he made no secret of his conviction that "the business of America is business."

The 1920s were also a decade of stern intolerance. As President Wilson lay paralyzed, his attorney general, A. Mitchell Palmer, mercilessly hunted foreign-born "Reds." In laws of 1921 and 1924, under the guise of immigration quotas, Congress extended to southern and eastern Europeans the policy of exclusion adopted earlier against Chinese and Japanese. The Ku Klux Klan revived, and lynched blacks and Jews. And after 1917, temperance crusaders dragooned the state legislatures into ratifying an Eighteenth Amendment that prohibited "the manufacture, sale, and transportation of alcoholic beverages."

Prohibition—not repealed until 1933 —was in part revenge of rural and Protestant America upon the great cities and their immigrants. But Prohibition also took revenge on its supporters. The Eighteenth Amendment and the Volstead Act of 1919 that enforced it created an immense illegal beer and liquor industry under the control of the very immigrants whom the temperance movement had sought to discipline.

License accompanied intolerance. War, Prohibition, and prosperity broke down inherited standards. Prohibition, an unenforceable law, led to contempt for all laws; it also increased the appeal of alcohol. Relief from the strain of war, the growing emancipation of women not

1913		1921	1923		1929	1933		1945
Wilson (D)		Harding (R)	Coolidge (R)			Hoover (R)	FDR (D) and the "New Deal"	

merely politically but sexually, and the freedom that affluence and automobiles conferred created a hectic and exhilarating "Jazz Age." But all things end. The 1920s ended in an economic catastrophe that appeared to put capitalism itself in question.

THE GREAT DEPRESSION

The collapse of the New York stock market in October 1929 helped trigger a depression that lasted until the next great war, for which it was partially responsible. The Great Depression's ultimate causes, a subject of much dispute, were essentially three.

First, the war distorted the fabric of world trade, and politics prevented readjustment after 1918. Britain and Germany had hurled the products of their industries at each other for four years. When they resumed peacetime production the result was worldwide overcapacity, thanks to a vast economic expansion in the United States and Japan that had filled the wartime gap in the world market. The same process operated in agriculture: the United States, Canada, Argentina, Australia, and New Zealand had multiplied their agricultural production after 1914. After 1919, governments dared not permit the free market to slash the resulting surpluses. Industrialists and bankers made their money talk; workers and farmers voted. Instead of allowing production to fall, most states chose price subsidies and tariffs—a choice that simply prolonged overproduction. Despite the best efforts of the bureaucrats, agricultural prices soon dropped, and kept on dropping. Cotton peaked in 1923, and grain in 1924–25; by 1927 the slide in prices was general.

Second, the war burned up the capital needed to propel Europe's growth. France lost more than half its 1914 foreign investments—a quarter had been in Russia. Brit-

ain took on a debt of $1 billion in paying for U.S. supplies. Britain's allies owed it $1.7 billion. The resumption of economic growth depended on renewed U.S. lending.

And the policies of the United States—the third major cause of the Great Depression—were irresponsible and self-contradictory. During the war, America had replaced Britain as the world's greatest creditor. U.S. foreign investments rose from $2 billion in 1913 to $15 billion in 1930. But the isolationist United States of the 1920s refused to play the role that its wealth thrust upon it, the role of leader and ultimate guarantor of the stability of the world market. It rejected any thought of canceling the crushing burden of war debts, incurred in a common cause, under which its allies labored. Coolidge well expressed the implacable American view of those debts in a famous remark in his Vermont twang: "They hired the money, didn't they? Let them pay it!"

The age of jazz: King Oliver's Jazz Band in Chicago (1922), with the young Louis Armstrong (*center*).

Worse, the United States barricaded itself behind the Fordney-McCumber tariff in 1922. High tariffs were traditional in the United States, but now they deprived Europe of a market desperately needed to earn profits with which to pay its war debts. As the president of the Chase National Bank remarked: "The debts of the outside world to us are ropes about their necks, by means of which we pull them towards us. Our trade restrictions are pitchforks pressed against their bodies, by which we hold them off."

The United States nevertheless had a foreign economic policy of sorts. Well-meaning emissaries such as Dawes and Young attempted to stabilize Europe economically. But in the absence of tariff reduction and debt cancellation they merely produced a financial merry-go-round. U.S. short-term loans fueled the German economic expansion that underwrote reparations to France, which in turn paid war debts to Britain. Both Britain and France then paid war debts to the United States. But what if Europe's economy turned downward, or U.S. lending ceased?

Both began to happen 1927–28. Germany's agricultural prices crumbled and its industrial growth stopped. In the United States the Federal Reserve System, an innovation of Wilson's first administration designed to stabilize the banking system, made economic instability worse. Since 1921 the "Fed" had happily pumped in credit, creating hectic growth. In mid-1927, sensing a possible downturn, it pumped harder than before. Easy credit helped stimulate an already foolhardy stock market to the greatest speculative boom in history. The Dow Jones index doubled in value, from 191 to 381, between early 1928 and September 1929. The Wall Street boom put pressure on Europe by siphoning off money from foreign lending. It squeezed U.S. banks and industry by sucking funds out of bank savings, industrial investment, and consumer spending.

In spring and summer 1929, U.S. economic activity turned downward. Production outran demand as speculative mania drained cash from the pockets of businesses and consumers. The market contin-

ued giddily upward. Then the bubble burst. Wall Street slipped on October 3, 1929. By the end of the month, after "Black Thursday" (October 24) and "Black Tuesday" (October 29), the Dow index was falling free. Investors who had bought stocks on credit trampled each other to sell, or leapt from high windows onto Wall Street. Business activity, commodity prices, foreign trade, and the vital lending to Europe all collapsed.

Congress reacted predictably. In March–June 1930, it passed the notorious Smoot-Hawley Tariff, the highest in U.S. history. Coolidge's successor, the unlucky and unloved Herbert Hoover, signed that tariff into law despite a monster petition from a thousand U.S. economists begging him to veto it. The tariff and the cut-off of American short-term credit on which Europe depended were the principal forces that transformed the Wall Street crash into the Great Depression.

All nations sought to keep their own industries and farmers afloat by barring imports. In spring and summer of 1931, the year of wrath, the banking system of central Europe collapsed. A subversive German scheme for economic union with Austria—a disguised annexation—provoked French financial retaliation. An already frail Austrian bank, the Credit Anstalt, failed. The resulting sudden flight of U.S. short-term loans from Germany almost destroyed a banking system enfeebled by agricultural depression and industrial malaise. The German economy, the motor of central Europe, stalled; 17,000 industrial enterprises shut down.

Britain also came under pressure. In September 1931 London suspended payments in gold, which it had discontinued during the war and had painfully reestablished in 1925 only with U.S. help. The pound sterling became just another paper currency, rather than the unchanging world standard it had been throughout the nineteenth century. That was the end of Britain's already shattered claim to world economic leadership. Hoover belatedly and half-heartedly tried to fill Britain's role by proposing a one-year moratorium on reparations and war-debt payments in June 1931. Cancellation would have been more appropriate, but U.S. opinion would not permit it. Regardless of U.S. wishes, war-debt and reparations payments effectively ceased, although negotiations lingered until 1932–33.

Governments sought to promote economic recovery by drastic expenditure cuts to balance their budgets. That further depressed their economies by lessening demand. Tariff and currency-devaluation wars escalated, further deepening and widening the Depression. Britain, formerly the world bastion of free trade, adopted tariffs in 1932. The United States left the gold standard and devalued the dollar in 1933. In Germany and the United States, the worst-hit powers, roughly one worker in four was unemployed by the time the Depression reached bottom in 1932. The Great Depression cut world industrial production by almost a third and world trade by two-thirds. The world market almost ceased to exist (see Figure 31-1). Then the precarious peace of 1919 collapsed.

THE WEST AND THE WIDER WORLD, 1919–39

The war discredited the concept of empire, as well as destroying empires. The victors received German colonies, chunks of the Ottoman Empire, and Pacific islands not as outright possessions, but as "mandates" from the League of Nations. In theory, the purpose of colonialism was now to prepare the subject peoples for independence. That colonialism now needed political fig-leaves was a sign of its coming collapse.

Especially in Asia and the Middle East, war and Bolshevism encouraged the ultimate agent of that collapse—nationalism. Japan's economic expansion encouraged it to press its claim to domination in East Asia. China's reaction and the Great Depression soon moved Japan to make good that claim by force. Japanese defiance of the West undermined the essential foundation of colonialism everywhere, the prestige won in the nineteenth century through the West's effortless domination of the wider world.

FIGURE 31-1   **Down the Drain: The Contracting Spiral of World Trade 1929–33**

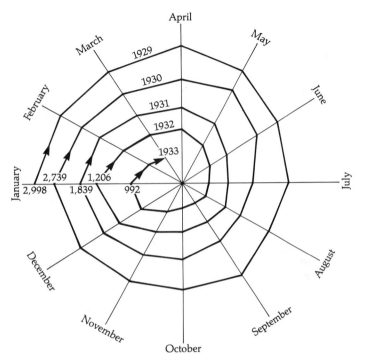

Millions of Dollars

From Charles P. Kindleberger, The World in Depression, 1929–1939 *(Berkeley: University of California Press, 1973), p. 172.*

Culmination and Twilight of the Colonial Empires: Britain and France

In 1919, Britain appeared more supreme outside Europe than at any time since the 1870s. Along with its South African and Australian dominions, Britain had taken the lion's share of the war's colonial booty. It had at last secured the east coast of Africa from the Cape to Cairo. It had triumphantly completed the partition of the Ottoman Empire that the Balkan nationalities had begun in 1878. Its major rivals were out of the running. Germany was defeated, Russia was in chaos, and the United States had no desire for further colonial acquisitions; in 1933–34 it pledged to give the Philippines independence by 1945 and unilaterally gave up its treaty right to intervene in Cuba. Britain's only remaining competitors were its allies, France and Japan.

But Britain's position was hollow. By May 1920 the chief of the general staff, Sir Henry Wilson, noted despairingly that "in no single theater are we strong enough—not in Ireland, nor England, not on the Rhine, not in Constantinople, nor Batoum, nor Egypt, nor Palestine, nor Mesopotamia, nor Persia, nor India." Nationalist revolts, Britain's shattered economic position, and the domestic priorities of its mass electorate made it impossible to hold either the immense gains of 1914–18 or Britain's first colony, Ireland.

At Easter 1916 a band of Irish nationalists had risen in Dublin with German promises of support. British troops put the rebels down and tactlessly executed the movement's leaders. That "blood sacrifice" destroyed the position of the Irish moderates and made the radical nationalist Sinn Fein a mass movement. In 1919 an offshoot of Sinn Fein, the "Irish Republican Army," launched a campaign of assassination and urban guerrilla war. The British responded. The feared "Black and Tans," former western-front desperadoes, reinforced the Royal Irish Constabulary. Anonymous gangs caused suspected I.R.A. members and sympathizers to disappear. Even partition in 1921–22 between an Irish Free State in the south and Protestant Ulster in the north did not end "the troubles." I.R.A. diehards refused to accept partition, continued to assassinate

British officials, and forced on the Free State itself a civil war more savage than the one the British had waged. A semblance of peace did not return until 1923, and in Ulster sporadic violence has continued to the present.

In Egypt, nationalist riots and assassinations in March 1919 likewise showed the limits of British power. Britain gave Egypt nominal independence in 1922 while retaining control of foreign policy, defense, and the all-important Suez Canal. In Iraq the British conceded sham-independence, inexpensively enforced by punitive raids with the fighter-bombers of the infant Royal Air Force.

Palestine was more difficult. The Balfour declaration of 1917 and the world war itself speeded Jewish emigration from Europe to Palestine. The ideal of a Jewish state was the creation of Theodor Herzl, who in 1897 had founded a Zionist Organization to promote it. Jewish immigation and aspirations to statehood inevitably cut across the claims of Palestine's Arab inhabitants, many of whom, paradoxically, had moved to Palestine to benefit from the economic upsurge the Jews had brought. In 1929 Arab-Jewish conflict erupted in the "Wailing Wall" riots in Jerusalem. After 1933, thanks to Adolf Hitler, Jewish immigration to Palestine doubled the Jewish population in three years. After 1936–37, a guerrilla struggle between Arabs and Jews tied down two British divisions sorely needed elsewhere. A British

The Easter Rising, 1916: ruins in central Dublin after British artillery bombardment.

ban on Jewish immigration in 1939 failed to placate the Arabs and aroused the fierce hostility of the Zionists.

Worse still for Britain, India repeatedly erupted in violence. Among the many ambiguous British promises of the dark year of 1917—when a mere 15,000 troops upheld British rule on the subcontinent—was a pledge of "responsible government" as reward for India's notable contribution to the war effort. Postwar British conduct appeared to betray that pledge. In April 1919, after a series of attacks on British civilians at Amritsar in the Punjab, General Reginald Dyer ordered his troops to disperse a crowd with rifle fire. In this "Amritsar Massacre" at least 379 died and more than 1,200 suffered wounds. The massacre, and the ensuing celebration of Dyer in British Conservative circles as the man who had prevented a second Indian Mutiny, opened an unbridgeable gulf between Britain and educated Indian opinion.

Amritsar impelled Mohandas K. Gandhi, a Hindu lawyer who had made his name as a leader of the Indian community in South Africa, to launch the Congress party on a campaign of nonviolent civil disobedience. That agitation collapsed in 1922, but British concessions did not follow. Gandhi revived his movement in 1930. The imprisonment of 60,000 demonstrators and Gandhi's rejection of British compromise offers again led to the movement's collapse; Gandhi had outrun Indian opinion. Then Britain gave in. The Government of India Act of 1935 gave India a constitution and a firm promise of independence, despite fierce opposition in London from Conservative diehards such as Winston Churchill. The Congress party swept the 1937 elections. But by that point, despite Gandhi's charismatic appeal, Indian nationalism had divided along the Hindu-Moslem line, A Westernized Moslem lawyer-politician, Mohammed Ali Jinnah, created a Moslem League that by 1940 was demanding partition of the subcontinent into Hindu and Moslem states.

India's movement toward independence was only one sign of the British Empire's decline; not even the white Do-

The Balfour Declaration

Foreign Office
November 2nd, 1917

Dear Lord Rothschild,

I have much pleasure in conveying to you, on behalf of His Majesty's Government, the following declaration of sympathy with Jewish Zionist aspirations which has been submitted to, and approved by, the Cabinet.

"His Majesty's Government view with favour the establishment in Palestine of a National Home for the Jewish people, and will use their best endeavors to facilitate the achievement of this object, it being clearly understood that nothing shall be done which may prejudice the civil and religious rights of existing non-Jewish communities in Palestine, or the rights and political status enjoyed by Jews in any other country."

I should be grateful if you would bring this declaration to the knowledge of the Zionist Federation.

Yours sincerely,
(Signed) Arthur James Balfour

Quoted in L. Stein, Zionism *(London: Ernest Benn, 1925) p. 377.*

Gandhi (1931) in his everyday garb as a Hindu holy man.

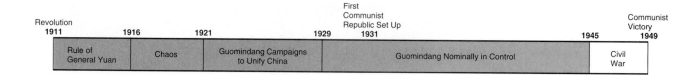

Revolution 1911		1916		1921		1929	First Communist Republic Set Up 1931		1945	Communist Victory 1949

Rule of General Yuan	Chaos	Guomindang Campaigns to Unify China	Guomindang Nominally in Control	Civil War

minions showed the unquestioning loyalty for which British imperialists had hoped. Their share in Britain's 1914–18 sacrifices and victory gave the Dominions claims on Britain. With Canada and South Africa in the lead, they sought full sovereignty at the Imperial Conference of 1926. By the Statute of Westminster of 1931 they received it. The British Empire adopted the ambiguous title of "British Commonwealth of Nations." And in 1932, Eamon De Valera, sole survivor of the rebel leaders of Easter 1916, became prime minister of the Irish Free State. In 1937 he took the Free State out of the Commonwealth in everything but name and set a powerful example.

France preferred the Foreign Legion bayonet to the subtleties of negotiation. It was little more successful than Britain. Its 1919 booty, Syria and Lebanon, proved hostile and unrewarding; the French battered Damascus with artillery as late as 1925. The Berbers of Morocco destroyed a Spanish army in 1921 and attacked the French. It took Pétain, tanks, and four years of fighting to reestablish colonial order. Algeria and Tunisia were intermittently restless.

In Indochina, beneath a placid surface, nationalist and Communist clandestine organizations spread, with encouragement from China. The Depression brought starvation to the Vietnamese peasantry and the first serious insurrections since French conquest in the nineteenth century. At Yen Bay, north of Hanoi, nationalists rose in 1930; Communists organized strikes and risings. Ho Chi Minh ("the bringer of enlightenment"), agent of the Communist International for Southeast Asia, founded a Communist Party of Indochina. French reprisals were brutal even by French standards. Ho escaped to China and Moscow, and dryly observed that had the nonviolent Gandhi been born in a French colony he "would

long since have entered heaven." France's control appeared unshaken. But soon white power everywhere in East Asia was at risk.

The Struggle for Mastery in East Asia Renewed: China and Japan

The Depression unleashed a struggle for supremacy in Asia that pitted Japanese imperial claims against both Chinese nationalism and the remnants of European domination.

In 1911–12 military revolt in southern and central China had at last overthrown the decrepit Qing dynasty. The leading proponent of a Western-style Chinese nationalism, Sun Yat-sen, supported that outcome—which destroyed what little prospect remained for a Japanese-style revolution from above that would harness dynastic loyalty to the task of transformation. Sun instead helped found a political party, the Guomindang, and strove to give China constitutional government.

But power in the new China—as in most other societies whose traditional order collapsed under the impact of the West—now came from the barrel of a gun. The end of the Qing dynasty and the crumbling of Confucianism in the face of Western ideas left no other form of legitimacy. Yuan Shikai, most successful leader of the Western-armed provincial armies, had the most guns. He attempted to make himself emperor. Regional warlords resisted; Yuan fell ill and died in 1916. After that, warlord armies fought obscure struggles the length and breadth of China. Those around Beijing (Peking) contended for the honor of manipulating a sham parliament. Chinese nationalism, outraged at continuing European and Japanese encroachments, sought in vain for a political vehicle.

Two contenders arose. Sun discarded parliamentary government for Leninism

Sun Yat-sen, theorist of Chinese nationalism (1923).

without Marxism. The Soviet Union, seeking a sphere of influence in China, delightedly offered advisers and arms. With the help of Michael Borodin, the Communist International's man in China, Sun drafted a new statute for the Guomindang that made it a centralized "vanguard party"— but one without a coherent ideology. Sun's military assistant, Chiang Kai-shek, created a party army in southern China with Soviet rifles and advisers, and inherited the Guomindang after Sun's death in 1925. But the Soviet Union had a second string to its bow: the Chinese Communist Party (CCP), founded in 1920–21 with Soviet advice by groups of Beijing and Shanghai intellectuals. Those groups included the sturdy and pugnacious son of a rich peasant, Mao Zedong (Mao Tse-tung).

In 1927, as Chiang extended Guomindang control to central China, collaboration between the Communists and the Guomindang broke down. Chiang crushed the Communists in Shanghai and elsewhere with much slaughter. Soon the CCP had lost its original base, the small working classes of the industrializing coastal cities. Mao escaped to the hills on the Jiangxi-Hunan border, created a Party army of peasants and bandits, and ultimately purged his remaining rivals in the Party leadership. Lenin had adapted Marxism to a largely peasant country but had kept Marx's notion of the industrial proletariat as chosen people. Mao discarded even that; his Marxism for Chinese conditions was to be an ideology of peasant revolt *against* the cities.

After temporarily suppressing the Communists, Chiang Kai-shek defeated the northern warlords and seized Beijing in 1928. That nominally unified China. But Chiang's rule was precarious; the Guomindang absorbed a variety of quarrelsome warlords as it expanded. The Communists in the hills remained a threat, despite five Guomindang "bandit-extermination campaigns." In 1934–35 Mao's forces escaped from south-central China and in an epic "Long March" of 6,000 miles sought refuge at Yenan in the remote north-west.

By then, Chiang had another enemy to occupy him. Japan had given up most of its claims on China in the Washington treaties of 1922. The Western-style political parties permitted under Japan's Bismarckian constitution of 1889 were at the height of their influence in the early and middle 1920s, despite occasional assassinations of politicians by ultra-nationalist sects. But internal and external pressures made Japan's era of liberalism at home and peace abroad a brief one. At Paris the powers had humiliated Japan by refusing its request to incorporate into the Versailles Treaty a declaration on racial equality. The corollary of that refusal was the banning of Japanese immigration to the United States and to Australia. Simultaneously, U.S. tariffs squeezed Japanese exports, and U.S. pressure dictated in 1921–22 the end of the alliance with Britain that had tied Japan to the international status quo.

Inside Japan itself, by the late 1920s, explosive economic growth, population increase, and radical ideologies pressed against that status quo. Economic growth between 1900 and 1929, at 4.2 percent a year, was faster than that of any other power. Population grew from 43.8 million in 1900 to 71.1 million in 1940. American tariffs and immigration restrictions pushed Japan toward dependence on mainland raw materials and emigration outlets, especially in coal- and iron-rich Manchuria.

Ultra-nationalist sects, a feature of the Japanese scene since the "men of spirit" of the 1850s, proliferated. Ideologues such as Kita Ikki (1883–1939) proposed vague syntheses of Marxism and Japanese nationalism, and looked forward to a world-dominating Japan with vast colonial possessions and a population of 250 million. Such ideas prospered in the military, especially among middle-level and junior officers with rural backgrounds. Ishiwara Kanji, most formidable of the middle-level officers, foresaw world conquest by stages. Japan would seize Manchuria, and would then fight Russia, Britain, and the United States in turn. Each victory would bring Japan the resources needed for the next step: "war can maintain war." Ishiwara was no isolated dreamer; he had the ear of the army's chiefs. And the army, like its German counterpart during the Hindenburg-Ludendorff dictatorship,

Rivals for the mastery of China: Chiang Kai-shek (*above*) and Mao Zedong (*below*).

Mao Proposes a Peasant Revolution   1927

Mao's "Report on an Investigation of the Agrarian Movement in Hunan" of March 1927 was his earliest attempt to persuade his Party that it must either lead China's peasantry or succumb to it.

The force of the peasantry is like that of the raging winds and driving rain. It is rapidly increasing in violence. No force can stand in its way. The peasantry will tear apart all nets which bind it, and hasten along the road to liberation. They will bury beneath them all forces of imperialism, militarism, corrupt officialdom, village bosses and evil gentry. Every revolutionary party, every revolutionary comrade will be subjected to their scrutiny and be accepted or rejected by them. Shall we stand in the vanguard and lead them or stand behind them and oppose them? Every Chinese is free to pick his answer. However, destiny will force us to pick an answer soon. . . .

From Benjamin I. Schwartz, Chinese Communism and the Rise of Mao *(Cambridge: Harvard University Press, 1964), pp. 74–75.*

soon became the decisive force in the state, responsible only to a figurehead emperor.

Chiang's conquest of northern China almost coincided with the Depression. Together they triggered this explosive mixture. Chinese nationalist boycotts of Japanese goods, Chinese aspirations to regain full control of Manchuria, and the collapse of Japan's already stagnant peasant economy in the Depression drove the Japanese army officer corps to strike, to

The rising sun, 1931: Japanese infantry in Manchuria await the order to attack the Chinese.

secure Japan's vital Manchurian hinterland before it was too late. In September 1931, Ishiwara and a group of like-minded officers planted explosives on Japan's railway in Manchuria and blamed the Chinese. The army swiftly cleared Manchuria of Chinese forces and created the puppet state of Manchukuo. The navy attacked the Chinese at Shanghai and ruthlessly bombarded the Chinese quarters of the city—in front of Western newsreel cameras. The cabinet in Tokyo, divided and terrified of assassination, backed the army. When the League of Nations mildly criticized Japan in February 1933, the Japanese delegation stalked out, never to return.

The West failed to do anything effective, despite its outrage over Shanghai. Britain now faced the same unpleasant situation that Russian occupation of northern China had created in 1900. London could not realistically fight a great war to preserve distant China; no vital British interest was at stake. In 1901–02 London had therefore taken on Japan as junior partner. But now Japan itself was the threat, and its strength was far greater than in 1902. This time Britain's only potential allies were the Soviet Union and the United States. But the Soviets were as great a threat as Japan to British interests in China. And while Washington sternly refused to recognize Japan's conquest of Manchuria, it refused with equal sternness to back its moralistic talk with economic reprisals, much less with force. Britain therefore soothed the Japanese and attempted to limit the damage.

Japan made that difficult. Its navy began a massive new building program; in 1934 Japan withdrew from the Washington naval treaty. The elaborate structure of interwar naval disarmament came crashing down. Japanese politicians increasingly submitted to the demands of the military. Those slow to submit risked the fate suffered by prime minister Inukai Tsuyoshi in 1932: assassination. In 1936 junior officers, with the collaboration of Kita Ikki, launched a coup in Tokyo and slaughtered several ministers. The high command reasserted itself with loyal troops and executions.

That ended the day of junior officers and freelance ideologues. Senior generals such as Tōjō Hideki increasingly directed Japanese policy in rivalry with the admirals. And in July 1937 a brush with Guomindang forces near Beijing swiftly escalated into an open-ended China war. A militarized Japan, fighting under the unintentionally ironic slogan of "Asia for the Asians," sought to make China a Japanese colony. The first of the wars that ultimately converged to make the Second World War had begun.

THE THIRTIES: THE DEMOCRACIES FALTER

The Japanese threat caught the democracies just as the Depression and their own demoralization touched bottom. Japan's success soon emboldened others. Fascist Italy, the Germany of Adolf Hitler, and ultimately even the Soviet Union broke the peace (see pp. 833–54). They met little opposition until very late.

Britain: Highmindedness and Decline, 1931–37

The Depression destroyed Ramsay MacDonald's second Labour government, which had taken office in 1929. Labour, trembling at the displeasure of the financial markets and lacking imagination, met the Depression by imposing balanced budgets. That required cuts in unemployment payments and provoked a cabinet and labor-union revolt in the catastrophic month of August 1931. MacDonald stayed on at the head of a "National Coalition" with Liberal and Conservative backing; Labour went into opposition.

As in Lloyd George's coalition, the Conservatives were the dominant partner. Baldwin flattered Parliament and the public; Neville Chamberlain provided the efficiency and drive. He was Austen Chamberlain's unlovable and iron-willed younger brother, in Lloyd George's unkind words "a good mayor of Birmingham in an off-year." In 1935 an enfeebled MacDonald retired, and Baldwin led the Conservatives to victory over Labour by

pretending to block Italy's conquest of Ethiopia (see p. 837). Then Baldwin left his iron-clad House of Commons majority to Chamberlain in 1937.

By that point Britain's world position was precarious. Japan's thrust into Manchuria had moved London to scrap the "ten year rule" and create a committee to look into defense needs—but nothing more concrete. MacDonald, a quasi-pacifist during the First World War, delayed while the World Disarmament Conference met in 1932–34, just as the revolt of the discontented powers took shape. Not until March 1934, after the Conference's inevitable collapse, did the British cabinet begin to debate rearmament. And only Winston Churchill, ceaselessly harassing the cabinet from outside, viewed the German threat with any urgency. Conservative opinion considered Churchill "unsound" since his association with the Dardanelles fiasco in 1915 (which others had mismanaged). His fierce opposition to the government over independence for India had not enhanced his reputation.

Churchill Warns MacDonald and Baldwin 1932

On November 23, 1932, in the House of Commons, Churchill denounced MacDonald's continued pursuit of Western disarmament in the face of the growing German threat:

Do not delude yourselves. Do not let His Majesty's Government believe—I am sure they do not believe—that all Germany is asking for is equal status. . . . That is not what Germany is seeking. All these bands of sturdy Teutonic youths, marching through the streets and roads of Germany, with the light of desire in their eyes to suffer for their Fatherland, are not looking for status. They are looking for weapons, and, when they have the weapons, believe me they will then ask for the return of lost territories and lost colonies, and when that demand is made it cannot fail to shake and possibly shatter to their foundations every one of the countries I have mentioned [France, Belgium, Poland, Rumania, Czechoslovakia, Yugoslavia], and some other countries I have not mentioned. . . .

From Martin Gilbert, Winston S. Churchill, *Vol. V, 1922–1939.* The Prophet of Truth *(Boston: Houghton Mifflin, 1977), p. 451.*

Baldwin's sloth and Chamberlain's niggling defense of financial orthodoxy triumphed. Large-scale British rearmament did not begin until 1936–37. It was too little and too late.

France: Cynicism and Decline, 1932–37

Highminded professions of faith in the League and disarmament accompanied the decline of Britain. The French were more cynical. The only disarmament that interested them was that of Germany, which collapsed in 1932–33. Yet France did not react. The Depression struck France later than Britain or Germany, mainly because France was less industrialized. But it hit hard and kept hitting. Industrial production stagnated at between 80 and 90 percent of its 1928 level from 1931 to mid-1939 (see Figure 31-2). Economic stagnation worsened the central vice of French politics, ideological polarization. The Third Republic, always disorganized, began to totter.

The Communists polled a million votes in 1928 and had gained another half million by 1936. A further sharpening of Moscow's anti-Socialist line in 1928 pro

duced open war between French Communists and Socialists. That conflict stopped the Socialists from collaborating for long with the Radical-Socialists to their right, for fear of losing yet more voters and union members to the Communists. Nor were the deputies of the center numerous enough to command the Chamber. And alongside the old Right of the Dreyfus era and the "two hundred families" that supposedly controlled French industry, a new populist right emerged. The "Leagues," bands of trench-coated anti-Semitic thugs with lead pipes and revolvers, supported ideologies ranging from monarchism to extreme nationalist authoritarianism.

In January 1934, after two years of weak governments of the Left that rivaled the merry-go-round of 1925–26, one of the Republic's characteristic scandals erupted. A shady financier of eastern European extraction, Alexander Stavisky, committed suicide or was murdered after the exposure of frauds apparently committed with the backing of prominent politicians. The Republic seemed even less reputable than usual. On February 6, 1934, the Leagues attacked parliament while Communists rioted in the industrial suburbs of Paris. Police firepower saved the Republic amid

FIGURE 31-2   **Depression and Recovery: Failure and Success**
(Industrial Production as a Percentage of 1928 Production)

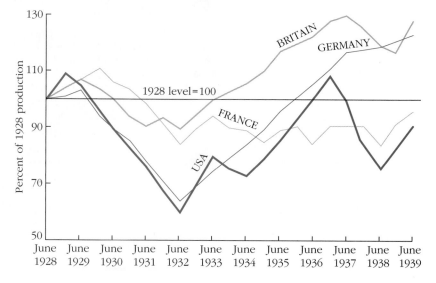

tension not seen in Paris since Boulanger and Dreyfus. The *"six février"* served notice that the Republic lived on borrowed time.

A change of line in Moscow gave the Left a second wind. In 1935 the Communist International, faced with the rise of Hitler's Germany, reversed its previous attempt to stamp out its Socialist rivals. In France the result was a "Popular Front" coalition of Radical-Socialists, Socialists, and Communists. Léon Blum, a vacillating Socialist intellectual, led the government that emerged from the Popular Front's election triumph of April–May 1936. Blum suppressed the Leagues. To the accompaniment of sit-in strikes and industrial turmoil he decreed paid vacations, the forty-hour week, and other concessions that French workers considered long overdue. Those restrictions on industry slowed rearmament and caused French investors to move their capital into harder currencies than the franc. Capital flight in turn brought Blum down in June 1937. The Left could win elections but could not govern.

Nor did Blum, torn between his own horror of war and the pressing need for rearmament to face Germany, find a coherent foreign policy. Not that the Right would have necessarily performed better; much of it mouthed the slogan "Better Hitler than Blum." Blum's foremost successor, Edouard Daladier, was a Radical of Napoleonic appearance but less than Napoleonic strength. His minister of finance, Paul Reynaud, saved the franc in the manner of Poincaré. But that success proved irrelevant. Under Daladier and Reynaud, France first abandoned its eastern allies, then itself collapsed.

The United States: Political Success and Economic Failure of the New Deal, 1933–38

Hoover appeared helpless as the economic fabric of the United States disintegrated. Stock prices continued to slide, wiping out much of the savings of a generation. By 1932, U.S. industrial production had dropped to half of its 1929 level. Only unemployment rose: from 5 million in December 1930 to 13 million in December 1932. The unemployed and their families sought refuge in shantytowns, named with bitter irony "Hoovervilles."

Hoover lost the 1932 election. His threadbare claims that prosperity was "just around the corner" were unconvincing. His spending on public works, although far greater than that of any previous administration, was not enough to spark the economy. His Democratic opponent, the New York grandee Franklin Delano Roosevelt, accepted the nomination with a pledge of a "new deal for the American people." But before Roosevelt could take office the overstrained banking system followed the rest of the economy, as panicked depositors stormed the tellers' windows. On inauguration day, March 4, 1933, Roosevelt shut the remaining banks before they collapsed. Capitalism itself seemed in ruins.

Roosevelt brought a short-term remedy that had eluded Hoover: force of conviction. "So first of all let me assert my firm belief that the only thing we have to fear is fear itself—nameless, unreasoning, unjustified terror . . . ," rang his presidential address. In a mere five days he pushed through Congress a Hoover plan to shore up the banks. In the first of a series of radio "fireside chats" that gave the nation back some of its lost self-confidence, he announced that the banks would reopen. By June 1933 he had averted the threat of total economic collapse. Industrial production briefly equaled the level of 1929.

Roosevelt and his "brain trust" of young intellectuals directed at Congress a torrent of legislation that established public works programs far more vast than those of Hoover and recruited the unemployed into a quasi-military Civilian Conservation Corps. The first New Deal administration created 6 million jobs. To raise agricultural prices, the government paid farmers not to plant crops. Government extended to farmers and householders some protection from the mortgage foreclosures that meant economic ruin and gave unemployment benefits to workers. Government ultimately guaranteed the right to organize unions and created the compulsory pension plan known as Social Security. And thanks to the free-

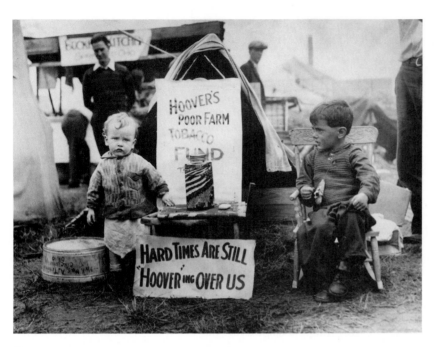

The impact of the Depression.

trade convictions of Roosevelt's otherwise ineffectual Secretary of State, Cordell Hull, U.S. trade barriers dropped after 1934. That was too late to save the fragmented world market—but better late than not at all.

The New Deal's European-style welfare-state measures seemed revolutionary—and aroused the bitter enmity of business interests. Soon the Republican establishment was denouncing Roosevelt as a "dictator" and traitor to his class. Labor, blacks, and most middle-class Americans took a different view. Roosevelt won his second term in 1936 by an unprecedented margin of 11 million votes; his Republican opponent carried only Maine and Vermont.

But stability and prosperity failed to return. Production briefly surpassed 1928 levels in 1936–37, then dropped again catastrophically (see Figure 31-2 on p. 814). By December 1937, the largest steel industry in the world was operating at 26 percent of capacity. Roosevelt had vastly increased the role of government in the economy—but until 1938 he held to the Hoover line of balanced budgets. Unfortunately, unbalanced budgets were precisely what the economy required to stimulate demand. Not until his 1938 recovery plan did Roosevelt halfheartedly endorse deficits. Necessity, not New Deal economic policies, led to recovery after 1939. Armament production for global war dragged the United States out of the Depression, just as the revolt of the discontented powers in Europe and Asia dragged it unwillingly back into world affairs.

THE AGE OF UNCERTAINTY: SCIENCE, SOCIETY, AND CULTURE BETWEEN TWO WARS

The twenty-year truce was not merely a time of demoralization for the democracies or of triumph for savage dictatorships—a theme taken up in the following chapter. It was also an era of disorienting intellectual, social, and cultural change. Science continued its rapid expansion of knowledge of the cosmos and of the building blocks of matter itself. Technology transformed everyday life. The state took on vast new duties. The war had accelerated the rise of workers' parties and the political, economic, and sexual emancipation of women. It had speeded the breakdown, among much else, of previous notions of what constituted art. A new writing, art, and architecture, reflecting disenchantment with the certainties of the pre-1914 era and rejection of the war, flourished. The mass culture born before the war reached maturity, especially in the United States, to the horror of many traditionalist intellectuals. And the war acted as catalyst for new and terrifying ideologies.

Science: The End of Certainty

By 1900, and still more by 1919, phenomena had emerged that were puzzling or inexplicable to physicists. Neither electromagnetism nor light precisely fitted the traditional Newtonian framework. Worse, the theorists soon had to cope with X rays (1895), radioactivity (1896), and Ernest Rutherford's 1911 discovery that atoms were not solid, as had been assumed since the first atomic theories had emerged in ancient Greece. Atoms apparently contained electrons, nuclei, and much empty space. A chemist discovered radioactive decay in 1913; uranium and thorium, it appeared, turned into lead. Atomic nuclei might contain additional particles.

Further experiment showed that the elements were not the unchangeable basic building blocks in which scientists had believed since the birth of modern chemistry in the eighteenth century. In 1919 Rutherford bombarded nitrogen with helium nuclei and produced oxygen. Researchers discovered neutrons and positrons in 1932 and 1933. The "cyclotron" or racetrack-like particle accelerator first proposed in 1932 allowed laboratory creation of the "transuranic" heavy elements. The first were neptunium and plutonium in 1940.

The theorists soon attempted to explain some of what the researchers were finding. Max Planck of Berlin suggested in 1900 that energy from warm bodies did not radiate at uniform levels across the spectrum but jumped in steps or *quanta;* the amount of energy released varied with its wavelength. Albert Einstein, at that point an obscure patent examiner in Switzerland, suggested in 1905 that light too was "quantized." Niels Bohr of Denmark applied the quantum concept in 1913 to Rutherford's new atom and explained both atomic structure and the differing spectra that various elements emitted. In 1927 Werner Heisenberg of Leipzig, in the course of researches on quantum theory, suggested that the very act of measuring the position, velocity, or mass of a particle interacted with the particle, introducing uncertainty into the measurement. Prediction of the action of subatomic particles fell back on mere statistics—a most un-Newtonian and disquieting state of affairs.

By that point Einstein had established the theory of relativity, the foundation, along with quantum theory, of modern physics. In 1905, in a paper that outlined his "Special Theory of Relativity," Einstein asserted that time and space were not absolute entities, as Newtonian physics required; rather, they varied relative to the observer's velocity and location. The only absolute in Einstein's new universe was the speed of light—186,300 miles per second—which was the absolute limit of velocity. Mass increased with velocity, and mass, multiplied by a constant squared, was equivalent to energy: $E = mc^2$. That fateful notion as yet lacked empirical confirmation.

By 1916 Einstein had incorporated gravitation into his theory, which now became the "General Theory of Relativity." And in 1919 an eclipse permitted the first confirmation of the General Theory. Starlight passing through the sun's gravitational field bent by the amount Einstein's theory predicted. Newton's tidy universe gave way to a four-dimensional and curved "space-time continuum." Attempts to unify the General Theory of Relativity with quantum theory, and to explain everything from gravitation to the birth and death of the cosmos and the ever-expanding world of subatomic particles, soon followed.

It also emerged that Einstein's insights had dramatic practical application. In January 1939, building on work by Niels Bohr, Enrico Fermi, and others, Otto Hahn and Fritz Strassmann of Berlin announced that they had split the nuclei of uranium atoms by bombarding them with neutrons. The process transmuted the uranium into barium and a small amount of the uranium's original mass into an astounding amount of energy, as Einstein's formula suggested. The race to create a self-sustaining atomic chain reaction—and weapons of unprecedented destructive power—began.

Biology and medicine experienced the same accelerated pace of advance that was visible in physics. Even before the First World War, the first crude antibiotics—organic poisons that killed disease organisms but not their human hosts—had appeared. Salvarsan, an arsenic compound that revolutionized the treatment of syphilis, became available as early as 1909. The sulfonamides, effective against pneumonia and gangrene, followed in 1935–38. Penicillin emerged in the laboratory in 1929; its first medical use in 1940 proved it startlingly effective against a wide range of diseases and infections.

Advances in immunization had in 1914–18 at least spared western Europe

Giant of the new physics: Albert Einstein in Berlin, 1920.

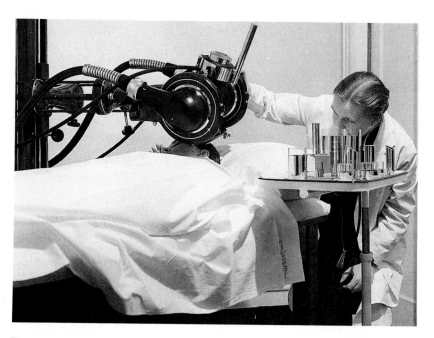

The beginnings of radiation therapy: X-ray treatment for skin cancer, 1930.

the typhoid epidemics that had accompanied previous great wars. In the interwar period inoculations for diphtheria, yellow fever, typhus, and bubonic plague became available. The discovery of hormones, such as insulin (1922) and cortisone (1936), permitted the development of therapies for previously untreatable conditions such as diabetes. The identification and isolation of vitamins helped eradicate deficiency diseases such as pellagra. Thanks to improvements in blood typing, transfusions became normal procedure after 1940. And insecticides, especially DDT (1939), showed promise of eliminating insect carriers of disease. For the Germans, who first developed them, the new insecticides also showed promise of another sort. In 1936 the great German chemical trust, I. G. Farben, began a crash program to develop, from a family of insecticides that killed by disrupting nerve impulses, a weapon for use against humans: the first nerve gas.

Technology: Steel, Oil, and Electricity

The war and the interwar period accelerated dramatic changes in materials and energy sources that were already under

way. Steel remained king, thanks to a bewildering variety of new stainless or extremely hard alloys with metals such as chromium, vanadium, tungsten, nickel, and molybdenum. Concrete, reinforced with steel rods, came into its own as a structural material that permitted the most astounding architectural shapes. Aluminum, refined with electric power, found its way into everything from aircraft to cooking pots. Plastics developed rapidly; by 1939 they provided transparent canopies and windows for aircraft and flexible insulation for electrical cables. Synthetic rubber, another German innovation, became vitally important both to Germany and to the United States after 1939. Artificial fibers such as rayon made possible garments even less expensive than cotton. But artificial yarns made from wood or cellulose fibers were only the first step. In the 1930s the first truly synthetic fiber, derived from oil, became available— nylon. Its great strength made it ideal for everything from stockings to parachutes.

In the realm of energy sources, oil and electricity now triumphed. The First World War had made demands for transport that only the internal combustion engine could meet, and had immensely accelerated motorization. Trucks, tanks, and tractors supplemented and in many cases replaced the horse. Oil-fired high-compression steam turbines or diesel engines replaced clumsy coal, which required stokers and prevented refueling at sea. By the mid-1920s aircraft had ceased to be underpowered kite-like objects of wood, cloth, and wire. By the early 1930s the first multi-engine all-metal airliners were carrying passengers rich and daring enough to try them. Even humanity's oldest form of combustion-propelled projectile revived. In 1926 the visionary Robert Goddard developed the first practical liquid-fueled rocket. His work attracted little attention in his native United States, but observers in Russia and Germany found it intriguing.

Electricity revolutionized communications and created new mass media: motion pictures, sound recordings, radio, and television. Motion-picture technology originated in the 1890s in the United States and France; by 1914 "movie houses" were common. Record players and radios, thanks to Lee DeForest's triode amplifier tube (1906–07), were widespread by 1928, the year of the first "talkie." Television—images electronically scanned, transmitted by radio, and displayed on a cathode ray tube—emerged in U.S. and British laboratories in the mid-1920s, although it did not reach the public for another two decades.

Electronics had more deadly uses: the detection of submarines by sound ranging (sonar) and especially of aircraft and surface ships by radio ranging (radar). After 1935 Britain and Germany raced one another for mastery over those vital auxiliaries to air and sea warfare. As the interwar truce ended, science was developing a potential it had not possessed in 1914: the potential to decide the outcome of war between great powers.

The State in Crisis

The First World War ended for good the state that governed best by governing least. The state now took responsibility for guaranteeing the survival and welfare of the individual. Prewar programs such as old-age pensions and industrial-accident insurance expanded. Unemployment benefits became law. In Germany, workers briefly gained a state-sanctioned voice in management decisions. The United States of Coolidge and Hoover resisted such allegedly socialist measures; then Roosevelt adopted many of them.

The war had also introduced management of currency and foreign exchange, and vast bureaucracies to plan investment and allocate raw materials. Peace had dismantled that planning machinery, but the example of the Hindenburg Program lived on in the Soviet Union (see pp. 830–32). The Depression, a crisis in some ways more severe than the war, gave the state back its wartime role—in "peacetime." The state grudgingly took responsibility for the fate of the economy.

Most democracies adopted some kind of economic planning. But as Roosevelt's confused experiments suggest, they lacked a theory. In 1936, John Maynard

Keynes at last provided a theory for an era in which *laissez-faire* appeared to lead ever deeper into depression. In his *General Theory of Employment, Interest, and Money*, Keynes argued that government deficit financing—the creation of money by decree—was the obvious antidote to deflation and unemployment. Government spending put people to work; their spending, through the "multiplier effect," put others to work. Ideas require time to penetrate, and Keynes's arrived too late. The old orthodoxy dominated as late as 1937, when a tax increase and a tightening of the money supply produced a renewed economic nosedive in the United States. To recover, Roosevelt adopted by trial and error a mild version of deficit financing. Within a decade, Keynes's theories had become conventional wisdom, the charter for continuous state management of market economies.

Workers: Expectations Disappointed

At the outbreak of war in 1914, Britain's Liberal foreign secretary, Sir Edward Grey, dolefully foretold its political and social consequences: "There will be Labour governments everywhere after this." Britain, France, and Weimar Germany indeed received governments led or dominated by workers' parties. But those governments, and the labor unions that supported them, operated under severe limitations.

First, the workers were themselves divided. Regional and craft quarrels fractured the unions of Britain and the United States; racial and ethnic lines also divided U.S. workers. On the Continent, Communists sought to destroy Socialists in the unions as well as in the political arena. In Germany, as described in Chapter 32, the Communist offensive after 1928 helped kill the Weimar Republic; both Socialist and Communist parties perished in the common ruin.

Second, the Depression dramatically lowered worker morale. Especially in Europe, it weakened the main weapon of industrial workers, the strike. Few can strike when one worker in four has no job. Finally, industrial workers, contrary to the predictions of Marx, found themselves in the minority in advanced capitalist societies. Except in egalitarian Scandinavia, political parties claiming to represent workers consistently failed to achieve more than a third of the vote. Insuperable social and ideological barriers prevented further growth—a profoundly demoralizing situation.

If workers accepted democratic rules, socialism was clearly impossible, for the "bourgeoisie" would hardly vote its own demise. But if the workers chose the path of revolution, the other two-thirds of society, with the help of the state apparatus, would inevitably crush them. That threat and the moderate instincts of western Europe's social democrats forced unions and workers' parties in the interwar period to fight a "war of position"—a trench struggle for gradual reform of the economic system rather than for its overthrow. Given their minority status, workers' parties that did achieve power rarely governed long. In the Depression many even failed to prevent their political opponents from reducing unemployment benefits and state employee salaries.

Women: New Predicaments for Old

Women in Britain, Germany, Scandinavia, and the United States likewise discovered that the vote and the workings of the political system changed their lives only slowly. Giving women the vote prevented a repetition of the prewar confrontations in Britain. It channeled women's political activities into the existing parties. It helped women's groups to lobby for full equality before the law and for legislation protecting mothers and children. But the onset of the Depression and the coming of a new war soon diverted politically active women from "women's issues" to more general ones.

Many countries, among them France, Italy, Belgium, and Switzerland, did not even give women the vote, thanks to the weight of male opinion and of the Church. And women's economic position between the wars was even more precarious than that of men. Demobilization of the mass armies and conversion to peacetime pro-

duction led to mass dismissals of women from industry. Structural changes—the continuing decline of peasant agriculture and of "mom and pop" retailing—likewise narrowed women's employment possibilities.

But women were unwilling to give up their new-found economic independence. Many had no choice: their husbands were dead. The interwar growth of business bureaucracies and of that temple of consumer goods, the department store, offered a substitute for industrial employment. Women entered the professions at a greater rate than before, especially in the United States, Britain, and Scandinavia. They maintained their positions in fields such as nursing, primary-school teaching, and librarianship. They nevertheless usually received less money than men—for the same work.

In one vital area the interwar period was the scene of truly dramatic change—control of reproduction. During and immediately after the war, pioneers such as the American Margaret Sanger (1883–1966) and Englishwoman Marie Stopes (1880–1958) made contraceptive information available to a mass audience for the first time in human history. A Dutch invention, the diaphragm, joined the condom, an eighteenth-century device popularized—like cigarettes—in the First World War.

Women thus for the first time acquired effective means to determine when and by whom they had children. Improved childbirth techniques and nutrition ensured that fewer of those children died. Fewer children in turn meant that the average woman now spent four years or less—instead of fifteen or more—pregnant or nursing. That historic achievement allowed some women, for the first time, to aspire to have both a career and a family.

Most men still objected. And the new science of the mind offered small improvement over nineteenth-century medical notions of female inferiority. In Freud's view, woman's unconscious yearning for a penis allegedly led her to seek a penis-substitute: babies. Above all, the course of interwar politics menaced emancipated women; Fascists and Nazis sought to crush all challenges to male su-

Margaret Sanger, pioneer of birth control for the masses, about to appear in court (1917).

premacy. The mission of the allegedly "inferior sex of the master race" was to breed large broods of heroes. But even those regimes failed to reverse the decline of the birth rate brought by industrialization and accelerated by contraception.

The High Culture of Disenchantment

The war broke down inhibitions in literature and art as well as in life. William II had insisted that "an art that transgresses the laws and barriers recognized by me ceases to be an art." Now he was gone; censorship, both formal and informal, diminished in intensity throughout northern Europe. Avant-garde literary and artistic trends that had originated before 1914 now became dominant, at least in high culture.

The prevailing mood was one of disenchantment. The war was the formative experience of an entire generation. Its apparent futility marked their writing, especially in highminded Britain, where the sordid brutality of war had come as a greater shock than elsewhere. British "war poets," including Wilfred Owen and Siegfried Sassoon, wrote eloquent verse that damned the war and the western front. The peculiar conditions of the war, the stark contrast between apparently futile slaughter at the front and almost complete safety beyond artillery range, engendered a fierce hatred of all symbols of authority. Sassoon, a highly decorated officer, railed with particular bitterness at generals, staffs, politicians, and civilians. French war writing, especially *Under Fire* (1917) by Henri Barbusse, who later became a Communist, reflected France's immense losses. Even German war literature occasionally sounded a despondent note, as in Erich Maria Remarque's *All Quiet on the Western Front* (1929).

But Germany was different from the West. There, heroic nihilists of the Ernst Jünger stamp dominated. Works such as *Battle as an Inner Experience* (1922) and *Fire and Blood* (1925) convinced the German young that they had missed something. Jünger spoke or claimed to speak for his generation: "War, the father of all

things, is also our father; it has hammered, hewn, and tempered us into what we are. And so long as the spinning wheel of life turns within us, this war will be the axis about which it whirls."

In England, the aesthetes of the "Bloomsbury Group" devoted themselves to the destruction of what little remained of Victorian morality in their own private lives. Freud appeared to suggest that conventional morality was an elaborate hypocritical cloak over unconfessable desires. He appeared to legitimate not merely confessing those desires, but advertising and gratifying them as well. And his doctrines were an inexhaustible source of small talk. Freud's works now became a popular success.

Bloomsbury also attacked the symbols of Victorianism. Lytton Strachey's *Eminent Victorians* (1918), with its inaccurate but compelling demolitions of Florence Nightingale, "Chinese" Gordon, and other British national totems, was an instant success. John Maynard Keynes, a Bloomsburyite by adoption, atoned for his guilt— in Bloomsbury's eyes—at having worked for the government during the war by savaging his former chief, Lloyd George, in *The Economic Consequences of the Peace* (1919).

In poetry, two transplanted Americans and an Irishman—T. S. Eliot (1888–1965), Ezra Pound (1885–1972), and William Butler Yeats (1865–1939)—gave English poetry a modern shape that ultimately derived from the French Symbolists: loose in structure and playing on layer upon layer of symbolism and allusion to mythology and literature. Eliot's greatest work, a manifesto for the new English poetry, was *The Waste Land* (1922). Its bleak vision of London and modern life as Dante's *Inferno* fitted precisely the postwar mood among intellectuals:

> *Unreal City,*
> *Under the brown fog of a winter*
>   *dawn,*
> *A crowd flowed over London Bridge, so*
>   *many,*
> *I had not thought death had undone*
>   *so many.*

Pound, more difficult and allusive even than Eliot, eventually succumbed to an obsessive anti-Semitism and took Fascist Italy as his adopted country. Yeats, like the others, wove symbols and bizarre occult or cosmological references into his poems. But he also wrote some of the most lucid and musical English verses of the twentieth century, such as the famous lines of "The Second Coming" (1921) that prophesied the triumph of political barbarism:

Things fall apart; the centre cannot
   hold;
Mere anarchy is loosed upon the
   world,
The blood-dimmed tide is loosed, and
   everywhere
The ceremony of innocence is
   drowned;
The best lack all conviction, while the
   worst
Are full of passionate intensity.

In the novel, a new technique, the "stream of consciousness," prevailed briefly. Marcel Proust pioneered it in his monumental *Remembrance of Things Past* (1913–27), in which he abandoned narrative in favor of an apparent reconstruction of the thoughts and memories of the novel's protagonist. Virginia Woolf, the one great literary talent of Bloomsbury, experimented with it. But its greatest master was the Irish expatriate, James

Joyce. His *Ulysses* (1921) was a minute reconstruction of a day in the life of a Dublin salesman, Leopold Bloom, organized around themes from Homer's *Odyssey*. Its occasional passages about sex at first prevented it from appearing in England or the United States, much less in Ireland. Banning, and its spread through copies smuggled from Paris, only enhanced its reputation. It was the most influential English novel of the century. In its sequel, *Finnegan's Wake* (1939), Joyce pushed his language beyond comprehensibility and left his audience behind.

On the Continent, Thomas Mann confirmed his position, acquired before the war, as Germany's greatest living man of letters. His monumental symbolic novel, *The Magic Mountain* (1924), was an ambiguous saga of good and evil that conveyed despair in the power of reason in human affairs. Despair in reason was a step forward for Mann. During the war, he had actively urged the rejection of reason, democratic politics, and the West in a massive tract entitled *Reflections of an Unpolitical Man* (1918).

German writers of the "Expressionist" school experimented with a drama of unbridled emotion, Freudian symbolism, and Left politics. Expressionist sons messily murdered their fathers and the other figures of authority discredited by the lost war. The greatest talents of the school were Bertolt Brecht (1898–1956), and the novelist and short-story writer Franz Kafka (1883–1926). Brecht soon exchanged Expressionism for Leninism. Kafka constructed a symbolic world in which fear, guilt, and merciless, incomprehensible forces torture the isolated individual. Kafka's novella, *The Metamorphosis* (1915), sums up Kafka's view of humanity's fate in the modern world. His hero, Gregor Samsa, wakes up one morning and discovers that he has inexplicably become a giant cockroach.

In the visual arts and architecture, new schools multiplied. The Great War slaked Italian Futurism's thirst for violence and change; Futurism emerged enfeebled. "Dada," a Parisian fashion of the teens and twenties, poked fun at art itself and celebrated the absurd and the unpredict-

The Bauhaus school of architecture and design, Dessau, Germany (1926).

able. Its progeny, "Surrealism," sought to represent inner reality in paintings strewn with half-melted pocket watches and Freudian symbols. The center of excitement in the visual arts moved briefly from Paris to Berlin and Munich, thanks to Expressionist masters such as Paul Klee (1879–1940). And in architecture, Walter Gropius, Mies van der Rohe, Bruno Taut, and others secured the first large-scale commissions for the new functional architecture, the "international style." The architects at least were optimists; they sought to remake humanity by remaking its environment. That was too ambitious a project—but they did revolutionize architecture and design.

Mass Culture and Its Critics

One source, beside the shock of the great war, of the despondency that afflicted many intellectuals in the 1920s was the appalling discovery that this was indeed the "age of the masses." A variety of German thinkers stigmatized democracy as the "rule of the inferior." Ortega y Gasset, a Spanish philosopher and literary critic, won immediate fame with his denunciation of *The Revolt of the Masses* (1929). Ortega complained that the unwashed legions, half-educated through universal primary schooling and given power through the vote, were besieging the citadel of Western civilization. The liberal elites born in the nineteenth century had ceased to lead; chaos had resulted.

The reason for that failure of leadership was obscure to Ortega. But it was plain enough. Liberals deplored as an affront to their own cultural standards or to human dignity the methods seemingly needed to exert leadership. Others were less squeamish. Georges Sorel, the pre-1914 French seer of revolution, had developed the concept of "political myths" that mobilized the masses. The French psychologist Gustave Le Bon (1841–1931) had argued that "the crowd" was "feminine" and had claimed that it demanded the domination of a charismatic male. In the Anglo-Saxon countries, vast engines of publicity sold everything from soap to vacuum cleaners to wartime hatred of "the

Hun." The foremost characteristic of the operators of that machinery was their contempt for the public they manipulated.

The "age of the masses" was thus to be an age of emotion, not reason. Advertising used the same techniques to sell a charismatic leader or a Lucky Strike. New media such as film, radio, and illustrated magazines proved especially effective at conveying and appealing to emotion. Politics in Fascist Italy and in Germany after 1933 took on quasi-religious overtones as vast regimented throngs hailed their leaders.

What most critics of interwar mass culture forgot was that, historically speaking, the alternative to semiliteracy had been no literacy at all. Until the nineteenth century only narrow elites had fully enjoyed the written word. Its extension to the majority of the population inevitably involved a lowering of standards, by the standards of the elite. But that was not the end of the world. One answer to semiliteracy was better mass education. Nor was the thrust of the mass market toward the lowest common denominator an all-encompassing and uniform thrust.

The continuing rise in living standards, except during the Depression, did not only foster mediocrity and uniformity. It also permitted excellence and diversity. Bauhaus architecture and design was a genuine popular success. In film, German directors before 1933 created popular successes that were also works of art. Even Hollywood, which established an absolute dominance over the world film industry in the 1930s, occasionally made movies that were not totally frivolous. And in politics, as Roosevelt's radio talks demonstrated, genuine democrats could mobilize a mass public as effectively as the new barbarians.

The Revolt against Reason

War and Depression unleashed those barbarians. In Germany above all, defeat and revolution made anti-Semitic conspiracy theories seem plausible to a wide audience. The wartime propaganda of Tirpitz's *Vaterlandspartei* against the West, the Left, and the Jews found its logical continuation in scores of radical nationalist prophets and sects.

An eccentric Munich schoolmaster, Oswald Spengler (1880–1936), provided a pseudo-historical justification for the new barbarism of the racists and of the visionaries of "soldierly nationalism" such as Jünger. In the summer of 1918, Spengler published the first volume of a turgid 900-page work entitled *The Collapse of the West*. For Spengler, history was a vast cyclical process in which civilizations, the products of creative minorities of Nietzschean supermen, rose, decayed, and collapsed. The West was nearing the end of its cycle. Amid chaos and the brutal self-assertion of new creative minorities, a new civilization might soon be born.

As history, Spengler's grandiose vision was oddly compelling although sometimes laughably distorted. As prophecy it proved almost self-fulfilling. The book's coincidence with Germany's defeat ensured its success. To many Germans, war and an unwanted revolution indeed seemed like the collapse of civilization. And in ensuing years, in works such as *Prussianism and Socialism* (1920) and "The Political Duties of German Youth" (1924), Spengler spelled out in detail the ruthless commitment he thought the new age demanded.

German philosophy added its authority to the chorus of unreason. Nietzsche had denounced Judeo-Christian values as a "slave morality" and had subordinated all morality to "life." His most prominent successor, Martin Heidegger (1889–1976), altogether denied that moral values had a rational basis. In Heidegger's *Being and Time* (1927), the individual was utterly alone, imprisoned in time. The only certainties were *Angst* (usually translated, too strongly, as "dread") and death. Only by living in full awareness of *Angst* and death could a select few define themselves and live "authentically"—a claim that ironically smacked of moral judgment.

This quest for authenticity—in a world where values apparently have no foundation or validity outside the individual—had curious consequences. It often led to self-affirmation through radical poli-

tics: the more radical, the more self-affirming. Heidegger himself made his choice in 1933. Academic freedom, he announced in his inaugural speech as rector of Freiburg University, was "inauthentic." Like Spengler, he enthusiastically urged German youth to serve German radical nationalism and a great leader. Unlike Spengler, Heidegger had a specific leader in mind—Adolf Hitler.

Others chose different leaders. Bertolt Brecht and the literary critic György Lukács (1885–1971) picked Stalin, to whom Lukács made embarrassing obeisance. Lukács's commitment to an irrational political faith did not make him self-conscious; he later wrote an entire volume lovingly demolishing German "irrationalism" from the romantics to Heidegger and Hitler. Brecht, in one of his Depression plays, used his unmatched command of German to celebrate the omniscience and ruthlessness of the Leninist "vanguard of the masses" in verses that the German Communist Party found excessively enthusiastic and frank.

Even in strongholds of middle-class values such as Britain and the United States, the war, the Depression, and the crises of the 1930s prompted intellectuals to irrational enthusiasms. Freud, although he claimed to be a rationalist, undermined reason through his faith in the overwhelming power of the savage forces he saw in the unconscious mind. Those who nevertheless retained a faith in "progress" and reason tended to lean leftward. Lincoln Steffens, a crusading American journalist, returned in 1919 from Russia with a jubilant announcement: "I have been over into the future, and it works!" He was the first of many. Widespread loss of faith in the future of Western society engendered an irrational desire to believe in progress *somewhere*. Visiting Western liberals noisily embraced the Soviet Union and resolutely ignored all evidence that contradicted the facade behind which their jolly Soviet hosts hid the reality of mass executions and starvation. In the mid-1930s American Communism successfully wooed some ˜disenchanted liberals; it claimed to be "twentieth-century Americanism."

War and Depression together created a disorienting and demoralizing world. Empires fell. Political and social landmarks crumbled. Religious, moral, political, and even scientific certainties undermined in the nineteenth century now collapsed. An exaggerated faith in the power of reason gave way to the fanatical celebration and cynical manipulation of emotion. The "best," the defenders of Western civilization and of democracy, lacked the conviction to squarely face the "passionate intensity" of their enemies, the nationalist-racist and Marxist-Leninist dictatorships. The 1920s were no golden age, even in western Europe. The 1930s opened with war in East Asia. They closed with the greatest war in history.

Suggestions for Further Reading

Interwar Politics

For a good introduction to interwar Europe, see especially R. J. Sontag, *A Broken World, 1919–1939* (1971). S. Marks, *The Illusion of Peace, International Relations in Europe, 1918–1933* (1976), is excellent on the peace settlement and its aftermath; for eastern Europe see C. A. Macartney and A. W. Palmer, *Independent Eastern Europe* (1962). On Britain, A. J. P. Taylor, *English History, 1914–1945* (1965), is highly readable, but see also M. Muggeridge, *The Thirties* (1940) and G. Orwell, *The Road to Wigan Pier* and *Down and Out in Paris and London.* On France, see especially P. Bernard and H. Dubief, *The Decline* of the Third Republic, 1914–1938 (1985), and A. Adamthwaite, *France and the Coming of the Second World War* (1977). On the United States, W. E. Leuchtenburg, *The Perils of Prosperity, 1914–1932* (1958), is still rewarding, but see also E. W. Hawley, *The Great War and the Search for a Modern Order* (1979); for the 1930s, R. S. McElwaine, *The Great Depression: America, 1929–1941* (1984), is excellent. A. J. Nicholls, *Weimar and the Rise of Hitler* (1968), and E. Kolb, *The Weimar Republic* (1988), offer useful summaries of Germany's brief democratic experiment.

The Great Depression

For the causes and course of the Great Depression, J. K. Galbraith, *The Great Crash, 1929* (1955), and C. Kindleberger, *The World in Depression, 1929–1939* (1973), are useful; D. Landes, *The Unbound Prometheus* (1972), places the event in long-term perspective. For events in the colonial empires, see especially E. Monroe, *Britain's Moment in the Middle East, 1914–1956* (1963); A. Williams, *Britain and France in the Middle East and North Africa, 1914–1967* (1968); B. N. Pandey, *The Break-up* of British India (1969); and J. M. Brown, *Modern India: the Origins of an Asian Democracy* (1985). On China, see J. K. Fairbank, *The Great Chinese Revolution, 1800–1985* (1986) and *The Cambridge History of China,* vol. 12, part I (1983), and J. E. Sheridan, *China in Disintegration* (1975). For Japan, see especially W. G. Beasley, *Japanese Imperialism, 1894–1945* (1987), and J. B. Crowley, *Japan's Quest for Autonomy* (1966).

Culture between Two World Wars

On the intellectual impact of the war, see the wonderful M. Eksteins, *Rites of Spring: The Great War and the Birth of the Modern Age* (1989); also R. Wohl, *The Generation of 1914* (1979). For the sharp contrast between Germany and the West, compare the German outlook depicted in E. Jünger, *The Storm of Steel* (1920; tr. 1929), with that of the writers discussed in P. Fussell, *The Great War and Modern Memory* (1975). For Germany's decisive contributions to interwar high culture, see especially P. Gay, *Weimar Culture* (1968); J. Willett, *Art and Politics in the Weimar Period: The New Sobriety, 1917–1933* (1979); and B. M. Lane, *Architecture and Politics in Germany, 1918–1945* (1968). For the many interwar intellectuals who despaired of their own societies and sought consolation in Moscow, see P. Hollander, *Political Pilgrims: the Travels of Western Intellectuals to the Soviet Union, China, and Cuba, 1928–1978* (1981).

-32-

THE TOTALITARIAN STATES

*B*y 1933 the demoralized democracies faced not only a militant Japan but three great dictatorships: the Soviet Union of Joseph Stalin, the Fascist Italy of Benito Mussolini, and the National Socialist Germany of Adolf Hitler. Dictatorship was not new. Lenin, an expert, defined it as "a power that is not limited by any laws, not bound by any rules, and based directly on force." Despots from the god-emperors of the ancient world to the tsars of Russia had ruled without laws or rules that limited the sovereign. But custom, the merciful inefficiency of their bureaucracies, and the inadequacies of the technologies at their command had limited their power.

Robespierre and the Committee of Public Safety had briefly wielded, in the name of the General Will, power more total than that of any preceding European state. Now, in the twentieth century, war and revolution made possible the perfection of the dictatorship of the General Will sketched out in 1793–94. It soon acquired a name. Giovanni Amendola, an Italian liberal later murdered by the thugs of the Italian dictatorship, coined in 1923–24 the adjective *"totalitario"* to describe Fascist election methods. Mussolini happily plagiarized it in 1925; he relished its brutal sound.

"Totalitarianism" thus became a generic term for the dictatorship of the age of mass politics, a dictatorship that set itself a limitless goal: *total power over the individual*. That goal distinguished it from traditional despotisms, and from "authoritarian" regimes such as the dictatorships of interwar eastern Europe or Latin America, which sought mainly to preserve their power. The totalitarian states sought instead to create a "new man," to remodel humanity. And their external goals were

(OPPOSITE) TOTALITARIAN RITUAL: ADOLF HITLER *(FRONT RANK, CENTER)* PAYS HOMAGE TO HIS PARTY'S DEAD ON THE FIFTEENTH ANNIVERSARY OF THE 1923 "BEER HALL PUTSCH."

almost equally limitless, for the example of freedom anywhere was a mortal threat for all such regimes.

Yet the three regimes were far from identical, despite their habit of imitating one another and their ultimate cooperation in launching the Second World War. Russia, the only Marxist-Leninist state of the three, was also the most economically and socially backward. Russia's middle class was small and its Orthodox Church relatively weak even before the Bolsheviks decided to exterminate the one and virtually abolish the other. Bolshevik power came from victory in a merciless civil war; from the beginning it rested "directly on force." Lenin and his successor Stalin faced none of the constitutional or social obstacles to total power present in the more developed societies of the West.

Mussolini and Hitler, by contrast, came to power with apparent legality in societies that had parliamentary regimes. They faced mighty entrenched interests and institutions—armies, industrialists, and churches—whose assistance was necessary for the consolidation and expansion of their power. In Russia the regime was free from birth to begin the total transformation of Russian society accomplished by the late 1930s. All it lacked was an implacable will. Stalin supplied that. In Italy and Germany the dictators had to buy their freedom. The method they chose was war.

RUSSIA: FROM REVOLUTION TO GENOCIDE

From Tsarist to Communist Autocracy

Within five years of the collapse of tsarism in 1917, Russia was once again an autocracy. After October 1917, Lenin systematically crushed all opposition—the short-lived Constitutional Assembly, the other left-wing parties, and the counter-revolutionary "Whites." The grass-roots workers' Soviets withered; the secret police (CHEKA) swelled to 30,000 and the Red Army to 5.3 million. Soon all that remained of the workers' Soviets was the name, which the Party took over for its new state: the Union of Soviet Socialist Republics.

The Bolsheviks defeated the Whites by 1921, only to face economic crisis and internal revolt. War, revolution, and civil war had cost Russia more than 10 percent of its 1913 population of 159 million. At least 2 million had died in the First World War, a million had emigrated, up to 10 million had died in the civil war and accompanying famines, and as many as 5 million had perished in drought and famine in 1921–22. Between 1917 and 1920, food shortages, Bolshevik brutality and mismanagement, and civil-war chaos had cut Russia's "proletariat" in half, from 3 million to 1.5 million. The industrial work force, recently recruited from the peasantry, simply returned to its villages. The peasantry itself fiercely resented the ruthless Bolshevik confiscation of crops to feed the cities. Externally, defeat in Poland in 1920 and the failure of world revolution to materialize meant isolation and apparent danger.

In February 1921 strikes against the self-proclaimed "workers' state" swept Petrograd. In March, sailors at Kronstadt, the nearby naval base that had once furnished fanatical recruits to Bolshevism, rose against Bolshevism on behalf of the half-starved remnant of Russia's workers. Millions of peasants in central Russia were already in armed revolt against the exactions of "war communism," the forced requisition of food. The regime appeared close to collapse.

Lenin and the Party acted. Mass arrests clamped Petrograd down. Trotsky besieged Kronstadt and annihilated the sailors at the cost of 10,000 Red Army casualties. Lenin outlawed "factionalism" in the Party and attacked those comrades who still took seriously the Party's claim to represent the *existing* Russian proletariat. In the Party's eyes, those workers and Kronstadt sailors who demanded free elections to the Soviets had ceased to be proletarians.

To placate the peasantry, the only great social group the Party was not yet strong enough to crush by force alone, Lenin and his associates retreated from "war communism." The "new economic policy" or NEP of 1921–28 restored some free enterprise to the countryside and even to industry. It was a recognition of reality—external isolation and internal weakness—that ended for the moment Lenin's attempt to force the pace of history and leap directly from tsarism to Communism.

The NEP was an economic success. Agricultural production passed 1913 levels in 1924. Enterprising peasants prospered. By 1926–27 even the cities had begun to revive. But the NEP proved a brief respite. In May 1922, Lenin suffered the first of a series of deadly strokes. In January 1924 he died. By that point the struggle for the succession had already begun: Trotsky was the leading candidate. But his Menshevik past, Red Army ties, and lack of modesty alienated a fiercely clannish Party that feared "Bonapartism"—the rule of a successful general. Trotsky's rival was a self-effacing bureaucrat from Georgia in the Caucasus, Joseph Stalin, a former seminary pupil and revolutionary bank robber. Lenin had placed Stalin in charge of the central Party machine, and thus of recruitment. Stalin soon allied himself with Trotsky's rivals on the Party "Left," Grigorii Zinoviev and Lev Kamenev.

Stalin craftily cloaked his ambition in mock humility and easily deflected Lenin's dying demand that the Party demote the uncouth Georgian, who was "too rude," a fault "insupportable in a general secretary." Stalin's foolish allies from the "Left" found him less threatening than Trotsky. And the new Party rank and file with whom Stalin was rapidly swamping the "Old Bolsheviks" owed their careers to him alone.

Stalin was careful to speak in the name of the Party, while consolidating his own power. Since Lenin had forbidden "factionalism," opponents of Stalin automatically became opponents of the Party. They forfeited both legitimacy and self-confidence; Stalin used the Party's cult of unity against them to force humiliating recantations and "self-criticisms." The CHEKA, renamed GPU, then OGPU, and finally NKVD, became Stalin's ally and in-

Trotsky, victorious Commissar for War, reviews his troops (1920).

strument; it soon overshadowed the Party. And Stalin had Lenin embalmed and placed on exhibit as a holy relic of the new state religion: "Leninism." Petrograd became Leningrad; all across the Soviet Union statues of the prophet arose. The cult of Lenin legitimated Bolshevik power and created the role that Stalin himself was soon to fill.

In 1925 Zinoviev and Kamenev led the attack on Trotsky, and expelled him from his Party and army offices. In 1926 Stalin turned on his allies and in turn demoted them with the help of the Party "Right" formed around the theorist Nikolai Bukharin. Trotsky had urged continued conflict: "permanent revolution" abroad and, at home, increased pressure on the peasants to squeeze from them capital for a crash industrialization program to achieve the Communist utopia. Stalin and Bukharin triumphed within the Party by asserting a seemingly more moderate course: "socialism in one country" and continuance of the NEP.

But once Trotsky, Zinoviev, and Kamenev were disposed of, Stalin took over their domestic policy. The naive Bukharin suddenly discovered that Stalin was "an unprincipled intriguer who . . . changes his theories depending on whom he wants to get rid of at any particular moment." Terrified, Bukharin sought alliance with Kamenev and Zinoviev: Stalin was "a new Ghenghis Khan; he will strangle us all."

Stalin's ambitions extended far beyond the death of his Party rivals. The world, he told the Party in 1926, had "two centers of gravity," the Soviet Union for socialism and "Anglo-America" for capitalism. "To win conclusively," the Soviet Union must replace its present "capitalist encirclement" with a "socialist encirclement" by a ring of satellites. And Stalin also foresaw a new world war; the Soviet Union, he predicted, would enter last of all, "in order to throw a decisive weight onto the scales."

To survive the coming war and to expand Soviet power, Stalin needed arma-

ments before anything else. A war scare that he invented in 1927–28 helped make the case for a Five-Year Plan of crash industrialization. The NEP was already failing to provide enough grain for the towns, as the peasantry resisted Party attempts to keep agricultural prices artificially low. Stalin could therefore argue that the NEP, if it continued, would make it impossible to extract from the peasants the surplus needed to finance industrialization and feed a larger factory work force. Party and OGPU pressure on the most prosperous peasants—the so-called *kulaks* ("fists")—increased.

By early 1929, Stalin had forced Trotsky into exile (and had him murdered in 1940, after erasing his name from the history of the Bolshevik Revolution). Stalin then demoted Bukharin and the "Right" by exposing their attempts to ally themselves with the discredited "Left." And he put an end to the NEP.

Lenin's party had erected a new autocracy over Russia. Stalin, whom the Soviet press increasingly hailed as the "Great Leader," was now close to erecting an autocracy over the Party. In the absence of laws and rules, Bolshevik dictatorship over the proletariat was swiftly becoming the dictatorship of an individual. And that individual, because he controlled the instrument of terror and claimed to embody the will of the proletariat and the supposed laws of history, could do anything he pleased.

The Great Famine, 1929–34

On December 27, 1929, as the first Five-Year Plan went into effect, Stalin informed Russia of its fate: "either we go backward to capitalism or forward to socialism. What does this mean? It means that after a policy that consisted in limiting the exploitative tendencies of the *kulaks,* we have switched to a policy of liquidating the *kulaks* as a class."

In Stalin's view, crash military-industrialization and the consolidation of Soviet power required making the landowning peasantry into a rural proletariat—serfs of the Soviet state—to work the land with state-owned machinery. The goal of

Stalin Demands Crash Industrialization

Stalin shrewdly blended Marxism-Leninism and Russian nationalism in his rationale for crash industrialization. He advanced his thesis most forcefully in a speech of early 1931.

To reduce the tempo [of industrialization] would mean to fall behind. And those who fall behind get beaten. But we do not want to be beaten. No, we refuse to be beaten! One feature of the history of old Russia was the continual beating she suffered because of her backwardness. She was beaten by the Mongol Khans. She was beaten by the Turkish beys. She was beaten by the Swedish feudal lords. She was beaten by the Polish and Lithuanian gentry. She was beaten by the British and French capitalists. She was beaten by the Japanese barons. All beat her—because of her backwardness, military backwardness, cultural backwardness, industrial backwardness, and agricultural backwardness. They beat her because to do so was profitable and could be done with impunity. . . . It is the jungle law of capitalism. You are backward, you are weak—therefore you are wrong; hence, you can be beaten and enslaved. You are mighty—therefore you are right. . . . We are fifty or a hundred years behind the advanced countries. We must make good this distance in ten years. Either we do it, or we shall be crushed.

From Basil Dmytryshyn, USSR: A Concise History *(New York: Charles Scribner's Sons, 1978), p. 158.*

"complete collectivization" that Stalin announced in December 1929 would end forever the mortal internal threat that Lenin had feared: "Capitalism begins in the village marketplace." It would also provide external might, to defend and advance the Revolution. With collectivization, Stalin made good his claim to be Lenin's true heir—despite the doubts Lenin had expressed about Stalin's manners. Stalin proposed to force the pace of history and complete the revolution that Lenin had launched in 1917.

Nor was Stalin's choice of the word *liquidate* an accident. The Party activists, army, and OGPU troops who forced the peasants into state-controlled collective farms received orders to select fixed quotas of *kulaks* and "*kulak* henchmen" for removal. Between 5 and 20 percent of the rural population, depending on the area, were deported to Siberia and central Asia. Most of them died, either on the march or under the care of the OGPU's newly established "Main Administration of Corrective Labor Camps," best known by its sinister acronym, GULAG. The peasants who remained resisted. They slaughtered and ate their livestock rather than deliver it to the collective farms. They refused to plant more than a bare minimum of crops. Villages and entire regions defied the regime. Red Army sweeps and mass executions gradually subdued them.

Stalin's war on the Soviet Union's 120 million peasants culminated in a devastating famine in the Ukraine and elsewhere in 1932–33. Stalin barred food relief shipments, to bring home to the peasantry the cost of defying him; Soviet food *exports* during the famine exceeded those during the prosperous years of the NEP. With macabre relish Stalin publicly commanded merriment: "Life has become more joyous, comrades; life has become gayer." Privately he remarked much later, to Winston Churchill, that 10 million had suffered death or deportation. Soviet demographers later admitted a population loss of 7.5 million; the true figure may have been as high as 15 million.

Stalin's war on the peasantry so devastated Soviet agriculture that in per capita terms it produced scarcely more in 1953

The "Mutability of the Past"

In his novel 1984, *published in 1949, the British essayist and novelist George Orwell (1903–50) depicted a nightmare totalitarian future that drew on Stalin's attempts to control the past.*

The mutability of the past is the central tenet of Ingsoc [Orwell's fictional state ideology]. Past events, it is argued, have no objective existence, but survive only in written records and in human memories. The past is whatever the records and the memories agree upon. And since the Party is in full control of all records, and in equally full control of the minds of its members, it follows that the past is whatever the Party chooses to make it. It also follows that though the past is alterable, it never has been altered in any specific instance. For when it has been recreated in whatever shape is needed at the moment, then this new version *is* the past, and no different past can ever have existed. . . . At all times the Party is in possession of the absolute truth, and clearly the absolute can never have been different from what it is now. . . .

From George Orwell, 1984 *(New York: Signet, 1961), p. 176.*

than it had in 1913. The catastrophic losses to agriculture probably exceeded the gains of the rapidly expanding industrial sector. But the terror-famine achieved its political purpose. The Party broke the one great social force in Russia. By 1932 the state had seized 88 percent of Russia's farmland; by 1937 collectivization was almost total.

And Stalin did extract the labor and some of the needed capital for the Five-Year Plan. According to some estimates, "de-kulakized" slave laborers furnished more than 5 percent of the Soviet labor force by 1933. Peasants fled the land for the industrial cities and mines of the Don Basin and the Urals. Food extracted from the peasantry at gunpoint helped the regime to more than triple Russia's industrial work force. Terror and propaganda whipped the exhausted workers onward, amid immense waste and confusion. Vast hydroelectric dams, steel mills, and armaments factories rose, based on technology bought from the West with exported grain and with gold that GULAG inmates dug from the arctic tundra. The first Five-Year

Joseph Stalin (1937): "To choose one's victims, to prepare one's plans minutely, to slake an implacable vengeance, and then to go to bed . . . there is nothing sweeter in the world."

1917   1924   1928   1953

| Lenin | Stalin against Trotsky | Stalin |

Plan multiplied Soviet capital-goods production by two and a half. At the "Party Congress of Victors" in January 1934 Stalin savored a success bought through the crippling and stunting of his society: "The line of the Party has triumphed."

The Great Terror, 1934–39

As the crisis of collectivization passed, Stalin nevertheless found himself under attack. In 1932 opponents circulated a long document full of devastating criticism of his wasteful and erratic economic leadership, and of the Party's alienation of the working class it claimed to incarnate. Stalin responded with orders to scrutinize the Party membership and purge those suspected of opposition. But he failed to persuade his colleagues on the Party's ruling committee, the Politburo, to redefine dissent within the Party as "counterrevolutionary activity," which carried the death penalty.

That impasse ended on December 1, 1934. A dissident Party member, with the apparent complicity of the NKVD, assassinated Sergei Kirov, boss of Leningrad and rising young star of the Party. Much later, after Stalin's death, Soviet leaders hinted broadly that Stalin was behind the murder. It gave him a pretext to clamp down once more. Having enserfed the peasantry, he now set as his goal the destruction of all doubters and *potential* sources of opposition. Hitler had set the example in June 1934 with a massacre of associates who had become politically inconvenient (see p. 842).

In the aftermath of Kirov's assassination, the NKVD under Stalin's personal direction received the power to shoot summarily anyone it pleased. It soon discovered a mythical "terrorist center" in Leningrad. In early 1935 it dredged up Zinoviev and Kamenev for the first of a series of show trials, an art form already perfected in trials of Socialist Revolution-

aries, Mensheviks, and foreign engineers falsely accused of sabotage. Calls went out to the Party to unmask "Trotskyites" and "Zinovievites." Soviet law soon provided swift death not only for alleged spies and "parasites," but also for those who had knowledge of their activities and failed to denounce them—including children of twelve years or older. The families and children of those arrested became hostages, liable to punishment—a further extension of the genocidal notion of "class justice" that Dzerzhinsky and Latsis of the CHEKA had pioneered. *Pravda,* the Party newspaper, began to carry stories praising children who had reported their parents to the NKVD.

In August 1936, amid mounting anxiety, Stalin announced a new Soviet constitution that contained lavish guarantees of individual freedoms. But woe to those who failed to exercise those freedoms "in accordance with the interests of the workers and for the purpose of strengthening the socialist system." That same month Zinoviev and Kamenev obligingly admitted to having planned Stalin's assassination; the court had them shot. Terror became all-pervasive.

But Stalin was not content. He accused the NKVD leaders of footdragging and replaced them with a new man, the "bloodthirsty dwarf," Nikolai Yezhov. In January 1937 Yezhov mounted yet another Moscow show trial, of the fancifully named "terrorist counterrevolutionary Trotskyite-Zinovievite bloc." Mass arrests and lesser trials occupied the rest of the year. The NKVD and its informers feverishly invented conspiracies, beat prisoners into confessions that implicated ever more suspects, and shot in the prison cellars those who were no longer of use.

Stalin also turned on the Red Army, which he apparently feared might threaten his power in the event of an ever more probable European war. The generals were tougher than the Party; they refused to confess to being in league with Germany and Japan. Stalin had his own high command shot in secret in June and July 1937 and announced the executions after the event.

The last great trial, in March 1938, was that of the so-called "bloc of anti-Soviet rightists and Trotskyites." It included a wide range of victims, from Bukharin to Genrikh Yagoda, the former head of the NKVD whom Stalin had replaced in 1936 for insufficient zeal. Old Bolsheviks confessed to sabotaging butter production with ground glass and to conspiring with Trotsky, Germany, Japan, Britain, and Poland. Western observers, including Roosevelt's ambassador and the correspondent of the *New York Times,* swallowed these absurd tales whole. Bukharin was puzzling, however. He confessed to almost everything, then hinted he was not guilty. Above all, he refused to admit to having plotted Lenin's murder, as Stalin's vindictive prosecutor, Andrei Vishinsky, claimed. The court had Bukharin shot with the rest, but he had marred the illusion of guilt that Stalin sought to create.

The great terror, like the terror-famine that preceded it, accomplished its objective. It remade the Party. Seventy percent of the Central Committee of 1934 perished; Stalin wiped out the leading Old Bolsheviks and any alternative within the Party to his own domination. Terror remade the armed forces. Half of the officer corps, 35,000 men, fell victim. And only 10 percent of those destroyed in the great terror were members of the Party or army. The rest were victims of chance associations, of neighbors' denunciations, of family relationships to suspects, of the envy of subordinates at work, of membership in national minorities. The victims of Stalin's genocide died not because of anything they had done but because of what they were. They perished *by categories,* from *kulaks* and "*kulak* henchmen," to Ukrainians, to Old Bolsheviks, to suspects of "Trotskyism," to relatives of suspects, to individuals whose only "crime" was that they belonged to a generation that remembered Russia before 1917.

The replacements of those "purged" were younger, with fewer memories than their predecessors. They were unlikely to question Stalin's leadership. Above all they were bound to Stalin: they owed their rapid promotions to the vacancies he and his NKVD had created. In many cases they had helped, with a word to the NKVD about their superiors—for Stalin was not the sole author of the terror. He had millions of helpers, bound forever to their master by fear, gratitude, and complicity. Stalin had created a new ruling class in his own image.

The cost was high. The secret 1937 census, according to some accounts, showed that the Soviet Union had 21.5 million people fewer than the second Five-Year Plan had forecast. Stalin, furious, had the demographers shot or sent to GULAG for having allegedly "exerted themselves to diminish the numbers of the population of the Soviet Union." Stalin reserved that privilege to himself. By 1939, the GULAG concentration camps held an estimated 10.4 million people—10 percent of the Soviet labor force. The death rate in the camps was as high as 10 percent a year. By 1940, Stalin's genocide had through famine, terror, and slave labor killed between 12.7 and 22.1 million people—on top of the immense losses between 1914 and 1922. Stalin had also signed a pact with Hitler.

ITALY: FROM DICTATORSHIP TO EXPANSION, 1922–40

To achieve total power in a developed Western society was a challenge more difficult than that facing Stalin. But the First World War created conditions that made it thinkable. For war—a war the rulers had imposed on a resentful parliament and a divided public—caught Italy at a particularly dangerous moment, as the coming of universal male suffrage in 1912–13 launched it into the age of mass politics.

The Crisis of Liberal Italy, 1919–22

War and the example of the Russian revolution mobilized the Italian masses; the 1919 election destroyed the dominance of the Liberals. Two great mass parties, the Catholic People's Party (*Popolari*) and the Socialists, now commanded between them a majority in parliament. But unlike Weimar Germany, the mass parties refused to cooperate and rule. Socialists embraced the half-understood example of Lenin. The *Popolari,* under Vatican influence, had entered politics partly to counter the Socialists. Parliamentary deadlock and a series of weak Liberal cabinets resulted. And for the Right, the Liberal regime had lost its small stock of prestige when the Allies at Paris had "mutilated" Italy's victory by refusing to concede its far-reaching Balkan and colonial claims.

Outside parliament, the Socialists took the offensive in the "two red years" of 1919–20. Their agricultural unions and political machines organized the landless laborers and were soon ruling Italy's richest farming region, the Po Valley. Landowners who refused to hire labor at the rates and in the numbers that the Socialists decreed suffered boycotts, arson, mutilation of livestock, and worse. Factory and transport workers struck repeatedly. But the Socialists' incessant talk of revolution, their violence against landowners, and their abuse of veterans as warmongers and capitalist dupes inevitably backfired.

In October 1914 Benito Mussolini, whom Lenin had seen as the future revolutionary leader of Italian Socialism, had quarreled with the party over its refusal to support war. Mussolini, the brutal and charismatic son of a village blacksmith, had agitated for war and had served in the infantry until he was wounded. In March 1919, he founded a movement to carry the war into politics: the *Fasci di Combattimento* ("combat leagues"). Its first recruits were a curious mixture of former assault troops, wartime junior officers, nationalist students, and socialists who had chosen war in 1914–15. "Fascist" ideology was and remained amorphous, but its principal components were a fierce hostility to the Left and a resentful and expansionist nationalism.

The Socialist offensive in the Po Valley flatlands and agitation by the Slovenes of newly annexed Trieste made the summer of 1920 "the hour of Fascism." Fascist *squadre,* gangs in black shirts or wartime field-gray, attacked Socialists and Slovenes with clubs, knives, pistols, and hand grenades. Landowners and a few industrialists happily contributed funds. Army units secretly provided trucks and weapons. The numerous landowning peasants, whom the Socialists had alienated with talk of collectivization of the land, joined the Fascist *squadre*. Some Liberals in Rome deplored Fascist violence but lacked the resolve to restore order. Other Liberals, among them Giovanni Giolitti, saw the Fascists as a healthy patriotic reaction against the excesses of the Socialists and the encroachments of the *Popolari* on the Liberal state.

By the summer of 1921 the Fascists had smashed the Socialists in the Po Valley and Tuscany, and had set themselves the task of conquering Italy. In Rome, Fascist deputies took the battle into parliament after Giolitti offered an electoral alliance. In the countryside, motorized "punitive expeditions" by the "blackshirts" grew ever larger and more ferociously effective. But hostility between the Socialists and the *Popolari* prevented them from joining hands against the Fascist threat.

By October 1922 Liberal Italy was finished. Right Liberals such as Salandra sought to co-opt Mussolini, to tame him by bringing him into the government. In a two-track maneuver that combined an insurrectionary "March on Rome" with negotiations with Salandra and others, Mussolini demanded to be named prime minister. The last Liberal cabinet feebly urged the King to bring in the army to restore order. Victor Emmanuel III consulted his generals, who answered that the army would do its duty, but that it would be better not to put it to the test. King, army, and Right Liberals chose Mussolini over a civil war they feared would strengthen the Left. They made Mussolini prime minister of Italy on October 31, 1922.

The Fascist State, 1922–29

As Mussolini admitted privately in 1924, the "March on Rome" was no revolution: "The revolution comes later." He had no

1859	1870		1922 1925		1943 1946
Period of Unification	Kingdom of Italy			Mussolini	

1945

majority in parliament and therefore had to take fellow-traveling Liberals and *Popolari* into his first cabinet. He depended on Italy's industrialists and on foreign bankers to shore up the economy. And to the end his authority ultimately derived from the king who had appointed him. The Fascist regime remained a "dyarchy," with dictator and king sharing power. The regime was thus the least "totalitarian" of the three great dictatorships: Mussolini's "NEP" lasted until 1935–36.

But Mussolini nevertheless aspired to total power, and moved to achieve it by stages. From the beginning he chipped away both at opponents and at conservative "flankers" who sought to use him merely to tame the Left. Fascist violence continued in the provinces; a new electoral law guaranteed a Fascist majority in the 1924 elections.

That victory led Mussolini to overreach. Fascism's most conspicuous opponent, Giacomo Matteotti of the Socialists, claimed in parliament that the new regime rested on force and fraud. Then he vanished. It soon emerged that the "CHEKA," as Mussolini only half-jokingly called his bodyguard of thugs, had taken Matteotti for a fatal ride in the country.

Mussolini himself preserved what a later age was to call "plausible deniability." Pressure for his resignation nevertheless mounted among Liberals in the cabinet and in parliament. Mussolini privately railed at the Italian people's "absurd fuss" over the death of one man. Then and later he secretly envied the Bolsheviks, who faced no such limits.

Socialists, *Popolari,* and Left Liberals, united at last, seceded from parliament in protest. That was suicidal; it split the opposition between those who seceded and those who stayed. Mussolini bought off with concessions some of the Liberals who remained. He faced down waverers in the cabinet by threatening to fight the opposition in the streets rather than yield power. As in 1922, he offered the Italian establishment a simple choice: him or civil war.

On January 3, 1925, with the King's silent support, Mussolini announced that he would remain in power indefinitely. The police shut down the opposition press. A succession of botched attempts to assassinate Mussolini soon gave him welcome pretexts to rule by decree and outlaw all opposition parties. Within the Fascist party, Mussolini abolished the few shreds of internal democracy that had survived from 1919–21: "The Revolution has one Leader." By 1928 he had grafted the party onto the state and had given the party's highest organ, the Grand Council of Fascism, power to regulate the succession to the throne. He created a Fascist youth movement to permeate the coming generations with a brutish nationalism and a pagan "sense of virility, of power, of conquest."

Mussolini, surrounded by the commanders of the "March on Rome," strikes a pose before assuming power in 1922.

Mussolini also secured a prize that had eluded his Liberal predecessors: a settlement of Italy's festering quarrel with the Church. The Lateran Pact of February 1929 created a Vatican City mini-state and gave the Vatican a large sum in Italian state bonds as compensation for the territory seized in 1870; a Concordat between Church and state made Catholicism the state religion. In return, Pope Pius XI hailed Mussolini as "the man whom Providence has placed in Our path." That blessing and the rural clergy's enthusiastic support for the regime made Mussolini's position unassailable. A plebiscite and a one-party election in March 1929 gave Mussolini an overwhelming and mostly genuine majority, and a black-shirted parliament. The dictatorship rested on monarchy, army, and police, but also on the acclamation of the masses and the blessings of the Church.

Mussolini Breaks Through to Empire: Ethiopia and after, 1935–40

Yet control of government and the growing cult of the *Duce* was not enough. In 1925 Mussolini had expressed many of his ultimate goals in a speech to the party. Fascism's "fierce totalitarian will" would " 'fascistize' the nation, so that tomorrow Italian and Fascist, more or less like Italian and Catholic, will be the same thing." He also had a method for achieving that goal. Like the Girondin orator Isnard (see p. 592), who in 1792 had foreseen a war "indispensable for completing the revolution," Mussolini saw a connection between war and revolution. In 1914–15 he had demanded a "revolutionary war." That war had destroyed Liberal Italy and placed him in power. Only more war could make that power total.

And from the extremists of Italy's Nationalist party and from his navy, Mussolini acquired a vision of Italy's goals in that war. "A nation," he informed a group of high officers in 1926–27, "that has no free access to the sea cannot be considered a free nation; a nation that has no free access to the oceans cannot be considered a great power. Italy must become a great power." Britain and France, and Italy's ties to the world market, stood in the way of Mediterranean domination and of what Mussolini later described as Italy's "march to the ocean." By 1923–24, if not before, Mussolini had already foreseen that a vengeful nationalist Germany would be Italy's most promising ally in that march.

Waiting for Germany was tedious. Between 1922 and 1931 Mussolini crushed with massacres and concentration camps the Arabs of Libya, whom the Liberal state had been unable to subdue. He dabbled with plans for attacking Turkey and sponsored Croat and Macedonian terrorist attacks on neighboring Yugoslavia. But British disapproval, Italy's economic and financial weakness, and the Depression forced Mussolini to pretend he had a deep love for peace—although the Depression also ended the foreign trade and loans that bound Fascist Italy to the international status quo.

In early 1933, as Hitler came to power, Mussolini briefly thought he had blackmailed the French into abandoning their support of their Yugoslav ally, a Mussolini target since the 1920s. Then the king and

---

Mussolini: War, Revolution, and Empire   1925

At times I look with favor on the idea of [creating] generations in the laboratory, of creating, in other words, the class of the warriors, who are always ready to die, the class of the inventors, who pursue the secrets of the mysteries [of nature]; the class of judges; the class of the great captains of industry; of the great governors. It is through this sort of methodical selection that one creates the great elites that in turn establish empires. . . . War and revolution are two terms that are almost always linked. Either war produces revolution or it is revolution that leads to war. Even the strategy of the two movements is alike: as in war, in revolution you do not always attack. Sometimes you must make more or less strategic retreats. Sometimes you must rest for long periods on positions you have conquered. But the goal is there: empire.

Speech to the Fascist party congress, June 22, 1925, from Opera Omnia di Benito Mussolini *(Florence: La Fenice, 1956), Vol. 21, pp. 362–63 (translation by M. Knox).*

the generals vetoed a Balkan war that would risk French retaliation and "a lesson that would last us for a century." France, terrified at the rise of Hitler, nevertheless soon gave Mussolini the opening he sought. In July 1931 France's prime minister, the unscrupulous and gullible Pierre Laval, had suggested to an Italian emissary that Italy might quench its thirst for expansion in Ethiopia. France would stand aside in return for Italy's help in maintaining the status quo in Europe against Germany.

Mussolini had at first rejected this offer as a French trick to bog Italy down in Africa just as Germany was opening up possibilities in Europe. Then, in early 1934, he reversed himself. He had quarreled with his would-be ally, Hitler, over Austria. If war in Europe was impossible, war in Africa might yet serve his purpose. The king, the military, and the Italian establishment were lukewarm rather than actively hostile, as they had been over Yugoslavia. They were willing to "avenge Adowa" if Mussolini insisted and if no great power objected.

In January 1935, Mussolini and Laval signed the Rome Agreements, which conceded Italy a "free hand" in East Africa in return for the abandonment of longstanding Italian colonial claims on France and for Italian backing for France in Europe. The last part of the bargain Mussolini regarded skeptically; to Berlin he confided through intermediaries that "he would exploit the French, if they offered him anything, without becoming dependent upon them."

Large Italian forces, the first of almost half a million troops and laborers, began shipping out for East Africa in March 1935. Britain feebly objected. War in Africa would make cooperation with Italy against the German threat impossible, and in an election year Baldwin could not abandon the League of Nations, of which Ethiopia was a member. When Mussolini rejected British efforts at compromise, London reluctantly sent more battleships to the Mediterranean to deter him. The League, impotent in the Manchurian crisis because no great power had been willing to fight Japan, now rallied behind Britain—and the overwhelming power of the

British fleet. But Baldwin's foreign secretary secretly assured Mussolini that Britain did not intend war. That pledge, together with intercepted British radio messages suggesting the fleet was short of ammunition, enabled Mussolini to overrule his hesitant military and the King. On October 3, 1935, Italy attacked Ethiopia.

Britain reacted with economic sanctions against Italy organized through the League of Nations. Sanctions proved easy to evade, and thanks to a British failure of nerve they did not cover the imported oil that fueled Italy's armed forces. Their main consequence was to cut Italian dependence on British coal—in favor of the coal of the Ruhr.

On the battlefield, the armies of emperor Haile Selassie of Ethiopia almost routed the Italians in December–January 1936; then Italy's lavish use of tanks, artillery, aircraft, and mustard gas crushed them. At the beginning of May 1936, Italian forces entered the Ethiopian capital, Addis Ababa. From his balcony, Mussolini hailed before a delirious crowd the "reappearance of empire, after fifteen centuries, on the fateful hills of Rome." War and the brutal Italian occupation of 1936–41 cost the lives of a million Ethiopians.

War also made Mussolini "founder of the Empire," with a prestige matching that of his conservative allies, the generals, and the king. Mussolini listened less and his advisers dared offer less and less advice. Sanctions inflamed Italian opinion against the West and made it easier for Mussolini to bully the industrialists and militarize the Italian economy under the banner of "autarky," the illusory pursuit of self-sufficiency in raw materials. And Italy's quarrel with the League and subsequent intervention in the Spanish Civil War in July–August 1936 gave him the opportunity to move closer to Berlin. In October 1936, he and Hitler inaugurated the "Rome-Berlin Axis." And in 1938 he imitated Hitler's anti-Semitic legislation.

On June 10, 1940, after a long struggle with the generals, king, and moderate opinion, Mussolini led Italy into the Second World War. Only war, he told a cheering crowd, would "resolve . . . the problem of our maritime frontiers" and "break the military and territorial chains that suffocate us in our sea, for a people of forty-five million souls is not truly free unless it has free access to the ocean." Victory would give him the prestige needed to smash the monarchy and to break the Church's grip on Italian society. Defeat instead hurled the Fascist regime and Italy itself into the abyss.

GERMANY: FROM WAR TO WAR

Adolf Hitler

The man who opened the road for Mussolini and invited Stalin into central Europe began as modestly as his fellow dictators. Son of an Austro-Hungarian customs official, Adolf Hitler absorbed pan-Germanism and anti-Semitism from his surroundings. After failing admission to the Vienna Art Academy in 1907–08, he drifted to Munich in 1913 rather than serve in the armies of the Habsburg dynasty he despised for its compromises with Slavs and Jews. War in 1914 he regarded as a deliverance (see p. 774). Always a loner, he found in the German army a home and in battle a vocation. From October 1914 to October 1918 he served at the front in the most dangerous job the infantry offered: battalion messenger. He earned two Iron Crosses, decorations rarely given to lance-corporals.

Word of the 1918 revolution and Germany's defeat reached him as he lay in hospital, temporarily blinded by British gas; the news roused him to fury. As the army demobilized, he remained in service at Munich for lack of anything better. The army's propaganda branch took him in. There he made a discovery that changed Europe and the world: "I could 'speak.'" In September 1919 his superiors sent him to observe a meeting of a radical rightist sect of Munich railway workers, the German Workers' Party (DAP).

Hitler immediately attracted attention and an invitation to join the Party. News of his talent as a speaker spread rapidly in Munich's right-radical circles. By July 1921 he had taken the DAP away from its founders, had changed its name to Na-

tional Socialist German Workers' Party (NSDAP), and had made himself its dictatorial leader. By late 1923 his party had 55,000 members and a paramilitary mass army, the brown-shirted SA (*Sturmabteilungen,* "storm troop sections"), under the leadership of Ernst Röhm, a fiercely politicized former army officer.

The *Führer,* as Hitler now became, spoke powerfully to a nation that had become convinced, however perversely, that it had suffered foreign aggression in 1914–18 and unmerited demotion to second-class power in 1919. Hitler's ideological delusions and those of his ever-larger audiences coincided, thanks to Germany's defeat. His starting point was the extremist form of social Darwinism that had long been popular in Germany. Following pseudo-biological prophets such as Ernst Haeckel (see p. 730), Hitler assumed that nature's laws—the "survival of the fittest" or the "free play of forces"—offered the only "healthy" rule for human conduct. Humanity was one with nature, not apart from it or above it; biology was supreme in all spheres of human activity.

That insight, Hitler insisted, was science. Like his rivals the Marxist-Leninists, Hitler and his followers combined pseudo-scientific materialism with bizarre ideological claims. For Communists, economics was the secret essence of human history, which was the history of class struggle. For Hitler, biology held the key: race—not class—was "the driving force of world history." And like the Marxist-Leninists, who saw "the capitalist" as demon, Hitler too saw a historic villain.

For Hitler, the Jewish people were a "race-tuberculosis of nations" who had supposedly lived "parasitically" throughout history from the labors of peoples that had given them shelter—especially the "Aryan" or "Nordic" peoples of Europe for whom Hitler claimed biological superiority. Throughout history, the Jews had allegedly sought the "eternal Jewish goal—world domination." They were responsible for Germany's internal weakness and thus for its defeat through the purported stab-in-the-back of 1918.

The Jewish threat, Hitler ranted to enthusiastic audiences, now placed before

"Vote National Socialist, or the sacrifices [of 1914–18] were in vain": the entire appeal of Hitler's party, born of war and bound for revenge, distilled into a single electoral slogan.

NATIONAL SOZIALIST ODER UMSONST WAREN DIE OPFER

the world a stark alternative: "either victory of the Aryan side or its annihilation and victory of the Jews." Only Germany could ensure "Aryan" victory; its "historic mission" was to found "an Aryan world order." And death awaited Germany's adversaries: as early as 1920 Hitler proclaimed his determination to "strike the [Jewish] evil at its root and exterminate it root and branch." His ultimate goal was racist world revolution.

Meanwhile, recovery from the lost war required a new state: "We need a dictator who is a genius, if we want to rise again." But in the age of mass politics, even dictatorship required pseudo-democratic phrases and mass enthusiasm or mass terror to make it work. Hitler therefore proclaimed that nationalist dictatorship was "Germanic democracy." His mass following, and many of Munich's social elite, seemed to agree.

The Ruhr crisis of 1923 shook Weimar's authority and led Hitler to bid for power before inaction drained away the enthusiasm of his increasingly fanatical following. On the night of November 8–9, 1923, Hitler and the SA seized key points in Munich and sought to launch a "March on Berlin" modeled on Mussolini's October 1922 exploit. But unlike Mussolini, Hitler failed to secure the support of army and police, who soon crushed this "Beer Hall *Putsch*." Hitler's oratory at his subsequent treason trial nevertheless turned defeat into victory. His allies, who included Ludendorff, sheepishly denied their responsibility. Hitler affirmed his own and appealed to a higher court: Weimar judges might condemn the rebels, but history would acquit them. He emerged from the trial as uncontested leader of German radical nationalism.

His short term in prison was a welcome rest, a chance to "confirm his ideas by the study of natural history." There he began a memoir and political tract entitled "A Four and One-Half Year Struggle against Lies, Stupidity, and Cowardice." A merciful editor later shortened the title to the catchier *Mein Kampf*—"My Struggle." Its 600 turgid pages included much wisdom about propaganda technique, expressed with a cynical frankness that

Hitler, Master of Propaganda   1925

Hitler set forth four mutually reinforcing principles for effective propaganda: it addressed "the most limited intelligence" in its audience, it appealed to emotion rather than intellect, it was relentlessly repetitive, and it displayed and fostered a fanatical one-sidedness.

All propaganda must be popular and its intellectual level must be adjusted to the most limited intelligence among those it is addressed to. . . . The more modest its intellectual ballast, the more exclusively it takes into consideration the emotions of the masses, the more effective it will be. . . . The art of propaganda lies in understanding the emotional ideas of the great masses and finding . . . the way to the attention and thence to the heart of the broad masses. . . .

The receptivity of the great masses is very limited, their intelligence is small, but their power of forgetting is enormous. In consequence . . . all effective propaganda must be limited to a very few points and must harp on these in slogans until the very last member of the public understands what you want him to understand. . . .

What . . . would we say about a poster that was supposed to advertise a new soap and that described other soaps as "good"? We would only shake our heads. Exactly the same applies to political advertising. The function of propaganda is . . . not to make an objective study of the truth . . . ; its task is to serve our own right, always and unflinchingly. . . . It does not have multiple shadings; it has a positive and a negative: love or hate, right or wrong, truth or lie, never half this way and half that way. . . .

From Adolf Hitler, Mein Kampf, *trans. by Ralph Manheim (Boston: Houghton Mifflin, 1943), pp. 180–83.*

distinguished Hitler from the theorists of commercial advertising. It also suggested that Hitler saw himself as that rare phenomenon, a combination of prophet and political leader.

Last but not least, *Mein Kampf* offered a foreign-policy program. In late 1922, Hitler had formulated in private how he proposed to go about fulfilling Germany's world mission: "We should attempt the carving up of Russia with English help." In *Mein Kampf* Hitler laid that program out in detail, beginning with a critique of William II's too ambitious foreign policy, which had alienated Britain, France, and Russia all at once. Germany should instead proceed to world domination by stages, smashing one adversary at a time: first the internal enemies, then France, and finally Russia, where Germany would seize the *Lebensraum* ("living space") it required, the vast blockade-proof empire Ludendorff had briefly grasped in 1918. Britain and Italy, both hostile to France during the Ruhr crisis, appeared available as allies; Hitler had inevitably conceived an admiration for Mussolini, who furnished a welcome prototype for nationalist dictatorship. In an unpublished "second book" of 1928 Hitler also discovered Germany's final adversary in the quest for world domination: the United States.

For the moment, these vistas were beside the point. Prosperity and the success of Stresemann's foreign policy lessened the appeal of radical nationalism. The NSDAP, which Hitler had reorganized as a tightly centralized "Führer-party" after his release from prison, received a mere twelve *Reichstag* seats in the 1928 election. But two things suggested that it was ready for further growth: its relentless emphasis on organization and propaganda, and its growing success with the hard-hit peasantry of north Germany as the agricultural depression deepened after 1927.

Hitler's Road to Power, 1929–33

Hitler's breakthrough into national politics came in 1929–30, even before the Depression hit Germany in full force. The press and film magnate Alfred Hugenberg, an extreme pan-German, had taken over the party of the traditional Junker Right, the German National People's Party (DNVP). Hugenberg, unlike the DNVP's earlier leaders, was fanatically committed to destroying the Weimar Republic. The Young Plan reparations settlement of 1929 offered him an occasion for a massive propaganda campaign against the Republic for allegedly consenting to the "enslavement of the German people" through reparations.

Hugenberg enlisted the help of Hitler and the NSDAP—and firmly established Hitler on the national political scene. Then the last Weimar coalition government collapsed because the SPD, like Labour in

Britain in 1931, rejected balancing the budget by cutting unemployment benefits. The government, under the authoritarian Center Party leader, Heinrich Brüning, lacked a firm *Reichstag* majority. Brüning therefore committed an act of folly. He called an election for September 1930.

The French had evacuated their last Rhineland occupation zone that June; the Germans were now free to vote their nationalist views without fear of consequences. Brüning's cost-cutting measures against the deepening Depression made him unloved. Hugenberg's campaign against the Young Plan had enabled Hitler to create an agitation and propaganda machine that utterly outclassed that of the other parties. The 1930 vote was an electoral earthquake: 107 Nazi *Reichstag* seats, and almost a fifth of the popular vote.

The NSDAP was now Germany's second largest party after the SPD. It tailored its appeals to every conceivable interest group, but its program was above all a name: Adolf Hitler. Hitler offered to fill the role that Bismarck had created and that William II had failed to fill, the role of national *Führer*. He symbolized a radical alternative to Weimar's economic misery, dreary indecisiveness, class and religious division, and national humiliation. The NSDAP, ranted one of Hitler's lieutenants, was "the opposite of everything that now exists." Increasing numbers of Germans found that deliberately vague appeal compelling.

The principal question in German politics after September 1930 was when, and under what conditions, Hitler would come to power. In the next two years, as the Depression shrank Brüning's authority, the Junker kitchen cabinet around Reich President Hindenburg became increasingly desperate. They applauded the NSDAP's nationalist fanaticism and sought to use it to buttress their own power, while resisting Hitler's increasingly pressing demands for the chancellorship. But like the similar efforts of Salandra and Giolitti in 1921–24, repeated conservative attempts to domesticate Hitler failed.

In spring 1932, Brüning sponsored Hindenburg's reelection for a second seven-year term, and Hitler unchivalrously ran against the "Old Gentleman." Hindenburg won, but only with the support of the SPD, which preferred even a Prussian field marshal to Hitler. After the election, Hindenburg dismissed Brüning, who had outlived his usefulness and had provoked Hitler by attempting to abolish the SA. The army, which played an increasingly political role, resisted curbs on what it naively perceived as the SA's violent young "idealists."

A *Reichstag* election in July 1932 gave the NSDAP an unprecedented 230 seats, amid SA violence that left hundreds dead. With the help of the 89 Communists, who opposed democracy as bitterly as the NSDAP, Hitler now had a *Reichstag* majority that was hostile not merely to any democratic or conservative cabinet or chancellor, but to Weimar democracy itself. NSDAP obstruction and Hitler's demand for the chancellorship produced parliamentary paralysis. Hindenburg still refused to hand over Germany "like a laboratory rabbit" to the bold experimenters of the NSDAP. But Brüning's two successors as chancellor failed to master the Depression, the *Reichstag,* the continuing Nazi street violence, and backbiting in the conservative camp. On January 30, 1933, Hindenburg gave in and made Adolf Hitler chancellor of the German Reich in a coalition cabinet with Hugenberg and numerous other conservatives.

The Nazi Revolution, 1933–37

Hitler soon showed his conservative allies that he was no puppet "hired" for the occasion, as they foolishly assumed. He established a direct alliance with the military high command on February 3 by promising to "exterminate Marxism root and branch," reawaken the German people's "will to arms," and create a new armed forces (*Wehrmacht*) once more based on universal military service. He extracted from Hindenburg permission to hold a new election, and emergency presidential powers that restricted press and other freedoms. The SA and its elite offshoot, the SS (*Schutzstaffel* or "security echelon"), terrorized political opponents and Ger-

man Jews with the approval of the Prussian police, which was now under the management of Hitler's close associate Hermann Göring.

On February 27, 1933, the *Reichstag* building in Berlin mysteriously burned; Hitler and his propaganda chief, the malevolent Joseph Goebbels, seized on this as evidence of a "Communist plot" that justified the suppression by presidential decree of all remaining constitutional freedoms. The election on March 5, 1933, gave the conservative-NSDAP coalition a majority. Hitler then bullied the new *Reichstag* into voting an "Enabling Act" that gave him as chancellor the power to make law by decree. That made him independent of both *Reichstag* and Hindenburg. By July 1933, Hitler had abolished all parties other than the NSDAP, including the DNVP of his conservative allies. He had purged the civil service of political opponents and Jews—a measure that began an intensifying effort to define who was a Jew and to isolate those so defined from the rest of the population.

Hindenburg and the army yielded. They approved heartily of Hitler's crushing of Communists and SPD, and swallowed whatever modest qualms they may have had over the anti-Jewish measures, which roused a storm of protest abroad. Hitler also received the blessings of the Vatican, which abandoned the Catholic Center party as it had the Italian Catholic *Popolari* and signed in July 1933 a Concordat with Hitler similar to its 1929 arrangement with Mussolini. In November 1933 a plebiscite and a *Reichstag* election gave Hitler a brown-shirted parliament and an 87.8 percent majority. Hitler had achieved in nine months what Mussolini, with far less mass support in 1922 than Hitler had in 1933, had needed seven years to accomplish.

But while the aged Hindenburg lived, Hitler still faced an authority higher than his own. In preparation for the "Old Gentleman's" death, Hitler consolidated his alliance with the army. That "state within the state" was equally indispensable to his domestic power and to his plans for war. When the SA under its chief Ernst Röhm challenged the army for leadership of the

On Hitler's order, the party organized a boycott of Jewish shops and offices in April 1933. The placard reads: "Germans! Defend yourselves! Don't buy from Jews!"

rearmament effort, Hitler chose the army. On June 30, 1934, with trucks and weapons the army provided, Hitler's SS forces rounded up and shot Röhm and more than 200 SA leaders. That "night of the long knives" sealed with blood Hitler's alliance with the military leadership. On August 2, after Hindenburg finally died, the *Wehrmacht* took an oath to Hitler personally. As "*Führer* and Reich Chancellor," a position that united his own powers with those of the Reich President, Hitler now enjoyed powers that far surpassed Mussolini's.

Hitler soon consolidated and extended that power. The NSDAP did its best to mobilize the population, including the industrial workers, who received membership in a Nazi "German Labor Front" in place of the smashed SPD trade unions. German youth, by 1936, was subject to compulsory membership in the "Hitler Youth" and "League of German Maidens." And the SS proved a far more formidable rival to the army than had Röhm's SA. Its fanatically loyal and fastidiously precise leader, Heinrich Himmler, had by 1934

Heinrich Himmler (*left*) and Ernst Röhm a few months before Himmler had Röhm shot at Hitler's order.

seized control of the Reich police forces, established a network of concentration camps outside the control of the normal judiciary, and set up a small but growing private army that included an SS bodyguard regiment for the *Führer*. By 1936, Himmler was officially "Reich leader of the SS and Chief of the German Police," a unique party-state hybrid.

And the regime struck once more at Germany's half-million Jews. In September 1935, at the annual Nuremberg party rally, Hitler proclaimed a "Reich citizenship law" that made the German Jews less than full citizens and forbade the intermarriage of "Germans" and "Jews." The definition and increasing segregation of the "racial enemy" proved a mighty step toward extermination.

By 1936–37, within the shell of the Weimar constitution, Hitler had created a system that German jurists described as a "*Führer*-state." Party organizations proliferated alongside the state bureaucracy and with Hitler's approval gradually usurped its powers. The SS, with Hitler's backing, encroached on both army and judiciary. "Political free enterprise," as one scholar has well described it, was the ruling principle of Hitler's Reich. From his villa in the Bavarian Alps, far above the struggle, Hitler encouraged the rivalries of his subordinates. Those rivalries strengthened his own power and served as a form of "natural selection" in molding the new National Socialist governing elite. The regime's dynamism was in part a consequence of Hitler's method of leadership, which contrasted with the more rigid top-down style of Stalin and even Mussolini. Hitler defined the goal of competition—to fulfill the *Führer's* will—and left it to his subordinates to guess that will and to strive frenetically to implement it. That was his most original contribution to the technique of total power.

Germany Rearms: "Everything for the Wehrmacht!"

Nazi Germany's road to total power led through massive rearmament and conquest. On February 3, 1933, five days after taking office, Hitler addressed a private meeting of his generals and admirals. As well as promising them the elimination of the Left and rearmament, he announced that the power of the new *Wehrmacht* would serve for "the conquest of new *Lebensraum* in the East and its ruthless Germanization." The generals did not take that statement seriously until much later. But they were delighted to rearm.

In the following year the army, Germany's dominant service, accelerated the clandestine rearmament plan that it had already begun under Weimar. When the Disarmament Conference of the League of Nations threatened to get in the way of that plan, Hitler left both the Conference and the League in October 1933, with the unanimous support of his generals, former conservatives, and diplomats. His establishment "flankers" enabled him to rearm and to launch the war that culminated in their own ruin.

Externally, rearmament inevitably led Germany into a "danger zone" in which it ran the risk of preventive war. Hitler warned his generals in February 1933 that they would soon find out "if France has statesmen; if so, it will not give us time but will attack us (presumably with [its] eastern hangers-on)." France had no statesmen, and Hitler neutralized Poland with a surprise non-aggression pact in January 1934. Each time Western outrage at Germany's anti-Jewish measures or its rearmament reached dangerous heights, Hitler soothed foreign opinion with a "peace speech" that played on the democracies' credulity and yearning for peace.

That tactic served even to cover Germany's March 1935 declaration that it had unilaterally torn up the disarmament provisions of Versailles. Germany, Hitler triumphantly announced, had an air force—the *Luftwaffe*—and would soon have a vast mass army based on universal service. London and Paris made feeble protests; then Britain legalized Germany's violations of the Versailles treaty by allowing Hitler a fleet a third the size of Britain's in the Anglo-German Naval Agreement of June 1935.

Internally, Hitler broke the opposition to breakneck rearmament that emerged in 1935–36, as the economy

Germany's first and last "Minister for Public Enlightenment and Propaganda," Joseph Goebbels.

achieved virtual full employment. Germany's steel barons, whose excess capacity had almost ruined them in the Depression, balked at investing in new plants. Big business leaders warned that the armament boom was overheating the economy; labor and raw material shortages would soon lead to massive inflation and financial ruin. Hitler treated the doubters with contempt. He was secretly confident that the loot that the *Wehrmacht* would seize in war would keep the economy going. He also had the support of the army leaders, who wanted armaments and did not share the industrialists' doubts. Hitler gave Hermann Göring, now chief of the *Luftwaffe* and second man in the Nazi state, full powers over the economy in mid-1936, and simple orders: "Within four years the German *Wehrmacht* must be ready to fight; within four years the German economy must be ready for war."

Rearmament itself proceeded rapidly, gobbling up an ever-greater portion of Germany's gross national product (see Figure 32-1). By 1939, despite the belated beginnings of rearmament in the democracies, Germany was out-spending all its Western rivals combined by a factor of almost two to one. Hitler's effort produced results: the most powerful air force and army in the world. All that remained was to use them. As Hitler remarked retrospectively in November 1939, "I did not create the *Wehrmacht* in order not to strike."

THE ROAD TO WAR, 1936–39

Germany's massive rearmament soon became the decisive driving force in world politics. But what did the *Wehrmacht* mean? The powers sought to guess Hitler's intentions but shrank from the obvious answer, that German rearmament served the purpose announced in *Mein Kampf,* the conquest of *Lebensraum.* To recognize Hitler's warlike intentions meant giving up a cherished myth: that World War I had been so terrible that another great war was unthinkable. It also meant war—

to stop Hitler before he grew too strong. The Western democracies shrank from that conclusion. Their reward was war— once Hitler was too strong to stop.

Diplomatic Revolution in Europe, 1936

By 1936, Germany's growing might and the Ethiopian quarrel between Italy and the League of Nations offered Hitler a unique opportunity. In February 1936 he sounded out the Italian attitude toward Locarno; Mussolini made clear that he would not object if Germany broke that treaty, of which Italy was a guarantor. On March 7, 1936, Hitler's forces occupied the demilitarized Rhineland without warning. Germany had broken not only the "dictated peace" of Versailles, but also Locarno, a treaty Germany had freely signed.

Hitler's action was by far the greatest risk he had so far taken. The German army was in the initial phases of massive expansion and was correspondingly disorganized. The French could have used overwhelming force. Victory would not have been bloodless; Hitler had given orders to fight, and to hold the line of the

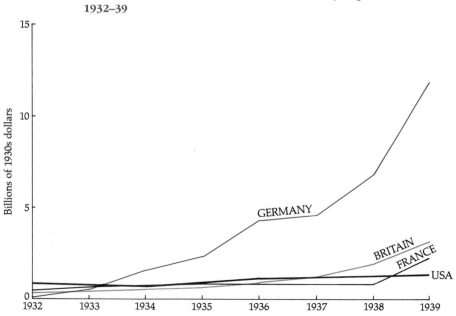

FIGURE 32-1   **Hitler Rearms, the Democracies Falter: Military Expenditure 1932–39**

Europe before the Second World War   1930–39

Germany in 1930

German acquisitions, 1930–39

German allies in 1939

0   MILES   200

Rhine. But Germany was not yet ready to fight for long.

In the event, it did not need to fight at all. Britain, with much of its navy tied up facing Italy, urged Paris not to take rash action. As *The Times* of London indulgently commented, Hitler's coup was no more than the occupation of "territory indisputably under German sovereignty." The French military made clear to its politicians that it likewise preferred inaction. The French politicians in turn happily seized on Britain's pusillanimity as an excuse for their own. Hitler, who launched the crisis despite doubts among his generals, saw the outcome as confirmation of his own superior judgment. He had now taken the measure both of the West and of his own timid high command.

The remilitarization of the Rhineland was a strategic and diplomatic revolution. Now Hitler could fortify Germany's western border and prevent France from defending its Polish and Czechoslovak allies by threatening to attack Germany. The smaller powers rushed to seek favor with the new master. Belgium, convinced of the futility of its French alliance, retreated into neutrality in November 1936. That move uncovered France's northeastern border, which the Maginot line did not protect. Austria, which Mussolini had quietly abandoned to Hitler in January 1936, signed a pact with Hitler in July that gave Germany the right to interfere in its foreign and domestic affairs. The Balkan states expanded their already close economic ties with Germany. Stalin, apparently after reading *Mein Kampf,* had in 1934 become a belated convert to the League of Nations and "collective security"—but he now intensified his efforts to tempt Hitler into a mutually profitable arrangement. Hitler saw no need to answer. He had the initiative.

Spain and China, 1936–39

Hitler found the quarrels of others tactically useful. Mussolini's Ethiopian adventure had distracted attention from German rearmament and had offered the opportunity to seize the Rhineland. New conflicts in Spain and China offered similar opportunities.

In July 1936, a group of traditionalist Spanish generals rose against the republic that had taken the place of Spain's enfeebled monarchy in 1931. Resistance by the population blocked the coup in most of Spain. Generals Francisco Franco and Emilio Mola then appealed for help to Fascist Italy and Nazi Germany. Help came. Mussolini had visions of dominating the western Mediterranean and saw Spain, like Ethiopia, as an opportunity to strengthen his power at home through what he described as the "permanent revolution" of warfare. He sent aircraft and a ground force that ultimately amounted to 50,000 men.

Hitler simply wanted a conflict in Spain that would divert the West from his doings in central Europe. He sent arms and *Luftwaffe* units. Even Stalin, who apparently saw the Spanish Civil War as a vehicle for keeping the "capitalist" powers at one another's throats, intervened on the side of the Republic with arms, advisers, and Communist-organized "International Brigades." Only Britain and France abstained. London viewed both sides with distaste and feared that the Spanish Civil War might lead to general war. Léon Blum's France offered hesitant unofficial assistance to the Spanish Republic but shrank from greater risks.

In the next three years, more than half a million Spaniards died in massacres of prisoners and civilians, in battles around Madrid in 1936–37, in bloody winter fighting in 1937–38, and in the final campaigns in southeastern Spain that ended with the collapse of the Republic in March–April 1939. The war became a symbol. For Germany and Italy, the battle against the Republic was a struggle against "Bolshevism"—a convenient propaganda theme to cloak the Italian and German threat to the status quo. For the Left of western Europe and the United States, the war was a struggle against "fascism"—a generic concept that the Communist International had invented to distinguish "capitalist" dictatorships from the dictatorship of Lenin and Stalin. Few recognized that this was above all a *Spanish* civil war, last of a long series of struggles between military-clerical Right and liberal or socialist Left that had convulsed Spain since Napoleon's invasion in 1808. It ended with the victory of the military dictatorship of Francisco Franco, who cannily outlasted his Nazi and Fascist patrons and died in power, and in bed, in 1975.

Full-scale war in East Asia soon overshadowed the events in Spain. In July 1937, a shooting incident between Japanese and Guomindang troops at the Marco Polo Bridge near Beijing (Peking) led both sides to escalate. Chiang Kai-shek had grudgingly agreed in 1936 to a temporary alliance with the Chinese Communists against the Japanese, and he now felt compelled to fight. The Japanese army welcomed the chance to reduce all China to colonial subjection. The Tokyo government, under a prime minister who had made his name as an expansionist ideologue, Prince Konoe Fumimaro, backed the army.

A Japanese landing force took Shanghai with much slaughter. In a series of swift campaigns, the Japanese forced Chiang southward. In December 1937, they seized Chiang's capital at Nanjing and massacred between 100,000 and 300,000 Chinese amid scenes of mass rape and displays of swordsmanship against unarmed prisoners. Almost simultaneously, Japanese aircraft sank the U.S. gunboat *Panay* on the Yangtze River. That seemed a warning to the West that China was Japan's preserve: "Asia for the Asians."

The West showed little resolve. Baldwin's successor, Neville Chamberlain, hoped to avoid provoking Japan until he had conciliated Hitler and Mussolini. American opinion, after abandoning Europe in the 1920s, had justified itself by creating the myth that bankers and armaments barons—rather than Ludendorff and Zimmermann—had forced the United States into war in 1917. Between 1935 and 1937 an isolationist Congress passed three "Neutrality Acts" to prevent U.S. sales of arms and ammunition to belligerents. Isolation would supposedly avoid another war.

When Roosevelt vaguely urged the democracies to "quarantine" the aggressors in an October 1937 speech, a fierce isolationist chorus attacked him. His modest rearmament plan of January 1938 provoked a furor in Congress but eventually passed. Roosevelt did join the British in January 1938 in secret naval talks directed against Japan. He contemplated imposing economic sanctions on Tokyo and eventually entering hostilities undeclared and by stages, bypassing the isolationists in Congress. Both notions came into their own in 1941. But Roosevelt was a master of ambiguity, of avoiding commitment until it was inescapable. Chamberlain found no reason to reverse his judgment of late 1937 that it was "always best and safest to count on *nothing* from the Americans except words."

Japan's war in China therefore went forward without Western interference. By 1939 the Guomindang had retreated to Chongqing (Chungking) in Sichuan province in the far southwest. Japan had won the war but could not end it. The "New Order in Asia" that Konoe proclaimed in November 1938 was upheld only by Japanese bayonets. Japan had neither subdued China nor secured the resources that its own economy lacked.

Alliances against the West, 1936–37

By late 1937, Hitler had reached a number of conclusions and decisions. He recognized that Britain was willing to accept the peaceful achievement of German aspirations in Austria, Czechoslovakia, and the Polish Corridor. But it was unlikely to tolerate the far wider program put forward in *Mein Kampf,* and become junior partner in a German quest for *Lebensraum* and world domination. Hitler therefore decided to seek alliances against Britain, to deter it or to distract it militarily.

In the fall of 1936, Mussolini's parallel search for allies against the West and Italo-German cooperation in Spain brought Hitler and Mussolini together in a "Rome-Berlin Axis." Footdragging by Mussolini's conservative flankers and fear of becoming a satellite of the Reich kept him from seeking a formal military alliance until early 1939. But he gave Hitler evidence of his good faith by ostentatiously adopting German-style laws against Italy's 50,000 Jews in the summer–fall of 1938, over opposition that included powerful elements within the Fascist party. Japan signed on with Hitler in November 1936, in an agreement publicly directed against the Communist International. That "Anti-Comintern Pact" in reality involved a secret military commitment against the Soviet Union and an unspoken hostility to Britain. Italy joined the Anti-Comintern Pact in November 1937 when it followed the German and Japanese example by leaving the dying League of Nations.

None of these "Hitler coalition" pacts as yet offered firm guarantees that Germany would have allies in war. But they scared London, which intensified—in the hope of binding Hitler to the status quo—its efforts to "appease" what it regarded as his legitimate claims in central Europe. Hitler inevitably viewed such efforts as signs of British weakness and as an invitation to further German coups. On November 5, 1937, he told his high command and his conservative foreign minister that Germany might have the opportunity to seize Austria or Czechoslovakia or both in the near future. War with Britain and France must in any event come before 1943–45. Germany was ready to move from rearmament to war.

His listeners, except for Göring of the *Luftwaffe* and Admiral Erich Raeder of the navy, found Hitler's resolve to launch a war of aggression imprudent. The generals grumbled that Germany's strategic situation was still unfavorable. Hitler took note. And in January–February of 1938 he exploited questions about the moral character of his minister of war and army commander in chief to dismiss them both, along with his conservative foreign minister. He himself became minister of war and chose new military subordinates pathetically eager to please their *Führer*. Joachim von Ribbentrop, the former champagne salesman and NSDAP foreign-policy pundit who had negotiated the

Anglo-German Naval Treaty and the Anti-Comintern Pact, became the new foreign minister. Hitler had cleared the way for further expansion by consolidating his control over the German army and the foreign office, the last preserves of the conservatives who had brought him to power.

Bloodless Conquests: Vienna, Munich, Prague, 1938–39

An opportunity for further expansion immediately arose. In February 1938 the prime minister of Austria, Kurt von Schuschnigg, visited Hitler, hoping to placate him. Hitler bullied Schuschnigg unmercifully and extorted his agreement to take two Austrian NSDAP leaders into his cabinet as minister of war and minister of the interior. Once back in Vienna, Schuschnigg thought better of his promise to hand Austria over to Hitler. But British and French support was not forthcoming, and Italy had given up its claim to be Austria's protector in 1936. On March 11–12, 1938 the *Wehrmacht* rolled bloodlessly across the Austrian border.

The Austrians received the *Wehrmacht* and its *Führer* with flowers and delirious applause. Hitler responded by proclaiming the immediate *Anschluss* ("merging") of Austria into Germany. Savage SS persecution of Vienna's Jews began immediately; the Austrian army received new uniforms and Prussian drill instructors. And "Greater Germany" now surrounded Czechoslovakia on three sides.

Unlike Austria, Czechoslovakia had a military alliance with France, 35 well-equipped divisions, and fortifications that in some areas rivaled the Maginot line. But like Austria, it lacked Western support. The France of Daladier shamefacedly sought a way of avoiding its alliance obligations. A prominent Englishman privately advised a German acquaintance not to shoot Czechoslovakia, but to strangle it.

Strangulation, or what his diplomats jokingly described as an ethnic "chemical solution," was indeed Hitler's first thought. The German minority of 3.25 million in Czechoslovakia's northern border area—the Sudetenland—was his chosen instru-

Anschluss, March 1938: The German army takes possession of Vienna.

ment. In April he instructed the political leadership of the Sudeten Germans to press Prague with a series of ever-escalating demands that would lead ultimately to the dissolution of the Czech state. "Autonomy" for the Sudetenland would render Czechoslovakia indefensible by depriving it of its border fortifications and industries.

When the Czechs mobilized their army in May 1938 in response to bogus rumors of an impending German attack, Hitler changed his policy. Force would replace subversion: "It is my unalterable intention to smash Czechoslovakia by military action in the near future." He set a target date of October 1, 1938, and intensified work on Germany's fortified *Westwall* to keep the French at bay while he crushed Czechoslovakia.

By early September, as Goebbels' propaganda about fictitious Czech atrocities against the Sudeten Germans reached a crescendo, a covert mobilization had readied the *Wehrmacht*. Sudeten Ger-

mans rioted on orders from Berlin, and Hitler demanded their "self-determination" at the close of the last annual Nuremberg party rally on September 12. Mussolini mocked the Czechs and pledged his support to Hitler. The Czechs, despite intense pressure from London and Paris, got ready to fight for their existence.

This crisis moved Neville Chamberlain to act, to carry to its logical conclusion the policy of active, preemptive "appeasement" he had followed since becoming prime minister in 1937. He flew to Germany twice and urged the dictator to accept the Sudetenland by slices rather than all at once. Hitler naturally responded to Chamberlain's attempts at conciliation with further demands: the entire Sudetenland by October 1. But Chamberlain failed to persuade his cabinet colleagues to accept that humiliating ultimatum. Hitler, in a speech at the Berlin Sports Palace on September 26, then raved at the Czechs and offered them a stark choice: "Peace or war!" Chamberlain's reply was a mournful

The Munich Conference, September 29–30, 1938. Chamberlain, Daladier, Hitler, Mussolini, and Ciano decide Czechoslovakia's fate.

"Peace for our time?" Chamberlain returns from Munich, 1938.

radio address in which he confessed his dismay over this "quarrel in a far away country between people of whom we know nothing." Chamberlain's colleagues displayed greater resolve; they ordered the Royal Navy mobilized and a blockade prepared. The French unhappily followed. Hitler's insistence on unilateral violent solutions appeared at last to have created a coalition capable of blocking Germany before it achieved European hegemony.

Then Hitler had second thoughts. German crowds greeted the approach of war with a sullen silence far different from the delirious enthusiasm of August 1914. Germany could crush the Czechs. But Czech fortifications would exact a stiff price and the army was still far from ready for general war; it was not scheduled to reach full strength until 1940–41. Finally, Germany in 1938 lacked the oil and raw materials required for a long war against Britain and France.

When Chamberlain proposed a further compromise through Mussolini, Hitler resentfully acquiesced to a four-power

conference at Munich on September 29–30, 1938. There Chamberlain and Daladier pressed on him a phased occupation of the Sudetenland by October 10. Roosevelt, from the background, urged London and Paris to avoid war. To save the West's face, the dictator agreed to an unenforceable four-power guarantee of the mutilated and militarily defenseless remnant of Czechoslovakia.

The Munich agreement was an immense moral, political, and strategic defeat for the West, a defeat that made possible Hitler's destruction of the European and world order in 1940–41. The West abandoned its one industrialized eastern European ally, and Germany's annexations in the Sudetenland included a rich booty: more than 70 percent of Czechoslovakia's major industries.

Chamberlain nevertheless returned from Munich with what he claimed was "peace with honor," "peace for our time." Churchill and a small band of dissident Conservatives thought otherwise. So did Hitler, who immediately and publicly rejected British attempts to hold him to the

Munich agreement: "We will suffer the tutelage of governesses no longer!" He was privately furious that his "entry into Prague had been spoiled." In a secret speech to his press representatives on November 10, he regretted that his peace speeches had misled the German people: "Force of circumstances was the reason I spoke for years only of peace." Now the task was to turn the *Volk* around: it must stand like "formed-up troops" behind his leadership. Doubters in the "intellectual strata" unfortunately still possessed necessary skills: "otherwise one could exterminate them, or whatever." As Hitler spoke, party activists devastated synagogues and Jewish shops all over Germany at his command, in the regime's last public attempt to mobilize the German people against the Jews.

By early 1939, Hitler had begun to see the realization of his program within his grasp. He inaugurated a new naval building plan: by the mid-1940s Germany would have an 800-ship fleet far superior to Britain's and capable of taking on the United States. He accelerated an immense construction plan to remake Germany's city centers within ten years. Huge domes and halls, designed so that their ruins would be impressive thousands of years hence, were to fit Berlin for its new status as capital of the world. To his officer corps, he insisted that Munich was not an end but a beginning; Germany was bound for world domination. It must move forward as it had since 1933, "without letup, exploiting every opportunity, however small, to move immediately toward a new success." And he publicly warned that "international Jewry" was the source of foreign accusations that he was seeking war. He promised retribution.

Convinced of the feebleness of Western resistance, Hitler saw no reason not to absorb the remainder of Czechoslovakia. On March 14–15, 1939, he bullied its helpless government into placing itself under German "protection." Hitler and the *Wehrmacht* entered Prague. Germany's overheated war economy received a new infusion of booty. But Hitler had at last gone too far. His conquest of territories inhabited almost entirely by Czechs disproved his claims that he sought only self-

---

Churchill on Munich   October 5, 1938

To the accompaniment of heckling from Chamberlain loyalists, Churchill sought unsuccessfully to convince the House of Commons that "peace for our time" was defeat without war.

CHURCHILL: . . . I will . . . begin by saying the most unpopular and most unwelcome thing. I will begin by saying what everybody would like to ignore or forget but which must nevertheless be stated, namely, that we have sustained a total and unmitigated defeat, and that France has suffered even more than we have.

VISCOUNTESS ASTOR: Nonsense.

CHURCHILL: When the Noble Lady cries "nonsense," she could not have heard the Chancellor of the Exchequer [Sir John Simon, speaking for the Chamberlain government] admit in his illuminating and comprehensive speech just now that Herr Hitler had gained in this particular leap forward in substance all he set out to gain. The utmost my right hon[orable] Friend the Prime Minister [Chamberlain] has been able to secure by all his immense exertions . . . the utmost he has been able to gain—[*Hon Members:* "Is peace."]. . . . The utmost he has been able to gain . . . has been that the German dictator, instead of snatching his victuals from the table, has been content to have them served to him course by course. . . .

From Martin Gilbert, Winston S. Churchill, *Vol. V, 1922–1939: The Prophet of Truth (Boston: Houghton Mifflin, 1977), p. 997.*

---

determination for Germans. His breach of the Munich agreement and of his September 1938 promise that the Sudetenland was his "last territorial demand in Europe" showed that he was utterly untrustworthy. The Prague coup crystallized opinion in Britain, which had turned increasingly against Germany after Munich and the November 1938 attack on Germany's Jews.

The Totalitarians United, and the Coming of Hitler's War

A storm of public protest enveloped Chamberlain, who had initially sought to avoid responding to the Prague coup. His answer, when it came on March 31, 1939, was ill-considered. Britain and France guaranteed Poland, which appeared to be

Hitler's likely next victim, against threats to its independence. The Western Allies soon extended similar guarantees to Rumania and to Greece, which Mussolini appeared to menace by his annexation of helpless Albania on April 7. Chamberlain, with Paris in tow, belatedly attempted to create a structure of diplomatic deterrence that would halt Hitler.

But Hitler played by war-fighting rules. Paper guarantees of states that the Western powers could not defend in war did not impress him. The Western pledge to Poland simply convinced him that the Poles, who had already resisted secret German demands for the German-inhabited city of Danzig and for West Prussian territory lost to Poland in 1918–19, should definitely be his next target. On April 3 he set September 1, 1939, as the planning date for an attack on Poland.

The Western guarantee to Poland also made Stalin the man of the hour: the "capitalist" powers were now pledged to fight among themselves. All Stalin had to do was to await bids for his support. Soviet participation in war might not even be necessary; the Soviet Union and Nazi Germany might exercise joint domination of

The morning after *Kristallnacht* ("plate glass night"), the Nazi party attack on synagogues, Jewish businesses, and Jews that Goebbels organized on November 9–10, 1938.

the Eurasian land mass. Stalin's daughter, who later defected to the West, testified to her father's conviction that "together with the Germans, we would have been invincible!"

In May 1939, Stalin dismissed his foreign minister, Maxim Litvinov, lest Litvinov's Jewish antecedents complicate negotiations with Berlin. Stalin's creature Vyacheslav Molotov took Litvinov's place and renewed Moscow's longstanding secret proposals for a German-Soviet political agreement. The British and French also explored cooperation with Russia, but they sent their negotiators to Leningrad by slow boat. Chamberlain had no enthusiasm for a Bolshevik alliance, and London, in view of Stalin's liquidation of half the Soviet officer corps, doubted the military usefulness of that alliance.

Hitler also moved to ensure that Italy would serve to distract Britain and France in the Mediterranean while he attacked Poland. The Axis powers concluded a war alliance, the so-called "Pact of Steel," on May 22, 1939. It was to operate automatically if either power "became . . . involved in warlike actions," regardless of who had provoked the conflict. Mussolini tried to limit his commitment by pointing out that Italy needed another three years to strengthen its armaments; Hitler was silent.

The day after the signing of the Pact of Steel, Hitler addressed his generals. The German-Polish border dispute over Danzig and West Prussia was merely the pretext for war. The real issue was "the enlargement of *Lebensraum* in the East." That must come soon; Germany faced a choice between continuing rise, and decline. And this action would be different from Czechoslovakia: "There will be fighting." If Britain and France objected, he would fight them as well.

By mid-August, as the Goebbels propaganda machine blasted the Poles, the *Wehrmacht* had again covertly mobilized. Talks with Moscow progressed well: Hitler and Stalin spoke the same language. On August 20 Hitler wrote urging Stalin to receive Ribbentrop to put the finishing touches on a Russo-German "non-aggression" pact. Stalin agreed. The British and French negotiators were in essence offering Stalin war with Germany, and no gains. Hitler was offering him no war, and a division of eastern Europe into Nazi and Soviet spheres. Stalin thus achieved objectives sought since the beginning of the Soviet state. The foundation of the non-aggression pact, Stalin later informed the British ambassador with amazing openness, was the common Russo-German aim of destroying the "old balance" of power that had existed in Europe.

On the night of August 23–24, in the Kremlin, Ribbentrop and Molotov signed the Nazi-Soviet Non-Aggression Pact in Stalin's presence. Its name was misleading: it promised benevolent neutrality in the event that either power became involved in war, even a war of aggression. And its secret protocol drew a line through eastern Europe and Poland that divided the two parties' respective booty. At the close of the negotiations, Ribbentrop ventured a joke: Berlin humorists were saying that Stalin was about to join the Anti-Comintern Pact. Stalin too offered a witticism: "The Germans wanted peace. . . ." And Stalin then toasted both Hitler and Heinrich Himmler, that "guarantor of order in Germany."

Even before Ribbentrop had closed his deal with the Russians, Hitler again spoke to his generals: "We must act." Now was the point of Germany's greatest relative strength. His own leadership was irreplaceable, and he could "at any time be removed by an idiot or criminal." In a few years British and French armaments would begin to catch up, while Germany's war economy would run down for lack of raw materials. Hitler's sole fear, according to one account of his remarks, was "that Chamberlain or some other swine [*Saukerl*] might arrive at the last moment" with peace proposals. He ordered the attack on Poland for August 26.

Hitler wavered briefly on August 25, when Britain signed a military alliance with Poland and Mussolini shamefacedly confessed that Italy was too weak to fight. Then, surrounded by SS advisers, he confirmed his decision for war. Germany's long-term situation was "very difficult, perhaps hopeless." But as he had written

Hitler "Foresees" the Holocaust   1939

In his Reichstag *anniversary speech of January 30, 1939, Hitler made clear publicly that he reserved a special fate for Europe's Jews.*

I have in my life very often been a prophet, and was generally laughed at. In the period of my struggle for power it was the Jewish people who first of all received my prophecies exclusively with laughter, [when I said] that I would one day take over the leadership of the state and thus of the entire German people, and that I would among many other things also bring to solution the Jewish problem. I believe that the laughter of German Jewry that then resounded has since died in their throats.

I will today once more be a prophet: if international finance Jewry inside and outside Europe succeeds in plunging the nations into a new world war, the outcome will not be the Bolshevization of the earth and thus the victory of Jewry, but the extermination [*Vernichtung*] of the Jewish race in Europe.

From Hitler: Reden und Proklamationen 1932–1945, *ed. Max Domarus (Munich, 1965), Vol. 2:1, p. 1058 (translation by M. Knox).*

Stalin and Ribbentrop enjoy a joke at the signing of the Nazi-Soviet Pact, August 23–24, 1939.

in *Mein Kampf,* Germany would "either be a world power, or would cease to be."

At 4:45 A.M., German summer time on September 1, 1939, the *Wehrmacht* attacked Poland from north, west, and south. In the next two days a sorrowing Chamberlain and the fearful French sought to promote, with Italian help, yet another conference. But the House of Commons refused. The Labour opposition and dissident Conservatives combined to "speak for England" and demand that Chamberlain honor Britain's pledge to Poland.

The March guarantee had perhaps been a tactical diplomatic error, but it had one great virtue at the end. Hitler, by challenging it, forced Chamberlain to declare war or suffer the collapse of his government. Britain's ultimatum to Germany expired at 11:00 A.M. on September 3. The Second World War had begun.

The causes of the war of 1939 have generated less dispute than those of World War I, of which it was a continuation. Britain, France, and the United States made a second war possible by failing either to dismember or conciliate Germany in 1919. Subsequently, their supine inaction and preemptive concessions permitted Hitler to rearm and strike. The Prusso-German conservatives helped Hitler to power and collaborated enthusiastically with him in creating the *Wehrmacht* that destroyed the European and world balance. Stalin sought alliance with Hitler for the overthrow of the European balance and the extension of Soviet power. Stalin gave Hitler the chance to strike when he did. But in the end, it was Hitler's drive toward total power and his vision of racist world revolution that made this greatest of wars: "The decision to strike was always in me."

Suggestions for Further Reading

Totalitarianism

H. Arendt, *Totalitarianism* (1951), remains the classic description of the phenomenon, but is often eccentric. W. Laqueur, *The Fate of the Revolution,* rev. ed. (1987), conveniently summarizes debate about the concept of totalitarianism and about the Soviet regime. G. Orwell, *1984* (1949) and *Animal Farm* (1946), offers biting analysis in fictional form of totalitarianism in general and of Stalin in particular.

Stalin

On the Soviet Union, M. Heller and A. Nekritch, *Utopia in Power* (1982), is a lively introduction; B. Dmytryshyn, *USSR: A Concise History* (1978), provides a brief narrative and key documents. H. Carrère d'Encausse, *Lenin: Revolution and Power* (1981) and *Stalin: Order Through Terror* (1981), offer clearsighted analysis. On Stalin, see especially A. Ulam, *Stalin* (1973), and R. Conquest, *Stalin, Breaker of Nations* (1991). On Stalin's consequences, see R. Conquest, *The Harvest of Sorrow* (1986), *The Great Terror* (1968), *Kolyma: the Arctic Death Camps* (1978), and A. I. Solzhenitsyn, *The GULAG Archipelago* (1973). The numbers Stalin killed remain a subject of hot debate; for useful estimates, see S. Rosefielde, "An Assessment of the Sources and Uses of GULAG Forced Labour, 1929–56," "Excess Mortality in the Soviet Union," and "Incriminating Evidence: Excess Deaths and Forced Labour Under Stalin," *Soviet Studies,* 1:1981, 3:1983, 2:1987. On Stalin's foreign policy, see above all A. Ulam, *Expansion and Coexistence* (1968).

Mussolini

The Italian dictatorship is insufficiently studied. C. Seton-Watson, *Italy from Liberalism to Fascism* (1967), offers an excellent introduction to the circumstances that made it possible. A. Lyttelton, *The Seizure of Power* (1973), ably describes its first decade. M. Knox, *Mussolini Unleashed, 1939–1941* (1982) and "Conquest, Foreign and Domestic, in Fascist Italy and Nazi Germany," *Journal of Modern History,* 56:1 (1984), explores where it was going.

Hitler and War

The best introduction to Nazi Germany remains K. D. Bracher, *The German Dictatorship* (1970). K. Hildebrand, *The Third Reich* (1984), and P. Ayçoberry, *The Nazi Question* (1981), are excellent on the interpretive issues. On Hitler himself, see first of all his own words: A. Hitler, *Mein Kampf* (Ralph Manheim translation, 1943), and *Hitler's Second Book* (1961). J. Fest, *Hitler* (1975), is by far the best biography. On the inner workings of the regime, M. Broszat, *The Hitler State* (1981), is outstanding. W. Deist, *The Wehrmacht and German Rearmament* (1981), is the best introduction to Hitler's war preparations. K. Hildebrand, *The Foreign Policy of the Third Reich* (1973), and G. Weinberg, *The Foreign Policy of Hitler's Germany* (1970, 1980), are excellent on foreign policy. W. Murray, *The Change in the European Balance of Power, 1938–39* (1984), provides outstanding analysis of the strategic consequences of Munich and dissects the West's failure to stop Hitler before he became too strong. On Hitler's responsibility for and movement toward genocide, see especially G. Fleming, *Hitler and the Final Solution* (1982), and R. Hilberg's classic, *The Destruction of the European Jews* (1961; revised and expanded, 1985).

Finally, A. J. P. Taylor's *The Origins of the Second World War* (1961), raised a storm by arguing that Hitler had no long-term vision and that war in 1939 was simply a result of opportunism and miscalculation. That view has found few supporters; Hitler's words, both public and private, demonstrate otherwise. P. M. H. Bell, *The Origins of the Second World War in Europe* (1986), provides a useful summary of recent research; G. Martel, ed., *The Origins of the Second World War Reconsidered* (1986), offers mostly hostile retrospective comment on Taylor.

FROM SECOND WORLD WAR TO COLD WAR 1939–1949

*I*n the next two and a half years, the war that began on September 1, 1939, grew into a global conflict. Hitler destroyed Poland, invaded Scandinavia, and crushed France. Those victories opened Mussolini's road to a Mediterranean and Balkan war. They encouraged Japan to move south on a collision course with Britain and the United States. And they gave Hitler the strategic and economic base he needed to begin "his" war for *Lebensraum* in the East and for racist world revolution.

On June 22, 1941, Germany attacked Soviet Russia. That at last brought into existence an "anti-Hitler coalition"—Britain, Russia, and a still reluctant United States—powerful enough to bring the Reich down. On December 7, 1941, Japan completed that coalition by forcing the United States into war. Hitler and Japan made the European war of 1939–41 into a global struggle that destroyed Europe's independence.

Only Hitler united his enemies. As the Reich faltered in its desperate struggle against the three allied world powers, the allies began to break up. Stalin sought an empire stretching far beyond the eastern European sphere gained from Hitler in 1939. Britain and America hesitantly sought Stalin's cooperation in a postwar system of world order, a successor to the defunct League of Nations. Given the underlying incompatibility between the Soviet Union and the Western Allies, "cold war" predictably followed world war once Hitler was dead. By 1947–48, the peoples of eastern Europe, already ruined by Hitler, had suffered a second—Soviet style—revolution from above. But this time the United States did not withdraw as it had in 1919. It reluctantly committed forces to hold in "peacetime" against Stalin the positions it had stormed in war against Hitler. Global war gave way to global confrontation between the American and

(OPPOSITE) THE FACE OF A NEW WORLD WAR: GERMAN MECHANIZED INFANTRY DESTROYS A RUSSIAN VILLAGE, 1941.

Russian superpowers, under the shadow of weapons of unimaginable power, atomic and then thermonuclear bombs.

THE NEW WARFARE

Technology and Science at War

The internal combustion engine restored the battlefield mobility that industrial firepower had taken away in 1914–18. The second German war was a war of movement; its pace sometimes rivaled or exceeded that of Napoleon's campaigns. Only in fortified areas or when evenly matched forces met head-on did the fighting congeal for months at a time into something that resembled Verdun.

The tank came into its own. In the 1920s British theorists had suggested that the future of war on land resembled war at sea: vast armored formations sweeping across the battlefield like great fleets. But the conservatism of Britain's cavalrymen, Chamberlain's budget stringency, and his government's resolve never to fight again on the Continent killed innovation in Britain. In Germany the tank caught on during the *Wehrmacht*'s rapid expansion after 1933; in 1935 the German army set up its first *Panzerdivisionen*—armored divisions. By September 1939 it had six of them.

Contrary to myth, Germany's armored forces were not a response to a demand by Hitler for weapons with which to implement a "*Blitzkrieg*" or "lightning war" strategy of short decisive campaigns. Until 1938, Hitler let the German army do its own planning. He was fortunate—and the world unfortunate—that his generals successfully combined motors, armor, radios, and the German deep-penetration tactics of 1917–18 into an instrument that could smash the European balance of power.

At sea, oil-fired turbines and diesel engines gave the fleets far greater range than the coal-fired navies of the First World War. A new capital ship, the aircraft carrier, rivaled and soon replaced the Dreadnought as the backbone of sea power. By 1941 the aircraft of the fast fleet carriers of the Imperial Japanese and U.S. navies could reach out hundreds of miles beyond the horizon to rain armor-piercing bombs on the enemy. Refueling at sea

Fleet carrier: the USS *Lexington* in 1939.

gave the fleets ranges of thousands of miles. And the amphibious techniques pioneered by the U.S. Marine Corps—partly to defend its budget between the wars—enabled Americans and British to fight their way back after the early Allied disasters.

In the air, the scene had also changed. Airpower was no longer in its infancy. Aircraft were now capable of tasks ranging from "strategic" bombing of the enemy's homeland to transport of troops and supplies, dropping of parachute or glider infantry, close support of ground troops, deep photo-reconnaissance, attack on surface fleets, antisubmarine patrol, and air defense. Air superiority was the key to rapid movement by land or sea. Only the Germans, in the last phases of the war, were tough and expert enough to fight successfully for long without air cover.

The greatest novelty of all was the contribution of science. Fritz Haber's nitrate process had given Germany the explosives that enabled it to fight on until 1918. But in World War I science had in other respects been a mere auxiliary to warfare. By 1939 that was no longer true. The development and production of decisive or potentially decisive weapons such as radar, computers to decipher enemy signals, liquid-fuel ballistic missiles, jet aircraft, and the atomic bomb required a high level of scientific skill, technological expertise, and economic power.

The bomb—the first nuclear weapon— was the result of an unprecedented commitment of scientific talent and resources, a commitment only the United States could make. The spur for this first example of "command science"—a vast government-directed research project aiming at a goal—was fear that Hitler would get the bomb first. Fortunately, German physicists advanced slowly and hesitantly, and Hitler gave priority to projects that promised quick results. The U.S. "Manhattan Project" spent a staggering $2 billion and drained the hydroelectric power of the Tennessee Valley and Pacific Northwest. But by July 1945 it had produced the uranium and plutonium bombs used against Japan. Science made possible—and war appeared to demand—weapons of mass destruction that were potentially capable, for the first time, of annihilating all humanity.

The Industrial and Geographic Balance

Even more than 1914–18, the Second World War was a struggle between war economies as well as between armed forces. Germany began at a slight disadvantage in total industrial potential compared to Britain and France. But its unassailable geographic position, control of Rumania's oil, and economic aid from Stalin more than made up for that shortcoming. Much of Germany's rubber supply flowed in through Vladivostok. Soviet oil fueled Hitler's U-boats, aircraft, and tanks. Turkey's chrome and Finland's nickel hardened the armor of the *Panzer* divisions. In 1940 Sweden provided almost half of Hitler's iron ore through the Baltic and the coastal waters of Norway. This time, the British blockade was ineffectual.

The collapse of France brought Germany much military and economic booty, and France's industries, which now worked for the Reich rather than against it. But Italy's simultaneous entry into the war extended Germany's military and economic risks without compensation; Britain now had an enemy it could defeat in Africa and the Mediterranean. And by the fall and winter of 1940, the economic power of the United States had begun to swing against Germany.

That threat helped decide Hitler for war against the Soviet Union, which he expected to crumble swiftly. But the Soviets held, although barely. Germany thereafter faced a coalition of world powers with at least three times Germany's industrial potential. The addition of Japan to the Axis powers in December 1941 was only a small gain; Britain, the United States, and the Soviet Union still had more than two and a half times the industrial potential of the "Hitler-coalition" of Germany, Italy, and Japan (see Figure 33-1). Soviet Russia's refusal to collapse and Hitler's rejection of Stalin's secret bids for an armistice led to the destruction of the

FIGURE 33-1   **The Axis Defeated: War Production**   **1940–43**

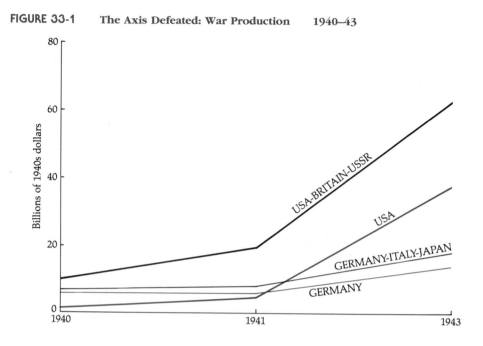

FROM EUROPEAN TO GLOBAL WAR, 1939–41

Poland: Defeat and Occupation

Poland fought bravely, but not for long. By September 15 the most serious fighting was over; German armor and airpower had sliced the Polish forces into helpless fragments. Stalin attacked the Poles from the rear on September 17 and claimed the Polish territories promised him under the secret protocol to the Nazi-Soviet pact.

In their occupation of Poland, Soviets and Nazis showed remarkable similarities in their methods. As Stalin remarked much later to a Yugoslav Communist, "This war is not as in the past; whoever occupies a territory also imposes on it his own social system. . . . It cannot be otherwise." Beginning in September 1939, Stalin deported to the GULAG more than a million Polish civilians and prisoners of war. To decapitate any future Polish national resistance, Stalin and the Politburo ordered the NKVD to shoot more than 20,000 Polish officers, members of the upper classes,

Reich under a rain of fire and steel from the east, the west, and the skies.

and clergy in March–April 1940; many of their bodies turned up in 1943 in a mass grave in Katyn forest in western Russia. The Baltic states suffered similar treatment when the Soviet Union swallowed them in June–July 1940. And Stalin, who so loved foreign Communists that he had liquidated many of them in the Great Terror, also handed over to Himmler hundreds of German and Austrian Communists who had sought refuge in the Soviet Union. Stalin was not joking when he publicly hailed "Russo-German friendship, cemented by blood."

Himmler and his sinister subordinate Reinhard Heydrich lacked Stalin's long experience in truly large-scale killing. They found Poland a splendid training ground. With the advancing German army came *Einsatzkommandos* ("task forces") of SS and Police whose mission was to kill Jews and educated Poles, especially priests. Thousands perished in experimental massacres; German army protests led to a brief halt. Then the army sheepishly handed over control of occupied Poland to the Party and the SS.

Hitler himself, on October 18, made clear to his subordinates what he expected from Poland: "cheap slaves." Himmler herded the Jews of Poland into newly created ghettos as a "first prerequisite" for an as yet unspecified "final goal." He also shipped in ethnic Germans from the Baltic and carpetbaggers from the "Old Reich" to settle the areas cleared of Poles and Jews. And war freed Hitler even inside Germany. In October 1939 he ordered—in secret—the killing of mental patients and the handicapped to rid the "race" of "worthless life." The totalitarian reshaping of Europe had begun.

"Greater Germany" Triumphant, 1940

The West made no attempt to help the Poles, despite repeated French pledges to attack Germany from the west. The French instead peered fearfully from their Maginot Line bunkers and sent out a few inept patrols. By the end of September 1939 the Germans were happily redeploying their forces from Poland to the French and Belgian borders.

Hitler immediately demanded that his generals attack in the West. Time was against Germany. The British were at last creating a mass army; Allied war production was rising; America "was still not dangerous to us because of her neutrality laws," but that might change. The generals grumbled that they needed more time. Some hesitantly plotted against the regime.

Unfortunately for the West, bad weather repeatedly forced Hitler to postpone the attack. The breathing space gave the German army time to add more vehicles, draw lessons from the fighting in Poland, and train relentlessly. It also gave Hitler and a brilliant junior general, Erich von Manstein, time to replace the army staff's uninspired copy of the Schlieffen Plan (see p. 762) with a surprise armored thrust through the hills around Luxembourg.

Distractions in Scandinavia also dogged Germany throughout the winter. Stalin had misjudged the Finns: unlike the defenseless Baltic states, they did not tamely give in to Soviet demands for military bases and territory. On November 30 Stalin therefore attacked Finland and set up a puppet Finnish Communist government in a captured border town. The League of Nations, in its last memorable act, expelled the Soviet Union as an aggressor. But the Finns and the great powers, not world opinion, determined the outcome. Soviet numerical superiority finally wore the Finns down in February–March 1940, but by that time Stalin's amateurishly led troops had suffered several hundred thousand dead and wounded. Fearing that Soviet occupation of all of Finland would lead to continued fighting and Allied intervention in Scandinavia, Stalin settled for the small annexations he had demanded at the outset.

War in Scandinavia indeed attracted Allied and German hopes and fears. Paris hoped to divert the war away from the plains of northern France. Winston Churchill, whom Chamberlain had unwillingly taken into the cabinet as chief of the Royal Navy, urged attacks on Germany's vulnerable iron ore supply line from neutral Sweden. The Germans also prepared; they longed for a window on the Atlantic in Norway for their submarines and commerce raiders.

The Germans moved first. On April 9, using the *Luftwaffe* to compensate for their naval inferiority, they seized key points in Norway with brilliantly executed amphibious and airborne attacks. German ground troops swiftly seized Denmark. Britain and France belatedly landed forces in central and northern Norway. But German speed, skill, and air superiority drove them out by early June.

Defeat in Scandinavia destroyed the mournful Chamberlain as a war leader. On May 10, 1940, Winston Churchill came to power as prime minister at the head of an all-party coalition. Labour, which had damned Churchill in earlier years for his uncompromising hostility to striking miners, Gandhi, and Hitler, now staunchly agreed to share with Churchill the responsibility for leading Britain's war effort. Churchill had been right about Hitler.

But Churchill arrived almost too late. The day of his appointment was the day on which the Germans launched their long-awaited offensive against France and the Low Countries. They had prepared well. The *Luftwaffe,* despite heavy losses, swept the skies of French aircraft and savagely bombed Rotterdam to terrorize the Dutch. German infantry swiftly crushed the small and inexperienced armies of Holland and Belgium. Seven *Panzerdivisionenen* and three motorized infantry divisions struck through Luxembourg and the Ardennes hills, and reached the Channel on May 20, cutting off in the Low Countries forty of the best-equipped Allied divisions. Of that huge force, 1.2 million fell prisoner; only 226,000 British and 112,000 French escaped to Britain from the beaches of Dunkirk.

On June 17, after the Germans had seized Paris, a new French government under the aged Marshal Pétain sued for armistice. By June 24 France was out of the war; only small "Free French" forces under the command of a charismatic junior general, Charles de Gaulle, fought on with British help. Hitler occupied the north and west of France, leaving Pétain only an enclave in the south with its capital at Vichy. Greater Germany—*Grossdeutschland*—now controlled Europe from the North Cape of Norway to the Spanish border. Hitler had succeeded where William II and Ludendorff had failed. In the intoxication of victory and looted champagne, the German generals and Hitler's conservative allies forgot their earlier doubts. War, as Hitler had hoped, had made him *Führer* indeed.

Britain, America, Russia and the German Strategic Impasse, 1940–41

But the war did not end in France; victory there proved a strategic dead end. Hitler expected Britain to "see reason" and join the Reich as a junior partner, but Churchill refused to give in: "Nations that went down fighting rose again but those which surrendered tamely were finished." Chamberlain and Halifax sought negotiations from weakness in the name of "realism," but Churchill beat them down in cabinet debate. He was confident that Britain's rising production of fighter aircraft would prevent the Germans from achieving air superiority and invading Britain.

Churchill also bid ruthlessly for the American support Britain needed to fight on; better Roosevelt as senior partner than Hitler. On May 20 Churchill secretly warned Roosevelt that failure to support Britain might lead to a new British government committed to surrender. That government might swing the British fleet to the Axis side and mortally threaten the United States in the North Atlantic. And to show Roosevelt and the world that Britain would fight so long as he was in command, Churchill's navy on July 3 sank or captured in harbor much of the fleet of Britain's former ally, France. The Axis could no longer gain naval superiority by seizing French battleships from the Pétain government.

The fall of France at last galvanized American opinion and freed Roosevelt to

The victor: Hitler tours Paris, 1940.

respond to Churchill's polite blackmail and to his display of resolve. The U.S. Congress ordered America's first peacetime military draft in August 1940; America's dwarf army of 280,000 could now once more become a serious force—in a few years. Roosevelt also defied the spirit of a congressional ban on weapons sales. In September 1940 he traded fifty obsolete U.S. destroyers for the right to use British bases in Newfoundland, Bermuda, and the Caribbean, and for a pledge that Britain would never turn its fleet over to the Germans. In November 1940 he trounced his Republican opponent, Wendell Willkie, and won an unprecedented third term as president.

Hitler saw the coming American threat—and a possible remedy—as early as July 31: "England's hope is Russia and America. If hope in Russia falls away, America too falls away, for after elimination of Russia an immense increase in Japan's power in east Asia follows." If Germany destroyed Soviet Russia, Hitler assumed, Japan would be free of threat on its northern flank and could keep the Americans busy in the Pacific. Hitler therefore sought an immediate attack on the Soviet Union. War in the East was not only "his" war, the war he had looked for since 1922 to secure for Germany a vast blockade-proof eastern empire, a "German India." It was also the answer to the growing support of the United States for Britain. A German "world *Blitzkrieg*" in Russia would make Germany unassailable by conquering Eurasia before Roosevelt could bring to bear the immense economic and military potential of the United States.

But Hitler's planners soon told him that Russia's harsh climate would prevent an eastern campaign that fall. He therefore fell back on stopgaps. Germany launched a sea and air war against Britain's Atlantic supply lines, but a strategy of attrition offered no promise of immediate results, and threatened to speed up Roosevelt's drift toward war. A second possibility was operation SEA LION, an invasion of Britain for which the Germans began to prepare in July. But in the vast "Battle of Britain" that reached its climax over southern Eng-

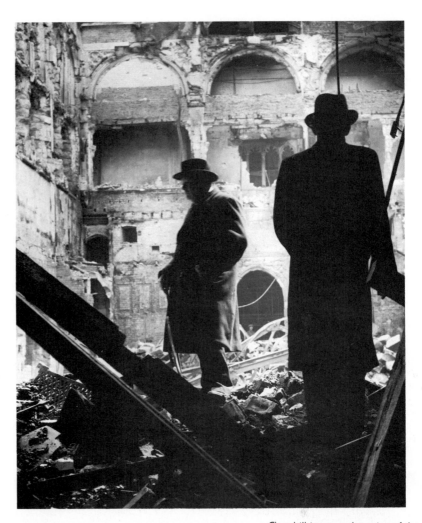

Churchill inspects the ruins of the House of Commons after a German attack.

land on September 15, the Spitfires and Hurricanes of the Royal Air Force (RAF) denied the *Luftwaffe* air superiority. The Germans then switched to night bombing in the "Blitz" of winter 1940–41. Their raids flattened large areas of London and killed civilians by the thousands, but failed to break British morale.

The German navy and Ribbentrop offered other options. The navy pressed for a Mediterranean campaign: seizing Britain's outpost at Gibraltar with the help of Franco's Spain and galvanizing the Italians to take Suez. Ribbentrop tried to fashion a world coalition from Madrid to Tokyo

Spitfire!

against Britain and the United States. On September 27, 1940, he succeeded in enlisting the Japanese and Mussolini in a "Tripartite Pact" in which all three pledged to come to each other's aid in the event of war with the United States.

St. Paul's Cathedral, London, under *Luftwaffe* bombardment, January 23, 1941.

Franco and Mussolini between them wrecked both the German navy plan and the European part of Ribbentrop's coalition. The price Franco set for Spain's intervention was higher, in supplies and territory, than Hitler was willing to pay; Gibraltar remained British. And Mussolini threw the Mediterranean theater into chaos by attacking Greece at the end of October 1940. The Greeks hurled the ill-trained Italians back into Albania. British torpedo bombers then sank three Italian battleships at anchor, and British armored forces from Egypt crushed the large but poorly led Italian army in Libya between December 1940 and February 1941.

Italy's disasters forced Hitler to intervene in the Mediterranean not to achieve final victory over Britain, but merely to rescue his ally. U-boats, a *Luftwaffe* air corps, and armored units under the brilliant but erratic Erwin Rommel arrived in time to prevent the collapse of Italy's position in Africa, and of Mussolini's regime. In spring 1941 Hitler ended Mussolini's Balkan war by striking south into Greece through Rumania and Bulgaria, and by bloodily dismantling a potentially hostile Yugoslavia.

But these new victories offered Hitler no way to end the war. German triumphs in the Mediterranean or Middle East could not force Britain to negotiate so long as it controlled the North Atlantic and had the support of the United States. And Roosevelt, despite a continuing isolationist opposition which trumpeted that "the British, the Jew[s], and the Roosevelt administration" were seeking to force America into war, was at last achieving results. In February–March 1941, Anglo-American staff talks secretly laid down the strategy governing the future U.S. war effort: *Germany first*. If and when the United States entered the war, it would concentrate its power against the West's most dangerous enemy. In March 1941 Congress passed a "Lend-Lease Act" which offered to a financially exhausted Britain, and thereafter to other U.S. allies, an almost unlimited supply of arms on long-term credit. Credits later turned into outright gifts, and ultimately amounted to $43 billion.

Racist War of Annihilation: *BARBAROSSA*

Even before Lend-Lease made clear that the United States was moving toward Britain, Hitler had decided on his response: "his" war, the war in the East. Ribbentrop had invited the Soviets to explore the possibility of Soviet participation in the Tripartite Pact. But the uncouth Molotov's visit to Berlin on November 12 and 13, 1940, wrecked that project. To Ribbentrop's fantasies about a Soviet Russian outlet to ice-free oceans through Iran and British India, Molotov replied with a long shopping list in Europe—*Germany's* chosen sphere. Stalin wanted Soviet bases at the Turkish Straits, the addition of Bulgaria to the Soviet "security zone," the removal of German protection over Finland, and joint Soviet-Danish—but not Soviet-German—control over the exits from the Baltic. Molotov also stressed the Soviet Union's "interest" in Rumania, Hungary, Yugoslavia, Greece, and even the portion of Poland currently assigned to Germany under the Nazi-Soviet Pact. The tactlessness and extravagance of Molotov's demands suggested that Stalin expected the Anglo-Saxon powers to defeat Germany, and was claiming his booty in advance.

Hitler was relieved. Stalin had "let the cat out of the bag." The Soviet-German "marriage of convenience" was over. On December 18, Hitler issued a directive for the greatest land war in history, Operation BARBAROSSA: "The German *Wehrmacht* must be prepared to *overthrow Soviet Russia in a swift campaign,* even before the end of the war with England." BARBAROSSA would annihilate all Soviet forces in European Russia and seize all Soviet territory up to a line that stretched from Archangel on the Arctic Ocean to Astrakhan on the Caspian Sea. That stroke, Hitler and his generals assumed, would crush the Soviet regime and give Germany world mastery.

The German military planners shared Hitler's racist contempt for the Red Army, and regarded the destruction of the Soviet Union as an "intriguing" operational problem. But for Hitler it was more than that.

"The coming campaign," he told his subordinates on March 3, "is more than a mere armed conflict; it also entails a struggle between two ideologies." And since, by Hitler's racist logic, Bolshevism was an outgrowth of Judaism, the ideological struggle required "racial" measures: "the Jewish-Bolshevik intelligentsia . . . must be removed."

What that meant soon became clear. Hitler's military assistants issued orders empowering Himmler of the SS to carry out "special tasks" in the coming area of operations. *Einsatzgruppen* ("task groups") of the SS and Police, with army help, were to take "executive measures with respect to the civilian population" of Russia. The army itself, under the "Commissar Order" of May–June 1941, became for the first time a direct extension of Hitler's racial goals. That order required shooting upon capture all Red Army political officers and Communist party members. The *Wehrmacht* estimated that it would take 3.5 million prisoners of war but allocated rations for only 790,000; the rest would presumably starve. And the experts of Göring's economic planning staff decided that the conquered territories would have to feed the *Wehrmacht*—leaving no food for the cities of European Russia. "X millions of people will die out," noted the bureaucrats dispassionately. BARBAROSSA was to be a racial and ideological war of extermination that trampled underfoot all limits on interstate violence established in Europe since the Thirty Years' War. Colonial war had come home to Europe.

On June 22, 1941, the *Wehrmacht*'s three million men attacked the Soviet Union on a front that stretched from the Baltic to the Black Sea. Stalin had received numerous warnings, but had spurned them as "capitalist provocations" designed to trick him into an unwanted and unnecessary war with Hitler. He had preferred to believe rumors planted by the Germans that the *Wehrmacht* deployment was a gigantic attempt to extort more raw materials from the Soviet Union. German deception worked; until the last, Stalin apparently expected a German ultimatum.

What he got instead was war. "What shall we do?" he reportedly asked the Politburo before suffering a nervous collapse. Not until July 3 did he belatedly take to the radio and urge his Soviet "brothers and sisters" in a broken voice to resist to the end. Stalin evidently had difficulty believing that those he had terrorized would fight for him. They fought above all for biological survival and for Great Russian nationalism. Wholesale massacres by the Germans of Soviet prisoners of war and Jews stiffened Soviet resistance. And the Soviet regime now appealed not to "proletarian internationalism" but to something far deeper. It invoked the Russian traditions that Stalin had promoted through the historical rehabilitation, in the 1930s, of past rulers whose methods resembled his own: Ivan the Terrible and Peter the Great.

The Germans advanced swiftly, thanks to strategic surprise and to their overwhelming advantages in military doctrine, experience, and *Luftwaffe* airpower. By early August they had taken Smolensk, halfway to Moscow, and had killed or captured more than a million Soviets. Hitler looked to the future; he believed he had won. He ordered German armament efforts shifted to air and sea warfare against the British. Subordinates drafted a directive for German thrusts through the Caucasus to the Middle East oilfields in the coming "period after BAR-BAROSSA." Germany, Hitler privately declared, would raze Moscow and Leningrad to the ground, exterminate much of the population of European Russia, and replace it with German settlers. The term "Greater German World Empire," which Goebbels had banned from his press in 1940 as premature, no longer seemed inappropriate.

July–December 1941: The Culmination of the War

Others saw the future differently. Churchill and Roosevelt immediately offered aid to a surprised Stalin, who accepted it in the spirit in which it was offered; as he once remarked, "In war I would deal with the Devil and his mother." But the Western powers nevertheless assumed that the Germans would destroy Soviet Russia. Roosevelt and Churchill met on shipboard near Newfoundland in mid-August 1941, and produced an "Atlantic Charter," a declaration of war aims in the style of Woodrow Wilson.

The Charter implied that the United States would eventually enter the war. It proclaimed that Britain and the United States sought "no aggrandizement, territorial or other" and desired "no territorial changes that [did] not accord with the freely expressed wishes of the people concerned." It announced that both powers would seek free markets, freedom of the seas, and "freedom from fear and want" for all humanity. But it made no reference to the third member of the new "Grand Alliance," or to that power's entirely different principles and methods. Roosevelt and Churchill evidently expected that they alone would dictate the outcome of the war. The United States began to ready an army that would surpass the *Wehrmacht:* a projected 215 divisions of which 61 would be armored.

The Newfoundland meeting was the outward expression of a halting change in Roosevelt's policy. In the conviction that the aid "short of war" promised with Lend-Lease was not enough to defeat Hitler, he began to move toward war itself. Without the formal approval of Congress, Roosevelt began between July and September 1941 an undeclared naval war in the North Atlantic. U.S. forces took over Iceland, an outpost Hitler coveted, from the British. Roosevelt agreed to convoy British shipping from Canada to Iceland. In September, after the inevitable clash between a U-boat and a U.S. destroyer, he gave the U.S. Navy orders to "shoot on sight" at Hitler's navy.

Before sailing to meet Churchill, Roosevelt had also moved against Japan. Hitler's May–June 1940 victory in Europe had encouraged Tokyo to turn southward toward the vital oil of the Dutch East Indies. Then a Soviet-Japanese nonaggression pact signed in April 1941, coupled with Hitler's attack on the Soviet Union in June, had ended Tokyo's fear of a Soviet threat on its northern flank in Manchuria.

In July 1941 Japan occupied bases in the southern part of French Indochina in preparation for a further jump southward. Roosevelt reacted by freezing all Japanese assets in the United States and by restricting the U.S. oil exports on which Japan depended. The Dutch took similar measures. In the space of a week, Japan had lost 90 percent of its oil supply. Roosevelt himself seems to have intended only to cut back U.S. oil exports as a warning, but zealous subordinates announced a total cutoff.

Tokyo then offered to moderate its activities in China and Indochina. But Roosevelt and his advisers judged Japan's offer insincere; the Japanese army in any event privately refused to give up its Chinese colony. In September 1941, Tokyo decided to go to war with the United States while its navy still had oil reserves and before the United States completed its naval rearmament—unless a breakthrough occurred in negotiations. None did. In mid-October the military rulers of Japan dropped their facade; Prince Konoye's civilian cabinet gave way to the government of General Tōjō Hideki. On November 26, as Roosevelt again insisted on Japanese withdrawal from China, Japan's fast carrier forces secretly sailed.

In Russia, the Germans at last closed on Moscow. In July and August Hitler had diverted armored forces south to the Ukraine, where they took another 650,000 prisoners in a great encirclement at Kiev. The Ukraine operation, troop exhaustion, and supply difficulties delayed the final drive on Moscow until early October. But once launched, operation TYPHOON made dramatic progress. The Germans demolished yet another Soviet army group and seized a further 600,000 prisoners in great battles at Vyazma and Bryansk.

In Moscow, the NKVD disappeared from the street corners. Bonfires in the ministry courtyards consumed mountains of files. Bureaucrats fled for Kuibyshev on the Volga River, which had been designated as the alternative capital. An announcement that Stalin remained in the Kremlin and a few NKVD shootings stabilized the situation briefly—but the Soviet regime appeared close to collapse. Then

Pearl Harbor, December 7, 1941.

the fall rains bogged the *Panzerdivisionen* and their supply echelons in Russian mud. The freeze that followed briefly speeded the advance once more, but Soviet resistance stiffened. German reconnaissance units reached the outskirts of Moscow; they could see the flashes of the antiaircraft guns on the Kremlin roof. But the Germans were desperate. By early December, only a quarter of their original tank force could move; 23 of every 100 German soldiers who had invaded the Soviet Union were dead, wounded, or missing. On December 5–6, fresh Soviet troops launched a counteroffensive that threw the Germans into confusion. Hitler had failed to destroy the Soviet Union.

The following day, December 7, 1941, the Japanese naval air arm struck at Hawaii, and crippled the battleship force of the U.S. Pacific Fleet at Pearl Harbor. The military logic of the Japanese attack was as impeccable as its execution was flawless—except that it missed the fleet carriers, which were at sea. Because the U.S. fleet was the main obstacle to Japan's southward advance to the oil of the Dutch

East Indies, a preemptive strike to eliminate that fleet had seemed essential. But the Japanese in their desperation had ignored the political and strategic consequences of attacking Pearl Harbor. Japan's "date which will live in infamy"—as Roosevelt described December 7—freed him of the delicate task of persuading Congress to declare war in defense of the British and Dutch colonial empires. And Pearl Harbor produced instant unanimity in the United States. Isolationists, many of whom saw themselves as defenders of American ethnic purity against contamination from the outside world, took up with a fierce racism the cause of crushing Japan. Nor had Tokyo—given its own racist disdain for outsiders and consequent underestimation of American resolve—thought how to end the war it had begun against an enemy with at least ten times its military-industrial power.

Hitler closed the circle on December 11, 1941, by declaring war on the United States. He apparently hoped that a two-ocean war would prevent America from concentrating its power decisively in either theater. His decision, like that of the Japanese, handed the United States an immense political-strategic victory. Roosevelt now had no need to persuade Congress to declare the war on Germany needed to implement his long-decided strategy of "Germany first." Hitler's declaration forced America to fight in Europe and guaranteed that it would fight hard. Hitler and Tokyo between them made certain the defeat of the Axis and the end of Europe's independence.

THE "FINAL SOLUTION"

The realization that Germany might lose spurred Hitler to greater military efforts. It also led him to make sure of one thing: the accomplishment of the "historic mission" he had long ago defined for Germany, the elimination of the alleged threat of "Jewish world domination."

The "executive measures" of the SS against the civilian population of Russia that Hitler ordered in March–April 1941 took effect during the headlong *Wehrmacht* advance from June to December. SS and Police *Einsatzkommandos* rounded up and shot as many of European Russia's 4.7 million Jews as they could catch. The *Wehrmacht* protested far less now than it had over the 1939 killings in Poland. Hitler's victories had immeasurably reinforced his authority and the prestige of his ideology, and the army itself had inherited from the *Freikorps* of 1918–21 (see p. 793) the tradition of shooting Bolsheviks "while attempting to escape." Until the war turned in December 1941, high German commanders had no qualms about ordering their units to massacre Soviet prisoners and Jews: "The [German] soldier must be fully convinced of the necessity of harsh, but just expiation by the Jewish-Bolshevik subhumans."

But the Jews of Russia were only part of Hitler's target. At the height of his victories in July 1941, Hitler remarked that "if any [European] state . . . permits a Jewish family to remain, that [family] will become the bacteria-breeding-ground for a new

---

Hitler Gloats Openly over the Extermination of the Jews   1942

Few Germans later admitted to having known about it, but Hitler publicly boasted in scarcely veiled language about the "Final Solution" on four occasions in 1942 (January 30, February 24, September 30, and November 8):

I told the *Reichstag* session [January 30, 1939; see p. 853] two things: First, that once they had forced the war upon us, neither armed force nor passage of time would bring us down, and second, that if Jewry were to unleash an international world war for the purpose of exterminating the Aryan peoples of Europe, then it would not be the Aryan peoples that would be exterminated, but Jewry. . . . The Jews in Germany once upon a time laughed at my prophesying. I do not know if they still laugh, or whether their laughter has already ceased. I can however now assure you that they will never laugh again [*es wird ihnen das Lachen überall vergehen*]. And *that* prophecy of mine will also be confirmed.

Hitler speech at Berlin, September 30, 1942, in Hitler: Reden und Proklamationen 1932–1945; ed. Max Domarus (Munich, 1965), Vol. II:2, p. 1920 (translation by M. Knox).

infection." On July 31, 1941, Himmler's subordinate Reinhard Heydrich received orders to organize, "with the participation of all necessary German central bureaucracies, all preparations for a general solution of the Jewish Question in Europe."

Hitler himself was apparently careful not to sign a document authorizing what soon became known in the SS and the German ministries as the "Final Solution of the Jewish Question." But both his public remarks and his private actions leave little doubt that he was the driving force behind it. He repeatedly demanded reports of the progress of the killings, and in November 1941 he promised the Grand Mufti of Jerusalem, leader of the Palestinian Arabs, that when Germany conquered the Middle East he would "annihilate" the Jews there as well.

In September–October 1941 the SS began deporting to Poland and occupied Russia the German and Austrian Jews. The SS shot many of them in mass executions. But that method soon proved cumbersome. In the fall, winter, and spring of 1941–42, Himmler and his subordinates therefore set up camps in occupied Poland designed as factories of death, with gas chambers and crematoria: Auschwitz-Birkenau, Treblinka, Lublin, Sobibor, Belzec, Chelmno. In January 1942, at a conference in the flossy Berlin suburb of Wannsee, Heydrich tasked the major Reich ministries to assist him in deporting the Jews—men, women, and children— to these death camps: "Europe will be combed through from west to east."

The "Final Solution" did not end until November 1944, when Himmler, on his own initiative, suspended it as the Reich neared collapse. Its consequence was the murder of more than 6 million Jews, including a quarter of a million from Germany, more than 1 million from Russia, 3 million from Poland, 200,000 from western Europe, and at least 750,000 from eastern Europe.

The Jews were the victims with the highest priority. But the Gypsies of Europe also suffered deportation to the death camps on "racial" grounds; hundreds of thousands perished. German experts tested killing-factory techniques on Soviet

The "Final Solution": Jewish deportees arrive at Auschwitz.

prisoners and on German mental patients and handicapped as well as on Jews. Between 1941 and 1945 the SS and the German army between them killed the staggering total of 3.3 million Red Army prisoners by shooting or maltreatment. More than 2 million Poles died during German conquest and occupation. And Hitler's intention, in the event of victory, was to exterminate most of the population of eastern Europe and European Russia. Hitler's genocide was more than a Holocaust of the Jewish people. It was the first step in a pseudo-biological attempt to remodel humanity—a racist world revolution.

It also went almost unchallenged, except on distant battlefields and in a doomed 1943 Jewish uprising in the Warsaw ghetto. French police and Dutch SS helped round up Jews for deportation. Slovaks, Greeks, and Hungarians cooperated with greater or lesser enthusiasm. Rumania and Germany's Croat puppet-state vigorously organized their own massacres of Jews; Latvians, Lithuanians, and Ukrainians provided the SS with valuable helpers. The major exceptions were Denmark, Norway, Bulgaria, and even Fascist Italy, which baffled the Germans with bureau-

The "Final Solution"

The first train arrived . . . 45 freight cars with 6,700 people, of whom 1,450 were already dead on arrival. . . . A large loudspeaker blares instructions: undress completely, take off artificial limbs, glasses, etc. Hand in all valuables. Shoes to be tied together (for the clothing collection). . . . Women and girls to the barber, who cuts off their hair in two or three strokes and stuffs it into potato sacks.

Then the line starts moving. . . . At the corner a strapping SS-man announces in a pastoral voice: Nothing will happen to you! Just breathe deeply inside the chambers, that stretches the lungs; this inhalation is necessary against the illnesses and epidemics. When asked what would happen to them, he replies: Well, of course the men will have to work, build houses and roads, but the women won't have to work. If they want to they can help in the household or the kitchen. For a few of these unfortunates a small glimmer of hope which suffices to have them take the few steps to the chambers without resistance—the majority knows what is ahead, the stench tells their fate. . . .

The wooden doors are opened. . . . Inside the chambers, the dead are closely pressed together, like pillars of stone. . . . Even in death one recognizes the families. They still hold hands, so they have to be torn apart to get the chambers ready for the next occupants. The corpses are thrown out—wet with sweat and urine, covered with excrement, menstrual blood. Children's bodies fly through the air. . . . Two dozen workers use hooks to pry open mouths and look for gold. . . . Others search genitals and anuses for gold, diamonds, and valuables. Wirth [an SS guard] motions to me: Just lift this can of gold teeth, this is only from today and the day before! . . .

From an eyewitness account of mass gassings, in Vierteljahrshefte für Zeitgeschichte *(1953), Vol. 1, pp. 190–91.*

cratic roadblocks and passive resistance, and saved many of their Jews.

The churches and the Allies did little. Most Protestants, except in Scandinavia, were silent. Pope Pius XII, despite excellent information about the death camps, offered only general condemnations of the killing of civilians. Even the October 1943 deportation of Roman Jews to Auschwitz—"from under his windows," as the German ambassador put it—did not move Pius XII to public protest, although the Church secretly helped to hide Jews. Stalin was himself a longstanding and virulent anti-Semite, and many high British and American bureaucrats harbored a poorly concealed distaste for Jewish refugees.

At first the Allies discounted the reports of the killings; deliberate, mechanized mass murder seemed too monstrous an act even for Hitler. Britain did issue a declaration describing the deportations in December 1942, and Churchill pressed for air attacks on the rail lines leading to Auschwitz. But the great distances to the target, the military demands of the air war and of the Normandy invasion, and bureaucratic sabotage by his subordinates prevented action.

This time Churchill did not use the public threats with which he had answered rumors in early 1942 that Hitler planned to use poison gas against Britain's Soviet ally. Then Churchill had promised reprisals: a deluge of mustard gas from the air upon Germany. That entirely credible threat had deterred Hitler, although he had secretly stockpiled large quantities of nerve gas, a weapon far more deadly than anything in the Allied chemical arsenal. But unlike the Soviet Union, the Jews of Europe were not a state—or an ally of Britain and the United States. They had last call on Allied resources. The victims of Hitler's genocide, like those of Stalin's, perished without even token assistance from that elusive force, world public opinion.

THE HOME FRONT: BUREAUCRACY, PROPAGANDA, TERROR, DEATH

On the home fronts, the war followed some of the precedents laid down in the First World War and the Great Depression. All the major belligerents mobilized immense masses of men for war and industry. Women again joined the work force in vast numbers, even in Germany, where the regime's ideology supposedly dictated that they remain at home. The Reich also mobilized up to 12 million Soviet prisoners of war, slave laborers, and foreign workers.

The totalitarian states had acted even in "peacetime" as if they were at war. Their economies, even when "capitalist" in formal terms, were largely state-directed even before 1939. War provided justification in Germany for still greater state and Nazi Party intervention in the economy and in daily life, and the occasion for ever-more intense barrages of lies from Goebbels' "Ministry of Public Enlightenment and Propaganda."

As the ring around Germany drew tighter, terror itself became a key ingredient in the war effort; Hitler was fanatically determined to prevent a repetition of Germany's 1918 political collapse. Civilians who expressed doubts about "final victory" disappeared into Himmler's camps. Military personnel guilty of "subverting the will to fight" perished by the thousands on portable *Wehrmacht* gallows. Conversely, Stalin in 1941 and 1942 gave survival priority even over domestic terror. NKVD pressure on the population and the army briefly relaxed. But once the Soviet Union gained the upper hand after 1943, arrests increased once more.

The democracies, as in 1914–18, improvised vast wartime bureaucracies to guide public opinion and to ration food, raw materials, and labor. Press, radio, and film became an arm of the war effort. Censorship, often voluntary, prevented the publication of news deemed harmful to morale. Photographs of American battle dead rarely appeared. And as in 1914–18, public discussion of war aims aroused extravagant expectations. At home, especially in Britain, those expectations spurred the planning of a postwar "welfare state" that would banish the misery of the Great Depression. In international politics, similar hopes accompanied the "United Nations"—a new and better League that would replace that supposed evil, the balance of power, and secure peace through universal goodwill without effort by the democracies. British and American war propaganda also encouraged illusions about the lovable nature and supposed agreement with the principles of the Atlantic Charter of jovial, pipe-smoking "Uncle Joe" Stalin.

Traditional democratic freedoms also suffered partial eclipse, especially for groups that appeared somehow linked with the enemy. Churchill's government rounded up 30,000 German and Italian "enemy aliens" during the great invasion emergency of 1940 and imprisoned them not for offenses committed but for *suspected* disloyalty. Although the United States faced an external threat far less immediate than Germans across the Channel, Pearl Harbor nevertheless triggered a hysterical racist clamor against the Japanese-American minority on the West Coast. Roosevelt ordered 112,000 of them deported to the interior; many lost farms and businesses. Deportees of military age shamed those responsible for this shabby treatment by volunteering to fight. Many served as linguists in the Pacific. Their unit in Europe, the 442nd Regimental Combat Team, terrified the Germans and earned more decorations for valor than any other American force of its size and time in combat.

Except for fortunate North America and distant Australia and New Zealand, all major belligerents suffered either foreign military occupation or devastation from the air. Many suffered both. That was the most striking difference between the two world wars. In the first, those behind the front had been almost immune from violent death. In the second, scorched earth and famine, guerrilla warfare and assassinations, reprisals and massacres, and the rain of high explosive, magnesium, white phosphorus, and napalm from the skies bound "front" and "rear" in shared danger. This was a "total war" far more total than its predecessor.

GLOBAL WAR, 1941–45

The global war of December 1941 turned swiftly against the Axis. By summer–fall 1942, Germany and Japan were stalled everywhere, from the Russian steppes to the South Pacific. Then Allied counterattacks drove the Axis back while air bombardment and submarine blockade wrecked the economies that sustained the Axis forces. And as the Allies advanced, discord between them became increasingly visible.

The Last Successes of the Axis, 1942

While the Germans sought to rebuild the forces shattered in the 1941–42 winter fighting in Russia, Japan seized a perimeter from India's western border to Wake Island, west of Hawaii (see the map on p. 873). Hong Kong, the Philippines, Singapore, and the Dutch East Indies swiftly fell to air and amphibious attack. Douglas MacArthur, photogenic commander of U.S. forces in the Philippines, left for Australia in March at Roosevelt's order. His troops fought on until the Japanese overwhelmed them in May. The inglorious surrender on February 15 of more than 80,000 British and Empire troops at Singapore—to a smaller Japanese force—was the deathblow to "white" imperial prestige in Asia. By summer 1942, Japan appeared poised to attack India from Burma, while Gandhi (see p. 809) inspired a new wave of demonstrations and riots against British rule.

But after a thrust southward toward New Guinea that led to a first indecisive action between carrier fleets, Japan struck at Midway Island, west of Hawaii. U.S. decipherment of Japanese signals enabled Chester Nimitz, the U.S. theater commander, to lay an ambush. On June 3–6, 1942, the two fleets traded air attacks near Midway—and the outnumbered U.S. Navy almost miraculously destroyed four Japanese fleet carriers and their highly trained pilots. The Battle of Midway tore the heart from the Japanese naval air force and made Japan's far-flung perimeter untenable.

By June 1942, Hitler was himself ready for a last major thrust, toward the oil of the Caucasus region. The *Panzerdivisionen* once again ripped immense gaps in the Soviet front. But as in 1941 Hitler failed to choose one objective and stick to it. As the Soviets crumbled, he ordered a second major thrust at Stalingrad, the key Soviet communications point on the Volga. There the Germans soon found themselves locked in street fighting in the rubble, where German armor and skill were of little use. The Red Army's bitter resistance made Stalin's city the Verdun of the Second World War.

Hitler had lost the strategic initiative in December 1941. He now lost even the operational initiative; Germany had no more troops or equipment for wide-ranging offensives. Even in Africa, where Rommel had improvised a modest *Blitzkrieg* at the end of a long and precarious supply line, Germany halted in July 1942 at El Alamein, 75 miles short of Alexandria.

The Allies Strike Back, 1942–43

Allied counterblows soon came. In the Pacific, a U.S. Marine Corps landing on Guadalcanal, at the southern tip of the Solomon Islands, countered the Japanese threat to the U.S. supply line to Australia. In a savage land, sea, and air battle of attrition that lasted from August 1942 to February 1943, the Marines and the U.S. Army forced the Japanese out. U.S. submarines began a ruthless campaign against Japanese merchant shipping that cut Japan's seaborne empire into isolated fragments.

Rivalry between MacArthur and the Navy prevented the concentration of U.S. effort on a single thrust back across the Pacific. Instead, MacArthur laboriously ascended the Solomons and New Guinea toward the Philippines, to which he had theatrically promised to return. Further north, the Navy—using Marine and U.S. Army landing forces backed by battleship gunfire and carrier aircraft—seized a succession of bloodstained central Pacific islands: Tarawa, Kwajalein, Eniwetok, Saipan, Guam, Ulithi, Palau. In fall 1944 MacArthur and the Navy joined to invade the Philippines. From Saipan, Tinian, and Guam, the shining new B-29s, the largest and farthest-ranging bombers in existence, could now batter the Japanese homeland.

British and U.S. troops soon drove the Germans from North Africa. In October–November 1942 the British desert commander, Bernard Montgomery, at last attacked Rommel at El Alamein. Montgomery deliberately fought a methodical 1918-style battle. Weight of fire, not skill, crushed his nimbler opponent. Rommel escaped, but then faced an unexpected attack from the rear after an American-British task force landed in French North

The Road to Tokyo Bay   1942–45

Africa on November 9, 1942. The slow-footed Allies failed to take Tunis before the Germans, but then they laid siege to Rommel and his Italian allies by land, sea, and air. In May 1943, the Axis bridgehead around Tunis collapsed; Hitler and Mussolini had lost North Africa and almost a quarter of a million irreplaceable veterans. In July, the Allies leapt to Sicily. As Mussolini's regime crumbled and Italy fled the war, Americans and British seized positions south of Rome in September–October.

On the eastern front, the Soviets launched the greatest counteroffensive of all. On November 19, 1942, the Red Army struck from the north and southeast of Stalingrad and encircled 300,000 Germans and German allies in and around the city. Hitler, as was his habit, ordered implacable resistance: no withdrawal, no breakout, no surrender. At the end, in February 1943, only 93,000 Germans remained alive to surrender as food and ammunition ran out. In July 1943 Hitler ventured a last local offensive at Kursk, south of Moscow.

Counterattack! Soviet infantry in the ruins of Stalingrad, 1943.

Surprise was lacking, and Soviet antitank guns smashed the Germans in the greatest armored battle of the war. Germany had lost even the tactical initiative in the East.

In the Atlantic, the U-boats that had savaged British and U.S. shipping in 1941–42 soon found themselves under siege. British microwave radar, British decipherment of German navy communications, and the addition of U.S. escorts and airpower to those of Britain won the "Battle of the Atlantic" by May 1943. In that month the Germans sank 50 merchant ships at too steep a price: 41 U-boats and crews. The defeat of the U-boats made possible the American build-up in Britain for the coming assault on Hitler's "Fortress Europe."

That fortress, as Churchill had pointed out in a speech, had no roof. Stalin's increasingly bitter demands for an Allied "second front" in Europe had led Britain to pour vast resources into heavy bomber forces; only in the air could Britain strike directly at Germany. Since German fighters made daylight bombing suicidal, RAF Bomber Command concentrated on night raids. And at night, it was clear by summer

1941, British bombers could hit no target smaller than a German city. The bomber offensive, for lack of alternatives, therefore sought to dislocate the German economy indirectly through what the chief of RAF Bomber Command described with relish as "de-housing" the Germans.

The Reich now paid dearly for having trampled on all the conventions of "civilized" European warfare, including inhibitions against bombing cities; the *Luftwaffe* had done its best to flatten Warsaw, Rotterdam, London, Coventry, and Belgrade. From March 1942 on RAF massed bomber raids devastated the cities of western and central Germany: Lübeck, Rostock, Cologne, Essen, Bremen, Düsseldorf. In July–August 1943, the RAF burned most of Hamburg, killing 50,000 civilians and de-housing 800,000 others. The *Luftwaffe*, overcommitted on all fronts, took the bombers on in a bitter struggle of attrition. But fresh Allied aircraft and crews joined the battle faster than the Germans could shoot them down.

Hitler and Goebbels used the fall of Stalingrad and the coming of the bombers to demand total mobilization for "total war" from the German people. SS terror, loyalty to a still revered *Führer,* and fear of retribution for Germany's war of extermination in the East thereafter kept the German people in the war to the bitter end. War production, thanks to fanatical German efforts and to the mobilization of millions of foreign workers, slave laborers, and prisoners of war, rose until 1944. New "reprisal" weapons, such as the V-1 "buzz-bomb" and the V-2 ballistic missile, poured from slave-built underground factories. Jet-propelled fighters, by late 1944, briefly challenged Allied control of the skies. But the Reich failed to overcome the combined forces of the coalition it had created.

The "Grand Alliance": Stalin and the West, 1941–43

That coalition, by fall 1943, had begun to define its war aims. By December 1941, when Churchill's foreign secretary, Sir Anthony Eden, visited Moscow, Stalin had recovered from his panic of the previous summer. The Soviet Union was going to survive. Eden discovered, as Hitler and Ribbentrop had before him, that Stalin had ambitions. He insisted, for example, on keeping the Baltic states he had acquired in his 1939 bargain with Hitler. That was a violation of the Atlantic Charter's promise of self-determination, which the Soviet Union had accepted, although with reservations, in September 1941. But Stalin jovially sought to reassure Eden: he was different from Hitler, whose "fatal defect" was that "he does not know where to stop. . . . I can assure you that I will always know where to stop."

Stalin shrewdly capitalized on the Soviet Union's immense casualties and on the prestige gained as the only ally fighting large German land forces. He ceaselessly demanded that Roosevelt and Churchill establish a "second front" in Europe—the front that had existed in 1939–40 and had collapsed thanks in part to Stalin's support for Hitler. Stalin also played masterfully on Anglo-American fears that Germany and the Soviet Union would conclude a separate peace that would leave the Western Allies facing Hitler alone. He repeatedly approached Hitler in secret with offers of an armistice that would restore the borders of 1939 and the Russo-German quasi-alliance against the Western powers.

Roosevelt and Churchill failed to counter Stalin effectively. Almost apologetically—and unsuccessfully—they asked him to declare war on Japan, with whom the Soviet Union had signed a non-aggression pact in April 1941. Roosevelt, too anxious to please, promised a second front in Europe in 1942, a logistical and military impossibility. Partly to placate Stalin, Roosevelt also proclaimed at a January 1943 conference with Churchill at Casablanca that the Allies would accept nothing less than "unconditional surrender" from Germany, Italy, and Japan. A further purpose of that policy, which Roosevelt derived from the implacable Union war aim in the U.S. Civil War, was to prevent a repetition of 1918–19. This time the Western Allies planned to smash Germany for good, stamping out "stab-in-the-back" legends and any desire for yet another rematch. Stalin responded with an inexpensive gesture: in May 1943 he announced the dissolution of the Communist International, which had become redundant now that he had placed his own men firmly at the head of the International's "fraternal parties."

As with Chamberlain's 1939 guarantee to Poland, Roosevelt's assurances that the "capitalists" would fight Hitler to the bitter end only encouraged Stalin to continue his secret courtship of Hitler. What the Anglo-Americans apparently did not know was that Hitler flatly refused to compromise; Germany's *Lebensraum* was at stake. Hitler would have willingly struck a deal with the Anglo-Americans—but *they* demanded Germany's total defeat. Stalin offered Hitler a chance for survival—but Hitler refused to bargain in the East. That deadlock ensured that the war would continue until Germany either won or ceased to exist.

By November–December 1943, when the ill-assorted Allies met for the first "Big Three" conference at Teheran in occupied Iran, Stalin held the advantage. The British and Americans were stalled in bloody

D-Day: Normandy, June 6, 1944.

fighting against a handful of German divisions south of Rome, while the Red Army was driving back some 2.5 million Germans. Lend-Lease aid, which gave the Red Army the 700,000 U.S. and British trucks it needed for the far-ranging offensive thrusts of 1944–45, was no substitute for a second front in the West. The United States drastically weakened its diplomatic position by scaling down its projected army from the 215 divisions planned in 1941 to a mere 89 by early 1944. Roosevelt sought to avoid war-weariness and his own defeat in the 1944 election. But that decision meant that the Western Allies now *needed* the Soviet Union to defeat Germany, and perhaps even Japan.

Churchill therefore offered preemptive concessions. To give Stalin back the western border he had secured in the Nazi-Soviet Pact of 1939, Churchill proposed that Poland "move westward" into Germany. Stalin, for his part, agreed to enter the Pacific war after the defeat of Germany. That was a prize the Anglo-Americans need not have paid for, since

the Soviet Union was certain in any event to seek booty in Manchuria and Korea after Germany's defeat.

The Reconquest of Europe, 1944–45

Throughout 1943 Germany had been strong enough to throw into the sea any green American or British troops landed on the mined and fortified shores of "Fortress Europe." By spring 1944, that had changed. The campaigns in North Africa and Italy had taught the U.S. Army about the Germans and about amphibious landings, the most difficult operation in war. The long-range P-51 Mustang fighters of the U.S. Army Air Corps had secured daylight air superiority over France and the western parts of Germany. British decipherment of German signals (code-named ULTRA) gave the Allies advance warning of German moves. A massive Allied deception operation persuaded Hitler and his generals that the main Allied landing on the Continent would come near Calais—or as far north as Norway.

On June 6, 1944, British, Canadian, and U.S. forces under the supreme command of an American, Dwight D. Eisenhower, landed on the Normandy beaches. Three airborne divisions descended on the German rear. Overwhelming air superiority, Allied logistical mastery, and messy ground fighting resembling that of 1918 expanded the Allied beachhead. Then, in late July, the U.S. First Army broke through at St. Lô and launched the Third Army of George S. Patton around the German western flank. Patton, unlike his cautious superior Eisenhower, understood mobile warfare as well as his German adversaries. By August he had overrun Paris and was reaching toward the German border. Charles de Gaulle, now head of a sizable Free French army, returned to claim the presidency of a new French republic. Even Montgomery, commanding the British and Canadians, showed unexpected speed in pursuit of a thoroughly beaten enemy. For a brief moment Hitler's subordinates despaired of halting the Allies short of the Rhine. In the East, the *Wehrmacht*'s Army Group Center folded up, crushed by a massive Soviet summer offensive that advanced more than 400 miles, from Smolensk to the outskirts of Warsaw, and cost the Germans half a million troops.

But Hitler held on, despite an assassination attempt on July 20 by a conspiracy of anti-Nazi staff officers. Himmler received the welcome task of purging the army and the bureaucracy. The Prussian conservatives who had invited Hitler into power—and then regretted it—now perished in the concentration camps they had made possible. Goebbels and the Nazi Party spurred the German population to fanatical resistance.

Eisenhower reined Patton in and gave Montgomery most of the shrinking stream of supplies reaching the Allied armies from their beachheads and improvised ports in Normandy. In mid-September Montgomery launched three U.S. and British airborne divisions in a straight line across Holland toward the Ruhr Valley and sent his armored divisions forward to link up. But the purpose of the attack was obvious, and Montgomery's armor was slow. An SS *Panzer* division resting near the northernmost drop zone at Arnhem crushed the British paratroops and de-railed the Allied thrust. Bitter positional fighting amid the minefields and camouflaged bunkers of Hitler's *Westwall* ran on into winter.

Hitler still hoped that a last stunning blow at the Western Allies would break the unnatural Grand Alliance and leave him to fight Stalin alone. In mid-December 1944, at the scene of his May 1940 victory in the Ardennes, he flung a last offensive at the Americans, whom he considered soft. His luck was no better than Ludendorff's in 1918, despite a penetration of fifty miles and a massacre of U.S. prisoners by SS troops. The U.S. 101st Airborne division, outnumbered and ringed by German armor, defiantly held the key road junction at Bastogne. Patton spun the U.S. Third Army around by ninety degrees on icy roads and within a week struck northward at the vulnerable German flank. As the skies cleared, Allied fighter-bombers hunted the roads clear of German tanks and trucks. This "Battle of the Bulge" consumed most of Germany's reserves of armor, ammunition, and gasoline, just as U.S. precision bombing of Germany's synthetic petroleum plants eliminated its sole source of fuel.

Allied airpower in the Bulge: a supply drop to the 101st Airborne Division at Bastogne, December 1944.

The Road to Berlin   1942–45

In the East, Stalin had by that point gone far toward the objectives staked out in 1939–40. By late July, the great Soviet drive that crushed Hitler's Army Group Center had seized the Polish city of Lublin. There Stalin established a Communist puppet regime (the "Lublin Committee") like the one he had tried to force on Finland in the 1939 Winter War. On August 1, 1944, as the Red Army approached Warsaw for the second time in a quarter-century, the Polish resistance movement rose against the Germans inside the city in a desperate effort to liberate the capital before the Red Army and the NKVD arrived.

Stalin halted his army across the Vistula River and gave Himmler's pitiless counterinsurgency forces time to crush the Poles in a two-month struggle. The SS eliminated on Stalin's behalf much of the remaining national leadership of Poland. Stalin met Churchill's protests by denouncing the Polish resistance fighters as "criminals." He denied to British and American aircraft the use of his airfields to drop supplies to the Poles. Despite pleas from Churchill, Roosevelt refused to use the considerable leverage over Stalin that the great Allied victories in France now gave. And while it marked time in Poland, the Red Army drove Rumania and Finland from the war, overran Bulgaria, and slowly conquered Hungary. Soviet troops seized Belgrade, but the Yugoslav Communist guerrilla army of Josip Broz Tito largely cleared the rest of Yugoslavia of Germans by its own efforts—a fact of much political importance later.

As Stalin carved out a Soviet empire, Churchill made a last attempt to secure a modest measure of independence for eastern Europe. He faced Stalin in the Kremlin in October 1944 and reached an agreement—to which Roosevelt never subscribed—that divided Europe into spheres of influence. By this informal "percentage deal" Stalin conceded Britain a 90 percent preponderance in Greece, where Communist partisans were soon to attack the British and the Greek government that had returned from exile in London. Stalin received a similar predominance in Rumania and slightly less in Bulgaria. Yugoslavia was to be split "50-50." On Poland, Churchill failed to shake Stalin from his support of the Lublin Poles.

When the "Big Three" met for the second time, at Yalta in the Crimea in February 1945, Stalin's position was even stronger than it had been the preceding fall. Roosevelt was mortally ill, and even in good health lacked Stalin's relentless mastery of detail. Churchill was now totally dependent on the United States; Britain was financially and militarily exhausted.

Above all, the Red Army now held practically all of Poland. It was advancing into East Prussia amid the rape and slaughter of civilians, while the Anglo-Americans were still grinding their way painfully through Hitler's *Westwall* fortifications. Roosevelt's advisers assumed that the United States still needed Stalin's assistance against Japan and that they must pay for that assistance with concessions both in Europe and Asia. Finally, Roosevelt himself, although no zealot for world government, assumed that only a new and better League, the United Nations, could prevent a second American retreat into isolationism. The success of the United Nations clearly required Soviet postwar cooperation.

Yalta was thus the masterpiece of Soviet wartime diplomacy. Stalin had already brushed aside Western objections and had recognized his Lublin Committee as Poland's government. At Yalta he agreed that a few Poles from the London government-in-exile could enter the Lublin government as individuals—and as hostages to the Red Army and the NKVD. And he secured a firm commitment to the division of Germany into occupation zones, one for each major ally. He also presumably noted with interest Roosevelt's unguarded remark that United States troops would probably remain in Europe less than two years after the war.

The "Big Three" at Yalta, February 1945.

In Asia, Roosevelt capitulated to Stalin's demands for Russia's pre-1904 privileges and more: railroad rights in Manchuria, the vital warm-water base of Port Arthur, and the annexation of southern Sakhalin and the Kurile islands north of Japan. Roosevelt even accepted the delicate task of securing the agreement of Chiang Kai-shek to this renewal of tsarist colonialism. In return, Stalin generously promised to enter the war against Japan three months after Germany's defeat. He pledged Soviet cooperation in founding the United Nations, which eventually came into being at a conference at San Francisco between April and June 1945. Finally, Stalin agreed at Yalta to a vaguely worded "Declaration on Liberated Europe" promising free elections in all countries the Allies occupied. Within a month of that promise, Stalin's tanks forced on Rumania a Communist-led government, while NKVD roundups and deportations in Poland intensified.

In early March 1945 Americans and British at last fought their way across the Rhine at several points; it was the Soviet turn to mark time while the Red Army cleared up the Baltic coast. British in the north and Americans to the south swiftly encircled 325,000 German troops in the Ruhr Valley. Patton drove across central Germany toward Czechoslovakia. The U.S. Ninth Army reached the Elbe River, sixty miles from Berlin, two weeks before the Soviets surrounded the city. Two battle-tried U.S. airborne divisions stood ready to descend on the rubble of Hitler's capital.

But Eisenhower and his superiors in Washington, in the disarray of Roosevelt's final illness and death on April 12, failed to seize Berlin. George Marshall, the U.S. chief of staff, opposed the sacrifice of American lives for "purely political purposes"—an oddly innocent remark, given that war *is* politics. Marshall and Eisenhower abandoned to the Red Army the symbol of victory over Germany, along with vital German territory. The United States ignored Churchill's desperate urging that it counter Stalin's all too obvious appetites by pushing as far east as possible.

The Red Army took Berlin against fanatical SS and *Wehrmacht* resistance, while Hitler committed suicide on April 30 in his bunker under the Reich chancellory. Mussolini had preceded him on April 28; the Italian Communist partisans who captured the *Duce* shot him "in the name of the Italian people." On May 7 and 9, the *Wehrmacht* surrendered unconditionally to the United States, Britain, and the Soviet Union. Germany, as Hitler had half-promised, had for the moment ceased to exist.

Japan in Ashes, 1945

As the members of the "anti-Hitler coalition" faced one another across the rubble of central Europe, the United States readied itself for the final assault on Japan. Hundreds of B-29 bombers were now in action. On the night of March 9–10 they turned central Tokyo into a sea of fire, and killed between 80,000 and 120,000 civilians. By July 1945 the United States had burned out half of the surface area of Japan's cities.

In February–March and April–June, two huge and bloody amphibious landings seized first Iwo Jima and then Okinawa, within fighter range of the Japanese home islands. Japanese pilots, following a tactic tested in the Philippines the previous fall, crashed explosive-laden *kamikaze* ("divine wind") suicide aircraft into U.S. carriers, transports, and escorts. They sank 21 U.S. ships and damaged more than 60 others. On land, the Japanese were equally merciless—toward themselves and toward the prisoners they rarely took. The Marines replied in kind; only 212 of the 22,000 Japanese troops on Iwo Jima ended as prisoners of war. The coming landings on the Japanese home islands, in the view of U.S. military planners, might cost as many as a million U.S. casualties, and many millions of Japanese. The war might last until mid-1946.

The Japanese cabinet saw defeat coming. But Japan's army, the decisive force now as before, refused to accept defeat. It still held southeast Asia, much of China, and Manchuria, Korea, and Japan. Japanese peace feelers through Moscow, deciphered by U.S. intelligence, suggested that Tokyo's diplomats now sought peace. But feverish military preparation for a last-ditch defense of the home islands sent a different signal. And Allied insistence on "unconditional surrender," which suggested the removal of the Emperor, gave the military diehards an apparently unanswerable argument for a fight to the death.

This difficult situation fell to Harry S. Truman, Roosevelt's vice president and successor. Truman, a man of personal and political courage ("The buck stops here."), underestimated by his contemporaries, entered the presidency with no experience of foreign affairs. He gradually turned against Stalin, but too slowly to affect the outcome in Europe. After July 1, 1945, the U.S. Army, despite continuing pleas from Churchill, withdrew from the wide areas it had conquered east of the planned Western zones of occupation.

On July 17, at Potsdam in the center of conquered Prussia-Germany, Truman met Stalin and Churchill at the last major wartime conference. Stalin confirmed his promise to enter the war in Asia. He secured half of a scheduled $20 billion in German reparations for the Soviet Union but pledged in return to deliver food from agricultural eastern Germany to the industrial Western zones. He also demanded a voice in the Ruhr occupation; the Western Allies refused. And he voiced a series of disquieting desires: naval bases in Greece, a United Nations mandate over the Italian colony of Libya, an interest in French Syria and Lebanon, and a role in the international administration of Tangier in Morocco. When Churchill congratulated Stalin on his military successes, Stalin grumpily remarked that at least one predecessor in the Kremlin had done better: in 1814 "Tsar Alexander got to Paris." That was an aspiration far beyond anything the Soviets had disclosed to Hitler in the Berlin talks of November 1940.

During the Potsdam conference an ungrateful British electorate replaced Churchill with the leader of the Labour party, Clement Attlee. That redoubled the burden on Truman. But Truman had discovered that the United States possessed a weapon that Roosevelt had concealed

Stalin, radiating self-confidence, with Churchill and Truman at Potsdam, July 1945.

from him—the still highly secret atomic bomb. Hitler had died before it was ready for use, but it might speed Japan's collapse. Stalin, informed of it officially for the first time at Potsdam, pretended indifference and expressed the hope that it would be used on the Japanese. His own atomic bomb project had begun secretly in 1942–43, after Soviet intelligence had alerted him to the British, American, and German nuclear efforts.

Truman shared the impatience of most citizens of the democracies. The war must end soon, so that "our boys" could return and happily demobilize. Neither Truman nor his planners explored the possibility of persuading Japan to surrender by siege, without an invasion; that would require too much time. Nor, despite advice from some State Department experts, was Truman willing to abandon publicly the demand for unconditional surrender. That formula had long outlived its supposed usefulness in soothing Stalin—but the public overwhelmingly supported it as a fitting revenge for Pearl Harbor.

The ruins of Hiroshima, August 1945.

Truman and Churchill did attempt to warn Tokyo with a declaration that promised "prompt and utter destruction" unless Japan surrendered, but hinted at Allied flexibility about Japan's postwar form of government. Japan ignored the hint. Truman therefore ordered that the first two operational bombs be dropped on Japanese industrial cities containing military installations. He could not "disinvent" the weapon on which the United States had spent $2 billion. U.S. opinion, from extreme Left to far Right, was in 1945 virtually unanimous in approving the use of the bomb to end the war. Most thankful of all were the infantry awaiting orders to storm the mined and barbed-wired beaches of Japan.

On August 6 and 9, B-29s from Tinian island dropped two atomic weapons on Hiroshima and Nagasaki, in southwestern Japan. Roughly 120,000 Japanese perished outright and many died later from long-term radiation injuries. The Hiroshima bomb failed to persuade, but the shock of the Nagasaki bomb and the simultaneous Soviet declaration of war and *Blitzkrieg* in Manchuria produced crisis in Tokyo. The

prime minister, Suzuki Kantarō, urged acceptance of the Potsdam declaration before worse followed. The war minister, General Anami Korechika, demanded continued resistance; most of the high command agreed. To break the deadlock, Suzuki made an unprecedented appeal to Emperor Hirohito, who by ancient but disused custom could in exceptional circumstances decide vital issues.

The Emperor, speaking softly, reproached his military for a wartime performance that had fallen far short of its promises. He insisted that Japan had no choice; it must "bear the unbearable." On August 15, after the suppression of a diehard military revolt, Japan's god-emperor broadcast to a people who had never before heard his voice and revealed that Japan would end the war. On September 2, 1945, Japan surrendered unconditionally to MacArthur and Nimitz on the deck of the battleship *Missouri,* at anchor in Tokyo Bay.

After six years and a day, the Second World War was over. It had cost the Soviet Union roughly 17 million military and civilian dead. Germany had lost 6.2 million; Poland, 6 million including its Jews; China, perhaps 4 million, not counting victims of famine and disease; Japan, 2 million; Yugoslavia 1.7 million; France somewhat more than and Italy somewhat less than half a million. Britain lost 325,000; the United States escaped with combat losses of only 292,000. More than 50 million people had perished in the most destructive conflict in history. Germany and Japan lay in ruins; tens of millions of destitute refugees, prisoners of war, slave laborers, and concentration camp survivors thronged central Europe. Economic chaos and political vacuum followed the defeat of the Axis in both Europe and Asia.

THE COLD WAR

As in 1918, victory did not bring peace. In bringing order out of chaos, the United States and the Soviet Union collided. The "Cold War" that followed divided Europe and the world for the next four decades. Its origins, chronological boundaries, and nature later provoked bitter debate, at least in the West. But its origins were no mystery. Conflict between great powers of differing aims, interests, and ideologies was neither new nor startling. What was surprising about the Cold War was the slowness of its coming. It took two years of ever more brutal Soviet measures in eastern Europe, of Soviet demands and encroachments in divided Germany, and of Soviet pressure on Europe's flanks to provoke the United States to a coherent response.

Before the Cold War: 1945–46

As in 1939–41, Stalin imposed the Soviet system on his new territories. And as in his destruction of his domestic rivals in the 1920s, he proceeded by stages, keeping his goals deliberately ambiguous. These "salami tactics," as Stalin's man in Hungary, Matyás Rákosi, described them, also owed a debt to Mussolini and Hitler, who had pioneered the technique of "legal" revolution through the power of the state apparatus. Stalin's relative caution, as Rákosi explained to a secret party meeting in May 1945, resulted above all from the need to divide Britain and the United States. If he did not provoke the United States, Stalin apparently thought, it might follow Roosevelt's prediction at Yalta and soon withdraw its troops from Germany. That would leave the Soviet Union dominant in Europe.

The Sovietization of eastern Europe therefore proceeded cautiously, in three phases. First came Red Army and NKVD control in 1944–45, then in 1945–47 a slow slicing away of the non-Communist parties. Finally, after the United States showed that it was prepared to stay in Europe and resist, came the creation of one-party Communist dictatorships in 1947–49.

In Rumania and Bulgaria, Stalin's lieutenants rapidly imposed Communist-dominated coalition governments. Churchill had in effect left both countries to Stalin in the "percentage deal" of fall 1944, and Stalin rightly assumed that action there would not unduly provoke the United States. Stalin was almost equally dictatorial in Poland, his vital land bridge

to the Soviet occupation zone in Germany; leaders of the Polish resistance who surfaced in March 1945 disappeared into NKVD custody. But Stalin was nevertheless careful to maintain a façade. Until 1947 he permitted the leader of the London Poles, Stanislaw Mikolajczyk, to remain as "second deputy prime minister" in the puppet government of Stalin's Lublin Committee.

Territorial Adjustments after the Second World War   1945

The boundaries shown on this map date from the beginning of World War II.

■ Axis states after World War II

□ Lands that changed hands after World War II

The Soviet flag rises over the *Reichstag*, April 1945.

Reichstag, a small group of German Communist émigrés under the leadership of the ice-cold and ruthless Walter Ulbricht landed in Berlin from Moscow. The Western Allies at first shut down German political activity in their zones and gave priority to the large-scale hunt for war criminals that culminated in the trials of the surviving Nazi leaders at Nuremberg in 1945–46. The Soviets shot a few prominent Nazis but gave priority in their zone to the creation of a regime around Ulbricht.

In early 1946, Ulbricht's resurrected German Communist Party cajoled and coerced the much larger SPD organizations in the Soviet zone into a merger that produced a "Socialist Unity Party," the SED. That tactic, which Stalin attempted to apply unsuccessfully through other Communist parties in western as well as eastern Europe, ultimately aimed at a united Communist Germany—a goal Stalin and his associates disclosed to Yugoslav and Bulgarian Communist leaders in early 1946.

Stalin's gradual destruction of non-Communist forces both in the Soviet zone of Germany and elsewhere in east-central Europe was not the only Soviet policy that aroused alarm in the West. Stalin insisted on receiving reparations from the western zones of Germany without in turn delivering the food from eastern Germany that he had pledged at Potsdam. He continued to demand a Soviet share in the occupation of the Ruhr while blocking with unacceptable conditions the fitful inter-allied negotiations over a German peace treaty. That provoked the United States, in September 1946, to announce that its occupation force would remain in Germany indefinitely.

On the Soviet Union's other borders, Stalin sought gains far beyond those the Red Army had already secured. He pressed the Norwegians for bases on their island outpost of Spitzbergen and repeatedly demanded Dardanelles bases and parts of the Caucasus from Turkey. In Greece, the Communist guerrilla movement, defeated in December 1944 after it had attacked the British in Athens, renewed the struggle in May 1946. Tito, the

Hungary and Czechoslovakia enjoyed relatively free elections in 1945–46. Especially in Czechoslovakia, Stalin did not at first need to use force. The Czech government-in-exile of President Beneš chose to collaborate from the beginning; unlike the Poles, the Czechs had no prior experience of Russian occupation. The Czech Communist Party of Kliment Gottwald achieved a plurality of 38 percent in the 1946 election.

In his zone of Germany, which he rightly regarded, even in ruins, as Europe's greatest power, Stalin applied similar methods. The day after the Red Army hoisted its flag on the remains of the leader of newly Communist Yugoslavia, provided weapons and supplies. Stalin remained in the background but at first made no objection. Communist victory in Greece would isolate Turkey and assure the Soviet Union the foothold in the eastern Mediterranean that Stalin had demanded in vain from Britain and the United States.

In three areas Stalin made tactical retreats. He held back from Sovietizing his occupation zone in Austria, probably for fear of provoking an *Anschluss* of the western zones of Austria with the western zones of Germany. In Finland, he contented himself with imposing a military alliance that left Finland's parliamentary institutions intact. That compromise, which rested on Finland's proven determination to resist Soviet invasion, Finland's political caution, and Sweden's continuing neutrality, lasted until the Cold War's end. Finally, in March 1946 Stalin suddenly agreed to honor his Teheran promise to evacuate the northern parts of Iran that he had occupied in 1941.

That swift—and unique—postwar withdrawal was symptomatic of Stalin's policy. Churchill, out of office but still forceful, had just spoken eloquently under Truman's sponsorship of an "Iron Curtain" that had descended across Europe. U.S. protests over the Soviet creation of satellite "republics" in Iran, together with Churchill's call for a new Anglo-American alliance to block further Soviet expansion apparently made a temporary retreat seem advisable to Stalin. It was his last.

"Containment" against Soviet Expansion, 1946–47

Within Washington's disorganized policy machinery, those who distrusted Soviet intentions gradually gained the upper hand after 1945. Truman, who had remarked in June 1941 that he hoped that Nazis and Soviets would kill each other off, was from the beginning inclined to resist Soviet demands. But in the absence of Soviet acts of direct hostility toward the United States, domestic opinion prevented the translation of sentiment into policy. U.S. wartime propaganda stressing Stalin's amiability

---

Churchill: "The Iron Curtain"   March 1946

In a speech given at Fulton, Missouri, with Truman in the audience, Churchill sought to educate the American public.

From Stettin in the Baltic to Trieste in the Adriatic, an iron curtain has descended across the Continent. Behind that line lie all the capitals of the ancient states of Central and Eastern Europe. Warsaw, Berlin, Prague, Vienna, Budapest, Belgrade, Bucharest and Sofia, all these famous cities and the populations around them lie in what I must call the Soviet sphere, and all are subject in one form or another, not only to Soviet influence but to a very high and, in many cases, increasing measure of control from Moscow. . . .

The Russian-dominated Polish government has been encouraged to make enormous and wrongful inroads upon Germany, and mass expulsions of millions of Germans on a scale grievous and undreamed-of are now taking place. The Communist parties, which were very small in all these Eastern States of Europe, have been raised to pre-eminence and power far beyond their numbers and are seeking everywhere to obtain totalitarian control. Police governments are prevailing in nearly every case. . . . These are sombre facts for anyone to have to recite on the morrow of a victory gained by so much splendid comradeship in arms and in the cause of freedom and democracy; but we should be most unwise not to face them squarely while time remains. . . . I do not believe that Soviet Russia desires war. What they desire is the fruits of war and the indefinite expansion of their power and doctrines.

From Lewis Broad, Winston Churchill 1874–1951 *(London: Hutchinson & Co., 1951), pp. 574–75.*

---

and promising world peace through the United Nations had succeeded too well. That "Uncle Joe" was as merciless though more cautious than Hitler and that no disunited "United Nations" could repeal the balance of power came as a rude shock.

While the political education of the American public proceeded with help from both Churchill and Stalin, the military power of the United States shrank dramatically. The 12.1 million men under arms in August 1945 demanded release. By June 1946 those vast and battle-hardened forces had dwindled to 3 million, and a year later stood at a mere 1.4 million, most of them without combat experience. Possession of the bomb led to complacency.

And Stalin's demobilization was far less rapid than that of the United States. By 1948–49 the Soviet armed forces were the largest in the world, with roughly 4 million men. An estimated thirty or more Soviet divisions under unified command in eastern Europe faced a scratch assortment of two U.S. and nine British, French, and Belgian divisions in western Europe. The West lacked a high command, and Soviet tank forces held a crushing edge in numbers and quality.

In the United States, the Republicans achieved majorities in both houses of Congress in November 1946, paralyzing Truman. But to the surprise of the doomsayers, the U.S. economy, which now briefly accounted for half of world industrial production, did not relapse into depression. Global war had forced the United States to take up at last the world economic leadership it had spurned in 1919. At the Bretton Woods Conference of July 1944, the Western powers agreed under U.S. sponsorship to a new international economic order, complete with a World Bank and International Monetary Fund. The Bretton Woods system offered a framework for world trade and the expansion of U.S. exports that had not existed between the wars. But a prerequisite for that expansion was the recovery of Europe. By the bitter winter of 1946–47 that recovery was disturbingly overdue.

Stalin's appetites and Europe's distress, which might strengthen the large Communist parties in France and Italy and choke off world trade once again, finally moved Truman to act. Britain, besieged as in 1919 with nationalist revolts from Egypt to India, furnished the occasion. In February 1947 Britain confessed that it could no longer back Turkey against Soviet pressure or support the Greek government against the Communist partisans. The collapse of the British position in the eastern Mediterranean left a power vacuum. If Truman did not fill it, Stalin clearly would.

On March 12, 1947, after gaining promises of Republican support in Congress, Truman announced the "doctrine" that bears his name. The United States would help Greece, Turkey, and all "free peoples" against "armed minorities or . . . outside pressures." The Republicans, under the leadership of Senator Arthur Vandenberg, enlisted with enthusiasm. But Vandenberg and U.S. public opinion exacted a price. As Vandenberg explained to Truman, Congress would spend money only if Truman "scared hell out of the American people." Truman therefore transformed an essentially pragmatic decision to support two strategic countries into something entirely different: a worldwide ideological struggle between light and darkness. And Truman's choice of words inadvertently placed an intolerable burden on many of America's allies-to-be. To qualify for U.S. aid, they now had to seem virtuous and "free," rather than merely strategically important.

In the short term, the Truman Doctrine succeeded brilliantly; aid to Greece and Turkey passed Congress. In June 1947 Truman's new secretary of state, the wartime chief of staff George Marshall, announced a second major initiative. The United States offered to both western and eastern Europe, including the Soviet Union, a massive infusion of economic aid to set the postwar recovery in motion at last. Although Congress would never have approved aid to the Soviets, the authors of the Marshall Plan left to Stalin the burden of refusal.

A senior State Department official, George Kennan, meanwhile supplied a much-needed statement of the Truman Doctrine's rationale. Writing as "Mr. X" in the July 1947 issue of *Foreign Affairs,* Kennan urged a "policy of firm containment, designed to confront the Russians with unalterable counterforce at every point where they show signs of encroaching upon a peaceful and stable world." Containment, Kennan argued, would ultimately lead "either [to] the break-up or the gradual mellowing of Soviet power." He later explained with embarrassment that by "counterforce" he had not necessarily meant the use of force, and that not *"every* point" at which the Soviet Union might seek expansion was equally vital to the United States. But his article, and other semiofficial and official pronouncements from Washington, in theory made U.S. commitments almost unlimited.

To uphold those commitments, the United States reorganized its armed forces in July 1947, creating a nuclear-armed air force independent of army and navy, and a Department of Defense. It also acquired new institutions that until now, alone of the great powers, it had disdained. Permanent peacetime secret services, the Central Intelligence Agency (CIA) for foreign intelligence and "covert action" (1947) and the National Security Agency (NSA) for codebreaking (1952), arose from the debris of the wartime intelligence effort.

Europe Divided, 1947–49

Stalin did not disappoint the framers of the Marshall Plan. Molotov attended the conference held in Paris to launch the Plan but soon uttered his characteristic stone-faced "*Nyet.*" Stalin commanded his satellites to refuse Marshall aid and ordered the Communist parties of western Europe to oppose the Plan with strikes and riots.

In fall and winter 1947–48 Stalin swiftly completed his "revolution by conquest" in the Soviet Union's new central and eastern European empire. In Hungary, Rákosi had already arrested key opposition leaders in May 1947. In October, Mikolajczyk fled Poland in fear of his life. In December King Michael of Rumania abdicated. In Czechoslovakia, Kliment Gottwald and his Communist Party seized control in February 1948 from inside the popularly elected government. Jan Masarcyk, the protégé of Beneš at the foreign ministry, fell, jumped—or was pushed—from a window to his death. Beneš, as in 1938, declined to fight; Gottwald shunted him aside. The new Communist regimes took the remarkable name of "people's democracies"—Stalin too was a master of packaging dictatorship for the age of mass politics.

The United States, Britain, and France now went ahead rapidly to restore economic and political life in their sectors of Germany. When they attempted to include the Western part of Berlin in the

The Berlin airlift, June 1948–May 1949.

creation of a new currency that foreshadowed a West German state, Stalin reacted angrily. In June 1948, in violation of the wartime inter-allied agreements providing for free access to Berlin, he blockaded the western sectors with Soviet tanks.

Truman and his advisers thought of sending their own—desperately few—tanks down the *Autobahn*. But in the face of the Soviet Union's crushing ground superiority (roughly twenty Soviet against two U.S. divisions in Germany), they chose in characteristically American fashion an engineering remedy for a political or military problem. To keep alive the same West Berliners they had bombed three years before, the Allies organized an endless chain of transport aircraft that delivered millions of tons of food, coal, and gasoline. In November 1948, Truman won reelection against heavy odds. In May 1949 Stalin abandoned the Berlin blockade.

Its effects, however, were lasting. The blockade led to the founding in April 1949 of the North Atlantic Treaty Organization

(NATO), the military alliance of the United States and the western European democracies that Wilson had failed to create in 1919. The blockade also pushed the United States and its Allies into speeding the transformation of the western zones into a "Federal Republic of Germany." That new German state adopted a constitution in May 1949 and held its first election that August. In the Soviet zone Ulbricht received Stalin's permission to proclaim a "German Democratic Republic" (DDR). The two superpowers now confronted each other with unbending hostility from northern Norway to the Turkish Caucasus.

As well as provoking—in the form of NATO—the "unalterable counterforce" Kennan had prescribed, Stalin also failed to Sovietize one key nation in east-central Europe. In 1947–48 he attempted to reduce Yugoslavia to the same subservience as his other eastern European satellites. When Tito fought back by purging Soviet agents from his party, Stalin expelled Yugoslavia from the international Communist movement for "nationalist tendencies." Then he sought to orchestrate a pro-Soviet coup: "I shall shake my little finger and there will be no Tito." But Tito remained. That first split in the international Communist movement scuttled the Greek Communist insurgency. Stalin had already told the Yugoslavs that the Greek civil war should be "rolled up" as unprofitable now that Truman was backing the Greek government. After the break with Moscow, Tito abandoned the Greek guerrillas; he needed Western economic support to survive.

Increased tension with the United States and the quarrel with Yugoslavia gave Stalin a chance to tighten further his control at home. Alleged external threat and genuine internal terror went together, as after 1927, to force the population to accept the privation caused by Stalin's military-economic priorities. In war and its aftermath, Stalin deported to Siberia and central Asia millions from nationalities—Crimean Tartars, Volga Germans, and the Baltic and Caucasus peoples—that he accused of collaboration with the German

invaders. He vengefully transferred to his own concentration camps all returned Soviet prisoners of war ("In Hitler's camps there are no Russian prisoners of war, only Russian traitors, and we shall do away with them when the war is over.") He demoted prominent military leaders now that he no longer needed them, and arrested many whose sole crime was having seen with their own eyes the wealth of the world west of the Soviet borders. The GULAG had suffered a labor shortage after 1941; by 1950 it once more held an estimated 8 to 10 million prisoners.

After war's end, Stalin's lieutenant Andrei Zhdanov began a purge of Soviet writers and scientists that continued even after Zhdanov died a sudden and perhaps unnatural death in 1948. Zhdanov's rival Georgi Malenkov and Yezhov's sinister successor at the NKVD, Lavrenty Beria, subsequently had Zhdanov's former associates in the Leningrad party apparatus eliminated. The gradually intensifying purge, which Stalin extended to the new eastern European satellites, soon took on an overtly anti-Semitic character. "Rootless cosmopolitanism" and "Zionism" were the chief charges under which prominent satellite leaders, many of them of Jewish descent, went to gallows or execution cellars after show trials in 1951–52. Stalin thus applied to the satellites the remedy imposed at home after Kirov's murder in 1934: the removal of all who were not his creatures and the creation of a new ruling class of grateful accomplices.

As Tocqueville had foreseen in the 1830s, America and Russia had each come to "sway the destinies of half the globe." Their confrontation in 1947–49 resulted from and ended a century of ever more destructive European national struggles. Hitler, the most extreme of all nationalist prophets, had invited the superpowers onto the scene. Then he had created chaos and destruction so vast that at the end only superpowers could master it.

That they proceeded to do—with methods that were mutually exclusive. Here too Tocqueville had seen clearly: "The principal instrument of [America] is freedom; of [Russia], servitude." The democracies of western Europe, despite occasional grumbling, conceded hegemony to Washington. They repeated, against Stalin, the choice Churchill had made in 1940: better to serve as the junior partner to another democracy, the United States, than to suffer the domination of a continent-wide slave state. In east-central Europe, Stalin's new multinational empire replaced the Habsburg order that had

collapsed in 1918. Supranational American-Soviet confrontation dwarfed and repressed Europe's nationalisms and froze the borders of 1945. But outside Europe both geography and the alignment of forces were far different. There Stalin failed to discern "where to stop," and nationalism, Europe's most successful export, opened new worlds of violent conflict.

Suggestions for Further Reading

The Second World War

As with the First World War, there is no comprehensive, up-to-date, and readable one-volume history of the war of 1939–45. G. Wright, *The Ordeal of Total War, 1939–1945* (1968), is a useful survey. J. Lukacs, *The Last European War, September 1939/December 1941* (1976), offers a brilliant synthesis of everything from grand strategy to the intellectual impact of the first two years of war. K. Hildebrand, *The Foreign Policy of the Third Reich* (1973), and A. Hillgruber, *Germany and the Two World Wars* (1981), lay out German strategy and objectives, but see also H. R. Trevor-Roper, ed., *Hitler's Secret Conversations, 1941–1944* (1953), and N. Rich, *Hitler's War Aims* (1973–74). G. Fleming, *Hitler and the Final Solution* (1982), and R. Hilberg, *The Destruction of the European Jews* (1961; revised and expanded, 1985), cover the "Final Solution" and Hitler's responsibility for it in chilling detail. On Germany's "barbarization of warfare" in the East and the army's role in genocide, see especially the brilliant book of O. Bartov, *Hitler's Army: Soldiers, Nazis, and War in the Third Reich* (1991); Bartov and M. van Creveld, *Fighting Power* (1982), also suggest why the Germans were so hard to defeat. Among the many excellent books on

aspects of the war, W. Murray, *Luftwaffe* (1984), and M. Hastings, *Overlord: D-Day and the Battle for Normandy* (1984), stand out.

Of Hitler's principal enemies only Churchill left memoirs: his wonderfully readable *The Second World War,* 6 vols. (1948–1953), remains the best history of the war as seen from London. On Roosevelt and American policy, see R. Sherwood, *Roosevelt and Hopkins* (1950); R. A. Divine, *The Reluctant Belligerent: American Entry into World War II* (1965); and G. Smith, *American Diplomacy in the Second World War, 1941–1945* (revised, 1985). On the Pacific war, see especially A. Iriye, *The Origins of the Second World War in Asia and the Pacific* (1987) and *Power and Culture: The Japanese-American War, 1941–1945* (1981); H. P. Willmott, *Empires in the Balance: Japanese and Allied Pacific Strategies to April 1942* (1982); R. H. Spector, *Eagle Against the Sun: The American War Against Japan* (1985); C. Thorne, *Allies of a Kind: The United States, Britain, and the War Against Japan, 1941–1945* (1978); and H. Feis, *The Atomic Bomb and the End of World War II* (1966).

The Cold War

On wartime diplomacy and the origins of the Cold War, H. Feis, *Churchill, Roosevelt, Stalin* (1957), still provides useful narrative; D. S. Gaddis, *The United States and the Origins of the Cold War, 1941–1947* (1972), and V. Mastny, *Russia's Road to the Cold War* (1979), use a wider selection of sources. H. Seton-Watson, *The East European Revolution* (1951, 1956), still offers

a useful overview of the Communist seizure of power in eastern Europe; A. Ulam, *The Rivals: America and Russia Since World War II* (1971), is a succinct and witty narrative; P. Seabury, *The Rise and Decline of the Cold War* (1967), introduces some of the interpretive issues.

·34·

THE AGE OF CONTAINMENT
1949–1975

The Prague coup and the Berlin Blockade marked the beginning of the "classic" Cold War, the fiercest phase of the superpower confrontation around which international politics pivoted for the next forty years. In Europe, the war remained cold. In Asia, by Stalin's choice, cold war became a shooting war in Korea in June 1950. Then military stalemate and Stalin's death in March 1953 ended the most acute period of hostility between the United States and the Soviet Union.

But truces in Korea and elsewhere in Asia did not end the superpower conflict. Anti-Soviet revolts in the east European satellites and recurrent Soviet threats over Germany repeatedly interrupted the post-Stalin "thaw." Tension between the superpowers culminated in 1962 with the attempt of Stalin's successor, Nikita Sergeyevich Khrushchev, to tilt the strate-gic balance by placing nuclear missiles in Cuba. Khrushchev's shamefaced withdrawal and U.S. distraction in Vietnam then inaugurated a period of gradual superpower "détente" or relaxation of tension, despite wars between U.S. and Soviet allies or clients in the Middle East. The Soviet Union looked on in masterful inactivity as the United States, convulsed at home, ultimately abandoned "containment" in Vietnam in 1972–75.

Unheard-of prosperity in the United States, western Europe, and a resurgent Japan accompanied superpower conflict. American-style material culture—appliances and automobiles, Hollywood films, television serials, and rock and roll—enveloped the world. A new generation arose in the West that remembered neither Depression nor war, and fiercely attacked its elders. A transnational women's movement that originated in France and the

United States at last pushed women's rights beyond the vote. For the democracies, the age of containment was an era of unprecedented technological advance and of wealth and well-being that spread far down the social scale. But as in earlier ages, the price of change and economic growth was unease and discontent.

CONFRONTATION IN EUROPE AND ASIA, 1949–53

Stalin's Temptation in Asia

Japan left the Western Allies a difficult legacy. Its slogan of "Asia for the Asians" had masked its own colonialism. But that slogan, together with the inglorious defeat of the British at Singapore in February 1942, mightily encouraged Asian nationalism. Thanks to the "Germany first" strategy of the United States, southeast Asia had enjoyed the lowest priority of all the Allied theaters of war. In August 1945, when Imperial Japan collapsed, the British had only half reconquered Burma. The Guomindang was still hiding in a remote enclave in southeast China. Indochina—Vietnam, Laos, and Cambodia—and the Dutch East Indies were still under Japanese control. Japan handed that control over not to the former colonial masters, but to armed native movements.

Cold War Europe

The Dutch gave up in 1949 under U.S. pressure, and granted the East Indies—renamed Indonesia—its independence. In Vietnam, Ho Chi Minh's Communist Party of Indochina destroyed its non-Communist nationalist rivals and in September 1945 declared Vietnam's independence from France. France's effort at reconquest led to fierce guerrilla conflict after November 1946.

To the north, the Soviets took Manchuria in their twelve-day war of August 1945 and remained there until 1946. They took only half of the former Japanese colony of Korea; the United States, warned by Stalin's drive for total control of occupied eastern Europe, insisted on dividing the strategically vital Korean peninsula into Soviet and U.S. zones at the 38th parallel. By 1947–48, two Korean states, one Communist and one with American "advisers," were locked in bitter hostility and intermittent border conflict. Japan itself fell to the United States alone. Douglas MacArthur, installed in Tokyo as a sort of American Shōgun, contemptuously dismissed Soviet bids to share in the occupation. In the Pacific, Moscow had contributed little to victory.

In China, the Guomindang of Chiang Kai-shek and the Chinese Communist Party (CCP) of Mao Zedong (Mao Tsetung) ended the war against Japan as nominal allies. Their marriage of convenience inevitably turned to renewed civil war in July 1946. China could not have *two* dictatorships. Truman and his advisers wavered between trying to revive the Guomindang-CCP coalition, backing the Guomindang, and abstaining. Washington tried all three policies in succession. Stalin at first sought to maintain a balance between the CCP and the Guomindang favorable to the Soviet Union, as in the 1920s. But once CCP victory seemed certain, Stalin bet on Mao.

In January 1949, Mao's "People's Liberation Army" entered Beijing (Peking), and in October Mao proclaimed the People's Republic of China (PRC). Chiang and the remnants of the Guomindang took refuge on the offshore island of Taiwan. Mao traveled to Moscow and after difficult negotiations signed a "treaty of friendship" with Stalin in February 1950; it promised the return to China of the Manchurian railway and Port Arthur, and allied China and the Soviet Union against Japan. After almost forty years of war, turmoil, and famine, something resembling a new dynasty had at last replaced the Qing.

The "loss" of China and the concurrent explosion of the first Soviet atomic bomb in August 1949 created turmoil in the United States. Truman now paid for having "scared hell out of the American people" and for having funded resistance to Soviet expansion in Europe by a pledge of aid to opponents of "armed minorities" everywhere. The Republican Right, in the unsavory person of Senator Joseph McCarthy of Wisconsin, attacked the president by claiming that he was not anti-Communist enough.

McCarthy and his many supporters were convinced of American omnipotence. For them neither Chinese Communists nor Soviets were serious enemies. Only treason at home by U.S. officials could have delivered China to Mao and the secret of the atomic bomb to Moscow. They saw and relentlessly pursued a largely imaginary internal menace—"Caaamunism" (as McCarthy and his supporters pronounced it) at the State Department and in the academic world. The public's sudden realization that it faced a

The Cold War comes home: McCarthy at work, October 1951.

Soviet nuclear threat added to the hysteria. The pattern of ideological witch-hunts and populist-isolationist demagogy visible in the 1920s and 1930s reasserted itself. Not until 1954 did McCarthy's wild charges discredit him; in the long term he gave resistance to Communism a bad name.

In response to the threatening new situation of 1949–50, Truman decided to build a thermonuclear, or hydrogen, bomb. Stalin, unknown to the Americans, had initiated his own H-bomb research in 1948. The new weapons were hundreds or even thousands of times more destructive than the Hiroshima bomb, which had been equivalent to a mere 20,000 tons of high explosive. Truman also ordered a review of U.S. defense preparations and strategy; his advisers embodied their conclusions in National Security Council paper NSC-68 of April 1950. It urged a major U.S. conventional as well as nuclear build-up to maintain a balance of power threatened by the Soviet Union's bomb, its ever-growing military, and its alliance with China. But the recommendations of NSC-68 were politically impractical. The

Republicans in Congress continued to demand budget cuts—while at the same time attacking the administration for being "soft on Caaamunism."

Then Stalin, by yet another ill-timed display of appetite, gave Truman the domestic support he needed to counter the Soviet build-up. Defeat in the Berlin Blockade turned Stalin toward Asia; in mid-1949 he secured Mao's help for an accelerated military build-up of the Soviet-sponsored North Korean state. At the end of 1949 (as Stalin's successor Nikita Khrushchev disclosed in his memoirs), Stalin received Kim Il-Sung, the former Red Army major who led the North, and authorized him to attack South Korea. Mao apparently agreed. On June 25, 1950, Kim's T-34 tanks—the weapon that had opened Stalin's road to Berlin—crossed the 38th parallel and rolled over the South Korean army.

The Korean War: Armed Containment in Asia, Rearmament in Europe

Truman scarcely hesitated. On June 30, 1950, he ordered American ground troops from Japan into combat. U.S. control of Japan and the credibility of the U.S. defense of Europe appeared to be at stake. Like Roosevelt in the Atlantic in 1941, Truman acted without a congressional declaration of war—and without congressional opposition. At the United Nations, a Soviet walkout ordered by Stalin allowed the Security Council, for the first time in its history, to vote with the necessary unanimity to fight in defense of a member. The United States provided supplies and a force that eventually grew to 350,000, alongside 400,000 South Koreans and 44,000 troops from fourteen other nations fighting under the U.N. flag.

The North Koreans, well-trained by their Soviet and Chinese advisers, stormed south and almost swallowed the peninsula in one gulp. But by early August, with much air and naval support, an Army, Marine, and South Korean force ground them to a halt around the vital port of Pusan, in the far southeastern corner of Korea. Then MacArthur landed the Marines and

One of Kim Il-Sung's T-34s meets the U.S. Marine Corps (1950).

the U.S. Army at Inchon, halfway up the Korean peninsula, cut the North Koreans to shreds, and reached the old border along the 38th parallel. Truman and the United Nations imprudently gave MacArthur permission to conquer North Korea, unless Chinese or Soviet intervention appeared likely. Containment briefly became "rollback." To MacArthur, who knew neither doubts nor humility, permission to cross the parallel was a blank check. As winter deepened, he drove headlong for the Yalu River that divides Korea and China, and strung his forces out on North Korea's icy mountain roads.

China made clear that it would fight to drive MacArthur back from its borders. In mid-October MacArthur disregarded a sudden appearance of Chinese "volunteers." In mid-November a massive Chinese counteroffensive took him completely by surprise and flung the U.N. forces back below the 38th parallel. Only the Marines, who walked out grimly from Chosin reservoir near the Yalu—through snow and seven Chinese divisions—emerged with credit from the disaster.

MacArthur, to redeem his reputation, demanded the bombing and blockade of China itself. In a letter to a Republican congressman, he criticized his commander in chief by insisting that "in war there is no substitute for victory." Truman dismissed him in April 1951 for insubordination; the president and his advisers saw no profit in a wider war against China that would pin down an ever-increasing proportion of U.S. forces and might lead to a direct U.S.-Soviet clash. That would be "the wrong war, at the wrong place, at the wrong time, and with the wrong enemy," and might damage Washington's ultimate Cold War goal of keeping the Soviets out of western Europe and Japan, the largest non-Communist concentrations of economic power and talent in the world beside the United States.

After MacArthur's defeat, Truman therefore fought a "limited war" in Korea, using U.S. reinforcements and firepower to push the Chinese back above the parallel. By July 1951, U.S. and allied forces had inflicted immense casualties on the Chinese and had stabilized the front. Bitter

Korea   1950–53

truce talks began, while trench raids and local offensives continued on Korea's bare and jagged hills. Chinese and North Koreans sought to wear down the resolve of an impatient and peacefully inclined democracy by talking and fighting at the same time. Stalin willed the continuation of the war. In January 1951, immediately after MacArthur's disaster, Stalin had told a secret meeting of his satellite leaders that the United States was so feeble militarily that a Soviet attack on western Europe would become feasible in the next three to four years. Wearing U.S. forces down in Asia would help guarantee success.

But Stalin was not immortal. He apparently began in 1952 to orchestrate one last purge, based on false charges that the Kremlin doctors—most of whom were of Jewish descent—had plotted to murder the Soviet leadership. The doctors' coming trial, like that of Zinoviev and Kamenev in 1936, promised to unleash a flood of denunciations, arrests, and liquidations. Stalin's associates trembled for their heads. "The Boss" was apparently about to inaugurate yet another round of social mobility, Soviet style.

But on March 5, 1953, Stalin died of a stroke. His heirs joined in a "collective leadership" that sought hesitantly to retreat from Stalin's terror within and from confrontation without. In the United States, impatience with the Korean stalemate ("die for a tie") carried the Republican candidate, Dwight D. Eisenhower, to victory in the 1952 presidential election. Eisenhower promised to apply his military experience to ending the war. Stalin's death gave the Communist side flexibility, and Eisenhower's expressed willingness to use nuclear weapons in Korea helped concentrate minds in Beijing. On July 27, 1953, the two sides finally signed an armistice that established a de facto boundary separating North and South Korea. After three years and the death of a million Chinese, perhaps 2 million Koreans, and 52,246 Americans, the war was over. Only a little more than a third of the 10,000 Americans whom the Communists had captured returned alive.

Containment in northeast Asia had succeeded, but at a price. Part of that price was that Washington began to perceive all Communist actions, even unrelated ones, as part of a grand design framed in Moscow. Truman sent the U.S. Navy to shield Taiwan from Mao's forces on the mainland, although Washington had earlier shunned Chiang Kai-shek. The United States looked on approvingly as Britain tamed a Communist insurgency among the overseas Chinese of Malaya. Mao's victory in China had already led Truman in May 1950 to order aid to France in Indochina, a cause of which Washington had earlier disapproved. The North Korean attack the following month led Washington to flood Indochina with weapons and funds that amounted to $1 billion a year by 1954.

But Ho Chi Minh skillfully identified Vietnamese Communism with national resistance to colonial rule. The Vietnamese Communist regular army that Mao's forces trained and equipped in southern China after 1949 showed unparalleled fighting power. U.S. prodding drove Paris to create non-Communist nationalist forces in Vietnam, Laos, and Cambodia, and to promise eventual independence; more Vietnamese indeed fought on the French side than on

Ho Chi Minh's. But few of them fought as hard. In late 1953 the French staked everything on luring Ho's forces to attack an isolated French outpost on the Laotian border at Dien Bien Phu. There the excellent artillery that the United States had given Chiang, who had lost it to Mao, who had given it to Ho, trapped the French instead. Dien Bien Phu fell in May 1954. France agreed to withdraw from Indochina, subject to a satisfactory truce. The United States, Soviet Union, China, France, and Britain met at Geneva in the first major East-West conference since 1947 and agreed to a cease-fire and the division of Vietnam at the 17th parallel. Laos and Cambodia were to be independent and neutral. The First Indochina War was over.

Contrary to later claims, the powers at Geneva did not formally agree on free elections and the reunification of all Vietnam by 1956. The United States rejected elections without United Nations supervision to ensure a fair vote. Neither Ho's newly minted "Democratic Republic of Vietnam" (DRV) north of the 17th parallel nor its southern counterpart supported the conference's unsigned face-saving declaration calling for elections. Ho and his associates were the least satisfied of the parties at Geneva; they felt that Beijing and Moscow had sold them out by failing to deliver all of Indochina. An unquiet truce nevertheless descended in Asia.

The attack by Stalin's North Korean clients on South Korea thus had worldwide consequences. It helped entangle the United States in southeast as well as in northeast Asia. And it at last roused the United States to remedy the military imbalance created by its hasty demobilization in 1945–46. Truman persuaded Congress to commit additional U.S. divisions and substantial military aid to Europe. The United States acquired its first large-scale peacetime draft, and built a standing military establishment twice the size of that of 1949, with a network of bases ringing the Soviet Union. Thanks to Stalin, Washington was able to implement many of the recommendations of NSC-68.

And Stalin also spurred the United States to look for allies among its former enemies. In 1952 Washington restored

Ho Chi Minh ("the Bringer of Enlightenment"), architect of Vietnamese Communism (1954).

sovereignty to a partially democratized Japan, linked to the United States by military bases and a security treaty. West Germany received back its sovereignty in a peace treaty with the Western powers in 1954, and began to rearm in 1955. By the late 1950s, NATO at last had enough forces, both American and German, to stop a Soviet armored thrust short of the Rhine. The Soviet Union answered with more armored divisions, intermediate-range nuclear missiles, and an alliance against NATO founded in 1955, the Warsaw Pact.

THE ADVENTURES OF NIKITA SERGEYEVICH KHRUSHCHEV, 1953–64

In Moscow, Stalin's death apparently prevented the last great purge, a new stage in his remodeling of Soviet society. Instead, the Soviet Union fell back into a drab bureaucratic "failed totalitarianism." The messianic claim to remake humanity remained, but the will to do so by terror was now gone. And without terror, the system was doomed to economic stagnation and collapse.

"Thaw" at Home and Abroad

Stalin's heirs fought to take credit for the "thaw" that set in after March 1953. Lavrenty Beria, master of the secret police, moved first. But his rivals united, called on the Red Army for support, and had him shot. The new "collective leadership," under Georgi Malenkov for the state bureaucracy and Nikita S. Khrushchev for the Communist Party, then announced implausibly that Beria had been a British intelligence agent since 1919. Some of Stalin's habits survived him.

Beria's liquidation was nevertheless the last. When Khrushchev displaced Malenkov in 1955, he merely demoted him. When Malenkov, Molotov, and Stalin's most bloodstained surviving associate, Lazar Kaganovich, allied themselves against Khrushchev in 1957, he merely dismissed them from their posts in the Party and government. Thanks to Khrushchev, the new Soviet ruling class that Stalin had created at last achieved job security. Amnes-

Khrushchev on Stalin   **February 24–25, 1956**

Khrushchev sought above all to differentiate between Lenin and Stalin, to present Stalin's terror and "cult of personality" as an accident rather than as a logical consequence of Lenin's party autocracy.

Lenin used severe methods only in the most necessary cases, when the exploiting classes were still in existence and were vigorously opposing the revolution, when the struggle for survival was decidedly assuming the sharpest forms, even including a civil war.

Stalin, on the other hand, used extreme methods and mass repressions at a time when the revolution was already victorious, when the Soviet state was strengthened, when the exploiting classes were already liquidated. . . . It is clear that here Stalin showed in a whole series of cases his intolerance, his brutality and his abuse of power. Instead of proving his political correctness and mobilizing the masses, he often chose the path of repression and physical annihilation, not only against actual enemies, but also against individuals who had not committed any crimes against the party and the Soviet Government.

From Basil Dmytryshyn, USSR: A Concise History *(New York: Charles Scribner's Sons, 1978), p. 501.*

ties gradually thinned the population of the GULAG after a series of bloody prisoner revolts.

And Khrushchev, whose deliberately uncouth peasant exterior concealed both shrewdness and a moral courage he had been careful to repress while Stalin had lived, soon set about destroying the legacy of his former "Boss." As the Twentieth Party Congress of February 1956 approached, all mention of the former "great leader" and "guide of progressive humanity" dropped from the Soviet press. At the Congress, Khrushchev attacked Stalin in a secret speech that shook the foundations of the Soviet system.

Khrushchev was careful to brand Stalin's "cult of personality" and his "extreme methods and mass repressions" as an exception, a historical accident that owed nothing to Lenin, much less to Marx. But Marx had justified dictatorship and terror, and Lenin had authorized terror against the "class enemy," and had erected the dictatorship of a Party that he insisted must be monolithic. Stalin had merely followed that logic to its conclusion and had attempted to make the Party monolithic through terror.

Khrushchev's secret speech nevertheless contained a wealth of information about the purges, from the technique of extorting false confessions to the startling numbers of victims in the higher ranks of the Party. Its text soon leaked to the outside world and devastated Communist parties and their sympathizers everywhere. Some left the Party, disillusioned with Communism. Others attacked Khrushchev for betraying the faith. In the Soviet Union, as Khrushchev had apparently intended, the speech made a return to Stalin's methods difficult. Dissidents now risked years in labor camps or torture in psychiatric hospitals, but executions were increasingly rare. Khrushchev replaced mass terror with subtle and calculated repression by the post-Beria secret police and intelligence service, the Committee for State Security (KGB).

Externally, "de-Stalinization" made Soviet policy less rigid. Khrushchev announced that "war was not fatalistically inevitable" between the "socialist camp" and the Western "capitalist" powers. In a belated attempt to woo German and European public opinion, he agreed to withdraw Soviet forces from Austria in 1955. He visited Tito that same year and apologized for Stalin's vindictiveness against Yugoslavia; the Soviet Union thus recognized that the "Soviet path" was not the sole road to Communism.

But de-Stalinization had limits abroad as well as at home. In the Soviet Union, the "great patriotic war" of 1941–45 and Stalin's rehabilitation of the tsarist past had partially merged Great Russian nationalism with Communism. But in the satellites, Communism was a Red Army import and nationalism was from the beginning its mortal enemy. The "people's democracies" consequently suffered repeated waves of unrest throughout the Cold War era. In East Berlin, Stalin's death and Ulbricht's imposition of wage cuts in June 1953 had triggered a new Kronstadt 1921—a desperate workers' revolt, soon crushed by Ulbricht's "People's Police" and Soviet armor.

Khrushchev's secret speech led to further ferment. In Poland, workers at Poznán demonstrated against wage cuts in June 1956. Street fighting between workers and troops then triggered a struggle within the Polish Communist Party between Stalinists and "moderates." But instead of sending tanks, Khrushchev grudgingly accepted assurances from the chief of the "moderates," Wladyslaw Gomulka, that Poland would remain within the Soviet empire. Gomulka then persuaded the population to subside in the name of national survival.

In Hungary, similar events led to tragedy. Rákosi, Stalin's man in Budapest, clung to power until Khrushchev ordered him to resign in July 1956. But his successor was another lesser Stalinist. When Hungary's equivalent to Gomulka, Imre Nagy, finally came to power in late October, the Hungarian Communist regime was disintegrating in the face of spontaneous national revolt. Demonstrators toppled the immense statue of Stalin in Budapest. Communist leaders hid or ran for the Soviet border. A small force of Soviet tanks withdrew from Budapest in the

Soviet tanks dominate the streets of Berlin after crushing the East German workers' revolt (June 1953).

face of popular fury. Nagy tried to persuade Moscow to hold back, while he calmed popular demands for multiparty democracy and for withdrawal from the Warsaw Pact.

Nagy failed. Like the Habsburgs whose role he now filled, Khrushchev could not permit the defection of one nationality, for fear the others might follow. Simultaneous Western disarray over the Suez crisis (see p. 927) made the decision to act easier. On November 4, 1956, Moscow flooded Budapest with tanks and crushed the revolt. During the fighting and aftermath, the Soviets and their collaborators killed thousands of Hungarians; 190,000 refugees fled west. Khrushchev had saved Stalin's empire with Stalin's methods.

The Sino-Soviet Split

To the east, where the Soviet Union faced a new phenomenon, a second Communist great power, those methods were less effective. Stalin had preserved an uneasy dominance over Mao even after 1949. Khrushchev and his colleagues could not. Mao was his own Lenin and Stalin; he regarded Stalin's puny successors with poorly concealed contempt. The Chinese also resented having to carry the military burden of Stalin's misjudgment in Korea, and grumbled about the poor quality and small quantity of Soviet economic aid. They nevertheless tolerated Khrushchev, despite de-Stalinization, which Mao read as unspoken criticism of his own thriving "cult of personality."

The parting of the ways, the greatest single defeat to Soviet policy since 1941, soon came. In October 1957, in a final bid to keep Beijing as a loyal vassal, Khrushchev signed a secret treaty providing China with assistance in developing the atomic bomb. But the following year, Mao staked a claim to world ideological leadership of the Communist movement. He launched an economic "Great Leap Forward" complete with collectivization and crash industrialization. The "attainment of Communism in China is no longer a remote future event," Mao's Central Committee trumpeted. That statement was a

Stalin dethroned: Budapest, November 2, 1956.

direct challenge to Moscow, which had never dared to promise the rapid attainment of Communism—the blissful end of history amid untold abundance—to its long-suffering subjects. And to add to the horror of the Soviets, Mao also challenged the United States by seeking war—unsuccessfully—in the Taiwan straits in the fall of 1958.

In June 1959, Soviet aid to China's nuclear program abruptly ended. Khrushchev decided not to give the bomb to his over-mighty and reckless vassal, and recalled his military and industrial experts from China. By 1960 the Sino-Soviet split was almost public. By the summer of 1963 the two "fraternal parties" were trading mortal insults and staging mass displays of ritual hatred. Moscow damned Beijing for its fanatical rigidity ("dogmatism"). Beijing denounced Moscow for betraying the Marxist-Leninist gospel ("modern revisionism"). The international Communist movement had irrevocably split.

From Berlin to Cuba

On the Soviet Union's western front, Khrushchev took the offensive. His objective was probably to settle the German question through a peace treaty that recognized as an international border the 1945 boundary between the western and Soviet occupation zones, and ended the West's nonrecognition of Ulbricht's shaky puppet regime. That would consolidate Soviet control of East Germany and east-central Europe.

But Khrushchev lacked subtlety. He had already, in the Suez crisis of 1956,

Kennedy: "Ask not . . ."   1961

Kennedy's inaugural address contained some of the most stirring phrases ever spoken by an American president. It also unwisely proclaimed a willingness to "pay any price."

Let the word go forth from this time and place, to friend and foe alike, that the torch has been passed to a new generation of Americans, born in this century, tempered by war, disciplined by a hard and bitter peace, proud of our ancient heritage, and unwilling to witness or permit the slow undoing of those human rights to which this nation has always been committed, and to which we are committed today at home and around the world.

Let every nation know, whether it wishes us well or ill, that we shall pay any price, bear any burden, meet any hardship, support any friend, oppose any foe to assure the survival and the success of liberty. . . .

In the long history of the world, only a few generations have been granted the role of defending freedom in its hour of maximum danger. I do not shrink from this responsibility; I welcome it. I do not believe that any of us would exchange places with any other people or any other generation. The energy, the faith, the devotion which we bring to this endeavor will light our country and all who serve it, and the glow from that fire can truly light the world.

And so, my fellow Americans, ask not what your country can do for you; ask what you can do for your country.

From Theodore C. Sorensen, Kennedy *(New York: Harper & Row, 1965), pp. 245–48.*

gleefully brandished the Soviet Union's small but growing arsenal of nuclear missiles. In October 1957 the Soviet Union's triumphant launching of the first artificial satellite, *Sputnik,* suggested that Soviet military technology was surpassing that of the United States. In November Khrushchev delivered an ultimatum to the West demanding a German peace treaty within six months.

The ultimatum became a rolling one, always extended. The exuberant Khrushchev accompanied it with a drumfire of nuclear threats that punctuated four years of steadily increasing superpower tension. His declared commitment to "peaceful co-existence" did not inhibit him from occa-

sionally predicting in ominous tones the ultimate triumph of Communism: "We will bury you." In September 1959 Khrushchev nevertheless became the first Soviet ruler to visit the United States, for an inconclusive summit with Eisenhower. After a Soviet antiaircraft missile knocked down one of the CIA's U-2 high-altitude reconnaissance aircraft over central Russia, Khrushchev canceled the return visit in May 1960 by staging a propaganda circus complete with personal slurs against Eisenhower.

The 1960 U.S. presidential election brought in a new Democratic administration under the debonair young Boston-Irish grandee, John Fitzgerald Kennedy. That offered Khrushchev new opportunities. Kennedy inherited from Eisenhower a Caribbean problem: Cuba. There a revolutionary adventurer, Fidel Castro, had come to power when the military regime of the incompetent Fulgencio Batista had collapsed in January 1959. Castro, who later claimed—not implausibly—to have been a lifelong Marxist-Leninist, immediately began to court Moscow. Khrushchev happily responded during a visit to the United Nations at which he distinguished himself by pounding his shoe on his desk during a General Assembly speech by Britain's prime minister.

Along with the Cuban problem, Kennedy inherited from Eisenhower a solution: an amateurish CIA-organized invasion of Cuba by anti-Communist Cuban exiles seeking to trigger an uprising against Castro. The invasion force landed at the Bay of Pigs on Cuba's south coast on April 17, 1961. But Kennedy refused to authorize the naval air support that would have given the lightly armed attackers a chance of survival; Castro swiftly crushed them with his Soviet tanks.

In the aftermath of that delicious humiliation of the "*Yanquis,*" Castro consolidated his dictatorship. He took over for his own purposes the Cuban Communist Party, won increased military, police, and economic aid from the Soviet Union, and hastened the departure of the best-educated and most articulate 15 percent of Cuba's population to southern Florida. The Soviet Union acquired a Caribbean satellite, complete with Leninist vanguard party, secret police, and GULAG; the United States received in the course of the decade up to a million enterprising new citizens.

Kennedy, sheepish over failure, met Khrushchev at a summit at Vienna in June 1961. There Khrushchev bullied him unmercifully and apparently concluded that Kennedy was soft. On August 13, Khrushchev proceeded to solve his German difficulties on his own. East German forces backed by Soviet armor sealed East Berlin off from the Western sectors with a massive wall of prefabricated concrete and electrified barbed wire. This "Berlin Wall" closed the last avenue of escape from Ulbricht's "German Democratic Republic" (DDR), which had lost 3 million citizens to the West in the preceding decade.

Kennedy and other Western leaders failed to respond to that unexpected Soviet stroke, although Kennedy called up U.S. reserve forces as a warning to Khrushchev not to press his luck. Worse followed. Khrushchev ordered nuclear tests that violated assurances he had given to Kennedy as well as a moratorium on atmospheric testing to which he had subscribed in 1958. In October 1961 the Soviet Union triumphantly detonated a bomb twice as large as any U.S. weapon, with a force equivalent to 58 million tons of high explosive.

In mid-1962, with Ulbricht's DDR at last on its way to consolidation behind barbed wire, the irrepressible Khrushchev launched a spectacular Caribbean gamble. In July he persuaded the Cubans to accept a Soviet garrison of 43,000 ground troops and technicians, armed with 48 medium-range and 32 intermediate-range ballistic missiles capable of striking most of the United States. The missiles would triple Soviet capacity to deliver thermonuclear warheads to United States targets. A *fait accompli* might also make possible the deployment of additional missiles that would give the Soviet Union parity or superiority. And success would shift the psychological superpower balance in favor of the Soviet Union. Khrushchev had evidently failed to learn one lesson from Korea—that the United States, if and when aroused, acted unpredictably.

The "New Frontier": Kennedy takes office (1961).

By early September 1962, the Cuban missile sites were under construction and were clearly visible from the air. Khrushchev and his diplomats lied repeatedly to Kennedy: the Soviet Union was merely installing antiaircraft rockets, not offensive missiles. But on October 14, 1962, photographs from a high-flying U-2 showed patterns already familiar from intermediate-range missile sites in the Soviet Union. Khrushchev's gamble that he could install the weapons before the United States noticed had failed.

Kennedy and his advisers consulted feverishly. The more militant urged an immediate air strike and an airborne and amphibious invasion of Cuba. Others pleaded for a predictably futile appeal to

Berlin divided by concrete and barbed wire: the Berlin Wall.

Khrushchev makes a point (1962).

the United Nations. Kennedy chose a naval blockade that would give Khrushchev time to retreat without too great a humiliation. But Kennedy also prepared for air strikes and an invasion, should they be necessary to prevent the missiles from becoming operational. His televised announcement on October 22 of a U.S. Navy "quarantine" of Cuba initiated a week of crisis that many feared was the prelude to "nuclear holocaust." But only Castro seems to have sought war; at the height of the crisis, he reportedly urged Khrushchev to launch a nuclear strike against the United States and proclaimed that "the Cuban people [were] prepared to sacrifice themselves for the cause of the destruction of imperialism and the victory of world revolution."

When the blockade took effect on October 24, Soviet ships loaded with additional missiles halted on their way to Cuba. Khrushchev belatedly admitted having placed offensive nuclear forces in Cuba but retreated behind the improbable claim that he had acted only to prevent a United States invasion—a threat the Bay of Pigs fiasco had dissipated, and which the Soviet missiles themselves had revived. He offered to withdraw them in return for a U.S. pledge not to invade Cuba. Work on the missile sites in Cuba meanwhile con-

tinued feverishly; the first missiles were apparently approaching operational readiness, and up to 45 nuclear warheads (it later became known) had reached the island.

On October 27, Kennedy sent his brother Bobby, the administration's enforcer, to tell the Soviet ambassador sternly that "the point of escalation was at hand." If Moscow did not agree to withdraw the missiles, the United States would remove them itself. That threat, backed with a strategic nuclear superiority of 10 to 1 or better and by overwhelming air, sea, and ground power in the Caribbean, at last persuaded Khrushchev to back down. The Soviet Union withdrew its missiles. But it left behind advisers, intelligence listening posts, and a mechanized brigade based near Havana. The United States pointedly avoided making a formal promise not to invade.

Like Stalin's death, the Cuban Missile Crisis marked the end of a major phase in the Cold War. It was the closest that Soviet and U.S. forces had come to fighting since the Berlin blockade—but on that occasion the United States had possessed a nuclear monopoly. In the aftermath of the far more dangerous Cuban crisis, both powers sought to curb their mutual hostility. A 1963 treaty banning nuclear tests in the atmosphere and in space was the first and most durable result of that effort.

But in other respects the two rivals drew entirely different lessons from the confrontation. The United States, reassured about the superpower balance, overcommitted itself in Asia. It also sought to limit nuclear weapons, and by 1969 had by deliberate inaction discarded the superiority that had helped checkmate Khrushchev in Cuba. Nuclear "parity," U.S. leaders theorized, would lead the Soviets to embrace arms control and eventual reductions. Thermonuclear weapons, U.S. academics suggested, were so destructive that their only use was to deter their use by others.

The Soviets took a different view. "You Americans will never be able to do this to us again." a Soviet negotiator grimly informed his American counterpart in the aftermath of the crisis. Khrushchev's col-

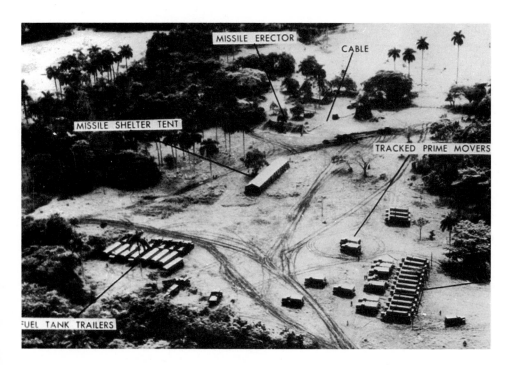

MISSILE ERECTOR

CABLE

MISSILE SHELTER TENT

TRACKED PRIME MOVERS

FUEL TANK TRAILERS

The Soviet ballistic missile site at San Cristóbal, Cuba (October 1962).

leagues forcibly retired him in October 1964, in part because he had begun to threaten the privileges of the Party elite, but also for mishandling the missile crisis. Under the stone-faced new leadership of Leonid Brezhnev and Alexei Kosygin, the Soviet regime tightened KGB controls at home and increased its defense budget from an already heavy 10 percent of gross national product in 1965 to 25 percent or more by 1980.

The Soviet goal was nuclear superiority (see Figure 34-1). Unlike Western academics, Soviet leaders saw nuclear weapons as militarily decisive and politically useful. The United States and its allies relied on the U.S. nuclear "umbrella" to hold back superior Soviet ground forces. If the Soviet Union could threaten the United States itself with nuclear destruction, U.S. threats to use nuclear weapons against the Soviet Union if the Soviet armies attacked U.S. allies would lose credibility. Nuclear superiority would also give the Soviet Union a global reach and greater freedom to support "wars of national liberation" that indirectly undermined the West's position. Finally, the growth of Soviet power

would presumably intimidate the Europeans and the Japanese, and divide them from the United States.

PEACE AND WAR IN THE SHADOW OF THE COLD WAR

While the superpowers struggled, Japan and the once-great powers of Europe enjoyed unprecedented economic growth. Not so the Middle East, where after 1945 the West no longer filled the vacuum created by Ottoman collapse. The foundation of a Jewish state and the conflicting ambitions of the Arabs led to two generations of bitter wars.

The Mid-Sized Powers in Eclipse

The revival of world trade was essential for the recovery of Europe and Japan. In the previous long peace, from 1871 to 1914, world trade had grown at an average annual rate of 3.4 percent; then the German bid for world mastery had pushed growth down to an average of 1 percent per year from 1913 to 1938. But after 1948,

Figure 34-1   After Cuba: Missile Power   1962–72

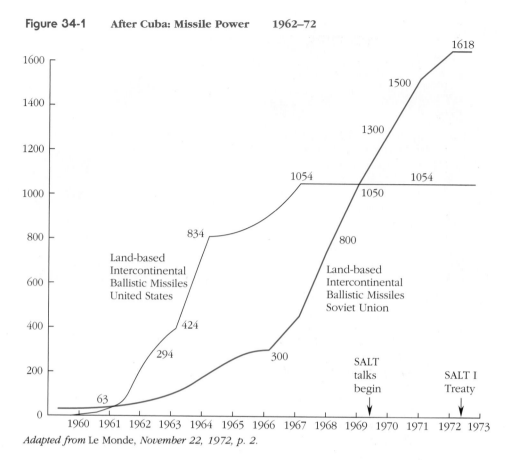

Adapted from Le Monde, *November 22, 1972, p. 2.*

more than $20 billion in Marshall Plan and other U.S. aid, together with a boom caused by the Korean War, galvanized the world economy. The Bretton Woods system installed in 1944–47 brought the stability and predictability that had been lacking in the 1920s and 1930s.

The result was astonishing growth. From 1950 to 1960, the volume of world trade grew by 6.4 percent each year. Europe and Japan rebuilt their economies under the military protection and economic leadership of the United States. The West German "economic miracle" was the most dramatic in Europe, with a growth rate of 7.7 percent per year. France followed, then Italy, which started as a far poorer country. Britain's longstanding failure to channel its best brains into industry and commerce helped condemn it to last place, with a growth rate of 2.6 percent per year.

But despite the aspirations of Europe's technocratic visionaries, no "United States of Europe" emerged. The European Community (EC) or European common market, founded at Rome in 1957, slowly developed a transnational political superstructure and a European parliament. But its powers remained small. The nation-state remained the principal focus of loyalty. And France crippled the EC for a decade by checkmating a halfhearted British attempt to enter it in 1963.

In Britain after 1945, Labour and Conservatives alternated in government with their customary decorum. Labour under Clement Attlee nationalized major industries, thereby protecting them from much-needed rationalization and modernization. Government health care and social insurance extended "cradle to grave" security to the entire population. When the aging Churchill returned to

Fall of France
1940

Provisional Government
under de Gaulle

1958

| Vichy Government and German Occupation | | Fourth Republic | Fifth Republic |

1945 1946

power in 1951, he left the welfare state intact but sold off some of Britain's nationalized industries. His foreign secretary and successor, Anthony Eden, resigned in disarray after the Suez crisis of 1956 (see p.927), but the reassuring leadership of Harold Macmillan kept the Conservatives in office until 1963–64. Labour then returned under the bland Harold Wilson, Labour's answer to Stanley Baldwin. Both parties pursued roughly similar policies: the welfare state at home, a "special relationship" with the United States abroad, and the retention of as much empire as Britain could hold without excessive effort.

France, as usual, was livelier. The Fourth Republic was similar in political habits and alignments to the Third Republic that had died in 1940. The founders of the new republic pushed de Gaulle, the savior of France, into premature retirement in early 1946. He repaid the compliment by damning the vagaries of the Chamber of Deputies as "the convolutions of this absurd ballet." His successors halfheartedly waged the Indochina war into which de Gaulle's emissaries had blundered in 1945–46. The Fourth Republic's one hour of glory was the 1954–55 premiership of Pierre Mendès-France, who set a deadline for French withdrawal from Indochina and made it stick.

But the Mendès-France government soon collapsed over the Algerian insurrection against France (see pp. 929–31) that erupted less than six months after the Indochina settlement. That second great colonial war wrecked the Fourth Republic. The French Right supported NATO but claimed that Algeria was part of France, although nine-tenths of Algeria's inhabitants were Moslems. Left-wing opinion and a strong Communist Party opposed NATO but—after some hesitation—favored Algerian independence. Parliamentary

deadlock followed. The army in Algeria was already restless; those who had served in Indochina grimly reproached the politicians for France's long record of defeat. A sense of betrayal impelled the army to swing its support behind de Gaulle's tumultuous return in a quasi-coup in May 1958.

De Gaulle demanded and received from parliament the right to draft a new constitution. His Fifth Republic was more durable than its predecessor; de Gaulle as president assumed stronger powers than any French executive since Napoleon III. And he used those powers wisely. He led France out of the Algerian war in 1962 without splitting the highly politicized army or provoking the bloody civil war between Right and Left that had seemed imminent in 1958. He gave France unprecedented economic growth. The France of landowning peasants consolidated in the Revolution of 1789 at last became a land of urban workers.

Italy surprised everyone. It achieved stability and unprecedented prosperity. Because of its collaboration with Mussolini, the monarchy failed to win a majority in a 1946 referendum. Italy became a republic, under the leadership of the political parties that reemerged after the collapse of Fascism. The Catholic *Popolari,* renamed Christian Democrats, were the largest; they faced small middle-class parties and a Socialist-Communist alliance. By 1947–48, as the lines of the Cold War hardened, Italy's new political system had also set. Alcide De Gasperi, a Catholic politician whom Mussolini had once persecuted and imprisoned, led the Christian Democrats and the government. The Communist-Socialist alliance lost heavily in the decisive election of April 1948, which De Gasperi fought with massive U.S. and Vatican support and with a remarkable platform: "For or Against Christ."

DeGaulle in Algiers (1958).

After 1953 a series of revolving-door governments followed De Gasperi. But even more than in France, the "absurd ballet" in parliament cloaked underlying continuity. Italy's Communist Party, western Europe's largest, formed a permanent "disloyal opposition" capable of overthrowing the system--if permitted to enter the government. By parliamentary arithmetic, only a coalition of the political center around the Christian Democrats could govern. With adjustments such as the addition of the Socialists to the coalition in 1963 after they broke with the Communists, that formula gave Italy forty years of remarkably stable although increasingly corrupt government. And the economy of Italy's industrial north grew with breakneck speed from the mid-1950s to the late 1960s, thanks to the skill of its entrepreneurs. That economic "miracle" enabled Italy, by the 1970s, to challenge Britain and France for economic primacy. That was an astounding achievement for a society that in 1913 had possessed less than a quarter of Britain's industrial power.

West Germany was western Europe's most dramatic success. Bonn—the Federal Republic's provisional capital, chosen in the expectation of an eventual move to Berlin—was not Weimar. The West German constitution of 1949 barred from parliament any party that received less than 5 percent of the vote. That "five-percent hurdle" restrained the political fragmentation that had helped destroy the first German republic. The new presidency, unlike the presidency of Weimar that had made Hitler chancellor, was a purely ceremonial position. And Hitler, through war, terror, and defeat, had destroyed—along with much else—the conservative elites that had so despised Weimar democracy that they had helped bring the Nazis to power.

The new Republic's first chancellor was an aged but vigorous former mayor of Cologne and pre-1933 opponent of Hitler, Konrad Adenauer. His party, the Christian Democratic Union/Christian Social Union (CDU/CSU), was a successor to the Catholic Center party that also appealed to Protestants. It became the mass party of the German urban and rural middle classes,

"In the beginning, there was Adenauer": Konrad Adenauer (chancellor, 1949–63), founder of West German democracy.

and ruled uninterruptedly from 1949 to 1966 in coalition with a small liberal party, the Free Democrats (FDP).

The Social Democratic Party (SPD), the only major party to survive from Weimar, opposed the CDU/CSU. After publicly discarding Marxism in 1959, the SPD at last broke the class barrier that had stunted its growth before 1933. Like the CDU/CSU, it appealed to an ever-larger and more prosperous middle and working class; it offered "good government" and the welfare state. Under Willy Brandt, a dynamic mayor of Berlin who had passed the Hitler years in political exile, the SPD achieved by 1966 a share of power in coalition with Adenauer's successors in the CDU/CSU. In 1969, in alliance with the FDP, Brandt and the SPD replaced the CDU/CSU in power. West Germany had achieved an orderly alternation between two large coherent parties. Antidemocratic fringe groups survived on the far Right and Left, but their clamor was infinitely greater than their influence. And the West German economy had grown into the largest in western Europe and the fourth largest in the world.

Finally, Japan amazed its American occupiers. MacArthur's democratic revolution from above, the greatest internal upheaval since the Meiji Restoration of 1868, was a qualified success. Drawing on the precedents of the parliamentary 1920s, Japanese politicians created a powerful machine of electoral consensus, the Liberal Democratic party. Its ruling oligarchy achieved and maintained a parliamentary majority based on the votes of Japan's peasantry and urban middle classes. That majority permanently excluded from power a fragmented opposition that included Communists, Socialists, and a Buddhist political cult. This "half democracy," as Japanese critics described it, provided a political stability that fostered spectacular economic growth.

The United States provided other ingredients as well: the technology offered by U.S. corporations to their Japanese subsidiaries, and markets and raw materials to replace Japan's lost empire in China and southeast Asia. Direct U.S. aid to Japan after 1954 totaled about $2 billion, but the expenditure by 1970 of more than $10 billion in orders by the U.S. military for the wars in Korea and Vietnam was more significant. The goods the U.S. armed forces ordered were mostly civilian; their production fostered the manufacturing techniques that Japan used to storm the world's export markets after the mid-1960s. In Japan, the United States provided the catalyst for the "economic miracle" of the 1950s and 1960s even more than it had in Europe. But it was the relentless hard work of the highly skilled and well-educated Japanese labor force that by the 1970s had made Japan the third largest economy in the world, after the United States and the Soviet Union.

The New Eastern Question, 1947–73

Hitler failed to kill all the Jews of Europe. Instead, paradoxically and unintentionally, he made possible the first Jewish state since the Roman reconquest of Jerusalem in A.D. 70. His genocide inspired a disgust for Europe among many of the Jews who survived, and led to a flood of emigration to Palestine. His genocide taught the lesson that only a Jewish state, weapons in hand, could ensure Jewish survival. His genocide temporarily discredited anti-Semitism in western Europe and the United States, and inspired guilt in those who had failed to aid the Jews of Europe in time. That unspoken guilt dissipated with time, but it was a powerful source of international support for the creation of a Jewish state.

In the aftermath of Hitler's war, Britain tried to uphold its 1939 ban on further Jewish immigration to Palestine (see p. 809). British interests in the Arab world—the world of oil—seemed to demand that Britain block the Zionist aspiration to found a Jewish state. But by 1945 the 600,000 Jews of Palestine constituted a third of the population, and many of them had fought for Britain against Hitler. They now resisted Britain as they had resisted the Arabs in the guerrilla conflict after 1936. By 1946 Zionist guerrilla groups, the Irgun and the "Stern Gang," were at war with both Arabs and British.

Chaim Weizmann, the Zionist leader who had secured Balfour's promise in 1917, tirelessly lobbied the powers for his cause.

By 1946, Britain's position was untenable. As in Ireland after 1919, the British army could not control a spreading guerrilla war without using methods that no democracy could defend. Truman backed the creation of a Jewish state. Even Stalin, who despite his anti-Semitism saw the Jews of Palestine as possible allies against Britain, did not oppose it. In 1947 Attlee's Labour government thankfully handed the poisoned gift of Palestine over to the United Nations, which proposed partition along ethnic-religious lines. The Jewish organizations accepted, but the Palestinian Arabs and their supports in the Arab states refused. An Arab "Liberation Army" attacked Jewish communities. In May 1948, as in Greece and India (see pp. 886 and 926), the exhausted British departed.

That left Palestine to anyone who could conquer it. On May 14, 1948, David Ben-Gurion, charismatic veteran of the Jewish settler communities, proclaimed a Jewish state—the state of Israel. The armies of Egypt, Jordan, Syria, Lebanon, and Iraq invaded Palestine with the announced intention of driving the Jews into the sea. Israel, outnumbered and outgunned, fought that "Arab League" to a standstill and drew Israel's precarious borders by force. Many Palestinian Arabs obeyed calls from their leaders to leave the Jewish-controlled areas, expecting a swift return with the Arab armies. In some cases Jewish forces drove Arab civilians out. Defeat left some 600,000 embittered Palestinian refugees in Jordan and Egypt, and made the Arab states more determined than ever to destroy the Jews.

The core of the new "Eastern Question"—the struggle between the successor states of the Ottoman Empire—was the irreconcilable conflict between the Palestinian Arabs, the Arab states, and Israel. But the antagonism also drew nourishment from a broader and more ancient conflict. The Arabs regarded Israel as yet another intrusion by the West, a successor to the Crusader kingdoms of the twelfth and thirteenth centuries and to the European imperialism of the nineteenth. Israel was a galling symbol of the Islamic world's humiliating weakness, first exposed by Napoleon's 1798–99 campaign in Egypt. Only Israel's destruction, many Arabs increasingly felt, could restore their self-respect.

Arab hostility was self-defeating. The fierce external threat welded Israel's disparate inhabitants together and consolidated its parliamentary system under Ben-Gurion's Labor party. A modern economy took shape, the result of native ingenuity and money from Jewish organizations abroad. In 1951 the gross national product of Egypt, the most prosperous of the Arab states, was three to four times that of Israel; by 1966–67 the ratio had declined to 1.6 to 1.

War had given birth to Israel, a Jewish state, the only democracy in the Middle East. Only war could preserve it, for the Arab powers refused to recognize the "Zionist entity" as a state and made no secret of their continuing desire to destroy it and its inhabitants. Egypt took the lead. Abdel Gamal Nasser, a visionary who dreamed of uniting the Arabs from the Atlantic to the Persian Gulf, emerged as dictator of Egypt after an army coup in 1952. From 1955 on, he secured lavish supplies of arms from the Soviet Union.

Twice, in 1956 and 1967, Nasser provoked Israel with Palestinian guerrilla raids from Gaza and closure of the straits of Tiran that commanded access to Israel's Red Sea port of Eilat. Twice Israel struck first and routed the Egyptians in short but devastating wars in the Sinai Peninsula. Indefensible borders and immense numerical odds left Israel no alternative to preemptive war. Nasser's proclaimed desire for a "war of annihilation" suggested that the price of failure would be a new "Final Solution."

In 1956, thanks to the sheepish withdrawal of its British and French allies, Israel had to leave the conquered Sinai to a United Nations "peacekeeping" force that later failed to keep the peace. In 1967, Israel therefore refused to withdraw after victory—and not only from the Sinai and Gaza. Syria and Jordan had joined Egypt in that "Six Days' War" and had lost the west bank of the Jordan River and the

strategic Golan heights from which Syrian artillery had shelled the farming settlements of northern Israel. The conquests of 1967 brought a measure of security, but with it a dangerous gift: the million new Arabs of the "occupied territories" of the West Bank and Gaza.

The Palestinian guerrilla organizations drew a lesson from the 1967 war: they could not look to the Arab states for victory. In 1968 the "Palestine Liberation Organization" (PLO) and its offshoots therefore launched a campaign of terror against soft targets such as Israeli airliners. Israel replied with air strikes against Palestinian refugee camps and open season on PLO leaders. Israeli reprisals against Jordan for Palestinian raids prompted Jordan's King Hussein to discipline the armed Palestinians who constituted a state within his state. In "Black September" 1970, Hussein's highly professional army crushed them. Lebanon, a state too weak to defend itself, became the last stronghold of the PLO.

An embarrassed Soviet Union soon replenished Nasser's arms and manned his radars, antiaircraft missiles, and fighters. In 1969–70 Nasser and the Soviets waged a "war of attrition" against Israel's forward defenses along the Suez Canal. Negotiations sponsored by the United Nations and United States proved predictably futile. Nasser died of a heart attack in September 1970. By that time Egypt had suffered 30,000 casualties, and Washington and Moscow—embarrassed still—had together imposed a cease-fire along the Canal. Nasser's successor, Colonel Anwar Sadat, prepared for yet another round against Israel. The increasing economic power of the Arab oil states had begun to isolate Israel from the timid and oil-dependent western Europeans. But this time, instead of a "war of annihilation," Sadat planned a limited attack to take back the east bank of the Canal and bloody the Israelis.

The Soviet Union supplied advanced antiaircraft and antitank missiles by the shipload. But Sadat was careful to distance himself from his Soviet patrons, who for their part perhaps feared that too close association with a new Arab war might damage the developing "détente" with the United States (see below). In July 1972 Sadat asked for the withdrawal of most of his Soviet "advisers." In 1973, with Egypt's army mobilized and deployed and with Syrian armor drawn up opposite the Golan heights, Sadat attacked. The date he chose was Yom Kippur, the Jewish Day of Atonement, October 6, 1973.

As Sadat had hoped, Israel's political isolation deterred it from repeating its pre-emptive strikes of 1956 and 1967. Sadat's carefully planned crossing of the Canal broke through Israel's thinly held fortifications, and his Soviet antitank missiles shattered the first hasty Israeli armored counterattacks. But then the Egyptians strayed inland from the Canal and into a battle of movement which the Israelis dominated with their usual skill and drive. In the north, outnumbered Israeli forces in the Golan routed more than 1,000 Syrian and Iraqi tanks and advanced to within artillery range of Damascus. In the south, Israel at last crossed the Canal into Egypt and encircled one of Sadat's two armies. The road to Cairo lay open. Then the superpowers imposed a cease-fire, although not before an unprecedented Soviet threat to commit paratroops in support of Egypt had provoked the United States to alert its nuclear forces.

Militarily the Yom Kippur War was yet another crushing defeat for the Arab cause. But unlike 1967, it was not a total humiliation. Sadat's initial success along the Canal allowed him to claim a moral victory. That made Egypt—although not the Palestinians or the other Arab states—more willing to negotiate. Israel's near disaster also compelled rethinking in Jerusalem. The ultimate result of 1973 was a first break in the wall of Arab hostility surrounding Israel and the transition from war to grudging peace between Israel and Egypt (see p. 964).

And yet the international implications of the Yom Kippur War were ominous. It encouraged the oil-producing states of OPEC (Organization of Petroleum Exporting Countries) to more than double the real (inflation-adjusted) price of oil from October 1973 to 1975—while placing a total embargo on the United States in revenge for its support of Israel. The Europeans cowered. They cut off trade with Israel and, except for Portugal, refused to allow the United States to use NATO bases in support of the massive airlift of ammunition that the beleaguered Jewish state needed to survive. Only Holland failed to comply swiftly enough with Arab demands; it suffered both Arab oil embargo and ostracism by its EC partners. That display of NATO and European disunity inevitably encouraged adversaries of the West to whom events in southeast Asia had already given heart.

THE AGONY OF CONTAINMENT: AMERICA IN VIETNAM

The United States emerged from the Cuban Missile Crisis convinced that nothing was impossible. Then Kennedy's brilliant rhetoric, the self-confidence of the academic elite he had drawn into government, and the pressures of domestic politics combined to commit the United States to a second war of containment in Vietnam.

The Illusion of Omnipotence, 1962–68

Containment by war had proved an effective though costly answer to Stalin's adventure in Korea. Against indirect methods, against insurgency, it was less successful. That familiar technique was the ultimate choice of Ho Chi Minh and his associates, who ruled the "Democratic Republic of Vietnam" (DRV) north of the 17th parallel from their capital at Hanoi. They had consolidated their control in the north in 1955–56 by killing as many as 50,000 peasants who resisted collectivization. They had also maintained their network of party cadres south of the 17th parallel, in South Vietnam.

There Ngo Dinh Diem, a Catholic anti-Communist from the precolonial Mandarin ruling class, established a "Republic of Vietnam" at Saigon, the capital of the South. Diem's regime rested on the traditional landowning elite and on the Vietnamese army France had organized to fight the Communists. The regime had little support among the South's peasants, whose loyalty Ho's party had secured during the war against the French by driving out landlords and redistributing land.

Eisenhower, after much hesitation, committed the United States to support Diem. If South Vietnam fell to Hanoi and to its apparent backers in Beijing, Eisenhower theorized, other southeast Asian "dominoes"—Laos, Cambodia, Thailand, Malaya, and Indonesia—would also fall. The United States had first tolerated France's Indochina war, and then, after 1950, had funded it. After 1954 the United States gradually took France's place. But Washington failed to foresee the sacrifices that policy might entail, or to understand

that Vietnam was unlike Korea in three essential ways. South Vietnam lacked a government or leader with even the frayed legitimacy of a Syngman Rhee. Vietnam was not a peninsula surrounded on three sides by a sea dominated by the U.S. Navy. And Vietnam was only distantly related to the fundamental American Cold War goal of maintaining its major allies in Europe and Japan.

In January 1959 Ho Chi Minh and his Party's inner circle decided to resume "armed struggle" in South Vietnam with the aim of annexing it to the DRV. A party-dominated army, called "Viet Cong" (Vietnamese Communists) by its enemies, took shape in the South. Between 1961 and 1963 it assassinated more than 3,000 Diem

War in Southeast Asia   1954–88

administrators or civilians connected with the government. Hanoi announced in December 1960 the creation of a political cover for that army, the "National Liberation Front" (NLF), a "popular front" that included many non-Communists but secretly took its orders from Hanoi. It was important that NLF and Viet Cong activities appear to Western public opinion as a Southern revolt against what Hanoi described as the "U.S.-Diem dictatorship."

Diem's shaky regime crumbled by 1962–63. His Catholicism, his autocratic manner, and his sinister brother and minister of police, Ngo Dinh Nhu, alienated the influential Buddhist clergy, some of whom burned themselves to death in acts of protest well-publicized on U.S. television. Diem's association with the Americans offended South Vietnam's urban, educated elites. His closeness to the landowners estranged the peasants. The NLF offered the city-dwellers a romantic nationalism and false assurances that its victory would mean autonomy for the South. To the peasants the NLF offered land, but made no mention of the fate of the collectivized peasants of the north. Viet Cong units and political cadres established control over ever-wider areas.

Kennedy, an enthusiast for spy novels and unconventional warfare, increased the number of U.S. military advisers in Vietnam from the 900 he had inherited from Eisenhower to more than 15,000, including helicopter and fighter-bomber units. They were not enough to stave off approaching defeat, and Kennedy apparently concluded that winning the war required Diem's removal. When Diem's confrontation with the Buddhists provoked unrest among his generals, Washington quietly encouraged them to plan a coup. Kennedy made it known in Saigon that if Diem did not dismiss Nhu "we must face the possibility that Diem himself cannot be preserved." That was a green light to the Vietnamese military plotters, who overthrew Diem on November 1, 1963. Contrary to Kennedy's intentions, but all too predictably, the coup forces shot Diem and Nhu.

The United States, confident that it could control events in a society of which

Lyndon Baines Johnson takes the oath of office after Kennedy's assassination, November 22, 1963.

it was deeply ignorant, in this way took total responsibility for the fate of South Vietnam. Kennedy himself died three weeks after Diem, on November 22, 1963, assassinated in Dallas in circumstances that later generated endless conspiracy theories. His vice president and successor, Lyndon Baines Johnson of Texas, proved wily and resourceful in his domestic policy. He accomplished what Kennedy had begun, the belated abolition of the "Jim Crow" segregation laws of the southern United States and the launching of a federal "war on poverty." But his confused attempts to cope with the disaster that he had inherited in Vietnam wrecked his presidency.

The coming 1964 presidential election and the legacy of the Chinese-American war in Korea made disengagement from Vietnam almost unthinkable. "Who lost Vietnam?" was a question Johnson dreaded as much as Eisenhower and Kennedy before him. Looming behind Hanoi was Beijing, where Mao and associates were proclaiming a worldwide peasant revolutionary war against the urban capitalism of the West. And China seemed all the more menacing after it exploded its first atomic bomb in October 1964. Withdrawal from Vietnam, the Washington elite and press assumed, would weaken the credibility of U.S. guarantees to its other allies and unleash a wave of Communist expansion that would engulf "dominoes" from the rice fields of Thailand to the oilfields of Indonesia.

Johnson therefore sought to dissuade Hanoi from pursuing its ambitions. The academic strategists whom Kennedy had brought from Harvard to Washington offered a method: carefully calibrated air and sea pinpricks by U.S. and South Vietnamese forces that would convince Hanoi to give up its attempt to annex the South. The DRV was not convinced; it sent ever-larger forces southward through Laos. By early 1965 South Vietnam seemed on the verge of collapse.

With congressional authorization to "prevent further aggression" in southeast Asia in his pocket, and with victory in the 1964 presidential election safely behind him, Johnson launched a major air campaign against the North in March 1965. But fear of provoking Chinese intervention—as in Korea—and the illusion that bombing by increments would "send a message" kept U.S. bombing safely below the level needed to cripple Hanoi's economy, society, and Soviet-supplied air-defense network.

The air war might eventually have worn the North down, but it could not save South Vietnam in the critical early months of 1965. Between March and May 1965 Johnson therefore committed U.S. Marines and paratroopers to the South. They were the first units of an expeditionary force that grew to 543,000 men and women by spring 1969. That force—or rather the roughly 75,000 infantrymen and 50,000 artillerymen and helicopter crewmen who actually did the fighting—had almost everything: apparently limitless firepower on call, helicopter medical evacuation, lavish supplies, and rotation back to the United States if they survived their 365 allotted days in Vietnam.

What they lacked was a strategy. Washington sought only to force Hanoi to negotiate; that was even less inspiring to the troops than "dying for a tie" in Korea. The U.S. Army command in the South sought to defeat the Viet Cong and the North Vietnamese through attrition. The U.S. Navy and Air Force competed to see which service could drop more bombs on strategically irrelevant targets in and around the North. Both air and ground wars maximized *American* attrition, without bringing a decision closer.

The U.S. ground war did buy time, however. Saigon's battlefield performance and political stability slowly improved. In January–February 1968 the victor of Dien Bien Phu, General Vo Nguyen Giap, launched Viet Cong and North Vietnamese forces at the cities of the South. Timed for Têt, the Vietnamese lunar new year, Giap's "General Uprising" was a stinging operational and tactical reverse for Hanoi. U.S. troops held and counterattacked. Saigon's troops, their backs to the wall, stood and fought. Contrary to Giap's expectation, the population of the cities did not join his troops; at Hue on the central coast, retreating North Vietnamese took revenge by massacring 2,800 civilians. Yet out of tactical defeat Hanoi gained strategic victory. The confusion and bloodshed of Têt shocked the American press and television reporters in Saigon, who interpreted fighting in the cities as a massive U.S. defeat.

Under a rough and profane exterior, Johnson concealed a fatal desire to be loved. Increasing fire from the press and the growth in 1967–68 of raucous student demonstrations against the war effort ("Hey, hey, LBJ, how many kids did ya kill today?") deeply wounded him. The Têt fighting and the strong showing of an "antiwar" candidate in the New Hampshire presidential primary broke what little nerve he had left. He had failed to define a war aim and to lead; now he concurred with his critics.

On March 31, 1968, Johnson appeared on television and announced three things: that the United States would cease bombing the North except for the area immediately north of the 17th parallel, that it would seek a negotiated withdrawal from the war, and that he himself would not run for reelection in the fall. Assassination had brought Johnson to power; he departed by committing political suicide.

His public confession that he thought the war unwinnable changed the terms of debate. After March 1968, Americans battled over how to leave Vietnam, not over how to win or whether to fight.

Defeat, 1968–75

Johnson's ill-fated vice president, Hubert Humphrey, lost the 1968 presidential election. On the Right, a racist third-party revolt against Johnson's domestic policies deprived the Democrats of their usually solid Southern vote. From the Left, violent student demonstrations against Humphrey outside the Democratic Convention in Chicago and the abstention of many "dovish" voters—in protest against Johnson's Vietnam policy—likewise cut into the Democratic vote. To the horror of most "doves," the victor was the Republican candidate, Richard M. Nixon, a former associate of Senator McCarthy.

Nixon had claimed during the campaign that he had a "secret peace plan." It remained secret. In spring 1969 he announced the "Vietnamization" of the war and the gradual withdrawal of American troops; by late 1972 fewer than 25,000 remained. To buy time, Nixon launched in May–June 1970 a last brief offensive thrust, an attack on the elaborate bases the North Vietnamese had established in Cambodia.

Nixon and his devious National Security Adviser, Henry Kissinger of Harvard, may had deluded themselves as well as others that "Vietnamization" would achieve a Korea-style stalemate. More probably, they aimed from the beginning at a gradual retreat from Vietnam in the style of de Gaulle's withdrawal from Algeria. But Hanoi refused to negotiate. Its delegates to the Paris talks that began in May 1968 demanded instantaneous and total withdrawal by the United States and the dismantling of its ally in Saigon. Hanoi also refused to promise the release of U.S. prisoners, mostly Navy and Air Force aircrews, from its concentration camps. The death of Ho Chi Minh in September 1969 made no difference. The Leninist party he had created lived on.

Têt, 1968: Marines advance warily through the ruins of Hue.

But by now the international situation surrounding the U.S. plunge into Vietnam had entirely changed. A Communist coup attempt in Indonesia had failed in 1965; the Indonesian military and Islamic militants retaliated with the massacre of hundreds of thousands of Indonesian Communists and sympathizers. *That* vital domino and its oil was not going to fall.

As for China, it had ironically ceased to need containment. Mao had reduced it to chaos with his "Great Proletarian Cultural Revolution" of 1966–69 (see p. 934), and the Sino-Soviet split had ripened into full-scale military confrontation between the two Communist giants along their 7,000-mile border.

In the spring and summer of 1969 Soviet and Chinese troops fought bitterly on the Ussuri River, north of Vladivostok. A Soviet journalist with close ties to the KGB reported ominously in the British press that "Marxist theoreticians" were discussing the possibility of a full-scale Sino-Soviet war. Soviet spokesmen secretly approached the United States, suggesting that a Soviet strike against China's infant nuclear weapons program would serve the interests of both superpowers. But Nixon sternly warned Moscow off. Kissinger secretly visited Beijing in July 1971 for talks with the shrewd Zhou Enlai, the second man in China. Nixon sought to exploit the mutual fears and hatreds of the Communist great powers to put pressure on Hanoi, to promote arms control, and to secure a Berlin settlement.

In February 1972, Nixon visited Beijing in person and ended the Chinese-American enmity that had endured since war in 1950. Ideology took a back seat to power relationships. As a Middle Eastern saying put it, the enemy of my enemy is my friend. The U.S. "opening to China" so worried Brezhnev that he agreed to a Nixon visit and retreated both in negotiations over Berlin and over strategic arms limitation.

Immediately before the Moscow summit of May 1972, Nixon blocked the vital North Vietnamese port of Haiphong with air-dropped mines, in reprisal for a failed North Vietnamese offensive aimed at Saigon. The mines and the fact that Brezhnev—like Mao—greeted Nixon warmly, apparently provoked second thoughts in Hanoi. But even Nixon's landslide reelection in November failed to persuade Hanoi to settle for less than Saigon's swift collapse. In December 1972 Nixon therefore ordered attacks on vital targets in and around Hanoi with the full firepower of the B-52 heavy bombers of the U.S. Air Force. Following that "Christmas bombing," Hanoi at last consented to release the United States from the war on terms short of utter humiliation.

On January 27, 1973, the DRV representatives signed a peace agreement in Paris providing for the return of U.S. prisoners, the withdrawal of U.S. advisers still in South Vietnam, and a precarious truce. Publicly, Nixon and Kissinger claimed they had achieved "peace with honor," a phrase rich in historical irony. Privately they apparently hoped for a "decent interval" between U.S. withdrawal and South Vietnamese collapse.

The interval was indecently short. Nixon, like Johnson, wanted to be loved. Unceasing personal attacks by his domestic opponents and frequent leakages to the press from within his administration warped his sometimes eccentric judgment. During the 1972 election campaign he ordered the "plumbers," a secret White House unit formed to combat the leaks, to plant electronic listening devices in the national Democratic Party headquarters at Washington's Watergate Hotel. In June 1972, an alert security guard caught the inept "plumbers" as they attempted to break in, and in spring–summer 1973

The opening to China: Nixon and Mao (1972).

Nixon's frantic attempts to cover up his own role in this "Watergate Affair" collapsed. Televised hearings before Congress left his administration in a shambles. On August 9, 1974, he left the presidency by a unique route—resignation to escape impeachment, criminal prosecution, and probable imprisonment.

Internally, the outcome of Watergate was a triumph for the rule of law. Externally, it enabled Congress to seize control of foreign policy and cut off aid to South Vietnam and to anti-Communist forces in Laos and Cambodia. Fierce congressional opposition paralyzed Nixon's vice president and successor, Gerald R. Ford. In January 1975 the North Vietnamese Politburo took the measure of Congress and of Ford: "Having withdrawn from Vietnam, the United States could hardly return." Hanoi, newly reequipped with Soviet tanks and heavy weapons, prepared a North Korean-style offensive across South Vietnam's northern and western borders.

In April 1975, DRV armor overran the exhausted and demoralized South Vietnamese army. The United States watched impotently and then organized one last operation: the evacuation from Saigon of all remaining Americans and some of the many South Vietnamese who had worked for the United States. The North annexed the South and renamed Saigon "Ho Chi Minh City." The Second Indochina War was over. It had cost the lives of roughly 725,000 North Vietnamese, 525,000 South Vietnamese, and 58,000 Americans. Its end brought not peace, but massacres in Vietnam and Cambodia, millions of refugees, and a Third Indochina War between the Communist victors (see pp. 957–58).

A "Generation of Peace"? Détente and Arms Control, 1968–75

As they disengaged from Vietnam, Kissinger and Nixon proclaimed that a new international order was being born. The opening to China would not only release the United States from southeast Asia. It would also open the road to a lasting "détente," or relaxation of tensions, between Moscow and Washington.

Talk of détente was not new. The atmospheric test ban treaty of 1963 was its first monument. In 1968 Johnson had signed with Moscow a nuclear nonproliferation treaty—which China and France rejected in favor of exploding their own hydrogen bombs. Strategic arms talks and a 1968 summit with Brezhnev proved abortive. But in Europe, the West Germans abandoned Adenauer's rigid policy of nonrecognition of Ulbricht's East German regime. Willy Brandt of the SPD, upon his entrance into Bonn's governing coalition in 1966, inaugurated a new "eastern policy." Brandt's *Ostpolitik* sought to lessen tensions both with the DDR and with the nations of eastern Europe on which Germany had trampled in 1938–45. Extreme versions of *Ostpolitik* looked forward to an end to NATO and the Warsaw Pact, and the reunification of Germany.

As a French intellectual once remarked, Germany's neighbors loved Germany so much that they were delighted to have two of them. *Ostpolitik* was nevertheless a modest success. It suffered a setback in August 1968, when the Soviet Union and its Warsaw Pact allies invaded Czechoslovakia to crush the "Prague Spring," a liberalization movement in the Czech Communist party. But embarrassment at Soviet brutality did not long deter Brandt, Johnson, or Nixon from seeking further negotiations.

Brandt became Chancellor of West Germany in 1969 and concluded nonaggression treaties with the Soviet Union, Poland, Czechoslovakia, and the DDR in 1970–73. Kissinger's opening to China helped move the Soviet Union in 1971 to sign a treaty with the United States, Britain, and France that formally guaranteed Western access to Berlin. In theory that prevented a renewal of Stalin's blockade or of Khrushchev's threats to West Berlin.

Kissinger judged that Brezhnev badly needed reinsurance against Beijing and an infusion of Western technology and money to bolster Soviet economic growth, which had peaked in the 1950s and declined thereafter. He assumed, in essence, that the West could bribe the Soviets. Economic ties and arms control would in good

Cobdenite fashion (see p. 743) enmesh Moscow in a structure of "interdependence." As Kennan had hoped in 1947, the Soviet Union would at last "mellow" and become a status quo power. The need for containment would end, and the world, in Nixon's self-inflating phrase, would enjoy a "generation of peace."

The Soviet view was quite different. Despite Moscow's sensitivity about Kissinger's flirtation with Beijing, the Soviets did not consider China a near-term threat. The vast bulk of Soviet divisions continued to menace western Europe. Brezhnev sought détente as a tool for achieving Soviet objectives, not as an occasion to abandon them. Western money, technology, and grain would shore up a flagging economy and upgrade Soviet weapons technology. Détente need not hold the Soviet Union back outside Europe, as the Soviet Union immediately demonstrated by backing Sadat's October 1973 war. Nor did détente mean the end of ideological struggle.

Soviet reservations thus undermined the two greatest monuments of détente, the strategic arms limitation treaty of May 1972 (SALT I) and the Helsinki security treaty of 1975. SALT I and its accompanying "ABM Treaty" limiting antimissile defenses wrote into international law the quantitative advantage that the Soviet buildup had gained since 1962. The Soviets retained 1,618 land-based and 950 submarine-launched intercontinental ballistic missiles to the 1,054 and 710 of the United States. But SALT I limited numbers of missiles only; it placed no restrictions on the "multiple independently targeted" warheads (MIRVs) that soon equipped those missiles. The treaty appeared to make the superpower arms competition more predictable than before but did little to end it. And its duration was only five years.

The Helsinki treaty of 1975, the final cap on the eastern treaties of 1970–73, was equally ambiguous. The West, in a Europe-wide conference at Helsinki that included neutral powers, at last bestowed legitimacy on Stalin's conquests of 1944–45. In return, Moscow offered cultural exchanges, and promises, immediately vi-olated, of respect for human rights and of free movement of people and ideas across the borders of the Soviet empire.

MASS CULTURE AND "COUNTERCULTURE"

Socially and politically, the 1950s were placid times in the West. Sociologists prematurely hailed the "end of ideology," the demise of messianic political faiths in the wake of Khrushchev's 1956 revelations. Then worldwide communications, anti-American discontents, a student generation of unprecedented size and wealth, and the twin catalysts of the Vietnam War and the independence struggles in the "Third World" (see pp. 926–32) created a wave of disturbances unprecedented since 1848.

The Americanization of the World

The growth of the world market amid undreamed-of prosperity also meant the rapid worldwide spread of the mass culture of the leading state. Two things speeded up that process: the dying British Empire's legacy of English as the universal language of commerce, and a new revolution in transportation and communications that paralleled the coming of steam and the telegraph in the nineteenth century. In 1950, almost all intercontinental travel was by ship. By 1960 four-engined jet aircraft had cut the trip from Paris to New York to eight hours; no spot on the globe was more than 24 hours away. By the 1970s, satellite television relays provided instantaneous transmission of pictures and sound from anywhere on Earth.

American film and television conveyed sparkling images of affluence and made few intellectual demands on their audiences. When dubbed into local languages, they acquired a wide following wherever governments allowed their citizens to view them. They also aroused appetites for wealth and growth that most societies found difficult to satisfy. Even the relatively rich Europeans did not duplicate the credit-card prosperity of the American middle classes until the 1970s.

Along with Hollywood movies and television serials came the gray legions of corporate America, from General Electric to ITT to Coca Cola. They established or widened beachheads for American commerce in Europe, Japan, and the "Third World." That massive expansion of America's cultural and economic visibility aroused a variety of reactions. European business at first gratefully embraced the Marshall Plan and private American investment in Europe. Welcome turned to distrust by the 1960s. U.S. capital export was so massive that Europeans feared losing control of their economies to America's allegedly sinister "multinational corporations." Then the burden of Vietnam undermined U.S. economic performance. Europeans created multinationals of their own and invested in the United States.

Culturally, reaction was likewise mixed. The defeated nations of Germany, Italy, and Japan embraced some elements of American democracy or industrial organization. But especially in Britain, France, and the Islamic world, native traditions resisted fiercely. Britons like the philosopher and unilateral-disarmament crusader Bertrand Russell looked down their noses at what they took to be American provincialism and irresponsibility. Conservative critics, from traditionalist Catholics to stern Gaullists to Shiite Moslems, decried "Coca-colonization" and the moral laxity that American wealth allegedly brought. The academic Left, from Mexico City and Tokyo to the cafés of the Left Bank in Paris, turned withering Marxist scorn on America, the leading capitalist state.

Student Revolt and Middle-Class Terrorism

After 1945 the United States sought to create the first society in history in which a majority of citizens had some higher education. In the 1960s much of western Europe began to follow. The rapid expansion of colleges and universities created a shortage of faculty that consigned students to boredom in immense factory-like classrooms. Affluence apparently removed any pressing need to work. Leisure and the outrageous example of "beat generation" rebels of the 1950s fostered the

The Americanization of the world: the supermarket comes to France.

rise in the early 1960s of a youth "counterculture." Its adherents were passionately contemptuous of inherited standards of behavior and dedicated to the joys that contraceptive pills, mind-distorting drugs, and the electric guitar had recently made available.

The rebellion of the youthful rich began appropriately enough in the richest country, the United States. In 1964, the University of California at Berkeley exploded in violent confrontation between a rigid central administration and a radical "Free Speech Movement" determined to shock and provoke. Vietnam loomed on the horizon as early as 1963, but it was Johnson's plunge into full-scale war in 1965 that gave the rebels their cause and mass base. College students received draft deferments, but those who graduated or flunked out faced army service unless they discovered a convenient medical condition.

In these circumstances a "New Left" arose that mocked predictions of the "end of ideology." From 1964–65 on, it savaged the American political and academic establishment from the Left with a zeal that recalled the 1950s attacks of Senator McCarthy from the Right. It proclaimed a "second American revolution" against "imperialism" in Vietnam and against middle-class society at home. Student insurrections paralyzed Columbia, Harvard, and other campuses in 1967–68. Nixon's 1970 thrust into Cambodia inspired an immense wave of protest.

By then the most determined student radicals had formed a terrorist group that called itself the "Weathermen." The name came from a line of the folk-rock cult figure Bob Dylan: ". . . you don't need a weatherman to know which way the wind blows." The Weathermen sought to "bring the war home," to imitate the "armed struggle" of the Viet Cong and of urban guerrillas like the Tupamaros in Uruguay (see p. 941). Their most striking achievement was the accidental demolition in 1970 of a Greenwich Village townhouse and bomb factory belonging to the parent of a member. And the broader "Movement" deflated swiftly after 1970, thanks

to the end of the draft and to the inherent contradiction between Leninist commitment and countercultural hedonism. Not "armed struggle" but drugs, sex, rock and roll, and imported Buddhist or Hindu mysticism were the most widespread forms of protest against middle-class America.

The American example helped inspire disturbances in Europe far more serious than mere campus revolts. The European rebels had inherited a tradition of romantic student radicalism stretching back into the nineteenth century. They also drew on the discipline and doctrine of their countries' Communist parties, although they condemned those parties as stodgy. Even more than their American counterparts they found inspiration in "Third World" revolutionary movements.

The Paris "days" of May 1968 turned back the clock to the Paris Commune of 1871; urban insurrection once more seemed to be practical politics. A student uprising with support from the industrial workers briefly controlled the Left Bank of Paris. Hundreds of thousands marched demanding de Gaulle's overthrow. The General flew off in disgust ("reforms yes; bed-messing no") to visit his army and to secure the support of the officer corps. He then returned to Paris and rallied the "forces of order" with a television speech that brought millions into the streets singing the "Marseillaise"—a revolutionary anthem transmuted into a call to arms against revolution. The student movement deflated. The Left lost votes in the election that followed. De Gaulle resigned in 1969 when a referendum went against him, but he resigned in favor of a hand-picked successor. The modern state had again shown its ability to tame upheavals from below.

In Germany, student revolt was in deadly earnest—as it had been under Weimar, when the Nazis had captured the student movement long before they seized the state. Some German "New Left" radicals, Freudian-Marxist in ideology and Stalinist in practice, turned to "armed struggle" in the late 1960s. Their most prominent group, the "Red Army Faction" or "Baader-Meinhof gang," attacked U.S. bases in West Germany and assassinated industrialists, judges, and politicians with ruthless precision. But computerized tracking of suspects eventually demolished the guerrillas. In 1976–77 Andreas Baader, Ulrike Meinhof, and other "Red Army Faction" leaders committed suicide in prison to embarrass "the system." Bombings, assassinations, and revolution by suicide failed to inspire the placid West German "masses" to revolt. After 1979, the German student Left largely abandoned "armed struggle" for ecological and anti-nuclear protest (see p. 961).

Italy's student radicals mounted the most determined challenge to the democratic state. Students and industrial workers combined in 1969 to make a deadly serious "hot autumn" of riots, strikes, and factory or university occupations. Throughout the 1970s terrorist groups of former students from both leftist and Catholic backgrounds sought to provoke the Italian parliamentary regime into revealing its allegedly "Fascist" nature. Some had received training in KGB-sponsored schools in Czechoslovakia, others with the PLO in Lebanon. Their instrument was the "knee-capping" or assassination of judges, factory managers, journalists, and politicians. In 1978 the terrorist "Red Brigades" kidnaped and killed a former prime minister, the Christian Democrat Aldo Moro. That stroke united Italian opinion against the terrorists and galvanized police and prosecutors. The "Red Brigades" and their offshoots ended in prison. Throughout the West youthful rebellion gave way to middle-class careers.

The Feminist Revolution

Among the movements that flourished in the 1960s alongside student and "counter-cultural" protest was a renewed and militant feminism. The vote, the Depression, and two world wars had damped feminist agitation from the 1920s to the 1950s. But in the intoxicating atmosphere of the 1960s, the continuing growth of women's share in the work force—often in poorly paid part-time or temporary jobs—helped ignite protest. The contradiction between women's claims to rights and the facts of

The power of the state: French police beat Paris students, May 1968.

male power in the family, at work, and in politics inspired radical theorists, especially in the United States and France. Precursors such as Simone de Beauvoir, France's leading female intellectual and author of *The Second Sex* (1949), soon appeared insufficiently militant. Beauvoir's elegant and learned analysis of "the slavery of half of humanity" appeared to lack a political program.

Numerous theorists and groups sought to supply one. In the United States, where women entered the labor force earlier and in greater numbers than in Europe, a broad front of women's organizations had arisen by the mid-1960s. It sought to open hitherto male professions to women and to secure "reproductive freedom": the removal of restrictions on contraception and abortion. This "first wave" of feminists ranged from mild liberalism to New Left radicalism. But in practice it flowed from the Lockean natural rights tradition, as Harriet and John Stuart Mill (see p. 644) had applied it in the nineteenth century— women should enjoy by right the same autonomy as men. To at last assert that autonomy, women now had to learn to compete successfully with men in all fields of human activity. The most radical "first wave" theorists concluded that women's autonomy demanded the destruction of the "patriarchal" family and the liberation of women from childbirth and childrearing.

As the euphoria of the 1960s subsided, a "second wave" of American feminist theorists began to celebrate—rather than seeking to eliminate—women's differences from men. The new "woman-centered" school had counterparts in western Europe and was related to the "equal but different" tradition of the nineteenth century (see p. 654). It asserted the superiority of women's nature, which was allegedly more intuitive, warm, compassionate, "nurturing," peace-loving, and practical than that of the purportedly cold, calculating, competitive, violent, power-mad male. It dismissed masterful women leaders from Margaret Thatcher of Britain to Indira Gandhi of India (see pp. 937 and 960) as victims who had in effect become men. It proclaimed that women were a "sex class" whose shared nature and experience overrode all ideological, social, national, and racial divisions. "Universal sisterhood" would inaugurate a new and purely female culture that would ultimately save humanity. Ironically, that vision caught on just as ideological, social, ethnic, and racial divisions fractured the women's movement—and as a counteroffensive by fiercely antifeminist "pro-family" women sought to roll it back.

But despite internal struggles and external opposition, the feminist revolt had decisive consequences. In the United States and western Europe, it spurred reforms that gave women a greater measure of formal equality than ever before in history. It inspired the creation of institutions such as day-care centers that helped to free women to join the work force in ever-greater numbers. Above all, it provided middle-class women with encouragement to pursue careers equivalent to those of men, encouragement that their mothers had lacked. Demographically, the consequence was later marriages and fewer children. Emotionally, the attempt to "have it all," to pursue a career and raise a family, sometimes provoked intolerable strain. Men inevitably proved slow to adjust to the equality in practical matters that the new "two-career family" demanded. But change was nevertheless perceptible. The feminist revolution brought closer to reality than ever before the nineteenth-century ideal of equality between the sexes.

Protests within the West were merely one sign of the passing of the "age of containment." The Middle East explosion of 1973 revealed the full extent of Western disunity. The swift escalation of oil prices that followed struck a stinging blow to the world economy. U.S. foreign policy succumbed temporarily to paralysis as Congress sought to demolish the "imperial presidency" that it blamed for Vietnam. Geography and political circumstances had favored containment in Korea, at a price. The agony of containment in Vietnam hastened the end of America's strategic dominance over the Soviet Union and of its economic edge over Japan. By the mid-1970s, commentators saw a new age of another kind emerging. Détente, they proclaimed, had ended the Cold War. In place of superpower conflict they saw a growing international class struggle between rich and poor states.

Career woman of the 1970s: the strain of family and work.

Suggestions for Further Reading

The Superpower Conflict

Few intelligent syntheses cover the post-1945 period. Recent events arouse too much retrospective passion and carry too heavy a weight of current hopes and fears. Sources are simultaneously too wide and too shallow. Much remains buried in the archives, especially the former Soviet archives. A. Ulam, *The Rivals: America and Russia Since World War II* (1971), is nevertheless excellent on the central U.S.-Soviet conflict. P. Seabury, *The Rise and Decline of the Cold War* (1967), is acute on that conflict's nature and dimensions. R. Aron, *The Imperial Republic: The United States and the World, 1945–1973* (1974), is both brilliant and detached. On the Soviet Union, see first the inside views of M. Djilas, *Conversations with Stalin* (1962), and (with caution) N. Khrushchev, *Khrushchev Remembers* (1974). A. Ulam, *The Communists* (1992), traces the entire post-1945 trajectory of the Communist powers, but see also his *Expansion and Coexistence* (1968) and *Dangerous Relations: the Soviet Union in World Politics, 1970–1982* (1983). For the Cuban Missile Crisis, G. Allison, *Essence of Decision* (1971), is still rewarding, despite much new evidence from the Soviet and Cuban side.

The Mid-Sized Powers

W. Laqueur, *Europe in Our Time: A History, 1945–1992* (1992), is a masterful synthesis. M. Schaller, *The American Occupation of Japan* (1985), traces the process that put Japan back on the road to supremacy in East Asia; K. van Wolferen, *The Enigma of Japanese Power* (1989), offers a compelling (and depressing) analysis of Japanese politics and society; H. C. Hinton, *Three and a Half Powers: The New Balance in Asia* (1975), places Japan in its international context.

The Middle East

The Middle East arouses even more passion than the Cold War; no reliable narrative history of the area since 1945 exists. L. C. Brown, *International Politics and the Middle East* (1984), is a fine introduction to how it got the way it is. P. Mansfield, *The Middle East: A Political and Economic Survey* (1980), is a useful handbook. Y. Harkabi, *Arab Strategies and Israel's Response* (1977), offers one Israeli view; for Arab difficulties with Israel and the modern world, see especially F. Ajami, *The Arab Predicament: Arab Political Thought and Practice Since 1967* (1992). W. Laqueur, *Confrontation: The Middle East War and World Politics* (1974), remains the best book on the Yom Kippur War.

From Korea to Vietnam

Few dispassionate accounts of America's wars of containment exist, but see D. Rees, *Korea: the Limited War* (1964), and G. Lewy, *America in Vietnam* (1978). G. Race, *War Comes to Long An* (1972), and E. M. Bergerud, *The Dynamics of Defeat* (1991), explain the perplexities—and the enemy—encountered in America's longest war. *Dispatches* (1978) conveys the atmosphere of Vietnam with unparalleled skill. P. Braestrup, *Big Story* (1977), describes with candor and irony the role of the U.S. press. H. Summers, *On Strategy* (1982), is a not always successful attempt to figure out what went wrong. For détente and the opening to China, see (with caution) H. Kissinger, *White House Years* (1979) and *Years of Decision* (1982).

Students and Feminists

The transnational student revolt still awaits its historian. D. Caute, *The Year of the Barricades. A Journey Through 1968* (1988); R. V. Daniels, *The Year of the Heroic Guerrilla. World Revolution and Counterrevolution in 1968* (1989); and R. Johnson, *The French Communist Party Versus the Students* (1972), are nevertheless useful. On the women's movement, see especially J. Mitchell and A. Oakley, *What Is Feminism?* (1986); C. Duchen, *Feminism in France* (1986); and H. Eisenstein, *Contemporary Feminist Thought* (1983).

35

THE NON-WESTERN WORLD FROM THE FORTIES TO THE NINETIES

Under the shadow of superpower conflict, an entire world of "new nations" arose in the years after 1945. The collapse of the European empires under the pressure of that most successful of European exports, nationalism, ultimately created more than 120 new states. Most of them were poor compared to the developed West. But that was almost the only characteristic they had in common. For despite claims that all non-Western societies shared a common "Third World" or southern-hemisphere heritage, the new states were dramatically different in history, culture, politics, economic structure, and wealth. By the 1990s it was clear that the notion of a unified "Third World" with interests that were implacably opposed to those of the West—or "North"—was misleading. For increasing numbers of non-Western states were making the leap from poverty to wealth that the West had made in the nineteenth century. One prerequisite for that leap—but no guarantee of success—was independence, achieved in the era of "decolonization" that gave birth to the vast majority of non-Western states.

DECOLONIZATION: IDEOLOGICAL WINDS OF CHANGE

The force of ideas was the most powerful of the "winds of change" that swept over the Western colonial empires in the two decades after Britain's defeat at Singapore in 1942. Nationalism, the political religion of the nation-state, arose spontaneously in the non-Western world whenever native ruling classes sought to resist Western power by acquiring Western ideas.

(OPPOSITE) WARS OF DECOLONIZATION: SUSPECTED GUERRILLAS UNDER GUARD DURING THE MAU MAU UPRISING IN KENYA (1952).

From China to Ghana, nationalism offered an ideology to replace the old communities and beliefs that Western power had shattered in the nineteenth century. The creation of nation-states, independent and sovereign externally and the focus of *all* loyalties internally, would wipe out the humiliation that Western domination had brought, provide a sense of belonging—and help nationalist intellectuals to power and wealth.

Some parts of the world took to the new ideas more readily than others. The societies of east Asia were cultural units of long standing. That eased their conversion into nation-states on the European pattern. In the Islamic world, loyalties were simultaneously too wide and too narrow to fit the new pattern easily. "Arab unity," "Islamic solidarity," or "Islamic Revolu-

tion" coexisted uneasily with centuries-old tribal, religious, and linguistic-ethnic rivalries. In Latin America, the world's oldest group of "new nations" except for Holland and the United States, the persistence of stratification by blood—Creole, *mestizo*, Indian, African—meant that the elites were often closer to their counterparts in neighboring states than to their own peasants. And in black Africa, state borders bore little relationship to the ethnographic map.

As an ideology of revolt against the West, nationalism inevitably had competitors—of which Marxism-Leninism was the most successful. Although in theory an ideology of class war, in practice it often merged—outside Europe—with nationalism. As Sun Yat-sen of China had recognized (see p. 810), nationalism and

South and East Asia since the Second World War

Leninist organizational techniques were a powerful combination. In the "Third World" as in the Soviet Union, Marxism-Leninism provided legitimation for "cults of personality" and for the almost unlimited power of Party elites. The resulting regimes were the most regimented and fiercely nationalist in history: China, North Vietnam, North Korea, Cuba, and Ethiopia from the 1970s to the 1980s. But those strange offspring of the European traditions of nationalism and Marxism were nationalist with a difference. Paradoxically, they also belonged to the "socialist camp"—a multinational Soviet empire based on the denial of nationalism. Only China, Yugoslavia, and Albania developed Marxist-Leninist nationalisms *opposed to* Moscow.

An assortment of "pan-movements" also competed with nationalism. The Islamic world gave birth to two mutually contradictory ones—Arab nationalism and pan-Islamism. Arab nationalism, whose chief manifestation was the Arab League of states with its periodic meetings and communiqués, proved weak indeed. Even when wielded by charismatic figures such as Gamal Abdel Nasser, it failed to unify the Arab world politically. Its religious counterpart, pan-Islamism, suffered from even greater weaknesses. Of Islam's close to a billion adherents, roughly a quarter were Arabs. The rest, from Senegal through Iran, Pakistan, and India to Indonesia and the Philippines, included such a wide variety of linguistic and ethnic groups that common action even in the United Nations rarely proved possible. Islam itself, like Christianity, also had internal divisions, especially the hostility between the minority Shiites—10 percent of all Moslems—and the majority Sunni (see p. 201). South of Islam, "pan-Africanism" found expression in 1963 in an "Organization of African Unity"; the organization endured but unity remained absent.

A final contender was—for lack of a better term—"Third Worldism": the ideology that proclaimed the division of humanity into a rich, oppressive, capitalist "North" and an innocent, victimized, agrarian "South." In 1955, at Bandung in Indonesia, 29 African and Asian states met and inaugurated a series of "Third World" meetings that promoted the notion of "nonalignment" in the Cold War and made increasingly insistent demands that the West atone for its "imperialist" past.

Third Worldism, as it developed in the 1960s and 1970s, was a powerful mixture. First of its ingredients was the notion that the reduction of the "Third World" to poverty had been the result of Western development and wealth. Second was a romantic faith in revolution and its supposed modernizing effects; that faith rested in part on a misreading of Soviet history. The final component was the claim that the "Third World" was a cohesive unit, that its solidarity against "imperialism" overrode all its many linguistic, ethnic, religious, and cultural divisions. Those were powerful myths, but they proved less powerful than nationalism, the cult of the nation-state.

DECOLONIZATION: BIRTH OF THE NEW NATIONS

The empires that survived the Second World War were doomed by demography, once the colonized peoples revolted. Britain, with roughly 41 million inhabitants in 1939, dominated an empire of more than 500 million. The colonial empires of France, Holland, Belgium, and Portugal were less disproportionate in size to the European powers that held them. But even there colonial rule rested on the continuing willingness of the colonized to submit and collaborate.

Overwhelming European power, the power of the Maxim gun, had produced submission and collaboration in the past. But now the balance of forces had changed. The rise and widening reach of the Soviet Union and of Mao's China gave colonial nationalists powerful allies. The dependable Soviet AK-47 assault rifle, copied from a German weapon of 1943–44, became the Maxim gun of *de*colonization. Economic growth and Western schooling produced native intellectuals who sought both peaceful and violent ways to force the colonizers to go. These intellectuals created nationalist mass movements far better at reconquering independence than the pre-colonial native rulers had been at keeping it. In Europe, the vast bloodletting of the two world wars and the economic uselessness of many of the colonies persuaded most European democracies to abandon their empires once native nationalists mounted a serious challenge.

Britain: The Long Retreat

British decolonization began first and lasted longest, given the British Empire's size and bizarre variety. It was also the least traumatic, thanks to London's pragmatic willingness to concede, graciously or not, what it no longer had the power to withhold. Ireland went first in 1921–37 (see p. 808). Its leader, the former rebel Eamonn De Valera, was the first of many nationalist leaders whose road to power led through British jails.

In the aftermath of the Second World War, the British empire found itself under even more determined siege than in 1919–21. Mohandas Gandhi—fortunately for India—had failed to drag down British rule in 1942 when the Japanese were at the gate. But after 1945 the Labour government of Clement Attlee had no choice but to quit India; Britain lacked the troops and money to hold by force a subcontinent of more than 400 million inhabitants.

Two mass movements had arisen that fought both Britain and each other: Gandhi's Congress Party and Mohammed Ali Jinnah's Moslem League. The Congress Party claimed all India by right of Hindu nationalism; the Moslem League claimed a Moslem state—Pakistan—around Karachi and in Bengal, east and west of the Hindu majority. By March 1947, in the words of a subordinate of Britain's last viceroy, the Indian empire was "a ship on fire in mid-ocean with ammunition in the hold." In August 1947 the British simply left. Then the excellent British-trained armies of the two successor states, India and Pakistan, went to war over the province of Kashmir. Hindu and Moslem populations on the

The partition of British India, 1947: Moslem refugees on a road near New Delhi strewn with Moslem dead.

wrong side of the partition lines fled for their lives. Independence brought 15 million refugees and 500,000 to 750,000 dead in religious-ethnic massacres.

Keeping India secure had moved Britain to conquer Ceylon, Burma, Malaya, and the north coast of Borneo. The end of empire in India led London to give independence to Burma and Ceylon (later Sri Lanka) in early 1948. Britain stayed on until 1957 in Malaya and Singapore to quell a Communist insurgency that sprang from Malaya's overseas Chinese minority. In 1963 Britain gave independence to its possessions in Borneo. It kept only Hong Kong, which it pledged in 1984 to transfer to China in 1997.

In the Middle East, around the oilfields essential to Britain and western Europe, London tried to hang on. It left Egypt in 1945 and gave up its thankless task in Palestine in 1948. But until the mid-1950s it managed to hold the irreducible minimum: the vital base of Cyprus, the oil states of the Persian Gulf, and a zone around the Suez Canal through which the oil passed to Europe. But soon the sad tale of 1882 repeated itself—with a different outcome. Like the Khedive before him, Britain's Egyptian client King Farouk was unseated in 1952 by a nationalist officers' revolt. After Farouk's overthrow, a charismatic figure on the model of Arabi Pasha took command: Colonel Abdel Gamal Nasser.

Nasser proposed to unify "the Arabs" from Morocco to Iraq. As a first step, he sought to evict Britain from the Suez Canal and lead the Arabs against Israel. In June 1956, weary of terrorist attacks on British sentries, Britain withdrew its last troops from the Canal Zone—and Nasser almost immediately confiscated the Canal from its European owners. He also challenged Israel by organizing guerrilla raids from the Gaza Strip, and provoked the United States by purchasing arms from the Soviet Union. Anthony Eden, Churchill's wartime foreign secretary and successor, took up the challenge: Nasser was another Hitler. Had Nasser not written a booklet, *Philosophy of the Revolution* (1953)? Was the Suez Canal in 1956 not the Rhineland of 1936? (But in 1936 Eden had merely thought

Hitler's action "deplorable.") The French, bogged down in war against the Algerian rebels and convinced that Nasser the pan-Arab zealot was behind it, were happy to help.

British and French airborne and amphibious forces, in secret coordination with Israel's conquest of the Sinai, seized the Mediterranean end of the canal on November 5–6, 1956. But Eden failed to understand that Washington sought to woo "Arab nationalism" and would not tolerate a British and French reconquest of Egypt. Eisenhower and his Secretary of State, John Foster Dulles, panicked Eden by suspending U.S. support for the stability of Britain's currency. That forced British withdrawal. The French, fuming over British timidity, resentfully followed.

Nasser claimed victory, although his army had suffered a worse rout than in 1948–49 and Cairo was defenseless against the British, French, and Israelis. Suez, a British military victory, ended Britain's prestige in the Middle East as defeat at Singapore had done in Asia. A coup against the British-backed Arab monarchy in Iraq, unrest in Jordan, and the beginnings of a civil war between Moslems and Maronite Christians in Lebanon followed in 1958. Iraq bloodily left the British orbit; British paratroops and U.S. Marines briefly landed in Jordan and Lebanon to maintain "stability." In Cyprus, a campaign launched by Greek guerrillas in 1955 led to Britain's departure in 1959–60. A low-intensity war within Cyprus between the Greek majority and the Turkish minority followed; it ended only in 1974, with a Greek coup that provoked a Turkish invasion and the forcible partition of the island.

If the 1940s were Britain's decade of decolonization in south Asia, and the 1950s the decade of Middle East, the 1960s were the decade of sub-Saharan Africa and the Caribbean. Harold Macmillan, Eden's successor, spoke grandly in January 1960 of the "wind of change" sweeping the African continent. In the next five years, in a "scramble for Africa" like that of the 1880s and 1890s but in reverse, Britain and France gave their African empires away. In 1956–57 Britain had already

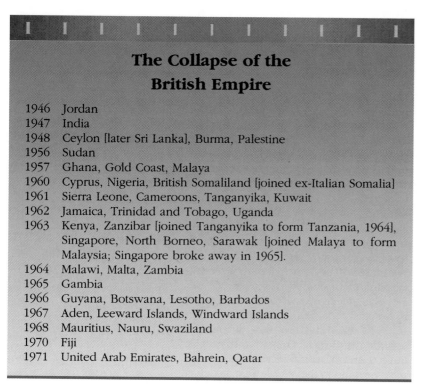

The Collapse of the British Empire

1946	Jordan
1947	India
1948	Ceylon [later Sri Lanka], Burma, Palestine
1956	Sudan
1957	Ghana, Gold Coast, Malaya
1960	Cyprus, Nigeria, British Somaliland [joined ex-Italian Somalia]
1961	Sierra Leone, Cameroons, Tanganyika, Kuwait
1962	Jamaica, Trinidad and Tobago, Uganda
1963	Kenya, Zanzibar [joined Tanganyika to form Tanzania, 1964], Singapore, North Borneo, Sarawak [joined Malaya to form Malaysia; Singapore broke away in 1965].
1964	Malawi, Malta, Zambia
1965	Gambia
1966	Guyana, Botswana, Lesotho, Barbados
1967	Aden, Leeward Islands, Windward Islands
1968	Mauritius, Nauru, Swaziland
1970	Fiji
1971	United Arab Emirates, Bahrein, Qatar

Harold Wilson's Labour government and the United Nations, and fought to maintain control over the black majority. The settlers were too few, and too isolated internationally to win; negotiations transformed Rhodesia into black-ruled Zimbabwe in 1978–79.

South of Rhodesia, the Union of South Africa under Boer leadership had achieved virtual independence after the First World War, but its politics remained balanced precariously between English-speakers, pro-British Boers, and vengeful backwoods *Trekboers*. In 1948 the *Trekboers* came to power, and imposed through laws a rigid system of racial oppression called *Apartheid* ("apartness") that already existed in fact. The Boers crushed black demonstrations, like the one at Sharpeville in 1960, with gunfire. In 1961 South Africa withdrew from the British Commonwealth rather than tolerate further criticism of its peculiar institutions.

Britain took the final steps in its abandonment of empire in the late 1960s and early 1970s. Its vital naval base at Aden, at the entrance to the Red Sea, went in 1967 after a bloody guerrilla war with Arab tribal "Marxists." Soviet warships in its harbor replaced those of the Royal Navy. Aden mutated into a "People's Democratic Republic of Yemen," complete with AK-47 massacres at Politburo meetings. And in 1971 Britain in effect handed over to the mercy of the Shah of Iran (see pp. 965–67) its oil-rich clients in the Gulf, from

given independence to the Sudan and to Ghana and the Gold Coast in west Africa. Independence for Nigeria, Africa's richest and most populous "new nation," came in 1960. In south-central Africa, Britain delayed for a while out of concern for its white settler population in Rhodesia. But in 1965 the whites unilaterally declared their independence from Britain, defied

The Sharpeville massacre, 1960: Blacks flee the guns of the South African police.

Kuwait in the north to the United Arab Emirates in the south.

All that remained of the British Empire were a few small Caribbean, Atlantic, and Pacific islands along with outposts whose populations feared that independence would lead to annexation by grasping neighbors: Hong Kong, Gibraltar, and the Falkland Islands off Argentina. The Commonwealth, in which many of Britain's former colonies remained, became a debating society.

France: The Suitcase or the Coffin

France did not give up as easily as Britain. Its second colonial empire, acquired after defeat by Germany in 1870–71, was a symbol of national vitality. French schoolteachers had zealously propagated the political myth of France's "civilizing mission" in Africa and Indochina. French politicians, Right, Center, and Left, refused to give up their empire. De Gaulle began in 1945 the failed attempt to reconquer Indochina. Socialists such as prime minister Guy Mollet, who later dispatched France's task force to Suez, sought at least to hold Algeria. The French army, miserably defeated by the *Wehrmacht* in 1940, committed its soul to victory in Indochina. But it failed at Dien Bien Phu (see p. 896), and the survivors returned in 1954 convinced that the Fourth Republic's politicians had stabbed the army in the back: "*On nous a fait le coup*" ("They shafted us").

In November 1954, Algerian rebels who took the name of the National Liberation Front (FLN) attacked French settlers and police stations. The war that followed was both colonial and civil; it destroyed the Fourth Republic and created an Algerian nation. For Algeria was not simply a colony. Its population included, in addition to 140,000 Jews and a swiftly growing Moslem population of 9 million, slightly more than 1 million European settlers, the *pieds-noirs* ("black-feet"): privileged immigrants from France, Spain, Italy, Malta. Administratively, Algeria was part of France.

France reacted to the Algerian revolt by reinforcing its army there, bombing

Apartheid defied (South Africa, 1970).

Moslem villages, and cutting its commitments elsewhere. It gave Tunisia and Morocco their independence in 1956. The FLN, with some arms from outside but more captured from the French, soon found a winning strategy. At Philippeville in August 1955, FLN guerrillas and Arab crowds killed some 70 *pieds-noirs*; the French obligingly killed more than 1,200 Moslems in reprisals. FLN assassination teams sought out and eliminated all Moslems who maintained contacts with the French. FLN enforcers amputated the noses of Moslems who smoked tobacco, a French monopoly. The FLN divided the European and Moslem communities with a river of blood; that polarization gave the FLN domination of the Algerian "camp."

By 1955–56, the two communities were at war. *Pieds-noirs* launched vengeful "rat-hunts" against any and all Moslems, even those who had nothing to do with the insurgents. FLN time bombs shredded young Europeans in the cafés of the once-pleasant city of Algiers. To end the bloodshed, the Fourth Republic abdicated to the army. In January 1957 it called in the *paras*, the pride of the army, and made them secret policemen. In the ensuing "Battle of Algiers" the paratroops took over the Arab quarters, swept up suspects at random, tortured them with electric shock and water, and gradually tracked down the FLN bomb networks. Many thousands of Algerian suspects simply "disappeared."

Torture won the Battle of Algiers but helped lose the war. In France, intellectuals of the Left but also of the Center and the Right denounced the army. Officers resigned in disgust. FLN spokesmen abroad and states sympathetic to the FLN—including the United States—denounced French methods. And the civilian ministers who had ordered the army to win by any and all means were already

seeking negotiations with the FLN. The army had vowed that *this* time it would win; if winning required the removal of the politicians before they "betrayed" the army, so be it. In May 1958, as *pied-noir* and military plots simmered, the theater commander in Algeria, General Raoul Salan, demanded that Charles de Gaulle be recalled to power.

De Gaulle came once more, as he had in 1940–45, to save France. But to the fury of the army and of the *pieds-noirs*, he soon gave signs of a hidden agenda. In 1958–59 the army decimated what remained of the FLN in the countryside and sought to win Moslem loyalty with promises

Africa and Southeast Asia in 1988

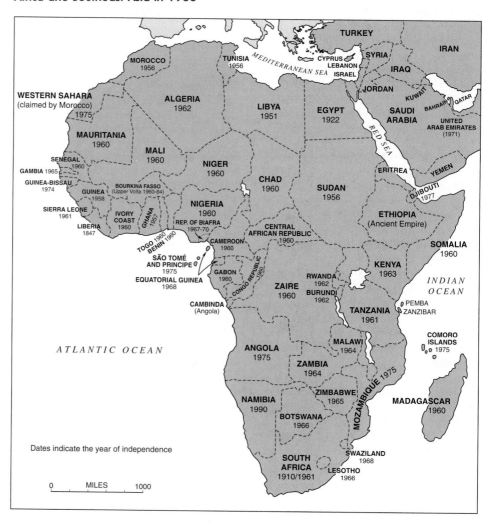

Dates indicate the year of independence

0   MILES   1000

of "integration." More Moslems, indeed, fought for France than against it. But the FLN maintained its political organization and its claim to represent the Moslem majority. At last it began to dawn on the French that winning through "integration" would mean a large and ever-growing Moslem presence in the French parliament; the Moslem birthrate was ten times that of the *pieds-noirs.* De Gaulle, with perfect timing, said the magic word in a speech of September 1959: "self-determination."

Pieds-noirs and army reacted. In 1961 the high command in Algiers, the *paras,* and the Foreign Legion revolted against de Gaulle as they had revolted against the Fourth Republic. But de Gaulle held fast. He appealed by radio to the half million draftees in Algeria and convinced the generals that they were isolated. The Algiers *Putsch* collapsed. In 1962, despite a *pied-noir* terrorist campaign and an uprising in the European quarter of Algiers, de Gaulle achieved a negotiated settlement. In effect, he conceded Algerian independence unconditionally, and left the *pieds-noirs* to choose "the suitcase or the coffin." Most chose the suitcase.

The Algerian war was traumatic for France, and still more so for the Algerians, who suffered the vast majority of the war's million or so casualties. It demonstrated the lengths to which communities driven by nationalism would go to defend or assert control of territory. It also stripped France of its African empire. During the course of the war, de Gaulle gave independence to almost all of France's colonies in sub-Saharan Africa: Guinea in 1958, and Cameroon, Chad, the Central African Republic, Congo-Brazzaville, Dahomey, Gabon, Ivory Coast, Mali, Niger, Senegal, and Togo in 1960.

Holland, Belgium, Portugal

The lesser empires of Holland and Belgium passed more quietly than did that of France. The Dutch found a "Republic of Indonesia" barring their return to the East Indies in 1945. Its leader was Achmet Sukarno, a charismatic nationalist who had collaborated with the Japanese to gain In-

Chaos in the Congo, 1963: Government paratroopers chase a mutinous policeman.

donesian independence. Four years of intermittent negotiations and "police actions" by the Dutch armed forces ultimately led—under U.S. pressure—to an agreement in November 1949 that granted independence. The Dutch kept only West Irian (the Dutch half of New Guinea) until Sukarno seized it in 1962–63.

The Belgians gave the most spectacular example of irresponsible decolonization. Their Congo empire, which the Berlin Conference of 1884–85 had assigned to King Leopold, had long been a byword for relentless brutality. Its rubber plantations, worked by native forced labor, were the subject of international protest even before the First World War. And the Belgian state, which took the colony over from Leopold's private Congo Company, did far less than other colonizers to create a Western-educated elite. When the approaching independence of the neighboring French Congo (Congo Republic) inspired nationalist riots, the Belgians panicked, packed up, and left in mid-1960. The Congolese army mutinied. A multi-cornered civil war and massacres of both tribal enemies and whites followed. Belgian mining companies hired mercenaries to hold the copper-rich province of Katanga. It took four years and 20,000 United Nations troops to restore even a semblance of order. The ultimate victor was the head of the Congolese army, Joseph Mobuto, who established a corrupt but durable dictatorship in 1966 and changed the country's name to Zaire.

Portugal's colonies were the first European seaborne empire; they were also the last. The Portuguese military-clerical dictatorship of Antonio Salazar (1932–68) lost its Indian enclave of Goa to an unprovoked Indian attack in 1961. In Africa—in Angola, Mozambique, and the west African mini-colony of Guinea-Bissau—Portugal chose to fight. But the commitment of 150,000 troops from the early 1960s until 1974 bled Portugal's already backward economy. In the end, Salazar gave way to a less-effective successor. The Portuguese army, politicized by its long struggle in Africa, overthrew the government in Lisbon in 1974 and dismantled Portugal's empire.

A bloody scramble followed. Indonesia invaded the Portuguese island of East Timor and killed as much as a third of its almost 700,000 people. In Angola, Portugal's withdrawal led to the flight of most of the remaining white settlers, economic collapse, civil war between rival groups, and intervention by the Soviet Union, Cuba, and South Africa (see p. 950). In Mozambique, the Marxist-Leninist *Frelimo* ("Front for the Liberation of Mozambique") of Samora Machel took power. In Guinea-Bissau, the Lisbon-educated Amilcar Cabral, the most skillful of Portugal's opponents, built a movement that achieved independence in 1973–74. But by then Cabral himself had perished by assassination, a victim of rivalries within his own movement. As he had foreseen, the real test of that movement—and of the rulers of all "new nations"—came after independence.

Losers and Winners, 1965–90

The two halves of the table illustrate the striking differences in rates of economic growth within the non-Western world. Some states stagnated or regressed. Others grew with startling rapidity.

	1990 pop-ulation (millions)	Per cap-ita GNP (1990 dollars)	Average annual growth rate in per cap-ita GNP, 1965–90 (percent)	Life ex-pectancy at birth, 1990	Adult illiteracy, 1990 (percent)
Tanzania	24.5	110	−0.2	48	54
Ethiopia	51.2	120	−0.2	48	na
Somalia	7.8	120	−0.1	48	76
Zaire	37.3	220	−2.2	52	28
Uganda	16.3	220	−2.4	47	52
Madagascar	11.7	230	−1.9	51	20
Niger	7.7	310	−2.4	45	72
Bolivia	7.2	630	−0.7	60	23
Jamaica	2.4	1,500	−1.3	73	2
Libya	4.5	1,760	−3.0	62	36
Argentina	32.3	2,370	−0.3	71	5
Venezuela	19.7	2,560	−1.0	70	12
China (PRC)	1,133.7	370	5.8	70	27
Indonesia	178.2	570	4.5	62	23
Cameroon	11.7	960	3.0	57	46
Thailand	55.8	1,420	4.4	66	7
South Korea	42.8	5,400	7.1	71	4
Singapore	3.0	11,160	6.5	74	na
Hong Kong	5.8	11,490	6.2	78	na

From World Bank, World Development Report 1992 *(New York: Oxford University Press, 1992), pp. 218–19.*

AFTER INDEPENDENCE: THE "THIRD WORLD" DIVIDED

In the 1960s, the poorest of the newly independent states had annual per capita levels of gross national product (GNP)—the best indicator of a society's overall wealth or poverty—of 100 or fewer 1965 dollars. Yet some very poor states grew swiftly, and some richer ones stagnated or regressed. Breaking the non-Western world into its major component parts—the Chinese cultural area, south Asia and its island offshoots, the Islamic Middle East, Latin America, and Africa south of the Sahara—makes that wide variety of outcomes easier to understand.

Confucian East Asia

Culturally, China had influenced its neighbors—Vietnam to the south and Korea and Japan to the northeast—from the beginning of recorded history. The Confucian pattern that China exemplified placed a high value on literacy, hierarchy, and the subordination of the individual to the group. Those qualities made east Asia's densely populated rice-growing economies work. But that pattern may initially have retarded economic growth in China by its very success and durability. Japan, which rose to the nineteenth-century Western challenge most readily, was always less Confucian than China, thanks to its hereditary warrior ruling caste. China and its neighbors, highly developed cultures with an ethos of literacy, duty, and relentless hard work, were nevertheless the best equipped for economic growth of all the non-Western world.

But politics and geography imposed differing outcomes. Japan's small size helped its consolidation as a modern state. And a fortunate combination of centralization (the Tokugawa shogunate and the traditions of the Imperial house) and decentralization (the "feudal" domains) gave innovators both a political and military vehicle for change and an opportunity to seize power. In China, the empire's unwieldiness, the rigidity of its Manchu rulers, and its choice of armed resistance rather than accommodation to the "barbarians" all led to a collapse that seemed to follow the cyclical pattern of dynastic decline hallowed by Chinese tradition. The immense Taiping rebellion of the 1850s and 1860s foreshadowed the far greater upheaval of the twentieth century: four decades (1911–53) of devastating civil war, invasion by Japan, and war in Korea against the United States.

Mao Zedong and his Communist Party mobilized the peasantry by appealing to their land hunger and roused the urban intellectuals by offering a vehicle for nationalism. That was a winning combination. But Mao, intoxicated with revolutionary messianism, soon sought to pioneer in economic development as he had in adapting Marxism-Leninism to a peasant society. In two disastrous experiments, the "Great Leap Forward" (1958–59) and the "Great Proletarian Cultural Revolution" (1966–69), he almost destroyed both the Chinese economy and his own Party. "Politics in command!" was Mao's guiding principle; the death by famine of as many as 25 million in the "three lean years" of 1959–61 was the result. The forcing of China's peasantry into "communes" and a crash industrialization

---

Why Maoism?

Lu Xun (Lu Hsün, 1881–1936), China's greatest twentieth century short-story writer and social critic, wrote bitter pages in the 1920s that suggest some of the ingredients of Mao's success.

It has never been granted to the Chinese people that they are human beings; at best, they have been raised to the level of slaves, and this is still the case today. In the past, they were often lower than slaves. The Chinese masses are neutral; in time of war they do not know what faction they belong to, and in fact they belong to any faction. Come the rebels: considering the people as being the government's, they loot and murder. Comes the regular army: instead of recognizing its own, it loots and murders too, as if the people belonged to the rebels. At this point, the only wish of the population is to find a Master, a Master who would deign to accept them as his people—no, not even that—who would deign to accept them as his cattle. The people would be ready to eat grass if necessary; all they ask is that the Master point out in what direction they must trot. . . .

As a rule, after each period of anarchy, when chaos reaches its climax, some personality appears—more powerful, more clever, more cunning (sometimes a foreigner)—to unify the empire and grant it some measure of order. . . .

In the end, the simplest and most adequate way of describing the history of China would be to distinguish between two types of periods: (1) the periods when the people wish in vain to enjoy a stable slave condition; and (2) the periods when the people manage to enjoy a stable slave condition. The alternation of these two states is what our old scholars called "the cycle of chaos and order."

From Simon Leys (Pierre Ryckmans), Chinese Shadows *(New York: Penguin Books, 1978), pp. 200–201.*

based on amateur backyard blast furnaces reduced the economy to a shambles. Mao's comrades then removed him from direct control of Party and state while retaining him as a living symbol of the Revolution and of the Party's legitimacy.

But Mao was not ready to be embalmed and placed on display like the dead Lenin. With the help of Jiang Qing, the former Shanghai film actress who had become his second wife, and of the Red Army political leader Lin Biao, Mao took power back in 1966 through a coup in Beijing. Then he mobilized China's youth for a unique all-out struggle against his *own* Party and government bureaucracy. Only rebellion could ensure the "continued development of the Revolution towards communism."

The cult of Mao: National Day celebrations, 1966.

Mao's "Great Proletarian Cultural Revolution" of 1966–69 delighted revolutionary enthusiasts in the West; to China, it brought chaos. The force behind it was the sudden release from totalitarian control that Mao offered his millions of youthful and fanatical "Red Guards": "To rebel is justified!" He urged them to take charge of China's destiny, and of their own. They took him at his word, and beat and murdered foreigners, high Party figures, government bureaucrats, and one another. The economy again threatened to disintegrate. Perhaps half a million Chinese perished in Red Guard purges and widespread fighting. The army ultimately restored order by force; Mao himself lost his grip on power with increasing age and died in 1976.

The final defeat of the radicals followed swiftly. Deng Xiaoping, the most cunning of the Party leaders who had attempted to cage Mao in the early 1960s, outmaneuvered Mao's designated successor, Hua Guofeng. With the apparent toleration of Deng and his faction, urban intellectuals posted slogans and essays on a "Democracy Wall" in Beijing in 1979. Deng then exploited the unrest to oust Hua in 1980–81.

In the saddle at last at the age of 76, Deng impartially destroyed both the democratic dissidents and the radical "Gang of Four," Jiang Qing and her three principal allies. He also hastened the "de-Maoization" of the economy. China's survival as a great power and the Party's own legitimacy demanded the adoption of the capitalist methods pioneered by China's small neighbors, Hong Kong, Singapore, South Korea, and the hated "Guomindang remnants" on Taiwan (see p. 936). China's peasants now received the right to sell their surpluses in free markets. The state leased back the farmland it had swallowed up during Mao's collectivization drives. Factory managers gained some measure of freedom from central planning. Around Hong Kong and other coastal cities, huge "free enterprise zones" arose to attact foreign investors. China's GNP growth in the 1980s and early 1990s surged to between 8 and 12 percent per year, recovering much of the ground that Mao had lost and giving China, by some estimates, the world's third largest economy.

Yet the Party retained control of heavy industry, and relaxed its grip on the rest of the economy only with great reluctance. It also soon found itself—like autocrats elsewhere—caught between the contradictory requirements of economic growth and those of political self-preservation. Deng's first choice as successor, Hu Yaobang, raised the hopes of China's intellectuals. In 1985 he denounced Mao for having plunged China into chaos through "radical leftist nonsense." In December 1986 the students of China took the new leadership at its word and demonstrated massively for Western-style democratic freedoms. The police contained the demonstrations.

Deng removed Hu Yaobang and party zealots campaigned against the pestilence of "bourgeois liberalism" spreading into China from the West. But Deng nevertheless held to his economic policies, despite inflation, corruption, a growing regional split between the booming coastal cities and the poor inland countryside, and the dangerously close contact between ordinary Chinese and Westerners that swift economic growth required.

A further explosion inevitably followed in April–June 1989. Beijing crowds of as many as a million people repeatedly demanded reforms. Students occupied Tienanmen Square ("The Square of Heavenly Peace") at the center of the capital and refused to leave until the government granted democracy. Deng knew that unless he crushed this open defiance, his authority would collapse. He brought in army units manned by grim-faced peasants from remote provinces and smashed the students with machine-gun fire and tanks on June 4, 1989. Demonstrators who survived joined the 15 million inmates of China's GULAG. A brief international outcry followed, but the pace of foreign investment scarcely slackened.

The Party had covertly abandoned Marxism, but not Leninism. Deng was clearly a believer in Lenin's axiom that "a regime that is prepared to use limitless terror cannot be overthrown." Yet in the long run, the course that Deng had set for China offered no relief from the contradiction between Leninist autocracy and capitalist economic revolution. At best, his successors might hope to preside over China's evolution into an unstable capitalist authoritarian regime like that of South Korea or Taiwan. But more and greater bloodshed—internal and possibly external—seemed equally likely.

North Korea and Vietnam, although they began under foreign rule rather than under informal Western domination, followed the Stalinist-Maoist pattern. The North Korean Communist "monarchy" of the aged Kim Il-Sung, who in 1984 appointed as his successor his son Kim Jong-Il, remained into the 1990s one of the world's most closed and Stalinist states. Its army remained poised to attack South Korea, its clandestine atomic bomb program threatened all of northeast Asia, and its only noteworthy export was weaponry—including primitive V-2 style ballistic missiles—and advice on war and terrorism to states as far afield as Iran, Iraq, Libya, Syria, Zimbabwe, Grenada, and Nicaragua. Vietnam imposed on South Vietnam after April 1975 the same Stalinist system that had already proven an economic failure in the North. The result was a decade of economic stagnation and hunger; politics and economics together led

---

Democracy Wall: A Chinese Dissident Speaks — 1978

Wei Jingsheng was the most daring of those who wrote on the wall in Beijing; he then disappeared into prison. His 1978 essay, "Democracy, the Fifth Modernization," shows the bitterness of the generation that suffered the full force of Mao's "Great Proletarian Cultural Revolution."

Today, it is perfectly irrelevant to try to determine the balance account of Mao Zedong's achievements and mistakes. . . . The question which the people should now be asking is this: without Mao Zedong's personal despotism, could China ever have fallen as low as we see her today? Or are we to believe that Chinese people are stupid, or lazy, or devoid of any desire to improve their lot? We know very well that this is not the case. Then what happened? The answer is obvious: the Chinese have taken a path they should never have entered; if they followed it, it is because a despot, who knew how shrewdly to peddle his trash, simply took them for a ride. . . .

German fascism, of stinking memory, was actually called "national socialism." It too was led by a tyrant; it too told the people to tighten their belts; it too deceived the people, assuring them: "You are a great nation!" Above all, it too suppressed basic democracy, because it clearly saw that democracy was for it the greatest danger, the most frightful enemy. Stalin and Hitler could shake hands and sign the famous German-Soviet pact, and on this basis the German and Russian peoples were condemned to suffer slavery and misery. Do we, too, need to continue suffering such slavery and misery? If we wish to break away from it, there is only one way: democracy.

From Simon Leys, The Chairman's New Clothes: Mao and the Cultural Revolution *(London: Allison and Busby Limited, 1981), pp. 260–61.*

---

to a flood of refugees, the million or million and a half "boat people" who risked death from drowning or from Thai pirates rather than remain in Vietnam. A younger generation of leaders came to power in 1986 and announced a sort of NEP (see p. 829): a grudging latitude for private enterprise "within the socialist system." Yet as late as 1988 much of the North suffered famine. Despite a modest economic upturn and foreign capitalist investment in the early 1990s, no loosening of Leninist party control seemed in sight.

The individual against the party-state: A lone Chinese democrat pleads with a platoon of tanks on the day after the Tienanmen massacre, June 1989.

By contrast, the non-Communist states of the Chinese cultural area of east Asia and southeast Asia prospered mightily. Malaysia, politically Malay but with an economy under the control of its large overseas Chinese minority, grew at a per capita rate of more than 4 percent. Thailand, the one south or southeast Asian state that had avoided colonial occupation, grew at a comparable rate, thanks to its Chinese minority and relatively literate population. It benefited both from an infusion of dollars during the Vietnam War and a subsequent boom in Pacific trade.

In South Korea, Japanese colonialism (1905–45) and United States patronage helped provide an industrial infrastructure and a Western-educated and technologically expert elite capable of swiftly following Japan's example. Politically, South Korea enjoyed enforced stability. The harsh domination after 1948 of a Harvard-educated politician, Syngman Rhee, gave way in 1960–61 to almost thirty years of military dictatorship. In 1986–87 the new

middle class that Korea's industrialization had created began to demand political rights; the authoritarian solutions of the past no longer worked. The military loosened its grip and permitted an election. The military candidate won, but offered an increasing measure of democratization; the presidency passed to a civilian in 1991–93.

A similar absence of democracy, but likewise mellowed by a gradual loosening of single-party or British colonial control, accompanied the spectacular per capita growth rates of culturally Chinese and economically capitalist Taiwan, Singapore, and Hong Kong. Their economic growth outstripped all other contenders including Japan, and suggested in miniature the world-shaking potential of China itself.

South Asia and the Islands

Four of the lands of south Asia—India, Pakistan, Bangladesh (East Pakistan until

1971), and Sri Lanka (Ceylon until 1972)—were closely linked by geography and history. They were the ultimate successors, after the British interlude, to the Mughal empire. To the east lay Burma, a borderland between south Asian and Chinese culture. Indonesia, dominated by Islam, and the Philippines, a compound of Malay, Islamic, Spanish, and U.S. influences, were unique, but their village-based societies were similar in many ways to the pattern of south Asia. They were Asian but not Confucian.

India and Pakistan remained locked in struggle after 1947–48. Pakistan, split between the dominant Punjab to the west and East Bengal to the east, failed to consolidate itself. When Gandhi's violent successor, Jawaharlal Nehru, quarreled with China over border areas in Tibet in 1961–62, the Chinese army gave India a sharp and persuasive defeat. Fighting between India and Pakistan erupted once more in 1965–66, and the Soviet Union, seeking favor with India as a counterweight to Mao's increasingly hostile China, brokered a compromise. In 1970–71, when the East Bengalis sought autonomy from Pakistan, the generals who ruled West Pakistan answered with massacres. Under Nehru's combative daughter, Indira Gandhi (unrelated to Mohandas Gandhi either by blood or political philosophy), India went to war and swiftly dismembered Pakistan. East Bengal became independent Bangladesh. India was now supreme on the subcontinent and confirmed that status by exploding in 1974 what it whimsically described as a "peaceful nuclear device." Secret Pakistani acquisition of Western nuclear fuel technology and China's apparent gift in the early 1980s of a tested bomb design apparently evened the contest. Endless friction over Kashmir offered ready occasions for renewed war.

Yet despite the Indian-Pakistani wars and periodic ethnic-religious riots and massacres, economic growth in south Asia was steady, although post-colonial "socialist" red tape slowed growth in India until the 1990s. In per capita terms, India grew between 1965 and 1990 at a rate of 1.9 percent per year, Pakistan at 2.5 percent; Bangladesh, one of the world's poorest states, stagnated at .7 percent. In the north Indian plain, new strains of rice and wheat and the entrepreneurship of India's Sikh minority brought an agricultural "Green Revolution" that promised to give India self-sufficiency in food. A powerful industrial economy arose around Bombay and other cities. By the early 1990s a growing proportion of India's 850 million people had achieved a standard of living approaching that of southern Europe.

Pakistan, except for brief periods in the 1950s and 1970s, remained a military dictatorship with parliamentary trimmings. But India persisted for a time in the democratic traditions it had inherited from Britain. An attempt at dictatorship in 1975–77 by Indira Gandhi collapsed amid universal condemnation, although she returned with a parliamentary majority in 1980 after promising not to repeat the experiment. Her eventual downfall was the Sikh minority, whose extremists sought an independent Sikh state, "Khalistan," carved from the Punjab, India's agricultural heart. When heavily armed Sikh militants seized the Sikh Golden Temple at Amritsar in 1984, Indira Gandhi evicted them using the Indian army. Sikhs assassinated her in retaliation; Hindus then killed many thousands of Sikhs living in Hindu areas. Indira Gandhi's son Rajiv Gandhi, third and last of the Congress Party dynasty that Nehru founded, ruled as her successor until defeat in a 1989 election. Then he too died by assassination, blown up by Tamil guerrillas in revenge for Indian intervention in Sri Lanka (see the following paragraphs). And by the early 1990s, a Hindu radical nationalist movement had emerged as a contender for power. It offered India's 100 million Moslems a stark choice: "The cemetery or Pakistan." And it sought to force that choice on the Moslems by riot and massacre. Nationalism and religion seemed poised to destroy India's parliamentary experiment and tear the subcontinent apart.

To the south, Sri Lanka showed great promise. Its peoples were 60 percent literate at independence; its agricultural export economy grew rapidly until the 1960s. Then nationalism caught up with

Indira Gandhi (prime minister, 1966–77, 1980–84), daughter of Nehru and architect of India's hegemony over South Asia.

it. Alongside the majority Sinhalese, who were Buddhist in religion and made up 70 percent of the population, lived a Hindu Tamil minority that had originally immigrated from southern India. Under British rule, the two communities had lived together in relative peace. But the creation of an independent sovereign state in 1948 brought with it a struggle for mastery over that state. By the mid-1950s, Sinhalese politicians had imposed Sinhalese as the official language, and ideologues were proclaiming Sinhalese superiority as the descendants of conquerors from the north in the sixth century B.C.

The Tamils, and enterprising group that dominated commerce and the professions, responded first with riots and then, after 1983, with guerrilla war and demands for a separate Tamil state around the city of Jaffna in northern Sri Lanka. A cycle of terror and reprisal similar to that in Algeria after 1954 locked Sinhalese and Tamil nationalisms into seemingly irreconcilable conflict for land and power. Indian army intervention in 1987 to broker a peace in turn goaded the "Tamil Tiger" guerrillas to savage attacks on the Indians and to further massacres of Sinhalese civilians. Despite the war, Sri Lanka maintained a growth rate from 1980 to 1990 of 4 percent, but continued growth remained hostage to the possibility of further bloodshed.

To the east, Burma retreated into resentful isolation after independence; in 1974 its most durable leader, General Ne Win, proclaimed a non-aligned "Burmese Road to Socialism" that led to poverty for all except bureaucrats and black marketeers. In 1988 the military government, which had in the interim changed the country's name to "Myanmar," killed as many as 2,000 pro-democracy protesters. It then lost an election in 1990, but predictably failed to hand power over to the democrats. Despite a gradual opening of the economy to Japanese investment, Burma's cycle of poverty and government violence seemed likely to continue.

Indonesia, further south, enjoyed the massive advantage of oil. Sukarno ruled until the late 1960s and squandered that wealth on palaces, monuments, and mistresses. His successor, General Suharto,

took power in the aftermath of the failed Communist coup of 1965 and the wholesale massacre of Communists that followed. His regime began to realize Indonesia's economic potential, thanks to close economic ties with Japan, but showed few signs of movement toward parliamentary government.

The Philippines suppressed a Communist insurgency after receiving independence in 1947, and then succumbed to military dictatorship under General Ferdinand Marcos (1965–86). A second and exceedingly bloody Communist insurgency followed. Marcos' power disintegrated after 1983, when his associates arranged the assassination of a key opponent, Benigno Aquino. When Marcos sought to steal the 1986 election, the dead man's widow, Corazon Aquino, took power in 1986 in a largely bloodless "people power" uprising backed by key army figures, the Catholic Church, U.S. public opinion, and the overwhelming majority of politically active Filipinos. Aquino's presidency was a qualified success, despite a series of military coup attempts and continued attacks by the Communist guerrillas of the New People's Army. But economic growth remained agonizingly slow.

The Islamic Middle East

Deep fissures divided the newly independent states of the Middle East from one another. The most important were two: the ideological and political antagonisms between different types of regime, and the envies and hatreds between states that lacked oil and those that had it. Hostility between tribes and between branches of Islam created further tensions both between and within the Middle Eastern states.

The region contained three main types of regime. First came the traditional monarchies and sheikdoms, usually based on Bedouin or other tribal loyalties: Saudi Arabia, Morocco, Jordan, the Gulf states from Kuwait to Oman, and the Iranian monarchy of the Pahlavi dynasty (1921–79). Egypt, Iraq, and Libya had also originally been monarchies—until military coups in 1952, 1958, and 1969 respectively. The second category was the "secular" states—Egypt, Syria, Iraq, Tunisia, Algeria, Libya. The Turkey of Kemal Atatürk provided the model: a military-dominated state dedicated to introducing Western technology and ideas. Like Turkey, most of the secular states tried to use the state bureaucracy as the chief motor of economic development. And most of them claimed to embody an "Arab socialism" that in practice meant deadening bureaucratic controls that fathered corruption and black markets. Finally, a third model, a revolutionary "Islamic Republic" based on Shiite Islam, arose in Iran after 1979 (see pp. 965–67).

Throughout the Cold War era, the Middle Eastern states tended to tilt in their foreign relations toward one of the two superpowers. Conservative states such as the traditional monarchies normally favored the United States. Roosevelt took over Britain's patronage of Saudi Arabia and of its oil in 1943–45—a relationship that endured. Morocco, under its durable monarch King Hassan II (1961–), also maintained close ties with Washington, as did moderate secular states such as Tunisia under Habib Bourguiba (1956–87) and Egypt after Anwar Sadat broke with Moscow in 1976. Algeria, "non-aligned" in rhetoric but less so in practice, also tended to tilt toward western Europe and the United States, valued customers for its natural gas and oil. Iran, until its 1978–79 revolution, posed as a bulwark of Western influence in the Gulf to mask its monarch's megalomaniacal ambitions.

The Soviets tended to recruit the most expansionist Middle Eastern states—Nasser's Egypt, Libya after the revolution of Colonel Muammar al-Qaddafi in 1969, Syria under the merciless Hafez al-Assad (1970–), the Iraq of Assad's equally remorseless counterpart Saddam Hussein (1979–), and the Marxist-Leninist "People's Democratic Republic of Yemen." Lavish shipments of arms, the Soviet Union's only major industrial export, along with numerous military and "police" advisers, cemented these ties. Yet Soviet influence was sometimes brief. Moscow never regained the position in the region that it had held before the loss of Egypt in 1972–76 (see p. 964).

The possession or lack of oil also divided the Middle Eastern states into two groups. Saudi Arabia, Libya, Algeria, Iran, Iraq, Kuwait, the Gulf sheikdoms, and even Egypt after its recovery of Sinai in 1982 all enjoyed the bounty of oil in varying degrees. After 1973, when the Arab and other oil-producing states of the OPEC cartel more than doubled the real price of oil within a year, that bounty increased markedly. But the newly rich were slow to convert their oil wealth into modern economies. The small populations of Saudi Arabia and the sheikdoms were still in part wedded to their desert traditions. Some of the secular states, such as Egypt and Algeria, had some oil but not enough. Others smothered initiative beneath layers of bureaucracy or tried to ban enterprise entirely, as did Qaddafi's Libya.

Religious and ethnic fractures likewise divided the Islamic Middle East. Iran, after its 1978–79 revolution, emerged as the world's only Shiite state; religion and Iranian nationalism combined to set it at odds with its Sunni Arab neighbors. Iraq, although Arab in population, was mostly Shiite in religion; the cleavage between Shiite and Sunni was a major source of internal weakness. Turkey, Iraq, Iran, and even Syria had sizable armed minorities of Kurds, a mountain warrior people who had fought all their neighbors for more than 2,000 years. Syria contained large Christian communities, and its officer corps and rulers were Alawites, a small Shiite sect that ruthlessly dominated the Sunni majority.

In Lebanon, five major communities struggled for mastery. The last census (1932) showed that 29 percent of the population was Maronite Christian, 22 percent Sunni Moslem, 20 percent Shiite Moslem, and 7 percent Druze, a heretical and combative Moslem sect. The French, on their departure in 1946, left a parliamentary regime that gave the presidency to the Maronites, the prime ministership to the Sunni, and the office of army chief of staff to the Druzes. But demography soon shifted the religious-ethnic balance, and a fifth group, the Palestinian refugees, entered the arena

Traditional monarchs and secular rulers: King Faisal of Saudi Arabia (1964–75, *above*) and (*below, left to right*) a 1970 encounter between Gaafar Mohammed Nimeiri of the Sudan (1969–85), Muammar al-Qaddafi of Libya (1969–), and Nasser of Egypt (1954–70).

after 1970. By 1984, the Shiites made up an estimated 31 percent of the population, the Maronites 25 percent, the Sunni 20 percent, and the Druzes only 6 percent. By 1975 the PLO's creation of a state within a state, at war with Israel, ignited a religious-ethnic civil war throughout Lebanon that continued, despite Israeli and Syrian intervention, until 1991.

Finally, nationalism divided rather than united the Middle Eastern states, even though all except Iran and Turkey were Arab. Efforts at union between Arab states, such as Nasser's attempt to absorb Syria into a "United Arab Republic" (1958–61) or Qaddafi's federations with Egypt (1972–73), Tunisia (1974), and Morocco (1984–86), all collapsed. The rulers of Syria, for instance, had no desire to become a mere province of Egypt; they possessed their own national consciousness and sense of mission, the creation of a "Greater Syria" that included Lebanon and Palestine. Nasser also failed to subjugate the Arabs of North Yemen between 1962 and 1968 despite massive use of Soviet tanks and mustard gas.

The multiple divisions between sects, tribes, and states tended to stunt the states of the region both politically and econom-ically. And the state machines and armies of the secular states also provided a classic arena for assassinations and coups. In the absence of settled political traditions and long-established legitimacy, as elsewhere in the "Third World," power grew out of the barrel of a gun. Those with the guns and the smattering of Western technical knowledge needed to use them saw no reason why they should not rule the state and direct the economy. The resulting one-party regimes ranged from the merely inefficient (Egypt, Tunisia, Algeria) to the terrifying (Libya, Syria, Iraq). Hafez al-Assad of Syria and his Soviet advisers dealt with Sunni unrest in 1982 by shelling flat much of the city of Hama and killing as many as 30,000. The monarchies tended to be less aggressive, somewhat less oppressive, and better economic performers than the secular states—but economic development undermined the traditions on which their stability rested. No lasting order to replace the Ottoman Empire or the Anglo-French domination that had followed it seemed in sight, and the rise of Islamic militance generated new and savage conflicts.

The Three Latin Americas

The "new nations" of Latin America had received their independence between 1811 and 1839, long before the post-1945 waves of decolonization. Yet the colonial conquest that had created them had marked them forever. Spain had ruled through a centralized bureaucracy that had prevented the Creoles, native-born of Spanish descent, from gaining experience in self-government—in sharp contrast to the pattern of the British settlement colonies from North America to Australia. After independence, narrow landed oligarchies and a disproportionately powerful land-owning Church had taken Spain's place as the rulers. And Spain had imposed on its colonial economies a pattern similar to that in politics—centralized controls and ruinous taxation that stunted enterprise. Anarchy and despotism, economic stagnation or regression had in most cases followed independence (see pp. 703–4).

But not all of the new states suffered the same misfortunes; Latin America was almost as divided as the Islamic Middle East or the Third World itself. With the exception of miscellaneous small states such as Guyana and Suriname, the former British and Dutch colonies between Venezuela and Brazil, the states of the region fell into three principal categories. First were those with a Creole or European majority: Costa Rica, Uruguay, and Argentina. They began as classic settler economies: Europe transported to the New World. They thrived throughout the nineteenth and early twentieth centuries on commodity exports such as coffee, beef, hides, wool, and grain. But—as elsewhere—politics intervened to decide their fate in the post-1945 world market.

Costa Rica's parliamentary regime rested on a base of prosperous small landowners, and maintained an enviable degree of stability and prosperity after the late 1940s. In Uruguay, however, a drop in world commodity prices and an economy crippled by bureaucratic bloat brought stagnation and massive inflation by the 1960s. Soon a Marxist-Leninist urban guerrilla movement, the "Tupamaro National Liberation Front," arose among the disaffected young of the upper classes. It sought to destroy parliamentary democracy by provoking the state to violent reprisals that would "unmask" its "true nature" as an organ of repression in the service of domestic "capitalism" and foreign "neocolonialism." The Tupamaros duly brought down the parliamentary regime in 1973–74. The military dictatorship that followed erased the guerrillas with torture and "disappearances." Parliamentary democracy had perished, but implacable Rightist dictatorship—not the Marxist millennium—had replaced it. Civilian government returned hesitantly in 1985.

Argentina traveled a road similar to Uruguay's, but even more savage. Its settler population had been overwhelmingly Spanish and Italian, with large German, British, French, and Jewish communities; in 1900 the country had appeared poised to become another Australia. But the Great Depression ended what little political stability it had enjoyed. Oligarchic military regimes gave way in 1944–46 to the populist dictatorship of Colonel Juan Perón, admirer of Mussolini and husband of the charismatic Eva (Evita) Duarte, patron saint of Argentina's "shirtless" dispossessed. An army coup destroyed Perón's regime in 1955, but his Peronist party lived on as Argentina's most powerful political force. Although it was too weak and disunited to overthrow the military, it was strong enough to make Argentina ungovernable until the army wearily permitted Perón to return to power in 1973. Then Perón died in 1974. His third wife, Isabel Martínez Perón, a former cabaret dancer, sought to rule with advice from the Peronist party and her astrologer. Inflation and Tupamaro-style Leftist guerrillas reduced Argentina to a shambles.

In 1976 the military again seized power and destroyed the guerrillas with torture and mass murder, dumping planeloads of drugged prisoners into the South Atlantic. Between 5,000 and 20,000 suspects "disappeared." The military killed with such abandon that fear of retribution then locked it into power. Finally the inglorious defeat of its 1982 attempt to seize the Falkland Islands from Britain (see p. 960) led to its fall, and to elections that returned Raul Alfonsín, a genuine democrat, as president. Alfonsín ruled until hyperinflation brought on by economic mismanagement chased him from office in 1989. His successor, the moderate Peronist Carlos Menem, sold off many inefficient state industries, balanced the budget, and by 1992 had tamed inflation. Argentina, for the first time in decades, seemed ready for economic growth. It was time; between 1965 to 1990 Argentina's GNP per capita had declined at an average annual rate of -0.3 percent.

The second category of Latin American states were the former colonies of Spain with a majority of Indians or *mestizos*—those of mixed blood. Of these states, Chile had the largest Creole population, at around 25 percent. There and in most other states from Bolivia through Central America to Mexico, large *mestizo* or Indian groups remained permanently excluded from a share in power. In Peru

Central and South America in 1993

and Bolivia, between 30 and 55 percent of the population consisted of Indians speaking Quechua or Aymara rather than Spanish; literacy in many of these states was relatively low.

They nevertheless traveled diverse paths. Mexico and Ecuador, thanks in part to their oilfields, enjoyed relatively high rates of growth from the 1950s to the 1980s, although Mexico's ruling "Institutional Revolutionary Party" (PRI) slowed the economy through corruption, state ownership of industry, and unpredictable banking policies. Growth accelerated after

the disputed 1988 presidential election of a Harvard-trained economist, Carlos Salinas de Gortari. Salinas sold off wasteful state-owned firms, loosened controls on foreign investment, and in 1992 defied Mexican nationalist sentiment by joining the United States and Canada in the North American Free Trade Agreement (NAFTA). Mexico seemed close at last to sustained economic growth.

Colombia also prospered relative to many other Latin American states, despite a long-running "*violencia*" or permanent civil war between political parties, Leftist guerrillas, and cocaine lords. But oil did not save Venezuela, nor did copper save Chile. Generals ruled Venezuela for much of the twentieth century; the most conspicuous and brutal were Juan Vincente Gomez (1908–35) and Marcos Peréz Jiménez (1952–58). Then a succession of weak parliamentary regimes nationalized more and more of the economy. A drop in world oil prices after 1982 cut Venezuela's per capita GNP by a quarter, and triggered repeated riots and military coup attempts.

The government of Chile, the oldest stable parliamentary regime on the continent, collapsed in 1973. For many years its politics had been deadlocked between a Marxist Left, a Catholic Christian Democratic center, and a conservative Right. In 1969 the candidate of the Left, Salvador Allende, took power as president on the strength of a plurality of 36.3 percent, less than two points ahead of his closest rival. Despite promises to the contrary—made to opposition parties that represented a majority of Chileans—Allende attempted to transform the economy in a "socialist" direction. He also invited Fidel Castro for a long and lavish state visit. Both the Nixon administration and the Chilean middle classes objected.

Allende's policies produced massive inflation and economic paralysis—in an economy already vulnerable because it rested on one commodity, copper, and on inefficient protected industry. Politically, Allende remained intent on a Marxist revolution for which he had no mandate; enthusiasts from the Latin American and European Left flocked to Chile. In September 1973, with the support of the Right and even of some Christian Democrats, the armed forces rocketed and stormed the presidential palace, and rounded up the Left. Allende apparently killed himself with a treasured machine pistol, a gift of Castro. Allende's supporters accused Nixon, Henry Kissinger, and the CIA of complicity in the coup. Washington had indeed subsidized Allende's political opponents and had tried in 1970 to provoke the Chilean army to remove him. But no firm evidence of U.S. involvement in the 1973 coup surfaced, despite lengthy congressional investigations. In any event, the generals and admirals who overthrew Allende had a domestic mandate.

Their leader, General Augusto Pinochet, soon converted that mandate into one of Latin America's most ruthless dictatorships. In the months after the coup, the military shot between 3,000 and 10,000 Leftists. Too late, the Christian Democrats and moderate Rightists realized that Pinochet, like Allende, was a man with a mission. But his mission was to eradicate Chilean Marxism rather than bring it to power. Pinochet privatized the state-owned firms, put down protests with unyielding brutality, and left the presidency on his own terms in 1988, while remaining commander of the armed forces. His Christian Democratic successor, Patricio Aylwin, reaped the benefits of Pinochet's economic reforms.

To the north, in Peru and Bolivia, military regimes predominated until the early 1980s. The Peruvian military, which ruled from 1968 to 1980, adopted Third Worldist notions of economic development, and nationalized banks and foreign firms. The result was prolonged stagnation. The civilian governments that followed presided over hyperinflation and an implacable insurgency of Quechua-speaking Indians led by university-educated Maoists, the *Sendero Luminoso* or "Shining Path" to revolution. *Sendero* grew swiftly, thanks

The face of military dictatorship: Augusto Pinochet (1986).

to Peru's economic failure and the socio-economic chasm between the Indian population and Peruvians of Spanish descent. In 1992 President Alberto Fujimori imposed a dictatorship that he described as a temporary measure against the guerrillas. The capture of *Sendero*'s leader, Abimael Guzmán Reynoso, a former philosophy professor also known as "the Fourth Sword of Marxism," gave the government a momentary advantage. But Peru's situation remained precarious.

Bolivia too acquired a civilian government in the 1980s, but showed little sign of stability or economic growth. The Central American states of Guatemala, El Salvador, and Nicaragua, already among the poorest in Latin America, suffered in the 1980s from civil wars between landowners and peasants, Creoles and Indians, Left and Right—and extremely low or negative per capita growth rates.

Finally, the largest of all Latin American states, Brazil, was in a category by itself. Its ethnic mixture, a unique compound of Portuguese, Africans, Italians, Germans, Slavs, East Indians, Japanese, Chinese, and native Indians, defies categorization; blacks remained at the bottom of the social scale, although color lines were less sharp than in Spanish America. Above all, Portugal had left its colonial subjects far more freedom for local and individual initiative than had Spain. The result was a society capable of growth—despite the extremes of wealth and poverty common elsewhere in Latin America, foreign debts of $122 billion (1990), a bloated state bureaucracy, repeated bouts of hyperinflation, and political turmoil that led to military rule between 1964 and 1985 and the dismissal of a president for corruption in 1992. By the 1980s, Brazil had become the world's tenth-largest economy. Its per capita growth rate from 1965 to 1990 was 3.3 percent, and its industries had achieved dramatic export successes. But political and economic mismanagement could yet slow or halt development.

The Sorrows of Africa

No wretchedness in Latin America compared with the misery found between the fringes of the Sahara and the Cape of Good Hope. Of the 23 states in the world with populations of more than 1 million and negative per capita growth between 1965 and 1990, 15 were in sub-Saharan Africa. The region's 450 million people produce roughly as much annually as Belgium's 10 million.

Africa's states were poorest of all the "new nations" at independence. All suffered from a variety of disabilities. Literacy in some of them was below 30 percent, and those who learned to read in government or missionary schools lost touch with their still non-literate societies. Traditional animist cults, based on magic, did little to prepare their followers to function in the cold "disenchanted" world of cause and effect, profit and loss. Islam, Africa's fastest-growing religion, carried a hostility to the "Christian" West that often extended to Western economic ideas. And the Christian missionaries who remained after independence to teach often had priorities other than economic development.

Independence came within boundaries drawn by figures such as Bismarck, Lord Salisbury, and Leopold of Belgium, which cut across tribal zones and traditional economic units. Pre-colonial political structures, a rich jumble of city-states and small kingdoms, interspersed with larger tribal confederations and empires that tended to expand rapidly for several generations and then crumble from lack of cohesion, offered little precedent for the creation of European-style nation-states. Independence led to bloody inter-tribal competition for control of the guns and money of the new post-colonial state machines. One-party (or one-tribe) dictatorships and short-lived parliamentary regimes fractured by ethnically based parties were the norm.

Economies tended toward subsistence agriculture or export-oriented one-crop systems. Only Nigeria with its massive oil reserves and large population, Botswana with its diamonds, and Rhodesia and South Africa with their European economies based on the labor of the black majority appeared to have solid economic prospects in the 1960s. Most black African states worsened their economic plight by ill-conceived "socialist" measures, such as requiring that peasants sell their produce to the state at fixed prices that were often below the cost of production. That destroyed incentives to farm; much of the African continent had been self-sufficient in food at independence, but soon imported it. And food-price subsidies swelled government debts and encouraged migration to the continent's growing shantytowns.

Some states appeared poor prospects from the beginning. Uganda and the Central African Republic succumbed to terrifying dictatorships by former army sergeants, Idi Amin Dada and Jean-Bedel Bokassa. Amin killed as many as 300,000 Ugandans between 1971 and 1979, and left behind a civil war from which the country recovered only slowly. In Liberia, a West African state founded in the early nineteenth century by freed slaves from the United States, a bloody coup led by a Sergeant Samuel Doe of the Krahn tribe overthrew the descendants of the founders in 1980. Doe's tribal adversaries rebelled, and in 1990 seized the capital and killed Doe. Anarchy—the collapse of the Liberian state amid bloodshed and mass suffering—followed, despite intervention by forces from neighboring African states. Inland from Liberia, the cruelty of nature replaced or reinforced the effects of war. The Saharan fringe—Mali, Burkina Faso, Niger, Chad, and the Sudan—suffered repeated disasters from drought and from population pressure on their fragile semi-desert environment.

Ethiopia, east and south of the Sudan, suffered both from drought and from the backward-looking monarchy of Haile Selassie—until its overthrow in 1974. His successors, the Marxist-Leninist zealots of the *Derg* ("Provisional Military Administrative Council"), proved far more terrifying than the aged "Lion of Judah." In 1977–78, amid purges and massacres, a Lieutenant Colonel Mengistu Haile Mariam took command of state and army. With Soviet aid, he sought to subjugate the Eritreans, the people of the former Italian colony whom the United Nations had forced into federation with Ethiopia in 1952. Mengistu pursued a Stalinist program of collectivization ("villagization") that ruthlessly dispossessed and displaced millions of peasants, and in 1987 he proclaimed Ethiopia a Communist "People's Democratic Republic." Between 1977 and the collapse of Mengistu's regime in 1991, war, purges, collectivization, and famine between them killed more Ethiopians and Eritreans than had Mussolini. Neighboring Somalia, under the dictatorship of Siad Barre (1969–91), passed from Soviet to U.S. clientage in the late 1970s; Barre's overthrow in 1991 led—as in Liberia—to the collapse of the state. A bloody civil war between rival clans and gangs followed, while hundreds of thousands of Somalis starved. Belated United States and United Nations military intervention helped guarantee the delivery of food, but could not force the Somalis to form a stable government.

Other sub-Saharan states adopted forms of "African socialism" less extreme than that of Ethiopia, but with little better results. The Marxist regimes of Angola and Mozambique pressed nationalization and collectivization schemes with similar economic consequences, although less drastic human ones. Ghana achieved independence under Kwame Nkrumah, who styled himself "the Redeemer," established a dictatorship, invited in East German and Chinese advisers, and cut a bold figure at "nonaligned" meetings until Ghana's army removed him in 1966. Ghana's economy fell steadily further behind that of its similar but more "capitalist" neighbor, the Ivory Coast, until the dictatorship of an air force lieutenant, Jerry Rawlings, imposed free-market reforms in

Famine and the state: A Sudanese policeman drives back a hungry crowd (1985).

Mobuto in 1965, shortly after taking power.

the late 1980s. Tanzania's experiment with village collective farming supposedly based on traditional African practices proved an economic disaster. Its "capitalist" northern neighbor, Kenya, enjoyed relative success. Zambia's nationalization of industries and land in the 1970s, along with drought, produced negative per capita growth. Guinea-Bissau's one-party "socialist" dictatorship and self-inflicted economic failures exasperated even the Swedes, those most patient donors of development aid.

Sub-Saharan Africa's largest and most populous states, Nigeria and Zaire, also failed to live up to post-independence expectations. Nigeria's British-style parliamentary regime fell victim to tribal strains and religious conflict between the Moslem north and the Christian and animist south (a conflict also found in the Sudan). An attempt by the Ibo people of southeast Nigeria to create an independent "Biafra" in 1967–70 met with defeat in a pitiless civil war; more than a million died. The army then ruled Nigeria until a brief parliamentary interlude in 1979–83, which ended in yet another coup. Nigeria's oil wealth prompted it to build prestige projects such as a useless $4 billion steel mill, and to found a new capital—a common symbol of state power and national integration, from St. Petersburg and Washington to Brasilia and Islamabad (Pakistan).

But heavy bureaucratic controls and the resulting corruption slowed economic growth.

Zaire profited from its huge mineral wealth even less than Nigeria did from its oil. Belgian and French military intervention helped the dictatorship of Mobutu survive numerous challenges from the provinces. The regime proved skillful at borrowing from Western banks and spending the money on prestige projects and its own pleasures. Opposition groups forced Mobutu to give up some of his powers after disturbances in 1991, but eventual chaos seemed as likely as orderly reform.

Finally, Rhodesia-Zimbabwe and South Africa, the European economies in Africa, survived. Defeat in 1978 did not mean "the suitcase or the coffin" for Zimbabwe's whites. The Marxist victor, Robert Mugabe, pursued a unique course: he convinced the white minority to remain provisionally and run the economy. In South Africa, despite increasing political isolation and worldwide economic sanctions, the Boer "white tribe" maintained its racial domination throughout the 1970s and 1980s. But the sanctions drastically slowed economic growth. In 1989–90, after a change of leadership in the ruling National Party, the Boer government moved with surprising speed to conciliate the black majority and regain international respectability. President Frederik W. De Klerk abolished most *Apartheid* restrictions, released Nelson Mandela of the opposition African National Congress (ANC) from prison, and began negotiations with the ANC over a new constitution that would bring the black majority to power. Talks continued despite widespread fighting—covertly encouraged for a time by the government's security forces—between the Zulus and the Xhosa, the tribe most closely associated with the ANC. But it remained unclear how to reconcile white demands for guarantees of life and property with the ANC's insistence on majority rule.

Nelson Mandela addresses his followers after his release from almost three decades of imprisonment by the Boer regime (1990).

From the 1940s to the 1970s the forces that had once driven Europe's expansion into the wider world operated in reverse.

Europe's demographic outward thrust had ended, thanks to industrialization and the carnage of the World Wars. The colonized peoples had learned to resist with Europe's own weapons and military-political techniques. And the rise of native nationalisms made empire unprofitable or untenable. Yet despite their common origins as formal or informal dependencies of Europe, the new nations traveled widely divergent paths through the Cold War era. The capitalist states of east Asia set an example that forced China to discard Marxist-Leninist economics, even while it sought to keep Marxist-Leninist politics.

South Asia, amid religious wars and stifling bureaucratic controls, gradually advanced. The warring states of the Middle East failed to find a new balance to replace the Ottoman and colonial orders. Many of the older new nations of Latin America missed the path to sustained economic growth. And in Africa south of the Sahara a few states prospered, many regressed, and some lapsed into chaos or civil war. Politics, culture, and responsiveness to the capitalist world market seemed to determine—for good or ill—which states were capable of making the perilous leap from poverty to power and wealth.

Suggestions for Further Reading

General Works

No adequate survey of the post-1945 "Third World" exists; few reliable or readable works cover even parts of it. G. Chaliand, *Revolution in the Third World* (1978, revised 1988), offers a lively guided tour that is now in some respects dated. It nevertheless provides an excellent analysis of the wide cultural differences within the "Third World." See also C. Rangel, *Third World Ideology and Western Reality* (1986). The World Bank's annual *World Development Report* offers comprehensive statistical data with which to test generalizations about the "Third World." E. Luttwak, *Coup d'Etat: A Practical Handbook* (1969, 1979), analyzes its dominant method of political change.

Decolonization

Nor is there any adequate comparative history of decolonization. E. Monroe, *Britain's Moment in the Middle East, 1914–1956* (1963); A. Williams, *Britain and France in the Middle East and North Africa, 1914–1967* (1968); W. R. Louis, *The British Empire in the Middle East, 1945–1951* (1984); and A. Horne, *A Savage War of Peace: Algeria 1954–1962* (1977), are useful on the Middle East and North Africa. B. N. Pandey, *The Break-up of British India* (1969) and *South and Southeast Asia, 1945–1979* (1980), ably cover south and southeast Asia.

The Diversity of the Non-Western World

For the varied cultures of the "Third World" and for post-1945 events, see—for East Asia—H. C. Hinton, *Three and a Half Powers: the New Balance in Asia* (1975); S. Leys, *Chinese Shadows* (1978) and *The Chairman's New Clothes: Mao and the Cultural Revolution* (1981); and R. MacFarquhar and J. K. Fairbank, eds., *The Cambridge History of China*, vols. 14 and 15 (1987, 1991). On South Asia, see Pandey (listed earlier) and J. M. Brown, *Modern India: The Origins of an Asian Democracy* (1985). V. S. Naipaul, *India: A Wounded Civilization* (1977), offers pessimistic cultural criticism; N. Maxwell, *India's China War* (1970), is an eye-opening case study in Indian foreign policy. On the Middle East, D. Pipes, *In the Path of God: Islam and Political Power* (1983), is useful on the force of ideas; P. Slugett and M. Farouk-Slugett, eds., *Tuttle Guide to the Middle East* (1992), imparts basic facts. On Latin America, see especially L. E. Harrison, *Underdevelopment Is a State of Mind: The Latin American Case* (1985); P. Sigmund, *The Overthrow of Allende and the Politics of Chile, 1964–1976* (1977); M. Falcoff, *Modern Chile, 1970–1989* (1989); C. Rangel, *The Latin Americans: Their Love-Hate Relationship with the United States* (1986); and V. S. Naipaul, *The Return of Eva Perón* (1980). On Africa, see D. K. Fieldhouse, *Black Africa 1945–1980. Economic Decolonization and Arrested Development* (1986), and the informed popular account of S. J. Unger, *Africa: People and Politics of an Emerging Continent* (1986); C. Young and T. Turner, *The Rise and Decline of the Zairian State* (1985), provide a depressing case study.

-36-

THE END OF
THE COLD WAR ERA

The 1975 Helsinki security treaty and other symbols of dé-tente did not change the un-derlying realities of the Cold War. The international order born in 1941–47 in the struggle between the two superpowers re-mained the pivot of international politics. But within the framework of the Cold War order, other powers went about their business. Japan's industries stormed the world's markets. Western Europe suffered stagnation, unemployment, and disorien-tation in the late 1970s and early 1980s, and then acquired new purpose in at-tempts to construct a European super-power. In the Middle East, an "Islamic Revolution" swept Iran in 1978–79, gener-ating potent new strains of terrorism and triggering the most destructive war be-tween non-Western states in the Cold War era. The victor in that struggle, the Arab national socialist dictatorship of Iraq,

then pressed on toward collision with the United States and much of the rest of the world in 1990–91. That collision coincided with a seemingly unthinkable event: the end of the Cold War through Soviet col-lapse. But as in 1918, the fall of empires unleashed not peace but savage ethnic-religious conflict.

In the realm of knowledge, the last half of the century was a period of stag-gering advance and growing bewilder-ment about the foundations and purposes of science and scholarship. The geometric expansion of human knowledge brought fragmentation. No single mind could fully grasp more than a small range of subjects. The gap between high culture and popu-lar culture inherited from the late nine-teenth century grew wider, just as the popular culture of the West swept the non-Western world with tides of unprece-dented intensity. In this disoriented condition, as the momentum of population growth drove humanity's numbers relentlessly upward, the world prepared to meet the third millennium of the Western era.

THE SOVIET EMPIRE FROM EXPANSION TO COLLAPSE, 1975–91

The Soviet Union seemed well launched on an upward trajectory by 1970, the year it surpassed the United States in numbers of intercontinental nuclear missiles. American indecision in the wake of Vietnam and the continued growth of Soviet military power then tempted Brezhnev to seek a second Soviet empire far beyond the "Yalta line" of 1945. That expansion in the end met determined resistance. Soviet economic growth, which had turned downward after Stalin's death, slowed and stopped. Then the Soviet empire and the Soviet Union itself crumbled under Western counterpressure, external defeat, eastern European unrest, economic and ecological catastrophe, and the demoralization of the Soviet rulers themselves.

The Culmination of Soviet Power, 1975–79

Détente was brief. The 1973 Yom Kippur war and the Arab oil embargo revealed western Europe's lack of resolve. In Washington, the Nixon administration self-destructed. Congress turned against America's "imperial presidency" and sought to bring the executive branch to heel. North Vietnam's victory in April 1975 suggested that the United States was paralyzed. Simultaneously, new openings tempted the Soviet Union in Europe, Africa, Asia, and the Caribbean.

In Portugal, a power vacuum opened up after the 1974 military revolution that put an end to its colonial empire. The Portuguese Communist Party, with Soviet money and advice, sought power through the "salami tactics" that Stalin had applied in eastern Europe in the late 1940s. But without Red Army backing, those tactics failed. Portugal was a member of NATO, which was unwilling to see it pass into

the Soviet orbit. Aid from western Europe and the United States helped Portugal's Socialist party to defeat its Communist rival, and to found a parliamentary democracy.

In Africa, the Soviets skillfully drew Portugal's former colonies, Mozambique and Angola, into their orbit. In Angola they helped to victory their chosen ally among the three guerrilla armies contending for power in the wake of Portuguese withdrawal. But putting the Marxist-Leninist MPLA ("Popular Movement for the Liberation of Angola") in power and keeping it there against rivals backed by the United States, Zaire, China, and South Africa required an ocean-spanning airlift, as many as 50,000 Cuban troops, and fifteen costly years of war (1976–91).

Further north, the Soviets established two other bridgeheads, at Aden and in Somalia, commanding the entrance to the Red Sea. They also wooed Somalia's rival, Mengistu Haile Mariam of Ethiopia. In 1977–78, Mengistu received over $1 billion in Soviet arms, Soviet and Cuban advisers, and a Cuban armored brigade under Soviet command. That help won a war in the Ogaden desert against Somalia—which then drifted toward the United States. But even with Soviet arms, Mengistu was unable to crush resistance in Eritrea. Ceaseless purges, general famine, and ever-growing ethnic revolt all around Ethiopia's periphery ultimately made Mengistu a Soviet burden rather than an asset.

In Asia, Soviet patronage of North Vietnam continued after Hanoi's conquest of the South in March–April 1975. In return the Soviets secured the huge U.S. base at Cam Ranh Bay for air and sea forces capable of threatening both southern China and Japan's sea lanes to the oil of the Middle East. But that patronage cost Brezhnev several billion dollars a year after 1979, when Vietnam opened a Third Indochina War (see p. 957) by seizing Cambodia.

In the Caribbean, two events in 1979 offered further openings. On the tiny island of Grenada, a shaky post-colonial regime fell victim to a coup by Marxist-Leninist enthusiasts, the "New Jewel Party." Their attempts to politicize the Grenadan "masses" and their appetite for weapons soon led them into close ties with the Soviet Union, East Germany, Cuba, Nicaragua, Bulgaria, North Korea, and the PLO.

On the Central American mainland, in Nicaragua, the withdrawal of U.S. support for the dictatorship of Anastasio Somoza Debayle led to his regime's collapse and the seizure of power in July 1979 by a Cuban-educated insurgent movement, the "Sandinista National Liberation Front" (FSLN). Within a month the new FSLN regime had clinched relations with the Soviet Union, Bulgaria, and Libya. It soon acquired ties to the PLO and North Korea. Cuban and Soviet bloc advisers poured in, and the FSLN proclaimed the United States "the enemy of all humanity." Shipments of Soviet-bloc arms soon arrived not only for the "Sandinista Armed Forces" (as the new party-army called itself) but also for insurgencies kindled or rekindled in El Salvador and Guatemala.

Swift expansion of the Soviet Navy, which gained a global reach from bases that stretched from Cuba to Cam Ranh Bay, accompanied the Soviet Union's disturbing military activism in the non-Western world. But most alarming of all was the swift buildup of Soviet conventional and nuclear forces aimed at western Europe. Brezhnev's decision to ratchet military spending upward toward a quarter of Soviet GNP—a figure similar to that of Nazi Germany in 1939—paid off. The Soviet Union had already achieved a numerical advantage of 2 to 1 or better over NATO in deployed divisions, tanks, and artillery; now it seemed to be catching up to the West in the sophistication of its armored vehicles, aircraft, and electronics.

And despite the cap on most strategic forces established by an unratified U. S.–Soviet SALT II treaty signed in 1979, the Soviets pressed their build-up of intermediate, or theater, nuclear forces. From 1978 onward they deployed an entirely new class of intermediate-range ballistic missiles, the three-warhead SS-20. These truck-mounted behemoths were easily hidden, reasonably accurate, and could reach Iceland, Portugal, Japan, and China from deep within the USSR. They also could fire with a minimum of preparation, in keeping with the Soviet emphasis on preemptive surprise attack. By 1979 the Soviet Union had deployed 120 SS-20s, and no limit appeared in sight. NATO had nothing remotely similar.

But then Brezhnev succumbed to a further—fatal—temptation. On December 27, 1979, KGB commandos and Soviet paratroops descended on Kabul, the capital of Afghanistan, and approximately 100,000 Soviet troops rumbled across the Afghan borders. This latest and most violent expansion of Soviet power, like its predecessors, was an outgrowth of events not entirely of Moscow's making. In 1978 a Marxist-Leninist Afghan party, the "Democratic Party of the People of Afghanistan" (DPPA), had overthrown the five-year-old Afghan republic and had provoked the fiercely independent and devoutly Islamic Afghan tribes with talk of secularism and land "reform." By spring 1979, despite the commitment of additional Soviet arms and advisers, a powerful insurgency was under way that drew on Afghanistan's proud nineteenth-century tradition of ferocious resistance to both Britain and Russia. A factional struggle within the DPPA replaced its original leader with Hafizullah Amin, a bloodthirsty figure whom Moscow regarded as untrustworthy.

Amin's seizure of power and the spreading revolt apparently led to the drastic Soviet measures of December 1979: Amin's assassination by the KGB and Red Army occupation of Afghanistan. But unlike Angola and Ethiopia, where the Cubans had done most of the Soviet Union's fighting, this was no proxy war. The Red Army's DPPA auxiliaries numbered only 30,000 and were so unreliable that they normally fought with Soviet tanks watching them from the rear. The Soviet Union had begun a war that it could neither win, nor end without giving up its claim to represent humanity's future. The Soviet empire had reached its point of culmination, and was about to enter a swift and final descent.

The Fall of Empires, 1979–91

As in Korea in June 1950, the unpredictable American reaction stunned the Soviets. Gerald Ford's Democratic successor as president, James E. ("Jimmy") Carter,

Afghanistan and the Persian Gulf

had in 1977 condemned the foreign policy of his predecessors for its "inordinate fear of Communism." The Soviet invasion of Afghanistan, he now confessed, proved that they had been right. He slapped an embargo on U.S. grain sales to the Soviet Union. He sought to humiliate the Soviets with a boycott of the 1980 Moscow Summer Olympics. He spurred U.S. defense spending. And he announced a "Carter Doctrine" to bar further Soviet expansion southward from Afghanistan: the United States would use military force to block attempts "by any outside force to gain control of the Persian Gulf region." Détente was dead.

Carter's successor, Ronald Reagan, proved an even more dangerous and unpredictable adversary. He announced— and seemed to believe—that the Soviet Union was an "Evil Empire." He doubled the U.S. national debt from $1 trillion in 1981 to $2.1 trillion in 1986 to rebuild the U.S. armed forces at a pace and in a style the Soviets could not match. He promoted an antiballistic missile shield project, the Strategic Defense Initiative (SDI), based on computer and optical technologies that the Soviet Union did not possess and could not develop. News of SDI, together with the demonstration—in 1982 air fighting between Israelis and Syrians in Lebanon—of the effortless superiority of the latest generation of U.S. fighters over their Soviet counterparts, provoked near-panic in Moscow. And Reagan followed through on a pledge by Carter to the NATO allies to deploy a force of U.S.

medium-range nuclear missiles in Europe to counter Brezhnev's SS-20s.

But that was not all. For the first time since MacArthur's drive to the Yalu in 1950, the United States replaced containment with "rollback." Reagan proclaimed a policy soon known as the "Reagan Doctrine": the United States would support *anti-Communist* insurgencies around the world. The CIA received orders to furnish the Afghan rebels with arms, including advanced antiaircraft missiles. That paralyzed the Soviets' main asset in Afghanistan, command of the air. From 1981–82 on, the CIA also organized and supported a growing insurgency, the *contras,* or "counter-revolutionaries," against the Sandinista regime in Nicaragua. And when the leaders of Grenada's New Jewel Party split into warring factions in October 1983, and the widening bloodshed seemed to threaten American citizens on the island, Reagan swiftly sent U.S. Marines and paratroops. Small parties of Cuban troops offered fierce but short-lived resistance; most Grenadans seemed happy to see the Americans. For the first time since 1917, a Western democracy had deposed a Marxist-Leninist regime.

Even the inner empire in eastern Europe that Stalin had conquered in 1945 was now far from secure. Of all the satellites, Poland had plunged most deeply into debt to Western bankers during détente. Misconceived industrial investments and rising inflation struck at the living standards of Poland's downtrodden workers, whose riots had toppled Gomulka in 1970 as they had toppled his predecessor in 1956. In summer 1980 Polish workers at Gdansk—once known as Danzig—went on strike: a class struggle against a Marxist-Leninist state. Poland's intellectuals and the Catholic Church, the historic vehicle of Polish nationalism, backed the strike. Against all precedent, the workers won the right to replace their Party-run sham unions with an independent national trade union, *Solidarnosc* ("Solidarity"). The demoralized Polish Communist Party lost control even of the press, and began to disintegrate. Poland, the largest and most strategically vital of all the satellites, appeared about to crumble—with dangerous repercussions in the DDR, Czechoslovakia, and Hungary.

Brezhnev and his associates found the answer: a Polish general. Moscow

A Solidarity demonstration defies martial law (1982).

placed the Polish Communist Party in the hands of Wojciech Jaruzelski, a prim and ruthless military figure with a long record of absolute obedience to the Soviet Union. In December 1981 Jaruzelski crushed Solidarity with riot police and the army; Soviet tank forces in East Germany, Poland, and western Russia stood ready to back him up. Jaruzelski placed before the Polish people a grim choice: either his dictatorship, or a Soviet intervention that would endanger the survival of the nation. Solidarity survived underground and Polish workers began a permanent although unspoken slowdown strike.

The Soviet domestic scene was by now at least as threatening as the foreign and imperial one. Soviet military procurement at last ceased to grow in the early 1980s; the economy was floundering. The annual rate of GNP increase had fallen inexorably from roughly 5 percent in the 1950s to negative growth by the early 1980s. Without terror—which Stalin's successors lacked the ideological conviction to wield—growth was apparently no longer possible. The diversion of up to a third of Soviet industrial and research resources to the military, the inefficiency of central planning, the rewarding of political loyalty over brains, and a demoralized work force ("they pretend to pay us, we pretend to work") meant that even massive investment produced only stagnation.

Rudimentary medical services, a rising industrial accident rate, intense chemical pollution, radiation from more than a hundred underground nuclear blasts in mines and oilfields, astounding levels of vodka consumption, and widespread hopelessness made the Soviet Union the only industrialized society in history to experience a long-term decline in the life expectancy of its population. Male life expectancy dropped from age 65 in 1965 to an estimated 61 or worse in 1981; the life expectancy of Soviet women from 73 in the early 1970s to 69 in 1985.

Nor did the Soviet Union—one of Europe's last two multinational empires—escape the demographic trends that had sapped its former imperial rivals. By 1970 only 51 percent of the Soviet population were Great Russians, the ruling nationality. The subject peoples, especially the Moslems of Central Asia, were growing at rates of up to three times that of the peoples of European Russia. Great Russians probably ceased to be a majority in the early 1980s, although they remained the largest single nationality within the Soviet Union. Nationalist unrest in Soviet Central Asia and the Caucasus accompanied the shift in numbers; demonstrations erupted whenever KGB pressure relaxed.

These trends clearly threatened the Soviet Union with the loss of superpower status by Brezhnev's death in 1982. Two

Soviet industrial pollution: a paper pulp plant near Archangel, 1990.

transitional figures, Yuri Andropov of the KGB and the colorless Konstantin Chernenko, followed Brezhnev to the grave after brief spells in power. Then in March 1985 the Politburo chose a far younger man, Mikhail Gorbachev. Andrei Gromyko, Molotov's pupil and heir at the foreign ministry, reportedly put Gorbachev over the top by remarking that he had a very nice smile and very hard teeth.

Gromyko was wrong. Gorbachev immediately revealed a genius for disastrous half-measures. His goal was to preserve and consolidate his own power, that of the Party, and that of a revived "socialism." But from the beginning he faced the same contradiction that had snared earlier autocrats from Peter the Great onward. Success in inter-state competition—the preservation of the Soviet Union's superpower status—was only possible in the long run through the development of a society and economy on the Western model. But that society would demand an end to autocracy. And failure in interstate competition likewise led, as Nicholas the Last had discovered in 1917, to autocracy's collapse.

Gorbachev's economic reform, *perestroika* (restructuring) soon developed into "catastroika." Gorbachev's reforms broke Stalin's central planning mechanism without creating functioning markets to replace it. Gorbachev failed to follow the Chinese example of reversing Stalinism in agriculture first, buying off the peasantry with profits and swamping urban discontent with food. Worse still—given his aim of preserving his own power and that of the Party—he also failed to follow the Chinese in keeping an iron grip on politics. To checkmate the opponents of *perestroika,* the remaining Stalinists in the Party, the military, and military-industry, he loosened Party and KGB control over the press, over broadcasting, and over access to the Western media. He naively intended this new policy of *Glasnost* (openness) as the decisive blow for *perestroika.* Instead, *Glasnost* destroyed Gorbachev, the Party, and the Soviet Union.

Glasnost, together with the 1986 meltdown and fire in a Soviet nuclear reactor at Chernobyl in the Ukraine, demolished the Party's claim that it held the key to history.

The accident contaminated livestock, milk, and crops from Lapland to Portugal, killed 31 outright and thousands more in the following years from radiation-induced illnesses. Large areas of the Ukraine and Byelorussia remained contaminated. And *Glasnost* mercilessly exposed the regime's incompetence in everything from reactor design to medical countermeasures to post-accident cleanup. Over the next three years the Soviet press and an increasingly vocal public opinion stripped away the legitimacy of the Soviet state.

Gorbachev had already begun the destruction of that legitimacy by blaming economic stagnation on Brezhnev. Then Stalin came under attack, as massive new evidence of his genocide leaked from the archives into the Soviet press. The term "totalitarianism," long banned as Western Cold War rhetoric, became the preferred description of the Soviet past. Finally, the public and the new free press turned on Lenin—the regime's embalmed saint—and damned him as the author of a historic wrong turning that had led Russia and its subject peoples to misery and ruin. By May 1990, demonstrators were appearing in Red Square carrying placards that certified the regime's death: "Socialism? No Thanks!" "Seventy-Two Years on the Road to Nowhere." "Down with the Red Fascist Empire."

By that point, the Soviet external empire was gone. Gorbachev sought throughout 1986–89 to trade his steady retreat for Western concessions. But his rising dependence on Western—and especially German—loans to finance *perestroika* stripped him of his bargaining power. Between 1987 and 1990 he agreed to scrap his SS-20s and other theater nuclear weapons, and to limit the Soviet Union's nuclear and conventional forces on terms virtually dictated by the United States. Between 1988 and 1991 he wound up Brezhnev's second Soviet empire—withdrawing the Red Army from Afghanistan, pledging to withdraw it from Cuba, helping to ease the Cubans out of Angola and the Vietnamese out of Cambodia and abandoning Ethiopia.

But once defeat in Afghanistan had destroyed the Red Army's aura of invincibility, and once the Soviet regime had confessed its failures and its dependence on the West, Stalin's inner eastern European empire began to crumble as well. Poland and Hungary led the way toward independence; Solidarity and the Hungarian opposition won the right to exist legally in early 1989. That fall, after Hungary tore down the stretch of fortified Iron Curtain along its border with Austria, East Germans flooded westward through Budapest to seek asylum in West Germany. Massive demonstrations against the East German regime in the East German city of Leipzig then threw the DDR leaders into panic. Erich Honecker, their chief, called Gorbachev to ask permission to shoot the demonstrators. But Gorbachev, although faced with the collapse of the DDR and the loss of the symbol of Soviet victory in the Second World War, advised Honecker to avoid bloodshed. This time, unlike 1953, 1956, and 1968, Soviet tanks did not roll.

Gorbachev's gesture, whatever its motives, earned him a Nobel Peace Prize. It also ended the eastern European empire that Stalin had created and that his successors had maintained by force. The collapsing DDR opened the Berlin Wall on November 9, 1989, and happy crowds surged through the Brandenburg Gate. Of

the satellite leaders, only Nicolae Ceausescu of Rumania chose to fight it out when Party and army rivals hijacked popular disturbances and launched a coup in December 1989. But the Rumanian army's tanks prevailed over Ceausescu's secret police. The new rulers named themselves the "Council of National Salvation," shot their former boss, and set up an ex-Communist dictatorship. Elsewhere the collapse of the satellite regimes was largely peaceful and led to freely elected non-Communist governments and the withdrawal of the Red Army. The "former DDR," after free elections, chose reunification with West Germany on October 3, 1990.

By that point the Soviet Union itself was in crisis. The inner ring of subject peoples, conquered by the tsars and reconquered by Stalin, began a slow-motion revolt: demonstrations, declarations of independence, appeals to the West. Soviet troops crushed demonstrators in Lithuania and elsewhere, but by spring 1991 United States warnings set limits on Gorbachev's use of force. Party and KGB diehards whom he had placed in key positions then sought to remove Gorbachev himself in a bungled coup d'état in August 1991. The protests of Reagan's successor George Bush, the incompetence of the plotters, and the resistance of Boris Yeltsin, recently elected president of the Russian Republic, led to the collapse of the coup and the banning of the Communist Party.

The failed coup and the death of the Party made the Soviet Union ungovernable. Between August and December 1991 the multinational empire of Lenin and the tsars dissolved into its national component parts. Fourteen new states split off in an arc around Russia: Estonia, Latvia, and Lithuania on the Baltic, Byelorussia (Belarus), Ukraine, Moldavia (Moldova) in the west; Georgia, Armenia, and Azerbaijan in the Caucasus; and the five predominantly Moslem republics of what had been Soviet Central Asia. At the initiative of Yeltsin and the Ukraine, a ramshackle "Confederation of Independent States" (CIS) emerged as heir-apparent to the Soviet Union's military establishment, nuclear arsenal, and defense policy. At the end of December

Boris Yeltsin of Russia (1991): from Communist bureaucrat to democratic reformer?

1991 Gorbachev resigned as president of a state that no longer existed. The white, blue, and red Russian tricolor replaced the red flag of Communism over the Kremlin's towers. The Cold War had ended with the dissolution of the Soviet superpower.

WAR AND PEACE IN ASIA

The final phase of the Cold War was a time of sharp contrasts in Asia. U.S. withdrawal in 1973–75 removed war in southeast Asia from American television screens. But it did not end war there. Japan and the smaller states within Japan's economic orbit prospered mightily. The island empire became an economic superpower, the world's second largest economy. But it showed few signs of taking up the responsibilities that accompanied that power.

Cambodian Genocide and Third Indochina War

North Vietnam's conquest of the South in March–April 1975 led to direct annexation. Hanoi abolished what was left of the southern "National Liberation Front" in 1976. Hundreds of thousands of former Saigon officials and soldiers disappeared into "re-education camps." Many thousands died.

In Cambodia, Hanoi had long sponsored a Communist guerrilla movement, the Khmer Rouge, that soon showed itself even more terrifying than its patrons. The Khmer Rouge leaders, Pol Pot (born Saloth Sar), Ieng Sary, and Khieu Samphan had acquired their Maoism at Left Bank cafés while studying in Paris in the 1940s and 1950s. There they conceived a utopian goal of a kind common among uprooted intellectuals: the forging of a unique "Cambodian Road to Socialism" through the elimination of the old society and the breaking of all ties between Cambodia and the outside world.

Pol Pot and his associates followed that road with pitiless consistency when they seized power in Cambodia in the wake of Hanoi's conquest of South Vietnam. In a few days in April 1975 they

Bones of victims of the Khmer Rouge, Tonle Bati, Takeo Province, Cambodia.

forcibly emptied Phnom Penh, a capital city containing perhaps 3 million inhabitants and refugees; many starved. The teenage peasant zealots of the Khmer Rouge hunted and killed all Cambodians with an education and anyone whose support for the collectivized and "ruralized" new order seemed less than total. In 1970, Cambodia's population had stood at an estimated 8 million. By 1980 the population of "Democractic Kampuchea" had fallen to between 5.5 and 6.5 million. Perhaps 750,000 of the 1.5 to 2.5 million missing people had fled across the minefields to Thailand. The rest had died.

World opinion showed its usual paralysis. Many in the West at first dismissed the accounts of torture, massacre, and starvation conveyed by refugees. Nor did Khmer Rouge genocide (or "autogenocide") play any part in Pol Pot's downfall; that followed instead from his fierce nationalist resentment of his former patrons in Hanoi. In 1977–78 Khmer Rouge forces clashed savagely with the Vietnamese along the Cambodia-Vietnam border. In December 1978 more than 100,000 Vietnamese troops launched a classic mechanized *Blitzkrieg* that dispersed the Khmer Rouge armies and seized Phnom Penh.

That "Third Indochina War" did not remain entirely isolated. China had long objected to Hanoi's close ties with Moscow. Hanoi likewise had no love for Beijing. In 1978 Vietnam began to expel its 900,000 to 1.2 million overseas Chinese. That brutal measure, together with the invasion of Cambodia, prompted a brief Chinese attack on North Vietnam in February–March 1979. China's inexperienced army did poorly, however, and Brezhnev apparently cautioned Beijing against pressing the attack. Vietnam proceeded to impose a semicolonial regime on Cambodia, complete with hundreds of thousands of Vietnamese settlers. Nearly 200,000 troops stayed on until 1988–89 to fight both Khmer Rouge and anti-Communist guerrillas. Not until Soviet backing faltered did Hanoi agree to withdraw, and a precarious truce, brokered and supervised by the United Nations, descended in 1991. The Third Indochina War had cost tens of thousands of dead beyond those who had perished by Khmer Rouge genocide, and the Khmer Rouge still held much of Cambodia.

Japan: The Fragility of Success

While the United States was floundering in Indochina, Japan was emerging as the "workshop of Asia." Its gross national product swelled from roughly 13 percent of U.S. GNP in 1965 to 54 percent in 1990. Its economy rested overwhelmingly on industry rather than agriculture or mining, for Japan's narrow, poor and mountainous islands had almost no oil and few minerals. As in the United States, the production of automobiles and electrical devices led the way. Unlike the United States, Japan's industries immediately targeted export markets from the United States to southeast Asia to Europe; to import food and oil, Japan had to export. By the mid-1970s Japan had conquered the U.S. market for television sets and seized a bridgehead in the automobile market. By the 1980s even the manufacturers of the United States' most innovative product, the computer chip, were complaining of "unfair" Japanese competition. Europe reacted with even greater hostility. Japan even took over the U.S. role as the world's greatest creditor—a position Washington had held since 1914–18.

Japanese success flowed in part from thirty years of relentless hard work and attention to detail by Japanese management and by Japan's highly educated and dedicated work force. It also derived in part from a social and political system in

The face of Japanese industry: Robots weld automobile bodies at a factory near Tokyo.

which big business, the government bureaucracies, and the ruling Liberal Democratic Party acted in unison to promote limitless economic growth.

But with growth came perplexities that the Japanese system was ill-prepared to master. Defeat in 1945 had not changed the fundamental nature of the Meiji state. Army and navy had ceased to count in decision-making, but the vacuum at the center, the lack of steering and of brakes that had led Japan to ruin in 1931–45, persisted. Internal debate on Japan's course, on the possible reactions abroad to Japan's seemingly ever-widening share of its trading partners' domestic markets, was strangely absent. Japanese government spokesmen routinely pledged to consume and import more, and to export less. Yet throughout the 1970s and 1980s, Japan's trade surpluses with Europe and the United States continued to swell.

Japan was nevertheless extremely vulnerable. The pacifist constitution that MacArthur had imposed in 1947 kept the island empire partially disarmed, unable to defend its shipping lanes to the oil of the Persian Gulf or to the vast "co-prosperity sphere" stretching southward to Thailand, Malaysia, and Indonesia which it had at last acquired under United States protection. Nor did its neighbors want it rearmed. Beijing repeatedly reminded Tokyo of the immense massacres committed during Japan's attempt to conquer China in 1937–45.

And so great was Japan's dependence on foreign trade that a severe downturn could easily unhinge both society and government. For Japan's defeat in 1945 had largely failed to produce the rethinking and repentance found in West Germany. The nationalist myths of racial and cultural superiority that had propelled Japan toward the conquest of Asia had survived the Pacific War. Many Japanese continued to view Pearl Harbor as a justified response to American economic aggression. And unlike West Germany and the other Western democracies, Japan's social and political order did not derive its strength from religious or legal-ethical principles—such as Locke's notions of inherent rights for individuals—that were

independent of government or society. The foundation of "Japan, Inc." was simply the collective will of the ruling elites, a will legitimized by success alone. Yet Japan's pace of economic growth had gradually slowed since the 1960s. And in the early 1990s Japan's inflated land and stock prices collapsed dramatically, the economy tipped into recession, and the resistance of Japan's trading partners intensified. Recurring corruption scandals crippled the Liberal Democratic Party; it splintered in mid-1993 and lost its long-standing parliamentary majority. Political paralysis seemed possible, just as the economic success required for social and political stability was less assured than in the past.

WESTERN EUROPE IN SEARCH OF ITSELF

The sharp rise in the world price of oil in 1973–75, a further oil-price shock in 1979–80, and the simultaneous collapse of superpower détente shook western Europe. Yet its states remained stable, relatively prosperous, and increasingly bent on achieving greater economic and political unity within the European Community (EC). Then came the end of the Cold War, and rising uncertainty.

Britain, France, and Italy from the Seventies to the Nineties

Britain in the 1970s was still recognizably the class-ridden society of the past. Workers voted Labour; the middle and upper-middle classes supported Conservatives or Liberals. Ineffectual governments alternated, while Britain's slow relative economic decline continued. The bland Edward Heath of the Conservatives (1970–74) followed Labour's even blander Harold Wilson (1964–70); Labour returned with Wilson in 1974–76; Wilson's tougher successor James Callaghan hung on until 1979.

Then came an electoral and ultimately a social earthquake. Margaret Thatcher, the daughter of a provincial grocer, led the Conservatives to a landslide victory on a radical platform: the dismantling of inefficient state-owned industry and the freeing of Britain's markets from bureaucratic controls and high taxes. Thatcher's ready wit in debate, immense capacity for work, bloody-minded persistence, and political courage made her Britain's longest-ruling prime minister (1979–90) since the early nineteenth century. She temporarily crushed the upper-class "old-school-tie" elements within her own party, and forced competition and efficiency on Britain's obstinate labor unions and unimaginative businessmen. She crushed Argentina as well in a brief war when its military rulers foolishly seized the Falkland Islands from Britain in 1982.

She also largely accomplished her self-proclaimed mission of changing welfare-state Britain from a "dependent to a self-reliant society—from a give-it-to-me to a do-it-yourself nation." The state's share of GNP dropped. Britain's industrial productivity leapt upward. Strikes declined dramatically. Stockholders, by 1989, outnumbered union members for the first time in Britain's history. Families bought their state-owned apartments. Profits became socially respectable. Class ceased to be the decisive barrier to achievement; Thatcher at last brought to Britain the revolutionary "career open to talent." Yet her grip on power proved fragile amid the economic storms of the late 1980s. In late 1990, as Britain slid into a deep recession, her own party ungraciously dumped her. The background of Thatcher's successor nevertheless showed the depth of her mark on British politics. John Major, who went on to defeat Labour narrowly in 1991, came from a working-class family.

In France, voter boredom and the worldwide economic slowdown of the late 1970s brought a turning point similar to that in Britain, but from the Left rather than the Right. De Gaulle's first two successors as president of France, Georges Pompidou (1969–74) and Valéry Giscard d'Estaing (1974–81), were men of the moderate Right. But in 1981 the elder statesman of the Socialist party, François Mitterand, took power in coalition with a Communist Party that still held almost a sixth of the vote.

Yet by mid-decade, France's politics had set in a new mold. Mitterand and his party tried "socialist" economics with dismal results, then rapidly reversed course away from nationalized industry and state planning. They surrendered to local government many of the powers that Paris had wielded—since Napoleon I—through its representatives in the provinces, the prefects (see p. 601). Prosperity, its last-ditch defense of Stalinist dogma, and its stout support of the Soviet invasion of Afghanistan shrank the Communist Party toward electoral insignificance. A new anti-immigrant party, the National Front, rose on the far Right. And the longstanding gap between the parties of the political center—the moderate Right and the Socialists—narrowed dramatically. In 1986–88 Mitterand as president successfully "cohabited" with a prime minister and parliamentary majority drawn from his Center-Right opponents. The ideological gulf between great blocs on the Left and Right that had poisoned French politics since 1789–94 had finally closed—leaving the Socialists without a distinctive political message and dooming them to defeat in the 1993 elections. The Revolution, French historians and political commentators gratefully concluded, was over. France seemed at last to have become a stable industrial society.

Italy's road from the 1970s to the 1990s was less smooth than that of Britain or France. Northern Italy's dynamic private firms gave Italy more overall growth in the 1980s than France or West Germany, and made it by 1990 the world's seventh-largest economy, ahead of Britain and level with France. In the early 1980s the Italian state defeated the terrorists of the Left, the "Red Brigades" and their offshoots. But it also failed in other vital respects. The state's deadening hand controlled a larger share of industry and commerce than in any other major capitalist economy. Italy's politics revolved around the division of patronage in the government bureaucracies and state-controlled firms, the buying off of interest groups with pensions and bribes, and the financing of the governing parties through massive kickbacks by industry. In 1990, total national debt surpassed annual GNP.

And the state had less luck against a far greater threat than the Red Brigades: the criminal empires of the Mafia (Sicily), Camorra (Naples), and 'Ndrangheta (Calabria) that dominated the economics and politics of the South, diverting economic development aid and making their wishes known through terror-bombings and the assassination of government prosecutors, police officials, and politicians. By the early 1990s, the apparent complicity of the Christian Democratic ruling party with organized crime in the South and the exposure of widespread political corruption in the North utterly discredited the parliamentary regime that had ruled Italy since 1948. Italy's party system crumbled, as crusading prosecutors investigated or jailed national leaders of the Christian Democrats and Socialists. Soviet collapse also split the Communists, the traditional alternative to the ruling system, into would-be social democrats and diehard Leninists. And an anti-Southern backlash made the North-South divide, unbridged since Garibaldi and Cavour had annexed the South in 1860–61, into a political as well as a social and economic divide. A new regional party, the "Northern League," denounced Rome's bloated government bureaucracies, state subsidies for the South, southern migrants, non-European immigrants, and the very notion of Italy's unity. Electoral reforms demanded by an irate public seemed likely to split Italy into a North dominated by the Northern League, a Center under the ex-Communists, and a Christian Democratic South and islands. As so often in the past, Italy's survival seemed in doubt.

Germany Reunited

The end of détente in 1979 hit West Germany harder than it hit its European partners. Willy Brandt's successor as chancellor, Helmut Schmidt (1974–82), practically led NATO during the Carter era. The socialist "Iron Chancellor" was the main force behind the alliance's 1979 decision to counter—with the deployment in western Europe of U.S. Pershing and cruise missiles—the Soviet Union's ever-increasing SS-20 missile force. But Schmidt's own party, the SPD, proved less cooperative than NATO. It abandoned him and turned against the Western alliance; in vain Schmidt urged his critics to "stop behaving as if the Americans were your enemies and the Soviets your friends!" A new ecological and antinuclear party, the Greens, appealed to German nationalism—from the Left—against the United States. Hundreds of thousands of West Germans demonstrated repeatedly against U.S. nuclear weapons, but not against Soviet ones. The SS-20s seemed to be driving a wedge into the heart of NATO.

But West Germany's political center held. The small liberal party, the FDP, after concluding that the SPD was abandoning the Western alliance, abandoned its Socialist coalition partners and joined the Christian Democrats (CDU/CSU) in 1982. That move brought Schmidt's government down. Under the leadership of Helmut Kohl, a bear-like provincial figure whose enemies unfailingly underestimated him, the CDU/CSU-FDP coalition won the 1983 "missile election" decisively. In 1983–84 the first American missiles deployed—and the world did not end, as the protesters had insisted it would. Instead, NATO's apparent resolve to defend itself further demoralized the Soviet leadership.

Despite a talent for spectacular verbal gaffes that rivaled that of Ronald Reagan, Kohl dominated German politics into the 1990s. His durable FDP foreign minister, Hans-Dietrich Genscher, detected Soviet weakness earlier than most Western leaders. Genscher went to work with determination and tact, offering ever-increasing loans that tied Gorbachev to West German goodwill while flattering him shamelessly. By 1989–90, as the Soviet empire crumbled, Genscher and Kohl moved swiftly to secure the primary goal of West German foreign policy ever since 1949, the annexation of East Germany. George Bush offered firm support. By summer 1990, after a majority of East Germans had voted to join the West, Gorbachev was in no position to refuse.

But once East Germany had merged with West Germany on October 3, 1990,

The end of the East German economy.

and immigrants that flooded Germany at the Cold War's end, heightened the appeal of the far Right. Shaved heads, black leather, combat boots, racist slogans, and the murder of refugees, Jews, Gypsies, and Turkish immigrants became the order of the day in 1991–92 among disaffected working-class youth in both East and West Germany. Kohl belatedly mobilized against these new barbarians the police apparatus that had demolished leftist terrorism in the 1970s and early 1980s. The great majority of Germans rejected *Fremdenhass*—hatred of foreigners. West Germany's constitutional order had successfully resisted neo-Nazi revivals in the past. But the financial and social strains of reunification seemed likely to put that order to a lengthy test.

The European Community—An Emerging European Superpower?

Germany's trials were also the trials of its neighbors, thanks to the growing importance of the European Community. In 1986 France's bureaucrats at the EC's headquarters in Brussels launched a far-reaching initiative toward greater economic and ultimately political unity among the Community's twelve states. Their target was the creation by January 1, 1993, of a unified European market embracing 325 million people. The unspoken purpose of the initiative was to tame Germany for the future by embedding it in a unitary European economic and political structure.

Despite the large income gap between the EC's rich states (West Germany, France, and northern Italy) and poor states (Greece, Portugal, Ireland, and even Britain), and the slowness of some states to bend their legal and commercial systems to fit EC standards, the "single market" initiative enjoyed general approval. Other EC projects were less immediately successful. Germany's refugee crisis led it to freeze implementation of a 1990 agreement with France and seven other EC states to abolish passport checks along their mutual borders. EC attempts to peg Europe's currencies to the German mark led to a spectacular crisis in 1992 when

The power of symbols: the new German Right (1992).

the bill came due. Four-fifths of the DDR's industry was uncompetitive, fit only for the scrap heap. Pools of toxic waste dotted a bleak landscape beneath clouds of soft-coal smog. The work force, after 45 years of socialism, had lost the habits of initiative and efficiency that West Germans took for granted. It soon emerged that a wide cultural gap had opened between the two German societies of the Cold War era. To the "Wessis," their "Ossi" counterparts seemed caught in a time warp, a people at once incompetent, dim-witted, and lazy. To the "Ossis," their rich West German cousins seemed overworked, self-important know-it-alls.

Worse still, the economic recovery of the East seemed likely to take a generation, rather than the few years that Kohl had counted on in pushing for unification. The former DDR sucked in hundreds of billions of marks in West German aid but remained economically stagnant. Yet funding that aid forced on Bonn increasing budget deficits, higher taxes, high interest rates, and inflation. The German economy slowed amid fierce protests from Germany's suffering EC partners.

And East German unemployment, along with the million or more refugees

Germany's high interest rates, a consequence of the need to raise vast sums to save the former DDR, drove Germany's partners into a deepening recession.

Above all, the road seemed far from clear for implementing the EC's most far-reaching initiative, the Maastricht treaty of 1991. That agreement foresaw a single European currency, a central European bank and monetary policy, a common European citizenship, and a common defense and foreign policy before the year 2000. But the voters had other ideas; public hostility to bureaucratic centralization, growing dissatisfaction with western Europe's governing parties, and economic recession threatened to wreck Maastricht. Denmark's citizens at first voted against the treaty; France's approved it by a narrow majority; Britain's seemed hostile. Germans did not fancy exchanging the sacred German mark for European "Esperanto money." Nationalist intellectuals bemoaned the likely loss of national traditions and peculiarities. And Maastricht raised a further perplexity. Prospective new EC members, from Norway, Sweden, Finland and Austria to Turkey, Poland, and Hungary, pressed to join. Yet widening the EC by admitting further members might damage the Maastricht attempt to deepen unity among the original twelve members.

Finally, the external crises that accompanied the end of the Cold War showed how little the EC had changed Europe politically; it still remained a continent of national states. In the Second Gulf War (see the next section) the EC split; Britain, France, and Italy, although with wide differences in enthusiasm, sent forces to fight Iraq under United States command in 1990–91. Germany, whose industrialists had aided Saddam's nerve gas and missile programs, offered only cash. Belgium refused even to sell ammunition to its NATO ally, Britain. Saddam's threat to one of the EC's most vital interests, its supply of oil, failed to produce a common European policy.

In the savage conflicts between the peoples of Yugoslavia that broke out in summer 1991, the EC likewise split along lines ordained by history: France for the Serbs, Germany for the Slovenes and Croats. Britain vetoed military action: experience in Northern Ireland showed that it was easy to send troops in, but hard to get them out. Germany's postwar constitution restricted the EC's most powerful army to self-defense, and Germany's 1941–45 sponsorship of Croat genocide and its brutal occupation of Serbia ruled out any German military role in the Balkans. Serbs and Croats therefore simply ignored EC-brokered ceasefires; "EC threatens Serbia with lengthy debate," ran an ironic German headline. Soon the EC gratefully handed the Balkan wars over to the United Nations and the United States. Europe had the makings of a superpower, but whether its peoples were ready to sacrifice their historic traditions and national independence for the sake of unity was uncertain.

European unity at risk: frenzied London currency traders during the crisis of the European exchange rate mechanism, 1992.

WAR AND PEACE IN THE MIDDLE EAST, 1975–93

The final phase of the Cold War era was a time of ever-fiercer conflict in the Middle East. The Arab world seemed incapable of creating stable regimes except by force. Even the traditional monarchies, from Saudi Arabia and Jordan to Morocco, relied on all-pervasive internal security machines. In the secular states, families, clans, tribes, and sects fought one another for survival—the control of the army and the police. The failure of states without oil to generate enough economic growth to outpace their swelling populations undermined what little legitimacy those regimes possessed. From Algeria to Egypt and Jordan, Islamic zealots attacked their governments at the grass-roots. Israeli-Arab conflict continued. But a second strand of the new "Eastern Question," a series of conflicts between Arabs and Iranians, Arabs and Arabs, and Arabs and the West over the immense oil riches of the Persian Gulf generated violence that far surpassed the struggle for Palestine.

Israel and its Neighbors, 1975–93

A brief relaxation followed the Yom Kippur War of October 1973. Anwar Sadat of Egypt cut his last Soviet ties and aligned himself with the United States in 1976. In 1977 he broke all precedent and flew to Jerusalem in search of peace with Israel; Egypt was war-weary and economically desperate. At a 1978 summit meeting at Camp David near Washington, Carter pushed Menachem Begin of Israel into a peace agreement underwritten with lavish United States aid for both Egypt and Israel. In March 1979 Egypt and Israel signed a treaty that ended thirty years of war. Despite Sadat's assassination by Islamic militants in October 1981, Israel returned the last slice of Sinai to Egypt in 1982. At least one of the Middle East's many borders was momentarily at peace.

Peace did not descend on Israel's northern border. The PLO and its offshoots in their "state-within-a-state" in southern Lebanon repeatedly bombarded and raided northern Israel. Israel replied with air strikes and armored thrusts. In 1982 it intervened in the multi-cornered civil war that had simmered since 1975–76 between Lebanon's principal communities, the Maronite Christians, Sunni Moslems, Shiite Moslems, Druzes, and Palestinians. Israeli forces brushed the Syrians aside and drove for Beirut, seeking to stamp out the PLO for good.

Snipers and terrorists soon convinced Israel that it could not hold Lebanon; it withdrew in 1983. An ill-considered U.S. and European attempt to prop up the Maronite Christian-dominated Lebanese central government followed, but came to grief when suicide truck-bombers penetrated the U.S. and French perimeters and killed 241 U.S. Marines and 58 French paratroopers. The Marines and the European forces withdrew sheepishly in February–March 1984, while Lebanese Shiites took Western hostages and attacked targets in Europe. Western retreat left the mastery of Lebanon to Syria, if it could conquer it. Syria sought first to destroy all armed Palestinians not loyal to itself. Yasser Arafat, the chief political leader of the Palestinian movement, fled for his life. Many of his followers perished. Syria then moved into Beirut and by late 1990 had ended Lebanon's civil war.

PLO defeat in Lebanon did not mean the end of Palestinian militance. Israel had been from the beginning a demographic time bomb. Several hundred thousand Palestinians had remained within Israel's borders in 1948–49; by the 1980s they were twice as prolific as Israel's Jewish population. Israel acquired a further one million Arabs on the west bank of the Jordan and in the Gaza Strip through its great victories in the Six Days' War of 1967. By the mid–1980s, 3.6 million Jews faced 2.1 million Arabs within the post–1967 borders of "greater Israel." Demographic trends, if continued, would have given the Arabs close to a majority by 2005. And rapid population growth inevitably increased the numerical weight of the young, the most easily aroused and least tolerant segment of any population.

The Palestinians had no intention of waiting until the next century; they wanted all of Palestine now. In December 1987, the young of the occupied Gaza Strip took on Israel's police and army with rocks and firebombs in an uprising or "*Intifada*" that attracted global television coverage and sympathy. But then Palestinian support for Iraq and Iraqi defeat in the Second Gulf War (see pp. 968–70) undermined the *Intifada*'s reputation and morale, and the rise of Islamic extremist groups split the movement. By 1991–92 fighting among the PLO, the Islamic movement Hamas, and other Arab groups was killing more Palestinians than the Israeli army. Fear of Hamas ultimately drove Yasser Arafat, most of the PLO, and Israel together in a dramatic September 1993

Sadat, Carter, and Begin clasp hands at the signing of the Israeli-Egyptian peace treaty, March 26, 1979.

agreement to establish self-governing Palestinian enclaves in Gaza and the West Bank. Peace and a Palestinian state seemed conceivable at last, although violent rejection of the accord by Hamas and PLO splinter groups foreshadowed further bloodshed.

The Iranian Revolution and the First Gulf War, 1978–88

Anwar Sadat had died by assassination in 1981, a victim of the widespread upsurge of religious militance of which he had once remarked, "This is not Islam, this is madness." The source of that "madness" was the Islamic world's impotence in the face of nineteenth- and twentieth-century Western power, and the failure of the secular states of the Middle East to catch up with the West—or even to defeat the Jewish state, the West's Middle Eastern outpost. The main trigger of that "madness" was the 1978–79 revolution that convulsed Iran.

Shah Mohammed Reza Pahlavi, "King of Kings" and ruler of Iran from 1941 to 1979, was a man of large ambitions. He sought to use Iran's oil wealth to force his subjects into the twentieth century. Land reform, Western education, and the partial emancipation of women outraged the powerful landowning Shiite clergy. In 1963 one of the clergy's most influential figures, the Ayatollah Ruhollah Khomeini of the holy city of Qum, attacked the Shah and all his works. Khomeini went first to jail and then into exile. There he ceaselessly reviled the Shah as an "unclean" tool of the "satanic" West.

The Shah for his part relied increasingly on his secret police, the dreaded SAVAK. He faced the same desperate choice as other "modernizing" autocrats. The introduction of Western ideas and economic practices soon created an intelligentsia that rejected the autocracy—just as those same ideas and practices alienated or shrank the traditional sectors of society on which the autocracy rested. The Shah nevertheless pressed on. With Kissinger's encouragement, he took over from Britain the role of lord of the Persian Gulf after 1971. In 1973–74 he led OPEC's

Israel in 1993

assault on the world economy, and used Iran's fabulous oil profits to buy the latest in tanks, ships, and aircraft from the United States and Europe.

But the Shah failed to spread the profits from the oil boom widely enough to defuse the resentments of his urban lower classes. His apparent sponsorship of the invasion of Iran by European and United States goods and customs, from alcohol to tailored blue jeans for women, outraged the devout. The intelligentsia deplored his refusal to offer them parliamentary government. In January 1978 the Shiite clergy led riots at Qum against the regime. Disorder spread across Iran. The Shah, ill with cancer and irresolute, failed to crush the unrest while his conscript soldiers were still loyal. In the Teheran riots of September 1978, the army began

The *Intifada*.

Militant Islam: Religious
extremists assassinate President
Sadat, October 1981.

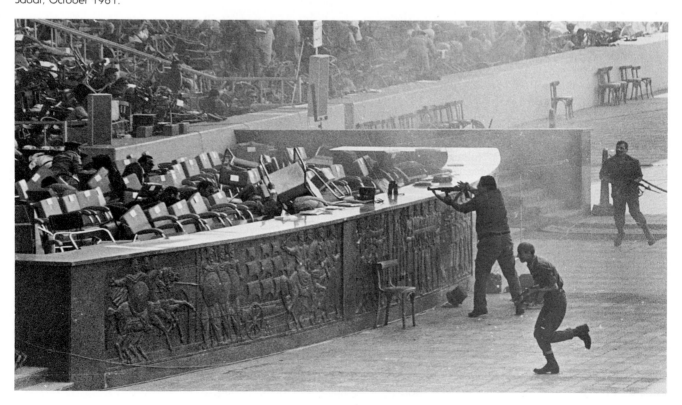

to crack. Khomeini's unarmed zealots taunted the troops to make them martyrs; the troops deserted or shot their sergeants and officers. The Shah's nerve shattered along with a cherished illusion: that his people loved him. In January 1979, he fled.

Khomeini arrived from Paris—a stern medieval figure alighting from a jumbo jet—to sweep a feeble provisional government from office. He then established a form of government never before seen, a theocratic "Islamic Republic" under the rule of Shiite clergy. Student militants, revolutionary committees, "Revolutionary Guards," and the shaven-headed zealots of Hezbollah (the "Party of God") enforced political conformity. They also ruthlessly reimposed Islamic dress on Iran's women. Teheran crowds enthusiastically chanting "Death to America" filled the West's television screens. When Carter allowed the dying Shah to visit New York in October 1979 for cancer treatment, Khomeini's "Islamic students" violated diplomatic tradition and seized the United States embassy in Teheran with its staff of over fifty.

Khomeini may not have originated the embassy coup, but he swiftly exploited it. What better way to mobilize domestic support, dramatize the Islamic Revolution abroad, and humiliate the "Great Satan" America than to hold its diplomats hostage? The Iranians had learned from North Vietnam, which had tied American negotiators in knots over the release of U.S. prisoners. The American television networks rose to the occasion. Soon each evening news broadcast began with an announcement of the number of days the hostages had been imprisoned.

The crisis placed intolerable pressure on Carter; 1980 was an election year. Iran's position between the Soviet Union and the Gulf deterred him from taking military action, lest Moscow use United States intervention as a pretext to expand its Afghan bridgehead southward. In April 1980 Carter nevertheless launched an ineptly planned hostage rescue mission that broke down in the Iranian desert; fierce interservice rivalry and Carter's eccentric insistence on the *minimum* use of force

had made failure likely. The hostage crisis decided the 1980 election against Carter; Iran packed the hostages onto an Air France jet as Ronald Reagan took the oath of office in January 1981.

By then Khomeini had a greater and more immediate worry than the "Great Satan." Like other revolutionary leaders before him, he aspired to world revolution—and he repeatedly called for Islamic upheavals throughout the Middle East. Among his preferred targets was Saddam Hussein, ruthless and fanatical Sunni ruler of the Shiite majority of neighboring Iraq. The Iraqi dictator, apparently thinking that revolutionary chaos had undermined Iranian military power, in return launched an armored thrust into Iran's oilfields in September 1980. Iran's 3 to 1 advantage in population soon began to tell. This was no war of maneuver between sophisticated opponents, but a tropical Somme 1916, a demolition derby of military ineptitude.

In early 1982 Iraq lost the oilfields it had seized. By 1985–86 it was close to losing Basra, its second city after Baghdad. Iranian "Revolutionary Guards," many of them adolescents carrying toylike plastic "keys to Paradise" furnished by the clergy, pressed the attack at immense cost. "Fountains of blood" foamed with red dye at Teheran cemeteries in macabre commemoration of the fallen. Religious war, an "Islamic" successor to SAVAK, and mass executions silenced opponents and doubters.

Iraq responded to defeat by appealing to other Arab regimes for aid against the Iranian Shiite menace. If Iraq went under, Kuwait and Saudi Arabia might follow. Iran secured clandestine assistance from Israel, which considered Saddam Hussein a worse threat than Khomeini. Israel also struck a blow against Iraq's nuclear ambitions by sending its F-16 fighter-bombers to destroy Iraq's French-built reactor in June 1981.

As Iran advanced, Iraq in desperation expanded the war by air and sea. It drenched Iranian troops and Kurdish villages with mustard gas, nerve gas, and hydrogen cyanide. Its air force attacked Iranian cities and the oil exports that fi-

The return of the Ayatollah: Khomeini in Teheran, February 1979.

nanced Iran's war. Iran in reply struck at international shipping bound for the oil ports of Iraq's Persian Gulf allies and launched missiles at Baghdad in the manner of Hitler's V-2 bombardment of London in 1944. Iraqi missiles in turn flattened entire blocks in Teheran and Qum.

In 1987, Washington responded to an appeal from Kuwait to escort its tankers through the Gulf. Britain, France, and Italy likewise committed ships to the Gulf. In spring 1988 the Iranians imprudently challenged the U.S. fleet and lost much of their navy in a flurry of U.S. cruise missiles. The Western navies hemmed Iran in, while Iraqi offensives forced a bitter Khomeini to accept a ceasefire in July–August 1988. The First Gulf War had cost up to a million dead and had lasted longer than any other twentieth century war between major states.

The Second Gulf War: Iraq against the World, 1990–91

Victory over the hated Iranians inspired Saddam Hussein to further conquests. By profession a political assassin and secret policeman, he had held undisputed power since 1979 by killing all potential rivals in the army and the ruling Ba'th ("Arab Renaissance") Party. His regime, like those of his models, Hitler and Stalin, rested on terror with an admixture of propaganda. It had to, for its ethnic-religious base, the Sunni Arabs in Iraq's center, was a mere fifth of Iraq's population. Dissident Kurds made up another fifth and Shiite Arabs the other three-fifths. Saddam's ultimate aim was to unite all Arabs from Morocco to Iran into a super-power based on control of oil, armed with nuclear weapons, and capable of destroying Israel and defying the "imperialist" West. Iraq, the self-proclaimed "Prussia of the Arabs," was for Saddam the foreordained core of that coming superpower.

Saddam had played skillfully on Western and Arab hopes and fears during his eight-year war with Iran. He posed as the protector of Saudi Arabia, Sunni Islam, and the oil of the Gulf against the Iranian Shiite threat. The Gulf Arabs responded with long-term loans; the West sold him arms and military technology that included equipment for his secret nerve gas, ballistic missile, and nuclear bomb projects. France, West Germany, Switzerland, Holland, Britain, and the United States were conspicuous suppliers. Saddam's longstanding friends in Moscow also provided arms and military advice. Within a decade or less, Iraq would be ready.

But Saddam lacked the necessary patience. In spring 1990 he boasted publicly of his chemical weapons and declared that he could "make the fire eat up half of Israel." He also convinced himself that no power stood between him and mastery of the Gulf. His army was the world's fourth largest, and decadent America would never accept "10,000 dead in one battle" to stop him. On August 2, 1990, on the pretext of settling a financial and territorial dispute, his armored divisions invaded and brutally occupied his small neighbor, Kuwait.

Like Kim Il-Sung before him, Saddam had gone too far. Iraq already owned a tenth of the world's oil reserves. After conquering Kuwait, it controlled almost a fifth. Had Saddam's tanks continued southward and seized the Saudi oilfields— as they seemed poised to do—he would control 45 percent of the world's oil and more than two-thirds of the Gulf's. He could then dictate the world price of oil and extort limitless deliveries of arms and technology from the West. The resulting economic chaos might plunge the world into depression and destroy the domestic political stability of the industrial democracies.

The Americans once again proved unpredictable. George Bush, with backstage prodding from Margaret Thatcher, answered the threat from Saddam that United States and European policies had helped create. Despite widespread press criticism of his daring commitment, Bush pledged almost immediately that "this [aggression] will not stand." He convinced Saudi Arabia to accept the deployment on its territory of a quarter of a million U.S. and allied troops. With Soviet support guaranteed by Gorbachev's desperate need for Western aid, Bush led the U.N. to declare Saddam's annexation of Kuwait "null and void." Through the U.N. he imposed on Iraq economic sanctions and a blockade enforced by the U.S. and allied navies. His Gulf coalition ultimately included 37 states, with troop contingents or ships and aircraft from much of NATO, Hungary, Poland, the Gulf Arabs, Egypt, Morocco, Pakistan, Bangladesh, and even the Syria of Hafez al-Assad. Only Jordan, Yemen, Cuba, and the Palestinians stood with Saddam.

When Saddam failed to withdraw from Kuwait, Bush ordered a further 250,000 American troops—including armored divisions no longer needed for a Third World War in central Europe—to the Gulf. Britain sent 43,000 soldiers, sailors, and airmen, and France 16,000. On November 29, 1990, the United States pushed through the U.N. Security Council a resolution authorizing the use of "all means necessary" to liberate Kuwait if Saddam did not withdraw by January 15, 1991. That resolution, and Saddam's continued defiance, checkmated opponents of war in the United States. Economic sanctions might evict Saddam from Kuwait at some distant future date, or they might not. U.S. air power and armor clearly would, although some feared the possible human cost. Bush pledged that the United States would use its full power from the outset rather than the "graduated pressure" that had failed in Vietnam. The U.S. Senate endorsed the U.N. resolution by a small majority, the House of Representatives by a far larger one. Saddam, perhaps deceived by memories of Vietnam and by the images of antiwar protest outside the White House conveyed by global television, answered with defiance.

On January 16–17, 1991, the first moonless night of the new year, the U.S. Air Force and Navy struck at Baghdad and at targets throughout Iraq. Effortless technological and tactical superiority stripped away Iraq's many-layered air defenses, wrecked chemical and nuclear plants, broke Saddam's communications with his ill-trained and poorly led army, and starved that army of food, water, and ammunition before bombing much of it to shreds. Saddam replied with a missile bombardment of Israel aimed at turning

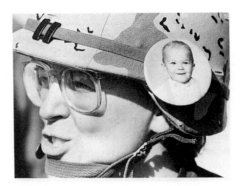

America in the Gulf: one of the 35,000 U.S. women who served in the war against Saddam Hussein.

the war into an Arab-Israeli struggle and splitting the Western-Arab coalition. But Israel's leaders refused to rise to the bait; they did not retaliate against Iraq. Not even ecological terrorism—the burning of Kuwait's oil wells and the dumping of crude oil into the Gulf at Saddam's orders—halted the allied air campaign. On February 23 the coalition launched a long-prepared ground attack that swept by surprise around the Iraqi army's unprotected

"First we're going to cut it off, and then we're going to kill it." General Colin L. Powell, chairman of the Joint Chiefs of Staff, predicts that the United States will destroy Saddam's invasion force in Kuwait (January 23, 1991).

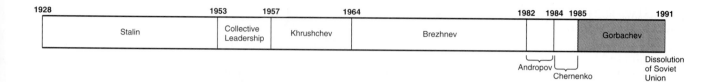

| 1928 | | 1953 | 1957 | 1964 | | 1982 | 1984 | 1985 | | 1991 |

Stalin — Collective Leadership — Khrushchev — Brezhnev — Andropov — Chernenko — Gorbachev — Dissolution of Soviet Union

desert flank, drove it from Kuwait, and pinned its battered remnants against Basra. U.S. casualties, at 148 killed in action, were wildly disproportionate to the many thousands of Iraqi dead.

Yet at the very end, Bush held back. He apparently feared that demolishing Iraq entirely would make Iran the master of the Gulf. Saudi and Turkish fears that Iraq's disintegration would create troublesome Kurdish and Shiite ministates on their borders also influenced U.S. policy. Bush spared Saddam—after the U.S. Air Force had destroyed several bunkers where the Iraqi leader was thought to be hiding. The ground war ended after 100 hours, leaving Saddam enough tanks and helicopters to put down bloodily the risings by Kurds and Shiites that immediately followed the coalition's victory. A belated U.S. and NATO humanitarian mission in northern Iraq helped save hundreds of thousands of Kurdish refugees. An even more belated "no-fly zone" shielded the Shiites in the south from Saddam's air force. U.N. inspectors picked over the remains of Iraq's chemical, missile, and nuclear projects, and economic sanctions remained in effect. Yet Saddam remained defiantly in power, while his Iranian neighbor rearmed with an eye to future opportunities. The United States and its allies had restored order to the Gulf for a few years.

NEW WORLD DISORDER

The "New World Order" that Bush proclaimed would follow the Cold War proved long on novelty but short on order. From 1947–48 until 1989–90 the superpowers had generally maintained discipline among their respective clients. They had also avoided—with the exception of Khrushchev's adventure in Cuba—direct

challenges to each other's vital interests. Before Soviet collapse, Saddam would probably have lacked the freedom to challenge the West for control of oil. The United States would undoubtedly also have hesitated before attacking a Soviet client so close to the USSR's borders. The end of the Cold War ended all such restraints. And as relations between Moscow and Washington thawed, so too did ancient European quarrels. States and peoples reveled in their newly recovered freedom. Some used it to seek conquest or revenge. And new mechanisms for restraining those violent impulses seemed absent.

Nationalism, the Final Stage of Communism

History had divided Europe into three bands or zones. In west and west-central Europe, great wars and the building of nation-states had settled—one way or another—all major religious-ethnic quarrels. In east-central Europe and the Balkans, the second zone, the two world wars and Hitler's genocide had only partially disentangled historic patterns of mixed settlement. Finally, the rubble of the Soviet multinational empire made up a third zone in which colonial Great Russian outposts planted by the tsars or by Stalin overlaid an already complex ethnic-religious pattern ordained by history.

The quarrels and potential quarrels of east-central Europe intensified from north to south. Soviet collapse stranded between independent Lithuania and Poland a Russian military enclave around Kaliningrad (formerly Königsberg) in what until 1945 had been East Prussia. Poland had seized and held Lithuania's capital, Vilnius, throughout the interwar period, and a sizable Polish minority remained in Lithuania. Poles and Germans coexisted un-

Saddam Hussein, in a favorite pose, celebrates the election defeat of George Bush, November 1992.

easily along the Oder-Neisse line that Stalin had laid down in 1945. Czechoslovakia split into separate Czech and Slovak states in 1992–93, leaving Slovakia with a disgruntled Hungarian minority of more than half a million. Hungary looked to its minorities not only in Slovakia, but also in Serbia and above all in Rumania, where the 2.1 million Hungarians of Transylvania lamented Romanian maltreatment that stretched back to 1918–20.

The quarrels that divided the peoples of Yugoslavia generated the greatest immediate violence. There the old border between the eastern and western Roman empires had become the border between Catholicism and Orthodoxy, between Croats and Slovenes on the one hand and Serbs on the other. Ottoman conquest had imposed an overlay of Islam. The many nationalities and groups each regarded their neighbors as mortal enemies; usually they were correct. In the interwar era, Serb royal dictatorship had welded them together in a miniature multinational empire. In the Cold War era, Tito's Communist autocracy and fear of Soviet invasion had done likewise. But like Stalin, Tito was mortal. He died in 1980, and the collapse of Communism and of the Soviet threat in 1989–91 freed Yugoslavia's peoples—for civil war. Ex-Communist leaders, Franjo Tudjman of Croatia and Slobodan Milosevic of Serbia, played the nationalist card. Tudjman denied that Hitler's Croat puppet-state had massacred more than half a million Serbs in 1941–45. Milosevic announced that "borders . . . are always dictated by the strong."

The Serbs were indeed strong. Their population, at roughly 9 million, was larger and more widely scattered than that of the other peoples within Yugoslavia's borders. They also controlled most of the Yugoslav army's artillery and tanks. Fear of a repetition of the massacres of 1941–45 and ambition for a "Greater Serbia" led them to take the offensive against Slovenia and Croatia when fighting broke out in June 1991 between Croat police and Serb militiamen. Slovenia defeated the Serbs and asserted its independence, thanks to geography and smuggled antitank rockets. Croatia fought doggedly but lost the

The Ethnic Groups of East-Central Europe

	Majority presence (50% or more)	Minority presence
Poles		Po
Czechs		—
Slovaks		Sk
Hungarians		Hu
Rumanians		—
Bulgarians		—
Slovenes		—
Croats		Cr
Serbs		Sb
Muslims		Mu
Montenegrins		—
Albanians		Al
Macedonians		Ma
Turks		Tk
Germans	—	Ge
Greeks	—	Gk
Ukrainians	—	Uk

No majority present, but more than one minority.

third of its territory that was partially inhabited by Serbs. Milosevic's army and Serb freebooters massacred, raped, and drove Croats from their homes in the conquered areas. Croats massacred Serbs when they could catch them.

In April 1992 Yugoslavia's breakup forced independence upon Bosnia-Hercegovina, a region split among Moslem Slavs, Serbs, and Croats. Serb offensives and massacres then "cleansed" two-thirds of Bosnia of Moslems and Croats. The Serbs scornfully ignored repeated but purely verbal protests from the

Europeans, the U.N., and Bush's Democratic successor, President Bill Clinton; they remained confident that no outside power would go to war to stop them. More than 150,000 died and 3 million fled their homes in the first two years of this Third Balkan War—by far the most massive violence in Europe since 1945. And the precarious Serb position in the southern province of Kosovo, historic "cradle of Serb civilization" but inhabited overwhelmingly by Albanian Moslems, threatened further war with Albania and with other Balkan states.

Europe's easternmost zone of ethnic-religious conflict was almost equally active. Soviet collapse stranded almost 26 million Great Russian colonists outside Russia and more than 27 million non-Russians inside it. Great Russian outposts, from Estonia and Latvia to Moldova to the

Crimea to Kazakhstan, coexisted uneasily with newly independent peoples divided from them by language and religion. Fighting tore Moldova. Festering disputes between Russia and Ukraine over ownership of the ex-Soviet Black Sea Fleet and of the Crimea threatened for the future. In the Caucasus, Georgians fought their national minorities and each other. Armenia and Azerbaijan battered each other over enclaves within their territories inhabited by minorities from the other. The shadowy "Confederation of Independent States" had neither the will nor the force to reimpose order.

Only Great Russian nationalism could do that. Communism's collapse left it the only idea—the only imperial ideology—that might claim to unite the vast spaces stretching from Poland to the Pacific. And as in the past the fall of empires generated

The Soviet Successor States

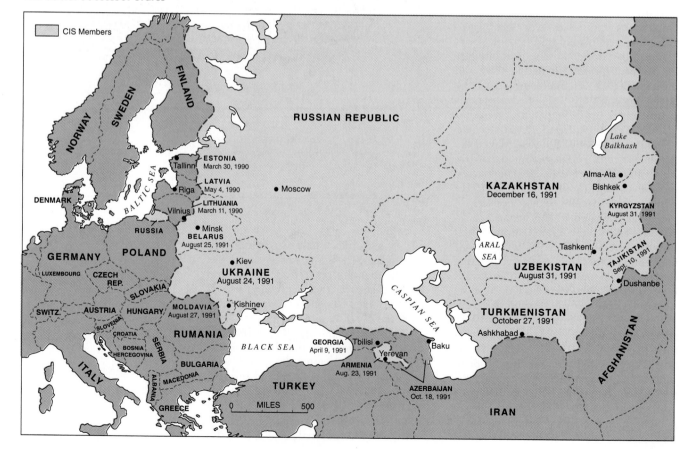

towering resentments. Great Russian nationalist prophets spun vengeful anti-Semitic and anti-Western conspiracy theories to explain the empire's collapse. Radical newspapers quoted Hitler with approval, and demanded a ruler with Stalin's iron hand. Ex-Communist ideologues demanded alliance with China—and support for the Orthodox Serbs—against the West. Uncertainty, inflation, unemployment, the suffering of Great Russians stranded outside Russia, and the separatist agitation of the non-Russian nationalities locked within it unsettled a politically naive population. Powerful interests and structures inherited from the Soviet "old regime," from the nuclear-armed armed forces and the KGB to military-industry, repeatedly embarrassed Gorbachev's successor in the Kremlin, Boris Yeltsin of the Russian Republic. If the Russian democratic experiment collapsed, Great Russian nationalism might yet seek to re-establish the empire of the tsars and of Stalin.

New Worlds Emerging

Prospects for controlling the bloodshed and disorder of the post-Cold War world seemed to rest in part with a revived United Nations. From Angola to Cambodia to Bosnia, U.N. observers and U.N.-flagged peacekeeping forces sought earnestly—and often vainly—to bridge mortal enmities. Other post-Communist struggles, such as the collapse of Liberia and of Ethiopia, the tribal wars that engulfed Afghanistan in the wake of Soviet withdrawal, and the endless civil war and famine in the Sudan, seemed so intractable that the United Nations largely ignored them.

The United Nations was and remained a bureaucracy, not a power. Only the military forces of the great powers could repel attempts by "the strong" to dictate their borders, or force peace on ethnic groups bent on mutual slaughter. The U.N.'s contribution to world order appeared to depend in part on how much its richer member states were willing to pay—in money and in blood—to enforce that order. National sovereignty

"Borders . . . are always dictated by the strong": A Serb patrol searches for Bosnian Moslems, 1993.

also remained a barrier to action. All states, but especially non-Western states, looked on interference in their "internal affairs" with continued suspicion. The United Nations still functioned mainly as a forum for agreement—when its member states did agree—on issues such as the protection of the environment and famine relief.

And the United Nations was powerless against a further side-effect of Soviet collapse, the accelerated spread of deadly technologies that promised to multiply many-fold the dangers of ethnic-religious conflict. At the very moment that Western governments and industrialists began to realize the risks they had run in arming Saddam, the defense establishment and black market of the defunct Soviet Union opened an immense bankruptcy sale. Amid the ruins of the Soviet empire, hard currency could buy virtually anything, from scientific and technical brainpower to tactical nuclear warheads, radioactive materials, submarines, missiles, advanced aircraft, and tanks. The Soviet Union, China, and North Korea had long sold ballistic missiles to powers such as Iran, Iraq, Syria, Libya, and Egypt. Algeria, Libya, Iran and North Korea concealed nuclear ambitions of varying intensities. India and Pakistan had both nuclear weapons and missiles to carry them; Pakistan allegedly owed its bomb design to China. Brazil and Argentina, which had also helped arm Saddam, waited in the wings. China loomed on the horizon as the Asian superpower of the twenty-first century—or as an unparalleled source of chaos. All had presumably learned from Saddam's lack of patience and stealth.

The world that faced this explosive mixture of new technologies and old hatreds was by the early 1990s so closely knit that a shock to any of its key economies might drag the others down as well. Computers and instantaneous communications had welded the world's stock, currency, and commodity exchanges into a seamless 24-hour world market. The electronic transfer of financial information and funds sent trillions of dollars, marks, yen, and lesser currencies sloshing from market to market. Automatic stock and futures trading driven by computer programs turned market hiccups into jagged ascents or hair-raising plunges.

Since 1944–45 the United States had acted as stabilizer for the entire system. But by the 1980s the rise of Japan and Europe, the fiscal hangover from Reagan's debt binge, and the failure of U.S. primary and secondary education to keep pace with competing societies had shrunk America's margin of superiority. The passage of world economic leadership from Britain to America in 1914–44 had been stormy. World depression or the division of the world into hostile economic blocks—Japan and Asia, German-Europe, and the Americas—might also accompany the relative loss of U.S. economic power. Yet for a moment, Soviet collapse left the United States in a stronger relative position than at any time since the 1920s. For good or ill, it still surpassed or even dwarfed possible rivals in all three dimensions of

power: overall economic strength, political leadership, and military might.

TOWARD THE TWENTY-FIRST CENTURY

Broad and swift scientific and technological advance paralleled the expansion of the world economy under the umbrella of U.S. power after 1945. Simultaneously, the proliferation of knowledge in innumerable highly specialized scientific and scholarly subdisciplines posed a threat already visible in the nineteenth century—that educated people, each locked in the jargon of a specialty, would cease to speak a common language. Especially in the social sciences and humanities, skepticism about the possibility of establishing truth corroded all established standards. And as the Americanization of the world through television proceeded, high culture retreated into a cloistered existence in the universities.

The Thrust of Science and Technology

"Command science," the systematic mobilization by governments of scientific knowledge for a specific purpose, came into its own after 1945. The Manhattan Project had shown the way. Its successors were the postwar programs of the great powers that created thermonuclear bombs, and atomic reactors to generate electricity and to power submarines and surface ships.

Yet by the 1980s reactor accidents had lessened enthusiasm for nuclear power. A power reactor at Three Mile Island in Pennsylvania partially melted in 1979; its containment vessel held, and only small amounts of radioactivity reached the atmosphere. The far worse Soviet nuclear accident at Chernobyl in 1986 seemed a portent of the limits of technology. The many similarly constructed reactors still functioning in the former Soviet territories struck many Western experts as potential time bombs. Yet increasing fear of ecological catastrophe through nuclear power intersected with claims that burning coal and oil would lead to a dangerous rise in global temperatures through the "greenhouse effect."

Command science was also the instrument of the conquest of space—a dream entertained since the seventeenth century, but now suddenly practical. The Soviet effort that launched *Sputnik* in 1957 put Yuri Gagarin into Earth orbit in 1961. Kennedy responded with a pledge to put an American on the moon by the end of the decade. The National Aeronautics and Space Administration (NASA), which Eisenhower had established after *Sputnik,* assembled the largest community of scientific talent ever mobilized for a single purpose, and spent up to $40 billion. On July 20, 1969, Neil Armstrong of the United States became the first human to walk on the Moon. The Soviet Union stuck closer to Earth; its space program was military in inspiration and priorities. After its moon voyage triumph, NASA bet virtually its entire shrinking budget on one program, the reusable "space shuttle." The explosion after launch of the shuttle *Challenger* in January 1986 temporarily paralyzed both civilian and military space programs. NASA ultimately pressed on in hopes of building a permanent orbital space station and sending missions to Mars in the twenty-first century.

Command science, despite its magnitude and its many spin-offs, was only a small part of the continuing scientific and technological revolution. During and after the Second World War, new materials came into their own. Plastics and glass fiber increasingly replaced steel and other metals. Composites of plastic and boron or carbon fiber, lighter and stronger than steel, became available in the 1970s. Titanium, almost 50 percent lighter than steel and with a higher melting point than aluminum, found innumerable uses in supersonic jet aircraft, nuclear reactors, and submarines.

But the most spectacular advances—a wave of innovation as potentially powerful as the "second industrial revolution" of steel, chemicals and electricity—came in electronics and biology. Semiconductors, materials such as germanium and silicon that conducted current only hesi-

tatingly at room temperature, had been a subject of curiosity since the primitive germanium diodes of the early radio receivers. In 1947 William Shockley, John Bardeen, and Walter H. Brattain of Bell Laboratories invented the transistor, the first semiconductor amplifying device. By the early 1960s the transistor had evolved into the integrated circuit, or "chip," consisting of innumerable microscopic transistors linked in complex patterns and imprinted on a silicon wafer.

The arrival of the transistor coincided with the birth, speeded by wartime cryptographic needs, of the new discipline of computing. Its theoretical roots reached back into the nineteenth century; its two leading theoreticians were Alan Turing (1912–54) of Cambridge, who played a leading role in Britain's decipherment of the *Wehrmacht*'s supposedly uncrackable codes, and the Hungarian refugee physicist-mathematician John von Neumann (1903–57) of Princeton. By the 1960s their successors had created theories, computer languages, and machines capable of the unimaginably complex and rapid calculations needed to model thermonuclear explosions, solve engineering problems through simulation, predict the paths of space vehicles, guide missiles and robots, and store and manipulate ever-greater masses of information.

From 1959 to the 1990s, chips and therefore computers doubled in computing power each year. The cost per transistor decreased over twenty years by a factor of more than *1 million.* That pace of advance showed no signs of slowing. As chip fabricators approached the apparent limits that silicon places on computer speed, those limits receded, and other faster materials such as gallium arsenide emerged. The invention in the 1960s of lasers, devices that generated focused light of a single frequency, added to the potential of semiconductors. Lasers offered innumerable applications from surgery to weaponry, and allowed long-distance transmission of information through glass fibers at densities far exceeding the limits of electrical or microwave circuits.

Potentially even more powerful than semiconductors and lasers were

The structure of life: the computer display of an automatic DNA-sequencing machine.

the new techniques of molecular biology. In 1951–53 James D. Watson of the United States and Francis H. C. Crick of Britain jointly deciphered the "double helix," the complex molecular structure of deoxyribonucleic acid, or DNA, the material in which cells encode their genetic information. That research led eventually to the beginnings of an understanding of evolution at the molecular level and to the manipulation of plant and animal genes to make bizarre hybrids that crossed species lines. The mapping of the entire human genetic code—all 100,000 genes, each consisting of 1,500 subunits—appeared a realistic prospect by the end of the century.

Molecular biology opened immense possibilities for good, for the eradication of most diseases and the understanding and possible slowing of aging. It provided the most powerful weapons for fighting the great viral pandemic of the 1980s and 1990s, AIDS (Acquired Immune Deficiency Syndrome). The virus, against which conventional medical techniques were almost as powerless as those of the Middle Ages against the Black Death, spread mainly through sexual intercourse and the sharing of unsterilized drug hypodermics by addicts. By the early 1990s it threatened tens of millions of victims around the world.

But together with hope and life, the new biology also appeared to offer death, through biological weapons of unprecedented subtlety and power—and transfiguration, through "human perfectibility" in a quite literal sense: the genetic reengineering of the human species. Nuclear weapons had given humanity a chance to annihilate itself, but also the long European peace after 1945. Molecular biology held out the prospect both of healing and of a new kind of annihilation, the transformation of humanity into something less or more than human.

The Disintegration of Scholarship and High Culture

In the realm of ideas, specialization and the triumph of the relativism that had flourished since the Enlightenment furthered the fragmentation already visible as the twentieth century began. Especially in the Anglo-Saxon countries, most philosophers abandoned speculation. The new "analytical" philosophers scorned metaphysics—the exploration through imagination of the nature of existence. They sought instead what Bertrand Russell (1872–1970), an early leader of the analytical school, described as the "unattainable ideal of impeccable knowledge." Their method was the close examination of language and meaning through logic and mathematics. Their quest led them to narrow increasingly the domain of truth to establish certainty.

Ultimately they so narrowed the domain of truth that it vanished. The reclusive Ludwig Wittgenstein (1889–1951), perhaps the greatest of twentieth-century philosophers, abandoned all attempts to describe the world and retreated acerbically into the analysis of language. His taunt that "the belief in the causal nexus is superstition" denigrated all forms of knowledge about nature and human affairs. But as Wittgenstein's eighteenth-century percursor David Hume had pointed out, the philosopher's study was the place for skepticism. Survival in the hard outside world that Wittgenstein shunned still required such "superstitions" as cause and effect.

On the Continent, after Heidegger, traditional forms of philosophy still prospered. The Left Bank sage Jean-Paul Sartre (1905–80) was Heidegger's principal heir. After 1945, Sartre's "existentialism" became a cult phenomenon from Paris to San Francisco that endured until the 1960s. Its basis was Heidegger's call for "authenticity" and his denial of a rational foundation for values. For Sartre, individuals were utterly free to choose their values. Any denial that such freedom existed was inauthentic, was an evasion of responsibility, was "bad faith." But Sartre offered no advice on what values to choose, for advice would constrict freedom and constitute "bad faith." He merely commanded choice, for only heroic choice was "authentic." Heidegger had chosen Nazism. Sartre, whose only gestures against Nazism had been literary, chose Marxism, which he described as the "unsurpassable philosophy of our time."

French intellectual fashions change as rapidly and wield as powerful an influence throughout the West as the hemlines of Paris designers. After the collapse of the May 1968 student revolt that Sartre's doctrines of heroic commitment had helped inspire, new preoccupations emerged. The most important was an intellectual tendency known as "structuralism." It had originated in linguistics between the world wars and thence had spread to anthropology, literary criticism, history, sociology, psychoanalysis, and philosophy. Its lowest common denominator was the claim that the *structure* of a language, myth, or literary or historical "text" was a more fundamental characteristic than other attributes such as its origin, history, purpose, or content.

In linguistics, its point of origin, structuralism was largely the product of the insights of the Swiss scholar Ferdinand de Saussure (1857–1913), who suggested that meaning was a product of oppositions or differences between the "signs" that made up language. Meaning was thus entirely relative. "Signs" had meaning only by virtue of their structural relationship to other "signs." An influential American scholar, Noam Chomsky (1928–), added a fruitful conjecture of his own—that *all* languages shared a common "deep structure" that grew out of the structure of the human mind itself. Chomsky's apparent biological determinism clashed with his politics; a combative Left-utopian, he rejected the "capitalist" West and implicitly demanded faith in the perfectibility of humanity, a perfectibility doubtful indeed if the human mind was as "hard-wired" as Chomsky the linguist assumed.

In anthropology, Claude Lévi-Strauss (1908–), investigated the myths of Brazilian and American Indians as clues to the structures of the "primitive mind." Structure was primary, content far less important; meaning existed only as part of a structure. Critics like Roland Barthes (1915–80) carried similar notions into literary criticism. The literary "text" became a subject for a decipherment or "deconstruction" that deliberately ignored the "text's" author, historical context, literary excellence or lack of it, and commonsense meaning. For the structuralist critic, the interpreter not the author gave meaning. That doctrine allowed the interpreter to give a "text" any meaning at all. And the implication that all "texts" were of equal value frequently produced bizarre results. Structuralist critics examined with deep seriousness works that few non-structuralists even considered to be literature.

Historians, beginning in France, took a Lévi-Straussian interest in the "collective mentalities" of past social groups. Analysis of social or intellectual "structures" began to supersede narrative. The study of long-term change—climatic, economic, and demographic—triumphed for a time over short-term "event history" and the history of ideas. Devotees of economics subjected small portions of the past to "cliometric" statistical examination. Historians increasingly though not always wisely borrowed methods from sociology and psychology. Marxism revived, until the ruin of Soviet "real socialism" left many of its adherents disoriented. For the first time in history, historians wrote works incomprehensible to the educated public.

Structuralism and the disciplines it influenced mirrored the disorientation of the age. If *all* truths were relative, tolerance even of bizarre claims was the highest virtue. In the humanities and social sciences few dared affirm that some "truths" were less relative than others and that the test of all generalizations was confrontation with empirical evidence. The natural sciences proved more resistant to bewilderment; experiment remained the test of truth or falsehood, and mathematics offered an empirically effective means of describing nature.

In the arts, disintegration was almost total as the century drew toward its end. In the visual arts the last undisputed master was Pablo Picasso (1881–1973). In the 1940s, with Europe at war, abstract expressionist painters such as Jackson Pollock and Willem de Kooning seized artistic leadership for New York. Yet some American experiments, such as the "pop art" of the 1960s that took its images from advertising, appeared almost self-consciously sterile. In architecture, the "international style" persisted, although architects increasingly adorned their buildings with "post-modernist" classical flourishes. In music, few composers after Igor Stravinsky (1882–1971) and Sergei Prokofieff (1891–1953) commanded mass audiences. Dissonance and disjointed rhythms bored or repelled all except specialists. Symphony orchestras and opera companies made do with the time-honored works of Mozart, Beethoven, Wagner, and other eighteenth- and nineteenth-century giants. In literature, especially in the United States, poetry and the serious novel fled to the universities to be embalmed in "creative writing" courses. Even Paris began to flag as a fountainhead of novelty. Soviet-bloc dissident and emigré writers, along with those of Latin America, showed more life than their European or American counterparts. Western high culture increasingly lacked the vitality and self-confidence of earlier ages.

One world? Japanese youth, Western mass culture (1989).

THE WIDENING AND NARROWING OF THE WEST

As the century drew to a close, Western ideas dominated the globe as never before. In the nineteenth century, the zenith of the West's relative power, its culture had only touched the surface of non-European societies. By the late twentieth century, instant communications relentlessly drove forward the economic and cultural integration of the world. That drive generated fierce reactions, above all from Islam. The Western conception of government resting on and limited by the right of the governed—*democratic government*—found few successful imitators. But the extension of the West's scientific and industrial revolution to all humanity appeared likely to continue. As James Watt's partner had boasted of the new steam-engines, "I sell, Sir, what all the world desires to have—power." The West offered power over nature and over the conditions of human existence to those willing to learn. That temptation has so far proved almost irresistible.

Yet the West has also narrowed in relative terms. By the 1980s the birth rate of Europe from France to the Urals had fallen to roughly equal the death rate. The United States continued to grow, but at a rate lower than ever before. Not so the other continents. As China passed the 1.1 billion mark in the 1980s, its growth slowed only slightly despite ruthless post-Mao laws against unlicensed births. South Asia's relentless rise hardly slowed. Africa's population expanded at a pace faster than that of any other continent, although the AIDS pandemic seemed to be slowing it—tragically—by the 1990s. World population was 4 billion in 1975 and will probably surpass 6.1 billion by the year 2000. Thereafter either economic development will reduce birth rates or natural catastrophes, overcrowding, environmental degradation, epidemics, and wars will increase death rates. Projections suggest that world population may finally level off at around 12.5 billion in the middle of the twenty-second century. East and South Asia would have more than 6 billion, sub-Saharan Africa 2.5 billion, North Africa and the Middle East 1 billion, Latin America and the Caribbean 1 billion, and North America and Europe together less than 1 billion. The West's share of the human species is contracting as the West's influence as the "mainstream of civilization" expands to embrace all humanity.

Suggestions for Further Reading

The Superpowers

As the present approaches, perspective vanishes and perceptive works become ever more sparse. *The New York Times* and *The Economist* (London) offer a better guide to how the world works than jargon-ridden books by policy gurus. J. Keegan and A. Wheatcroft, *Zones of Conflict: An Atlas of Future Wars* (1986), offer a military and political geography of the antagonisms of the 1980s. A. Ulam, *Dangerous Relations: The Soviet Union in World Politics, 1970–1982* (1983), dissects superpower relations in the Brezhnev period. Ronald Reagan's foreign policy still awaits a balanced assessment; some of the essays in J. L. Gaddis, *The United States and the End of the Cold War* (1992),

offer a start. H. Carrère d'Encausse, *Confiscated Power: How Soviet Russia Really Works* (1982) and *The End of the Soviet Empire* (1993), are excellent on the dynamics of Soviet collapse. M. Feschbach, *Ecocide in the Soviet Union* (1992), provides chilling data on the system's effects on its peoples. A. Ulam, *The Communists* (1992), covers its entire post-1948 trajectory. J. F. Brown, *Surge to Freedom* (1992), describes the fall of Stalin's east-European empire. On the ethnic struggles let loose by the end of the Cold War, see especially M. Glenny, *The Fall of Yugoslavia: The Third Balkan War* (1992).

East Asia and Europe

Nguyen Van Canh, *Vietnam Under Communism, 1975–1982* (1983), describes the fate of South Vietnam after the departure of the United States. The Khmer Rouge are still poorly understood, but see F. Ponchaud, *Cambodia Year Zero* (1978); W. Shawcross, *The Quality of Mercy: Cambodia, Holocaust, and Modern Conscience* (1984); and K. D. Jackson, ed., *Cambodia, 1975–1978: Rendezvous with Death* (1992). K. van

Wolferen, *The Enigma of Japanese Power* (1989), offers deep and sometimes disturbing insights. For Europe, see W. Laqueur, *A Continent Astray: Europe, 1970–1978* (1979) and *Europe in Our Time: A History, 1945–1992*. J. Herf, *War by Other Means: Soviet Power, West German Resistance, and the Battle of the Euromissiles* (1991), explains the NATO crisis of the early 1980s.

The Middle East from Peace to War

On the Middle East and Islamic militance, see especially D. Pipes, *In the Path of God: Islam and Political Power* (1983); F. Ajami, *The Arab Predicament: Arab Political Thought and Practice Since 1967* (1992); S. Bakhash, *The Reign of the Ayatollahs* (1984); G. Sick, *All Fall Down: America's Tragic Confrontation with Iran* (1985); and I. Rabinovich, *The War for Lebanon, 1970–1983* (1984). S. al-Khalil (Kanan Makiya), *Republic of Fear* (1989), analyzes Saddam's Iraq with unparalleled penetration and foresight; his *Cruelty and Silence* (1933) offers further

evidence on Saddam's domestic terror, and explores the complicity of Arab intellectuals with the Ba'athist regime. D. Hiro, *The Longest War* (1991) and *Desert Shield to Desert Storm: The Second Gulf War* (1992), cover Saddam's two wars; R. Hallion, *Storm Over Iraq: Air Power and the Gulf War* (1992), helps explain why the Second Gulf War was not Vietnam. P. Slugett and M. Farouk-Slugett, eds., *Tuttle Guide to the Middle East* (1992), offer an up-to-date area handbook.

Technology and Culture

W. A. McDougall, *The Heavens and the Earth: A Political History of the Space Age* (1985), offers analysis of one great monument of "command science." For intellectual developments since the Second World War, see especially J. A. Passmore, *A Hundred Years of Philosophy* (1968) and *Recent Philosophers* (1985); N. Cantor, *Twentieth-Century Culture: Modernism to Decon-*

struction (1988); R. N. Stromberg, *After Everything: Western Intellectual History Since 1945* (1975); and the merciless G. Himmelfarb, *The New History and the Old* (1987). D. Ravitch, *What Do Our 17-Year-Olds Know?* (1987), documents America's educational collapse.

ILLUSTRATION CREDITS

108 Kunsthistorisches Museum, Vienna
111 Hirmer Fotoarchiv
114 Giraudon/Art Resource, New York
116 Harcourt Brace Picture Library
118 Alinari/Art Resource, New York

Chapter 5

122 Hirmer Fotoarchiv
126 *(top)* Harcourt Brace Picture Library; *(bottom)* Harcourt Brace Picture Library
127 German Archeological Institute, Rome
128 Librarie Hachette, Paris
130 *(top)* Courtesy of the Trustees of the British Museum; *(bottom)* Courtesy of the Trustees of the British Museum
132 Metropolitan Museum of Art, purchase, 1895
133 Giraudon/Art Resource, New York
134 *(left)* Metropolitan Museum of Art, purchase, 1895; *(right)* Metropolitan Museum of Art, purchase, 1895
135 The Victoria & Albert Museum, London
138 Biblioteca Nationale Vittorio Emunele III, Naples
139 Staatsbibliothek, Bamberg
140 Courtesy of the Trustees of the British Museum
141 Dean & Chapter of Westminster

Chapter 6

144 Courtesy of the Freer Gallery of Art, Smithsonian Institution, Washington, D.C.
146 Zimmer: Princeton
149 Raghubir Singh/Woodfin Camp & Associates
151 Courtesy of the Freer Gallery of Art, Smithsonian Institution, Washington, D.C.
152 Archeological Survey of India, New Delhi
155 *(top)* United Nations; *(bottom)* Courtesy of the Freer Gallery of Art, Smithsonian Institution, Washington, D.C.
157 *(top left)* From Chian Yee's *Chinese Calligraphy: An Introduction to Its Aesthetic and Technique,* 3rd ed., revised and enlarged, copyright © 1973 by the President and Fellows of Harvard College; *(top right)* Courtesy of the Trust-

ees of the British Museum; *(bottom)* John R. Freeman and Co.
158 Harcourt Brace Picture Library
159 Harcourt Brace Picture Library
161 Courtesy of the Consulate General of the People's Republic of China
163 The Victoria & Albert Museum, London
164 University of California

Chapter 7

166 Hirmer Fotoarchiv
171 *(top)* Historical Pictures/Stock Montage; *(bottom)* Byzantine Visual Resources, © 1993, Dumbarton Oaks, Washington, D.C.
172 *(top)* G. E. Kidder-Smith; *(bottom)* Dmitri Kessel, Life Magazine © Time, Inc.
176 Alinari/Art Resource, New York
177 Historical Pictures/Stock Montage
179 Bibliotheque Nationale, Paris
181 Culver Pictures
183 The Bettmann Archive
191 The Metropolitan Museum of Art, The Cloisters Collection, 1966
192 The Metropolitan Museum of Art, gift of J. Pierpont Morgan, 1917

Chapter 8

194 The Metropolitan Museum of Art, Rogers Fund, 1940 (40.170.15)
198 Arabian American Oil Co. (ARAMCO)
200 University of Edinburgh Library
201 *(top)* New York Public Library; *(bottom)* American Numismatic ociety
202 Robert Harding Picture Service
203 Karen Collidge
204 Berlin Museum
206 The Metropolitan Museum of Art
208 Harcourt Brace Picture Library
210 Robert Harding Picture Service
216 Vanni/Art Resource, New York

Chapter 9

220 Harcourt Brace Picture Library
222 The Metropolitan Museum of Art, gift of J. Pierpont Morgan, 1917
226 Osterreichische Nationalbibliothek, Vienna
227 *(top)* Louvre, Paris; *(bottom)* Stadtbibliothek, Schaffhausen
230 *(top)* Foto Marburg/Art Resource,

New York; *(bottom)* Courtesy of the Trustees of the British Museum
231 Osterreichische Nationalbibliothek, Vienna
232 Bibliotheque Nationale, Paris
233 *(top)* Bibliotheque Nationale, Paris; *(bottom)* Antikvarisktopografiska Arkivet, Stockholm
234 Norwegian Information Service
236 Foto Marburg/Art Resource, New York
239 The Metropolitan Museum of Art, gift of George Blumenthal, 1941
241 Museo del Castello, S. Forzesco, Milan
242 *(top left)* Hirmer Fotoarchiv; *(top right)* Bayerische Staatsbibliothek; *(bottom)* Courtesy of the Trustees of the British Museum
244 Photo: Hinz
246 *(top)* SEF/Art Resource, New York; *(bottom)* Scala/Art Resource, New York
247 Historical Pictures/Stock Montage

Chapter 10

250 Courtesy of the Trustees of the British Museum
252 The Bettmann Archive
253 The Bettmann Archive
254 Harcourt Brace Picture Library
256 Scala/Art Resource, New York
259 The Bettmann Archive
260 Photo Bulloz
261 The Bettmann Archive
262 The Bettmann Archive
264 *(top)* Barnaby's Picture Library; *(bottom)* Courtesy of the Trustees of the British Museum
265 Harcourt Brace Picture Library
268 The Granger Collection
270 *(top)* Foto Biblioteca, Vatican, Rome; *(bottom)* Harcourt Brace Picture Library
272 Musee Municipale, Dijon
274 The Pierpont Morgan Library, New York. M638, f.23v.

Chapter 11

278 The Metropolitan Museum of Art, The Cloisters Collection, 1947 (47.101.33)
280 Museo di Roma
281 Vatican: Archivo Segreto
283 Alinari/Art Resource, New York
285 Giraudon/Art Resource, New York

842   The Bettmann Archives
843   AP/Wide World Photos
849   AP/Wide World Photos
850   *(top)* AP/Wide World Photos; *(bottom)* The Bettmann Archive/BBC Hulton
852   UPI/Bettmann Newsphotos
853   Stefan Lorant

Chapter 33

856   The Bettmann Archive/BBC Hulton
858   AP/Wide World Photos
862   AP/Wide World Photos
863   Times Newspapers, Ltd.
864   *(top)* AP/Wide World Photos; *(bottom)* UPI/Bettmann Newsphotos
867   The Bettmann Archive
869   Bettmann Newsphotos
874   Sovfoto
876   AP/Wide World Photos
877   Robert Capa/Magnum
879   UPI/Bettmann Newsphotos
881   UPI/Bettmann Newsphotos
882   U.S. Army Photo
884   The Bettmann Archive
887   The Bettmann Archive

Chapter 34

890   AP/Wide World Photos
893   AP/Wide World Photos

894   AP/Wide World Photos
896   UPI/Bettmann Newsphotos
898   AP/Wide World Photos
899   UPI/Bettmann
901   AP/Wide World Photos
902   *(top)* The Bettmann Archive/BBC Hulton; *(bottom)* Sergio Larrain/Magnum
903   AP/Wide World Photos
905   AP/Wide World Photos
906   David Seymour/Magnum
911   AP/Wide World Photos
913   David McCullin/Magnum
914   AP/Wide World Photos
917   © Didier Maillac/REA/Impact Photos
919   UPI/Bettmann Newsphotos
920   Harcourt Brace Picture Library

Chapter 35

922   Popperfoto
926   AP/Wide World Photos
928   John Berry/Magnum
929   UPI/Bettmann Newsphotos
931   UPI/Bettmann Newsphotos
934   Eastfoto
936   AP/Wide World Photos
937   UPI/Bettmann
940   *(top)* Guy LeQuerrec/Magnum; *(bottom)* AP/Wide World Photos

943   Reuters/Bettmann Newsphotos
945   Reuters/Bettmann
946   *(top)* AP/Wide World Photos; *(bottom)* AP/Wide World Photos

Chapter 36

948   Reuters/Bettmann
953   UPI/Bettmann
954   © Morgan/Greenpeace
956   Reuters/Bettmann
957   Bob Nicklesburg/Gamma Liaison
958   Reuters/Bettmann
962   *(top)* AP/Wide World Photos; *(bottom)* Cham/Sipa Press
963   AP/Wide World Photos
964   UPI/Bettmann Newsphotos
966   *(top)* Copyright by P. Kern/Sygma; *(bottom)* Nakram Gadelkarim-Al Akhbar/Gamma Liaison
967   UPI/Bettmann
969   *(top)* Reuters/Bettmann; *(bottom)* Reuters/Bettmann
970   Reuters/Bettmann
973   Art Zamur/Gamma Liaison
976   © Applied Biosystems/Peter Arnold, Inc.
978   © 1989 Roger Ressmeyer—Starlight

INDEX